# GALE
# ENCYCLOPEDIA OF
# MULTICULTURAL
## AMERICA

# GALE
# ENCYCLOPEDIA OF
# MULTICULTURAL
## AMERICA

### volume 1
#### Acadians – Iranian Americans

Contributing Editor
## RUDOLPH J. VECOLI

Edited by
### JUDY GALENS
### ANNA SHEETS
### ROBYN V. YOUNG

Endorsed by *EMIE Bulletin* of the Ethnic Materials
Information Exchange Round Table,
American Library Association.

*An International Thomson Publishing Company*

Changing the Way the World Learns

NEW YORK • LONDON • BONN • BOSTON • DETROIT • MADRID
MELBOURNE • MEXICO CITY • PARIS • SINGAPORE • TOKYO
TORONTO • WASHINGTON • ALBANY NY • BELMONT CA • CINCINNATI OH

## STAFF

Judy Galens, Anna Sheets, Robyn V. Young, *Editors*

Neil Schlager, *Managing Editor, Multicultural Team*
Sharon Malinowski, *Editor*
Dawn R. Barry, Melissa Walsh Doig, Jeffrey Lehman, *Associate Editors*

Victoria B. Cariappa, *Research Manager*
Barbara McNeil, *Research Specialist*
Maria Bryson, *Research Associate*

Mary Beth Trimper, *Production Director*
Evi Seoud, *Assistant Production Manager*
Shanna Heilveil, *Production Assistant*

Marlene H. Lasky, *Permissions Manager*
Diane Cooper, *Permissions Associate*

Cynthia Baldwin, *Product Design Manager*
Tracey Rowens, *Art Director*

♾™ This book is printed on acid-free paper that meets the minimum requirements
of American National Standard for Information Sciences-
Permanence Paper for Printed Library Materials, ANSI Z39.48-1984.

♻ This book is printed on recycled paper that meets Environmental Protection Agency Standards.

ISBN 0-8103-9163-5
Vol 1 ISBN 0-8103-9164-3

**Library of Congress Cataloging-in-Publication Data**

Gale encyclopedia of multicultural America / Judy Galens, Anna J.
Sheets, Robyn V. Young, editors.
 p. cm.
 Includes bibliographical references and index.
 ISBN 0-8103-9164-3. -- ISBN 0-8103-9165-1 (pbk.)
 1. Ethnology--United States--Encyclopedias. 2. Pluralism (Social
sciences)--United States--Encyclopedias. I. Galens, Judy, 1968-
. II. Sheets, Anna J. (Anna Jean), 1970- . III. Young, Robyn V.,
1958- .
E184.A1G14 1995                                            95-23341
305.8'00973--dc20                                              CIP

I T P ™  Gale Research Inc., an International Thomson Publishing Company.
        ITP logo is a trademark under license.

10 9 8 7 6 5 4 3 2

# CONTENTS

## Volume 2

# PREFACE

Based upon a need for comprehensive reference sources in the area of multiculturalism in public, high school, and academic libraries, Gale presents the *Gale Encyclopedia of Multicultural America*. This source contains over one hundred signed original essays, each addressing a distinct ethnic, ethnoreligious, or Native American group in the United States. The articles, which range from 5,000 words to 20,000 words in length, are arranged alphabetically.

## SCOPE

The groups included in the *Gale Encyclopedia of Multicultural America* were selected according to two principal criteria: the magnitude of each ethnic group based on the 1990 U.S. Census, and the recommendations of an advisory board regarding widely studied groups in high schools and universities. To meet the needs of students and researchers, the editors and advisory board therefore chose to include some groups that have relatively small populations. The majority of the articles were written by scholars and writers with a special interest in and knowledge of the ethnic groups about which they were writing. Once the essays were completed, additional scholars were asked to review the essays for comprehensiveness, factual accuracy, and objectivity.

The editors have attempted to make the *Gale Encyclopedia of Multicultural America* as inclusive as possible. Its scope encompasses peoples from Africa, Asia, the Caribbean, Central America, Europe, the Middle East, North America, the Pacific Islands, and South America; thus the *Gale Encyclopedia of Multicultural America* recognizes the history, culture, and contributions of established ethnic groups, such as English Americans and French Americans, as well as newer Americans who have been previously overlooked in studies of American ethnic groups, like Hmong Americans and Guatemalan Americans. Moreover, certain ethnoreligious groups, such as the Amish, are included as well.

Because America's cultural diversity is not limited to immigrant groups, the *Gale Encyclopedia of Multicultural America* also contains essays on Native American groups, representing regions

The *Gale Encyclopedia of Multicultural America* has been endorsed by *EMIE Bulletin* of the Ethnic Materials Information Exchange Round Table, American Library Association.

from throughout the United States. The richness of their heritage and the importance of their historical role in the United States require their inclusion in any discussion of multiculturalism. As a full-scale treatment of Native Americans was not possible in this publication, twelve groups were chosen for inclusion based on their cultural diversity, geographical representation, and the recommendations of the advisory board.

There are two chapters devoted to peoples from Subsaharan Africa. Because the vast majority of people in the United States from this region identified themselves as African American in the 1990 U.S. Census, there is a lengthy essay entitled "African Americans" that represents persons of multiple ancestry. An essay on Nigerian Americans, who are a relatively recent immigration group and therefore have a history in the United States that is quite different from other African immigrants, is included as well. According to the 1990 U.S. Census, there were 91,688 people of Nigerian descent in the United States that year, making Nigerians the single largest American immigrant group from a specific country in Subsaharan Africa.

## FORMAT

While each essay contained in the *Gale Encyclopedia of Multicultural America* includes information on the country of origin and circumstances surrounding major immigration waves (if applicable), the primary focus of these essays is on that group's experiences in the United States, specifically in the areas of acculturation and assimilation, family and community dynamics, language, religion, employment and economic traditions, politics and government, and significant contributions. Wherever possible, each entry also features directory listings of periodicals, radio and television stations, organizations and associations, and museums and research centers to aid the user in conducting additional research. Each entry also contains sources for further study that are both useful and accessible. Every essay is designed for ease of use by students, teachers, librarians, and the general public, with the articles divided into clearly marked headings and subheadings. This method of organization makes it easy to find specific types of information within an essay, and it also facilitates comparisons between groups.

## ADDITIONAL FEATURES

In addition to a general subject index, which provides reference to significant terms, people, places, movements, events, and organizations, the *Gale Encyclopedia of Multicultural America* contains a general bibliography of over 100 books and periodicals, compiled by Vladimir Wertsman of the Ethnic Materials Information Exchange Round Table, American Library Association. These sources do not replicate those listed in each entry; rather, they are concerned with more general works in the field of multicultural studies. The text is highlighted by 171 photographs.

## ACKNOWLEDGEMENTS

The editors gratefully acknowledge contributing editor and author of the introduction Rudolph J. Vecoli, as well as the members of the advisory board, especially Vladimir Wertsman for his relentless enthusiasm and support; Neil Schlager and the Multicultural Team, particularly Sharon Malinowski for her guidance, skill, and generous spirit; Jeffrey Muhr and Roger Valade for their technical expertise; Wiley M. Woodard for his extensive research; and the many scholars who reviewed the essays, including Arnold Alanen, Wanni Anderson, Kay A. Averette, Carlota Cárdenas de Dwyer, Araxie Churukian, Oralia Garza de Cortés, Lou Gretch-Cumbo, Kyung-Sun Lim, Joel Monture, Kirin Narayan, Chia Ning, Sorya Poc, Claire Quintal, Martha Ratliff, Akiko Tani, Robert Thacker, Nadeen M. Thomas, Rudolph J. Vecoli, and Vladimir Wertsman. Although we are indebted to these individuals for their efforts, we also recognize that the ultimate responsibility for this publication is ours as the editors.

## SUGGESTIONS ARE WELCOME

The editors welcome your suggestions on any aspect of this work. Please send comments to: The Editor, *Gale Encyclopedia of Multicultural America*, Gale Research Inc., 835 Penobscot Bldg., 645 Griswold St., Detroit, MI 48226-4094; or call 1-800-347-GALE; or fax to (313) 961-6741.

# CREDITS

The editors wish to thank the permissions managers of the companies that assisted us in securing reprint rights. The following list acknowledges the copyright holders who have granted us permission to reprint material in this edition of the *Gale Encyclopedia of Multicultural America*. Every effort has been made to trace the copyright holders, but if omissions have been made, please contact the editors.

## COPYRIGHTED PHOTOGRAPHY

The photographs and illustrations appearing in the *Gale Encyclopedia of Multicultural America* were received from the following sources:

Cover Photographs: **UPI/Bettmann**: The Joy of Citizenship; Against the Sky: **The Bettmann Archive**: Leaving Ellis Island.

**Courtesy of Village Historique Acadien**: page 3; **Courtesy of David Richmond**: page 7; **AP/Wide World Photos, Inc.**: pages 27, 47, 58, 67, 85, 90, 102, 106, 132, 153, 229, 232, 267, 286, 333, 505, 571, 599, 644, 727, 737, 830, 860, 924, 1050, 1132, 1151, 1168, 1175, 1218, 1278, 1303, 1316, 1369, 1413, 1425; **Courtesy of Skip Mason/Digging It Up Photo Archives**: page 32; **The Bettmann Archive**: pages 44, 660, 769, 1119, 1231, 1337; **UPI/Bettmann**: pages 73, 272, 305, 317, 386, 391, 398, 432, 436, 487, 568, 636, 652, 694, 732, 753, 801, 871, 873, 881, 890, 943, 955, 1011, 1019, 1026, 1092, 1138, 1146, 1163, 1245, 1276, 1285, 1301, 1366, 1381, 1384; © **Ann Trulove/Unicorn Stock Photos**: page 76; A Project Save Photograph Courtesy of Kay Danielian Megerdichian: page 112; © **Michael Newman/PhotoEdit**: page 118; **Courtesy of Rudi VonBriel**: page 127; © **Frances M. Roberts/Levine & Roberts**: pages 166, 330, 722, 1045, 1182; **Courtesy of The Gousse Family Photographs**: page 189; © **Suzanne L. Murphy**: pages 200, 1190, 1235, 1328; © **Richard B. Levine/Levine & Roberts**: pages 205, 902, 978, 1062, 1078; **Courtesy of Culver Pictures**: page 212; © **Robert Ginn/PhotoEdit**: page 275; © **Oscar C. Williams**: pages 290, 792, 1356; © **Gary Conner/PhotoEdit**: pages 303, 520, 605, 803, 842, 1332; © **Elaine S. Queery**: pages 321, 1121; © **1975 The Saul Zaentz Company**: page 355; © **Aneal Vohra/Unicorn Stock Photos**: pages 376, 401, 415, 713, 716, 788, 1074, 1224; **Courtesy of Dr. John M. Nielsen, Professor at Dana College**: page 413; © **Charlotte Kahler**: pages 428; © **Dennis MacDonald/PhotoEdit**: 440; © **Audrey Gottlieb**: pages 452, 457, 494, 580, 587, 1059; © **Gale Zucker**: pages 478, 1110; © **Rick Baker/Unicorn Stock Photos**: page 481; **Courtesy of Tyler Photo Illustrators**: pages 509, 1193; **Courtesy of The Tuomi Family Photographs/Balch Institute for Ethnic Studies**:

# ADVISORY BOARD

# CONTRIBUTORS

Nabeel Abraham
Professor of Anthropology
Henry Ford Community College
Dearborn, Michigan

June Granatir Alexander
Adjunct Assistant Professor
Russian and East European Studies
University of Cincinnati
Cincinnati, Ohio

Donald Altschiller
Freelance Writer
Cambridge, Massachusetts

Diane Andreassi
Freelance Writer
Livonia, Michigan

Carl L. Bankston III
Professor, Department of Sociology
Louisiana State University
Baton Rouge, Louisiana

Diane Benson
Tlingit Actress and Writer
Eagle River, Alaska

Barbara Bigelow
Freelance Writer
White Lake, Michigan

D.L. Birchfield
Editor and Writer
Oklahoma City, Oklahoma

Herbert Brinks
Professor, Department of History
Calvin College
Grand Rapids, Michigan

Sean Buffington
Professor, Department of Ethnic Studies
University of Michigan
Ann Arbor, Michigan

Phyllis Burson
Independent Consultant
Silver Spring, Maryland

Helen Caver
Associate Professor and Librarian
Jacksonville State University
Jacksonville, Alabama

Cida S. Chase
Professor of Spanish
Oklahoma State University
Stillwater, Oklahoma

Clark Colahan
Professor of Spanish
Whitman College
Walla Walla, Washington

Robert J. Conley
Freelance Writer
Tahlequah, Oklahoma

Jane Cook
Freelance Writer
Green Bay, Wisconsin

Paul Cox
Dean, General Education and Honors
Brigham Young University
Provo, Utah

Ken Cuthbertson
*Queen's Alumni Review*
Queen's University
Kingston, Ontario, Canada

Rosetta Sharp Dean
Counselor and Writer
Anniston, Alabama

Stanley E. Easton
Professor of Japanese
Jacksonville State University
Jacksonville, Alabama

Lucien Ellington
Professor of Japanese
University of Tennessee-Chattanooga
Chattanooga, Tennessee

Jessie L. Embry
Oral History Program Director
Charles Redd Center for Western Studies
Brigham Young University
Provo, Utah

Allen Englekirk
Professor of Spanish
Gonzaga University
Spokane, Washington

Marianne Fedunkiw
Freelance Writer
Toronto, Ontario, Canada

Mary Gillis
Freelance Writer
Huntington Woods, Michigan

Edward Gobetz
Executive Director
Slovenian Research Center of America, Inc.
Willoughby Hills, Ohio

Mark A. Granquist
Assistant Professor of Religion
Saint Olaf College
Northfield, Minnesota

Derek Green
Freelance Writer
Ann Arbor, Michigan

Paula Hajar
Freelance Writer
New York, New York

Loretta Hall
Freelance Writer
Albuquerque, New Mexico

Sheldon Hanft
Professor, Department of History
Appalachian State University
Boone, North Carolina

Evan Heimlich
Assistant Coordinator
Multicultural Resource Center
The University of Kansas
Lawrence, Kansas

Mary A. Hess
Teaching Assistant
Integrated Arts and Humanities
Michigan State University
Lansing, Michigan

Laurie Hillstrom
Freelance Writer
Pleasant Ridge, Michigan

Maria Hong
Freelance Writer
Austin, Texas

**Ed Ifkovic**
Writer and Lecturer
Hartford, Connecticut

**Alphine Jefferson**
Professor, Department of History
The College of Wooster
Wooster, Ohio

**Syd Jones**
Freelance Writer and Novelist
Aptos, California

**Jane Jurgens**
Assistant Professor
Learning Resources Center
St. Cloud State University
St. Cloud, Minnesota

**Jim Kamp**
Freelance Writer and Editor
Royal Oak, Michigan

**Oscar Kawagley**
Assistant Professor of Education
College of Liberal Arts, UAF
Fairbanks, Alaska

**Vituat Kipel**
Librarian, Slavic and Baltic Division
The New York Public Library
New York, New York

**Donald B. Kraybill**
Professor, Department of Sociology
Elizabethtown College
Elizabethtown, Pennsylvania

**Ken Kurson**
Freelance Writer
New York, New York

**Odd S. Lovoll**
Professor of Scandinavian American Studies
Saint Olaf College
Northfield, Minnesota

**Jacqueline A. McLeod**
Freelance Writer
Michigan State University
East Lansing, Michigan

**Paul Robert Magosci**
Director and Chief Executive Officer
Multicultural History Society of Ontario
Toronto, Ontario, Canada

**William Maxwell**
Contributing Editor
*A Gathering of the Tribes Magazine*
New York, New York

**H. Brett Melendy**
University Archivist
San Jose State University
San Jose, California

**Mona Mikhail**
Professor, Department of Near Eastern Languages
    and Literatures
New York University
New York, New York

**Christine Molinari**
Manuscript Editor
The University of Chicago Press
Chicago, Illinois

**Lloyd Mulraine**
Professor of English
Jacksonville State University
Jacksonville, Alabama

**Jeremy Mumford**
Assistant News Editor
Courtroom Television Network
New York, New York

**N. Samuel Murrell**
Professor of Religion and Black Studies
The College of Wooster
Wooster, Ohio

**Amy Nash**
Freelance Writer
Minneapolis, Minnesota

**John Mark Nielson**
Professor of English
Dana College
Blair, Nebraska

**Ernest E. Norden**
Professor, Division of Spanish and Portuguese
Baylor University
Waco, Texas

**John F. Packel, II**
Freelance Writer
Brooklyn, New York

**Tinaz Pavri**
Freelance Writer
Columbus, Ohio

Richard Perrin
Librarian, Reference and Instructional Services
Timme Library
Ferris State University
Big Rapids, Michigan

Peter L. Peterson
Professor of History
West Texas A&M
Canyon, Texas

George E. Pozzetta
Professor, Department of History
University of Florida
Gainesville, Florida

Brendan Rapple
Reference Librarian/Education Bibliographer
O'Neill Library
Boston College
Boston, Massachusetts

Megan Ratner
Freelance Writer
New York, New York

La Vern J. Rippley
Professor of German
Saint Olaf College
Northfield, Minnesota

Julio César Rodríguez
Freelance Writer
Walla Walla, Washington

Lorene Roy
Associate Professor and Minority Liaison Officer
The University of Texas at Austin
Austin, Texas

Kwasi Sarkodie-Mensah
Chief Reference Librarian
O'Neill Library
Boston College
Boston, Massachusetts

Leo Schelbert
Professor, Department of History
University of Illinois at Chicago
Chicago, Illinois

Mary C. Sengstock
Professor, Department of Sociology
Wayne State University
Detroit, Michigan

Stefan Smagula
Freelance Writer
Austin, Texas

Bosiljka Stevanovic
Principal Librarian
Donnell Library Center
World Languages Collection
The New York Public Library
New York, New York

Andris Straumanis
Freelance Writer
New Brighton, Minnesota

Pamela Sturner
Freelance Writer
New Haven, Connecticut

Mark Swartz
Manuscript Editor
The University of Chicago Press
Chicago, Illinois

Harold T. Takooshian
Professor, Division of Social Sciences
Fordham University
New York, New York

Felix Unaeze
Head Librarian
Reference and Instructional
        Services Department
Timme Library
Ferris State University
Big Rapids, Michigan

Steven Béla Várdy
Professor and Director,
        Department of History
Duquesne University
Pittsburgh, Pennsylvania

Ling-chi Wang
Professor, Asian American Studies
Department of Ethnic Studies
University of California, Berkeley
Berkeley, California

K. Marianne Wargelin
Freelance Writer
Minneapolis, Minnesota

Vladimir Wertsman
Chair of Publishing in Multicultural Materials
Ethnic Materials Information Exchange
American Library Association
New York, New York

**Mary T. Williams**
Associate Professor
Jacksonville State University
Jacksonville, Alabama

**Elaine Winters**
Freelance Writer
Berkeley, California

**Eveline Yang**
Manager, Information Delivery Program
Auraria Library
Denver, Colorado

**Eleanor Yu**
Deputy News Editor
Courtroom Television Network
New York, New York

# INTRODUCTION

**RUDOLPH J. VECOLI**

The term multiculturalism has recently come into usage to describe a society characterized by a diversity of cultures. Religion, language, customs, traditions, and values are some of the components of culture, but more importantly culture is the lens through which one perceives and interprets the world. When a shared culture forms the basis for a "sense of peoplehood," based on consciousness of a common past, we can speak of a group possessing an ethnicity. As employed here, ethnicity is not transmitted genetically from generation to generation; nor is it unchanging over time. Rather, ethnicity is invented or constructed in response to particular historical circumstances and changes as circumstances change. "Race," a sub-category of ethnicity, is not a biological reality but a cultural construction. While in its most intimate form an ethnic group may be based on face-to-face relationships, a politicized ethnicity mobilizes its followers far beyond the circle of personal acquaintances. Joined with aspirations for political self-determination, ethnicity can become full-blown nationalism. In this essay, ethnicity will be used to identify groups or communities that are differentiated by religious, racial, or cultural characteristics and that possess a sense of peoplehood.

The "Multicultural America" to which this encyclopedia is dedicated is the product of the mingling of many different peoples over the course of several hundred years in what is now the

United States. Cultural diversity was characteristic of this continent prior to the coming of European colonists and African slaves. The indigenous inhabitants of North America who numbered an estimated 4.5 million in 1500 were divided into hundreds of tribes with distinctive cultures, languages, and religions. Although the numbers of "Indians," as they were named by Europeans, declined precipitously through the nineteenth century, their population has rebounded in the twentieth century. Both as members of their particular tribes (a form of ethnicity), Navajo, Ojibwa, Choctaw, etc., and as American Indians (a form of panethnicity), they are very much a part of today's cultural and ethnic pluralism.

Most Americans, however, are descendants of immigrants. Since the sixteenth century, from the earliest Spanish settlement at St. Augustine, Florida, the process of repeopling this continent has gone on apace. Some 600,000 Europeans and Africans were recruited or enslaved and transported across the Atlantic Ocean in the colonial period to what was to become the United States. The first census of 1790 revealed the high degree of diversity that already marked the American population. Almost 19 percent were of African ancestry, another 12 percent Scottish and Scotch-Irish, ten percent German, with smaller numbers of French, Irish, Welsh, and Sephardic Jews. The census did not include American Indians. The English, sometimes described as the "founding people," only comprised 48 percent of the total. At the time of its birth in 1776, the United States was already a "complex ethnic mosaic," with a wide variety of communities differentiated by culture, language, race, and religion.

The present United States includes not only the original thirteen colonies, but lands that were subsequently purchased or conquered. Through this territorial expansion, other peoples were brought within the boundaries of the republic; these included, in addition to many Native American tribes, French, Hawaiian, Inuit, Mexican, and Puerto Rican, among others. Since 1790, population growth, other than by natural increase, has come primarily through three massive waves of immigration. During the first wave (1841-1890), almost 15 million immigrants arrived: over four million Germans, three million each of Irish and British (English, Scottish, and Welsh), and one million Scandinavians. A second wave (1891-1920) brought an additional 18 million immigrants: almost four million from Italy, 3.6 million from Austria-Hungary, and three million from Russia. In addition, over two million Canadians, Anglo and French, immigrated prior to 1920. The intervening decades, from 1920 to 1945, marked a hiatus in immigration due to restrictive policies, economic depression, and war. A modest post-World War II influx of refugees was followed by a new surge subsequent to changes in immigration policy in 1965. Totalling approximately 16 million—and still in progress, this third wave encompassed some four million from Mexico, another four million from Central and South America and the Caribbean, and roughly six million from Asia. While almost 90 percent of the first two waves originated in Europe, only 12 percent of the third did.

Immigration has introduced an enormous diversity of cultures into American society. The 1990 U.S. Census report on ancestry provides a fascinating portrait of the complex ethnic origins of the American people. Responses to the question, "What is your ancestry or ethnic origin?," were tabulated for 215 ancestry groups. The largest ancestry groups reported were, in order of magnitude, German, Irish, English, and African American, all over 20 million.

Other groups reporting over six million were Italian, Mexican, French, Polish, Native American, Dutch, and Scotch-Irish, while another 28 groups reported over one million each. Scanning the roster of ancestries one is struck by the plethora of smaller groups: Hmong, Maltese, Honduran, Carpatho-Rusyns, and Nigerian, among scores of others. Interestingly enough, only five percent identified themselves simply as "American"—and less than one percent as "white."

Immigration also contributed to the transformation of the religious character of the United States. Its original Protestantism (itself divided among many denominations and sects) was both reinforced by the arrival of millions of Lutherans, Methodists, Presbyterians, etc., and diluted by the heavy influx of Roman Catholics—first the Irish and Germans, then Eastern Europeans and Italians, and more recently Hispanics. These immigrants have made Roman Catholicism the largest single denomination in the country. Meanwhile, Slavic Christian and Jewish immigrants from Central and Eastern Europe established Judaism and Orthodoxy as major American religious bodies. As a consequence of Near Eastern immigration—and the conversion of many African Americans to Islam—there are currently some three million Muslims in the United States. Smaller numbers of Buddhists, Hindus, and followers of other religions have also arrived. In many American cities, houses of worship now include mosques and temples as well as churches and synagogues. Such religious pluralism is an important source of American multiculturalism.

The immigration and naturalization policies pursued by a country are a key to understanding its self-conception as a nation. By determining who to admit to residence and citizenship, the dominant element defines the future ethnic and racial composition of the population and the body politic. Each of the three great waves of immigration inspired much soul-searching and intense debate over the consequences for the republic. If the capacity of American society to absorb some 55 million immigrants over the course of a century and a half is impressive, it is also true that American history has been punctuated by ugly episodes of nativism and xenophobia. With the possible exception of the British, it is difficult to find an immigrant group that has not been subject to some degree of prejudice and discrimination. From their early encounters with Native Americans and Africans, Anglo-Americans established "whiteness" as an essential marker of difference and superiority. The Naturalization Act of 1790, for example, specified that citizenship was to be available to "any alien, being a free white person." By this provision not only were blacks ineligible for naturalization, but also future immigrants who were deemed not to be "white." The greater the likeness of immigrants to the Anglo-American type (e.g., British Protestants), the more readily they were welcomed.

Not all Anglo-Americans were racists or xenophobes. Citing Christian and democratic ideals of universal brotherhood, many advocated the abolition of slavery and the rights of freedmen—freedom of religion and cultural tolerance. Debates over immigration policy brought these contrasting views of the republic into collision. The ideal of America as an asylum for the oppressed of the world has exerted a powerful influence for a liberal reception of newcomers. Emma Lazarus's sonnet, which began "Give me your tired, your poor, your huddled masses yearning to breathe free, the wretched refuse of your teeming shore," struck a responsive chord among many Anglo-Americans. Moreover, American capitalism depended upon the rural workers of Europe, French Canada, Mexico, and Asia to man its factories and mines. Nonetheless, many Americans have regarded immigration as posing a threat to social stability, the jobs of native white

workers, honest politics, and American cultural—even biological—integrity. The strength of anti-immigrant movements has waxed and waned with the volume of immigration, but even more with fluctuations in the state of the economy and society. Although the targets of nativist attacks have changed over time, a constant theme has been the danger posed by foreigners to American values and institutions.

Irish Catholics, for example, were viewed as minions of the Pope and enemies of the Protestant character of the country. A Protestant Crusade culminated with the formation of the American (or "Know-Nothing") Party in 1854, whose battle cry was "America for the Americans!" While the Know-Nothing movement was swallowed up by sectional conflict culminating in the Civil War, anti-Catholicism continued to be a powerful strain of nativism well into the twentieth century.

Despite such episodes of xenophobia, during its first century of existence, the United States welcomed all newcomers with minimal regulation. In 1882, however, two laws initiated a progressive tightening of restrictions upon immigration. The first established qualitative health and moral standards by excluding criminals, prostitutes, lunatics, idiots, and paupers. The second, the Chinese Exclusion Act, the culmination of an anti-Chinese movement centered on the West Coast, denied admission to Chinese laborers and barred Chinese immigrants from acquiring citizenship. Following the enactment of this law, agitation for exclusion of Asians continued as the Japanese and others arrived, culminating in the provision of the Immigration Law of 1924, which denied entry to aliens ineligible for citizenship (those who were not deemed "white"). It was not until 1952 that a combination of international politics and democratic idealism finally resulted in the elimination of all racial restrictions from American immigration and naturalization policies.

In the late nineteenth century, "scientific" racialism, which asserted the superiority of Anglo-Saxons, was embraced by many Americans as justification for imperialism and immigration restriction. At that time a second immigrant wave was beginning to bring peoples from eastern Europe, the Balkans, and the Mediterranean into the country. Nativists campaigned for a literacy test and other measures to restrict the entry of these that "inferior races." Proponents of a liberal immigration policy defeated such efforts until World War I created a xenophobic climate which not only insured the passage of the literacy test, but prepared the way for the Immigration Acts of 1921 and 1924. Inspired by racialist ideas, these laws established national quota systems designed to drastically reduce the number of southern and eastern Europeans entering the United States and to bar Asians entirely. In essence, the statutes sought to freeze the biological and ethnic identity of the American people by protecting them from contamination from abroad.

Until 1965 the United States pursued this restrictive and racist immigration policy. The Immigration Act of 1965 did away with the national origins quota system and opened the country to immigration from throughout the world, establishing preferences for family members of American citizens and resident aliens, skilled workers, and refugees. The unforeseen consequence of the law of 1965 was the third wave of immigration. Not only did the annual volume of immigration increase steadily to the current level of one million or more arrivals each year, but the majority of the immigrants now came from Asia and Latin America. During the 1980s, they accounted for 85 percent of the total number of immigrants, with Mexicans, Chinese, Filipinos, and Koreans being the largest contingents.

The cumulative impact of an immigration of 16 plus millions since 1965 has aroused intense concerns regarding the demographic, cultural, and racial future of the American people. The skin color, languages, and lifestyles of the newcomers triggered a latent xenophobia in the American psyche. While eschewing the overt racism of earlier years, advocates of tighter restriction have warned that if current rates of immigration continue, the "minorities" (persons of African, Asian, and "Hispanic" ancestry) will make up about half of the American population by the year 2050.

A particular cause of anxiety is the number of undocumented immigrants (estimated at 200,000-300,000 per year). Contrary to popular belief, the majority of these individuals do not cross the border from Mexico, but enter the country with either student or tourist visas and simply stay—many are Europeans and Asians. The Immigration Reform and Control Act (IRCA) of 1986 sought to solve the problem by extending amnesty for undocumented immigrants under certain conditions and imposing penalties on employers who hired undocumented immigrants, while making special provisions for temporary agricultural migrant workers. Although over three million persons qualified for consideration for amnesty, employer sanctions failed for lack of

effective enforcement, and the number of undocumented immigrants has not decreased. Congress subsequently enacted the Immigration Act of 1990, which established a cap of 700,000 immigrants per year, maintained preferences based on family reunification, and expanded the number of skilled workers to be admitted. Immigration, however, has continued to be a hotly debated issue. Responding to the nativist mood of the country, politicians have advocated measures to limit access of legal as well as undocumented immigrants to Medicare and other welfare benefits. A constitutional amendment was even proposed that would deny citizenship to American-born children of undocumented residents.

Forebodings about an "unprecedented immigrant invasion," however, appear exaggerated. In the early 1900s, the rate of immigration (the number of immigrants measured against the total population) was ten per every thousand; in the 1980s the rate was only 3.5 per every thousand. While the number of foreign-born individuals in the United States reached an all-time high of almost 20 million in 1990, they accounted for only eight percent of the population as compared with 14.7 per cent in 1910. In other words, the statistical impact of contemporary immigration has been of a much smaller magnitude than that of the past. A persuasive argument has also been made that immigrants, legal and undocumented, contribute more than they take from the American economy and that they pay more in taxes than they receive in social services. As in the past, immigrants are being made scapegoats for the country's problems.

Among the most difficult questions facing students of American history are: how have these tens of millions of immigrants with such differing cultures incorporated into American society?; and what changes have they wrought in the character of that society? The concepts of acculturation and assimilation are helpful in understanding the processes whereby immigrants have adapted to the new society. Applying Milton Gordon's theory, acculturation is the process whereby newcomers assume American cultural attributes, such as the English language, manners, and values, while assimilation is the process of their incorporation into the social networks (work, residence, leisure, families) of the host society. These changes have not come quickly or easily. Many immigrants have experienced only limited acculturation and practically no assimilation during their lifetimes. Among the factors that have affected these processes are race, ethnicity, class, gender, and character of settlement.

The most important factor, however, has been the willingness of the dominant ethnic group (Anglo-Americans) to accept the foreigners. Since they have wielded political and social power, Anglo-Americans have been able to decide who to include and who to exclude. Race (essentially skin color) has been the major barrier to acceptance; thus Asians and Mexicans, as well as African Americans and Native Americans, have in the past been excluded from full integration into the mainstream. At various times, religion, language, and nationality have constituted impediments to incorporation. Social class has also strongly affected interactions among various ethnic groups. Historically, American society has been highly stratified with a close congruence between class and ethnicity, i.e., Anglo-Americans tend to belong to the upper class, northern and western Europeans to the middle class, and southern and eastern Europeans and African Americans to the working class. The metaphor of a "vertical mosaic" has utility in conceptualizing American society. A high degree of segregation (residential, occupational, leisure) within the vertical mosaic has severely limited acculturation and assimilation across class and ethnic lines. However, within a particular social class, various immigrant groups have often interacted at work, in neighborhoods, at churches and saloons, and in the process have engaged in what one historian has described as "Americanization from the bottom up."

Gender has also been a factor since the status of women within the general American society, as well as within their particular ethnic groups, has affected their assimilative and acculturative experiences. Wide variations exist among groups as to the degree to which women are restricted to traditional roles or have freedom to pursue opportunities in the larger society. The density and location of immigrant settlements have also influenced the rate and character of incorporation into the mainstream culture. Concentrated urban settlements and isolated rural settlements, by limiting contacts between the immigrants and others, tend to inhibit the processes of acculturation and assimilation.

An independent variable in these processes, however, is the determination of immigrants themselves whether or not to shed their cultures and become simply Americans. By and large, they are not willing or able to do so. Rather, they cling, often tenaciously, to their old world traditions, languages, and beliefs. Through chain migrations, relatives and friends have regrouped in cities, towns, and the countryside for mutual assistance and to maintain their customary ways. Establishing churches, societies, newspapers, and other institutions, they have built communities and have developed an enlarged sense of peoplehood. Thus, ethnicity (although related to nationalist movements in countries of origin) in large part has emerged from the immigrants' attempt to cope with life in this pluralist society. While they cannot transplant their Old Country ways intact to the Dakota prairie or the Chicago slums, theirs is a selective adaptation, in which they have taken from American culture that which they needed and have kept from their traditional culture that which they valued. Rather than becoming Anglo-Americans, they became ethnic Americans of various kinds.

Assimilation and acculturation have progressed over the course of several generations. The children and grandchildren of the immigrants have retained less of their ancestral cultures (languages are first to go, customs and traditions often follow) and have assumed more mainstream attributes. Yet many have retained, to a greater or lesser degree, a sense of identity and affiliation with a particular ethnic group. Conceived of not as a finite culture brought over in immigrant trunks, but as a mode of accommodation to the dominant culture, ethnicity persists even when the cultural content changes.

We might also ask to *what* have the descendants been assimilating and acculturating. Some have argued that there is an American core culture, essentially British in origin, in which immigrants and their offspring are absorbed. However, if one compares the "mainstream culture" of Americans today (music, food, literature, mass media) with that of one or two centuries ago, it is obvious that it is not Anglo-American (even the American English language has undergone enormous changes from British English). Rather, mainstream culture embodies and reflects the spectrum of immigrant and indigenous ethnic cultures that make up American society. It is the product of syncretism, the melding of different, sometimes contradictory and discordant elements. Multiculturalism is not a museum of immigrant cultures, but rather this complex of the living, vibrant ethnicities of contemporary America.

If Americans share an ideological heritage deriving from the ideals of the American Revolution, such ideals have not been merely abstract principles handed down unchanged from the eighteenth century to the present. Immigrant and indigenous ethnic groups, taking these ideals at face value, have employed them as weapons to combat ethnic and racial prejudice and economic exploitation. If America was the Promised Land, for many the promise was realized only after prolonged and collective struggles. Through labor and civil rights movements, they have contributed to keeping alive and enlarging the ideals of justice, freedom, and equality. If America transformed the immigrants and indigenous ethnic groups, they have also transformed America.

How have Americans conceived of this polyglot, kaleidoscopic society? Over the centuries, several models of a social order, comprised of a variety of ethnic and racial groups, have competed for dominance. An early form was a society based on caste—a society divided into those who were free and those who were not free. Such a social order existed in the South for two hundred years. While the Civil War destroyed slavery, the Jim Crow system of racial segregation maintained a caste system for another hundred years. But the caste model was not limited to black-white relations in the southern states. Industrial capitalism also created a caste-like structure in the North. For a century prior to the New Deal, power, wealth, and status were concentrated in the hands of an Anglo-American elite, while the workers, comprised largely of immigrants and their children, were the helots of the farms and the factories. The caste model collapsed in both the North and the South in the twentieth century before the onslaught of economic expansion, technological change, and geographic and social mobility.

Anglo-conformity has been a favored model through much of our history. Convinced of their cultural and even biological superiority, Anglo-Americans have demanded that Native Americans, African Americans, and immigrants abandon their distinctive linguistic, cultural, and religious traits and conform (in so far as they are capable) to the Anglo model. But at the same time that they demanded conformity to their values and lifestyles, Anglo-Americans erected barriers that severely limited social intercourse with those they regarded as inferior. The ideology of Anglo-conformity has particularly influenced educational policies. A prime objective of the American public school system has been the assimilation of "alien" children to Anglo-American middle class values and behaviors. In recent years, Anglo-conformity has taken the form of opposition to bilingual education. A vigorous campaign has been waged for a constitutional amendment that would make English the official language of the United States.

A competing model, the Melting Pot, symbolized the process whereby the foreign elements were to be transmuted into a new American race. There have been many variants of this ideology of assimilation, including one in which the Anglo-American is the cook stirring and determining the ingredients, but the prevailing concept has been that a distinctive amalgam of all the varied cultures and peoples would emerge from the crucible. Expressing confidence in the capacity of America to assimilate all newcomers, the Melting Pot ideology provided the rationale for a liberal immigration policy. Although the Melting Pot ideology came under sharp attack in the 1960s as a coercive policy of assimilation, the increased immigration of recent years and the related anxiety over national unity has brought it back into favor in certain academic and political circles.

In response to pressures for 100 percent Americanization during World War I, the model of Cultural Pluralism has been offered as an alternative to the Melting Pot. In this model, while sharing a common American citizenship and loyalty, ethnic groups would maintain and foster their particular languages and cultures. The metaphors employed for the cultural pluralism model have included a symphony orchestra, a flower garden, a mosaic, and a stew or salad. All suggest a reconciliation of diversity with an encompassing harmony and coherence. The fortunes of the pluralist model have fluctuated with the national mood. During the 1930s, when cultural democracy was in vogue, pluralist ideas were popular. Again during the period of the "new ethnicity" of the 1960s and the 1970s, cultural pluralism attracted a considerable following. In recent years, heightened fears that American society was fragmenting caused many to reject pluralism for a return to the Melting Pot.

As the United States approaches the twenty-first century its future as an ethnically plural society is hotly contested. Is the United States more diverse today than in the past? Is the unity of society threatened by its diversity? Are the centrifugal forces in American society more powerful than the centripetal? The old models of Anglo-conformity, the Melting Pot, and Cultural Pluralism have lost their explanatory and symbolic value. We need a new model, a new definition of our identity as a people, which will encompass our expanding multiculturalism and which will define us as a multiethnic people in the context of a multiethnic world. We need a compelling paradigm that will command the faith of all Americans because it embraces them in their many-splendored diversity within a just society.

## SUGGESTED READINGS

On acculturation and assimilation, Milton Gordon's *Assimilation in American Life: The Role of Race, Religion, and National Origins* (1964) provides a useful theoretical framework. For a discussion of the concept of ethnicity, see Kathleen Neils Conzen, et al. "The Invention of Ethnicity: A Perspective from the USA," *Journal of American Ethnic History,* 12 (Fall 1992). *Harvard Encyclopedia of American Ethnic Groups,* ed. Stephan Thernstrom (Cambridge, MA, 1980) is a standard reference work with articles on themes as well as specific groups; see especially the essay by Philip Gleason. "American Identity and Americanization." Roger Daniels' *Coming to America: A History of Immigration and Ethnicity in American Life* (New York, 1991) is the most comprehensive and up-to-date history. For a comparative history of ethnic groups see Ronald Takaki's *A Different Mirror: A History of Multicultural America* (1993). On post-1965 immigration, David Reimers' *Still the Golden Door: The Third World Comes to America* (1985), is an excellent overview. A classic work on nativism is John Higham's, *Strangers in the Land: Patterns of American Nativism: 1860-1925* (1963), but see also David H. Bennett's *The Party of Fear: From Nativist Movements to the New Right in American History* (1988). On the Anglo-American elite see E. Digby Baltzell's *The Protestant Establishment: Aristocracy and Caste in America* (1964).

# ACADIANS

by
**Evan Heimlich**

*Acadians brought a solidarity with them to Louisiana. As one of the first groups to cross the Atlantic and adopt a new identity, they felt connected to each other by their common experience.*

## OVERVIEW

Acadians are the descendants of a group of French-speaking settlers who migrated from coastal France in the late sixteenth century to establish a French colony called Acadia in the maritime provinces of Canada and part of what is now the state of Maine. Forced out by the British in the mid-sixteenth century, a few settlers remained in Maine, but most resettled in southern Louisiana and are popularly known as Cajuns.

### HISTORY

Before 1713, Acadia was a French colony pioneered mostly by settlers from the coastal provinces of Brittany, Normandy, Picardy, and Poitou—a region that suffered great hardships in the late sixteenth and early seventeenth centuries. In 1628, famine and plague followed the end of a series of religious wars between Catholics and Protestants. When social tensions in coastal France ripened, more than 10,000 people left for the colony founded by Samuel Champlain in 1604 known as "La Cadie" or Acadia. The area, which included what is now Nova Scotia, New Brunswick, Prince Edward Island, and part of Maine, was one of the first European colonies in North America. The Company of New France recruited colonists from coastal France as indentured servants. Fishermen, farmers, and trappers served for five years to repay the company with their labor for the transportation and materials it had provided. In the New World, colonists forged alliances with local Indians, who generally preferred the settlers from France over those from Britain because, unlike the British who took all the land they could, the coastal French in Acadia did not invade Indian hunting grounds inland.

The early French settlers called themselves "Acadiens" or "'Cadiens" (which eventually became Anglicized as "Cajuns") and were among the first Old World settlers to identify themselves as North Americans. The New World offered them relative freedom and independence from the French upper class. When French owners of Acadian lands tried to collect seignorial rents from settlers who were farming, many Acadians simply moved away from the colonial centers. When France tried legally to control their profit from their trade in furs or grain, Acadians traded illegally; they even traded with New England while France and England waged war against each other.

As French colonial power waned, Great Britain captured Acadia in 1647; the French got it back in 1670 only to lose it again to the British in the 1690s. Acadians adapted to political changes as their region repeatedly changed hands. Before the British took the Nova Scotia region, they waged the Hundred Year War against French colonial forces in a struggle over the region's territory. The Treaty of Utrecht in 1713, which failed to define realistic boundaries for the French and English territories after Queen Anne's War, converted most of the peninsula into a British colony. Despite British attempts to impose its language and culture, Acadian culture persisted. Large families increased their numbers and new settlers spoke French. The British tried to settle Scottish and other Protestant colonists in Acadia to change the region's French-Catholic culture to a British-Protestant one. The French-speaking Acadians, however, held onto their own culture.

In 1745 the British threatened to expel the Acadians unless they pledged allegiance to the King of England. Unwilling to subject themselves to any king (especially the King of England who opposed the French and Catholics), Acadians refused, claiming that they were not allied with France. They also did not want to join the British in fights against the Indians, who were their allies and relatives. To dominate the region militarily, culturally, and agriculturally without interference, the British expelled the Acadians, dispersing them to colonies such as Georgia and South Car-

olina. This eventually led the British to deport Acadians in what became known as *Le Grand Dérangement*, or the Expulsion of 1755.

The roundup and mass deportation of Acadians, which presaged British domination of much of North America, involved much cruelty, as indicated by letters from British governor, Major Charles Lawrence. In an attempt to eliminate the Acadians from Acadia, the British packed them by the hundreds into the cargo holds of ships, where many died from the cold and smallpox. At the time, Acadians numbered about 15,000, however, the Expulsion killed almost half the population. Of the survivors and those who escaped expulsion, some found their way back to the region, and many drifted through England, France, the Caribbean, and other colonies. Small pockets of descendants of Acadians can still be found in France. In 1763 there were more than 6,000 Acadians in New England. Of the thousands sent to Massachusetts, 700 reached Connecticut and then escaped to Montreal. Many reached the Carolinas; some in Georgia were sold as slaves; many eventually were taken to the West Indies as indentured servants. Most, however, eventually made their way down the Mississippi River to Louisiana. At New Orleans and other southern Louisiana ports, about 2,400 Acadians arrived between 1763 and 1776 from the American colonies, the West Indies, St. Pierre and Miquelon islands, and Acadia/Nova Scotia.

According to *Cajun Country*, after Spain gained control of Louisiana in the mid-1760s, Acadian exiles "who had been repatriated to France volunteered to the king of Spain to help settle his newly acquired colony." The Spanish government accepted their offer and paid for the transport of 1,600 settlers. When they arrived in Louisiana in 1785, colonial forts continued Spain's services to Acadian pioneers (which officially began with a proclamation by Governor Galvez in February of 1778). Forts employed and otherwise sponsored the settlers in starting their new lives by providing tools, seed corn, livestock, guns, medical services, and a church.

A second group of Acadians came 20 years later. Louisiana attracted Acadians who wanted to rejoin their kin and Acadian culture. After decades of exile, immigrants came from many different regions. The making of "Acadiana" in southern Louisiana occurred amid a broader context of French-speaking immigration to the region, including the arrival of European and American whites, African and Caribbean slaves, and free

Reenactment of an early
Acadian dining-room
scene at the Babineau
House in Caraquet, New
Brunswick, Canada.

Blacks. Like others, such as Mexicans who lived in annexed territory of the United States, Cajuns and other Louisianans became citizens when the United States acquired Louisiana from Napoleon through the Louisiana Purchase in 1803.

### SETTLEMENT PATTERNS

The diaspora of Acadians in the United States interweaves with the diaspora of French Canadians. In 1990, one-third as many Americans (668,000) reported to the U.S. Census Bureau as "Acadian/Cajun" as did Americans reporting "French Canadian" (2,167,000). Louisiana became the new Acadian homeland and "creolized," or formed a cultural and ethnic hybrid, as cultures mixed. French settlers in Louisiana adapted to the subtropics. Local Indians taught them, as did the slaves brought from Africa by settlers to work their plantations. When French settlers raised a generation of sons and daughters who grew up knowing the ways of the region—

unlike the immigrants—Louisianans called these native-born, locally adapted people "Creoles." Louisianans similarly categorized slaves—those born locally were also "Creoles." By the time the Acadians arrived, Creoles had established themselves economically and socially.

French Creoles dominated Louisiana, even after Spain officially took over the colony in the mid-eighteenth century and some Spanish settled there. Louisiana also absorbed immigrants from Germany, England, and New England, in addition to those from Acadia. Spanish administrators welcomed the Acadians to Louisiana. Their large families increased the colony's population and they could serve the capital, New Orleans, as a supplier of produce. The Spanish expected the Acadians, who were generally poor, small-scale farmers who tended to keep to themselves, not to resist their administration.

At first, Spanish administrators regulated Acadians toward the fringes of Louisiana's non-Indian settlement. As Louisiana grew, some

Cajuns were pushed and some voluntarily moved with the frontier. Beginning in 1764, Cajun settlements spread above New Orleans in undeveloped regions along the Mississippi River. This area later became known as the Acadian coast. Cajun settlements spread upriver, then down the Bayou Lafourche, then along other rivers and bayous. People settled along the waterways in lines, as they had done in Acadia/Nova Scotia. Their houses sat on narrow plots of land that extended from the riverbank into the swamps. The settlers boated from house to house, and later built a road parallel to the bayou, extending the levees as long as 150 miles. The settlement also spread to the prairies, swamps, and the Gulf Coast.

### INTERNAL MIGRATION

Soon after the Louisiana Purchase, the Creoles pushed many Acadians westward, off the prime farmland of the Mississippi levees, mainly by buying their lands. Besides wanting the land, many Creole sugar-planters wanted the Cajuns to leave the vicinity so that the slaves on their plantations would not see Cajun examples of freedom and self-support.

After the Cajuns had reconsolidated their society, a second exodus, on a much smaller scale, spread the Cajuns culturally and geographically. For example, a few Acadians joined wealthy Creoles as owners of plantations, rejecting their Cajun identity for one with higher social standing. Although some Cajuns stayed on the rivers and bayous or in the swamps, many others headed west to the prairies where they settled not in lines but in small, dispersed coves. As early as 1780, Cajuns headed westward into frontier lands and befriended Indians whom others feared. By the end of the nineteenth century, Cajuns had established settlements in the Louisiana-Texas border region. Texans refer to the triangle of the Acadian colonies of Beaumont, Port Arthur, and Orange as Cajun Lapland because that is where Louisiana "laps over" into Texas.

Heading westward, Cajuns first reached the eastern, then the western prairie. In the first region, densely settled by Cajuns, farmers grew corn and cotton. On the western prairie, farmers grew rice and ranchers raised cattle. This second region was thinly settled until the late 1800s when the railroad companies lured Midwesterners to the Louisiana prairies to grow rice. The arrival of Midwesterners again displaced many Cajuns; however, some remained on the prairies in clusters of small farms. A third region of Cajun settlement, to the south of the prairies and their waterways, were the coastal wetlands—one of the most distinctive regions in North America and one central to the Cajun image. The culture and seafood cuisine of these Cajuns has represented Cajuns to the world.

### CAMPS

Life for Cajuns in swamps, which periodically flood, demanded adaptations such as building houses on stilts. When floods wrecked their houses, Cajuns rebuilt them. In the late 1800s, Cajun swamp dwellers began to build and live on houseboats. Currently, mobile homes with additions and large porches stand on stilts ten feet above the swamps. Cajuns and other Louisianans also established and maintained camps for temporary housing in marshes, swamps, and woods. For the Acadians, many of whom were hunters and trappers, this was a strong tradition. At first, a camp was only a temporary dwelling in order to make money. Eventually, Cajuns did not need to live in camps, because they could commute daily from home by car or powerboat. By that time, however, Cajuns enjoyed and appreciated their camps. As settlements grew, so did the desire to get away to hunt and fish; today, many Cajun families maintain a camp for recreation purposes.

# ACCULTURATION AND ASSIMILATION

Cajuns have always been considered a marginal group, a minority culture. Language, culture, and kinship patterns have kept them separate, and they have maintained their sense of group identity despite difficulties. Cajun settlement patterns have isolated them and Cajun French has tended to keep its speakers out of the English-speaking mainstream.

Acadians brought a solidarity with them to Louisiana. As one of the first groups to cross the Atlantic and adopt a new identity, they felt connected to each other by their common experience. Differences in backgrounds separated the Acadians from those who were more established Americans. Creole Louisianans, with years of established communities in Louisiana, often looked down on Acadians as peasants. Some

Cajuns left their rural Cajun communities and found acceptance, either as Cajuns or by passing as some other ethnicity. Some Cajuns became gentleman planters, repudiated their origins, and joined the upper-class (white) Creoles. Others learned the ways of local Indians, as Creoles before them had done, and as the Cajuns themselves had done earlier in Acadia/Nova Scotia.

Because Cajuns usually married among themselves, as a group they do not have many surnames; however, the original population of Acadian exiles in Louisiana grew, especially by incorporating other people into their group. Colonists of Spanish, German, and Italian origins, as well as Americans of English-Scotch-Irish stock, became thoroughly acculturated and today claim Acadian descent. Black Creoles and white Cajuns mingled their bloodlines and cultures; more recently, Louisiana Cajuns include Yugoslavs and Filipinos.

Economics helped Cajuns stay somewhat separate. The majority of Cajuns farmed, hunted, and/or fished; their livelihoods hardly required them to assimilate. Moreover, until the beginning of the twentieth century, U.S. corporate culture had relatively little impact on southern Louisiana. The majority of Cajuns did not begin to Americanize until the turn of the twentieth century, when several factors combined to quicken the pace. These factors included the nationalistic fervor of the early 1900s, followed by World War I. Perhaps the most substantial change for Cajuns occurred when big business came to extract and sell southern Louisiana's oil. The discovery of oil in 1901 in Jennings, Louisiana, brought in outsiders and created salaried jobs. Although the oil industry is the region's main employer, it is also a source of economic and ecological concern because it represents the region's main polluter, threatening fragile ecosystems and finite resources.

Although the speaking of Cajun French has been crucial to the survival of Cajun traditions, it has also represented resistance to assimilation. Whereas Cajuns in the oilfields spoke French to each other at work (and still do), Cajuns in public schools were forced to abandon French because the compulsory Education Act of 1922 banned the speaking of any other language but English at school or on school grounds. While some teachers labeled Cajun French as a low-class and ignorant mode of speech, other Louisianans ridiculed the Cajuns as uneducable. As late as 1939, reports called the Cajuns "North America's last unassimi-

lated [white] minority;" Cajuns referred to themselves, even as late as World War II, as "*le français*," and all English-speaking outsiders as "*les Americains*."

The 1930s and 1940s witnessed the education and acculturation of Cajuns into the American mainstream. Other factors affecting the assimilation of the Cajuns were the improvement of transportation, the leveling effects of the Great Depression, and the development of radio and motion pictures, which introduced young Cajuns to other cultures. Yet Cajun culture survived and resurged. After World War II, Cajun culture boomed as soldiers returned home and danced to Cajun bands, thereby renewing Cajun identity. Cajuns rallied around their traditional music in the 1950s, and in the 1960s this music gained attention and acceptance from the American mainstream. On the whole, though, the 1950s and 1960s were times of further mainstreaming for the Cajuns. As network television and other mass media came to dominate American culture, the nation's regional, ethnic cultures began to weaken. Since the 1970s, Cajuns have exhibited renewed pride in their heritage and consider themselves a national resource. By the 1980s, ethnicities first marginalized by the American mainstream became valuable as regional flavors, however, while Cajuns may be proud of the place that versions of their music and food occupy in the mainstream, they—especially the swamp Cajuns—are also proud of their physical and social marginality.

### TRADITIONS, CUSTOMS, AND BELIEFS

Cajun society closely knits family members and neighbors who tend to depend on each other socially and economically, and this cooperation helps to maintain their culture. According to *Cajun Country*, "The survival—indeed the domination—of Acadian culture was a direct result of the strength of traditional social institutions and agricultural practices that promoted economic self-sufficiency and group solidarity." Cajuns developed customs to bring themselves together. For example, before roads, people visited by boat; before electrical amplification and telephones, people sang loudly in large halls, and passed news by shouting from house to house. And when Cajuns follow their customs, their culture focuses inwardly on the group and maintains itself.

Cajuns maintain distinctive values that predate the industrial age. Foremost among these, perhaps, is a traditional rejection of protocols of social hierarchy. When speaking Cajun French, for instance, Cajuns use the French familiar form of address, *tu*, rather than *vous* (except in jest) and do not address anyone as *monsieur*. Their *joie de vivre* is legendary (manifested in spicy food and lively dancing), as is their combativeness. Cajun traditions help make Cajuns formidable, mobile adversaries when fighting, trapping, hunting, or fishing. Cajun boaters invented a flatboat called the *bateau*, to pass through shallow swamps. They also built European-style luggers and skiffs, and the *pirogue*, based on Indian dugout canoes. Cajuns often race *pirogues*; or, two competitors stand at opposite ends on one and try to make each other fall in the water first. Fishermen hold their own competitions, sometimes called "fishing rodeos."

Cajuns value horses, too. American cowboy culture itself evolved partly out of one of its earliest ranching frontiers on Louisiana's Cajun prairies. Cajun ranchers developed a tradition called the barrel or buddy pickup, which evolved into a rodeo event. Today, Cajuns enjoy horse racing, trail-riding clubs, and Mardi Gras processions, called *courses*, on horseback.

Cajuns also enjoy telling stories and jokes during their abundant socializing. White Cajuns have many folktales in common with black Creoles—for example, stories about buried treasure abound in Louisiana. One reason for this proliferation was Louisiana's early and close ties to the Caribbean where piracy was rampant. Also, many people actually did bury treasure in Louisiana to keep it from banks or, during the Civil War, from invading Yankees. Typically, the stories describe buried treasure guarded by ghosts. Cajuns relish telling stories about moonshiners, smugglers, and contraband runners who successfully fool and evade federal agents.

Many Cajun beliefs fall into the mainstream's category of superstition, such as spells (*gris-gris*, to both Cajuns and Creoles) and faith healing. In legends, Madame Grandsdoigts uses her long fingers to pull the toes of naughty children at night, and the werewolf, known as *loup garou*, prowls. Omens appear in the form of blackbirds, cows, and the moon. For example, according to *Cajun Country:* "When the tips of a crescent moon point upward, [the weather] is supposed to be dry for a week. A halo of light around a full moon supposedly means clear weather for as many days as there are stars visible inside the ring."

## CUISINE

Cajun cuisine, perhaps best known for its hot, red-pepper seasoning, is a blend of styles. Acadians brought with them provincial cooking styles from France. Availability of ingredients determined much of Cajun cuisine. Frontier Cajuns borrowed or invented recipes for cooking turtle, alligator, raccoon, possum, and armadillo, which some people still eat. Louisianans' basic ingredients of bean and rice dishes—milled rice, dried beans, and cured ham or smoked sausage—were easy to store over relatively long periods. Beans and rice, like gumbo and crawfish, have become fashionable cuisine in recent times. They are still often served with cornbread, thus duplicating typical nineteenth-century poor Southern fare. Cajun cooking is influenced by the cuisine of the French, Acadian, Spanish, German, Anglo-American, Afro-Caribbean, and Native American cultures.

Gumbo, a main Cajun dish, is a prime metaphor for creolization because it draws from several cultures. Its main ingredient, okra, also gave the dish its name; the vegetable, called *"guingombo,"* was first imported from western Africa. Cayenne, a spicy seasoning used in subtropical cuisines, represents Spanish and Afro-Caribbean influences. Today Louisianans who eat gumbo with rice, usually call gumbo made with okra *gumbo févi*, to distinguish it from *gumbo filé*, which draws on French culinary tradition for its base, a *roux*. Just before serving, *gumbo filé* (also called *filé gumbo*) is thickened by the addition of powdered sassafras leaves, one of the Native American contributions to Louisiana cooking.

Cajuns thriftily ate many animals and parts of animals. *Gratons*, also known as cracklings, were made of pig skin. Internal organs were used in the sausages and *boudin*. White *boudin* is a spicy rice and pork sausage; red *boudin*, which is made from the same rice dressing but is flavored and colored with blood, can still be found in neighborhood *boucheries*. Edible pig guts not made into *boudin* were cooked in a *sauce piquante de débris* or entrail stew. The intestines were cleaned and used for sausage casings. Meat was carefully removed from the head and congealed for a spicy *fromage de tête de cochon* (hogshead cheese). Brains were cooked in a pungent brown sauce. Other Cajun specialties include *tasso*, a spicy Cajun version of jerky, smoked beef and pork sausages (such as *andouille* made from the large intestines), *chourice* (made from the small intestines), and *chaudin* (stuffed stomach).

Perhaps the most representative food of Cajun culture is crawfish, or mudbug. Its popularity is a relatively recent tradition. It was not until the mid-1950s, when commercial processing began to make crawfish readily available, that they gained popularity. They have retained a certain exotic aura, however, and locals like to play upon the revulsion of outsiders faced for the first time with the prospect of eating these delicious but unusual creatures by goading outsiders to suck the "head" (technically, the thorax). Like lobster, crawfish has become a valuable delicacy. The crawfish industry, a major economic force in southern Louisiana, exports internationally. However, nearly 85 percent of the annual crawfish harvest is consumed locally. Other versions of Cajun foods, such as pan-blackened fish and meats, have become ubiquitous. Chef Paul Prudhomme helped bring Cajun cuisine to national prominence.

Cooking is considered a performance, and invited guests often gather around the kitchen stove or around the barbecue pit (more recently, the butane grill) to observe the cooking and comment on it. Guests also help, tell jokes and stories, and sing songs at events such as outdoor crawfish, crab, and shrimp boils in the spring and summer, and indoor gumbos in winter.

## MUSIC

The history of Cajun music goes back to Acadia/Nova Scotia, and to France. Acadian exiles, who had no instruments such as those in Santo Domingo, danced to *reels à bouche*, wordless dance music made by only their voices at stopping places on their way to Louisiana. After they arrived in Louisiana, Anglo-American immigrants to Louisiana contributed new fiddle tunes and dances, such as reels, jigs, and hoedowns. Singers also translated English songs into French and made them their own. Accordi to *Cajun Country*, "Native Americans contributed a wailing, terraced singing style in which vocal lines descend progressively in steps." Moreover, Cajun music owes much to the music of black Creoles, who contributed to Cajun music as they developed their own similiar music, which became zydeco. Since the nineteenth century, Cajuns and black Creoles have performed together.

Not only the songs, but also the instruments constitute an intercultural gumbo. Traditional Cajun and Creole instruments are French fiddles, German accordians, Spanish guitars, and an

assortment of percussion instruments (triangles, washboards, and spoons), which share European and Afro-Caribbean origins. German American Jewish merchants imported diatonic accordians (shortly after they were invented in Austria early in the nineteenth century), which soon took over the lead instrumental role from the violin. Cajuns improvised and improved the instruments first by bending rake tines, replacing rasps and notched gourds used in Afro-Caribbean music with washboards, and eventually producing their own masterful accordians.

During the rise of the record industry, to sell record players in southern Louisiana, companies released records of Cajun music. Its high-pitched and emotionally charged style of singing, which evolved so that the noise of frontier dance halls could be pierced, filled the airwaves. Cajun music influenced hillbilly/country music; moreover, for a period, Harry Choates' string band defined Western swing music. Beginning in 1948, Iry Lejeune recorded country music and renditions of Amée Ardoin's Creole blues, which Ardoin recorded in the late 1920s. Lejeune prompted "a new wave of old music" and a postwar revival of Cajun culture. Southern Louisiana's music influenced Hank Williams—whose own music, in turn, has been extremely influential. "Jambalaya" was one of his most successful recordings and was based on a lively but unassuming Cajun two-step called "Grand Texas" or "L'Anse Couche-Couche." In the 1950s, "swamp pop" developed as essentially Cajun rhythm and blues or rock and roll. In the 1960s, national organizations began to try to preserve traditional Cajun music.

## HOLIDAYS

Mardi Gras, which occurs on the day before Ash Wednesday, the beginning of Lent, is the carnival that precedes Lent's denial. French for "Fat Tuesday," Mardi Gras (pre-Christian Europe's New Year's Eve) is based on medieval European adaptations of even older rituals, particularly those including reversals of the social order, in which the lower classes parody the elite. Men dress as women, women as men; the poor dress as rich, the rich as poor; the old as young, the young as old; black as white, white as black.

While most Americans know Mardi Gras as the city of New Orleans celebrates it, rural Cajun Mardi Gras stems from a medieval European procession in which revelers traveled through the countryside performing in exchange for gifts. Those in a Cajun procession, called a *course* (which traditionally did not openly include women), masquerade across lines of gender, age, race, and class. They also play at crossing the line of life and death with a ritual skit, "The Dead Man Revived," in which the companions of a fallen actor revive him by dripping wine or beer into his mouth. Participants in a Cajun Mardi Gras *course* cross from house to house, storming into the yard in a mock-pillage of the inhabitant's food. Like a trick-or-treat gang, they travel from house to house and customarily get a series of chickens, from which their cooks will make a communal gumbo that night. The celebration continues as a rite of passage in many communities.

Carnival, as celebrated by Afro-Caribbeans (and as a ritual of ethnic impersonation whereby Euro- and Afro-Caribbean Americans in New Orleans chant, sing, dance, name themselves, and dress as Indians), also influences Carnival as celebrated in southern Louisiana. On one hand, the mainstream Mardi Gras celebration retains some Cajun folkloric elements, but the influence of New Orleans invariably supplants the country customs. Conversely, Mardi Gras of white, rural Cajuns differs in its geographic origins from Mardi Gras of Creole New Orleans; some organizers of Cajun Mardi Gras attempt to maintain its cultural specificity.

Cajun Mardi Gras participants traditionally wear masks, the anonymity of which enables the wearers to cross social boundaries; at one time, masks also provided an opportunity for retaliation without punishment. *Course* riders, who may be accompanied by musicians riding in their own vehicle, might surround a person's front yard, dismount and begin a ritualistic song and dance. The silent penitence of Lent, however, follows the boisterous transgression of Mardi Gras. A masked ball, as described in *Cajun Country*, "marks the final hours of revelry before the beginning of Lent the next day. All festivities stop abruptly at midnight, and many of Tuesday's rowdiest riders can be found on their knees receiving the penitential ashes on their foreheads on Wednesday."

Good Friday, which signals the approaching end of Lent, is celebrated with a traditional procession called "Way of the Cross" between the towns of Catahoula and St. Martinville. The stations of the cross, which usually hang on the walls of a church, are mounted on large oak trees between the two towns.

On Christmas Eve, bonfires dot the levees along the Mississippi River between New Orleans and Baton Rouge. This celebration, according to *Cajun Country*, has European roots: "The huge bonfires ... are descendants of the bonfires lit by ancient European civilizations, particularly along the Rhine and Seine rivers, to encourage and reinforce the sun at the winter solstice, its 'weakest' moment." Other holidays are uniquely Cajun and reflect the Catholic church's involvement in harvests. Priests bless the fields of sugar cane and the fleets of decorated shrimp boats by reciting prayers and sprinkling holy water upon them.

## HEALTH AND MENTAL HEALTH ISSUES

Professional doctors were rare in rural Louisiana and only the most serious of conditions were treated by them. Although the expense of professional medical care was prohibitive even when it was available, rural Cajuns preferred to use folk cures and administered them themselves, or relied on someone adept at such cures. These healers, who did not make their living from curing other Cajuns, were called *traiteurs*, or treaters, and were found in every community. They also believed that folk practitioners, unlike their professional counterparts, dealt with the spiritual and emotional—not just the physiological—needs of the individual. Each *traiteur* typically specializes in only a few types of treatment and has his or her own cures, which may involve the laying-on of hands or making the sign of the cross and reciting of prayers drawn from passages of the Bible. Of their practices—some of which have been legitimated today as holistic medicine—some are pre-Christian, some Christian, and some modern. Residual pre-Christian traditions include roles of the full moon in healing, and left-handedness of the treaters themselves. Christian components of Cajun healing draw on faith by making use of Catholic prayers, candles, prayer beads, and crosses. Cajuns' herbal medicine derives from post-medieval French homeopathic medicine. A more recent category of Cajun cures consists of patent medicines and certain other commercial products.

Some Cajun cures were learned from Indians, such as the application of a poultice of chewing tobacco on bee stings, snakebites, boils, and headaches. Other cures came from French doctors or folk cures, such as treating stomach pains by putting a warm plate on the stomach, treating ringworm with vinegar, and treating headaches with a treater's prayers. Some Cajun cures are unique to Louisiana: for example, holding an infection over a burning cane reed, or putting a necklace of garlic on a baby with worms.

Cajuns have a higher-than-average incidence of cystic fibrosis, muscular dystrophy, albinism, and other inherited, recessive disorders, perhaps due to intermarriage with relatives who have recessive genes in common.

# LANGUAGE

Cajun French, for the most part, is a spoken, unwritten language filled with colloquialisms and slang. Although the French spoken by Cajuns in different parts of Louisiana varies little, it differs from the standard French of Paris as well as the French of Quebec; it also differs from the French of both white and black Creoles.

Cajun French-speakers hold their lips more loosely than do the Parisians. They tend to shorten phrases, words, and names, and to simplify some verb conjugations. Nicknames are ubiquitous, such as "'*tit* joe" or "'*tit* black," where "'*tit*" is slang for "*petite*" or "little." Cajun French simplifies the tenses of verbs by making them more regular. It forms the present participle of verbs—e.g., "is singing"—in a way that would translate directly as "is after to sing." So, "Marie is singing," in Cajun French is "*Marie est apres chanter*." Another

distinguishing feature of Cajun French is that it retains nautical usages, which reflects the history of Acadians as boaters. For example, the word for tying a shoelace is *amerrer* (to moor [a boat]), and the phrase for making a U-turn in a car is *virer de bord* (to come about [with a sailboat]).

Generally, Cajun French shows the influence of its specific history in Louisiana and Acadia/Nova Scotia, as well as its roots in coastal France. Since Brittany, in northern coastal France, is heavily Celtic, Cajun French bears "grammatical and other linguistic evidences of Celtic influence." Some scattered Indian words survive in Cajun French, such as "bayou," which came from the Muskhogean Indian word, "*bay-uk*," through Cajun French, and into English.

Louisiana, which had already made school attendance compulsory, implemented a law in the 1920s that constitutionally forbade the speaking of French in public schools and on school grounds. The state expected Cajuns to come to school and to leave their language at home. This attempt to assimilate the Cajuns met with some success; young Cajuns appeared to be losing their language. In an attempt to redress this situation, the Council for the Development of French in Louisiana (CODOFIL) recently reintroduced French into many Louisianan schools. However, the French is the standard French of Parisians, not that of Cajuns. Although French is generally not spoken by the younger generation in Maine, New England schools are beginning to emphasize it and efforts to repeal the law that made English the sole language in Maine schools have been successful. In addition, secondary schools have begun to offer classes in Acadian and French history.

In 1976, Revon Reed wrote in a mix of Cajun and standard French for his book about Cajun Louisiana, *Lâche pas la patate*, which translates as, "Don't drop the potato" (a Cajun idiom for "Don't neglect to pass on the tradition"). Anthologies of stories and series of other writings have been published in the wake of Reed's book. However, Cajun French was essentially a spoken language until the publication of Randall What-ley's Cajun French textbook (*Conversational Cajun French I* [Baton Rouge: Louisiana State University Press, 1978]).

In the oilfields, on fishing boats, and other places where Cajuns work together, though, they have continued to speak Cajun French. Story-tellers, joke tellers, and singers use Cajun French for its expressiveness, and for its value as in-group communication. Cajun politicians and businessmen find it useful to identify themselves as fellow insiders to Cajun constituents and patrons by speaking their language.

# FAMILY AND COMMUNITY DYNAMICS

Cajuns learned to rely on their families and communities when they had little else. Traditionally they have lived close to their families and villages. Daily visits were usual, as were frequent parties and dances, including the traditional Cajun house-party called the *fais-dodo*, which is Cajun baby talk for "go to sleep," as in "put all the small kids in a back bedroom to sleep" during the party. Traditionally, almost everyone who would come to a party would be a neighbor from the same community or a family member. Cajuns of all ages and abilities participated in music-making and dancing since almost everyone was a dancer or a player.

In the 1970s, 76 percent of the surnames accounted for 86 percent of all Cajuns; each of those surnames reflected an extended family which functioned historically as a Cajun subcommunity. In addition to socializing together, a community gathered to do a job for someone in need, such as building a house or harvesting a field. Members of Cajun communities traditionally took turns butchering animals and distributing shares of the meat. Although *boucheries* were essentially social events, they were a useful way to get fresh meat to participating families. Today, *boucheries* are unnecessary because of modern refrigeration methods and the advent of supermarkets, but a few families still hold *boucheries* for the fun of it, and a few local festivals feature *boucheries* as a folk craft. This cooperation, called *coups de main* (literally, "strokes of the hand"), was especially crucial in the era before worker's compensation, welfare, social security, and the like. Today such cooperation is still important, notably for the way it binds together members of a community.

A challenge to a group's cohesiveness, however, was infighting. Fighting could divide a community, yet, on the other hand, as a spectator sport, it brought communities together for an activity. The *bataille au mouchoir*, as described in *Cajun Country*, was a ritualized fight "in which the challenger offered his opponent a corner of his handkerchief and the two went at each other with fists or knives, each holding a corner, until one gave up." Organized bare-knuckle fights persisted at least until the late 1960s. More recently, many Cajuns have joined boxing teams. Neighboring communities maintain rivalries in which violence has historically been common. A practice called *casser le bal* ("breaking up the dance") or *prendre la place* ("taking over the place") involved gangs starting fights with others or among themselves with the purpose of ending a dance. Threats of violence and other difficulties of travel hardly kept Cajuns at home, though. According to *Cajun Country*, "As late as 1932, Saturday night dances were attended by families within a radius of fifty miles, despite the fact that less than a third of the families owned automobiles at that time."

Cajun family relations are important to all family members. Cajun fathers, uncles, and grandfathers join mothers, aunts, and grandmothers in raising children; and children participate in family matters. Godfathering and godmothering are still very important in Cajun country. Even non-French-speaking youth usually refer to their godparents as *parrain* and *marraine*, and consider them family. Nevertheless, traditionally it has been the mother who has transmitted values and culture to the children. Cajuns have often devalued formal education, viewing it as a function of the Catholic church—not the state. Families needed children's labor; and, until the oil boom, few jobs awaited educated Cajuns. During the 1920s many Cajuns attended school not only because law required it and jobs awaited them, but also because an agricultural slump meant that farming was less successful then.

## COURTSHIP

Although today Cajuns tend to date like other Americans, historically, pre-modern traditions were the rule. Females usually married before the age of 20 or risked being considered "an old maid." A young girl required a chaperon—usually a parent or an older brother or uncle, to protect her honor and prevent premarital pregnancy, which could result in banishment until her marriage. If a courtship seemed to be indefinitely prolonged, the suitor might receive an envelope from his intended containing a coat, which signified that the engagement was over. Proposals were formally made on Thursday evenings to the parents, rather than to the fiancee herself. Couples who wanted to marry did not make the final decision; rather, this often required the approval of the entire extended family.

Because Cajuns traditionally marry within their own community where a high proportion of residents are related to one another, marriages between cousins are not unusual. Pairs of siblings frequently married pairs of siblings from another family. Although technically forbidden, first-cousin marriages have occurred as well. Financial concerns influenced such a choice because intermarriage kept property within family groupings. One result of such marriages is that a single town might be dominated by a handful of surnames.

## WEDDINGS

Cajun marriage customs are frequently similar to those of other Europeans. Customarily, older unmarried siblings may be required to dance barefoot, often in a tub, at the reception or wedding dance. This may be to remind them of the poverty awaiting them in old age if they do not begin families of their own. Guests contribute to the new household by pinning money to the bride's veil in exchange for a dance with her or a kiss. Before the wedding dance is over, the bride will often be wearing a headdress of money. Today, wedding guests have extended this practice to the groom as well, covering his suit jacket with bills.

One rural custom involved holding the wedding reception in a commercial dance hall and giving the entrance fees to the newlyweds. Another Cajun wedding custom, "flocking the bride," involved the community's women bringing a young chick from each of their flocks so that the new bride could start her own brood. These gifts helped a bride establish a small measure of independence, in that wives could could sell their surplus eggs for extra money over which their husbands had no control.

## RELIGION

Roman Catholicism is a major element of Cajun culture and history. Some pre-Christian traditions seem to influence or reside in Cajun Catholicism. Historians partly account for Cajun Catholicism's variation from Rome's edicts by noting that historically Acadians often lacked contact with orthodox clergymen.

Baptism of Cajun children occurs in infancy. Cajun homes often feature altars, or shrines with lawn statues, such as those of Our Lady of the Assumption—whom Pope Pius XI in 1938 declared the patroness of Acadians worldwide—

in homemade grottoes made of pieces of bathtubs or oil drums. Some Cajun communal customs also revolve around Catholicism. For decades, it was customary for men to race their horses around the church during the sermon. Wakes call for mourners to keep company with each other around the deceased so that the body is never left alone. Restaurants and school cafeterias cater to Cajuns by providing alternatives to meat for south Louisiana's predominantly Catholic students during Ash Wednesday and Lenten Fridays. Some uniquely Cajun beliefs surround their Catholicism. For example, legends say that "the Virgin will slap children who whistle at the dinner table;" another taboo forbids any digging on Good Friday, which is, on the other hand, believed to be the best day to plant parsley.

## EMPLOYMENT AND ECONOMIC TRADITIONS

Coastal Louisiana is home to one of America's most extensive wetlands in which trapping and hunting have been important occupations. In the 1910s extensive alligator hunting allowed huge increases in *rat musqué* (muskrat) populations. Muskrat overgrazing promoted marsh erosion. At first the muskrats were trapped mainly to reduce their numbers, but cheap Louisiana muskrat pelts hastened New York's capture of America's fur industry from St. Louis, and spurred the rage for muskrat and raccoon coats that typified the 1920s. Cajuns helped Louisiana achieve its long-standing reputation as America's primary fur producer. Since the 1960s, Cajuns in the fur business have raised mostly nutria.

The original Acadians and Cajuns were farmers, herders, and ranchers, but they also worked as carpenters, coopers, blacksmiths, fishermen, shipbuilders, trappers, and sealers. They learned trapping, trading, and other skills for survival from regional Indians. Industrialization has not ended such traditions. Workers in oilfields and on oil rigs have schedules whereby they work for one or two weeks and are then off work for the same amount of time, which allows them time to pursue traditional occupations like trapping and fishing.

Because present-day laws ban commercial hunting, this activity has remained a recreation, but an intensely popular one. Louisiana is located at the southern end of one of the world's major flyways, providing an abundance of migratory birds like dove, woodcock, and a wide variety of ducks and geese. A wide range of folk practice is associated with hunting—how to build blinds, how to call game, how to handle, call and drive packs of hunting dogs, and how to make decoys. Cajun custom holds that if you hunt or fish a certain area, you have the clear-cut folk right to defend it from trespassers. Shooting a trespasser is "trapper's justice." Certain animals are always illegal to hunt, and some others are illegal to hunt during their off-season. Cajuns sometimes circumvent restrictions on hunting illegal game, which is a practice called "outlawing."

According to some claims, the modern American cattle industry began on the Cajun prairie almost a full century before Anglo-Americans even began to move to Texas. Learning from the Spanish and the Indians, Cajuns and black Creoles were among the first cowboys in America, and they took part in some of this country's earliest cattle drives. Cattle rearing remains part of prairie Cajun life today, but the spread of agriculture, especially rice, has reduced both its economic importance and much of its flamboyant ways. In the nonagricultural coastal marshes, however, much of the old-style of cattle rearing remains.

Cajuns catch a large proportion of American seafood. In addition to catching their own food, many Cajuns are employees of shrimp companies, which own both boats and factories, with their own brand name. Some fisherman and froggers catch large catfish, turtles, and bullfrogs by hand, thus preserving an ancient art. And families frequently go crawfishing together in the spring.

The gathering and curing of Spanish moss, which was widely employed for stuffing of mattresses and automobile seats until after World War II, was an industry found only in the area. Cajun fishermen invented or modified numerous devices: nets and seines, crab traps, shrimp boxes, bait boxes, trotlines, and frog grabs. Moss picking, once an important part-time occupation for many wetlands Cajuns, faded with the loss of the natural resource and changes in technology. Dried moss was replaced by synthetic materials used in stuffing car seats and furniture. Now there is a mild resurgence in the tradition as moss is making a comeback from the virus which once threatened it and as catfish and crawfish farmers have found that it makes a perfect breeding nest.

Cajuns learned to be economically self-reliant, if not completely self-sufficient. They learned many of southern Louisiana's ways from local Indians, who taught them about native edible foods and the cultivation of a variety of melons, gourds, and root crops. The French and black Creoles taught the Cajuns how to grow cotton, sugarcane, and okra; they learned rice and soybean production from Anglo-Americans. As a result, Cajuns were able to establish small farms and produce an array of various vegetables and livestock. Such crops also provided the cash they needed to buy such items as coffee, flour, salt, and tobacco, in addition to cloth and farming tools. A result of such Cajun agricultural success is that today Cajuns and Creoles alike still earn their livelihood by farming.

Cajuns traded with whomever they wanted to trade, regardless of legal restrictions. Soon after their arrival in Louisiana, they were directed by the administration to sell their excess crops to the government. Many Cajuns became bootleggers. One of their proudest historical roles was assisting the pirate-smuggler Jean Lafitte in an early and successful smuggling operation.

In the twentieth century, the Cajuns' trading system has declined as many Cajuns work for wages in the oil industry. In the view of some Cajuns, moreover, outside oilmen from Texas—or "Takes-us"—have been depriving them of control over their own region's resource, by taking it literally out from under them and reaping the profits. Some Cajun traders have capitalized on economic change by selling what resources they can control to outside markets: for example, fur trappers have done so, as have fishermen, and farmers such as those who sell their rice to the Budweiser brewery in Houston.

# POLITICS AND GOVERNMENT

Cajuns, many of whom are conservative Democrats today, have been involved at all levels of Louisiana politics. Louisiana's first elected governor, as well as the state's first Cajun governor, was Alexander Mouton, who took office in 1843. Yet perhaps the most well known of Louisiana's politicians is Cajun governor Edwin Edwards (1927-), who has served for more than ten years in that office—the first French-speaking Catholic to do so in almost half a century. In recent decades, more Cajuns have entered electoral politics to regain some control from powerful oil companies.

## MILITARY

Historically, Cajuns have been drafted and named for symbolic roles in pivotal fights over North America. In the mid-1700s in Acadia/Nova Scotia, when the French colonial army drafted Acadians, they weakened the Acadians' identity to the British as "French Neutrals," and prompted the British to try to expel all Acadians from the region. In 1778, when France joined the American Revolutionary War against the British, the Marquis de Lafayette declared that the plight of the Acadians helped bring the French into the fight. The following year, 600 Cajun volunteers joined Galvez and fought the British. In 1815, Cajuns joined Andrew Jackson in preventing the British from retaking the United States. Cajuns were also active in the American Civil War; General Alfred Mouton (1829-1864), the son of Alexander Mouton, commanded the Eighteenth Louisiana Regiment in the Battle of Pittsburgh Landing (1862), the Battle of Shiloh (1863), and the Battle of Mansfield (1864), where he was killed by a sniper's bullet.

# INDIVIDUAL AND GROUP CONTRIBUTIONS

## ACADEMIA

Thomas J. Arceneaux, who was Dean Emeritus of the College of Agriculture at the University of Southwestern Louisiana, conducted extensive research in weed control, training numerous Cajun rice and cattle farmers in the process. A descendent of Louis Arceneaux, who was the model for the hero in Longfellow's *Evangeline*, Arceneaux also designed the Louisiana Cajun flag. Tulane University of Louisiana professor Alcé Fortier was Louisiana's first folklore scholar and one of the founders of the American Folklore Society (AFS). Author of *Lâche pas la patate* (1976), a book describing Cajun Louisiana life, Revon Reed has also launched a small Cajun newspaper called *Mamou Prairie*.

## ART

Lulu Olivier's traveling "Acadian Exhibit" of Cajun weaving led to the founding of the Council for the Development of French in Louisiana (CODOFIL), and generally fostered Cajun cultural pride.

## CULINARY ARTS

Chef Paul Prudhomme's name graces a line of Cajun-style supermarket food, "Chef Paul's."

## MUSIC

Dewey Balfa (1927- ), Gladius Thibodeaux, and Louis Vinesse Lejeune performed at the 1964 Newport Folk Festival and inspired a renewed pride in Cajun music. Dennis McGee performed and recorded regularly with black Creole accordionist and singer Amédé Ardoin in the 1920s and 1930s; together they improvised much of what was to become the core repertoire of Cajun music.

## SPORTS

Cajun jockeys Kent Desormeaux and Eddie Delahoussaye became famous, as did Ron Guidry, the fastballer who led the New York Yankees to win the 1978 World Series, and that year won the Cy Young Award for his pitching. Guidry's nicknames were "Louisiana Lightnin'" and "The Ragin' Cajun."

# MEDIA

## PRINT

### Acadiana Catholic.
Formerly *The Morning Star*, it was founded in 1954 and is primarily a religious monthly.

**Contact:** Barbara Gutierrez, Editor.
**Address:** 1408 Carmel Avenue, Lafayette, Louisiana 70501-5215.
**Telephone:** (318) 261-5511.
**Fax:** (318) 261-5603.

### Acadian Genealogy Exchange.
Devoted to Acadians, French Canadian families sent into exile in 1755. Carries family genealogies, historical notes, cemetery lists, census records, and church and civil registers. Recurring features include inquiries and answers, book reviews, and news of research.

**Contact:** Janet B. Jehn.
**Address:** 863 Wayman Branch Road, Covington, Kentucky 41015.
**Telephone:** (606) 356-9825.

### Acadiana Profile.
Published by the Acadian News Agency since 1969, this is a magazine for bilingual Louisiana.

**Contact:** Trent Angers, Editor.
**Address:** Acadian News Agency, Inc., Box 52247, Oil Center Station, Lafayette, Louisiana 70505.
**Telephone:** (800) 200-7919.

### Cajun Country Guide.
Covers Cajun and Zydeco dance halls, Creole and Caju restaurants, swamp tours, and other sites in the southern Louisiana region.

**Contact:** Macon Fry or Julie Posner, Editors.
**Address:** Pelican Publishing Co., 1101 Monroe Street, P.O. Box 3110, Gretna, Louisiana 70054.
**Telephone:** (504) 368-1175; or, (800) 843-1724.
**Fax:** (504) 368-1195.

### Mamou Acadian Press.
Founded in 1955, publishes weekly.

**Contact:** Bernice Ardoin, Editor.
**Address:** P.O. Box 360, Mamou, Louisiana 70554.
**Telephone:** (318) 363-3939.
**Fax:** (318) 363-2841.

### Rayne Acadian Tribune.
A newspaper with a Democratic orientation; founded in 1894.

**Contact:** Steven Bandy, Editor.
**Address:** 108 North Adams Avenue, P.O. Box 260, Rayne, Louisiana 70578.
**Telephone:** (318) 334-3186.
**Fax:** (318) 334-2069.

### The Times of Acadiana.
Weekly newspaper covering politics, lifestyle, entertainment, and general news; founded in 1980.

**Contact:** Richard Baudouin, Editor.
**Address:** 201 Jefferson Street, P.O. Box 3528, Lafayette, Louisiana 70502.
**Telephone:** (318) 237-3560.
**Fax:** (318) 233-7484.

## RADIO

### KAFB-FM (97.7).
This station, which has a country format, plays "Cajun and Zydeco Music" from 6:00 a.m. to 9:00 a.m. on Saturdays.

**Contact:** Johnny Bordelon, Station Manager.
**Address:** 100 Chester, Box 7, Marksville, Louisiana 71351.
**Telephone:** (318) 253-9331.

### KDLP-AM (1170).
Country, ethnic, and French-language format.

**Contact:** Paul J. Cook.
**Address:** 182 Pluto Street, Bayou Vista, Louisiana 70381.
**Telephone:** (504) 395-2853.

### KJEF-AM (1290), FM (92.9).
Country, ethnic, and French-language format.

**Contact:** Bill Bailey, General Manager.
**Address:** 122 North Market Street, Jennings, Louisiana 70545.
**Telephone:** (318) 824-2934.
**Fax:** (318) 824-1384.

### KQKI-FM (95.3).
Country, ethnic, and French-language format.

**Contact:** Paul J. Cook.
**Address:** 182 Pluto Street, Morgan City, Louisiana 70380.
**Telephone:** (504) 395-2853.
**Fax:** (504) 395-5094.

### KROF-AM (960).
Ethnic format.

**Contact:** Garland Bernard, General Manager.
**Address:** Highway 167 North, Box 610, Abbeville, Louisiana 70511-0610.
**Telephone:** (318) 893-2531.
**Fax:** (318) 893-2569.

### KVOL-AM (1330), FM (105.9).
Blues, ethnic format.

**Contact:** Roger Cavaness, General Manager.
**Address:** 123 East Main Street, Lafayette, Louisiana 70501.
**Telephone:** (318) 233-1330.
**Fax:** (318) 237-7733.

### KVPI-AM 1050.
Country, ethnic, and French-language format.

**Contact:** Jim Soileau, General Manager.
**Address:** 809 West LaSalle Street, P.O. Drawer J, Ville Platte, Louisiana 70586.
**Telephone:** (318) 363-2124.
**Fax:** (318) 363-3574.

# Organizations and Associations

**The Center for Acadian and Creole Folklore.**
Located at the University of Southwestern Louisiana (*Université des Acadiens*), the center organizes festivals, special performances, and television and radio programs; it offers classes and workshops through the French and Francophone Studies Program; it also sponsors musicians as adjunct professors at the university.

**The Council for the Development of French in Louisiana (CODOFIL).**
A proponent of the standard French language, this council arranges visits, exchanges, scholarships, and conferences; it also publishes a free bilingual newsletter.

**Address:** *Louisiane Française, Boite Postale* 3936, Lafayette, Louisiana 70502.

**The International Relations Association of Acadiana (TIRAA).**
This private-sector economic development group funds various French Renaissance activities in Cajun country.

**The Madawaska Historical Society.**
Promotes local historical projects and celebrates events important in the history of Acadians in Maine.

# Museums and Research Centers

Visitors can see preservations and reconstructions of many nineteenth-century buildings at the Acadian Village and Vermilionville in Lafayette; at the Louisiana State University, Rural Life Museum in Baton Rouge, and at the Village Historique Acadien at Caraquet.

Researchers can find sources at Nichols State University Library in Thibodaux; at the Center for Acadian and Creole Folklore of the University of Southwestern Louisiana; and at the Center for Louisiana Studies at the University of Southwestern Louisiana.

# Sources for Additional Study

Ancelet, Barry, Jay D. Edwards, and Glen Pitre (with additional material by Carl Brasseaux, Fred B. Kniffen, Maida Bergeron, Janet Shoemaker, and Mathe Allain). *Cajun Country.* Jackson: University of Mississippi Press, 1991.

Ancelet, Barry, and Elemore Morgan, Jr. *The Makers of Cajun Music.* Austin: University of Texas Press, 1984.

Brasseaux, Carl. *Founding of New Acadia, 1765-1803; In Search of Evangeline: Birth and Evolution of the Myth.* Thibodaux, Louisiana: Blue Heron Press, 1988.

*Cajuns: Essays on Their History and Culture,* edited by Glenn Conrad. Lafayette, Louisiana: Center for Louisiana Studies, University of Southwestern Louisiana, 1978.

Comeaux, Malcolm. *Attchafalaya Swamp Life: Settlement and Folk Occupations.* Baton Rouge: Louisiana State University, Geoscience Publications, 1972.

*The First Franco-Americans: New England Life Histories From the Federal Writers Project, 1938-1939,* edited by C. Stewart Doty. Orono: University of Maine at Orono Press, 1985.

Griffiths, Naomi Elizabeth Saundaus. *The Acadians: Creation of a People.* New York, McGraw-Hill Ryerson, 1973.

Hallowell, Christopher L. *People of the Bayou: Cajun Life in Lost America,* illustrations by Joe Deffes. New York: Dutton, 1979.

Reed, Revon Reed. *Lâche pas la patate.* Montreal: Parti Pris, 1976.

Rushton, William Faulkner. *The Cajuns: From Acadia to Louisiana.* New York: Farrar, Straus, Giroux, 1979.

About 70 percent of
blacks are making
progress in nearly
every aspect of
American life: the
black middle-class is
increasing, white-
collar employment is
on the rise, and
although the growth
of black political and
economic power is
slow, it remains
steady.

# AFRICAN AMERICANS

by
Barbara C. Bigelow

## OVERVIEW

The continent of Africa, the second largest on the globe, is bisected by the equator and bordered to the west by the Atlantic Ocean and to the east by the Indian Ocean. Roughly the shape of an inverted triangle—with a large bulge on its northwestern end and a small horn on its eastern tip—it contains 52 countries and six islands that, together, make up about 20 percent of the world's land mass, or 11.5 million square miles.

Africa is essentially a huge plateau divided naturally into two sections. Northern Africa, a culturally and historically Mediterranean region, includes the Sahara desert—the world's largest expanse of desert, coming close to the size of the United States. Sub-Saharan, or Black Africa, also contains some desert land, but is mainly tropical, with rain forests clustered around the equator; vast savanna grasslands covering more than 30 percent of continent and surrounding the rain forests on the north, east, and south; some mountainous regions; and rivers and lakes that formed from the natural uplifting of the plateau's surface.

Africa is known for the diversity of its people and languages. Its total population is approximately 600 million, making it the third most populous continent on earth. Countless ethnic groups inhabit the land: it is estimated that there are nearly 300 different ethnic groups in the West

African nation of Nigeria alone. Still, the peoples of Africa are generally united by a respect for tradition and a devotion to their community.

Most of the flags of African nations contain one or more of three significant colors: red, for the blood of African people; black, for the face of African people; and green, for hope and the history of the fatherland.

## HISTORY

Some historians consider ancient Africa the cradle of human civilization. In *Before the Mayflower*, Lerone Bennett, Jr., contends that "the African ancestors of American Blacks were among the major benefactors of the human race. Such evidence as survives clearly shows that Africans were on the scene and acting when the human drama opened."

Over the course of a dozen centuries, beginning around 300 A.D., a series of three major political states arose in Africa: Ghana, Mali, and Songhay. These agricultural and mining empires began as small kingdoms but eventually established great wealth and control throughout Western Africa.

African societies were marked by varying degrees of political, economic, and social advancement. "Wherever we observe the peoples of Africa," wrote John Hope Franklin in *From Slavery to Freedom*, "we find some sort of political organization, even among the so-called stateless. They were not all highly organized kingdoms—to be sure, some were simple, isolated family states—but they all ... [established] governments to solve the problems that every community encounters." Social stratification existed, with political power residing in a chief of state or a royal family, depending on the size of the state. People of lower social standing were respected as valued members of the community.

Agriculture has always been the basis of African economics. Some rural African peoples worked primarily as sheep, cattle, and poultry raisers, and African artisans maintained a steady trade in clothing, baskets, pottery, and metalware, but farming was a way of life for most Africans. Land in such societies belonged to the entire community, not to individuals, and small communities interacted with each other on a regular basis. "Africa was ... never a series of isolated self-sufficient communities," explained Franklin. Rather, tribes specialized in various economic endeavors, then traveled and traded their goods and crops with other tribes.

Slave trade in Africa dates back to the mid-fifteenth century. Ancient Africans were themselves slaveholders who regarded prisoners of war as sellable property, or chattel, of the head of a family. According to Franklin, though, these slaves "often became trusted associates of their owners and enjoyed virtual freedom." Moreover, the children of slaves could never be sold and were often freed by their owners.

Throughout the mid-1400s, West Africans commonly sold their slaves to Arab traders in the Mediterranean. The fledgling system of slave trade increased significantly when the Portuguese and Spanish—who had established sugar-producing colonies in Latin America and the West Indies, respectively—settled in the area in the sixteenth century. The Dutch arrived in Africa in the early 1600s, and a large influx of other European traders followed in ensuing decades with the growth of New World colonialism.

## MODERN ERA

Much of Africa's land is unsuitable for agricultural use and, therefore, is largely uninhabited. Over the centuries, severe drought and periods of war and famine have left many African nations in a state of agricultural decline and impoverishment. Still, most nations in Africa tend to increase their rate of population faster than the countries on any other continent.

Agriculture, encompassing both the production of crops and the raising of livestock, remains the primary occupation in Africa. The more verdant areas of the continent are home to farming communities; male members of these communities clear the farmland and often do the planting, while women usually nurture, weed, and harvest the crops.

Africa is very rich in oil, minerals, and plant and animal resources. It is a major producer of cotton, cashews, yams, cocoa beans, peanuts, bananas, and coffee. A large quantity of the world's zinc, coal, manganese, chromite, phosphate, and uranium is also produced on the continent. In addition, Africa's natural mineral wealth yields 90 percent of the world's diamonds and 65 percent of the world's gold.

Much of Africa had become the domain of European colonial powers by the nineteenth century. But a growing nationalistic movement in the mid-twentieth century fueled a modern African revolution, resulting in the establishment of independent nations throughout the continent. Even South Africa, a country long gripped by the injustice of apartheid's white supremacist policies, held its first free and fair multiracial elections in the spring of 1994.

## THE FIRST AFRICANS IN AMERICA

Most Africans transported to the New World as slaves came from sub-Saharan Africa's northwestern and middle-western coastal regions. This area, located on the continent's Atlantic side, now consists of more than a dozen modern nations, including Gabon, the Republic of the Congo, Cameroon, Nigeria, Benin, Togo, Ghana, Upper Volta, the Ivory Coast, Liberia, Sierra Leone, Guinea, Gambia, and Senegal.

Africans are believed to have traveled to the New World with European explorers—especially the Spanish and the Portuguese—at the turn of the fifteenth century. They served as crew members, servants, and slaves. (Many historians agree that Pedro Alonzo Niño, who accompanied Christopher Columbus on his expedition to the New World, was black; in addition, it has been established that in the early 1500s, blacks journeyed to the Pacific with Spanish explorer Vasco Núñez de Balboa and into Mexico with Cortéz.) The early African slave population worked on European coffee, cocoa, tobacco, and sugar plantations in the West Indies, as well as on the farms and in the mines that operated in Europe's South American colonies.

Later, in the seventeenth and eighteenth centuries, the Dutch, the French, and the English became dominant forces in New World slave trade, and by the early eighteenth century, colonization efforts were focusing on the North American mainland. In August of 1619, the first ship carrying Africans sailed into the harbor at Jamestown, Virginia, and so began the history of African Americans.

During the early years of America's history, society was divided by class rather than skin color. In fact, the first Africans in North America were not slaves, but indentured servants. At the dawn of colonial time, black and white laborers worked together, side by side, for a set amount of time before earning their freedom. According to Lerone Bennett, "The available evidence suggests that most of the first generation of African Americans worked out their terms of servitude and

were freed." Using the bustling colony of Virginia as an example of prevailing colonial attitudes, Bennett explains that the coastal settlement, in its first several decades of existence, "was defined by what can only be called equality of oppression.... The colony's power structure made little or no distinction between black and white servants, who were assigned the same tasks and were held in equal contempt."

But North American landowners began to face a labor crisis in the 1640s. Indians had proven unsatisfactory laborers in earlier colonization efforts, and the indentured servitude system failed to meet increasing colonial labor needs. As Franklin reflected in *From Slavery to Freedom*, "Although Africans were in Europe in considerable numbers in the seventeenth century and had been in the New World at least since 1501, ... the colonists and their Old World sponsors were extremely slow in recognizing them as the best possible labor force for the tasks in the New World."

By the second half of the 1600s, however, white colonial landowners began to see slavery as a solution to their economic woes: the fateful system of forced black labor—achieved through a program of perpetual, involuntary servitude—was then set into motion in the colonies. Africans were strong, inexpensive, and available in seemingly unlimited supplies from their native continent. In addition, their black skin made them highly visible in the white world, thereby decreasing the likelihood of their escape from bondage. Black enslavement had become vital to the American agricultural economy, and racism and subjugation became the means to justify the system. The color line was drawn, and white servants were thereafter separated from their black comrades. Slave codes were soon enacted to control almost every aspect of the slaves' lives, leaving them virtually no rights or freedoms.

## SIGNIFICANT IMMIGRATION WAVES AND SETTLEMENT OF THE BLACK POPULATION

Between 10 and 12 million Africans are believed to have been imported to the New World between 1650 and 1850. The process began slowly, with an estimated 300,000 slaves brought to the Americas prior to the seventeenth century, then reached its peak in the eighteenth century with the importation of more than six million Africans. These estimates do not include the number of African lives lost during the brutal journey to the New World.

Slave trade was a profitable endeavor: the more slaves transported to the New World on a single ship, the more money the traders made. Africans, chained together in pairs, were crammed by the hundreds onto the ships' decks; lying side by side in endless rows, they had no room to move or exercise and barely enough air to breathe. Their one-way trip, commonly referred to as the Middle Passage, ended in the Americas and the islands of the Caribbean. But sources indicate that somewhere between 12 and 40 percent of the slaves shipped from Africa never completed the Middle Passage: many died of disease, committed suicide by jumping overboard, or suffered permanent injury wrestling against the grip of their shackles.

By the mid-1700s, the majority of Africans in America lived in the Southern Atlantic colonies, where the plantation system made the greatest demands for black labor. Virginia took and maintained the lead in slave ownership, with, according to Franklin, more than 120,000 blacks in 1756—about half the colony's total population. Around the same time in South Carolina, blacks outnumbered whites. To the North, the New England colonies maintained a relatively small number of slaves.

The continued growth of the black population made whites more and more fearful of a black revolt. An all-white militia was formed, and stringent legislation was enacted throughout the colonies to limit the activities of blacks. It was within owners' rights to deal out harsh punishments to slaves—even for the most insignificant transgressions.

The fight against the British during the Revolutionary War underscores a curious irony in American history: the colonists sought religious, economic, and political freedom from England for themselves, while denying blacks in the New World even the most basic, human rights. The close of the American Revolution brought with it the manumission, or release, of several thousand slaves, especially in the North. But the Declaration of Independence failed to address the issue of slavery in any certain terms.

By 1790, the black population approached 760,000, and nearly eight percent of all blacks in America were free. Free blacks, however, were bound by many of the same regulations that applied to slaves. The ratification of the U.S. Constitution in 1788 guaranteed equality and "certain inalienable rights" to the white population, but not to African Americans. Census reports counted each slave as only three-fifths of a person when determining state congressional representation; so-called free blacks—often referred to as "quasi-free"—faced limited employment opportunities and restrictions on their freedom to travel, vote, and bear arms.

It was in the South, according to historians, that the most brutal, backbreaking conditions of slavery existed. The invention of the cotton gin in 1793 greatly increased the profitability of cotton production, thereby heightening the demand for slaves to work on the plantations. The slave population in the South rose with the surge in cotton production and with the expansion of plantations along the western portion of the Southern frontier. But not all slaves worked on Southern plantations. By the second half of the nineteenth century, nearly half a million were working in cities as domestics, skilled artisans, and factory hands.

A growing abolitionist movement—among both blacks and whites—became a potent force in the 1830s. After a century of subjugation, many blacks in America who could not buy their freedom risked their lives in escape attempts. Antislavery revolts first broke out in the 1820s, and uprisings continued for the next four decades. Black anger, it seemed, could only be quelled by an end to the slave system.

Around the same time, a philosophy of reverse migration emerged as a solution to the black dilemma. The country's ever-increasing African American population was cause for alarm in some white circles. Washington D.C.'s American Colonization Society pushed for the return of blacks to their fatherland. By the early 1820s, the first wave of black Americans landed on Africa's western coastal settlement of Liberia; nearly 1,500 blacks were resettled throughout the 1830s. But the idea of repatriation was largely opposed, especially by manumitted blacks in the North: having been "freed," they were now subjected to racial hatred, legalized discrimination, and political and economic injustice in a white world. They sought equity at home, rather than resettlement in Africa, as the only acceptable end to more than two centuries of oppression.

The political and economic turbulence of the Civil War years intensified racial troubles. Emancipation was viewed throughout the war as a military necessity rather than a human rights issue. In December of 1865, eight months after the Civil

War ended, the Thirteenth Amendment to the Constitution was adopted: slavery was abolished. But even in the late 1800s and early 1900s, the black population in the United States saw few changes in its social, political, and economic condition.

With no money, land, or livestock, freed slaves were hardly in a position to establish their own farming communities in the South. Thus began the largely exploitative system of tenant farming, which took the form of sharecropping. A popular post-slavery agricultural practice, sharecropping allowed tenants (most of whom were black), to work the farms of landlords (most of whom were white) and earn a percentage of the proceeds of each crop harvested. Unfortunately, the system provided virtually no economic benefits for the tenants; relegated to squalid settlements of rundown shacks, they labored as if they were still bound in slavery and, in most cases, barely broke even.

The price of cotton fell around 1920—a precursor to the Great Depression. Over the next few decades, the mass production and widespread use of the mechanical cotton picker signaled the beginning of the end of the sharecropping system. At the same time, the United States was fast becoming an industrial giant, and a huge labor force was needed in the North. This demand for unskilled labor, combined with the expectation of an end to the legal and economic oppression of the South, attracted blacks to northern U.S. cities in record numbers. On Chicago's South Side alone, the black population quintupled by 1930.

Migration to the North began around 1920 and reached its peak—with an influx of more than five million people—around World War II. Prior to the war, more than three-quarters of all blacks in the United States lived in the southern states. In all, between 1910 and 1970, about 6.5 million African Americans migrated to the northern United States. "The black migration was one of the largest and most rapid mass internal movements of people in history—perhaps *the* greatest not caused by the immediate threat of execution or starvation," wrote Nicholas Lemann in *The Promised Land*. "In sheer numbers it outranks the migration of any other ethnic group—Italians or Irish or Jews or Poles—to this country."

But manufacturing jobs in the northern United States decreased in the 1960s. As the need for unskilled industrial laborers fell, hundreds of thousands of African Americans took government service jobs—in social welfare pro-grams, law enforcement, and transportation sectors—that were created during President Lyndon Baines Johnson's presidency. These new government jobs meant economic advancement for some blacks; by the end of the decade, a substantial portion of the black population had migrated out of the urban ghettos.

The U.S. Census Bureau projects that by the year 2050, minorities (including people of African, Asian, and Hispanic descent) will comprise a majority of the nation's population. In 1991 just over 12 percent of the U.S. population was black; as of 1994, about 32 million people of African heritage were citizens of the United States. Within six decades, blacks are expected to make up about 15 percent of the nation's population (U.S. Bureau of the Census, 1993).

# ACCULTURATION AND ASSIMILATION

History casts a dark shadow on the entire issue of black assimilation in the United States. For hundreds of years, people of African descent were oppressed and exploited purely on the basis of the blackness of their skin. The era of "freedom" that began in the mid-1780s in post-Revolutionary America excluded blacks entirely; black Americans were considered less than human beings and faced discrimination in every aspect of their lives. Many historians argue that slavery's legacy of social inequality has persisted in American society—even 130 years after the post-Civil War emancipation of slaves in the United States.

Legally excluded from the white world, blacks were forced to establish their own social, political, and economic institutions. In the process of building a solid cultural base in the black community, they formed a whole new identity: that of the African American. African Americans recognized their African heritage, but now accepted America as home.

In addition, African Americans began to employ the European tactics of petitions, lawsuits, and organized protest to fight for their rights. This movement, which started early in the nineteenth century, involved the formation and utilization of mutual aid societies; independent black churches; lodges and fraternal organizations; and educational and cultural institutions designed to fight black oppression. As Lerone Bennett stated in *Before the Mayflower*: "By 1837 ... it was plain that Black people were in America to stay and that room had to be made for them."

Some observers note that the European immigrants who streamed into America during the nineteenth and twentieth centuries also faced difficulties during the assimilation process, but these difficulties were not insurmountable; their light skin enabled them to blend more quickly and easily with the nation's dominant racial fabric. Discrimination based on race appears to be far more deeply ingrained in American society.

## TRADITIONS, CUSTOMS, AND BELIEFS

In *Superstition and the Superstitious*, Eric Maple provides examples of common African folklore and beliefs. For example, when a pregnant woman walks under a ladder, she can expect to have a difficult birth. When someone sneezes, an African wishes that person "health, wealth, prosperity, and children." In Nigeria it is believed that sweeping a house during the night brings bad luck; conversely, all evil things should be expelled from the house by a thorough sweeping in the morning. If a male is hit with a broom he will be rendered impotent unless he retaliates with seven blows delivered with the same broom. In Africa, ghosts are greatly feared because, according to Maple, "all ghosts are evil." One Yoruba tribesman was quoted as saying: "If while walking alone in the afternoon or night your head feels either very light or heavy, this means that there is a ghost around. The only way to save yourself is to carry something that gives off a powerful odor."

## PROVERBS

A wealth of proverbs from African culture have survived through the generations: If you want to know the end, look at the beginning; When one door closes, another one opens; If we stand tall it is because we stand on the backs of those who came before us; Two men in a burning house must not stop to argue; Where you sit when you are old shows where you stood in youth; You must live within your sacred truth; The one who asks questions doesn't lose his way; If you plant turnips you will not harvest grapes; God makes three requests of his children: Do the best you can, where you are, with what you have now; You must act as if it is impossible to fail.

## MISCONCEPTIONS AND STEREOTYPES

African Americans have struggled against racial stereotypes for centuries. The white slaveholding class rationalized the institution of slavery as a necessary evil: aside from playing an integral part in the nation's agricultural economy, the system was viewed by some as the only way to control a wild, pagan race. In colonial America, black people were considered genetically inferior to whites; efforts to educate and Christianize them were therefore regarded as justifiable.

The black population has been misunderstood by white America for hundreds of years. The significance of Old World influences in modern African American life—and an appreciation of the complex structure of traditional African society—went largely unrecognized by the majority of the nation's nonblacks. Even in the latter half of the twentieth century, as more and more African nations embraced multiparty democracy and underwent massive urban and industrial growth, the distorted image of Africans as an uncivilized lot continued to pervade the consciousness of an alarmingly high percentage of white Americans. As social commentator Ellis Cose explained: "Theories of blacks' innate intellectual inadequacy provided much of the rationale for slavery and for Jim Crow [legal discrimination based on race]. They also accomplished something equally pernicious, and continue to do so today: they caused many blacks (if only subconsciously) to doubt their own abilities—and to conform to the stereotype, thereby confirming it" (Ellis Cose, "Color-Coordinated Truths," *Newsweek*, October 24, 1994, p. 62).

For decades, these images were perpetuated by the American media. Prime-time television shows of the 1960s and 1970s often featured blacks in demeaning roles—those of servants, drug abusers, common criminals, and all-around threats to white society. During the controversial "blaxploitation" phase in American cinema—a period that saw the release of films like *Shaft* and *Superfly*—sex, drugs, and violence prevailed on the big screen. Though espoused by some segments of the black artistic community as a legitimate outlet for black radicalism, these films were seen by many critics as alienating devices that glorified urban violence and drove an even greater wedge between blacks and whites.

African American entertainment mogul Bill Cosby is credited with initiating a reversal in the tide of media stereotypes. His long-running situation comedy *The Cosby Show*—a groundbreaking program that made television history and dominated the ratings throughout the 1980s—helped to dispel the myths of racial inferiority. An intact family consisting of well-educated, professional parents and socially responsible children, the show's fictional Huxtable family served as a model for more enlightened, racially-balanced programming in the 1990s.

## CUISINE

Most African nations are essentially agricultural societies. For centuries, a majority of men have worked as farmers and cattle raisers, although some have made their living as fishermen. Planting, sowing, and harvesting crops were women's duties in traditional West African society. The task of cooking also seems to have fallen to women in ancient Africa. They prepared meals like fufu—a traditional dish made of pounded yams and served with soups, stew, roasted meat and a variety of sauces—over huge open pits.

Many tribal nations made up the slave population in the American South. Africans seem to have exchanged their regional recipes freely, leading to the development of a multinational cooking style among blacks in America. In many areas along the Atlantic coast, Native Americans taught the black population to cook with native plants. These varied cooking techniques were later introduced to southern American society by Africans.

During the colonial period, heavy breakfast meals of hoecakes (small cornmeal cakes) and molasses were prepared to fuel the slaves for work from sunup to sundown. Spoonbread, crab cakes, corn pone (corn bread), corn pudding, greens, and succotash—cooked over an open pit or fireplace—became common items in a black cook's repertoire in the late 1700s and the 1800s.

African Americans served as cooks for both the northern and southern armies throughout the Civil War. Because of the scarcity of supplies, the cooks were forced to improvise and invent their own recipes. It was during this time that Creole and Cajun cooking developed. Some of the dishes that sprang from this period of culinary creativity include jambalaya (herbs and rice cooked with chicken, ham, sausage, shrimp, or oysters), bread pudding, dirty rice, gumbo, and red beans and rice—all of which remain favorites on the nation's regional cuisine circuit.

The late 1800s and early 1900s saw the establishment of many African American-owned eateries specializing in southern fried chicken, pork chops, fish, potato salad, turkey and dressing, and rice and gravy. In later years, this diet—which grew to include pigs' feet, chitlins (hog intestines), collard greens (a vegetable), and ham hocks—became known as "soul food."

Food plays a large role in African American traditions, customs, and beliefs. Nothing underscores this point more than the example of New Year's Day, a time of celebration that brings with it new hopes for the coming months. Some of the traditional foods enjoyed on this day are black-eyed peas, which represent good fortune; rice, a symbol of prosperity; greens, which stand for money; and fish, which represents the motivation and desire to increase wealth.

## A REVIVAL OF OTHER TRADITIONS

Over the centuries, various aspects of African culture have blended into American society. The complex rhythms of African music, for instance, are evident in the sounds of American blues and jazz; a growth in the study of American folklore—and the development of American-style folktales—can be linked in part to Africa's long oral tradition. But a new interest in the Old World began to surface in the 1970s and continued through the nineties. In an effort to connect with their African heritage, some black Americans have adopted African names to replace the Anglo names of their ancestors' slaveowners. In addition, increasing numbers of African American men and women are donning the traditional garb of their African brothers and sisters—including African-inspired jewelry, headwear, and brightly colored, loose-fitting garments called *dashikis*—to show pride in their roots.

## HOLIDAYS CELEBRATED BY AFRICAN AMERICANS

In addition to Christmas, New Year's Day, Easter Sunday, and Martin Luther King, Jr. Day, other dates throughout the calendar year hold a special significance for African Americans. For example, on June 19th of each year, many blacks celebrate a special day known as Juneteenth. Although the Emancipation Proclamation, which declared an end to slavery in the Confederacy, took effect on January 1, 1863, the news of slavery's end did not reach the black population in Texas until June 19, 1865. Union General Gordon Granger arrived outside Galveston, Texas, that day to announce the freedom of the state's 250,000 enslaved blacks. Former slaves in Texas and Louisiana held a major celebration that turned into an annual event and spread throughout the nation as free blacks migrated west and north.

From December 26th to January 1st, African Americans observe *Kwanzaa* (which means "first fruits" in Swahili), a nonreligious holiday that celebrates family, culture, and ancestral ties. This week-long commemoration was instituted in 1966 by Dr. Maulana Karenga to promote unity and pride among people of African descent.

Kwanzaa comes directly from the tradition of the agricultural people of Africa, who gave thanks for a bountiful harvest at designated times during the year. In this highly symbolic celebration, *mazeo* (crops) represent the historical roots of the holiday and the rewards of collective labor; *mekeka* (a mat) stands for tradition and foundation; *kinara* (a candleholder) represents African forebears; *muhindi* (ears of corn) symbolize a family's children; *zawadi* (gifts) reflect the seeds sown by the children (like commitments made and kept, for example) and the fruits of the parents' labor; and the *kikombe cha umoja* functions as a unity cup. For each day during the week of Kwanzaa, a particular principle or *nguzo saba* ("n-goo-zoh sah-ba") is observed: (Day 1): *Umoja* ("oo-moe-ja")—unity in family, community, nation, and race; (Day 2): *Kujichagulia* ("coo-gee-cha-goo-lee-ah")—self-determination, independence, and creative thinking, (Day 3): *Ujima* ("oo-gee-mah")—collective work and responsibility to others; (Day 4): *Ujamaa* ("oo-jah-mah")—cooperative economics, as in the formation and support of black businesses and jobs; (Day 5): *Nia* ("nee-ah")—purpose, as in the building and development of black communities; (Day 6): *Kuumba* ("coo-oom-bah")—creativity and beautification of the environment; (Day 7): *Imani* ("ee-mah-nee")—faith in God, parents, leaders, and the righteousness and victory of the black struggle.

For African Americans, the entire month of February is set aside not as a holiday, but as a time of enlightenment for people of all races. Black History Month, first introduced in 1926 by historian Carter G. Woodson as Negro History Week, is observed each February as a celebration of black heritage. A key tool in the American educational system's growing multicultural movement, Black History Month was designed to foster a better understanding of the role black Americans have played in U.S. history.

## HEALTH AND MENTAL HEALTH ISSUES

African Americans are at a high risk for serious health problems, including cancer, diabetes, and hypertension. Several studies show a direct connection between poor health and the problem of underemployment or unemployment among African Americans. One-third of the black population is financially strapped, with an income at or below the poverty level. Illnesses brought on by an improper diet or substandard living conditions are often compounded by a lack of quality medical care—largely a result of inadequate health insurance coverage.

Statistics indicate that African Americans are more likely to succumb to many life-threatening illnesses than white Americans. This grim reality is evident even from birth: black babies under one year of age die at twice the rate of white babies in the same age group. "When you collect all the information and search for answers, they usually relate to poverty," noted University of Iowa pediatrics professor Dr. Herman A. Hein in 1989 (Mark Nichols and Linda Graham Caleca, "Black Infant Mortality," *Indianapolis Star*, August 27, 1989, p. A-1). A lack of prenatal care among low-income mothers is believed to be the greatest single factor in the high mortality rate among African American infants.

A 1992 medical survey found that black Americans were more likely to die from cancer than white Americans: the age-adjusted cancer mortality rate was a full 27 percent higher for the nation's black population than the white population. African Americans also had a significantly lower five-year survival rate—only 38 percent compared to 53 percent for whites—even though the overall cancer incidence rates are actually *lower* for blacks than for whites. Black Americans who suffer from cancer seem to be receiving inferior medical treatment, and they are much more likely to have their cancer diagnosed only after the malignancy has metastasized, or spread to other parts of the body (Catherine C. Boring and others, "Cancer Statistics for African Americans," *CA 42*, 1992, pp. 7-17).

Hypertension, or high blood pressure, strikes a third more African Americans than whites. Although the Public Health Service reports that the hypertension is largely inherited, other factors such as poor diet and stress can play a key role in the development of the disorder. The effects of hypertension are especially devastating to the black population: blacks aged 24 to 44 are reportedly 18 times more likely than whites to suffer kidney failure as a complication of high blood pressure (Dixie Farley, "High Blood Pressure: Controlling the Silent Killer," *FDA Consumer*, December 1991, pp. 28-33). A reduction in dietary fat and salt are recommended for all hypertensive patients. African Americans are believed to be particularly sensitive to blood pressure problems brought on by a high-salt diet.

Sickle cell anemia is a serious and painful disorder that occurs almost exclusively in people of African descent. The disease is believed to have been brought to the United States as a result of African immigration, and by the last decade of the twentieth century it had found its way to all corners of the world. In some African nations, two to three percent of all babies die from the disease. In the United States, one in every 12 African Americans carries the trait; of these, about one in 600 develops the disease. Sickle cell anemia is generally considered to be the most common genetically determined blood disease to affect a single ethnic group (Katie Krauss, "The Pain of Sickle Cell Anemia," *Yale-New Haven Magazine*, summer 1989, pp. 2-6).

Normal red blood cells are round, but the blood cells of sickle cell victims are elongated and pointed (like a sickle). Cells of this shape can clog small blood vessels, thereby cutting off the supply of oxygen to surrounding tissues. The pain associated with sickle cell anemia is intense, and organ failure can result as the disease progresses. By the late 1980s, researchers had begun to make strides in the treatment and prevention of some of the life-threatening complications associated with sickle cell anemia, including damage to the heart, lungs, immune system, and nervous system.

Although the threats to the health of African Americans are numerous and varied, the number one killer of blacks in the United States is violent crime. In the early 1990s, the Center for Disease Control and Prevention (CDC) in Atlanta, Georgia, began viewing violence as a disease. In an October 17, 1994 press conference, CDC director David Satcher noted that homicide is the leading cause of death among black Americans aged 15 to 34. The severity of the problem has led the CDC to take an active role in addressing violence as a public health issue.

In November of 1990, the National Center for Health Statistics reported that while life expectancy for whites increased in the 1980s, life expectancy actually fell among African Americans during the latter half of the decade. African American men have a life expectancy of only 65.6 years—more than seven years lower than that of the average white American male (U.S. Bureau of the Census, 1993). Census projections suggest that between 1995 and 2010, life expectancy should increase to 67.3 years for black men and 75.1 years for white men.

# LANGUAGE

More than 1,000 different languages are spoken in Africa, and it is often difficult for even the most studied linguistic scholars to differentiate between separate African languages and the dialects of a single language. The multitudinous languages of Africa are grouped into several large families, including the Niger-Congo family (those spoken mainly in the southern portion of the continent) and the Afro-Asiatic family (spoken in northern Africa, the eastern horn of Africa, and Southwest Asia).

Africa has a very long and rich oral tradition; few languages of the Old World ever took a written form. Literature and history in ancient Africa, therefore, were passed from generation to generation orally. After the fourteenth century, the use of Arabic by educated Muslim blacks was rather extensive, and some oral literature was subsequently reduced to a more permanent written form. But, in spite of this Arab influence, the oral heritage of Africans remained strong, serving not only as an educational device, but as a guide for the administration of government and the conduct of religious ceremonies.

Beginning with the arrival of the first Africans in the New World, Anglo-American words were slowly infused into African languages. Successive generations of blacks born in America, as well as Africans transported to the colonies later in the slave trading era, began to use standard English as their principal language. Over the years, this standard English has been modified by African Americans to encompass their own culture, language, and experience.

The social change movements of the 1960s gave birth to a number of popular black expressions. Later, in the 1980s and 1990s, the music of hip-hop and rap artists became a culturally significant expression of the trials of black urban life. In her book *Talkin & Testifyin*, linguistic scholar Geneva Smitherman offers this explanation of the formation of a very distinctive black English: "In a nutshell: Black Dialect is an Africanized form of English reflecting Black America's linguistic-cultural African heritage and the conditions of servitude, oppression, and life in America. Black Language is Euro-American speech with Afro-American meaning, nuance, tone, and gesture.

The Black Idiom is used by 80 to 90 percent of American Blacks, at least some of the time. It has allowed Blacks to create a culture of survival in an alien land, and as a by-product has served to enrich the language of all Americans."

As recounted in *Before the Mayflower*, scholar Lorenzo Turner found linguistic survivals of the African past in the syntax, word-formations, and intonations of African Americans. Among these words in general use, especially in the South, are "goober" (peanut), "gumbo" (okra), "ninny" (female breast), "tote" (to carry), and "yam" (sweet potato). Additionally, Turner discovered a number of African-inspired names among Americans on the South Side of Chicago, including: "Bobo," meaning one who cannot talk; "Geiji," the name of a language and tribe in Liberia; "Agona," after a country in Ghana; "Ola," a Yoruban word meaning that which saves; and "Zola," meaning to love.

# FAMILY AND COMMUNITY DYNAMICS

In *From Slavery to Freedom*, Franklin pointed out that "the family was the basis of social organization .... [and] the foundation even of economic and political life" in early Africa, with descent being traced through the mother. Historians have noted that Africans placed a heavy emphasis on their obligations to their immediate and extended family members and their community as a whole. In addition, according to Franklin, Africans are said to have believed that "the spirits of their forefathers had unlimited power over their lives"; thus a sense of kinship was especially significant in the Old World.

Slavery exerted an undeniable strain on the traditional African family unit. The system tore at the very fiber of family life: in some cases, husbands and wives were sold to different owners, and children born into servitude could be separated—sold—from their mothers on a white man's whim. But, according to Nicholas Lemann in *The Promised Land*, "the mutation in the structure of the black family" that occurred during slavery did not necessarily destroy the black family. Rather, the enduring cycle of *poverty* among African Americans seems to have had the strongest negative impact on the stability of the family.

As of March of 1992, the U.S. Bureau of the Census estimated that 32.7 percent of African Americans lived below the poverty level (with family incomes of less than $14,000). It is this segment of the underclass that defines the term "families in crisis." They are besieged by poverty and further challenged by an array of cyclical social problems: high unemployment rates; the issue of teenage pregnancy; a preponderance of fatherless households; inadequate housing or homelessness; inferior health care against a backdrop of high health hazards; staggering school drop-out rates; and an alarming incarceration rate. (One out of four males between the ages of 18 to 24 was in prison in the early 1990s.) Experts predict that temporary assistance alone will not provide long-term solutions to these problems. Without resolutions, impoverished black families are in danger of falling further and further behind.

Another third of all African American families found themselves in tenuous financial positions in the mid-1990s, corresponding with the prevailing economic climate of the United States in the late 1980s and early 1990s. These families faced increasing layoffs or job termination as the nation's once-prosperous industrial base deteriorated and the great business boom of the early 1980s faded. Still, they managed to hold their extended family units together and provide support systems for their children.

At the same time, more than 30 percent of African American families were headed by one or two full-time wage earners. This middle- and upper-middle-class segment of the nation's black population includes men and women who are second, third, or fourth generation college graduates—and who have managed to prosper within a system that, according to some observers, continues to breed legalized racism in both subtle and substantive ways. As models of community action and responsibility, these African American families have taken stock in an old African proverb: "It takes a whole tribe to raise one child."

## EDUCATION

As early as the 1620s and 1630s, European missionaries in the United States began efforts to convert Africans to Christianity and provide them with a basic education. Other inroads in the black educational process were made by America's early white colonists. The Pennsylvania Quakers (members of a Christian sect known as the Society of Friends) were among the most vocal advocates of social reform and justice for blacks in the first century of the nation's history. Staunch opponents of the oppressive institution of slavery, the Quakers began organizing educational meetings for people of African heritage in the early 1700s; in 1774, they launched a school for blacks in Philadelphia. By the mid-1800s, the city had become a center for black learning, with public, industrial, charity, and private schools providing an education for more than 2,000 African American students.

After the Civil War and the abolition of slavery, groups known as Freedmen's organizations were formed to provide educational opportunities to former slaves. Under the Freedmen's Bureau Acts passed by Congress in the 1860s, more than 2,500 schools were established in the South.

Over the next decade or so, several colleges opened for black students. In the late 1870s, religious organizations and government-sponsored land-grant programs played an important role in the establishment and support of many early black institutions of higher learning. By 1900, more than 2,000 black Americans would graduate from college.

The end of the nineteenth century saw a surge in black leadership. One of the best-known and most powerful leaders in the black community at this time was educator and activist Booker T. Washington. A graduate of Virginia's Hampton Normal and Agricultural Institute, Washington set up a similar school in Tuskegee, Alabama, in 1881, with a $2,000 grant from the Alabama legislature. Committed to the ideal of economic self-help and independence, the Tuskegee Institute offered teachers' training—as well as industrial and agricultural education—to young black men and women.

Activist Mary McLeod Bethune, the most prominent black woman of her era, also had a profound impact on black education at the turn of the twentieth century. In 1904, with less than two dollars in savings and a handful of students, she founded the Daytona Normal and Industrial Institute in Florida. Devoted mainly to the education of African American girls, the Daytona Institute also served as a cornerstone of strength for the entire black community. The school later merged with Cookman's Institute, a Florida-based men's college, to become Bethune-Cookman College.

Bethune's efforts, and the struggles of dozens of other black educational leaders, were made in the midst of irrefutable adversity. In 1896 the U.S. Supreme Court sanctioned the practice of racial segregation: the court's ruling in the case of

*Plessy vs. Ferguson* upheld the doctrine of "separate but equal" accommodations for blacks—and schools were among these accommodations. It took more than half a century for the *Plessy* decision to be overturned; in 1954, a major breakthrough in the fight for black rights came when the Supreme Court handed down its decision in the *Brown vs. Board of Education of Topeka* case: "To separate [black] children from others of similar age and qualifications solely because of their race generates a feeling of inferiority as to their status in the community that may affect their hearts and minds in a way unlikely ever to be undone.... Segregation with the sanction of law, therefore, has a tendency to [retard] the educational and mental development of Negro children and to deprive them of some of the benefits they would receive in a racially integrated school system.... In the field of public education the doctrine of 'separate but equal' has no place. Separate educational facilities are inherently unequal" (from the decision of the U.S. Supreme Court in the case of *Brown vs. Board of Education of Topeka*, May 17, 1954, 347 U.S. 483).

*Brown* was clearly a landmark decision that set the tone for further social advancements among African Americans, but its passage failed to guarantee integration and equality in education. Even four decades after *Brown*, true desegregation in American public schools had not been achieved. The school populations in cities like Detroit, Chicago, and Los Angeles remain almost exclusively black, and high school drop-out rates in poor, urban, predominantly black districts are often among the highest in the nation—sometimes reaching more than 40 percent.

U.S. Census reports suggest that by the year 2000, the country will witness a change in the face of school segregation. Hispanics, unprotected by the *Brown* decision, will outnumber blacks in the United States; the Hispanic community, therefore, will need to battle side by side with African Americans for desegregation and equity in education. As Jean Heller put it in the *St. Petersburg Times*, "The *Brown* decision outlawed *de jure* segregation, the separation of races by law. There is no legal remedy for *de facto* segregation, separation that occurs naturally. It is not against any law for whites or blacks or Hispanics to choose to live apart, even if that choice creates segregated school systems" (Jean Heller, A Unfulfilled Mission," *St. Petersburg Times* (Florida), December 10, 1989, p. 1A).

Not all attempts at school desegregation have failed. Heller points out that the East Harlem

Shalewa Crowe stands before her students as they participate in the "Unity Pledge" at the New Concept Development Center in Chicago. This school is one of many in the United States that provides an Afro-centric curriculum.

school district, formerly one of the worst in New York City, designed such an impressive educational system for its black and Hispanic students that neighboring whites began transferring into the district. Educational experts have suggested that the key to successful, nationwide school integration is the establishment of high quality educational facilities in segregated urban areas. Superior school systems in segregated cities, they argue, would discourage urban flight—thereby increasing the racial and economic diversity of the population—and bring about a natural end to segregation.

In 1990 the U.S. Department of Commerce reported that the gap between black and white high school graduation rates was closing. The department's census-based study showed an encouraging increase in the overall percentage of black high school graduates between 1978 and 1988. Only 68 percent of blacks and 83 percent of whites graduated from secondary school in 1978; ten years later, 75 percent of blacks and 82 percent of whites had graduated.

But studies show that fewer blacks than whites go on to college. Between 1960 and 1991, the percentage of black high school graduates who were enrolled in college or had completed at least one year of college rose from 32.5 to 46.1 percent, compared to a rise of 41 to 62.3 percent for white graduates (U.S. Bureau of the Census, 1993). As the United States completes its move from a manufacturing society to an information-based, technological society, the need for highly educated, creative, computer-literate workers continues to grow.

In response to perceived inadequacies in black American education, a progressive philosophy known as Afrocentrism developed around 1980. An alternative to the nation's Eurocentric model of education, Afrocentrism places the black student at the center of history, thereby instilling a sense of dignity and pride in black heritage. Proponents of the movement—including its founder, activist and scholar Molefi Kete Asante—feel that the integration of the Afrocentric perspective into the American consciousness will benefit students of all colors in a racially diverse society. In addition, pro-Afrocentric educators believe that empowered black students will be better equipped to succeed in an increasingly complex world.

## WEDDINGS

American tradition calls for the bride to have "something old, something new, something borrowed, and something blue" in her possession for luck on her wedding day. While modern African American couples marry in the western tradition, many are personalizing their weddings with an ancestral touch to add to the day's historical and cultural significance.

Among Africans, marriage represents a union of two families, not just the bride and groom. In keeping with West African custom, it is essential for parents and extended family members to welcome a man or woman's future partner and offer emotional support to the couple throughout their marriage. The bonding of the families begins when a man obtains formal permission to marry his prospective bride.

In the true oral tradition, Africans often deliver the news of their upcoming nuptials by word of mouth. Some African American couples have modified this tradition by having their invitations printed on a scroll, tied with raffia, and then hand-delivered by friends. The ancestral influence on modern ceremonies can also be seen in the accessories worn by the bride and groom. On African shores, the groom wears his bride's earring, and the bride dons an elaborate necklace reserved exclusively for her.

Because enslaved Africans in America were often barred from marrying in a legal ceremony, they created their own marriage rite. It is said that couples joined hands and jumped over a broom together into "the land of matrimony." Many twentieth-century black American couples reenact "jumping the broom" during their wedding ceremony or reception.

## THE ISSUE OF INTERRACIAL MARRIAGE

In the three decades between 1960 and 1990, interracial marriages more than quadrupled in the United States, but the number remains small. By 1992 less than one percent of all marriages united blacks with people of another racial heritage (U.S. Bureau of the Census, 1993).

"America has often been referred to as a melting pot, a heterogeneous country made up of diverse ethnic, religious, and racial groups," noted *Boston Globe* contributor Desiree French. But, in spite of the nation's diversity, it has taken more than 350 years for many Americans to begin to come to terms with the idea of interracial marriage (Desiree French, "Interracial Marriage," *Sun-Sentinel* (Fort Lauderdale), January 25, 1990, p.3E; originally printed in the *Boston Globe*). As late as 1967, antimiscegenation laws (laws that prohibited the marriage of whites to members of another race) were still on the books in 17 states; that year, the U.S. Supreme Court finally declared such laws unconstitutional.

Surveys indicate that young Americans approaching adulthood at the dawn of the twenty-first century are much more open to the idea of interracial unions than earlier generations. A decline in social bias has led experts to predict an increase in cross-cultural marriages throughout the 1990s.

Still, according to the 1994 National Health and Social Life Survey, 97 percent of black women are likely to choose a partner of the same race (John H. Gagnon, Robert T. Michael, Edward O. Laumann, and Gina Kolata, *Sex in America: A Definitive Survey* [Boston: Little Brown, 1994]). *Newsweek* magazine quoted one young black woman as saying that "relationships are complicated enough" without the extra stress of interracial tensions (Michael Marriott, "Not Frenzied, But Fulfilled," *Newsweek*, October 17, 1994, p. 71). Conflict in the United States over black-white relationships stems from the nation's brutal history of slavery, when white men held all the power in society. More than a century after the abolition of slavery, America's shameful legacy of racism remains. According to some observers, high rates of abortion, drug abuse, illness, and poverty among African Americans seemed to spark a movement of black solidarity in the early 1990s. Many black women—"the culture bearers"—oppose the idea of interracial marriage, opting instead for racial strength and unity through the stabilization of the black family (Ruth Holladay, "A Cruel History of Colors Interracial Relationships," *Indianapolis Star*, May 6, 1990, p. H-1).

# RELIGION

In *From Slavery to Freedom*, John Hope Franklin described the religion of early Africans as "ancestor worship." Tribal religions varied widely but shared some common elements: they were steeped in ritual, magic, and devotion to the spirits of the dead, and they placed heavy emphasis on the need for a knowledge and appreciation of the past.

Christianity was first introduced in West Africa by the Portuguese in the sixteenth century. Franklin noted that resistance among the Africans to Christianization stemmed from their association of the religion with the institution of slave trade to the New World. "It was a strange religion, this Christianity," he wrote, "which taught equality and brotherhood and at the same time introduced on a large scale the practice of tearing people from their homes and transporting them to a distant land to become slaves."

In the New World, missionaries continued their efforts to convert Africans to Christianity. As far back as 1700, the Quakers sponsored monthly Friends meetings for blacks. But an undercurrent of anxiety among a majority of white settlers curbed the formation of free black churches in colonial America: many colonists felt that if blacks were allowed to congregate at separate churches, they would plot dangerous rebellions. By the mid-1700s, black membership in both the Baptist and Methodist churches had increased significantly; few blacks, however, became ordained members of the clergy in these predominantly white sects.

African Americans finally organized the first independent black congregation—the Silver Bluff Baptist Church—in South Carolina in the early 1770s. Other black congregations sprang up in the first few decades of the 1800s, largely as outgrowths of established white churches. In 1816 Richard Allen, a slave who bought his own freedom, formed the African Methodist Episcopal (AME) church in Philadelphia in response to an unbending policy of segregated seating in the city's white Methodist church.

An increase in slave uprisings led fearful whites to impose restrictions on the activities of black churches in the 1830s. In the post-Civil War years, however, black Baptist and Methodist ministers exerted a profound influence on their congregations, urging peaceful social and political involvement for the black population as Reconstruction-period policies unfolded.

But as segregation became a national reality in the 1880s and 1890s, some black churches and ministers began to advocate decidedly separatist solutions to the religious, educational, and economic discrimination that existed in the United States. AME Bishop Henry McNeal Turner, a former Civil War chaplain, championed the idea of African migration for blacks with his "Back to Africa" movement in 1895—more than twenty years before the rise of black nationalist leader Marcus Garvey. By the early 1900s, churches were functioning to unite blacks politically.

Organized religion has always been a strong institution among African Americans. More than 75 percent of black Americans belong to a church, and nearly half attend church services each week ("America's Blacks: A World Apart," *Economist*, March 30, 1991). Black congregations reflect the traditional strength of community ties in their continued devotion to social improvement—evident in the launching of youth programs, anti-drug crusades, and parochial schools, and in ongoing efforts to provide the needy with food, clothing, and shelter.

Today, the largest African American denomination in the country is the National Baptist Convention of the U.S.A., Inc. Many African Americans belong to the AME and CME (Christian Methodist Episcopal) churches, and the Church of God in Christ—a Pentecostal denomination that cuts across socioeconomic lines—also has a strong black following. The 1990s saw a steady increase in black membership in the Islamic religion and the Roman Catholic church as well. (A separate African American Catholic congregation, not sanctioned by the church in Rome, was founded in 1989 by George A. Stallings, Jr.) Less mainstream denominations include Louis Farrakhan's Nation of Islam, based on the black separatist doctrine of Elijah Muhammad. Though faulted by some critics for its seemingly divisive, controversial teachings, the Nation of Islam maintains a fairly sizeable following.

# EMPLOYMENT AND ECONOMIC TRADITIONS

When African Americans left the South in the early 1900s to move north, many migrants found jobs in manufacturing, especially in the automobile, tobacco, meat-packing, clothing, steel, and shipping industries; African Americans, were hit especially hard by the decline of the nation's manufacturing economy later in the century. In the 1960s, U.S. presidents John F. Kennedy and Lyndon Baines Johnson launched a "war on poverty." Some blacks were able to move out of the ghettos during these years, following the passage of the Civil Rights and Fair Housing Acts, the inauguration of affirmative action policies, and the increase of black workers in government jobs. But John Hope Franklin contended in *From Slavery to Freedom* that the Civil Rights Act of 1964, though "the most far-reaching and comprehensive law in support of racial equality ever enacted by Congress," actually reflected only "the illusion of equality."

Designed to protect blacks against discrimination in voting, in education, in the use of public facilities, and in the administration of federally-funded programs, the Civil Rights Act of 1964 led to the establishment of the Equal Employment Opportunity Commission and the institution of affirmative action programs to redress past discrimination against African Americans. Affirmative action measures were initiated in the mid-1960s to improve educational and employment opportunities for minorities; over the years, women and the handicapped have also benefited from these programs. But opponents of affirmative action have argued that racial quotas breed racial resentment.

A strong feeling of "white backlash" accompanied the passage of the Civil Rights Act of 1964; racial tensions sparked violence across the country as blacks tried to move beyond the limits of segregation—economically, politically, and socially—in the latter half of the twentieth century. Still, more than three decades after the act's passage, economic inequities persist in America.

The conservative policies of U.S. presidents Ronald Reagan and George Bush dealt a serious blow to black advancement in the 1980s and early 1990s. The percentage of Americans living in poverty "rose in the 1980s, when the government [cut] back its efforts" to support social programs (Nicholas Lemann, "Up and Out," *Washington Post National Weekly Edition*, May 24-June 4, 1989, pp. 25-26). The budget cuts made by these Republican administrations drastically reduced black middle-class employment opportunities.

According to the U.S. Census, in 1991 the median family income for African Americans was $18,807, nearly $13,000 less than the median income for white families; 45.6 percent of black children lived below the poverty level, compared to 16.1 percent of white children; and black unemployment stood at 14.1 percent, more than twice the unemployment rate among whites.

But the outlook for African American advancement is encouraging. Experts predict that by the year 2000, blacks will account for nearly 12 percent of the American labor force. A strong black presence is evident in the fields of health care, business, and law, and a new spirit of entrepreneurship is burgeoning among young, upwardly-mobile African Americans. About 70 percent of blacks are making progress in nearly every aspect of American life: the black middle-class is increasing, white-collar employment is on the rise, and although the growth of black political and economic power is slow, it remains steady (Joseph F. Coates, Jennifer Jarratt, and John B. Mahaffie, "Future Work," *Futurist*, May/June 1991, pp. 9-19). The other 30 percent of the black population, however, is trapped by a cycle of poor education, multigenerational poverty, and underemployment. The civil rights struggles of the 1990s and beyond, then, must be primarily economic in nature.

# POLITICS AND GOVERNMENT

The abolitionist movement of the 1830s joined a multiracial coalition in the quest for black emancipation and equality. In addition to agitating for civil rights through traditional legal means, the abolitionists took a daring step by operating the legendary Underground Railroad system, a covert network of safe havens that assisted fugitive slaves in their flight to freedom in the North. "Perhaps nothing did more to intensify the strife between North and South, and to emphasize in a most dramatic way the determination of abolitionists to destroy slavery, than the Underground Railroad," Franklin wrote in *From Slavery to Freedom*. "It was this organized effort to undermine slavery ... that put such a strain on intersectional relations and sent antagonists and protagonists of slavery scurrying headlong into the 1850s determined to have their uncompromising way." Around 50,000 slaves are believed to have escaped to the northern United States and Canada through the Underground Railroad prior to the Civil War.

The reality of the black plight was magnified in 1856 with the Supreme Court's decision in the case of *Dred Scott vs. Sandford*. A slave named Dred Scott had traveled with his master out of the slave state of Missouri during the 1830s and 1840s. He sued his owner for freedom, arguing that his journeys to free territories made him free. The Supreme Court disagreed and ruled that slaves could not file lawsuits because they lacked the status of a U.S. citizen; in addition, an owner was said to have the right to transport a slave anywhere in U.S. territory without changing the slave's status.

The Union victory in the Civil War and the abolition of slavery under President Abraham Lincoln consolidated black political support in the Republican party. This affiliation lasted throughout the end of the nineteenth century and into the early decades of the twentieth century—even after the Republicans began to loosen the reins on the Democratic South following the removal of the last federal troops from the area in 1876.

Earlier in the post-Civil War Reconstruction era, African Americans made significant legislative gains—or so it seemed. The Civil Rights Act of 1866 and the Fourteenth Amendment to the Constitution were intended to provide full citizenship—with all its rights and privileges—to all blacks. The Fifteenth Amendment, ratified in 1870, granted black American men the right to vote.

But the voting rights amendment failed in its attempts to guarantee blacks the freedom to choose at the ballot box. Poll taxes, literacy tests, and grandfather clauses were established by some state and local governments to deny blacks their right to vote. (The poll tax would not be declared unconstitutional until 1964, with the passage of the Twenty-fourth Amendment.) These legalized forms of oppression presented seemingly insurmountable obstacles to black advancement in the United States.

Around the same time—the 1870s—other forms of white supremacist sentiment came to the fore. The so-called "Jim Crow" laws of segregation—allowing for legal, systematic discrimination on the basis of race—were accepted throughout the nation. Voting rights abuses persisted. And violence became a common tool of oppression: between 1889 and 1922, nearly 3,500 lynchings took place, mainly in the southern states of Alabama, Georgia, Louisiana, and Mississippi, but also in some northern cities.

By the turn of the twentieth century, Booker T. Washington had gained prominence as the chief spokesperson on the state of black America and the issue of racial reconciliation. Recognized throughout the United States as an outstanding black leader and mediator, he advocated accommodationism as the preferred method of attaining black rights. His leading opponent, black historian, militant, and author W. E. B. Du Bois, felt it was necessary to take more aggressive measures in the fight for equality. Du Bois spearheaded the Niagara Movement, a radical black intellectual forum, in 1905. Members of the group merged with white progressives in 1910 to form the National Association for the Advancement of Colored People (NAACP). After Washington's death in 1915, the NAACP became a greater force in the struggle for racial reform.

The massive black migration to the North in the 1920s showed that racial tension was no longer just a rural, southern issue. Anti-black attitudes, combined with the desperate economic pressures of the Great Depression, exerted a profound effect on politics nationwide. Democrat Franklin Delano Roosevelt attracted black voters with his "New Deal" relief and recovery programs in the 1930s. For 70 years blacks had been faithful to the Republican Party—the party of Lincoln. But their belief in Roosevelt's "serious interest in the problem of the black man caused thousands of [African Americans] to change their party allegiance," noted John Hope Franklin in *From Slavery to Freedom*. Housing and employment opportunities started to open up, and blacks began to gain seats in various state legislatures in the 1930s and 1940s.

World War II ushered in an era of unswerving commitment to the fight for civil rights. According to Franklin, the continued "steady migration of [African Americans] to the North and West and their concentration in important industrial communities gave blacks a powerful new voice in political affairs. In cities like Chicago, Detroit, and Cleveland they frequently held the balance of power in close elections, and in certain pivotal states the [black vote] came to be regarded as crucial in national elections." Progress was being made on all fronts by national associations, political organizations, unions, the federal branch of the U.S. government, and the nation's court system.

President Harry S Truman, who assumed office on the death of Roosevelt in 1945, contributed to black advancement by desegregating the military, establishing fair employment practices in the federal service, and beginning the trend toward integration in public accommodations and housing. His civil rights proposals of the late 1940s came to fruition a decade later during President Eisenhower's administration. The Civil Rights Act of 1957, also known as the Voting Rights Act of 1957, was the first major piece of civil rights legislation passed by Congress in more than eight decades. It expanded the role of the federal government in civil rights matters and

This photograph is representative of the non-violent demonstrations for civil rights that occurred throughout the 1960s.

established the U.S. Commission on Civil Rights to monitor the protection of black rights.

But the Commission soon determined that unfair voting practices persisted in the South; blacks were still being denied the right to vote in certain southern districts. Because of these abuses, the Civil Rights Act of 1957 was followed three years later by a second act that offered extra protection to blacks at the polls. In 1965, yet another Voting Rights Act was passed to eliminate literacy tests and safeguard black rights during the voter registration process.

The postwar agitation for black rights had yielded slow but significant advances in school desegregation and suffrage—advances that met with bold opposition from some whites. By the mid- to late-1950s, as the black fight for progress gained ground, white resistance continued to mount. The Reverend Martin Luther King, Jr., took the helm of the fledgling civil rights movement—a multiracial effort to eliminate segregation and achieve equality for blacks through non-

violent resistance. The movement began with the boycott of city buses in Montgomery, Alabama, and, by 1960, had broadened in scope, becoming a national crusade for black rights. Over the next decade, civil rights agitators—black and white—organized economic boycotts of racist businesses and attracted front-page news coverage with black voter registration drives and anti-segregationist demonstrations, marches, and sit-ins. Bolstered by the new era of independence that was simultaneously sweeping through sub-Saharan Africa, the movement for African American equality gained international attention.

Around the same time, racial tensions—especially in the South—reached violent levels with the emergence of new white supremacist organizations and an increase in Ku Klux Klan activity. Racially-motivated discrimination on all fronts—from housing to employment—rose as Southern resistance to the civil rights movement intensified. By the late 1950s, racist hatred had once again degenerated into brutality and bloodshed: blacks were being murdered for the cause, and their white killers were escaping punishment.

In the midst of America's growing racial tragedy, Democrat John F. Kennedy gained the black vote in the 1960 presidential elections. His domestic agenda centered on the expansion of federal action in civil rights cases—especially through the empowerment of the U.S. Department of Justice on voting rights issues and the establishment of the Committee on Equal Employment Opportunity. Civil rights organizations continued their peaceful assaults against barriers to integration, but black resistance to racial injustice was escalating. The protest movement heated up in 1961 when groups like the Congress of Racial Equality (CORE), the Student Nonviolent Coordinating Committee (SNCC), and the Southern Christian Leadership Conference (SCLC) organized "freedom rides" that defied segregationist policies on public transportation systems. "By 1963," wrote John Hope Franklin, "the Black Revolution was approaching full tide."

Major demonstrations were staged that April, most notably in Birmingham, Alabama, under the leadership of King. Cries for equality met with harsh police action against the black crowds. Two months later, Mississippi's NAACP leader, Medgar Evers, was assassinated. Soon demonstrations were springing up throughout the nation, and Kennedy was contemplating his next move in the fight for black rights.

On August 28, 1963, over 200,000 black and white demonstrators converged at the Lincoln Memorial to push for the passage of a new civil rights bill. This historic "March on Washington," highlighted by King's legendary "I Have a Dream" speech, brought the promise of stronger legislation from the president.

After Kennedy's assassination that November, President Johnson continued his predecessor's civil rights program. The passage of the Civil Rights Act of 1964 sparked violence throughout the country, including turmoil in cities in New York, New Jersey, Pennsylvania, and Illinois. The Ku Klux Klan stepped up its practice of black intimidation with venomous racial slurs, cross burnings, firebombings—even acts of murder.

The call for racial reform in the South became louder in early 1965. King, who had been honored with the Nobel Peace Prize for his commitment to race relations, commanded the spotlight for his key role in the 1965 Freedom March from Selma to Montgomery, Alabama. But African Americans were disheartened by the lack of *real* progress in securing black rights. Despite the legislative gains made over two decades, John Hope Franklin noted that "between 1949 and 1964 the relative participation of [blacks] in the total economic life of the nation declined significantly."

Black discontent over economic, employment, and housing discrimination reached frightening proportions in the summer of 1965, with rioting in the Watts section of Los Angeles. This event marked a major change in the temper of the civil rights movement. Nearly a decade of nonviolent resistance had failed to remedy the racial crisis in the United States; consequently, a more militant reformist element began to emerge. "Black Power" became the rallying cry of the middle and late 1960s, and more and more civil rights groups adopted all-black leadership. King's assassination in 1968 only compounded the nation's explosive racial situation. According to Franklin, King's murder symbolized for many blacks "the rejection by white America of their vigorous but peaceful pursuit of equality." The Black Revolution had finally crystallized, and with it came a grave sense of loss and despair in the black community. The new generation of black leaders seemed to champion independence and separatism for blacks rather than integration into white American society.

Fear of black advancement led many whites to shift their allegiance to the Republican party in the late 1960s. With the exception of President Jimmy Carter's term in office from 1977 to 1981, Republicans remained in the White House for the rest of the 1970s and 1980s. But a new era of black activism arose with the election of Democratic president Bill Clinton in 1992. After a dozen years of conservatism under Presidents Reagan and Bush, Clinton was seen as a champion of "the people"—all people. Demonstrating a commitment to policies that would cut across the lines of gender, race, and economics, he offered a vision of social reform, urban renewal, and domestic harmony for the United States. Once in office, Clinton appointed African Americans to key posts in his Cabinet, and the black population began wielding unprecedented influence in government. For example, the 102nd Congress included 25 African American representatives; the elections in 1993 brought black representation in the 103rd Congress up to 38.

## MILITARY

Brave African American men and women have advanced the cause of peace and defended the ideals of freedom since the 1700s. As far back as 1702, blacks were fighting against the French and the Indians in the New World. Virginia and South Carolina allowed African Americans to enlist in the militia, and, throughout the eighteenth century, some slaves were able to exchange their military service for freedom. African American soldiers served in the armed forces during the American Revolution, the War of 1812, the Civil War, the Spanish-American War, World Wars I and II, the Korean War, the Vietnam conflict, the Persian Gulf War, and during peace-keeping ventures in Somalia and Haiti. For nearly two centuries, however, segregation existed in the U.S. military—a shameful testament to the nation's long history of racial discrimination.

On March 5, 1770, prior to the outbreak of the American Revolution, a crowd of angry colonists gathered in the streets of Boston, Massachusetts, to protest unjust British policies. This colonial rally—which would later be remembered as the Boston Massacre—turned bloody when British soldiers retaliated with gunfire. A black sailor named Crispus Attucks is said to have been the first American to die in the conflict. The death of Attucks, one of the earliest acts of military service by blacks in America, symbolizes the cruel irony of the revolutionary cause in America—one that denied equal rights to its African American population.

The American Revolution focused increased attention on the thorny issue of slavery. An underlying fear existed that enslaved blacks would revolt if granted the right to bear arms, so most colonists favored the idea of an all-white militia. Although some blacks fought at the battles of Lexington, Concord, and Bunker Hill in 1775, General George Washington issued a ban on the enlistment of slaves that summer; by November, he had extended the ban to all blacks, slave or free. However, the Continental Congress—apprehensive about the prospect of black enlistment in the British Army— partially reversed the policy in the next year. An estimated 5,000 blacks eventually fought in the colonial army.

Integration of the fledgling American Army ended in 1792, when Congress passed a law limiting military service to white men. More than half a century later, blacks were still unable to enlist in the U.S. military.

Many African Americans mistakenly perceived the Civil War, which began in April of 1861, as a war against slavery. But as Alton Hornsby, Jr., pointed out in *Chronology of African-American History*, "[President Abraham] Lincoln's war aims did not include interference with slavery where it already existed." Early in the struggle, the president felt that a stand "against slavery would drive additional Southern and Border states into the Confederacy," a risk he could not afford to take at a time when the Union seemed dangerously close to dissolving. By mid-1862, though, the need for additional Union Army soldiers became critical. The Emancipation Proclamation, issued by Lincoln in 1863, freed the slaves of the Confederacy. With their new "free" status, blacks were allowed to participate in the Civil War. By the winter of 1864-65, the Union Army boasted 168 volunteer regiments of black troops, comprising more than 10 percent of its total strength; over 35,000 blacks died in combat.

Between 300,000 and 400,000 African Americans served in the U.S. armed forces during World War I, but only ten percent were assigned to combat duty. Blacks were still hampered by segregationist policies that perpetuated an erroneous notion of inferiority among the troops; however, the stellar performance of many black soldiers during the era of the world wars helped to dispel these stereotypes. In 1940, for example, Benjamin O. Davis, Sr., became the first black American to achieve the rank of brigadier general. Over the next decade, his son, U.S. Air Force officer Benjamin O. Davis, Jr., distinguished himself as commander of the 99th Fighter Squadron, the 332nd Fighter Group, the 477th Bombardment Group, and the 332nd Fighter Wing.

Several hundred thousand blacks fought for the United States in World War II. Still, according to John Hope Franklin in *From Slavery to Freedom*, "too many clear signs indicated that the United States was committed to maintaining a white army and a black army, and ironically the combined forces of this army had to be used together somehow to carry on the fight against the powerful threat of fascism and racism in the world."

In an effort to promote equality and opportunity in the American military, President Truman issued Executive Order 9981 on July 26, 1948, banning segregation in the armed forces. Six years later, the U.S. Department of Defense adopted an official policy of full integration, abolishing all-black military units. The late 1950s and early 1960s saw a steady increase in the number of career officers in the U.S. military. By the mid-1990s, close to 40 percent of the American military was black. Some social commentators feel that this disproportionately high percentage of African Americans in the military—the entire black population in the United States being around 12 percent—calls attention to the obstacles young black people face in forging a path into mainstream American business.

# INDIVIDUAL AND GROUP CONTRIBUTIONS

African Americans have made notable contributions to American popular culture, to government policy, and to the arts and sciences. The following is a mere sampling of African American achievement:

## EDUCATION

Alain Locke (1886-1954) was a prolific author, historian, educator, and drama critic. A Harvard University graduate and Rhodes Scholar, he taught philosophy at Howard University for 36 years and is remembered as a leading figure in the Harlem Renaissance. For more than three decades, social scientist and Spingarn medalist Kenneth B. Clark (1914- ) taught psychology at New York's City College; his work on the psychology of segregation played an important part in the Supreme Court's 1954 ruling in the *Brown vs. Board of Education* case. In 1987 dynamic anthropologist and writer Johnnetta B. Cole (1936- ) became the first African American woman president of Spelman College, the nation's oldest and most esteemed institution of higher learning for black women. Henry Louis Gates, Jr. (1950- ), a respected literary scholar, critic, and the chairman of Harvard University's African American Studies Department, offers a fresh new perspective on the related roles of black tradition, stereotypes, and the plurality of the American nation in the field of education; he is best known for championing a multicultural approach to learning.

## FILM, TELEVISION, THEATER, AND DANCE

Actor Charles Gilpin (1878-1930) is considered the dean of early African American theater. In 1921, the former vaudevillian was awarded the NAACP Spingarn Award for his theatrical accomplishment. Richard B. Harrison (1864-1935) was an esteemed actor who gained national prominence for his portrayal of "De Lawd" in *Green Pastures*. For three decades Harrison entertained black audiences with one-man performances of William Shakespeare's *Macbeth* and *Julius Caesar*, as well as readings of poems by Edgar Allan Poe, Rudyard Kipling, and Paul Laurence Dunbar. Actor, writer, director, and civil rights activist Ossie Davis (1917- ) is committed to advancing black pride through his work. He has been a groundbreaking figure in American theater, film, and television for five decades.

Best known for her role as Mammy in *Gone with the Wind*, Hattie McDaniel (1895-1952) was awarded the 1940 Oscar for best supporting actress—the first Oscar ever won by an African American performer. Actress and writer Anna Deavere Smith (1950- ), a bold and intriguing new force in American theater, examines issues like racism and justice in original works such as *Fires in the Mirror* and *Twilight: Los Angeles 1992*.

Dancer and choreographer Katherine Dunham (1910?- ) has been called the mother of Afro-American dance. She is best known for blending elements of traditional Caribbean dance with modern African American rhythms and dance forms. Also a noted activist, Dunham went on a 47-day hunger strike in 1992 to protest U.S. policy on Haitian refugees.

## GOVERNMENT

Alexander Lucius Twilight, the first African American elected to public office, was sent to the Vermont legislature in 1836 by the voters of Orleans County. Less than a decade later, William A. Leidesdorf, a black political official, was named sub-consul to the Mexican territory of Yerba Buena (San Francisco); he also served on the San Francisco town council and held the post of town treasurer. Attorney and educator Charles Hamilton Houston (1895-1950) was a brilliant leader in the legal battle to erode segregation in the United States; his student, Thurgood Marshall (1908-1993), successfully argued against the constitutionality of segregation in the 1954 *Brown vs. Board of Education* case. A director of the NAACP Legal Defense and Educational Fund for more than two decades, Marshall went on to become a U.S. Supreme Court justice in 1967. Career military officer Colin Powell (1937- ) made his mark on American history as the first black chairman of the Joint Chiefs of Staff, a position he held from 1989 to 1993. Some political observers have pegged him as a U.S. presidential candidate in the 1996 elections. An early follower of Martin Luther King, Jr., Jesse Jackson (1941- ) became a potent force in American politics in his own right. In 1984 and 1988 he campaigned for the Democratic nomination for the U.S. presidency. Founder of Operation PUSH and the National Rainbow Coalition, Jackson is committed to the economic, social, and political advancement of America's dispossessed and disfranchised peoples. Attorney and politician Carol Moseley-Braun (1947- ) won election to the U.S. Senate in 1992, making her the first black woman senator in the nation. Kweisi Mfume (born Frizzell Gray; 1948- ), a Democratic congressional representative from Maryland for half a dozen years, became the chairman of the powerful Congressional Black Caucus in 1993.

## JOURNALISM

Frederick Douglass (1818-1875), the famous fugitive slave and abolitionist, recognized the power of the press and used it to paint a graphic portrait of the horrors of slavery. He founded *The North Star,* a black newspaper, in 1847, to expose the reality of the black condition in nineteenth century America. John Henry Murphy (1840-1922), a former slave and founder of the *Baltimore Afro-American,* was inspired by a desire to represent black causes with honor and integrity. Activist and journalist T. Thomas Fortune (1856-1928), a staunch defender of black rights during the late nineteenth and early twentieth centuries, used his editorial position at various urban newspapers in the North to crusade for an end to racial discrimination. Robert S. Abbott (1870-1940) was a key figure in the development of black journalism in the twentieth century. The first issue of his *Chicago Defender* went to press in 1905. Charlayne Hunter-Gault (1942- ) broke the color barrier at the University of Georgia, receiving her degree in journalism from the formerly segregated institution in 1963. A national correspondent for public television's *MacNeil/Lehrer NewsHour,* she has earned distinction for her socially-conscious brand of investigative reporting.

## LITERATURE

Langston Hughes (1902-1967) was a major figure of the Harlem Renaissance, a period of intense artistic and intellectual activity centered in New York City's black community during the early 1920s. The author of poetry, long and short fiction, plays, autobiographical works, and nonfiction pieces, Hughes infused his writings with the texture of urban African Americana. Pulitzer Prize-winning author Alex Haley (1921-1992) traced his African heritage, his ancestors' agonizing journey to the New World, and the brutal system of slavery in the United States in his unforgettable 1976 bestseller *Roots.* Playwright Lorraine Hansberry (1930-1965), author of the classic play *A Raisin in the Sun,* was the first black recipient of the New York Drama Critics Circle Award. Maya Angelou (1928- ), renowned chronicler of the black American experience, earned national acclaim in 1970 with the publication of the first volume of her autobiography, *I Know Why the Caged Bird Sings;* she presented her moving original verse, *On the Pulse of Morning,* at the inauguration of U.S. president Bill Clinton in January 1993. Cultural historian and novelist Toni Morrison (1931- ), author of such works as *The Bluest Eye, Tar Baby, Beloved,* and *Jazz,* was awarded the Nobel Prize for literature in 1993. In the late 1980s, Terry McMillan (1951- ) emerged as a powerful new voice on the literary scene; her 1992 novel *Waiting to Exhale* was a runaway bestseller.

## MUSIC

African Americans have made a profound impact on the nation's musical history. The blues and jazz genres, both rooted in black culture, exerted an unquestionable influence on the development of rock and soul music in the United States.

The blues, an improvisational African American musical form, originated around 1900 in the Mississippi Delta region. Some of its pioneering figures include legendary cornetist, bandleader, and composer W. C. Handy (1873-1958), often called the "Father of the Blues"; singing marvel Bessie Smith (1898-1937), remembered as the "Empress of the Blues"; and Muddy Waters (1915-1983), a practitioner of the urban blues strain that evolved in Chicago in the 1940s.

Jazz, a blend of European traditional music, blues, and Southern instrumental ragtime, developed in the South in the 1920s. Key figures in the evolution of jazz include New Orleans horn player and "swing" master Louis Armstrong ("Satchmo"; 1900-1971), who scored big with hits like "Hello, Dolly" and "What a Wonderful World"; Lionel Hampton (1909- ), the first jazz musician to popularize vibes; trumpeter Dizzy Gillespie (1917-1993) a chief architect of a more modern form of jazz called "bebop"; singer Ella Fitzgerald (1918- ), a master of improvisation who came to be known as "The First Lady of Song"; innovative and enigmatic trumpeter, composer, and bandleader Miles Davis (1926-1991), who pioneered the genre's avant-garde period in the 1950s and electrified jazz with elements of funk and rock—beginning the "fusion" movement—in the late 1960s; and Melba Liston (1926- ), trombonist, arranger, and leader of an all-female jazz group in the 1950s and 1960s.

Vocalist, composer, and historian Bernice Johnson Reagon (1942- ), founder of the female *a cappella* ensemble Sweet Honey in the Rock, is committed to maintaining Africa's diverse musical heritage.

In the field of classical music, Marian Anderson (1902-1993), one of the greatest contraltos of all time, found herself a victim of racial prejudice in her own country. A star in Europe for years before her American debut, she was actually barred from making an appearance at Constitution Hall by the Daughters of the American Revolution in April of 1939—an incident that prompted First Lady Eleanor Roosevelt to resign from the organization. Shortly thereafter, on Easter Sunday, Anderson sang on the steps of the Lincoln Memorial. Composer and pianist Margaret Bonds (1913-1972) wrote works that explore the African American experience. Her best known compositions include *Migration*, a ballet; *Spiritual Suite for Piano*; *Mass in D Minor*; *Three Dream Portraits*; and the songs "The Ballad of the Brown King" and "The Negro Speaks of Rivers."

## SCIENCE AND TECHNOLOGY

Granville T. Woods (1856-1910) was a trailblazer in the fields of electrical and mechanical engineering whose various inventions include a telephone transmitter, an egg incubator, and a railway telegraph. His contemporary, George Washington Carver (1861?-1943), was born into slavery but became a leader in agricultural chemistry and botany—and one of the most famous African Americans of his era. Inventor Garrett A. Morgan (1877-1963), a self-educated genius, developed the first gas mask and traffic signal. Ernest Everett Just (1883-1915), recipient of the first Spingarn medal ever given by the NAACP, made important contributions to the studies of marine biology and cell behavior. Another Spingarn medalist, Percy Lavon Julien (1889-1975), was a maverick in the field of organic chemistry. He created synthesized versions of cortisone (to relieve the pain and inflammation of arthritis) and physostigmine (to reduce the debilitating effects of glaucoma).

Surgeon and scientist Charles Richard Drew (1904-1950) refined techniques of preserving liquid blood plasma. Samuel L. Kountz (1930-1981), an international leader in transplant surgery, successfully transplanted a kidney from a mother to a daughter—the first operation of its kind between individuals who were not identical twins. He also pioneered anti-rejection therapy in transplant patients. Benjamin Carson (1951- ) is a pediatric neurosurgeon who gained international acclaim in 1987 by separating a pair of Siamese twins who were joined at their heads. Medical doctor and former astronaut Mae C. Jemison (1957- ) made history as the first black woman to serve as a mission specialist for the National Aeronautics and Space Administration (NASA). She was a crew member on the 1992 flight of the space shuttle *Endeavour*.

## SOCIAL ISSUES

Harriet Tubman (1820?-1913) was a runaway slave who became a leader in the abolitionist movement. A nurse and spy for the Union Army during the Civil War, she earned distinction as the chief "conductor" of the Underground Railroad, leading an estimated 300 slaves to freedom in the North. Attorney, writer, activist, educator, and foreign consul James Weldon Johnson (1871-1938) was an early leader of the NAACP and a strong believer in the need for black unity as the legal fight for civil rights evolved. He composed the black anthem "Lift Every Voice and Sing" in 1900. Labor and civil rights leader A. Philip Randolph (1889-1979) fought for greater economic opportunity in the black community. A presidential consultant in the 1940s, 1950s, and 1960s and a key organizer of the 1963 March on Washington, Randolph is probably best remembered for his role in establishing the Brotherhood of Sleeping Car Porters, the first black union in the country, in 1925.

Ella Baker (1903-1986), renowned for her organizational and leadership skills, co-founded the Southern Christian Leadership Conference, the Student Nonviolent Coordinating Committee, and the Mississippi Freedom Democratic Party—groups that were at the forefront of civil rights activism in the United States. Mississippi native Fannie Lou Hamer (1917-1977) was an impassioned warrior in the fight for black voter rights, black economic advancement, and women's rights. Rosa Parks (1913- ) sparked the Montgomery bus boycott in December of 1955 when her refusal to give up her seat to a white passenger landed her in jail. Malcolm X (born Malcolm Little; 1925-1965) advocated a more radical pursuit of equal rights than Martin Luther King, Jr. (1929-1968), the champion of nonviolent resistance to racism. A fiery speaker who urged blacks to seize self-determination "by any means necessary," Malcolm embraced the concept of global unity toward the end of his life and revised his black separatist ideas. In 1965 he was assassinated by members of the Nation of Islam—an organization with which he had severed earlier ties. Attorney and activist Marian Wright Edelman (1939- ) founded the Children's Defense Fund in 1973. Randall Robinson (1942?- ), executive director of the human rights lobbying organization TransAfrica, Inc., has played a key role in influencing progressive U.S. foreign policy in South Africa, Somalia, and Haiti.

### SPORTS

A Brooklyn Dodger from 1947 to 1956, Jackie Robinson (1919-1972) is credited with breaking the color barrier in professional baseball. In 1974 Frank Robinson (1935- ), a former National and American League MVP, became the first black manager of a major league baseball franchise. Phenomenal Cleveland Brown running back Jim Brown (1936- ), a superstar of the late 1950s and 1960s, helped change the face of professional football—a sport that for years had been dominated by whites. The on-court skills and charisma of two of the top NBA players of the 1980s and early 1990s, retired Los Angeles Laker Earvin "Magic" Johnson (1959- ) and Chicago Bull Michael Jordan (1963- ) left indelible marks on the game of basketball.

Track sensation Jesse Owens (1913-1980) blasted the notion of Aryan supremacy by winning four gold medals at the 1936 Olympics in Berlin. Wilma Rudolph (1940- ) overcame the crippling complications of polio and became the first American woman to win three Olympic gold medals in track and field. Always colorful and controversial, Olympic gold medalist and longtime heavyweight champion Muhammad Ali (born Cassius Clay; 1942- ) was a boxing sensation throughout the 1970s and remains one of the most widely recognized figures in the sport's history. Althea Gibson (1927- ) and Arthur Ashe (1943-1993) both rocked the tennis world with their accomplishments: Gibson, the first black player ever to win at Wimbledon, was a pioneer in the white-dominated game at the dawn of the civil rights era. Ashe, a dedicated activist who fought against racial discrimination in all sports, was the first African American to triumph at Wimbledon, the U.S. Open, *and* a Grand Slam tennis tournament.

### VISUAL ARTS

Sculptor Sargent Johnson (1888-1967), a three-time winner of the prestigious Harmon Foundation medal for outstanding black artist, was heavily influenced by the art forms of Africa. Romare Bearden (1914-1988) was a highly acclaimed painter, collagist, and photomontagist who depicted the black experience in his work. His images reflect black urban life, music, religion, and the power of the family. A series titled *The Prevalence of Ritual* is one of his best-known works. Jacob Lawrence (1917- ), a renowned painter, has depicted through his art both the history of racial injustice and the promise of racial harmony in America. His works include the *Frederick Douglass* series, the *Harriet Tubman* series, the *Migration of the Negro* series, and *Builders*.

Augusta Savage (1900-1962), a Harlem Renaissance sculptor, was the first black woman to win acceptance in the National Association of Women Painters and Sculptors. *Lift Every Voice and Sing*, *Black Women*, and *Lenore* are among her notable works. Multimedia artist and activist Faith Ringgold (1930- ) seeks to raise the consciousness of her audience by focusing on themes of racial and gender-based discrimination. Ringgold is known for weaving surrealist elements into her artworks; her storytelling quilt *Tar Beach* inspired a children's book of the same title.

# MEDIA

### PRINT

*African American Review.*
Founded in 1967, this quarterly publication contains interviews and essays on black American art, literature, and culture.

**Address:** Indiana State University, Department of English, Terre Haute, Indiana 47809.
**Telephone:** (812) 237-2968.

*Africa Report.*
Founded in 1937, this periodical covers current political and economic developments in Africa.

**Address:** African American Institute, 833 United Nations Plaza, New York, New York 10017.
**Telephone:** (212) 949-5666.

**Amsterdam News.**

Now known as the *New York Amsterdam News,* this source was founded in 1909 and is devoted to black community-interest stories.

**Address:** Powell-Savory Corp., 2340 Frederick Douglass Boulevard, New York, New York 10027.

**Telephone:** (212) 932-7400.

**Chicago Defender.**

Founded in 1905 by Robert S. Abbott as a black weekly newspaper, it is now a daily paper with a black perspective.

**Contact:** John H. Sengstacke, Editor.

**Address:** 2400 South Michigan Avenue, Chicago, Illinois 60616.

**Telephone:** (312) 225-2400.

**Crisis.**

The official publication of the National Association for the Advancement of Colored People, this monthly magazine, founded in 1910, features articles on civil rights issues.

**Contact:** Garland Thompson, Editor.

**Address:** Crisis Publishing Co., 260 Fifth Avenue, 6th Floor, New York, New York 10001.

**Telephone:** (212) 481-4100.

**Ebony and Jet.**

Both of these publications are part of the family of Johnson Publications, which was established in the 1940s by entrepreneur John H. Johnson. *Ebony,* a monthly magazine, and *Jet,* a newsweekly, cover African Americans in politics, business, and the arts.

**Contact:** *Ebony*—Lerone Bennett, Jr., Editor; *Jet*—Robert Johnson, Editor.

**Address:** Johnson Publishing Co., Inc., 820 South Michigan Avenue, Chicago, Illinois 60605.

**Telephone:** (312) 322-9200.

**Emerge.**

This monthly news and human interest magazine focuses on the African American perspective in a modern world.

**Contact:** George E. Curry, Editor.

**Address:** Emerge Communications, Inc., 170 Varick Street, New York, New York 10013.

**Telephone:** (212) 627-4157.

**Essence.**

First published in 1970, this monthly magazine targets a black female audience.

**Contact:** Susan L. Taylor, Editor.

**Address:** Essence Communications, Inc., 1500 Broadway, New York, New York 10036.

**Telephone:** (212) 642-0600.

**Freedomways.**

Founded in 1961, this source offers a quarterly review of progress made in the ongoing movement for human freedom.

**Contact:** Esther Jackson and Jean Carey Bond, Editors.

**Address:** 799 Broadway, Suite 542, New York, New York 10003.

**Telephone:** (212) 477-3985.

## RADIO

### WESL-AM (1490).

Founded in 1934; gospel format.

**Contact:** Doug Eason, Director of Operations.

**Address:** 149 South Eighth Sreet, East St. Louis, Illinois 62201.

**Telephone:** (618) 271-1490.

### WLIB-AM (1190).

Founded in 1942; news/talk format with a black ethnic focus.

**Contact:** Mark Riley, Director of Operations.

**Address:** 801 Second Avenue, New York, New York 10017.

**Telephone:** (212) 661-3344.

### WRKS-FM (98.7).

Founded in 1941; an ABC-affiliate with an urban/contemporary format.

**Contact:** Charles M. Warfield, Jr., Director of Operations.

**Address:** 1440 Broadway, New York, New York 10018.

**Telephone:** (212) 642-4340.

## TELEVISION

### Black Entertainment Television (BET).

The first cable network devoted exclusively to black programming, BET features news, public affairs and talk shows, television magazines, sports updates, concerts, videos, and syndicated series.

**Contact:** Robert Johnson, President and Chief Executive Officer.

**Address:** 1232 31st Street, N.W., Washington, D.C. 20007.

**Telephone:** (202) 337-5260.

**WGPR-TV, Channel 62, Detroit.**
Groundbreaking black-owned television station that first went on the air September 29, 1975; began as an independent network; slated in 1994-1995 to become a CBS-affiliate.

**Contact:** George Mathews, President and General Manager.
**Address:** 3146 East Jefferson Avenue, Detroit, Michigan 48207.
**Telephone:** (313) 961-8862.

# ORGANIZATIONS AND ASSOCIATIONS

### Black Filmmakers Foundation (BFF).
Founded in 1978 to support and promote independently produced film and video work for African American artists.

**Addresses:** Tribeca Film Center, 375 Greenwich St., New York, New York 10013; or, 2049 Century Park East, 42nd Floor, Los Angeles, California 90067.
**Telephone:** In New York—(212) 941-3944; in Los Angeles—(310) 201-9579.

### Black Resources, Inc.
A resource on race-related matters for corporations, government agencies, and institutions.

**Address:** 231 West 29th Street, Suite 1205, New York, New York 10001.
**Telephone:** (212) 967-4000.

### NAACP Legal Defense and Educational Fund (LDF).
A nonprofit organization founded in 1940 to fight discrimination and civil rights violations through the nation's court system. (Independent of the NAACP since the mid-1950s.)

**Contact:** Elaine R. Jones, Director-Counsel.
**Address:** 99 Hudson Street, 16th Floor, New York, New York 10013.
**Telephone:** (212) 219-1900.

### The National Association for the Advancement of Colored People (NAACP).
Founded in 1910, the NAACP is perhaps the best-known civil rights organization in the United States. Its goals are the elimination of racial prejudice and the achievement of equal rights for all people.

**Address:** Headquarters—4805 Mt. Hope Drive, Baltimore, Maryland 21215.
**Telephone:** For general information, contact New York office—(212) 481-4100.

### National Black United Fund.
Provides financial and technical support to projects that address the needs of black communities throughout the United States.

**Address:** 2271 Seventh Avenue, New York, New York 10020.
**Telephone:** (212) 234-1695.

### The National Urban League.
Formed in 1911 in New York by the merger of three committees that sought to protect the rights of the city's black population. Best known for piloting the decades-long fight against racial discrimination in the United States, the National Urban League and its regional branches are also active in the struggle for political and economic advancement among African Americans and impoverished people of all colors.

**Address:** 500 East 62nd Street, New York, New York 10021.
**Telephone:** (212) 310-9000.

### Southern Christian Leadership Conference (SCLC).
An educational service agency founded in 1957 (with Martin Luther King, Jr., as its first president) to aid in the integration of African Americans in all aspects of life in the United States. Continues to foster a philosophy of nonviolent resistance.

**Address:** 334 Auburn Avenue, N.E., Atlanta, Georgia 30312.
**Telephone:** (404) 522-1420.

# MUSEUMS AND RESEARCH CENTERS

### The Afro-American Historical and Genealogical Society.
Founded in 1977 to encourage scholarly research in Afro-American history and genealogy.

**Address:** P.O. Box 13086, T Street Station, Washington, D.C. 20009.
**Telephone:** (202) 234-5350.

**The Association for the Study of Afro-American Life and History (ASALH).**
Originally named the Association for the Study of Negro Life and History, this research center was founded by Dr. Carter G. Woodson in 1915. ASALH is committed to the collection, preservation, and promotion of black history.

**Address:** 1401 14th Street, N.W., Washington, D.C. 20005.
**Telephone:** (202) 667-2822.


**The Martin Luther King, Jr., Center for Nonviolent Social Change.**
Founded in 1969 by Coretta Scott King to uphold the philosophy and work of her husband, the slain civil rights leader.

**Contact:** Dexter Scott King, Chairman and Chief Executive Officer; or Coretta Scott King, President.
**Address:** 449 Auburn Avenue, N.E., Atlanta, Georgia 30312.
**Telephone:** (404) 524-8969.


**The Museum of African American Culture.**
Preserves and displays African American cultural artifacts.

**Address:** 1616 Blanding Street, Columbia, South Carolina 29201.
**Telephone:** (803) 252-1450.


**The Schomburg Center for Research in Black Culture.**
An arm of the New York Public Library, the Schomburg Center was founded at the height of the Harlem Renaissance by historian Arthur A. Schomburg to preserve the historical past of people of African descent. It is widely regarded as the world's leading repository for materials and artifacts on black cultural life.

**Contact:** Howard Dodson, Jr., Director.
**Address:** 515 Malcolm X Boulevard, New York, New York 10037-1801.
**Telephone:** (212) 491-2200.


# SOURCES FOR ADDITIONAL STUDY

Bennett, Lerone, Jr. *Before the Mayflower: A History of Black America—The Classic Account of the Struggles and Triumphs of Black Americans*, fifth revised edition. New York: Penguin, 1984.

*A Documentary History of the Negro People in the United States*, two volumes, edited by Herbert Aptheker. New York: Citadel Press, 1969 (originally published in 1951).

Estell, Kenneth. *African America: Portrait of a People*. Detroit: Visible Ink Press, 1994.

Franklin, John Hope. *Racial Equality in America*. Chicago: University of Chicago Press, 1976.

Franklin, John Hope, with Alfred A. Moss, Jr. *From Slavery to Freedom: A History of Negro Americans*, sixth edition. New York: Knopf, 1988 (originally published in 1947).

Harris, Joseph E. *Africans and Their History*. New York: Penguin, 1987.

Hornsby, Alton, Jr. *Chronology of African-American History: Significant Events and People from 1619 to the Present*. Detroit: Gale Research, 1991.

Lemann, Nicholas. *The Promised Land. The Great Black Migration and How It Changed America*. New York: Knopf, 1991.

Lynd, Staughton. *Class Conflict, Slavery, and the U.S. Constitution*. Westport, Connecticut: Greenwood Press, 1980 (originally published in 1967).

Mannix, Daniel Pratt. *Black Cargoes: A History of the Atlantic Slave Trade, 1518-1865*. New York: Viking, 1962.

Maple, Eric. *Superstition and the Superstitious*. A. S. Barnes, 1972.

McPherson, James M. *Blacks in America: Bibliographical Essays*. Garden City, N.Y., 1971. Out of print.

*The Negro American: A Documentary History*, edited by Leslie H. Fishel and Benjamin Quarles. [Glenview, Illinois], 1976.

Parham, Vanessa Roberts. *The African-American Child's Heritage Cookbook*. Sandcastle Publishing, 1993.

Smitherman, Geneva. *Talkin & Testifyin: The Language of Black America.* Boston: Houghton Mifflin, 1977.

Woodson, Carter G. *A Century of Negro Migration.* Chicago: Association for the Study of Negro Life and History, 1918.

———. *The Negro in Our History.* [Washington, D.C.], 1962 (originally published by Associated Publishers, 1922).

# ALBANIAN AMERICANS

by
**Jane Jurgens**

Albanians have succeeded in preserving a sense of communal identity, customs, and traditions in the numerous clubs, associations and coffee-houses (*vatra*) that have been organized wherever Albanians live.

## OVERVIEW

Albania is a mountainous country, 28,748 square miles in size, slightly larger than the state of Maryland. It is located in southeastern Europe and borders Montenegro, Serbia, and Macedonia on the north and east, Greece in the south and southeast, and the Adriatic Sea on the west. The name Albania was given by the Romans in ancient times (after a port called Albanopolis); but the Albanians themselves call their country Shiqiptarë ("Sons of the Eagle"). The majority of the country's population of 3,360,000 consists of Albanians (more than 85 percent) in addition to assorted minorities: Greeks, Bulgarians, Gypsies, Macedonians, Serbs, Jews, and Vlachs. More than two million Albanians live in neighboring Balkan countries (e.g., Kosovo Region in Yugoslavia, Macedonia, and Turkey) as well as in other countries. The country's capital is Tirana; the Albanian flag is red with a black double-edged eagle, the symbol of freedom. The national language is Albanian.

### HISTORY

Albanians descend from the ancient Illyrians. Conquered by the Romans in the third century A.D., they were later incorporated into the Byzantine Empire (395 A.D.) and were subjected to for-

This photograph was taken shortly after this young Albanian woman entered the United States.

eign invasions by Ghots, Huns, Avars, Serbs, Croats, and Bulgarians. In 1468 Albania became part of the Ottoman Empire despite strong resistance by Gjergj Kastrioti Skenderbeu (George Castrioti Skanderbeg, 1403-1468), who is the most outstanding hero of Albania's fight against foreign subjugation. At the beginning of the nineteenth century, Albania's fight for independence intensified under the leadership of Naim Frasheri (1846-1900), Sami Frasheri (1850-1904), and Andon Zaki Cajupi (1866-1930). During World War I, Albania became a protectorate of the Great Powers after a short period of independence in 1912. It once again gained full independence in 1920, first as a republic and since 1928 as a monarchy under King Ahmet Zogu (1895-1961). In 1939, Albania was invaded and occupied by Italy; it regained independence after World War II, but under a Communist regime (led by Enver Hoxha, 1908-1985) which outlawed religion and suppressed the people. After the collapse of communism in 1991, Albania became a free and democratic country with a multi-party parliamentarian system under President Sali Berisha.

### THE FIRST ALBANIANS

Few Albanians came to the United States before the twentieth century. The first Albanian, whose name is lost, is reported to have come to the United States in 1876, but soon relocated to Argentina. Kole Kristofor (Nicholas Christopher), from the town of Katundi, was the first recorded Albanian to arrive in the United States, probably between 1884 and 1886. He returned to Albania and came back to the United States in 1892. In *The Albanians in America*, Constantine Demo records the names of 16 other Albanians who either came with Kole or arrived soon after. They came from Katundi, located in southern Albania.

### SIGNIFICANT IMMIGRATION WAVES

Albanians are the most recent group of Europeans to immigrate to the United States and their numbers have remained small. Prior to World War I, Albanians migrated to America because of poor economic conditions, political concerns, or to escape military conscription in the Turkish army. Many Albanians (between 20,000 and 30,000) who fled Albania for political reasons returned to Albania between 1919 and 1925. Many of these same Albanians re-migrated to the United States, intending to remain permanently in America. Another wave immigrated after Albania came under Communist control in 1944. After the fall of communism, Albanians began entering the United States in increasing numbers between 1990 and 1991. There are no accurate immigration statistics on the most recent immigration.

According to U.S. immigration statistics, between the years 1931 and 1975, the total number of Albanians entering the United States was 2,438. After 1982, the official number of Albanians entering the United States is as follows: 1983 (22); 1984 (32); 1985 (45); 1986 (n/a); 1987 (62); 1988 (82) 1989 (69); 1990 (n/a); 1991 (141). These immigration figures do not reflect accurately the number of Albanians living in the United States. The 1990 population census reports the number of people claiming at least one ancestor as Albanian at 47,710, although the total population in the United States may range from 75,000 to 150,000 or more.

### SETTLEMENT PATTERNS

Early Albanian immigrants settled around Boston and then moved to other parts of Massachusetts where unskilled factory labor was plentiful. Prior to 1920, most of the Albanians who migrated to the United States were Orthodox Tosks from the city of Korce in southern Albania. Most were young males who either migrated for economic gain or were seeking political asylum and did not intend to remain permanently in the United

States. They lived in community barracks or *kon-aks*, where they could live cheaply and send money home. The *konak* gradually gave way to more permanent family dwellings as more women and children joined Albanian men in the United States. Early Massachusetts settlements were established in Worcester, Natick, Southbridge, Cambridge, and Lowell. The 1990 census reveals that the largest number of Albanians live in New York City with a high concentration in the Bronx, followed by Massachusetts, Michigan, New Jersey, Illinois, California, Ohio, and Pennsylvania. Settlements of Albanians can be found in Chicago, Los Angeles, Denver, Detroit, New Orleans, Miami, Pittsburgh, and Washington, D.C.

# ACCULTURATION AND ASSIMILATION

Current studies that fully record the experiences and the contributions of Albanian Americans in the United States do not exist. Albanian neighborhoods have tended to resist assimilation in the United States. The communities in New York and Massachusetts have tended to be restricted and interaction with other groups has been infrequent. Other groups of Albanians in the Midwest may have assimilated more quickly. In 1935, a newspaper reported that the Albanians were "not a clannish people ... [they] associate freely with other nationalities, do business with them, partake of their common culture, and participate in a typically middle class way to the general life of the city" (Arch Farmer, "All the World Sends Sons to Become Americans," *Chicago Sunday Tribune*, July 28, 1935). Albanians have often been confused with other ethnic groups, such as Greeks or Armenians. They have succeeded in preserving a sense of communal identity, customs, and traditions in the numerous clubs, associations and coffee-houses (*vatra*) that have been organized wherever Albanians live.

Most of the early Albanians who immigrated to the United States were illiterate. According to Denna Page in *The Albanian-American Odyssey*, it was estimated that of the 5,000 Albanians in America in 1906, only 20 of them could read or write their own language. Due to the strong efforts of community leaders to make books, pamphlets, and other educational materials (especially the newspaper, *Kombi*) available in the *konaks*, the rate of illiteracy declined significantly. By 1919, 15,000 of 40,000 Albanians could read and write their own language. Albanians remained suspicious of American ways of life and were often reluctant to send their children to American schools. Gradually, they accepted the fact that an education provided the foundation for a better way of life in America.

## CUISINE

Albanian dishes have been heavily influenced by Turkey, Greece, Armenia, and Syria. Recipes have often been adapted and altered to suit American tastes. Albanians enjoy a variety of appetizers, soups, casseroles, pilaf, pies, stews, and desserts. Salads (*sallate*) are made with cabbage, lettuce, onions, peppers, olives, and feta cheese. *Sallate me patate* is a potato salad. Soups are made with a variety of ingredients such as beans, chicken, lentils, and fish. *Pace*, a soup made with lamb's tripe, is served at Easter. Albanian pies, *lakror-byrek*, are prepared with a variety of *gjelle* ("filling"). Fillings may be lamb, beef, cabbage, leeks, onions, squash, or spinach, combined with milk, eggs, and olive oil. A *lakror* known as *brushtul lakror* is made with a cottage and feta cheese filling, butter and eggs. *Domate me qepe* is a *lakror* made with an onion and tomato filling. Stews are made with beef, rabbit, lamb, veal, and chicken, which are combined with cabbage, spinach, green beans, okra, or lentils. Favorites include *mish me patate* (lamb with potatoes), *comblek* (beef with onions) and *comblek me lepur* (rabbit stew). A popular dish with Albanian Italians living in Sicily is Olives and Beef Albanesi-Siciliano, which consists of brown, salted beef cubes in a sauce of tomatoes, parsley, garlic, olives, and olive oil and served with *taccozzelli* (rectangles of pasta and goat cheese). *Dollma* is a term applied to a variety of stuffed dishes, which consist of cabbage, green peppers, or vine leaves, and may be filled with rice, bread, onions, and garlic. An Albanian American variation of the traditionally Greek lasagna-like dish, *moussaka*, is made with potatoes and hamburger instead of eggplant. Albanians enjoy a variety of candies, cookies, custards, sweet breads, and preserves. They include *halva*, a confection made with sugar, flour, butter, maple syrup, water, oil, and nuts; *te matur*, a pastry filled with butter and syrup; *baklava*, a filo pastry made with nuts, sugar, and cinnamon; *kadaif*, a pastry made with shredded dough, butter, and walnuts; and *lokume*, a Turkish paste. Popular cookies include *kurabie*, a butter cookie made without liquid; *finique*, a filled cookie with many variations; and *kuluraqka-kulure*, Albanian "tea cookies." *Te dred-*

*hura, bukevale,* and *brustull* are hot sweet breads. Family members will announce the birth of a child by making and distributing *petulla,* pieces of fried dough sprinkled with sugar or dipped in syrup. Albanians enjoy Turkish coffee or Albanian coffee (*kafe*), Albanian whiskey (*raki*) and wine. *Kos,* a fermented milk drink, is still popular.

### TRADITIONAL COSTUMES

Albanian costumes have been influenced by Turkey, Greece, and Persian-Tartar designs. Albanian traditional costumes vary depending on the region. In countries where Albanians have established themselves, traditional costumes often distinguish the region in Albania from which the Albanian originally came. A man's costume from Malesia (Malcija Vogel area), for example, consists of close-fitting woolen trousers with black cord trim, an apron of wool with a leather belt buckled over it, and a silk jacket with long dull red sleeves with white stripes. A long sleeveless coat may be worn over the jacket along with an outer, short-sleeved jacket (*dzurdin*). The head and neck may be covered with a white cloth. A style of male dress most often seen in the United States is the *fustanella,* a full, white pleated skirt; a black and gold jacket; a red flat fez with a large tassel (*puskel*); and shoes with black pompoms.

Women's clothing tends to be more colorful than the men's clothing. Northern Albanian costumes tend to be more ornamental and include a distinctive metal belt. Basic types of costume include a wide skirt (*xhublete*), long shirt or blouse (*krahol*), and a short woolen jacket (*xhoke*). The traditional costume of Moslem women may include a tightly pleated skirt (*kanac*) or large woollen trousers (*brekeshe*). Aprons are a pervasive feature in every type of women's costume and great variety is seen in their shape and embroidery. Many Albanian Americans often wear traditional costumes during Independence Day celebrations and other special occasions and social events.

### HOLIDAYS AND CELEBRATIONS

Since Albanian Americans are members of either Roman Catholic, Orthodox, or Islamic faiths, many religious festivals and holy days are observed. November 28 is celebrated as Albanian Independence Day, the day that Albanians declared their independence from the Ottoman Empire in 1912. Many Albanian Albanians also recognize the Kosova declaration of independence from Serbia on July 2, 1990.

### MUSICAL TRADITIONS

Although the Albanian musical tradition has been influenced by neighboring countries such as Greece, much of the musical folklore remains distinct. Albania has had a rich tradition of musical and theatrical activities. In 1915, Albanian Americans organized the Boston Mandolin Club and the Albanian String Orchestra. They also had amateur groups perform plays by Albanian authors. Because the heroic sense of life has always been part of Albanian life, ballads are often recited and sung in an epic-recitative form that celebrates not only fantastic heroes of the past but also more recent heroes and their deeds in modern history. Songs may be accompanied by traditional instruments such as the two stringed *cifteli,* a lute instrument, and a*lahuta,* a one-stringed violin.

# LANGUAGE

Albanian is probably part of the Illyrian branch of eastern Indo-European. It is a descendant of Dacian, one of the ancient languages that were among the Thraco-Phrygian group once spoken in Anatolia and the Balkan Peninsula. Its closest modern relative is Armenian. Today, Albanian is spoken in two major dialects (with many subdialects) in Albania and in neighboring Kosova—*Tosk* (about two-thirds of the population) and *Gheg* (the remaining one-third). A third dialect (*arberesh*) is spoken in Greece and southern Italy. Throughout the centuries, Albania has endured numerous invasions and occupations of foreign armies, all of whom have left their influence on the language. Despite outside influence, a distinct Albanian language has survived. Albanians call their language "*shqip.*"

Until the early twentieth century, Albanians used the Greek, Latin, and Turko-Arabic alphabets and mixtures of these alphabets. In 1908, Albania adopted a standard Latin alphabet of 26 letters, which was made official in 1924. During the 1920s and 1930s, the government tried to establish a mixed Tosk and Gheg dialect from the Elbascan region as the official language. In 1952, a standardized Albanian language was adopted, which is a mixture of Gheg and Tosk but with a prevailing Tosk element. In addition to the letters of the Latin alphabet, the Albanian language adds: "dh," "gf," "ll," "nj," "rr," "sh," "th," "xh," and "zh." Albanian is taught at such universities as the University of California-San Diego, University of Chicago, University of North Carolina-

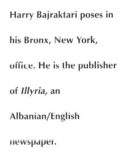

Harry Bajraktari poses in his Bronx, New York, office. He is the publisher of *Illyria,* an Albanian/English newspaper.

Chapel Hill, and Cleveland State University. Libraries with Albanian language collections include the Library of Congress, Chicago Public Library, Boston Public Library, New York Public Library (Donnel Library Center), and Queens Borough Public Library.

## GREETINGS AND OTHER POPULAR EXPRESSIONS

Some common expressions in the Albanian language include: *Po* ("Yes"); *Jo* ("No"); *Te falemnderit/Ju falemnderit* ("Thank you"); *Po, ju lutem* ("Yes, please"); *Miredita* ("Hello" or "Good day"); *Mire-mengjes* ("Good Morning"); *Si jeni?* ("How are you?"); *Gezohem t'ju njoh* ("Pleased to meet you" or "morning"); *Mirembrema* ("Good evening"); *Naten e mire* ("Good night"); *Mirupafshim* ("Goodbye"); *Me fal/Me falni* ("Excuse me"); *Ne rregull* ("All right" or "Okay"); *S'ka perse* ("Don't mention it"); *Gjuha vete ku dhemb dhembballa* ("The tongue follows the toothache"); *Shqiptare* ("Albanians").

# FAMILY AND COMMUNITY DYNAMICS

## THE CODE OF LEKE DUKAGJINI (*Kanuni I Leke Dukagjinit*)

The Kanun is an ancient set of civil, criminal, and family laws that still exerts influence on the lives of many Albanian Americans. The Kanun is traditionally ascribed to Leke Dukagjini (1460-1481), a compatriot and contemporary of Skanderberg. It sets forth rights and obligations regarding the church, family, and marriage. The code is based on the concepts of honor (*bessa*) and blood; the individual is obligated to guard the honor of family, clan, and tribe. The rights and obligations surrounding the concept of honor have often led to the blood feud (*gjak*), which frequently lasts for generations. At the time of King Zog in the 1920s, the blood feud accounted for one out four male deaths in Albania. This code was translated into English and published in a bilingual text in

1989 in the United States. American attorneys brought the code to the attention of Albanian lawyers to help Albania codify their new legislation after the collapse of communism. According to a newspaper article, the code is "the central part of their legal and cultural identity" (*New York Times*, November 11, 1994, p. B-20).

The Kanun defines the family as a "group of human beings who live under the same roof, whose aim is to increase their number by means of marriage for their establishment and the evolution of their state and for the development of their reason and intellect." The traditional Albanian household is a patriarchy in which the head of the household is the eldest male. The principal roles of the wife are to keep house and raise the children. The children have a duty to honor their parents and respect their wishes.

### THE ROLE OF WOMEN

Although the Kanun considers a woman a superfluity in the household, many Albanian American women in the United States would strongly disagree. Historically, Albanian American women have borne the responsibility of preserving the memories, customs, and traditions of the Albanian homeland. A woman's first obligation is to marry and raise a family. Girls have not been allowed as much freedom as boys and were not encouraged "to go out." Instead, girls have been kept at home and taught domestic skills. Girls were sent through high school but not encouraged to pursue higher education and a career. After graduation and before marriage, women have often helped with the family business. Albanian women have usually married at an early age.

During the 1920s and 1930s, Albanian men outnumbered Albanian women in the United States by about three to one. Many Albanian men considered their stay in America temporary and therefore left their wives in Albania with the intent of making enough money to return home. During this period, when Albanian women were in short supply, Albanian men in the United States began to "order" wives from Albania. The man usually supplied the dowry, which compensated the girl's parents for her fare to the United States.

Today many Albanian American women feel caught between two worlds. They often feel obligated to conform to the standards and mores of their community but, at the same time, are pressured to "Americanize." Although many Albanian American women have pursued higher education and careers outside the home, many in the community still view these pursuits as inappropriate.

Albanian American women have only recently begun to organize. The *Motrat Qirijazi* (Sisters Qirjazi), the first Albanian-American women's organization, was founded on March 27, 1993. The principal founder and current president is Shqipe Baba. This organization serves all Albanian women in the United States, assisting and supporting them in the pursuit of unity, education, and advancement.

### WEDDINGS

Traditionally, Albanian weddings are arranged by parents or by an intermediary or matchmaker. The festivities may begin a week before the wedding (*jav' e nuses*—"marriage week"). Usually, an engagement ceremony is held between the two families and the bride is given a gold coin as a token of the engagement. A celebration is held at the home of the bride's parents and the future bride is given gifts and sweets. Refreshments are usually served. A second celebration is given by the family of the groom and the bride's family attends. At these celebrations, small favors of candy-coated almonds (*kufeta*) are exchanged. In Albania, a dowry is usually given but this custom is not followed in the United States.

A week before the ceremony, wedding preparations began. During this week, relatives and friends visit the homes of the couple and food preparation begins. A chickpea bread (*buke me qiqra*) is usually prepared. Gifts to the groom and the bride's trousseau and wedding clothes are displayed. A party is given in which family and friends attend. Members of the groom's family come to the house of the bride and invite her to the festivities. They carry wine, flowers, and a plate of rice, almond candy, and coins with a cake on top. The groom also invites the *kumbare* (godfather) and *vellam* (best man). The bride gives similar gifts. The party is a time of great rejoicing with food, drink, dancing, and singing. Around midnight, the bride and groom, with family and friends, go in opposite directions to three different bodies of water to fill two containers. Coins are thrown into the air at each stop for anyone to pick up.

On the day of the wedding, the bride is dressed, given a sip of wine by her parents along with their good wishes. Other family members give her money. The *vellam* brings in the bride's shoes, filled with rice and almond candy, wrapped in a silk handkerchief. Accompanied by singing women, the *vellam* puts the shoes on the bride and gives money to the person who assisted the bride in dressing. The *vellam* is encouraged to give everybody money. He throws coins into the air three times and everyone tries to get one coin. The groom's family accompanies the bride to the ceremony. The ceremony is followed by a reception. On the following day, the bride may be visited by her family, who bring sweets (*me peme*). One week after the ceremony, the couple is visited by friends and relatives. This is called "first visit" (*te pare*). After a few weeks, the bride's dowry may be displayed (in Albania) and the bride, in turn, distributes gifts to the groom's family. The couple is sent off with good wishes: "*te trashegojen e te plaken; jete te gjate me dashuri*" or "a long, happy, healthy life together" ("Albanian Customs," *Albanian Cookbook* [Worcester, Massachusetts: Women's Guild, St. Mary's Albanian Orthodox Church, 1977).

## BIRTH AND BIRTHDAYS

Traditionally, the one who tells friends and relatives that a child has been born receives a *sihurik* (tip). Within three days after the birth, the family makes *petulla* (fried dough or fritters) and distributes them to friends and family. A hot sweet bread (*buevale*) may also be prepared for guests who visit the mother and child. A celebration is usually held on the third day where friends and relatives bring *petulla* and other gifts. In the Orthodox Church, this celebration may be delayed until the child is baptized. Traditionally, for Albanians of the Orthodox faith, the *kumbare* and *ndrikull* (godparents) choose the name of the child to be baptized. Many superstitions surround the birth of an Albanian child. Among older Albanian Americans may of these superstitions may still exist. Infants are especially vulnerable to the "evil eye" and many Albanian mothers will place a *kuleta* (amulet) on a new-born child. For Christians, the *kuleta* may be a small cross, and among Muslims, it may be a small triangular silver form (*hajmali*). Garlic may also ward off evil. A person who touches an Albanian child or offers a compliment is required say "*Mashalla*" (as God wishes) to ward off the misfortune of the evil eye.

Among Orthodox Christians, birthdays are not traditionally observed. Instead, the family observes a "name's day" for the saint after whom the person is named. Family and friends may gather together and wish the person a "happy name-day" and "good health and long life." The family may serve guests fruit preserves (*liko*), pastries (*te embla*), Albanian whiskey (*raki*), and coffee (*kafe*). Guests would be formally served in the reception room (*ode*) or the living room (*vater*). The guests are treated with great courtesy and all formalities are observed.

# RELIGION

Albanians in the United States are primarily Orthodox Christians, Roman Catholics, or Muslims. Currently, the Albanian Orthodox Church in the United States is divided into two ecclesiastical jurisdictions. The Albanian Orthodox Archdiocese in America (OCA) is an autocephalous church established in 1908 by Fan S. Noli, a major religious and political figure in the Albanian community. With a membership of around 45,000, it currently has 16 parishes nationwide. The current Primate is Metropolitan Theodosius. The headquarters of the Archdiocese, St. George Albanian Orthodox Cathedral, is located in South Boston. One of the oldest chapters of the St. George Cathedral was organized in Worcester, Massachusetts, in 1911. This chapter became the Church of Saint Mary's Assumption in 1915. The Albanian Orthodox Archdiocese of America, established in 1950 by Bishop Mark Lipa, is under the jurisdiction of the ecumenical Patriarch of Constantinople. This Archdiocese currently administers two churches, Saint Nicholas in Chicago and Holy Trinity in South Boston.

Albanian Roman Catholics began coming to the United States in the 1960s and 1970s. At present, three Albanian Catholic churches exist in the United States: Church of Our Lady of Shkodra, located in the Bronx, New York City, founded in 1969 and has a membership of 1,350; St. Paul Catholic Church, located in Warren, Michigan; and Our Lady of the Albanians, located in Beverly Hills, Michigan.

Albanian Muslims came to the United States around 1913. Currently, there are between 25,000 and 30,000 Albanian Muslims in the United States, primarily of the Sunni division within Islam. The Presidency of Albanian Muslim Community Centers in the United States and Canada was founded in 1992 by Imam Vehbi Ismail (1919- ) in an attempt to provide unity for Muslims of Albanian heritage. The Presidency comprises 13 community centers or mosques located in Connecticut, Philadelphia, Toronto, New

York, New Jersey, Florida, and Michigan. Albanian Americans of all faiths are welcome at these centers (for more information on Albanian Muslims, contact Imam Vehbi Ismail, Albanian Islamic Center, 20426 Country Club Road, Harper Woods, Michigan 48236).

A small sect of Muslims of the Bektaski Order, the First Albanian Teke Bektashiane in America, is located in Taylor, Michigan. The Order was founded in 1954. They have a small library and publish *The Voice of Bektashism*.

# EMPLOYMENT AND ECONOMIC TRADITIONS

The Albanians who came to the United States prior to 1920 were from rural backgrounds and worked as farmers, while others from the urban areas worked as small shopkeepers and tradesmen. The large population of Albanians who settled in Massachusetts found work with the American Optical Company of Southbridge and the textile mills of New Bedford. Others worked as cooks, waiters, and bellhops. Albanians soon began opening their own businesses. The most successful Albanian businesses were fruit stores and restaurants. "By 1925 ... most Albanians of Greater Boston could claim ownership of over three hundred grocery and fruit stores" (Dennis Lazar, *Ethnic Community as it Applies to a Less Visible National Group: The Albanian Community of Boston, Massachusetts* [Rensselaer Polytechnic Institute, doctoral dissertation, 1982], p. 6). Today Albanians are employed in a variety of professional and enterprises. The Ghegs and Kosovars have been especially successful in the Bronx area of New York City, selling and managing real estate.

# POLITICS AND GOVERNMENT

Albanian Americans have always felt a strong attachment to Albania and have supported events that occur in the homeland. Both the Orthodox church and the Albanian press have played important roles in the awakening of Albanian nationalism in the United States. The early political efforts of Albanian Americans centered upon furthering the cause of Albania's independence from the Ottoman Empire by instilling a sense of pride in Albanian heritage. Early names in the national-

ist movement were Petro Nini Luarasi, who founded the first Albanian national organization in America, the *Mali i Memedheut* ("Longing for the Homeland"), and Sotir Petsi, who founded *Kombi*, the first known Albanian weekly newspaper. *Kombi* actively supported an independent Albania, run by Albanians, within the Turkish empire. The circulation of this early newspaper was instrumental in reducing the rate of illiteracy among Albanians in the United States. Fan S. Noli was one of the most influential figures in the Albanian Nationalist movement in the United States. On January 6, 1907, he founded *Besa-Besen* ("Loyalty"), the first Albanian Nationalist organization in the United States. The founding of the Albanian Orthodox Church in America in 1908 was also a significant event in the life of Albanian Americans. To further Albania's freedom, Fan Noli began publication of *Dielli* ("The Sun") in 1909. A successor to *Kombi*, *Dielli* supported liberation for Albania. Faik Konitza became the first editor of *Dielli*. To further strengthen the cause, a merger of many existing Albanian organizations occurred in April 1912, becoming the Pan-Albanian Federation of America (*Vatra*). Vatra became the principal organization to instill Albanians with a sense of national purpose.

Since the end of World War II, Albanian Americans have shown an increasing interest in American politics, as the process relates to Albanian issues. The Albanian Congressional Caucus has recently been formed with the support of congressional members Elliot Engle (New York), Susan Molinare (New York), and others. Its purpose is to promote Albanian causes with a focus on the plight of Albanians in Kosova. With the defeat of communism in Albania, many new immigrants have arrived in the United States. Several new immigrant aid societies, such as the New England Albanian Relief Organization, Frosinia Organization, and the Albanian Humanitarian Aid Inc., have been organized to assist newly arrived Albanian immigrants. Such organizations have also worked to assist Albanians in Albania.

# INDIVIDUAL AND GROUP CONTRIBUTIONS

### ACADEMIA

Arshi Pipa (1920- ), born in Scutari, Albania, taught humanities, philosophy, and Italian at various colleges and universities in Albania and in the United States. Nicholas Pano (1934- ) is a professor of history and has served as the Dean of Arts and Sciences at Western Illinois University; he has made contributions to scholarly journals on the subject of Albania and is the author of *The People's Republic of Albania* (1968). Peter R. Prifti (1924- ), author and translator, has made significant contributions to Albanian studies and has published widely on a variety of Albanian topics; he is the author of *Socialist Albania Since 1944* (1978). Stavro Skendi (1906-1989), born in Korce, Albania, was Emeritus Professor of Balkan Languages and Culture at Columbia University from 1972 until his death.

## BUSINESS

Anthony Athanas (1912- ) is a community leader and has been a restauranteur for over 50 years.

## COMMUNITY LEADERS

Constantine A. Chekrezi, an early supporter of the nationalist movement in Albania, briefly served as editor of *Dielli* in 1914 and published *Illyria* from March to November 1916; he is the author of *Albania Past and Present* (1919), which is considered to be the first work in English on Albania written by an Albanian, *A History of Europe—Ancient, Medieval and Modern* (1921), an early history of Europe written in Albanian, and an English-Albanian Dictionary (1923). Christo Dako, an educator and a key figure in the early nationalist movement, is the author of *Albania, the Master Key to the Near East* (1919). Faik Konitza (1876-1942), was one of the more influential leaders of the Albanian community in America in the early twentieth century; he published the magazine *Albania* from 1897-1909 and was the editor of *Dielli* from 1909-1910, and 1921-1926; he also co-founded the Pan-American Federation of America in 1912, serving as its president from 1921-1926; he served as Minister Plenipotentiary of Albania from 1926-1939. Fan Stylian Noli (1865-1964) was one of the most well-known and distinguished historical personalities in the Albanian community; a major figure in the Albanian nationalist movement, Noli founded the Albanian Orthodox Church In America in 1908. Eftalia Tsina (1870-1953), the mother of physician Dimitra Elia, was an early promoter of Albanian social and cultural issues; in the 1920s, she founded *Bashkimi*, the first Albanian women's organization in Boston.

## ENTERTAINMENT

John Belushi (1949-1982), actor and comedian, is best known for his work on the original television series *Saturday Night Live* (1975-1979); his movies include: *Goin' South* (1978), *National Lampoon's Animal House* (1978), *Old Boyfriends* (1979), *The Blues Brothers* (1980), *Continental Divide* (1981), and *Neighbors* (1981). His brother, James (Jim) Belushi (1954- ) is an actor and comedian who has been in films since 1978; his best-known films include: *The Principal* (1987), *Red Heat* (1988), *K-9* (1989), *Mr. Destiny* (1990), *Only the Lonely* (1991), *Curly Sue* (1991), and *Diary of a Hitman* (1992). Stan Dragoti (1932- ) is a prominent director and producer who is best known for his work in movies and television; his best-known work as a movie director includes: *Dirty Little Billy* (1973), *Love at First Bite* (1979), *Mr. Mom* (1983), *The Man with One Red Shoe* (1985), *She's Out of Control* (1989), and *Necessary Roughness* (1991).

## JOURNALISM

Gjon Mili (1904-1984), a photographer for *Life* magazine and other magazines from 1939, is best known for his innovative and visionary work with color and high speed photography. His vivid images are well known to readers of *Life*; collections of his work are housed in the Museum of Modern Art (New York), Time-Life Library (New York), Massachusetts Institute of Technology (Cambridge), and the Bibliotheque Nationale (Paris). Donald Lambro (1940- ) is a writer, political analyst, and investigative reporter whose writings include *The Federal Rathole* (1975), *Conscience of a Young Conservative* (1976), *Fat City: How Washington Wastes Your Taxes* (1980), *Washington—City of Scandals: Investigating Congress and Other Big Spenders* (1984) and *Land of Opportunity: The Entrepreneurial Spirit in America* (1986).

## MEDICINE

Andrew and Dimitra Tsina Elia were early pioneers in the Albanian community in the field of medicine. Andrew Elia (1906-1991) graduated from Boston University Medical School in 1935 and was a practicing obstetrician and gynecologist in the Boston area. Dimitra Elia (1906-1965) was one of the first Albanian American women to practice general medicine in the United States.

## MUSIC

Thomas Nassi (1892- ), musician and composer, graduated from the New England Conservatory of

Music in 1918; he trained choirs for the Cathedral of St. George in Boston and for churches in Natick, Worcester, and Southbridge, Massachusetts, between 1916-1918. He also arranged Byzantine liturgical responses in Albanian for mixed choirs.

## POLITICS

Steven Peters (1907-1990) served as a research analyst in the U.S. State Department in 1945 and the Foreign Service in 1958; he is the author of *The Anatomy of Communist Takeovers* and the government publications, *Area Handbook for the Soviet Union* and *Area Handbook for Albania*. Rifat Tirana (c. 1907-1952), an economist, was a member of the staff of the League of Nations in the 1930s; at the time of his death, he was serving as deputy chief of the U.S. Security Agency Mission to Spain; he authored *The Spoil of Europe* (1941). Bardhyl Rifat Tirana (1937- ) served as co-chair of the Presidential Inaugural Committee (1976-1977) and director of the Defense Civil Preparedness Agency (1977-1979).

## SPORTS

Lee Constantine Elia (1937- ), baseball player, coach, and manager, managed the Chicago Cubs (1982-1983) and the Philadelphia Phillies (1987-1988).

## WRITERS

Shqipe Malushi, poet, essayist, media information specialist and an active community leader, has published fiction, nonfiction, translations, essays, and newspapers articles; her works of poetry, written in Albanian and in English, include: *Memories of '72* (1972, in Kosova), *Exile* (1981), *Solitude* (1985), *Crossing the Bridges* (1990), and *For You* (1993); she has published *Beyond the Walls of the Forgotten Land* (1992), a collection of short stories, and *Transformation* (1988), a book of essays. She has also written and collaborated on several plays and screenplays. Loretta Chase (1949- ), born in Worcester, Massachusetts, is a popular writer of romance novels for Regency and Avon Presses; her novels include: *Isabella* (1987), *Viscount Vagabond* (1988), and *Knaves Wager* (1990). Nexmie Zaimi is the author of *Daughter of the Eagle: The Autobiography of an Albanian Girl* (1937), which describes her immigrant experience, customs, and practices.

## PRINT

### Albanian Herald.
Albanian and English. Begun in 1993, the *Herald* is one the newest Albanian newspapers with a nationwide circulation. Less political than either *Liria* or *Illyria*, the paper covers a wide variety of cultural, social, and historical topics as well as political events.

**Contact:** Gjok Martini, Editor.
**Address:** 11661 Joseph Campau, Hamtramck, Michigan 48212.
**Telephone:** (313) 365-1133.

### Albanica.
Journal devoted to Albanian culture on a scholarly level.

**Contact:** Arshi Pipa, Editor.
**Address:** 134 G Street, N.W., Washington, D.C. 20024.
**Telephone:** (202) 479-0633.

### Dielli.
Albanian and English weekly, one of the oldest Albanian newspapers, published by the Pan Albanian Federation of America, *Vatra*. It publishes articles on social, cultural, and political events of interest to Albanians.

**Contact:** Agim Karagjozi, Editor.
**Address:** 167 East 82nd Street, New York, New York 10028.
**Telephone:** (718) 347-6470.

### Illyria.
Albanian and English bi-weekly published by the Illyrian Publishing Company featuring international news with a focus on news from the Balkans. Emphasis is currently on political events of interest to Albanian Americans; however, the paper is beginning to focus on local community events as well.

**Contact:** Hajdar Bajraktari.
**Address:** 232 Hughes Avenue, Bronx, New York 10452.
**Telephone:** (718) 220-2000.

### Liria.
Albanian and English monthly published by the Free Albania Organization. Features local and national news on Albanian community life and events and news from Albania.

Contact: Shkelqim Begari, Editor.
Address: 409 West Broadway, South Boston, Massachusetts 02127.
Telephone: (617) 269-5192.

## RADIO

### WCUW-FM.

"Albanian Hour" is the oldest continuous Albanian radio program in the country; it airs on Saturday from 8:30 to 9:30 p.m. It broadcasts local community news and events and international news from Albania. Lately, it focuses on concerns of new immigrants from Albania.

Contact: Demetre Steffon.
Address: 910 Main Street, Worcester, Massachusetts 01602.
Telephone: (508) 753-1012.

### WKDM-AM.

"LDK Radio Program" ("Democratic League of Kosova") airs on Friday, 7:00 to 8:00 p.m. It presents local news, community events, and international news.

Contact: Rooster Mebray, Producer.
Address: 449 Broadway, Second Floor, New York, New York 10013.
Telephone: (212) 966-1059; or (718) 933-6202.

### WKDM-AM.

"Voice of Malesia" airs on Monday from 7:00 to 8:00 p.m. It features community events, music, interviews, and news from Albania.

Contact: Gjeto Sinishtaj.
Address: 449 Broadway, Second Floor, New York, New York 10013.
Telephone: (212) 966-1059; or (718) 898-0107.

### WMEX-AM.

"Albanian Hour of Boston," formerly, "Voice of Albania," airs every Sunday evening from 8:00 to 9:00 p.m. It features local community news and events, music, and interviews as well as news from Albania.

Contact: David Kosta.
Address: P.O. Box 170, Cambridge, Massachusetts 02238.
Telephone: (617) 666-4803.

### WNWK-FM.

"Festival of the Albanian Music" airs on Sundays, 8:30 to 9:00 p.m. and features music from Albania.

Contact: Louis Shkreli.
Address: 449 Broadway, New York, New York 10013.
Telephone: (212) 966-1059; or (718) 733-6900.

## TELEVISION

### WNYE (Channel 25, Brooklyn, New York).

"T.V. Victoria" airs Sunday, 4:00 to 5:00 p.m. and features local and international news, local and community events, and sports. Commentary is provided in Albanian and English on news from Albania.

Contact: Terrence O'Driscoll, Station Manager; or Esat Osmani.
Address: 112 Tillary Street, Brooklyn, New York 11201.
Telephone: (718) 935-4480; or (718) 939-4838.

# ORGANIZATIONS AND ASSOCIATIONS

At present, Albania is undergoing rapid changes and Albanian Americans are responding. Since the fall of the Communist government in Albania (1990-1992), several new relief organizations such as the Frosina Organization (New York City), New England Albanian Relief Organization (Worcester, Massachusetts), and Albanian Humanitarian Aid Inc. (New York City) have been formed within the Albanian community to assist newly arrived immigrants. Second, many long standing Albanian organizations and associations in the United States are redefining their function in view of the new political order that now exists in Albania.

### Albanian American Civic League.

Founded in 1986, the organization is dedicated to informing the American public about the political and social problems in Albania.

Contact: Joseph DioGuardi.
Address: 717 Second Street, N.E., Washington, D.C. 20003.
Telephone: (202) 547-3637.

### Albanian American National Organization (AANO).

Founded in 1938 as the Albanian Youth Organization, it is a non-denominational cultural organization open to all Albanians and Americans of Albanian descent.

**Contact:** Andrew Tanacea.

**Address:** 22 Dayton Street, Worcester, Massachusetts 10609.

**Telephone:** (508) 754-9440.


### Albanian Catholic Institute (ACI).

Gathers and disseminates information on the state of religion in Albania; conducts research on Albania's religious and cultural history; maintains collection of materials pertaining to Albanian history.

**Contact:** Gjon Sinishta.

**Address:** University of San Francisco, Xavier Hall, San Francisco, California 94117-1080.

**Telephone:** (415) 666-6966.


### Albanian National Council.

Founded in 1988, the organization provides assistance to all people of Albanian descent regardless of religion.

**Contact:** Gjok Martini.

**Address:** 11661 Hamtramck, Michigan 48212.

**Telephone:** (313) 365-1133.


### Free Albania Organization (FAO).

A nonprofit organization that has kept the Albanian community informed about political and social events in Albania through the newspaper *Liria* since 1941.

**Contact:** William Johns, President.

**Address:** 409 West Broadway, South Boston, Massachusetts 02127.

**Telephone:** (617) 269-5192.


### Pan-Albanian Organization, "*Vatra.*"

Founded in 1912, *Vatra* is a national organization open to all Albanians 18 years of age and older. The organization is well known to all Albanians and has played an active political and cultural role in the community. It has sponsored many charitable, cultural, and social events and publishes books on Albanian culture. The organization has provided scholarships for students of Albanian descent. *Vatra* has recently relocated from South Boston to New York. It continues to publish the newspaper *Dielli*.

**Contact:** Agim Karagjozni.

**Address:** 167 East 82nd Street, New York, New York.

**Telephone:** (516) 354-6598 or (718) 482-2002.


# MUSEUMS AND RESEARCH CENTERS

**Fan S. Noli Library.**

The library and archives contain the papers of Fan S. Noli.

**Address:** Albanian Orthodox Archdiocese in America, St. George Albanian Orthodox Cathedral, 529 East Broadway, South Boston, Massachusetts 02127.

**Telephone:** (617) 268-1275.


# SOURCES FOR ADDITIONAL STUDY

Demo, Constantine. *The Albanians in America: The First Arrivals*. Boston: Society of Fatbardhesia of Katundi, 1960.

Federal Writers Project of Massachusetts. *The Albanian Struggle in the Old World and the New*. Boston: Federal Writers Project of Massachusetts, 1939.

Noli, Fan S. *Fiftieth Anniversary Book of the Albanian Orthodox Church in America, 1908-1958*. Boston: Pan-Albanian Federation of America, 1960.

Page, Denna L. *The Albanian-American Odyssey: A Pilot Study of the Albanian Community of Boston, Massachusetts*. New York: AMS Press, 1987.

Roucek, Joseph. "The Albanian and Yugoslav Immigrants in America," *Revue Internationale Des Etudes Balkaniques*, 3, 1938; pp. 499-519.

————. "Albanian Americans." In *One America*, edited by Francis Brown and Joseph S. Roucek. New York: Prentice Hall, 1952; pp. 232-239.

# AMISH

by
**Donald B.
Kraybill**

If the Amish can
educate and retain
their children, make
a living, and restrain
interaction with the
larger world, they
will likely flourish
into the twenty-first
century.

## OVERVIEW

The year 1993 marked the existence of 300 years
of Amish life. Extinct in their European homeland, today they live in more than 200 settlements in 22 states and the Canadian province of
Ontario. The Amish are one of the more distinctive and colorful cultural groups across the spectrum of American pluralism. Their rejection of
automobiles, use of horse-drawn farm machinery,
and distinctive dress set them apart from the
high-tech culture of modern life.

### HISTORY

Amish roots stretch back to sixteenth-century
Europe. Impatient with the pace of the Protestant
Reformation, youthful reformers in Zurich,
Switzerland, outraged religious authorities by baptizing each other in January 1525. The rebaptism
of adults was then a crime punishable by death.
Baptism, in the dissidents' view, was only meaningful for adults who had made a voluntary confession of faith. Because they were already baptized
as infants in the Catholic Church, the radicals
were dubbed Anabaptists, or rebaptizers, by their
opponents. Anabaptism, also known as the Radical Reformation, spread through the Cantons of
Switzerland, Germany, and the Netherlands.

The rapid spread of Anabaptist groups threatened civil and religious authorities. Anabaptist hunters soon stalked the Reformers. The first martyr was drowned in 1527. Over the next few decades, thousands of Anabaptists burned at the stake, drowned in rivers, starved in prisons, or lost their heads to the executioner's sword. A 1,200-page *Martyrs Mirror*, first published in Dutch in 1660 and later in German and English, records the carnage. Many Amish have a German edition of the *Martyrs Mirror* in their homes today.

The Swiss Anabaptists sought to follow the ways of Jesus in daily life, loving their enemies, forgiving insults, and turning the other cheek. Some Anabaptist groups resorted to violence, but many repudiated force and resolved to live peaceably even with adversaries. The flames of execution tested their faith in the power of suffering love, and although some recanted, many died for their faith. Harsh persecution pushed many Anabaptists underground and into rural hideaways. Swiss Anabaptism took root in rural soil. The sting of persecution, however, divided the church and the larger society in Anabaptist minds. The Anabaptists believed that the kingdoms of this world anchored on the use of coercion clashed with the peaceable kingdom of God.

By 1660 some Swiss Anabaptists had migrated north to the Alsace region of present-day France, which borders southwestern Germany. The Amish came into the picture in 1693 when Swiss and South German Anabaptists split into two streams: Amish and Mennonite. Jakob Ammann, an elder of the Alsatian church, sought to revitalize the Anabaptist movement in 1693. He proposed holding communion twice a year rather than the typical Swiss practice of once a year. He argued that Anabaptist Christians in obedience to Christ should wash each others' feet in the communion service. To promote doctrinal purity and spiritual discipline Ammann forbade fashionable dress and the trimming of beards, and he administered a strict discipline in his congregations. Appealing to New Testament teachings, Ammann advocated the shunning of excommunicated members. Ammann's followers, eventually called Amish, soon became another sect in the Anabaptist family.

### SIGNIFICANT IMMIGRATION WAVES

Searching for political stability and religious freedom, the Amish came to North America in two waves—in the mid-1700s and again in the first half of the 1800s. Their first settlements were in southeastern Pennsylvania. Eventually they followed the frontier to other counties in Pennsylvania, then to Ohio, Indiana, and to other Midwestern states. Today Amish settlements are primarily located in the mid-Atlantic and the Midwest regions of the United States. Very few Amish live west of the Mississippi or in the deep south. In Europe, the last Amish congregation dissolved about 1937.

### SETTLEMENT PATTERNS

Flowing with the rising tide of industrialization in the late nineteenth century, some clusters of Amish formed more progressive Amish-Mennonite churches. The more conservative guardians of the heritage became known as the Old Order Amish. In the twentieth century some Old Order Amish, hankering again after modern conveniences, formed congregations of New Order Amish in the 1960s. The small numbers of New Order Amish groups sometimes permit their members to install phones in their homes, use electricity from public utilities, and use tractors in their fields.

At the turn of the twentieth century the Old Order Amish numbered about 5,000 in North America. Now scattered across 22 states and Ontario they number about 150,000 children and adults. Nearly three quarters live in Ohio, Pennsylvania, and Indiana. Other sizeable communities are in Iowa, Michigan, Missouri, New York, and Wisconsin. A loose federation of some 900 Amish congregations, the Amish function without a national organization or an annual convention. Local church districts—congregations of 25 to 35 families—shape the heart of Amish life.

# ACCULTURATION AND ASSIMILATION

The Amish have been able to maintain a distinctive ethnic subculture by successfully resisting acculturation and assimilation. The Amish try to maintain cultural customs that preserve their identity. They have resisted assimilation into American culture by emphasizing separation from the world, rejecting higher education, selectively using technology, and restricting interaction with outsiders.

## TRADITIONS, CUSTOMS, AND BELIEFS

The word Amish evokes images of buggies and lanterns. At first glance Amish groupings across North America appear pressed from the same cultural mold. A deeper look reveals many differences among Amish groups. Some affiliations forbid milking machines while others depend on them. Mechanical hay balers widely used in some areas are taboo in others. Prescribed buggy tops are gray or black in many affiliations but other groups have white or yellow tops. Buttons on clothing are banished in many groups, but acceptable in others. The dead are embalmed in one settlement but not in another. Some bishops permit telephones in small shops, but others do not. Artificial insemination of livestock is acceptable in one district but not in another. In some communities virtually all the men are farmers, but in others many adults work in small shops and cottage industries. In still other settlements Amish persons work in rural factories operated by non-Amish persons. Practices vary between church districts even within the same settlement. Diversity thrives behind the front stage of Amish life.

Several distinctive badges of ethnic identity unite the Old Order Amish across North America: horse-and-buggy transportation; the use of horses and mules for field work; plain dress in many variations; a beard and shaven upper lip for men; a prayer cap for women; the Pennsylvania German dialect; worship in homes; eighth-grade, parochial schooling; the rejection of electricity from public utility lines; and taboos on the ownership of televisions and computers. These symbols of solidarity circumscribe the Amish world and bridle the forces of assimilation.

Amish life pivots on *Gelassenheit* (pronounced Ge-las-en-hite), the cornerstone of Amish values. Roughly translated, this German word means submission, yielding to a higher authority. In practice it entails self-surrender, resignation to God's will, yielding to others, self-denial, contentment, and a quiet spirit. The religious meaning of Gelassenheit expresses itself in a quiet and reserved personality and places the needs of others above self. It nurtures a subdued self, gentle handshakes, lower voices, slower strides, a life etched with modesty and reserve. Children learn the essence of Gelassenheit in a favorite verse: "I must be a Christian child, / Gentle, patient, meek, and mild, / Must be honest, simple, true, / I must cheerfully obey, / Giving up my will and way."

Another favorite saying explains that JOY means Jesus first, Yourself last, and Others in between. As the cornerstone of Amish culture, Gelassenheit collides with the bold, assertive individualism of modern life that seeks and rewards personal achievement, self-fulfillment, and individual recognition at every turn.

The spirit of Gelassenheit expresses itself in obedience, humility, and simplicity. To Amish thinking, obedience to the will of God is *the* cardinal religious value. Disobedience is dangerous. Unconfessed it leads to eternal separation. Submission to authority at all levels creates an orderly community. Children learn to obey at an early age. Disobedience is nipped in the bud. Students obey teachers without question. Adults yield to the regulations of the church. Among elders, ministers concede to bishops, who obey the Lord.

Humility is coupled with obedience in Amish life. Pride, a religious term for unbridled individualism, threatens the welfare of an orderly community. Amish teachers also remind students that the middle letter of pride is I. Proud individuals display the spirit of arrogance, not Gelassenheit. They are pushy, bold, and forward. What non-Amish consider proper credit for one's accomplishments the Amish view as the hankerings of a vain spirit. The Amish contend that pride disturbs the equality and tranquility of an orderly community. The humble person freely gives of self in the service of community without seeking recognition.

Simplicity is also esteemed in Amish life. Simplicity in clothing, household decor, architecture, and worship nurtures equality and orderliness. Fancy and gaudy decorations lead to pride. Luxury and convenience cultivate vanity. The tools of self-adornment—make-up, jewelry, wrist watches, and wedding rings—are taboo and viewed as signs of pride.

## AMISH SURVIVAL

The Amish do not actively evangelize. They do welcome outsiders, but few make the cultural leap. Membership in some settlements doubles about every 20 years. Their growth is fueled by a robust birth rate that averages seven children per family. The defection rate varies by settlement, but is usually less than 20 percent. Thus, six out of seven children, on the average, remain Amish.

Beyond biological reproduction, a dual strategy of resistance and compromise has enabled the Amish to flourish in the modern world. They have resisted acculturation by constructing social fences around their community. Core values are

This group of Amish boys is watching a horse and mule auction in Lancaster, Pennsylvania. This annual event attracts Amish farmers from throughout the Midwest.

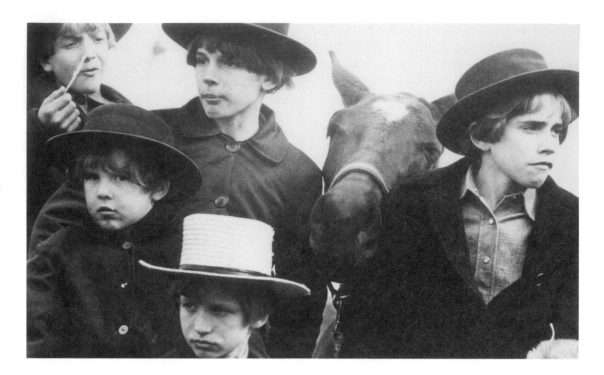

translated into visible symbols of identity. Badges of ethnicity—horse, buggy, lantern, dialect, and dress—draw sharp contours between Amish and modern life.

The Amish resist the forces of modernization in other ways. Cultural ties to the outside world are curbed by speaking the dialect, marrying within the group, spurning television, prohibiting higher education, and limiting social interaction with outsiders. Parochial schools insulate Amish youth from the contaminating influence of worldly peers. Moreover, ethnic schools limit exposure to threatening ideas. From birth to death, members are embedded in a web of ethnicity. These cultural defenses fortify Amish identity and help abate the lure of modernity.

Their survival strategy has also involved cultural compromises. The Amish are not a calcified relic of bygone days, for they change continually. Their willingness to compromise often results in odd mixtures of tradition and progress. Tractors may be used at Amish barns but not in fields. Horses and mules pull modern farm machinery in some settlements. God smiles on 12-volt electricity from batteries but not when it comes from public utility lines. Hydraulic and air pressure are used instead of electricity to operate modern machines in many Amish carpentry and mechanical shops. Members frequently ride in cars or vans, but are not permitted to drive them. Telephones, found by farm lanes and shops, are missing from Amish homes. Modern gas appliances fill Amish kitchens

in some states and lanterns illuminate modern bathrooms in some Amish abodes.

These riddles of Amish life often baffle and, indeed, appear downright silly to outsiders. In reality, however, they reflect delicate bargains that the Amish have struck between their desire to maintain tradition while enjoying the fruits of progress. The Amish are willing to change but not at the expense of communal values and ethnic identity. They use modern technology but not when it disrupts family and community stability.

Viewed within the context of Amish history, the compromises are reasonable ways of achieving community goals. Hardly foolish contradictions, they preserve core values while permitting selective modernization. They bolster Amish identity while reaping many benefits of modern life. Such flexibility boosts the economic vitality of the community and also retains the allegiance of Amish youth.

## CUISINE

Food preferences among the Amish vary somewhat from state to state. Breakfast fare for many families includes eggs, fried potatoes, toast, and in some communities, commercial cereals such as Cornflakes and Cheerios. Typical breakfast foods in Pennsylvania also include shoofly pie, which is sometimes dipped in or covered with coffee or milk, stewed crackers in warm milk, mush made from corn meal, and sausage. Puddings and scrapple are also breakfast favorites. The puddings consist of ground liver, heart, and kidneys from pork and beef. These basic ingredients are also combined with flour and corn meal to produce scrapple.

For farm families the mid-day dinner is usually the largest meal of the day. Noontime dinners and evening suppers often include beef or chicken dishes, and vegetables in season from the family garden, such as peas, corn, green beans, lima beans, and carrots. Mashed potatoes covered with beef gravy, noodles with brown butter, chicken potpie, and sauerkraut are regional favorites. For side dishes and deserts there are applesauce, corn starch pudding, tapioca, and fruit pies in season, such as apple, rhubarb, pumpkin, and snitz pies made with dried apples. Potato soup and chicken-corn-noodle soup are commonplace. In summer months cold fruit soups consisting of strawberries, raspberries, or blueberries added to milk and bread cubes appear on Amish tables. Meadow tea, homemade root beer, and instant drink mixes are used in the summer.

Food preservation and preparation for large families and sizeable gatherings is an enormous undertaking. Although food lies beyond the reach of religious regulations, each community has a traditional menu that is typically served at large meals following church services, weddings, and funerals. Host families often bake three dozen pies for the noontime meal following the biweekly church service. Quantities of canned food vary by family size and preference but it is not uncommon for a family to can 150 quarts of applesauce, 100 quarts of peaches, 60 quarts of pears, 50 quarts of grape juice, and 50 quarts of pizza sauce.

More and more food is purchased from stores, sometimes operated by the Amish themselves. In a more progressive settlement one Amishwoman estimates that only half of the families bake their own bread. The growing use of instant pudding, instant drinks, snack foods, and canned soups reflects growing time constraints. The use of commercial food rises as families leave the farm and especially as women enter entrepreneurial roles.

## TRADITIONAL COSTUMES

The Amish church prescribes dress regulations for its members but the unwritten standards vary considerably by settlement. Men are expected to wear a wide brim hat and a vest when they appear in public. In winter months and at church services they wear a black suit coat which is typically fastened with hooks and eyes rather than with buttons. Men use suspenders instead of belts.

Amish women are expected to wear a prayer covering and a bonnet when they appear in public settings. Most women wear a cape over their dresses as well as an apron. The three parts of the dress are often fastened together with straight pins. Various colors, including green, brown, blue, and lavender, are permitted for men's shirts and women's dresses, but designs and figures in the material are taboo. Although young girls do not wear a prayer covering, Amish children are typically dressed similar to their parents.

## HOLIDAYS

Sharing some national holidays with non-Amish neighbors and adding others of their own, the Amish calendar underscores both their participation in and separation from the larger world. As conscientious objectors, they have little enthusiasm for patriotic days with a military flair. Memorial Day, Veterans Day, and the Fourth of July are barely noticed. Labor Day stirs little interest. The witches and goblins of Halloween run contrary to Amish spirits: pumpkins may be displayed in some settlements, but without cut faces. And Martin Luther King, Jr.'s birthday slips by unnoticed in many rural enclaves.

Amish holidays earmark the rhythm of the seasons and religious celebrations. A day for prayer and fasting precedes the October communion service in some communities. Fall weddings provide ample holidays of another sort. Amish without wedding invitations celebrate Thanksgiving Day with turkey dinners and family gatherings. New Year's Day is a quiet time for family gatherings. In many communities a second day is added to the celebrations of Christmas, Easter, and Pentecost. The regular holiday, a sacred time, flows with quiet family activities. The following day, or second Christmas, Easter Monday, and Pentecost Monday, provides time for recreation, visiting, and sometimes shopping. Ascension day, the day prior to Pentecost, is a holiday for visiting, fishing, and other forms of recreation.

Christmas and Easter festivities are spared from commercial trappings. Families exchange Christmas cards and gifts. Some presents are homemade crafts and practical gifts, but are increasingly store bought. Homes are decorated with greens but Christmas trees, stockings, special lights, Santa Claus, and mistletoe are missing.

Although eggs are sometimes painted and children may be given a basket of candy, Easter bunnies do not visit Amish homes. These sacred holidays revolve around religious customs, family gatherings, and quiet festivities rather than commercial trinkets and the sounds of worldly hubbub. Birthdays are celebrated at home and school in quiet, pleasant ways, with cakes and gifts. Parents often share a special snack of cookies or popsicles with school friends to honor a child's birthday.

### HEALTH AND MENTAL HEALTH ISSUES

Contrary to popular misconceptions the Amish use modern medical services to some extent. Lacking professionals within their ranks, they rely on the services of dentists, optometrists, nurses, and physicians in local health centers, clinics, and hospitals. They cite no biblical injunctions against modern health care nor the latest medicine, but they do believe that God is the ultimate healer. Despite the absence of religious taboos on health care, Amish practices differ from prevailing patterns.

The Amish generally do not subscribe to commercial health insurance. Some communities have organized church aid plans for families with special medical costs. In other settlements special offerings are collected for members who are hit with catastrophic medical bills. The Amish are unlikely to seek medical attention for minor aches or illnesses and are more apt to follow folk remedies and drink herbal teas. Although they do not object to surgery or other forms of high-tech treatment they rarely employ heroic life-saving interventions.

In addition to home remedies, church members often seek healing outside orthodox medical circles. The search for natural healing leads them to vitamins, homeopathic remedies, health foods, reflexologists, chiropractors, and the services of specialized clinics in faraway places. These cultural habits are shaped by many factors: conservative rural values, a preference for natural antidotes, a lack of information, a sense of awkwardness in high-tech settings, difficulties accessing health care, and a willingness to suffer and lean on the providence of God.

Birthing practices vary in different settlements. In some communities most babies are born at home under the supervision of trained non-Amish midwives. In other settlements most children are born in hospitals or at local birthing clinics. Children can attend Amish schools without immunizations. Some parents follow the advice of family doctors or trained midwives and immunize their children, but many do not. Lax immunization is often due to cost, distance, misinformation, or lack of interest. Occasional outbreaks of German measles, whooping cough, polio, and other contagious diseases prompt public health campaigns to immunize Amish children. Amish elders usually encourage their people to cooperate with such efforts. In recent years various health providers have made special efforts to immunize Amish children.

Marriages within stable geographical communities and the influx of few converts restricts the genetic pool of Amish society. Marriages sometimes occur between second cousins. Such intermarriage does not always produce medical problems. When unique recessive traits are common in a closed community certain diseases simply are more likely to occur. On the other hand, a restricted gene pool may offer protection from other hereditary diseases.

A special type of dwarfism accompanied by other congenital problems occurs at an exceptionally high rate in some settlements. Higher rates of deafness have also been found. In the late 1980s, Dr. Holmes Morton identified *glutaric aciduria* in the Lancaster, Pennsylvania, Amish community. Unrecognized and untreatable before, the disease is a biochemical disorder with symptoms similar to cerebral palsy. Approximately one in every 200 Amish infants inherits the disease. By 1991, Dr. Morton had organized a special clinic that tested some 70 percent of Amish infants and treated those diagnosed with the disease in the Lancaster settlement.

# LANGUAGE

The Amish speak English, German, and a dialect known as Pennsylvania German or Pennsylvania Dutch. The dialect is the Amish native tongue and should not be confused with the Dutch language of the Netherlands. Originally a German dialect, Pennsylvania Dutch was spoken by Germanic settlers in southeastern Pennsylvania. The folk pronunciation of the word *German*, *Deutsche*, gradually became *Dutch* in English, and eventually the dialect became known as Pennsylvania Dutch. Even the Amish who live outside of Pennsylvania speak the Pennsylvania German dialect. In Amish culture, the dialect is used mainly as a form of oral communication: it is the language of work, family, friendship, play, and intimacy.

Young children live in the world of the dialect until they learn English in the Amish school. Students learn to read, write, and speak English from their Amish teachers, who learned it from their Amish teachers. But the dialect prevails in friendly banter on the playground. By the end of the eighth grade, young Amish have developed basic competence in English although it may be spoken with an accent. Adults are able to communicate in fluent English with their non-Amish neighbors. When talking among themselves, the Amish sometimes mix English words with the dialect, especially when discussing technical issues. Letters are often written in English, with salutations and occasional phrases in the dialect. Competence in English varies directly with occupational roles and frequency of interaction with English speakers. Ministers are often the ones who are best able to read German. Idioms of the dialect are frequently mixed with German in Amish sacred writings. Although children study formal German in school they do not speak it on a regular basis.

## GREETINGS AND OTHER POPULAR EXPRESSIONS

Common Pennsylvania Dutch greetings and other expressions include: *Gude Mariye*—Good morning; *Gut-n-Owed*—Good evening; *Wie geht's?*—How are you?; *En frehlicher Grischtdsaag*—a Merry Christmas; *Frehlich Neiyaahr*—Happy New Year; *kumm ball widder*—come soon again. When inviting others to gather around a table to eat, a host might say *Kumm esse*.

# FAMILY AND COMMUNITY DYNAMICS

The *immediate family*, the *extended family*, and the *church district* form the building blocks of Amish society. Amish parents typically raise about seven children, but ten or more children is not uncommon. About 50 percent of the population is under 18 years of age. A person will often have more than 75 first cousins and a typical grandmother will count more than 35 grandchildren. Members of the extended family often live nearby, across the field, down the lane, or beyond the hill. Youth grow up in this thick network of family relations where one is rarely alone, always embedded in a caring community in time of need and disaster. The elderly retire at home, usually in a small apartment built onto the main house of a homestead. Because the Amish reject government aid, there are virtually no families that receive public assistance. The community provides a supportive social hammock from cradle to grave.

## SOCIAL ORGANIZATION

A church district comprises 25 to 35 families and is the basic social and religious unit beyond the family. Roads and streams mark the boundaries of districts. Members are required to participate in the geographic district in which they live. A district's geographic size varies with the density of the Amish population. As districts expand, they divide.

A bishop, two preachers, and a deacon share leadership responsibilities in each district without formal pay or education. The bishop, as spiritual elder, officiates at baptisms, weddings, communions, funerals, ordinations, and membership meetings. The church district is church, club, family, and precinct all wrapped up in a neighborhood parish. Periodic meetings of ordained leaders link the districts of a settlement into a loose federation.

The social architecture of Amish society exhibits distinctive features. Leisure, work, education, play, worship, and friendship revolve around the immediate neighborhood. In some settlements, Amish babies are born in hospitals, but they are also born at home or in local birthing centers. Weddings and funerals occur at home. There are frequent trips to other settlements or even out of state to visit relatives and friends. But for the most part the Amish world pivots on local turf. From home-canned food to homemade haircuts, things are likely to be done near home. Social relationships are multi-bonded. The same people frequently work, play, and worship together.

Amish society is remarkably informal and the tentacles of bureaucracy are sparse. There is no centralized national office, symbolic national figurehead, or institutional headquarters. Apart from schools, a publishing operation, and regional historical libraries, formal institutions simply do not exist. A loosely organized national committee handles relations with the federal government for all the settlements. Regional committees funnel the flow of Amish life for schools, mutual aid, and historical libraries, but bureaucracy as we know it in the modern world is simply absent.

The conventional marks of modern status (education, income, occupation, and consumer goods) are missing and make Amish society relatively homogeneous. The agrarian heritage places everyone on common footing. The recent rise of cottage industries in some settlements and factory work in others threatens to disturb the social equality of bygone years, but the range of occupations and social differences remains relatively small. Common costume, horse and buggy travel, an eighth-grade education, and equal-size tombstones embody the virtues of social equality.

The practice of mutual aid also distinguishes Amish society. Although the Amish own private property, like other Anabaptists they have long emphasized mutual aid as a Christian duty in the face of disaster and special need. Mutual aid goes beyond barn raisings. Harvesting, quilting, birthing, marriages, and funerals require the help of many hands. The habits of care encompass all sorts of needs triggered by drought, disease, death, injury, bankruptcy, and medical emergency.

## GENDER ROLES

Amish society is patriarchal. Although school teachers are generally women, men assume the helm of most leadership roles. Women can nominate men to serve in ministerial roles but they themselves are excluded from formal church roles; however, they can vote in church business meetings. Some women feel that since the men make the rules, modern equipment is permitted more readily in barns and shops than in homes. In recent years some women have become entrepreneurs who operate small quilt, craft, and food stores.

Although husband and wife preside over distinct spheres of domestic life, many tasks are shared. A wife may ask her husband to assist in the garden and he may ask her to help in the barn or fields. The isolated housewife is rarely found in Amish society. The husband holds spiritual authority in the home but spouses have considerable freedom within their distinctive spheres.

## SOCIAL GATHERINGS

Various social gatherings bring members together for times of fellowship and fun beyond biweekly worship. Young people gather in homes for Sunday evening singing. Married couples sometimes gather with old friends to sing for shut-ins and the elderly in their homes. Work frolics blend work and play together in Amish life. Parents gather for preschool frolics to ready schools for September classes. End-of-school picnics bring parents and students together for an afternoon of food and games.

Quilting bees and barn raisings mix goodwill, levity, and hard work for young and old alike. Other moments of collective work (cleaning up after a fire, plowing for an ill neighbor, canning for a sick mother, threshing wheat, and filling a silo) involve neighbors and extended families in episodes of charity, sweat, and fun. Adult sisters, sometimes numbering as many as five or six, often gather for a sisters day, which blends laughter with cleaning, quilting, canning, or gardening.

Public auctions of farm equipment are often held in February and March and attract crowds in preparation for springtime farming. Besides opportunities to bid on equipment, the day-long auctions offer ample time for farm talk and friendly fun. Games of cornerball in a nearby field or barnyard often compete with the drama of the auction. Household auctions and horse sales provide other times to socialize. Family gatherings at religious holidays and summer family reunions link members into familial networks. Single women sometimes gather at a cabin or a home for a weekend of fun. Special meetings of persons with unique interests, often called reunions, are on the rise and attract Amish from many states: harnessmakers, cabinetmakers, woodworkers, blacksmiths, businesswomen, teachers, the disabled, and the like. The disabled have gathered annually for a number of years.

Among youth, seasonal athletics are common: softball, sledding, skating, hockey, and swimming. Volleyball is a widespread favorite. Fishing and hunting for small game are preferred sports on farms and woodlands. In recent years some Amishmen have purchased hunting cabins in the mountains where they hunt white-tailed deer. Deep-sea fishing trips are common summertime jaunts for men in Pennsylvania. Others prefer camping and canoeing. Pitching quoits is common at family reunions and picnics.

Leisure and pleasure have long been suspect in Amish life. Idleness is viewed as the devil's workshop. But the rise of cottage industries and the availability of ready cash has brought more recreational activities. Amish recreation is group oriented and tilted more toward nature than toward taboo commercial entertainment. The

Amish rarely take vacations but they do take trips to other settlements and may stop at scenic sites. Some couples travel to Florida for several weeks in the winter and live in an Amish village in Sarasota populated by winter travelers from settlements in several states. Trips to distant sites in search of special medical care sometimes include scenic tours. Although some Amish travel by train or bus, chartered vans are by far the most popular mode. Traveling together with family, friends, and extended kin these mobile groups bond and build community life.

## INTERACTION WITH OTHER ETHNIC GROUPS

Amish culture and religion stresses separation from the world. Galvanized by European persecution and sanctioned by scripture, the Amish divide the social world into two pathways: the straight, narrow way to life, and the broad, easy road to destruction. Amish life embodies the narrow way of self-denial. The larger social world symbolizes the broad road of vanity and vice. The term world, in Amish thinking, refers to the outside society and its values, vices, practices, and institutions. Media reports of greed, fraud, scandal, drugs, violence, divorce, and abuse confirm that the world teems with abomination.

The gulf between church and world, imprinted in Amish minds by European persecution, guides practical decisions. Products and practices that might undermine community life, such as high school, cars, cameras, television, and self-propelled farm machinery, are tagged worldly. Not all new products receive this label, only those that threaten community values. Definitions of worldliness vary within and between Amish settlements, yielding a complicated maze of practices. Baffling to outsiders, these lines of faithfulness maintain inter-group boundaries and also preserve the cultural purity of the church.

## WEDDINGS

The wedding season is a festive time in Amish life. Coming on the heels of the harvest, weddings are typically held on Tuesdays and Thursdays from late October through early December. The larger communities may have as many as 150 weddings in one season. Fifteen weddings may be scattered across the settlement on the same day. Typically staged in the home of the bride, these joyous events may involve upwards of 350 guests, two meals, singing, snacks, festivities, and a three-hour service. The specific practices vary from settlement to settlement.

Young persons typically marry in their early twenties. A couple may date for one to two years before announcing their engagement. Bishops will only marry members of the church. The church does not arrange marriages but it does place its blessing on the pair through an old ritual. Prior to the wedding, the groom takes a letter signed by church elders to the bride's deacon testifying to the groom's good standing in his home district. The bride's deacon then meets with her to verify the marriage plans.

The wedding day is an enormous undertaking for the bride's family and for the relatives and friends who assist with preparations. Efforts to clean up the property, paint rooms, fix furniture, pull weeds, and pave driveways, among other things, begin weeks in advance. The logistics of preparing meals and snacks for several hundred guests are taxing. According to custom, the day before the wedding the groom decapitates several dozen chickens. The noontime wedding menu includes chicken roast—chicken mixed with bread filling, mashed potatoes, gravy, creamed celery, pepper cabbage, and other items. Deserts include pears, peaches, puddings, dozens of pies, and hundreds of cookies and doughnuts.

The three-hour service—without flowers, rings, solos, or instrumental music—is similar to an Amish worship service. The wedding includes congregational singing, prayers, wedding vows, and two sermons. Four single friends serve the bride and groom as attendants: no one is designated maid of honor or best man. Amish brides typically make their own wedding dresses from blue or purple material crafted in traditional styles. In addition to the groom's new but customary black coat and vest, he and his attendants often wear small black bow ties.

Several seatings and games, snacks, and singing follow the noon meal. Young people are paired off somewhat randomly for the singing. Following the evening meal another more lively singing takes place in which couples who are dating pair off—arousing considerable interest because this may be their first public appearance. Festivities may continue until nearly midnight as guests gradually leave. Some guests, invited to several weddings on the same day, may rotate between them.

Newly married couples usually set up housekeeping in the spring after their wedding. Until then the groom may live at the bride's home or continue to live with his parents. Couples do not take a traditional honeymoon, but visit relatives on weekends during the winter months. Several newlywed couples may visit together, sometimes staying overnight at the home of close relatives. During these visits, family and friends present gifts to the newlyweds to add to the bride's dowry, which often consists of furniture. Young men begin growing a beard, the functional equivalent of a wedding ring, soon after their marriage. They are expected to have a "full stand" by the spring-time communion.

## FUNERALS

With the elderly living at home, the gradual loss of health prepares family members for the final passage. Accompanied by quiet grief, death comes gracefully, the final benediction to a good life and entry into the bliss of eternity. Although funeral practices vary from community to community, the preparations reflect core Amish values, as family and friends yield to eternal verities.

The community springs into action at the word of a death. Family and friends in the local church district assume barn and household chores, freeing the immediate family. Well-established funeral rituals unburden the family from worrisome choices. Three couples are appointed to extend invitations and supervise funeral arrangements: food preparation, seating arrangements, and the coordination of a large number of horses and carriages.

In the Lancaster, Pennsylvania, settlement a non-Amish undertaker moves the body to a funeral home for embalming. The body, without cosmetic improvements, returns to the home in a simple, hardwood coffin within a day. Family members of the same sex dress the body in white. White garments symbolize the final passage into a new and better eternal life. Tailoring the white clothes prior to death helps to prepare the family for the season of grief. Women often wear the white cape and apron worn at their wedding.

Friends and relatives visit the family and view the body in a room on the first floor of the home for two days prior to the funeral. Meanwhile, community members dig the grave by hand in a nearby family cemetery as others oversee the daily chores of the bereaved. Several hundred guests attend the funeral in a barn or home typically on the morning of the third day after death. During the simple hour-and-a-half-long service,

ministers read hymns and scriptures, offer prayers, and preach a sermon. There are no flowers, burial gowns, burial tents, limousines, or sculpted monuments.

The hearse, a large, black carriage pulled by horses, leads a long procession of other carriages to the burial ground on the edge of a farm. After a brief viewing and graveside service, pallbearers lower the coffin and shovel soil into the grave as the bishop reads a hymn. Small, equal-sized tombstones mark the place of the deceased in the community of equality. Close friends and family members then return to the home for a meal prepared by members of the local congregation. Bereaved women, especially close relatives, may signal their mourning by wearing a black dress in public settings for as long as a year. A painful separation laced with grief, death is nevertheless received gracefully as the ultimate surrender to God's higher ways.

## EDUCATION

The Amish supported public education when it revolved around one-room schools in the first half of the twentieth century. Under local control, the one-room rural schools posed little threat to Amish values. The massive consolidation of public schools and growing pressure to attend high school sparked clashes between the Amish and officials in several states in the middle of the twentieth century. Confrontations in several other states led to arrests and brief stints in jail. After legal skirmishes in several states, the U.S. Supreme Court gave its blessing to the eighth-grade Amish school system in 1972, stating that "there can be no assumption that today's majority is 'right' and the Amish and others are 'wrong.'" The court concluded that "a way of life that is odd or even erratic but interferes with no rights or interests of others is not to be condemned because it is different."

Today the Amish operate more than 850 parochial schools for some 24,000 Amish children. Many of the schools have one room with 25 to 35 pupils and one teacher who is responsible for teaching all eight grades. A few Amish children attend rural public schools in some states but the vast majority go to parochial schools operated by the Amish.

A scripture reading and prayer opens each school day, but religion is not formally taught in the school. The curriculum includes reading, arithmetic, spelling, grammar, penmanship, history, and geography. Both English and German are taught. Parents want children to learn German to enhance their ability to read religious writings, many of which are written in formal German. Science and sex education are missing in the curriculum as are the other typical trappings of public schools: sports, dances, cafeterias, clubs, bands, choruses, computers, television, guidance counselors, principals, strikes, and college recruiters.

A local board of three to five fathers organizes the school, hires a teacher, approves curriculum, oversees the budget, and supervises maintenance. Teachers receive about $25 to $35 per day. The cost per child is roughly $250 per year, nearly 16 times lower than many public schools where per pupil costs often top $4,000. Amish parents pay public school taxes and taxes for their own school.

Schools play a critical role in the preservation of Amish culture. They not only reinforce Amish values, but also shield youth from contaminating ideas. Moreover, schools restrict friendships with non-Amish peers and impede the flow of Amish youth into higher education and professional life. Amish schools promote practical skills to prepare their graduates for success in Amish society. Some selective testing indicates that Amish pupils compare favorably with rural peers in public schools on standardized tests of basic skills.

Amish teachers, trained in Amish schools, are not required to be certified in most states. Often the brightest and best of Amish scholars, they return to the classroom in their late teens and early twenties to teach. Amish school directors select them for their ability to teach and their commitment to Amish values. Frequently single women, they typically drop their occupation if wed. Periodic meetings with other teachers, a monthly teachers' magazine, and ample common sense prepare them for the task of teaching 30 students in eight grades. With three or four pupils per grade, teachers often teach two grades at a time. Pupils in other classes ponder assignments or listen to previews of next year's lessons or hear reviews of past work. Classrooms exhibit a distinct sense of order amidst a beehive of activity. Hands raise to ask permission or clarify instructions as the teacher moves from cluster to cluster teaching new material every ten or 15 minutes. Some textbooks are recycled from public schools while others are produced by Amish publishers. Students receive a remarkable amount of personal attention despite the teacher's responsibility for

eight grades. The ethos of the classroom accents cooperative activity, obedience, respect, diligence, kindness, and the natural world. Despite the emphasis on order, playful pranks and giggles are commonplace. Schoolyard play in daily recesses often involves softball or other homespun games.

Amish schools exhibit a social continuity rarely found in public education. With many families sending several children to a school, teachers may relate to as few as a dozen households. Teachers know parents personally and special circumstances surrounding each child. In some cases, children have the same teacher for all eight grades. Indeed, all the children from a family may have the same teacher. Amish schools are unquestionably provincial by modern standards. Yet in a humane fashion they ably prepare Amish youth for meaningful lives in Amish society.

# RELIGION

At first glance the Amish appear quite religious. Yet a deeper inspection reveals no church buildings, sacred symbols, or formal religious education even in Amish schools. Unlike most modern religions, religious meanings pervade all aspects of Amish life. Religion is practiced, not debated. Silent prayers before and after meals embroider each day with reverence. The Amish way of living and being requires neither heady talk nor formal theology.

The *Ordnung*, a religious blueprint for expected behavior, regulates private, public, and ceremonial behavior. Unwritten in most settlements, the Ordnung is passed on by oral tradition. A body of understandings that defines Amish ways, the Ordnung marks expected Amish behavior: wearing a beard without a mustache; using a buggy; and speaking the dialect. It also specifies taboos: divorce; filing a lawsuit; wearing jewelry; owning a car; and attending college. The understandings evolve over the years and are updated as the church faces new issues: embryo transplants in cattle; using computers and facsimile machines; and working in factories. Core understandings, such as wearing a beard and not owning a car, span all Old Order Amish settlements but the finer points of the Ordnung vary considerably from settlement to settlement.

Although ordained leaders update the Ordnung in periodic meetings, each bishop interprets it for his local congregation. Thus, dress styles and the use of telephones and battery-powered appliances may vary by church district. Once embedded in the Ordnung and established as tradition, the understandings rarely change. As new issues face the church, leaders identify those which may be detrimental to community life. Non-threatening changes such as weed-whackers and instant coffee may be overlooked and gradually slip into Amish life. Battery-powered video cameras, which might lead to other video entanglements with the outside world, would surely be forbidden.

Children learn the ways of the Ordnung by observing adults. The Ordnung defines the way things are in a child's mind. Teenagers, free from the supervision of the church, sometimes flirt with worldly ways and flaunt the Ordnung. At baptism, however, young adults between the ages of 16 and 22 declare their Christian faith and vow to uphold the Ordnung for the rest of their lives. Those who break their promise face excommunication and shunning. Those choosing not to be baptized may gradually drift away from the community but are welcome to return to their families without the stigma of shunning.

### WORSHIP SERVICES

Worship services held in Amish homes reaffirm the moral order of Amish life. Church districts hold services every other Sunday. A group of 200 or more, including neighbors and relatives who have an "off Sunday," gather for worship. They meet in a farmhouse, the basement of a newer home, or in a shed or barn. A fellowship meal at noon and informal visiting follow the three-hour morning service.

The plain and simple but unwritten liturgy revolves around congregational singing and two sermons. Without the aid of organs, offerings, candles, crosses, robes, or flowers, members yield themselves to God in the spirit of humility. The congregation sings from the *Ausbund,* a hymnal of German songs without musical notations that date back to the sixteenth-century Anabaptists. The tunes passed across the generations by memory are sung in unison without any musical accompaniment. The slow, chant-like cadence means a single song may stretch over 20 minutes. Extemporaneous sermons, preached in the Pennsylvania German dialect, recount biblical stories as well as lessons from farm life. Preachers exhort members to be obedient to Amish ways.

Communion services, held each autumn and spring, frame the religious year. These ritual high points emphasize self-examination and spiritual rejuvenation. Sins are confessed and members reaffirm their vow to uphold the Ordnung. Communion is held when the congregation is at peace, when all members are in harmony with the Ordnung. The six- to eight-hour communion service includes preaching, a light meal during the service, and the commemoration of Christ's death with bread and wine. Pairs of members wash each others feet as the congregation sings. At the end of the communion service members give an alms offering to the deacon, the only time that offerings are collected in Amish services.

### EXCOMMUNICATION

Baptism, worship, and communion are sacred rites that revitalize and preserve the Ordnung. But the Amish, like other human beings, forget, rebel, experiment, and stray into deviance. Major transgressions are confessed publicly in a members meeting following the worship service. Violations of the Ordnung—using a tractor in the field, posing for a television camera, flying on a commercial airline, filing a lawsuit, joining a political organization, or opening a questionable business—are confessed publicly. Public confession of sins diminishes self-will, reminds members of the supreme value of submission, restores the wayward into the community of faith, and underscores the lines of faithfulness which encircle the community.

The headstrong who spurn the advice of elders and refuse to confess their sin face a six-week probation. The next step is the *Meidung,* or shunning—a cultural equivalent of solitary confinement. Members terminate social interaction and financial transactions with the excommunicated. For the unrepentant, social avoidance becomes a lifetime quarantine. If their stubbornness does not mellow into repentance, they face excommunication.

# EMPLOYMENT AND ECONOMIC TRADITIONS

Amish life is rooted in the soil. Ever since European persecution pushed them into rural areas, the Amish have been farmers. The land has nurtured their common life and robust families. Since the middle of the twentieth century, some of the older and larger Amish settlements in Indiana,

Ohio, and Pennsylvania have shifted to nonfarm occupations because of the pressure of urbanization. As urbanization devoured prime farmland, prices soared. Land, for example, in the heart of Pennsylvania's Lancaster Amish settlement sold for $300 an acre in 1940. In the 1990s, the same land sold for $8,000 to $10,000 an acre. If sold for development, prices can double or even triple.

The shrinking and expensive farmland in some of the older settlements has forced a crisis in the Amish soul. The Amish have also contributed to the demographic squeeze with their growing population. The community has coped with the crisis in several ways. First, farms have been subdivided into smaller units with intensive cropping and larger concentrations of livestock. Second, some families have migrated to the rural backwaters of other states where farms could be purchased at much lower prices. Third, in some settlements a majority of families no longer farms, but works in small shops, rural factories, or in various trades. But even ex-farmers insist that the farm remains the best place to raise a family.

The rise of cottage industries and small shops marks an historic turn in Amish life. Mushrooming since the 1970s, these new enterprises have reshaped Amish society. Amish retail shops sell dry goods, furniture, shoes, hardware, and wholesale foods. Church members now work as carpenters, plumbers, painters, and self-trained accountants. Professionals, like lawyers, physicians, and veterinarians, are missing from Amish ranks because of the taboo on high school and college education. The new industries come in three forms. Home-based operations lodged on farms or by newly built homes employ a few family members and neighbors. Bakeshops, craft shops, hardware stores, health food stores, quilt shops, flower shops, and repair shops of all sorts are but a few of the hundreds of home-based operations. Work in these settings revolves around the family. A growing number of these small cottage industries cater to tourists but many serve the needs of Amish and non-Amish neighbors alike.

Larger shops and manufacturing concerns are housed in newly constructed buildings on the edge of farms or on commercial plots. These formal shops with five to ten employees manufacture farm machinery, hydraulic equipment, storage barns, furniture, and cabinetry. Some metal fabrication shops arrange subcontracts with other manufacturers. The larger shops are efficient and profitable. Low overhead, minimal advertising, austere management, modest wages, quality workmanship, and sheer hard work grant many shops a competitive edge in the marketplace.

Mobile work crews constitute a third type of industry. Amish construction groups travel to building sites for commercial and residential construction. The construction crews travel in hired vehicles and in some settlements they are permitted to use electric tools powered by portable generators and on-site electricity.

The rise of cottage industries may, in the long run, disturb the equality of Amish life by encouraging a three-tier society of farmers, entrepreneurs, and day laborers. Parents worry that youth working a 40-hour week with loose cash in their pockets will snub traditional Amish values of simplicity and frugality. The new industries also increase contact with the outside world which will surely prompt even more changes in Amish life. Despite the occupational changes, virtually no Amish are unemployed or receive government unemployment benefits.

# POLITICS AND GOVERNMENT

The Amish view government with an ambiguous eye. Although they support and respect civil government, they also keep a healthy distance from it. On the one hand, they follow biblical admonitions to obey and pray for rulers and encourage members to be law-abiding citizens. On the other hand, government epitomizes worldly culture and the use of force. European persecutors of the Anabaptists were often government officials. Modern governments engage in warfare, use capital punishment, and impose their will with raw coercion. Believing that such coercion and violence mock the gentle spirit of Jesus, the Amish reject the use of force, including litigation. Since they regulate many of their own affairs they have less need for outside supervision.

When civil law and religious conscience collide, the Amish are not afraid to take a stand and will obey God rather than man, even if it brings imprisonment. They have clashed with government officials over the use of hard hats, zoning regulations, Workers' Compensation, and building codes for schools. However, as conscientious objectors many have received farm deferments or served in alternative service programs during times of military draft.

The church forbids membership in political organizations and holding public office for several reasons. First, running for office is viewed as arrogant and out of character with esteemed Amish values of humility and modesty. Second, office-holding violates the religious principle of separation from the world. Finally, public officials must be prepared to use legal force if necessary to settle civic disputes. The exercise of legal force mocks the stance of non-resistance. Voting, however, is viewed as a personal matter. Although the church does not prohibit it, few persons vote. Those who do vote are likely to be younger businessmen concerned about local issues. Although voting is considered a personal matter, jury duty is not allowed.

The Amish pay federal and state income taxes, sales taxes, real estate taxes, and personal property taxes. Indeed, they pay school taxes twice, for both public and Amish schools. Following biblical injunctions, the Amish are exempt from Social Security tax. They view Social Security as a national insurance program, not a tax. Congressional legislation, passed in 1965, exempts self-employed Amish persons from Social Security. Amish persons employed in Amish businesses were also exempted by congressional legislation in 1988. Those who do not qualify for the exemption, Amish employees in non-Amish businesses, must pay Social Security without reaping its benefits. Bypassing Social Security not only severs the Amish from old age payments, it also closes the spigot to Medicare and Medicaid.

The Amish object to government aid for several reasons. They contend that the church should assume responsibility for the social welfare of its own members. The aged, infirm, senile, disabled, and retarded are cared for, whenever possible, within extended family networks. To turn the care of these people over to the state would abdicate a fundamental tenet of faith: the care of one's brothers and sisters in the church. Furthermore, federal aid in the form of Social Security or Medicare would erode dependency on the church and undercut its programs of mutual aid, which the Amish have organized to assist their members with fire and storm damages and with medical expenses.

Government subsidies, or what the Amish call handouts, have been stridently opposed. Championing self-sufficiency and the separation of church and state, the Amish worry that the hand which feeds them will also control them. Over the years they have stubbornly refused direct subsidies even for agricultural programs designed for farmers in distress. Amish farmers do, however, receive indirect subsidies through agricultural price-support programs.

In 1967 the Amish formed the National Amish Steering Committee in order to speak with a common voice on legal issues related to state, and especially, federal government. The Steering Committee has worked with government officials to resolve disputes related to conscientious objection, zoning, slow-moving vehicle emblems, Social

Security, Workers' Compensation, and the wearing of hard hats at construction sites. Informally organized, the Steering Committee is the only Amish organization which is national in scope.

## THE FUTURE OF AMISH SOCIETY

The future shape of Amish life escapes prediction. Particular outcomes will be shaped not only by unforeseen external forces, such as market prices, government regulations, and rates of urbanization, but also by internal politics and the sentiments of particular Amish leaders. Without a centralized decision-making process, let alone a strategic planning council, new directions are unpredictable. Migrations will likely continue to new states and to the rural areas of states where the Amish presently live.

The willingness of many Amish to leave their plows for shops and cottage industries in the 1970s and 1980s signalled a dramatic shift in Amish life. Microenterprises will likely blossom and bring change to Amish life as they increase interaction with the outside world. These business endeavors will probably alter the class structure and cultural face of Amish society over the years. But the love of farming runs deep in the Amish heart. Faced with a growing population, many families will likely migrate to more rural areas in search of fertile soil.

The cultural flavor of twenty-first century Amish life may elude forecast, but one pattern is clear. Settlements which are pressed by urbanization are the most progressive in outlook and the most updated in technology. Rural homesteads beyond the tentacles of urban sprawl remain the best place to preserve traditional Amish ways. If the Amish can educate and retain their children, make a living, and restrain interaction with the larger world, they will likely flourish into the twenty-first century. But one thing is certain: diversity between their settlements will surely grow, mocking the staid stereotypes of Amish life.

# MEDIA

## PRINT

### Arthur Graphic Clarion.
Newspaper of the Illinois Amish country.

Contact: Allen Mann, Editor.
Address: P.O. Box 19, Arthur, Illinois 61911.

Telephone: (217) 543-2151.
Fax: (217) 543-2152.

### Die Botschaft.
Weekly English newspaper with correspondents from many states that serves Old Order Mennonite and Old Order Amish communities.

Contact: Brookshire Publications, Inc.
Address: 200 Hazel Street, Lancaster, Pennsylvania 17608-0807.

### The Budget.
Weekly Amish/Mennonite community newspaper.

Contact: George R. Smith, National Editor.
Address: Sugarcreek Budget Publishers, Inc., 134 North Factory Street, P.O. Box 249, Sugarcreek, Ohio 44681-0249.
Telephone: (216) 852-4634.
Fax: (216) 852-4421.

### The Diary.
Monthly publication that lists migrations, marriages, births, and deaths. It also carries news and feature articles.

Contact: Pequea Publishers.
Address: P.O. Box 98, Gordonville, Pennsylvania 17529.

### Family Life.
Monthly family magazine printed in English.

Contact: Pathway Publishers.
Address: Route 4, Aylmer, Ontario, N5H 2R3 Canada.

### Mennonite Quarterly Review.
Scholarly journal covering Mennonite, Amish, Hutterian Brethren, Anabaptist, Radical Reformation, and related history and religious thought.

Contact: John E. Roth, Editor.
Address: Mennonite Historical Society, Goshen College, Goshen, Indiana 46526.
Telephone: (219) 535-7111.
Fax: (219) 535-7438.

### Young Companion.
Monthly magazine for young people printed in English.

Contact: Pathway Publishers.
Address: Route 4, Aylmer, Ontario N5H 2R3, Canada.

# ORGANIZATIONS AND ASSOCIATIONS

**Lancaster Mennonite Historical Society (LMHS).**
Individuals interested in the historical background, theology, culture, and genealogy of Mennonite and Amish related groups originating in Pennsylvania. Collects and preserves archival materials. Publishes the *Mirror* bimonthly.

**Contact:** Carolyn C. Wenger, Director.
**Address:** 2215 Millstream Road, Lancaster, Pennsylvania 17602-1499.
**Telephone:** (717) 393-9745.

**National Committee for Amish Religious Freedom (NCARF).**
Provides legal defense for Amish people, since the Amish are reluctant to defend themselves or seek court action.

**Contact:** Rev. William C. Lindholm, Chair.
**Address:** 30650 Six Mile Road, Livonia, Michigan 48152.
**Telephone:** (313) 427-1414.

# MUSEUMS AND RESEARCH CENTERS

**Heritage Historical Library.**
**Address:** Route 4, Aylmer, Ontario N5H 2R3, Canada.

**Mennonite Historical Library.**
**Address:** Goshen College, Goshen, Indiana 46526.
**Telephone:** (219) 535-7000.

**Ohio Amish Library.**
**Address:** 4292 SR39, Millersburg, Ohio 44654.

**Pequea Bruderschaft Library.**
**Address:** P.O. Box 25, Gordonville, Pennsylvania PA 17529.

**The Young Center for the Study of Anabaptist and Pietist Groups.**
**Address:** Elizabethtown College, One Alpha Drive, Elizabethtown, Pennsylvania 17022.
**Telephone:** (717) 361-1470.

# SOURCES FOR ADDITIONAL STUDY

*The Amish and the State.* Baltimore: Johns Hopkins University Press, 1993.

*Amish Society,* fourth edition. Baltimore: Johns Hopkins University Press, 1993.

*The Amish Wedding and Other Special Occasions of the Old Order Communities.* Intercourse, Pennsylvania: Good Books, 1988.

Hostetler, John A. *Amish Life.* Scottdale, Pennsylvania: Herald Press, 1983.

Kline, David. *Great Possessions: An Amish Farmer's Journal.* San Francisco: North Point Press, 1990.

Kraybill, Donald B. *The Riddle of Amish Culture.* Baltimore: Johns Hopkins University Press, 1989.

Kraybill, Donald B., and Marc A. Olshan. *The Amish Struggle with Modernity.* Hanover, New Hampshire: University Press of New England, 1994.

Nolt, Steven M. *A History of the Amish.* Intercourse, Pennsylvania: Good Books, 1992.

*The Puzzles of Amish Life.* Intercourse, Pennsylvania: Good Books, 1990.

Scott, Stephen. *Why Do They Dress That Way?* Intercourse, Pennsylvania: Good Books, 1986.

# APACHES
### by
### D. L. Birchfield

While adhering strongly to their culture in the face of overwhelming attempts to suppress it, Apaches have been adaptable at the same time.

## OVERVIEW

Federally recognized contemporary Apache tribal governments are located in Arizona, New Mexico, and Oklahoma. Apache reservations are also located in Arizona and New Mexico. In Oklahoma, the Apache land was allotted in severalty under the General Allotment Act of 1887 (also known as the Dawes Act); Oklahoma Apaches became citizens of the new state of Oklahoma and of the United States in 1907. Apaches in Arizona and New Mexico were not granted U.S. citizenship until 1924. Since attempting to terminate its governmental relationship with Indian tribes in the 1950s, the United States has since adopted a policy of assisting the tribes in achieving some measure of self-determination, and the U.S. Supreme Court has upheld some attributes of sovereignty for Indian nations. In recent years Apache tribal enterprises such as ski areas, resorts, and lumber mills have helped alleviate chronically high rates of unemployment on the reservations, and bilingual and bicultural educational programs have resulted from direct Apache involvement in the educational process.

### HISTORY

Apaches have endured severe economic and political disruptions, first by the Spanish, then by the Comanches, and later by the United States government. Apaches became known to the Spanish during authorized and illegal Spanish exploratory expeditions into the Southwest during the sixteenth century, beginning with the Coronado expedition of 1540, but including a number of others, at intervals, throughout the century. It was not until 1598, however, that Apaches had to adjust to the presence of Europeans within their homeland, when the expedition of Juan de Onate entered the Pueblo country of the upper Rio Grande River Valley of the present state of New Mexico, with the intention of establishing a permanent Spanish colony. The Onate expedition successfully colonized the area, and by 1610 the town of Santa Fe had been founded. Until the arrival of the Spanish, the Apaches and the Pueblos had enjoyed a mercantile relationship. Pueblos traded their agricultural products and pottery to the Apaches in exchange for buffalo robes and dried meat. The annual visits of whole Apache tribes for trade fairs with the Pueblos, primarily at the pueblos of Taos and Picuris, were described with awe by the early Spaniards in the region. The Spanish, however, began annually to confiscate the Pueblo trade surpluses, thereby disrupting the trade. Nonetheless some Apaches, notably the Jicarillas, became friends and allies of the Spanish.

The historic southward migration of the Comanche Nation, beginning around 1700, was devastating for the Eastern Apaches. By about 1725 the Comanches had established authority throughout the whole of the Southern Plains region, pushing the Eastern Apaches (the Jicarillas north of Santa Fe, and the Mescaleros south of Santa Fe) into the mountains of the front range of the Rockies in New Mexico. Denied access to the buffalo herds, the Apaches turned to Spanish cattle and horses. When the Spanish were able to conclude a treaty of peace with the Comanches in 1786, they employed large bodies of Comanche and Navajo auxiliary troops with Spanish regulars, in implementing an Apache policy that pacified the entire Southwestern frontier by 1790. Each individual Apache group was hunted down and cornered, then offered a subsidy sufficient for their maintenance if they would settle near a Spanish mission, refrain from raiding Spanish livestock, and live peacefully. One by one, each Apache group accepted the terms. The peace, though little studied by modern scholars, is thought to have endured until near the end of the Spanish colonial era.

The Mexican Revolution of 1845 disrupted the peace, and by the time the United States moved into the Southwest at the conclusion of the Mexican War in 1847, the Apaches posed an almost unsolvable problem. The Americans, lacking both Spanish diplomatic skills and Spanish understanding of the Apaches, sought to subjugate the Apaches militarily, an undertaking that was not achieved until the final surrender of Geronimo's band in 1886. Some Apaches became prisoners of war, shipped first to Florida, then to Alabama, and finally to Oklahoma. Others entered a period of desultory reservation life in the Southwest.

## MODERN ERA

Apache populations today may be found in Oklahoma, Arizona, and New Mexico. The San Carlos Reservation in eastern Arizona occupies 1,900,000 acres and has a population of more than 6,000. The San Carlos Reservation and Fort Apache Reservation were administratively divided in 1897. In the 1920s the San Carlos Reservation established a business committee, which was dominated by the Bureau of Indian Affairs. The business committee evolved into a tribal council, which now runs the tribe as a corporation. The reservation lost most of its best farmland when the Coolidge Dam was completed in 1930. Mount Graham, 10,720 feet in elevation, is sacred land to the Apaches. It stands at the southern end of the reservation. The Tonto Reservation in east-central Arizona is a small community, closely related to the Tontos at Camp Verde Reservation.

The Fort Apache Reservation occupies 1,665,000 acres in eastern Arizona and has a population of more than 8,500. It is home to the Coyotero Apaches which include the Cibecue and White Mountain Apaches. Approximately half of the land is timbered; there is diverse terrain with different ecosystems depending upon the elevation, from 2,700 feet to 11,500 feet. Fort Apache was founded as a military post in 1863 and decommissioned in 1922. The Fort Apache Recreation Enterprise, begun in 1954, has created much economic activity, including Sunrise Ski Area, which generates more than $9 million in revenue annually.

The Camp Verde Reservation occupies approximately 500 acres in central Arizona. The reservation, in several small fragments, is shared by about an equal number of Tonto Apaches and Yavapai living in three communities, at Camp Verde, Middle Verde, and Clarksdale. About half of the 1,200 tribal members live on the reserva-

tion. Middle Verde is the seat of government, a tribal council that is elected from the three communities. The original tract of 40 acres, acquired in 1910, is at Camp Verde. By 1916, an additional 400 acres had been added at Middle Verde. In 1969, 60 acres were acquired at Clarksdale, a donation of the Phelps-Dodge Company when it closed its Clarksdale mining operation, to be used as a permanent land base for the Yavapai-Apache community that had worked in the Clarksdale copper mines. An additional 75 acres of tribal land surrounds the Montezuma Castle National Monument. Approximately 280 acres at Middle Verde is suitable for agriculture. The tribe has the highest percentage of its students enrolled in college of any tribe in Arizona.

The Jicarilla Reservation occupies 750,000 acres in north-central New Mexico. There are two divisions among the Jicarilla, the Olleros ("Mountain People") and the Llaneros ("Plains People"). Jicarilla is a Spanish word meaning "Little Basket." In 1907, the reservation was enlarged, with the addition of a large block of land to the south of the original section. In the 1920s, most Jicarilla were stockmen. Many lived on isolated ranches, until drought began making sheep raising unprofitable. After World War II, oil and gas was discovered on the southern portion of the reservation, which by 1986 was producing annual income of $25 million (which dropped to $11 million during the recession in the early 1990s). By the end of the 1950s, 90 percent of the Jicaril-

la had moved to the vicinity of the agency town of Dulce.

The Mescalero Reservation occupies 460,000 acres in southeast New Mexico in the Sacramento Mountains northeast of Alamogordo. Located in the heart of a mountain recreational area, the Mescaleros have taken advantage of the scenic beauty, bringing tourist dollars into their economy with such enterprises as the Inn of the Mountain Gods, which offers several restaurants and an 18-hole golf course. Another tribal operation, a ski area named Ski Apache, brings in more revenue. The nearby Ruidoso Downs horse racing track also attracts visitors to the area. From mid-May to mid-September, lake and stream fishing is accessible at Eagle Creek Lakes, Silver Springs, and Rio Ruidoso recreation areas. The Mescaleros, like the Jicarilla, are an Eastern Apache tribe, with many cultural influences from the Southern Great Plains.

Apaches in Oklahoma, except for Kiowa-Apaches, are descendants of the 340 members of Geronimo's band of Chiricahua Apaches. The Chiricahua were held as prisoners of war, first in 1886 at Fort Marion, Florida, then for seven years at Mount Vernon Barracks, Alabama, and finally at Fort Sill, Oklahoma. By the time they arrived in Fort Sill on October 4, 1894, their numbers had been reduced by illness to 296 men, women and children. They remained prisoners of war on the Fort Sill Military Reservation until 1913. In that year, a total of 87 Chiricahua were allotted lands on the former Kiowa-Comanche Reservation, not far from Fort Sill.

The Kiowa-Apache are a part of the Kiowa Nation. The Kiowa-Apache are under the jurisdiction of the Kiowa-Comanche-Apache Agency of the Anadarko Area Office of the Bureau of Indian Affairs. In the 1950s, the Kiowa-Apache held two seats on the 12-member Kiowa-Comanche-Apache Business Committee. Elections for the Kiowa-Apache seats on the Business Committee were held every four years at Fort Cobb. The Kiowas and the Comanches now have separate business committees, which function as the equivalent of tribal governments, and the Kiowa-Apaches have remained allied with the Kiowas. The Kiowa-Apache are an Athapascan-speaking people. They are thought to have diverged from other Athapascans in the northern Rocky Mountains while the Southern Athapascans were in the process of migrating to the Southwest. They became allied with the Kiowas, who at that time lived near the headwaters of the Missouri River in the high Rockies, and they migrated to the Southern Plains with the Kiowas, stopping en route for a time in the vicinity of the Black Hills. Since they first became known to Europeans, they have been closely associated with the Kiowas on the Great Plains. The Lewis and Clark expedition met the Kiowa-Apaches in 1805 and recorded the first estimate of their population, giving them an approximate count of 300. The Kiowas and the Kiowa-Apaches eventually became close allies of the Comanches on the Southern Plains. By treaty in 1868 the Kiowa-Apaches joined the Kiowas and Comanches on the same reservation. A devastating measles epidemic killed hundreds of the three tribes in 1892. In 1901, the tribal estate was allotted to individual tribal members, and the remainder of their land was opened to settlement by American farmers. The Kiowa-Apache allotments are near the communities of Fort Cobb and Apache in Caddo County, Oklahoma. Official population reports for the Kiowa-Apaches put their numbers at 378 in 1871, 344 in 1875, 349 in 1889, 208 in 1896, and 194 in 1924. In 1951, historian Muriel Wright estimated their population in Oklahoma at approximately 400.

### FIRST APACHES IN AMERICA

Apaches are, relatively speaking, new arrivals in the Southwest. Their language family, Athapascan, is dispersed over a vast area of the upper Western hemisphere, from Alaska and Canada to Mexico. Apaches have moved farther south than any other members of the Athapascan language family, which includes the Navajo, who are close relatives of the Apaches. When Spaniards first encountered the Apaches and Navajos in the sixteenth century, they could not tell them apart and referred to the Navajo as *Apaches de Navajo*.

Athapascans are generally believed to have been among the last peoples to have crossed the land bridge between Siberia and Alaska during the last interglacial epoch. Most members of the language family still reside in the far north. Exactly when the Apaches and Navajos began their migration southward is not known, but it is clear that they had not arrived in the Southwest before the end of the fourteenth century. The Southwest was home to a number of flourishing civilizations—the Anasazi, the Mogollon, the Hohokum, and others—until near the end of the fourteenth century. Those ancient peoples are now believed to have become the Papago, Pima, and Pueblo peoples of the contemporary Southwest. Scholars at one time assumed that the arrival of the Apaches and Navajos played a role in the abandonment of those ancient centers of civilization. It is now known that prolonged drought near the end of the fourteenth century was the decisive factor in disrupting what was already a delicate balance of life for those agricultural cultures in the arid Southwest. The Apaches and Navajos probably arrived to find that the Anasazi in the present-day Four Corners area had reestablished themselves near dependable sources of water in the Pueblo villages of the upper Rio Grande Valley in what is now New Mexico, and that the Mogollon in southwestern New Mexico and southeastern Arizona and the Hohokam in southern Arizona had likewise migrated from their ancient ruins. When Spaniards first entered the region, with the expedition of Francisco de Coronado in 1540, the Apaches and Navajos had already established themselves in their homeland.

### SETTLEMENT PATTERNS

The Grand Apacheria, as it was known, the homeland of the Apaches, was a vast region stretching from what is now central Arizona in the west to present-day central and south Texas in the east, and from northern Mexico in the south to the high plains of what became eastern Colorado in the north. This region was divided between Eastern and Western Apaches. Eastern Apaches were Plains Apaches. In the days before the horse, and before the historic southward migration of the Comanche Nation, in the early 1700s, the Plains Apaches were the lords of the Southern Plains. Western Apaches lived primarily on the western side of the Continental Divide in the mountains of present-day Arizona and western New Mexico. When the Comanches adopted the use of the horse and migrated southward out of what is now Wyoming, they displaced the Eastern Apaches from the Southern Great Plains, who then took up residence in the mountainous country of what eventually became eastern New Mexico.

# ACCULTURATION AND ASSIMILATION

While adhering strongly to their culture in the face of overwhelming attempts to suppress it, Apaches have been adaptable at the same time. As an example, approximately 70 percent of the Jicarillas still practice the Apache religion. When the first Jicarilla tribal council was elected, following the reforms of the Indian Reorganization Act of 1934, ten of its 18 members were medicine men and five others were traditional leaders from chiefs' families. In 1978, a survey found that at least one-half of the residents of the reservation still spoke Jicarilla, and one-third of the households used it regularly. Jicarilla children in the 1990s, however, prefer English, and few of the younger children learn Jicarilla today. The director of the Jicarilla Education Department laments the direction such changes are taking, but no plans are underway to require the children to learn Jicarilla. At the same time, Jicarillas are demonstrating a new pride in traditional crafts. Basketry and pottery making, which had nearly died out during the 1950s, are now valued skills once again, taught and learned with renewed vigor. Many Apaches say they are trying to have the best of both worlds, attempting to survive in the dominant culture while still remaining Apache.

## TRADITIONS, CUSTOMS, AND BELIEFS

The most enduring Apache custom is the puberty ceremony for girls, held each summer. Clan relatives still play important roles in these ceremonies, when girls become Changing Woman for the four days of their *nai'es*. These are spectacular public events, proudly and vigorously advertised by the tribe.

## EDUCATION

Many Apache children were sent to Carlisle Indian School in Pennsylvania not long after the school was founded in 1879 by Richard Henry Pratt; a large group of them arrived in 1887. Government and mission schools were established among the Apaches in the 1890s. These schools pursued vigorous assimilationist policies, including instruction only in English. By 1952, eighty percent of the Apaches in Arizona spoke English. Today, Apaches participate in decisions involving the education of their young, and this has resulted in exemplary bilingual and bicultural programs at the public schools at the San Carlos and Fort Apache reservations, especially in the elementary grades. In 1959, the Jicarilla incorporated their school district with the surrounding Hispanic towns. Within 30 years, its school board included four Jicarilla members, including the editor of the tribal newspaper. In 1988, the Jicarilla school district was chosen New Mexico School District of the Year.

Some Apache communities, like the Cibecue community at White Mountain Reservation, are more conservative and traditional than others, but all value their traditional culture, which has proven to be enduring. Increasingly, especially in communities such as the White Mountain Reservation, education is being used as a tool to develop human resources so that educated tribal members can find ways for the tribe to engage in economic activity that will allow more of its people to remain on the reservation, thus preserving its community and culture.

## CUISINE

Baked mescal, a large desert agave plant, is a uniquely traditional Apache food and is still occasionally harvested and prepared. The proper season for harvesting is May or June, when massive red flowers begin to appear in the mescal patches; it requires specialized knowledge just to find them. The plant is dug out of the ground and stripped, leaving a white bulb two to three feet in circumference. A large cooking pit is dug, about 15 feet long, four feet wide, and four feet deep, large enough to cook about 2,000 pounds of mescal. The bottom of the pit is lined with stones, on top of which fires are built. The mescal is layered on top of the stones, covered with a layer of straw, and then with a layer of dirt. When cooked, the mescal is a fibrous, sticky, syrupy substance with a flavor similar to molasses. Portions are also

This photograph of Apache Mountain Spirit dancers was taken in Mescalero, New Mexico.

dried in thin layers, which can last indefinitely without spoiling, and which provide the Apaches with lightweight rations for extended journeys.

### TRADITIONAL CRAFTS

Reconstructed traditional houses of the Apache, Maricopa, Papago, and Pima are on display at the Gila River Arts and Crafts Museum in Sacaton, Arizona, south of Phoenix. The gift shop at the museum sells arts and crafts from more than 30 tribes in the Southwest. Gift shops selling locally made traditional crafts can also be found at visitor centers, museums, or the tribal complex on the Apache reservations in Arizona and New Mexico. San Carlos Apache women are famous for their twined burden baskets. They are made in full size and in miniature. Another specialty is coiled basketry, featuring complex designs in black devil's claw. Mescalero Apache women can fashion sandals and bags from mescal fibers in hardly any time at all.

### APACHE DANCES AND SONGS

Charlotte Heth, of the Department of Ethnomusicology, University of California, Los Angeles, has noted in a chapter in *Native America: Portrait of the Peoples* that "Apache and Navajo song style are similar: tense, nasal voices; rhythmic pulsation; clear articulation of words in alternating sections with vocables. Both Apache Crown Dancers

and Navajo Yeibichei (Night Chant) dancers wear masks and sing partially in falsetto or in voices imitating the supernaturals."

The White Mountain Apache Sunrise Dance is a girls' puberty ceremony. The Crown Dance or Mountain Spirit Dance is a masked dance in which the participants impersonate deities of the mountains—specifically the *Gans,* or mountain spirits. The Apache Fire Dance is also a masked dance. Instruments for making music include the water drum, the hand-held rattle, and the human voice. Another traditional instrument still used in ritual and ceremonial events is the bullroarer, a thin piece of wood suspended from a string and swung in a circle. Not all dances are open to the public. Visitors should call the tribal office to find out when dances are scheduled at which they will be welcome. The Yavapai-Apache, Camp Verde, Arizona, occasionally present public performances of the Mountain Spirit Dance. Oklahoma Apaches sometimes perform the Fire Dance at the annual American Indian Exposition in Anadarko, Oklahoma; and the San Carlos Apache, San Carlos, Arizona, and the White Mountain Apache, Whiteriver, Arizona, perform the Sunrise Dance and Mountain Spirit Dance throughout the summer, but their traditional dances are most easily observed at the San Carlos Tribal Fair and the White Mountain Tribal Fair.

### HOLIDAYS CELEBRATED BY APACHES

Apaches celebrate a number of holidays each year with events that are open to the public. The San Carlos Apache Tribal Fair is celebrated annually over Veterans Day weekend at San Carlos, Arizona. The Tonto Apache and Yavapai-Apache perform public dances each year at the Coconino Center for the Arts, Flagstaff, Arizona, on the Fourth of July. The White Mountain Apache host The Apache Tribal Fair, which usually occurs on Labor Day weekend, at Whiteriver, Arizona. The Jicarilla Apache host the Little Beaver Rodeo and Powwow, usually in late July, and the Gojiiya Feast Day on September 14-15 each year, at Dulce, New Mexico. The Mescalero Apache Gahan Ceremonial occurs each year on July 1-4 at Mescalero, New Mexico. Apaches in Oklahoma participate in the huge, week-long American Indian Exposition in Anadarko, Oklahoma, each August.

### HEALTH AND MENTAL HEALTH ISSUES

Apaches have suffered devastating health problems from the last decades of the nineteenth century and throughout most of the twentieth century. Many of these problems are associated with malnutrition, poverty, and despair. They have suffered incredibly high rates of contagious diseases such as tuberculosis. Once tuberculosis was introduced among the Jicarilla, it spread at an alarming rate. The establishment of schools, beginning in 1903, only gave the tuberculosis bacteria a means of spreading rapidly throughout the entire tribe. By 1914, 90 percent of the Jicarillas suffered from tuberculosis. Between 1900 and 1920, one-quarter of the people died. One of the reservation schools had to be converted into a tuberculosis sanitarium in an attempt to address the crisis. The sanitarium was not closed until 1940.

Among nearly all Native peoples of North America, alcohol has been an insidious, destructive force, and the Apache are no exception. A recent study found that on both the Fort Apache Reservation and the San Carlos Reservation, alcohol was a factor in more than 85 percent of the major crimes. Alcohol, though long known to the Apache, has not always been a destructive force. Sharing the traditional *telapi* (fermented corn sprouts), in the words of one elder, "made people feel good about each other and what they were doing together." Alcohol as a destructive force in Apache culture is a phenomenon that dates from colonization, and it has been a byproduct of demoralization and despair. Tribal leaders have attempted to address the underlying health problems by trying to create tribal enterprise, by fostering and encouraging bilingual and bicultural educational opportunities, and by trying to make it possible for Apaches to gain more control over their lives.

# LANGUAGE

The Athapascan language family has four branches: Northern Athapascan, Southwestern Athapascan, Pacific Coast Athapascan, and Eyak, a southeast Alaska isolate. The Athapascan language family is one of three families within the Na-Dene language phylum; the other two, the Tlingit family and the Haida family, are language isolates in the far north, Tlingit in southeast Alaska, and Haida in British Columbia. Na-Dene is one of the most widely distributed language phyla in North America. The Southwestern Athapascan language, sometimes called Apachean, has seven dialects: Navajo, Western Apache, Chiricahua, Mescalero, Jicarilla, Lipan, and Kiowa-Apache.

# FAMILY AND COMMUNITY DYNAMICS

For the Apaches, the family is the primary unit of political and cultural life. Apaches have never been a unified nation politically, and individual Apache tribes, until very recently, have never had a centralized government, traditional or otherwise. Extended family groups acted entirely independently of one another. At intervals during the year a number of these family groups, related by dialect, custom, intermarriage, and geographical proximity, might come together, as conditions and circumstances might warrant. In the aggregate, these groups might be identifiable as a tribal division, but they almost never acted together as a tribal division or as a nation—not even when faced with the overwhelming threat of the Comanche migration into their Southern Plains territory. The existence of these many different, independent, extended family groups of Apaches made it impossible for the Spanish, the Mexicans, or the Americans to treat with the Apache Nation as a whole. Each individual group had to be treated with separately, an undertaking that proved difficult for each colonizer who attempted to establish authority within the Apache homeland.

Apache culture is matrilineal. Once married, the man goes with the wife's extended family, where she is surrounded by her relatives. Spouse abuse is practically unknown in such a system. Should the marriage not endure, child custody quarrels are also unknown: the children remain with the wife's extended family. Marital harmony is encouraged by a custom forbidding the wife's mother to speak to, or even be in the presence of, her son-in-law. No such stricture applies to the wife's grandmother, who frequently is a powerful presence in family life. Apache women are chaste, and children are deeply loved.

# EMPLOYMENT AND ECONOMIC TRADITIONS

Apaches can be found pursuing careers in all the professions, though most of them must leave their communities to do so. Some are college faculty; others, such as Allan Houser, grand-nephew of Geronimo, have achieved international reputations in the arts. Farming and ranching continue to provide employment for many Apaches, and Apaches have distinguished themselves as some of the finest professional rodeo performers.

By 1925, the Bureau of Indian Affairs had leased nearly all of the San Carlos Reservation to non-Indian cattlemen, who demonstrated no concern about overgrazing. Most of the best San Carlos farmland was flooded when Coolidge Dam was completed in 1930. Recreational concessions around the lake benefit mostly non-Natives. By the end of the 1930s, the tribe regained control of its rangeland and most San Carlos Apaches became stockmen. Today, the San Carlos Apache cattle operation generates more than $1 million in sales annually. Cattle, timber, and mining leases provide additional revenue. There is some individual mining activity for the semiprecious peridot gemstones. A chronic high level of unemployment is the norm on most reservations in the United States. More than 50 percent of the tribe is unemployed. The unemployment rate on the reservation itself is about 20 percent.

A number of tribal economic enterprises offer some employment opportunities. The Fort Apache Timber Company in Whiteriver, Arizona, owned and operated by the White Mountain Apache, employs about 400 Apache workers. It has a gross annual income of approximately $30 million, producing 100 million board feet of lumber annually (approximately 720,000 acres of the reservation is timberland). The tribe also owns and operates the Sunrise Park Ski Area and summer resort, three miles south of McNary, Arizona. It is open year-round, and contributes both jobs and tourist dollars to the local economy. The ski area has seven lifts and generates $9 million in revenue per year. Another tribally owned enterprise is the White Mountain Apache Motel and Restaurant. The White Mountain Apache Tribal Fair is another important event economically.

The Jicarilla Apache also operate a ski enterprise, offering equipment rentals and trails for a cross-country ski program during the winter months. The gift shop at the Jicarilla museum provides an outlet for the sale of locally crafted Jicarilla traditional items, including basketry, beadwork, feather work, and finely tanned buckskin leather.

Many members of the Mescalero Apache find employment at their ski resort, Ski Apache. Others work at the tribal museum and visitor center in Mescalero, Arizona. A large Mescalero enterprise, the Inn of the Mountain Gods, has a gift shop, several restaurants, and an 18-hole golf course, and offers horseback riding, skeet and trap shooting, and tennis.

For the Yavapai-Apache, whose small reservation has fewer than 300 acres of land suitable for agriculture, the tourist complex at the Montezuma Castle National Monument—where the tribe owns the 75 acres of land surrounding the monument—is an important source of employment and revenue.

Tourism, especially for events such as tribal fairs and for hunting and fishing, provides jobs and brings money into the local economies at a number of reservations. Deer and elk hunting are especially popular on the Jicarilla reservation. The Jicarilla also maintain five campgrounds where camping is available for a fee. Other campgrounds are maintained by the Mescalero Apache (3), the San Carlos Apache (4), and the White Mountain Apache (18).

# POLITICS AND GOVERNMENT

The Apache tribes are federally recognized tribes. They have established tribal governments under The Indian Reorganization Act of 1934 (25 U.S.C. 461-279), also known as the Wheeler-Howard Act, and they successfully withstood attempts by the U.S. government to implement its policy during the 1950s of terminating Indian tribes. The Wheeler-Howard Act, however, while allowing some measure of self-determination in their affairs, has caused problems for virtually every Indian nation in the United States, and the Apaches are no exception. The act subverts traditional Native forms of government and imposes upon Native people an alien system, which is something of a mix of American corporate and governmental structures. Invariably, the most traditional people in each tribe have had little to say about their own affairs, as the most heavily acculturated and educated mixed-blood factions have dominated tribal affairs in these foreign imposed systems. Frequently these tribal governments have been little more than convenient shams to facilitate access to tribal mineral and timber resources in arrangements that benefit everyone but the Native people, whose resources are exploited. The situations and experiences differ markedly from tribe to tribe in this regard, but it is a problem that is, in some measure, shared by all.

## RELATIONS WITH THE UNITED STATES

Apaches were granted U.S. citizenship under the Indian Citizenship Act of 1924. They did not legally acquire the right to practice their Native religion until the passage of The American Indian Religious Freedom Act of 1978 (42 U.S.C. 1996). Other important rights, and some attributes of sovereignty, have been restored to them by such legislation as The Indian Civil Rights Act of 1966 (25 U.S.C. 1301), The Indian Self-Determination and Educational Assistance Act of 1975 (25 U.S.C. 451a), and The Indian Child Welfare Act of 1978 (25 U.S.C. 1901). Under the Indian Claims Commission Act of 1946, the Jicarillas have been awarded nearly $10 million in compensation for land unjustly taken from them, but the United States refuses to negotiate the return of any of this land. In *Merrion v. Jicarilla Apache Tribe*, the U.S. Supreme Court ruled in favor of the Jicarillas in an important case concerning issues of tribal sovereignty, holding that the Jicarillas have the right to impose tribal taxes upon minerals extracted from their lands.

# INDIVIDUAL AND GROUP CONTRIBUTIONS

## LITERATURE, ACADEMIA, AND THE ARTS

Apaches are making important contributions to Native American literature and the arts. Lorenzo Baca, of Mescalero Apache and Isleta Pueblo heritage, is not only a writer, but also a performing and visual artist who does fine art, sculpture, video, storytelling and acting. His poetry has been anthologized in *The Shadows of Light: Poetry and Photography of the Motherlode and Sierras* (Jelm Mountain Publications), in *Joint Effort II: Escape* (Sierra Conservation Center), and in *Neon Powwow: New Native American Voices of the Southwest* (Northland Publishing). His audio recording, *Songs, Poems and Lies*, was produced by Mr. Coyote Man Productions. An innovative writer, his circle stories entitled "Ten Rounds" in *Neon Powwow* illustrate his imagination and capacity to create new forms of poetic expression. Jicarilla Apache creative writers Stacey Velarde and Carlson Vicenti present portraits of Native people in the modern world in their stories in the *Neon Powwow* anthology. Velarde, who has been around horses all her life and has competed in professional rodeos since the age of 13, applies this background and knowledge in her story "Carnival Lights," while Vicenti, in "Hitching" and "Oh Saint Michael," shows how Native people incorporate traditional ways into modern life.

White Mountain Apache poet Roman C. Adrian has published poetry in *Sun Tracks*, *The New Times*, *Do Not Go Gentle*, and *The Remembered Earth*. The late Chiricahua Apache poet Blossom Haozous, of Fort Sill, Oklahoma, was a leader in the bilingual presentation of Apache traditional stories, both orally and in publication. One of the stories, "Quarrel Between Thunder and Wind" was published bilingually in the *Chronicles of Oklahoma*, the quarterly scholarly journal of the Oklahoma Historical Society.

Jose L. Garza, Coahuilateca and Apache, is not only a leading Native American poet but a leading Native American educator as well. His poetry has appeared in such publications as *Akwe:kon Journal*, of the American Indian Program at Cornell University, *The Native Sun*, *New Rain Anthology*, *The Wayne Review*, *Triage*, and *The Wooster Review*. Garza is a professor at Edinboro University in Pennsylvania and is a regional coordinator of Wordcraft Circle of Native American Mentor and Apprentice Writers. In Wordcraft Circle, he organizes and helps conduct intensive writing workshops in which young Native writers from all tribes have an opportunity to hone their creative skills and learn how they can publish their work.

Other Apache writers include Lou Cuevas, author of *Apache Legends: Songs of the Wild Dancer* (Naturegraph); Jicarilla Apache scholar Veronica E. Velarde Tiller, the author of *The Jicarilla Apache Tribe* (University of Nebraska Press); and Michael Lacapa, of Apache, Hopi, and Pueblo heritage, the author of *The Flute Player* (Northland Publishing) and *The Mouse Couple* (Northland). Throughout the Apache tribes, the traditional literature and knowledge of the people is handed down from generation to generation by storytellers who transmit their knowledge orally.

## VISUAL ARTS

Chiricahua Apache sculptor Allan Houser has been acclaimed throughout the world for his six decades of work in wood, marble, stone, and bronze. Houser was born June 30, 1914, near Apache, Oklahoma. He died on August 22, 1994, in Santa Fe, New Mexico. His Apache surname was Haozous, which means "Pulling Roots."

In the 1960s, Houser was a charter faculty member at the Institute of American Indian Arts in Santa Fe, where he began to cast statues in bronze. He taught until 1975. After retirement from teaching, he devoted himself full-time to his work, creating sculptures in bronze, wood, and stone. In April 1994, he presented an 11-foot bronze sculpture to first lady Hillary Rodham Clinton in Washington, D.C., as a gift from the American Indians to all people.

Houser was known primarily for his large sculptures. Many of these could be seen in a sculpture garden, arranged among pinon and juniper trees, near his studio. His work is included in the British Royal Collection, at the Metropolitan Museum of Art in New York City, the Heard Museum in Phoenix, Arizona, the Denver Art Museum, Denver, Colorado, the Museum of Northern Arizona at Flagstaff, Arizona, the Linden Museum in Stuttgart, Germany, the Fine Arts Museum of the Museum of New Mexico in Santa Fe, New Mexico, the Apache Tribal Cultural Center in Apache, Oklahoma, the Gilcrease Museum in Tulsa, Oklahoma, the University Center in Tulsa, Oklahoma.

Houser's work has won many awards, including the Prix de West Award in 1993 for a bronze sculpture titled "Smoke Signals" at the annual National Academy of Western Art show at the National Cowboy Hall of Fame in Oklahoma City, Oklahoma. "Smoke Signals" is now a part of the permanent collection of the National Cowboy Hall of Fame.

One of his best known works, a bronze statue of an Indian woman, titled "As Long as the Waters Flow," stands in front of the state capitol of Oklahoma in Oklahoma City. At the University of Oklahoma, in Norman, two large Houser sculptures were on loan to the university and on display on the grounds of the campus at the time of his death. At the Fred Jones Jr. Museum on campus, were several Houser pieces from private Oklahoma collections on view. Upon his death, the University of Oklahoma Student Association announced the creation of the Allan Houser Memorial Sculpture Fund. The fund will be used to purchase a major Houser sculpture for permanent display on the University of Oklahoma campus.

# MEDIA

## PRINT

### American Indian Law Newsletter.
Address: 1915 Roma Avenue, N.E., Albuquerque, New Mexico, 87106.

### Americans Before Columbus.
Address: 318 Elm Street, Albuquerque, New Mexico 87012.

### Apache Drumbeat.
Address: Bylas, Arizona 85530.

### Apache Junction Independent.
Community newspaper.

Contact: Jim Files, Editor.
Address: Independent Newspapers, Inc., 11000 North Scottsdale Road, Suite 210, Scottsdale, Arizona 85254.
Telephone: (602) 483-0977.
Fax: (602) 948-0496.

### Apache News.
Community newspaper founded in 1901.

Contact: Stanley Wright, Editor.
Address: Box 778, Apache, Oklahoma 73006.
Telephone: (405) 588-3862.

### Apache Scout.
Address: Mescalero, New Mexico 88340.

### Bear Track.
Address: 1202 West Thomas Road, Phoenix, Arizona 85013.

### Center for Indian Education News.
Address: 302 Farmer Education Building, Room 302, Tempe, Arizona 85287.

### Drumbeat.
Address: Institute of American Indian Arts, Cerrillos Road, Santa Fe, New Mexico 87501.

### Fort Apache Scout.
Address: Box 898, Whiteriver, Arizona 85941.

### Four Directions.
Address: 1812 Las Lomas, N.E., Albuquerque, New Mexico 87131.

### Gila River Indian News.
Address: Box 97, Sacaton, Arizona 85247.

### Graduate Indian Center Newsletter.
Address: 4520 Montgomery, N.E., Suite 1B, Albuquerque, New Mexico 87109.

**Indian Arizona.**
Address: 4560 North 19th Avenue, Suite 200, Phoenix, Arizona 85015-4113.

**Indian Education Update.**
Address: 2121 South Mill Avenue, Suite 218, Tempe, Arizona 85282.

**Indian Extension News.**
Address: New Mexico State University, Las Cruces, New Mexico 88001.

**Indian Life.**
Address: 1664 East Campo Bello Drive, Phoenix, Arizona 85022.

**Indian Programs.**
Address: University of Arizona, Tucson, Arizona 85721.

**Indian Quest.**
Address: 708 South Lindon Lane, Tempe, Arizona 85281.

**Indian Resources Development Newsletter.**
Address: P.O. Box 30003, Las Cruces, New Mexico 88003-0003.

**Indian Trader.**
Address: P.O. Box 1421, Gallup, New Mexico 87301.

**Indian Voice.**
Address: 9169 Coors Road, N.W., Box 10146, Albuquerque, New Mexico 87184.

**Institute of American Indian Arts Newsletter.**
Address: P.O. Box 20007, Santa Fe, New Mexico 87504.

**Jicarilla Chieftain.**
Address: P.O. Box 507, Dulce, New Mexico 87528.

**Native American Smoke Signals.**
Address: 13282 Central Avenue, P.O. Box 515, Mayer, Arizona 86333.

**Native Images.**
Address: P.O. Box 1624, Tempe, Arizona 85280.

**Native Peoples Magazine.**
Address: 1833 North Third Street, Phoenix, Arizona 85004.

**San Carlos Moccasin.**
Address: P.O. Box 775, San Carlos, Arizona 85550.

**Smoke Dreams.**
Address: Riverside Indian School, Anadarko, Oklahoma 73005.

**Southwest Native News.**
Address: P.O. Box 1990, Tuba City, Arizona 86045.

**Southwind Native News.**
Address: P.O. Box 40176, Albuquerque, New Mexico 87196.

**Thunderbird.**
Address: Albuquerque Indian School, 1000 Indian School Road, N.W., Albuquerque, New Mexico 87103.

**UTS'ITTISCTAAN'I.**
Address: Northern Arizona University, Campus Box 5630, Flagstaff, Arizona 86011.

**RADIO**

**KCIE-FM (90.5).**
Address: P.O. Box 603, Dulce, New Mexico 87528.

**KENN.**
Address: P.O. Box 1558, Farmington, New Mexico 87499-1558.

**KGAK.**
Address: 401 East Coal Road, Gallup, New Mexico 87301-6099.

**KGHR-FM (91.5).**
Address: P.O. Box 160, Tuba City, Arizona 86519.

**KHAC-AM (1110).**
Address: Drawer F, Window Rock, Arizona 86515.

**KNNB-FM (88.1).**
Eclectic and ethnic format 18 hours daily.

Contact: Phoebe L. Nez, General Manager.
Address: Highway 73, Skill Center Road, P.O. Box 310, Whiteriver, Arizona 85941.
Telephone: (602) 338-5229.
Fax: (602) 338-1744.

**KPLZ.**

**Address:** 816 Sixth Street, Parker, Arizona 85344-4599.

**KRPT.**

**Address:** P.O. Box 1360, Anadarko, Oklahoma 73005.

**KSHI-FM (90.9).**

**Address:** P.O. Box 339, Zuni, New Mexico 87327.

**KTDB-FM (89.7).**

**Address:** P.O. Box 89, Pine Hill, New Mexico 87321.

**KTNN-AM.**

**Address:** P.O. Box 2569, Window Rock, Arizona 86515.

**TELEVISION**

**KSWO-TV.**

**Address:** P.O. Box 708, Lawton, Oklahoma 73502.

# ORGANIZATIONS AND ASSOCIATIONS

**Apache Tribe of Oklahoma.**

**Address:** P.O. Box 1220, Anadarko, Oklahoma 73005.
**Telephone:** (405) 247-9493.
**Fax:** (405) 247-9232.

**Arizona Commission for Indian Affairs.**

**Address:** 1623 West Adams, Phoenix, Arizona 85007.

**Fort Sill Apache Tribe of Oklahoma.**

**Address:** Route 2, Box 121, Apache, Oklahoma 73006.
**Telephone:** (405) 588-2298.
**Fax:** (405) 588-3313.

**Indian Education Center.**

**Address:** Arizona State University, Tempe, Arizona 85281.

**Jicarilla Apache Tribe.**

**Address:** P.O. Box 147, Dulce, New Mexico 87528.
**Telephone:** (505) 759-3242.
**Fax:** (505) 759-3005.

**Kiowa Tribe of Oklahoma.**

**Address:** P.O. Box 369, Carnegie, Oklahoma 73015.

**Telephone:** (405) 654-2300.
**Fax:** (405) 654-2188.

**Mescalero Apache Tribe.**

**Address:** P.O. Box 176, Mescalero, New Mexico 88340.
**Telephone:** (505) 671-4495.
**Fax:** (505) 671-4495.

**New Mexico Commission on Indian Affairs.**

**Address:** 330 East Palace Avenue, Santa Fe, New Mexico 87501.

**New Mexico Indian Advisory Commission.**

**Address:** Box 1667, Albuquerque, New Mexico 87107.

**San Carlos Apache Tribe.**

**Address:** P.O. Box O, San Carlos, Arizona, 85550.
**Telephone:** (602) 475-2361.
**Fax:** (602) 475-2567.

**Tonto Apache Tribal Council.**

**Address:** Tonto Reservation No. 30, Payson, Arizona 85541.
**Telephone:** (602) 474-5000.
**Fax:** (602) 474-9125.

**White Mountain Apache Tribe.**

**Address:** P.O. Box 700, Whiteriver, Arizona 85941.
**Telephone:** (602) 338-4346.
**Fax:** (602) 338-4778.

**Yavapai-Apache Tribe.**

**Address:** P.O. Box 1188, Camp Verde, Arizona.
**Telephone:** (602) 567-3649.
**Fax:** (602) 567-9455.

# MUSEUMS AND RESEARCH CENTERS

Apache museums and research centers include: Albuquerque Museum in Albuquerque, New Mexico; American Research Museum in Santa Fe, New Mexico; Art Center in Roswell, New Mexico; Bacone College Museum in Muscogee, Oklahoma; Black Water Draw Museum in Portales, New Mexico; Coronado Monument in Bernalillo, New Mexico; Ethnology Museum in Santa Fe;

Fine Arts Museum in Santa Fe; Gilcrease Museum in Tulsa, Oklahoma; Great Plains Museum in Lawton, Oklahoma; Hall of the Modern Indian in Santa Fe; Heard Museum of Anthropology in Phoenix, Arizona; Indian Hall of Fame in Anadarko, Oklahoma; Institute of American Indian Arts in Santa Fe; Maxwell Museum in Albuquerque; Milicent Rogers Museum in Taos, New Mexico; Northern Arizona Museum in Flagstaff; Oklahoma Historical Society Museum in Oklahoma City; Philbrook Museum in Tulsa; Southern Plains Indian Museum in Anadarko; State Museum of Arizona in Tempe; Stovall Museum at the University of Oklahoma in Norman.

# SOURCES FOR ADDITIONAL STUDY

Buskirk, Winfred. *The Western Apache*. Norman: University of Oklahoma Press, 1986.

Eagle/Walking Turtle (Gary McLain). *Indian America: A Traveler's Companion*, third edition. Santa Fe, New Mexico: John Muir Publications, 1993.

Forbes, Jack D. *Apache, Navajo, and Spaniard*. Norman: University of Oklahoma Press, 1969, 1994.

Goodwin, Grenville. *The Social Organization of the Western Apache*. Chicago: University of Chicago Press, 1942.

Kenner, Charles L. *A History of New Mexican-Plains Indian Relations*. Norman: University of Oklahoma Press, 1969, 1994.

Marquis, Arnold. *A Guide to America's Indians: Ceremonials, Reservations, and Museums*. Norman: University of Oklahoma Press, 1974.

Melody, Michael E. *The Apaches: A Critical Bibliography*. Bloomington: Indiana University Press, 1977.

Moorhead, Max L. *The Apache Frontier: Jacobo Ugarte and Spanish-Indian Relations in Northern New Spain, 1769-1791*. Norman: University of Oklahoma Press, 1968.

Opler, Morris Edward. *An Apache Life-way: The Economic, Social, and Religious Institutions of the Chiricahua Indians*. Chicago: University of Chicago Press, 1941.

Perry, Richard J. *Apache Reservation: Indigenous Peoples and the American State*. Austin: University of Texas Press, 1993.

Stockel, H. Henrietta. "Ceremonies and Celebrations," in *Women Of the Apache Nation. Voices of Truth*. Reno: University of Nevada Press, 1991.

"Traditional and Contemporary Ceremonies, Rituals, Festivals, Music, and Dance," in *Native America: Portrait of the Peoples*, edited by Duane Champagne. Detroit: Gale Research, 1994.

Trimble, Stephen. *The People: Indians of the American Southwest*. Santa Fe: New Mexico: Sar Press, 1993.

Wright, Muriel H. *A Guide to the Indian Tribes of Oklahoma*, foreword by Arrell Morgan Gibson. Norman: University of Oklahoma Press, 1951, 1986.

In the 1950s and
1960s the Arab
countries resonated
with nationalist
ideologies, and the
Arab world was
filled with promise
and hope, especially
regarding the
question of Palestine
and Arab national
unity—two of the
burning issues of the
day.

# ARAB AMERICANS

**by**
Nabeel Abraham

## OVERVIEW

Arab Americans trace their ancestral roots to several Arab countries. Lebanon is the homeland of a majority of Arab Americans, followed by Syria, Palestine, Iraq, Egypt, Yemen, and Jordan. The Arab world consists of 21 countries that span from North Africa to the Persian Gulf.

### HISTORY

Ethnic Arabs inhabited the Arabian Peninsula and neighboring areas. With the rise of Islam in the seventh century A.D. and its phenomenal expansion over parts of Asia, Africa, and Europe, Arabic culture and language spread to the newly conquered peoples. Over time the Arab identity lost its purely ethnic roots as millions in the Middle East and North Africa adopted the Arabic language and integrated Arab culture with that of their own.

### MODERN ERA

Today, the term Arab is a cultural, linguistic, and to some extent, political designation. It embraces numerous national and regional groups as well as many non-Muslim religious minorities. Arab Christians, particularly in the countries of Egypt and the Fertile Crescent (Syria, Iraq, Palestine,

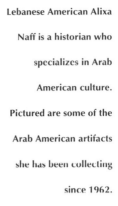

Lebanese American Alixa Naff is a historian who specializes in Arab American culture. Pictured are some of the Arab American artifacts she has been collecting since 1962.

and Jordan) constitute roughly ten percent of the population. In Lebanon, Christians of various sects approach just under half of the population, while in Egypt, Christians comprise between ten and 15 percent of the population.

## ARABS IN AMERICA

According to the 1990 census, there were 870,000 persons in the United States who identified themselves as ethnically Arab or who emigrated from one of the 21 countries that constitute the contemporary Arab world. Previous estimates by scholars and Arab American community organizations placed the number of Arab Americans at between one and three million. The discrepancy is partly due to the standardization of Arabs in the United States, leading many to conceal their ethnic affiliation. The traditional suspicion of Middle Easterners toward government authorities seeking information of a personal nature compounds this problem. These two factors along with standard problems in collecting census data probably explain the discrepancy between the estimates of scholars and the actual census count. Considering these factors, a revised estimate would probably place the number of Arab Americans in the range of one to two million.

The 1990 census indicates that most Arab Americans are U.S. citizens (82 percent) even though only 63 percent were born in the United States. Arab Americans are geographically con-centrated in a handful of cities and states. According to an essay in *American Demographics* by Samia El-Badry, over two-thirds of Arab Americans live in ten states while just three metropolitan areas (Detroit, New York, and Los Angeles-Long Beach) account for over one-third of the population.

Arab immigrants represent a tiny fraction of the overall migration to the United States, constituting less than three percent of the total. In her study of the census data, El-Badry found that more than 27,000 people from Arab countries immigrated to the United States in 1992, 68 percent more than those who arrived ten years earlier, not including Palestinians from Israel or Israeli-occupied territory. Approximately 20 percent of the 78,400 Arab immigrants who arrived in the United States between 1990 and 1992 were Lebanese. The remainder were from Egypt, Jordan, Syria, and Iraq. The figures for Sudan and Yemen, though small in comparison, indicated rapid growth from these politically unstable countries.

## SIGNIFICANT IMMIGRATION WAVES

Arabic-speaking immigrants arrived in the United States in three major waves. The first wave between the late 1800s and World War I consisted mainly of immigrants from Greater Syria, an Arab province of the Ottoman Empire until the end of World War I. Following the breakup of the Empire, the province was partitioned into the separate political entities of Syria, Lebanon, Palestine, and Transjordan. The vast majority of immigrants in this wave were members of Christian minorities. Although some writers claim that these immigrants left their native countries for religious or political reasons, the evidence suggests that they were drawn to the United States and other countries by economic opportunity.

Of the approximately 60,000 who emigrated to the United States between 1899 and 1910, approximately half were illiterate, and 68 percent were single males. The early immigrants were mostly unskilled single men who had left their families behind. Like many economically motivated immigrants during this period, Arabs left with the intention of earning money and returning home to live out the remainder of their lives in relative prosperity.

The major exception to this pattern was a small group of Arab writers, poets, and artists who took up residence in major urban centers such as New York and Boston. The most famous of the group was Kahlil Gibran (1883-1931), author of *The Prophet* and numerous other works. Curiously, this literary circle, which came to be known as the Pen League (*al-Rabita al-Qalamiyya*) had a negligible influence on the early Arab American communities in the United States. The Pen League's greatest impact was on arts and letters in Lebanon, Egypt, and other Arab countries.

Early immigrants settled in the urban areas of the Northeast and Midwest, in states like New York, Massachusetts, Pennsylvania, Michigan, and Ohio. By 1940, a fifth of the estimated 350,000 Arabs resided in three cities—New York, Boston, and Detroit. In these urban areas, the immigrants clustered in ethnic neighborhoods. Although many found work in the industrial factories and textile mills that propelled the U.S. economy in the first half of the twentieth century, some also chose the life of itinerant salesmen, peddling dry goods and other sundry items across the American heartland. Others homesteaded on the Great Plains and in rural areas of the South.

Very few Arabic-speaking immigrants made their way across the Atlantic during the interwar period marked by the Great Depression and anti-immigrant sentiment. Immigration resumed, however, after the close of World War II, especially from the 1950s to the mid-1960s. Unlike the earlier influx, this second wave included many more Muslims. It also included refugees who had been displaced by the 1948 Palestine War that culminated in the establishment of Israel. This period also witnessed the arrival of many Arabic-speaking professionals and university students who often chose to remain in the United States after completion of their training. Immigrants of the second wave tended to settle where jobs were available. Those with few skills drifted to the established Arab communities in the industrial towns of the East coast and Midwest, while those with professional skills ventured to the new suburbs around the major industrial cities or to rural towns.

In the mid-1960s, a third wave of Arab immigration began which continues to the present. According to El-Badry, more than 75 percent of foreign-born Arab Americans identified in the 1990 census immigrated after 1964, while 44 percent immigrated between 1975 and 1980. This influx resulted in part from the passage of the Immigration Act of 1965 which abolished the quota system and its bias against non-European immigration.

The third wave included many professionals, entrepreneurs, and unskilled and semi-skilled laborers. These immigrants often fled political instability and wars engulfing their home countries with their families. They included Lebanese Shiites from southern Lebanon, Palestinians from the Israeli-occupied West Bank, and Iraqis of all political persuasions. But many professionals from these and other countries like Syria, Egypt, and Jordan, and unskilled workers from Yemen also emigrated in search of better economic opportunities. Had conditions been more hospitable in their home countries, it is doubtful that many of these immigrants would have left their native countries.

## RELATIONSHIP WITH ESTABLISHED AMERICANS

Relations with the host society have been mixed. Early immigrants went largely unnoticed by the general population. They tended to settle in economically vibrant areas, which drew similar immigrants. Those who opted to homestead in the Midwest or farm in the South also blended into their surroundings. This same pattern carried over after the Second World War to the second wave of Arab immigration.

Relations, however, soured for members of the third wave and for native-born Arab Americans after the June 1967 Arab-Israeli War. This situation worsened after the Arab oil embargo and the quadrupling of world oil prices that followed in the wake of the October 1973 Arab-Israeli

War. Arabs and Muslims were vilified as blood-thirsty terrorists, greedy oil sheiks, and religious fanatics by the mass media, politicians, and political commentators. With the fall of the Shah and the rise of Ayatollah Khomeini to power in Iran (a large, non-Arab country) in 1979 came another oil shortage and price shock that further exacerbated anti-Middle Eastern sentiment in the United States.

For the better part of the 1980s, Arab Americans lived in an increasing state of apprehension as the Reagan Administration waged a war on international terrorism, and tensions ensued from the two U.S. attacks against Libya and U.S. involvement in Lebanon following Israel's 1982 invasion of that country. The hijacking of an American passenger plane in Europe en route to Lebanon triggered a backlash against Arab Americans, Muslims, and Middle Easterners in the United States. After another hijacking in 1985, on the morning of Friday, October 11, a bomb went off at the Los Angeles office of the American Arab Anti-Discrimination Committee (ADC), killing the organization's regional director, 41-year-old Alex Odeh. The previous day Odeh had appeared on a local television news program, where he opined that the Palestine Liberation Organization (PLO) and its leader, Yasir Arafat, were not behind the hijacking of the *Achille Lauro* cruise liner in the Mediterranean. The Federal Bureau of Investigation (FBI) strongly hinted that the Jewish Defense League (JDL), or a similar Jewish extremist group, was behind the bombing and considered Odeh's murder the top terrorist act of 1985. The murder of Alex Odeh was clearly political and continues to be highly significant for Arab Americans.

The mid-1980s were the peak of anti-Arab hate crimes. In comparison, the Gulf crisis of 1991-1992 was relatively less lethal. Although there were many reports of assaults against Arab Americans, few incidents resulted in serious injuries and no one was killed. No Arab or Islamic community organizations were bombed, though many received threats and an incendiary device that apparently failed to explode was discovered at the American Muslim Council in San Diego. A few incidents during this period can be traced to the assassination in November 1990 of Rabbi Meir Kahane, the former leader of the Jewish Defense League. His murder triggered a rash of death threats and harassment against prominent Arab Americans.

U.S. law enforcement agencies also violated the civil liberties of Arab Americans. Beginning in the 1960s, the FBI, the Immigration and Naturalization Service (INS), and other federal and local law enforcement agencies began surveillance of Arab student and community activities. The surveillance, code-named Operation Boulder, was the result of an executive order signed by President Richard Nixon. The special measures included entry restrictions on foreign nationals, surveillance, information gathering on political activities and organizations, and even restrictions on Arab access to permanent resident status. Ostensibly the measures were designed to prevent Arab terrorists from operating in the country. This argument rang hollow as there had been no instances of Arab terrorism in the United States until that time. In fact, no incidents occurred for the next 25 years until the 1993 bombing of the World Trade Center by Arab Muslim immigrants. Ironically, much of the FBI surveillance and questioning focused on constitutionally guaranteed activities involving the exercise of free speech and association.

On the morning of January 26, 1987, scores of INS, FBI, and police agents raided several houses in Los Angeles, arresting six Palestinians and the Kenyan wife of one of the arrested men. Several days later another Palestinian was arrested while sitting for an exam at a local community college. The eight were held in detention for nearly three weeks. The arrests reportedly were the culmination of a three-year-long FBI probe into the activities of Arab American activists. The L.A. Eight, as they came to be known, were originally charged under a little-used section of the 1952 McCarran-Walter Immigration Act. This law allowed the government to deport aliens who "knowingly circulate, distribute, print or display" material that advocates the overthrow of the U.S. government or who advocate or teach the "doctrines of world communism." In court, attorneys for the government could produce nothing incriminating except magazines and other printed literature linking the defendants to the Popular Front for the Liberation of Palestine, a nationalist guerilla group with Marxist overtones. Unable to make the subversion charge stick, the government moved to deport six of the Arab Americans on visa technicalities and tried to invoke other clauses of the McCarran-Walter Act. These attempts were thrown out of court as unconstitutional.

The L.A. Eight's ordeal continued into 1994, as the government insisted on deporting them even though it failed to produce any evidence that the defendants had done anything illegal.

Many civil libertarians who rallied to their defense feared the arrests were a blatant attempt by the government to chill the political activities of Arab Americans and others who opposed U.S. foreign policy in the Middle East. Their concern was heightened when a copy of a secret INS plan was obtained by the *Los Angeles Times* shortly after the arrests occurred. The plan revealed the existence of an interagency contingency plan to apprehend, detain, and deport large numbers of Arab and Iranian students, permanent residents, and American citizens, in the event the President declared a state of emergency. According to the plan, a target group of less than 10,000 persons was scheduled for detention and deportation.

# ACCULTURATION AND ASSIMILATION

Early Arab immigrants assimilated easily into American society facilitated by the fact that the majority were Christian. Aside from barely discernable Arabic names beneath anglicized surnames and a preference for some Old World dishes, they retained few traces of their ethnic roots. Many were successful, some achieving celebrity status.

At the turn of the century when the first wave immigrated, the Arab world still languished under Ottoman Turkish rule, then four centuries old. Arab and regional national consciousness was still nascent. By the time the second wave immigrants arrived in mid-century, the Arab world was in the process of shaking off the European colonial rule that had carved up much of the Middle East after the breakup of the Ottoman Empire at the end of World War I. In the 1950s and 1960s the Arab countries resonated with nationalist ideologies, and the Arab world was filled with promise and hope, especially regarding the question of Palestine and Arab national unity—two of the burning issues of the day. These ideological currents profoundly influenced many second-wave immigrants. The second wave of Arab immigrants was able to assimilate into mainstream society without much resistance. This wave tended to retain some distinctive features of its ethnic past because many of the newcomers were Muslim, contributing to the retention of a distinct cultural identity. The establishment of cultural clubs, political committees, and Arabic language schools helped maintain a cultural identity and a political awareness among many new arrivals and their children.

Arriving in the 1970s and 1980s, the third wave of Arab immigrants encountered a negative reception from the host society. Instead of assimilating, these new immigrants often opted to remain on the outskirts of society, even while adopting many American cultural mores. The third wave has been the driving force behind the recent upsurge in the establishment of Muslim schools, mosques, charities, and Arabic language classes.

Collectively many Arab Americans have experienced cultural marginalization. Arabs, Muslims, and Middle Easterners generally have been vilified in the news media, in Hollywood productions, in pulp novels, and in political discourse. Arab Americans cope with their marginality in one of three different ways: denying their ethnic identity; withdrawing into an ethnic enclave; or engaging mainstream society through information campaigns aimed at the news media, book publishers, politicians, and schools. The theme of these campaigns centers on the inherent unfairness of, and pitfalls in, stereotyping Arabs, Muslims, and Middle Easterners.

The types of Arab Americans who choose to deny their ethnic background cover the spectrum: recent arrivals, assimilated immigrants, and native-born. Among the American-born, denial takes the form of a complete break with one's ethnicity in favor of wholesale adoption of American culture. Others, particularly immigrants, tend to stress their distinctiveness from Arab and Islamic culture, as when Iraqi Christians stress their Chaldean identity as opposed to their Iraqi affiliation.

Arab Americans who opt to withdraw into an ethnic enclave tend to be recent immigrants. Running the gamut from unskilled workers to middle-class professionals, this group prefers to live in ethnic neighborhoods, or close to other members of the same group in the suburbs. They believe that their ethnic culture and religious traditions are alien to American culture, and hence need to minimize assimilation. Cultural marginalization is the price of living in American society.

Those who advocate engaging society head-on seek to win societal acceptance of Arab Americans as an integral part of America's cultural plurality. The integrationists adopt several strategies. Some stress the common bonds between Arab or Islamic values and American values, emphasizing strong family ties. They also focus on the commonalities between Christianity and Islam. Others seek to confront anti-Arab stereotyping and racism by emphasizing that they are Americans who happen to be of Arab ancestry. Along with well-assimilated, native-born Arab Americans, this group also consists of foreign-born professionals who wish to maintain their ethnic identity free from stigmatization by the wider culture.

Foremost among the key issues facing the Arab American community is dealing with the rising numbers of new immigrant inflow. The current stream of Arab immigrants is expected to increase as political instability and civil conflict within various Arab countries grows.

## TRADITIONS, CUSTOMS, AND BELIEFS

Customs center on hospitality around food, socializing with family and friends, and a preference to reside close to relatives. Arab Americans generally harbor negative attitudes toward dating and pre-marital sex, especially for females. Educational achievement and economic advancement are viewed positively, as are the maintenance of strong family ties and the preservation of female chastity and fidelity. Arab American beliefs about the United States are extremely positive, particularly regarding the availability of economic opportunities and political freedoms. Socially, however, Arab Americans feel that American society is highly violent, rather promiscuous, too lenient toward offenders, and somewhat lax on family values.

A common American stereotype about Arabs emphasizes that they are by definition Muslims and therefore are bloodthirsty, fanatical, and anti-Western. Another misconception is that Iranians are Arabs, when most Iranians are Persians who speak Farsi, an Indo-European language, which uses Arabic script. Arabic, on the other hand, belongs to the Semitic language family. Other misconceptions and stereotypes include: Arabs are desert nomads; however, only two percent of contemporary Arab society is nomadic; and, Arabs oppress women. While formal laws protecting women's equality are fewer in Arab countries than the United States, the prevalence of rape and physical abuse of women in the Arab world appears to be lower than in American society.

Stereotypes of Arab culture and society abound in Western literary works, scholarly research, and in the news and entertainment media. Typical of the fiction genre is Leon Uris's celebrated novel *Exodus* (1958), in which the Arab country of Palestine is repeatedly depicted as a "fruitless, listless, dying land." Arabs opposed to the creation of the State of Israel are described as the "dregs of humanity, thieves, murderers, highway robbers, dope runners and white slavers." More generally, Arabs are "dirty," "crafty," and "corrupt." Uris amplified these characterizations in his 1985 work, *The Haj*. These and other examples are examined in Janice J. Terry's *Mistaken Identity: Arab Stereotypes in Popular Writing* (1985). A study of the cultural antecedents of Arab and Muslim stereotyping in Western culture is found in Edward W. Said's highly acclaimed work, *Orientalism* (1978). News media coverage is critiqued in Said's *Covering Islam* (1981); television portrayals of Arabs are examined in Jack Shaheen's *The TV Arab* (1984).

## CUISINE

The most pronounced dietary injunction followed by Arab Muslims is the religious prohibition on the consumption of pork. Many Arab Christians also disdain the consumption of pork, but for cultural reasons. Muslims are required to consume meat that is ritually slaughtered (*halal*). In response to the growing demand for *halal* meats, many enterprising Arab American grocers have in recent years set up *halal* meat markets.

Arab Americans have a distinctive cuisine centered on lamb, rice, bread, and highly seasoned dishes. The Middle Eastern diet consists of many ingredients not found in the average American kitchen, such as chick peas, lentils, fava beans, ground sesame seed oil, olive oil, olives, feta cheese, dates, and figs. Many Arab dishes, like stuffed zucchini or green peppers and stuffed grape or cabbage leaves, are highly labor-intensive.

## TRADITIONAL COSTUMES

Virtually no items of traditional clothing are worn by Arab Americans. The exception is the tendency of some immigrant women, particularly those from peasant stock, who wear traditional dress. Among the most dramatic are the colorfully embroidered dresses worn by some Palestinian women in certain neighborhoods of Detroit and Dearborn. More common are the plain-colored head scarfs worn by many Lebanese and other Arab Muslim females. Some Arab and other Muslim women occasionally don long, shapeless dresses, commonly called Islamic dresses, in addition to the head scarf.

Men rarely wear traditional garb in public. At some traditional wedding parties individuals might don an Arab *burnoose*. Many foreign-born

These Arab American family members are standing in front of the Yemën Cafe in Brooklyn, New York. Many Arab Americans live within an Arabized subculture that has enabled them to maintain their distinct ethnic culture.

men of all ages are fond of carrying worry beads, which they unconsciously run through their fingers while engaging in conversation or while walking.

## LANGUAGE

The Arabic language retains a classical literary form which is employed on formal occasions (oratory, speeches, and university lectures) and in most forms of writing, some novels and plays excepted. Everyday speech is the province of the many and varied regional and local dialects. It is these dialects, and in the case of highly assimilated Arab Americans, their remnants, that a visitor among Arab Americans is likely to encounter.

Each national group (Lebanese, Palestinian, Syrian, Egyptian, Yemeni, etc.) has its particular dialect, and within each group regional and local subdialects are found. For the most part, speakers of different dialects can make themselves understood to speakers of other dialects. This is especially true when closely related dialects (Lebanese, Syrian, Palestinian, Jordanian) are involved, and less so among geographically distant dialects. The great exception is the Egyptian dialect which is familiar to most speakers of Arabic because of the widespread influence of the Egyptian movie and recording industries, and the dominant cultural role Egypt has traditionally played in the Middle East.

### GREETINGS AND OTHER POPULAR EXPRESSIONS

Some basic Arabic greetings include: *marhaba* ("mar-ha-ba")—hello, and its response *ahlen* ("ah-len")—welcome (colloquial greetings in Lebanese, Syrian, Palestinian, and Jordanian dialects). Egyptians would say: *Azayyak* ("az-zay-yak")—How are you? and its response *quwayyas* ("qu-whey-yes")—fine. A more formal greeting, readily understood throughout the Arabic-speaking world is: *asalaam 'a laykum* ("a-sa-lamb ah-laykum")—greetings, peace be upon you. The proper response is *wa 'a laykum asalaam* ("wa-ah-laykum a-sa-lamb")—and, peace be upon you, too.

## FAMILY AND COMMUNITY DYNAMICS

In Arab society members of two or three generations dwell in a single household or, in wealthier families, in a family compound. This extended household centers around a married man and some of his adult sons and their families. A grandparent may also reside in the household. A variation on this structure is for several brothers and their respective families to reside in a compound with a grandparent and other elderly relatives.

Among Arab Americans, the large extended family constituting a single household is found only among recent immigrants. As families acculturate and assimilate they tend to form nuclear families with, occasionally, the addition of an elderly grandparent, and an unmarried adult child. In less assimilated communities, adult married children set up a household near their parents and married siblings. This arrangement allows the maintenance of extended family networks while enjoying the benefits of living in a nuclear family.

## DATING AND MARRIAGE

American-style dating is virtually non-existent among all but the most assimilated Arab Americans. Dating conflicts with strict cultural norms about female chastity and its relationship to the honor of the woman and her family. The norm stipulates that a female should be chaste prior to marriage and remain faithful once wed. Similar standards apply to males, but expectations are reduced and the consequences of violations are not as severe. The ethics relating to female chastity cut across social class, religious denomination, and even ethnic lines, as they are found with equal vigor in virtually every Middle Eastern ethnic and national group. Real or alleged violations of the sexual mores by a female damages not only her reputation and diminishes her chances of finding a suitable marriage partner, but also shames her family, especially her male kinsmen.

Among Arab American Muslims a type of dating is allowed after a woman undergoes a ritual engagement. In Islam, the enactment of the marriage contract (*kitb al-kitab*) amounts to a trial period in which the couple become acquainted with one another. This period can last months or even a year or more. If successful, the marriage will be consummated after a public ceremony. During this period, the family of an engaged woman will permit her to go out with the fiance but only with a chaperon. The fiance will pay her visits and the couple may be allowed to talk privately together, but this will be the only time they are allowed to be alone until the wedding. It is perfectly acceptable for one or both parties to terminate the engagement at this point rather than face the prospect of an unhappy marriage.

Arab culture prefers endogamous marriages—marriages between cousins. This preference is, however, not uniform throughout Arab society. It is not strong among some Christian groups like Egypt's Copts, and among certain educated elite. In general, the ideal marriage in Arab society is for a man to marry the daughter of his paternal uncle. The ideal is achieved in only a small percentage of all marriages. Marriages among cousins on either the paternal and maternal side are relatively common. The preference for cousin endogamy is found among immigrant families, but declines among highly assimilated and native-born Arab Americans.

Arranged marriages are common among recent immigrants. Arranged marriages run the gamut from the individual having no voice in the matter and no prior acquaintance with a prospective marriage partner to the family arranging a meeting between their son or daughter and a prospective mate they have selected. In the latter situation, the son or daughter will usually make the final decision. This pattern is prevalent among assimilated immigrant and native-born families, especially if they are educated or have high aspirations for their children. Some working-class immigrant families in Dearborn, Michigan, for example, arrange the marriage of their daughters, who are sometimes legal minors, to men in the home country. This practice seems to be limited to a small minority.

While not all Arab Americans practice cousin endogamy or engage in arranged marriages, most demonstrate a strong preference for religious endogamy in the selection of marriage partners. In this Arab Americans retain a deeply-rooted Middle Eastern bias. Middle Easterners do not approve of inter-religious marriages. However, interdenominational marriages are not uncommon among educated Arab Americans. Arab Americans find it easier to marry a non-Arab of a different religious background than enter into an inter-religious marriage with a fellow Arab American. This is especially true of Arab American men, who unlike women, find it easier to marry an outsider. There is a powerful familial resistance to letting Arab American women marry outside the group. An Arab Muslim woman who was unable to find a mate from within her group, could marry a non-Arab Muslim (e.g., Pakistani, Indian, or Iranian). Arab Christian women facing a similar situation would opt to marry an outsider as long he was Christian.

In selecting a marriage partner, attention is paid to family standing and reputation. Since dating and other forms of mixing are virtually non-existent, there are few opportunities for prospective mates to meet, let alone learn about each other. Thus parents and other interested relatives must rely heavily on community gossip about a prospective suitor or bride. Under such conditions, the family standing of the prospective mate will be of major interest.

The strict segregation of the sexes is inevitably weakening because American society poses many opportunities for unrelated males and females to meet at school or on the job. Consequently, there is a detectable increase in the number of cases of romantic involvement among young Arab Americans in cities where large numbers of Arab Americans reside. But many of these relations are cut short by families because they fail to win their approval.

Divorce, once unheard of in Arab society, is increasingly making a presence among Arab Americans although it is nowhere near the epidemic proportions found among mainstream Americans. Recent immigrants appear less likely than assimilated Arab Americans to resolve marital unhappiness through divorce.

### CHILDREN

Boys and girls are reared differently, though the degree is determined by the level of assimilation. Boys are generally given greater latitude than girls. At the extreme end of the spectrum, girls are expected to marry at a relatively young age and their schooling is not considered as important as that of boys. High school is the upper limit for girls in very traditional immigrant homes, though some post-high school education is expected among educated households. The daughters of professionals are usually encouraged to pursue careers. Middle Eastern families tend to favor boys over girls, and this preference extends to wide segments of the Arab American community. In a few traditional homes, girls are not allowed to ride bicycles or play certain sports, while boys are otherwise indulged. The oldest son usually enjoys a measure of authority over younger siblings, especially his sisters. He is expected to eventually carry the mantle of authority held by the father.

### THE ROLE OF WOMEN

Formal authority lies with the husband/father as it does in Arab society. Women play important roles in socializing children and preserving kinship ties and in maintaining social and religious traditions. The degree of hospitality in the home is held up as a measure of a family's standing among Arabs everywhere, and in this respect Arab Americans are no different. Guests are given a special place at the dinner table where they are feted in a ritual display of hospitality arranged by the women of the household.

Outside the home, the role of Arab American women has fluctuated with the ebb and flow of the immigration tide. As communities become assimilated, women tend to assume leadership roles in community organizations in the mosque or church, or in community-wide endeavors like the organization of parochial schools. With each new influx of immigrants, assimilated women tend to lose ground in those institutions that attract new immigrants (e.g. the mosque). Quickly women who at one time were among the leadership find themselves taking a back seat or even ousted from the institution.

### EDUCATION

Education is highly valued among wide segments of the community. Affluent households prefer private schools. Working class and middle class members tend to send their children to public schools. A recent trend in some Arab American Muslim communities is the growth of Islamic parochial schools. These schools, favored by recent immigrants of all classes, are still in their infancy.

In her analysis of the 1990 census data, El-Badry found that Arab Americans are generally better educated than the average American. The proportion of those who did not attend college is lower than the national average, while the number of those attaining master's degrees or higher is twice that of the general population. Foreign-born Arab professionals overwhelmingly prefer the fields of engineering, medicine, pharmacy, and the sciences in general. Although native-born Arab Americans can be found working in virtually every field, there is a preference for careers in business, medicine, law, and engineering.

There are few formalized traditions of philanthropy in the community. Arab Muslims, like all Muslims, are enjoined to give a certain percentage of their annual income to charity as a *zakat* (tithe). But large contributions to community projects are not part of the community's tradition.

### HOLIDAYS CELEBRATED BY ARAB AMERICANS

The three religious holidays celebrated by Arab American Muslims are also celebrated by Muslims everywhere. They are *Ramadan, Eid al-Fitr,* and *Eid al-Adha. Ramadan* is a month-long dawn-to-dusk fast that occurs during the ninth month of the Islamic calendar. Ramadan is a month of self-discipline as well as spiritual and physical purification. The fast requires complete abstinence from food, drink (including water), tobacco, and sex, from sunrise to sunset during the entire month. *Eid al-Fitr* marks the end of Ramadan. A cross between Thanksgiving and Christmas, the *Eid* is a festive and joyous occasion for Muslims everywhere. *Eid al-Adha,* the Feast of the Sacrifice, commemorates the Prophet Abraham's willingness to sacrifice his son Ishmael in obedience to God. According to the Quran, the Muslim holy book which is considered to be the word of God, the Angel Gabriel intervened at the last moment, substituting a lamb in place of Ishmael. The holiday is held in conjunction with the *Hajj,* the Pilgrimage to Mecca, in which increasing numbers of American Muslims are participating.

Some Arab Muslim families celebrate the birth of Jesus at Christmas. Muslims recognize Jesus as an important prophet, but do not consider him divine. They use the occasion of Christmas to exchange gifts, and some have adopted the custom of decorating a Christmas tree. Arab American Christians observe major Christian holidays. Followers of Eastern rite churches (Egyptian Copts, Syrian Orthodox, Greek Orthodox) celebrate Christmas on the Epiphany, January 6. Easter is observed on the Sunday after Passover, rather than on the date established by the Roman church. In addition, the Eastern Churches, particularly the Coptic church, mark numerous religious occasions, saints' days, and the like, throughout the year.

# RELIGION

Christians still comprise the majority of Arab Americans nationally. The Muslim component is growing fast, however, and in some areas, Muslims constitute an overwhelming majority of Arab Americans. Arab Christians are divided between Eastern rite churches (Orthodox) and the Latin rite (Uniate) churches (Maronites, Melkite, and Chaldean). In the beginning, all Middle Eastern churches followed Eastern rites. Over the centuries, schisms occurred in which the seceders switched allegiance to Rome, forming the Uniate churches. Although the Uniate churches formally submit to the authority of the Roman pope and conform to Latin rites, they continue to maintain their own patriarchs and internal autonomy. Like the Eastern churches, the Uniates also allow priests to marry (though monks and bishops must remain celibate). The Middle East churches retain distinct liturgies, which are recited in ancient Coptic, Aramaic, Syriac, or Chaldean depending upon the particular sect.

Arab Muslims are nominally divided between Sunni and Shiite (*Shia*), the two major branches of Islam. The schism dates to an early conflict in Islam over the succession of the *Caliphate*—leader—of the religious community following the death of the Prophet Muhammad. The Sunni faction won out, eliminating leaders of the opposing faction lead by the Prophet's nephew, Ali, and his sons. Ali's followers came to be known as the *Shia*—the partisans. Over time the Shiites developed some unique theological doctrines and other trappings of a distinct sect, although to Sunnis, the differences appear inconsequential. The majority of Arab American Muslims are Sunni. Arab Shiite Muslims are mostly from Lebanon and Iraq, as well as northern Yemen.

The most significant change Muslims make in adapting Islamic ritual to life in the United States is moving the Friday sabbath prayer to Sunday. For decades, Arab American Muslims have resigned themselves to the fact that, because of job and school obligations, they would not be able to observe Friday communal prayers, or *jumaa.* Recently, however, growing numbers of worshippers attend *jumaa.* Arab American Muslims also forego some of the five daily prayers devout Muslims are obligated to perform because of a lack of facilities and support from mainstream institutions. Technically, Muslims can pray at work or school if the employer or school authorities provide a place. Increasing numbers of devout Muslims insist on meeting their ritual obligations while on the job.

Religious disputes tend to be confined largely to competition between groups *within* the same sect rather than between sects. Thus, for example, in Dearborn, Michigan, which has a large population of Lebanese Shiites, competition is rife among various Shiite mosques and religious centers for followers from the Shiite community. Sunnis in the area generally belong to Sunni congregations, and are not viewed as potential recruits by the Shiites. Similarly, Arab Christian denominations tend to remain insular and eschew open rivalry with other denominations.

# EMPLOYMENT AND ECONOMIC TRADITIONS

In her review of the 1990 census data El-Badry estimated that 60 percent of Arab Americans work as executives, professionals, salespeople, administrative support, or service personnel, compared to 66 percent of the general population. Many Arab Americans are entrepreneurs or self-employed (12 percent versus seven percent of the general population).

Arab Americans are concentrated in sales; one out of five works in the retail sales industry, slightly higher than the U.S. average of 17 percent. Of these, El-Badry observes, 29 percent work in restaurants, from managers to busboys. Another 18 percent work in grocery stores, seven percent in department stores, and six percent in apparel and accessory outlets.

Data on Arab Americans receiving unemployment benefits are nonexistent. However, in the Southend neighborhood of Dearborn, where several thousand mostly recent Yemeni and Lebanese immigrants reside, many felt the brunt of the early 1980s economic recession which hit Detroit's automobile industry particularly hard.

# POLITICS AND GOVERNMENT

Although politically marginalized, Arab Americans have attempted to gain a voice in U.S. foreign policy since the late 1960s. The first national organization dedicated to such a purpose was the Association of Arab American University Graduates, Inc. (AAUG). Founded in the aftermath of the devastating Arab defeat by Israel in the June 1967 war, the AAUG sought to educate Americans about the Arab, and especially the Palestinian, side of the conflict. The group continues to serve as an important forum for debating issues of concern to Arab Americans. The early 1970s saw the establishment of the first Arab American organization devoted exclusively to lobbying on foreign policy issues. Named the National Association of Arab Americans, the organization continues to function at present.

After a decade of increasing stereotypes of Arabs in the United States, a group of Arab Americans led by former Senator James Abourezk (1931- ) of South Dakota founded the American Arab Anti-Discrimination Committee (ADC) in 1980. While not a lobby, ADC sensitizes the news media to issues of stereotyping. The organization has had less success with the entertainment media. More recently, the Arab American Institute (AAI) was established to encourage greater participation of Arab Americans in the electoral process as voters, party delegates, or candidates for office.

Arab American influence on local and state government is limited mainly to Dearborn and a few other localities where their numbers are sufficiently large to be felt by the political establishment. Get-out-the-vote campaigns have been moderately successful in this mostly immigrant, working-class community. Participation in unions is limited to the working class segment of the Arab American community. While the history of this participation remains sketchy and incomplete, individual contributions have not escaped notice. As early as 1912 an Arab striker was killed in the famous Industrial Workers of the World (IWW)-led strike in Lawrence, Massachusetts. In the 1930s, another Arab American labor activist, George Addes, played an important role in the left coalition inside the United Auto Workers leadership. In August 1973 Nagi Daifallah, a Yemeni farm worker active in the United Farm Workers Union, was brutally gunned down with another organizer by a county sheriff. At the time, California was emerging as a center for Yemeni immigrant workers. Yemeni and other Arab automobile workers were also active in union activities in the Detroit area in the 1970s. During the October 1973 Arab Israeli War, an estimated 2,000 Arab workers protested the purchase of Israeli government bonds by the United Auto Workers union. Arab auto workers boycotted work on November 28, 1973, forcing the closing of one of two lines at a Chrysler assembly plant.

# INDIVIDUAL AND GROUP CONTRIBUTIONS

Arab Americans have made important contributions in virtually every field of endeavor, from government to belles lettres.

### ACADEMICS

Among the many Arab American academics, Edward W. Said (1935- ) stands out as a world-class intellectual. Born in Jerusalem, Palestine, and educated at Princeton and Harvard universities, Said has achieved international renown as a scholar in the fields of literary criticism and comparative literature.

## EDUCATION

Christa McAuliffe (1948-1986) was a teacher and crew member on the ill-fated flight of the Challenger space shuttle.

## ENTERTAINMENT

In the entertainment field several Arab Americans have achieved celebrity status, including singers Paul Anka (1941- ) and Paula Abdul (1962- ), actors Danny Thomas (1914-1991), Vic Tayback (1930-1990), and Oscar winner F. Murray Abraham (1939- ). No list of Arab American entertainers would be complete without mention of Casey Kasem (1933- ), the popular radio personality who grew up in Detroit, and Moustapha Akkad, producer of the blockbuster *Halloween* thrillers.

## FASHION

Joseph Abboud is winner of several prestigious design awards.

## GOVERNMENT

A number of Arab Americans have played prominent roles in government at the federal level. The first Arab American to be elected to the U.S. Senate was James Abourezk (1931- ) of South Dakota. Abourezk earned a reputation as a fighter for native American and other minority rights while in Congress. Current Senate majority leader, George Mitchell, Democrat from Maine (1933- ) is the offspring of a Lebanese mother and an Irish father. The most prominent Arab American woman in national government is Donna Shalala (1941- ). Prior to her appointment to a cabinet post as Secretary of Health and Human Services in the Clinton Administration, Shalala headed the University of Wisconsin. In the preceding administration, another Arab American, John Sununu (1941- ), the son of Lebanese Palestinian immigrants, served as George Bush's White House Chief of Staff. Beyond the official circles of government, consumer advocate Ralph Nader ranks as one of the most prominent Arab Americans in the public eye. His activism has had a lasting impact on national policy.

## LITERATURE

In the field of poetry, several Arab Americans have achieved recognition. Sam Hazo (1928- ) is an established American poet, as well as founder of the International Poetry Forum in Pittsburgh. Palestinian American Naomi Shihab Nye (1952- ), and Lebanese American Lawrence Joseph are also well-known poets.

## MEDICINE

The most prominent Arab American in medicine is Michael De Bakey (1908- ), the famous heart surgeon.

## SPORTS

Arab American Doug Flutie won the Heisman Trophy.

# MEDIA

The Arab American community has traditionally supported a number of local electronic (radio, cable and broadcast TV programs) and print media. The Arab American community is increasingly relying on nationally-produced programming

## PRINT

Currently there is only one national, bilingual Arabic-English publication produced in the United States. First published in 1992, *Jusoor* ("Bridges") is a new quarterly, which includes poetry and essays on politics and the arts. For a number of years a bilingual weekly newspaper, known as *Sada al-Watan* was published in Dearborn, Michigan, but recently fell on hard times. Listed below are several national publications of long standing that enjoy wide Arab American readership.

*Action.*
International Arabic newspaper (English and Arabic).

**Contact:** Raji Daher, Editor.
**Address:** P.O. Box 416, New York, New York 10017.
**Telephone:** (212) 972-0460.
**Fax:** (212) 682-1405.

*American-Arab Message.*
Religious and political weekly printed in Arabic and English; founded in 1937.

**Contact:** Imam M. A. Hussein.

**Address:** 17514 Woodward Avenue, Detroit, Michigan 48203.

**Telephone:** (313) 868-2266.

**Fax:** (313) 868-2267.


### Arab Studies Quarterly.

Magazine covering Arab affairs, the Middle East, and U.S. foreign policy.

**Contact:** Jamal Nassar, Editor.

**Address:** P.O. Box 408, Normal, Illinois 61761-0408.

**Telephone:** (309) 438-2493.


### Journal of Arab Affairs.

**Contact:** Tawfic E. Farah, Editor.

**Address:** M E R G Analytica, Box 26385, Fresno, California 93729-6385.

**Fax:** (209) 323-4758.


### Jusoor.

**Contact:** Munir Akash, Editor.

**Address:** P.O. Box 34163, Bethesda, Maryland 20817.

**Telephone:** (301) 869-5853.


### The Link.

**Contact:** John F. Mahoney, Executive Director.

**Address:** Americans for Middle East Understanding, Room 241, 475 Riverside Drive, New York, New York 1025-0241.

**Telephone:** (212) 870-2053.


### Middle East International.

**Contact:** Michael Wall, Editor.

**Address:** 1700 17th Street, N.W., Suite 306, Washington, D.C. 20009.

**Telephone:** (202) 232-8354.


### Middle East Report.

**Contact:** Joe Stork, Editor.

**Address:** Suite 119, 1500 Massachusetts Avenue, N.W., Washington, D.C. 20005.

**Telephone:** (202) 223-3677.


### News Circle/Halqat al-Akhbar.

Monthly periodical that presents issues and news of the Arab American community and the Arab world.

**Contact:** Joseph Haiek, Editor.

**Address:** Box 3684, Glendale, California 91201.

**Telephone:** (818) 545-0333.

**Fax:** (818) 242-5039.


### Washington Report on Middle East Affairs.

**Contact:** Richard H. Curtiss, Executive Editor.

**Address:** P.O. Box 53062, Washington, D.C. 20009.

**Telephone:** (800) 368-5788.


## RADIO

### Arab Network of America (ANA).

A national network that broadcasts Arab language programming in six metropolitan areas (Washington, D.C., Detroit, Chicago, Pittsburgh, Los Angeles, and San Francisco).

**Contact:** Eptisam Malloulti, Radio Program Director.

**Address:** 150 South Gordon Street, Alexandria, Virginia 22304.

**Telephone:** (800) ARAB-NET.


## TELEVISION

### The Arab Network of America.

**Contact:** Laila Shaikhli, TV Program Director.

**Address:** 150 South Gordon Street, Alexandria, Virginia 22304.

**Telephone:** (800) ARAB-NET.


# ORGANIZATIONS AND ASSOCIATIONS

### American Arab Anti-Discrimination Committee (ADC).

Founded in 1980 by former Senator James Abourezk to combat negative and defamatory stereotyping of Arab Americans and their cultural heritage. This is the country's largest grass-roots Arab American organization.

**Contact:** Albert Mokhiber, President.

**Address:** 4201 Connecticut Avenue, N.W., Suite 500, Washington, D.C. 20008.

**Telephone:** (202) 244-2990.


### Arab American Historical Society.

Encourages the preservation of Arab American history, publications, and art. Publishes quarterly *Arab American Historian*.

**Contact:** Joseph Haiek, Chair.

**Address:** P.O. Box 27278, Los Angeles, California 90027.

**Fax:** (818) 242-5039.

**Arab American Institute (AAI).**

Dedicated to involving Arab Americans in electoral politics, mobilizing votes and funds behind Arab American candidates at various levels of government. The Institute also encourages Americans to become involved in the Democratic and Republican parties.

**Contact:** James Zogby, President.
**Address:** 918 16th Street, N.W., Suite 601, Washington, D.C. 20006.
**Telephone:** (202) 429-9210.

**Arab Women's Council (AWC).**

Seeks to inform the public on Arab women and their culture.

**Contact:** Najat Khelil, President.
**Address:** P.O. Box 5653, Washington, D.C. 20016.

**Association of Arab American University Graduates, Inc. (AAUG).**

The oldest national Arab American organization. Founded in the aftermath of the Arab defeat in the June 1967 Arab-Israeli War to inform Americans of the Arab viewpoint. AAUG's membership consists mostly of academics and other professionals. The organization sponsors intellectual forums and conferences, and publishes books as well as the journal *Arab Studies Quarterly*.

**Contact:** Ziad Asali, President.
**Address:** P.O. Box 408, Normal, Illinois 61761-0408.
**Telephone:** (309) 452-6588.

**Attiyeh Foundation (AF).**

Cultural and educational organization conducting projects about the Middle East. Works to promote awareness of Arab culture and history through people-to-people contact. Publishes *Ethnic Heritage in North America*.

**Contact:** Michael Saba, President.
**Address:** P.O. Box 288, Champaign, Illinois 61824-0288.
**Telephone:** (217) 352-1661.

**Najda: Women Concerned About the Middle East.**

Promotes understanding between Americans and Arabs by offering educational programs and audiovisual presentations on Middle Eastern history, art, culture, and current events.

**Contact:** Alice Kawash, President.
**Address:** P.O. Box 7152, Berkeley, California 94707.
**Telephone:** (510) 549-3512.

**National Association of Arab Americans (NAAA).**

The major Arab American political lobby in Washington devoted to improving U.S.-Arab relations. Like ADC, NAAA also combats negative stereotypes of Arabs.

**Contact:** Khalil E. Jahshan, Executive Director.
**Address:** 1212 New York Avenue, N.W., Suite 300, Washington, D.C. 20005.
**Telephone:** (202) 842-1840.

## MUSEUMS AND RESEARCH CENTERS

There are two archives devoted to collecting the papers and related memorabilia of Arab Americans. There are no research centers or museums dedicated to Arab Americans.

**The Faris and Yamna Naff Family Arab American Collection.**

**Contact:** Alixa Naff.
**Address:** Archives Center, National Museum of History, Smithsonian Institution, Washington, D.C.
**Telephone:** (202) 357-3270.

**The Near Eastern American Collection.**

**Contact:** Rudolph J. Vecoli, Director.
**Address:** Immigration History Research Center, University of Minnesota, 826 Berry Street, St. Paul, Minnesota 55114.
**Telephone:** (612) 627-4208.

## SOURCES FOR ADDITIONAL STUDY

Abraham, Nabeel. "Anti-Arab Racism and Violence in the United States," in *The Development of Arab-American Identity*, edited by Ernest McCarus. Ann Arbor: University of Michigan Press, 1994.

———. "The Gulf Crisis and Anti-Arab Racism in America," in *Collateral Damage: The 'New World Order' at Home and Abroad*, edited by Cynthia Peters. Boston: South End Press, 1992.

*Arab Americans: Continuity and Change*, edited by Baha Abu-Laban and Michael W. Suleiman. Normal, Illinois: Association of Arab American University Graduates, Inc., 1989.

*Arabic-Speaking Immigrants in the U.S. and Canada: A Bibliographical Guide with Annotation*, edited by Mohammed Sawaie. Lexington, Kentucky: Mazda Publishers, 1985.

*Arabs in the New World*, edited by Sameer Y. Abraham and Nabeel Abraham. Detroit: Center for Urban Studies, Wayne State University, 1983.

*Crossing the Waters: Arabic-Speaking Immigrants to the United States before 1940*, edited by Eric J. Hooglund. Washington, D.C.: Smithsonian Institution Press, 1987.

El-Badry, Samia. "The Arab Americans," *American Demographics*, January 1994, pp. 22-30.

*The Immigration History Research Center: A Guide to Collections*, compiled by S. Moody and J. Wurl. Westport, Connecticut: Greenwood Press, 1991.

Naff, Alixa. *Becoming American: The Early Arab Immigrant Experience*. Carbondale: Southern Illinois University Press, 1985.

Orfalea, Gregory. *Before the Flames*. Austin: University of Texas Press, 1988.

# ARGENTINEAN AMERICANS

by
Julio Rodriguez

Argentina's ethnically diverse population challenges any attempt to ethnically classify Argentinean Americans.

## OVERVIEW

The word Argentina is derived from the Latin word "argentum," which in English means silver. For this reason Argentina is sometimes called "The Land of Silver." The official name of the country is the Republic of Argentina. Located in the southernmost section of South America, the Republic of Argentina comprises 2,791,810 square kilometers, just over 15 percent of the continent's surface. Its area, including the South Atlantic islands and the Antarctic sector, covers 2.35 million square miles, which is about one-third the size of the United States. The 1991 Argentinean census counted more than 32 million people residing in the country. This amounts to 12 percent of the total South American population, making it the third most populous country on the continent after Brazil and Colombia. Approximately 90 percent of the Argentineans are born Roman Catholics. About two percent of the population is Protestant and, according to recent Argentinean statistics, about 400,000 Jews live in Buenos Aires.

An ethnically diverse country, about 90 percent of the Argentinean population consists of immigrants from Italy and Spain and their descendants. In the late nineteenth and twentieth centuries, other ethnic groups, including Germans, Poles, Welsh, Irish, Lebanese, Hungarians,

Czechs, Danish, French, Jews, Japanese, Koreans, and Swiss also chose Argentina for settlement. Almost half of the immigrants who arrived during that period eventually returned to their countries of origin. For many of them, Argentina was only a transitory haven. Motivated by the desire to escape the violence and poverty that plagued Europe during World War I, many immigrants set sail with the idea of improving their lot and eventually returning to Europe. In many cases, however, these immigrants remained in Argentina, either because they decided they had worked too hard to sell what had taken them so many years to obtain, or because their families and children had made Argentina their home. As a result, an atmosphere of nostalgia stemming from the impossibility of the immigrants' return to their homeland is deeply rooted in Argentinean culture, especially in its music. About 760,000 immigrants from Uruguay, Chile, Bolivia, Peru, and Paraguay are also living in Argentina today.

## GEOGRAPHICAL SETTING

Argentina is often considered a land with four geographical sections. The northwestern border lies in the Andes Mountains. South of the mountains, the country begins to flatten toward the tip of the continent, becoming rocky grassland. A high plateau region lies east of the Andes and slopes into a large, grassy area. This grassy area is drained by the Río Paraguay and Río Paraná, which themselves drain into the baylike Río de la Plata (River of Silver), the widest river on earth. The climate is mild in this region, the pampas, where two thirds of the people live.

## EARLY HISTORY

About 300,000 American Indians were scattered throughout the large area that is now Argentina when the Spaniards arrived in the sixteenth century. These Indians fell into at least ten distinct groups with various lifestyles. The Guaraní, for example, farmed the fertile river valleys. More typical in the south were the Onas who lived by hunting animals such as the ostrich and seal and by gathering mollusks. Farther north, the Araucanians roamed the grasslands in bands of one to two hundred families, living off the wild animals that abounded in the area. Other tribes populating the area included the Incas in the northwest, the Charrúas in the east, and the Quechuas, Tehuelches, and Huarpes in the central and west-

ern regions. The Pampas inhabited the plains of the same name.

## SPANISH RULE

The arrival of explorer Juan Díaz de Solís in 1516 marked the beginning of 300 years of rule by Spain. More than 50 years would pass before Buenos Aires was founded in 1580, and it was to remain little more than a village for the next two centuries. There were a sufficient number of Spanish women to generate pure Spanish families, and thus began the Creole (Spanish born in the New World) elite. Unions between Spanish men and Indian women produced mestizo offspring, who grew into the artisans and laborers of colonial towns or the herdspeople and wagoners of the early countryside. Black slaves entered the country in the seventeenth and eighteenth centuries, becoming servants and artisans, caring for livestock, and planting or harvesting.

In 1776 political leadership of the large area claimed by the Spanish crown was centered at Buenos Aires. British troops tried to seize Buenos Aires in 1806, but residents fought them off and a decade later, in 1816, declared independence from Spain at the urging of the national hero José de San Martín. Buenos Aires was made the country's capital in 1862.

## MODERN ERA

In 1930 the national government experienced a military takeover, an event that would repeat itself time and again in the coming years. In 1943 Argentinean soldiers seized control while Colonel Juan Domingo Perón Sosa began to muster support from the lower classes. In 1946 Perón was elected president and proceeded to become the workers' champion, backing labor unions, social security, shorter hours, higher medical benefits, and so on. His charismatic second wife, Eva (Evita) Duarte, inspired the masses as well, but in the long run Perón's policies raised expectations that remained unfulfilled. Exiled in 1955, he returned to lead the country again in 1973, then died and was succeeded by his third wife, vice president María Estela Martínez de Perón, who was deposed in 1976. There began a period of fierce repression that is sometimes labeled the "dirty war." Lasting until 1983, this period was characterized by imprisonment, torture, and murder of opponents to the military. An alleged 15,000 to 30,000 Argentineans, many of them

Jews, "disappeared" during this period, giving rise to the charge of antisemitism. Meanwhile the Argentinean military was defeated by Britain in a 1982 war over ownership of the Islas Malvinas (Falkland Islands).

The Argentineans demonstrated against their government in 1982 and 1983, managing to elect Raúl Alfonsín president in 1983. Alfonsín's record as a champion of human rights and his reputation as a lawyer boded well for the people. Still, they are threatened by a history of military takeovers and the rising cost of living; the rise in prices was over a thousand percent in 1985.

## SIGNIFICANT IMMIGRATION WAVES

Prior to the 1970s, Argentinean immigrants were classified by the U.S. government within the broad category of "Other Hispanics," and immigration statistics from before that time do not exist. Nonetheless, Argentinean immigrants to the United States are a relatively new group. In 1970 there were 44,803 Argentinean immigrants in the United States. The 1990 U.S. Census, which counted 92,563 Argentineans, indicates that nearly half of all Argentinean immigrants arrived in the United States in the last two decades alone.

Early Argentinean immigrants came to the United States, primarily during the 1960s, for greater economic opportunities. The majority of these immigrants were well-educated professionals, including a substantial number of medical doctors and scientists. Later immigrants—those who began to immigrate to the United States during the mid- to late-1970s—fled their homeland to escape political persecution during the "dirty war." This group was more diverse and less educated than their predecessors, although their educational attainment tended to be higher than that of Argentina's overall population.

In the 1970s, 20 percent of the Argentineans in the United States resided in the New York metropolitan area. In the 1980s, this percentage increased to just over 23 percent. This is partially due to the fact that New York City already had a large Argentinean population as well as many Italian immigrants from other countries. (It is therefore expected that New York would attract Italian-Argentineans.) New York City also has a number of organizations created to assist its large Argentinean population, including the Argentine-American Chamber of Commerce, which promotes business ventures between Argentina and the United States, and the Argentine-North

American Association for the Advancement of Science, Technology and Culture. Overall, Argentinean Americans seem to prefer metropolitan areas, such as New York City, where 17,363 Argentinean Americans were counted in the 1990 U.S. Census, and Los Angeles, home for 15,115 Argentinean immigrants. The least preferred destinations are North Dakota and Montana, where only 15 Argentineans were counted in each state.

# ACCULTURATION AND ASSIMILATION

Statistics show that Argentinean American immigrants, as a group, have fewer children than Argentineans; young Argentinean Americans make up between 17 and 19 percent of the Argentinean American population. There are also a higher proportion of married Argentinean American individuals at all ages, particularly between 20 and 29. Likewise, the number of separated and divorced individuals is significantly higher in the United States.

Argentina's ethnically diverse population challenges any attempt to ethnically classify Argentinean Americans. Some common terms applied to the peoples of South America are "Hispanic" and "Latino." These terms present problems when they are used to define Argentinean Americans as well as many other peoples from the Americas. The word "Hispanic" derives from the Latin word "Hispania," a proper name in Latin that describes the area also known as the Iberian Peninsula (Spain and Portugal). To apply this term to Argentinean Americans, as does the questionnaire for the 1990 U.S. Census, excludes almost half of their population, most of whom are Italian born or of Italian descent. The term "Latino" also presents some major difficulties in describing the cultural and ethnic diversity of South America, which extends far beyond its Latin European heritage. The term Latin America bluntly excludes the native peoples of Central and South America, as well as its numerous immigrant groups who have little in common with the Latin European countries.

## CUISINE

Argentinean cuisine is very rich and includes a variety of traditional recipes that have been

Geraldo Hernandez waves from the "Centro Argentino of New Jersey" float as it coasts down New York City's Fifth Avenue in the 1988 Hispanic American Parade.

passed on from generation to generation. Traditional Argentinean cuisine is based on dishes made with vegetables and meat, such as the *mazamorra* (made with corn), *locro* (a meat and vegetable soup), and *empanadas* (meat turnovers).

Argentina is perhaps best known for its beef. As John Hamill wrote: "There is this secret place, south of the border, where polite society hasn't totally surrendered to the body sculptors and cholesterol cops. Down there, people in restaurants, perfectly respectable people, still openly order huge, rare steaks" ("Where the 'Bife' Is," *Travel Holiday* 174 [March 1991]: 36-38). The excellence of Argentinean beef is known worldwide. Traditional Argentinean specialties are *asado* (grilled meat and ribs), *parrillada,* (Argentinean mixed barbecue), and *empanadas*.

Immigrant groups have significantly contributed to the Argentinean cuisine. Along with the traditional dishes, Italian pasta is often the main course on the Sunday table. There is a popu-

lar belief that on the 29th of each month eating *ñoquis* (Italian pasta) brings good fortune. A ritual has evolved out of this belief and consists in placing money, usually a flattened bill that is tied up into a bow, under the plate. The Spanish settlers also contributed to the wealth of the Argentinean cuisine. Typically Spanish dishes are derived from pork, such as *chorizo* (sausage), bacon, and *jamón serrano* (pork ham cooked in salt).

Another Argentinean specialty is the *dulce de leche,* a type of thick caramel made with highly condensed milk. One of the most popular sweet treats in Argentina, it is usually eaten on toast spread over butter. Argentinean cuisine has evolved a variety of desserts and pastries based on this product.

### MATE

A traditional Argentinean beverage is *mate,* a type of tea grown in the north of the country. The tea is prepared in a small potlike container, called a *mate*, which is usually made from a carved, dried gourd. Curing techniques, intended to protect the gourd from cracking when water is poured into it, vary according to the region of the country and determine the taste of the beverage. Probably the two most widely known curing techniques use milk or ashes. After being cured, *mate* is then prepared in the gourd by adding the tea, called *yerba mate*, and water. The tea is sipped directly from the gourd with a straw.

*Mate* is a highly traditional beverage, and with the passing of time it has developed a unique symbology. For example, a host that provides cold and bitter *mate* expresses rejection or hard feelings toward the guest. Contrarily, *mate* served sweet and hot expresses friendship, welcome, or affection. *Mate* also differs according to region. In central Argentina, for example, *mate* is usually prepared with boiling water and sugar. In the northeast, a particular form of *mate*, known as the *tereré*, consists of *mate* prepared with cold water and usually without any sugar.

### LA SOBREMESA

A traditional Argentinean custom following meals is the *sobremesa*. This word lacks a precise equivalent in English, but it describes the time spent sitting at the table after a meal in conversation, providing family members a chance to exchange ideas and discuss various issues. Argentinean meals usually consist of a light breakfast, and a hearty lunch and dinner. Dinner is usually served after 9:00 p.m. In some regions of the country people still take a *siesta* after lunch. Even in rather big cities, such as Mendoza, this custom is still observed. Business hours have been adapted to this custom. Most activities cease soon after midday and restart at about 4:00 p.m. Even the street traffic significantly wanes during these hours.

### TRADITIONAL CLOTHING

The most popular Argentinean character, often presented as a symbol of Argentinean tradition, is the *gaucho*. Although the *gaucho* is almost extinct, his attire is sometimes worn for parades and national celebrations such as the Day of Tradition. The attire of the *gaucho* has evolved with time. Originally, it consisted of a simple garment known as the *chiripá*, a diaperlike cloth pulled over lacy leggings, which was usually worn with a *poncho*. The *gaucho's* traditional pants became baggy

trousers that were fastened with a leather belt adorned with coins and silver and an elaborate buckle. A neckerchief and a short-brimmed straw hat were also occasionally worn. A traditional Argentinean woman, or *china*, would typically wear a long loose dress, fastened at the waist and sleeves. Sometimes the material of the dress would have colorful patterns, typically flowery ones, which would match the flowers in her hair.

### HOLIDAYS CELEBRATED BY ARGENTINEAN AMERICANS

One of the more popular Argentinean holidays is the Day of Tradition, celebrated on November 10. This festivity includes parades in the towns and cities of the country and folkloric shows known as *peñas*. In these *peñas* folkloric music is played by regional groups and traditional food, such as *asado* or *impends*, is sold at small stands. In some *peñas* it is possible to attend a rodeo, where skillful horse riders, usually dressed as *gauchos*, display their equestrian abilities.

Due to the influence of immigrant groups, Christmas in Argentina is usually celebrated much like it is in Spain or Italy. A Christmas tree, usually artificial and covered by cotton snow, is set up in every home. Often, a manger is arranged under the tree to evoke the time when Jesus Christ was born. The nativity is also dramatized by religious groups at churches, theaters, or public squares during the week preceding Christmas. This practice is called *Pesebre Viviente* ("Living Manger"). Like Americans, Argentineans celebrate the coming of Santa Claus (called "Papá Noel"), who is said to travel in a deer-driven sleigh with Christmas presents for the children. The two most important family reunions take place during Christmas and New Year's. Christmas is traditionally considered a religious celebration, whereas New Year's is a national celebration. Among young people it is customary to have dinner with their families, participate in the toast, which is often made at midnight, and afterward meet friends and dance until dawn. The Christmas dinner typically consists of a very rich meal, high in calories. The immigrant tradition has totally neglected the seasonal change and kept the traditional Christmas diet of the cold European winter, commonly serving *turron* and *panetone* (Italian).

Another important religious celebration is Epiphany, which in Argentina is known as the Day of the Three Wise Men. It is celebrated on the sixth of January. Children are instructed by their parents to leave their shoes at the foot of the bed or under the Christmas tree. By their shoes, they are also supposed to leave a glass of water for the wise men, and some grass for the camels they ride. The children usually write a letter with their requests for presents and leave it with the shoes, water, and grass. The night of the fifth of January children typically go to bed very early in the evening, expecting to get up early to receive their presents. On the following morning, the sidewalks and public squares are filled with children playing with their new toys.

# LANGUAGE

The official language of Argentina is Castilian Spanish. Nevertheless, other languages and dialects are still in use in some communities of the country. Among the native languages Guaraní is probably the most widespread; it is spoken mainly in the north and northeast of Argentina. Among the Spanish and Italian communities, some people speak their native tongues. In Buenos Aires, newspapers are published in English, Yiddish, German, and Italian. The variety of Spanish spoken in Argentina is referred to as "Spanish from the Río de la Plata." This variety extends throughout Argentina and Uruguay and has some particular characteristics regarding phonology, morphology, and vocabulary.

Differences in phonology (pronunciation) can usually be associated with the geographic location of the speaker. For example, in the metropolitan area of Buenos Aires the letters "y" and "ll" in Spanish are pronounced similarly to the English "j" in "John." Elsewhere in the Americas or Spain those letters tend to be pronounced as the English "y" in "yawn."

Probably the most significant morphological characteristic of Argentinean Spanish is the verb form for the second person singular pronoun, which in standard Spanish is *tú* ("you" singular, in informal conversational style), and in Argentinean Spanish is *vos*. The verb form accompanying this personal pronoun is different from its equivalent in standard Spanish. For example: *tú juegas* (you play) in standard Spanish, is *vos jugás* in Argentinean Spanish. In the present tense, this form can be derived from the conjugated verb of the second person plural used in Spain: *vosotros* (you all). The use of *vos* in Argentinean Spanish is known as *voseo*, and it is still the source of some controversy. Some Argentineans believe this form to be incorrect and sometimes disrespectful. It has even been considered a national disgrace. The argument is that the use of the *voseo* form unnecessarily separates the Argentineans and Uruguayans who use it from other Spanish-speaking peoples.

As in other South and Central American countries, local Spanish language has been enriched by numerous terms borrowed from native languages. For example, the words *vicuña* (vicuna) and *choclo* (corn, or *maíz* in standard Spanish) have been borrowed from the Quechua language. Immigrants have also made important linguistic contributions to the variety of Spanish spoken in Argentina, especially the Italians. In "Lunfardo" (Argentinean slang) there are countless words derived from Italian. Their usage is widespread in informal, everyday language. For example, the verb *laburar* (to work) in Lunfardo comes from the Italian word *laborare*. The standard Spanish verb is *trabajar*. The common Argentinean greeting *Chau*, which in Argentina is used to say "bye-bye," comes from word *ciao*, which in Italian means "hello."

In some cases, the linguistic influence of Castilian Spanish upon a community of speakers of a different language has given rise to a new language variety. For example in Belgrano (Buenos Aires) there is an important community of German immigrants. The variety of German spoken there is known as "Belgrano-Deutsch," which uses terms such as the verb *lechen* (to milk; from *melken* in standard German), derived from the Spanish word *leche* (milk).

# FAMILY AND COMMUNITY DYNAMICS

Because of their strong Spanish and Italian heritage, the Argentinean family is characterized by the close relationships traditionally maintained by these peoples. The family often extends to cousins, aunts, uncles, in-laws, and sometimes even the families of the in-laws. Grandparents play an important role within the family. In Argentina, family reunions are usually carried out on a weekly basis. Sundays and observed national holidays are often spent with relatives and friends, and typically an "asado" (Argentinean barbecue) or Italian pasta become the favorite choice for lunch. The family is often the focus of social life in Argentina, especially after marriage. Children usually spend a longer time living with their parents than they do in the United States. Sometimes they stay with them until they get married. Although this situation is at times imposed by economic necessity, there are also some gender biases in this respect. Women who live alone, for example, run the risk of being negatively labeled. In the cities this situation is better tolerated but it is still seen as odd. Argentinean families are usually not as geographically widespread as their American counterparts.

## WEDDING CEREMONIES

The wedding ceremony commonly consists of three main events. The first is the bride and bridegroom's shower party, which varies according to the social class and region of the country. In the middle class it usually consists of parties separately organized for the bride and bridegroom by their friends. In most cases the parties are organized so as to surprise them with tricks and *prendas*. The second event is the formal wedding, which is held before a state officer, usually a judge of the peace at the local civil registry. This establishes the matrimonial contract and the legal rights of the couple. Both the bridegroom and bride usually wear formal clothes for this event, which usually takes place in the morning during a business day. Two witnesses—commonly friends of the couple—are required to sign the entry in the book of civil matrimony. After the ceremony, the people present throw rice on the couple as they leave the building. Rice stands as a symbol for wishes of prosperity and fertility.

The third celebration consists of the church wedding ceremony, attended by the families and friends of bride and bridegroom. It is customary for the bridegroom not to see the bride before this ceremony. The belief is that if he does, it could bring bad luck to the couple. Therefore, the bride and bridegroom usually get dressed at their homes and meet in the church. After the ceremony, the newlywed couple greets friends and family at the entrance of the church and again rice is thrown on the couple, symbolizing economic prosperity and a fruitful marriage. Afterwards there is usually a party that is often very structured. The wedding pictures of almost any couple include these ritualized customs: cutting the cake, dancing the waltz, and changing the *liga*. The bride puts quite a few ligas on, which during the party are to be taken off by the bridegroom. He then puts them on the single girls present at the party.

## BAPTISMS

Children have a very important role in Argentinean culture. Traditionally they are protected in the family from the world of adults. There are many celebrations that are actually intended for children, such as Epiphany, Christmas, the Day of the Children, and baptism. In a Catholic family baptism is the first ceremony in which children participate. During this ceremony the newborn is assigned its godparents, who are usually relatives or friends of the family. Traditionally, the Argentinean President becomes the godfather of the seventh son, which is a rare occurrence. The commitment that the godparents make includes providing advice and spiritual guidance to the godchild. Sometimes they are also expected to look after the children in case of the parents' unexpected death. To be a godparent today is more a symbol of the confirmation of the close bond or friendship between the parents and the selected godparents. It is also very common to have a set of godparents for the wedding ceremony in Catholic families. Usually the godparents are another couple whose function is to give advice to the newlyweds on matrimonial matters.

## LOS QUINCE

Another traditional party celebration, representing the turning point between adolescence and womanhood, is informally known as *Los Quince*. Held on a girl's fifteenth birthday, the celebration is usually organized by the relatives and friends of the teenage girl. She wears a dress similar to the white dress worn by brides, although the color can be other than white, like pink or light blue. Customarily, the father dances a waltz with his daughter after dinner, followed by the girl's godfather and her friends, while the rest of the guests stand in a circle. In some cases the whole family attends mass in church before the party.

## THE ROLE OF WOMEN

The role of women in Argentinean society has changed in the last few decades. While daily tasks such as cooking, laundry, care of the children, and shopping are still the domain of women, the number of women who pursue careers in addition to fulfilling their roles as mothers and wives is increasing. Little by little, women are entering typically male-dominated fields such as politics, economics, engineering, and law. Argentina was, in fact, the first American country to have a woman president.

Luis and Estela Genesoni serve lunches from their food cart, named after their children, in Manhattan, New York.

The situation of the Argentineans in the United States seems to be somewhat different. Married women seem to be more restricted in American society. In a recent study about migrant Argentinean women called "Migrant Careers and Well Being of Women," one of the interviewed subjects affirmed: "I only go out with my husband," "I live locked up," "I'm afraid to go out." In this report it is further stated that "for those married women who wanted to return to Argentina there was family conflict, since most husbands wished to remain permanently in the United States." Yet, "the unmarried seemed better adjusted and reported more freedom and less family pressure than in Argentina. 'A woman in the United States can live alone, work, travel, and nobody thinks anything bad of her. In Argentina they would think I am crazy.' 'As a single woman, I would have a more restricted life in Argentina—there is more machismo.'"

In Argentina it is very usual for couples to ask their parents or a sibling to babysit for their children. These conveniences are often unavailable to immigrant women who may find it necessary to look after the children and postpone their own work or professional career. For example, in the report quoted above, an Argentinean immigrant woman stated: "I miss the family. I have to do everything at home by myself. If I lived in Argentina my mother, sister or friend would take care of the children sometimes. Here even when I don't feel well I have to continue working."

## EDUCATION

Education is still praised by Argentineans as one of the most important assets an individual can have. In Argentina, private and public institutions offer a wide range of possibilities for elementary, high school, and university education. The choice between a public or private institution often depends on the economic capabilities of the family. In the last few years there has been a significant surge in the number of bilingual schools. Perhaps the most common combination is Spanish and English, but there are also very renowned elementary and high schools that offer bilingual instruction in Spanish and Italian, or Spanish and German. Religious schools are also widespread, and during the last two decades they have started to open to coed education.

In Argentina education is mandatory from six to 14 years of age. Elementary school ranges from the first to the seventh year, while high school is optional and can comprise between five to seven years of study in some vocational schools. Universities are either private or government-financed. Government-financed universities are free and often the only admission requirement is completion of a high school degree, although some universities may request an entrance examination. Careers that enjoy a certain social prestige, like medicine, law, engineering, and economics, are prevalent career choices among young students. Because of such educational attainment, most Argentinean immigrants have assimilated relatively well in the United States, particularly in careers associated with science and academia.

# RELIGION

The rituals and ceremonies of the Catholic church are widespread throughout Argentina. The Declaration of Rights, which prefaces the Argentinean Constitution, states that the Roman Catholic religion shall be protected by the state since the majority of Argentineans profess this faith. Furthermore, the Constitution provides that the president of the country be a Roman Catholic. During the last decades the Argentinean Catholic church has undergone a significant crisis, reflected not only in absenteeism in the churches but also in the small number of seminary students and novices. It is therefore common for many Argentineans to affirm their religious beliefs and simultaneously confess their lack of involvement within the church. Among Argentinean immigrants in the United States there seems to be a corresponding trend.

# EMPLOYMENT AND ECONOMIC TRADITIONS

Many Argentineans in the United States are characterized by their high level of education: technicians, skilled workers, and professionals in general make up the majority of Argentinean immigrants in the United States. However, statistics show about 50 percent of the Argentineans who entered the United States from 1965 to 1970 were manual workers. Possibly this increase is due to the fact that periods of economic and political stability in Argentina had limited prospects not only for professionals but also for people involved in other occupations. Immigration then became more massive and included people from different social classes. The statistics showed that by 1970, the percentage of Argentineans with ten or more years of education was four times higher in the United States than in Argentina. According to the 1990 U.S. Census, about 21 percent of the Argentinean immigrants residing in the metropolitan areas of Los Angeles and New York had a bachelor's degree or higher education.

The percentage of Argentineans between 25 and 59 years old in the workplace has been increasing. In 1980, 58 percent of Argentinean women immigrants between 25 and 59 years old could be found in the workplace, compared with 52 percent of the general female U.S. population and 24 percent in other South and Central American countries. The United States seems to offer women increased opportunities for employment. Male Argentinean Americans tend to participate in activities such as manufacturing industries, commerce, transportation, communication, and construction. They have a lower participation in activities such as agriculture, hunting, fishing, and silviculture.

# INDIVIDUAL AND GROUP CONTRIBUTIONS

### ACADEMIA

Leopoldo Maximo Falicov is a physicist at the University of California, Berkely and the author of *Group Theory and Its Physical Applications* (1966). Mathematician Luis Angel Caffarelli teaches at the Institute for Advanced Study in Princeton, New Jersey. Harvard graduate Enrique Anderson-Imbert teaches Hispanic literature and has written several works on such Argentinean figures as Rubén Darío and Domingo Faustino Sarmiento. Dermatologist Irma Gigli is a director at the University of California, San Diego, who has also taught at Harvard Medical School and New York University Medical Center.

### THE ARTS

Composer Lalo Schiffrin wrote the music for the television series *Mission Impossible*. Opera director Tito Capobianco founded the San Diego Opera Center and the Pittsburgh Opera Center. Geny Dignac is a sculptor whose award-winning works have appeared in exhibits throughout the world.

### SPORTS

Verónica Ribot-Canales became a U.S. citizen in September 1991. In April 1992 she switched her sports nationality from Argentina to the United States. She has competed in three Olympics, winning 12 South American titles for Argentina. Ribot-Canales will represent the United States in 1996.

## MEDIA

Television in Spanish is available from Mexican broadcasts, which very rarely include any material for Argentineans. One of the most popular Argentinean Television channels is available through the Television Station SUR, in Miami, Florida.

## ORGANIZATIONS AND ASSOCIATIONS

**Argentine-American Chamber of Commerce.**
Located in New York City, this organization promotes business ventures between Argentina and the United States.

**Argentine Association of Los Angeles.**
Provides information on Argentina and supports Argentinean American activities. Located in Los Angeles.

**Argentine-North American Association for the Advancement of Science, Technology and Culture.**
Supports professional groups and cultural events. Located in New York City.

**Club Tango.**
Gathers to learn and dance Argentinean tangos.

**Contact:** Art Hemenway, Director.
**Address:** 2019 Fairview Avenue East, No. 10, Seattle, Washington 98102.
**Telephone:** (206) 323-2143.

**Embassy of Argentina.**
Provides information on Argentina.

**Address:** 1600 New Hampshire Avenue, N.W., Washington, D.C. 20009.

## MUSEUMS AND RESEARCH CENTERS

**Argentinean Information Service Center (AISC).**
This center provides information about conditions in Argentina to governmental and non-governmental institutions. AISC has also compiled a list of individuals who were abducted, imprisoned, or killed in Argentina during the late 1970s. Supports organizations and activities that internationally promote respect for human rights and democracy. Holds bimonthly meetings.

**Contact:** Víctor Penchaszadeh, M.D., Executive Secretary.
**Address:** 32 West 82nd Street, Suite 7-B, New York, New York 10024.
**Telephone:** (212) 496-1478.

**San Martín Society of Washington, D.C.**
This society promotes study and historic research on Argentinean General José de San Martín's (1778-1850) life and work. Sponsors periodic commemorative ceremonies, including San Martín's birthday (February 25), Argentinean Independence Day (July 9, 1816), and the anniversary of San Martín's death (August 17). Holds annual meetings and publishes periodicals.

**Contact:** Christian García-Godoy, President.
**Address:** P.O. Box 33, McLean, Virginia 22101.
**Telephone:** (703) 883-0950.
**Fax:** (703) 883-0950.

## SOURCES FOR ADDITIONAL STUDY

Cattan, Peter. "The Diversity of Hispanics in the U.S. Work Force." *Monthly Labor Review*, August 1993, p. 3.

Centro Editor de América Latina. *Dinámica migratoria argentina (1955-1984): democratización y retorno de expatriados*, second edition, edited by Alfredo E. Lattes and Enrique Orteiza, 1987.

Freidenberg, Judith, et al. "Migrant Careers and Well Being of Women." *International Migration Review*. 22, No. 2, p. 208.

# ARMENIAN AMERICANS

by
**Harold
Takooshian**

The U.S. Armenian
community is best
viewed as the
product of two sets
of intense, opposing
forces—centripetal
pressures binding
Armenians closer
together, and
centrifugal pressures
pushing them apart.

## OVERVIEW

The estimated 700,000 Americans of Armenian ancestry are descended from an ancient nation located at the borders of modern Russia, Turkey, and Iran. Through much of the past 4,000 years, Armenians have been a subjugated people with no independent state until September 23, 1991, when the Soviet Union dissolved and the 3,400,000 people in that area voted to form a new Republic of Armenia.

### HISTORY

The Armenian homeland lies at the crossroads of Asia Minor, which links Europe with the Middle and Far East. The plateau's original settlers, beginning about 2800 B.C., were the various Aryan tribes of Armens and Hayasas who later melded to form the Urartu civilization and kingdom (860-580 B.C.). These settlers developed advanced skills in farming and metal work. The Armenian civilization managed to survive despite a steady succession of wars and occupations by much larger groups, including the Hittites, Assyrians, Parthians, Medes, Macedonians, Romans, Persians, Byzantines, Tartars, Mongols, Turks, Soviet Russians, and now Azerbaijanis, in the 25 centuries that followed. The capital city of Armenia today, Yerevan (population 1.3 million), celebrated its 2,775th anniversary in 1993.

The long history of the Armenian nation has been punctuated by triumphs over adversity. In 301 A.D., the small kingdom of Armenia became the first to adopt Christianity as its national religion, some 20 years before Constantine declared it the state religion of the Roman empire. In 451, when Persia ordered a return to paganism, Armenia's small army defiantly stood firm to defend its faith; at the Battle of Avarair, Persia's victory over these determined martyrs proved so costly that it finally allowed Armenians to maintain their religious freedom. By the time European Crusaders in the twelfth century entered the Near East to "liberate" the Holy Land from the Moslems, they found prosperous Armenian communities thriving among the Moslems, while maintaining the Holy Sepulchre in Jerusalem and other Christian sites. Under 400 years of Ottoman Turkish rule (1512-1908), the Christian Armenian minority—an industrious, educated elite within the Sultan's empire—had risen to a position of trust and influence. One such subject of the Sultan, Calouste Gulbenkian, later became the world's first billionaire through negotiations with seven Western oil companies that sought Arabian oil in the 1920s.

During World War I (1915-1920), with the collapse of the Ottoman empire and the rise of Pan-Turkish nationalism, the Turkish government attempted to eradicate the Armenian nation in

"I should like to see any power of the world destroy this race, this small tribe of unimportant people, whose history is ended, whose wars have been fought and lost, whose structures have crumbled, whose literature is unread, whose prayers are no longer answered.... For when two of them meet anywhere in the world, see if they will not create a new Armenia!"

William Saroyan, 1935.

what is now termed "the first genocide of the twentieth century." One million Turkish Armenians were slaughtered, while the other million survivors were cast from their Anatolian homeland into a global diaspora that remains to this day.

### THE ARMENIAN REPUBLIC

On May 28, 1918, facing death, some Armenians declared an independent Armenian state in the northeast corner of Turkey. Facing the stronger Turkish army, the short-lived Republic quickly accepted Russian protection in 1920. In 1936 it became the Armenian Soviet Socialist Republic (ASSR), the smallest of the Union's 15 republics, occupying only the northeastern ten percent of the territory of historic Armenia. (The remaining 90 percent in Eastern Turkey lies empty of Armenians today.) Though Stalin successfully encouraged some 200,000 diaspora Armenians to "return" to Soviet Armenia after World War II, the Stalin years were marked by political and economic oppression. On September 23, 1991, with the Soviet Union dissolving, citizens of Armenia overwhelmingly voted to form another independent republic. As of 1995, Armenia is one of only two of the 15 former Soviet states not headed by a former communist, now maintaining a free press and vigorous new multi-party system that it has not had before. It is still recovering from a severe 1988 earthquake that destroyed several cities and killed some 50,000 people. Also since 1988, Armenia has been embroiled in a painful armed conflict with larger, Moslem Azerbaijan, resulting in a blockade of Armenia, and dire shortages of food, fuel, and supplies. Meanwhile, the four million Armenians in the diaspora energetically extend their support for Armenia's survival.

Among the 15 Soviet republics, Armenia was the smallest; its 11,306 square miles would rank it 42nd among the 50 U.S. states (it is about the size of Maryland). It was also the most educated (in per capita students), and the most ethnically homogeneous, with 93 percent Armenians, and 7 percent Russians, Kurds, Assyrians, Greeks, or Azeris. The capital city of Yerevan (population 1,300,000) was nicknamed the Silicon Valley of the USSR because of its leadership in computer and telecommunications technology. The huge statue of Mother Armenia, sword in hand, facing nearby Turkey from downtown Yerevan, symbolizes how citizens in the Armenian republic historically see themselves as stalwart guardians of the homeland, in the absence of the far-away *spiurk* (diaspora Armenians).

Although the independent Republic of Armenia has existed since 1991, it is misleading to term it a homeland like, for example, Sweden is for Swedish Americans, for a few reasons. First, for almost all of the past 500 years, Armenians have had no independent state. Second, communism's avowed policy of quashing nationalists within its 15 republics rendered the status of the previous Soviet republic and its citizens as questionable among most diaspora Armenians. Third, this Republic occupies only the northeastern ten percent of the territory of historic Armenia, including only a few of the dozen largest Armenian cities of pre-1915 Turkey—cities now empty of Armenians in Eastern Turkey. Only a small fraction of the ancestors of today's Armenian Americans had any contact with the Russified northern cities of Yerevan, Van, or Erzerum. A recent survey finds that 80 percent of U.S. Armenian youth express an interest to visit the Republic, yet 94 percent continue to feel it important to regain the occupied part of the homeland from Turkey. Modern Turkey does not allow Armenians into parts of Eastern Turkey, and less than one percent of American Armenians have "repatriated" to the Armenia Republic.

## ARMENIAN IMMIGRATION TO AMERICA

Like ancient Phoenicians and Greeks, Armenians' affinity for global exploration stretches back to the eighth century B.C. By 1660, there were 60 Armenian trading firms in the city of Amsterdam, Holland, alone, and Armenian colonies in every corner of the known earth, from Addis Ababa to Calcutta, Lisbon to Singapore. At least one old manuscript raises the possibility of an Armenian who sailed with Columbus. More documented is the arrival of "Martin the Armenian," who was brought as a farmer to the Virginia Bay colony by Governor George Yeardley in 1618—two years before the Pilgrims arrived at Plymouth Rock. Still, up to 1870, there were fewer than 70 Armenians in the United States, most of whom planned to return to Anatolia after completing their training in college or a trade. For example, one was pharmacist Kristapor Der Seropian, who introduced the class book concept while studying at Yale. In the 1850s, he invented the durable green dye that continues to be used in printing U.S. currency. Another was reporter Khachadur Osganian, who wrote for the *New York Herald* after graduating from New York University; he was elected President of the New York Press Club in the 1850s.

The great Armenian migration to America began in the 1890s. During these troubled final years of the Ottoman Empire, its prosperous Christian minorities became the targets of violent Turkish nationalism and were treated as *giavours* (non-Moslem infidels). The outbreaks of 1894-1895 saw an estimated 300,000 Turkish Armenians massacred. This was followed in 1915-1920 by the government-orchestrated genocide of a million more Armenians during World War I. This tumult

caused massive Armenian immigration to America in three waves. First, from 1890-1914, 64,000 Turkish Armenians fled to America before World War I. Second, after 1920, some 30,771 survivors fled to the United States until 1924, when the Johnson-Reed Immigration Act drastically reduced the annual quota to 150 for Armenians.

The third wave to America began following World War II, as the 700,000 Armenians who earlier had been forced from Turkey into the Middle East faced paroxysms of rising Arab/Turkish nationalism, Islamic fundamentalism, or socialism. The large and prosperous Armenian minorities were driven westward to Europe and America—first from Egypt (1952), then Turkey again (1955), Iraq (1958), Syria (1961), Lebanon (1975), and Iran (1978). Tens of thousands of prosperous, educated Armenians flooded westward toward the safety of the United States. Though it is hard to say how many immigrants constituted this third wave, the 1990 U.S. Census reports that of a total of 267,975 Americans who have Armenian ancestry, more than 60,000 came in the decade of 1980-1989 alone, and over 75 percent of them settled in greater Los Angeles (Glendale, Pasadena, Hollywood). This third wave has proven the largest of the three, and its timing slowed the assimilation of the second-generation Armenian Americans. The influx of fiercely ethnic Middle Eastern newcomers caused a visible burgeoning of Armenian American institutions starting in the 1960s. For instance, Armenian day schools began appearing in 1967, and numbered eight in 1975, the first year of the Lebanese civil war; since then, they have increased to 33 as of 1995. A 1986 survey confirmed that the foreign-born are the spearhead of these new ethnic organizations—new day schools, churches, media, political, and cultural organizations—which now attract native as well as immigrant Armenians (Anny P. Bakalian, *Armenian-Americans: From Being to Feeling Armenian* [New Brunswick, NJ: Transaction, 1992]; cited hereafter as Bakalian).

## ARMENIAN SETTLEMENTS IN AMERICA

The first wave of Armenians in America flooded into greater Boston and New York, where some 90 percent of the immigrants joined the handful of relatives or friends who had arrived earlier. Many Armenians were drawn to New England factories, while others in New York started small businesses. Using their entrepreneurial backgrounds and multilingual skills, Armenians often found quick success with import-export firms and acquired a dis-

torted reputation as "rug merchants" for their total domination of the lucrative oriental carpet business. From the East Coast, growing Armenian communities soon expanded into the Great Lakes regions of Detroit and Chicago as well as the southern California farming areas of Fresno and Los Angeles. Armenian communities may also be found in New Jersey, Rhode Island, Ohio, and Wisconsin.

Since the 1975 Lebanese civil war, Los Angeles has replaced war-torn Beirut as the "first city" of the Armenian diaspora—the largest Armenian community outside of Armenia. The majority of Armenian immigrants to the United States since the 1970s has settled in greater Los Angeles, bringing its size up to 200,000 or 300,000. This includes some 30,000 Armenians who left Soviet Armenia between 1960 and 1984. The Armenian presence in Los Angeles makes this U.S. city one of the few that is noticeable to the general public. Though the community has no full-time television or radio station, it currently supports about a dozen local or syndicated television or radio programs designed for Armenian-speaking audiences. Since 1979, UniArts Publications has published a bilingual Armenian Directory White/Yellow Pages that lists 40,000 households, thousands of local businesses, and hundreds of Armenian organizations among its 500 pages. The community bustles with Armenian media and publishers, some 20 schools and 40 churches, one college, and all sorts of ethnic spe-

cialty shops and businesses. The community also has its problems. The number of LEP (Limited English Proficiency) Armenian students in local public schools has leapt from 6,727 in 1989 to 15,156 in 1993, creating a shortage of bilingual teachers. Even more perturbing is the growing involvement of Armenian youth with weapons, gangs, and substance abuse. Some of the thousands of newcomers from the former Soviet Union have been accused of bringing with them a *jarbig* (crafty) attitude that evokes embarrassment from other Armenians and resentment and prejudice from *odars* (non-Armenians). In response, the Armenian community has tried to meet its own needs with two multiservice organizations: the Armenian Evangelical Social Service Center and the Armenian Relief Society.

Armenians estimate their own number to be between 500,000 and 800,000 in the United States plus 100,000 in Canada. These estimates include all those with at least one Armenian grandparent, whether or not they identify with Armenians. Assuming an estimate of 700,000, the four largest U.S. concentrations are in southern California (40 percent, or 280,000), greater Boston (15 percent, or 100,000), greater New York (15 percent, or 100,000), and Michigan (10 percent, or 70,000). Since so few Armenians entered America prior to World War I, and so many since World War II, the majority of U.S. Armenians today are only first-, second-, or third-generation Americans, with very few who have all four grandparents born on U.S. soil. Official U.S. Census figures are more conservative than Armenian estimates. The 1990 Census counted 308,096 Americans who cite their ancestry as "Armenian," up from 212,621 in 1980. One hundred fifty thousand report Armenian as the language spoken at home in 1990, up from 102,387 in 1980.

## RELATIONS WITH OTHER AMERICANS

The majority of Armenians were not so much "pulled" to America by opportunity as they were "pushed" to America by bloodshed within their native country. Still, traditional Armenian culture so closely resembles American values that many Armenian feel they are "coming home" to America and make an easy transition to its free-market economy and social values. A large percentage of immigrants become wealthy businesspeople or educated community leaders within a decade or two of arrival, and feel a kinship with U.S. natives.

American society's reception of Armenians is equally friendly. Armenians have experienced little prejudice in the United States. Armenians are a tiny minority, barely noticed by most Americans because Armenian newcomers are typically multilingual, English-speaking Christians arriving in tight-knit families in which the head of household is an educated professional, skilled craftsman, or businessperson readily absorbed into the U.S. economy. Armenian culture encourages women's education (dating back to its fifth century Canon Law), so many women also have training or work experience. Since most move in a "chain migration," with families already in the United States to receive them, new arrivals have assistance from their families or from the network of U.S. Armenian organizations. In their personal values too, Armenians were dubbed "The Anglo-Saxons of the Middle East" by British writers of the 1800s, because they have the reputation of being industrious, creative, God-fearing, family-oriented, frugal businesspeople who lean towards conservatism and smooth adaptation to society. Examples of anti-Armenian sentiment are few.

# ACCULTURATION AND ASSIMILATION

Throughout the diaspora, Armenians have developed a pattern of quick acculturation and slow assimilation. Armenians quickly acculturate to their society, learning the language, attending school, and adapting to economic and political life. Meanwhile, they are highly resistant to assimilation, maintaining their own schools, churches, associations, language, and networks of intramarriage and friendship. Sociologist Anny Bakalian observes that across generations, U.S. Armenians move from a more central "being Armenian" to a more surface "feeling Armenian," expressing nostalgic pride in their heritage while acting fully American.

The U.S. Armenian community is best viewed as the product of two sets of intense, opposing forces—centripetal pressures binding Armenians closer together, and centrifugal pressures pushing them apart. Centripetal forces among Armenians are clear. More than most U.S. nationalities, diaspora Armenian youth and adults feel like the proud guardians charged with protecting their ancient, highly-evolved culture—its distinctive language, alphabet, architecture, music, and art—from extinction. This sense of duty makes them resist assimilation. They tenaciously maintain their own schools, churches, associations, language, local *hantesses* (festivals) and networks of intramarriage and friendship. Today's U.S. Armenian community is bound together by a network of Armenian groups including, for example, some 170 church congregations, 33 day schools, 20 national newspapers, 36 radio or television programs, 58 student scholarship programs, and 26 professional associations. Anthropologist Margaret Mead has suggested that over the centuries, diaspora Armenians (like Jews) have developed a tight-knit family structure to serve as a bulwark against extinction and assimilation (*Culture and Commitment* [New York: Columbia University Press, 1978]). There is merit to the sentiment expressed by some Armenians that America's culture has evolved for less than 400 years since the 1600s, at a time when Armenian culture was already 2,500 years into its evolution.

Meanwhile, centrifugal forces also can be strong, driving Armenians out of their community. Due to political and religious schisms, the many groups often duplicate or even compete with one another, creating ill feelings. The American-born and youths, in particular, often view organization leaders as "out-of-touch," while others avoid Armenian organizations due to the plutocratic tendency to allow their wealthy sponsors to dictate organization policy. Unlike most U.S. nationalities, there is no coordinating body at all among the many wealthy Armenian groups, often leading to discord and a vying for leadership. The few recent efforts at community coordination (like the compilation of the *Armenian Almanac*, *Armenian Directory*, and *Who's Who*) are the efforts of well-intentioned individuals, not funded community groups. Since 1991, perhaps the emergence of a stable Armenian Republic for the first time in 500 years may serve as a stabilizing force within the diaspora. Meanwhile, it is not clear how many U.S. Armenians have left behind their community, if not their heritage, due to divisive forces within it.

## PROVERBS

The Bible is the source of most Armenian adages. Armenians also share with their Moslem Turkish neighbors the sayings of "Hojah," a mythical character who teaches listeners by his sometimes foolish, sometimes wise example. Other popular Armenian sayings are: We learn more from a clever rival than a stupid ally; It burns only where the fire falls; Wherever there are two Armenians there are at least three opinions; Mouth to mouth, the splinter becomes a log; The older we get, the more our parents know; Jealousy first hurts the jealous; Money brings wisdom to some, and makes others act foolish; In marriage, as in death, you go either to heaven or to hell; I'm boss, you're boss. So who grinds the flour?; Lock your door well: don't make a thief of your neighbor; The evil tongue is sharper than a razor, with no remedy for what it cuts; The fish begins to smell from its head; Fear the man who doesn't fear God; A narrow mind has a broad tongue; A sweet tongue will bring the snake from its hole; See the mother, marry the girl.

## CUISINE

The Armenian woman is expected to take pride in her kitchen, and pass this skill on to her daughters. Nutritionally, the Armenian diet is rich—emphasizing dairy, oils, red meats. It emphasizes subtlety of flavors and textures, with many herbs and spices. It includes nonmeat dishes, to accommodate Lent each spring. Since so much time and effort is needed—for marinating, stuffing, stewing—U.S. Armenian restaurants lean toward the expensive multi-course evening fare, not fast food or take-out. Traditional Armenian foods fall into two categories—the shared, and the distinctive.

The shared part of the Armenian diet is the Mediterranean foods widely familiar among Arabs, Turks, Greeks. This includes appetizers like *humus*, *baba ganoush*, *tabouleh*, *madzoon* (yogurt); main courses like *pilaf* (rice), *imam bayildi* (eggplant casserole), *foule* (beans), *felafel* (vegetable fritters), meat cut into cubes called *kebabs* for barbecue (*shish kebab*) or boiling (*tass kebab*), or ground into *kufta* (meatballs); bakery and desserts like pita bread, *baklawa*, *bourma*, *halawi*, *halvah*, *mamoul*, *lokhoom*; and beverages like espresso, or *oghi* (raisin brandy).

The distinctive part of the Armenian diet is unlikely to be found outside an Armenian home or restaurant. This includes appetizers like Armenian string cheese, *manti* (dumpling soup), *tourshou* (pickled vegetables), *tahnabour* (yogurt soup), *jajik* (spicy yogurt), *basterma* (spicy dried beef), *lahmajun* (ground meat pizza), *midia* (mussels); main courses like *bulghur* (wheat), *harisse* (lamb pottage), *boeregs* (flaky pastry stuffed with meat, cheese, or vegetables), *soujuk* (sausage), *tourlu* (vegetable stew), *sarma* (meat/grain fillings wrapped by grape or cabbage leaves), *dolma* (meat/grain fillings stuffed into squash or tomatoes), *khash* (boiled hooves); bakery and desserts like *lavash* (thin flat bread), *katah* (butter/egg pastry), *choereg* (egg/anise pastry), *katayif* (sweets), *gatnabour* (rice pudding), *kourabia* (sugar cookies), *kaymak* (whipped cream); and beverages like *tahn* (a tart yogurt drink).

Traditional recipes go back 1,000 years or more. Though demanding, their preparation has become almost a symbol of national survival for Armenians. A vivid example of this occurs each September in the Republic of Armenia. Armenians gather by the thousands at the outdoor grounds of Musa Ler to share *harrise* porridge for two days. This celebrates the survival of a village nearly exterminated in the Turkish genocide in 1918 (as described in Franz Werfel's novel, *Forty Days of Musa Dagh*).

## HOLIDAYS CELEBRATED BY ARMENIAN AMERICANS

Traditional holidays celebrated by Armenian Americans include January 6: Armenian Christmas (Epiphany in most other Christian churches, marking the three Magi's visit to Christ); February 10: St. Vartan's Day, commemorating martyr Vartan Mamigonian's battle for religious freedom against the Persians in A.D. 451; religious springtime holidays such as Lent, Palm Sunday, Maundy Thursday, Good Friday, Easter; April 24: Martyrs' Day, a day of speeches and marches remembering the first day in 1915 of the Turkish genocide of some one million Armenians in Anatolia; May 28: Independence Day, celebrating the short-lived freedom of the Republic of Armenia from 1918-1920, after 500 years of Turkish suzerainty; and September 23: the Declaration of independence from the Soviet Union in 1991.

# LANGUAGE

The Armenian language is an independent branch of the Indo-European group of languages. Since it separated from its Indo-European origins thousands of years ago, it is not closely related to any other existing language. Its syntactical rules make it a concise language, expressing much meaning in few words. One unique aspect of Armenian is its alphabet. At the time Armenians converted to Christianity in 301, they had their own language but, with no alphabet, they relied on Greek and Assyrian for writing. One priest, Mesrob Mashtots (353-439), resigned his high post as the royal Secretary to King Vramshabouh when he received God's call to become an evangelist monk. With inspired scholarship, in 410 he literally invented the unique new characters of an alphabet that captured the array of sounds of his language in order to pen the Holy Scriptures in his own Armenian tongue. Immediately, his efforts ushered in a golden age of literature in Armenia, and the nearby Georgians soon commissioned Mesrob to invent an alphabet for their language. Armenians today continue to use Mesrob's original 36 characters (now 38), and regard him as a national hero.

The spoken Armenian of Mesrob's era has evolved over the centuries. This classical Armenian, called *Krapar*, is used now only in religious services. Modern spoken Armenian is now one language with two dialects world-wide. The slightly more guttural "Eastern" Armenian is used among 55 percent of the world's 8 million Armenians—those in Iran, in Armenia, and in the post-Soviet nations. "Western" is used among the other 45 percent in every other nation throughout the diaspora—the Middle East, Europe, and the Americas. With effort, speakers of the two dialects can understand each other's pronunciation, much the way Portuguese can comprehend Spanish.

Because over half of this ancient people now live dispersed outside their homeland, the intense fear of cultural extinction among diaspora Armenians has resulted in a lively debate. Many Armenians wonder if the speaking of Armenian is essential for future national survival. A recent U.S. survey found that 94 percent of Armenian immigrants to the United States feel their children should learn to speak Armenian, yet the actual percentage who can speak Armenian dropped dramatically from 98 percent among the first generation to just 12 percent among third-generation Americans (Bakalian, p. 256). The Armenian day school movement is not nearly sufficient to reverse or even slow this sharp decline in Armenian-language speakers. The 1990 U.S. Census found that 150,000 Americans report speaking Armenian at home.

Armenian is taught at several American colleges and universities, including Stanford University, Boston College, Harvard University, the University of Michigan, and the University of Pennsylvania to name a few. Library collections in the Armenian language may be found wherever there is a large Armenian American population. Los Angeles, Chicago, Boston, New York, Detroit, and Cleveland public libraries all have good Armenian language holdings.

### GREETINGS AND OTHER POPULAR EXPRESSIONS

Some common expressions in Armenian are: *Parev*—Hello; *Inch bes es?*—How are you? *Pari louys*—Good morning; *Ksher pari*—Good night, *Pari janabar*—A good trip!; *Hachoghootiun*—Good luck; *Pari ygak*—Welcome; *Ayo*—Yes; *Voch*—No; *Shnor hagalem*—Thank you; *Pahme che*—You're welcome; *Abris*—Congratulations!; *Oorish or ge desnevink*—See you again; *Shnor nor dari*—Happy new year; *Shnor soorp dznoort*—Merry Christmas; *"Kristos haryav ee merelots"*—Easter greeting "Christ is risen!"; *"Ortnial eh harutiun Kristosi!"*—Easter reply "Blessed is Christ risen!"; *Asvadz ortne kezi*—God bless you; *Ge sihrem*—I like you/it; *Hye es?*—Are you Armenian?

# FAMILY AND COMMUNITY DYNAMICS

In her book *Culture and Commitment*, anthropologist Margaret Mead singled out Jewish and Armenian nationalities as two examples of cultures in which children seem unusually respectful and less rebellious towards their parents, perhaps because these groups had come so close to extinction in the past. In 1990, the President of the Armenian International College in California surveyed a representative sample of 1,864 Armenians in public and private schools in 22 states, ages 12 to 19, to derive this snapshot of "the future of the Armenian community in America: More speak English at home (56 percent) than Armenian (44 percent). Some 90 percent live with two parents, and 91 percent report excellent or good relations with them. Some 83 percent plan for college. Some 94 percent feel it important to have faith in God. Among those involved in an Armenian church, 74 percent are Apostolic, 17 percent Protestant, seven percent Catholic. Only five percent do not identify as "Armenian" at all. Some 94 percent felt somehow affected by the 1988 earthquake in Armenia. These findings confirm a positive view of Americans proud of their heritage.

Education has been a high priority in Armenians' ancestral culture. One Canadian sponsor of hundreds of young Armenians into Canada later described them as "school crazy" in their eagerness to complete an education. A 1986 survey of 584 Armenian Americans found that 41 percent of immigrants, 43 percent of first generation, and 69 percent of second-generation Armenians had completed a college degree. Another survey of Armenian adolescents in 1990 found 83 percent plan to attend college. The 1990 U.S. Census similarly found that 41 percent of all Armenian-ancestry adults reported some college training—with a baccalaureate completed by 23 percent of men and 19 percent of women. Though these data vary, they all confirm a picture of a people seeking higher education.

Armenian day schools now number 33 in North America, educating some 5,500 pupils. Though their prime goal was to foster ethnic identity, evidence also documents their academic excellence in preparing students, in at least two ways. These schools achieve unusually high averages on standardized national tests like the California Achievement Tests, even though the majority of their pupils are foreign-born ESL (English as a Second Language) students. Graduates of these schools typically go on to scholarships and other successes in their higher education.

Notable here is the growth of Armenian studies within U.S. universities over the past 30 years. Some 20 U.S. universities now offer some program in Armenian studies. As of 1995, over a half-dozen of these have established one or more endowed chairs in Armenian studies within a major university: University of California, Berkeley; University of California, Los Angeles;, California State University—Fresno; Columbia University, Harvard University, and the Universities of Michigan and Pennsylvania.

## SURNAMES

Armenians have distinctive surnames, which their familiar "ian" endings make easily recognizable. Most Armenians in Anatolia took surnames with "ian" meaning "of"—such as Tashjian (the tailor's family) or Artounian (Artoun's family)—in about the eighteenth century. A U.S. survey found that 94 percent of traditional Armenian surnames today end in "-ian" (like Artounian), with only six percent ending in "yan" (Artounyan), "-ians" (Artounians), or the more ancient "-ooni" (Artooni). In still other cases, Armenians can often detect surnames just by their Armenian root, despite some other suffix adjusted to fit a diaspora Armenian into a local host nation—such as Artounoff (Russia), Artounoglu (Turkey), Artounescu (Romania). Of course, with intermarriage or assimilation in the United States, more Armenians are shedding their distinctive surnames, typically for briefer ones. The "ian" suffix is especially common among East European Jews (Brodian, Gibian, Gurian, Millian, Safian, Slepian, Slobodzian, Yaryan), perhaps indicating some historic link in this region.

# RELIGION

When Christ's apostles Thaddeus and Bartholemew came to Armenia in 43 and 68 A.D., they found a pagan nation of nature-worshippers; the land was dotted with temples for a pantheon of gods resembling those of nearby Greece and Persia. Armenian authorities eventually executed the two preachers, in part because of Armenian listeners' receptivity to the Gospel. In 301 King Trdates III was the last Armenian king to persecute Christians, before his dramatic conversion to Christianity by the miracles of "Gregory the Illuminator." Armenia thus became the world's first Christian nation, a major breakthrough for those early believers, and a source of continuing pride to Armenians today. Trdates III appointed Gregory the Church's first Catholicos in 303, and the Cathedral he erected in Echmiadzin, Armenia, continues today as the seat of the supreme Catholicos of the worldwide Armenian Apostolic Church. In 506 doctrinal differences caused the Armenian and Constantinople churches to divide, and the Armenian Apostolic Church remains an orthodox church today. Few nations have been so transfixed by their religion as Armenians. With the single exception of some 300 Jews in Armenia, there is no other known group of non-Christian Armenians today, making Christianity practically a defining feature of being Armenian. Moreover, Armenians' Christian heritage had led not only to repeated martyrdoms, but also to a number of key elements of their modern culture.

Today, practicing Christian Armenians fall into one of three church bodies—Roman Catholic, Protestant, or Orthodox. The smallest of these is the Armenian Rite of the Roman Catholic Church, which includes nearly 150,000 worldwide members. Of these, an estimated 30,000 Armenian Catholics are in one of the ten U.S. parishes within the relatively new North American Diocese, established in 1981 in New York City. It was back in the twelfth century that Western Europe and the Armenians re-established contact, when Middle East Armenians extended hospitality to the passing Crusaders. In the late 1500s the Vatican's Congregation for the Propagation of the Faith began the Roman Catholic Church's outreach to its "separated" Armenian brethren. In 1717 Father Mekhitar of Sebaste (1675-1749) began forming the Mekhitarist Order's Armenian seminary and research center on the Isle of San Lazzaro in Venice, Italy, which remains known today for its erudition on Armenian affairs. The Church also formed the Armenian Sisters of the Immaculate Conception in Rome in 1847, an order best known today for the 60 Armenian schools it has opened around the world. The current Superior General of the Vatican's Jesuit Order, Hans Kolvenbach, is an expert in Armenian studies, further indicating the close relationship between Roman Catholic and Armenian Christianity.

In the United States Armenian priests are elected by laymen and ordained by bishops, but confirmed by the Patriarch, who resides in Armenia. There are lower priests (called *kahanas*) who are allowed to marry. The Armenian Catholic Church also has higher servants of God (called *vartabeds*) who remain celibate so that they may become bishops. The liturgy is conducted in classical Armenian and lasts three hours, but the sermons can be delivered in both English and Armenian.

Protestantism among Armenians dates back to American missionary activity in Anatolia, beginning in 1831. At that time, there was a fundamentalist reform movement within the ranks of the highly traditional Armenian orthodox Church, which closely paralleled the theological views of American Protestants. In this way, missionaries indirectly inspired reform-minded Armenians to form their own Protestant denominations, principally Congregationalist, Evangelical, and Presbyterian. Today, ten to 15 percent of U.S. Armenians (up to 100,000) belong to one of 40 Armenian Protestant congregations, most of them in the Armenian Evangelical Union of North America. These Armenians have a reputation as an unusually educated and financially prosperous segment within the U.S. Armenian community.

By far the largest church group among U.S. Armenians is the original orthodox Apostolic Church founded by Saint Gregory in 301, and currently includes 80 percent of practicing Armenian Christians in the United States. Many non-Armenians admire the beauty of its Divine Liturgy, spoken in old Armenian (*Krapar*). The Church has some 120 parishes in North America. Due to the division following Archbishop Tourian's assassination in 1933, 80 of these are under the Diocese, the other 40 under the Prelacy. Compared with other denominations, there are two points to note about this Church. First, it typically does not portend to influence its members on social issues of the day—like birth control, homosexuality, or school prayer. Second, it does not proselytize among non-Armenians. A 1986 survey found that only some 16 percent of U.S. Armenians have joined a non-Armenian church—a figure that increases in proportion to their length of stay on U.S. soil (Bakalian, p. 64).

# EMPLOYMENT AND ECONOMIC TRADITIONS

Due to the quick assimilation and divided nature of the Armenian American community, precise data on the demographics of this group—their education, occupations, income, family size, and dynamics—is lacking. Still, there is a wealth of fairly uniform impressionistic information on the Armenian community's tendencies. The majority of early Armenian immigrants took unskilled jobs in wire mills, garment factories, silk mills, or vineyards in California. Second-generation Armenian Americans were a more professional lot and often obtained managerial positions. Third-generation Armenian Americans, as well as Armenian immi-

grants who came after World War II, were well-educated and largely attracted to careers in business; they also have a penchant toward engineering, medicine, the sciences, and technology. One Armenian group, which sponsored some 25,000 Armenian refugees into the United States from 1947-1970, reports that these refugees tended to do well economically, with a surprisingly large fraction achieving affluence within their first generation in the United States, primarily by working long hours in their own family businesses.

Though U.S. Census data is admittedly imprecise, especially on ethnic issues, this picture of the Armenian community emerges from the 1990 reports: Of the total of 267,975 Americans who report their ancestry as Armenian, fully 44 percent of these are immigrants—21 percent prior to 1980, and fully 23 percent in 1980-1990. The self-reported mean household income averaged $43,000 for immigrants and $56,000 for native-born, with eight percent of immigrants and 11 percent of natives reporting in excess of $100,000 annually. Eighteen percent of immigrant families and three percent of native families fell below the poverty line.

Another profile is yielded in a 1986 sociological survey of 584 New York Armenians: Some 40 percent were immigrants, four out of five of these from the Middle East. Their three largest occupations were business owners (25 percent), professionals (22 percent), and semi-professionals (17 percent). Median income was about $45,000

annually. Only 25 percent sympathized with one of the three Armenian political parties (primarily Dashnags), with the remaining 75 percent neutral or indifferent (Bakalian, p. 64).

# POLITICS AND GOVERNMENT

As the Armenian American community swelled after World War I, so did tensions within it. A few Armenian political parties—Dashnags, Ramgavars, Hunchags—disagreed over acceptance of the Russian-dominated Armenian republic. This conflict came to a head on December 24, 1933 in New York's Holy Cross Armenian Church, when Archbishop Elishe Tourian was surrounded and brutally stabbed by an assassination team in front of his stunned parishioners during the Christmas Eve service. Nine local Dashnags were soon convicted of his murder. Armenians ousted all Dashnags from their Church, forcing these thousands to form their own parallel Church structure. To this day, there continues to be two doctrinally identical yet structurally independent Armenian Church bodies in America, the original Diocese and the later Prelacy. As of 1995, efforts continue to reunite them.

With regard to American politics, Armenian Americans have been active in almost every level of government. Notable politicians include

Steven Derounian (1918- ), a U.S. congressman who represented New York form 1952 to 1964 and Walter Karabian (1938- ) who was a California State Senator for several years.

# INDIVIDUAL AND GROUP CONTRIBUTIONS

Over the years, diaspora Armenians have been fortunate to contribute to the economies and cultures of the nations in which they live, including the United States. Their most visible contributions seem to be in the arts, science and technology (particularly medicine), and business. Up to now they have been least involved in law and the social sciences. In 1994, the first *Who's Who among Armenians* in North America was published in the United States. Among notable Armenian Americans, three clearly stand out for the visibility of their Armenian heritage. First and foremost is author William Saroyan (1908-1981) who, among other things, declined the 1940 Pulitzer Prize for his play "The Time of Your Life," because he felt such awards distract artists. Another is George Deukmejian (1928- ), the popular Republican governor of California from 1982-1990, who in 1984 was among those considered as a vice-presidential running-mate for his fellow Californian Ronald Reagan. Third is Vartan Gregorian (1935- ), the director of the New York Public Library from 1981-1989, who went on to become the first foreign-born President of an Ivy-League college—Brown University.

## ACADEMIA

Armenian American university presidents have included Gregory Adamian (Bentley), Carnegie Calian (Pittsburgh Theological), Vartan Gregorian (Brown), Barkev Kibarian (Husson), Robert Mehrabian (Carnegie Mellon), Mihran Agbabian (the new American University of Armenia, affiliated with the University of California system).

## ARTS

Visual artists include painter Arshile Gorky (Vostanig Adoian, 1905-1948); photographers Yousef Karsh, Arthur Tcholakian, Harry Nalchayan; and sculptors Reuben Nakian (1897-1986) and Khoren Der Harootian. Musical notables include singer/composers Charles Aznavour,

Raffi, Kay Armen (Manoogian); sopranos Lucine Amara and Cathy Berberian, and contralto Lili Chookasian; composer Alan Hovhaness; violin maestro Ivan Galamian; and Boston Pops organist Berj Zamkochian. Entertainers in film and television include many Armenians who have changed their distinctive surnames—Arlene Francis (Kazanjian), Mike Connors (Krikor Ohanian), Cher (Sarkisian) Bono, David Hedison (Hedisian), Akim Tamiroff, Sylvie Vartan (Vartanian), director Eric Bogosian, and producer Rouben Mamoulian (who introduced the modern musical to Broadway, with *Oklahoma!* in 1943).

## COMMERCE

Business leaders today include tycoon Kirk Kerkorian (of Metro Goldwyn-Mayer [MGM]), Stephen Mugar (founder of Star Markets in New England), industrialist Sarkis Tarzian, and Alex Manoogian, founder of the Masco Corporation, a conglomerate of building products companies.

## LITERATURE

In addition to William Saroyan, notable Armenian American writers include novelist Michael Arlen (Dikran Kouyoumdjian), his son Michael J. Arlen, Jr., and Marjorie Housepian Dobkin.

## MEDICINE

Within science and technology, noted physicians are Varaztad Kazanjian (1879-1974, "the father of plastic surgery"), Raymond Damadian (inventor of Magnetic Resonance Imaging [MRI]), and Jack Kevorkian, physician and controversial proponent of doctor-assisted suicide.

## PUBLIC AFFAIRS

In addition to Governor Deukmejian are Edward N. Costikyan (1924-) of New York City, and Garabed "Chuck" Haytaian of New Jersey. Lawyers include activist Charles Garry (Garabedian), and Raffi Hovanissian, the recent Foreign Minister of Armenia.

## SPORTS

Sports figures include athletes Garo Epremian, Chuck Esegian, Andre Agassi (winner of the 1994 U.S. Tennis Open); coaches Ara Parseghian, Jerry Tarkanian; race-car sponsor J. C. Agajanian, and chess grandmaster Gary Kasparov.

# MEDIA

### PRINT

**Armenian International Magazine.**

Founded in 1989, this unprecedented monthly newsmagazine seems modeled after *Time* in content and format. *AIM* has quickly become a unique source of current facts and trends among Armenians worldwide, offering up-to-date news and features.

**Contact:** Vartan Oskanian, Editor.
**Address:** Fourth Millenium, 207 South Brand Boulevard, Glendale, California 91204.
**Telephone:** (818) 246-7979.
**Fax:** (818) 246-0088.

**Armenian Mirror-Spectator.**

Community newspaper in Armenian and English founded in 1932.

**Contact:** Ara Kalaydjian, Editor.
**Address:** Baikar Association, Inc., 755 Mt. Auburn Street, Watertown, Massachusetts 02172.
**Telephone:** (617) 924-4420.
**Fax:** (617) 924-3860.

**Armenian Reporter.**

Since 1967, an independent, English-language Armenian news weekly, considered by some the newspaper of record for the diaspora.

**Contact:** Edward K. Boghosian, Editor.
**Address:** Box 600, Fresh Meadows, New York 11365.
**Telephone:** (718) 380-3636.

**Armenian Review.**

Since 1948, a quarterly academic journal on Armenian issues, published by the largest Armenian political party, the Armenian Revolutionary Federation.

**Address:** 80 Bigelow Avenue, Watertown, Massachusetts 02172.
**Telephone:** (617) 926-4037.

**Armenian Weekly.**

Periodical on Armenian interests in English.

**Contact:** Vahe Habeshian, Editor.
**Address:** Hairenik Association, Inc., 80 Bigelow Avenue, Watertown, Massachusetts 02172-2012.

**Telephone:** (617) 926-3974.
**Fax:** (617) 926-1750.

**California Courier.**

English language ethnic newspaper covering news and commentary for Armenian Americans.

**Contact:** Harut Sassounian, Editor.
**Address:** P.O. Box 5390, Glendale, California 91221.
**Telephone:** (818) 409-0949.

**UniArts Armenian Directory Yellow Pages.**

Founded in 1979. An annual directory of the entire Armenian community in southern California—listing 40,000 families and thousands of businesses, and listing a bilingual reference section listing hundreds of community organizations and churches.

**Contact:** Bernard Berberian, Publisher.
**Address:** 424 Colorado Street, Glendale, California 91204.
**Telephone:** (818) 244-1167.
**Fax:** (818) 244-1287.

### RADIO

**KTYM-AM (1460).**

Armenian American Radio Hour offers two bilingual programs totalling three hours per week in greater Los Angeles.

**Contact:** Harry Hadigian, Director.
**Address:** 14610 Cohasset Street, Van Nuys, California 91405.
**Telephone:** (213) 463-4545.

### TELEVISION

**KRCA-TV (Channel 62).**

Armenia Today, a daily half-hour show describing itself as "the only Armenian daily television outside Armenia;" it is carried on 70 cable systems in southern California.

**Address:** Thirty Seconds Inc., 520 North Central Avenue, Glendale, California 91203.
**Telephone:** (818) 244-9044.
**Fax:** (818) 244-8220.

# ORGANIZATIONS AND ASSOCIATIONS

**Armenian Assembly of America (AAA).**

Founded in 1972, AAA is a nonprofit public affairs office that tries to communicate the

Armenian voice to government, increase the involvement of Armenians in public affairs, and sponsor activities fostering unity among Armenian groups.

**Contact:** Ross Vartian, Executive Director.
**Address:** 122 C Street, Washington, D.C. 20001.
**Telephone:** (202) 393-3434.

### Armenian General Benevolent Union (AGBU).

Founded in 1906 in Egypt by statesman Boghos Nubar, this wealthy service group operates internationally, with some 60 chapters in North America. AGBU resources are targeted onto specific projects chosen by its Honorary Life President and Central Committee—sponsoring its own schools, scholarships, relief efforts, cultural and youth groups, and, since 1991, a free English-language newsmagazine. More than any major diaspora group, AGBU has had close ties with Armenia, in both the Soviet and post-Soviet eras.

**Contact:** Louise Simone, President.
**Address:** 31 West 52nd Street, New York, New York 10019-6109.
**Telephone:** (212) 765-8260.
**Fax:** (212) 765-8208/9.

### Armenian Network of America (ANA).

Founded 1983. A nonpolitical social organization with chapters in several U.S. cities, ANA is of special appeal to young adults in the professions.

**Address:** P.O. Box 1444, New York, New York 10185.
**Telephone:** (914) 693-0480.

### Armenian Revolutionary Federation (ARF).

Founded in 1890 in Turkey, the ARF, or Dashnags, is the largest and most nationalistic of the three Armenian political parties.

**Address:** 80 Bigelow Street, Watertown, Massachusetts 02172.
**Telephone:** (617) 926-3685.

### Diocese of the Armenian Apostolic Church of America.

The largest of the several independent Christian churches among Armenians, directly under the supreme Catholicos in Echmiadzin, Armenia.

**Contact:** Archbishop Khajag Barsamian.
**Address:** 630 Second Avenue, New York, New York 10016.
**Telephone:** (212) 686-0710.

### National Association for Armenian Studies and Research (NAASR).

Fosters the study of Armenian history, culture, and language on an active, scholarly, and continuous basis in American institutions of higher education.

**Contact:** Manoog S. Young, Board Chair.
**Address:** 395 Concord Avenue, Belmont, Massachusetts 02178-3049.
**Telephone:** (617) 489-1610.

### Society for Armenian Studies (SAS).

Promotes the study of Armenia and related geographic areas, as well as issues related to the history and culture of Armenia.

**Contact:** Dr. Dennis Papazian, Chair.
**Address:** University of Michigan Armenian Research Center, 4901 Evergreen Road, Dearborn, Michigan 48128-1491.
**Telephone:** (313) 593-5181.

# MUSEUMS AND RESEARCH CENTERS

The three premier collections of Armenian materials are outside the United States. Certainly the largest is the Matenadaran, overlooking downtown Yerevan, Armenia—the Armenian national depository for over 1,500 years. Second, the Gulbenkian Library in Jerusalem vigorously collects Armenian materials from around the world. Third, the Calouste Gulbenkian Museum in downtown Lisbon houses an especially rich Armenian collection among its trove of global holdings. The 1990 Armenian American Almanac identified 76 libraries and research collections in the United States, scattered among public and university libraries, Armenian organizations and churches, and special collections. Of special value are the university collections at the University of California, Los Angeles (21,000 titles), Harvard University (7,000), Columbia University (6,600), University of California, Berkeley (3,500), and the University of Michigan, as well as two outstanding special collections.

### Armenian Library and Museum of America (ALMA).

ALMA houses a library of over 10,000 volumes and audiovisual materials, and several permanent and visiting collections of Armenian artifacts dating as far back as 3000 B.C.

**Address:** 65 Main Street, Watertown, Massachusetts 02172.

**Telephone:** (617) 926-ALMA.

**National Association for Armenian Studies and Research (NAASR).**

NAASR provides a newsletter, *Journal of Armenian Studies*, and a building housing its large mail-order bookshop, and a library of over 12,000 volumes, 100 periodicals, and diverse audio-visual materials.

**Address:** 395 Concord Avenue, Belmont, Massachusetts 02178.

**Telephone:** (617) 489-1610.

# SOURCES FOR ADDITIONAL STUDY

*Armenian American Almanac*, third edition, edited by Hamo B. Vassilian. Glendale, California: Armenian Reference Books, 1995.

Bakalian, Anny P. *Armenian-Americans: From Being to Feeling Armenian*. New Brunswick, New Jersey: Transaction, 1992.

Malcolm, M. Vartan. *The Armenians in America*. Boston: Pilgrim, 1919; reprinted, San Francisco: R & E, 1969.

Mirak, Robert. *Torn between Two Lands*. Cambridge, Massachusetts: Harvard University Press, 1983.

Takooshian, Harold. "Armenian Immigration to the United States Today from the Middle East," *Journal of Armenian Studies*, 3, 1987, pp. 133-55.

Waldstreicher, David. *The Armenian Americans*. New York: Chelsea House, 1989.

Wertsman, Vladimir. *The Armenians in America, 1616-1976: A Chronology and Fact Book*. Dobbs Ferry, New York: Oceana Publications, 1978.

# ASIAN INDIAN AMERICANS

by
Tinaz Pavri

Asian Indians have quietly permeated many segments of the American economy and society while still retaining their Indian culture.

## OVERVIEW

India, the most populous country in South Asia, is a peninsula. Bounded by Nepal and the Himalaya mountains to the north, Pakistan to the northwest, the Indian Ocean to the south, the Arabian Sea to the west, and the Bay of Bengal to the east, India occupies about 1,560,000 square miles.

Second in population only to China, India is home to around 900 million people of diverse ethnicity, religion, and language. About 82 percent of all Indians are Hindus. Approximately 12 percent are Muslims, while smaller minorities include Christians, Sikhs, Buddhists, Jains, and Zoroastrians. Over 300 languages are spoken in India, as well as hundreds of dialects. The official Indian languages include Hindi, which is spoken by about 30 percent of the population, and English.

India's capital is the modern city of New Delhi in northern India, and its flag is the "tricolor," which boasts three equal stripes of orange, white, and green. The white stripe is in the middle, and has at its center a wheel or *chakra*. The *chakra* symbolizes the spinning wheel and was popularized by India's revered leader Mahatma Gandhi as a sign of self-reliance and pride during the Indian independence movement.

## HISTORY

One of the world's oldest civilizations, the Indus Valley civilization (2500-1700 B.C.), flourished across present-day India, Bangladesh, and Pakistan. Dravidians comprised India's earliest ethnic group. They were gradually pushed to the south by invading Aryan tribes who established many empires, including the Nanda and Gupta kingdoms in northern India. Alexander the Great invaded northern India in the fourth century B.C.

Around the tenth century A.D., Islamic raiders began their invasions of India. The earliest invaders were the Turks, followed by the Moghuls in about 1500 A.D. The Moghuls established a thriving empire in North India. These Muslim invasions resulted in the conversion of a section of the populace to Islam, establishing forever a significant Muslim society in India.

## MODERN ERA

By 1600 the British had established a presence in India through the East India Company, a trading company that exported raw materials like spices out of India to the West. Britain then strengthened its hold over its Indian colony by installing a parliament, courts, and bureaucracy. Several independent Hindu and Muslim kingdoms, however, continued to exist within the broader framework of British rule. The British army existed to maintain internal order and control uprisings against the colonizing government by the Indian people.

In 1885 the British sanctioned the formation of the Indian National Congress, of which an offshoot, the Congress party, remains one of India's most important political parties. The British hoped that this political party would serve to quell growing resistance to British rule by co-opting some of India's most politically aware and educated individuals into working within the bounds of British rule. Instead, the Indian National Congress became the vehicle through which Indians coordinated their struggle for freedom from British rule. An indigenous independence movement spearheaded by men like Mahatma Gandhi and Jawaharlal Nehru—later free India's first prime minister—gained strength in the early twentieth century.

India's movement for independence was marked by nonviolence as hundreds of thousands of Indians responded to Mahatma Gandhi's call for *satyagraha*, or nonviolent protest. *Satyagraha* involved passive noncooperation with the British at every level. Indians simply refused to participate in any activity over which there was British supervision, thus making it impossible for the British to continue to govern India.

Britain formally relinquished its hold over India in 1947, and two sovereign countries, India and Pakistan, were created out of British India. The partition was a result of irreconcilable differences between Hindu and Muslim leadership. It was decided that India was the land of the Hindus and Pakistan would be the land of the Muslims. Modern India, however, is a secular nation.

Nehru and his political party, the Congress, remained in power until his death in 1964. Leaving a lasting legacy, Nehru molded independent India's economy, society, and polity. Lal Bahadur Shastri became India's second prime minister, and upon his death was succeeded by Nehru's daughter Indira Gandhi, who remained in power until 1977 when, for the first time, the Congress lost in parliamentary elections to the opposition Janata party. Indira's loss was largely due to the increasingly authoritarian tactics she had adopted before she was voted out of power. Morarji Desai, the leader of the Janata party, then became India's fourth prime minister.

Indira Gandhi and the Congress were returned to power in 1980, and upon her assassination in 1984, her son, Rajiv Gandhi, was elected prime minister. In 1994 the Congress, with Narasimha Rao as the prime minister, is once again in office, and is instituting unprecedented and far-reaching economic reforms in the country. The Rao government has succeeded in some measure in dismantling the old Nehruvian, socialist-style restrictions on the economy and on private industry. Today, India's exports have increased significantly, its foreign exchange reserves are at their highest levels in decades, and the economy appears robust.

Economic liberalization, however, has caused widening discrepancies between the wealthy and the poor in India. Moreover, a rising tide of religious fundamentalism and intolerance in recent years are threatening India's otherwise promising future. For the first time in decades, a powerful political party, the Bharatiya Janata Party (Bharateeyah Juntah) or the Indian People's Party, has challenged the prevalent belief in and acceptance of India's secularism, maintaining instead that India is a Hindu state. The party has found widespread support in some areas of India and in some sections of the Asian Indian community in the United States and Europe. Thus far, however, the government has functioned within the parameters of India's democratic institutions.

## THE FIRST ASIAN INDIANS IN AMERICA

In many accounts, immigrants to the United States from India, Pakistan, and Bangladesh are referred to as Asian Indians. The first Asian Indians or Indian Americans, as they are also known, arrived in America as early as the middle of the nineteenth century. By the end of the nineteenth century, about 2,000 Indians, most of them Sikhs (a religious minority from India's Punjab region), settled on the west coast of the United States, having come in search of economic opportunity. The majority of Sikhs worked in agriculture and construction. Other Asian Indians came as merchants and traders; many worked in lumber mills and logging camps in the western states of Oregon, Washington, and California, where they rented bunkhouses, acquired knowledge of English, and assumed Western dress. Most of the Sikhs, however, refused to cut their hair or beards or forsake the wearing of the turbans that their religion required. In 1907 about 2,000 Indians, alongside other immigrants from China, Japan, Korea, Norway, and Italy worked on the building of the Western Pacific Railway in California. Other Indians helped build bridges and tunnels for California's other railroad projects.

Between 1910 and 1920, as agricultural work in California began to become more abundant and better paying, many Indian immigrants turned to the fields and orchards for employment. For many of the immigrants who had come from villages in rural India, farming was both familiar and preferable. There is evidence that Indians began to bargain, often successfully, for better wages during this time. Some Indians eventually settled permanently in the California valleys where they worked. Despite the 1913 Alien Land Law, enacted by the California legislature to discourage Japanese immigrants from purchasing land, many Asian Indians bought land as well; by 1920 Asian Indians owned 38,000 acres in California's Imperial Valley and 85,000 acres in the Sacramento Valley. Because there was virtually no immigration by Indian women during this time, it was not unheard of for Indian males to marry Mexican women and raise families.

At the beginning of the twentieth century, about 100 Indian students also studied in universities across America. During the summers, it was not uncommon for Indian students in California to work in the fields and orchards alongside their countrymen. A small group of Indian immigrants also came to America as political refugees from British rule. To them, the United States seemed the ideal place for their revolutionary activities. In fact, many of these revolutionaries returned to India in the early part of the twentieth century to assume important roles in the struggle for India's independence.

The turn of the century also saw increasing violence against Asian Indians in the western states. Expulsions of Indians from the communities in which they worked were occasionally organized by other Euro-American workers. Some Indians who had migrated for economic reasons returned to India after they had saved respectable sums of money in America; others stayed, putting down roots in the West. The immigration of Indians to America was tightly controlled by the American government during this time, and Indians applying for visas to travel to the United States were often rejected by U.S. diplomats in major Indian cities like Bombay and Calcutta. The Asiatic Exclusion League (AEL) was organized in 1907 to encourage the expulsion of Asian workers, including Indians. In addition, several pieces of legislation were introduced in the United States, specifically the congressional exclusion laws of 1917 and 1923, that attempted either to restrict the entry of Indians and other Asians or to deny them residence and citizenship rights in America. Some of these were defeated while others were adopted. For instance, a literacy clause was added to a number of bills, requiring that immigrants pass a literacy test to be considered eligible for citizenship, thus effectively barring many Indians from consideration for citizenship.

## SIGNIFICANT IMMIGRATION WAVES

In July 1946, Congress passed a bill allowing naturalization for Indians and, in 1957, the first Asian Indian senator, Dalip Saund, was elected to Congress. Like many early Indian immigrants, Saund came to the United States from Punjab and had worked in the fields and farms of California. He had also earned a doctorate at the University of California, Berkeley. While more educated and professional Indians began to enter America, immigration restrictions and tight quotas ensured that only small numbers of Indians entered the country prior to 1965. Overall, approximately 6,000 Asian Indians immigrated to the United States between 1947 and 1965.

From 1965 onward, a second significant wave of Indian immigration began, spurred by a change in U.S. immigration law that lifted prior quotas and restrictions and allowed significant numbers of Asians to immigrate. Between 1965 and 1974, Indian immigration to the United States increased at a rate greater than that from almost any other country. This wave of immigrants was very different from the earliest Indian immigrants—Indians that emigrated after 1965 were overwhelmingly urban, professional, and highly educated and quickly engaged in gainful employment in many U.S. cities. Many had prior exposure to Western society and education and their transition to the United States was therefore relatively smooth. More than 100,000 such professionals and their families entered the U.S. in the decade after 1965.

Almost 40 percent of all Indian immigrants who entered the United States in the decades after 1965 arrived on student or exchange visitor visas, in some cases with their spouses and dependents. Most of the students pursued graduate degrees in a variety of disciplines. They were often able to find promising jobs and prosper economically, and many became permanent residents and then citizens.

## SETTLEMENT PATTERNS

The 1990 U.S. census reports 570,000 Asian Indians in America. About 32 percent are settled in the Northeast, 26 percent in the South, 23 percent in the West, and 19 percent in the midwestern states. New York, California, and New Jersey are the three states with the highest concentrations of Asian Indians. In California, where the first Indian immigrants arrived, the cities of San Francisco and Los Angeles are home to the oldest established Asian Indian communities in the United States.

In general, the Asian Indian community has preferred to settle in the larger American cities rather than smaller towns, especially in New York City, Los Angeles, San Francisco, and Chicago. This appears to be a reflection of both the availability of jobs in larger cities, and the personal preference of being a part of an urban, ethnically diverse environment, one which is evocative of the Indian cities that many of the post-1965 immigrants came from. Still, there are sizeable Asian Indian communities in suburban areas, including Silver Springs (Maryland), San Jose and Fremont (California), and Queens (New York).

# ACCULTURATION AND ASSIMILATION

Asian Indians have quietly permeated many segments of the American economy and society while still retaining their Indian culture. Most Asian Indian families strive to preserve traditional Indian values and transmit these to their children. Offspring are encouraged to marry within the community and maintain their Indian heritage. The occupational profile presented by the Asian Indian community today is one of increasing diversity. Although a large number of Asian Indians are professionals, others own small businesses or are employed as semi- or nonskilled workers. Asian Indian are sometimes stereotyped in American society as industrious, prosperous, and professionally and educationally advanced. To an extent, the stereotypes are based in reality. In comparison with other ethnic groups in the United States, Asian Indians enjoy relatively high standards of living, attain high levels of education, and are well employed.

The Asian Indian community in the United States is an ethnically diverse one. One can distinguish among subgroups who trace their roots to different regions or states within India, who speak different languages, eat different foods, and follow distinct customs. Some of the most populous Indian groups within the United States are Gujaratis, Bengalis, Punjabis, Marathis, and Tamils. They come from a number of the Indian states, or regions, each of which has its own language. It is more likely that these subgroups will interact socially and celebrate important occasions with members of their own subcommunity rather than the larger Indian community. Indians are also encouraged to marry within their subgroups. However, there are occasions, like the celebration of India's day of independence and the Hindu New Year, when the Asian Indian community will come together as one.

## TRADITIONS, CUSTOMS, AND BELIEFS

Traditionally, Asian Indians believe in astrology and consider certain days in the year more conducive to the conclusion of business deals or to the purchase of new houses or cars. They make ceremonial offerings of flowers or sweets to the gods on important days like the beginning of a new job, the commencement of college, or the birth of a child. Many of these traditions are followed more strongly by Asian American immigrants than their offspring, and vary among the different subgroups.

## CUISINE

The majority of Asian Indian Americans have retained diets rooted in Indian cuisine. Indian food is prepared with a variety of spices, including cumin, turmeric, chili powder, ginger, and garlic. All Asian Indians eat a variety of *dals* (lentils), beans, and *chaval* (rice) dishes. Hindus generally will not eat beef for religious reasons, while Muslims eschew pork. Second-generation Asian Indians are more likely to ignore these religious taboos.

*Tandoori,* clay-baked chicken or fish marinated in yogurt and spices, is a popular North Indian dish. *Biryani,* or flavored rice with vegetables and meats, is served on festive occasions, often accompanied by a cooling yogurt sauce called *raita* (ryetah). Southern Indian dishes like *masala,* crepes filled with spiced potatoes or *idlis* (idlees), and steamed rice cakes, are also popular. Indian cuisine is largely dependent on the region of India from which a subcommunity traces its roots. Caste also plays a role.

Green chutneys made of mint or coriander accompany a variety of savory fritters like the triangular, stuffed *samosas.* Pickled vegetables and fruits like lemons or mangoes are popular accompaniments to meals. A variety of unleavened breads like *naans, rotis* (roetees), and *parathas* are also widely eaten. Finally, "sweetmeats" like halva and burfi can often round off a festive meal.

Traditional Indian cooking tends to be a time-consuming process, and Asian Indians in the United States have developed shortcuts involving mechanical gadgets and canned substitutes in preparing Indian meals. However, most families continue to eat freshly-prepared Indian food for the main meal of the day. Indeed, the evening meal often serves as the time when the family will get together to discuss their daily activities. The average Asian Indian family tends not to eat out as often as other American families because of the importance accorded to eating together at the family table. Meal preparation still tends to be the domain of the females of the house, and while daughters are often expected to help, sons are not generally expected to assist in the kitchen.

## TRADITIONAL COSTUMES AND ACCESSORIES

Many Asian Indian women wear the sari—yards of colorful embroidered or printed silk or cotton

Asian Indian dancers perform at the India Cultural Festival at Middlesex College in Edison, New Jersey.

wrapped around the body—at community functions and celebrations like weddings. At such occasions, both men and women might also wear the *kameez,* also made of silk or fine cotton, a long shirt worn over tight-fitting leggings. Shawls made of silk or wool and elaborately embroidered or woven with gold or silver threads or beads and draped around the shoulders are an added touch to women's costumes. Women might wear a *bindi,* or ornamental dot, which signifies marriage, but is also worn as a fashion accessory, on their foreheads at celebrations.

Indians are very fond of gold jewelry, and many women wear simple gold ornaments like rings, earrings, bangles, and necklaces daily, and more elaborate ones at special occasions. Jewelry is often passed down through the generations from mother to daughter or daughter-in-law.

## DANCES AND MUSIC

Asian Indian preferences in music range from Indian classical music, which might include instruments such as the stringed sitar, the tabla, or drums, and the harmonium, to popular music from Indian films and the West. Indian classical music dates back several thousand years, and has its roots in divine temple music. Indian classical music came into its own and gained a wide Indian audience only after India's independence, and today enjoys an international following. Indian film music, often a fusion of Indian and Western rock or pop music, also has a widespread following both in India and within the community in the United States.

Carnatic music, the classical music of south India, commonly employs such musical instruments as the *veena*, a stringed instrument, and a range of violins. Carnatic music usually accompanies Bharata Natyam, a classical dance in which dancers perform portions of mythological tales, emulating ancient temple carvings of men and women with their body, hand, and eye movements.

Indian folk dances like the exuberant Bhangra from the Punjab region are popular at celebratory gatherings of the community. In this dance, dancers throw their arms in the air and simulate the actions of the farmer at work with his sickle. Traditional Bhangra music is increasingly being fused with elements of hip-hop, rap, and reggae, and bands like Alaap or Toronto's Dhamak are popular with younger members of the community.

## RELIGIOUS HOLIDAYS AND CELEBRATIONS

In addition to universal celebrations like International New Year's Day, Asian Indians celebrate India's day of independence from the British on August 15 and Republic Day on January 26. Many religious celebrations are also observed, the most important being *Diwali* (deevalee), the festival of lights celebrating the return home of the Lord Rama, and *Holi* (hoelee), the Hindu festival of colors celebrating spring. On these days, sweets are distributed among friends and family. Oil lamps, or *diyas*, are lit on *Diwali*. The community often organizes a traditional dinner with entertainment to mark the holiday. Major festivals for Muslims include *Eid-ul-Fitr*, which marks the end of *Ramadan*, the month of fasting. It is celebrated with prayers and visits with friends. Asian-Indian Christians celebrate Christmas and Easter.

## HEALTH AND MENTAL HEALTH ISSUES

Most Asian Indians accept the role of modern medicine and pay careful attention to health matters. Ayurvedic medicine has many adherents within the community. Ayurveda emphasizes spiritual healing as an essential component of physical healing and bases its cures on herbs and natural ingredients such as raw garlic and ginger. Ayurveda also focuses on preventive healing. One of its most famous proponents is Deepak Chopra,

an India-born doctor whose book *Ageless Body, Timeless Mind* makes a case for the practice of Ayurveda and has sold over a million copies in the United States. Homeopathic medicine also has adherents among the community.

Yoga is also commonly practiced by members of the Asian Indian American community. The ancient practice of Yoga dates back several thousand years. It combines a routine of exercise and meditation to maintain the balance between body and mind. Practiced correctly, Yoga is said to enable the individual to relieve him or herself of daily stresses and strains and to achieve his or her full potential as a human being. Various *asanas* or poses are held by the individual in practicing Yoga.

Asian Indians are less inclined to seek out assistance for mental health problems than they are for physical health problems. This relates to the low levels of consciousness about, and prevailing stigmas attached to mental health issues in India. The traditional Indian belief has been that mental problems will eventually take care of themselves, and that the family rather than outside experts should take care of the mentally ill. This attitude might change as prevailing societal beliefs about mental health are assimilated by the community.

# LANGUAGE

India is a multi-lingual country with over 300 languages. About 24 of these have over a million speakers. This diversity is reflected in the Asian Indian community in America. First-generation Indians continue to speak their native language within the family—with spouses, members of the extended family, and friends within the community. Most also speak English fluently, which has made the transition to American society easier for many Indian immigrants.

Regional differences are prevalent. Hindi is spoken mostly by immigrants from northern India, although almost all first-generation Asian Indians have a working knowledge of it. Immigrants from the states of southern India speak regional languages like Tamil, Telegu, or Malayalam. A substantial number of immigrants from western India, particularly those from the state of Gujarat, continue to speak Gujarati, while those from the region of Bengal speak Bengali. Most second- and third-generation Asian Indians understand the language spoken by their parents and extended family, but tend not to speak it themselves. Many Indians are multilingual and speak several Indian languages. Thus, a Gujarati speaker is likely to know Hindi as well.

## GREETINGS AND OTHER POPULAR EXPRESSIONS

Common Asian Indian greetings tend to be in Hindi or Hindustani, and include such greetings as *Namaste* (Namastay), the equivalent of "hello." This greeting is usually accompanied by the palms of one's hands pressed together against the chest. *Aap kaise hai* is the equivalent of the universal query "How are you?" *Theek* (fine), would be the response. For Muslims, the traditional Islamic greetings of *inshallah* ("insha-allah")—God willing, or *Salaam Aleikum* ("sullahm allaykum")—God be with you, are the most common.

# FAMILY AND COMMUNITY DYNAMICS

For the most part, Asian Indians tend to live in nuclear families in the United States, although it is common for members of the extended family, particularly grandparents, to visit for months at a time. It has also been fairly common, particularly from 1965 on, for Asian Indians to encourage their siblings to emigrate from India, and to provide them with financial and emotional support until they are well settled in the United States. Family ties are very strong, and it is considered the responsibility of more prosperous members to look after their less well-to-do relatives. Relatively low percentages of Asian Indian families receive public assistance. This is due to both relative affluence in the community and the tendency for extended family members to provide financial support in times of need.

Dating is not a traditional Indian custom, and Asian Indian parents tend to frown upon the practice, although they are slowly yielding to their offspring's demands to be allowed to date. The preference is still for the selection of a marriage partner from within the subgroup of the larger community and with the full approval and consent of the parents. Family or community members are often involved in the selection of a suitable mate. The family and educational backgrounds of the potential partner are thoroughly examined before introductions are made. Asian Indians believe that their children will be happier if they are married to someone who shares the same history, tradition, religion, and social customs and who will be able to impart these values to their children, thus ensuring the continuity of the community. They believe that such marriages made within the community tend to be more stable and longer lasting than those that cross community borders.

Asian Indians value education highly. A great percentage of all Asian Americans attend college for a minimum of four years. This percentage is much higher than any other ethnic group in America. Many also attend graduate school and pursue such professions as medicine, business administration, and law.

Asian Indian women have made great progress in recent years in both India and the United States. In India Indira Gandhi once held the highest seat in government—that of the Prime Minister. In the United States, while many women continue to perform the traditional household tasks of cooking and caring for children, a greater number of Asian Indian women, particularly second- and third-generation women, are pursuing their own professional careers and life choices.

## WEDDINGS

Weddings in the Indian community are often elaborate affairs, sometimes stretching over several days. In traditional Hindu ceremonies the bride and groom exchange garlands of flowers and circle a ceremonial fire three to seven times. The bride often wears a red sari and gold ornaments. She might also have her hands and feet painted in intricate designs with henna, a tradition called *mehendi*. The groom might wear the traditional North Indian dress of a *churidar kameez*, or tight leggings made of silk or fine cotton, and a long shirt, or opt for a western-style suit. A Brahman priest conducts the ceremony.

Weddings are normally held at party centers or halls, not in temples. Dancing and music is fairly common at Indian American weddings, a result of the assimilation of American customs. Some weddings might include *shehnai* music, or a thin, wailing music played on an oboe-like instrument. This music is traditionally played at Hindu weddings in India. Feasts of traditional foods are prepared for guests and traditional Hindu or Muslim rites are observed. Often, family members prepare the feast themselves, although it is increasingly common to engage professional caterers.

## FUNERALS

Asian Indian families can expect a lot of community support upon the death of a family member. Members of the community provide both comfort and material help in times of bereavement. After priests offer prayers, the Hindu dead are cremated. In India the cremation traditionally takes place on a wooden pyre and the body, which is often dressed in gold-ornamented clothing, burns over several hours. Garlands of flowers, incense sticks, and *ghee* (purified melted butter) are placed on the stretcher along with the body. In India as well as in the United States, it is traditional for the males of the family play the primary roles in the final rites; women play smaller roles during this ceremony. Asian Indian Muslims are buried in cemeteries according to Islamic tradition and Christians in accordance with Christian beliefs.

# RELIGION

The earliest Hindu *mandir,* or temple, the "old temple," existed in San Francisco as early as 1920, but in general the religious needs of Hindu Asian Indians prior to the 1950s were served mainly through ethnic and community organizations like the Hindu Society of India. Since the 1950s, Hindu and Sikh temples have increasingly been built for worship in cities with high concentrations of Asian Indians like New York, Los Angeles, and Chicago, while Asian Muslims worship at mosques and Christians at existing churches. There are now more than a hundred places of worship for Asian Indians around the United States.

All Hindus, regardless of their regional differences and the particular gods they worship (Hinduism being a polytheistic religion), tend to worship at available temples. Brahman priests typically lead the service and recite from the scriptures. Services can be conducted in either Sanskrit, Hindi, or the regional languages. *Poojas,* or religious ceremonies that celebrate auspicious occasions like the birth of a child, are also performed by the priests. While some priests serve full time, others might have a second occupation in addition to performing priestly duties.

While some Asian Indians visit temples regularly, others limit their visits to important religious occasions. Since Hinduism tends to be less formally organized than other religions like Christianity, prayer meetings can also be conducted at individuals' homes. It is also quite common for Asian Indian homes to have a small room or a part of a room reserved for prayer and meditation. Such household shrines are central to a family's religious life.

Many Asian Indians practice Islam, meaning "submission to God." Similar to Christianity, followers of Islam believe in the prophet Muhammad, who was ordered by the angel Gabriel in A.D. 610 to spread God's message. Muhammad recorded the angel's revelations in the *Koran,* the Muslim holy book. There are five requirements, or Pillars, of Islam: (1) Confession that there is "no god but God" and Muhammad is the messenger of God; (2) Pray five times daily; (3) Giving of alms; (4) Fasting in daylight hours for the Muhammadan month of Ramadan; and (5) Pilgrimage to Mecca at least once in a lifetime. While Muslims regard the message of Islam as eternal and universal, their individual lives have demonstrated a variety of orientations toward traditional and popular patterns.

The Asian Indian community in America also includes small numbers of Buddhists, followers of Gautama Buddha, and Jains, followers of Mahavira. The most unique feature of the Jain religion, which was founded in the sixth century B.C., is its belief in the doctrine of *ahimsa,* or nonviolence. This belief leads Jains to practice strict vegetarianism, since they cannot condone the killing of animals. The Jains in the United States have their own temples for worship. Both Buddhism and Jainism place a great value on personal austerity and are concerned with the final escape from the cycle of birth and rebirth known as reincarnation.

Small but significant Zoroastrian or Parsi communities have settled in cities such as New York and Los Angeles. The Parsees came to India as refugees from Arab-invaded Persia in the ninth and tenth centuries. They are about 100,000 strong in India and have made significant economic and social contributions to the country. Earliest reports of Parsi immigrants to the United States date from the turn of this century, when groups of Parsees entered this country as merchants and traders.

Of all the Asian Indian religious communities, the Sikhs are the oldest and tend to be the most well organized in terms of religious activity. Sikhism is different from Hinduism in its belief in one God. Sikhs follow the teachings of Guru Nanak, the founder of the religion, and worship in temples called *Gurudwaras* (Gurudwaaras). Services in *Gurudwaras* are held about once a week as well as on religious occasions. Tenets of the Sikh religion include wearing a turban on the head for males and a symbolic bangle called a *Kara* around their wrists. In addition, Sikh males are required not to cut their hair or beards. This custom is still followed to by many in the community; others choose to give up the wearing of the turban and cut their hair.

# EMPLOYMENT AND ECONOMIC TRADITIONS

The economic profile of Asian Indians has changed dramatically. While the first immigrants were agricultural and manual laborers, today, significant numbers of Asian Indians are engaged in professions such as medicine, accounting, and engineering. Many Asian Indians who entered the United States as students remained and became respected professors and academics. In fact, a recent study indicates that a higher percentage of Asian Indians is engaged in managerial positions today than any other ethnic group in the United States.

Indian immigrants to the United States sometimes have been unable to practice the profession for which they were trained in India due to either a lack of employment opportunities or the lack of American certification. In such cases, like law, for instance, they have either chosen alternative occupations or have retrained themselves in another field. Doctors and engineers have been among the most successful in finding employment in the field within which they were trained.

Many Asian Indians own small businesses like travel agencies, Indian groceries, and garment stores, particularly in neighborhoods like Flushing, in Queens, New York, where a strong Asian Indian community exists. Asian Indians own or operate about 27 percent of all hotels and motels in the United States. It is common for extended families to become involved in these business ventures.

# POLITICS AND GOVERNMENT

Indian immigrants were actively involved in the struggle for residence and citizenship rights in the early part of the twentieth century. Inspiring leaders like Dalip Saund, who later became a congressman in 1957, and rebels like Taraknath Das mobilized the Indian community in California to strike back against anti-Indian violence and exclusion. The Ghadar Party, organized by Indians and Sikhs, was formed in San Francisco between 1913 and 1914 to realize the goal of revolution in India; it then organized in the United States around the immigration issue.

Later generations of Asian Indians have tended not to play particularly active roles in modern American politics. Only about 25 percent of the community are registered voters and some Asian Indians continue to identify themselves with the politics of India rather than America. There are signs, however, that this noninvolvement is changing. Since the 1980s, the community has actively raised funds for their candidates of choice. Many young Asian Indians are working on Capitol Hill and in state legislatures gaining valuable experience for the future, and some politicians are now beginning to realize the power of the community to raise capital. During the 1988 presidential campaign, the Asian Indian community raised hundreds of thousands of dollars for candidates in both parties. The Association of Indians in America launched a successful campaign to have Asian Indians included within the "Asian or Pacific Islander" category rather than the "Caucasian/White" category in the census, believing that the conferring of this minority status would bring benefits to the community. Accordingly, Asian Indians are today classified under the "Asian or Pacific Islander" category.

Geographically dispersed as they are, the residence patterns of Asian Indians has generally prevented them from forming powerful voting blocs. Historically, a greater percentage of Asian Indians has tended to vote for Democratic rather than Republican candidates.

### RELATIONS WITH INDIA

Asian Indians have retained close ties to India, maintaining contact with friends and relatives and often travelling to India at regular intervals. They have remained interested in Indian politics because of these ties, and have contributed to the election campaigns of Indian politicians. Contributions from the Asian Indian community to different political parties in India are also quite common, as is the phenomenon of Indian political party leaders travelling to the United States to make their case to the community.

India considers its Indian communities abroad very important. Even though there has been concern over the years of a "brain drain"

from India, or a phenomenon where India's best talent moved to America and Europe, the feeling today is that India can still gain both economically and culturally from its emigrants. Indians who have emigrated abroad are viewed as ambassadors for India, and it is hoped that their achievements will make the country proud. Indeed, unique achievements by Asian Indians in America and Europe are often showcased by the Indian media.

In times of natural disaster like floods or earthquakes in India, the Asian Indian community has sent generous contributions. Second generation Asian Indian students have demonstrated an interest in travelling to India on study projects. In recent times, Asian Indians are watching the liberalizing economic reforms unfurled by the Narasimha Rao government in India with great interest and noting potential avenues for trade and investment. Many Asian Indians maintain nonresident (NRI) savings accounts in India through which they are able to make investments in private businesses in different parts of the country.

# INDIVIDUAL AND GROUP CONTRIBUTIONS

## ACADEMIA

Asian Indians serve as distinguished faculty members at prestigious universities and colleges all over the United States. The following constitute only a handful of the many Asian Indians who have made names for themselves in academia. Arjun Appaduravi is an anthropologist with Chicago University and editor of *Public Culture*. Jagdish Bhagwati (1934- ), a renowned economist specializing in the economics of underdevelopment, has also written several books on the subject. He is currently a faculty member at the Massachusetts Institute of Technology. Shyam Bhatiya (1924- ) is a geographer on the faculty of the University of Wisconsin–Oshkosh. Pramod Chandra is an art history professor at Harvard. Kuldeep Prakash Chopra (1932- ), a physicist, teaches at Old Dominion University and has served as a science advisor to the governor of Virginia. Shanti Swarup Gupta (1925- ), a statistician, has taught statistics and mathematics at Stanford and Purdue universities and is the recipient of numerous awards in the field. Jayadev Misra (1947- ), a computer science educator and winner of several national awards in software and hardware design, is a professor of computer science at the University of Texas at Austin. Rustum Ray (1924- ) has been a member of the faculty at Pennsylvania State University since 1950 and has held many visiting positions, including that of science policy fellow at the Brookings Institution during 1982-83. Gayatu Chakravarti Spivak is a respected literary critic and professor at Columbia University. Ramesh Tripathi (1936- ) has been on the ophthalmology faculty at the University of

Chicago since 1977 and has earned numerous awards in his field.

## ART

Natvar Bhavsar (1934- ) is a painter who has held a number of one-man shows at galleries like the Max Hutchinson Gallery in New York and the Kenmore Gallery in Philadelphia. His work is part of the permanent collections of museums such as the Boston Fine Arts Museum, the Metropolitan Museum of Art, and the Whitney Museum of American Art in New York.

## CULINARY ARTS

Madhur Jaffrey is the author of several popular books on Indian cuisine and the broader cuisine of East Asia. She has written, among others, *Madhur Jaffrey's World-of-the-East Vegetarian Cooking*, *An Invitation to Indian Cooking*, and *A Taste of India*. Her book *A Taste of the Far East* won the James Beard award for cookbook of the year in 1994. She has also appeared on the television series "Indian Cookery and Far Eastern Cookery."

## FILM

Ismail Merchant is a world-renowned film producer. Along with his partner James Ivory, the Merchant-Ivory team has produced and directed such award-winning films as *A Room with a View* (1986), *Howard's End* (1990), and *The Remains of the Day* (1993). In his own right, Merchant has produced *The Courtesans of Bombay* and *In Custody*. Merchant is also a successful cookbook author, having written *Ismail Merchant's Indian Cuisine*, which was named by the *New York Times* as one of the best cookbooks of the year, and, more recently, *Ismail Merchant's Passionate Meals*. Director Mira Nair has directed *Mississippi Masala*, starring Denzel Washington, and *Salaam, Bombay*. Both films deal with the adjustments Asian Indians must make while living in the United States.

## GOVERNMENT AND POLITICS

Dalip Saund (1899-1973) became a U.S. congressman in 1957. Born in the Punjab region of India, he immigrated to the United States in 1920. He earned a Ph.D. in Mathematics from the University of California, Berkeley and was one of the earliest activists fighting for the citizenship and residence rights of Asian Indians in the United States.

Many Asian Indian Americans have been appointed to administrative positions. Joy Cherian was Equal Employment Opportunities Commissioner from 1990 to 1994. Cherian was first appointed by President Ronald Reagan to the Equal Employment Opportunities Commission in 1987. In 1982 Cherian founded the Indian American Forum for Political Education and today runs a consulting firm. Sambhu Banik, a Bethesda psychologist, was appointed in 1990 as executive director of the President's Committee on Mental Retardation. Kumar Barve (1958- ), a Democrat from Maryland, was elected vice chairman of the Montgomery County's House delegation in 1992. Barve became the first Asian Indian in the country to be elected to a state legislature. Bharat Bhargava was appointed assistant director of Minority Business Development Authority by President George Bush. Dinesh D'Souza, a graduate of Dartmouth and an outspoken conservative, was appointed a domestic policy advisor in the Reagan administration. He is a first generation Asian Indian, having come to the United States as an undergraduate student, and is the author of *Illiberal Education: Politics of Sex and Race on Campus*. D'Souza is a fellow at the American Enterprise Institute (AEI). T.R. Lakshmanan was head of the Bureau of Statistics in the Transportation Department. Arthur Lall (1911- ) has been involved in numerous international negotiations, has written extensively on diplomacy and negotiations, including the 1966 book *Modern International Negotiator*, and has taught at Columbia University. President Bush named Gopal S. Pal a member of the board of regents, Uniformed Services University of the Health Sciences under the U.S. Defense Department. Arati Prabhakar served as research director of the National Institute of Standards and Technology, Department of Commerce. Zach Zachariah of Florida was President Bush's 1992 finance committee chairman in that state, and had the distinction of raising the most funds of any one person in that campaign. Three Asian Indians have won elections as mayors: John Abraham in Teaneck, New Jersey, David Dhillon in El Centro, California; and Bala K. Srinivas in Holliwood Park, Texas.

## JOURNALISM

Pranay Gupte was born in India. He has served as a foreign correspondent for the *New York Times* and is the author of a number of books, including *Vengeance* (1985), which chronicled the years immediately after the assassination of the Indian

Prime Minister Indira Gandhi, and *The Crowded Earth: People and the Politics of Population.*

## LITERATURE

Notable nonfiction writers include Dinesh D'Souza, author of the 1991 best-seller *Illiberal Education: The Politics of Race and Sex on Campus,* and Ravi Batra, an economist whose *The Great Depression of 1990* and *Surviving the Great Depression of 1990* also attained best-seller status. Deepak Chopra, an endocrinologist turned ayurvedic practitioner, has published a series of highly successful books, including *Ageless Body, Timeless Mind: The Quantum Alternative to Growing Old* (1993).

Asian Indian American fiction writers include such figures as Bharati Mukherjee (1940- ), professor of English at Columbia University, who was awarded the National Book Critics Circle Award for *The Middleman and Other Stories* (1988), Gita Mehta, whose works include *Karma Cola: Marketing the Mystic East* (1979) and the novel *A River Sutra* (1993), and Vikram Seth, whose *A Suitable Boy* (1993) has been compared to the works of Austen and Tolstoy. Shashi Tharoor wrote *Reasons of State* (1982) and *The Five-Dollar Smile and Other Stories* (1993) and Anita Desai's *In Custody* (1985) was made into a film in 1994. Folklorist and poet A.K. Ramamijan wrote *Speaking of Siva.* Kirin Narayan is the author of *Love, Stars, and All That* (1994), a novel about Asian Indian experiences in the United States.

Dhan Gopal Mukerji was one of the first Asian Indian Americans to write for children. His works include both animal fantasies like *The Chief of the Herd* (1929) and novels, such as *Gay Neck: The Story of a Pigeon,* which won the Newbery Medal in 1927.

## MUSIC

Zubin Mehta (1936- ), musician and conductor, was born in Bombay, India. He was born in the Zoroastrian faith, the religious minority in India that traces its ancestry to ninth-century Persia. He has served as music director of a number of orchestras, including the Los Angeles Philharmonic, the Israel Philharmonic, and the New York Philharmonic. Most recently, he has been engaged in gala productions with the "three tenors," Luciano Pavarotti, José Carerras, and Plácido Domingo. He has won the New York City Mayor's Liberty Award. Several Indian musicians have established schools in the United States to keep Indian culture alive among young Asian Indians. One such musician is Ali Akbar Khan, a North Indian classical musician who formed a school in California's Bay Area.

## SCIENCE AND TECHNOLOGY

Asian Indians have made numerous advancements in science and technology. The following individuals only represent a small sample. Har Gobind Khorana (1922- ) won the 1968 Nobel Prize in Medicine for the United States. He has held professorships at many distinguished universities worldwide. Vijay Prabhakar practiced medicine for many years with the Indian Health Service, a branch of the U.S. Department of Health and Human Services, which provides health care to Native Americans. He is the recipient of numerous awards, including the Public Service Health Award. Subrahmanyam Chandrasekhar (1910- ), a theoretical astrophysicist, won the 1983 Nobel Prize in Physics. He has also held professorships at many prestigious institutions.

# MEDIA

## ELECTRONIC NEWSGROUPS

The following newsgroups are available on the Internet: The newsgroup alt.india.progressive provides information on events in the United States geared toward promoting ethnic and religious harmony within the Indian community in the United States and in India; the newsgroup soc.culture.indian.info provides information on cultural and social events of interest to Asian Indians; the newsgroup clari.world.asia.india provides up-to-date news on events in India.

## PRINT

*India Abroad.*

This weekly newspaper was first published in 1970, making it the oldest Asian Indian newspaper in the United States. It focuses on news about the community in the United States, on issues and problems unique to the community, and on news from India.

**Contact:** Gopal Raju, Editor and Publisher.
**Address:** 43 West 24th Street, New York, New York 10010.
**Telephone:** (212) 929-1727.

*India Currents.*

This is a monthly newsmagazine focusing on issues of interest to the Asian Indian community.

**Contact:** Arvind Kumar, Editor.

**Address:** P.O. Box 71785, San Jose, California 95151.

**Telephone:** (408) 774-6966.

*News India.*

This weekly newspaper features articles and news on India and the Asian Indian community.

**Contact:** John Perry, Editor.

**Address:** Hannah Worldwide Publishing, 244 Fifth Avenue, New York, New York 10001.

**Telephone:** (212)-481-3110.

**Fax:** (212) 889-5774.

## RADIO

There are many FM and AM radio programs broadcast in Hindi across the United States. In addition, there are some programs that are broadcast in other regional Indian languages like Gujarati, Marathi, or Tamil. Most of these originate in cities with significant Asian Indian populations. Some Hindi radio programs include KEST-AM in San Francisco, California; WSBC-AM in Chicago, Illinois; WEEF-AM in Highland Park, Illinois; WAIF-FM in Cincinnati, Ohio; and KPFT-FM in Houston, Texas.

## TELEVISION

Asian Indian programs are common on cable channels in U.S. cities with large communities like New York, Los Angeles, and Chicago. In addition, TV Asia telecasts news and feature programs of interest to the Indian community nationally on the International Channel.

**Address:** TV Asia, c/o The International Channel, 12401 West Olympic Boulevard, Bethesda, Maryland 20814.

**Telephone:** (310) 826-2426.

# ORGANIZATIONS AND ASSOCIATIONS

A distinction must be made between organizations that base membership upon an encompassing Asian Indian identity and those that are linked more closely to different regions and states within India, such as the Maharashtrian or Tamil organizations in different U.S. states. In addition, religion-based groups like the Sikh or Zoroastrian organizations also exist. The following is a list of organizations that serve all Asian Indians without distinction of religion, language, or region.

**Association of Asian Indians in America (AAIA).**

Serves the larger Asian Indian community in the United States. Promotes Indian cultural events and represents Asian Indian interests in Congress.

**Contact:** Dr. H. Janardhana, President.

**Address:** 300 Clover Street, Rochester, New York 14610.

**Telephone:** (716) 288-3874.

**National Association of Americans of Asian Indian Descent (NAAAID).**

Primary membership is business and professional Asian Indians. Protects and promotes economic, social, and political rights and interests of Asian Indians.

**Address:** 221 Park Avenue, Swarthmore, Pennsylvania 19081.

**Telephone:** (215) 544-0550.

**National Federation of Indian American Associations (NFIAA).**

Represents interests of Asian Indians in the United States and promotes Indian culture and values. Attempts to influence legislation in favor of the community.

**Contact:** Thomas Abraham, Chair.

**Address:** P.O. Box 462, Wakefield Station, Bronx, New York 10466.

**Telephone:** (718) 329-8010.

# SOURCES FOR ADDITIONAL STUDY

*An Immigrant Success Story: East Indians in America,* edited by Arthur Helwig and Usha Helwig. Philadelphia: University of Pennsylvania Press, 1990.

Jensen, Joan. *Passage from India: Asian Indian Immigrants in North America.* Princeton: Yale University Press, 1988.

Leonard, Karen. *Making Ethnic Choices: California's Punjabi Mexican Americans*. Philadelphia: Temple University Press, 1992.

Melendy, H. Brett. *Asians in America: Filipinos, Koreans and East Indians*. Boston: Twayne, 1977.

*The New Ethnics: Asian Indians in the United States*, edited by Parmatma Saran and Edwin Eames. New York: Praeger, 1990.

# Australian and New Zealander Americans

by
Ken Cuthbertson

Australians and New Zealanders in the United States assimilate easily because they are not a large group and they come from advanced, industrialized areas with many similarities to the United States in language, culture, and social structure.

## OVERVIEW

Since immigration statistics usually combine information about New Zealand with that of Australia, and because similarities between the countries are great, they are linked in this essay also. The Commonwealth of Australia, the world's sixth largest nation, lies between the South Pacific and the Indian Ocean. Australia is the only country in the world that is also a continent, and the only continent that lies entirely within the Southern Hemisphere. The name Australia comes from the Latin word *australis*, which means southern. Australia is popularly referred to as "Down Under"—an expression that derives from the country's location entirely below the equator. Off the southeast coast lies the island state of Tasmania; together they form the Commonwealth of Australia. The capital city is Canberra.

Australia covers an area of 2,966,150 square miles—almost as large as the continental United States, excluding Alaska. Unlike the United States, Australia's population in 1994 was 17,800,000; the country is sparsely settled, however, with an average of just six persons per square mile of territory as compared to more than 70 in the United States. This statistic is somewhat misleading, though, because the vast Australian interior—known as the "Outback"—is mostly flat desert or arid grassland with few settlements. A person standing on Ayers Rock, in the middle of the continent, would have to travel at least 1,000 miles in any direction to reach the sea. Australia is very dry. In some parts of the country rain may not fall for years at a time and no rivers run. As a result, most of the country's 17.53 million inhabitants live in a narrow strip along the coast, where there is adequate rainfall. The southeastern coastal region is home to the bulk of this population. Two major cities located there are Sydney, the nation's largest city with more than 3.6 million residents, and Melbourne with 3.1 million. Both cities, like the rest of Australia, have undergone profound demographic change in recent years.

New Zealand, located about 1,200 miles to the southeast of Australia, comprises two main islands, North Island and South Island, the self-governing Cook Island and several dependencies, in addition to several small outlying islands, including Stewart Island, the Chatham Islands, Auckland Islands, Kermadec Islands, Campbell Island, the Antipodes, Three Kings Island, Bounty Island, Snares Island, and Solander Island. New Zealand's population was estimated at 3,524,800 in 1994. Excluding its dependencies, the country occupies an area of 103,884 square miles, about the size of Colorado, and has a population density of 33.9 per square mile. New Zealand's geographical features vary from the Southern Alps and fjords on South Island to the volcanoes, hot springs, and geysers on North Island. Because the outlying islands are scattered widely, they vary in climate from tropical to the antarctic.

The immigrant population of Australia and New Zealand is predominantly English, Irish, and Scottish in background. According to the 1947 Australian census, more than 90 percent of the population, excluding the Aboriginal native people, was native-born. That was the highest level since the beginning of European settlement 159 earlier, at which time almost 98 percent of the population had been born in Australia, the United Kingdom, Ireland, or New Zealand. Australia's annual birth rate stands at just 15 per 1,000 of population, New Zealand at 17 per 1,000. These low numbers, quite similar to U.S. rates, have contributed only nominally to their population, which has jumped by about three million since 1980. Most of this increase has come about because of changes in immigration policies. Restrictions based on a would-be immigrant's country of origin and color were ended in Australia in 1973 and the government initiated plans to attract non-British groups as well as refugees. As a result, Australia's ethnic and linguistic mix has become relatively diversified over the last two decades. This has had an impact on virtually every aspect of Australian life and culture. According to the latest census data, the Australian and British-born population has dropped to about 84 percent. Far more people apply to enter Australia each year than are accepted as immigrants.

Australia enjoys one of the world's highest standards of living; its per capita income of more than $16,700 (United States) is among the world's highest. New Zealand's per capita income is $12,600, compared with the United States at $21,800, Canada at $19,500, India at $350, and Vietnam at $230. Similarly, the average life expectancy at birth, 73 for an Australian male and 80 for a female, are comparable to the U.S. figures at 72 and 79, respectively.

## HISTORY

Australia's first inhabitants were dark-skinned nomadic hunters who arrived around 35,000 B.C. Anthropologists believe these Aborigines came from Southeast Asia by crossing a land bridge that existed at the time. Their Stone Age culture remained largely unchanged for thousands of generations, until the coming of European explorers and traders. There is some evidence that Chinese mariners visited the north coast of Australia, near the present site of the city of Darwin as early as the fourteenth century. However, their impact was minimal. European exploration began in 1606, when a Dutch explorer named Willem Jansz sailed into the Gulf of Carpentaria. During the next 30 years, Dutch navigators charted much of the northern and western coastline of what they called New Holland. The Dutch did not colonize Australia, thus in 1770 when the British explorer Captain James Cook landed at Botany Bay, near the site of the present city of Sydney, he claimed the whole of the east coast of Australia for Britain, naming it New South Wales. In 1642, the Dutch navigator, A. J. Tasman, reached New Zealand where Polynesian Maoris were inhabitants. Between 1769 and 1777, Captain James Cook visited the island four times, making several unsuccessful attempts at colonization. Interestingly, among Cook's crew were several Americans from the 13 colonies; the American connection with Australia did not end there.

It was the 1776 American Revolution half a world away that proved to be the impetus for large-scale British colonization of Australia. The government in London had been "transporting" petty criminals from its overcrowded jails to the North American colonies. When the American colonies seized their independence, it became necessary to find an alternate destination for this human cargo. Botany Bay seemed the ideal site: it was 14,000 miles from England, uncolonized by other European powers, enjoyed a favorable climate, and it was strategically located to help provide security for Great Britain's long-distance shipping lines to economically vital interests in India.

"English lawmakers wished not only to get rid of the 'criminal class' but if possible to forget about it," wrote the late Robert Hughes, an Australian-born art critic for *Time* magazine, in his popular 1987 book, *The Fatal Shore: A History of Transportation of Convicts to Australia, 1787-1868*. To further both of these aims, in 1787 the British government dispatched a fleet of 11 ships under the command of Captain Arthur Phillip to establish a penal colony at Botany Bay. Phillip landed January 26, 1788, with about 1,000 settlers, more than half of whom were convicts; males outnumbered females nearly three to one. Over the 80 years until the practice officially ended in 1868, England transported more than 160,000 men, women, and children to Australia. In Hughes' words, this was the "largest forced exile of citizens at the behest of a European government in premodern history."

In the beginning, most of the people exiled to Australia from Great Britain were conspicuously unfit for survival in their new home. To the Aborigines who encountered these strange white people, it must have seemed that they lived on the edge of starvation in the midst of plenty. The relationship between the colonists and the estimated 300,000 indigenous people who are thought to have inhabited Australia in the 1780s was marked by mutual misunderstanding at the best of times, and outright hostility the rest of the time. It was mainly because of the vastness of the arid Outback that Australia's Aboriginal people were able to find refuge from the bloody "pacification by force," which was practiced by many whites in the mid-nineteenth century.

Australia's population today includes about 210,000 Aboriginal people, many of whom are of mixed white ancestry; approximately a quarter of a million Maori descendants currently reside in New Zealand. In 1840, the New Zealand Company established the first permanent settlement there. A treaty granted the Maoris possession of their land in exchange for their recognition of the sovereignty of the British crown; it was made a separate colony the following year and was granted self-governance ten years later. This did not stop white settlers from battling the Maoris over land.

Aborigines survived for thousands of years by living a simple, nomadic lifestyle. Not surprisingly the conflict between traditional Aboriginal values and those of the predominant white, urbanized, industrialized majority has been disastrous. In the 1920s and early 1930s, recognizing the need to protect what remained of the native population, the Australian government established a series of Aboriginal land reserves. Well-intentioned though the plan may have been, critics now charge that the net effect of establishing reservations has been to segregate and "ghettoize" Aboriginal people rather than to preserve their traditional culture and way of life. Statistics seem to bear this out, for Australia's native population has shrunk to about 50,000 full-blooded Aborigines and about 160,000 with mixed blood.

Many Aborigines today live in traditional communities on the reservations that have been set up in rural areas of the country, but a growing number of young people have moved into the cities. The results have been traumatic: poverty, cultural dislocation, dispossession, and disease have taken a deadly toll. Many of the Aboriginal people in cities live in substandard housing and lack adequate health care. The unemployment rate among Aborigines is six times the national average, while those who are fortunate enough to have jobs earn only about half the average national wage. The results have been predictable: alienation, racial tensions, poverty, and unemployment.

While Australia's native people suffered with the arrival of colonists, the white population grew slowly and steadily as more and more people arrived from the United Kingdom. By the late 1850s, six separate British colonies (some of which were founded by "free" settlers), had taken root on the island continent. While there still were only about 400,000 white settlers, there were an estimated 13 million sheep—*jumbucks* as they are known in Australian slang, for it had quickly become apparent that the country was well suited to production of wool and mutton.

## MODERN ERA

On January 1, 1901, the new Commonwealth of Australia was proclaimed in Sydney. New Zealand joined the six other colonies of the Commonwealth of Australia: New South Wales in 1786; Tasmania, then Van Diemen's Land, in 1825; Western Australia in 1829; South Australia in 1834; Victoria in 1851; and Queensland. The six former colonies, now refashioned as states united in a political federation that can best be described as a cross between the British and American political systems. Each state has its own legislature, head of government, and courts, but the federal government is ruled by an elected prime minister, who is the leader of the party that wins the most seats in any general election. As is the case in the United States, Australia's federal government consists of a bicameral legislature—a 72-member Senate and a 145-member House of Representatives. However, there are some important differences between the Australian and American systems of government. For one thing, there is no separation of legislative and executive powers in Australia. For another, if the governing party loses a "vote of confidence" in the Australian legislature, the prime minister is obliged to call a general election.

King George V of England was on hand to formally open the new federal parliament at Melbourne (the national capital was moved in 1927 to a planned city called Canberra, which was designed by American architect Walter Burley Griffin). That same year, 1901, saw the passage by the new Australian parliament of the restrictive immigration law that effectively barred most Asians and other "colored" people from entering the country and ensured that Australia would remain predominantly white for the next 72 years. Ironically, despite its discriminatory immigration policy, Australia proved to be progressive in at least one important regard: women were granted the vote in 1902, a full 18 years before their sisters in the United States. Similarly, Australia's organized labor movement took advantage of its ethnic solidarity and a shortage of workers to press for and win a range of social welfare benefits several decades before workers in England, Europe, or North America. To this day, organized labor is a powerful force in Australian society, far more so than is the case in the United States.

In the beginning, Australians mainly looked west to London for commerce, defense, political, and cultural guidance. This was inevitable given that the majority of immigrants continued to come from Britain; Australian society has always had a distinctly British flavor. With Britain's decline as a world power in the years following World War I, Australia drew ever closer to the United States. As Pacific-rim neighbors with a common cultural ancestry, it was inevitable that trade between Australia and the United States would expand as transportation technology improved. Despite ongoing squabbles over tariffs and foreign policy matters, American books, magazines, movies, cars, and other consumer goods began to flood the Australian market in the 1920s. To the dismay of Australian nationalists, one spinoff of this trend was an acceleration of the "Americanization of Australia." This process was slowed only somewhat by the hardships of the Great Depression of the 1930s, when unemployment soared in both countries. It accelerated again when Britain granted former colonies such as Australia and Canada full control over their own external affairs in 1937 and Washington and Canberra moved to establish formal diplomatic relations.

As a member of the British Commonwealth, Australia and America became wartime allies after the Japanese attack on Pearl Harbor. Most Australians felt that with Great Britain reeling, America offered the only hope of fending off Japanese invasion. Australia became the main American supply base in the Pacific war, and about one million American G.I.s were stationed there or visited the country in the years 1942 to 1945. As a nation considered vital to U.S. defense, Australia was also included in the lend-lease program, which made available vast quantities of American supplies with the condition that they be returned after the war. Washington policymakers envisioned that this wartime aid to Australia also would pay huge dividends through increased trade between the two countries. The strategy worked; relations between the two nations were never closer. By 1944, the United States enjoyed a huge balance of payments surplus with Australia. Almost 40 percent of that country's imports came from the United States, while just 25 percent of exports went to the United States. With the end of the war in the Pacific, however, old antagonisms resurfaced. A primary cause of friction was trade; Australia clung to its imperial past by resisting American pressure for an end to the discriminatory tariff policies that favored its traditional Commonwealth trading partners. Nonetheless, the war changed the country in some fundamental and profound ways. For one, Australia was no longer content to allow Britain to dictate its foreign policy. Thus when the establishment of the United Nations was discussed at the San Francisco Conference in 1945, Australia rejected its former role as a small power and insisted on "middle power" status.

In recognition of this new reality, Washington and Canberra established full diplomatic relations in 1946 by exchanging ambassadors. Meanwhile, at home Australians began coming to grips with their new place in the post-war world. A heated political debate erupted over the future direction of the country and the extent to which foreign corporations should be allowed to invest in the Australian economy. While a vocal segment of public opinion expressed fear of becoming too closely aligned with the United States, the onset of the Cold War dictated otherwise. Australia had a vested interest in becoming a partner in American efforts to stem the spread of communism in Southeast Asia, which lies just off the country's northern doorstep. As a result, in September 1951 Australia joined the United States and New Zealand in the ANZUS defense treaty. Three years later, in September 1954, the same nations became partners with Britain, France, Pakistan, the Philippines, and Thailand in the Southeast Asia Treaty Organization (SEATO), a mutual defense organization which endured until 1975.

From the mid-1960s onward, both of Australia's major political parties, Labor and Liberal, have supported an end to discriminatory immigration policies. Changes to these policies have had the effect of turning Australia into something of a Eurasian melting pot; 32 percent of immigrants now come from less-developed Asian countries. In addition, many former residents of neighboring Hong Kong have begun relocating to Australia along with their families and their wealth in anticipation of the 1997 reversion of the British Crown colony to Chinese control.

It comes as no surprise that demographic diversification has brought with it changes in Australia's economy and traditional patterns of international trade. An ever-increasing percentage of this commerce is with the booming Pacific-rim nations such as Japan, China, and Korea. The United States still ranks as Australia's second largest trading partner—although Australia no longer ranks among America's top 25 trading partners. Even so, Australian American relations remain friendly, and American culture exerts a profound impact on life Down Under.

## THE FIRST AUSTRALIANS AND NEW ZEALANDERS IN AMERICA

Although Australians and New Zealanders have a recorded presence of almost 200 years on American soil, they have contributed minimally to the total immigration figures in the United States. The 1970 U.S. Census counted 82,000 Australian Americans and New Zealander Americans, which represents about 0.25 percent of all ethnic groups. In 1970, less than 2,700 immigrants from Australia and New Zealand entered the United States—only 0.7 percent of the total American immigration for that year. Data compiled by the U.S. Immigration and Naturalization Service indicates that about 64,000 Australians came to the United States in the 70 years from 1820 to 1890—an average of just slightly more than 900 per year. The reality is that Australia and New Zealand have always been places where more people move to rather than leave. While there is no way of knowing for certain, history suggests that most of those who have left the two countries for America over the years have done so not as political or economic refugees, but rather for personal or philosophical reasons.

Evidence is scarce, but what there is indicates that beginning in the mid-nineteenth century, most Australians and New Zealanders who immigrated to America settled in and around San Francisco, and to a lesser extent Los Angeles, those cities being two of the main west coast ports of entry. (It is important to remember, however, that until 1848 California was not part of the United States.) Apart from their peculiar clipped accents, which have always sounded vaguely British to undiscerning North American ears, Australians and New Zealanders have found it easier to fit into American society than into British society, where class divisions are much more rigid and as often as not anyone from "the colonies" is regarded as a provincial philistine.

## PATTERNS OF IMMIGRATION

There is a long, albeit spotty, history of relations between Australia and New Zealand and the United States, one that stretches back to the very beginnings of British exploration. But it was really the California gold rush in January 1848 and a series of gold strikes in Australia in the early 1850s that opened the door to a large-scale flow of goods and people between the two countries. News of gold strikes in California was greeted with enthusiasm in Australia and New Zealand, where groups of would-be prospectors got together to charter ships to take them on the 8,000-mile voyage to America.

Thousands of Australians and New Zealanders set off on the month-long transpacific voyage; among them were many of the ex-convicts who had been deported from Great Britain to the colony of Australia. Called "Sydney Ducks," these fearsome immigrants introduced organized crime into the area and caused the California legislature to try to prohibit the entry of ex-convicts. Gold was but the initial attraction; many of those who left were seduced upon their arrival in California by what they saw as liberal land ownership laws and by the limitless economic prospects of life in America. From August 1850 through May 1851, more than 800 Aussies sailed out of Sydney harbor bound for California; most of them made new lives for themselves in America and were never to return home. On March 1, 1851, a writer for the *Sydney Morning Herald* decried this exodus, which had consisted of "persons of a better class, who have been industrious and thrifty, and who carry with them the means of settling down in a new world as respectable and substantial settlers."

When the Civil War raged in America from 1861 to 1865, immigration to the United States all but dried up; statistics show that from January 1861 to June 1870 just 36 Australians and New Zealanders made the move across the Pacific. This situation changed in the late 1870s when the American economy expanded following the end of the Civil War, and American trade increased as regular steamship service was inaugurated between Melbourne and Sydney and ports on the U.S. west coast. Interestingly, though, the better the economic conditions were at home, the more likely Australians and New Zealanders seem to have been to pack up and go. When times were tough, they tended to stay home, at least in the days before transpacific air travel. Thus, in the years between 1871 and 1880 when conditions were favorable at home, a total of 9,886 Australians immigrated to the United States. During the next two decades, as the world economy faltered, those numbers fell by half. This pattern continued into the next century.

Entry statistics show that, prior to World War I, the vast majority of Australians and New Zealanders who came to America did so as visitors en route to England. The standard itinerary for travelers was to sail to San Francisco and see America while journeying by rail to New York. From there, they sailed on to London. But such a trip was tremendously expensive and although it was several weeks shorter than the mind-numbing 14,000-mile ocean voyage to London, it was still difficult and time-consuming. Thus only well-to-do travelers could afford it.

The nature of relations between Australians and New Zealanders with America changed dramatically with the 1941 outbreak of war with Japan. Immigration to the United States, which had dwindled to about 2,400 persons during the lean years of the 1930s, jumped dramatically in the boom years after the war. This was largely due to two important factors: a rapidly expanding U.S. economy, and the exodus of 15,000 Australian war brides who married U.S. servicemen who had been stationed in Australia during the war.

Statistics indicate that from 1971 to 1990 more than 86,400 Australians and New Zealanders arrived in the United States as immigrants. With few exceptions, the number of people leaving for the United States grew steadily in the years between 1960 and 1990. On average, about 3,700 emigrated annually during that 30-year period. Data from the 1990 U.S. Census, however, indicates that just over 52,000 Americans reported having Australian or New Zealander ancestry, which represents less than 0.05 percent of the U.S. population and ranks them ninety-seventh among ethnic groups residing in the United States. It is unclear whether all of those 34,400 missing persons returned home, migrated elsewhere, or simply did not bother to report their ethnic origin. One possibility, which seems to be borne out by Australian and New Zealander government statistics, is that many of those who have left those countries for the United States have been people born elsewhere—that is, immigrants who moved on when they did not find life in Australia or New Zealand to their liking. In 1991, for example, 29,000 Australians left the country permanently; 15,870 of that number were "former settlers," meaning that the rest were presumably native-born. Some members of both groups almost certainly came to the United States, but it is impossible to say how many because of the dearth of reliable data on Australian and New Zealander immigrants in the United States, where they live or work, or what kind of lifestyles they lead.

What is apparent from the numbers is that for whatever reason the earlier pattern of staying in their homeland during hard times has been reversed; now whenever the economy slumps, more individuals are apt to depart for America in search of what they hope are greener pastures. During the 1960s, just over 25,000 immigrants from Australia and New Zealand arrived in the United States; that figure jumped to more than 40,000 during the 1970s, and more than 45,000 during the 1980s. In the late 1980s and early 1990s a deep worldwide recession hit the resource-based economies of Australia and New Zealand hard, resulting in high unemployment and hardship, yet immigration to the United States remained steady at about 4,400 per year. In 1990, that number jumped to 6,800 and the following year to more than 7,000. By 1992, with conditions improving at home, the number dropped to about 6,000. Although U.S. Immigration and Naturalization service data for the period does not offer a gender or age breakdown, it does indicate that the largest group of immigrants (1,174 persons) consisted of homemakers, students, and unemployed or retired persons.

## SETTLEMENT PATTERNS

About all that can be said for certain is that Los Angeles has become the favorite port of entry into the country. Laurie Pane, president of the 22-chapter Los Angeles-based Australian American Chambers of Commerce (AACC), suspects that as many as 15,000 former Australians live in and around Los Angeles. Pane surmises that there may be more Australians living in the United States than statistics indicate, though: "Australians are scattered everywhere across the country. They're not the sort of people to register and stay put. Australians aren't real joiners, and that can be a problem for an organization like the AACC. But they're convivial. You throw a party, and Australians will be there."

Pane's conclusions are shared by other business people, academics, and journalists involved with the Australian or New Zealander American community. Jill Biddington, executive director of the Australia Society, a New York-based Australian American friendship organization with 400 members in New York, New Jersey, and Connecticut notes that without reliable data, she can only guess that the majority live in California because it is similar to their homeland in terms of lifestyle and climate.

Dr. Henry Albinski, director of the Australia-New Zealand studies center at Pennsylvania State University, theorizes that because their numbers are few and scattered, and because they are neither poor nor rich, nor have they had to struggle, they simply do not stand out—"there aren't stereotypes at either end of the spectrum." Similarly, Neil Brandon, editor of a biweekly newsletter for Australians, *The Word from Down Under,* says he has seen "unofficial" estimates that place the total number of Australians in the United States at about 120,000. "A lot of Australians don't show up in any legitimate census data," says Brandon. Although he has only been publishing his newsletter since the fall of 1993 and has about 1,000 subscribers all across the country, he has a firm sense of where his target audience is concentrated. "Most Aussies in the U.S. live in the Los Angeles area, or southern California," he says. "There are also fair numbers living in New York City, Seattle, Denver, Houston, Dallas-Forth Worth, Florida, and Hawaii. Australians aren't a tightly knit community. We seem to dissolve into American society."

According to Harvard professor Ross Terrill, Australians and New Zealanders have a great deal in common with Americans when it comes to outlook and temperament; both are easy going and casual in their relationships with others. Like Americans, they are firm believers in their right to the pursuit of individual liberty. He writes that Australians "have an anti-authoritarian streak that seems to echo the contempt of the convict for his keepers and betters." In addition to thinking like Americans, Australians and New Zealanders do not look out of place in most American cities. The vast majority who immigrate are Caucasian, and apart from their accents, there is no way of picking them out of a crowd. They tend to blend in and adapt easily to the American lifestyle, which in America's urban areas is not all that different from life in their homeland.

# ACCULTURATION AND ASSIMILATION

Australians and New Zealanders in the United States assimilate easily because they are not a large group and they come from advanced, industrialized areas with many similarities to the United States in language, culture, and social structure. Data about them, however, must be extrapolated from demographic information compiled by the Australian and New Zealander governments. Indications are that they live a lifestyle strikingly similar to that of many Americans and it seems reasonable to assume that they continue to live much as they always have. Data show that the average age of the population—like that of the United States and most other industrialized nations—is growing older, with the median age in 1992 at about 32 years.

Also, there has been a dramatic increase in recent years in the number of single-person and two-person households. In 1991, 20 percent of Australian households had just one person, and 31 percent had but two. These numbers are a reflection of the fact that Australians are more mobile than ever before; young people leave home at an earlier age, and the divorce rate now stands at 37 percent, meaning that 37 of every 100 marriages end in divorce within 30 years. While this may seem alarmingly high, it lags far behind the U.S. divorce rate, which is the world's highest at 54.8 percent. Australians and New Zealanders tend to be conservative socially. As a result, their society still tends to be male-dominated; a working father, stay-at-home mother, and one or two children remains a powerful cultural image.

## TRADITIONS, CUSTOMS, AND BELIEFS

Australian historian Russell Ward sketched an image of the archetypal Aussie in a 1958 book entitled *The Australian Legend.* Ward noted that while Aussies have a reputation as a hard-living, rebellious, and gregarious people, the reality is that, "Far from being the weather-beaten bushmen of popular imagination, today's Australian belongs to the most urbanized big country on earth." That statement is even more true today than it was when it was written almost 40 years ago. But even so, in the collective American mind, at least, the old image persists. In fact, it was given a renewed boost by the 1986 movie *Crocodile Dundee*, which starred Australian actor Paul Hogan as a wily bushman who visits New York with hilarious consequences.

Apart from Hogan's likeable persona, much of the fun in the film stemmed from the juxtaposition of American and Aussie cultures. Discussing the popularity of *Crocodile Dundee* in the *Journal of Popular Culture* (Spring 1990), authors Ruth Abbey and Jo Crawford noted that to American eyes Paul Hogan was Australian "through and through." What is more, the character he played resonated with echoes of Davy Crockett, the fabled American woodsman. This meshed comfortably with the prevailing view that Australia is a latter-day version of what American once was: a simpler, more honest and open society. It was no accident that the Australian tourism industry actively promoted *Crocodile Dundee* in the United States. These efforts paid off handsomely, for American tourism jumped dramatically in the late 1980s, and Australian culture enjoyed an unprecedented popularity in North America.

## INTERACTIONS WITH OTHER ETHNIC GROUPS

Australian and New Zealander society from the beginning has been characterized by a high degree of racial and ethnic homogeneity. This was mainly due to the fact that settlement was almost exclusively by the British, and restrictive laws for much of the twentieth century limited the number of non-white immigrants. Initially, Aboriginals were the first target of this hostility. Later, as other ethnic groups arrived, the focus of Australian racism shifted. Chinese goldminers were subject to violence and attacks in the mid-nineteenth century, the 1861 Lambing Riots being the best known example. Despite changes in the country's immigration laws that have allowed millions of non-whites into the country in recent years, an undercurrent of racism continues to exist. Racial tensions have increased. Most of the white hostility has been directed at Asians and other visible minorities, who are viewed by some groups as a threat to the traditional Australian way of life.

There is virtually no literature or documentation on the interaction between Australians and other ethnic immigrant groups in the United States. Nor is there any history of the relationship between Aussies and their American hosts. This is not surprising, given the scattered nature of the Australian presence here and the ease with which Aussies have been absorbed into American society.

## CUISINE

It has been said that the emergence of a distinctive culinary style in recent years has been an unexpected (and much welcomed) byproduct of a growing sense of nationalism as the country moved away from Britain and forged its own identity—largely a result of the influence of the vast number of immigrants who have come into the country since immigration restrictions were eased in 1973. But even so, Australians and New Zealanders continue to be big meat eaters. Beef, lamb, and seafood are standard fare, often in the form of meat pies, or smothered in heavy sauces. If there is a definitive Australian meal, it would be a barbecue grilled steak or lamb chop.

Two dietary staples from earlier times are *damper,* an unleavened type of bread that is cooked over a fire, and *billy* tea, a strong, robust hot drink that is brewed in an open pot. For dessert, traditional favorites include peach melba, fruit-flavored ice creams, and *pavola,* a rich meringue dish that was named after a famous Russian ballerina who toured the country in the early twentieth century.

Rum was the preferred form of alcohol in colonial times. However, tastes have changed; wine and beer are popular nowadays. Australia began developing its own domestic wine industry in the early nineteenth century, and wines from Down Under today are recognized as being among the world's best. As such, they are readily available at liquor stores throughout the United States, and are a tasty reminder of life back home for transplanted Aussies. On a per capita basis, Aussies drink about twice as much wine each year as do Americans. Australians also enjoy their ice cold beer, which tends to be stronger and darker than most American brews. In recent years, Australian beer has earned a small share of the American market, in part no doubt because of demand from Aussies living in the United States.

## TRADITIONAL COSTUMES

Unlike many ethnic groups, Australians do not have any unusual or distinctive national costumes. One of the few distinctive pieces of clothing worn by Australians is the wide-brimmed khaki bush hat with the brim on one side turned up. The hat, which has sometimes been worn by Australian soldiers, has become something of a national symbol.

## AUSTRALIAN DANCES AND SONGS

When most Americans think of Australian music, the first tune that springs to mind tends to be "Waltzing Matilda." But Australia's musical heritage is long, rich, and varied. Their isolation from western cultural centers such as London and New York has resulted, particularly in music and film, in a vibrant and highly original commercial style.

The traditional music of white Australia, which has its roots in Irish folk music, and "bush dancing," which has been described as similar to square-dancing without a caller, are also popular. In recent years, home-grown pop vocalists such as Helen Reddy, Olivia Newton-John (English-born but raised in Australia), and opera diva Joan Sutherland have found receptive audiences around the world. The same holds true for Australian rock and roll bands such as INXS, Little River Band, Hunters and Collectors, Midnight Oil, and Men Without Hats. Other Australian bands such as Yothu Yindi and Warumpi, which are not yet well known outside the country, have been revitalizing the genre with a unique fusion of mainstream rock and roll and elements of the timeless music of Australia's Aboriginal peoples.

## HOLIDAYS

Being predominantly Christian, Australian Americans and New Zealander Americans celebrate most of the same religious holidays that other Americans do. However, because the seasons are reversed in the Southern Hemisphere, Australia's Christmas occurs in midsummer. For that reason, Aussies do not share in many of the same yuletide traditions that Americans keep. After church, Australians typically spend December 25 at the beach or gather around a swimming pool, sipping cold drinks.

Secular holidays that Australians everywhere celebrate include January 26, Australia Day—the country's national holiday. The date, which commemorates the 1788 arrival at Botany Bay of the first convict settlers under the command of Captain Arthur Phillip, is akin to America's Fourth of July holiday. Another important holiday is Anzac Day, April 25. On this day, Aussies everywhere pause to honor the memory of the nation's soldiers who died in the World War I battle at Gallipoli.

# LANGUAGE

English is spoken in Australia and New Zealand. In 1966, an Australian named Afferbeck Lauder published a tongue-in-cheek book entitled, *Let Stalk Strine*, which actually means, "Let's Talk Australian" ("Strine" being the telescoped form of the word Australian). Lauder, it later turned out, was discovered to be Alistair Morrison, an artist-turned-linguist who was poking good-natured fun at his fellow Australians and their accents— accents that make lady sound like "lydy" and mate like "mite."

On a more serious level, real-life linguist Sidney Baker in his 1970 book *The Australian Language* did what H. L. Mencken did for American English; he identified more than 5,000 words or phrases that were distinctly Australian.

## POPULAR EXPRESSIONS

A few words and expressions that are distinctively "Strine" are: *abo*—an Aborigine; *ace*—excellent; *billabong*—a watering hole, usually for livestock; *billy*—a container for boiling water for tea; *bloke*—a man, everybody is a bloke; *bloody*—the all-purpose adjective of emphasis; *bonzer*—great, terrific; *boomer*—a kangaroo; *boomerang*—an Aboriginal curved wooden weapon or toy that returns when thrown into the air; *bush*—the Outback; *chook*—a chicken; *digger*—an Aussie soldier; *dingo*—a wild dog; *dinki-di*—the real thing; *dinkum, fair dinkum*—honest, genuine; *grazier*—a rancher; *joey*—a baby kangaroo; *jumbuck*—a sheep; *ocker*—a good, ordinary Aussie; *Outback*—the Australian interior; *Oz*—short for Australia; *pom*—an English person; *shout*—a round of drinks in a pub; *swagman*—a hobo or bushman; *tinny*—a can of beer; *tucker*—food; *ute*—a pickup or utility truck; *whinge*—to complain.

# FAMILY AND COMMUNITY DYNAMICS

Again, information about Australian or New Zealander Americans must be extrapolated from what is known about the people who reside in Australia and New Zealand. They are an informal, avid outdoor people with a hearty appetite for life and sports. With a temperate climate all year round, outdoor sports such as tennis, cricket, rugby, Australian-rules football, golf, swimming, and sailing are popular both with spectators and participants. However, the grand national pastimes are somewhat less strenuous: barbecuing and sun worshipping. In fact, Australians spend so much time in the sun in their backyards and at the beach that the country has the world's highest rate of skin cancer. Although Australian and New Zealander families have traditionally been headed by a male breadwinner with the female in a domestic role, changes are occurring.

# RELIGION

Australian Americans and New Zealander Americans are predominantly Christian. Statistics suggests that Australian society is increasingly secular, with one person in four having no religion (or failing to respond to the question when polled by census takers). However, the majority of Australians are affiliated with two major religious groups: 26.1 percent are Roman Catholic, while 23.9 percent are Anglican, or Episcopalian. Only about two percent of Australians are non-Christian, with Muslims, Buddhists, and Jews comprising the bulk of that segment. Given these numbers, it is reasonable to assume that for those Australian emigrants to the United States who are churchgoers, a substantial majority are almost certainly adherents to the Episcopalian or Roman

Catholic churches, both of which are active in the United States.

# EMPLOYMENT AND ECONOMIC TRADITIONS

It is impossible to describe a type of work or location of work that characterizes Australian Americans or New Zealander Americans. Because they have been and remain so widely scattered throughout the United States and so easily assimilated into American society, they have never established an identifiable ethnic presence in the United States. Unlike immigrants from more readily identifiable ethnic groups, they have not established ethnic communities, nor have they maintained a separate language and culture. Largely due to that fact, they have not adopted characteristic types of work, followed similar paths of economic development, political activism, or government involvement; they have not been an identifiable segment of the U.S. military; and they have not been identified as having any health or medical problems specific to Australian Americans or New Zealander Americans. Their similarity in most respects to other Americans has made them unidentifiable and virtually invisible in these areas of American life. The one place the Australian community is flourishing is on the information superhighway. There are Australian groups on several online services such as CompuServe (PAC-FORUM). They also come together over sporting events, such as the Australian rules football grand final, the rugby league grand final, or the Melbourne Cup horse race, which can now be seen live on cable television or via satellite.

# POLITICS AND GOVERNMENT

There is no history of relations between Australians or New Zealanders in the United States with the Australian or New Zealand governments. Unlike many other foreign governments, they have ignored their former nationals living overseas. Those who are familiar with the situation, say there is evidence that this policy of benign neglect has begun to change. Various cultural organizations and commercial associations sponsored directly or indirectly by the government are now working to encourage Australian

Americans and American business representatives to lobby state and federal politicians to be more favorably disposed toward Australia. As yet, there is no literature or documentation on this development.

# INDIVIDUAL AND GROUP CONTRIBUTIONS

### ENTERTAINMENT

Paul Hogan, Rod Taylor (movie actors); Peter Weir (movie director); Olivia Newton-John, Helen Reddy, Rick Springfield, (singers).

### MEDIA

Rupert Murdoch, one of America's most powerful media magnates, is Australian-born; Murdoch owns a host of important media properties, including the *Chicago Sun Times*, *New York Post*, and the *Boston Herald* newspapers, and 20th Century-Fox movie studios.

### SPORTS

Greg Norman (golf); Jack Brabham, Alan Jones (motor car racing); Kieren Perkins (swimming); Pat Cash, Evonne Goolagong, Rod Laver, John Newcombe (tennis).

### WRITERS

Germaine Greer (feminist); Thomas Keneally (novelist, winner of the 1983 Booker Prize for his book *Schindler's Ark*, which was the basis for Stephen Spielberg's 1993 Oscar winning film *Schindler's List*), Patrick White (novelist, and winner of the 1973 Nobel Prize for Literature).

# MEDIA

### PRINT

*The Word from Down Under: The Australian Newsletter.*
Address: P.O. Box 5434, Balboa Island, California 92660.
Telephone: (714) 725-0063.
Fax: (714) 725-0060.

### RADIO

**KIEV-AM (870).**
Located in Los Angeles, this a weekly program called "Queensland" is aimed mainly at Aussies from that state.

# ORGANIZATIONS AND ASSOCIATIONS

There are a number of organizations and associations in the United States that serve Australian Americans and New Zealander Americans in this country.

**Australia-New Zealand Study Center.**
Established in 1982, the organization establishes exchange programs for undergraduate students, promotes the teaching of Australian-New Zealand subject matter at Pennsylvania State University, seeks to attract Australian and New Zealand scholars to the university, and assists with travel expenses of Australian graduate students studying there.

Contact: Dr. Henry Albinski, Director.
Address: 161 North Burrowes Building, University Park, Pennsylvania, 16802-6200.
Telephone: (814) 863-1591.
Fax: (814) 865-3336.

**Australia Society.**
This is primarily a social and cultural organization that fosters closer ties between Australia and the United States. It has 400 members, primarily in New York, New Jersey, and Connecticut.

Contact: Jill Biddington, Executive Director.
Address: 630 Fifth Avenue, Fourth Floor, New York, New York 10111.
Telephone: (212) 265-3270.
Fax: (212) 265-3519.

**Australian American Association.**
This organization encourages closer ties between the United States and Australia.

Contact: Peter M. St. Germain, Treasurer.
Address: 1251 Avenue of the Americas, New York, New York 10020.
Telephone: (212) 703-7250.
Fax: (212) 703-4790.

**Australian American Chamber of Commerce.**
With 22 chapters around the country, the organization promotes business, cultural, and social relations between the United States and Australia.

**Contact:** Mr. Laurie Pane, President.
**Address:** 611 Larchmont Boulevard, Second Floor, Los Angeles, California 90004.
**Telephone:** (213) 469-6316.
**Fax:** (213) 469-6419.

**Australian-New Zealand Society of New York.**
Seeks to expand educational and cultural beliefs.

**Contact:** Eunice G. Grimaldi, President.
**Address:** 51 East 42nd Street, Room 616, New York, New York 10017.
**Telephone:** (212) 972-6880.

**Australian Studies Association of North America.**
This academic association promotes teaching about Australia and the scholarly investigation of Australian topics and issues throughout institutions of higher education in North America. Internet E-mail: Hudzik@ssc.msu.cdu.au.

**Contact:** Dr. John Hudzik, Associate Dean.
**Address:** College of Social Sciences, Michigan State University, 203 Berkey Hall, East Lansing, Michigan. 48824.
**Telephone:** (517) 353-9019.
**Fax:** (517) 355-1912.

**Edward A. Clark Center for Australian Studies.**
Established in 1988, this center was named after a former U.S. Ambassador to Australia from 1967 to 1968; it conducts teaching programs, research projects, and international outreach activities that focus on Australian matters and on U.S.-Australia relations.

**Contact:** Dr. John Higley, Director.
**Address:** Harry Ransom Center 3.362, University of Texas, Austin, Texas 78713-7219.
**Telephone:** (512) 471-9607.
**Fax:** (512) 471-8869.

**Melbourne University Alumni Association of North America.**
This association is primarily a social and fund raising organization for graduates of Melbourne University.

**Contact:** Mr. William G. O'Reilly.
**Address:** 106 High Street, New York, New York 10706.

**Sydney University Graduates Union of North America.**
This is a social and fund raising organization for graduates of Sydney University.

**Contact:** Dr. Bill Lew.
**Address:** 3131 Southwest Fairmont Boulevard, Portland, Oregon. 97201.
**Telephone:** (503) 245-6064
**Fax:** (503) 245-6040.

# SOURCES FOR ADDITIONAL STUDY

Arnold, Caroline. *Australia Today*. New York: Franklin Watts, 1987.

*Australia*, edited by George Constable, et al. New York: Time-Life Books, 1985.

*Australia*, edited by Robin E. Smith. Canberra: Australian Government Printing Service, 1992.

*Australians in America: 1876-1976*, edited by John Hammond Moore. Brisbane: University of Queensland Press, 1977.

Bateson, Charles. *Gold Fleet for California: Forty-Niners from Australia and New Zealand*. [Sydney], 1963.

Forster, John. *Social Process in New Zealand*. Revised edition, 1970.

Hughes, Robert. *The Fatal Shore: A History of The Transportation of Convicts to Australia, 1787-1868*. New York: Alfred Knopf, 1987.

# AUSTRIAN AMERICANS

by
Syd Jones

During the years 1901-1910 alone, over 2.1 million Austrian citizens arrived on these shores to become one of the ten most populous immigrant groups in the United States.

## OVERVIEW

A mountainous landlocked country located in south-central Europe, Austria encompasses an area of 32,377 square miles, roughly the size of the state of Maine. Bordered to the west by Switzerland and Liechtenstein, to the south by Italy and the former Yugoslavia, to the east by Hungary, and to the north by the Czech and Slovak Republics as well as Germany, Austria lies at the center of political and geographic Europe. Two-thirds of Austria's land mass is located in the Alpine region, with its highest peak, the Grossglockner, reaching 12,457 feet.

With a population of 7,587,000, Austria has maintained zero population growth in the last half of the twentieth century. It is a German-speaking country. Eighty-five percent of its population are Roman Catholic while only six percent are Protestant. Vienna, the capital of the Federal Republic of Austria, also doubles as one of the nine autonomous provinces that constitute the federation. The Austrian flag is a simple red-white-red arrangement of horizontal stripes with the Austrian coat of arms in the center.

### HISTORY

Austria's very name denotes its history. Ostmark or Ostarichi ("eastern provinces" or "borderland") as it was known in the time of Charlemagne, became over time the German Österreich, or Austria in Latin. As an eastern kingdom—more bulwark than principality, more fortress than palace—Austria bordered the civilized world. The first human inhabitants of this rugged environment were Stone Age hunters who lived 80,000 to 150,000 years ago. Permanent settlements were established in early Paleolithic times. Though little remains of that distant period, an early Iron Age settlement was unearthed at Hallstatt in the western lake district of present-day Austria. The Celts arrived around 400 B.C., and the Romans, in search of iron ore deposits, invaded 200 years later. The Romans established three provinces in the area by 15 B.C. They introduced the grape to the hills surrounding the eastern reaches of the Danube near a settlement they called Vindobona, later known as Wien, or Vienna in English.

For the next four centuries the Romans fought Germanic invasions, eventually losing, but establishing a fortification line along the Danube River, upon which many modern Austrian cities are built. With the fall of Rome, barbarian tribes such as the Bavarians from the west and Mongolian Avars from the east settled the region, bringing new cultural influences. One Germanic tribe, the Franks, were particularly interested in the area, and by the end of the eighth century, Charlemagne succeeded in subduing the other claimants, Christianizing the region and creating a largely Germanic province for his Holy Roman Empire. This Ostmark, or eastern borderland, did not hold long. Incursions from the east by the Magyars around 900 A.D. unsettled the region once again, until the Magyars too were subdued.

The political and territorial concept of Austria came about in 976 when the eastern province was granted to the house of Babenberg. For the next three centuries that family would rule the eastern borderland, eventually choosing Vienna as their seat. By the twelfth century Austria had become a duchy and a flourishing trade center. With the death of the line of Babenberg in 1246, the duchy was voted first to Ottokar II, king of Bohemia, who was defeated in battle by a member of a Swiss noble house, Rudolf IV of Habsburg. The Habsburgs would rule not only Austria, but large parts of Europe and the New World as well until 1918. The Habsburgs created a central European empire around the region of Austria and extending into Bohemia, Hungary, Yugoslavia, Poland, Spain, and the Netherlands. Throughout their rule, the empire acted as a bulwark against eastern invasion by Turks and Magyars, and through both diplomacy and strategic marriages, the Habsburgs established a civilization that would be the envy of the world. Under such emperors as Rudolf, Charles V, and the empress Maria Theresa, universities were established and Vienna became synonymous with music, fostering such composers as Franz Haydn, Wolfgang Mozart, Ludwig van Beethoven, Franz Schubert, and Johannes Brahms.

When the Napoleonic Wars ended the power of the Holy Roman Empire, the Austrian or Habsburg Empire took its place in central Europe and its foreign minister, Clemens Metternich-Winneburg, consolidated power to make a unified German state. The democratic revolutions of 1848 temporarily destabilized the country, but under the rule of Franz Joseph a strong government again rose to power. The Austrian Empire faced increasing nationalistic pressure, however. First the Magyars in Hungary won a compromise with Vienna, creating the Austro-Hungarian Empire in 1867. Other ethnic minorities in the polyglot empire pressed for independence, and eventually, with the assassination of Archduke Ferdinand in Sarajevo in 1914 by a Serbian extremist, the world was plunged into a war that destroyed the Austrian Empire.

In 1918, with the abdication of the last Habsburg, Karl I, the modern Republic of Austria was founded. Now a smaller country, it comprised only the original Germanic provinces with seven million inhabitants. Operating under severe economic hardship, Austria was annexed by Germany in 1938 led by Adolf Hitler, a former Austrian who had become chancellor of Germany. Until 1945, Austria was part of the Third Reich, an ambivalent ally to Germany in the Second World War. With the defeat of Germany, the republic was again restored in Austria, but the country was occupied jointly by the United States, Britain, France, and the Soviet Union until the state treaty of 1955 ensured Austria's permanent neutrality. Austria was no longer a bulwark against the east, but a buffer state between two competing ideologies. As a neutral country, Austria became the site of many United Nations organizations, and blending a market economy with a state partnership, its economy flourished. With the fall of the Soviet empire, Austria has rediscovered its former role as the geographic center of a new and revitalized Europe.

## THE FIRST AUSTRIANS IN AMERICA

Austrian emigration patterns have been difficult to determine. There was no state known as Austria until 1918; prior to then the sprawling Habsburg Empire, an amalgam of a dozen nationalities, encompassed the idea of Austria. Thus Austrian immigration can rightly be seen as the immigration of Czech, Polish, Hungarian, Slovenian, Serbian, and Croatian peoples as well as a plethora of other national and ethnic groups. Additionally, immigrants themselves were often unclear about their countries of origin. A German-speaking person born in Prague in 1855, for example, was Czech, but also part of the larger Austrian Empire—Austrian, in fact, but may have considered himself German. Immigrants thus may have listed Czech, Austrian, and/or German as their country of origin. This study will confine itself to German Austrian emigration patterns.

The earliest documented German Austrian settlers in America were some 50 families of Protestants from Salzburg who arrived in the colony of Georgia in 1734 after fleeing religious persecution. Granted free passage and land, they established the settlement of Ebenezer near Savannah. Despite initial difficulties with poor land, sickness, and a relocation of their community, they grew and prospered as new families of immigrants arrived. Although the Revolutionary War witnessed the destruction of their settlements, one of these Austrian settlers, Johann Adam Treutlen, became the first elected governor of the new state of Georgia.

Few Austrians immigrated to the United States during the first half of the nineteenth century; fewer than 1,000 Austrians were listed in official surveys by 1850. Those who did come settled in Illinois and Iowa and were supported by 100 to 200 Catholic priests sent from both Germany and Austria to oversee the settlers' religious training and education. The Leopoldine Stiftung, an Austrian foundation that supported such missionaries, funded priests not only for the newly emigrated, but also for the Native Americans. Priests such as Francis Xavier Weninger (1805-1888) spread the Gospel to Austrian immigrants in the Midwest and black slaves in New Orleans. Bishop Frederic Baraga (1797-1868) was one of the most active priests among the Native Americans, working and preaching in northern Michigan. John Nepomuk Neumann (1811-1860) established numerous schools in the Philadelphia area and was a proponent of the retention of German culture and language.

Tyroleans provided a further segment of early nineteenth-century immigration to America. Mostly peasants, these Tyroleans came to the new world in search of land, yet few had the money they needed to turn their dreams into reality. Other early emigrants fled the oppressive Metternich regime, such as Dr. Samuel Ludvigh (1801-1869), a democratic intellectual who eventually founded *Die Fackel,* a well-known German-language periodical in Baltimore. The 1848 revolutions in Austria saw a small but influential tide of political refugees. These so-called Forty-eighters were mostly anticlerical and held strong antislavery views as well. Though they were few in number, they had a lasting influence on not only politics and journalism, but also in medicine and music. They were mostly free-thinking, well-educated liberals who found assimilation a wearisome process in their newly adopted country. Their presence also upset the conservative Americans. Among these Forty-eighters were many Austrian Jews. Most of the Forty-eighters became abolitionists in America, joining the new Republican party despite the fact that the Democratic party traditionally showed more openness to immigrants. It has been conjectured that their votes helped Abraham Lincoln win the 1860 presidential election.

## SIGNIFICANT IMMIGRATION WAVES

Immigration statistics are difficult to interpret for the years between 1861 and 1910, as the U.S. Bureau of Immigration categorized all the inhabitants of the Austro-Hungarian Empire together. During these decades immigration swelled, with estimates of German-speaking Austrians in the United States reaching 275,000 by 1900. Immigrants were encouraged by relaxed emigration laws at home; by the construction of more railways, which allowed easy access to the ports of Europe from their mountainous homeland; by general overpopulation in Europe; and by migration from the farm to the city as Western society became increasingly industrialized. America thus became a destination for displaced Austrian agrarian workers. Many Austrians found employment in the United States as miners, servants, and common laborers. Others flocked to the cities of the Northeast and Midwest—New York, Pittsburgh, and Chicago—where many first- and second-generation Austrians still live. The 1880s witnessed massive immigration to the United States from all parts of Europe, Austria included, with over five million coming to America in that ten-year period. But if peasants were being displaced from the land in Austria, much the same situation was at play in the American midwest where mechanization was revolutionizing agriculture. Thus, newly arrived immigrants, dreaming of a plot of farm land, were largely disappointed. Many of these new arrivals came from Burgenland, an agricultural province to the southeast of Vienna.

During the years 1901-1910 alone, over 2.1 million Austrian citizens arrived on these shores to become one of the ten most populous immigrant groups in the United States. The Austrians—Catholic or Jewish and cosmopolitan—avoided rural Protestant conservative America. Fathers left families behind in Austria, hoping to save money working in Chicago stockyards and Pennsylvania cement and steel factories. More than 35 percent of them returned to their native home with their savings.

With the onset of the First World War, Austrian immigration stopped for a time. Even during the postwar period of 1919 to 1924, fewer than 20,000 Austrians came to the United States, most of them from Burgenland. The passage of a restrictive immigration law in 1924 further curtailed Austrian immigration, first to a limit of 785 and then to 1,413 persons per year. Austrian immigration slowed to a trickle during the years of the Depression.

A new wave of immigrants from Austria began arriving in the late 1930s. Unlike earlier immigrants who were largely unskilled laborers from the provinces, these new arrivals were mostly well-educated urban Jews fleeing Hitler's new regime. In 1938 Austria had become incorporated into the Third Reich and anti-Semitism had become a daily fact of life. In the three-year period between the *Anschluss*, or annexation by Germany, and the outbreak of all-out war in 1941, some 29,000 Jewish Austrians emigrated to the United States. These were generally highly skilled professionals in medicine, architecture, law, and the arts and included men of international renown: composers Arnold Schoenberg (1874-1951) and Erich Korngold (1897-1957); author Franz Werfel (1890-1945); and stage and film directors such as Max Reinhardt (1873-1943) and Otto Preminger (1906-1986). The Jewish Austrian intellectual elite was, in fact, scattered around the globe in the diaspora caused by the Second World War.

Some 40,000 Austrians entered the United States from 1945-1960. U.S. immigration quotas again limited and diverted immigration to other countries such as Canada and Australia. Recent Austrian immigration has been negligible, as Austria has built itself into a wealthy industrial state. The 1990 U.S. census listed 948,558 citizens of

Austrian ancestry, only 0.4 percent of the total population. However, it is estimated that in the years from 1820 to 1960, 4.2 million or ten percent of the immigrants who arrived in America came from Austro-Hungary and the states succeeding it.

## SETTLEMENT

The first sizable wave of Austrian immigrants tended to settle in the urbanized centers of the northeastern United States, especially in New York City. They were also populous in New Jersey, Pennsylvania, and Connecticut. Allentown, Pennsylvania, for example, had an Austrian-born population of 6,500 in 1930, the largest single ethnic minority in that town. Recent emigration has changed this trend somewhat. The 1990 census reports the largest single concentration in New York, followed by large contingents in both California and Florida.

# ACCULTURATION AND ASSIMILATION

In general, Austrian immigrants have quickly assimilated in America. Part of a multi-ethnic melange in their original homeland, Austrians were accustomed to the melting pot and were quick to pick up new languages and customs once in America. Dr. Harry Zohn (1922- ), professor of German literature at Brandeis University, voices a sentiment typical of many Austrian Americans: "I'm an American who just happened to be born in Vienna." Zohn, a refugee from Nazism, was one of the fortunate few whose entire family managed to escape. Once in the United States, Zohn quickly adapted to the culture and language, though never losing his intellectual and spiritual ties to Middle Europe, writing in both German and English about Austrian literature and culture (E. Wilder Spaulding, *The Quiet Invaders: The Story of Austrian Impact upon America* [Vienna: Österreichische Bundesverlag, 1968]).

On the whole, Austrians tend to differentiate themselves strongly from German immigrants whom they see as more chauvinistic and domineering. Austrians in America like to think of themselves as more cosmopolitan, sophisticated, and tolerant than their German neighbors. As a group, Austrian immigrants have not drawn attention to themselves. Moreover, they are, somewhat to their dismay, often lumped together with German immigrants and have thus suffered

Austrian American Arnold Schwarzenegger, in his role as president of the President's Council on Physical Fitness and Sports, meets with President George Bush at the White House in January 1990.

from the same stereotypes as the Germans in America. Both world wars of this century resulted in Americans often having negative attitudes toward Germany. In the First World War, the two groups were derogatorily called Dutchy, from the German word *Deutsch*. Names sounding German, such as Braun and Schmidt, were changed overnight to Brown and Smith. Austrians and Germans became, for many Americans, the enemy within. Other stereotypes persisted even in peacetime, including the beer-swilling Austrian, and the pleasure-loving, wine-sipping, charming proponents of *Gemütlichkeit* or coziness.

## TRADITIONS, CUSTOMS, AND BELIEFS

Austrian traditions, maintained most faithfully by those living in the mountainous region of Western Austria, center mainly around the seasons. *Fasching* is an old winter custom that traditionally takes place in February. In its pagan form, it was an attempt to drive out the evil spirits of winter

and prepare for spring. Processions of villagers dressed in varieties of masked costumes and ringing cow bells symbolized the fight of spring against winter. Some of these processions still take place in parts of Tyrol and Styria, but the *fasching* has generally evolved into a procession of carnival balls linked with Lent and the passion of Easter.

Similarly, the old spring festivals wherein village children would parade with boughs decorated with ivy and pretzels to celebrate the reawakening of the sun, have been replaced by Palm Sunday and Corpus Christi celebrations. May Day and the dance around the maypole is still a much-celebrated event in villages all over Austria. The festival of the summer solstice, announced by bonfires on the hills, still takes place in parts of Salzburg, under the name of St. John's Night.

Harvest festivals of autumn, linked with apple and wine gathering, have a long tradition throughout Austria. Harvest fairs are still a vital part of the autumn season, and the wine harvest, from grape picking and pressing through the various stages of wine fermentation, is an affair closely monitored by many Austrians. The pine bough outside a winery signals customers that new wine is available. The thanksgiving festival of St. Leonard, patron saint of livestock, is a reminder of a pagan harvest celebration.

Perhaps best known and most retained by Austrian immigrants in America are traditions of the Christmas season, the beginning of which is marked by St. Nicholas Day on December 6. Good children are rewarded with apples and nuts in their stockings, while bad ones receive only lumps of coal. Caroling and the Christmas tree are but two of the Austrian and German contributions to the American celebrations of yuletide. One of the best-known Christmas carols, "Silent Night," was written by an Austrian.

As many customs and beliefs from Austria have been incorporated by the Catholic Church, many Austrian Americans have retained the feast days of their native country, though without the pageantry or connection to their original purpose. The Austrian custom of placing a pine tree atop newly constructed houses has become a traditional ceremony for American ironworkers as well, many of whom were of Central European origin. The fir tree, as mentioned, has become a staple of American Christmas. Yet overall, Austrian customs have become barely recognizable in America.

### CUISINE

Austrian cuisine relies heavily on meat, especially pork. The famous dish *wienerschnitzel*, pork or veal fried in bread crumbs, is among the many recipes that were imported along with the immigrants. *Goulasch*, a spicy Hungarian stew, is another item that has found its way onto the American table, as has *sauerkraut*, both a German and Austrian specialty. Sausages, called *wurst* in German, have become so popular in America that names such as wiener (from *wienerwurst*) and frankfurter (from Frankfurt in Germany) are synonymous with a whole class of food. Pastries and desserts are also Austrian specialties; Austrian favorites include cake such as *Sachertorte*, a heavy chocolate concoction closely connected with Vienna's Hotel Sacher; *linzertorte*, more of a tart than cake, stuffed with apricot jam; and the famous pastry *apfelstrudel*, a flaky sort of pie stuffed with apples. The list of such sweets is lengthy, and many of them have found places, under different names, as staples of American cuisine. Breads are another Austrian contribution to the world's foods: the rye breads of both Germany and Austria are dense and longlasting with a hearty flavor.

Austrian beer, such as the light lagers and heavier *Bock*—brewed for Christmas and Easter—is on par with the better known German varieties. Early immigrants of both nationalities brought the fondness for barley and hops with them, and many Austrians founded breweries in the United States. Wines, especially the tart white wines of the Wachau region of the Danube and the refined, complex varietals of Gumpoldskirchen to the south of Vienna, have become world famous as well. The Austrian love for the new wine, or *heuriger*, is witnessed by dozens of drinking songs. The simple wine tavern, owned and operated by the vintner and his family, combines the best of a picnic with dining out.

### TRADITIONAL COSTUMES

In Austria, the traditional costumes or *trachten*, are still fashionable, not only for the rural population, but for city-dwellers as well. Most typical and best known by those outside Austria is the *dirndl*. Both village girls and Viennese matrons can be seen wearing this pleated skirt covered by a brightly colored apron and surmounted by a tight-fitting bodice. White blouses are worn under the bodice, sometimes embroidered, sometimes with lace. For men the typical *trachten* is the *steirer anzug*, a collarless variation of a hunting costume, usually gray with green piping and trim, which can be worn for both formal and informal occasions. The *wetterfleck*, a long loden cape, is also still worn, as are knickers of elk hide or wool. *Lederhosen*, or leather shorts, associated with both Germany and Austria, are still typical summer wear in much of Austria.

### AUSTRIAN MUSIC AND DANCES

From simple *lieder*, or songs, to symphonies and operas, Austrian music has enriched the cultural life of the Western world. Vienna in particular was the home of native Austrian and German composers alike who created the classical idiom. Men such as Haydn, Mozart, Beethoven, Schubert, and Brahms developed symphony and chamber music. More modern composers such as Anton Bruckner, Gustav Mahler, and Arnold Schoenberg—the latter immigrated to the United States—expanded the boundaries of tonality and structure in music composition.

Austria is also synonymous with the waltz, developed from an earlier peasant dance and made famous through the music of Johann Strauss and Joseph Lanner. The Viennese operetta has also influenced the musical taste of the world, helping to develop the form of the modern musical. Johann Strauss, Jr., is only one of many who pioneered the form, and a Viennese, Frederick Loewe, helped to transform it on Broadway by writing the lyrics to such famous musicals as *My Fair Lady* and *Camelot*.

## HOLIDAYS CELEBRATED BY AUSTRIAN AMERICANS

Beyond such traditional holidays as Christmas, New Year's, and Easter, Austrian Americans cannot be said to celebrate various feast and seasonal days as a group. The more cosmopolitan immigrants from Vienna, for example, were and are much more internationalist in outlook than fellow Austrian immigrants from Burgenland, who hold to more traditional customs even in the United States. This latter group, former residents of a rural, agricultural area and generally Catholic, are more likely to observe such traditional feasts as St. Leonard's Day in November, St. Nicholas Day on December 6, and Corpus Christi in June, as well as such seasonal festivities as harvest festivals for wine in October.

## HEALTH AND MENTAL HEALTH ISSUES

The medical tradition in Austria is long and noteworthy. The Viennese have contributed medical innovations such as antisepsis and new therapies such as psychoanalysis to the world. Austrian Americans place a high value on health care. They also bring with them the idea of medical care as a birthright, for in Austria such care has been part of a broad government-run social program during much of the twentieth century. There are no documented congenital diseases specific to Austrian Americans.

# LANGUAGE

Austria and Germany are, to paraphrase Winston Churchill's famous quip about England and America, two countries separated by a common language. That Austria is a German-speaking country seems to come as a surprise to many Americans. Germans also have great fun scratch-

ing their heads over Austrianisms (e.g., the German *kartoffel* becomes *erdapfel*, or apple of the earth, in Austria). However, Austrian German, apart from a lighter, more sing-song accent and some regional words, is no different from true German than Canadian English is from American English. The umlaut (ä, ö, ü) is the primary diacritical mark over vowels, and is sometimes expressed by an "e" after the vowel instead of employing the diacritic.

As English is an offshoot of Old German, there are enough similarities between the two languages to make language assimilation a reasonably easy task for Austrian Americans. The "v" for "w" confusion is an especially difficult phonetic problem, as German has no unaspirated pronunciation of "w." Another pronunciation difficulty is the English diphthong "th" for which German has no equivalent, resulting in the thick "s" so caricatured by stage and screen actors.

## GREETINGS AND OTHER POPULAR EXPRESSIONS

Typical Austrian greetings and farewells include the more formal Germanisms such as *Guten Tag* ("gooten tahg")—Good day; *Guten Abend* ("gooten ahbend")—Good evening; and *Auf Wiedersehen* ("ouf veedersayen")—Good-bye. More typically Austrian are *Grüss Gott* ("groos gote")—literally Greetings from God, but used as Hello or Hi; and *Servus* ("sairvoos")—both Hello and Good-bye, used by younger people and between good friends. Other polite expressions—for which Austrian German seems to have an overabundance—include *Bitte* ("bietuh")—both Please and You're welcome; *Danke Vielmals* ("dahnka feelmahls")—Thanks very much; and *Es tut mir sehr leid* ("es toot meer sair lied")—I'm very sorry. Seasonal expressions include *Frohe Weihnachten* ("frohuh vienahkten")—Merry Christmas; and *Prosit Neujahr* ("proezit noy yahr")—Happy New Year. *Zum wohl* ("tzoom vole")—To your health—is a typical toast.

# FAMILY AND COMMUNITY DYNAMICS

Initially, many of the immigrants from Austria were males who came to America to earn and save money and then to return home. Most often, these early immigrants would live together in crowded rooming houses or primitive hostels in urban centers of the industrial northeastern United States. As permanent immigration patterns replaced this more nomadic style, the structure of the Austrian family became transplanted to America. Typically a tight nuclear family that seldom included a grandmother, the Austrian family has few of the characteristics of the extended Mediterranean family. The father ruled the economic life of the family, but the strong matriarch was boss at home. As in Austria, male children were favored. Sundays were a sacrosanct family time together. In general, few outsiders were allowed the informal "Du" greeting or even invited into the home.

This tight structure soon broke down, however, in the more egalitarian American environment. Austrian immigrants tended overall to assimilate rapidly into their new country, adapting to the ways of America and being influenced by the same cultural trends that affected native-born Americans: the increasing importance of the role of women in the twentieth century; the decline of the nuclear family, including a rising divorce rate; and the mobility of citizens—both geographically and economically. The variety of Austrian immigrants also changed in this century. Once mainly agrarian workers who congregated in urban areas despite their desire to settle on the land, immigrants from Austria—especially after the First World War—tended to be better educated with a larger world view. The flight of the Jewish Austrian intelligentsia during the Nazi period especially affected the assimilation patterns. These professional classes placed a high premium on education for both male and female children. Thus Austrian immigrants became skilled workers and professionals.

## RELIGION

Mostly Roman Catholic, Austrians brought their religion with them to America. Austrian missionaries, mainly Jesuits, baptized Native Americans and helped chart the New World from the seventeenth century on. But by the nineteenth century that mission had changed, for newly arrived Austrian immigrants, disdained by Irish Catholic priests who spoke no German, were clamoring for Austrian priests. Partly to meet this need and partly to convert new souls to Catholicism, the Leopoldine Stiftung or Foundation was established in 1829. Collecting weekly donations throughout the Habsburg Empire, the foundation sent money and priests into North America to bring faith to the frontier. Through such contributions over 400 churches were built on the East Coast, in the Midwest, and in what was then known as Indian country further west. The Jesuits were especially active during this period in cities such as Cincinnati and St. Louis. The Benedictines and Franciscans were also represented by both priests and nuns. These priests founded bishoprics and built congregations in the thousands. One unfortunate reaction to this was an intensification of nativist tendencies, or anti-immigrant sentiments. This influx of priests was looked upon as a conspiracy to upset the balance of the population in America with Roman Catholics imported from Europe. For many years such nativist sentiments made it difficult for Austrian immigrants to fully assimilate into American society.

On the whole, the formal traditions and rights of the Church in the United States and in Austria were the same, but external pressures differed. Thus, as with the U.S. population in general, Austrian Americans in the twentieth century have become more secular, less faith-bound. New waves of Austrian immigrants, especially those fleeing Nazism, also changed the religious makeup of the groups as a whole. For the most part, arrivals between 1933 and 1945 were Jewish, and largely assimilated Jews.

## EMPLOYMENT AND ECONOMIC TRADITIONS

As with all examinations of Austrian immigration, occupational statistics suffer from the inconsistent distinction between ethnic groups among the Austro-Hungarian immigrants. German-speaking Austrians did settle in the center of the country to become farmers, but in what numbers is unclear. Prior to 1900 Austro-Hungarian immigrants were also laborers, saloon keepers, waiters, and steel workers. Statistics that are available from 1900, however, indicate that a high proportion of later arrivals found work as tailors, miners, and peddlers. By the mid-twentieth century, these same occupational trends still prevailed, with tailoring and the clothing industry in general employing large numbers of Austrian Americans. The food industry was also heavily weighted with Austrians: bakers, restaurateurs, and meat packers. Mining was also a predominant occupation among Austrians.

In the half-century since then, Austrian Americans have branched out into all fields: medicine, law, entertainment, management, and technology, as well as the traditional service industries where many of them started as new immigrants.

# POLITICS AND GOVERNMENT

The earliest notable political influence that Austrian Americans wielded came through the pens and the votes of the Forty-eighters. These liberal refugees from the failed revolts of 1848 were strongly abolitionist and pro-Lincoln. Later arrivals during the half-century of mass immigration from Austro-Hungary (1860-1910) packed the ranks of unskilled labor and of America's fledgling labor movement. Indeed, the deaths of ten Austro-Hungarian laborers during the 1897 mining strike in Lattimer, Pennsylvania, prompted a demand for indemnity by the embassy of Austro-Hungary.

Immigrants in the 1930s and 1940s tended to have strong socialist beliefs and formed organizations such as the American Friends of Austrian Labor to help promote labor issues. During World War II an Austrian government in exile was attempted in the United States, but fighting between factions of the refugees, specifically between Social Democrats and Christian Socialists, prevented any concerted action on that front. The creation of the Austrian battalion—the 101st Infantry Battalion—became the center of a debate that raged among Austrian Americans. Groups such as Austria Action and the Austrian Labor Committee opposed such a formation, anxious lest it become the vanguard of the restoration of the Habsburg monarchy under Otto von Habsburg after the war. On the other side, the Free Austrian Movement advocated such a battalion, even if it meant aligning the right with the left among the recruits. A scant six months after its formation, the Austrian battalion was disbanded. Despite this failure, the debate occasioned by the creation of the battalion had helped to bring to the forefront of American discussion the role of Austrian Americans and of Austria itself in the Second World War. Not only were Austrian Americans not interned, but Austria itself, in the Moscow Declaration of November 1, 1943, was declared one of the first victims of Nazism, and the restoration of its independence was made an Allied war aim.

Little information on Austrian American voting patterns exists, though early Jewish Austrian immigrants and Austrian socialists tended to vote Democrat rather than Republican. Interesting in this context is the career of Victor Berger (1860-1929), an Austrian who not only influenced Eugene V. Debs in becoming a socialist, but also became the first socialist to sit in the House of Representatives in Washington.

Austrians of the first generation, on the whole, maintain close links with Austria, returning periodically to their place of birth. Even Jewish Austrians who had to flee the Holocaust return to visit and sometimes to retire in their homeland.

# INDIVIDUAL AND GROUP CONTRIBUTIONS

Austrian Americans have made lasting contributions in all fields of American life, though seldom is the emphasis on the fact of their Austrian roots. From the arts to the world of science, this immigrant population has made its mark.

### ACADEMIA

Joseph Alois Schumpeter (1883-1950) was a well-known critic of Marxism and an authority on business cycles. Another notable Austrian American economist was Ludwig von Mises (1881-?), a critic of the planned economies of socialist countries. Other Austrian Americans in the fields of literature and history have done much to generate interest in Austria and Central Europe: Harry Zohn is a much-published professor of German literature at Brandeis University, and the Viennese Robert A. Kann's (1906-?) *A History of the Habsburg Empire* has become a standard reference. R. John Rath helped to centralize Austrian studies with his center at Rice University and then at the University of Minnesota. These are only a few of the many notable Austrian American historians at work in this country.

### ART AND ARCHITECTURE

Austrian artists who came to the United States include the painter George Peter (1860-?), who immigrated to Milwaukee, Wisconsin, in 1885, painted Civil War themes, and eventually became director of the Milwaukee museum. Others include the artist and architect Joseph Urban (1872-1933); the sculptor and architectural designer Karl Bitter (1867-1915); Joseph Margulies, born in Austria in 1896, who painted and etched scenes of the New York ghetto; and René d'Harnoncourt (1901-?) from Vienna, who eventually became director of contemporary art at the Museum of Modern Art in New York. Max Fleischer (1885-?) was one of the pioneers of the animated cartoon on film whose creations include Betty Boop and Popeye. The exodus from Austria caused by the rise of Hitler brought to the United States such distinguished painters as the modernist Wilhelm Thoeny (1888-1949); the expressionist painters Franz Lerch (1895-?) and Max Oppenheimer (1885-1956); and the graphic artist, John W. Winkler (1890-?). Among architects of note are Karl Bitter, mentioned above, and John L. Smithmeyer (1832-1908), who was the architect of the Library of Congress. Best known of all Austrian American architects was Richard Neutra (1892-1970), whose name is synonymous with the steel and concrete structures he pioneered in California. Other more modern architects include R. M. Schindler (1887-1953) and Victor Gruen (1903-?), who emigrated in 1938 and whose environmental architecture helped transform such cities as Los Angeles, Detroit, and Fort Worth. Frederick John Kiesler (1896-1965) was known as an innovative architect, whose set designs, interiors, and bold floating architectural designs earned him a reputation as a maverick and visionary.

## BUSINESS

Franz Martin Drexel (1792-1863), a native of Voralberg, founded the banking house of Drexel and Company in Philadelphia, which later gave rise to the House of Morgan. Another immigrant from Voralberg, John Michael Kohler (1844-1900), built one of the largest plumbing outfitters in the United States and introduced the enamel coated bathtub. August Brentano (1831-1886) was an impoverished Austrian immigrant who turned a newspaper stand into a huge bookshop chain. The development of department stores in America also owes a debt to Austrian Americans Nathan M. Ohrbach (1885-?), founder of the Ohrbach stores, and Joe Weinstein (1894-?), founder of the May stores. John David Hertz (1879-1961), an Austrian Czech, made his name synonymous with rental cars. Austrian American fashion designers have included Nettie Rosenstein (1893-?), a winner of the prestigious Coty award for clothing design, and the Vienna-born Rudi Gernreich (1922- ) who created the topless

bathing suits of the 1960s. In the world of publishing, Frederick Ungar, a refugee from the Hitler era, created a well-respected New York house, as did Frederik Amos Praeger (1915- ). Tourism in the United States has also been enhanced by the Austrian-style ski resorts and schools in Sun Valley developed by Felix Schaffgotsch, with a ski school operated by Hans Hauser. The Arlberg technique in skiing was promoted by Hannes Schneider (1890-1955) in Jackson, New Hampshire, and later resorts such as Aspen and Heavenly Valley were made famous by their Austrian instructors. In technology, the 1978 invention of a text scanner by the Austrian American Ray Kurzweil (1948- ) has opened a new world for blind readers.

## JOURNALISM

Among journalists, the foremost name is Joseph Pulitzer (1847-1911). Though claimed by both Hungarians and Austrians, Pulitzer spoke German and had a Hungarian father and an Austrian mother. The founder of the *St. Louis Post-Dispatch* and owner of the *New York World*, Pulitzer's name is remembered for the prize in journalism that he endowed. He was one of many Austro-Hungarians involved in journalism in nineteenth-century America. Others include Gustav Pollak (1848-1919), a contributor to *The Nation* and the *Evening Post*, and Joseph Keppler (1838-1894), an innovator in color cartoons and owner of the humorous magazine *Puck*. A more recent publishing venture involving an Austrian American is the *New Yorker*, whose founding president, Raoul H. Fleischmann (1885-1969), was born in Bad Ischl, Austria. Other more current Austrian American journalists include the one-time associate editor of the *Boston Globe*, Otto Zausmer; an editor for the *Christian Science Monitor*, Ernest S. Pisko; and Erwin Knoll (1928-1994), a Vienna-born journalist and longtime editor of *The Progressive*.

## LAW AND SOCIETY

One of the best-known Austrian Americans in the law was Felix Frankfurter (1882-1965), a native of Vienna, who was a justice on the Supreme Court for 23 years. The Spingarn Medal, awarded yearly to an outstanding African American leader, was created by Joel Elias Spingarn (1875-1939), one of the founders of the National Association for the Advancement of Colored People (NAACP) and the son of an Austrian immigrant.

## LITERATURE

Franz Werfel (1890-1945), though born in Prague, was a thoroughly Austrian writer. He and his wife fled the Nazis and came to the United States in 1940. His *Song of Bernadette* became a best seller in the United States, and the Werfels settled in Beverly Hills. The children's writer and illustrator Ludwig Bemelmans (1898-1962) was born in South Tyrol and settled in New York as a youth. His famous Madeline stories continue to charm young readers. Hermann Broch (1886-1951), one of the most influential of modern Austrian writers, known for such novels as *The Sleepwalkers* and *The Death of Virgil*, was another refugee from Hitler's Europe and taught at both Princeton and Yale. Frederic Morton (1925- ), born in Vienna and educated in New York, has written many nonfiction books of renown, among them *The Rothschilds* and *A Nervous Splendor: Vienna 1888-1889*.

## MEDICINE

Among Austrian American Nobel laureates in medicine were Karl Landsteiner (1868-1943), the discoverer of blood types, and the German Austrian Otto Loewi (1873-1961), a co-winner of the Nobel for his work in the chemical transmission of nerve impulses. Loewi came to New York University after he was driven out of Graz by the Nazis. Many other Austrian Americans have also left their mark in the United States both as practitioners and educators, but perhaps none so methodically as the psychoanalysts who spread Sigmund Freud's work to America. These include A. A. Brill (1874-1947), the Columbia professor and Freud translator; Heinz Werner (1890-1964); Paul Federn; Otto Rank (1884-1939), a Freud disciple; and Theodor Reik (1888-?), the New York psychoanalyst. This group of immigrants was not limited to Freudians, however. Alexandra Adler (1901-?), daughter of Alfred Adler, who is generally known as the second great Viennese psychoanalyst, came to the United States to work at both Harvard and Duke. Bruno Bettelheim (1903-1990) was also a native of Vienna; he became known for his treatment of autistic children and for his popular writings. The list of those both in medicine and mental health who were driven out of Austria during the reign of Hitler is long and impressive.

## MUSIC

Arnold Schoenberg (1874-1951), creator of the 12-tone system and a pioneer of modern music,

fled the rise of Nazism in 1933 and continued composing and teaching at both the University of Southern California and the University of California, Los Angeles. Erich Wolfgang Korngold (1897-1957), a Viennese composer best known for his opera *Die tote Stadt*, immigrated to the United States in 1934 and composed and conducted film scores in Hollywood. Ernst Křenek (1900-1991), also a Viennese, was a modernist whose fame was built through his incorporation of jazz and opera in his *Jonny spielt auf*. He taught at Vassar for many years. Frederick Loewe (1904-?), a native Viennese, was the lyricist in the team of Lerner and Loewe who helped transform the American musical. The folk singer and actor Theodore Bikel (1924- ) was born in Vienna and came to the United States via Israel and London. Paul Wittgenstein (1887-1961), brother of the philosopher and a pianist of note, settled in New York after 1938. Having lost his right arm in the First World War, Wittgenstein became famous for playing with one hand, and major composers such as Maurice Ravel wrote music for the left hand for him. The longtime general manager of New York's Metropolitan Opera, Rudolf Bing (1902-?), was also Austrian, born in Vienna. Bruno Walter (1876-1962), a German conductor who became a naturalized Austrian and then fled Hitler, was famous for his recordings of Mahler and Mozart and his conducting at the Met and with the New York Philharmonic. Another conductor, Erich Leinsdorf (1912-1993), also found fame in America with a longtime association with the Boston Symphony.

## SCIENCE

Three of Austria's four Nobel Prize winners in physics immigrated to the United States. They include Victor Franz Hess (1883-1964), the discoverer of cosmic rays; Isidor Isaac Rabi (1898-1988), a physicist at Columbia; and Wolfgang Pauli (1900-1958). George Paul Sutton (1920- ) immigrated to the United States in 1920 and contributed greatly in the development of rockets and missiles. Otto Halpern (1899-?) also contributed to the defense effort of his new homeland by his invention of a counter-radar device. A fair assortment of world class mathematicians also arrived in America from Austria. Among these, Richard von Mises (1883-1953) had a distinguished career at Harvard. Distinguished biologists include Spaeth Hauschka (1908-?) and Erna Altura Werber; among chemists are Ludwig F. Andrieth (1901-?), Oskar Paul Wintersteiner (1898-?), Ernst Berl

(1877-1946), who came to the United States to work on explosives and chemical warfare, and Hermann Francis Mark (1895-?), whose work in synthetic plastics led to the development of such materials as nylon and orlon.

### STAGE AND SCREEN

The earliest contribution of Austrian Americans is found in the theater. Many of the earliest theater houses in this country were built by Austrian immigrants who brought their love for theater with them. Prominent arrivals from Austria include the impresario Max Reinhardt (1873-1943). Famous for his *Everyman* production at the Salzburg Festival and for a school of dramatics in Vienna, Reinhardt worked in Hollywood and New York after immigrating to escape the Nazis. Other Austrian Americans include such well-known stage and screen actors as Rudolph Schildkraut (1895-1964), who starred for De Mille in Hollywood, Paul Muni (1895-1967), Hedy Lamarr (1915- ), Oscar Homolka (1898-1978), and Arnold Schwarzenegger (1947- ). An impressive group of film directors also hail from Austria: Erich von Stroheim (1885-1957), whose film *Greed* is considered a modern masterpiece; Joseph von Sternberg (1894-1969), the father of gangster films; Fred Zinnemann (1907- ), the director of *High Noon*; Billy Wilder (1906- ) whose many accomplishments include *The Apartment* and *Sunset Boulevard*; and Otto Preminger (1906-1986), a boyhood friend of Wilder's in Vienna and director of such film classics as *Exodus* and *Anatomy of a Murder*.

# MEDIA

### PRINT

*Austria Kultur.*

This bimonthly publication is published by the Austrian Cultural Institute, an agency funded by the Austrian government to represent Austrian culture in the United States. It concentrates on cultural affairs such as exhibitions and exchanges.

**Contact:** Wolfgang Waldner, Editor.

**Address:** 11 East 52nd Street, New York, New York, 10022.

**Telephone:** (212) 759-5165.

Other regional German-language newspapers and magazines such as California's *Neue Presse* and the *Staats Zeitung* operate throughout the United States, though none are specifically oriented to or targeted at an Austrian readership.

### RADIO AND TELEVISION

Though the short-wave broadcasts of the Austrian Broadcasting Company, ORF, can be picked up in the United States, and various cable networks air German-language programming on their international channels, there is no domestically produced programming that targets the Austrian American audience.

# ORGANIZATIONS AND ASSOCIATIONS

In general, Austrian Americans, because of diverse interests and ethnic backgrounds, have tended to favor small regional organizations and clubs over national ones. Most of these societies are organized by province of origin, and those of the Burgenland contingent are the most pervasive. In addition, urban areas such as Chicago, New York, Los Angeles, and Miami Beach tend to have associations for the promulgation of Austrian culture. Other Austrian societies and organizations are united by such common themes as music or literature, or by shared history as with those who fled Austrian Nazism or Hitler. The following are a sampling of regional fraternal and cultural associations.

**Austrian-American Federation, Incorporated.**

**Contact:** Dr. Clementine Zernik, President.

**Address:** 31 East 69th Street, New York, New York, 10021.

**Telephone:** (212) 535-3261.

**Austrian American Council Northeast.**

The six chapters of this nonprofit organization have a common goal: to deepen the friendship and understanding between the United States and Austria. To this end, members facilitate cultural and educational exchange between the two countries and also participate in humanitarian efforts such as SOS *Kinderdorf*, an outreach to disadvantaged children in both Europe and the United States.

**Contact:** Juliana Belcsak, President.

**Address:** 5 Russell Terrace, Montclair, New Jersey 07042.

**Telephone:** (201) 783-6241.

**Austrian American Council West.**

Contact: Veronika Reinelt, Vice-President.

Address: 2701 Forrester Drive, Los Angeles, California 90064.

Telephone: (310) 559-8770.

**Austrian American Council Midwest.**

Contact: Gerhard Kaes, President.

Address: 5411 West Addison Street, Chicago, Illinois 60641-3295.

Telephone: (312) 685-4166.

**Austrian American Council Southwest.**

Contact: Christa Cooper, President.

Address: 1535 West Loop South, Suite 319a, Houston, Texas 77027.

Telephone: (713) 623-2233.

**Austrian American Council Southeast.**

Contact: Alfred Marek, President.

Address: P.O. Box 337, 33 Monsell Court, Roswell, Georgia 30077.

**Austrian American Club, Los Angeles.**

Contact: Othmar Friedler, President.

Address: P.O. Box 4711, North Hollywood, California 91607.

Telephone: (310) 634-0065

**Austrian-American "Enzian" Club, Colorado Springs.**

Contact: Helga Jonas, President.

Address: 29 Circle Sea Road, Fountain, Colorado 80817.

Telephone: (719) 382-7639.

**Austrian Society of Arizona.**

Contact: Wolfgang Klien, President.

Address: 4501 North 22nd Street, Phoenix, Arizona 85016.

Telephone: (602) 468-1818.

# MUSEUMS AND RESEARCH CENTERS

**Austrian Cultural Institute.**

Part of the cultural affairs section of the Austrian Consulate General, the institute is responsible for cultural and scientific relations between Austria and the United States. It maintains a reference library specializing in Austrian history, art, and folklore, and organizes lectures and panel discussions as well as educational exchanges.

Contact: Dr. Eichinger, Director; or, Friederike Zeitlhofer, Librarian.

Address: 11 East 52nd Street, New York, New York 10022.

Telephone: (212) 759-5165.

**Center for Austrian Studies.**

Located at the University of Minnesota, the center conducts research on Austrian history and publishes both a newsletter, three times annually, as well as the *Austrian History Yearbook*.

Contact: David Good.

Address: University of Minnesota, 314 Social Sciences Building, Minneapolis, Minnesota 55455.

Telephone: (612) 624-9811.

**Society for Austrian and Habsburg History.**

Focuses on central European history, and on Austria in particular. For scholars interested in research.

Contact: Ronald Coons.

Address: Department of History, University of Connecticut, 241 Glenbrook Road, Storrs, Connecticut 06269-2103.

Telephone: (203) 486-3722.

**International Arthur Schnitzler Research Association.**

Maintains a Schnitzler archive at the University of California, Riverside, and encourages and conducts research on that Austrian playwright and novelist as well as contemporaries of Schnitzler. It publishes the quarterly *Modern Austrian Literature*.

Contact: Professor Donald G. Daviau.

Address: Department of Literature and Languages, University of California, Riverside, Riverside, California 92521.

Telephone: (909) 787-5603.

# SOURCES FOR ADDITIONAL STUDY

Goldner, Franz. *Austrian Emigration 1938 to 1945*. New York: Frederick Ungar, 1979.

Spaulding, E. Wilder. *The Quiet Invaders: The Story of the Austrian Impact upon America*. Vienna: Österreichische Bundesverlag, 1968.

# BARBADIAN AMERICANS

by
Lloyd E. Mulraine

## OVERVIEW

Proudly referred to as "Little England" by her islanders, Barbados, a small Caribbean country, is the easternmost island in the West Indies island chain, which stretches from southeast Florida to the northern coast of South America. Its nearest neighbor, St. Vincent, is due west. The island is one-sixth the size of Rhode Island, the smallest of the United States; it is 21 miles (30 km.) long and 14 miles (22 km.) across at its widest point, with a surface area of 166 square miles (431 sq. km.). Although relatively flat, Barbados is composed mostly of coral, rising gently from the west coast in a series of terraces to a ridge in the center. Its highest point is Mt. Hillaby, reaching 1,104 feet (336 m.).

According to the *1994 Caribbean Basin Commercial Profile*, the population of Barbados in December 1992 was 258,000—52.1 percent of which was female, and 47.9 percent male. Ninety-two percent were of African ethnic origin, four percent white, one percent Asian Indian, and three percent of mixed race. About 70 percent live in the urban area that stretches along the sheltered Caribbean Sea side of the island from Speightstown in the north, to Oistins in the south, and St. Philip in the southeast. The remainder live in villages scattered throughout the countryside, ranging in size from 100 to 3000 persons. Population density is among the highest in the world at 1589.7 people per square mile. The official language of Barbados is English, and the capital is Bridgetown.

There are over 100 denominations and religious sects in Barbados. Seventy percent of the population nominally belongs to the Anglican/Episcopal church, an important heritage of the island's long, unbroken connection with England. The rest belong to such religious groups as Methodist, Moravian, Roman Catholic, Church of God, Seventh-day Adventist, Pentecostal, and a host of others. Adult literacy is approximately 99 percent. The national flag, flown for the first time at midnight November 29/30, 1966, consists of three equal vertical stripes of ultramarine, gold, and ultramarine with a broken trident in the center of the gold stripe.

## HISTORY

The word Barbados (pronounced "bar-bay-dos") comes from Las Barbadas, the name given to the island by the Portuguese who landed there in the early sixteenth century. They named it after the fig tree that grew in abundance on the island, and whose branches had great mats of twisted fibrous roots looking like beards hanging to the ground. Barbados is a derivative of barbudo, the Portuguese name for one who has a thick beard.

According to historical accounts, from c. 350 A.D. to the early sixteenth century, various Amerindian civilizations flourished in Barbados. The first wave of settlers, now called Barrancoid/Saladoid, occupied the island from c. 350-650 A.D. The Spaniards in the sixteenth century referred to them as Arawaks. They originated in the Orinoco basin in South America. Archeological findings reveal that they were skilled in farming, fishing, and ceramics. In about 800 A.D. a second wave of Amerindian migrants occupied the island. They were expert fishermen and grew crops of cassava, potato, and maize. They also produced cotton textile goods and ceramics. A third wave of migrants settled on the island during the mid-thirteenth century. The Spaniards called them Caribs. More materially developed and politically organized, they subdued and dominated their predecessors.

In 1625, when the first English ship, the *Olive Blossom*, on a return visit from Brazil to England, accidentally arrived in Barbados, Captain John Powell and his crew claimed the island on behalf of King James I. They found the island uninhabited. The Amerindians had long departed. During the early sixteenth century, they were victims of the Spaniards' slave raiding missions, and were forced to work on the sugar estates and in the mines of Hispaniola and elsewhere.

## MODERN ERA

The party of English mariners who arrived in Barbados on May 14, 1625, were the first Europeans to begin its colonization. On February 17, 1627, the *William and John*, bearing English settlers and ten African slaves captured from the Portuguese at sea, landed at the present site of Holetown village, and planted the second British colony in the Caribbean, the first being St. Kitts in 1623. The 80 pioneer settlers who disembarked the ship survived on subsistence farming, and exported tobacco and cotton. John Powell, Jr., served as the colony's first governor from April to July 1627. During that same year, Powell also brought 32 Indians from Guiana. They were to live as free people while teaching the English the art of tropical agriculture and regional political geography.

Powell's expedition was financed by Sir William Courteen, an Englishman, but later it was argued that Courteen had no settlement rights to Barbados since he received no royal patent. On July 22, 1627, Charles I granted a patent to James Hay, the first Earl of Carlisle, for the settlement of Barbados. He assumed the status of Lord Proprietor. This Proprietary Patent of 1627 gave the Earl authority to make laws for Barbados with the consent, assent, and approbation of the freeholders.

Due to an error, another royal patent was issued to the Earl of Pembroke, giving him legal ownership of Barbados but creating conflict and confusion on the island. As Carlisle and Pembroke contended for political supremacy over Barbados, the Powell faction, through bold defiance of both contenders, managed to stay in charge of the government. On April 1, 1628, a second patent was issued to Carlisle, revoking that of Pembroke, and Charles Wolverton was appointed Governor of Barbados. When he arrived there, he appointed a group of 12 men to assist him in the administration of the infant colony. In later years a ruling council was appointed by the English government, generally in accordance with the advice of the governor, and its members were usually chosen from the wealthiest and most influential planters. Barbados experienced much political turmoil and instability from 1627 to 1629. On

June 30, 1629, Henry Hawley arrived on the island and assumed the governorship. He was a strong, ruthless ruler whose leadership helped to establish political and economic conditions for the development of a society dominated by a small landed elite.

In 1636 Hawley issued a proclamation that henceforth all blacks and Indians brought to the island, and their offspring, were to be received as lifelong slaves, unless there existed prior agreements to the contrary. Barbados thus developed into the first successful English slave plantation society in the New World. Negroes and Indians who worked for white landowners were considered heathen brutes and were treated as chattel. At the same time, there developed a white underclass of indentured servants consisting of voluntary workers, political refugees, transported convicts, and others. By 1640 the social structure of the island consisted of masters, servants, and slaves. The slaves and their posterity were subject to their masters forever, while servants were indentured for five years. After serving their terms, most indentured servants were released from any commitment to their masters. Many were supplied with money and land to start their own farms. The population of the colony grew rapidly, and by 1640 there were 40,000 people living in Barbados, mostly English yeomen farmers and indentured servants drawn there by the opportunity to acquire cheap land and to compete in an open economic system. Fifteen percent of the population were African slaves.

In 1637 sugar cane cultivation was introduced from Brazil. Production of tobacco, the island's main crop, declined as a result of competition from the American colonies, heavy duties imposed by England, and falling prices. Barbadian soil was ideal for the new crop, and the sugar industry prospered, attracting white planters and merchants from a number of European countries. By 1650 Barbados was considered the richest colony in the New World. Planters discovered that African slaves could work much harder in the tropical climate than white indentured servants. In the 1630s the island's black population was less than 800. By 1643 this number increased to slightly less than 6,000 and by 1660, a mere 20 years after the introduction of sugar cane to the island, Barbados developed into a plantation-dominated society in which slaves outnumbered whites by a two-to-one margin. It is estimated that between 1640 and 1807, the year the British Parliament abolished the slave trade in British territory, including Barbados, that some 387,000

African slaves were brought to Barbados as victims of the slave trade. Many of these African slaves were the ancestors of present day Barbadians. The history of Barbados is to a great extent a history of oppression and resistance, the toil and struggles of African Barbadians toward a just and free society.

The slaves were never content under oppression, and they yearned for freedom. In the seventeenth century, several planned rebellions were aborted because of negro informants. For example, in 1675 two slaves planning rebellion were overheard by a slave woman named Anna, also known as Fortuna, who immediately told her master about the plan. It is recorded that she was recommended for freedom as recompense for her great service to her country, but there is no record that this freedom was ever granted. In 1692 another near rebellion was aborted. Many slaves were executed or died in prison after plots were discovered. The only actual outbreak of armed revolt was the rebellion of 1816.

During the seventeenth century, a new breed of Barbadians—mulattos fathered by white masters and their black slave women—began to populate the colony. They were called coloreds, and many of them were freed by their masters/fathers. By the eighteenth century a small community of free persons of mixed racial identity existed in the colony.

Free-coloreds were a problem both for white Barbadians who were determined to exclude them from white society, and for the slaves whom the free-coloreds despised. Whites made every effort to attach the stigma of racial and genetic inferiority to them. As a result, discriminatory legislation was passed in 1721 that stated that only white male Christian citizens of Great Britain who owned at least ten acres of land or a house having an annual taxable value of ten pounds could vote, be elected to public office, or serve on juries.

Despite exclusion by whites, free-coloreds sought to distance themselves from their slave ancestry, sometimes even from their own mothers, and took a strong pro-slavery stand when imperial legislative action at the beginning of the nineteenth century tended toward improvement of the slaves' condition. By 1831 the franchise was extended to free-colored men; however, the property-owning requirements continued to apply to all voters. Thus, only a small minority gained voting rights. With the advent of a general emancipation, the free-colored people lost their status as a separate caste.

In 1833 the British Parliament passed a law that would free the slaves in the West Indies the following year. The Barbados House of Assembly was hostile to the new law, but finally passed it, and the slaves in Barbados, like the rest of the West Indies, became free on August 1, 1834. However, the emancipated people were not entirely free; they were subjected to a four-year apprenticeship period. In addition, the Contract Act was passed in 1840, which in essence gave the planters a continued hold on the emancipated slaves, a condition that lasted well into the next century.

Samuel Jackman Prescod, the first colored man to hold office in Barbados, was elected to the House of Assembly in 1843. Prescod was one of the leading political figures of nineteenth-century Barbados. He became associated with the antislavery movement, and by 1838 he was the most popular spokesman for the emancipated people who were still denied the privileges of true freedom. He was editor of *The Liberal*, a radical newspaper that expressed the grievances of the disadvantaged colored people and of the black working class. He fought for franchise reform, but the country did not gain universal adult suffrage until 1950, almost a century later.

In 1958, Barbados and nine other British Caribbean territories joined together to form the West Indian Federation, a separate nation within the British Commonwealth. Grantley Adams, the first premier of Barbados, became the Prime Minister of the Federation. This new nation hoped to achieve self-government, economic viability, and independence, but the Federation collapsed in 1962. Barbados finally gained its independence on November 30, 1966, under Prime Minister Errol Barrow. Presently, Barbados is a sovereign and independent state within the British Commonwealth.

## THE FIRST BARBADIANS IN AMERICA

Barbadian connection with America dates back to the 1660s, when close links were established between Barbados and the Carolinas. Sir John Colleton, a prominent Barbadian planter, was among the first to suggest the establishment of a colony there, and in 1670 a permanent colony was established in what is known today as Charleston, South Carolina. Many prominent Barbadian merchants and planters subsequently migrated to Carolina, among them, Sir John Yeamans, who became governor. These Barbadians contributed knowledge, lifestyle, and sugar econo-

my, along with place names, and dialect to Carolina. For example, Gullah, the dialect of the Carolina coast and islands, resembles Barbadian dialect. After the nineteenth-century Emancipation, Barbadians became a part of the flow of West Indian immigrants into the United States.

## SIGNIFICANT IMMIGRATION WAVES

The first major wave of West Indian immigrants, including Barbadians, to the United States took place between 1901 and 1920, with a total of 230,972 entering the country. The majority were unskilled or semi-skilled laborers who came in search of economic opportunities. A substantial number were employed in low-paying service occupations and menial jobs that nonetheless offered higher wages than they could earn at home.

Between 1931 and 1950 West Indian immigration to the United States declined, due partly to an immigration restriction law that imposed a quota system heavily weighted in favor of newcomers arriving from northern and western European countries. The Great Depression was another factor in the drop in West Indian immigration, which reached a significant low in the 1930s.

A second wave began in the 1950s and peaked in the 1960s, when 470,213 immigrants arrived in the United States. More West Indians entered the United States during this decade than the total number that entered between 1891 and 1950 (See table 2). Between 1965 and 1976 a substantial number of immigrants from the Caribbean entered the United States, Barbados alone accounting for 17,400 of them. A large percentage of this wave of immigrants consisted of professional and technical workers forced to leave home because of limited economic opportunities in the Caribbean.

## SETTLEMENT PATTERNS

Most Barbadian immigrants settled in the New York metropolitan area. *The 1990 Census of Population Report* shows that over 82 percent live in the Northeast, with over 62 percent in New York. More than 11 percent live in the South, approximately four percent live in the West, and almost two percent live in the Midwest. The five states with the highest Barbadian populations are New York, with 22,298; Massachusetts, with 3,393; Florida, with 1,770; New Jersey, with 1,678; and California, with 1,160. Unlike Chinese Americans

Barbadian American children are dressed in traditional costumes for the Children's Festival at the World Trade Center in New York City.

or Italian Americans, Barbadians—or West Indians, for that matter—do not occupy small enclaves in the cities of America where they live. They instead tend to settle wherever they can find jobs or affordable housing, and they strive for upward mobility and opportunities to improve their lives.

## ACCULTURATION AND ASSIMILATION

Although Barbadian Americans do not necessarily choose to live in close proximity to fellow Barbadians, they share a bond no matter where they locate. That bond is their pride in, and loyalty to, Barbados—no matter how long they might live in America, they look to Barbados as home. They maintain their connection with Barbados by reading its newspapers, by keeping abreast of events at home, and by remaining actively involved in the politics of the island.

Barbadians have a culture that is uniquely their own. It might be described as Euro-African, although ten years after England outlawed the slave trade, only seven percent of emancipated Barbadians were African-born, significantly less than in most of the other British Caribbean colonies. Thus the relative loss of much of the African culture perhaps accounts for the prominence of European culture on Barbados. Although vestiges of African dialects remain in the lan-

guage, proverbs, tuk band, folk music, and foods such as *conkie* and *coucou*, there is a noticeable absence of African religions such as Voodoo and Shango, or Kele found on other Caribbean islands. Fewer words of African origin have become part of the Barbadian vocabulary than of those of other West Indian islands.

Barbadian Americans also maintain a number of organizations that help to unite them. Chief of these are the Barbados Associations, which meet annually. In addition, Barbadians belong to cricket clubs, social clubs, student clubs, and professional organizations. Unfortunately, the social class differences upheld in Barbados have been transferred to America and affect these organizations. However, one event transcends all class barriers: the annual West Indian Carnival celebrated in some large American cities. The West Indian Carnival is a celebration of national costumes, food, drink, music, and dancing in the streets as well as an occasion when all class barriers are removed, at least for the moment.

Although Barbadian Americans fit well into mainstream American life and culture, they usually prefer to marry partners from Barbados. Second in choice is another West Indian, followed by an American of West Indian parentage or another foreign non-white. Most Barbadian-Americans raise their children with Barbadian values, such as respect for elders and concern for family members, especially siblings. Education is high on their list of priorities, and industry and responsibility follow close behind. In education and employment Barbadians make worthwhile contributions to American society.

## TRADITIONS, CUSTOMS, AND BELIEFS

Barbadians have a variety of traditions that are handed down from generation to generation, especially by word of mouth. Many traditions may be traced to Africa or Europe. For example, one Barbadian custom that was influenced by English settlers is the belief that saying "rabbit rabbit" on the first day of every month will ensure good luck for that month. Many Barbadian beliefs, however, are rooted in the country's own distinct culture. For example, a baby should be allowed to cry at times because crying is believed to help develop the voice. Children should not cry during the night though, because a duppy (ghost) might steal the infant's voice, making it hoarse the next day. It is believed that first born children, or children born on Christmas day, are destined to be stupid.

There are also many customs regarding funerals. It is traditional to bury the dead without shoes so that, when the duppy is walking around, it will not be heard. It is also considered unwise to enter a graveyard if one has a sore, as this will make it very difficult for the sore to heal. After returning home from a funeral, one should enter the house backwards to stop duppies from entering the house as well. Walking backwards is effective because once the duppy walks in your footsteps, it will be facing away from the door, and will be fooled into leaving. Opening an umbrella indoors is another method for inviting duppies into the house. Therefore, an umbrella should be placed unopened in a corner to dry.

## CUISINE

The national dish of Barbados is *coucou* and flying fish. *Coucou* is a corn flour paste prepared exactly as it was done in some parts of Africa, where it was called *foo-foo*. Sometimes it is prepared with okra, which is allowed to boil into a slimy sauce. The corn flour is then added and stirred in, shaped into balls, and served with flying fish steamed in a rich gravy. Flying fish may also be fried in a batter or roasted.

Another traditional Barbadian meal is *conkie*, which is a delicacy in Ghana, where it is known as *kenkey*. *Conkie* is a form of bread made of Indian corn flour with sweet potato, pumpkin, and other ingredients. The dough is wrapped in the broad leaf of the banana plant, which is singed in boiling water and allowed to steam until cooked. Although *conkie* can be eaten at any time of the year, it is now eaten mainly at Independence time. Pepper-pot is another Barbadian specialty. It is a concoction of hot pepper, spice, sugar, cassareep, and salted meat, such as beef and/or pork, and is eaten with rice or another starch. This dish, too, originated in Ghana.

Another popular Barbadian dish is pudding and souse, traditionally a special Saturday meal. The intestines of the pig are meticulously cleaned and stuffed with such ingredients as sweet potatoes, pepper, and much seasoning and allowed to boil until cooked. Sometimes the blood of the pig is included in the ingredients. When this occurs, the dish is called black pudding. Souse is made from the head and feet of the pig pickled with breadfruit or sweet potatoes and cooked into a stew. It is usually served with the pudding.

## TRADITIONAL BARBADIAN DANCES

Barbados is an island rich in forms of entertainment; songs and dance are the chief forms of amusement. Some of Barbados's traditional dance forms such as the Joe and Johnny dance no longer exist on the island, but the Maypole dance can still be found there. Many modern dance groups, influenced to some extent by African culture, have sprung up across the island. Nightly entertainment at hotels and clubs consists of a floor show of limbo dancing, folk dance, and live bands. Many talented performers dressed in colorful costumes provide professional and enjoyable productions at local theaters. The Crop Over festival features costume bands, folk music, and calypso competitions. Barbadian Americans often return home for these festivities, and they carry on these traditions in America whenever they have the opportunity to do so.

## HOLIDAYS CELEBRATED BY BARBADIAN AMERICANS

Barbadians refer to all of their holidays as "Bank Holidays." These include New Year's Day, January 1; Errol Barrow Day, January 21; Good Friday, late March or early April; Easter Monday; May day, May 2; Whit Monday, usually in May; Kadooment Day, August 1; United Nations Day, October 3; Independence Day, November 30; Christmas Day, December 25; and Boxing Day, December 26. Many of these holidays are clearly religious holidays, influenced by the presence of the Anglican Church on the island. Good Friday is an especially important holiday in Barbados.

Until recently, almost everyone attended church services on Good Friday, which normally lasted from noon until three o'clock in the afternoon. All secular activities, such as card playing, dominoes, and swimming were avoided on that day. Women attending church wore black, white, or purple dresses as a sign of mourning for Christ's crucifixion.

There are many beliefs associated with Good Friday. One tradition holds that if the bark of a certain kind of tree is cut at noon on that day, blood oozes from the tree; another holds that before sunrise animals can be seen kneeling in prayer. Still another tradition teaches that if one breaks a fresh egg into a glass of water at noon and sets the glass in the sun for awhile, the egg white will settle into a certain formation, such as a coffin, a ship, or a church steeple. Each of these shapes is a sign of major importance for the future of the one who broke the egg: A coffin signifies death; the ship means travel; and the church indicates upcoming marriage.

Perhaps one of the most festive celebrations in Barbados is Crop Over, which was most likely influenced by the Harvest Festival of the Anglican church and the Yam Festivals of West Africa. Historical evidence indicates that as early as 1798 a manager of Newton Plantation in Barbados held a dinner and dance for the slaves, in celebration of the completion of the sugar-cane harvest. It was revived in 1973 as a civic festival.

Crop Over takes place during the last three weeks of June through the first week of July. The early portion of the festival is dominated by events in the rural areas: fairs, cane-cutting competitions, open-air concerts, "stick licking," native dancing, and handicraft and art displays. On the first Saturday in July, the celebration moves to Bridgetown. Sunday is known as Cohobblepot, and is marked by various cultural events and the naming of the Crop Over Queen. The finale occurs on Monday, or Kadooment, during which there are great band competitions and a march from the National Stadium to the Garrison Savannah. There Barbadians burn an effigy of a man in a black coat and hat called Mr. Harding, which symbolizes the ending of hard times.

It is not practical for Barbadians living in America to observe many of these holidays, but Christmas and New Year's, which are also holidays in America, are celebrated much the same way as they are in Barbados with overeating, drinking, dancing, and the exchange of gifts. Many Barbadian Americans return to Barbados for Crop Over.

## PROVERBS

It is said that at one time a Barbadian hardly spoke a dozen sentences without speaking a proverb. Barbadians still, without conscious effort, decorate their speech with proverbs. A few examples of these appear below. They were preserved by G. Addison Forde in his work *De Mortar-Pestle: A Collection of Barbadian Proverbs*, 1987: Duh is more in de mortar dan de pestle; If crab don' walk 'bout, crab don' get fat; Cockroach en' had no right at hen party; De higher de monkey climb, de more 'e show 'e tail; Donkey en' have no right in horse race; Don' wait till de horse get out to shut de stable door; Play wid puppy an' 'e lick yuh mout.

# LANGUAGE

The average Barbadian—known as "Bajan"—will undoubtedly boast that he or she speaks "the Queen's English," presumably standard English, but nothing can be further from the truth. Barbadians have a unique dialect, and it is said that no matter how many years a Bajan spends away from Barbados, he or she never loses the dialect, which is also called "Bajan." The use of standard English depends to a great extent on the level of education of the speaker, but even many highly educated Bajans use certain colloquialisms that are not used by other speakers in the Caribbean. In ordinary social settings, Bajans prefer to speak Bajan, but when the occasion warrants it, they slip into a language that is more nearly standard English. There are also regional differences in speech on the island. Especially noticeable is the difference in speech of those who live in the parishes of St. Lucy and St. Philip.

Bajan is a language much like the creole spoken in other areas of the Caribbean or in West Africa. Some creoles have an English base, while others have a French base, but each is a language and an adequate tool for communication. Some educators discourage the use of Bajan, but to discontinue its use is to rob Barbadians of a vital part of their cultural heritage. Even after spending many years abroad, Barbadian Americans continue to speak Bajan. Bajan has a distinctive accent whether spoken by white or black, or by educated or uneducated Barbadian. Among certain peculiarities of the language, pointed out by linguists, is the use of compounds that in standard English are redundant. Examples are "boar-hog," meaning boar; "sparrow-bird," meaning a sparrow; and "big-big," meaning very large. Although there are fewer words of African origin in the language than in some of the other creoles, such words as *coucou, conkie, wunnah,* and *backra* are definitely African in origin.

## FAMILY AND COMMUNITY DYNAMICS

Like most West Indians, Barbadians are family oriented. Sometimes the parents in a home are not legally married to each other, but this makes very little difference to the family members. Any disruption to the family affects all concerned. Typically, the father is head of the home—he is the "boss." The roles of family members are clearly defined, and Barbadians follow them rigorously. There is man's work, woman's work, and children's work. Even though both parents might work outside the home, the woman is responsible for all domestic chores such as cooking, grocery shopping, laundering, and keeping the family clean. Children's chores include washing dishes, sweeping the house and yard, getting rid of garbage, and taking care of domestic animals. The father brings home the money to feed and keep the family, and he is often revered by the rest of the family.

The extended family is also a vital part of family life. Often, grandparents live in the home with their children and grandchildren. Aunts, uncles, and cousins, along with godparents and even close friends, may make up a family unit. Any disruptions, problems, or family changes affect all the members of the family. For example, a family member's departure because of marriage, a family feud, or to travel abroad is an occasion of tremendous concern for everyone.

Barbadians who immigrate to America do so for social, political, educational, or economic reasons. All come "to better themselves." Most Barbadian Americans leave behind spouses and/or children with promises to send for them as soon as possible. The separation puts a tremendous emotional strain on the family members, especially children who are often left behind with grandparents, other family members, or friends. Often it is the male head of the home who precedes the fam-

ily, and when he arrives, he is faced with a reality that falls short of his expectations. The job he thought he would get evades him, and he must settle for one far below his abilities and qualifications, which places him in a lower wage bracket. Sometimes he finds himself doing menial jobs among disgruntled and even racist coworkers. He may become disillusioned and humiliated, and his self-esteem may sink to an extremely low level. Worst of all, the anticipated reunion of the family, instead of taking place as soon as possible, may have to be postponed indefinitely because of lack of funds and other problems. Despite these hardships, the Barbadian typically does not seek public assistance. He works hard to achieve his goal, and eventually, he is able to have his family join him. The younger members quickly adapt to their new environment and American lifestyles, while the older members maintain the values of home.

Many Barbadian Americans, however, arrive professionally and technically prepared for the job market. Others enter trade-schools, colleges, universities, and professional schools to be trained, and afterwards fill many professional and technical positions in this country. Some become lawyers, physicians, university professors, accountants, nurses, and professional counselors. They make outstanding contributions to American life and culture. Barbadian Americans, like other West Indians, are friendly people. They will go out of their way to render assistance to others. They interact well with such minorities as Puerto Ricans, Haitians, Central Americans, South Americans, Asians, and Europeans. On the whole, they integrate well into mainstream American society.

### WEDDINGS

Most weddings in Barbados are performed in a church. Weddings are always held on Saturday because it is considered bad luck to get married on Friday. Traditionally, the bride wears a white gown and a veil. The groom, who arrives before the bride, sits in the front of the church with his best man. He is not supposed to look back until the bride arrives inside the church, at which time he stands and waits until she arrives at his side. A minister then performs the ceremony, which varies according to the wishes of the couple or the status of the family. At the end of the ceremony, the wedding party leaves the church and drives in a procession to the reception hall or house, honking their horns as they drive along. The uninvited guests usually leave their businesses and hang around the church or on the side of the road to see the bride. Several superstitions are associated with marriage. The bride must never make her own wedding dress, and it should remain unfinished until the day of the wedding; the gown's finishing touches should be done while the bride is dressing for the wedding. It is bad luck if the bridegroom sees the wedding dress before the day of the wedding; if it rains on the day of the wedding (especially if the bride gets wet); or if a cat or a dog eats any of the wedding cake.

# RELIGION

Because there is no record of the religion of the first settlers on Barbados, the Amerindians, the first documented religion on the island was the Anglican church. It is almost certain that the early slaves brought their religions from Africa to the island, but the absence of records deprives us of this information. At the time of settlement of Barbados by the English, Anglicanism was the state religion in England. It is not surprising that this religion was brought to the island and became the dominant church in Barbados for many years. The island was divided into 11 parishes in the seventeenth century, and today these parishes still exist. There is a church in each parish, along with other meeting places. Until

"I left Barbados because the jobs were scarce. I decided to take a chance and come to this new country. There were a lot of us from the West Indies. We heard this was a good, new country where you had the opportunity to better your circumstances."

Lyle Small in 1921, cited in *Ellis Island: An Illustrated History of the Immigrant Experience,* edited by Ivan Chemayeff et al. (New York: Macmillan, 1991).

1969 the church was fully endowed and established by the government, and it enjoyed the privileges of a state church, with its bishops and clergy paid from general tax receipts.

In the seventeenth century, Irish indentured servants brought Roman Catholicism to Barbados, and Jews and Quakers were among other religious groups that also arrived on the island, followed by Moravians and Methodists in the late eighteenth century. In the late nineteenth century the Christian Mission and other revivalist religions appeared, and today there are over 100 Christian religions as well as Judaism, Islam, and

Hinduism in Barbados. Anglicanism has lost much of its religious influence, although it still claims 70 percent of the population, most of whom are nominal members. Barbadians who emigrate do not leave their religion behind them.

# EMPLOYMENT AND ECONOMIC TRADITIONS

Like most immigrants, Barbadian Americans come to America to "better themselves" economically. At home, economic opportunities do not keep pace with population growth, and salaries and wages are deplorably low. Over 82 percent settle in the Northeast region of the United States, 76 percent in New York state alone. Some find occupation in professional and technical fields, but the vast majority work as clerical workers, operators, craftsmen, foremen, sales workers, private household workers, service workers, managers, officials, foremen, and laborers; a very few work as farm managers and laborers. To enter the job market, many accept low-paying jobs they would consider beneath them at home. Except for the professional and technical workers, Barbadians' income is usually much lower than that of many other immigrant groups. Nevertheless, they make much more than they would at home. Because they believe in upward mobility, many Barbadians attend technical and professional schools and colleges, and they quickly qualify themselves for better paying jobs.

# POLITICS AND GOVERNMENT

Unlike most of the other Caribbean islands settled by Britain, for almost 350 years Barbados experienced unbroken British colonial rule. The country's government is structured after the British Parliament. The Barbadian Parliament consists of a Senate and a House of Assembly. Twenty-one senators are appointed by the Governor-general (the Queen's representative), 12 on the advice of the prime minister, two recommended by the opposition, and seven at the governor's discretion. In the House of Assembly there are a speaker and 27 members who are elected by the people. The term of office is five years. The main political parties in Barbados are the Democratic Labor Party, Barbados Labor Party, and the National Democratic Party.

Associated with Barbados politics are the names of such leaders as Sir Grantley Herbert Adams (1898-1971), first premier of Barbados and Prime Minister of the Federation of the Indies; and Errol Walton Barrow (1920-1987), Premier and first prime minister of Barbados. These men influenced the politics of the island. In 1954, when a ministerial system of government was introduced, Adams became the first premier of Barbados, and the island gained internal self-government. On November 30, 1966, under Barrow, Barbados became an independent nation and a member of the British Commonwealth of Nations.

Barbadians have a passion for politics, especially Barbados politics. At home or abroad, two very important topics of discussion in which the vast majority of Barbadians engage are politics and cricket. It seems that the average Barbadian is more politically literate and involved than other West Indians. Their passionate love for their country is no doubt a major factor in their political involvement. Because of their pride in, and attachment to, their homeland, Barbadian Americans remain actively involved in the politics of Barbados. Many zealously continue to monitor changes and developments in government, and to support financially their favorite parties at home while demonstrating a passive interest in American politics.

## RELATIONS WITH BARBADOS

Barbadian Americans passionately love their homeland. A Barbadian never truly leaves home and keeps abreast of developments there by purchasing American editions of Barbadian newspapers or by having copies mailed to him from Barbados. They actively correspond with family and friends at home who inform them of the latest events on the island. They also maintain ties with relatives and friends, many of whom they financially assist, and whenever possible, they spend vacations in Barbados.

# INDIVIDUAL AND GROUP CONTRIBUTIONS

## ACTIVISM

Prince Hall (1735?-1807) was an important black leader in the eighteenth century. Accounts of his birth, parentage, early life, and career vary, but it is widely accepted that Hall was born in Bridgetown, Barbados, in about 1735 to an English man and a woman of African descent, and that he came to America in 1765. Prince Hall was both an abolitionist and a Masonic organizer. Because of his organizing skill, a charter for the establishment of a lodge of American Negroes was issued on April 29, 1787, authorizing the organization in Boston of African Lodge No. 459, a "regular Lodge of Free and accepted Masons, under the title or denomination of the African Lodge," with Prince Hall as master. Prince Hall was also an abolitionist and spokesman. He was one of eight Masons who signed a petition on January 13, 1777, requesting the Massachusetts state legislature to abolish slavery and declaring it as incompatible with the cause of American independence. He was later successful in urging Massachusetts to end its participation in the slave trade. He established the first school for colored children in his home in Boston in 1800. Hall ranks among the most significant black leaders in his day.

## GOVERNMENT AND POLITICS

As early as the 1670s, Barbadians have contributed to American government. Many prominent Barbadians immigrated to Carolina during that decade, among them was Sir John Yeamans, who became governor of the colony that is known today as South Carolina.

In the twentieth century, Shirley Chisholm, born in 1924 to Barbadian parents, became a politician of great stature in America. Although Chisholm was born in Brooklyn, New York, she spent the first ten years of her life in Barbados, where she received much of her primary education under the strict eye of her maternal grandmother. She gave credit for her later educational success to the well-rounded early training she received in Barbados. In 1964 Chisholm ran for the New York State Assembly and won the election. She fought for rights and educational opportunities for women, blacks, and the poor. She served in the State Assembly until 1968, then she ran for the United States Congress. Chisholm won the election to the U.S. House of Representatives and became the first black woman ever to be elected to the House, where she served with distinction from 1969 to 1982. In 1972 Chisholm made an unprecedented bid for the Presidential nomination of the Democratic party. She was the first black and first woman to run for the presidency. She is also the founder of the chair of the National Political Congress of Black Women.

## JOURNALISM

Robert Clyve Maynard (1937-1993), newspaper editor and publisher, was the son of Barbadian parents who immigrated to the United States in 1919. Robert was born in Brooklyn, New York, where he grew up in the Bedford-Styvesant section. Although his parents insisted on sound study habits and strong work ethic, Maynard dropped out of high school. Nevertheless, at an early age, he developed an interest in writing, which he pursued. After a series of jobs with various newspapers, he became the first black person in the United States to direct editorial operations for a major daily newspaper in 1979, when the Gannett Company appointed him editor of the *Oakland Tribune*. As editor, Maynard also launched a well-received morning edition of the paper. In 1983 Maynard bought the Oakland Tribune, Inc. from Gannett, becoming the first black person in the United States to own a controlling interest in a general-circulation city daily, and the first big-city editor of any race in recent times to buy out his paper. His contributions to the field of journalism in America place him in the ranks of outstanding Americans.

## LITERATURE

Paule Marshall, daughter of Barbadian parents, occupies a prominent place in black literature. Shortly after the First World War, Paule Marshall's parents migrated from Barbados to Brooklyn, New York, where Paule was born in 1929. After graduating from college, she became a writer. Marshall's writing combines her West Indian and Afro-American heritages. Her novel, *Brown Girl, Brownstones* is about a Barbadian girl growing up in Brooklyn. Much of her work deals with life in Barbados where, as a child, she spent time with her grandmother.

# MEDIA

## PRINT

*Carib News.*

In-depth weekly newspaper published for English-speaking Caribbean readers living in America.

**Contact:** Carl Rodney, Editor.
**Address:** 15 West 39th Street, 13th Floor, New York, New York 10018.

**Telephone:** (212) 944-1991.

## RADIO

Barbadian Americans do not own radio stations in America, but a few stations broadcast programs targeted toward English-speaking Caribbean audiences.

**WLIB-AM (1250).**

Located in New York City, this station broadcasts music, sports, and news from the Caribbean on Fridays and Saturdays from 7 a.m. to 7 p.m.

**Telephone:** (212) 447-1000.

**WNWK-FM (105.9).**

Located in Newark, New Jersey, WNWK broadcasts Reggae music, news, sports, and educational shows targeted to Caribbean audiences in the tristate area of New York, New Jersey, and Connecticut, 5 p.m. to midnight, Monday through Friday.

**Contact:** Emil Antonoff.
**Address:** One Riverfront Plaza, Suite 345, North Newark, New Jersey 07102.
**Telephone:** (212) 966-1059.

**WNJR-AM (1430).**

Also in Newark, New Jersey, this station broadcasts music, news, sports, and interviews with well-known Caribbean personalities. Focuses on Caribbean audiences, Saturday 9 a.m. to 12 noon.

**Contact:** Randy Dopwell.
**Address:** One Riverfront Plaza, Suite 345, North Newark, New Jersey 07102.
**Telephone:** (201) 642-8000.

# ORGANIZATIONS AND ASSOCIATIONS

Barbadian Americans maintain a limited number of local organizations in the larger cities where they live, and a national Barbados Association. Cricket is the national game of Barbados, hence in many communities in America cricket clubs compete on a friendly basis. There are also professional, social, and educational clubs organized by various groups. The Barbados Association has annual activities where Barbadians celebrate their Bajan heritage.

# Sources for Additional Study

Beckles, Hilary McD. *A History of Barbados: From Amerindian Settlement to Nation-State*. Cambridge: Cambridge University Press, 1990.

*Caribbean Basin Commercial Profile*, edited by Susan Kholer-Reed and Sam Skogstad III. Washington, D.C.: Caribbean Publishing Company, Ltd., 1994.

Frazer, Henry, et al. *A-Z of Barbadian Heritage*. Kingston, Jamaica: Heineman Publishers (Caribbean) Limited, 1990.

Hoyos, F. A. *Barbados: Our Island Home*. London: Macmillan Publishers, 1984.

LaBrucherie, Roger A. *A Barbados Journey*. Pine Valley, California: Imagenes Press, 1985.

Puckrein, Gary A. *Little England: Plantation Society and Anglo-Barbadian Politics, 1627-1700*. New York: New York University Press, 1984.

Schomburgh, Robert H. *The History of Barbados*. London: Frank Cass & Co., Ltd. 1971.

Tree, Ronald. *A History of Barbados*. New York: Random House, 1972.

# BELARUSAN AMERICANS

by
Vituat Kipel

## OVERVIEW

The Republic of Belarus is a newly independent country which, prior to August 25, 1991, was known as the Byelorussian Soviet Socialist Republic. Since 1922 it had formed part of the Soviet Union. Geographically it is located in what is virtually the center of Europe, occupying 80,154 square miles (207,600 square kilometers). It is bounded by Poland to the west, Russia to the east, Ukraine to the south, and Lithuania/Latvia to the north and northwest. Belarus's capital city, Minsk, is situated along the railroad route linking Warsaw and Moscow and has a population of about two million. Other major cities of Belarus are Brest, Grodno, Vitebsk, Gomel, Mogilev, Polotsk, Baranovichy, Pinsk, and Slutsk.

The population of Belarus is over ten million people; over two million more Belarusans live in other parts of the former Soviet Union. About 80 percent of Belarusans in the Republic profess the Eastern Orthodox faith; about 15 to 18 percent are Roman Catholics. The remaining population is divided among Eastern Rite Catholics, (Uniates), Baptists, and Old Believers. There are also strong Muslim and Jewish minorities.

Because the Belarusans' ethnic territory is divided among several neighboring states, it is difficult to present a clear picture of a Belarusan state, nationhood, and historical development.

Part of the confusion stems from terminology. As political concepts, the terms "Byelorussia," "Byelorussian," and since 1991, "Belarus" and "Belarusans," are all relatively new. For most Americans, the term "Byelorussia" was not known until the end of World War II, when the then Byelorussian Soviet Socialist Republic became a charter member of the newly forming United Nations. Prior to World War II the terms more familiar to Americans were "White Russia" and "White Russians" or "White Ruthenia" and "White Ruthenians." The term "White" in these various formulations is simply the literal translation of "byelo-" or "byela-."

## HISTORY

The tribes who were the antecedents of present-day Belarusans began to organize into individual principalities around such cities as Polotsk, Smalensk, and Turov as early as the ninth and tenth centuries. During the twelfth century these principalities moved closer, forming a unified structure and establishing the core of the Grand Duchy of Lithuania, which became an important political power as a commonwealth in eastern Europe over the next several centuries. As these Belarusan principalities gave rise to the Grand Duchy of Lithuania, Belarusan became recognized as the official language of this state. The city of Navahradak, in the earlier period, and the city of Vilna, in the later period, served as the capitals of this large, multinational, influential state.

Gradually the Grand Duchy of Lithuania came under the strong cultural influence of Poland. The upper strata of society became dissociated from the broader mass of the population, in part, by embracing Roman Catholicism, largely accepting the Polish forms of Catholicism, which in turn created religious inequality and social unrest. These factors destabilized the Grand Duchy, weakening it militarily and politically. Meanwhile in the east, the state known as Muscovy grew stronger and began its expansion westward. During the seventeenth and eighteenth centuries Muscovy moved into the territory of the Grand Duchy and farther west into Poland.

## BELARUS UNDER RUSSIAN OCCUPATION

The beginnings of Russian domination over the Belarusan territories go back to the sixteenth and seventeenth centuries when the easternmost parts of Belarus were incorporated into the Russian Empire. Then, in a series of successful advances, Russia invaded and annexed the core of ethnic Belarusan lands in 1772, 1793, and 1795. Russian policies towards Belarus were uncompromising in their call for the territories to undergo Russian acculturation. Such Russification was systematically justified and encouraged. This approach remained vigorous through the reigns of successive tsars and the decades of the Soviet regime.

The nineteenth century witnessed an active implementation of Russian policies in Belarus. The term *Belarus* was abolished and replaced by the deliberately vague geographical concept, "Northwest Territory." The use of the Belarusan language was outlawed and all communication was ordered to be exclusively in Russian. Beginning in the 1830s the government adopted a policy of forced deportation of Belarusans to the northern regions of the Empire. Uprisings in Belarus in 1831 and 1863 to 1864 provoked policies of unprecedented harshness regarding Russification, exploitation of the land, and oppression of the populace. The result of these policies was the reduction of Belarus to the status of a colony; it was denied its own governmental bodies and was supervised in all things by appointed administrators. A further result was the creation of an enormous surplus of the local labor force which, in turn, caused a large wave of emigration. Thus, beginning with the last two decades of the nineteenth century and into the early years of World War I, hundreds of thousands of Belarusan peasants migrated out of their homeland to Siberia and the United States.

Although the Russian administrators exerted considerable effort to uproot any characteristics of Belarusan separateness—political or cultural—an ethnic awareness among Belarusans began to emerge toward the last quarter of the nineteenth century. From there on, the revival in self-awareness gained in numbers and in strength. In 1902 the first Belarusan political party, the Belarusan Revolutionary *Hramada,* was established. This was soon followed by numerous cultural and religious organizations, publishing groups, and a teachers' union. However, the real impetus for a widespread revival of Belarusan consciousness and development of a mass movement was the appearance of Belarusan-language newspapers: first, the short-lived *Nasa Dola* (1906), and then its successor, *Nasa Niva* (1906-15), both published in Vilna. This latter newspaper played a particularly important role in assembling the most active leaders of the Belarusan intelligentsia.

## MODERN ERA

The high point of Belarusan political activities during the pre-war period and the World War I years was the convening of the all-Belarusan Congress in December 1917 in the capital city of Minsk. The Council, elected at this Congress in 1918, adopted a resolution declaring the independence of Belarus in the form of the Belarusan Democratic Republic. This new democratic state was short-lived, however. Bolshevik armed forces interrupted the Congress and overran the Republic.

The Bolsheviks moved quickly to catch up with the national aspirations of the people. On January 1, 1919, they proclaimed the Belarusan Soviet Socialist Republic (abbreviated as the BSSR). This event had a positive influence on the general populace as the leadership of the newly established Belarusan Soviet Republic improved the economy, political administration, educational system, and cultural life. Many Belarusan emigrants from Western Europe and the United States returned to their homeland. Unfortunately, according to the terms of the Treaty of Riga, signed in 1921, a significant part of Belarusan ethnic territory was given over to the new Polish state.

Belarusan national life in both halves—the eastern, under the Soviets, and the western, under the Poles—flourished during the early and mid-twenties. In both areas there were hundreds of Belarusan schools, publishing houses, and other expressions of cultural life. The Belarusan national movement reached its peak in eastern and western Belarus during the 1920s.

Uncomfortable with the growth of the Belarus national movement, Polish administrators in the middle of the 1920s began to curb Belarusan political activities, close Belarusan schools, outlaw Belarusan-language newspapers, and harass their religious communities. By the beginning of the 1930s the Belarusan movement in Poland had been totally crushed, with its leaders either imprisoned or emigrated—primarily to Soviet Belarus. The systematic persecution of nationally conscious Belarusan in Soviet Belarus began several years later. Soviet Belarus experienced several waves of intermittent purges, the peak years being 1930, 1933, and 1937 to 1938. The official explanation for these pogroms was that the party was struggling with the "National Democrats," i.e., with the Belarusan intelligentsia and nationally democratically minded citizens.

The major parts of the Belarusan nation—the Belarusan Soviet Socialist Republic and Western Belarus—were reunited into a single state in September 1939 when Soviet troops occupied the eastern part of the Polish state. The occupation of Western Belarus by the Soviet armed forces proved costly to the Belarusans: thousands of Belarusans were deported to Siberia, numerous leaders were shot, and all Belarusan activities were suppressed.

The German *Wehrmacht* occupied Belarusan territory within a few weeks after the beginning the German-Soviet War, on June 22, 1941. A number of Belarusan political leaders cooperated with the German occupiers, but any hope of new political freedom under German rule was dashed by the spring of 1944 when the Soviet army advanced westward and occupied Belarusan territory.

World War II devastated Belarus. Over nine thousand villages, two hundred towns, and approximately six million Belarusans were lost. The territory of Belarus was once again balkanized. Parts of Belarusan ethnic territory were included in Poland, Lithuania, and Latvia, with the largest portion given to the Russian Federation. Hundreds of thousands of Belarusans were resettled in Siberia, while thousands of others emigrated as a result of the war. Almost two decades would pass before Belarus could heal the material wounds resulting from World War II.

Surprisingly, despite the denigration and mistreatment of Belarusan culture, a sizable segment of the population and the intelligentsia resisted Russification. A powerful revival process became evident by 1985. Belarusan schools began to open, the Supreme Soviet adopted a Constitution proclaiming the Belarusan language the official language of the Republic, and numerous societies fostered a new esteem for the language and culture. The national revival also led to the emergence of the Belarusan Popular Front, a national political movement functioning as a democratic opposition party in the parliament of the republic. Many obstacles remain, however, before Belarus becomes a truly democratic state, as envisioned in the proclamation of August 25, 1991.

## BELARUSAN IMMIGRANTS IN AMERICA

Some believe that the earliest Belarusan immigrants in America settled in the Colony of Virginia in the early 1600s. The reason is that Captain John Smith, who became the first Governor of Virginia in 1608, had visited Belarus in 1603. In his *True Travels*, Captain Smith recalls that he came to "Rezechica, upon the River Niper in the confines of Lithuania," and then he narrates how he traveled through southern Belarus, as Zora Kipel related in her article (*Zapisy*, Volume 16, 1978). Thus, it is possible that Smith brought Belarusans with him to Virginia, together with Polish or Ukrainian manufacturing specialists.

Mass emigration from Belarus began slowly during the final decades of the nineteenth century and lasted until World War I. At the outset emigration from Belarus was directed toward the industrial cities in Poland, to Riga, St. Petersburg, the mines in Ukraine and Siberia, and later, to the United States. Libava and northern Germany were the main points of departure while New York, Philadelphia, Boston, and Baltimore were the main gates of entry to the United States. Slightly over a million Belarusans came to the shores of America, but only about 650,000 immigrants settled here permanently. Unfortunately for the Belarusan immigrants, their ethnicity was not properly registered when they arrived. They were routinely registered as Russians (having Russian Imperial passports and being of the Eastern Orthodox religion) or as Poles, if they were Roman Catholics. Thus, American bureaucracy is partly responsible for creating "the Russian immigrant masses." Research has demonstrated that the majority of those "Russian masses" were of Belarusan background.

Belarusans who arrived in the United States after World War I were predominantly political immigrants, mainly from western Europe and Poland. They numbered only a few thousand persons but were able to found several Belarusan organizations. A few Belarusans, mainly the children of Jewish Belarusan marriages, came to the United States between the late 1930s and the end of 1941.

## POSTWAR IMMIGRATION

Belarusans arrived in sizable numbers in the post-World War II period, from 1948 to the early 1950s. During this period about 50,000 Belarusans immigrated to the United States; for the most part, they were people with "displaced person" status who had left Europe for political reasons. They represented a very broad spectrum of the Belarusan nation, sharing one trait in common: fervent anti-Communism. The great majority of them were nationally conscious Belarusans filled with the political resolve to reestablish an independent democratic Belarusan state, the Belarusan Democratic Republic. They came from a variety of countries, the majority of them from West Germany and Austria, but many from Great Britain, France, Italy, Belgium, Denmark, and other countries in South America and north Africa. These lands had been their first stop-overs after the events of World War II had prompted them to leave Belarus. These immigrants represented several distinct categories: former prisoners of war of the Polish and Soviet armies; former emigres who had left Belarus shortly after World War I or in 1939, when the Soviets invaded Poland; persons who had worked in Germany during the war as *Ostarbeiters*; refugees who had fled Belarus in 1943 or 1944; and post-World War II defectors and dissidents.

Emigration waves from Belarus during the 1980s and 1990s have been relatively small as compared with previous waves. People have emigrated for various reasons: political, economic, and filial (to reunite with families). Most of these immigrants are of Jewish Belarusan background. The political and economic situation in Belarus in the mid 1990s suggests that immigration should continue and increase in size, especially by individuals who are rejoining family members in the United States.

Because official databases in the United States are unable to provide accurate numbers of Belarusans entering the country, widely varying figures have appeared in print. Attempts have been made in Belarus by various researchers to calculate the number of Belarusans emigrating to the United States. While such calculations and estimates vary, they tend to range between one-half million to one million. The Belarusan Institute of Arts and Sciences in the United States has studied the problem and concluded that the total number of Belarusan immigrants who settled in the United States is somewhere between 600,000 and 650,000 persons.

## SETTLEMENT

Since no one mapped the distribution of Belarusan immigrants to America when they arrived, it is impossible to reconstruct precise settlement patterns. Only general outlines are possible. The criteria for distribution and settlement tended to be based on the availability of unskilled jobs, proximity to landsmen, and the decision of the sending agent as to which port in the United States the immigrant should be sent. There is evidence of Belarusan settlement all over the United States, from Alaska to Florida, with the greatest numbers concentrated in the states between Illinois and New York. Belarusan population tends to be heaviest in industrial cities and mining regions. For the majority of immigrants, their first stops were New York City; Jersey City, Bayonne, the Amboys, Passaic, Newark, South River, and other small towns in New Jersey; cities such as Cleveland and Akron in Ohio; and Gary, Indiana, Chicago, Illinois, Detroit, Michigan, and Pittsburgh, Pennsylvania. A smaller number of Belarusans went to farms in New York, New Jersey, Connecticut, and Massachusetts.

# ACCULTURATION AND ASSIMILATION

The Belarusan American Association, together with a number of other groups, developed a system of supplementary secondary schools in Belarusan communities where the American-born generations receive education in the language, culture, and religious traditions of Belarus. The task of representing Belarusan culture at various venues throughout the United States has been assumed by choirs, theatrical groups, musical and dance ensembles. One such dance ensemble, located in the New York metropolitan area, is headed by Dr. Alla Romano, a faculty member at the City University of New York. This group, *Vasilok*, has performed widely and often in the United States as well as in the Bielastok region and in Belarus itself.

## TRADITIONS, CUSTOMS, AND BELIEFS

Many customs with roots in Belarus (some of which are shared with neighboring Slavic nations) are observed by Belarusan Americans. Belarusan customs typically interweave elements of nature, especially agriculture, with pagan and Christian components. Most customs are related to the calendar, ceremonial events, and games. Although the life styles of our modern, technological age are not conducive to maintaining many of these folk traditions, it is remarkable how many of them have survived. This is especially evident when one examines the 36 volumes on Belarusan ethnography published as *Bielaruskaja Narodnaja Tvorcasc* by the Academy of Sciences in Minsk, Belarus, between 1977 and 1993.

## CUISINE

Cuisine plays an important role in manifesting the hospitality, cordiality, and friendliness implic-

it in the traditional Belarusan greeting, "A guest in the house is God in the house." Since Belarus is located in the forest, grain, and potato belts of eastern Europe, Belarusan cooking reflects the riches of the land. Favorite dishes include a wide variety of grains, a diversity of mushrooms, meats, and many kinds of fish dishes. There are, of course, a number of items which Belarusans share in common with their Slavic neighbors: *halubcy* (stuffed cabbage), borscht, and *kaubasa* (kielbasy). One popular comestible well known to many Americans is the bagel. The traditional bagel comes from the town of Smarhon in the northwestern part of Belarus. But unquestionably the most famous food of Belarus is the potato. The Belarusan housewife has close to one hundred ways of preparing potato dishes for every occasion. Traditional dishes are especially popular at holiday time in Belarusan American homes.

## TRADITIONAL COSTUMES

The most visible and expressive Belarusan folk art is found in national apparel, where the predominant colors are red, white, black, and occasionally green. Symmetric and geometric designs are the most common features of Belarusan decorative patterns.

There are distinct patterns, designs, and materials for men and women. A woman's holiday dress of homespun material consists of a white linen blouse, always ornamented with embroidery or a woven design; an apron, usually of white linen with embroidery; a long pleated skirt of colorful woolen material; a vest, laced or buttoned in the front, often with slits from the waist down; and a headdress. The man's costume is composed of linen trousers and a shirt. The shirt is long, always embroidered, and worn with a hand-woven belt or sash.

## SONGS AND DANCES

Scholars trace the origins of Belarusan music to pagan times. A national characteristic is the tendency to form instrumental groups. Every village in the home country has its own musicians and that pattern has been replicated in the United States, with virtually every Belarusan community having its own orchestra. The most commonly used instruments are the violin (*skrypka*), accordion (*bajan*), cymbals, pipe (*dudka*), and the tambourine.

An important part of the Belarusan musical heritage is the huge repertoire of songs, suitable for every occasion, including birth, marriage, death, entering military service, the change of seasons, work, and leisure. Belarusans sing solos, duets, and harmonize in ensembles and choirs. The rich and elaborately lyrical songs which form the basis of Belarusan folk music have a special appeal for Belarusans. Singing is often accompanied by one or more instruments, very often the *husli* (psaltery). The lullaby is especially popular in Belarusan families. Generations of children have grown up learning the lyrics to these songs sung to them by their mothers and grandmothers.

Dancing has similarly enjoyed a millennium-long life span in Belarus and this tradition continues in America. Belarusan folk dancing is characterized by the richness of its composition, uncomplicated movements, and small number of rapid steps. Folk dances are often accompanied by song expressing the feelings, work habits, and life style of the people. Ethnographers have identified over one hundred Belarusan folk dances, many of which are performed in America. The legacy of song and dance is an aspect of the native culture that is shared by both old and new immigrants, transcending chronological barriers.

## HOLIDAYS

Holiday seasons are filled with traditional Belarusan practices and customs. The Christmas season, for example, includes many unique customs. One of the most cherished and carefully preserved traditions is the celebration of *kuccia*, a very solemn and elaborate supper on Christmas Eve. Twelve or more dishes are prepared and served. Each dish is served in a specific order, with a portion set aside for the ancestors. The pot holding the *kuccia* (a special barley confection) is placed in the corner of the room, under the icons. After the family says grace, the *kuccia* is the first course served. Another widely observed custom is the decoration of the Christmas tree with hand-made Belarusan ornaments. As a rule, the entire family takes part in the ceremony, with the oldest family members contributing most of the craftsmanship. Caroling, an old Christmas tradition, is solidly maintained by Belarusan Americans both of the older and younger generations, with the latter employing this custom as a means of fundraising for organizational purposes.

The Easter season is another occasion for the observance of many traditional customs. The season begins with a period of fasting, followed by *Vierbnica* (Palm Sunday), and a competition of flower bouquets. Following the Easter Liturgy, the priest blesses colored eggs, sausage, *babka* (special Easter bread), and cheese. An Easter breakfast, *Razhavieny*, is held in the parish hall where traditional foods are served. Easter Sunday is given over to visiting friends and relatives, and to playing various games, such as cracking the Easter eggs.

Other "double-faith" observances include the celebration of *Kupalle*, marking the end of Spring and beginning of Summer. *Dziady* commemorates the departed and is one of four such feasts celebrated each year. Many Belarusan communities preserve the tradition of honoring army recruits. A special liturgy is celebrated, followed by a party where traditional draftee songs are sung. An Autumn observance, *Dazynki*, the harvest festival, is a joyous event concluding with a community dinner.

The most widely observed sanctified feastday is that of St. Euphrosynia of Polacak, the Patron Saint of Belarus. Her feast day, May 23, is traditionally celebrated by all Belarusans. Belarusan Americans also have a special devotion to St. Cyril of Turdu, whose feastday falls on April 28. The Mother of God of Zyrovicy is the patroness of many Belarusan churches. Her patronal feast is May 20. Other church-related customs and anniversaries observed by Belarusan Americans are the Smalensk Marian icon, *Adzihitrya* (Guide), observed on August 10, the Feast of Pentecost/Whitsunday, and the Feast of All the Saints of Belarus (the third Sunday after Pentecost). Belarusan Roman Catholics observe the feast of Our Lady of Vostraja Brama in Vilna on November 16; and St. Mary of Budslau on July 2, among others.

## CRAFTS

Among the Belarusan crafts that are widespread in the United States are woven rugs and embroidered table covers and bedspreads. Hand-woven belts and embroidered towels are perhaps most prized. Towels have particular significance because of the numerous solemn occasions when they are employed—weddings, christenings, and adorning icons. Belarusan American families have dozens of towels for all types of events. Pottery, straw incrustations, and woodcarving are also popular age-old Belarusan crafts practiced throughout the United States. These items are typically adorned with simple geometric designs and are put to more practical uses, rather than kept as *objets d'art*.

# LANGUAGE

The Belarusan language is a part of the East Slavic group of languages which includes Ukrainian and Russian. The language of Belarusan Americans has specific features. In everyday use many Americanisms have entered the Belarusan language, but are often so assimilated to the lexical and phonological patterns of Belarusan that they do not seem foreign to the language. A peculiar phenomenon is the language of thousands of Belarusan immigrants who came prior to World War I. These people claimed to speak Russian but were in fact speaking a Russified Belarusan, often with the admixture of Yiddish words. Unfortunately, because of the lack of language professionals working for the U.S. Census, this melange of languages stemming from a Belarusan base was recorded as Russian.

# FAMILY AND COMMUNITY DYNAMICS

As in other Slavic cultures, the earlier Belarusan family was a large, communal group. Incorporating distant relatives or even strangers, the family was held together by the work each contributed to the farm rather than by blood relationships. A stranger (*zdolnik*) might join a family for life or for an agreed period; he and his heirs were accorded equal status with other members. Most often the father or grandfather acted as family head. He assigned the men jobs and acted as trustee for the family property, which was collectively owned. In modern times, such families have become rare, but some of the family leader's authority remains. At family gatherings, for example, the head sits in the place of honor, with the other men grouped by rank around him. Women sit at the other end of the table. The family head blesses the meal and serves himself first.

The sexes are also divided with respect to the jobs each performs. Washing clothes or preparing food, for example, is traditionally considered women's work, and no man would consider doing these tasks. Women also enjoy financial independence, within the limitations of family obligations. Like the men, they keep the money made from the sale of surplus vegetables. The women have unquestioned authority in the household, with complete responsibility for children younger than 14 years. As the male head of the household supervises the men, his wife directs the work of women within the parameters of the farm community. Belarusan women have long been respected for their willingness and ability to work.

## FAMILY NAMES

Widespread and recognizable, Belarusan surnames include such names as Barsuk, Kalosha, Kresla, Savionak, and Sienka. Belarusan surnames are often based on geographical origin, e.g., Babruiski, Minskii, Mogilevskii, Slutski, Vilenski. Many others derive from baptismal names, e.g., Jakubau, Haponau, Kazimirau, or such diminutives as Jakubionak and Hapanionak. The most typical Belarusan surnames are those with the suffixes "ovich" or "ievich," such as Dashkievich, Mickievich, Zmitrovich. Others derive from occupations, e.g., Dziak, Hrabar, Mular.

# RELIGION

Approximately 80 percent of modern-day Belarusans are Eastern Orthodox, about 15 to 18 percent are Roman Catholic, and the remaining population is divided among Eastern Rite Catholics, (Uniates), Baptists, and Old Believers. There are also strong Muslim and Jewish minorities.

Only after World War II did groups of believers begin to establish distinctly Belarusan churches in America. The majority of Belarusan immigrants were of the Eastern Orthodox faith. The formal organization of Belarusan Orthodox activities dates from 1949 to 1950, when parishes began to be founded as parishes of the Belarusan Autocephalous Orthodox Church (BAOC). Organizational work for the BAOC began in North America under the guidance of Archbishop Vasil, who established his residence in New York City. Archbishop Mikalaj of Toronto has become the Primate of this jurisdiction, which includes parishes in the states of New York, New Jersey, Ohio, and Michigan. Several Belarusan parishes in Illinois, New Jersey, and New York are within the jurisdiction of Archbishop Iakovos, the Exarch of the Ecumenical Patriarch for North and South America. The BAOC conducts an extensive school program and is involved in providing aid to Chernobyl victims. The liturgical services are conducted in Belarusan.

Belarusan Catholics of the Latin Rite have not formed parishes of their own in the United States. Consequently, Belarusan American Roman Catholics have devoted themselves to civic activities within the Belarusan Orthodox communities, while occasionally enjoying a visiting Catholic priest of Belarusan descent. Belarusan Catholics of the Byzantine-Slavic Rite (Uniates), organized their own parish in Chicago, primarily through the efforts of two Belarusan activists, Rev. John Tarasevich and his nephew Rev. Uladzimir Tarasevich.

# POLITICS AND GOVERNMENT

## RELATIONS WITH BELARUS

The idea of Belarusan statehood and separateness began to surface in non-Belarusan publications such as the newspapers *Novyi Mir*, *Russkii Golos*, and *Novoye Russkoye Slovo*. These Ukrainian American newspapers not only published materials of interest to Belarusan immigrants, but wholeheartedly supported Belarusan independence and the establishment of Belarusan ethnic organizations. In these ways—contacts with the homeland and through the printed word—the concepts of national separateness, national self-awareness, and Belarusan independence were communicated to the Belarusan American immigrant communities, inspiring them to come together and form specifically Belarusan ethnic organizations.

The political activities of Belarusan groups consist mainly of lobbying various political groups and individual political leaders to support the idea of a democratic and independent Belarusan state. The Belarusan American Association is a champion in this undertaking. For more than forty years this group has written thousands of memoranda and visited hundreds of legislators at all levels, soliciting political support for Belarus's movement for independence. During the past 20 years, under the leadership of Anton Shukeloyts, this organization has achieved an outstanding record of support for political dissidents and for the Belarusan National Front in the homeland.

# INDIVIDUAL AND GROUP CONTRIBUTIONS

Several Belarusan Americans have made noteworthy contributions to American society and to the Belarusan community. An early attempt to form a Belarusan landsmen's circle was made by Dr. Aleksandr Sienkievich and some of his friends in Baltimore, Maryland, between 1910 and 1912. Although he recognized the need for such an organization, he soon became involved with the anarchist movement in the United States and was lost to the Belarusan movement. Viable Belarusan organizations were established in Chicago in the 1920s by such people as Anton and Jan Charapuks, Jazep Varonka, Rev. John Tarasevich, Makar Ablazhej, and a number of others who maintained contact with the Belarusan national movement in the homeland. Varonka, in particular, had already distinguished himself in Belarus by serving as the prime minister of the Belarusan National Republic before coming to the United States in 1923. He also started the first Belarusan newspaper in the United States, *The White Ruthenian Tribune* (1926) and pioneered radio broadcasts in the Belarusan language (1929).

# MEDIA

## PRINT

### *Bielarus/The Belarusan.*
A monthly Belarusan-language newspaper, established in 1950 by the Belarusan American Association, that chronicles the Belarusan presence in the United States and promotes the idea of Belarusan independence.

**Contact:** Dr. Jan Zaprudnik, Editor.
**Address:** 166-34 Gothic Drive, Jamaica, New York 11432.
**Telephone:** (516) 627-0902.

### *Bielaruski Holas (Byelorussian Voice).*
Byelorussian interest magazine.

**Contact:** Marian Ziniak, Editor and Publisher.
**Address:** 24 Tarlton Road, Toronto, Ontario, Canada, M5P 2M4.

Journals include *Belarusan Thought* (South River, New Jersey), *Polacak* (Cleveland, Ohio), and *Bielarusan Review* (Torrance, California).

# ORGANIZATIONS AND ASSOCIATIONS

Immigrants arriving after World War II were anxious to establish organizations that would promote

Belarusan consciousness and maintain their heritage here. They were active and vocal proponents of an independent Belarusan state and an independent Belarusan religious community. Among the first secular and religious organizations established by these immigrants were: United Whiteruthenian American Relief Committee, headquartered in South River, New Jersey (established in 1949); Belarusan American Association, Inc. (established in New York City in 1949 and chartered in Albany, New York, in 1950); the Byelorussian American Youth Organization (established in Cleveland, Ohio in 1951 and affiliated with the Belarusan American Association); the Belarusan American Congress Committee (established in 1951); the Belarusan American Academic Society, a student organization (established in 1951); the Association of Bielarusians in Illinois (established in 1953); several dozen women's organizations, veterans, various professional groups (physicians, poets, and writers); the Belarusan American Union (established in New York in 1965); and other smaller youth groups, such as scouts, YMCA groups, and several religious societies. These Belarusan organizations offer social, political, cultural, educational, recreational, and religious programs and activities. Over the past 40 years or more, about one hundred new Belarusan groups have been formed in dozens of states. These diverse organizations share two common characteristics: their anti-Communist stance; and their commitment to the goal of an independent and democratic Belarusan state.

The following is a list of some of the more prominent Belarusan organizations:

### Belarusan American Association.

Address: 166-34 Gothic Drive, Queens, New York 11432.

### Belarusian Congress Committee of America (BCCA).

Provides information about Belarus and Americans of Belarusian descent; supports the development of independent Belarus.

Contact: Russell R. Zavistovich, President.
Address: 724 West Tantallon Drive, Fort Washington, Maryland 20744.
Telephone: (301) 292-2610.

### Belarusan Institute of Arts and Sciences.

Address: 230 Springfield Avenue, Rutherford, New Jersey 07070.

Telephone: (201) 933-6807.
Fax: (201) 438-4565.

### Bielarusian American Union of New York.

Address: 104-29 Atlantic Avenue, Richmond Hill, New York 11419.
Telephone: (718) 625-9352.

### Byelorussian American Women Association (BAWA).

Aims to preserve national identity, cultural heritage, and traditions.

Contact: Vera Bartul, President.
Address: 146 Sussex Drive, Manhasset, New York 11030.
Telephone: (516) 627-9195.

### Byelorussian Autocephalous Orthodox Church.

Address: 9 River Road, Highland Park, New Jersey 08904.
Telephone: (908) 247-4490.

### Byelorussian Congress Committee.

Address: Byelorussian American Community Center, South Whitehead Avenue, South River, New Jersey 08882.
Telephone: (908) 254-9594.

# SOURCES FOR ADDITIONAL STUDY

*Belarus: Then and Now* (series). Minneapolis, Minnesota: Lerner Publications, 1993.

*Byelorussian Cultural Tradition in America.* New Brunswick, New Jersey: Rutgers University, 1983.

Kipel, Vitaut. "Byelorussians in the United States," *Ethnic Forum*, Volume 9, Nos. 1-2, 1989, pp. 75-90.

Novik, U. *Belarus: A New Land of Opportunity.* Minsk: Technology, 1993.

Zaprudnik, Jan. *Belarus: At a Crossroads in History.* Boulder, Colorado: Westview Press, 1993.

# BELGIAN AMERICANS

by
Jane Stewart
Cook

Belgian Americans have excelled in many fields, especially in music, science, medicine, education, and business.

## OVERVIEW

Belgium, whose official name is the Kingdom of Belgium, is a densely populated country not much larger than the state of Maryland. It covers an area of 11,781 square miles (30,519 square kilometers), bounded on the north by The Netherlands, on the west by France, and on the east by Germany. The tiny nation of Luxembourg lies to the south. This strategic location has earned Belgium the sobriquet, "crossroads of Europe." Brussels, its capital city, is just a three-hour drive to The Hague, the capital of The Netherlands, and Paris, and the capital of France.

The country is divided into three regions: Northern Lowlands, Central Lowlands, and Southern Hilly Region. Its highest point is the Botrange Mountain (2,275 feet), and its major rivers are the Schelde, the Sambre, and the Meuse, which are important transportation routes. Approximately ten million people call Belgium home. The Flemish, those residing in Flanders, the northern half of the country, speak Dutch. They make up the majority of Belgium's population. Wallonia, the region closest to France, is occupied by the French-speaking Walloons. About one percent of the population speaks German, principally those who reside near the former West German border. About 98 percent of Belgians are Catholic. Protestants and those of the

Jewish and Muslim faiths make up the remainder. Belgium's political system is that of a constitutional monarchy, with the monarch having limited powers. The national flag, adopted in 1830, is a vertical tricolor of black, yellow, and red.

## HISTORY

From approximately 57 B.C. to A.D. 431, Rome ruled over Gaul, an area of what is now France, Belgium, Luxembourg, and Germany. The land was then inhabited by independent tribes of Celtic origin. Julius Caesar's account of his efforts to subdue the area gives us the first written record of what came to be called Belgium. The Romans looked on Belgium as a defensive barrier to the Franks, Germanic tribes that eventually settled in what is now Flanders. Language patterns followed the settlement patterns. Germanic speech evolved into Dutch in the north, and the Latin of Rome developed into French in the south. These language patterns, which were established by the third century, A.D., have altered only slightly up to the present day.

With the collapse of the Roman Empire in the fifth century, the Franks held sway for more than 550 years. With the death of Charlemagne in 814, the country was divided into France, the Holy Roman Empire (Germany), and the "Middle Kingdom," a buffer state comprised of the Lowlands and Belgium. Feudal states developed, and in the later Middle Ages the dukes of Burgundy ruled the Low Countries. In 1516, Belgium became a possession of Spain and remained so until 1713, when the country was given to Austria as settlement in the War of the Spanish Succession. Belgium was annexed by France in 1795, and placed under the rule of The Netherlands after Napoleon's defeat in the Battle of Waterloo in 1815. In 1830, Belgium declared its independence, adopted a constitution, and chose its first king, Leopold I. He was succeeded in 1865 by his son, Leopold II.

## MODERN ERA

During World War I, Belgium was overrun by Germany. More than 80,000 Belgians died. Under the personal command of their "soldier king," Albert I, Belgians managed to hold on until the arrival of the Allied forces in 1918. History repeated itself in World War II when Hitler bombed Belgium into submission and took its king, Leopold III, prisoner. The arrival of Allied

forces in 1944 was followed by the Battle of the Bulge, which would decide the war's outcome. Belgium rebuilt its war-torn country, became a founding member of the United Nations and the North Atlantic Treaty Organization, and by the 1960s was enjoying a prosperous economy. Belgium has been a leader in the movement toward European economic integration, and in 1958 became a founding member of the European Economic Community.

## THE FIRST BELGIANS IN AMERICA

It is said that when Henry Hudson sailed up the New York river that now bears his name, three Flemings were aboard the ship. Certainly the Belgians participated in the early settlement (seventeenth century) of what is now Manhattan. Many historians believe that Peter Minuit, who acted as purchasing agent for the West Indian Company when Manhattan Island was bought from the resident Native Americans, was a Walloon, or at least of Belgian heritage. And it is known that his secretary, Isaac de Rasiers, was a Walloon.

Henry C. Bayer, in his *The Belgians, First Settlers in New York and in the Middle States*, discusses Belgian settlements at Wallabout, Long Island, and Staten Island, as well as in Hoboken, Jersey City, Pavonia, Communipaw, and Wallkill, New Jersey. These place names are derived from both the Walloons who settled there, as well as from the Dutch version of Walloon words used to describe a locale. For example, Hoboken is named after a town in Belgium. Pavonia got its name when a Fleming, Michael Pauw, purchased land on the Jersey shore. Translating his own name, Pauw (which in Flemish and Dutch means "peacock") into Latin, he got "Pavonia." Wallkill is the Dutch word for "Walloon's Stream." Elsewhere, the Walloomsac River in Vermont derives its name from the Walloons who settled on the east branch of the Hoosac River in New York. Belgian settlements were also established during the seventeenth century in Connecticut, Delaware, and Pennsylvania. These were settled primarily by Walloons, many of whom came to America on ships owned by the West India Company, whose founder, William Usselinx, was Flemish.

A notable name connected with America's early history is Lord Baltimore, whose family were prominent aristocrats in Flemish Belgium. Belgian officers also fought during the Revolutionary War. To note a few: Charles De Pauw, a Fleming who accompanied Lafayette to America; Ensign

Thomas Van Gaasbeck, Captain Jacques Rapalje, and Captain Anthony Van Etten, all of New York; and Captain Johannes Van Etten of Pennsylvania.

## SIGNIFICANT IMMIGRATION WAVES

Belgians came to America in greatest numbers during the nineteenth century. They came for reasons no different than many other Western Europeans—financial opportunity and a better life for their families. Belgian immigration records do not appear until 1820. From 1820 to 1910, immigration is listed at 104,000; from 1910 to 1950, 62,000 Belgians came to the United States. During the period 1847 to 1849, when disease and economic deprivation were the lot for many in Belgium, emigration numbers of those leaving for America reached 6,000 to 7,000 a year. During this time, most of those coming to the United States were small landowners (farmers), agricultural laborers, and miners; crafts people such as carpenters, masons and cabinetmakers; and other skilled tradespeople, such as glass blowers and lace makers. In later years, especially after the two World Wars, many middle class and urban professionals left Belgium for this country, seeking work in our universities, laboratories, and industrial corporations. Altogether, it is estimated that from 1820 to 1970, approximately 200,000 Belgian immigrants settled in the United States. Each year since 1950, a fixed quota of 1,350 has remained unfilled, and it is calculated that by 1981, Belgians represented no more than 0.4 percent of the foreign-born population.

## SETTLEMENT PATTERNS

Nineteenth-century settlement patterns followed work opportunities. For example, the glass industry in the East attracted many to West Virginia and Pennsylvania. Detroit, Michigan, attracted building tradespeople. Door, Brown, and Kewaunee Counties in Wisconsin attracted those seeking farmland. Considerable numbers came to Indiana. Substantial pockets of Belgian Americans can also be found in Illinois, Minnesota, North Dakota, Ohio, Kentucky, Florida, Washington, and Oregon. Many towns and cities across the United States bear the names of their counterparts in Belgium: Liege, Charleroi, Ghent, Antwerp, Namur, Rosiere, Brussels.

Michigan and Wisconsin have the largest population of Belgian Americans, with the above-named Wisconsin counties having the largest rural settlement in the United States. The Belgian American settlement in Detroit took place mainly between 1880 and 1910. Most of these new arrivals were skilled Flemish crafts people. Detroit's early industrial and manufacturing growth was fueled in great part by their skills in the building trades and transportation. According to Jozef Kadijk, whose 1963 lecture at Loyola University in Chicago appears in *Belgians in the United States*, approximately 10,000 residents of Detroit at that time were born in Belgium. Taking their descendants into account is said to increase that figure to 50,000. Most of the Wisconsin Belgians were Walloons from the areas of Brabant and Liege, Belgium. They began arriving in substantial numbers by 1853, following the lure of farmland that could be purchased from 50 cents to $1.25 an acre. Here they cleared fields, felled trees, and built rude log shelters to house their families. Writing back home of their satisfaction with their new lives, they soon were joined by thousands of their fellow countrymen. The 1860 census shows about 4,300 foreign-born Belgians living in Brown and Kewaunee Counties.

# ACCULTURATION AND ASSIMILATION

Belgians are also Western Europeans, and as such, presented a familiar religious and cultural background to others in their new homeland. Stereotypical notions as to traits of character often depict the Dutch-influenced Fleming as reserved, stubborn, practical, and vigorous, while the passion of France is observed in the Walloon's wit, extroversion, and quickness of mind and temper. It is true that whether Flemish or Walloon, the influences of The Netherlands, Germany and France upon their language, religion, and social customs were evident. This helped to make their assimilation easier—although they sometimes met with a strong anti-Catholic sentiment, which equated allegiance to the Church with disloyalty to America, and was prevalent in many parts of the United States. However, the Walloons who settled in Northeast Wisconsin found their way made easier because of the established French Catholic communities. In general, the Flemings, with higher education levels and sought-after job skills, suffered less prejudice than the Walloons, the majority of whom were poor, unskilled, and illiterate. But through their industry and thrift, these poor farmers soon won the respect of their neighbors. In time, Belgian Americans became admired not only for their industry and down-to-earth outlook, but also for their sociable character and friendly manner. Belgian hospitality and the retention of many old-world customs and traditions gave color and vitality to the communities in which they resided. Another factor which both hastened assimilation and fostered ethnic pride was the tragic experience of Belgium during the World Wars. The sympathy extended to Belgian Americans by others led them to re-emphasize their origins and culture.

## TRADITIONS, CUSTOMS, AND BELIEFS

It is said that a Belgian, whether Fleming or Walloon, is an inveterate hand shaker. On meeting, greeting, and parting, prolonged handshakes are the rule. This custom is thought to stem from ancient times, when a man's handshake proved he held no weapon. The Belgians' belief in the value of the community and their sturdy outlook on life have helped them recover from plague, famine, two World Wars, and economic depression. Those characteristics have also contributed to the progress and well-being of Belgian Americans. For example, in 1871, a devastating forest fire in Wisconsin (known as the "Peshtigo Fire") destroyed land, farms, and residences in an area six miles wide and 60 miles long. The Belgian communities of northeast Wisconsin were swept away, leaving 5,000 homeless to face the coming winter. It is significant of their determination and resilience that by 1874 these communities were completely rebuilt. An interesting architectural variant can be found in Door County, Wisconsin, as a direct result of the disastrous fire. Up to that time, most homes were built of wood, because it was plentiful and cheap. Red brick homes and buildings began to appear—sturdy and square in design, trimmed in white, and reminiscent of the Belgium homeland. Even today, many fine examples of this form of architecture can be found throughout the Belgian farming communities in Wisconsin.

Many Belgian Americans lived long distances from hospitals or doctors; many could not afford medical services. Therefore folk remedies and home cures were common. A poultice made of flax seed and applied to the chest was thought to help with fever and colds. "King of Pain" liniment for aches and sprains, "Sunrise Herb Tea" for constipation, and cobwebs placed on wounds to stop bleeding were other remedies used.

Every ethnic group that came to America in the nineteenth century could not help but be influenced by other cultures. As ties with the old country weakened, these groups became more and more "Americanized." And, for the most part, they were eager to do so. But all groups, to some degree, kept land-of-origin customs and beliefs alive through religious and social practices. Belgian Americans have been very successful in preserving their secular and religious traditions.

## INTERACTIONS WITH OTHER ETHNIC MINORITIES

In the early days, rural populations tended to remain homogeneous, separated mainly by distance from other communities. They relied on others of their own group to help them survive. Strong identification with one's own kind gave comfort and protection to those sharing a common language and heritage. Because of proximity, urban populations began to interact with other ethnic groups (mainly Catholics) earlier than those in rural areas. In time, greater access to transportation, employment and education, and the settlement of other nationalities nearby caused the sociable Belgians to seek interaction with others outside their group. Proud of their heritage, they have used it to enlighten and enrich their encounters with others.

## CUISINE

Belgians have a love affair with food and revere the act of eating. To rush through a meal is thought to be uncivilized behavior. Belgian food is hearty and rich and often accompanied by beer. Indeed, there are more than 300 varieties of beer brewed in Belgium and the amount of beer consumed, per capita, is second only to Germany. Although many dishes in Belgian cooking are the same for the Flemish and the Walloons, there are differences. For example, Flemish cooking features sweet-salt and sweet-sour mixtures (sauerkraut and pickles). Nutmeg is a favored spice in Flemish cooking. Walloon cuisine is based on French techniques and ingredients. Garlic is a favored seasoning. As in Belgium, a typical Belgian American family meal begins with a thick vegetable soup, followed by meat and vegetables. Pork sausages made with cabbage and seasonings are called *tripes à l'djote* (or Belgian tripe); *boulettes* are meatballs. *Djote*, or "jut" is cooked cabbage and potatoes seasoned with browned butter, pepper, salt, and nutmeg, while *potasse* is a dish of potatoes, red cabbage and side pork. A homemade cottage cheese called *kaset* is often included with the meal. This spreadable cheese is cured in crocks and used like butter. For dessert, there is Belgian pie, which is an open-faced tart filled with custard or cottage cheese, then topped with layers of prunes or apples. A pastry called *cougnou* and shaped like the baby Jesus is a special Christmas treat for Walloons. A waffle-like cookie called *bona* or *guilette* is made with a special baking iron and is also served by Walloons at Christmas. The Belgian waffle, called *gället*, although a traditional food eaten on New Year's Day, has been Americanized and is commonly found on restaurant menus. Some traditional Flemish foods include: *geperste kop,* or head cheese, which is not cheese but the renderings from a pig's head, ears, and stomach made into a jelly-like product; *olie bollen,* a raised doughnut made with apples, and *advocaat,* a liqueur made of grain alcohol, vanilla, eggs, milk, and sugar.

Belgian women are known for their expertise in bread baking. Long ago, huge outdoor ovens were used for baking. The bakehouse was made of masonry and fieldstone, with walls two feet thick. The oven protruded from one end, and was also made of masonry and stone. The bakehouse chimney and interior of the oven were red brick. These whitewashed structures were often trimmed in green and their walls supported grape vines, whose fruit was used for making jelly. Their large ovens could bake as many as 50 loaves of bread at one time. And, after the bread was finished baking, the oven was just hot enough for baking pies. Some of these picturesque ovens still exist in rural Belgian American communities, although few of them are still in use.

### TRADITIONAL COSTUMES

Wooden shoes called *sabots* (Walloon) or *klompen* (Flemish) were traditional footwear for men, women, and children. Like the people of Belgium, they wore these shoes outdoors; they were left by the door when entering the house. Some immigrants brought the knowledge and the tools for making wooden shoes with them from Belgium. Belgian Americans who could afford them wore wooden shoes decorated with carvings of leaves and flowers. Children sometimes used their wooden shoes as skates or sleds. The early immigrants were usually clothed in homespun cloth and caps. Belgian lace, the fine handwork which originated in sixteenth-century Flanders, was often used to trim religious vestments, altar cloths, handkerchiefs, table cloths, napkins, and bed linens. This fine art was practiced by Belgian immigrants in every area of settlement in the United States. When celebrating the Kermiss, which is a Belgian harvest festival, the organizers of the Kermiss wore red, white, and blue sashes while leading the people of the community in a procession to the church to give thanks.

### BELGIAN DANCES AND SONGS

At the Kermiss festivities (described below), revolutionary songs of the old country were sung, such as the Brabanconne and the Marseillaise. During the procession to the church, a dance called "Dance of the Dust" would be done on the dirt road. This dance honors the soil from which the harvest is reaped. At social get-togethers, drinking songs such as the Walloon song, "Society of the Long Clay Pipe," and songs of Belgium towns and cities, such as "Li Bia Bouquet," which honors the province of Namur, are sung. The local band, which usually consisted of cornets, slide trombone, violin, clarinet, and bass drum, played at weddings, festivals, and other social occasions, offering waltzes, quadrilles, and two-steps.

### RECREATION

Archery clubs, pigeon racing, and bicycling clubs were forms of organized recreation for many Flemish Belgians. Gradually these organizations died out, but some existed until the 1960s and 1970s. Bowling, music societies, and drama clubs were formed by both Flemish and Walloon communities. Bowling is still a favorite form of recreation. A card game called "conion" was a popular pastime in taverns. The men fished, trapped, and hunted. Informally, women met to socialize and do needlework and sewing. Their work took on an additional aspect during World Wars I and II, when they supplied the Red Cross with articles of clothing and other needed materials for the war effort. Children skated, sledded, and played ball. Both boys and girls enjoyed games of chase and hide and seek. For rural children, berry picking in the company of their mothers was also recreation. Women enjoyed the preserving of fruits and berries, often gathering together as they did with their sewing groups.

### HOLIDAYS CELEBRATED BY BELGIAN AMERICANS

The festival of Kermiss (also Kermis or Kermess) celebrates the abundant harvest. It generally lasted for six consecutive weeks. It is said that the first Kermiss in America was initiated in 1858 by Jean Baptiste Macaux, a native of Grand-Leez, Belgium. Masses were held to give thanks, and there was much feasting, dancing, and singing. Games were played—among them the card game called "conion" and a greased pole climb. The celebration of Kermiss has persisted to the present day in rural Belgian American communities.

Assumption Day on August 15 honors the Virgin Mary and her ascension into heaven. In the rural areas, a field mass was part of the celebration. This holiday celebration began in the morning, with clergy clad in white vestments and a choir singing Gregorian chant.

On the last Monday in May, people gathered to petition the Virgin for her blessings on their new plantings. This solemn holiday is called Rogation Day. A procession would be made to the church or shrine honoring the Virgin Mary. Young girls dressed in white with long veils would strew flowers along the way.

Belgian Americans celebrate traditional religious holidays such as Christmas and Easter. They also celebrate St. Nicholas Day, which comes on December 6. In the early days, men of the community would dress up like St. Nicholas (the Dutch version of our Santa Claus) and go from house to house, leaving candy and small presents for the children. Today, for many Belgian Americans, this holiday marks the beginning of the Christmas season.

## HEALTH AND MENTAL HEALTH ISSUES

There are no documented physical or mental afflictions that affect Belgians any more than affect the general population. They have access to health and life insurance through their employers, or at their own expense. However, in the early days, beneficial societies were formed to provide this coverage, usually for a nominal monthly fee. These benefits often exist in some form today, to the extent that membership is held in various Belgian fraternal and religious organizations.

# LANGUAGE

In Belgium, geographic circumstances determine which language is spoken. Those residing in northern Belgium speak Flemish, which is derived from Dutch and German. Those Belgians from the south speak Walloon, which is a French patois derived from Latin. Because of their proximity to France, Walloons hold the French language in high regard, using it as the standard for their own. On the other hand, the Flemings share many of the customs and beliefs, as well as the Dutch language, with the people of The Netherlands. A minority—about one percent of Belgium's population—speak German.

Because of geographic and cultural circumstances, a natural language boundary exists in Belgium. In the past, attempts to force an official adoption of either French or Dutch by towns along the language boundary caused great dissension among the people. To settle these disputes, laws were passed in the early 1960s making the language boundary permanent. As a result, both Dutch and French are the official languages, and two distinct cultures flourish side by side. Many Belgians switch back and forth between the two languages, using their native dialect with family and friends and either Dutch or French in public or formal situations. But even though both Dutch and French are the official languages of the country, they are still not regarded by Belgians as equal in value. The following proverbs illustrate how the two are viewed: French in the parlor, Flemish in the kitchen; You speak the language of the man whose bread you eat; It is necessary to cease being Flemish in order to become Belgian. Flemish proverbs include: *Stel niet uit tot morgen wat je heden kunt doen* (Delay not until tomorrow what you can do now); *Wie hierbinnen komt zijn onze vrienden* (Those who enter here are our friends); *Avondrood brengt water in de sloot* (Red sky at night brings water in the stream); *Beter een half ei dan een lege dop* (Better half an egg than an empty shell); *Zwijgen en denken kan niemand krenken* (Silence and thinking hurts no one).

Belgian immigrants in the United States used the primary language of their homeland in Belgium. The Flemish and Walloon languages were commonly used by first-generation Belgians until World War I. Gradually, most Belgian Americans lost the ability to speak either Walloon or Flemish. Immigrant parents were eager to have their children learn English, and today few retain more than a word or two in the old language. Individuals who were at least 50 years old in the middle 1970s spoke the Walloon language in a family environment but had to speak English in school. Punished by teachers when they did speak Walloon, they raised their own children to speak English and spoke Walloon with themselves only with people of their own generation (Françoise Lempereur, "The Walloon Settlement of North-East Wisconsin," in *Belgians in the United States*, [Brussels, Belgium: Ministry of Foreign Affairs, 1976).

## GREETINGS AND OTHER POPULAR EXPRESSIONS

The following greetings and expressions are in Dutch or French, depending upon whether the Belgian speaker is Flemish or Walloon. Dutch: *Goedemorgen* ("ghooderMORghern")—Good morning; *Goedemiddag* ("ghooderMIddahkh")—Good afternoon; *Dank u* ("dahnk ew")—Thank you; *Ja/Nee* ("yaa/nay")—Yes, No; *Vrolijk Kerstfeest* ("VROAlerk KEHRSTfayst")—Merry Christmas; *Veel geluk* ("vayl gherLURK")—Good luck. French: *Bonjour* ("bohng-zhoor")—Hello, good day; *Au revoir* ("ohr-vwahr")—Good bye; *Bonsoir* ("bohng-swahr")—Good evening; *A demain* ("ah duh-mahng")—Until tomorrow; *Eh bien* ("ay b'yahng")—Well; *Très bien* ("treh b'yahng")—Very well; *Voilà* ("vwah-lah")—Here you are; *Bon* ("bohng")—Good.

# FAMILY AND COMMUNITY DYNAMICS

Belgian immigrants who arrived in America during the nineteenth century were immediately concerned with survival. Those who settled in the Midwest often came with only a few meager possessions. Often, they set down in what was then wilderness, and they needed all their mental and physical resources to make it through their first winter. The fact that there was no way for them to return to their homes in Belgium, and the comfort and assistance of the Catholic clergy pulled them through. These early families set to work clearing the land, building shelters, and planting crops. Men, women, and children all worked in the fields and tended the animals. Others, who lived in cities, took work where they could find it to support their families. The most fortunate were those that came with craft skills—a growing America needed these workers, and they readily found employment. As they became established in their new country, they began to form organizations to help the sick and poor among them. They also maintained ties with those they left behind in Belgium. As a result, many more came to join their friends and relatives in the new land. As years went by, the crude homesteads and rocky fields became productive family farms; job opportunities

This portrait of Maria Valvert Goussé and her daughter, Marthe, was taken in Antwerp, Belgium in 1909. In 1910 they immigrated to the United States; Marthe died the following year of diphtheria.

in the cities led many Belgian Americans to become business owners or to enter a profession.

Belgian American families tended to be large. There were strong social and religious taboos against divorce. Rural women were expected to work in the fields as well as in the home. Traditional roles for men and women were observed, and any deviation was often censured. Even though it was not uncommon for widows to carry on their deceased husband's occupation, especially that of farming, it was frowned upon if women assumed a community leadership role, except on a social basis. Children also had chores to do at an early age, and gender-based chores were commonly assigned. On farms, they also helped with planting and harvest, and as a result, were often absent from school during those times of the year. However, these early immigrants respected teachers and education. Parochial schools were established, but they also sent their children to the public schools. While most second-generation young women attended elementary school, most did not go on to high school. However, teaching was an approved vocation for women.

Belgian American populations are heavily concentrated in the Midwest. Whether rural or city dwelling, the second and third generations tended to carry on the work traditions of their forebears. Detroit, for example, has many Belgian descendants employed in the building and related trades. Well-kept Belgian farms dot small Wisconsin communities, even though many farmers may work second jobs at paper mills or at other occupations for their main source of income. As with most ethnic groups that arrived here during the nineteenth century, Belgian Americans have taken advantage of what America had to offer, combined it with their own unique talents and strengths, and enriched it with their contributions. Today, the grandchildren and great-grandchildren of nineteenth-century Belgian immigrants have assimilated fully into the educational and occupational roles of twentieth-century society.

### WEDDINGS

The young (16 to 20 years was a common marrying age) bride prepared for her wedding by filling her hope chest with hand made quilts, tablecloths, and linens. Her friends often gave her a bridal shower. It was taken for granted that she would marry within the Catholic religion. Rural communities often held twilight wedding masses so the men would have time to be out of the fields.

A typical wedding celebration lasted all day and all night. It was common for 300 to 600 people to be invited. In the old days, the wedding couple went from house to house, extending a personal invitation. Once held in the bride's family home, the celebration is now often held at a local hall or country club. It was customary for neighbor women to help prepare the food, and preparation took many days. A very festive atmosphere surrounded the entire event. The guests ate and drank all day, and in the evening there was a wedding dance. The gift opening took place after the wedding dinner, and gifts were displayed for all the guests to see. Money was rarely given as a gift. Many of these same customs apply today, especially in the more homogeneous Belgian communities.

### CATECHISM AND FIRST COMMUNION

Religious instruction for young people begins early. Catechism studies prepare children for first communion, which usually takes place at age 12. Children study under the guidance of a priest for about three years, and are confirmed in their teens. Boys often served as altar boys when they became communicants. Today, girls are allowed this privilege in some Catholic churches as well. These religious rites of passage are celebrated by family and friends with parties and gift-giving.

### FUNERALS

After announcement of a death, a wake is held for friends and family. It is customary to have an open casket for viewing of the deceased. The body is taken to the church for a Catholic mass the following day. Funeral masses in memory of the dead person are held throughout the year, having been paid for by relatives and friends. A funeral dinner is held for all mourners. The dinner is usually put on by a group of church women, whose special task is supplying this service to members of the church. It is customary for friends and neighbors to send food to the home of the deceased. Other funeral customs from the past still persist in some form today. The rosary is still said at the wake. A procession of vehicles from the church to the cemetery is a usual occurrence. The wearing of dark, or black, clothing is observed today by only the most traditional mourners, but once was an expected ritual for the family. This usually went on for at least one year. During this time family members did not attend festive or social events. Tying a purple or black ribbon on the door of the dead person's home and the wearing of a black arm band by men in the family were other mourning customs of an earlier time.

# RELIGION

The majority of Belgian Americans are of the Roman Catholic faith, although some are Presbyterians and Episcopalians. By 1900, Belgian religious orders were thriving in 16 states. The Sisters of Notre Dame, from Namur, Belgium, were successful in establishing bilingual schools in 14 of those states; the Benedictines built missions in the western part of the country, and the Jesuits, who founded St. Louis University in 1818, were able to expand the reach of the University through the use of Belgian teachers and benefactors. But Belgian immigrants often were without churches of their own, mainly because they assimilated at a faster rate in the more populous areas, attending Catholic churches founded by other ethnic Catholics, such as the German or French. However, two of the more homogeneous groups, those in Door County, Wisconsin, and those in Detroit, Michigan, were successful in establishing churches of their own.

In 1853, a Belgian missionary, Father Edward Daems, helped a group of immigrants establish a community in Northeast Wisconsin in an area called Bay Settlement. They called it *Aux premiers Belges*—The first Belgians. By 1860, St. Hubert's Church in Bay Settlement and St. Mary's in Namur were built. Other Belgian churches established during the nineteenth century in Door County were St. Michael's, St. John the Baptist, and St. Joseph's. In 1861, the French Presbyterian Church was established in Green Bay. Small roadside chapels were also built to serve those who lived too far away to attend parish churches regularly. The chapels were named by worshipers in honor of patron saints.

In 1834, Father Bonduel of Commnes, Belgium, became the first priest to be ordained in Detroit. The first Catholic College (1836) was operated by Flemish Belgian priests, and the first school for girls was founded by an order of Belgian nuns in 1834. By 1857, Catholics in Detroit were a sizable group. However, they had still had no church of their own and were, at that time, worshipping with other Catholics at St. Anne's Church. This was remedied in 1884, when the first Belgian parish was established.

With the consolidation of many Catholic parishes throughout the United States, even Belgian Americans in small, stable communities may no longer attend an ethnically affiliated church. As with, for example, the German Catholic and the French Catholic parish churches, many Belgian Catholic parishes have died out or have merged with other parishes in this age of priest shortages and financial hardship.

# POLITICS AND GOVERNMENT

At first, little heed was paid to the American system of government. Exercising the right to vote and to have an influence in local affairs came gradually, as Belgian Americans learned the English language and began to establish leadership among themselves. Soon they began to draw upon these leaders for various offices—town assessor, justice of the peace, superintendent of schools. As a group, they realized the power of their vote, and as time went on, began to exert great influence in the communities where they resided. Independent of spirit, they were prone to band together politically to solve their problems, rather than passively waiting for outsiders to order their affairs.

On a national scale, Belgian Americans responded as a distinct group to Belgium's tragic experience during the two World Wars. The Flemings, especially, made a strong effort to avoid being associated in people's minds with the Germans. In general, assimilation was hastened by wartime experiences. Belgian American veterans'

and fraternal organizations came into being during this time.

## MILITARY

Belgian Americans fought in America's War of Independence. The Civil War came shortly after the greatest influx of Belgian immigrants; and as American citizens, many were called to serve. In rural communities this caused great hardship, as women and children struggled to support themselves by working the farms alone. Belgian Americans fought in both World Wars. Their efforts were made more poignant by the fact that, in both Wars, Belgium was devastated by the German army. It is noted that during World War I, Belgian Americans gave so generously to the children who were victims of that war, that an official delegation from Belgium was sent to the United States in 1917 to honor their efforts. In a reverse effort, Edgar Sengier, the director of the Union Mine in Belgium, showed foresight in shipping all of Belgium's supply of radium and uranium ore to the United States. This kept this valuable material out of Hitler's hands. This ore was of tremendous value in the Manhattan project—America's plan to build the atomic bomb. Belgian Americans also served in subsequent military engagements in Korea and Vietnam.

## RELATIONS WITH BELGIUM

Very few immigrants returned to Belgium, but the tie between the old country and the new has never been severed. From the beginning, letters went back and forth, telling of conditions in America and urging those left behind to join the new arrivals. As years went by, Belgians gradually became "Americanized." But even so, the connection with Belgium remained. The outpouring of aid from Belgians in the United States during World War I and World War II is certainly proof of that. Organizations such as the World War Veterans sent groups to Belgium and also received official delegations from there—often at the highest political and governmental levels. The Belgian American Educational Foundation grew out of the World War I Commission for the Relief of Belgium. This organization promotes and facilitates exchanges among the academic, artistic, and scientific communities of Belgium and the United States. The religious connection between the two countries remains strong, basically because of the ongoing work of Catholic missions in the United States by such Belgian Catholic orders as the

Norbertines and the Crosiers (Holy Cross Fathers). Even more so, the modern-day interest in researching one's forebears has led many Belgian Americans to reconnect with their mother country. Whether Walloon or Fleming, pride in one's ancestry and customs is reflected in this interest. Since the 1970s, librarians across the country, and especially in the Midwest, note the rise in requests for genealogical information in this search for Belgian roots.

# INDIVIDUAL AND GROUP CONTRIBUTIONS

Belgian Americans have excelled in many fields, especially in music, science, medicine, education, and business. Many are unsung, appreciated, and lauded only by their peers and in their own communities. Others have received national, and in some instances, international, recognition for their achievements. Some of their accomplishments are listed in the following sections.

## ACADEMIA

Charles Raw was an important nineteenth-century archaeologist and museum curator whose career centered on the study of American archeology; in 1881, he was appointed curator of Archeology at the National Museum, where he established his reputation as the foremost American archaeologist. George Sarton (1884-1956) was a brilliant science historian, who traced the cultural and technical evolution of science from its beginnings to modern day. Others who made significant contributions to their academic specialty are economist Robert Triffin (b. 1911) and economic historian Raymond de Roover (1904-1972).

## BUSINESS AND INDUSTRY

Washington Charles De Pauw (b. 1822) was an industrialist whose method of manufacturing plate glass secured his fortune; much of his wealth was used to benefit the city of New Albany, Indiana, where his plant was located. Peter Corteville (1881-1966) founded the Belgian Press, a Detroit printing company that published a prominent Belgian American weekly newspaper, the *Gazette van Detroit*, which at one point attained a circulation of almost 10,000.

## EXPLORERS AND MISSIONARIES

Catholic missionary-explorers were active across America from the seventeenth century on. Two of the most notable are Father Louis Hennepin, a Franciscan, and Father Pierre-Jean de Smet, a Jesuit. Father Hennepin (1614-1705) joined the 1678 La Salle expedition to explore the Mississippi River; he was the first European to sketch and describe the Niagara Falls. In 1683, he wrote a comprehensive treatment of the Upper Mississippi Valley; 60 editions of this book were published in most of the major European languages. Father de Smet (1801-1873) was a notable pioneer in the exploration of the nineteenth-century frontier. From 1845 to 1873, he traveled thousands of miles in undeveloped Western territory. As a missionary, perhaps his most important work was with the Native Americans, and he played a prominent role in the final peace treaty with the Sioux leader, Sitting Bull.

## LITERATURE

Georges Simenon (1903- ) is famous for his psychological detective stories and is the creator of the popular Inspector Maigret. He is the author of more than 200 works. He came to the United States during World War II, and later lived in Switzerland.

## MEDICINE

Father Joseph Damien De Veuster (1840-1889) devoted his life to the care of lepers in Hawaii; better known as Father Damien, he contracted leprosy himself in 1885. He was beatified by the Catholic Church in 1993, 104 years after his death. Albert Claude (1898-1983) was a joint recipient in 1974 of the Nobel Prize in Medicine for his work on the structure of the cell; he was also a pioneer in the development of the electronic microscope. Of more recent note: Charles Schepens (1919- ) has made important contributions in the field of ophthalmology. Emile Boulpaep (1938- ) discovered physicochemical characteristics of cell membranes that provided insight into a number of kidney and heart disorders. He was awarded the prestigious Christoffel Plantin prize in 1992, which honors the achievements of Belgians living in other countries.

## MUSIC

Practitioners of the carillon art have flourished in the United States. The carillon is a bell tower comprised of fixed chromatically tuned bells which are sounded by hammers controlled from a keyboard. More than 150 carillons are located across the United States, on university campuses, botanical gardens, parks, and cathedrals. The 52-bell carillon in Ghent, Belgium, is 700 years old and was the largest in the world until it was surpassed in 1925 by the 53-bell carillon at the Park Avenue Baptist Church in New York City. Its present carillonneur, Jos D'hollander is one of the foremost in the country. Other famous carillonneurs were Antoon Brees, Riverside Church of New York and Cranbrook Church in the Detroit area, and Camiel Lefevre of Bok Tower in Florida. Lefevre was the first graduate of the world's first carillon school in Mechelen, Belgium, which was founded in 1922 and funded by the Belgian American Education Foundation. F. Gorden Parmentier, a Green Bay, Wisconsin native, is a world-recognized composer of symphonies and opera. Robert Gorrin (b. 1898) was a French language poet who lived in the United States during World War II. He created the National Jazz Foundation, and was one of the world's foremost jazz authorities.

## SCIENCE AND TECHNOLOGY

Karel J. Van de Poele (1846-1895) is known as "the father of the electric trolley." By 1869, his electrical streetcars were operating in Detroit. He founded the Van de Poele Electric Light Company and invented the dynamo, which served to power American industry in its early days. Jean-Charles Houzeau de Lehaie (1820-1888) has been called the "Belgian von Humboldt" for his work in the fields of astronomy, mathematics, physics, botany, politics, journalism, and literature. He was born in Belgium and arrived in New Orleans in 1857. He was actively involved in politics at the time of the Civil War and campaigned against slavery. Ernest Rebecq Solvay (1838-1922) invented the process of manufacturing sodium carbonate with ammoniac. He built his first factory in a town named in his honor, Solvay, New York. Leo Baekeland (1863-1944) was a chemist who invented the substance bakelite, a synthetic resin which ushered in an industrial design revolution and was the forerunner of the modern plastics industry. He also invented the photographic paper called Velox. Karel Bossart (1904-1975) was called the father of the Atlas missile. His engineering work in the missile field culminated in 1958, when he received the U. S. Air Force's Exceptional Civilian Award for developing the first intercontinental ballistic missile. He was a graduate of Massachusetts Institute of Technology. Gaston De Groote (b. 1915) was the commander of the *Savannah*, the world's first nuclear-powered cargo passenger ship. George Washington Goethals (1858-1928) is known as the builder of the Panama Canal. An engineer, administrator, and soldier, he spent seven years overseeing its construction, and was the Canal Zone's first civil governor. Georges Van Biesbroeck (1880-1974) was an astronomer at Yerkes Observatory in Wisconsin. He is noted for verifying Einstein's theory that light is slightly distorted in the area of the solar corona.

# MEDIA

## PRINT

Two Flemish newspapers, the *Gazette van Moline* and *Gazette van Detroit*, were the largest Belgian publications in the early twentieth century. The *Gazette van Moline*, founded in 1907, was the first Flemish newspaper in the United States. It ceased publication in 1921. The *Gazette van Detroit* was founded in 1914, and was still publishing into the 1980s, although at a greatly reduced circulation. In 1964, the year of its fiftieth anniversary, its circulation was approximately 5,000. Newsletters are prevalent among Belgian associations and heritage societies in the United States. Listed below are two examples of the type:

**Belgian Laces.**
Official quarterly bulletin of the Belgian Researchers, Inc., and the Belgian American Heritage Society. Described as "the link between people of like ancestry and like interest on both sides of the ocean.

**Contact:** Leen Inghels, Editor.
**Address:** Fruitland Lane, LaGrande, Oregon 97850.
**Telephone:** (503) 963-6697.

*Gazette Di Waloniye Wisconsin.*
A French-language quarterly periodical that serves to connect the Belgian Americans of Northeastern Wisconsin with those in Belgium.

**Contact:** Willy Monfils, Editor.
**Address:** 770 Chemin de la Boscaille, B-7457, Walhain, Belgium.

## RADIO AND TELEVISION

**Belgian Radio and Television.**
Broadcasts daily and frequency can be tuned in for listening anywhere in the United States and Canada.

**Address:** P.O. Box 26, B-1000, Brussels, Belgium.

# ORGANIZATIONS AND ASSOCIATIONS

Belgian American Societies exist in areas of Belgian settlement throughout the United States. Most of these associations came into being in the early decades of the twentieth century, and served as social and cultural outlets for those of Belgian descent. In time, these local and state organizations formed regional federations, such as the Federation of Belgian American Societies of the Midwest and the United Belgians Societies. Many of these societies are still active, and the following state organization serves as an example of the type:

**Belgian American Association.**
Founded in 1945, the association has a membership of 4,000 individuals and firms united to better relationships between the United States and Belgium. Its focus is to foster awareness and appreciation between the two countries. Activities include a cultural conference, roundtable talks, organization of meetings for business people, film showings, luncheons and dinners in honor of important American visitors to Belgium, and organization of trips to the United States. The Association maintains liaison with similar groups abroad, informs members of available travel and education opportunities, operates exchange programs, sponsors fund raising and relief activities, and participates in related legislative activities. The Association also publishes a monthly newsletter.

Contact: Collette-Anne Stassey, Secretary General.
Address: 1201 Pennsylvania Avenue, N.W., Suite 500, Washington, D.C. 20044.

**Belgian American Chamber of Commerce.**
Founded in 1925, it has a membership of 500 Belgian exporters and American importers of Belgian products. It publishes the *Belgian American Trade Review*, a quarterly journal that contains company profiles, information on Belgian products, new members list, and Port of Antwerp news.

Contact: Robert Coles, Executive Director.
Address: Empire State Building, 350 Fifth Avenue, Suite 1322, New York, New York, 10118.
Telephone: (212) 967-9898.

**Belgian American Education Foundation.**
Founded in 1920, the foundation has 250 members. It promotes closer relations and exchange of intellectual ideas between Belgium and the United States through fellowships granted to graduate students of one country for study and research in the other. Assists higher education and scientific research. Commemorates the work of the Commission for Relief in Belgium and associated organizations during World War I.

Contact: Emile Boulpaep, President.
Address: 195 Church Street, New Haven, Connecticut 06510.
Telephone: (203) 777-5765.

**Belgian American Heritage Society of West Virginia.**
Founded in 1992, has as its purpose the social and intellectual advancement of West Virginia Belgians. Serves as a resource for those interested in Belgian genealogy, history, and culture.

Contact: Rene V. Zabeau, President.
Address: P.O. Box 195, Clarksburg, West Virginia 26302-0195.
Telephone: (304) 624-4464.

**Belgian Tourist Office.**
Founded in 1947, it promotes travel and tourism to Belgium. It also provides information services and maintains a speakers bureau and publishes *Belgium Newsbreaks* five times yearly.

Address: 745 Fifth Avenue, New York, New York 10151.
Telephone: (212) 758-8130.

# MUSEUMS AND RESEARCH CENTERS

**The Belgian Researchers.**
Provides books, periodicals, and other materials for genealogical research. Principal objective: "Keep our Belgian heritage alive in our hearts and in the hearts of our posterity." Publishes *Belgian Laces*, the official quarterly newsletter.

Contact: Pierre L. Inghels, President and Editor.
Address: Fruitland Lane, LaGrande, Oregon 97850.
Telephone: (503) 963-6697.

**Center for Belgian Culture of West Illinois.**
Promotes Flemish history and culture, and provides leadership in perpetuating Belgian heritage and teaching the values of Belgian culture.

Contact: Mary Morrissey, Archivist.
Address: 712 Eighteenth Avenue, Moline, Illinois 61265.
Telephone: (309) 762-0167.

**Genealogical Society of Flemish Americans.**
Provides information and library materials pertaining to Flemish genealogical research. Publishes *Flemish American Heritage*.

Address: 18740 Thirteen Mile Road, Roseville, Michigan 48066.

**University of Wisconsin—Green Bay Special Collections Library/Belgian American Ethnic Resource Center.**
The center is a cooperative project of the State Historical Society of Wisconsin and the University of Wisconsin—Green Bay. Of special interest in the Center's holdings are materials on persons of Belgian descent, whose families originally settled in Brown, Kewaunee, and Door counties. These materials include family papers, church records, photographs, oral history interviews, and records of school districts and towns.

Contact: Debra L. Anderson, Special Collections Librarian.
Address: 2420 Nicolet Drive, Green Bay, Wisconsin, 54311-7001.
Telephone: (414) 465-2539.

# SOURCES FOR ADDITIONAL STUDY

Amato, Joseph. *Servants of the Land: God, Family and Farm, the Trinity of Belgian Economic Folkways in Southwestern Minnesota*. Marshall, Minnesota: Crossings Press, c. 1990.

Bayer, Henry C. *The Belgians, First Settlers in New York and in the Middle States*. New York: Devin-Adair Company, 1925.

*Belgians in the United States*. Brussels, Belgium: Ministry of Foreign Affairs, 1976.

Bernardo, Stephanie. *The Ethnic Almanac*. Garden City, New York: Dolphin Books, Doubleday & Company, 1981.

Holand, Hjalmer Rued. *Wisconsin's Belgian Community; An Account of the Early Events in the Belgian Settlement in Northeastern Wisconsin with Particular Reference to the Belgians in Door County*. Sturgeon Bay, Wisconsin: Door County Historical Society, 1933.

Sabbe, Philemon D., and Leon Buyse. *Belgians in America*. Belgium: Lannoo, Tielt, 1960.

Santiago, Chiori. "Carillons: Making Heavy-Metal Music with Staying Power," *Smithsonian*, November 1994; pp. 113-124.

Brazilian

immigration to the

United States did not

begin on a

significant scale until

the mid-1980s.

# BRAZILIAN AMERICANS

by

**Alphine W.**
**Jefferson**

## OVERVIEW

The country of Brazil, officially called the Federative Republic of Brazil (or República Federativa do Brasil), is located in central eastern South America. A vast country, it covers 3,290,000 square miles—nearly 45 percent of South America's land mass. Brazil is bounded by French Guinea, Guyana, Venezuela, and Suriname to the north, Columbia to the northwest, Peru, Bolivia, Paraguay, and Argentina to the west, Uruguay to the south, and the Atlantic Ocean to the east. The nation is divided into 23 states, three territories, and one federal district, the last of which includes its capital, Brasília.

According to United Nations estimates for 1995, Brazil has a population of approximately 165 million people of various ethnicities. Like the United States, Brazil is a land of immigrants. People of Portuguese descent make up a slight majority of the population; among the other ethnic groups in the country are Africans, Italians, Germans, Japanese, and Native Americans (primarily of the Tupi and Guarani linguistic families). More than a third of all Brazilians are of mixed racial heritage. Racial identification in Brazil, as in much of Latin America, is rather nebulous. Latin Americans with some white blood often claim a "white" racial identity.

Eighty-nine percent of Brazilians are Roman Catholic. Other Brazilians subscribe to various forms of Protestantism. There are also very small Islamic and Jewish communities in the country. Many Brazilians who subscribe to one of the mainline religions also practice other religious traditions, including Spiritism, Candomblé, Macumba, Umbanda, or Santería. These religious practices are informed by Christianity and traditional African and Amerindian religious ceremonies.

Brazil's official language is Portuguese, although a variety of other languages, such as Japanese, German, and various Native American languages, are spoken. The nation's capital, Brasília, is in the interior of the country; large coastal cities, including São Paulo, Rio de Janeiro, Belo Horizonte, Recife, and Salvador, are important to Brazilian trade. The national flag of Brazil is a yellow diamond centered on a green field. In the middle of the diamond is a blue globe bearing 23 white stars and a banner with the words "Ordem e Progresso," which means "order and progress." The green and the yellow represent Brazil's forest and mineral wealth, while the blue represents both the sky and the vastness of Brazil's states and capital.

## HISTORY

Recent archaeological evidence suggests that Brazil may have been inhabited as early as 40,000 years ago. Various Native American groups are known to have lived in Brazil for thousands of years. The first European to lay claim to the region was Pedro Cabral, who discovered the land for Portugal in 1500. The next year, Italian explorer Amerigo Vespucci traveled along the South American coast. Brazil's first settlement was established at Salvador da Bahia. Salvador was Portugal's most important city—after its own capital of Lisbon—for 300 years. In the nineteenth century, colonization of Brazil by Portuguese settlers began in earnest.

Brazil was ruled by Lisbon as a colony until 1808, and during these years the early Brazilians helped to frame the development of the country. Native American groups living on the coast of Brazil were pushed to the interior of the country by the Portuguese as early as 1616. The coast of the country was then settled by the Portuguese. In 1533 the first Africans were forcibly brought to Brazil to be used as slaves, primarily on coffee and sugar plantations. Slavery was abolished in Brazil in 1888, by a law that was signed by the regent Princess Isabel. Finally, the Treaty of Madrid, signed in 1750, definitively drew Brazil's borders, which were remarkably similar to the nation's contemporary boundaries.

In 1808 French emperor Napoleon Bonaparte invaded Portugal, touching off the bloody Peninsular War. The Portuguese royal family, led by King Dom João VI, fled from Napoleon's army and reestablished its kingdom in Brazil, first in Salvador and later in Rio de Janeiro. Dom João returned to Portugal in 1821, leaving his son Dom Pedro I as regent. Pedro I declared Brazil's independence on September 7, 1822. His son, Dom Pedro II, succeeded him in 1831 and ruled until 1889.

## MODERN ERA

A federal republic was established following an 1889 coup, and for the next 41 years the Brazilian government was a constitutional democracy with a limited franchise. Getúlio Vargas, a member of the revolutionary Liberal Alliance, staged a military coup in 1930, establishing a dictatorship and ruling as governor for the next 15 years. During World War II, Brazil underwent considerable economic growth. A series of elected presidents followed Vargas, but in 1964, as a result of popular frustration with steadily rising inflation, economic stagnation, and various other social problems, the military staged yet another coup. Then-president João Goulart was deposed, and Army Marshall Humberto Castelo Branco officially became president on April 11, 1964.

The military continued to choose government officials until 1982, when a period of liberalization began in Brazil. In 1989 Fernando Collor de Mello became president in the nation's first direct presidential election in decades. However, Collor de Mello, famed for his wide-reaching economic reforms, was accused of accepting bribes in 1992, and on September 29th of that year, was impeached by the Brazilian government for political corruption. He was succeeded by his vice president, Franco Itmar, who officially took office on October 2, 1992. Two years later, former foreign and finance minister Fernando Henrique Cardoso won a hotly contested presidential election against the favored candidate, populist Luis Inacio "Lula" da Silva, a trade union leader. This election signaled stability for Brazil's fragile democratic institutions and validated Cardoso's stringent financial policies and reforms.

## SIGNIFICANT IMMIGRATION WAVES

Some sources claim that the earliest immigrants from Brazil to the United States were probably eight Jewish Brazilians who entered the country in 1654. But Brazilian American immigration information is not very reliable; the U.S. Immigration and Naturalization Service did not tabulate Brazilians as a separate group entering the States until 1960. Before that, Brazilians were counted in a group that included all South Americans. It is known that between 1820 and 1960, 234,761 people of South American descent entered the United States, with peak waves of South American immigrants entering from 1841 to 1850 and 1911 to 1930. It is impossible to tell how many of these South Americans were actually from Brazil. According to the 1960 U.S. Census Bureau report, however, 27,885 people of Brazilian ancestry were living in the United States.

From 1960 until the mid-1980s, there was a relatively even pattern of Brazilian immigration to the United States; estimates suggest that between 1,500 and 2,300 Brazilians immigrated each year, mainly from southern and south-central Brazil, including the states of Espírito Santo, Minas Gerais, Rio de Janeiro, São Paulo, Paraná, Santa Catarina, and Rio Grande do Sul. The majority of these immigrants were of European heritage and came from the middle- and upper-middle-classes of Brazilian society.

During the mid-1980s, Brazil's economy began to deteriorate rapidly; in 1990 inflation reached 1,795 percent annually. Despite the economic reforms of President Collor de Mello, incomes continued to drop by nearly 30 percent, and many Brazilians lost faith in their government. The Brazilian government estimates that between 1986 and 1990, 1.4 million Brazilians left the country permanently—many of them immigrating to the United States, others heading for Japan and various countries in South America and Europe.

According to Maxine Margolis in *Little Brazil: An Ethnography of Brazilian Immigrants in New York City*, Brazilian immigration to the United States did not begin on a significant scale until the mid-1980s. Between 1987 and 1991, 20,800 Brazilians immigrated to America; however, 8,133 Brazilians entered the country in 1991 alone. Again, the majority of these immigrants were middle- or upper-middle-class members of Brazilian society, and most of them came from southern or south-central Brazil. The 1990 U.S. Census Bureau report indicates that there are about 60,000 Brazilians living and working in the United States, but because Brazilian Americans were only counted in the census if they wrote "Brazil-

ian" in the "Other Hispanic" category—Brazilians are not Hispanic—this number is most likely too small. Other sources suggest that there are approximately 100,000 Brazilians, documented and undocumented, living in the New York area alone. In addition, there are sizable Brazilian communities in Boston, Washington, D.C., Los Angeles, Miami, and Phoenix.

As Brazil's economic conditions worsened, the American consulate found that many more Brazilians wanted to immigrate to the United States than quotas legally allowed. Consequently, since the mid-1980s, a significant percentage of all Brazilian immigration to the United States has been illegal. The most common way for Brazilians to illegally enter the United States is to overstay a tourist visa, fade into established Brazilian communities, and obtain low-skill, low-wage work. A riskier method of gaining entry is with "doctored" or fake passports and/or green cards. A number of professional immigration services—legitimate and otherwise—operate in both the United States and Brazil to assist those wishing to come to America. Some Brazilians enter the United States on their own via the Mexican border, but this is extremely time-consuming, dangerous, and expensive. Undocumented persons make up a large percentage of the Brazilian population in the United States, thereby skewing census and immigration data. Margolis notes that there may be as many as 350,000 Brazilians living in the United States without proper documentation.

## SETTLEMENT PATTERNS

Nearly half of all Brazilian Americans live in the northeastern United States, primarily in the states of New York, New Jersey, and Massachusetts; sizable populations also reside in California, Florida, Pennsylvania, and Washington, D.C. First generation Brazilians tend to congregate in areas where other Brazilian Americans are living—such as Little Brazil in Manhattan or Astoria in Queens—especially if they speak little or no English. However, second- and third-generation Brazilian Americans are more likely to have gained financial independence and therefore may relocate to areas with fewer or no other Brazilian Americans. These neighborhoods do not preserve Brazilian cultural heritage as many first generation neighborhoods do. It is estimated that the majority of illegal Brazilian immigrants live in New York City; however, because these people are largely undocumented, their exact places of residence are difficult to ascertain.

# ACCULTURATION AND ASSIMILATION

Margolis cites some of the misconceptions and stereotypes held by many Americans about Brazil and Brazilians, the most common being that Brazilians are Hispanic and therefore speak Spanish. The term Hispanic, when used correctly, refers to people of Spanish or Spanish-speaking origin from Central America, South America, and the Caribbean. Although people of many nationalities live in Brazil, it is primarily a country of Portuguese origin, and its official language is Portuguese. There is little published information on Brazilian Americans as an ethnic group, even though Brazilian immigration to New York City is rapidly rising and has been since the mid-1980s.

Because of the lack of information about Brazilian Americans, many "established" Americans seem to have stereotyped them as an ethnic group. Media portrayals of Brazil and its citizens contribute to the erroneous belief that Brazilians are less than industrious laborers who favor a good party over a hard day's work. Movies, television, and theatrical productions depict Brazilians as doing little else than dancing the *lambada* and the *samba* (popular Brazilian dances) and participating in their world famous street parties. Indeed, participants in the nation's annual *Carnaval* celebration are hardly inhibited. Moreover, grandly produced and suggestively staged variety shows—featuring Brazilian entertainers such as *Brazil Alive!*, *Oba! Oba!*, *Rio Ecstasy*, and *Fantasy Brazil*—shock the generally more reserved and puritanical North American audiences. Even sporting events reveal a distinctly Brazilian gusto: when Brazil captured the coveted Copa do Mundo (soccer's World Cup) in 1994, sports fans thought nothing of dancing in the streets. Despite the misconceptions these stereotypes create, Brazilian Americans maintain pride in their cultural traditions and continue to celebrate their Brazilian heritage.

## TRADITIONS, CUSTOMS, AND BELIEFS

Brazilians have many traditions, customs, and beliefs that have existed for hundreds of years and are woven into Brazilian culture. Though common throughout much of the country and observed by all racial groups, many of these practices can be traced to the traditional beliefs and behaviors of Africans, Amerindians, and European folk culture. Indeed, some scholars observe that the fusion of different cultural beliefs finds its greatest expression in Brazil. Religious rituals, military and political rallies, festivals, and family celebrations are important parts of Brazilian society. Brazilians also give parties to celebrate such events as soccer (*futebol*) victories; soccer is such an important part of Brazilian and Brazilian American life that it is not uncommon to see hundreds of people gathered around a single small television set watching a game.

Brazilian Americans have preserved their cultural heritage by maintaining some of Brazil's customs, traditions, and beliefs, including the value and importance of the extended family and the observance of Brazilian festivals and holidays, which celebrate Brazilian culture. These cultural traditions have changed over time as more and more Brazilian Americans are assimilated into mainstream American life.

## CUISINE

Brazil is a country filled with people of many different backgrounds and origins; its cooking reflects its multicultural roots. Brazilian cooking has been influenced by African, Native American, Spanish, Portuguese, Italian, German, and even Japanese cuisines. In particular, Brazilian cooking reflects the cooking styles of the African slaves who were brought to Brazil beginning in the sixteenth century. *Dendê* (palm oil), coconut milk, spicy peppers, *feijão* (black beans), and *farinha* (manioc flour) are principal ingredients in Brazilian dishes. The national dish of Brazil, *feijoada*, consists of a variety of smoked or sun-dried meats and sausages, black beans, and a sauce made from the juices of the beans and the meats. It is usually served with sliced oranges, shredded kale or collard greens, *farofa* (toasted manioc flour), and various hot sauces and condiments. Popular beverages include *Brahma*, a Brazilian beer; *caipirinhas* and *batidas*, tropical drinks made with rum and *cachaça*; and *Guaraná*, a popular Brazilian soft drink made from the berries of the *guaraní* tree.

Other Brazilian foods that are popular among Brazilian Americans and can be found in many Brazilian restaurants in the States include *churrasco à rodízio*, a meal of barbecued chicken, pork, and beef served with rice, black beans, French fries, and potato salad; *frango à passarinho* (literally, "chicken in the style of a little bird"), small pieces of chicken wrapped in garlic leaves; *moqueca*, a fish stew native to the Brazilian state of Bahia; and *bacalhau*, or codfish casserole. During

Brazilian parties or street festivals, a variety of Brazilian snack foods are served. Among them are *kibe*, fried snacks of Lebanese origin; *acarajé*, a deep-fried black bean fritter filled with spicy sauces, shrimp, green peppers, and chiles; and *pasteis*, a pastry filled with meat, shrimp, or olives.

## TRADITIONAL COSTUMES

There are different traditional costumes for different states and regions of Brazil. One such costume—often worn during street fairs and at other Brazilian American events—comes from the Brazilian state of Bahia. For women, it consists of a huge, hooped white skirt, a white bodice with elaborate sleeves, strings of colorful looped beads worn around the neck, and elaborately wrapped white turbans. Tiny string bikinis, called *fio dental*, or "dental floss," are worn by many Brazilian women on the beach. For everyday wear, most Brazilians and Brazilian Americans dress in American-style clothing. Indeed, the influence of the United States is so great that many Brazilian and Brazilian American youth wear "hip-hop" or "rap" style garb. Poorer Brazilians may wear western clothing, reflecting their rural or *gaúcho* ("cowboy") traditions.

## HOLIDAYS CELEBRATED BY BRAZILIAN AMERICANS

For the many states, cities, and communities in Brazil with patron saints, it is customary to hold festivals for these saints each year. During Holy Week—the week before Easter, which is seen as one of the most important weeks of the year—Brazilians recreate the passion and the resurrection of Jesus Christ. Some Brazilian communities also recreate the events of the birth of Jesus during the Christmas season. Military parades are common in Brazil as a way of celebrating state holidays, such as Brazilian Independence Day, which occurs during Fatherland Week. Two other major Brazilian festivals are *Carnaval*, a huge, nationwide, annual celebration that takes place the week before Lent, and *Festa do Iemenja*, a solemn ceremony held on New Year's Eve. The *Festa do Iemenja*, dedicated to the "Queen of the Sea," is a major rite in Rio de Janeiro and Bahia. Flowers, perfumes, fruits, and even jewelry are tossed into the sea to please the mother of the waters and gain her protection for a new year. Moreover, this is the time when many Brazilians place on their wrists a cloth bracelet bearing the words: "Lembra do Senghor do Bonfim," which translates as "remember the bishop of the good end." (This is a reference to a famous church in Bahia, Igreja so Senghor do Bonfim, built in 1745 and famous for its healing powers.)

Brazilian Americans celebrate secular American holidays, such as the Fourth of July, Thanksgiving Day, and New Year's Day, and Christian Brazilian Americans also celebrate such holidays as Christmas and Easter by attending church services and having special meals and ceremonies at home. Many of these services are held in Portuguese with Brazilian music.

On Brazil's Independence Day, there are feasts in many Brazilian American communities, particularly in large cities in the northeast region of the country, such as Boston, New York City, and Newark, New Jersey. Independence Day, celebrated each September 7th, marks Brazil's liberation from Portugal. The largest celebration by far is the Brazilian Independence Day Parade and Street Fair, which has been held annually since 1985 on New York's West 46th Street ("Little Brazil"). The all-day street festival attracts thousands of people, predominantly Brazilian Americans, from throughout the Northeast; participants wear green and gold, Brazil's colors, dance to Brazilian music, and enjoy Brazilian food and drinks.

Brazilian American communities also celebrate *Carnaval*. In Brazil, *Carnaval* takes place during the four days before the beginning of Lent, but many pre-festival events start up to two months earlier. In many ways, *Carnaval* is considered to be the quintessential expression of Brazilian culture, and Brazilian Americans are proud to celebrate the event. *Carnaval* festivities are also becoming increasingly popular among non-Brazilians in America.

## HEALTH AND MENTAL HEALTH ISSUES

There are no documented health or mental health problems specific to Brazilian Americans. Brazilian Americans generally obtain health insurance at their own expense or through their employers. Most Brazilian Americans who live illegally in the United States have no health insurance and enter the health bureaucracy at risk. Many also rely on "faith healers," associated with one or more of their religious traditions.

Brazilian American Spiritists practice alternative or homeopathic approaches to health and medicine. Instead of traditional medical techniques, Spiritists use such practices as past-lives therapy, dispossession and exorcism therapies, acupuncture, chromotherapy, yoga therapy, and homeopathy. Back in Brazil, some Spiritists have set up psychiatric hospitals that utilize the aforementioned healing methods.

## LANGUAGE

Although Portuguese is not the only language spoken in Brazil, it is the official language of the nation and the native language of most Brazilian immigrants. Portuguese is a Romance language, similar in some ways to Spanish, and is spoken by about 200 million people worldwide. There are two major differences between Brazilian Portuguese and the Portuguese spoken in Portugal: firstly, the Brazilian vocabulary is larger by several thousand words; secondly, the pronunciation is softer. Brazilian Portuguese has "adopted" words and phrases from the Tupí-Guaraní languages, spoken by many Native Americans in Brazil, and also from the various languages spoken by African slaves who were brought to Brazil. These African languages influenced the softening of the Brazilian Portuguese pronunciation. In 1992 Brazilian Portuguese became the international standard for textbook production and writing because Brazilians comprise 75 percent of the world's Portuguese speakers.

Of the 57,108 people recorded in the 1990 U.S. Census Bureau report (41,395 of whom were first-generation and 15,713 of whom were second-

or third-generation), 52,292 people spoke English, although 22,587 said that they did "not speak English very well." Because Brazilian Americans often retain close ties with their old world culture and language, several urban areas with high concentrations of Brazilian immigrants feature radio broadcasts in Portuguese and publish Portuguese-language newspapers and periodicals.

### GREETINGS AND OTHER EXPRESSIONS

Common greetings and expressions in Brazilian Portuguese include: *Bom dia*—Good morning; *Boa tarde*—Good afternoon; *Boa noite*—Good night; *Como vai?*—How are you?; *Obrigado*—Thank you (masculine); *Obrigada*—Thank you (feminine); *De nada*—You're welcome; *Pois não*—Certainly; or, Don't mention it; *Passe bem*—Goodbye; *Até amanhã*—See you tomorrow; *Que horas são?*—What time is it?; *Como se chama a senhora (a senhorita)?*—What's your name?

## FAMILY AND COMMUNITY DYNAMICS

Brazilian social life centers around the family. It is not uncommon for Brazilians to see members of their extended families—married siblings, grandparents, aunts, cousins, and other relations—on a daily basis. Family is also very important to Brazilian Americans. Many Brazilians are encouraged to immigrate to the States by family members who have already made the journey; new immigrants often live with other family members or close friends until they find homes of their own. Especially in larger Brazilian American communities, family members almost always live near one another. Many Brazilian Americans travel to Brazil as often as they can in order to maintain contact with extended family members who remain in the homeland. Even for Brazilian Americans who have lived in the United States for many years, the social and cultural value placed on the family usually remains intact.

In Brazil, social status is very important. Educated Brazilians are socialized from an early age to show respect in speech and conduct to those of higher social status. Individualism in many forms is generally dismissed by Brazilians as egotistical behavior, since Brazilians tend to focus on the family and the community rather than on the individual. Each step in the life cycle—christening, going to school, confirmation, beginning outside work—is viewed as a rite of passage. In making these significant transformations, Brazilians often have many mediators—usually older family members and friends—who counsel them in understanding the ways of the world.

Economic and social necessity have chipped away at the traditional extended family structure in immigrant communities throughout the United States. Many Brazilian immigrants to America are single; married men and women often leave their spouses and children at home until they can afford to send for them. Until they find their own houses or apartments, Brazilians commonly stay with friends or at cheap boarding houses (often Brazilian-run) in cities with large Brazilian communities, such as New York or Newark. After a single family member has established himself or herself in the States, that person is able to facilitate the immigration of other family members. Brazilian Americans often help each other find jobs and adequate housing, and they share cultural information and news from Brazil. Of course, some Brazilians move to the United States with their immediate families—particularly those who have jobs before they arrive or enough money to last until they can find employment.

As the standard of living for Brazilian immigrants begins to rise, many invest in such modern conveniences as television sets, microwave ovens, and stereo equipment. (These items are seen as luxuries because they are so expensive in Brazil.) A common concern for many Brazilian Americans seems to be the welfare of those still living in Brazil. Many Brazilian Americans send money to friends and family back home, and charitable organizations sponsor drives to collect money and clothing for the poor in Brazil. There is little organized charitable work by Brazilian Americans, however, to help other Brazilian Americans in need. This can be explained partially by the fact that many are undocumented—and therefore live in fear of detection and deportation.

## THE ROLE OF WOMEN

Many married, middle-class women in Brazil do not work outside of the home, even if they have advanced university degrees. It is common—even among the lower-middle-class in the old country—for households to employ servants and maids. Many Brazilian women must adapt to new roles and obtain outside employment when they immigrate to the United States, as it is usually a financial necessity. According to Margolis, these adjustments in roles can cause many problems for immigrants, particularly for married couples in which the woman is making more money than the man. Moreover, middle-class women who had maids and servants in Brazil are somewhat disheartened at the thought of assuming those same roles in America in order to find employment.

## WEDDINGS

In Brazil, wedding customs conform to the major practices of each religious denomination. The road to matrimony starts with a large engagement reception, where the families of the intended come together; the man gives the woman a simple gold wedding band, which is worn on the right hand prior to the marriage. During the wedding ceremony, the ring is placed on the left hand. Western traditions have influenced weddings in Brazil, making services similar to those in North America. The upper-class in Brazil, however, looks to France for many of its cultural manifestations.

In general, the bride wears white and the groom dons formal wear. Bridesmaids and groomsmen are replaced by the *padrinho* (godfather) and *madrinho* (godmother) of both the bride and groom. The service follows the traditional liturgical rites of the Catholic or Protestant church.

The reception is a gala, cross-generational affair, with plenty of food, liquor, music, and dancing. Usually, an older male relative will discreetly gather small monetary donations and present them to the couple before they leave for the honeymoon. Depending on the status of the family, honeymoons can range from a simple night in a room of a crowded house to a week on the beach—a favorite honeymoon spot.

## BAPTISMS

Baptismal traditions are determined by the religious denomination of the family. For Catholics, the child is baptized in infancy and later, after reaching the "age of understanding" (usually between eight and 12), he or she is formally confirmed. The child's godparents play an important role, taking vows to love, protect, and, if necessary, provide for the child. White baptismal clothing is absolutely essential; poor parents reportedly spend food money on the appropriate dress. After the actual baptismal service, the child is showered with presents at a lavish reception.

## FUNERALS

The death of beloved Brazilian race car driver Aytron Senna (1960-1994) allowed all the world to see how Brazilians deal with death. Within minutes of his demise in the Grand Prix in Italy, thousands of Brazilians flocked to his home in São Paulo, stood outside on the walls, and cried. Senna's funeral service went on for hours; every major Brazilian political and religious leader eulogized him.

In Brazil, the color of mourning is black. Usually, a large picture of the deceased is on display at the funeral service. Generally speaking, bodies in Brazil are not embalmed. Thus, most burials occur within 24 hours. In addition to mourning, funerals function as vehicles for public displays of emotion, belonging, and connection. Women are expected to wear heavy veils and to actively mourn the dead. Sociological sources indicate that unrestrained displays of raw emotion are such a basic part of Brazilian culture that they are expected and encouraged. Thus, it is customary to give fainting mourners a mixture of sugar water to calm them.

Funeral customs vary from place to place and are informed by the religious traditions of the deceased. In the northeastern part of Brazil, the dead are paraded throughout the streets in their coffins, with family and friends walking behind as they leave the *necrotério* (morgue and funeral home) and proceed to the cemetery. Among the middle- and upper-classes in urban areas, cars and hearses are used. For many Catholics, a special mass is held 15 days after the burial; this signifies the final act of public mourning.

## EDUCATION

Many Brazilian immigrants to the United States have university degrees and held skilled jobs in Brazil. However, these immigrants often have difficulty finding desirable jobs in the United States because the requirements for degrees are different in Brazil—and because many Brazilian Americans, even those with advanced education, are not fluent in English. Illegal immigrants are largely excluded from the American labor market, since they pose a legal risk to perspective employers. Overall, second-and third-generation immigrants are more likely to have skilled, high-paying jobs, as they have been educated in the United States, are more likely to be fluent in English, and have legal permanent resident status.

# RELIGION

Although the vast majority—nearly 90 percent—of Brazilian Americans are Roman Catholic, others belong to fundamentalist Protestant churches. In addition, a small number of Brazilian Americans practice Spiritism, a faith based on communication with the spirits of the dead; Umbanda, a combination of Spiritism, folk Catholicism, and African-Brazilian beliefs and rituals; and Candomblé, an African-Brazilian religion that originates from the Brazilian state of Bahia. Little is known about the existence of these religions in the United States because their practitioners fear censure from both Brazilians and Americans.

Brazil is the world's largest Roman Catholic country. The Brazilian Catholic church is seen as radical by more conservative Catholics and has been instrumental in pushing for social change in Brazil—often in direct opposition to the state. Most Brazilian Americans are affiliated with the Roman Catholic Church. In areas of the United States with large Brazilian immigrant communities, Catholic churches offer services in Portuguese or have Brazilian or Portuguese-speaking clerics to assist parishioners. In New York City, the largest and best-known Roman Catholic church with services in Portuguese is Our Lady of Perpetual Help in Manhattan. This church features a prominently displayed statue of Nossa Senhora Aparecida, a Brazilian saint, and serves as a center for many Brazilian Americans to congregate and worship together.

About ten percent of Brazilian Americans belong to one of several Protestant churches. In the United States, particularly in the Northeast, most Brazilian American Protestants are either Pentecostals or Baptists. Pentecostal Brazilian Americans tend to socialize primarily with members of the Pentecostal church, and therefore Pentecostal churches—several of which have services in Portuguese—often become the center of the social lives of most members. Baptist Brazilian Americans, on the other hand, tend to socialize more outside of the church. Some Baptist churches in the United States, such as the Baptist Church of the Portuguese Language in Queens, New York, offer services in Portuguese. In addition to the Pentecostal and Baptist denominations, the Universal Church (a Protestant sect which is Brazilian in origin) and Seventh-Day Adventist churches also attract Brazilian American believers.

Spiritism is a Brazilian practice that combines science, philosophy, and Christian morality and follows the teachings of Allan Kardec, a nineteenth-century French philosopher who set forth his principles in two books: *The Book of the Spirits* and *The Book of the Mediums*. Spiritists, who tend to be white and middle-class, believe in communication with the dead via spirit mediums. Small groups of Brazilian American Spiritists meet in communities with large Brazilian American populations.

# EMPLOYMENT AND ECONOMIC TRADITIONS

Because Brazilian immigrants who entered the United States prior to 1960 were not documented separately, little information exists on their employment history. According to the 1990 census, of the 43,190 Brazilian Americans who were over the age of 16, 31,662 were a part of the labor force. The majority of Brazilian American workers are members of one of four categories: service occupations; technical, sales, and administrative support occupations; managerial and professional specialty occupations; or operators, fabricators, and laborers.

Margolis conducted research on Brazilian immigrant workers in New York City. (The majority of the people with whom she worked were illegal immigrants.) She found that restaurant work is the most common form of work for male Brazilians who have recently immigrated to the United States. Many other undocumented Brazilian males take jobs in construction or with small companies that pay wages in cash; others work as street vendors or as shoe shiners. The vast majority of female Brazilian immigrants to the United States, both legal and illegal, take jobs in domestic service and in child care, usually for private households. Margolis notes that other Brazilian women take jobs as restaurant workers, street vendors, or even go-go dancers. Her findings also indicate that illegal immigrants tend to take positions where they can be paid "under the table," avoiding possible detection or deportation from immigration authorities.

# POLITICS AND GOVERNMENT

Hardly any information exists about Brazilian American participation in the U.S. voting process.

However, Brazilian Americans are actively involved with politics in Brazil. First-generation immigrants, Brazilian Americans who remain close to family members still living in Brazil, and business people with ties to Brazil, are especially interested in the political situation in the homeland.

## RELATIONS WITH BRAZIL

During the 1989 Brazilian presidential election—the first direct presidential election since 1964—many Brazilian Americans became involved in the election process. Brazilian Americans who were still eligible to vote through the Brazilian consulate organized themselves in support of each of the candidates. Fernando Collor de Mello, who won the election and was later impeached, was supported most heavily by business people and wealthier Brazilian Americans. Collor de Mello ran against Luis Inacio "Lula" da Silva, a trade union leader and Labor party candidate who received support from many middle-class Brazilian American merchants and newer immigrants.

Despite the fact that many Brazilian Americans were very interested and involved in the presidential campaign, relatively few of the eligible immigrants voted through the Brazilian consulate; the consulate apparently did not advertise the necessity of registering in June for the November election. Illegal Brazilian immigrants to the United States, who were eligible to vote in their elections at home, generally did not do so because they feared being reported to immigration authorities. Of the Brazilian Americans who did cast ballots, da Silva won the majority.

Two years after Collor de Mello's impeachment, former government minister Fernando Henrique Cardoso won the 1994 presidential election against "Lula" da Silva, the favored candidate. Cardoso's financial policies have improved the Brazilian economy considerably.

# INDIVIDUAL AND GROUP CONTRIBUTIONS

Several Brazilian Americans have made significant contributions to American culture. Brazilian American journalist Jota Alves founded the New York monthly newspaper *The Brazilians* and also started the tradition of the New York City Brazilian Independence Day Parade and Street Fair in 1985. Jazz musician Airto Moreira and jazz singers

Brazilian Americans voice their discontent with recent elections in New York City's Brazilian Street Fair.

Astrud Gilberto, Flora Purim, and Tania Maria are well known among Brazilian Americans and jazz enthusiasts. In addition, numerous Brazilian American professors and students have contributed to American colleges and universities. Anthropologist Roberto DaMatta teaches at the University of Notre Dame. He has written many books about Brazilian culture and society.

# MEDIA

## PRINT

### Brasil/Brazil.

A scholarly journal of Brazilian literature with text in English and Portuguese.

**Contact:** Nelson H. Vieira or Regina Zilberman, Editors.
**Address:** Brown University, Department of Portuguese and Brazilian Studies, Box O, Providence, Rhode Island 02912.
**Telephone:** (401) 863-3042.
**Fax:** (401) 863-7261.

### Brazil Watch.

Biweekly newsletter that focuses on political, economic, and business events in Brazil.

**Contact:** Richard W. Foster, Editor.
**Address:** Orbis Publications, Inc., 1924 47th Street, N.W., Washington, D.C. 20007.
**Telephone:** (202) 625-2702.

### The Brazilians.

Monthly magazine published in both Portuguese and English. It seeks to promote Brazilian culture and includes business information, news, and articles on Brazilian music, art, and traditions.

**Contact:** Eddie Mendes, Editor.
**Address:** 15 West 46th Street, New York, New York 10036.
**Telephone:** (212) 382-1630.

### Brazilian Monthly.

Published in both Portuguese and English, this magazine covers cultural issues in Brazil and in Brazilian American communities and provides information on news, politics, and sports.

**Contact:** Flavia Smith or Heloisa Souza, Editors.
**Address:** P.O. Box 93, Brookline, Massachusetts.
**Telephone:** (617) 566-3651.

### Capital to Capital.

Weekly newspaper published in Portuguese, English, and Spanish. Its primary goal is to provide information about the Brazilian American community, but it also includes news, religion, and sports coverage. It is available by subscription or on newsstands in a few areas, including Washington, D.C.

**Contact:** Dario Santos, Editor.
**Address:** P.O. Box 9861, Washington, D.C. 20016.
**Telephone:** (202) 723-5854.

### The Florida Review.

Biweekly newspaper published in Portuguese (with a small section in Spanish). Designed to meet the needs of both Brazilian Americans and Brazilians visiting the United States, it provides world and community news, cultural information from Brazil, and other services, and is distributed throughout the United States and in major Brazilian cities.

**Contact:** Marcos Ommati, Editor.
**Address:** 801 Bayshore Drive, Box 19, Miami, Florida 33131.
**Telephone:** (305) 374-5235.

### Luzo—Brazilian Review.

Devoted to the culture of the Portuguese speaking world. Text in English, Portuguese, and Spanish.

**Address:** University of Wisconsin Press, Journal Division, 114 North Murray Street, Madison, Wisconsin 53715.
**Telephone:** (608) 262-4952.
**Fax:** (608) 262-7560.

### News From Brazil.

Monthly magazine that covers current events and culture in Brazil, including movies, books, music, politics, ecology, and the economy. It is published in English—with a short story every month in Portuguese—and is distributed through subscriptions and on newsstands in the Los Angeles area.

**Contact:** Rodney Mallo, Editor.
**Address:** P.O. Box 42536, Los Angeles, California 90050.
**Telephone:** (213) 255-4953.

### RADIO

### KLBS.

A Portuguese-language station with daily broadcasts from 6:30 a.m. to 8:00 p.m. Programming includes news, community information, Brazilian music, and interviews.

**Contact:** J. J. Encarnacao.
**Address:** P.O. Box 1428, Los Banos, California 93635.
**Telephone:** (209) 826-0578.

### KSTN-FM.

Features two hours of Brazilian-centered news, commentary, and music, Monday through Friday. On Sundays, the station broadcasts a Catholic mass in Portuguese.

**Contact:** Knox Larue.
**Address:** 2171 Ralph Avenue, Stockton, California 95206.

**Telephone:** (209) 948-5786.

### WRYM-AM.

Broadcasts a two and one-half hour program each week in Portuguese, featuring music and community and world news.

**Contact:** Albino Baptista.
**Address:** 1056 Willard Avenue, Newington, Connecticut 06111.
**Telephone:** (203) 666-5646.

### TELEVISION

One Spanish-language channel in New York City broadcasts a weekly two-hour program in Portuguese for the Brazilian American community, featuring a popular situation comedy, sports highlights, and news. In addition, several of the world famous Brazilian "soap operas," called *novellas,* are shown on Spanish-language stations around the country. Satellite technology allows some educational institutions to tune into SCOLA, which carries some programs from Brazil.

# ORGANIZATIONS AND ASSOCIATIONS

**Brazilian American Chamber of Commerce.**
This organization, which was founded in 1968, has over 300 members, many of which are corporate. The Chamber of Commerce promotes the interests of business in Brazil and in the United States. It publishes a newsletter and the *Brazilian American Business Review Directory.*

**Contact:** Tony Sayegh, President.
**Address:** 22 West 48th Street, New York, New York 10036.
**Telephone:** (212) 575-9030.

**Brazilian American Cultural Institute (BACI).**
Seeks to foster an understanding between Brazil and the United States through cultural exchange. Operates art gallery for American and Brazilian works.

**Contact:** Dr. Jose M. Neistein, Executive Director.
**Address:** 4103 Connecticut Avenue, N.W., Washington, D.C. 20008.
**Telephone:** (202) 362-8334.

**Brazilian American Cultural Center (BCC).**
The mission of the Cultural Center is to promote the culture and art of Brazil and Brazilian Ameri-

ca. It also sponsors programs and exhibits about Brazilian history, art, and music and publishes *The Brazilians*.

**Address:** 20 West 46th Street, New York, New York 10036.
**Telephone:** (212) 730-0515.

## MUSEUMS AND RESEARCH CENTERS

**Brazilian American Cultural Institute.**
Founded in 1964, this institute focuses on the promotion of Brazilian culture and art in the United States. It has 1,000 members and sponsors films, shows, exhibits, and Portuguese-language courses, all of which are open to the public. The institute also has an art gallery, a concert hall, and an extensive library. The library holds some 6,000 books relating to Brazil—many written in Portuguese by Brazilian authors—and more than 3,000 recordings of Brazilian music.

**Contact:** Dr. José Neistein.
**Address:** 4103 Connecticut Avenue, Washington, D.C. 20008.
**Telephone:** (202) 362-8334.

## SOURCES FOR ADDITIONAL STUDY

Crowley, David J. *African Myth and Black Reality in Bahian Carnaval*. Museum of Cultural History, UCLA, Monograph Series No. 25, n.d.

DaMatta, Roberto. *Carnavals, Rogues, and Heroes: An Interpretation of the Brazilian Dilemma*, translated by John Drury. Notre Dame, Indiana: University of Notre Dame Press, 1991.

*Family, Household, and Gender Relations in Latin America*, edited by Elizabeth Jelin. London, England: Kegan Paul International Ltd., 1991.

Freyere, Gilberto. *The Mansions and the Shanties: The Making of Modern Brazil*. New York: Knopf, 1963.

Harris, Jessica B. "Brazil: A Cornucopia of Culture," *Black Enterprise*, August 1987, p. 84.

Hess, David J. *Spirits and Scientists: Ideology, Spiritism, and Brazilian Culture*. University Park: Pennsylvania State University Press, 1991.

Hewitt, W. E. *Base Christian Communities and Social Change in Brazil*. Lincoln: University of Nebraska Press, 1991.

Kessner, Thomas, and Betty Boyd Caroli. *Today's Immigrants, Their Stories: A Look at the Newest Americans*. New York: Oxford University Press, 1981.

Margolis, Maxine L., and William E. Carter. *Brazil: Anthropological Perspectives—Essays in Honor of Charles Wagley*. New York: Columbia University Press, 1979.

Margolis, Maxine L. *Little Brazil: An Ethnography of Brazilian Immigrants in New York City*. Princeton, New Jersey: Princeton University Press, 1994.

Rodrigues, José Honório. *The Brazilians: Their Character and Aspirations*. Austin: University of Texas Press, 1967.

U.S. Department of State, Bureau of Public Affairs. *Background Notes on Brazil*. Washington, D.C.: Government Printing Office, October 1990.

Aside from the rare
adventurer, few
Bulgarians settled in
the United States
before the great
immigration wave of
the early twentieth
century, in which
thousands of
southern and eastern
Europeans altered
the country's ethnic
cast.

# BULGARIAN AMERICANS

by
Eleanor Yu

## OVERVIEW

Bulgaria is a small country on the east coast of the Balkan Peninsula in southeastern Europe. Its land area is approximately 42,823 square miles, or 110,550 square kilometers, making it slightly larger than the state of Tennessee. It boasts a varied topography, with flatlands in the north (the Danubian Plateau) and center (the Thracian Plain) and two large mountain ranges spanning the country from west to east—the Balkans across the center and the Rhodopes across the south. The Danube River separates Bulgaria from Romania and forms the country's northern border. Bulgaria shares its western border with Serbia and Macedonia and its southern border with Greece and Turkey. The Black Sea coastline bounds the country to the east.

Bulgaria's population numbered about 8.9 million in 1990. Two-thirds of the populace is urban, with over one million people living in the capital city, Sofia. In 1991, ethnic Bulgarians accounted for 85.3 percent of the population, ethnic Turks represented 8.5 percent, Gypsies 2.6 percent, Macedonians 2.5 percent, and Armenians, Russians, and Greeks each accounted for less than one percent. About 85 percent of the population belongs to the Bulgarian Orthodox Church. Smaller numbers are Muslim (13 percent), Jewish (0.8 percent), Roman Catholic (0.5

percent), and Protestant. Since the country cast off Soviet-sponsored Communism in late 1989, Bulgarians have increasingly turned to public worship, and religious observance has been on the upswing.

The official state language is Bulgarian. Turkish has survived several waves of repression during Communist rule and is the primary language of about eight percent of citizens. The Bulgarian flag is composed of three horizontal stripes, white, green, and red in color.

The country's main agricultural regions—the Danubian and Maritsa plains—grow large quantities of corn, tomatoes, tobacco, wheat, barley, grapes, sugar beets, oil-seeds, potatoes, and soybeans. The famous crop of the dry and dusty Tundzha Valley, or the "Valley of the Roses," makes Bulgaria the world's largest exporter of attar, or extract, of roses.

## HISTORY

The ancient Thracians were one of the original civilizations of the eastern Balkans. For much of the first millennium B.C., they inhabited large parts of modern Bulgaria, northern Greece, and European Turkey. Over the centuries, however, Thrace's lack of a strong, central leadership made it an attractive target for various conquering armies, from the Persians in the sixth century B.C., to the Macedonians, who settled the region under Alexander the Great, to the Romans, who overpowered the Thracians in 50 A.D. When the attenuated Roman Empire divided itself into two parts, Thrace fell under the administration of the eastern, or Byzantine, empire.

By the sixth century A.D., migrant Slavic tribes, encountering little opposition from Byzantine troops, had established themselves south of the Danube and absorbed the smaller Thracian population. Almost two centuries later, the Bulgars, a Turkic tribe from central Asia, began their conquest of the region. They, too, assimilated into the larger Slavic population; over time the culture of the warlike, nomadic Bulgar conquerors fused with the ways of the Christianized, agricultural Slav. What evolved was a unified kingdom whose cultural and military achievement, at its height, rivalled that of Byzantium.

The First Bulgarian Kingdom arose in the early ninth century. Aggressive warfare against Byzantium had pushed the borders of Bulgaria to the Carpathian Mountains in the north and to the Aegean Sea in the south. In 865, Bulgarian czar Boris I, perhaps seeking to stabilize relations with Byzantium, made Eastern Orthodox Christianity the official state religion. Shortly after, Bulgaria established its own patriarchate, independent of the Eastern Orthodox Church in Constantinople. Not only did this mean the Bulgarian Orthodox Church could conduct its services in the Slavic language, but it also kept ecclesiastical authority within the country's borders. The close identification of the Bulgarian Orthodox religion with the nation was a thread that wove through much of the country's history, as the Church repeatedly found itself shouldering the burden of nation-building and acting as sanctuary to Bulgarian culture.

Under the reign of Boris I's son, Czar Simeon (893-927), the First Bulgarian Empire reached its maximum size and its golden age of art, literature, and commerce. A handful of monasteries still bear frescoes dating from this period. After Simeon's reign, the empire began to decline. It was plagued by constant warfare against the Byzantines, the Magyars, and the Kievan Russians and by internal disarray. In 1014, the Bulgarian czar Samuel lost a decisive battle to the Byzantine Emperor Basil II, who ordered the mass blinding of 14,000 Bulgarian prisoners. By 1018, the whole of Bulgaria had fallen once more under the sway of Byzantine rule.

The Second Bulgarian Empire began in 1185, when the brothers Asen and Peter forced the weakening Byzantine Empire to recognize an independent Bulgarian state. The brothers made Turnovo their capital. With the ascension of Asen II (1218-41), medieval Bulgaria reached its zenith in cultural development and in territorial growth. The kingdom extended from the Adriatic to the Black Sea, touching the Aegean at its southern frontier and enveloping Belgrade in the north. Trade flourished, as did learning, religion, and the arts. Bulgaria entered a second and more brilliant "golden age," and Turnovo was the seat of Slavic culture.

This period of relative tranquility ended around 1240, when Tartar invaders were cutting a swath through Europe. Bulgaria, torn by internal dissension and unable to repel the Tartars' frequent raiding parties, was forced to pay tribute to the invaders. The Tartars were driven out in 1300, and there followed another period of expansion and prosperity. But as the fourteenth century neared its end, a new threat stood poised at the southern frontier of the Bulgarian kingdom—the armies of the Ottoman Empire, which had already gained a foothold on the European shores of the Aegean.

In 1385 Sofia became the first major Bulgarian city to fall to the Ottoman Empire. The turning point in the half-century-long Ottoman offensive in the Balkans was the defeat of the powerful Serbian army at the battle of Kosovo Polje in 1389. With this victory, the Turks were able to gain control of the Balkan Peninsula. They wasted no time in crushing what remained of Bulgarian resistance and imposed a five-century-long rule over Bulgaria.

Turkish colonization had profound short- and long-term effects on the development of the Bulgarian nation. While looting Orthodox monasteries, Turkish troops destroyed great masterpieces of Bulgarian culture, including scores of paintings, frescoes, and manuscripts from the golden ages. Stripped of its independence as well as its riches, the Bulgarian Orthodox Church was made a sub-patriarchate of the Greek Orthodox Church for four centuries. Many Bulgarians were enslaved, forced to convert to Islam, or exiled to other parts of the Ottoman Empire. The Turks replaced the existing social structure with a more oppressive form of feudalism, rewarding Turkish landlords and converts to Islam with the most fertile land, while burdening Bulgarian peasants with heavy local and state taxes.

However, Turkish subjugation was not absolute. Bulgarians were permitted a limited form of local self-government. They spoke their native tongue among themselves without restriction. The Bulgarian artisan and merchant classes prospered as they sold food and cloth to the rest of the Ottoman Empire. The empire's centralized government left remote mountain villages and monasteries untouched. As a result, the villages were able to preserve Bulgarian culture, while the monasteries served as a refuge for literature and religious learning.

From the monasteries, a wave of nationalist feeling fanned out to the rest of the country in the 1760's. At the same time the Ottoman Empire, increasingly plagued by corruption and misrule, was sliding ever closer to its eventual disintegration. One monk in particular, Father Paisii of Hilendar, is credited with stoking the flames of the Bulgarian "National Revival. " His history of the Bulgarian people encouraged his compatriots to agitate for Bulgarian-language schools and ecclesiastical independence from the Greek Orthodox Church.

In 1870, worn down by revolts and European enemies, the Ottoman sultan conceded the autonomy of the Bulgarian church and mandated the creation of the Bulgarian Exarchate. Meanwhile, Bulgarian expatriates in Serbia and Romania, dissatisfied by the slow pace of Turkish reform, were forming armed, revolutionary groups that sought the violent overthrow of the Turks. In 1876, the Bucharest-based Bulgarian Revolutionary Central Committee organized the "April Uprising" against the Turks. Although that revolt failed, the brutal Ottoman reprisals, which killed 30,000 Bulgarians, drew Europe's attention to what had previously been considered an Ottoman backwater.

### INDEPENDENCE AND THE MODERN ERA

Outraged on behalf of its little "Slavic brother" and backed by international public opinion, Russia led the clamor for Bulgarian autonomy. The major European powers tried to secure reforms from the sultan through diplomacy. Negotiations foundered, however, on the question of autonomous Bulgarian provinces, and Czar Alexander II of Russia declared war on Turkey in April 1877.

The eight-month War of Liberation ended in Turkish defeat. In March of 1878, Russia imposed upon the Turks the Treaty of San Stefano, which created a Russian-protected "Big Bulgaria" that encompassed Bulgaria proper and most of Macedonia and Thrace. Fearing Russia's growing influence in the Balkans, the western European powers dismantled the treaty within months. In July 1878, the Congress of Berlin reduced the size of Bulgaria by two-thirds and confined the new nation to the area between the Danube River and the Balkan Mountains. Although they were largely populated by ethnic Bulgarians, Macedonia, Thrace, and Southern Bulgaria (called Eastern Rumelia) were returned to Turkey. The new treaty also gave the Ottoman state the right to invade Bulgaria in times of civil unrest.

Pro-Bulgarian sentiment simmered in the Turkish provinces of Macedonia, Thrace, and Eastern Rumelia. Uprisings persisted in Macedonia, in particular, where a large portion of the populace spoke a Bulgarian dialect and adhered to the Bulgarian Orthodox faith. Formed in 1893, the Internal Macedonian Revolutionary Organization (IMRO) dedicated itself to armed rebellion. The IMRO's most memorable revolt, the Ilinden, or St. Ilya's Day uprising, on August 2,

1903, ended in the deaths of thousands of Macedonians and the destruction of entire villages at the hands of the Turkish army.

Bulgaria's territorial ambitions led it into the successive Balkan Wars of 1912 and 1913. Covetous of its lost territories, Bulgaria joined Serbia and Greece in 1912 in a successful offensive against Turkey. Then, when Greece and Serbia each claimed large portions of Macedonia, Bulgaria turned on its erstwhile allies, only to lose to them in 1913. Although forced to yield some land, Bulgaria finished the wars with a net gain in territory.

In World War I, the promise of Serbian Macedonia enticed Bulgaria into an alliance with the losing Central Powers (Germany, Austria-Hungary, and Ottoman Turkey). In the 1930's, the authoritarian King Boris III cemented Bulgaria's relationship with fascist Germany and Italy. Hoping to recover Thrace and Macedonia, Bulgaria again allied itself to the losing side in World War II. It declared war on the United States, Great Britain, and France on December 13, 1941. However, Boris successfully resisted sending Bulgarian troops to bolster Germany's eastern front, arguing that the troops were needed at home as a deterrent to attack. Nor did the Bulgarian people support Nazi Germany's anti-Jewish policies; although Boris acquiesced to a number of repressive measures against Jews, he staved off the Nazi-ordered deportation of 50,000 Bulgarian Jews.

The Soviet army invaded Bulgaria in September 1944, only hours after the Soviet Union declared war on the Balkan country. Shortly afterward, a coalition of Bulgarian resistance groups, dominated by the Communists, seized control of the government. Under the eye of the occupying Soviet army, the Bulgarian Communists abolished the monarchy and established the People's Republic in September 1946. A new constitution, modelled on the Soviet constitution, was drafted in 1947. Soviet troops withdrew from Bulgarian soil that same year.

The Communists consolidated their power over the next four decades, earning Bulgaria a reputation as Moscow's most loyal Warsaw Pact ally. Under the leadership of Vulko Chervenkov (1949-1956) and Todor Zhivkov (1956-1989), Bulgarian foreign and domestic policy rarely strayed from the Soviet Union's. Evidence indicates that the Bulgarian state security police, the Durzhavna Sigurnost, often acted in lieu of the KGB, accepting assignments from which Moscow wanted to distance itself.

As the 1980's drew to a close, the shock waves of Soviet *perestroika* reverberated across eastern Europe. Bulgarians articulated their unhappiness with the regime through public protests and increasingly visible dissident activity. On November 10, 1989, one day after the fall of the Berlin Wall, reformers within the Communist party forced the resignation of Zhivkov.

Post-Communist politics in Bulgaria is dominated by two major parties—the Bulgarian Socialist Party, as the Communist party renamed itself, and the Union of Democratic Forces, which won the new government's first election, only to lose power 11 months later. The country's transition to capitalism has been uncertain, with the privatization of state-run enterprises proceeding slowly. A soaring crime rate and economic crisis have led some to call for the restoration of the monarchy and others to call for a return to Communism.

## THE FIRST BULGARIANS IN AMERICA

Aside from the rare adventurer, few Bulgarians settled in the United States before the great immigration wave of the early twentieth century, in which thousands of southern and eastern Europeans altered the country's ethnic cast. The earliest documented Bulgarian immigrants were converts to Protestantism, who arrived around the middle of the nineteenth century to pursue higher education in America, as Nikolay G. Altankov notes in *The Bulgarian-Americans*, published by Ragusan Press in 1979. Their passages were funded by American Protestant groups intent on grooming talented natives for missionary work back in Bulgaria. Although some Bulgarian students did return home to spread the gospel, others chose to remain in the States, settling in their adopted country with their families.

Early Bulgarian Americans included Ilya S. Iovchev, who arrived in 1870 and became a journalist, and Hristo Balabanov, who came to the States in 1876, earned an M.D., then established a medical practice in Tacoma, Washington, in 1890.

## SIGNIFICANT IMMIGRATION WAVES

Bulgarians have a long tradition, dating to the Byzantine period, of migrating to flee political turmoil. Every unsuccessful revolt against the Turks in the eighteenth and nineteenth centuries was accompanied by mass migrations of Bulgarians to Russia, the Ukraine, Moldavia, Hungary, Romania, Serbia, and other Balkan nations.

Bulgarian refugees begin their journey to the United States.

Expatriate Bulgarian communities formed and thrived in some of those countries. Today, an estimated two million ethnic Bulgarians live beyond the country's borders, with the vast majority residing in Russia and Romania.

Bulgarians first started immigrating to the United States in large numbers between 1903 and 1910. During this period, approximately 50,000 Bulgarians from Turkish-occupied Macedonia and from Bulgaria proper, or "the kingdom," arrived in the United States. Economic opportunity was the primary attraction for Bulgarians from "the kingdom," who were escaping overpopulation and unemployment in their native regions. Macedonian-Bulgarians had an additional impetus to emigrate; the unsuccessful St. Ilya's Day revolt of 1903 drew brutal reprisals from the Turkish army, which laid waste to three Macedonian provinces and killed 5,000 revolutionaries and villagers. Some 30,000 homeless Macedonians fled to Bulgaria. Within months, the largest wave of Bulgari-

an and Macedonian Bulgarian emigration had begun.

After 1910, political developments continued to influence the ebb and flow of emigration from Bulgaria. Territorial loss following the Balkan Wars and the First World War drove between 400,000 and 700,000 ethnic Bulgarians from Aegean Thrace, Macedonia, and Dobrudzha into Bulgaria proper. Their arrival strained the already limited economic resources of the country and led many Bulgarians, in turn, to seek work abroad.

For the typical Bulgarian immigrant of the early twentieth century, passage to the United States was not obstacle-free. With little of value to his name, a peasant would sell his land and livestock, mortgage his farm, or take a high-interest loan from a steamship agent in order to fund his transatlantic trip. Such a costly outlay meant there was no turning back. Some immigrants began their journeys at Danube River ports, traveling to

Vienna and continuing overland by train to any number of European port cities (Hamburg, Le Havre, Trieste), where they spent up to a week or more in detention camps before boarding a ship to New York. Others embarked from the Greek ports of Piraeus or Salonika. Although their points of departure varied, most immigrants spent the month-long ocean voyage in steerage, in the hold of the ship, where crowded, unsanitary conditions and poor food encouraged the spread of disease. Many Bulgarians sought to avoid stringent entrance exams at Ellis Island, the immigration station in New York City, by entering the country illegally, through Canada or Mexico.

Bulgarian immigration never boomed the way immigration from other southern or eastern European countries did, and in 1924, the National Origins Immigration Act limited the number of Bulgarians who could enter the United States to a mere 100 a year. From 1924 until the lifting of the national origins quota restrictions in 1965, only 7,660 Bulgarians were officially admitted to the United States. Historians believe thousands more made America their home during this period, entering illegally via Canada or Mexico or with non-Bulgarian passports issued by the country of their last residence rather than the country of their birth. Many Bulgarians, it is believed, have been recorded as Turks, Greeks, Serbs, Romanians, Russians, or Yugoslavs. At one point, U.S. immigrations statistics did not distinguish Bulgarians from Serbs and Montenegrins. For these reasons, the actual number of people of Bulgarian ancestry living in the United States is believed to be significantly higher than the 1990 U. S. Census figure—slightly over 70,000 as opposed to the official 20,894.

The 1924 quota restrictions affected not only the dimension of Bulgarian immigration but its character as well. Most of the immigrants of the interwar years (1919-1939) were women and children joining husbands and fathers who had already established themselves in America. Otherwise, immigration from Bulgaria during these years had dwindled to a trickle.

The rise of the Communist state in 1945 precipitated a new wave of immigration. In contrast to the earlier immigrants, the postwar emigres were primarily political refugees and professionals who left Bulgaria with no expectation of returning. Thousands fled in the wake of the Soviet invasion of Bulgaria in 1944. Following retreating German troops to Germany or Austria, some Bulgarians settled in western European countries;

others entered the United States under the Displaced Persons Act of 1947. A handful became Americans under the auspices of a 1944 congressional act that granted citizenship to refugees who were accepted into U. S. military service overseas. Until the Bulgarian borders were sealed in 1949, refugees continued to leave by the thousands. The route to America was often circuitous, with refugees typically spending several years in non-Communist European countries—Greece, Turkey, Italy, Austria, Germany—or even in South America before finally making their way to the United States. After 1956, the flow of postwar refugees slowed to a mere 100 to 300 a year, but periodic relaxations on travel or border regulations continued to give the determined occasion to flee.

In 1989, the demise of single-party rule in Bulgaria brought an end to Communist restraints on travel and opened the country's borders. Many Bulgarians, fleeing economic instability under the new government, are once again leaving for western European countries or America. Since 1990, they have been immigrating to the United States at a rate of about 1,000 a year. Like those who emigrated during the Cold War, these immigrants are predominantly skilled workers and professionals.

## SETTLEMENT PATTERNS

The early immigrants tended to settle in Slavic or Balkan enclaves in the Midwest and the Northeast, where unskilled laborers could find work in factories, mills, and mines. The earliest recorded Bulgarian communities arose shortly after the turn of the century in the cities of Steelton and Philadelphia, Pennsylvania; Cleveland and Dayton, Ohio; Chicago, Illinois; St. Louis, Missouri; and New York City. Smaller numbers of Bulgarians settled in the American West or Northwest as farmers or railroad workers. Between 1910 and 1914, a group of ethnic Bulgarians from Bessarabia established a farming community in North Dakota. Another group established itself in Yakima, Washington, as fruit growers.

Nevertheless, the most popular destination for new arrivals was the Midwest, where, for instance, the twin cities of Granite City and Madison, Illinois counted over 6,000 Bulgarian inhabitants in 1907. As the automobile industry grew, Detroit became home to the largest concentration of Bulgarians in this country—there were 7,000 in the city alone in 1910, with an additional 1,500 scattered in nearby Michigan cities. An estimated 10,000 Bulgarian Americans continue to live in Michigan today. In contrast, only about three to four thousand Bulgarians reside in the New York metropolitan area. Other cities hosting large numbers of Bulgarian Americans include Gary, Fort Wayne, and Indianapolis, Indiana; Lorain, Toledo, Cleveland, Youngstown, and Akron, Ohio; and Los Angeles, California. Pittsburgh, once a hub for Bulgarian immigrants, has declined in importance in recent years, while the greater New York and Los Angeles areas have attracted growing numbers of recent immigrants.

# ACCULTURATION AND ASSIMILATION

As an ethnic group, Bulgarian Americans do not have a conspicuous or clearly defined image in the United States. Scholars have attributed the group's low profile to a number of factors. Bulgarian immigration, even at its height (1907-1910), never approached the magnitude of immigration by other comparable southern or eastern European nationalities. Practically nonexistent before 1900, Bulgarian immigration also occurred later. Those who did come led largely nomadic lives or were dispersed around the country and tended not to form distinct ethnic communities. There were no "little Bulgarias" from which the American public could draw its stereotypes.

"While I am not a whole American, neither am I what I was when I first landed here; that is, a Bulgarian.... I have outwardly and inwardly deviated so much from a Bulgarian that when recently visiting in that country I felt like a foreigner.... In Bulgaria I am not wholly a Bulgarian; in the United States not wholly an American."

Stoyan Christowe in 1919, cited in *Ellis Island: An Illustrated History of the Immigrant Experience,* edited by Ivan Chemayeff et al. (New York: Macmillan, 1991).

According to Nikolay Altankov, the first scholar to make an extensive study of Bulgarian Americans, the group's own attitudes may have encouraged the indifference of the general public. Far from being vocal or visible, Bulgarians tend to shy away from involvement in public life. With some exceptions, they prefer to devote their energies to friends and families rather than to politics or ethnic activities.

When the early immigrants did attract notice, their "Bulgarian-ness" was often obscured by their identification with other Slavs. During the heyday of Bulgarian immigration, outsiders might have recognized Granite City's "Hungary Hollow" as an eastern European enclave, but few bothered to distinguish Bulgarians from their Magyar or Slavic neighbors. Insofar as Bulgarians were confused with larger Slavic groups, they encountered the same prejudices as those immigrants. Their opportunities for employment were limited, and they took the low-paying, unskilled, and often dangerous work that the native-born refused. They faced the inevitable derogatory epithets. Established Americans looked down on the newcomers, whose unfamiliar customs and lack of English skills alienated them from the mainstream and whose poverty forced them to live in crowded, unsanitary conditions.

By contrast, immigrants who arrived during the Cold War as political refugees received a more welcome reception. Their strong anti-Communist stance inspired sympathy. They were better educated, more cosmopolitan, and more highly skilled than the earlier immigrants. As academics, doctors, engineers, and small business owners, they had stronger financial prospects in their adopted country. However, because their numbers were small and they were even less likely to settle in specifically Bulgarian neighborhoods, they failed to raise the profile of Bulgarian Americans.

The descendants of the early immigrants, the second generation, often chose to live in non-Bulgarian neighborhoods and marry out of their ethnicity. Educated in American schools and steeped in American culture, they were eager to cast aside the "differentness" that marked their parents. Increasingly, they spoke only English. Observance of Bulgarian customs went the way of regular attendance at a Bulgarian church. In short, second-generation Bulgarian Americans assimilated into American life, frequently at the expense of ethnic heritage. And yet, from the relatively comfortable vantage point as third-generation Americans, their children are feeling the draw of their past. Many Americans of Bulgarian descent are re-discovering their ethnic roots. Bulgarian folk dance and music, in particular, are enjoying a new popularity among Bulgarians and non-Bulgarians alike.

## TRADITIONS, CUSTOMS, AND BELIEFS

In Bulgaria, practice of traditions varies from region to region. A city dweller, for instance, might not adhere as strictly to tradition as a villager does. And the customs the urbanite follows differ from those practiced by the farmer, whose life is shaped by close ties to the land and a greater dependency on the vagaries of nature. Historical circumstance has exacted its tolls, somewhat estranging the postwar generations of Bulgarians, educated under Communism, from the beliefs of their ancestors. These tendencies are preserved among immigrants to the United States. Although immigrants bring their traditions to their adopted country, their American-born children, in their haste to assimilate, may be eager to shed long-held customs. Nonetheless, certain traditions marking rites of passage, such as baptisms, weddings, and funerals, have had tremendous staying power.

## PROVERBS

Bulgarian proverbs usually rhyme in the original language. Even in translation, however, they convey common Bulgarian values such as hard work and respect for friends: God gives, but doesn't put it in the cowshed; A group that gets along together will be able to raise a mountain; A clear account makes a good friend; Study brings success; Nothing is impossible to a Bulgarian.

## CUISINE

Like the cuisines of its Balkan neighbors, Bulgarian cooking has assimilated many elements of Turkish cuisine. There is an emphasis on dairy products, mainly yogurt and cheese; on nuts, especially the walnuts and sunflower seeds of the Tundzha Valley; and on fresh, seasonal fruits and vegetables. Traditional meat dishes—stews, sausages, kebabs (grilled meats)—are most often made of lamb, veal, or pork. Also popular are chicken, beef, brains, kidney, and liver. Bulgarian dishes are generally spicier than those of neighboring countries, and cooks are liberal in their use of herbs and strongly flavored condiments such as garlic and chili peppers.

Because many of the ingredients in Bulgarian cuisine are available in the United States, first- and second-generation Bulgarian Americans have continued cooking and consuming the dishes they enjoyed in Bulgaria. However, family meals often become more elaborate and meat more frequent if the family prospers in its adopted country. Con-

versely, the diets of poor, early immigrant laborers tended to match their humble living conditions.

Traditional breakfasts are simple, eaten at home before the work day begins. The breakfast usually consists of bread, fruit, and cheese—the most familiar being *sirene*, a salty, feta-like cheese, and *kashkaval*, a hard cheese similar to Cheddar—which are washed down with a glass of yogurt (*kiselo mlyako*) or *boza*, a millet drink. Mid-day meals tend to be soups or fried dishes, cooked in butter or oil, while grilled meat or spicy stews, preceded by a salad tossed in yogurt or in oil, are the mainstay of evening meals. Bulgarians have traditionally relied on numerous light snacks (fruit, cheese, bread, and other baked goods), eaten throughout the day, to sustain them as they labored in the fields or pastures or, later, in the factories and mines.

The classic Bulgarian dishes are simple and hearty. The "national soup," *tarator*, is a cold cucumber and yogurt soup seasoned with dill and garlic and topped with chopped walnuts. Another popular starter, the *salata shopska*, is a mixed salad of tomatoes, cucumbers, cabbage, peppers, and onions tossed in vinegar and sunflower oil and sprinkled with a light layer of crumbled cheese. Bulgarian meals are invariably accompanied by the oven-baked bread known as *pitka*, which is served with *ciubritsa*, an aromatic condiment with a native herb resembling tarragon at its base.

Of the traditional Bulgarian main dishes, *gyuvech* is the best known. Baked in an earthenware dish, it is a rich, spicy stew of various vegetables—usually some combination of peppers, chilies, onions, tomatoes, eggplant, and beans—cooked with meaty chunks of veal, pork, lamb, or beef, then slathered with a yogurt-egg sauce which bakes into a crust. Also popular, *sarmi* is made by stuffing cabbage leaves with minced meat and rice. Other common meat dishes are *kebabche*, a grilled patty of minced pork, lamb, and veal flavored with garlic, and *kyufte*, a meatball of the same ingredients, as well as the more universal chops and filets of veal and pork.

Desserts, too, reflect Bulgaria's history and its unique geopolitical position: the middle Eastern pastry *baklava*, a layered pastry of chopped nuts drenched in honey, is as common as *garash*, a chocolate layer cake with central European antecedents. Local fruits make another post-dinner favorite, the dessert varying with the season—strawberries, raspberries, plums, cherries, peaches, apples, and grapes. Coffee, or *kafe*, is consumed Turkish-style or as European *espresso*.

## DANCE AND MUSIC

Music and dance are central to Bulgarian culture. Music has bound together the community in times of oppression and in celebration. Significantly, there are few strictly solo performances of folk dance or music. Songs are used to commemorate religious occasions, traditional holidays, past wars, and historical events, births, marriages, deaths, departures, and harvests. Even religious services are chanted in song-like fashion rather than read. Song and dance are very much a part of the fabric of daily life, as well. Shepherds can still be heard in the Rhodope Mountains playing plaintive songs to their flocks, using the traditional goatskin bagpipe. In villages and cities alike, a Bulgarian youth will announce romantic intentions by challenging the object of his or her interests to a dance contest. And any given performance of the popular line dance, the *horo*, will include participants of all ages in its circle.

Because Bulgarian music and dance are communal in nature, they are preserved among immigrants only to the extent that there is a close-knit community. Early Bulgarian immigrants often held evening parties, or *vecherinka*, at Bulgarian-owned saloons or coffee houses, where workers sought release from their long, difficult days in song, dance, and drink. Saint's days and holidays were greeted with the greatest festivity, as men performed variations on the basic *horo*, or circular line dance. The immigrants could briefly forget their hardships in lively dances like the *ruchenitsa*, which allowed them to showcase their agility in leaps and squats, or the *kopenitsa*, with its tricky, rhythmically complex steps. Increasingly isolated from Bulgarian American daily life, however, traditional music and dance is relegated today to weddings and other special events or to the occasional performance at ethnic festivals.

Although its role in Bulgarian American life has perhaps declined, Bulgarian folk music has inspired a new generation of Western artists, from the American pop singers David Byrne and Paul Simon to the English singer-songwriter Kate Bush, to the ranks of non-Bulgarian Americans who have formed traditional Bulgarian folk dance and music groups in the United States. New York City alone boasts the women's singing group, Zhenska Pesen, and the Bosilek Bulgarian Dance Troupe. Contemporary music from Bulgaria is also enjoying an unprecedented popularity in the West, and many recordings are available on Western labels. The best known of these is *Le Mystere des Voix Bulgares*, performed by the Bulgarian State Radio and Television Female Vocal Choir.

Bulgarian music is distinguished by its rhythmic complexity, heavy ornamentation, and the stirring and slightly nasal sound of the "open-throated" singing style. Most traditional folk songs are ornately decorated solos performed by a woman against the steady drone of a bagpipe or another voice. (Songs for dancing, categorized as "useful" and, therefore, less artistic music, were simpler and less decorated.) In some villages, a polyphonic style arose in which the women sing in two- or three-part harmony and decorate their songs with whoops, vibrati, and slides. The female singers are sometimes accompanied by men playing traditional Bulgarian instruments; these include, most commonly, the *ghaida*, or goatskin bagpipe; the *kaval*, a sheperd's flute made of three wooden tubes; the *gadulka*, a stringed instrument with no frets or fingerboard on its neck; the *tambura*, a lute-like stringed instrument with a long, fretted neck; and the *tapan*, a large, two-sided drum.

## HOLIDAYS CELEBRATED BY BULGARIAN AMERICANS

Bulgarian Americans celebrate Christmas (Koleda), New Year's Day (Surva), and Easter (Velikden) and, to a greater or lesser degree, a smattering of prominent saints' days. These include St. Cyril and St. Methodius Day on May 11, St. Constantine and St. Elena Day on May 21, St. Elijah's Day (Ilinden) on July 20, the Birth of the Virgin on September 8, St. John of Rila's Day (Ivan Rilski) on October 19, St. Demetrius's Day (Dimitrovden) on October 26, the Day of the Archangels Michael and Gabriel (Arhangelovden) on November 8, and St. Nicholas's Day (Nikulden) on December 6. Arguably the most important secular holiday, March 3rd marks the liberation of Bulgaria from the Turks. Immigrant families also observe the standard American holidays, such as Thanksgiving and the Fourth of July.

Most saint's days are recognized simply by feasting or attendance at special church services, where candles are lit before the appropriate icon. Other saint's days coincide with seasonal celebrations of pagan origins and incorporate pre-Christian customs into a Christian framework. On New Year's or Saint Basil's Day, for instance, groups of young children carrying *survaknitsa*, bundles of twigs draped with colored thread and dried fruit, supposedly bring luck and prosperity to their neighbors by visiting their homes and lightly slapping them with the fruit-laden twigs. *Kukerov den* welcomes the start of the agricultural year. On the first Sunday before Lent, young men ensure fertility by parading and dancing in huge masks, or *kuker*, made of animal skins and fur. On March 1st, or *Baba Marta*, people celebrate the first day of spring by wearing or giving away *martenitsa*, a good luck charm made of two woolen balls, one red, symbolizing red cheeks, and the other white, for white skin. A second springtime fertility rite, in which unmarried women perform dances and songs, coincides with St. Lazar's Day, eight days before Easter. Summer begins on the day of St. Constantine and St. Elena, while St. Demetrius's Day, October 26, is a harvest holiday marking the end of the agricultural year. The extent to which Bulgarian American families observe these holidays is often determined by the presence or absence of ties to a larger Bulgarian American community.

# LANGUAGE

Bulgarian is a south Slavic language, closely related to Serbo-Croatian and Slovenian and more distantly to Russian. It is one of the oldest written languages in Europe. Like Russian, Bulgarian uses the 29-character Cyrillic alphabet, which was adapted from the Greek alphabet in the ninth century A.D. to accommodate the sounds of the Old Slavonic tongue. The Orthodox missionaries Cyril and Methodius created this alphabet for the spoken Slavic language, and their disciples Kliment and Naum translated religious texts into Old Church Slavonic using the script, which they named Cyrillic after its creator. The alphabet spread from early medieval Bulgaria to other Slavic civilizations. With substantial justification, Bulgarians consider their native tongue the ur-Slavic language that influenced all the other Slavic languages.

Bulgarian has gained by its contact with other civilizations. It retains over 2,000 words from the pre-Cyrillic Old Slavonic tongue. Four centuries of Greek Orthodox supervision over the Bulgarian church has added Greek religious terms, as well as some Greek words used in daily life, to the Bulgarian language. The Turks, then the Russians, donated vocabulary relating to political, economic, and day-to-day life. The postwar era introduced to Bulgarian a number of western European words, especially in the fields of technology and science.

Bulgarians in the United States have likewise incorporated many American English words into their daily speech. However, only the immigrant generation uses this mongrelized Bulgarian; their American-educated children are more likely to consider English their primary language.

## GREETINGS AND OTHER POPULAR EXPRESSIONS

*Zdravei*—Hello; *Kak ste?*—How are you?; *Blagodarya*—Thank you; *Nyama zashto*—You're welcome; *Molya*—Please; *Izvinete*—Excuse me; *Dobro utro*—Good morning; *Dobar den*—Good day; *Dobar vecher*—Good evening; *Leka nosht*—Good night; *Dovizhdane*—Goodbye; *Chestito*—Congratulations; *Chestit rozhden den*—Happy birthday; *Chestita nova godina*—Happy new year; *Nazdrava*—To your health.

# FAMILY AND COMMUNITY DYNAMICS

Bulgarian American communities took root slowly in the decades preceding the First World War. The unmarried men who first came to the United States believed their stay would be temporary. That perception, coupled with the mobile nature of their work, initially inhibited the creation of permanent communities. Nevertheless, immigrant social life came to organize itself around two types of institutions during the early part of this century: the *boort*, or boardinghouse, and the *kafene*, or cafe.

The *boort* was a Bulgarian-owned boardinghouse that allowed groups of immigrant men to save money by living together and pooling their household duties and expenses. It was usually run by a Bulgarian who had met with enough success in America to buy a house. Confining his private quarters to a single room or two, he would rent out the remaining room or rooms. The boardinghouse owner often held a factory job as well. If he was married, his wife and family might provide meals or other housekeeping services to the boarders for an additional fee. More often, the boarders chose to do their own chores. The typical *boort* was overcrowded and sparsely furnished. Boarders slept and ate in shifts, six or more to a single room. They often worked different rotations at the same factory or mine. Although conditions ran to the squalid, many immigrants preferred saving their earnings to living in comfort.

The *kafene* (cafe or coffeehouse) offered an escape from the rigors of work and crowded households. In addition to serving familiar food and drinks, it functioned as a center for recreation and socializing. The proprietor of a *kafene* was usually more educated and better established in his new country than was the boardinghouse owner. He had a better command of the English language than his customers and was often called upon to act as translator, attorney, travel agent, or in any number of other capacities. As a natural outgrowth of his multiple roles, he sometimes ran another business—a newsstand, a grocery store, a rooming house, an employment agency, a bank— on the side.

### FAMILY ROLES

Among the first generation, family relations adhered rather closely to the traditional Bulgarian model. The close-knit family was headed by a patriarch who made all pivotal decisions. The father's parents often lived in his household, caring for the children while the father and mother worked. Social life revolved around the extended family to a far greater degree than in western European societies. Marriages were arranged by family members or professional marriage brokers.

With assimilation, however, came the disintegration of this model. Because women were relatively scarce, they were more highly valued in the immigrant community than they were in Bulgaria. Bulgarian wives, realizing how essential their labor was to their families' survival in the new country, became more independent-minded. Immigrant women were forming their own organizations and clubs as early as 1913. Bulgarian men, lacking both fluency in English and status in American society, found their patriarchal roles somewhat diminished. Their children assumed an ambassadorial role, explaining and interpreting the society and language of America to their parents. And increasingly, second-generation children left home to attend college or go to work. In contrast, grown-up children in Bulgaria left their parents' homes only to marry, settling nearby even then. As families assimilated, the traditional hierarchies flattened, giving women and children a greater voice in their households.

### TRADITIONS OF EARLY LIFE

According to Orthodox tradition, a child born on the day of an important saint must take that saint's name, or face an unhappy life unprotected by the saint.

Baptism is considered an important rite that establishes individual identity before the eyes of God. The godparents bring the child, dressed in new clothes for the occasion, to church. Relatives and friends are invited to attend. If either godparent has not been baptized, he or she must be baptized at that time in order to be permitted to be godparent. The priest blesses the child and then bathes the child in a tub of warm water. Then he sprinkles with holy water a fragrant plant symbolic of good health, called the *zdravets*. After the baptism, there may be a celebratory dinner at the parents' home, to which guests typically bring gifts of money. Each year thereafter, the godmother goes to church and lights a candle on the child's baptism day.

*Proshtupulnik* is a non-religious tradition that celebrates a child's first step. Family and friends are invited to bring objects symbolic of various professions. These objects—a paint brush to symbolize art, scissors for the tailor, a pen for the writer, money for the banker, a globe for the world traveler, and so on—are arranged on a small table. The parents then roll a rounded loaf of bread toward the table and urge the newly ambulatory child to chase it. Once the bread falls at the foot of the table, the child is instructed to choose one of the objects on top. According to tradition, the child will choose the tool of his or her future profession.

### WEDDINGS

Typically a month in duration, the Bulgarian engagement period seems short to most Americans. Once a couple announces their intention to marry, the parents of the groom visit the bride's home. Bringing gifts and money for her parents, they formally invite the prospective bride to join their family. An engagement party takes place at the bride's home after she and her parents have agreed to the marriage. This practice has been modified in the United States, where it may be difficult to arrange wedding festivities in one month's time and where Bulgarians marry non-Bulgarians.

Shortly after the engagement, a maid of honor and a best man are chosen. Their roles are more than ceremonial; they are expected to aid the couple in the wedding preparations and to help them throughout their married life. Among other responsibilities, they are expected to be godparents to the couple's children. It is also understood that the maid of honor should buy or otherwise provide the bride's bouquet and wedding dress.

On the last night of the engagement—the night before the wedding—the bride's house resounds with sad songs of leavetaking. Far from celebrating the joys of marriage, these songs mourn the bride's imminent departure from her parents' home. Each subsequent part of the wedding is also characterized by appropriate music; folk songs mark the arrival of the groom's party at the bride's house, the emergence of the bride to join them, and the procession to the church. A traditional wedding band plays lively dance music throughout the festivities following the ceremony.

The wedding ceremony, which usually takes place early in the day, is similar to other Eastern Orthodox wedding services. The priest leads the service; he asks the couple if they wish to marry, blesses them, then declares them married. Husband and wife exchange rings, after which the priest places crowns on their heads to signify their future together as the joint rulers of their family. The couple then drinks wine or champagne from a common glass, thus ensuring their future prosperity. As the ceremony draws to a close, the guests line up to offer the bride fresh flowers. The couple might now engage in a folk custom that supposedly foretells which spouse will rule over the other in married life: each tries to be the first to step on the other's foot. Many modern couples, preferring to regard each other as equal partners, choose to forego this custom.

In cities, newlyweds visit and lay flowers at various monuments while the guests make their way to the reception. The purpose of this custom is to allow the bride and groom to be the last to arrive at the reception, which is usually held in a restaurant, hotel, or private home. Once they arrive, the couple finds, placed on a table, a round, home-baked loaf of bread and a bowl of honey. Before the assembled guests, the bride dips a chunk of bread in honey and puts it in the mouth of the best man while the groom follows suit with the maid of honor. Then the bride and groom feed each other pieces of honey-dipped bread, each trying to outdo the other with larger and more unmanageable chunks. A second loaf of bread is provided for another custom, in which the husband and wife each grip the bread and pull. Whoever breaks the larger piece will, according to tradition, be the dominant partner in the marriage.

At the reception, a feast of lavish dishes and wine is punctuated by live folk music. Guests of all ages join in the *horo*, a circular line dance, whose leader leaps and performs difficult steps while waving a long flagpole. Traditionally, the wedding band was composed of folk instruments; today it may be a union of Bulgarian folk and modern Western instruments. The band's playlist may also be divided between modern pop songs and folk music.

### FUNERALS

In Bulgaria today, a family announces a relative's death by issuing cards or fliers to acquaintances and posting notices in offices or on building walls. Funeral services are usually held inside a sermon hall at the cemetery rather than at the graveside. There, a priest or employee of the cemetery leads prayers for the dead and reads a short sermon. A band plays solemn music as the coffin is led to the grave. Guests bring flowers, making sure that each bouquet includes an even number of flowers, since odd-numbered bouquets are reserved for festive occasions. Close family members dress in black for the first 40 days following the funeral, and sometimes longer. Mirrors in the home of the deceased are covered with black cloth.

Forty days after the funeral, the family of the deceased holds another service to celebrate the soul's flight from the body. Followers of the Bulgarian Orthodox faith believe that the spirit leaves the body forty days after death; some say there is scientific proof the body becomes perceptibly lighter on that day. More fliers, bearing a photo of the deceased, are posted announcing the occasion. Guests congregate at the grave or at church, where they light candles for the deceased and are fed ceremonial foods. The most common dish eaten on this day is *zhito*, or boiled whole wheat topped with sugar and nuts.

# RELIGION

Most Bulgarian Americans belong, at least nominally, to the Bulgarian Orthodox Church, an independent national branch of Eastern Orthodoxy. The first Bulgarian Church in America was established in 1909 in Granite City, Illinois. Shortly after the founding of Granite City's St. Kyril and St. Methody, the Holy Synod, the church's Sofia-based ruling body, authorized the dedication of a second church, Holy Annunciation, in Steelton, Pennsylvania. In the succeeding decades, 30 additional Bulgarian churches were founded, all under the jurisdiction of the Holy Synod. (Many of these no longer exist.) Administratively, the churches belonged to the Bulgarian Eastern Orthodox Mission for the United States and Canada. In 1938, the mother church elevated the mission to the level of a diocese and installed Bishop Andrei Velichki (d. 1972) as its titular head. However, the rise of Communism in Bulgaria contributed to a growing friction between the American churches and the authorities in Sofia until nine churches finally broke relations with the Holy Synod in 1963. They established an independent diocese headed by Bishop Kyril Yoncheff.

In subsequent years, the Bulgarian American churchgoing community became increasingly polarized, as some continued to attend churches that recognized the authority of the Holy Synod in Bulgaria and others refused to go to churches which they believed were compromised by ties to the Communist regime. Even after the collapse of Communism a bitter divide still separates churches of the independent diocese from those of the loyalist diocese.

The church has nonetheless remained at the heart of community life. After attending services conducted entirely in Bulgarian, immigrants can attend social events organized by church groups or simply exchange gossip and argue politics. New immigrants may take advantage of English lessons or job counseling services.

# EMPLOYMENT AND ECONOMIC TRADITIONS

In the nineteenth century, it had become commonplace for Bulgarian peasants from poor, mountainous regions to leave their homes and seek temporary work abroad, usually in neighboring countries. These migrant workers, called *burchevii*, wandered to such countries as Turkey and Egypt, but always with the intention of returning home with their earnings. Most of the early immigrants in America were *burchevii*. They tended to be single men, usually uneducated peasants and laborers who found work in the industrial centers of America, in railroad construction, or in the steel mills, mines, and automobile factories of the Midwest and Northeast.

Between 1910 and 1929, the number of Bulgarians who returned to their native country outstripped the number who immigrated to the United States. Some returnees left to marry and buy plots of land with their savings. Others went back to serve in the Bulgarian army during the Balkan Wars and the First World War. Those who stayed continued working in factories and mines in order to save enough to money to enable second- and third-generation Bulgarian Americans to receive an education and enter the professional ranks of American society.

# POLITICS AND GOVERNMENT

The earliest Bulgarian American political organizations grew out of social need. Groups of immigrants who hailed from the same village formed mutual benefit societies in which members pledged to support each other in times of financial hardship. Patterned after similar organizations in the home country, the first-known Bulgarian organizations, founded by Macedonian Bulgarians, arose in the United States around 1902. They reflected the predominance of Macedonian Bulgarians among the early immigrant pool. In 1906, Iliia Iovchev, a Bulgarian-born employee of the Immigration Bureau at Ellis Island, started the Bulgarian and Macedonian Immigrant Society *Prishlets* (newcomer). Its purpose was to help immigrants through the admission procedures at Ellis Island and settle in the New World. A women's charitable organization called *Bulgarkata v Amerika* devoted itself to performing charity work on behalf of both the local community and the women's native villages in 1913. That same year, the Bulgarian People's Union, the first group with a national profile, emerged. By that time, nearly 30 mutual benefit societies had been organized around the country. Their numbers continued to mount, and by 1933 there were over 200 such organizations with a total of 10,000 members.

One of the longest-lived national organizations was the Macedonian Political Organization (MPO), founded in Fort Wayne, Indiana, in 1922. With branches in many cities, it supported the claim that Macedonians are ethnically Bulgarian and promoted the creation of an independent Macedonia. From 1926 onward, the MPO published a Bulgarian-language weekly called the *Makedonska Tribuna*. The group changed its name to the Macedonian Patriotic Organization in 1952.

Some immigrants were also involved in the national political scene. Before World War II, many Bulgarian American workers were active in leftist or labor causes; some belonged to the Bulgarian Socialist Labor Federation, a group founded in 1910 that later merged with the American Socialist Labor Party. Postwar immigrants, on the other hand, tended to belong to strongly anti-Communist organizations, such as the Bulgarian National Committee, set up in 1949 by former Bulgarian politician Georgi M. Dimitrov. Competing right-wing groups organized the royalist Bulgarian National Front in New York in 1958. In an attempt to unite a number of splinter groups, an anti-Communist umbrella organization calling itself the American Bulgarian League arose in 1944. Its goal was to promote understanding between Bulgaria and America.

The fall of communism in Bulgaria has led to a revival in organizational activity in America. As new groups arise to support specific political agendas in Bulgaria, existing groups have re-focused their activities to help newly arrived immigrants or to bridge cultural gaps between the United States and Bulgaria.

# INDIVIDUAL AND GROUP CONTRIBUTIONS

Although Bulgarian Americans are comparatively few in number, their contributions to American society have been significant. The list below provides a small sample of notable Bulgarian Americans.

## ART

The artist Christo Javacheff (1935- ), or "Christo," fled Bulgaria in 1956, and settled in New York several years later with his French-born wife and son. Before gaining admission to the United States, he studied and created art in Vienna, Geneva, and Paris. It was in Paris that Christo's signature style began to emerge, as he experimented with wrapping objects in lengths of cloth or string. Later, Christo focused on the design of monumental, non-permanent installations for public spaces. His art interacted with existing buildings, structures, or geographical features. For example, an early project marked the first anniversary of the construction of the Berlin Wall by blocking off a busy Parisian street for three hours with an "iron curtain" constructed of 204 oil drums. Later projects continued to provide oblique, but highly visible, social commentary.

Other accomplished Bulgarian American artists include Atanas Kachamakov, a sculptor who founded an art school in Los Angeles; Constantine Vichey, a Columbia-educated architect and the designer of the Varig and Aeroflot offices in New York City; and Nevdon Koumrouyan, a jewelry designer whose work has been exhibited at the Smithsonian Institution.

## BUSINESS

Arguably the most influential Bulgarian American businessman today, Frank Popoff has headed the chemical giant, The Dow Chemical Company, since he was named its Chief Executive Officer in December 1987 and its Chairman in December 1992. Born in Bulgaria, Popoff immigrated to the United States as a small child. He joined Dow Chemical in 1959, immediately after earning his M.B.A. from Indiana University, and rose quickly through the ranks. Popoff serves on the boards of several corporate and philanthropic organizations.

The banker Henry Karandjeff came from an earlier generation of immigrants and had a more local profile. Born in a Macedonian village in 1893, he arrived in the United States at the age of 13. He graduated from the St. Louis University in 1919 and later founded two savings and loans banks in Granite City, Illinois. When he retired, he left a successful business to his son.

## LITERATURE AND JOURNALISM

Peter Dimitrov Yankoff (1885-?) drew upon his immigrant experience to pen the 1928 novel, *Peter Menikoff: The Story of a Bulgarian Boy in the Great American Melting Pot*. Another Bulgarian immigrant, Boris George Petroff, wrote *Son of Danube* (1940).

The journalist Christ Anastasoff authored scores of articles, many of them about Bulgarian and Macedonian immigrants. His book *A Visit to Yugoslavia and Macedonia* was published in 1957. Boyan Choukanov catered to a primarily Bulgarian American audience as editor of the *American Bulgarian Review* and as host of the weekly cable television show "Balkan Echo" in New York City. Stephane Groueff, a New York-based reporter, published *Manhattan Project*, a book about the history of the development of the atomic bomb. On CNN International, the face and voice of Ralitsa Vassileva (1964- ) is beamed around the world by satellite as she anchors the news network's "Headline News" and "World Report" shows.

## MEDICINE

The psychiatrist George Kamen (1942- ) was still living in Bulgaria when he pioneered the idea of group therapy in the late 1960s. The revolutionary new treatment brought him both professional acclaim and political troubles. Because Kamen worked with groups of patients who discussed with each other their deepest thoughts and emotions, he inevitably attracted official scrutiny. Kamen soon became the target of a campaign of harassment, and decided to flee Bulgaria. After several unsuccessful attempts, he escaped to Vienna, and from there, to political asylum in West Germany. Kamen and his wife Katia, also Bulgarian, arrived in the United States in 1980. Today he has a private practice in New York City.

## POLITICS

A colorful and energetic writer and politician, Stoyan Christowe (1898- ) emigrated from his native Macedonia in 1911. The teenager first settled in St. Louis with a group of older men from his village. Christowe taught himself English and was admitted to Valparaiso University in Indiana. He became a reporter after graduating and, in 1928, was sent to the Balkans as a foreign correspondent for the *Chicago Daily News*. During the Second World War, Christowe served in Military Intelligence in the Pentagon. In 1961 he was elected a Vermont state representative, a post he held until his election to the State Senate in 1965. Running as a Republican, Christowe was re-elected to four more terms. He retired in 1972. Christowe's eventful life provided excellent material for his books, which include memoirs, novels, and a volume about Macedonia.

# MEDIA

## PRINT

### Good Luck Bulgarian Newspaper.

This Bulgarian-language monthly was first conceived as a newsletter in 1991. Its founders, two immigrants who had been journalists in their native Bulgaria, changed to a broadsheet format in 1993. Combining material from their native country and their adopted one, the editors dedicate the first three pages of each issue to Bulgarian news and the two succeeding pages to practical advice about living in the United States, such as the fundamentals of starting a business. The remaining three pages contain advertising and articles focusing on American news and culture.

**Contact:** Orlin Krumov or Sam Todorov, Editors.

**Address:** 338 West Miner Street, Apartment 3-B, Arlington Heights, Illinois 60005.

**Telephone:** (708) 632-1542.

### Makedonska Tribuna (Macedonian Tribune).

Biweekly general interest newspaper in Bulgarian and English.

**Contact:** A. A. Virginia N. Surso.

**Address:** Macedonian Patriotic Organization, 124 West Wayne, Fort Wayne, Indiana 46802.

**Telephone:** (219) 422-5900.

**Fax:** (219) 422-4379.

# ORGANIZATIONS AND ASSOCIATIONS

**Bulgarian American Chamber of Commerce.**
Founded in 1993, the Chamber of Commerce is a non-profit organization that promotes cooperation among Bulgarian-owned businesses in the English-speaking world. Its annual directory contains listings of businesses, services, churches, and social organizations located in the United States, Canada, and Australia. The Chamber also sponsors cultural events and visits from famous Bulgarians. Its guests have included the opera soprano Ghena Dimtrova, the Bulgarian President Zhelyu Zhelev, and the exiled Bulgarian king, Simeon.

**Contact:** Ogden Page, President.

**Address:** 6464 Sunset Boulevard, Suite 850, Hollywood, California 90028.

**Telephone:** (213) 962-2414.

**Bulgarian American Enterprise Fund.**
Created in 1989 under the aegis of the Bush administration, this private investment fund is interested in developing the Bulgarian economy. The Fund's activities are two-fold: it invests in Bulgarian businesses in Bulgaria and it encourages American companies to do business in Bulgaria.

**Contact:** Frank Bauer, President.

**Address:** 333 West Wacker Drive, Suite 2080, Chicago, Illinois 60606.

**Telephone:** 312-629-2500.

**Bulgarian National Front (BNF).**
Works to promote and defend the democratization of Bulgaria and the return to free market economy

and Western values, and to make known in America the culture and history of Bulgaria.

**Contact:** Dr. Ivan Docheff, President.
**Address:** P.O. Box 46250, Chicago, Illinois 60646.
**Telephone:** (609) 597-4605.

# SOURCES FOR ADDITIONAL STUDY

Altankov, Nikolay. *The Bulgarian-Americans*. Palo Alto, California: Ragusan Press, 1979.

Carlson, Claudia, and David Allen. *The Bulgarian Americans*. New York: Chelsea House Publishers, 1990.

Christowe, Stoyan. *The Eagle and the Stork, an American Memoir*. New York: Harper's Magazine Press, 1976.

Cambodian
Americans are
members of one of
the youngest ethnic
groups in American
society.

# CAMBODIAN AMERICANS

by
Carl L. Bankston III

## OVERVIEW

Cambodia is a country of about 8,000,000 people, approximately the size of the state of Missouri, located in Southeast Asia. It is bordered on the west and northwest by Thailand, on the north by Laos, on the east by the southern part of Vietnam, and on the south by the Gulf of Thailand. The climate is tropical, with monsoon rains from May to October and a dry season from December to March. There is little variation in temperature, which is hot most of the year. There are mountains in the southwest and north, but most of the country consists of low, flat plains. Three-quarters of the land are covered with forests and woodland, and much of the land is cultivated with rice paddies. Cambodia has few roads and bridges, and many of the existing roads and bridges are in poor condition due to years of war and political upheaval. Aside from rice, the main crop, Cambodia also produces rubber and corn.

The Cambodian people and their language are also known as "Khmer," a term that is much closer to their own word for themselves. About 90 percent of the people in Cambodia are ethnic Cambodians, or Khmer, five percent are Vietnamese, one percent are Chinese, and four percent belong to a variety of other ethnic groups, including the Cham (Muslims). Most Cambodians are wet-rice farmers in their ancestral land.

Eighty percent of them live in the countryside and practice subsistence farming. It is estimated that about 48 percent of Cambodian men and about 22 percent of Cambodian women can read and write. Cambodia is an overwhelmingly Buddhist country; 95 percent of the population practices Theravada Buddhism, the type of Buddhism found in many of the countries in southern Asia. Other faiths include Mahayana Buddhism, the type of Buddhism found most often in northern parts of Asia, Roman Catholicism, Islam, and tribal animistic religions. The flag of Cambodia contains two horizontal blue stripes divided by a wider, red stripe in the middle. In the center of the red stripe is a white temple.

## HISTORY

Before 1975, there were almost no people of Cambodian ancestry in the United States. They have settled in the United States as a result of the tragic events in their native country that followed the the Vietnam War in which the United States was deeply involved. Because Cambodian Americans are such a new part of this country, their history is especially important to them, and it is especially helpful to know something of Cambodian history in order to appreciate Cambodian culture and the unique situation of this ethnic group.

## ORIGINS

Cambodia is an ancient country with a long history that has been a source of pride and pain to the Cambodian people. The Cambodians probably lived originally in western China, but they migrated down the Mekong River valley into Indochina sometime before the common era. In Indochina, they came into contact with highly developed civilizations that had been heavily influenced by the culture of ancient India. From these civilizations, they took the religions of Hinduism and Buddhism and the idea of divine kingship. These religious and political ideas became the basis of the early Cambodian state. They also developed a sophisticated system of reservoirs and canals for irrigation, which relied on the power of the god-king to organize large numbers of people to build massive public works.

The greatest period in Cambodian history is known as the Angkorean period, after the huge complex of temples in northwestern Cambodia known as Angkor Wat, which literally means "city-temple." Most scholars place the Angkorean period as having lasted from about 802 to about 1431 A.D. During much of this time, Cambodia, or "Kambuja-Desa," as it is called in old inscriptions, was the most powerful kingdom in Southeast Asia, governing great expanses of territory that are now part of Thailand and southern Vietnam, as well as the land that remains a part of Cambodia today.

By the end of the Angkorean era, the kingdom of Kambuja-Desa came under increased pressure from the Siamese (Thai) on the west and the Vietnamese on the east. The ability of the royal bureaucracy to manage the complex irrigation system may also have weakened. Gradually, the capital and center of the kingdom shifted from Angkor Wat to Phnom Penh, which remains the capital today. Trade had become more important for the Cambodians, and Phnom Penh was located where the Mekong River and the Tonle Sap come together, an easier location from which to control trade from Laos and China.

From the 1400s on, the Cambodians lost territory to both the Siamese and the Vietnamese. By the 1800s, Cambodia had fallen almost entirely under the control of Vietnam and Siam, and Cambodia was sealed off from the outside influences that were beginning to affect other Southeast Asian countries. Vietnam, however, suffered from troubles of its own, since it had been split into northern and southern halves by rival ruling families. In 1788, the leader of a peasant rebellion managed to reunify Vietnam. One of the Vietnamese contenders for the throne, from the southern Nguyen family, sought help from the French, who, having entered Indochina, gradually established a colonial empire that became known as "French Indochina." In 1859, French Emperor Napoleon III sent troops to Vietnam. In 1984, Cambodia became a French protectorate.

## CAMBODIA UNDER THE FRENCH

King Norodom, the King of Cambodia at the time the French established control, appears to have seen French protection as a way of keeping his neighbors at bay and perhaps also as a help in defeating the numerous revolts against him by his own subjects. However, France gradually tightened its control over Cambodian political life. In 1904, Norodom died and the French made his half-brother, Sisowath, king instead of Prince Sisowath Monireth, his son, who the French considered too independent. Sisowath and the two kings who followed him were all hand-picked and placed in office by French officials.

While there was a steady growth of Cambodian nationalism, the country remained at peace through the early part of the twentieth century. When World War II broke out and France was occupied by Germany, the French remained in control in Indochina, with the agreement of Germany's allies in Asia, the Japanese. In 1941, Monivong, the king who had followed Sisowath, died, and the French made Monivong's grandson, Norodom Sihanouk, king. Sihanouk was only 19 years of age at the time. Although he was highly intelligent, artistically talented, and apparently sincere in wanting to be a good ruler, Sihanouk had had no training for the throne and relied heavily on his French advisors in the early years of his rule.

Sihanouk was to dominate Cambodian history for most of the half-century following his coronation. He also developed from a client of the French into a determined, if cautious, adherent to the cause of Cambodian independence. The victory of Japanese troops over the allies provided many Asian colonies with evidence that the European colonists could be defeated. Anti-French feelings intensified in Cambodia when the French attempted, in the 1940s, to replace the traditional writing system with a system based on the letters used by Europeans. In 1945, Japanese troops disarmed the French forces in Cambodia. Sihanouk, in the first of many changes in alliance, promised cooperation with the Japanese, changed the name of the country to "Kampuchea," and declared independence from France on March 12, 1945.

The French reestablished themselves in Cambodia after the defeat of Japan, but their power had been seriously weakened. Nationalist feelings continued to grow stronger in Cambodia. In France, some young Cambodian students, influenced by the French Communist Party, began to formulate ideas that combined extreme nationalism with Communist ideology. One of these students was Saloth Sar, who later became known as Pol Pot, the leader of the Khmer Rouge. All nationalists looked back to the time of Angkor Wat as a symbol and ideal of Cambodian greatness.

By 1953, the war in neighboring Vietnam was becoming a problem for the French, and it was unpopular in France. Sihanouk's resistance to colonial rule and the prospect of fighting another full-scale war in Cambodia led France to grant Cambodia independence on November 9, 1953, but France retained much control over the Cambodian economy. In 1954, after the French had failed to reimpose their rule on Vietnam, delegates to the Geneva Conference agreed that elections would be held in all three of the countries of Indochina. In order to participate in the elections, Sihanouk abdicated his throne in 1955 and was elected to the highest office in the country.

Sihanouk managed to keep his country neutral during many of the long years of war that raged in Vietnam and Laos. He was also, however, intolerant of Cambodian leftists, whom he labeled the "Khmer Rouge," or "Red Khmer," and many of these leftists fled into the countryside.

## CAMBODIA, THE VIETNAM WAR, AND THE UNITED STATES

The United States became involved in Southeast Asia to preserve a non-Communist regime in South Vietnam. In Laos, Cambodia's northern neighbor, there was something of an extension of the Vietnam war in the 1960s, in the form of a war between Lao guerilla forces allied with North Vietnam and the Royal government of Laos, which was pro-American. The policies of Prince Sihanouk were primarily aimed at keeping Cambodia out of these wars and, until about 1970, he was largely successful. His constant attempts to play the different sides in the Vietnam conflict against each other, though, resulted in hostility toward him by the pro-American governments of Thailand and South Vietnam and in a suspicious attitude toward him on the part of the Americans. By 1966, Sihanouk had forged a secret alliance with North Vietnam because he felt certain that the Vietnamese Communists would win the war and because the North Vietnamese agreed, under the treaty, to respect the borders of Cambodia, to leave Cambodian civilians alone, and to avoid conflicts with the Cambodian army.

War in the surrounding countries undermined the economy of Cambodia and threatened to spill across the border. In the secret treaty, Sihanouk agreed to allow the North Vietnamese to station troops inside of Cambodia and to receive weapons brought from China and North Vietnam through the port of Sihanoukville. South Vietnam and the United States, although they did not know about the secret treaty, were aware of the North Vietnamese troops.

In 1970, apparently with American support, the Cambodian general Lon Nol staged a coup while Sihanouk was in China. This was after the Americans had already begun the secret aerial bombing of North Vietnamese military sites in Cambodia, with devastating results. When the United States welcomed a more cooperative regime, the Vietnam War had finally overtaken Cambodia. In May, 1970, American and South Vietnamese forces invaded eastern Cambodia, driving the North Vietnamese forces further into the country.

Sihanouk, now out of power, joined forces with the Khmer Rouge guerrillas. Having the prince on their side gave the Khmer Rouge an enormous advantage in drawing support from the peasants, many of whom still regarded Sihanouk as an almost divine figure. At the same time, American aerial bombing in the Cambodian countryside, directed against both the North Vietnamese and the Khmer Rouge, caused enormous disruption of the traditional society. In the first half of 1973, before the U.S. Congress prohibited further bombing in Cambodia, American planes dropped over 100,000 tons of bombs on the country.

It is difficult to say to what extent the extreme radicalism of the Khmer Rouge was due to the bombing, or to far-left Maoist ideas developed by Khmer Rouge leaders as students in France, or to the carrying out of these ideas by generally very young and uneducated peasant soldiers. However, the Khmer Rouge appears to have already been uncompromising and brutal in the areas it controlled even before it took control of the whole country. In April, 1975, with the United States having pulled its troops out of Vietnam and Saigon about to fall to the Vietnamese Communists, the Khmer Rouge marched into Phnom Penh.

## REVOLUTION AND WAR

Democratic Kampuchea, as Cambodia was now called, became a bizarre experiment in revolutionary social change. In order to create a completely new society in which everyone would be equal, the Khmer Rouge, under the leadership of Pol Pot, ordered everyone, including the elderly and sick, out of the cities and towns of Cambodia and into the countryside. Family life, all traces of individualism, and all attachments to old institutions, including religion, were abolished. A new calendar for a new era was invented, with 1975 renamed "Year Zero." All Cambodians were put to work at agricultural labor in order to build up the agricultural surplus of the nation to finance rapid industrialization. In effect, these uncompromising ideals turned the entire country into a collection of forced labor camps, with young soldiers whose lives had consisted mainly of bitter warfare, as guards.

Estimates of the number of people who died under Pol Pot's Democratic Kampuchean regime vary from one million to over four million. It is not clear how many people were actually executed by the Khmer Rouge and how many people died of starvation and poor living conditions, some of which may have been the after-effects of war and U.S. bombing. Still, the period from 1975 to 1979 was traumatic for all Cambodians. Cambodians in the United States and elsewhere tell of seeing close friends and family members being killed by the Khmer Rouge and of enduring great suffering.

Democratic Kampuchea, in addition to espousing an extreme form of socialism, was also committed to extreme nationalism. The Khmer Rouge wanted to recreate the greatness of Cambodia in the Angkorean period, which meant retaking the areas that had become parts of Vietnam and Thailand. Border skirmishes between Cambodian and Vietnamese forces led Vietnam to invade Cambodia on Christmas Day in 1978, and by early January the Vietnamese held Phnom Penh. In the chaos of war, the rice crop went untended and thousands of Cambodians, starving and freed from the Khmer Rouge labor camps, began crossing the border into Thailand. Television cameras brought the images of these refugees into the homes of Americans and other westerners, and immigration from Cambodia to the United States began as a response to the "Cambodian refugee crisis."

Under pressure from the United States and other nations, the Vietnamese pulled their troops out of Cambodia in 1989, leaving the Cambodian government they had created in power. The United Nations sought to create a coalition government, including this Vietnamese-backed government, forces loyal to Sihanouk (who had broken with the Khmer Rouge almost immediately after they took power), and other factions. By 1993, a government had been elected under Sihanouk as constitutional monarch and head of state. The Khmer Rouge refused to take part in this election and continued to oppose the new government.

## IMMIGRATION

Large numbers of refugees from Cambodia have come to the United States only since 1979, when the U.S. refugee program began accepting Cambodians from refugee camps in Thailand. Most of these arrived in the early 1980s. Of the 118,823 foreign-born Cambodians identified by the 1990 Census in the United States, only 16,880 (or about 14 percent) had arrived before 1980. As thousands of refugees from Vietnam, Laos, and Cambodia began to come into the United States each year, the United States developed organizational procedures for resettlement. Voluntary agencies (or VOLAGS), many of which were affiliated with American churches, had been set up by 1975 to assist the first wave of Vietnamese refugees. These agencies had the task of finding sponsors, individuals, or groups who would assume financial and personal responsibility for refugee families for up to two years. By the early 1980s, refugee camps had been set up in various countries throughout Southeast Asia. Most Cambodians stayed in refugee camps in Thailand, but many who were being prepared for resettlement in the United States were sent to camps in the Philippines or elsewhere. Agencies under contract to the U.S. Department of State organized classes to teach English to familiarize refugees with American language and culture. In 1980 and 1981, 34,107 Cambodians entered the United States. From 1982 to 1984, the influx continued, with 36,082 Cambodians entering the United States. After that time, the numbers began to diminish. In 1985 and 1986, 19,921 Cambodians reached American soil, and from 1987 to 1990, only 11,843 Cambodians were admitted. By the early 1990s, prospects of a political settlement in Cambodia removed much of the perceived urgency of accepting Cambodian refugees, and immigration from Cambodia to the United States decreased to very small numbers.

**SETTLEMENT**

The 1990 U.S. Census found almost 150,000 Cambodian Americans in the United States, although those active in working with Cambodian immigrants warn that the Census may have undercounted this group, since the Cambodians are so new to American society and many may not have responded to the Census. The largest concentration of Cambodian Americans is in California, where close to 70,000, or nearly half of the people of Cambodian ethnicity, appear to have settled. The largest Cambodian community was Long Beach, California, where over 17,000, according to Census, made their home. Again, however, Cambodian American spokespersons

maintain that these estimates are dramatically low and that the actual number of Cambodian Americans was probably closer to twice that many. Nearby Los Angeles also had a significant population of Cambodians of at least 4,250. Stockton, California, had the second largest Cambodian community, numbering at least 10,000. Outside of California, the greatest number of Cambodian Americans were found in Massachusetts, where over 14,000 lived. About half of the Massachusetts Cambodians lived in the city of Lowell. Other states with large Cambodian populations include Texas (at least 6,000), Pennsylvania (at least 5,500, located mostly in Philadelphia), Virginia (at least 4,000), New York (at least 4,000, over two-thirds of whom lived in New York City), Minnesota (at least 4,000), and Illinois (over 3,000). Despite their large numbers, Cambodian Americans remained very much newcomers and often strangers in their adopted country. Only about one in every five foreign-born Cambodians in the United States had become a naturalized U.S. citizen by the early 1990s.

## ACCULTURATION AND ASSIMILATION

Cambodian Americans are members of one of the youngest ethnic groups in American society. According to the 1990 Census, the median age of people of Cambodian ancestry in the United States was only 19.4, compared to 34.1 for other Americans. Almost half of the Cambodian Americans counted in that Census year were under 18 years of age. About 42 percent of these Cambodian Americans below the age of 18 were born in the United States; most of the others arrived between 1980 and 1986.

Cambodian Americans also live in larger families than other Americans. The average number of people in their families was 5.03, compared to an average of 3.06 in white American families and 3.48 in black American families. Both the youth of Cambodian Americans and their large families indicate that, small though their numbers are, they will continue to grow as a proportion of American society.

Adjusting to American society has been difficult for most Cambodians, who come from rural areas and have few relevant job skills and little familiarity with mainstream American culture. One of the difficulties has been the problem of differences between generations, between older

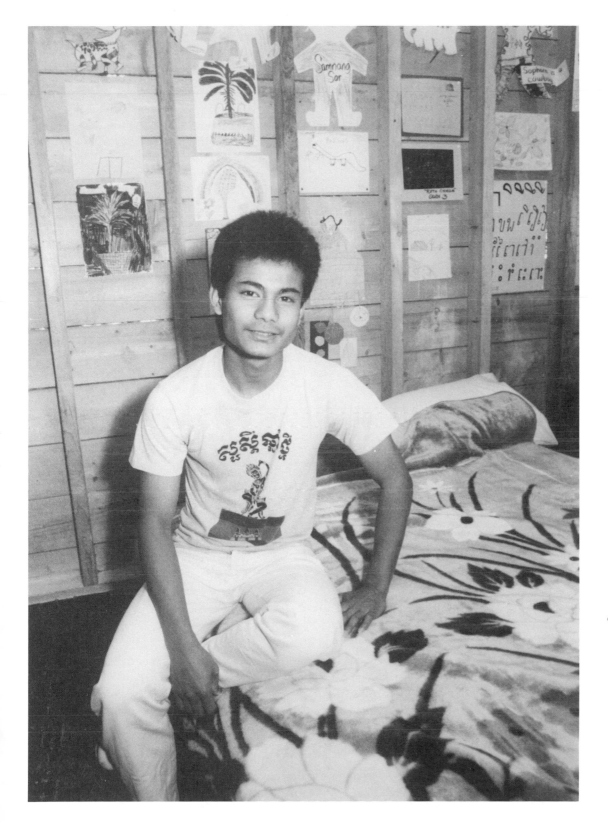

Actor Virak Ui is sitting on the set of a Cambodian home at Boston's Children's Museum. The exhibit, called "From Time to Time: Celebrating 75 Years at Our House," traces the city's diverse immigration history.

people who see themselves as Cambodians and sometimes speak little, if any English, and younger people who have either been born in the United States or have no memory of Cambodia and consider themselves entirely American.

According to Cambodian American scholar and activist Dr. Sam-Ang Sam, many Cambodian young people are plagued by identity problems, leading them to discard their Cambodian first names in favor of English first names, and they must often deal with racism from classmates and with being teased about their "foreignness." To help maintain a sense of ethnic identity, many Cambodian American Buddhist monks have set up classes in their native language for young people, and Cambodian language classes are offered by many Cambodian community organizations.

Cambodian Americans won the sympathy of many Americans in 1979 and in the early 1980s, when the plight of Cambodian refugees in Thailand became world news. Since their arrival in the United States, though, some unfortunate stereotypes of Cambodians have developed. Because Cambodian culture places a high value on courtesy and avoidance of direct confrontation, other Americans sometimes stereotype them as passive. Among older Cambodian Americans some of this appearance of passivity results from their unfamiliarity with the larger American society. Employers who give Cambodian Americans a chance, however, usually find that they are extremely hardworking, conscientious, and eager to adapt and make their way under any circumstances.

### CAMBODIAN MUSIC AND DANCE

Music is important to traditional Cambodian culture, and Cambodian Americans put a great deal of effort into maintaining this link with their heritage. Traditional music ensembles perform in almost all large Cambodian communities in the United States. There are six types of music ensembles, but the type known as *areak ka* is considered the most traditional and is used for popular religious ceremonies and wedding ceremonies. The instruments used in the *areak ka* ensemble are a three-stringed fiddle, a type of monochord, a long-necked lute, and goblet-drums. Other instruments that may be found in Cambodian ensembles include a quadruple-reed oboe, several types of gongs, a large barrel drum, a flute, a two-stringed fiddle, a three-stringed zither, hammered dulcimers, cymbals, and the xylophone. Although Cambodian music may sound somewhat strange at first to those who are unfamiliar with Asian music, most people of other ethnic backgrounds find, after a little exposure, that they can appreciate and enjoy this ancient yet vibrant art.

The best known Cambodian dance is called the "masked dance," because the dancers wear the masks of the characters they portray. The masked dance always tells the story of the *Ramayana*, an epic that the Cambodians took from ancient India. All parts in the masked dance, even those of

women, are played by men. Cambodian classical ballet, or "court dance," on the other hand, has traditionally been danced by women, although men have been entering classical ballet since the 1950s. There are a number of Cambodian dancers in the United States, and the art of dance is also beginning to revive in Cambodia. Bringing this part of the culture back to life, however, is difficult, since an estimated 90 percent of all trained dancers died during the Khmer Rouge regime.

### CAMBODIAN PROVERBS

Linguist Karen Fisher-Nguyen has observed that proverbs in Cambodia before 1975 were so important a means of educating the young that they could be found in almost all of the teaching materials of the public schools, and that studying proverbs was actually a part of the school curriculum. Many Cambodian Americans continue to treasure their proverbs as expressions of the traditional wisdom of their people. The sayings below reflect many of their values and ideals: The new rice stalk stands erect; the old stalk, full of grain, leans over; Travel on a river by following its bends, live in a country by following its customs; The small boat should not try to be a big boat; Don't let an angry man wash your dishes; don't let a hungry man guard your rice; Drop by drop, the vessel will fill; pour it, and everything will spill; Men have words—elephants have tusks; If you don't take your wife's advice, you'll have no rice seed next year; Don't rush to dump your rain water when you hear the sound of thunder; Losing money is better than wasting words; If you are an egg, don't bang against a rock; Gain knowledge by study, wealth by work.

### HOLIDAYS CELEBRATED BY CAMBODIAN AMERICANS

The most important Cambodian holiday, and the one celebrated most often in Cambodian American communities, is the New Year, or *Chaul Chnam*. The New Year's celebration is held on April 13 and lasts for three days. Many parties and dances are held during these three days, and traditional Cambodian music is usually heard at these events, although American popular music has also become part of these celebrations. One New Year's tradition that many Cambodian Americans still observe is that of the game of *bos chhoung*. In this game, young men and women stand facing each other, about five feet apart. A young man takes a scarf rolled into a ball and throws it at a young woman in whom he is interested. She must catch the scarf, and if she misses it, she must sing and dance for him. If she catches the scarf, she will throw it back to him. If he misses it, he must do the singing and dancing. For Buddhist Cambodians, the New Year Festival is an important time to visit the temple to pray, meditate, and plan for the coming year. The Water Festival, held in November when the flooding has stopped and the water starts to flow out of the Great lake into the river again, is celebrated in both Cambodia and the United States. It usually involves boat races and colorful, lighted floats sailing down the river.

## HEALTH AND MENTAL HEALTH ISSUES

In addition to the health problems faced by other poor groups in the United States, Cambodian Americans face special mental and physical health problems resulting from their tragic recent history. Most Cambodian refugees lived under the extreme brutality of the Khmer Rouge regime that ruled the country from 1975 to 1979, and their native country has been in a state of war both before and since that time. Most Cambodian refugees also spent time living in refugee camps in Thailand or other Southeast Asian countries. Health professionals and others who work with Cambodian Americans often note that these experiences have left Cambodians with a sense of powerlessness that affects many, even in America. Physical ailments often result from the emotional anguish they have suffered and continue to suffer. Among those who have been resettled in Western countries, there has appeared a strange malady often referred to as the "Pol Pot syndrome," after the leader of the Khmer Rouge. The "Pol Pot syndrome" includes insomnia, difficulty in breathing, loss of appetite, and pains in various parts of the body.

The stress that has led to such illnesses often tends to create a low general level of health for Cambodian Americans. In the entry on "Khmer" in *Refugees in the United States: A Reference Handbook*, May M. Ebihara reports that 84 percent of Cambodian households in California have reported that at least one household member was under the care of a medical doctor, compared to 45 percent of Vietnamese households and 24 percent of Hmong and Lao households. The syndrome known as "post traumatic stress disorder," a type of delayed reaction to extreme emotional stress that has been found to affect many Vietnam veterans, is also common among Cambodian refugees in the United States and other countries.

Traditional Cambodian healers, known as *krou Khmer*, may be found in many Cambodian American communities. Some of the techniques used by these healers are massages, "coining," and treatment with herbal medicines. "Coining," or *koh khchal*, is a method of using a copper coin dipped in tiger balm to apply pressure to acupuncture points of the body. Many Western doctors believe that this actually can be an effective means of pain relief. Coining does leave bruise marks, however, and these can alarm medical personnel and others not familiar with this practice.

# LANGUAGE

Cambodian, or Khmer, is classified by linguists as an Austro-Asiatic language, related to Vietnamese, Mon (a language spoken in Burma and western Thailand), and various tribal languages of Southeast Asia. Although many major Asian languages, including Vietnamese, are tonal languages, Cambodian is not tonal: as in the European languages, tones of voice may indicate emotion, but they do not change the meanings of words. The Cambodian alphabet, which has 47 letters, is derived from the alphabet of ancient India, and it is similar to the Thai and Laotian alphabets, as the Thai and Lao people borrowed their systems of writing from the Cambodians.

## CAMBODIAN GREETINGS AND OTHER COMMON EXPRESSIONS

Cambodian has many sounds that are quite different from those of English, and these are represented by the letters of the Cambodian alphabet. Linguists usually use a phonetic alphabet to write these sounds in the characters used by English and other European languages, but the phrases below are written in a fashion that should provide nonspecialist speakers of American English with a fairly close approximation to their actual pronunciation: *Som Chumreap Sur*—Good Day; *Loak sohk suh-bye jeeuh tay?*—Are you well, sir?; *Loak-srey sohk suh-bye jeeuh tay?*—Are you well, madame?; *Baht, knyom sohk suh-bye jeeuh tay*—I'm fine (from a man); *Jah, knyom sohk suh-bye jeeuh tay*—I'm fine (from a woman); *Som Aw Kun*—Thank-you; *Sohm toh*—Excuse me, or I'm sorry; *Meun uh-wye tay*—Don't mention it, or you're welcome; *Teuh nah?*—Where are you going?; *Niyeh piesah anglay bahn tay?*—Can you speak English?; *Sdap bahn tay*—Do you understand?; *Sdap bahn*—I under-

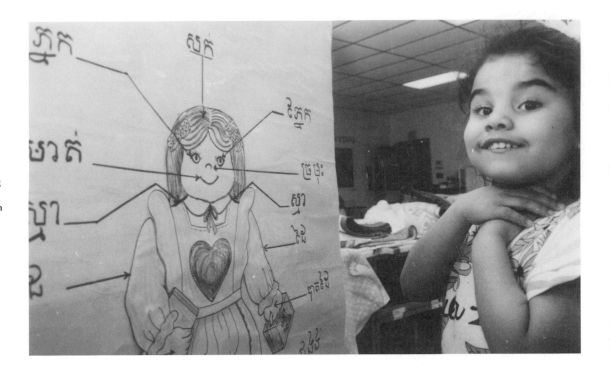

Four-year-old Angelina Melendez of Lowell, Massachusetts, is learning the parts of the body from a chart written in the Cambodian language of Khmer. Angelina attends the Demonstration School, which was developed by the University of Lowell to meet the educational needs of the area's Asian American and Hispanic American children.

stand; *Sdap meun bahn*—I don't understand; *Som Chumreap Lea*—Good-bye.

### LITERATURE

Much of the early literature of Cambodia is written in Sanscrit and known by modern scholars primarily from inscriptions on temples and other public buildings. Classical Cambodian literature is based on Indian models, and the *Reamker*, a Cambodian version of the Indian poem the *Ramayana*, is probably the most important piece of classical Cambodian literature. The *Reamker* is still known by Cambodians today. In the years before 1975, episodes from this poem were often acted out by dancers in the royal court or by villagers in village festivals. A collection of aphorisms, known as the *Chbab* (or "laws"), exists in both written and oral literature. Until recently, children were required to memorize the *Chbab* in school. Similar to the *Chbab* are the *Kotilok* (or "Art of Good Conduct"), which are fables designed to teach moral lessons.

European literary forms, such as novels, had taken root in Cambodia by the 1970s, but almost no literature was produced under the Khmer Rouge, and many intellectuals were killed during the Khmer Rouge regime. Since 1979, suffering under the Khmer Rouge has been a major theme in Cambodian literature, both in Cambodia and abroad. Among Cambodian Americans, also, the urge to bear witness to the horrors of the years

from 1975 to 1979 has inspired many to write, and as a result, the autobiography is the most commonly employed literary form. Many of these Cambodian American authors have taken coauthors, but some have mastered English sufficiently to write solely authored works.

# FAMILY AND COMMUNITY DYNAMICS

The family is extremely important to Cambodian Americans, in part because so many of them lost family members in their previous countries. They tend to have very large families. Children—especially young children—are treasured, and parents treat them with a great deal of affection. Despite the importance of family for Cambodian Americans, they have relatively high numbers of households headed by a single, female parent; in 1990 about 20 percent of Cambodian American households were headed by women, a factor that contributes to their poverty. This high proportion of female-headed households does not appear to be primarily the result of divorce, but rather of the fact that women outnumber men in the Cambodian population, due to years of war.

In Cambodia, men are responsible for providing for their families. Only men can occupy the prestigious status of the Buddhist monk. They also receive formal education, whereas Cambodian women are trained certain tasks in the home. Contrary to other Asian cultures, the Cambodian woman occupies a key position in the household. Generally, the wife budgets the family assets, and cares for the children. She is highly regarded by the men in her own family and by Cambodian society at large. In the refugee camps, many Cambodian women had their first taste of formal education. In the United States, young Cambodian American women are pursuing their educations in large numbers, and they have often become important as breadwinners for their families.

## WEDDINGS

Traditional Cambodian wedding ceremonies are still held by Cambodian Americans, and even members of other ethnic groups who have married Cambodians have celebrated these ceremonies. Although in Cambodia marriages are often arranged by the parents, it is becoming common for Cambodian American young people to choose their own partners. The bride in a Cambodian wedding wears a *sampot*, an ornate brocade wrap-skirt. She also wears many bracelets, anklets, and necklaces. Grooms sometimes wear the traditional *kben* (baggy pantaloons) and jacket, but western-style suits are becoming common.

A procession will bring gifts of food and drink to the bride's home. At the beginning of the wedding, the couple sits at a table covered with flowers, fruit, candles, and sometimes with a sword to chase evil spirits away. Friends and relatives take turns standing up in front of the crowd to talk about the new couple. A Buddhist monk cuts a lock of hair from the bride and the groom and mixes the two locks together in a bowl to symbolize the sharing of their lives. Gifts, frequently in the form of envelopes with money in them, are offered to the couple by the guests. At the end of the wedding, the couple goes through the ritual known as *ptem*, in which knots are tied in a white string bracelet to represent the elders' blessing.

## INTERACTION WITH OTHER ETHNIC MINORITIES

Because Cambodian Americans have settled most often in urban areas, they have frequent contacts with disadvantaged members of other minority groups. Often these contacts are troubled by cultural misunderstandings and by the social problems frequently found in poor communities. In some areas where there are large Cambodian communities, Cambodian youth gangs have developed, in part as a matter of self-protection. Older Cambodians often see that they have much in common with their poor Asian, black, and Hispanic neighbors and will frequently distinguish these areas of "poor people" from the comfortable middle-class neighborhoods of the "Americans." Most Cambodian Americans are fairly dark-skinned and they are acutely aware of prejudice in America. They sometimes internalize this prejudice and express feelings of inadequacy because of it.

It has been noted that Cambodian Americans in Texas have frequent contacts with Mexicans or Mexican Americans, and that the members of the two ethnic groups accommodate one another easily. Cambodians may frequently be found as participants in Mexican American weekend markets, and many Cambodians in Texas have learned Spanish and follow Mexican customs in interacting with their Spanish-speaking peers.

# RELIGION

Buddhism is the traditional religion of Cambodia. Before 1975, the ruler of the country was the official protector of the religion and the monks were organized into a hierarchy overseen by the government. Monasteries and temples were found in all villages, and monks played an important role in the education of children and in passing on Cambodian culture. The people also supported their local monasteries, through gifts and by giving food to monks. Monks were forbidden to handle money and had to show humility by begging for their food. Every morning, the monks would go from house to house, with their eyes downcast, holding out their begging bowls into which the lay people would spoon rice. Although the religion was attacked by the radical Khmer Rouge during their regime and many monks were killed, the vast majority of Cambodians remain Buddhists and the faith remains an important part of the national culture.

Buddhism in India is divided into two schools of thought. The "Northern School," known as Mahayana Buddhism, is found most often in China, Japan, Tibet, Korea, and Vietnam. The "Southern School," called Theravada (or Hinayana) Buddhism, predominates in Laos, Thailand, Cambodia, Burma, and Sri Lanka. Theravada Buddhists stress the importance of becoming a monk and achieving Nirvana, a state in which there is no self or rebirth, through one's own efforts. Mahayana Buddhists lay more emphasis on help from Bodhisattvas, enlightened beings who have delayed achieving Nirvana in order to help others become enlightened.

Fundamental to the Buddhist doctrine are the Four Noble Truths: (1) Existence inevitably leads to unhappiness which follows from the impermanence and disintegration of all living elements; (2) Unhappiness is caused by desire inherent in human nature; desire causes man to become attached to the impermanent; (3) Unhappiness can be avoided by the crushing of desire; and (4) Desire can be crushed by strict adherence to a prescribed moral path. In Buddhism all worldly things are considered changing and impermanent. Those who are not aware of the impermanent nature of the world become attached to worldly things, and this leads to suffering. The suffering will continue as the soul goes through a cycle of rebirths, continually drawn back to worldly desires. Meditation and a moral, disciplined life can enable a believer to overcome desires. The soul that successfully overcomes all desires may reach Nirvana.

The law of Karma (Kam in the Cambodian language) controls life and rebirth. This law may be seen as a kind of spiritual accounting; good deeds, or "merit," help the soul to be reborn in better circumstances and to earn rewards in the present life; bad deeds cause the soul to be reborn in worse circumstances and can bring about bad luck. For these reasons, "making merit" is a central part of religion for Cambodians. Cambodian Buddhists see making merit as more than simply piling up spiritual credits by performing good works. Correct behavior and merit-making activities such as attending religious ceremonies or donating money to temples and food to monks are seen as upholding the order of the universe. These beliefs have often led Cambodians to wonder if the sufferings of their people might be due to some collective fault of the nation.

Some Cambodian Americans have converted to Christianity, either in the refugee camps, or after arriving in the United States. Often these conversions have been the result of spiritual crises brought about by the tragedies of recent Cambodian history. In many cases, people felt that Buddhism had somehow failed because of the death and destruction that had occurred in their country. In other cases, Christianity has seemed attractive because it is the religion of the majority of Americans, and conversion has seemed a good way to conform to American society and to express gratitude to the religious organizations that played an important part in resettling refugees in the United States.

The majority of Cambodian Americans, however, continue the practice of their traditional religion. As more of them have settled in this country, and as they have established their own communities, observing their religious rituals has become easier. In 1979, there were only three Cambodian temples in the United States. By the early 1990s, more than 50 of these temples had been established in Cambodian communities throughout the United States. Even in those communities in which no temples exist, living around other Cambodian Americans has made it possible for Buddhists to observe their rites in private homes or in community halls and other meeting places. Monasteries, or places where Buddhist monks live, are usually attached to the temples, or places of worship, and the monks are in charge of the temples and the religious rituals held in them. Most American Buddhist temples are in houses or apartments, but there are some more traditionally styled temples, such as the large temple-monastery complex in Maryland.

## EMPLOYMENT AND ECONOMIC TRADITIONS

Adapting to the American economy has been difficult for many people of Cambodian ancestry in the United States. Most of them were farmers in their previous country, and in the United States they have generally been settled in cities. They have high rates of unemployment and the jobs found by first-generation Cambodian Americans are most often low-paying jobs in service and manual labor occupations.

Cambodian Americans are, for the most part, a poor group. According to the 1990 U.S. Census, 42 percent of the families of Cambodian ethnicity were living below the poverty level and 51 percent of all Cambodian households rely on public assistance income. The median household income of Cambodian Americans in 1990 was only $18,837, compared to $30,056 for Americans in general. Cambodian Americans have a high rate of unemployment: About ten percent of those in the labor force in 1990 were unemployed. This high rate of unemployment is largely a result of having arrived in this country so recently. If rates of unemployment are examined by years of arrival, it is clear that the longer Cambodian Americans have been in the United States, the higher the probability they will be employed. Nearly 17 percent of Cambodians in the labor force who arrived in the United States between 1987 and 1990 were unemployed in 1990. Among those who arrived in 1985 or 1986, though, only about 12 percent were unemployed. Among Cambodians who arrived between 1982 and 1984, the percentage of unemployed in the labor force dropped to 11 percent. Only about nine percent of those who arrived in 1980 and 1981 and only about seven percent of those who arrived before 1980 were unemployed. These figures provide evidence for a trait noticed by many familiar with Cambodians in the United States: their eagerness to find work, even low-paying work, as soon as they have acquired sufficient language skills and familiarity with American society.

Lack of formal education is a serious handicap for Cambodian Americans. Census statistics show that about 53 percent of Cambodian American men have a sixth grade education or less and 90 percent have less than 12 years of schooling. Women are faced with even more serious difficulties, since 66 percent of them have sixth grade educations or less and 95 percent have completed less than 12 years of schooling. Even when Cambodian Americans are from highly educated backgrounds, however, they often find that their educations are not relevant to the American workplace, and they are handicapped by their language skills. The author Someth May, for example, worked before the publication of his book as a janitor, despite his elite background in his home country. Despite the limited educations of their parents, however, Cambodian American young people often do quite well in school and show themselves dedicated to acquiring more education. Only about six percent of Cambodian Americans between the ages of 16 and 19 are high-school dropouts, compared to about ten percent of white Americans and about 14 percent of African Americans in the same age group.

# POLITICS AND GOVERNMENT

Most Cambodian Americans are concerned with questions of survival in the new country and are not actively involved in American politics. They remain keenly interested in the reconstruction of their native country, and some Cambodian American organizations, such as the Cambodian Network Council are contributing to the rebuilding of Cambodia by sending trained Cambodian Americans and people of other ethnicities to Cambodia as volunteers.

# INDIVIDUAL AND GROUP CONTRIBUTIONS

Cambodian Americans are beginning to make their marks in American society. Some notable examples follow:

### ACADEMIA

Im Proum is a prominent linguist who currently lives in Fairfax, Virginia; he formerly taught at Cornell University where he coauthored several of the standard texts on the Cambodian language with Dr. Franklin Huffmann. Sam Ang-Sam is a scholar, musician, and activist; he studied music at the University of Fine Arts in Phnom Penh and afterward continued his studies in the United States, where he received a Ph.D. in ethnomusicology from Wesleyan University; he later served on the faculty at the University of Washington in Seattle and is currently director of the Cambodian Network Council in Washington, D.C.; he travels around the world performing and teaching about Cambodian music. Chinary Ung is a scholar and musician who lives in Tempe, Arizona, and teaches about Cambodian culture at Arizona State University; as a musician, Dr. Ung specializes in playing the Cambodian xylophone.

### ACTIVISM

Maha Ghosananda is a Buddhist monk who lives in Rhode Island, but frequently travels to Cambodia; founder and director of the Khmer Society of New England, he is one of the world's most prominent peace activists and has organized two marches for peace in Cambodia; he has also been nominated for the Nobel Peace Prize. Vora Kanthoul is an authority on contemporary Cambodian issues and an influential figure in the Cambodian American community; he is executive director of the United Cambodian Community and teaches comparative world cultures at Long Beach City College; he studied in France, Russia, and Taiwan, and earned a Cambodian law degree in Phnom Penh and a Master's degree in political science from Southern Illinois University at Carbondale; from 1973 to 1975 he served in the Cambodian Foreign Service; in 1983 he served as minister and counselor of Cambodia's permanent mission to the United Nations.

### FILM

Haing Ngor is among the most famous Cambodian Americans; he is best known for his portrayal of the Cambodian interpreter and journalist Dith Pran in the film, *The Killing Fields*, for which Ngor won an Academy Award; born in rural Cambodia, he worked his way through medical school and became an obstetrician and surgeon in Phnom Penh; after the Khmer Rouge takeover in 1975, his family was killed by Khmer Rouge execution squads; he escaped to Thailand in 1979 and came in to the United States in 1980.

### JOURNALISM

Dith Pran, the subject of the film *The Killing Fields*, now works as a photographer in New York; before 1975 in Cambodia, he worked as an assistant and interpreter for *New York Times* correspondent Sydney Schanberg; when Pran's family escaped from Cambodia on the eve of the Khmer Rouge takeover, Pran stayed behind to help Schanberg, saving Schanberg and other journalists from execution; however, while Western journalists were able to leave, Pran himself was trapped in Cambodia under the Khmer Rouge from 1975 to 1979, when he escaped to Thailand, where he and Sydney Schanberg were reunited.

# MEDIA

### PRINT

**Angaor Borei News.**
Cambodian community newspaper in English.

**Contact:** Mr. Diep Ly, Manager.
**Address:** 2565 East Chapman Avenue, Suite F, Fullerton, California 92631.
**Telephone:** (714) 773-5519.

**Khosana.**
Semi-annual journal that contains academic news of Thai, Laotian, and Cambodian studies.

**Contact:** Michael R. Rhum, Editor.

**Address:** Association for Asian Studies, Thailand-Laos-Cambodia Studies Group, Department of Anthropology, Northern Illinois University, Dekalb, Illinois 60115.
**Telephone:** (815) 753-8577.

**Vatt Khmer.**
Newsletter that discusses Buddhism and Cambodian culture and civilization. Text is primarily in Khmer but partly in English.

**Address:** Cambodian Buddhist Society, Inc., 13800 New Hampshire Avenue, Silver Spring, Maryland 20904.
**Telephone:** (301) 622-6544.

# ORGANIZATIONS AND ASSOCIATIONS

Cambodian Americans have formed a wide variety of organizations during the short time they have been a part of American society. Most of these exist to help newly arrived Cambodians adjust to American society, but they also provide information about Cambodian American culture, business, and other aspects of Cambodian life in this country.

**Art of Apsara.**
Encourages the development and exhibition of contemporary Cambodian art. Runs a gallery in Long Beach, open to the general public.

**Contact:** Mon Duch, Director.
**Address:** Suite 105, 2338 East Anaheim, Long Beach, California 90804.
**Telephone:** (310) 438-3932.

**Cambodian Association.**
Serves Cambodian Americans in the Philadelphia area. Helps newly arrived Cambodians with problems in education and housing, assists in preserving Cambodian culture, acts as an advocate for the interests of Cambodian Americans.

**Contact:** Walter Chin, Director.
**Address:** 5412 North Fifth Street, Philadelphia, Pennsylvania 19121.
**Telephone:** (215) 324-4070.

**Cambodian Family.**
Serves Cambodian Americans in the Santa Ana area. Offers English language training to Cambo-

dian refugees, provides help in finding employment, gives classes in health education and parenting skills. Also offers programs for Cambodian American youth, including a gang prevention program, after-school classes, and Cambodian language classes.

**Contact:** Rivka Hirsch, Director.

**Address:** 1111 East Wakeham Avenue, D, Santa Ana, California 92705.

**Telephone:** (714) 542-2907.


### Cambodian Network Council (CNC).

The primary national organization of Cambodians in the United States. This is an umbrella organization that seeks to facilitate communication among local Cambodian organizations, to help set up new local organizations, and to build coalitions. The CNC hosts an annual convention of Cambodian American associations. It also maintains a data bank of Cambodian American professionals and runs an international program sending volunteers to Cambodia to help in rebuilding the country.

**Contact:** Dr. Sam-Ang Sam.

**Address:** 713 D Street, Washington, D.C. 20036.

**Telephone:** (202) 546-9144.


### Folsom Cordova School District.

Provides educational materials, such as bilingual texts for Cambodian Americans.

**Contact:** Ms. Judy Lewis.

**Address:** 2460 Cordova Lane, Rancho Cordova, California 95670.

**Telephone:** (916) 635-6815.


### National Association for the Education and Advancement of Cambodian, Laotian, and Vietnamese Americans (NAFEA).

Seeks to provide equal educational opportunities for and advance the rights of Indochinese Americans; encourage appreciation of Indochinese cultures, peoples, education, and language.

**Contact:** Ms. Ngoc Diep Nguyen, President.

**Address:** 1855 Mt. Prospect Road, Des Plaines, Illinois 60018.

**Telephone:** (708) 803-3112.


### United Cambodian Council (UCC).

The largest Cambodian agency in the United States, the United Cambodian Council is located in Long Beach, the site of America's largest Cambodian community. Organized in 1977 by a group of Cambodian intellectuals to serve the needs of the Cambodians in Long Beach, the agency now helps anyone who needs its services. Although most of its clients are Southeast Asians, it assists low-income Americans of all ethnicities. In addition to the employment and language training generally offered by Cambodian service organizations, the UCC is a partner with St. Mary's Church in the Long Beach Southeast Asian Health Project, which provides a wide variety of health services and information.

**Contact:** Mr. Vora Kanthoul, Executive Director.

**Address:** 2338 East Anaheim, Suite 200, Long Beach, California 90804.

**Telephone:** (310) 433-2490.


# SOURCES FOR ADDITIONAL STUDY

*Cambodian Culture Since 1975: Homeland and Exile*, edited May M. Ebihara, Carol A. Mortland, and Judy Ledgerwood. Ithaca, New York: Cornell University Press, 1994.


Chandler, David P. *A History of Cambodia.* Boulder, Colorado: Westview Press. 1992.


Criddle, Joan D., and Teeda Butt Mam. *To Destroy You Is No Loss: The Odyssey of a Cambodian Family.* New York: Atlantic Monthly Press, 1987.


May, Someth. *Cambodian Witness: The Autobiography of Someth May,* edited by James Fenton. New York: Random House.


Scott, Joanna C. *Indochina's Refugees: Oral Histories from Laos, Cambodia, and Vietnam.* Jefferson, North Carolina: McFarland and Company. 1989.


*Southeast Asian-American Communities*, edited by Kali Tal. Woodbridge, Connecticut: Viet Nam Generation, 1992.

From the 1930s to the 1980s, more than 2.3 million Canadians immigrated to the United States.

# CANADIAN AMERICANS

by
Marianne
Fedunkiw

## OVERVIEW

Canada is the largest country in the Western Hemisphere, covering 9,970,610 square kilometers including both land and freshwater areas. It is surrounded on three sides by oceans: the Pacific to the west, the Arctic to the north, and the Atlantic to the east. Its southern border with the United States, which stretches 5,525 miles, is the longest undefended border in the world.

Because Canada is such a large country (much of which is relatively uninhabitable), approximately 60 percent of its 1991 population of 26.9 million was concentrated in urban centers, particularly in the southeastern stretch between Windsor, Ontario, and Quebec City, Quebec. The largest cities are Toronto, with a population of 3.8 million, followed by Montreal, with 3.1 million, and Vancouver, with 1.6 million.

Unlike the United States, Canada is made up of provinces and territories. From west to east, these are: Yukon Territory and Northwest Territories, British Columbia (BC), Alberta, Saskatchewan, Manitoba, Ontario, Quebec, New Brunswick, Nova Scotia, Prince Edward Island (PEI), and Newfoundland and Labrador. Each province has its own provincial government, coat of arms, and provincial capital. The nation's capital is Ottawa, Ontario. Although there are provincial divisions, provinces tend to identify with one another by region. For example, Alberta, Saskatchewan, and Manitoba make up the prairie provinces, while New Brunswick, Nova Scotia, PEI, and Newfoundland make up the Atlantic provinces. The Canadian national flag, adopted in 1965, is a red maple leaf set against a white background and bordered on either side by wide, vertical bands of red.

## EARLY HISTORY

The first explorers to visit North America, as opposed to the indigenous peoples, were said to be the Vikings. Around 1000 A.D., Norwegian Leif Ericson's ship first landed in Labrador and went on to what is now Massachusetts, stopping on the coast of modern-day Nova Scotia along the way. However, there are those who believe there were earlier visitors to Canada: Celtic monks fleeing the Vikings, and African travellers. All those who visited found a harsh, cold land occupied by potentially hostile native peoples, and many suffered from scurvy and other afflictions. As a result, few early explorers survived or stayed very long.

## EUROPEAN EXPLORERS LAY CLAIM TO NEW LANDS

By the late 1400s, parts of North America were being claimed for European empires. Giovanni Gabotto, a native Italian who became known as John Cabot after he immigrated to England, landed at Cape Breton Island on the east coast of Canada on June 24, 1497, and claimed the land for his patron King Henry VII. Despite this fact, many French explorers and colonists traveled to Canada as well. Seeking a northern base along the route to the Far East, the French explorer Jacques Cartier gained renown for venturing into the Canadian mainland via the St. Lawrence River in 1535. Cartier made it as far west as Hochelaga, the native peoples' name for what became Montreal. Another famous French explorer, Samuel de Champlain, established his first trading post in 1608 in what is today Quebec City. The land's vast resources, particularly beaver pelts, became part of the draw for early visitors. In fact, the ripening fur trade led to the founding in 1670 of the Hudson Bay Company, which is still in operation today.

Settlement was not easy in the seventeenth century. By 1663 there were only 2,500 French settlers, most of whom were clustered in Montreal, Quebec City, and Trois Rivieres (Three Rivers). Vicious battles took place between the French settlers and the native Iroquois, and the European colonies were all but destroyed. In fact, relationships with indigenous peoples often determined the pace of settlement. Jesuit missionaries, who were sent to the new land to help colonize and convert the natives to Christianity, met with considerable opposition, for example, and in many cases missions were destroyed and missionaries killed.

## THE FRENCH AND THE ENGLISH

By 1713, the population of New France, as the Canadian colony was called, numbered less than 20,000, compared with some 400,000 English, Scottish, and Irish settlers in the Atlantic states. The French and English began fighting over the Canadian lands, particularly the valuable beaver country around Hudson's and James Bays. The early settlement of Port-Royal in Nova Scotia changed hands a number of times. The French set up strategic fortifications to prepare for British attacks, and the British countered by establishing their own fortifications. For example, the French built Louisbourg, a fortress which guarded the entrance to the St. Lawrence River, and in response the British built, in 1749, a base at Halifax.

The French and British were also battling over lands in the United States at this time. In 1753 French troops established Fort Duquesne, a base near present-day Pittsburgh, and controlled much of the Ohio Valley. War was declared between France and Britain in 1756, and two years later the French lost Fort Duquesne, upper Ohio (which tied the French colonies in Louisiana to Canada), and Niagara. In 1759—in a famous battle on the Plains of Abraham near Quebec City—the British gained a foothold in New France. Then on February 10, 1763, France signed the Peace of Paris treaty and Britain assumed control over all of North America except for New Orleans, which France ceded to Spain. All that was left for France were the small islands of St. Pierre and Miquelon, off the southern coast of Newfoundland, which are still French properties today.

## BRITISH NORTH AMERICA

Many early ties linked the areas that would become Canadian lands with those that, after 1776, would become states. At its zenith, British Canada included not only present-day territory, but also the states of Illinois, Indiana, Michigan, Ohio, and Wisconsin. In fact, after the British conquest of New France, the "Canadian" colonies had to determine whether they wished to join the Thirteen Colonies in their bid for independence or remain within the Empire. Newfoundland, Prince Edward Island, and Quebec opted relatively quickly to remain with Britain, while Nova Scotia deliberated. In 1776, almost two-thirds of Nova Scotia's population consisted of New England emigrants with strong ties to their former land. In the end, however, Nova Scotia decided to stay with England, too, rather than become the fourteenth state of the Union. American invaders did try to take part of British Canada in December 1775, when forces led by Benedict Arnold and Richard Montgomery unsuccessfully attacked Quebec. Furthermore, those Americans who supported British rule—the United Empire Loyalists—found refuge in the Atlantic provinces in the later eighteenth century.

The new British rule and pressure from the revolutionaries in the Thirteen Colonies did not make for a harmonious meld of lands and peoples in Canada. Concessions were made, however, to keep Quebec in the British Empire. The Quebec Act of 1774 returned to the French Canadians their civil law based upon Napoleonic code (still provincially applicable today) and the freedom to practice the Roman Catholic religion. To further accommodate both French and British interests, the Constitutional Act of 1791 allowed for two separate elective legislative assemblies within the distinct provinces of Upper Canada (the largely British area to the west of the Ottawa River) and Lower Canada (present-day Quebec).

## THE RIEL REBELLION

Tension between the French and English was not confined to the East. When the Canadian government acquired western lands from the Hudson Bay Company in 1869, Louis Riel led a group of Metis settlers in protest. The Metis, who were part French Canadian and part native, feared that the encroachment of other settlers would mean the loss of their freedom and identity.

Riel, an educated man who had studied for the priesthood, served as the spokesman for the Metis. They set up a "Provisional Government" of their own and denied entry to William McDougall, the newly appointed lieutenant-governor of the region. Further conflict ensued when a young Orangeman named Thomas Scott, who had fought against Riel's government, was executed.

The government of Ontario issued a warrant for Riel's arrest, and the Orangemen, who controlled much of Ontario, topped that with a $5,000 reward for his capture.

Riel was not overthrown, however, despite the fact that 1,200 government troops marched 500 miles to enforce peace in the West. In fact, Riel maintained considerable influence. In 1874, he was elected to the Dominion Parliament as a representative from Manitoba, but he never took his seat because he was exiled for five years and went south to live in Montana. He returned to Canada in 1884 and the next year led another Metis surprising. The rebellion was quashed, though, and Riel was tried and hanged for treason in 1885 at the age of 41.

## RELATIONS WITH THE AMERICAN NEIGHBORS

In addition to the Loyalists fleeing the American Revolution, Canada became a sought-after destination for American farmers in search of cheaper land. By 1812, about 60 percent of the population of Upper Canada was comprised of non-Loyalist colonists from the United States. Loyalists and British made up the remaining 40 percent in about even proportions.

The most significant relationship with Americans in the early nineteenth century, however, was one of war. Many Americans believed that the British were supporting Indian attacks in the United States, while other Americans, such as the expansionist "war hawks," favored going to war to seize Upper Canada for themselves. Americans also resented Britain's imposition of a naval blockade upon France, which hampered American trade with France, and Britain's seizure of thousands of British sailors found to be "deserters" on American ships. As a result of these mounting tensions, American President James Madison declared war on Britain on June 1, 1812.

## THE WAR OF 1812

The war went poorly for the Americans because they mistakenly concentrated their initial efforts on taking the eastern part of Upper Canada, including the Detroit River and Niagara. The Americans believed they would be welcomed by their compatriots who had moved to Canada, but they were wrong. The Americans lost not only Detroit, but all of the American territory west of Lake Erie to General Isaac Brock's troops, which were fewer in number, and his ally the Shawnee chief Tecumseh. The battles of the War of 1812 continued well into 1814 with both sides making advances, but victory was on the side of the British more often. In fact, in August 1814, the British advanced as far south as Washington, taking and burning the Capitol and President's House. The Americans whitewashed the walls to cover the burns, and it has since been called the White House.

In the end, the war changed little in terms of boundaries or national possessions. But ideologically, the war fostered anti-American sentiments and corresponding loyalty to the colony itself—making the settlers neither Loyalists nor British, but Upper Canadians.

## REBELLIONS TO CONFEDERATION

The 1830s was a decade of discontent in both Lower and Upper Canada, which culminated in the rebellions of 1837. Although relatively few people participated in the uprisings, they set the stage for changes in government that led to confederation in 1867. On July 1, 1867, Nova Scotia, New Brunswick, and the Canadas (Lower and Upper) joined together to form the Dominion of Canada.

Another major development in the relationship between Canada and the United States that helped propel Canada to independence centered around the American Civil War. Canada quickly opposed the war, particularly the thought of the South winning (although many Americans believed the British supported the South), and hostilities between the two countries grew. The situation grew worse when many American slaves fled to freedom in Canada via the "Underground Railroad," and when "The Fenian Brotherhood"—anti-British Irish Americans—attacked the Canadian village of Fort Erie in southern Ontario in the summer of 1866. The fear of annexation by the United States, either North or South, eventually led Canadians to forge the British North America Act, which established the Dominion of Canada. The first Prime Minister was Sir John A. Macdonald.

Although the prairies and outlying parts of Ontario and Quebec—then a huge area called Rupert's Land—were not part of Confederation, the same fear of American takeover led, first to an expansion of the railroad to the West, and then to an influx of settlers westward. Manitoba joined Canada as a province in 1870, followed by British Columbia in 1871, the Yukon Territory in 1898, and the trio of Alberta, Saskatchewan, and the Northwest Territories in 1905.

As for the remaining Maritime provinces, Prince Edward Island joined in 1873, and Newfoundland was the last to join in 1949. This reluctance perhaps explains why many Newfoundlanders who have moved to the United States identify themselves not as Canadian Americans, but as Americans of Newfoundland descent.

## MODERN ERA—WORLD WAR I AND BEYOND

The twentieth century has seen the tension between the French and English in Canada continue. English-speaking Canada continued to feel strong ties to Britain—it fought with England in the Boer War (1899-1902) and in World War I. The French-speaking Canadians, however, resented fighting in "English wars," and the issue of compulsory military service drove the two groups further apart.

Meanwhile, European and Asian immigrants continued to flow into Canada. Much of the still-open Canadian West was built up by new Canadians. The period between the two World Wars brought a greater sense of national autonomy. By 1939, English-Canadians made up only half of the 12 million population. Another 30 percent were French, and the rest consisted of Ukrainians, Poles, Germans, and Scandinavian immigrants. By the time the Second World War began, Canada made its own decision to take part, going to battle on September 10, 1939.

The years following World War II were ones of prosperity in Canada, particularly compared to those preceding the war, which devastated the country. The 1950s and 1960s saw decreasing trade with Britain and increasing exchange with the United States. Canada also achieved greater respect internationally. Lester B. Pearson, Canadian prime minister from 1963 to 1968, won the Nobel Peace Prize in 1957 for his work in the Middle East. Pearson also served as chairman of the North Atlantic Treaty Organization (NATO) in 1951-52, and as president of the United Nations General Assembly in 1952-53.

## SIGNIFICANT IMMIGRATION WAVES TO THE UNITED STATES

Although there has always been a flow of people between Canada and the United States, reliable data has only been kept since the 1910 census of the United States and the 1911 census of Canada. Migration is also somewhat seasonal: the Canadian American population swells in the winter months. States such as Florida and Arizona have strong seasonal populations of Canadians, which affects items such as media for Canadians in the United States. By 1990, almost 30 percent of Canadians in the United States were 65 and older, which lowers the average income level for the group.

The number of Canadians moving to the United States has climbed steadily since the 1850s. Based on the 1990 report *Migration between the United States and Canada*, migration between the two countries was relatively unrestricted until immigration laws were changed in the United States in 1965 and in Canada in 1976. In the early part of the twentieth century, for example, more than 1.2 million Canadians crossed the border to live in the United States. Interestingly, this was four times more than the number moving from the United States to Canada. The decade of

**"Can't you see the freedom in America? That it's not just political? Can't you see American liberty? Can't you see self-reliance and self-expression? That is the American atmosphere.... In America you can do anything you want, live anywhere you want, and, finally, do what it is that you most want to do very easily—perhaps not without what you might consider to be sacrifices, but they're not really sacrifices."**

Agnes Martin in 1931, cited in *American Mosaic: The Immigrant Experience in the Words of Those Who Lived It,* edited by Joan Morrison and Charlotte Fox Zabusky (New York: E.P. Dutton, 1980).

the 1920s set a record with nearly one million Canadians heading south, primarily to take advantage of the industrial boom in northeastern and north central states. The number of Canadians in the United States peaked at 1.3 million in 1930, after which the economic depression and World War II slowed emigration. The flow picked up markedly in the 1950s and early 1960s, however, because of greater job opportunities and higher wages in the United States. From the 1930s to the 1980s, more than 2.3 million Canadians immigrated to the United States. When the immigration laws began to tighten between 1960 and 1970, however, the annual number dropped by almost 60 percent.

This decline continued through the 1980s and had a marked effect on U.S. immigration. While in the early 1960s Canadians made up almost 12 percent of total immigrants to the United States, by the early 1980s that number fell to just two percent. In fact, almost 65 percent of the immigrants listed on the 1980 U.S. census immigrated before 1960.

During the period when immigration laws were less restrictive, crossing the border was less an international shift than a movement based upon economic influences—just like internal migration. When the laws tightened, the patterns became more controlled and more typical of long-distance international migration, according to *Migration between the United States and Canada.* Demographically, most Canadians who immigrated to the United States before 1960 live in the northern states, while those who came later tend to live in states further south.

**SETTLEMENT PATTERNS**

In the 1990 U.S. census, just over 500,000 people living in America, or .2 percent of the total population, cited Canadian as their ancestry group. Interestingly, this definition of "Canadian" excluded those from the provinces of Newfoundland and Nova Scotia, as well as French Canadians and Acadians. All of these ancestry groups are listed separately. The highest regional concentration of Canadian Americans was in the northeastern states, although the highest single-state population is found in California, with 86,341. In second place is Massachusetts, with 66,007, and in third place is New York, with 45,274.

# ACCULTURATION AND ASSIMILATION

Unlike other groups, there is almost no language barrier separating English-speaking Canadians and Americans. This is one reason why assimilation is relatively easy. Another factor is that the two countries are close neighbors, so many traditions and customs creep across the boundaries and become familiar. *Migration between the United States and Canada* states that "the ease with which Canadian and United States immigrants are assimilated is evident from the large population of naturalized U.S. citizens among Canadian-born immigrants.... In both countries, more than 80 percent of the immigrants prior to 1980 have become naturalized citizens of the destination country."

Ultimately, English-speaking Canadians who moved to the United States also enjoyed the benefit of settling relatively close to their home country. Unlike immigrants from European, Asian, or African countries, Canadians could visit relatives and receive news from Canada via newspapers, radio, or television rather readily. Unless they had recent ethnic ties to a country that was their home before Canada, assimilation was largely a smooth procedure. Aside from an abiding interest in all things British held by some Canadians, traditions tended to be more "North American" than distinctively different. The media plays a large role in this cultural mixing: most of Canada's population is concentrated in a thin band close to the American border, well within the range of American radio and television. In addition, many Canadian immigrants could still hear and see familiar programs and events.

Since Canadian nationalism historically was built upon a wariness of American control, a Canadian moving to the United States would do so in the face of this fear. The type of individual most likely to make the move would prefer American culture and want to assimilate into it.

## STEREOTYPES OF CANADIANS

Because of the many similarities between Canadians and Americans, common stereotypes either portray Canada as just another large state, or exaggerate the differences that do exist. An example of the former is an American referring to the provinces as "states," the Prime Minister as "the President of Canada," or Parliament or the House of Commons as "Congress" or "the Senate." The exaggeration of differences centers around weather, culture, and common pastimes. Some people envision all of Canada as a land of igloos and ice, where everyone is French Canadian (or at least fully bilingual) and plays ice hockey.

The main sources of these stereotypes are television and film. For example, Second City Television (SCTV) produced comedy sketches and a movie featuring beer-swilling, flannel-attired Canadian brothers Bob and Doug Mackenzie in the 1970s and early 1980s. Another more passive source of stereotypes is simply an incomplete knowledge of the vast and diverse country that is America's northern neighbor. Given the opportunity to tour all of Canada, it would be difficult to describe the Maritimes, the Prairies, northern Ontario or Quebec, and British Columbia using the same words.

Although it is difficult to outline hard and fast boundaries to define Canadians versus Americans, there are differences. In the *New York Times*, for example, Canadian novelist and nationalist Robertson Davies described basic differences in the underlying myths upon which each country is built: "The myth of America is a very powerful one and one that we in Canada look toward with envy. You have your heroes. You have your great men of the past, you have your myth of tradition, of the conquering of the West, and the pioneer life and the gold rush life and all that sort of thing, which is enormously romantic, and nations feed on the romantic tradition.... We don't go for heroes. As soon as a man begins to achieve some sort of high stature, we want to cut him down and get rid of him, embarrass him" (December 15, 1994).

## CUISINE

Differences in cuisine for Canadians who have immigrated to the United States depend upon where they grew up and to which area of the United States they moved. For example, Canadians from the Maritime provinces (Newfoundland, New Brunswick, Nova Scotia, and Prince Edward Island) and coastal British Columbia include a hearty amount of seafood in their diets, and this preference would not change if they immigrated to a seaboard state.

Like language and cultural traditions, however, other cuisine choices depend upon Canadians' ethnic origin and the degree to which they have assimilated into Canadian society before moving to the United States. Ethnocultural groups such as the Mennonites and Jewish peoples maintain an individual cuisine as part of their identity. This is also true of traditional clothing.

## HOLIDAYS

Canadians and Americans share many of the same national holidays, although they are not always celebrated on the same days. For example, while Americans celebrate the birth of their nation on July 4, Canadians celebrate Canada Day on July 1. Both countries observe Thanksgiving, although it is a holiday in Canada on the first Monday of October rather than the American holiday in November. In addition, there are Canadian provincial holidays which differ from province to province, and other ethnocultural holidays that citizens of either country may observe.

### HEALTH AND MENTAL HEALTH ISSUES

There are no documented health problems or medical conditions specific to Canadian Americans. Recent Canadian immigrants to the United States must adjust, however, from government-controlled health care to a private system. Canada's public system has been in place since the 1960s, and in comparison the cost of staying healthy in America seems steep. In Canada, workers and/or employers pay a special tax to the provincial government, which in turn pays for most medical services, up to an agreed-upon limit. Most health care practitioners are self-employed and bill the provincial government directly for their services.

Canadians in Canada or in the United States have access to sophisticated medical treatment using leading-edge technology. Some Canadian physicians, however, have become disenchanted with increasing levels of government control over medicine in Canada and have moved to the United States to practice.

# LANGUAGE

Canada has two official languages, English and French. These two languages are the mother tongue for more than 84 percent of Canadians, with 60 percent speaking primarily English and almost 24 percent French. Among the others languages that make up the remaining 16 percent are Italian, Chinese, German, Portuguese, Polish, and Ukrainian.

For the majority of Canadians who either speak English or are bilingual, moving to the United States was not a difficult transition in relation to language. Those who are Francophones, or French-speaking Canadians, are classified as a separate group. Other Canadians who are profiled separately include Acadians and a number of native groups, among them the Iroquois, Tlingit, and Inuit.

The Canadians who have another ethnic origin would not only be familiar with either English, French, or both, but might also retain their mother tongue to some degree after immigrating to America. They might, therefore, identify themselves as "German Americans" rather than "German Canadian Americans," which more accurately traces their roots through Canada on the way to America. Of the 836,000 Canadians who lived in the United States for five or more years, 79 percent spoke English at home, while 19 percent said they could speak English but spoke another language at home.

# FAMILY AND COMMUNITY DYNAMICS

Canada prides itself upon its multiculturalism, and this fact supplies a context for any discussion of family and community dynamics. An Italian Canadian who moves to the United States, for example, might maintain the customs, language, and community dynamics of Italy. Defining such a person as Canadian would obscure those traditions. For this reason, the section on a certain country of origin should be consulted for information on cultural and religious practices. Other factors, such as cuisine, traditional clothing, and special events, can differ based upon not only the ethnic background, but also the region of Canada from which an individual came. In fact, the U.S. census of 1990 excludes those from Newfoundland and Nova Scotia, as well as Acadians and French Canadians, from its overall consideration of the Canadian American population.

### MARRIAGE, DIVORCE, AND WIDOWHOOD

As of 1980, the percentage of female Canadians in the United States over 15 years of age who were married (58.9 percent), was very close to that for Canadians in Canada (at 59.7 percent). There are, however, twice as many divorced Canadian Americans (6.8 percent) as Canadians (3.1 percent). Although twice as many Canadian Americans were widowed than Canadians—20.5 percent versus ten percent—this may illustrate the disproportionately high number of people older than 65 living in the United States.

### EDUCATION

In 1991, Canada spent $54.2 billion on education to service the more than six million Canadians, or a quarter of the country's population, who were enrolled in full-time educational programs.

Enrollment in all schools, from pre-elementary to university, has been growing since the late 1980s. Total enrollment in Canadian universities was 757,497 undergraduates and 110,085 graduate students.

Canada also features a strong network of 201 community colleges which offer semi-professional or technical and vocational programs leading to a diploma rather than a university degree. For those who move to the United States, however, there are ten times as many post-secondary institutions to choose from, because the American population is around 10 times larger.

Other than certain private, single-sex schools, there are no appreciable differences in the education of Canadian boys and girls. There are, however, some differences in educational attainment between the sexes at the higher levels. For example, the number of female graduates of undergraduate university programs in Canada has been greater than that of males from 1990 to 1992, although slightly more men than women went on to complete master's and doctoral degrees.

Canadians who move to the United States obtain, overall, higher educational levels than native Canadians. In 1980, 20.5 percent of Canadian Americans held a university degree, two-thirds more than the 12.3 percent in Canada. The same is true, to a lesser extent, for women—10.3 percent of Canadian American women have completed post-secondary education, compared to 7.0 percent in Canada.

The most popular curricula college students enroll in can be derived from statistics on the sector in which most Canadian Americans work—namely, the tertiary or service sector—as well as the fact that a high percentage are professionals. The most significant growth in Canadian Americans who worked in highly skilled occupations occurred in the late 1960s and 1970s. By 1980, just over half of Canadian Americans were employed in highly skilled jobs, and the tertiary sector accounted for 70 percent of the Canadian American work force.

# RELIGION

Religion has been a building block of Canadian society since the French and British explorers arrived in the sixteenth century. The first Roman Catholic service in Canada was held in 1534, and the first Anglican service took place 44 years later. The most active churches in Canada, based upon recent figures, are the Roman Catholics and Anglicans, although there is also strong representation by the United Church of Canada, Jewish, Muslim, Evangelical Lutheran, and Pentecostal faiths. Protestant Canadians who immigrated to the United States encountered certain differences in the naming of denominations: for example, Canadian Anglicans would most closely resemble American Episcopalians.

# EMPLOYMENT AND ECONOMIC TRADITIONS

Generally, the types of jobs Canadians immigrants took upon arrival in the United States depended upon economic conditions at the time. In the early twentieth century, hundreds of thousands of Canadians sought jobs in booming American industries. More recent figures indicate that 60 percent of Canadian Americans work in highly skilled jobs, a number which has been growing since the late 1950s. These positions are classified as: administrative support including clerical, professional specialty, and executive administrative and managerial. In the latter two categories, the figures for Canadian Americans are higher than average for the United States.

The unemployment figures for Canadian Americans in the early 1980s were lower than for Canadians. Only 4.6 percent of Canadian American women were unemployed versus 8.6 percent in Canada, while 4.8 percent of Canadian men in the United States were unemployed versus 6.4 percent in Canada. However, labor force participation rates for Canadian Americans were highest for both sexes in the early 1960s and have been declining steadily since.

# POLITICS AND GOVERNMENT

With a few notable exceptions, Canadian Americans have initiated little conflict within the United States. In fact, relatively few Canadian Americans have become involved in American politics. One exception is Jerry Simpson (1842-1905), a Populist party representative who served three terms in Congress. Born in Westmoreland County, New Brunswick, Simpson was a self-educated man who began his career as a cook on a Great

Lakes boat at age 14 and rose to become captain. He established a farm and ranch in Kansas before entering politics. Amendments to American immigration laws in 1965 severely restricted the number of Canadians who could legally emigrate to the United States.

## LABOR ORGANIZATIONS

Canadians have a strong presence in both national labor organizations (such as the Canadian Labour Congress and Canadian National Federation of Independent Unions) and international trade unions with local chapters in both Canada and the United States. Some of the international trade unions with the largest Canadian participation are: United Steelworkers of America, with 875 locals in Canada; United Food and Commercial Workers International Union, with 175 locals in Canada; International Association of Machinists and Aerospace Workers, with 152 lodges in Canada; and International Brotherhood of Electrical Workers, with 121 locals in Canada.

Because Canadians tend to assimilate thoroughly into American life, it is difficult to identify group patterns in items such as voting and participation in the armed forces. One major difference Canadian immigrants would encounter in U.S. politics involves the dominance of two political parties. In Canada, there are three national political parties, the Progressive Conservatives, the Liberals, and the New Democratic Party. Of course, in different provinces there are other strong party representatives, such as the Social Democrats or Parti Quebecois.

Canadian Americans' quick rate of assimilation also affects their level of participation in the political issues of their home country. Although the English-language media in border states and the English-language seasonal newspapers in states such as Florida and Arizona do well in presenting current Canadian events, geographical distance often leads to a sense of isolation. Coupled with the many similarities between Americans and Canadians, achieving a distinct sense of identity becomes a challenge for immigrant Canadians. Groups such as French Canadians, who are already individuated by their separate language, culture, and long history in the United States, are better able to maintain their identity and ties to Canada. For example, this group would be very aware of the latest struggles for French independence in Canada and the rise of the separatist Parti Quebecois and Bloc Quebecois.

# INDIVIDUAL AND GROUP CONTRIBUTIONS

## ACADEMIA

Perhaps the most notable Canadian American academic is economist John Kenneth Galbraith (1908- ), born in Iona Station, Ontario; after completing his bachelor's degree in Ontario, he went to California to pursue graduate studies; he was a professional economist from 1949 to 1975 and held a number of teaching positions in North America and Europe; his many books include *American Capitalism* (1952), *The Great Crash* (1955), and *A Short History of Financial Euphoria* (1993); he received the Medal of Freedom in 1946. English professor Margaret Anne Doody (1939- ), born in St. John, New Brunswick, came to the United States in 1976 as an associate professor at the University of California at Berkeley, and has taught at Vanderbilt University in Nashville since 1989; she is the author of a number of books on Samuel Richardson and his writings.

## FILM, TELEVISION, AND THEATER

"America's Sweetheart," Mary Pickford (1893-1979), was really Canadian by birth; born Gladys Mary Smith in Toronto, she starred in silent screen versions of *Rebecca of Sunnybrook Farm*, *Tess of the Storm Country*, and *Coquette*, for which she won an Oscar, and became an early pioneer of film in the United States; she organized the Mary Pickford Corporation in 1916 to produce her work, and in 1919 joined Charlie Chaplin, D. W. Griffith, and her husband-to-be, Douglas Fairbanks, to establish United Artists Company. Another Canadian-born actor is Glenn Ford (1916- ), originally Gwyllyn Samuel Newton Ford; born in Quebec City, he attended high school in Santa Monica, California; his films include *Destroyer* (1943), *Cimarron* (1961), and *Superman* (1978); Ford served with the United States Marines Corp during World War II; in 1958, he was named "Number One Box Office Star in America" in a poll by the *Motion Picture Herald*. Film star Donald Sutherland (1935- ) was born in St. John, New Brunswick; his films include M*A*S*H (1970), *Ordinary People* (1980), and *JFK* (1991).

One of the best-known Canadian names in television was Lorne Greene (1915-1987); born in Ottawa, Ontario, he made his American debut on the New York stage in 1953; among his many credits of stage, screen, and television are the movies *Peyton Place* (1957) and *Earthquake* (1974), and the television western series "Bonanza" (1959-1973), in which he played the patriarch of the Ponderosa ranch, Ben Cartwright. Born in New Westminster, British Columbia, Raymond Burr (1917-1993) is perhaps best known for his role on the television series "Perry Mason" (1957-1966); he also performed in the series "Ironside" from 1967 to 1975. Another recognizable Canadian face on television and in film is William Shatner (1931- ); the Montreal native has appeared on Broadway but is famous for his role as Captain James T. Kirk of the Starship Enterprise in the television series "Star Trek" (1966-1969) and subsequent *Star Trek* films; Shatner followed this success with a leading role in the police series "T. J. Hooker" in the 1980s, and he wrote a series of science-fiction novels beginning in 1989 that were adapted for television as *TekWar*.

Two younger Canadian-born actors, well-known for their television work, are Michael J. Fox and Jason Priestley. Fox (1961-) was born in Vancouver, British Columbia; he received two Emmy Awards for his starring role in the television sitcom "Family Ties" (1982-1989), and has also appeared in films such as *Back to the Future* (1985) and *The Secret of My Success* (1987). Priestley, also born in Vancouver, is a leading actor in the television series "Beverly Hills 90210."

A group of Canadian-born comedians have found success in the United States on the television comedy series "Saturday Night Live." Mike Myers (1963- ), born in Toronto, also starred in the movie *Wayne's World*. Dan Aykroyd (1952- ), born in Ottawa, was the star and screenwriter for the film *Blues Brothers* (1980), and also appeared in *Ghostbusters* (1984) and *Driving Miss Daisy* (1989).

Among those Canadian Americans who often appeared on the Broadway stage were Hume Cronyn, Colleen Dewhurst, and Christopher Plummer. Actor, writer, and director Hume Cronyn (1911- ) was born in London, Ontario, and came to the United States in 1932; he starred in countless plays—many of them with his late wife, actress Jessica Tandy—including 1978 Pulitzer Prize winner *The Gin Game*; Cronyn has been named to the Theatre Hall of Fame (1979) and Kennedy Center Honors (1986) in addition to receiving a Tony Award in 1964 and an Emmy Award in 1992; his films include: *Lifeboat* (1944), *The Postman Always Rings Twice* (1946), and *Cocoon* (1985). Colleen Dewhurst (1926-1991)

was born in Montreal, Quebec; her Broadway appearances included: "Desire under the Elms" (1952), *Camille* (1956), *All the Way Home* (1960), and *Moon for the Misbegotten* (1974)—the latter two both earned her a Tony Award; she also directed plays and appeared in a number of films and television movies, including the 1986 series "Anne of Green Gables;" she played a guest role as Murphy Brown's mother in the television series "Murphy Brown;" her second husband was actor George C. Scott. Christopher Plummer (1929- ) was born in Toronto and made his Broadway debut in 1954 in *Starcross Story*; although he has done considerable stage work, particularly in the Shakespearean classics, he is best known for his role of Captain Von Trapp in the 1965 Academy Award-winning *The Sound of Music*; he has appeared in many television dramas, including the miniseries "The Thorn Birds" (1983); he has received many awards, among them a Theatre World Award (1955), two Drama Desk Awards (1973 and 1982), a Tony Award (1974), and an Emmy Award (1977).

### JOURNALISM

Television anchorman Peter Jennings (1938- ) is Canadian American; born in Toronto, Ontario, he began his career in Canada and then moved to ABC News in New York City in 1964; since 1983 he has been senior editor and anchorman of "World News Tonight;" he was named Best Anchor in the United States by the *Washington Journalism Review* in 1988 and 1989. Another Canadian American broadcast journalist, Robin MacNeil (1931- ) was born in Montreal, Quebec; after studying in Canada, he became a Washington correspondent in 1963; in 1975 he served as executive editor and co-anchor of the "MacNeil/Lehrer Report" on WNET-TV in New York City, and since 1983 has hosted the "MacNeil/Lehrer News Hour" on PBS; he has also authored or co-authored five books.

### MUSIC

Many Canadians continue to live in Canada while working in the United States, but singer/songwriter Paul Anka (1941- ) moved to the United States soon after achieving success; born in Ottawa, Ontario, Anka first made a hit with "Diana," composed in 1957; he followed it in 1959—the same year he moved to the United States—with the popular songs, "Put Your Head on My Shoulder," "Crazy Love," "Lonely Boy," and "Time to Cry;" Anka also composed the theme music for *The Tonight Show;* he has received 22 songwriting awards—18 for most-performed songs and four for songs performed more than one million times—and 15 gold records. Born in Fort Macleod, Alberta, singer/songwriter Joni Mitchell first captured attention in the United States with "Chelsea Morning" (1962); in 1970 she won a Grammy for her album *Clouds* (1969).

## SCIENCE AND TECHNOLOGY

Physicist Richard Edward Taylor (1929- ) was born in Medicine Hat, Alberta, and was one of three recipients of the Nobel Prize for Physics in 1990 for his work in demonstrating that protons and neutrons are made up of quarks; Taylor moved to the United States in 1952. Orthopaedic surgeon and educator John Emmett Hall (1925-) was born in Wadena, Saskatchewan, and has been a professor of orthopaedic surgery at Harvard University Medical School since 1971. Psychiatrist and educator Charles Shagass (1920- ) was born in Montreal and came to the United States in 1958; since 1991 he has been a professor at the Medical College of Philadelphia, Pennsylvania.

## SPORTS

Canada has been home to some of the world's greatest athletes—particularly in professional ice hockey. Wayne Gretzky (1961- ) was born in Brantford, Ontario, and holds the National Hockey League scoring title in addition to 12 league trophies; after nine years with the Edmonton Oilers, Gretzky moved to Los Angeles and has, since 1988, played with the Los Angeles Kings team. Gretzky's Edmonton teammate, Mark Messier (1961- ) was born in Edmonton; since 1991, Messier has been a star player for the New York Rangers. Brett Hull (1964- ), son of hockey great Bobby Hull, was born in Belleville, Ontario; he began his professional hockey career with the Calgary Flames, but since 1987 has been with the St. Louis Blues; he was the recipient of two league trophies (Lady Byng and Hart Memorial) and held the league scoring record for goals scored from 1989-92.

## VISUAL ARTS

Many Canadian artists, particularly women, have chosen to live in the United States. Henrietta Shore (1880-1963), born in Toronto, began spending half of each year in New York taking classes with the Art Students' League at the age of 20; she immigrated to California in 1913 and became an American citizen eight years later; her paintings of landscapes, figures, and abstract works led to a number of major solo exhibitions and a medal in the Panama-Pacific Exposition of 1915. Agnes Martin (1912-) was born in Macklin, Saskatchewan, but grew up in Vancouver; she left for the United States at age 20 and became an American citizen at 28; she earned a master's degree in fine arts from Columbia University, spent several years painting and teaching children in New York and New Mexico, and lived in a desert hut for six years (1967-1973) in New Mexico, meditating and writing; primarily an abstract artist, Martin often uses grids of pencil or paint on paper or canvas with various textures. Toronto-born Sylvia Stone (1928- ) immigrated to New York in 1945; Stone is known for her sculpture and painted aluminum reliefs; after she married abstract painter Al Held, her paintings became less figurative and more abstract; she also began to broaden her materials to include aluminum, plexiglass, metal, and mirrors; Stone has also taught at Brooklyn College. Jacqueline Winsor (1941- ) was raised in St. John's, Newfoundland, and became an artist after she found a career as a secretary was not what she wanted; she graduated from the Massachusetts College of Art in 1965 and went on to get her master's of fine arts from Rutgers in 1967; after settling in New York, this abstract sculptor experimented with hemp and rope and went on to create box-like structures of various materials in which the interiors are lit.

Other Canadian American artists include: Hartwell Wyse Priest (1901- ), born in Brantford, Ontario; sculptor Mary Abastenia Eberle (1878-1942), who was the daughter of Canadian parents living in Webster City, Iowa; and Canadian-born abstract artist Dorothea Rockburne (1934- ).

# MEDIA

## PRINT

There are no English-language daily newspapers for Canadian Americans. Those who desire Canadian news can get it either by subscribing to a Canadian newspaper or by reading the Canadian coverage in an American paper (more extensive in the border states). There are, however, a group of weekly newspapers serving the needs of "snowbirds" (Canadians who spend the winter in the United States),as well as resident Canadian Americans.

### The American-Canadian Genealogist.

Formerly *The Genealogist*, this publication of the American-Canadian Genealogical Society reports on the work of the society, which is devoted to the study of the genealogies of French Canadians and French Americans.

**Contact:** Anne-Marie Perrault, Editor.

**Address:** P.O. Box 668, Manchester, New Hampshire 03105-0668.

**Telephone:** (603) 622-1554.

### Canada News.

Founded in 1982, it is owned in part by publisher Bill Leeder and his wife Sally, although the majority owner is the *St. Catharines Standard*, a daily newspaper out of St. Catharines, Ontario. It is published weekly between November and April, with four summer issues and an annual travel publication in September, and boasts an average circulation of 20,400, mostly in Florida. The news coverage includes Canadian American events as well as news from Canada.

**Contact:** Joe Braddy, Editor.

**Address:** 2725 Thornhill Road, Auberndale, Florida 33823.

**Telephone:** (800) 535-6788.

### Canada This Week.

Founded in 1994, it is a seasonal weekly during the winter months which concentrates on news from Western Canada. An early print run was 8,700 copies.

**Contact:** Rob Irvine, Editor.

**Address:** 244 North Country Club Drive, Suite 103, Mesa, Arizona 85201.

**Telephone:** (602) 655-0846.

### Canadian News.

Founded in 1994, it serves the Canadian market out of Yuma, Arizona. It is a seasonal weekly running from November to March, which offers strictly Canadian coverage with a Western Canadian focus.

**Contact:** Barb Glen, Editor.

**Address:** 1769 West 26th Drive, P.O. Box 1024, Yuma, Arizona 85366.

**Telephone:** (602) 344-4003.

### The Sun Times of Canada.

Founded in 1990, it is a seasonal weekly from November to April with five preview issues in the months from July to November. With a circulation around 21,000, mostly in Florida, this newspaper offers Canadian news, entertainment, and business reports, including Canadian mutual fund and stock reports.

**Contact:** Geoffrey Stevens, Editor.

**Address:** 515 West Bay Street, Suite C, Tampa, Florida 33606.

**Telephone:** (813) 254-6620.

## RADIO

Because such a high percentage of Canadians settled in neighboring U.S. states, their needs for "news from home" could be best served by tuning in to Canadian stations as much as possible. American media, particularly in these border states, also devote significant coverage to Canadian developments. To serve the needs of Canadian Americans, there are both Canadian radio programs that are syndicated to American radio stations, and American radio programs that offer daily and weekly summaries of Canadian news.

### "Canada Calling" and "Canada This Week."

These radio programs cover Canadian news events, specifically packaged for Canadian Americans and "snowbirds" (Canadians who maintain a winter residence in southern states) in Florida and Arizona. "Canada Calling," first broadcast in 1952, is a five-and-a-half-minute daily radio news show broadcast on 30 stations in Florida and one station in Phoenix. "Canada This Week" is a 15-minute weekly summary of Canadian news events broadcast on Sundays. Both shows are broadcast from Lakefield, Ontario, just northeast of Toronto.

**Contact:** Prior Smith.

**Address:** P.O. Box 986, Lakefield, Ontario K0L 2H0.

**Telephone:** (705) 654-3901.

### Canadian Broadcasting Corporation's (CBC).

"As It Happens," "Sunday Morning," and "Quirks and Quarks" radio programs are distributed by Public Radio International (PRI). "As It Happens," a news commentary/documentary program, is fed to 22 of the 50 states. Ten cities in Minnesota alone carry the program, including KNOW-FM in St. Paul. "Sunday Morning" is heard in 17 states, again most frequently in Minnesota, but also on stations ranging from West Virginia (WVWV-FM in Huntington) to Alaska (KSKA-AM in Anchorage). The science program "Quirks and Quarks" is distributed by PRI to 16 states.

**Contact:** Ann Phi, Communication Assistant.
**Address:** Public Radio International, 100 North Sixth Street, Suite 900A, Minneapolis, Minnesota 55403.
**Telephone:** (612) 338-5000.

### TELEVISION

### CFCF-TV.
"Canada Pulse News," a half-hour weekly summary of Canadian news, is shown on WFLX Fox 29 in West Palm Beach and on WTMV 32 in Tampa/St. Petersburg. Produced by CFCF-TV in Montreal, Quebec, its first season was in 1993 and it runs 13 weeks each year.

**Contact:** George Goulakos, Sales Manager.
**Address:** CFCF-TV, 405 Ogilvy Avenue, Montreal, Quebec H3N 1M4.
**Telephone:** (514) 495-6100.

### "This Week in Canada."
This program airs a half-hour weekly in the winter season, in select states such as Florida, Maine, Michigan, Nebraska, New York, and Virginia, on the Public Broadcast System (PBS). It offers a selection of Canadian news events and is produced by World Affairs Television of Montreal, Quebec.

**Contact:** Colin Niven, Producer.
**Address:** World Affairs Television, 600 Maisonneuve West, Suite 3230, Montreal, Quebec H3A 3J2.
**Telephone:** (514) 847-2970.

# ORGANIZATIONS AND ASSOCIATIONS

### The Americas Society.
A business-funded group.

**Contact:** Stephen Blank, Director.
**Address:** North American/Canadian Affairs, 680 Park Avenue, New York, New York 10021.
**Telephone:** (212) 249-8950.

### Association for Canadian Studies in the United States (ACSUS).
Founded in 1971, ACSUS has a membership of 1,300 individuals and institutions, which include business and government officials as well as librari-

ans, professors, publishers, and students with an educational interest in Canada. The organization was brought together to promote scholarly activities about Canada at all educational levels. ACSUS publishes *The ACSUS Papers, American Review of Canadian Studies*, and the *Canadian Studies Update*, a quarterly newsletter. It also sponsors a biennial conference.

**Contact:** David N. Biette, Executive Director.
**Address:** 1 Dupont Circle, No. 620, Washington, D.C. 20036.
**Telephone:** (202) 887-6375.

### Committee on Canada-United States Relations.
Founded in 1933, the committee consists of 60 members, 30 from the Chamber of Commerce of the United States and 30 from the Canadian Chamber of Commerce. Its goal is to investigate problems, such as trade and investment challenges, which are common to both countries. Semiannual meetings are held in the spring and fall.

**Contact:** Wolf Brueckmann, Executive Secretary.
**Address:** c/o Chamber of Commerce of the U.S., 1615 H Street, N.W., Washington, D.C. 20062.
**Telephone:** (202) 463-5463.

### North American Committee (CAC).
This organization was founded in 1957, originally with just Canadian and American business leaders. The 110 current members are Canadian, American, and Mexican leaders in private-sector agricultural, business, labor, and professional positions. CAC is jointly sponsored by the C.D. Howe Research Institute in Canada and the National Planning Association in the United States. It studies issues related to expanding commerce and interdependence among Canada, the United States, and Mexico to build cooperation and minimize areas of conflict. Semiannual meetings are held in March in the United States and in September in Canada.

**Contact:** Dahlia Stein, Director.
**Address:** c/o National Planning Association, 1424 16th Street, N.W., Suite 700, Washington, D.C. 20036.
**Telephone:** (202) 884-7630.

# MUSEUMS AND RESEARCH CENTERS

### Canadian-American Center (National Northeast Resource Center on Canada).
This is a joint research facility made up of Canadian studies programs at the Universities of Maine

and Vermont and the State University of New York at Plattsburgh. Research is carried out in the fields of economics, humanities, international relations, law, and social sciences as they relate to Canada and the United States. In addition to publishing the *Canadian-American Public Policy Series* and *Borderlands Monograph Series*, the center sponsors professional meetings.

**Contact:** Dr. Stephen Hornsby, Director.

**Address:** University of Maine, Canadian-American Center, 154 College Avenue, Orono, Maine 04469.

**Telephone:** (207) 581-4220.

### Florida-Canada Institute.

Founded in 1987, it promotes cultural, business, and educational exchanges between Florida and Canada. It is supported by the Florida International Affairs Commission.

**Contact:** Dr. Elliot Vittes, Director.

**Address:** University of Central Florida, Department of Political Science, Orlando, Florida 32816-1356.

**Telephone:** (407) 823-2078.

### Johns Hopkins University Center of Canadian Studies.

Founded in 1969, it is part of the School of Advanced International Studies at Johns Hopkins. Its research areas include: Canadian/U.S. relations, the impact of foreign trade on Canadian culture and politics, and Canadian politics and government. Courses at the master's and doctoral degree levels are taught by resident faculty as well as visiting professors from Carleton University in Ottawa, Ontario, and Laval University in Quebec City, Quebec.

**Contact:** Dr. Charles F. Doran, Director.

**Address:** 1740 Massachusetts Avenue, N.W., Washington, D.C. 20036.

**Telephone:** (202) 663-5714.

# SOURCES FOR ADDITIONAL STUDY

Francis, R. Douglas, Richard Jones, and Donald B. Smith. *Origins: Canadian History to Confederation.* Toronto: Holt, Rinehart and Winston, 1988.

Long, John F., and Edward T. Pryor, et al. *Migration between the United States and Canada.* Washington, D.C.: Current Population Reports/Statistics Canada, February 1990.

Walton, Richard J. *Canada and the U.S.A.: A Background Book About Internal Conflict and the New Nationalism.* New York: Parents' Magazine Press, 1972.

After being cut off
from the European
homeland for nearly
half a century, Rusyn
American contacts
with the homeland
were renewed
following the
Revolution of 1989,
the fall of
communism, and the
collapse of the
Soviet Union.

# CARPATHO-RUSYN AMERICANS

by
Paul Robert
Magocsi

## OVERVIEW

Carpatho-Rusyns (also known in English as Ruthenians) come from an area in the geographical center of the European continent. Their homeland, known as Carpathian Rus' (Ruthenia), is located on the southern and northern slopes of the Carpathian Mountains where the borders of Ukraine, Slovakia, and Poland meet. Carpatho-Rusyns have never had their own state and have lived since the sixth and seventh centuries as a national minority, first in the kingdoms of Hungary and Poland, then from the late eighteenth century to 1918 in the Austro-Hungarian Empire. Since the end of World War I, borders have changed frequently, and Carpatho-Rusyns have found themselves living in several different countries: from 1919 to 1939 in Czechoslovakia and Poland; during World War II in Hungary, Slovakia, and Nazi Germany; and from 1945 to 1989 in the Soviet Ukraine, Czechoslovakia, and Poland. Since the Revolution of 1989 in East Central Europe and the fall of the Soviet Union two years later, the Carpatho-Rusyns have lived, for the most part, in three countries: Ukraine, Slovakia, and Poland. There are also smaller numbers in neighboring Romania, Hungary, the Czech Republic, in the Vojvodina region of Yugoslavia, and in nearby eastern Croatia.

As a people without their own state, Carpatho-Rusyns have had to struggle to be recognized as a distinct group and to be accorded rights such as education in their own language and preservation of their culture. At various times in the twentieth century, they have also tried to attain autonomy or self-rule. These efforts have met with varying degrees of success depending on the general political situation in the countries where they have lived. For example, during the interwar years (1919-1938) in Czechoslovakia, Carpatho-Rusyns did have their own province called Subcarpathian Rus', in which they enjoyed state support for education and culture as well as a degree of political autonomy. On the other hand, during the four decades of communist rule following World War II, Carpatho-Rusyns were not even recognized as a distinct people but were simply considered a branch of Ukrainians. Since the Revolution of 1989, they are recognized in Slovakia, Poland, Hungary, the Czech Republic, and Yugoslavia, but not in Ukraine.

Related to their status as a national minority is the problem of numbers. Since they are not recognized in countries like Ukraine, or have not been recorded in Poland, it is impossible to know with certainty how many Carpatho-Rusyns there are in the European homeland today. Informed estimates place their number possibly at 800,000 to one million. This includes 600,000 to 800,000 in Ukraine; 100,000 in Slovakia; 40,000 in Poland; 30,000 in Yugoslavia; 20,000 in Romania; and the rest in Hungary, Croatia, and the Czech Republic.

Minority status has also contributed indirectly to confusion regarding the very name used to describe the group. Traditionally, they have called themselves *Rusyns* or *Rusnaks*, but the states who have ruled them, and their own leaders, have used many other names, including *Carpatho-Russian*, *Carpatho-Ukrainian*, and *Uhro-Rusyn*. In Poland, Carpatho-Rusyns adopted the name Lemko at the outset of the twentieth century. In the United States, the group has also identified itself by many names: aside from Carpatho-Rusyn, the most popular have been *Carpatho-Russian*, *Lemko*, *Ruthenian*, or the vague and ethnically meaningless *Byzantine* or *Slavish*.

Carpatho-Rusyns began immigrating to the United States in the late 1870s and in the 1880s. By the outbreak of World War I in 1914, approximately 225,000 had arrived. This was to be the largest number of Carpatho-Rusyns ever to reach America. When emigration resumed after World War I, only about 20,000 came in the second wave during the interwar years. From World War II to the present, the numbers have been smaller still—at the most, 10,000. Upon arrival in the United States, the vast majority of Carpatho-Rusyns identified with the state that they had left. It is, therefore, impossible to know their exact number. Based on immigration statistics and membership records in religious and secular organizations, it is reasonable to assume that there are about 620,000 Americans who have at least one ancestor of Carpatho-Rusyn background.

At the time of the first and largest wave of immigration (1880s to 1914), the Carpatho-Rusyn homeland was located entirely within the Austro-Hungarian Empire. That empire was itself divided into two parts: about three-quarters of Carpatho-Rusyns lived in the northeastern corner of the Hungarian Kingdom, with the remainder in the Austrian province of Galicia. In both parts of Austria-Hungary, the economic situation for Carpatho-Rusyns was the same. Their approximately 1,000 villages were all located in hilly or mountainous terrain from which the inhabitants eked out a subsistence-level existence based on small-scale agriculture, livestock grazing (especially sheep), and seasonal labor on the richer plains of lowland Hungary. Their livelihood was always precarious, however, and following a growth in the population and shortage of land, many felt they had no choice but to emigrate to the United States.

Most of the earliest immigrants in the 1870s and 1880s were young males who hoped to work a year or so and then return home. Some engaged in seasonal labor and may have migrated back and forth several times between Europe and America in the decades before 1914. Others eventually brought their families and stayed permanently. Whereas before World War I, movement between Europe and America was relatively easy for enthusiastic young laborers, after World War II, communist rule in the European homeland put an effective end to virtually all cross-border emigration and seasonal migration.

Since earning money was the main goal of the immigrants, they settled primarily in the northeast and north central states, in particular the coal mining region around Scranton and Wilkes-Barre in eastern Pennsylvania, and in Pittsburgh and its suburbs in the western part of that state. Other cities and metropolitan areas that attracted Carpatho-Rusyns were New York City and northeastern New Jersey; southern Connecticut; the Binghamton-Endicott-Johnson City triangle in south central New York; Cleveland and Youngstown, Ohio; Gary and Whiting, Indiana; Detroit and Flint, Michigan; and Minneapolis, Minnesota.

By 1920, nearly 80 percent of all Carpatho-Rusyns lived in only three states: Pennsylvania (54 percent), New York (13 percent), and New Jersey (12 percent). This settlement pattern has been in large part retained by the second-, third-, and fourth-generation descendants of Carpatho-Rusyns, although most have left the inner cities for the surrounding suburbs. Since the 1970s, there has also been migration out of the northeast, in particular to the sunbelt states of Florida, Arizona, and California.

Like other eastern and southern Europeans, Carpatho-Rusyns were not discriminated against because of their color, although they were effectively segregated from the rest of American society because of their low economic status and lack of knowledge of English. They were never singled out as a group, but rather lumped together with other Slavic and Hungarian laborers and called by the opprobrious epithet, *Hunkies*. This was, however, a relatively short-term phase, since the American-born sons and daughters of the original immigrants had, by the late 1930s and 1940s, adapted to the host society and become absorbed into the American middle class. Effectively, Americans of Carpatho-Rusyn descent are an invisible minority within the white middle class majority.

# ACCULTURATION AND ASSIMILATION

The relationship of Carpatho-Rusyns toward American society has changed several times during the more than 100 years since they began to arrive in significant numbers in the United States. There are basically three phases, or periods, during which the attitudes of Carpatho-Rusyns toward American society have ranged from minimal adaptation to total assimilation and acceptance of the American norm.

During the first period, from the 1880s to about 1925, Carpatho-Rusyns felt estranged both linguistically and culturally from the American world surrounding them. Not only did they speak a foreign language, they were also members of a distinct Eastern Christian church that initially did not exist in the United States. Upon arrival, Carpatho-Rusyns were all Byzantine Rite Catholics, or Greek Catholics; that is, adherents of a church that followed Orthodox ritual but was jurisdictionally united with the Roman Catholic church. The American Roman Catholic hierarchy, however, did not accept-and in some cases did not even recognize-Greek Catholic priests. Since religion was a very important factor in their daily lives in Europe, where Greek Catholicism had become virtually synonymous with Carpatho-Rusyn culture and identity, the immigrants, after finding jobs to support themselves materially, sought ways to assure for themselves spiritual fulfillment.

Not finding their own church and being rejected by the American Roman Catholics, Carpatho-Rusyns built their own churches, invited priests from the European homeland, and created fraternal and mutual-benefit organizations to provide insurance and worker's compensation in times of sickness or accident as well as to support the new churches. The oldest and still the largest of these fraternal societies was the Greek Catholic Union, founded in 1892 in Wilkes-Barre, Pennsylvania and then transferred to the suburbs of Pittsburgh in 1906. The churches and fraternals each had their services and publications in the Carpatho-Rusyn language, as well as schools in which children were taught the language of their parents. In short, during this first period, the immigrants felt that they could not be accepted fully into American society, and so they created various kinds of religious and secular organizations that would preserve their old world culture and language.

The second period in Rusyn American life lasted from about 1925 to 1975. For nearly a half-century, the children of immigrants born in the United States increasingly rejected the old world heritage of their parents and tried to assimilate fully into American life. New youth organizations were founded that used only English, while the most popular sports clubs, even within the pre-World War I organizations, were devoted to baseball, basketball, bowling, and golf. By the 1950s, the formerly vibrant Rusyn-language press had switched almost entirely to English. Even the Byzantine Rite Catholic church, which in the intervening years developed into a recognized religious body, began in the 1950s to do away with traditions that were different from those in the Roman Catholic church. In short, Carpatho-Rusyns seemed to want to do everything possible—even at the expense of forgetting their ethnic and religious heritage—to be like "other" Americans. Even the international situation was helpful in this regard, since throughout virtually this entire period, Carpatho-Rusyn Americans were cut off from the European homeland by the economic hardships of the 1930s, World War II, and finally the imposition of communist rule and the creation of the Iron Curtain after 1945.

The third phase in Rusyn American life began about 1975 and has lasted to the present. Like many other "assimilated" Americans, the third-generation descendants of Carpatho-Rusyn immigrants have wanted to know what their grandparents knew so well but what their parents tried desperately to forget. The stimulus for this quest at ethnic rediscovery was the "roots fever" that surrounded the nationwide telecast of the African American saga *Roots* and the celebrations surrounding the bicentennial of the United States in 1976.

New organizations such as the Carpatho-Rusyn Research Center and several Rusyn folk ensembles were founded in the late 1970s, and several new publications began to appear that dealt with all aspects of Carpatho-Rusyn culture. Finally, the Revolution of 1989 and the fall of communism opened up the European homeland and provided new incentives for travel and opportunities for firsthand rediscovery of one's roots and ancestral family ties. Thus, since the 1970s, an increasing number of Americans of Carpatho-Rusyn background have begun to learn about and maintain, at the very least, nostalgic ties with an ancestral culture that they otherwise never really knew. Moreover, in contrast to earlier times, American society as a whole no longer stigmatized such interest in the old world, but actually encouraged the search for one's roots.

# LANGUAGE

Carpatho-Rusyns are by origin Slavs. They speak a series of dialects that are classified as East Slavic and that are most closely related to Ukrainian. However, because their homeland is located within a political and linguistic borderland, Carpatho-Rusyn speech has been heavily influenced by neighboring West Slavic languages like Slovak and Polish, as well as by Hungarian. Several attempts have been undertaken in the European homeland and in the United States to codify this unique speech pattern into a distinct Carpatho-Rusyn literary language. The most successful results have been in the Vojvodina region of Yugoslavia, where a local Rusyn literary language has existed since the early 1920s, as well as in present-day Slovakia where a Rusyn literary language was formally codified in 1995.

The early immigrants to the United States used Rusyn for both spoken and written communication. As early as 1892, the *Amerikansky russky viestnik* (American Rusyn Bulletin) began to appear in Mahanoy City and eventually Homestead, Pennsylvania as the weekly and, at times, three-times-weekly newspaper of the Greek Catholic Union. It was published entirely in Rusyn until 1952, after which it switched gradually and then completely into English. That newspaper was one of 50 weekly and monthly Rusyn-language publications that have appeared in the United States, including the daily newspaper *Den'* (*The Day*; New York, 1922-1926). Traditionally, the Rusyn language uses the Cyrillic alphabet. Cyrillic was initially also used in the United States, although by the 1920s a Roman-based alphabet became more and more widespread. Today only one newspaper survives, the bilingual weekly *Karpats'ka Rus'/Carpatho-Rus'* (Yonkers, New York, 1939- ), half of which is published in Rusyn using the Cyrillic alphabet.

First-generation immigrants, in particular, wanted to pass on the native language to their American-born offspring. Hence, church-sponsored parochial and weekend schools were set up, especially from 1900 to 1930. To preserve the native language, several Rusyn American grammars, readers, catechisms, and other texts were published. The language was also used on a few radio programs during the 1940s and 1950s in New York City, Pittsburgh, Cleveland, and other cities with large Rusyn concentrations. At present there are no radio programs, and the language is taught formally only to students attending the Byzantine Catholic Seminary in Pittsburgh and the Carpatho-Russian Orthodox Diocesan Seminary in Johnstown, Pennsylvania.

# FAMILY AND COMMUNITY DYNAMICS

In the Carpatho-Rusyn homeland, where there was a need for agricultural laborers, families were often large, with an average of six to ten children. Family homesteads might also house grandparents as well as a newly wedded son or daughter and spouse waiting to earn enough to establish their own home. Many villages comprised three or four extended families interrelated through blood or through relationships such as godparents.

The immigrants who came to the United States were initially males who lived in boarding houses. Those who remained eventually married in America or brought their families from Europe. The extended family structure typical of the European village was replaced by nuclear families living in individual houses or apartments that included parents and on average, three to four children.

Coming to the United States primarily before World War I, Carpatho-Rusyns entered a society in which there were little or no welfare programs or other forms of public assistance. The ideal was to take care of oneself, depending perhaps only on a fraternal insurance organization to which dues were paid. There was never any expectation that the government would assist individuals or families in what were considered their private lives. Such attitudes of self-reliance were passed on to the second and third generations, most of whom shunned public assistance even when it became available beginning in the 1930s. Only since the 1970s, with the widespread closing of steel mills and related industries in western Pennsylvania, where thousands suddenly found themselves out of work, have attitudes toward public assistance changed. This means that today third-, fourth-, and fifth-generation Carpatho-Rusyns are likely to accept unemployment insurance whenever their livelihood is threatened.

The traditional old world pattern of marriages arranged by parents, sometimes with the help of a matchmaker, was, with rare exceptions, not followed among Carpatho-Rusyn immigrants. Instead, individuals have courted and found their own partners. At least until the 1950s, parents did not urge their daughters to continue their education after high school, but instead to get married and serve as the homemaker for a family. Boys, too, were often encouraged to go to technical schools or to begin work as an apprentice in a trade. Since the 1960s, however, an increasing number of both young men and women are encouraged to attend colleges and universities, after which they work in fields such as communications, service industries, and medicine (especially nursing).

Whereas before the 1950s women were encouraged to become homemakers, they were always welcome to take an active part in community activity. At least since the 1930s, women have served on the governing boards of Rusyn American fraternals, have had their own sports clubs, and have been particularly effective in establishing ladies' guilds which, through social events, have been able to raise extensive funds to help local church parishes. To this day, many ladies' guilds operate catering and small food services from the basements of churches, cooking traditional Rusyn dishes like *holubky* (stuffed cabbage) and *pirohy* (three-cornered cheese- or potato-filled ravioli) and selling them to the community at large. The profits go to the church.

Carpatho-Rusyns had a vibrant community life during the first three decades of this century. Fraternal organizations, social clubs, political groups, and churches sponsored publications, theatrical and musical performances, public lectures, parades, and picnics, all of which were in part or wholly related to the preservation and promotion of a Carpatho-Rusyn culture and identity. Such activity virtually ceased or lost any specific Carpatho-Rusyn content in the decades immediately following World War II.

There has been a marked revival of activity, however, since the 1970s. Several new song and dance ensembles, the largest of which is Slavjane in Pittsburgh, were founded by third-, fourth-, and fifth-generation descendants of the pre-World War I immigrants. A scholarly organization, the Carpatho-Rusyn Research Center, was founded in 1978; it has distributed thousands of books about Rusyn culture and history, and publishes a quarterly, the *Carpatho-Rusyn American* (Fairview, New Jersey; Pittsburgh, Pennsylvania, 1978- ). Several other local cultural and social organizations were established or renewed in cities and towns where Rusyns have traditionally lived, such as Minneapolis (The Rusin Association), Yonkers, New York (Carpatho-Russian American Center), and Pittsburgh (Carpatho-Rusyn Society). This trend toward cultural renewal and the rediscovery of one's heritage has been enhanced by the political changes that have taken place in East Central Europe after 1989. As a result, visits to families and friends that were effectively cut off by the Iron Curtain are now becoming a common occurrence.

# RELIGION

Carpatho-Rusyns are Christians and, for the most part, they belong to various Eastern Christian churches. They trace their Christian origins back to the second half of the ninth century, when the Byzantine Greek monks Cyril and Methodius and their disciples brought Christianity from the East

Roman or Byzantine Empire to Carpathian Rus'. After 1054, when the Christian world was divided into Roman Catholic and Eastern Orthodox spheres, the Carpatho-Rusyns remained part of the eastern tradition. This meant that in Carptho-Rusyn churches, Church Slavonic (written in the Cyrillic alphabet) was used instead of Latin as the liturgical language, priests could marry, and after the sixteenth century the "old calendar" was maintained, so that nonmovable feasts like Christmas were celebrated about two weeks after they were celebrated according to the western calendar. Eastern Christians also recognized as the head of their church the ecumenical patriarch, who resided in Constantinople, the capital of the former Byzantine Empire.

The question of church jurisdiction changed in the mid-seventeenth century, when some Carpatho-Rusyn bishops and priests united with the Catholic church based in Rome. These Uniates, as they were first called, were at first allowed to keep all their eastern Orthodox traditions, but they were required to accept the authority of the Pope in Rome instead of the Orthodox ecumenical patriarch. Because the Uniates continued to use the eastern liturgy and follow eastern church practices, they were eventually called Greek Catholics, and today Byzantine Rite Catholics. Since the seventeenth century, Carpatho-Rusyns have been divided into two branches of Eastern Christianity—Orthodoxy and Byzantine Rite Catholicism.

Regardless of whether Carpatho-Rusyns were Orthodox or Byzantine Rite Catholic, the church remained a central feature of their life-cycle in the European homeland. Until well into the twentieth century, all rites of passage (birth/baptisms, weddings, funerals) and public events in Rusyn villages and towns were determined by the church calendar. In many ways, Carpatho-Rusyn culture and identity were synonymous with either the Byzantine Rite Catholic or Orthodox churches. Virtually all the early Carpatho-Rusyn cultural leaders, including the nineteenth-century "national awakener" Aleksander Dukhnovych, were priests.

Because religion was so important, it is not surprising that Carpatho-Rusyns tried to recreate aspects of their church-directed life after immigrating to the United States. From the very outset, however, the Byzantine Rite Catholics met with resistance from American Catholic bishops, who before World War I were intolerant toward all traditions that were not in accord with American Roman Catholic norms (especially those that used "foreign" languages and followed practices like a married priesthood). As a result, thousands of Byzantine Rite Catholics left the church and joined the Orthodox church. This "return to the ancient faith" began as early as 1892 and was led by a priest who at the time was based in Minneapolis, Father Alexis Toth.

Aside from losing members to Orthodoxy, the Byzantine Rite Catholic church was also having difficulty maintaining traditional practices. After 1929, Byzantine Rite Catholics were forced by Rome to accept the practice of celibacy for priests and to turn over all church property, which until then was generally held by laypersons who had built and paid for the buildings. This so-called "celibacy controversy" caused great dissatisfaction, and led to the defection of thousands more Byzantine Rite Catholics, who created a new American Carpatho-Russian Orthodox church. The Byzantine Rite Catholics also gave up other traditional practices, and by the 1950s and 1960s changed to the western calendar and used primarily English in their services.

The division between Orthodoxy and Byzantine Rite Catholicism in the European homeland has continued among Carpatho-Rusyns and their descendants in the United States. Today the Byzantine Rite Catholic church has four dioceses located in Pittsburgh, Pennsylvania, Passaic, New Jersey; Parma, Ohio; and Van Nuys, California. The American Carpatho-Russian Orthodox church has one diocese based in Johnstown, Pennsylvania. The Orthodox Church in America, with its seat in New York City, has 12 dioceses across the country. The approximate Carpatho-Rusyn membership in these churches is as follows: Byzantine Rite Catholics—195,000; Carpatho-Russian Orthodox—18,000; Orthodox Church in America—250,000.

In the early years of the immigration, when Carpatho-Rusyns did not yet have their own churches, many Byzantine Rite Catholics attended, and eventually joined, Roman Catholic churches. Subsequently, intermarriage increased the number of Carpatho-Rusyn Roman Catholics, who today may number as high as 80,000 to 100,000. The community's internal religious controversies and the proselytizing efforts of American Protestant churches, especially in the early decades of the twentieth century, have also resulted in the growth of several evangelical sects among Carpatho-Rusyns and conversions, especially to various Baptist churches.

# EMPLOYMENT AND ECONOMIC TRADITIONS

Although the vast majority of Carpatho-Rusyns who came to the United States during the major wave of immigration before World War I left small villages where they worked as small-scale subsistence-level farmers or as livestock herders, only a handful found jobs in agriculture in the United States. As one priest and community activist quipped earlier in the century: "Our people do not live in America, they live *under* America!" This remark reflects the fact that many of the earliest Carpatho-Rusyn immigrants found employment in the coal-mining belt in eastern Pennsylvania. Since they lacked industrial and mining skills upon arrival, they were given the most menial tasks, such as coal splitting and carting. Carpatho-Rusyns were also attracted to the iron mines in upstate Minnesota; the lead mines of south central Missouri; the coal mines of southern Oklahoma and Washington state; the gold, silver, and lead mines of Colorado; and the marble quarries of Vermont. Even more important than mining for Carpatho-Rusyns was the growing steel industry of Pittsburgh and its neighboring towns. The steel mills and associated industries employed most Carpatho-Rusyns who lived in western Pennsylvania and neighboring Ohio.

Already during the pre-World War I decades, women were obliged to work outside the home in order to supplement the family income. With limited English-language and work skills, at first they were only able to find work as cleaning women in offices or as servants and nannies in well-to-do households. The second-generation American-born were more likely to find work as retail salespersons, waitresses, and workers in light industries such as shoe, soap, and cigar factories.

Like women, the second-generation American-born men had moved slightly up the employment ladder to work as skilled and semi-skilled workers, foremen, or clerical workers. By the third and fourth generation, there was a marked increase in managerial and semi-professional occupations. In general, however, Carpatho-Rusyns and their descendants have preferred working in factories, mills, mines, and other industries, rather than trying to establish their own businesses.

A dependence on the existing American industrial and corporate structure has, in recent decades, had a negative effect on thousands of Rusyn Americans who thought the jobs or industries that they and their fathers and grandfathers worked in would always be there for themselves and their children. The widespread closing of coal mines in eastern Pennylvania and the collapse of America's steel industry put thousands of Rusyn Americans out of work. As a result, Carpatho-Rusyns, like other middle-class working Americans in the past two decades, have had to lower their expectations about economic advancement and to retrain themselves for, and especially to encourage their children to prepare for, jobs that are no longer in coal and steel, but in electronics, computers, and service-related industries.

# POLITICS AND GOVERNMENT

At least until World War I, Carpatho-Rusyns in the European homeland did not have any experience in politics. They were used to being ruled and not to participating in the governing process. The result was skepticism and a deep-seated mistrust toward politics which was to continue after immigration to the United States. Not surprisingly, first-generation Carpatho-Rusyns, and even their American-born descendants, have rarely become elected officials in the United States. It was not until the 1970s that the first individuals of Carpatho-Rusyn background were to be found in elected offices beyond the local level, such as Mark Singel, the lieutenant governor of Pennsylvania, and Joseph M. Gaydos, Democratic congressman from Pennsylvania. As for the majority of Carpatho-Rusyns, their relation to political life was limited to participation in strikes, especially in the coal fields and in steel and related industries during the decades of the 1890s to 1930s. While there were some Carpatho-Rusyn political clubs established during the 1930s and 1940s to support Democratic party candidates, these were generally few in number and short-lived.

On the other hand, Carpatho-Rusyn Americans have in the past played an active and, at times, a decisive role in homeland politics. This was particularly so during the closing months of World War I, when Carpatho-Rusyn Americans, like other immigrant groups from east central and southern Europe, proposed various options for the future of their homelands following what proved to be the imminent collapse of the Russian, Austro-Hungarian, and Ottoman Empires.

In the spring and summer of 1918, both Byzantine Rite Catholic and Orthodox religious and lay leaders formed political action committees, the most important of which was the American Council of Uhro-Rusyns in Homestead, Pennsylvania. The Homestead-based council chose a young, American-trained Carpatho-Rusyn lawyer, Gregory Zatkovich, to represent them. Under his leadership, the American Rusyns joined with other groups in the Mid-European Union in Philadelphia, lobbied the American government, and followed President Woodrow Wilson's suggestion that the Carpatho-Rusyn homeland might become part of the new state of Czechoslovakia. An agreement to join Czechoslovakia was reached in Philadelphia in November 1918, after which Zatkovich led a Rusyn American delegation to convince leaders in the homeland of the desirability of joining Czechoslovakia.

The "American solution" was indeed accepted in 1919 at the Paris Peace Conference. Only the Lemko Rusyns north of the mountains were left out; eventually they were incorporated into the new state of Poland. In recognition of his role, Zatkovich, while still an American citizen, was appointed by the president of Czechoslovakia to be the first governor of its eastern province called Subcarpathian Rus'.

During the 1920s and 1930s, the Rusyn American community closely followed political events in the homeland, and frequently sent protests to the League of Nations, calling on the Czechoslovak government to implement the political autonomy that had been promised, but not fully implemented, in the province of Subcarpathian Rus'. The United States government was now less interested in faraway East Central Europe, so that Rusyn American political influence on the homeland declined and eventually ended entirely, in particular after Subcarpathian Rus' was annexed to the Soviet Union in 1945 and the rest of East Central Europe came under Soviet-inspired communist rule.

After being cut off from the European homeland for nearly half a century, Rusyn American contacts with the homeland were renewed following the Revolution of 1989, the fall of communism, and the collapse of the Soviet Union. Both secular and church bodies began once again to provide moral and financial assistance to Rusyn organizations in the homeland. Rusyn Americans also became active in the World Congress of Rusyns, established in eastern Slovakia in March 1991.

Often related to contacts with the European homeland has been the question of national identity. Throughout their entire history in the United States, politics for most Carpatho-Rusyns has meant trying to decide and reach a consensus on the question: "Who are we?" At least until about 1920, most Carpatho-Rusyns in the United States considered themselves to form a distinct Slavic nationality called Rusyn or Uhro-Rusyn (that is, Hungarian Rusyn). By the 1920s, there was a strong tendency, encouraged especially by the Orthodox church, to consider Rusyns as little more than a branch of the Russian nationality. Hence, the term *Carpatho-Russian* became a popular term to describe the group. By the 1950s and 1960s, two more possible identities were added, Slovak and Ukrainian.

Since the 1970s, however, there has been a pronounced return to the original Rusyn identity, that is, the idea that Carpatho-Rusyns are neither Russian, nor Slovak, nor Ukrainian, but rather a distinct nationality. Several of the older religious and lay organizations have reasserted the Rusyn orientation, and it has been fully embraced from the outset by all the new cultural and scholarly institutions established in the United States since the 1970s. The Rusyn orientation in America has been encouraged further by the Rusyn national revival that has been occurring in all the European homeland countries (Slovakia, Ukraine, Poland, Hungary, Yugoslavia) since the Revolution of 1989.

# INDIVIDUAL AND GROUP CONTRIBUTIONS

### ART

Undoubtedly, the most famous American of Carpatho-Rusyn descent was Andy Warhol (born Andrew Warhola, 1928-1987), the pop artist, photographer, and experimental filmmaker. At the height of his career in the 1960s and 1970s, he had become as famous as the celebrities he was immortalizing. Recalling the idealized saintly images (icons) that surrounded him when he was growing up and attending the Byzantine Rite Catholic Church in Pittsburgh's Rusyn Valley (Ruska dolina) district, Warhol created on canvas and in photographs new "American icons" that epitomized the second half of the twentieth century. Since his untimely death in 1987, his older brothers, John and Paul Warhola, have become instrumental in perpetuating the Carpatho-Rusyn heritage of Andy and his family. That heritage figures prominently in the new Andy Warhol Museum in Pittsburgh. The Warhol Foundation, which funded the Pittsburgh museum, has also donated paintings and provided financial support for the Warhola Family Museum of Modern Art, founded in 1992 in Medzilaborce, Slovakia, just a few miles away from the Carpatho-Rusyn village where both Andy Warhol's parents were born.

## ENTERTAINMENT AND COMMUNICATIONS

In the 1940s and 1950s, Lizabeth Scott (born Emma Matzo, 1922) played the role of a sultry leading lady in several Hollywood films, while Sandra Dee (born Alexandra Zuk, 1942) was cast in roles that depicted the typical American teenage girl of the 1950s and 1960s. Her very name was later used as a nostalgic symbol of that era in the musical *Grease*. In more recent years, other Americans of Carpatho-Rusyn descent have been active in television, including the actor Robert Urich (1946- ) and the FOX Television newscaster, Cora-Ann Mihalik (1955- ).

## RELIGION

It is in the area of religion where Carpatho-Rusyns have made a particularly significant contribution to American life. Three individuals stand out for their work not only on behalf of Eastern Christianity, the traditional faith of Carpatho-Rusyns, but also of Roman Catholicism and American evangelical Protestantism.

The Russian Orthodox Church of America, today the Orthodox Church in America, is one of the oldest in the United States. It was founded as early as 1792, when Alaska was a colony of the Russian Empire. The real growth of that church was connected not to the Alaskan mission, however, but to its influence over thousands of immigrants from East Central Europe who settled in the northeastern United States during the decades before World War I. The expansion of Russian Orthodoxy during those years is attributable largely to Father Alexis Toth (1853-1909), a former Byzantine Rite Catholic priest who joined the Orthodox Church in 1891. Not only did he bring his own Minneapolis parish with him, he also set out on missionary activity in several northeastern states, converting nearly 25,000 Carpatho-Rusyns

and other East Slavic immigrants to Orthodoxy. The church grew so rapidly that it moved its headquarters from San Francisco to New York City. For his services, Toth was hailed as the "father of Orthodoxy in America," and in 1994 he was made a saint of the Orthodox Church of America.

The two other influential religious activists were both born in the United States of Carpatho-Rusyn parents. Miriam Teresa Demjanovich (1901-1927) converted to Roman Catholicism as a child, became a member of the Sisters of Charity, and devoted the rest of her years to a life of pure spirituality. A year after her death, a collection of her "spiritual conferences" was published, *Greater Perfection* (1928), which became so popular that they were translated into several languages, including Chinese. Her followers have established a Sister Miriam Teresa League in New Jersey, which is working to have her made a saint in the Roman Catholic church.

Perhaps the best known religious activist of Carpatho-Rusyn descent in American society as a whole is Joseph W. Tkach (b. 1927), since 1986 Pastor General of the Worldwide Church of God. Tkach is editor of the popular religious magazine *Plain Truth*, and he is the guiding force behind the church's syndicated news-oriented television series, "The World Tomorrow," rated as one of the top religious programs in the United States.

# MEDIA

## PRINT

### Carpatho-Rusyn American.
A forum on Carpatho-Rusyn ethnic heritage.

**Contact:** Patricia Krafcik, Editor.
**Address:** Carpatho-Rusyn American, P.O. Box 192, Fairfax, Virginia 22030.
**Telephone:** (703) 691-8585.
**Fax:** (703) 691-0513.

### Karpatska Rus'/Carpatho-Rus'.
A Carpatho-Russian newspaper of the Lemko Association.

**Contact:** Alexander Herenchak, Editor.
**Address:** 556 Yonkers Avenue, Yonkers, New York 10704.

### The New Rusyn Times.
A cultural-organizational publication of the Carpatho-Rusyn Society.

**Address:** 125 Westland Drive, Pittsburgh, Pennsylvania 15217.

**Telephone:** (412) 682-2869; or (216) 561-9418.

### Trembita.

The newsletter of the Rusin Association.

**Contact:** Lawrence Goga, Editor.
**Address:** 1115 Pineview Lane North, Minneapolis, Minnesota 55441.
**Telephone:** (612) 595-9188.

## ORGANIZATIONS AND ASSOCIATIONS

### Carpatho-Russian American Center.

A social and cultural center that caters primarily to Lemkos and their descendants.

**Contact:** John Ryzyk, President.
**Address:** 556 Yonkers Avenue, Yonkers, New York 10704.
**Telephone:** (914) 969-3954.

### Carpatho-Rusyn Research Center.

The main publishing house for materials on Carptho-Rusyns worldwide, it also supports research projects.

**Address:** Box 131-B-Main Street, Orwell, Vermont 05760.

### Carpatho-Rusyn Society.

Promotes Carpatho-Rusyn cultural activity in western Pennsylvania/eastern Ohio.

**Address:** 125 Westland Road, Pittsburgh, Pennsylvania 15217.
**Telephone:** (412) 682-2869.

### Lemko Association of the United States and Canada.

The oldest Rusyn American cultural/social organization concerned primarily with immigrants and their descendants from the Lemko Region in Poland.

**Contact:** Alexander Herenchak, President.
**Address:** 555 Province Lane Road, Box 156, Allentown, New Jersey 08501.
**Telephone:** (609) 758-1115.

## SOURCES FOR ADDITIONAL STUDY

Barriger, Lawrence. *Good Victory: Metropolitan Orestes Chornock and the American Carpatho-Russian Orthodox Greek Catholic Diocese.* Brookline, Massachusetts: Holy Cross Orthodox Press, 1985.

Dyrud, Keith. *The Quest for the Rusyn Soul: The Politics of Religion and Culture in Eastern Europe and America, 1890-World War I.* Philadelphia, London, and Toronto: Associated University Presses for the Balch Institute Press, 1992.

Gulovich, Stephen C. "The Rusin Exarchate in the United States," *Eastern Churches Quarterly* VI, 1946, pp. 459-485.

Magocsi, Paul Robert. *The Carpatho-Rusyn Americans.* New York and Philadelphia: Chelsea House Publishers, 1989.

———. *Opportunity Realized: The Greek Catholic Union's First One Hundred Years.* Beaver, Pennsylvania: Greek Catholic Union of the U.S.A., 1994.

———. *Our People: Carpatho-Rusyns and Their Descendants in North America,* third revised edition. Toronto: Multicultural History Society of Ontario, 1994.

*Orthodox America, 1794-1976: Development of the Orthodox Church in America,* edited by Constance J. Tarasar and John H. Erickson. [Syosset, New York], 1975.

Pekar, Athanasius B. *Our Past and Present: Historical Outlines of the Byzantine Ruthenian Metropolitan Province.* Pittsburgh, Pennsylvania: Byzantine Seminary Press, 1974.

Simirenko, Alex. *Pilgrims, Colonists, and Frontiersmen: An Ethnic Community in Transition.* New York: Free Press of Glencoe, 1964.

Warzeski, Walter C. *Byzantine Rite Rusyns in Carpatho-Ruthenia and America.* Pittsburgh, Pennsylvania: Byzantine Seminary Press, 1971.

Chaldean Americans
are a highly religious
people proud of
their Christian
heritage.

# CHALDEAN AMERICANS

by
Mary C.
Sengstock

## OVERVIEW

Chaldean Americans are descendants of people from the northern Tigris-Euphrates Valley, presently located in the Middle Eastern nation of Iraq. The majority of Chaldean Americans live in Detroit, Michigan, although there are also Chaldean Americans in Chicago, Illinois; El Cajon, San Jose, and Turlock, California; and Qaxaca, Mexico. It is difficult to determine the exact number of Chaldeans in the United States because they are not represented as such in the U.S. Census. According to statistical projections from previous data on the Chaldean American community, however, it is estimated that Chaldeans in the Detroit metropolitan area may number as many as 70,000 to 80,000; in California they are projected at 2,000 to 3,000 persons.

Although Chaldean Americans constitute the bulk of Iraqi immigrants living in the United States, they represent less than 10 percent of the population of Iraq. While the vast majority of Iraqis, like residents of other Arabic nations, are Muslim, Chaldeans are Roman Catholic, and practice one of the 18 to 20 separate rites of the Catholic Church. They also differ from other Iraqis in that their ancestral language is not Arabic but a dialect of Aramaic, also referred to as Chaldean, Assyrian, or Syriac. As a result of their religious and linguistic differences from other

Iraqi immigrants, Chaldeans tend not to identify themselves either with Iraq or the Arab world, but prefer being called Chaldean Americans.

## HISTORY

Chaldean Americans are a highly religious people proud of their Christian heritage. According to legend, they were converted to Christianity by the Apostle Thomas on one of his missionary journeys to the East. (St. Addai, an associate of Thomas, is revered as a Chaldean patron.) In the third century, they were followers of Nestorius, a patriarch of Constantinople who was declared a heretic by the Roman Church for teaching that Jesus Christ was not concurrently God and man. This division between the followers of Nestorius in the East and the Roman Church lasted until 1445, when some Chaldeans were received into the Roman Church by Pope Eugenius IV. They were permitted to retain their historic rituals and the Chaldean/Aramaic language for mass and other ceremonies. Searching for an appropriate name to call this new Catholic rite, the Pope focused on their historic homeland, which in ancient times had been the land of the Babylonians, Assyrians, and Chaldeans. It was also the historic homeland of the prophet Abraham, who came from Ur, a city of the Chaldeans. Hence, the Pope chose "Chaldean" as the name for the new Catholic rite.

Over 95 percent of Chaldeans in the Detroit community can trace their origin to a single town, Telkaif, which is one of several Christian towns in the northern Iraqi province of Mosul, near the ruins of the ancient city of Nineveh. Some of the earliest members of Detroit's Chaldean American community recall hearing stories from their grandparents about the conversion of their town from Nestorianism. This occurred in about 1830, when the town recognized the Roman Pontiff as the head of the Church.

## CHALDEAN MIGRATION TO THE UNITED STATES

While Chaldeans are believed to have immigrated to the United States as early as 1889, the first significant migration wave did not occur until around 1910, when Chaldeans began settling in metropolitan Detroit. At the time, Detroit was popular among a number of immigrant groups because of the growing automobile industry. It also had an established Middle Eastern community during this period, consisting primarily of Christian immigrants from Lebanon.

In 1943 community sources listed 908 Chaldeans in the Detroit area; by 1963, this number had tripled, to about 3,000 persons. An even greater number of Iraqi citizens immigrated to the United States due to changes in U.S. immigration laws during the mid-1960s, and growth in Detroit's Chaldean American community became even more dramatic, increasing to about 45,000 in 1986, and approximately 75,000 by 1992. (These figures are based on the statistical projections and estimates of Chaldean American community leaders.) This period also saw an increase in immigration to other parts of the country, particularly California.

The majority of Chaldean Americans left their homeland for economic and religious reasons. Telkaif in the early 1900s was a poor, nonindustrialized village. Many left the town for nearby cities such as Mosul, Baghdad, Basra, or Beirut. Only later did some of them decide to migrate to the United States, or simply to North America. At the time the earliest settlers came, the United States had not yet introduced restriction on immigration, making entry relatively easy. Migration at that time was largely a male phenomenon; women and children generally stayed behind until their husbands, fathers, and brothers became established.

Chaldeans also fled their homeland to escape religious persecution from the Muslim majority in the Middle East. The combination of religious freedom, an established Lebanese Moronite community, and economic opportunity made the United States, particularly metropolitan Detroit, inviting. Once members of the Telkaif community had settled in the area, they encouraged others from their homeland to join them. Thus began an immigration process, known as "chain migration," between Telkaif and Detroit, which continues to the present.

In this process, members of a community who have already established themselves in a new location assist relatives and friends left behind to migrate as well. The assistance they provide can take many forms, including the provision of jobs, a place to stay, or, at the very least, information and advisement. Close relatives may even provide money for passage. In a typical chain, a man migrates first; later he sends home for his wife and children, or if he is not married, he may return to find a bride. As he and his wife become citizens, they arrange for the migration of their parents and siblings as well. And these, in turn, arrange to assist their spouses, in-laws, and other relatives.

This type of assistance became especially important in the 1920s, after the passage of U.S. quota limitations on migration. Under quota restrictions, only 100 immigrants from Iraq were allowed to enter the United States each year. These quotas reinforced the chain migration process by giving preference to the families of persons already in America, under the assumption that such persons would have assistance in the United States and were less likely to become indigent and require public assistance.

Migration of all types largely ceased during World War II when travel became difficult. It commenced again following the war, particularly with the introduction of the student visa, which allowed migrants to enter the United States for educational purposes, on the assumption that they would return home following their training. Many Chaldean Americans entered as students and later married members of the community, thus allowing them to remain in the country.

The 1968 change in U.S. migration law allowed for a significantly larger number of immigrants from Iraq, and the migration of Chaldeans increased substantially. A steady stream of Chaldean immigrants came to the United States, until the onset of the Gulf War when the United States placed restrictions on immigration from Iraq.

# ACCULTURATION AND ASSIMILATION

The steady rate of Chaldean migration has had a profound effect on the assimilation of Chaldeans in American society because it has provided a constant influx of Chaldean culture. However, many changes have taken place in Iraq since the first Chaldean settlers came to the United States, which, in turn, has greatly altered Chaldean American communities.

Like most ethnic groups, Chaldean Americans have also been affected by cultural differences between the immigrant generation and their children and grandchildren born in the United States. Chaldean Americans reared in the United States are more comfortable speaking English than the language of their parents. They attend school with non-Chaldeans, watch television, and adopt an American life style.

Recent Chaldean immigrants were more likely to have been born and reared in one of modern Iraq's major cities, such as Baghdad, Mosul, or Basra. They are better educated and many have attended college or professional schools. The two groups differ socioeconomically as well; many of the earlier immigrants, and their children born in the United States, have prospered and moved into more affluent suburbs, while more recent immigrants, despite their educational background and general understanding of the English language, struggle among the nation's poor. Yet perhaps the most dramatic difference between older and newer Chaldean immigrant groups is language. Since World War II, Iraq has taught Arabic, the national language, in schools throughout the country. As a result, the Chaldean/Aramaic language of early immigrants has largely been replaced by the Arabic tongue of the newcomers. In fact, few immigrants today know Chaldean at all.

Chaldean Americans are often mistaken for other ethnic groups in the United States, specifically Arab Americans. Like Arab Americans, Chaldeans tend to have large families, own independent businesses such as grocery or party stores and gas stations, and they even share some foods. On a deeper level, however, there are important distinctions between the two immigrant groups. The large patriarchal families of Muslim Arabs have traditionally allowed a man to take multiple wives, a pattern forbidden for centuries in the Christian tradition. Chaldeans also contend that women are accorded a higher place in their social structure than in the Arabic tradition. In the Chaldean community today, many young women are encouraged to attain higher education. Even in the area of food there are important distinctions; Arabs do not consume alcohol and pork, which are forbidden in the Muslim faith. Chaldeans have no such restrictions. Many of these distinctions clearly flow from religious differences, but they are important distinctions in their own right.

# LANGUAGE

Most modern-day immigrants speak Arabic, the dominant language of the Iraqi nation, but the earliest Chaldean immigrants spoke only Chaldean, which they also call "Jesus language," since it is believed to be the language which Jesus Christ spoke during his life. Some Chaldeans resent the fact that they were forced to learn Arabic in Iraqi schools. Inquiring which language Chaldean American children should learn usually provokes a debate. Practical thinkers consider the Arabic language more useful in today's world. More nostalgic individuals assert the importance of learning their original tongue. Hence, while most Chaldean Americans speak Arabic, they do not necessarily take pride in it.

# FAMILY AND COMMUNITY DYNAMICS

The Chaldean American family is not limited to the nuclear family of husband, wife, and children. Rather, it includes grandparents, siblings, aunts, uncles, and cousins. Indeed, Chaldeans are quick to point out that their shared ancestry means that everyone is at least distantly related to everyone else. Family names are recognized by everyone and enable members of the community to place everybody in relation to everyone else. Therefore, a Chaldean's family ties constitute a major source of identity within the community.

Chaldeans tend to have large families, in keeping with Catholic tradition. In the past, the number of children per couple averaged from five to six, with some couples having as many as 12 or 15 children. This number has decreased with second and third generations, but Chaldean families continue to be somewhat larger than the national average.

Ties to one's extended family are close and involved. Visiting between a married couple and the parents and siblings of both husband and wife are frequent, occurring at least several times each week, even daily. Extended Chaldean American families also perform numerous functions together, such as cooking, child care, or cleaning. Cooking and eating together several times each week is common. Child care is often shared by sisters, sisters-in-law, or grandmothers. Yard work for older relatives may be managed by younger members of the extended family.

Because of the importance given to family and community, Chaldeans prefer to have their children be "endogamous," or marry within the community, as occurred in Telkaif. Today, many Chaldeans marry persons from outside the community. However, the rate of endogamy continues to be high, and even those who marry non-Chaldeans ("exogamy") usually continue to remain close to their parents and siblings. Among Chaldeans, most exogamous marriages bring an outsider into the community, rather than resulting in the loss of a member.

Chaldean families exercise great influence over the individual. As was just indicated, one example of this is the expectation that family preferences will be considered in the choice of a spouse. Chaldeans are also expected to open their homes to other members of the family, should that be necessary. This means that young people are expected to welcome their elderly parents or a visiting relative from Iraq into their homes, for periods which may last from a few weeks to several months or even years.

In its initial years, the Chaldean American community was a small and highly unified group. All but one or two families could trace their origin to the town of Telkaif; all were interrelated; and marriages were frequently arranged within the community or with persons in the original town. Moreover, they spoke a common language, Chaldean/Aramaic, which they shared with few other Americans. Common interests in the Church and a community economic system also served to draw the members into a closely knit unit.

Over the past eight decades, however, significant changes have occurred in the Chaldean American community. What was, in 1960, a community of about 3,000 members has now multiplied to nearly 25 times that size. Differences and divisions are inevitable. Many such divisions arise from the varying places of birth among Chaldeans. While early Chaldean immigrants were born in small, rural communities, more recent groups are from Iraq's large, industrialized cities. Moreover, many Chaldeans were born in the United States and are therefore heavily influenced by American culture. Other problems arise from economic wealth. Many established Chaldean families have obtained significant wealth in the United States. Several more recent immigrants, however, struggle well below the poverty level. Language too, tends to divide Chaldean American communities. Early immigrants maintain their ancestral Chaldean/Aramaic language, but more recent immigrants speak Arabic. At the same time, numerous American-born Chaldeans favor English. Such differences have torn communities, and even families apart. Nonetheless, Chaldean Americans remain somewhat unified by their common heritage and Catholic faith. Jobs, income, and other needs of recent immigrants are paramount in community priorities. Also, problems of the homeland, such as

Iraq's recent wars, first with Iran and then with the United States, assume a prominent role in community concerns.

## RELATIONS WITH OTHER ETHNIC GROUPS

Many Americans have difficulty distinguishing Chaldean Americans from other American ethnic groups, particularly Arab Americans and Iraqi Americans, much to the dismay of the members of these groups, who are quite aware of the differences among them. While they share similar physical traits, they differ linguistically, culturally, and most importantly, in terms of religion. During the early years of the twentieth century, a period about which many Chaldeans have heard from their parents and grandparents, Arabic-speaking Muslims were abusive oppressors of Christians in the area in which Telkaif was located. Many Chaldeans have negative memories of treatment by Iraqis as well. In fact, from a political standpoint, many Chaldeans are more supportive of Israel than Arab countries in the Middle East.

Many Chaldean Americans remain resentful of their constant identification with the Arab American community. Most simply reassert their identity as Chaldeans. Others, however, have attempted to develop links with groups that share their religious, linguistic, and cultural heritage, though not necessarily their Roman Catholic faith. Chaldeans who follow this tactic have attempted to link with other groups sharing the Aramaic language and the historic tie to the Assyrian or Babylonian heritage. Examples are Nestorian Christians in the Chicago Area, and a community of Assyrian Christians of several denominations, including Chaldean Catholics, living in Turlock, California.

For a variety of reasons, however, most Chaldean Americans have not embraced this identity. Perhaps the most important reason is the salience of the Roman Catholic faith for so many Chaldeans. For them it is preferable to relinquish the Chaldean identity for the dominant Roman Catholic designation, rather than exchange their religious tie for a linguistic one.

A more consequential factor, however, may lie in the size of the Chaldean American community in the Detroit area. Chaldean Americans do not need to find another group with which to link themselves. With over 70,000 of their background in a relatively limited geographic area, they are able to find many others who share not only a general but a very specific historic, linguistic, religious, and ancestral heritage. As the major concentration of Chaldeans in the United States, they need look no further than each other for a meaningful ethnic identity.

The media has recorded many cultural clashes between blacks and Chaldeans in the United States, which have resulted from Chaldean Americans operating stores in fundamentally urban, African American communities. The large grocery chains have found these areas unprofitable and have largely abandoned them, but they can be quite profitable when run as an extended family business. Many blacks feel that these stores overcharge, only hire Chaldeans, and neglect to reinvest into the community. The high prices usually result from having to make purchases in smaller quantities. Chaldeans also hire members of their own ethnic group because they are usually family members who demand less income. Some improvements have been made, however, as many Chaldean stores are increasingly hiring more African Americans, thus contributing to the community.

# RELIGION

Religion is of such importance in the Chaldean community that their name and identity derives from it. As full members of the Roman Catholic Church, Chaldeans follow the same rules and hold the same beliefs as other Catholics. However, they have their own leader, or patriarch, and the rituals used in their mass and other ceremonies are quite different from those practiced in the Western Church. Originally, they conducted services in the historic Chaldean/Aramaic language, but many services are now conducted in Arabic. Occasionally, masses are given in English for American-born persons of Chaldean ancestry.

The first Chaldean Church in the United States was founded in 1947 in Detroit. It was named "Mother of God," thus reaffirming the Chaldean split with their Nestorian heritage and their unity with Catholicism. More recently, the Church moved to Southfield, Michigan and was elevated to the status of a cathedral (Our Lady of Chaldeans Cathedral) when the Chaldean diocese of the United States was formed under the leadership of Chaldean Bishop Ibrahim Ibrahim. Prior to 1947, Chaldean immigrants usually attended services at Western rite Catholic Churches. For special events, such as weddings and holidays, many

Yousif Zallew, who has
lived in the United States
for 13 years, owns a small
grocery store in Detroit,
Michigan.

Chaldeans attended services at Lebanese Catholic Churches (of the Moronite Eastern rite), which share more in common with the Chaldean Church than Western rite Churches.

Chaldean children often attend Western rite Catholic Schools because the Chaldean rite does not offer such schools. This often requires parents to support two parishes, their own Chaldean church and the parish in which their children attend school. However, many children also attend special instruction in their own rite at the Chaldean Church.

According to Roman Catholic rules, members of the Catholic Church are expected to attend services and receive sacraments in their appropriate rite whenever possible. In practice, however, Catholics attend services at whichever Catholic Church is most convenient. Moreover, many priests of the Western rite can usually be persuaded to perform special ceremonies, such as weddings and funerals. Consequently, many Chaldeans have found it more convenient to

attend Western rite Catholic Churches, especially in areas where there is a small Chaldean population. As a result, many second and third generation Chaldean Americans are likely to prefer the more "American" services of Western Catholic Churches. Nonetheless, Chaldean Churches remains important for recent immigrants, for whom the Arabic language and the familiar rituals are still meaningful.

The Chaldean Church has also served as the center of community social life for the bulk of its existence. In addition to weddings, funerals, and baptisms, the Church offers special ceremonies for Chaldean children who received First Communion during the year and, in recent years, a graduation ceremony each spring honoring all Chaldean young people who graduated from high school or college during the year. Sunday services provide an opportunity for members of the community to meet one another and exchange greetings and gossip. The Church is also responsible for the formation of numerous organizations serving the community, including parish councils, family clubs, a men's club, a women's group, a business association, and youth groups.

# EMPLOYMENT AND ECONOMIC TRADITIONS

Chaldean Americans have traditionally owned and operated their own businesses, primarily grocery stores. As early as 1923, when only seven Chaldean men lived in the Detroit area, there were four Chaldean-owned stores. In the 1980s, it was estimated that over 1,000 Chaldean-owned grocery stores were located in Detroit and its environs. Because the grocery industry has become saturated, however, many Chaldean Americans have moved into related areas. Newer immigrants often own party stores and gas stations and immigrants who have been here many years, or their children and grandchildren, have moved into fields which serve the retail grocery trade, including wholesale food supply, marketing and maintenance of store fixtures (such as refrigeration equipment, freezers, burglar alarms), commercial real estate, business financing, and so on.

These are largely family-owned businesses. In some instances two stores owned by close relatives may work together in joint buying or advertising projects, but, for the most part, the stores are operated independently. These independent businesses are of extreme importance in the community as most family members assist in the family enterprise—even small children or immigrants who lack knowledge of English can make deliveries or stock shelves. This makes it unnecessary to hire other employees and helps to control business expenses. It also allows the family to assist other immigrants, who can be employed in the family business as soon as they arrive from the country of origin.

The role of these independent businesses in the welfare of the family and the growth of the ethnic community illustrates the influence of family over the individual. If the family store is to serve the purpose of assisting immigrants from the country of origin, then the family must be able to depend upon its members to play their role in its development. It cannot afford to have its most competent young people move into other lines of work. Consequently, many young Chaldeans who might have preferred other occupations were drawn into the grocery business. Most accepted this responsibility with little sense of loss, so great

is the influence of the Chaldean family over its members.

This pattern has changed somewhat as the second and third generations born in America have moved into different occupations. Many Chaldean Americans have joined such professions as medicine, dentistry, law, accounting, and teaching, to name a few. Some immigrants also come to this country with skills in other occupational areas. However, grocery stores continue to serve as a major meeting place for members of the community and concerns about the grocery business remain a major topic of conversation among Chaldean Americans. The time schedules of these stores also exert influence over community activities. For example, weddings, family gatherings, and Church activities tend to occur late in the evening in order to accommodate the late closing hour of most grocery and party stores.

# POLITICS AND GOVERNMENT

An established community, Chaldean Americans actively participate in local, state, and federal government by keeping abreast of government activity and voting regularly. They are also quite interested in events taking place in their homeland.

### EFFECT OF THE GULF WAR ON CHALDEAN AMERICANS

The most dramatic event to affect Chaldean Americans in some time occurred in 1991 and 1992, when hostilities broke out between Iraq and the United States. As the only major concentration of Iraqi immigrants in the United States, Chaldean Americans received a great deal of attention from the press, the military, and the general public. Reporters from throughout the world sought to interview community leaders concerning their views. Military representatives worried about the degree to which local Chaldeans might be security threats. Moreover, rumors spread that Chaldean Americans would be incarcerated in a camp in Louisiana as was done with the Japanese during the Second World War. Since Chaldean Americans and Arab Americans are linked together in the public mind, both were subjected to harassment by the general public, who saw them as local representatives of a hostile foreign power—in spite of the fact that many

Arab Americans immigrated from nations which were U.S. allies during the Gulf War.

For Chaldean Americans, who view themselves as committed Americans and do not identify strongly with either Iraq or the Arab World, the experience was distressing. The Gulf War was, in a real sense, a battle of brother against brother, since many families had sons in both the U.S. and Iraqi armies. Nearly all Chaldean Americans have relatives in Iraq; most had to wait weeks or months to learn whether they were safe. In particular, they were shocked by the carnival-type atmosphere of the War. The American public watched news reports of the hostilities like a sports event, and spoke of it in similar terms. Most distressing to Chaldean Americans, however, was the public's continued perception of their alliance with Arab Americans.

The Gulf War is likely to exert its effects on the Chaldean American community for some time. These effects will largely be seen in the areas of community growth and identity patterns. As a result of American resentment over the Gulf War, immigration from Iraq has slowed. If difficulties with Iraq continue, such restrictions will also endure, making it difficult for additional Chaldeans to join their families in this country.

# MEDIA

**PRINT**

*Arrafideyn Newspaper.*
Contact: Abdulk Halik Alfalah, Editor.
Address: 19204 Woodward, Detroit, Michigan 48203.
Telephone: (313) 893-3521.

*Chaldean Detroit Times.*
Contact: Amir Denha, Publisher and Editor.
Telephone: (313) 552-1989.

*Chaldean Voice Weekly Bulletin.*
Contact: Father Manuel Boji.
Address: 25585 Berg Road, Southfield, Michigan 48034.
Telephone: (810) 356-0565.

**RADIO**

**WCAR-AM (1090).**
Known as the Chaldean Voice, this station broadcasts to Michigan's large Chaldean American community.

Address: 32500 Parklane Boulevard, Garden City, Michigan 48135.
Telephone: (313) 525-1111.

**TELEVISION**

**WGPR-TV (Channel 62).**
Arab American Television.

Contact: Faisal Arabo, President.
Address: 3140 East Jefferson, Detroit, Michigan 48207.
Telephone: (313) 352-1343.

# ORGANIZATIONS AND ASSOCIATIONS

**Arab American & Chaldean Communities Social Council.**
Contact: Haifa Fakhouri, Director.
Address: 28551 Southfield Road, Lathrup Village, Michigan 48076.
Telephone: (313) 874-2320.

**Chaldean American Crusaders.**
Contact: Robert Garbara, President.
Address: 25626 Telegraph Road, Southfield, Michigan 48034.
Telephone: (810) 573-7499.

**Chaldean Federation of America.**
Functions as an umbrella organization for most Chaldean American groups.

Contact: Sam Yono, Chairman; or Kam Kewson, Director.
Address: 25626 Telegraph Road, Southfield, Michigan 48034.
Telephone: (810) 557-3200.

**Our Lady of Chaldeans Cathedral.**
Contact: Bishop Ibrahim Ibrahim.
Address: 25585 Berg Road, Southfield, Michigan 48076.
Telephone: (810) 356-0565.

# SOURCES FOR ADDITIONAL STUDY

Adeney, W. F. *The Greek and Eastern Churches.* Clifton, New Jersey: Reference Book Publishers, 1965.

Aswad, B. C. *Arabic-Speaking Communities in American Cities.* New York: Center for Migration

Studies and Association of Arab-American University Graduates, 1974.

Attwater, D. *Christian Churches of the East,* two volumes, revised edition. Milwaukee, Wisconsin: Bruce Publishing Co., 1947.

Ibrahim, S. E., and N. S. Hopkins. *Arab Society in Transition.* Cairo: The American University in Cairo, 1977.

Nolte, R. H. *The Modern Middle East.* New York: Atherton Press, 1963.

Rabban, R. "Chaldean Rite," in *New Catholic Encyclopedia* 3. New York: McGraw-Hill, 1967.

Sengstock, M. C. *The Chaldean-Americans: Changing Conceptions of Ethnic Identity.* New York: Center for Migration Studies, 1982.

# CHEROKEES

**by**

**Robert J. Conley**

The process of
acculturation began
early for the
Cherokees with the
introduction of
European trade
goods in 1673.

## OVERVIEW

The Cherokee Nation today occupies all or part of 14 counties of what is now the northeastern portion of the state of Oklahoma. Not considered a reservation, the land falls under what has been called "a checkerboard jurisdiction," with one farm or acreage falling under tribal jurisdiction while its neighbor is under that of the state. A second and separate federally recognized tribal government for Cherokees, the United Keetoowah Band of Cherokees in Oklahoma, exists in the same area. There is also a Cherokee reservation in North Carolina for the Eastern Band of Cherokees. In addition to the three federally recognized Cherokee governments, there are numerous groups throughout the United States who claim to be Cherokee bands or tribes. There are also thousands of individuals claiming Cherokee ancestry who are not associated with any group. Although the Cherokee people today are divided geographically, culturally, and politically, the vast majority of Cherokees—who number over 150,000—are affiliated with the Cherokee Nation.

## HISTORY

The word Cherokee is believed to have evolved from a Choctaw word meaning "Cave People." It was picked up and used by Europeans and eventu-

This portrait of a Cherokee man was taken on a North Carolina reservation on September 23, 1938.

ally accepted and adopted by Cherokees in the form of *Tsalagi* or *Jalagi*. Traditionally, the people now known as Cherokee refer to themselves as *ani-yun-wiya*, a name usually translated as "the Real People," sometimes "the Original People." Earliest historical data locates the Cherokees in a vast area of what is now the southeastern United States, with about 200 towns scattered throughout the present states of Alabama, Georgia, Kentucky, North Carolina, South Carolina, Virginia, and West Virginia. Cherokee oral tradition tells of a time when the Cherokees were ruled over by a powerful priesthood called the *ani-Kutani*. When the priests took away a young man's wife, he organized a revolt and all the priests were killed. Since then, according to the tale, the Cherokees have had a democratic government.

The Cherokees' first experience with the invading white man was almost certainly a brief encounter with the deadly expeditionary force of Spanish explorer Hernando DeSoto in 1540. English colonial traders began to appear among the Cherokees around 1673. Such interactions produced some mixed marriages, usually between a white trader and a Cherokee woman.

Three trends mark Cherokee history during the eighteenth and nineteenth centuries: war with the colonists (beginning in 1711); epidemics of European disease (primarily smallpox); and the continual cession of land (beginning in 1775). The Cherokees were forced to sign one treaty after another with the new United States govern-

ment, each one giving away more land to the new nation. As early as 1803, President Thomas Jefferson planned to move all eastern Indians to a location west of the Mississippi River, and signed an agreement with the state of Georgia promising to accomplish that deed as soon as possible. Andrew Jackson actually set the so-called "Removal Process" in motion. In the meantime the government had been doing everything in its power to convince Cherokees to move west voluntarily, and the first to do so were the faction known as Chickamaugans. Other migrations followed in the late eighteenth and early nineteenth centuries.

The vast majority of the Cherokees, however, remained in their ancestral homelands. In 1835 the United States Congress passed the Removal Act. The Cherokee Nation, by this time under the administration of Principal Chief John Ross, refused to recognize the validity or the legality of the Removal Act, and challenged it in court. The U.S. Supreme Court ruled in favor of the Cherokee Nation. President Jackson is reported to have said, "Justice Marshall has made his decision. Now let him enforce it." Jackson then sent negotiators into the Cherokee Nation to secure a treaty whereby they would give up all of their land in the east for land out west. Since the government of the Cherokee Nation refused to negotiate, the treaty was signed by other Cherokees without authorization. The United States called the treaty a legal document and proceeded to force the Cherokees to live up to its terms.

Jackson ordered the U.S. Army to forcibly remove the Cherokees from their homelands in 1838. People were taken out of their homes and herded like cattle into stockades to await removal. Conditions were crowded and unsanitary, and many died in these prisons. The forced march began later that same year. Approximately 20,000 Cherokees were marched west over what would soon be known as the "Trail of Tears." Along the way, approximately 4,000 people died. A few managed to escape by hiding out in the mountains. In the west, the Cherokee divided into two major factions. The Cherokees who had signed the removal treaty and all of their friends, allies, and associates had become known as the Treaty Party. They had moved west voluntarily in 1835 after having signed the treaty. The followers of Chief John Ross, who had suffered the forced removal, were known as the Ross Party. These two factions started a civil war that lasted until 1843. At the end of this domestic strife the Cherokees started over and rebuilt their Nation. Tahlequah was established as the capital city.

They built new homes, schools, and churches, and even though they had a treaty with the United States, which promised that they would be left alone, that was not to be.

The Cherokee Nation was dragged into the white man's Civil War. Chief John Ross begged the United States to send troops to protect its neutrality as promised in the treaty, but the troops never came. Under pressure from former Treaty Party members turned Confederate Cherokees, Ross was forced to sign a treaty with the Confederacy. Following the Civil War, the United States used that treaty as an excuse to punish the Cherokee Nation, forcing it to sign yet another treaty and to give up more land. Certain governmental powers were also taken away from the Cherokee Nation. The Cherokee Nation, along with the Choctaw Nation, the Chickasaw Nation, the Creek Nation, and the Seminole Nation were organized into "Indian Territory."

Over the next half century the powers of the so-called Five Civilized Tribes that made up the Indian Territory were further eroded by the United States. In 1907, against the wishes of nearly all of the traditional full-blood people of all five tribes, Indian Territory was combined with Oklahoma Territory to its west to form the new state of Oklahoma.

From the beginning, the United States had no intention of dealing with Indians in the new state. The tribal governments were all but abolished and likely would have been but for the complications of transferring land titles. The President of the United States began appointing Chiefs for the five tribes when the government had need of a signature to make the transfers legal. Several appointments were made only long enough to obtain the desired signature and these appointees became known as "Chiefs for a day."

### MODERN ERA

In 1973, President Richard Nixon indicated that the Cherokees had the right to vote, revitalizing the Cherokee Nation but creating the uncomfortable situation of having two Cherokee (the other, the United Keetoowan Band of Cherokee Indians in Oklahoma, was founded in the 1950s) governments in the same location, with the same jurisdiction, and basically the same constituency. A conflict over political issues developed, with both sides claiming to be the only legal government for Cherokees in Oklahoma. Since then, the Cherokee Nation has grown and prospered, making its most impressive strides under the leadership of Principal Chief Wilma P. Mankiller (1945- ).

The Cherokee Nation today operates under a constitution, with a chief executive called the Principal Chief, a legislature called the Tribal Council, and a judicial branch called a tribunal made up of three tribal justices. From its humble condition in the 1970s, the Cherokee Nation has grown to massive proportions, employing 1,300 people, 85 percent of whom are Cherokees with a $1.6 million monthly payroll.

# ACCULTURATION AND ASSIMILATION

The process of acculturation began early for the Cherokees with the introduction of European trade goods in 1673. Steel pots and knives, tomahawks, glass beads, manufactured cloth, guns, and gunpowder gradually replaced traditional products of native manufacture. Trade with Europeans also changed hunting practices, calling for large numbers of pelts and quickly endangering the population of many game animals. Clothing styles changed.

Intermarriage with whites caused a drastic change in family structure for many Cherokees. The Cherokees have a matrilineal clan structure, a family in which descent is traced through the female line. This type of family structure was undermined by the insistence of white males to be considered heads of households, and to pass along their own surnames to their offspring. They were supported in this by the efforts of the missionaries.

When pressure for removal became intense in the 1820s and 1830s, a significant portion of the Cherokees, believing that their white neighbors wanted them removed because they were "savage," began a conscious effort to make themselves over and become "civilized." They hired teachers from universities in the northeast and invited missionaries to come into the Cherokee country and teach and preach. These people became known as "Progressives," and their efforts, combined with the acculturation and assimilation process that had begun in 1673, accelerated and was tremendously successful in changing lifestyles.

The changes that occurred because of this effort were so pervasive that, following the Trail of Tears, with removal pressures no longer a factor, the Cherokees continued their new ways. In the west, they built homes more or less like the homes of white men. They built churches, divided the new country into voting districts, and wrote a new constitution.

Many Cherokees became farmers, ranchers, merchants, bankers, and lawyers. In many ways, the Cherokee Nation mirrored the larger United States. Some have said that the Cherokee Nation imitated the United States and then improved on it. The largest single item on the national budget was education. Cherokee legislators could not vote themselves a raise. The Cherokee Nation established the first free, compulsory public school system, established the first institution of higher learning west of the Mississippi River, and installed the first telephone west of the Mississippi. So successful was the Cherokee Nation and impressive were its accomplishments along these lines, that people have been heard to say that "the Cherokees all became white," or "everybody in Oklahoma is part Indian, usually Cherokee." Yet, age-old Cherokee beliefs and customs survived in traditional full-blood communities in remote locations almost completely unknown to the outside world.

## TRADITIONS, CUSTOMS, AND BELIEFS

Some Cherokees today are almost indistinguishable from white people, and their customs, habits, and beliefs reflect those of mainstream America. But traditional Cherokees gather at various "stomp grounds," which are consecrated, ceremonial grounds. Each ground has its own set of religious leaders. The ceremony performed there is a series of dances, done in a counter-clockwise direction around the sacred fire all night long. Attendance at the stomp grounds declined for many years, but since the 1970s it seems to have been increasing. Although stomp dancers were very secretive for years, there are now some groups who perform publicly to educate the general population, Cherokee and others, regarding traditional Cherokee ways and beliefs.

## INTERACTION WITH OTHER ETHNIC MINORITIES

Because of the long history of intermarriage, and because of the nature of the division of land in eastern Oklahoma, Cherokees have long been used to interacting with non-Cherokees. In fact, Cherokees always seem to have been willing to accept outsiders into their ranks, some might say, too willingly. Tahlequah, for example, appears to

have a large white population, but much of that population consists of old mixed-blood families, and many of them are officially tribal members. There are also Indians from other tribes who have moved into Tahlequah: Creeks, Kiowas, Osages, and even Navajos. Some of that is the result of intermarriage, some is not. There is a significant Hispanic population in Tahlequah today, and a small black population. Both of these groups have had trouble fitting in. They have not been readily accepted by the Cherokees, full- or mixed-blood, nor by the local whites, although there is seldom any overt racism displayed.

## EDUCATION

Before Oklahoma statehood took over or closed down almost all of its institutions, the Cherokee Nation had its own school system. The Cherokee Nation had produced more college graduates than its neighboring states of Arkansas and Texas combined. Oklahoma statehood and the state's public school system changed all that. According to the 1970 census, the average adult Cherokee had only five and one-half years of school. Fewer than 70 years of Oklahoma public schools had been devastating for Cherokees. Up until very recent times, Cherokee students, upon being enrolled in the first grade, were automatically placed in slow-learner classrooms. Cherokee high school students were not encouraged to apply for college and were not taken on trips with the white students to visit college campuses. Some Cherokee students attended government boarding schools for Indians, but the majority were in public schools.

Since the revitalization of the Cherokee Nation, there has been gradual, steady improvement in the area of education. Programs have been instituted in the public schools for Cherokee students because of pressures from the Cherokee Nation and because of the availability of federal funds for such programs. The Cherokee Nation has taken over Sequoyah High School, a former federally run boarding school, and is operating it for Indian students in Tahlequah. The Cherokee Nation also has established a complete pre-school program for Cherokee children from age three until they are ready to enter the first grade. There is also a Cherokee Nation higher education program to assist Cherokees in attending college. Many of the public schools that formerly discouraged Cherokee students now have Cherokee teachers, counselors, administrators, and other personnel on their staffs. Most Cherokees still attend public schools (several of which have up to

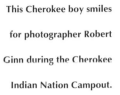
This Cherokee boy smiles for photographer Robert Ginn during the Cherokee Indian Nation Campout.

90 percent Cherokee enrollment), but over the last 20 years or so, the situation there for Cherokees has greatly improved.

## CUISINE

Cherokees were traditionally an agrarian people, maintaining a town garden and individual garden plots. The women did most of the tending of crops, but then the women owned the gardens and the homes. They planted a wide variety of beans, pumpkins, squash, and corn. In addition to the growing of crops, women gathered many wild plants for food, including wild onions and greens, mushrooms, berries, grapes, and nuts.

Deer was the main animal hunted for meat, but bear, buffalo, elk, squirrel, rabbit, opossum, and other animals were also killed for food. Early on, the Cherokees began raising cattle, hogs, chickens, and other domesticated animals acquired from Europeans. The contemporary Cherokee diet is not that much different from that of the general population of the United States, although at special gatherings one will find wild onions and eggs, bean bread, fry bread, grape dumplings, and possibly fried crawdads (crayfish). A special treat is *kanuche*, made by pounding whole hickory nuts, boiling them in water and straining the hulls out, resulting in a rich broth. *Kanuche* may be mixed with hominy, corn, or rice.

## TRADITIONAL COSTUMES

Cherokee men once wore only a breechcloth and moccasins in warm weather. In colder weather they added leggings and a fringed hunting jacket. Chiefs and priests wore long, full cloaks made of feathers and feather caps (not the traditional and popular plains Indian headdress). The men shaved their heads, leaving a topknot (sometimes called a scalplock), which they allowed to grow long, and often their bodies and faces were tattooed. In warm weather women wore only a short skirt and added a poncho-like top during the winter. Styles changed in the early nineteenth century as a result of trade with Europeans. Women began to make and wear long dresses and blouses of manufactured trade cloth, and men began wearing shirts and jackets of cloth. They also added colorful turbans. By the 1880s, most of that distinctive clothing had been abandoned and Cherokees dressed mostly like frontier whites.

Today, for special occasions, some Cherokee men will don ribbon shirts, a contemporary pan-Indian item. A few may even dress up in hunting jackets and turbans. Women may wear traditional "tear dresses," so named because the pattern calls for tearing the fabric along straight lines rather than cutting with scissors.

## CHEROKEE DANCES AND SONGS

The stomp dance, which has already been discussed, is a religious activity. No Cherokee social dances have survived, but some Cherokees have joined in the pan-Indian practice of pow wow dancing. When Cherokee singing is announced, it is almost always gospel singing in the Cherokee language. It is possible today, though, to hear stomp dance songs sung without actually attending a stomp dance. At least one old Cherokee lullaby has survived. Barbara McAlester, a Cherokee opera singer, sometimes performs it as part of her concerts.

## HOLIDAYS CELEBRATED BY CHEROKEE

In the old days, certain ceremonies were performed at specific times of the year, and they included songs and dances. The largest of these was the Green Corn Dance, celebrating the beginning of spring. Today, the Cherokee Nation observes one annual holiday on September 6, which marks the anniversary of the adoption of the new constitution following the Trail of Tears. It reunited those Cherokees who had moved west on their own before the Trail of Tears with the main body of the Cherokees under the administration of Chief John Ross. For convenience, this holiday is celebrated over the Labor Day weekend in Tahlequah, Oklahoma, and is attended each year by thousands of people from all over the world. Activities include a parade through downtown Tahlequah, a State of the Nation address by the Principal Chief, traditional games, concerts, and arts and crafts shows.

## HEALTH AND MENTAL HEALTH ISSUES

A traditional Cherokee says that there was a time long ago when there was no disease in the world. Then there came a time when human beings developed weapons. When the Cherokee got these new weapons, bows and arrows especially, they were able to kill many more animals than before. One day the animals called a council to discuss this problem. They all agreed that the people had to kill animals in order to obtain food for their survival but they also agreed that the Cherokees were killing too many animals too casually. They decided that a hunter should have to take his killing more seriously. He should pray and fast and go through a prescribed ritual. Then he should kill only what he needed and afterward he should apologize to the spirit of the slain animal. If a hunter failed to show the proper respect and neglected to do any of these prescribed things, the animal spirits would strike him with some dread-ful disease. So horrible were some of the diseases the animals came up with that the plants, having overheard the council, each decided to provide a cure for one of the specific diseases that the animals had proposed.

Traditional Cherokee healers, like those of other American Indian tribes, have always been expert at the medicinal use of plants. But a traditional Cherokee cure almost always involves more than just the use of the plant medicine. It involves the ritualistic use of words and sometimes specific actions. Many traditional Cherokees still go to these Indian doctors to cure their ills.

With the arrival of Europeans came European diseases that the Cherokee doctors did not know how to cure. A belief developed that it takes a white doctor to cure a white man's disease. Indian beliefs also were generally undermined by missionaries, school systems, government programs, and intermarriage. Many Cherokees began to depend for health care, either exclusively or in part, on white doctors.

For many years, the health of American Indians was in the hands of the United States government through its Indian Health Service (IHS). In recent years, however, tribes have begun contracting with the IHS to administer these services themselves. There are still two IHS hospitals in the Cherokee Nation, one in Claremore, Oklahoma, and one in Tahlequah. In addition, the Cherokee Nation has its own Health Division, which operates five rural health clinics and a number of other health programs.

Cherokees, like other American Indians, generally face the same health problems as anyone else. For example, heart disease is a major problem, and it has recently been projected that by the year 2000, Acquired Immune Deficiency Syndrome (AIDS) will be a matter of primary concern. Cherokees, again like other American Indians, have a high occurrence of diabetes, perhaps as a result of dietary habits fostered by outside influences such as government boarding schools and the government's food distribution program for Indians.

# LANGUAGE

The Cherokee language belongs to the Iroquoian family of languages and is therefore related to Mohawk, Seneca, Onondaga, Oneida, Cayuga, and Tuscarora, among others. It is a complex and difficult language; in his *Cherokee—English Dictio-*

*nary*, for example, Durbin Feeling lists 126 forms of a single verb. Cherokee has been a written language at least since 1821, when Sequoyah (c. 1770-1843), a Cherokee, produced a syllabary for that purpose. (A syllabary is a writing system in which each symbol stands for an entire syllable. In the Cherokee syllabary, for instance, the symbol "A" stands for the sound "go.") Although Sequoyah is credited with inventing the syllabary, some Cherokees have taken exception with that claim, maintaining that the syllabary is an ancient Cherokee writing system which was kept secret until Sequoyah decided to make it public. Soon afterward, almost the entire Cherokee population became literate, and in 1828, the Nation began publishing a bilingual newspaper, the *Cherokee Phoenix*.

Today, the Cherokee language is still in wide use. It is used in the Indian churches and at the stomp grounds, and many children still grow up with Cherokee as their first language, learning English when they go to school. Bilingual education programs in the public schools also encourage continued use of the language.

## GREETINGS AND OTHER POPULAR EXPRESSIONS

*Osiyo* or *'siyo* is usually translated as "hello" and it may be followed by *Tohiiu?*—How are you? (Are you well?). One response is *tohigwu*—I am well. *Wado* is "thank you." *Howa* means all right, or okay. "Man" is *asgaya*; "boy" is *achuja*. "Woman" is *agehyuh* and "girl," *agehyuja*. "Cherokee Nation" is translated as *Chalagihi Ayehli* (or *Jalagihi Ayehli*), using the "Cherokeeized" version of the word *Cherokee* (with the place ending "hi") and the versatile word *ayehli*, which can mean "center," "soul," or "nation."

# RELIGION

The ancient Cherokee belief system described a world that was flat and floating on water. This is the world that we live on. Above it is a Sky Vault made of stone, which might be pictured as a bowl turned upside down over a saucer. The original life forms, all spirit beings, and the souls of the departed live on top of the Sky Vault. Life up there is like that down here.

There is a world underneath the one we inhabit. It is the opposite of this one. When it is winter on earth, it is summer down there. When it is night here, it is daytime there. There are also many powerful and potentially destructive spirit forces below.

It would be a mistake to see these two Cherokee spirit worlds as heaven and hell. They are not defined as good and evil, although the one below is seen as tremendously chaotic. They are thought of simply as being opposed to one another. We live our lives between them in a constant state of precarious balance. Because of this dangerous situation, the most important aspect of life in this traditional Cherokee view is to maintain balance and harmony. Almost all old habits, rituals, and ceremonies are designed and practiced to that end. The world is seen as existing in pairs of opposites: light and dark; day and night; summer and winter; male and female; earth and sky; fire and water. All things must be kept in their proper place and in balance with their opposites. A mixture of opposites results in pollution and to avoid disaster, they must be followed by some sort of cleansing ceremony.

If the Cherokees are religious, in a Christian way, they might be Methodist, Presbyterian, Unitarian, or any other Christian denomination. Among the more traditional Cherokees is a large group of Cherokee Baptists. Cherokee Baptists attend what are called "Indian churches," in which they make use of a Cherokee-language New Testament and a Cherokee-language hymnal. Services are conducted in the Cherokee language. In fact, the Cherokee Baptist church has been credited with saving the Cherokee language from extinction, and although the truth of that claim is subject to debate, certainly the church has played a significant role in that area. Very often, when Cherokees talk about traditional people, they are talking about Cherokee Baptists.

# EMPLOYMENT AND ECONOMIC TRADITIONS

This discussion will focus on the more traditional Cherokees, those who live in Cherokee communities and are visibly Indian. Employment opportunities are limited for these people because they tend to stay at home. They would rather be around their families and friends and remain a part of their community than seek better opportunities elsewhere. For these Cherokees, unemployment figures are high. Major employers in the area are large nurseries in Cherokee County, Oklahoma, and large chicken processing plants in

Arkansas. The Cherokee Nation also has become a major employer in the area. But there still are not enough jobs to go around. Low-income people living in rural areas often lack dependable transportation, so even if they can secure jobs, they may not be able to hold on to them.

The Cherokee Nation offers job training programs, but once an individual is trained for a job, if there is no such opening in the area and he/she does not want to move, he/she is no better off than before. Some people have gone through several job training programs, becoming qualified carpenters, plumbers, and electricians, and yet remain unemployed. Many people mow lawns, cut firewood, and accept various odd jobs in order to support their families. They still hunt, and they still gather wild food plants.

# POLITICS AND GOVERNMENT

The governmental structure of the Cherokee Nation already has been described. This section will focus on political issues. Because membership in the Cherokee Nation has no blood percentage requirement but is based strictly on lineal descent from any person listed as Cherokee on the so-called Dawes Roll (the roll prepared by the United States government's Dawes Commission for purposes of land allotment in preparation for Oklahoma statehood) many Cherokees complain that too many white people (usually Cherokees with less than one-fourth Cherokee blood) take advantage of Cherokee programs.

The Indian Self-determination Act, known as PL 93-638, allows Indian tribes to contract with the federal government either through the Bureau of Indian Affairs or Indian Health Service to operate programs for themselves, which have been previously operated by either of these two government bureaus.

The Cherokee Nation has been taking advantage of this law since the 1970s and has contracted nearly all of the available government programs. There has been discussion for several years about the possibility of the Cherokee Nation's contracting to run the Indian hospitals within its jurisdiction. Some Cherokees, including some hospital employees, are strongly opposed to such a move, saying that the Cherokee Nation is not prepared to run the hospitals.

State governments seem to be almost constantly making attempts to encroach into the area of tribal jurisdiction. They want to impose state hunting and fishing regulations on tribal members. They want to collect various kinds of taxes from tribal members or from the tribes themselves. Indians do not pay income tax, federal or state, unless their income is derived strictly from business activity that takes place on land that is still held in trust by the federal government for the Indian owner. Issues of state infringement on tribal sovereignty, in which the Cherokee Nation has been involved in recent years, includes the state's attempt to tax tobacco sales at Indian smoke shops, and the state's attempt to regulate Indian gaming. The Cherokee Nation operates high stakes Bingo parlors.

In terms of American politics, there are Cherokee Democrats and Cherokee Republicans. There were Cherokee supporters of H. Ross Perot and, very likely, there are Cherokee Populists and Cherokee Anarchists. Cherokees are seldom if ever of one mind on any given issue. When it comes to national politics they will only come close to a consensus if the issue at hand is one of tribal sovereignty. For example, every so often a congressman will introduce a bill to abrogate all Indian treaties and terminate all tribal governments. Most likely, nearly all Cherokees would unite in opposing such a bill.

# INDIVIDUAL AND GROUP CONTRIBUTIONS

Although the Cherokee Nation is but one of over 300 American Indian tribes in the United States, the Cherokees have produced a significant number of prominent people in various areas. In addition to those individuals listed below, any number of other prominent Americans, and at least one Englishman, have claimed Cherokee descent at one time or another: Tom Mix, Monte Blue, John Nance Garner, Iron Eyes Cody, Walter Brennan, Johnny Cash, Burt Reynolds, James Garner, Willie Nelson, Oral Roberts, Cher, Anita Bryant, Loretta Lynn, Kevin Costner, Sir Winston Churchill, and President Bill Clinton.

## ART

Cherokee artists and artists of Cherokee descent include Cecil Dick (1915-1992); George Cochran (1911-1992); Willard Stone (1916-1990); Anna Mitchell; Bill Glass, Sr.; Bill Glass, Jr. (1950- ); Virginia Stroud (1951- ); Jeanne Walker Rorex

(1951- ); Bill Rabbit (1946- ); Robert Annesley (1943- ); Jane Osti; Bert Seabourne (1931- ); Joan Hill (1930- ); Murv Jacob (1945- ); and Janna Jacob (1976- ).

## FILM, TELEVISION, AND THEATER

Frank Boudinot (d. circa 1864) moved to New York City in the first half of the nineteenth century to become a professional actor; he used the stage name of Frank Starr; during the Civil War, he was an officer in the Union Army and died of wounds received during that conflict. Victor Daniels (1899-1955), using the professional name Chief Thundercloud, was a successful film actor for over 20 years; among other roles, he played Tonto in the early *Lone Ranger* films and Chiricahua Apache tribal leader Geronimo in a 1939 version of that story. Clu Gulager (1928-), whose first name is a version of *tlu-tlu*, the Cherokee word for a purple martin, is a veteran film and television actor, perhaps best remembered for his role of Deputy, later Sheriff, Ryker on the long-running television series "The Virginian," his first series was "The Tall Man," in which he played Billy the Kid, and his films include *The Killers* and *The Last Picture Show*. Wes Studi (1947- ), full-blood Cherokee, has received critical acclaim for his portrayals of Magua in *The Last of the Mohicans*, (1992) and of Geronimo in the 1994 film *Geronimo: An American Legend*. Arthur Junaluska (1918- ), Eastern Cherokee, was an actor, playwright, and theatrical director. Dennis Weaver (1924- ), film and television actor, known for his role as Chester on the long-running television series "Gunsmoke", and McCloud in the television series by that same name. Will Rogers (1879-1935) could be categorized in any number of ways; he was a performer in Wild West shows and on stage, later becoming a film actor, radio personality, and nationally syndicated newspaper columnist; during his lifetime, he was probably the best loved man in America, if not in the entire world.

## LITERATURE

Sequoyah, inventor of the Cherokee syllabary, was born in the old Cherokee country and moved west before the Trail of Tears, and he apparently died somewhere in Mexico. Contemporary Cherokee writers include Norman H. Russell (1921- ), poet and educator, author of *Indian Thoughts*; Robert J. Conley (1940- ), the award-winning author of *Mountain Windsong, Nickajack, The Real People* series of novels, and others; Marilou Awiakta

(1936- ), poet, storyteller, and author of *Abiding Appalachia, Rising Fawn and the Fire Mystery*, and *Selu: Seeking the Corn Mother's Wisdom*; Diane Glancy (1941- ), poet and novelist, and author of *Firesticks*; Jean Hager (1932- ), award-winning author of *Grandfather Medicine, Night Walker*, and others; Carroll Arnette/Gogisgi (1927- ), poet, and teacher, author of *Rounds, Tsalagi, South Line, Engine*, and others; Robin Coffee (1955- ), poet, and author of *Voices of the Heart, Sacred Seasons*, and others; Ralph Salisbury (1926- ), poet, teacher, and author of *A White Rainbow, Spirit Beast Chant, Pointing at the Rainbow*, and others; Gladys Cardiff (1942- ), Eastern Cherokee poet and author of *To Frighten a Storm*; Ron Rogers (1948- ), poet and writer of short fiction; Thomas King (1944- ), screenwriter, novelist, and author of *Green Grass and Running Water*; Rayna Green (1942- ), writer, folklorist, and editor of *That's What She Said: Contemporary Poetry and Fiction by Native American Women*; Geary Hobson (1941- ), educator, writer, critic, author of *Deer Hunting and Other Poems*, and editor of *The Remembered Earth: An Anthology of Contemporary American Indian Literature*; Lynn Riggs (1899-1954), playwright, and author of *Green Grow the Lilacs*, which later became the Rogers and Hammerstein musical, *Oklahoma*.

## MILITARY

Admiral Joseph James (Jocko) Clark (1893-1971), a World War II naval hero, was commander of the seventh fleet during the Korean conflict.

## MUSIC

Jack F. Kilpatrick (1915-1967) was a noted composer and long-time professor of musicology at Southern Methodist University; in addition, with his wife Anna, Kilpatrick wrote several books dealing with Cherokee tales and Cherokee language texts. Barbara McAlester is an opera singer who was born in Oklahoma and currently lives in New York City; she has performed around the world.

# MEDIA

## PRINT

### The Cherokee Advocate.
The official newspaper of the Cherokee Nation.

Contact: Lynn M. Howard, Editor.
Address: P.O. Box 948, Tahlequah, Oklahoma 74465.
Telephone: (918) 456-0671.
Fax: (918) 456-6485.

### The Cherokee One-Feather.

The official publication of the Eastern Band of Cherokee Indians featuring news of interest to the local Cherokee tribe and to American Indians in general.

Contact: Richard L. Welch, Editor.
Address: P.O. Box 501, Cherokee, North Carolina 28719.
Telephone: (704) 497-5513.
Fax: (704) 497-4810.

### Cherokee Tribune.

Community weekly newspaper founded in 1934.

Contact: Jim Hilliard, Publisher.
Address: Neighbor Newspaper, Inc. P.O. Box 449, Marietta, Georgia 30061.
Telephone: (404) 428-9411.

### Journal of Cherokee Studies.

Covers historical and cultural research of Cherokees.

Contact: Duane H. King, Editor.
Address: Museum of the Cherokee Indian, P.O. Box 1599, Cherokee, North Carolina 28719.
Telephone: (704) 497-3481.

### Twin Territories.

Privately published, it deals largely with historical material on the so-called Five Civilized Tribes.

Address: P.O. Box 1426, Muskogee, Oklahoma 74402.

# ORGANIZATIONS AND ASSOCIATIONS

**The Cherokee Nation.**
Address: P.O. Box 948, Tahlequah, Oklahoma 74465.

**Cherokee National Historical Society (CNHS).**
Seeks to interest the public in Cherokee history; operates Cherokee Heritage Center, which includes the Cherokee National Museum, and Cherokee Arboretum and Herb Garden (including trees and plants used traditionally by Cherokees for food, fiber, and medicines).

Contact: Troy Wayne Poteete, Executive Director.

Address: P.O. Box 515, Tahlequah, Oklahoma 74465.
Telephone: (918) 456-6007.

**The Eastern Band of Cherokee Indians.**
Address: P.O. Box 455, Cherokee, North Carolina 28719.

**The United Keetoowah Band of Cherokees in Oklahoma.**
Address: 2450 South Muskogee Avenue, Tahlequah, Oklahoma 74464.

# MUSEUMS AND RESEARCH CENTERS

Notable Cherokee museums include: The Cherokee Museum in Cherokee, North Carolina; the Cherokee National Museum and the Five Civilized Tribes Museum in Tahlequah, Oklahoma.

# SOURCES FOR ADDITIONAL STUDY

Bird, Traveller. *Tell Them They Lie: The Sequoyah Myth*. Los Angeles: Westernlore Press, 1971.

Brown, John P. *Old Frontiers: The Story of the Cherokee Indians from Earliest Times to the Date of Their Removal to the West, 1838*. Kingsport, Tennessee: Southern Publishers, 1938.

Collier, Peter. *When Shall They Rest? The Cherokees' Long Struggle with America*. New York: Holt, Rinehart, and Winston, 1973.

Conley, Robert J. *The Witch of Goingsnake and Other Stories*. Norman, Oklahoma: University of Oklahoma Press, 1988.

Cunningham, Frank H. *General Stand Watie's Confederate Indians*. San Antonio: Naylor Company, 1959.

Feeling, Durbin. *Cherokee-English Dictionary*. Tahlequah, Oklahoma: The Cherokee Nation, 1975.

Fogelson, Raymond D. *The Cherokees: A Critical Bibliography*. Bloomington: Indiana University Press, 1978.

Foreman, Grant. *Indians and Pioneers*. Norman: University of Oklahoma Press, 1930.

Kilpatrick, Jack Frederick, and Anna Gritts. *Walk in Your Soul: Love Incantations of the Oklahoma Cherokees*. Dallas: Southern Methodist University Press, 1964.

Mankiller, Wilma P., and Michael Wallis. *Mankiller: A Chief and Her People*. New York: St. Martin's Press, 1993.

Mooney, James. *Myths of the Cherokee*. Washington, D.C.: Seventh Annual Report of the Bureau of American Ethnology, 1891.

Many Chilean American immigrants were political exiles who, as a group, were well-educated and highly-skilled.

# CHILEAN AMERICANS

by
Phyllis J. Burson

## OVERVIEW

A country slightly larger than Texas, Chile is located on the west coast of South America. Its land mass measures 292,258 square miles (756,945 sq. km.) and is bounded by Peru on the north, Bolivia and Argentina on the east, and the South Pacific Ocean on the West. Chile is a long, narrow country, about 100 miles wide and 2,600 miles long.

The population is approximately 13.75 million. Ninety-five percent are of European-Indian (mestizo) and European origin. Three percent are Indian and two percent are of other descent. Over 80 percent of the people live in urban areas. Almost 90 percent of the population are Roman Catholic and about ten percent are Protestant. A small percentage are of the Judaic faith. Virtually all of the people speak Spanish. Santiago, in central Chile, is the capital city and Valparaíso is the largest port. Mining, agriculture, light manufacturing, and fish products are important to the economy. The national flag is based on the design of the U.S. flag and is divided in half horizontally. The upper left two-thirds contains a white star on a blue background, to the right of which is solid white. The lower half is red. The national flower is the copihue, a member of the rose family.

## HISTORY

The name Chile comes from an Indian word meaning "land's end," and indicates that Chile stretches to the tip of South America. Indian groups migrated into the area of modern Chile at least 10,000 years ago. In the early fifteenth century A.D. the Incan empire began to expand from its center in Peru into present-day Chile. At the height of the empire, it stretched 3,000 miles along the Andes, extending into what is now southern Chile. The Incan advance was halted by the Mapuche Indians, who still live in Southern Chile, and by the Spanish, who invaded the Incan capital in present-day Peru in 1532. The first Europeans began to explore Chile in 1535, claiming it for the Spanish crown in 1536 and founding Santiago in 1541. Over the next several years, the overwhelming majority of the Indian population died because they lacked immunity for diseases, such as measles, brought by the Europeans. As a result, most of the indigenous groups were easily defeated by the Spaniards, though the Mapuche Indians successfully resisted the invaders.

Extensive intermarriage occurred between Europeans and Indians, creating the mestizos (mixed) race that makes up two-thirds of the current Chilean population. The Spanish introduced Roman Catholicism and a land tenure system that created a small, wealthy landowning class and a large, landless, peasant class. Over time, those born in South America grew to resent foreign domination by Spain. On September 18, 1810, the day that is still celebrated as Independence Day, the Chileans set up a rebel government. After several battles, Bernardo O'Higgins (1778-1842) and José de San Martín (1778-1850) led the Chileans to victory. On February 12, 1818, they proclaimed their independence from Spain. Bernardo O'Higgins became the first head of government and is revered as the father of Chilean independence.

In the War of the Pacific (1879-1883) against Peru and Bolivia, Chile increased its area by one third and gained valuable mineral resources and deposits of nitrate, a natural fertilizer.

During the first half of the twentieth century, several governmental reforms took place. Church and state became separate, ensuring freedom of worship. Women gained the vote, and the government set up free, compulsory primary education. The Chileans were proud of their democratic tradition, with regular elections and freedom of the press. Many considered Chile to be the most stable democracy in South America and, thus, were unprepared for the violence of the 1970s.

In 1970, Salvador Allende (1908-1973), a Marxist and an organizer of the Socialist party in Chile, became president. He instituted far-reaching social reforms, but these contributed to an economic crisis and widespread dissatisfaction. The U.S. Central Intelligence Agency, fearful of Allende's Socialist policies, secretly supported groups hostile to the government. On September 11, 1973, Augusto Pinochet (1915- ), led a military coup and established an authoritarian government. During the coup, Allende lost his life.

Pinochet took strict control over the press, radio, television, and school system. The government repeatedly violated civil and human rights. Many journalists and other intellectuals were killed, imprisoned, or forced into exile. About one million people, almost a tenth of the population, left Chile during the Pinochet dictatorship. However, the government succeeded in building a strong economy. In 1990, after 16 years of military rule, Pinochet allowed an elected president, the moderate Patricio Aylwin (1918- ), to take office. Aylwin and the current president, Eduardo Frei, who took office in 1994, have moved Chile toward more freedom and openness, while maintaining economic growth.

## SIGNIFICANT IMMIGRATION WAVES

Because of its long coastline and its several major ports, there has long been an interchange of people between Chile and other seafaring countries. Few Chileans live more than 100 miles from the ocean. Because of its strategic position on world trade routes, a lively trade developed between North and South America. Until the Panama Canal was completed, many ships traveling between the east and west coasts of the United States made the long journey around Cape Horn at the southern tip of South America. They stopped in Valparaíso and other ports to sell goods and replenish their stores. Significant immigration to Chile did not end with the coming of the Spaniards. Because of economic hardship or political difficulties in their countries of origin, a significant number of Germans, Italians, Irish, English, Greeks, Yugoslavs, Lebanese, and others came to Chile during the nineteenth and twentieth centuries. For example, after each of the two world wars, a significant number of Germans and other Europeans came to Chile. During and after the Hitler era, both Nazis and the Jews they persecuted settled in Chile. Because of these many diverse groups, Chile has been called the United States of South America. The diversity is also reflected in the variety of surnames found in the country. Typical last names are Spanish, such as Lopez; German, such as Hahn; Irish, such as O'Connell; or English, such as Lee. Because more than two-thirds of the population is mixed European and Indian, the typical Chilean has brown eyes and dark brown, almost black, hair. However, some are blue-eyed blondes, have red hair, or even look middle-eastern.

The seaports were also a takeoff point for those wishing to emigrate from Chile. Indeed, leaving Chile by land was difficult until the advent of the airplane. The high Andes mountains and one of the driest deserts on earth separate Chile from its neighbors.

As early as the 1790s, merchant ships from Chile began to arrive at the California coast. The first large wave of immigrants from Chile to the United States occurred during the California gold rush of 1848-49. Carlos López, tells the story in his book *Chilenos in California; A Study of the 1850, 1852, and 1860 Censuses*. Ships arriving at the port of Valparaíso first brought the news of the discovery of the precious metal, along with samples of gold dust. The Chilean economy was in crisis and ship owners, hoping to create business, spread wild rumors about the abundance of gold in California. Thousands of Chileans crammed the ships to make their fortunes. Some of the first Chileans to arrive were experienced miners. They taught the "anglos" better techniques of panning for and extracting gold. In order to crush ore, these miners improved an existing device, expertly fashioning huge stone wheels to be used in what came to be called "Chili mills." Adventurers came, too, including the prominent Vicente Pérez Rosales (1807-1886), who kept a record of his trip in his diary. In San Francisco, the Chileans settled in an area called "Chilecito" (little Chile). When a new shipload of Chileans arrived, they were welcomed and instructed in the ways of California by the Chilecito community. On July 15, 1849, residents of Chilecito were attacked and robbed. Chileans suffered other discrimination; the government passed a foreign miner's tax. Further, in the summer of 1850 there was a move to expel foreigners, especially Chileans and Mexicans, from the mines. Thousands of Chileans returned to San Francisco, though many remained in the mining towns. Perhaps half of the Chilean `49ers eventually returned to Chile, disappointed with the difference between the romantic stories they had heard and the realities of nineteenth-century California.

The Chileans who remained in California retained an active ethnic identity for some time. They often lived in areas called "Chilitowns," speaking Spanish and cooking their traditional foods. To keep in contact, they established newspapers and local clubs. In 1867 a Chilean American newspaper appeared in San Francisco. In translation, its name was "The Voice of Chile and of the American Republics." Later, it merged with a Mexican American paper, providing news of interest to Chileans and Mexicans in San Francisco until 1883. Local organizations all over California provided a way for Chilean Americans to continue their traditions and support each other socially and financially.

Though many of the '49ers who settled permanently in California retained their interest in the mother country, the majority of them married non-Chileans. Over time, Chilean Americans spread out all over California and into neighboring states. As their children learned English in school and mixed with the wider society, the high rate of intermarriage with non-Chileans continued. The ethnic neighborhoods, newspapers, and clubs disappeared as the interests of Chilean Americans changed.

From the time of the gold rush until the 1960s, a small number of immigrants trickled into the United States from Chile. Young people from upper class Chilean families came to the United States to attend college or graduate school, and frequently remained. Single men whose companies sent them to Chile often returned with South American brides. Exporters, sailors, and professionals emigrated to the United States to increase their economic or career opportunities.

However, significant immigration into the United States did not begin to occur until the latter half of the 1960s. At that time, a larger number of Chileans began to emigrate in hopes of increasing their economic opportunities. They knew they could find better jobs and a higher standard of living in the United States.

The overthrow of Allende in 1973 and the establishment of a military dictatorship led to a large exodus of Chileans. Pinochet was determined to rid the country of divisive elements. Chief among his targets were journalists, radical students, intellectuals, and other professionals. Many fled for their lives to Europe, other parts of Latin America, the United States, and Canada. The size of the group that came to the United States was small in comparison to those who emigrated to other countries. Some countries persuaded Pinochet to exile Chilean dissidents rather than imprison or kill them. The United States offered to take Chilean refugees under a program for so-called "political parolees."

Many of the refugees were ill-prepared for the transition to life in North America. They lacked employment, housing, or contacts with Chileans already here to ease their entry into the United States. Some were sent in the middle of winter to areas of heavy snow, for which their California-like climate had not prepared them. A number of churches responded to these needs. In one well-known case, an Irish priest, Father Chouchulain Moriarty, heard of the plight of the immigrants. He dedicated himself to assisting the newly arriving Chileans to adjust to American life. Father Moriarty established a program in the Roman Catholic Church of the Sacred Heart in San Jose, California. New arrivals were housed in the church convent building, and helped to find jobs, secure permanent housing, and learn English. Because of the reputation of Father Moriarty's work, political parolees from all over California and as far away as the Midwest traveled to San Jose to become part of the program.

Throughout the Pinochet regime, Chileans continued to emigrate to the United States, for both political and economic reasons. Those who have come since 1990, when the military regime ended, are emigrating primarily for economic reasons. Though the Chilean economy is growing, there is still a large class of poor people in the country.

Beginning in 1988, Chilean exiles were allowed, and later encouraged, to return home. In that year President Pinochet decreed that all those in exile could return to Chile. After he came into office in 1990, President Aylwin established a generous program for Chileans who returned, including financial assistance and other benefits. A substantial number of those in exile did return, including some living in the United States, eager to reunite with their families and to be part of a more democratic Chile. In addition, Chilean Americans have been affected negatively by downturns in the U.S. economy. For this reason, some, especially those who have lost jobs in downsizing, decided to return to Chile. Many of the returning Chileans brought with them their children, who had been born abroad and were often not fluent in Spanish. There were so many such children that the Chilean government found it necessary to set up programs for "Spanish as a second language" in the schools.

Most of the Chilean American population has arrived during the past 25 years. As of 1990, the U.S. census indicated that there were about 61,465 persons of Chilean ancestry in the United States. About 55,681 of these had been born in Chile. Thus, less than one-tenth of all Chilean Americans were born here. The overwhelming majority are first-generation immigrants who retain close emotional ties to their country of origin. Many visit their families in Chile periodically or send their children there for vacations. A small percentage, especially academics and business people, spend some of their time in the United States and some in Chile, pursuing their careers on two continents.

### SETTLEMENT PATTERNS

Most Chileans who come to the United States settle in or around cities. They come from a highly urbanized country and find it compatible to settle in a metropolitan area. Cities provide the jobs they need and the opportunity to interact with other Chileans. They especially gravitate toward California, New York City, and Florida because of the large Spanish-speaking population in these areas. They know they will be able to find jobs where they can use their Spanish language and communicate with bosses. Furthermore, Chileans feel an emotional tie to states such as Florida, where there is a substantial Latin influence. By far, the largest number of Chilean Americans live in California. States with the next largest numbers of Chileans are, in order from greatest to fewest: New York, Florida, New Jersey, and Texas. Many settled in Canada, especially Toronto and Montreal, during the Pinochet regime. At that time, the Canadian government allowed them special entry visas for humanitarian reasons.

# ACCULTURATION AND ASSIMILATION

There are two major reasons why Chileans have come to the United States during the last 25 years. The first group, small in number, emigrated because of the political repression of the Pinochet regime. Many of these immigrants are of middle or upper class origin. A significant proportion of them arrived with advanced educations and well-developed skills. They had contacts with other Chilean exiles and a sense of identity from their shared commitment to a democratic Chile. After

a period of adjustment, many of them were able to pursue skilled jobs or professions. Unfortunately, others, who lacked skills or whose professional certifications were not recognized in the United States, were forced to take low-level jobs in which they were unable to use their skills. Some had been politically active students or union leaders in Chile who did not enter the United States with easily transferrable skills.

Most immigrants fall into the second group. They come to the United States searching for economic opportunities. Many of these are poorer, with less education and fewer skills than the group of political exiles. They often find it necessary to take jobs at the lower end of the pay scale. A typical pattern is to find a job as a babysitter or in the construction industry, where fluency in English is of limited importance. As time permits, they attend English classes or get secretarial or technical training, eventually acquiring more desirable jobs. Chilean Americans work hard to secure education and training so as to better themselves.

Because Chile is far away and does not share borders with the United States, immigrants cannot simply cross a border to enter the country. They must save money and work hard to get here. Such enterprising immigrants often have high motivation and additional skills, as well as American relatives or other contacts. These facts ease their transition into the American economy.

Because they share the Spanish language, Chileans often interact with other Latinos in church, at work, and around the neighborhood. This frequently leads to friendships and sometimes to marriage. Chileans also have a high rate of intermarriage with other U.S. citizens, which is contributing to their assimilation into mainstream society. Although most Chilean Americans are eager to learn or improve their English, some find it more comfortable to live and work in Spanish-speaking neighborhoods.

Chilean Americans find themselves in the position of being a minority within a minority. That is, Chileans make up a tiny part of the Latino population in the country, itself a minority group. Many Chileans feel quite separate from Central American or Caribbean people; they have never tasted Mexican food and their accents are quite different from Puerto Ricans. Yet the dominant white majority considers them all to be Latinos, making few distinctions. Indeed, most books about Latinos, such as Milton Meltzer's *Hispanic Americans* (1982), fail to discuss Chileans at all, focusing only on the larger Latino groups in the United States. Because Chilean Americans are such a small group numerically, most mainstream Americans do not know enough about Chileans to have well-defined ideas of how they differ from other Latinos. Thus, most discrimination that is specifically targeted to Chileans, as Chileans, comes from other South Americans who bring old grudges to the United States. In October, 1994, for example, Bolivians staged a protest at the performance of Bafochi, a Chilean ballet group, in Washington, D.C.

The Bolivians called the Chileans "thieves" and "pirates." They were objecting because some of the dances to be performed had originated in an area Bolivia lost to Chile during the War of the Pacific in the nineteenth century. To avoid open conflict during the performance, the ballet group omitted several controversial pieces.

## TRADITIONS, CUSTOMS, AND BELIEFS

Chileans have a reputation for being a friendly people and this tradition is maintained by Chilean Americans. According to a well-known folk song, "if you go to Chile, the country folk will come to greet you and you will see that Chileans love a friend from far away." Unlike certain other Latin countries, guests wait to be invited into the home. They usually greet the head of the family first to show respect. Visitors often spend time asking about the family, including the children.

When Chilean Americans come to the United States, they find the pattern of the regular work day not too different from their native country. Business people are accustomed to working from nine to five, perhaps staying a few hours extra to finish work. Although this has changed in the larger Chilean cities, many more Chileans are used to coming home for lunch hour than is true in the United States. Although some Chileans take a nap after lunch, the siesta is not as entrenched a tradition as it is in some other Latin American countries.

Chileans commonly eat four times a day. They have breakfast, a late lunch, tea at about five, and a late dinner. In Chile, lunch is typically the largest meal of the day. Afternoon tea is served in late afternoon around five or six o'clock. People eat sandwiches or, sometimes, cakes, and drink tea. Chile is one Latin country where tea is a more popular drink than coffee. Dinner is often eaten between eight-thirty and ten-thirty, but some Chilean Americans report they have, on occasion, left the table at two o'clock in the morning. Chilean Americans are often forced to change their eating patterns by the necessity of leaving for work early in the morning and taking coffee breaks at the times designated by their employers rather than by their traditions. Some Chileans are so poor that they can only afford one substantial meal a day. Chilean Americans from poor backgrounds often eat better in the United States, even when working at low-paying jobs, than they were able to do in Chile.

## PROVERBS AND SUPERSTITIONS

Chile's rich store of folk lore, sayings, and superstitions is derived from its European and Indian past, as well as its relation to the mountains and the ocean. One saying, related to the water, is that the shrimp who falls asleep is carried away by the current. Tuesday (not Friday) the 13th is considered to be an unlucky day. One saying is that faraway loves are loves of idiots. Some traditional Chilean superstitions are identical to those in the United States. For example, Chileans also say that breaking a mirror will bring seven years of bad luck.

Some believe that the spirits of the dead are responsible for strange noises. One superstition is that spirits of the dead will visit those who work late at night. There are some superstitions about the devil. For example, neighbors may say that someone who is suddenly lucky has entered into an agreement with the devil. Some of these superstitions are more common in the Chilean countryside than in the cities. Though many Chilean Americans repeat them, they do not always believe them.

## CUISINE

The fishing industry is larger in Chile than in any other Latin American country except Peru. Seafood has long been an important part of the diet, with approximately 200 types of fish available. Fish is inexpensive, so it is eaten by almost all Chileans. The types of seafood they eat include mussels, scallops, clams, crabs, lobsters, abalone, and sea urchins. The conger eel is a national specialty; there are many ways to prepare it in both simple and elegant dishes. Chilean Americans adapt their seafood cooking to the varieties of fish and shellfish that are available in North America. They enjoy soups, stews, and seafood combinations.

Many traditional dishes contain beans and corn, reflecting the Indian heritage of the country. Most Chilean bean recipes call for *porotos* or cranberry beans. The climate of the country allows beans to grow during most of the year, so they are a natural for inclusion in many dishes. Chilean corn is somewhat different from that grown in the United States. In some Chilean varieties, the ears are much larger than their North American cousins. One very popular dish, *porotos granados*, contains beans, corn, squash, garlic, and onion. Many recipes, such as *pastel de choclo* (corn and meat pie), call for unripe corn. In this dish, ground corn, sprinkled with sugar before baking, replaces the upper crust found in meat pies made in the United States. *Empanadas*—pockets of dough filled with meat or cheese, onions, olives, raisins, hardboiled eggs and spices, that are baked or fried—are one of the favorite traditional foods of Chilean Americans. They are eaten as snacks or one course of a meal, and are a favorite treat for holidays. *Humitas* are made from grated corn, onions, and spices. Traditionally, these are wrapped in corn husks and cooked in boiling water.

Wine is a popular drink among Chileans. South of Santiago lies a stretch of Chile's central valley that is superb wine-growing country. The early Spaniards introduced vineyards to Chile so that they could grow wine for use in the Catholic mass. From the time when a French winegrower was imported to improve the wine, Chileans have used European methods to make wine and have won prizes for their specialties. Another alcoholic drink, also made from grapes, is called *pisco.* A favorite drink is *pisco sour*, in which *pisco* is served with lemon juice, sugar, beaten egg whites, and ice. The Chileans also use fermented grapes to make another popular drink called *chica*.

## TRADITIONAL COSTUMES

For Chileans, appearance is important. They make an effort to appear neat and clean. Chileans are generally not attracted to the casualness and, what some consider to be sloppiness, of dress in the United States. Even those who are poor make an effort to avoid wearing tattered clothing. Styles generally follow fashion trends set in Europe. Chileans tend to be more dressed up for the same event than people in the United States. For example, men usually go to restaurants in suits. Over time, Chilean Americans tend to become more relaxed in their dress, while still enjoying more formal dress. Sometimes conflicts arise between immigrants and their children, who wish to adopt the sloppy appearance of other teenagers.

## DANCES

The so-called "national dance" of Chile is the *cueca*, which depicts the courting behavior of the rooster and the hen. Characteristic of this dance are stamping and use of scarves. The man may use the scarf to pull the woman toward him, and she may use it to cover her face in a flirtatious manner. The *cueca* may be performed in formal attire or a more rural outfit. The formal, ballroom attire for men is based on the traditional dress of the Chilean cowboy. This consists of black pants, a colorful sash, white shirt, and a black bolero jacket. A waist-length, brightly colored, handwoven woolen poncho is worn over the bolero, or sometimes thrown over the shoulder. The man wears fringed leggings and high, pointed leather boots with large decorative spurs. He wears a flat, wide-brimmed straw or, sometimes, fancy leather hat. Women wear a straight black skirt with a slit from which can be seen layers and layers of white lace. She wears a white blouse, black bolero jacket, and a hat like her partner's.

Alternatively, the *cueca* may be performed in a folk outfit. In this version, the man wears rural work pants with a shirt open at the neck with the sleeves rolled up. He wears the traditional woven straw hat and boots or sandals, depending on what part of the country is being represented. As in the more formal outfit, the man will wear a short, colorful poncho. The woman wears a dress gathered at the waist with a round collar and lace at the cuffs. The dress may be plaid or flowered, with white lace underneath.

Another popular dance is the *refalosa*. In this dance, scarves are also used, but the typical movements are sliding, rather than stamping, as in the *cueca*. Other dance traditions in Chile are those originating on Easter Island that feature pelvic thrusting, and the skimming dances characteristic of the fishing villages of the area of Chiloe.

Chilean Americans enjoy watching and performing dances. In some cities there are dance groups where people get together periodically to enjoy their traditional dances.

## HOLIDAYS CELEBRATED BY CHILEAN AMERICANS

Chilean Americans celebrate New Year's Eve with parties. On this night, as on most holidays, children are allowed to stay up as late as they wish. There is a tradition that it will be a lucky year if the first thing a person says in the New Year is "rabbit." New Year's Day in Chile falls in summer (because the country is south of the equator), so many families have a picnic or spend time at the beach.

Chileans celebrate Independence Day on September 18th. On that day in 1810, *criollos* (settlers born in Chile rather than Spain), began their struggle for independence from Spain and set up a government. In Chile fairs are held in cities and towns during the week before and the week after September 18th. People build booths with thatched roofs in which to sell food, exhibit crafts, and put on entertainment. In some parts of the United States, Chileans hold similar fairs on Independence Day. There is an annual Independence Day festival in northern Virginia, called *ramada*, referring to the branches that are used to make the booths of the *leantos* constructed for the celebration. Visitors to the fair enjoy traditional crafts, sing the national anthem, dance the *cueca*, listen to folk music from the Andes and other parts of the country, and eat plenty of *empanadas*.

Christmas is celebrated in Chile on December 25th, just as it is in the United States. In Chile, it too is a summer holiday. Children and adults stay up late on Christmas Eve to eat a big family meal. Some people go to mass. At midnight everyone opens presents, including small children who have stayed up for the event. This means that kids are running around outside in the summer weather until four o'clock in the morning. Santa Claus is popular in Chile. As in the traditional U.S. outfit, he has a beard, but he wears the traditional folk dance outfit of Chile with open shirt, rolled-up sleeves, woolen socks, and sandals. Chilean Americans have, in general, kept the tradition of opening presents at midnight and allowing children to stay up. Most Chilean Americans also continue the tradition of a relaxed Christmas Day, with perhaps an outing.

### HEALTH AND MENTAL HEALTH ISSUES

Health in Chile has improved in the last 20 years, with falling infant mortality and longer life expectancy. As other diseases decline in importance, Chileans give more attention to heart disease and cancer. There do not appear to be any special diseases specific to Chileans. Many Chilean Americans believe in the effectiveness of herbal teas for a variety of illnesses. They call such teas "little waters."

For many years, health care in Chile was nationalized, so that many Chilean immigrants have experience with, and are comfortable in accepting, such care. However, recently, health care in Chile has become largely privatized. Like other Americans, Chilean Americans vary in the type and amount of health care coverage they possess, largely depending on whether they receive benefits from their employer.

# LANGUAGE

Virtually all Chilean Americans speak Spanish, though some have come from parts of Chile where German, Italian, or another language was spoken in their homes. Their accent depends on social class and region of the country from which they came. Frequently, Chileans omit the "s" sound in words, and sometimes drop out the last syllable of a longer word. (In the greetings listed below, the "s" sound is retained, because it is used in conversation where there is reason to be formal.)

Chileans make great use of the word-ending that means "little." A friend named Norma may be referred to affectionately as Normita (nor-*mee*-tah"), literally meaning "little Norma."

### GREETINGS

Friends and family commonly greet each other with the *abrazo* (ah-bra-zoh). This is a handshake and hug, sometimes with a kiss on the right cheek. The *abrazo* is repeated upon parting. Other greetings include: *Hola! Qué hubo?* (oh-lah kay oo-boh)—How are you?; *Cómo está?* (koh-moh ess-tah)—How are you?; *Gusto de verte!* (goo-stoh day vehr-tay)—Nice to see you!; *Buenos Días!* (bway-nohs dee-ahs)—Good day!; *Chao!* (chow)—Goodbye!. To express appreciation for their host's food, Chileans say: *Es Rico!* (ess ree-koh)—It's delicious.

# FAMILY AND COMMUNITY DYNAMICS

Chileans have strong family ties. Traditionally, the father is the head of the family, but the mother makes many decisions within the home. Chilean women often speak out and take stands on both private and public issues. They have a tradition of being politically, as well as socially, active in their communities. In the United States they are an important part of the self-help and cultural groups that are active in many cities. Children are taught to give respect to their parents and the elderly. Young boys are typically given more freedom than girls. Teenagers are usu-

This Chilean American woman is preparing food for a family celebration.

ally allowed to date by about age 16, with the emphasis on group activities. It is common for children to live at home until they marry. Even after they have families of their own, children often return home to spend Sundays and holidays with their parents.

Machismo, the cult of male superiority and dominance, is still a fact of life in Chile. However, in comparison to some other Latin countries, women have more opportunities. Social customs reflect fairly egalitarian treatment of the sexes. An increasing number of women work outside the home. The majority of these are domestics, but there are also teachers, secretaries, social workers, and other professionals. Women make up 30 percent of the work force. There is some opportunity for women to gain career advancement. In 1970, for example, a higher percentage of women who worked outside the home had technical and professional jobs than was true in the United States. As in other Latin countries, Chileans typically retain two last names; the first is from their father and the second from their mother.

Children frequently have two parties a year, one for their birthday and one on the day of the saint for whom they were named. Since many children in Chile are named Juan or Juana, St. John's Day is a big day for parties. Chilean children usually have fewer toys than the typical child raised in the United States. Children are more likely to receive gifts of candy than toys from their friends at birthday parties.

## BAPTISMS

In Chile, baptisms are often performed when the child is about two months old. Godparents are chosen who agree to raise the child in the faith if the parents should die. At age eight, children take their First Communion. Another set of godparents may be added at this time; sometimes the child is allowed to choose them.

## WEDDINGS

Chileans often have two marriage ceremonies, one civil and the other religious. These are frequently performed on different days, with the civil ceremony perhaps several days before the church service. At weddings, the bride traditionally keeps the groom waiting. Everyone arrives at the church except the bride, who will have someone drive her around the city until she is ready to appear. After a half hour or, perhaps, an hour, she arrives at the church. The bride wears white, but the groom seldom wears a tuxedo unless it is a high-society wedding. There is not usually a wedding party; the bride and groom go through the ceremony without attendants. The reception is often a sit-down meal.

## FUNERALS

Funerals are usually held sooner than is the practice in the United States, because embalming is not common. Wakes are held in the homes and the funerals, usually relatively brief, in churches. Because the country is so long, many relatives never reach a funeral, because of travel time.

## EDUCATION

Chile has one of the best-educated populations in Latin America, with a literacy rate of 94 percent for men and 93 percent for women. Eight years of education are free and compulsory. Chileans value learning and are proud of their educational system; they consider education to be a way to a better life. Parents often urge their children to complete their education before marrying. If their means are limited and they must choose between educating sons or daughters, sons are often chosen. Many Roman Catholic parents prefer to send their children to religious schools. Several thousand Chilean American students are pursuing degrees in higher education. Although they are enrolled in a wide variety of programs, two particularly popular fields are natural science and engineering. These fields are seen as leading to promising careers. In addition, students are attracted by the well-equipped laboratories and other technical apparatus available at universities in the United States.

# RELIGION

Because such a high proportion of Chileans are Roman Catholic, most of those who emigrate to the United States are of this faith. The global nature of the church, with its shared beliefs and practices, eases the transition for a Catholic from Santiago to San Francisco or New York. Chileans find that, although the churches may look different and the congregation and priest may speak English, there are still the comfortable traditions, the same saints, candles, and order of the mass. Chileans often attend churches in which there are services in Spanish. Sometimes they organize local events especially attractive to other Chilean Catholics, such as those connected with patron saints.

Protestant immigrants often join the denominations in North America in which they had been active at home. Santiago has one of the world's largest Pentecostal churches, so many Chileans look for Pentecostal congregations in the United States. Many German Chileans join Baptist or Lutheran churches. Other Chileans join the Seventh Day Adventist church. Like the Roman Catholics, the Protestants often search for congregations where Spanish is used. A small group of Jewish Chileans have also come to the United States. Like the Roman Catholics, they have a worldwide sense of community with others who share the Jewish faith and traditions.

# EMPLOYMENT AND ECONOMIC TRADITIONS

Many Chilean American immigrants were political exiles who, as a group, were well-educated and highly-skilled. After a short period of adjustment, most became highly successful professionals in a variety of fields. More recent immigrants, who did not benefit from the same educational background as their predecessors, have had to take low-paying jobs—such as babysitting, construction, and maintenance—where their Spanish does not create communication problems. Over time, however, many of these individuals have obtained training in English and some technical training as well, therefore improving their economic status.

# POLITICS AND GOVERNMENT

The party preferences of Chilean Americans vary with their socioeconomic status and background. Most Chileans of upper class or business backgrounds favor the Republican party. Chileans of lower class backgrounds and those who fled Chile because of Pinochet generally favor the Democratic Party. Since the majority of Chileans have arrived during the last ten or 15 years, when union membership in the United States was declining, and since they are not entrenched in manufacturing jobs, Chileans have not been especially active in union politics. Those who have lost their jobs often do not feel comfortable using unemployment benefits; they have a strong desire to support themselves. Second-generation Chilean Americans, born and raised in this country, are becoming more involved in the issues of domestic Latino politics. Few Chilean Americans have been active in the military, but this will change as more native-born children grow up.

### RELATIONS WITH CHILE

Many Chileans are proud of and optimistic about their country of origin. When an airplane from another country lands in Santiago, the returning Chileans frequently applaud to express their pleasure at being back.

The Chilean American '49ers and their descendants took a strong interest in events in Chile. During the War of the Pacific, local organizations in California raised considerable money to support the Chilean war effort and help the needy back home. A century later, after the military coup, Chilean Americans took an active part in protesting the repressive actions of the Pinochet government. A number of writers in exile in the United States centered their work on themes related to political and social conditions in Chile. In addition, local groups raised money to help families of the "disappeared" Chilean citizens who simply vanished because Pinochet had decreed their death. One type of Chilean craft, the *arpillera,* is a wallhanging made with bits of cloth sewn together to create a picture. Beginning in 1974, women in Chile created *arpilleras* to show the cruelty of the Pinochet regime. These could not be sold openly in Chile, but some Americans help to sell them in the United States as a way of publicizing the human rights violations. Many local groups in the United States continue to raise funds for social programs in Chile, such as rural schools or children without homes.

# INDIVIDUAL AND GROUP CONTRIBUTIONS

Chilean Americans have contributed to American life in many realms, including literature, the arts, science, social science, music, and business.

## ACADEMIA

Many Chilean Americans are active in academic institutions. Cecilia Hidalgo (1941- ), the first woman to receive a Ph.D. in biochemistry in Chile, worked in research in Boston for many years before returning to South America. Arturo Valenzuela is the director of the Center of Latin American Studies at Georgetown University. A political scientist, Dr. Valenzuela is an expert on the political system in Chile. Alfonso Gómez-Lobo (1940- ) is a philosophy professor, also at Georgetown University. His specialty is ancient Greek philosophy. Gómez-Lobo states that his academic reputation helped him leave Chile after the coup.

## ART

Artistic expression is another strong tradition in Chilean culture. Many Chilean Americans contribute to art, sculpture, and photography in the United States.

Elena Castedo's sister, Montserrat Castedo (1941- ), is an artist and tapestry maker. She places bits of colored fabric, some of which she dyes herself, on a percale background stretched across an easel. Castedo focuses on the theme of peace and harmony in nature. After many years of residence in the United States, she has now returned to live in Chile. However, she has retained her ties with the United States and her work was recently exhibited in the United States.

Author and illustrator Fernando Krahn (1935- ) lived in New York for several years, providing cartoons for the *Atlantic Monthly*, *New Yorker*, *Esquire* and *The Reporter*. His books

include *Journeys of Sebastian*, *Hildegarde and Maximilian*, and *A Funny Friend from Heaven*. He has also illustrated books for his Chilean wife, who is a writer. The couple now lives in Spain.

Raimundo Rubio (1956- ) describes himself as a contemporary, avant-garde painter. He uses surrealistic techniques, placing unrelated objects together in the same picture. He comes from a family of Chilean intellectuals; his father and brother are poets. Trained in Chile as a painter, Rubio came to the United States in 1979. Exhibits of his work have appeared in Miami, Washington, D.C., and Spain. In October, 1994, he opened a one-person show in New York.

Soledad Salame (1954- ), came to the United States in 1982. She does painting, sculpture, and print making. Her work is closely tied to nature and the environment. For example, she has created murals that include living plants.

The sculptor and painter who signs her works with the name Pía (1953- ) works mostly with a variety of types of wood, but also in stone. She views her work as closely connected to Easter Island, a small land mass with ancient traditions off the shore of Chile. Photographer Luis Salvatierra (1948- ), born in Valparaíso, came to the United States in 1974 because of the military coup. He spent considerable time documenting the Latino community in Washington, D.C. More recently, he has been translating Pablo Neruda's poetry into photography.

## BUSINESS

Chileans are also involved in business, some at the national and international level. Andrés Bande (1944- ) is a business executive who was born in Santiago. Currently, he is president of Ameritech International, a worldwide telecommunications company based in Chicago. Previously, he was executive vice president of US West International, a regional Bell company, which he reorganized and expanded. Bande has been active in organizations for Latinos, including a group that promotes excellence in education.

## LITERATURE

Chile has a long tradition of poetry and other types of artistic expression. Two Chilean poets, Gabriela Mistral (1889-1957) and Pablo Neruda (1904-1973), have won Nobel prizes. In 1945 Gabriela Mistral was the first South American to win the prize. She was a teacher and lived for a time in Long Island, New York. Neruda is thought by many to be the greatest Spanish language poet in the twentieth century. Though neither of these were Chilean Americans, they have inspired a generation of writers who are.

Much of the work of Chilean American writers is concerned with the plight of those who suffered under the military rule of Pinochet. Indeed, many of the writers are themselves exiles, voluntarily or involuntarily, from the military regime. Isabel Allende (1942- ), whose diplomat father was a cousin of the ousted president, Salvador Allende, is a novelist. After the coup, she participated in getting information out of Chile about those whom Pinochet was torturing. Afterwards, fearing for her life, she fled the country, eventually moving to the United States in 1988. Her first novel, *House of the Spirits*, has been translated into 27 languages and released as a film in 1994. The novel is loosely autobiographical, drawing on her experiences of being raised by her grandfather and clairvoyant grandmother. Other novels include *Of Love and Shadows* and *Eva Luna*. She lives and writes in California.

Ariel Dorfman (1942- ) is a well-known author, journalist, and educator who has lived in exile from Chile for many years. His works include *Last Song of Manuel Sendero*, *My House Is on Fire*, *Mascara*, *Hard Rain*, and a play called "Death in Maiden." One of Dorfman's themes is the state of being in exile. He has been an outspoken critic of Pinochet.

Fernando Alegría (1918- ) is a poet and novelist, as well as a retired professor of Spanish American literature from Berkeley and Stanford University. His work reflects his commitment to his Chilean ancestry and to improving the lot of the poor and oppressed. As a young man, he wrote a book about Walt Whitman. One of his favorite themes is the hero; he published a book about the Mapuchan leader Lautaro (1943). His *Allende: A Novel* is a fictionalized biography of Salvador Allende. *Chilean Spring* is a fictionalized diary of a Chilean photographer killed after the 1973 coup. *The Funhouse* tells the story of a Latin American who came to the United States during the Vietnam War.

Writer and poet Marjorie Agosín grew up in Chile and now teaches literature at Wellesley College. Her writings express her concern about the social conditions of women and the political repression in Chile. Cecilia Vicuna is a young poet whose works are published by Grey Wolf Press in Minneapolis. Her work is highly mystical.

Elena Castedo is an author who lives in Boston. Her book entitled *Paradise* was one of five finalists for the National Book Award in 1993.

## MUSIC

Chileans in the United States continue a tradition called *peña*. This means getting together to play and listen to music, telling long, Chilean jokes, and enjoying food. For many years during the military regime of Pinochet, Violeta Parra, a well-known Chilean composer and singer, lived in a tent in Santiago and held a famous *peña* every weekend. She wanted Chileans to return to their traditional folk music and instruments, rather than merely to copy songs from the United States or other countries. Under her influence, many young musicians, some of whom later emigrated to the United States, began to play traditional Chilean folk music. They used instruments, such as the *quena*, a small Indian flute, and a stringed instrument from the Andes mountains. In the United States, *peña* is sometimes held in a local restaurant on a certain evening of the week. Chileans bring their guitars and other instruments; everyone enjoys the singing and the fellowship.

One type of traditional Chilean folk music that is shared by Bolivia and Peru is Andean music, sometimes called *altiplano*, to indicate that it originated high in the mountains. Chilean born Rene Iribarren plays Andean music in the United States with a group called Alborada, meaning dawn. Iribarren, who plays ten different instruments, is the composer for the group. They have released a recording called "Melodies from the Highlands of South America."

Many Chileans also excel in classical music. Pianist Claudio Arrao (1903-1991) is known throughout the world. A child prodigy, Arrao played for the president of Chile when he was only six years old. Later, Arrao went to Germany to study, where he remained for a number of years. In 1941 he moved to New York City and lived there until his death. Arrao traveled throughout the world giving concerts. He is considered to be one of the most outstanding interpreters of Beethoven's piano music.

A number of other Chilean Americans are classical musicians. Juan Pablo Tzyuierdo is the conductor for the Pittsburgh Symphony Orchestra. Maximiliano Valdés is conductor of the Buffalo Hill Harmonic Orchestra in Buffalo, New York. Juan Orrego Salas is a composer and a teacher at the Indiana University school of music in Bloomington, Indiana. Roberto Díaz, who comes from a Chilean musical family, is first violist for the National Symphony Orchestra at the Kennedy Center in Washington, D.C.

# MEDIA

### PRINT

*La Aurora del Sur.*

This periodical (which means "The Dawn of the South") is a monthly magazine with a national circulation that provides information to the Chilean American community.

**Contact:** Ines Yanec, Editor.
**Address:** P.O. Box 3891, Glendale, California 91221.
**Telephone:** (213) 666-3069.
**Fax:** (213) 660-4930.

### RADIO AND TELEVISION

There are hundreds of radio and television stations that broadcast in Spanish, so it is easy for Chilean Americans to get news and information in a language they understand. Most radio and television stations avoid regular programming that is specific to Chileans, because the stations want to appeal to a broad range of their Spanish-speaking audience.

One of the most highly rated programs on Spanish language television is "Sabado Gigante," or Giant Saturday. This variety program includes games, contests, interviews, and brief documentary pieces. Although the program features items of interest to Spanish speakers from many countries, the host was born in Chile. He uses the name Don Francisco, but his real name is Mario Kreutzberber. He originally produced the program in Santiago, but it is now produced in Miami. This popular show can be seen on stations in the Univision cable network every Saturday evening from 7:00 p.m. to 11:00 p.m., eastern standard time.

# ORGANIZATIONS AND ASSOCIATIONS

Perhaps because large-scale immigration has occurred only recently, Chilean American organizations are local, rather than national. Many such groups are oriented toward helping other Chileans with their adjustment to the United States. Some groups raise money to send to Chile to support social or political causes there. Another focus is the sponsorship of dance groups or other cultural activities to educate children and teenagers about Chilean traditions.

**San Martín Society.**

This national, historical society was founded in 1977 to commemorate the activities of the brilliant military tactician and independence fighter, José de San Martín, in Chile, Argentina and Peru. The society gives awards for civic or institutional leadership.

**Contact:** Cristian Garcia-Godoy, President.
**Address:** P.O. Box 33, McLean, Virginia 22101-0033.
**Telephone or fax:** (703) 883-0950.

# MUSEUMS AND RESEARCH CENTERS

**Embassy of Chile.**

The Embassy provides information about Chilean culture, business opportunities, and travel to the country. The Embassy sponsors cultural events and facilitates contacts with Chileans.

**Address:** 1732 Massachusetts Avenue, N.W., Washington, D.C., 20036.
**Telephone:** (202) 785-1746.

**Homer Babbidge Library.**

Located at the University of Connecticut, the library has about 2500 volumes, including many rare books, about the history, literature, and politics of Chile from the sixteenth to the twentieth centuries. Collections are open to the public. Services include copying and interlibrary loan.

**Contact:** Darlene Waller, Curator, Special Collections Department.
**Address:** Homer Babbidge Library, University of Connecticut, Storrs, Connecticut 06269-1005.
**Telephone:** (203) 486-2524.
**Fax:** (203) 486-3593.

**Natural History Museum.**

Part of the Smithsonian Institution, this museum owns a collection of approximately 168 ethnographic artifacts and 457 archaeological artifacts from Chile. The majority of the items in the ethnographic collection are about the Mapuche

Indians in the nineteenth and twentieth centuries. This collection can be seen by appointment.

**Contact:** Deborah Hull-Walski, Collections Manager, Museum Support Center.
**Address:** 4210 Silver Hill Road, Suitland, Maryland 20746.
**Telephone:** (301) 238-3529.

### Organization of American States.

Includes exhibits of Chilean American artists and sculptors in its Art Museum of the Americas.

**Contact:** Belgica Rodriguez, Director.
**Address:** Art Museum of the Americas, 201 18th Street, N.W., Washington, D.C. 20005.
**Telephone:** (202) 363-6336.

### The San Martín Society.

Maintains a historical collection focused on the contributions of José de San Martín. Holdings include 1300 books, dissertations, microfilms, speeches pamphlets, and other documents. Services include a copying center. The collection is open to the public by written request. Their major publication is the San Martín Papers, 1988.

**Contact:** Cristian Garcia-Godoy, President.
**Address:** P.O. Box 33, McLean, Virginia 22101-0033.
**Telephone or fax:** (703) 883 0950.

### University of California at Berkeley.

Contains a collection of documents relating to Chilean American history in California, particularly at the time of the gold rush, as well as material about Chilean history, politics, economics, culture, and the arts.

**Contact:** Reference librarian.
**Address:** Main Library, University of California at Berkeley, Berkeley, California 94720.
**Telephone:** (510) 642-6657.

# SOURCES FOR ADDITIONAL STUDY

*Chilean Writers in Exile: Eight Short Novels*, edited by Fernando Alegria. Trumansburg, New York: Crossing Press, 1982.

Faugsted, George Edward. *The Chilenos in the California Gold Rush*. San Francisco: R and E Research Associates, 1973.

Lopez, Carlos. *Chilenos in California: A Study of the 1850 and 1860 Censuses*. San Francisco: R and E Research Associates, 1973.

Maceoin, G. *No Peaceful Way*. New York: Sheed and Ward, 1974.

*Military Rule in Chile: Dictatorship and Oppositions*, edited by J. S. Valenzuela and A. Valenzuela. Baltimore: Johns Hopkins University Press, 1986.

Pike, F. B. *Chile and the United States: 1880-1962*. Notre Dame, Indiana: University of Notre Dame Press, 1963.

# CHINESE AMERICANS

by
L. Ling-chi Wang

## OVERVIEW

China, or *Zhongguo* (the Middle Kingdom), the third largest country in the world, occupies a significant portion of southeast Asia. The land mass, 3,657,765 square miles (9,700,000 sq. km.), or as big as all of Europe, is bounded to the north by Russia and Mongolia, to the west by Russia and India, to the southwest by the Himalayas, to the south by Indochina and the South China Sea, and to the east by the Yellow Sea and the Pacific Ocean. Three major rivers flow through China: the Huanghe (Yellow River) in the north; the Yangzi in the heartland; and the Zhujiang (Pearl River) in the south. Eighty-five percent of China's land is nonarable, and the rest is regularly plagued by flood and drought.

Upon this land, China now feeds its 1.3 billion people (1990), one-fifth of humanity. Ninety-four percent are Han Chinese; the remaining six percent are made up of the 55 non-Han minorities, the most prominent of whom are the Zhuang, Hui, Uighur, Yi, Tibetan, Miao, Mongol, Korean, and Yao. These minorities have their own history, religion, language, and culture.

The official language of China is *putonghua* or Mandarin (*guanhua*), spoken by over 70 percent of the Han Chinese. The remaining Chinese, living mostly in southern China, speak the other seven major Chinese dialects: *wu, xiang, gan*, northern *min*, southern *min, yue* (Cantonese), and *kejia* (Hakka). In spite of their mutual unintelligibility, all eight branches of Chinese share the same writing system, the only fully developed ancient system of writing still used. The earliest examples of this system of Chinese writing appear on thousands of animal bones and tortoise shells from the middle of the second millennium B.C., during the late Shang Dynasty. However, according to recent archeological evidence, some 32 inscribed symbols on painted pottery from an early Yangshao culture site near Xi'an in Shaanxi, suggest the existence of Chinese writing as early as 6,000 years ago.

## HISTORY

Chinese historians have estimated that Chinese civilization began about 5,000 years ago in the Huanghe (Yellow River) river basin and the middle Yangzi region. The voluminous history, *Shi Ji* ("Historical Records"), by Si Maqian (145 B.C.-?) and recent archeological finds support the validity of the assumption. For example, the neolithic sites of the Yangshao culture along the midsection of the Yellow River confirm the traditional view that the river basin was the cradle of the Chinese civilization.

Legends have it that Huangdi ("the Yellow Emperor") defeated his rival tribes, established the first Chinese kingdom, made himself *tienzi*, or "The Son of Heaven," and invented many things for the benefit of his people, including clothing, boats, carts, medicine, the compass, and writing. Following Huangdi, historians believe that the Xia Dynasty (2100-1600 B.C.) was the first dynasty of China and marked the beginning of Chinese history. Xia, weakened by corruption in its final decades, was eventually conquered by a Shang king to the east who established the Shang Dynasty (1600-1100 B.C.). The Shang achievements can be readily seen from the remnants of its spectacular palaces, well-crafted giant bronze cauldrons, refined jade carvings, and massive written records. During the Zhou Dynasty (1100 to 771 B.C.), the Chinese idea of the emperor, being the "Son of Heaven" who derived his mandate from heaven, was firmly established. In the highly organized feudal society, the Zhou royal family ruled over hundreds of feudal states.

Beginning in 770 B.C., Chinese history entered two periods of turmoil and war: the Spring/Autumn (770-476 B.C.) and the Warring States (475-221 B.C.). During these 550 years, the former feudal states engaged in perpetual wars and brutal conquests. During the same time, China witnessed unprecedented progress in agriculture, science, and technology and reached the golden age of Chinese philosophy and literature. Confucius (551-479 B.C.), founder of Confucianism; Lao-tzu (sixth century), the founder of Taoism; the egalitarian Mo-zi (480-420 B.C.); and Han-fei (280-233 B.C.), founder of legalism, defined the character of Chinese civilization and made profound and enduring contributions to the intellectual history of the world.

Qin Shi Huangdi of the Qin state finally crushed all the rival states and emerged as the sole ruler of the Chinese empire in 221 B.C. Qin extended the borders of China; imposed harsh laws; completed the Great Wall; built a transportation network; and standardized weights, measures, currency, and, most importantly, the Chinese writing system. The brutality of his rule soon led to widespread rebellion, and the Qin rule was eventually replaced by the Han Dynasty (206 B.C.-220 A.D.). The Han emperor firmly established the Chinese state under Confucianism and created an educational and civil service system that remained in use until 1911. During this period, China came into contact with the Roman Empire and with India.

During the Sui-Tang era, China traded extensively by land and by sea with the known world, and Islam, Judaism, Zoroastrianism, and Christianity were brought into China. But Tang began to decline toward the end of the eighth century, causing rebellions of warlords from within and invasions from without. After Tang, China was again divided. In 1211 Genghis Khan, a Mongolian leader, began the invasion into China from the north, but the conquest was not completed until 1279 under Kublai Khan, his grandson, who established the Yuan Dynasty (1271-1368) in China. During Mongolian rule, China traded extensively with Europe, and Marco Polo brought China's achievements to European attention.

The decline of the Ming Dynasty (1368-1644) led to the conquest of China for the second time by a foreign power, the Manchu, from the northeast. The Manchu established the Qing Dynasty (1644-1911) and again expanded China's borders. Like the Mongols, however, the Manchu conquerors were also conquered and absorbed by the Chinese. Failed reform within the Quing administration, internal pressure through various organized rebellions, external pressure from the major Western powers, and the military defeat by

Japan in 1895 all led China to become increasingly isolated and weak.

## MODERN ERA

The isolation was finally broken when the British defeated China in the Opium War (1839-1842), forcing China to open its ports to international trade and exposing China in the next 100 years to Western domination. Under the yoke of imperialism and mounting political corruption and internal unrest, especially the Taiping Uprising, the Qing Dynasty collapsed in a revolution led by Dr. Sun Yat-sen in 1911.

The new Republic of China, under the leadership of Sun, his dictatorial successor Chiang Kai-shek, and the Nationalist Party (Guomindang or Kuomintang), proved both weak and corrupt. From the invasion by Japan, which began in 1931, to a strong insurgent movement led by Communist Mao Tse-tung, the Chiang regime was severely undermined and eventually ousted from China in 1949, retreating to Taiwan under U.S. military protection. Mao established the People's Republic of China, free from foreign domination for the first time since the Opium War. His alliance with the Soviet Union in the 1950s, however, led to its isolation throughout the Cold War. His support of the wars in Korea and Vietnam made China the enemy of the United States. The United States-China detente was initiated in the historic meeting between President Richard Nixon and Mao Tse-tung and Chou Enlai in 1972. In 1978, under the leadership of Deng Xiaoping, China also undertook a series of bold economic reforms. In 1979 the United States broke ties with Taiwan and normalized its relations with China. Since the end of the Cold War, China has become a major political and economic power in an increasingly economically integrated, yet disorderly world.

## HISTORY OF CHINESE IMMIGRATION

In many respects, the motivations for Chinese to go to the United States are similar to those of most immigrants; some came to "the Gold Mountain" (*Jinshan* in Mandarin or *Gumsaan* in Cantonese), the United States, to seek better economic opportunity, while others were compelled to leave China either as contract laborers or refugees. They brought with them their language, culture, social institutions, and customs, and over time, they made lasting contributions to their adopted country and tried to become an integral part of the U.S. population.

However, their collective experience as a racial minority, since they first arrived in the mid-nineteenth century, differs significantly from the European immigrant groups and other racial minorities. Chinese were singled out for discrimination through laws enacted by states in which they had settled; they were the first immigrant group to be targeted for exclusion and denial of citizenship by the U.S. Congress in 1882. Their encounter with Euro-Americans has been shaped not just by their cultural roots and self-perceptions but also by the changing bilateral relations between the United States and China. The steady infusion of immigrants from China and Taiwan and easy access to traditional and popular cultures from China, Taiwan, and Hong Kong, through telecommunication and trans-Pacific travel, have helped create a new Chinese America that is as diverse as it is fast-changing. Chinese American influence in politics, culture, and science, is felt as much in the United States as it is in China, Taiwan, and Hong Kong.

The movement of the Chinese population within China (called the *han*, or *tang*, people in pre-twentieth century China and *huaqiao*, or *huaren*, in the twentieth century), has continued throughout the 5,000-year history of China. *Huaqiao* (literally, sojourning Chinese), or more accurately, *huaren* (persons of Chinese descent), is a term commonly used for Chinese residing outside of China proper or overseas. Today, about 35 million Chinese live outside of China in over 130 countries. Chinese immigration to the United States is part of this great historic process.

Even though ancient Chinese legends and writings, most notably the fifth-century account by Weishen of a land called Fusang, suggest the presence of Chinese in North America centuries before Christopher Columbus, and a few Chinese were reported to be among the settlers in the colonies in the east coast in the eighteenth century, significant Chinese immigration to the west coast of the United States (*Jinshan*) did not begin until the California Gold Rush.

Chinese immigration can be roughly divided into three periods: 1849-1882, 1882-1965, and 1965 to the present. The first period, also known as the first wave, began shortly after the Gold Rush in California and ended abruptly with the passage of the Chinese Exclusion Act of 1882, the first race-based immigration law. During this period, the Chinese could act like other pioneers of the West and were allowed to immigrate or travel freely between China and San Francisco. Thousands of Chinese, mostly young male peasants, left their villages in the rural counties around the Zhujiang, or Pearl River, delta in Guangdong Province in southern China to become contract laborers in the American West. They were recruited to extract metals and minerals, construct a vast railroad network, reclaim swamplands, build irrigation systems, work as migrant agricultural laborers, develop the fishing industry, and operate highly competitive, labor-intensive manufacturing industries in the western states. The term limit of their contracts, together with the strong anti-Chinese sentiment that greeted them upon their arrival, precluded most of them from becoming permanent settlers. Under these circumstances, most of the laborers had only limited objectives: to advance their own and their families' economic well-being during their sojourn and to return to their ancestral villages to enjoy the fruits of their labor during retirement. At the end of the first period, the Chinese population in the United States was about 110,000, or one-fifth of one percent, of the U.S. total.

When Chinese labor was no longer needed and political agitation against the Chinese intensified, the U.S. Congress enacted a series of very harsh anti-Chinese laws, beginning in 1882, designed to exclude Chinese immigrants and deny naturalization and democratic rights to those already in the United States. Throughout most of the second period (the period of exclusion; 1882-1965), only diplomats, merchants, and students and their dependents were allowed to travel between the United States and China. Occasional loopholes in the late 1940s and 1950s, created by special legislation for 105 Chinese immigrants per year in 1943, the presence of Chinese American war brides in 1946, and selected refugees in 1953 and 1961, allowed some Chinese to enter. Otherwise, throughout this period, Chinese Americans were confined largely to segregated ghettos, called Chinatowns, in major cities and isolated pockets in rural areas across the country. Deprived of their democratic rights, they made extensive use of the courts and diplomatic channels to defend themselves, but with limited success.

The Civil Rights movement in the 1960s, particularly the enactment of the Civil Rights Act of 1964 and the Immigration and Nationality Act of 1965, finally ushered in a new era, the third period in Chinese American immigration history. Chinese Americans were liberated from a structure of racial oppression. The former legisla-tion restored many of the basic rights denied Chinese Americans, while the latter abolished the racist law that severely restricted Chinese immigration and prevented Chinese Americans from being reunited with their loved ones. Under these new laws, thousands of Chinese came to the United States each year to reunite with their families and young Chinese Americans mobilized to demand racial equality and social justice.

Equally significant are two other types of Chinese immigrants who have been entering the United States since the early 1970s. The first type consists of highly select and well-educated Chinese. No less than 250,000 Chinese intellectuals, scientists, and engineers have come to the United States for advanced degrees. Most of them have stayed to contribute to U.S. preeminence in science and technology. The second type is made up of tens of thousands of Chinese immigrants who have entered the United States to escape either political instability or repression throughout East and Southeast Asia, the result of a dramatic reversal of the U.S. Cold War policies toward China in 1972 and toward Vietnam in 1975. Some of these are Chinese from the upper and middle classes of Taiwan, Hong Kong, and throughout Southeast Asia who want long-term security for themselves, their businesses, and their children. Others are ethnic Chinese from Vietnam and Cambodia who became impoverished refugees and "boat people," when Vietnam implemented its anti-Chinese or "ethnic cleansing" policies in 1978. It was this steady infusion of Chinese immigrants that accounted for the substantial increase of the Chinese American population, amounting to 1.6 million in the 1990 census, making them the largest Asian American group in the United States.

## SETTLEMENT PATTERNS

Economic development and racial exclusion defined the patterns of Chinese American settlement. Before the Chinese Exclusion Act of 1882, the patterns of Chinese settlement followed the patterns of economic development of the western states. Since mining and railway construction dominated the western economy, Chinese immigrants settled mostly in California and states west of the Rocky Mountains. As these industries declined and anti-Chinese agitation intensified, the Chinese retreated—and sometimes were forced by mainstream society—into small import-export businesses and labor-intensive manufacturing (garments, wool, cigars, and shoes) and service industries (laundry, domestic work, and restaurants) in such rising cities as San Francisco, New York, Boston, Philadelphia, Chicago, Los Angeles, and Seattle; into agriculture in rural communities in California; and into small retail business in black rural communities in the Deep South. Some Chinese found themselves systematically evicted from jobs, land, and businesses and their rights, privileges, and sanctuaries in mainstream society permanently suspended. By the early twentieth century, over 80 percent of the Chinese population were found in Chinatowns in major cities in the United States.

Chinatowns remained isolated and ignored by the American mainstream until after World War II. After the war, as the United States became a racially more open and tolerant society, emigration from the Chinatowns began. With new employment opportunities, a steady stream of Chinese Americans moved into new neighborhoods in cities and into sprawling suburbs, built around the rising military-industrial complex during the Cold War. As the new waves of postwar immigrants arrived, the poor moved into historic Chinatowns and the more affluent settled into new neighborhoods and suburbs, creating the so-called new Chinatowns in cities including San Francisco, Los Angeles, New York, and Houston, and a string of suburbs with strong Chinese American presence, such as the ones along Interstate 10 west of Los Angeles and Highway 101 between San Francisco and San Jose. The new immigrants brought new cultural and economic vitality into both the new and the old communities even as they actively interacted with their Euro-American counterparts.

From interactions under ghetto confinement, to the rise of a suburban Chinese American middle class, to the revitalization of historic Chinatowns, Chinese American communities across the United States have become more diverse, dynamic, and divided, with the arrival of new waves of immi-

**"I** myself rarely left Chinatown, only when I had to buy American things downtown. The area around Union Square was a dangerous place for us, you see, especially at nighttime before the quake [1906]. Chinese were often attacked by thugs there and all of us had to have a police whistle with us all the time."

Gim Chang, a Chinese resident of San Francisco, cited in *Ellis Island: An Illustrated History of the Immigrant Experience,* edited by Ivan Chermayeff et al. (New York: Macmillan, 1991).

grants creating new conflicts as well as opportunities that are uniquely Chinese American.

The growth and proliferation of the Chinese American population in the last three decades also aroused resentment and hostility in cities and suburbs and in the spheres of education and employment. For example, some neighborhoods and suburbs, most notably, San Francisco and Monterey Park, California tried to curb Chinese American population growth and business expansion by restrictive zoning. Chinese American achievements in education, seen with increasing apprehension in some cases, has led to the use of discriminatory means to slow down or reverse their enrollment in select schools and colleges. Since the early 1980s, there has been a steady increase in incidents of racial violence reported. These trends have been viewed with increasing alarm by Chinese Americans across the United States.

## ACCULTURATION AND ASSIMILATION

Throughout the second half of the nineteenth and early decades of the twentieth centuries, Chinatown was a permanent home for the Chinese who were cut off from China "like orphans" (*haiwai guer*) and yet disenfranchised from the Euro-American mainstream. Assimilation was never a viable choice for Chinese Americans, who were excluded and denied citizenship because they were deemed nonassimilable by the white mainstream.

In 1852 Governor John Bigler of California, demanded Chinese exclusion on the ground they were nonassimilable. In 1854 the California Supreme Court, in *Hall v. People,* ruled that Chinese testimony against whites was inadmissible in a court of law because, "the same rule which would admit them to testify, would admit them to all the equal rights of citizenship; and we might soon see them at the polls, in the jury box, upon the bench, and in our legislative halls." By congressional statutes and judicial decisions, Chinese immigrants were made ineligible for naturalization, rendering them politically disenfranchised in a so-called democracy and exposing them to frequent and flagrant violations of their Constitutional rights.

Chinese Americans could not understand how the United States could use gunboat diplomacy to open the door of China and at the same time use democracy to close the door to Chinese Americans. The bitter encounter with American democracy and hypocrisy planted a seed of modern Chinese nationalism, which led the Chinese Americans to fight for equal rights at home and to orient their collective will toward freeing China from imperialist domination. They linked the racial oppression of the Chinese in the United States to the impotence of China.

Life within the Chinatown ghetto, therefore, was hard but not stagnant. Legally discriminated against and politically disenfranchised, Chinese Americans established their roots in Chinatowns, fought racism through aggressive litigation and diplomatic channels, and participated actively in various economic development projects and political movements to modernize China. For the immigrant generation, there was only one choice, modernization for themselves and for China. Assimilation was seen as an impossibility. For the American-born generation, many members of which made a concerted effort to assimilate, mainstream society remained inhospitable.

In the nineteenth century, most Chinese immigrants saw no future in the United States and oriented their lives toward eventual return to China, *luoye-guigen*. With this sojourner mentality, they developed a high degree of tolerance for hardship and racial discrimination and maintained a frugal Chinese lifestyle, which included living modestly; observing Chinese customs and festivals through family and district associations; sending regular remittance to parents, wives, and children, and maintaining village ancestral halls and charities. Parents tried to instill Chinese language and culture in their children, send them to Chinese schools in the community or in China, motivate them to excel in American education, and above all, arrange marriages. The parents in Louis Chu's *Eat a Bowl of Tea* (1961) tried to find their sons brides in villages in the Zhujiang delta. For the most part, their sole aspiration was to work hard and save enough to retire in comfort back in the villages from which they came.

They also joined social organizations. District associations (*huiguan*) and family associations (*gongsuo*), respectively, represented the collective interest and well-being of persons from the same villages or counties and persons with the same family names. These ascriptive organizations provided aid and comfort to their members, arbitrated disputes, helped find jobs and housing, established schools and temples, and sponsored social and cultural events. Most of these organizations had branches in different Chinatowns, enabling members to travel from one city to another. Together,

these organizations formed the Consolidated Chinese Benevolent Association in each city, a de facto ghetto government, to settle disputes among individuals and organizations and to represent the community's interests with both U.S. and Chinese governments, at times through civil disobedience, passive resistance, and litigation, and at other times through diplomatic channels and grassroots protests instigated in China. Their activities brought mixed blessings to the community. At times, these organizations became too powerful and oppressive, and they also obstructed social and political progress. Without question, they left an enduring legacy in Chinese America.

Into these uniquely American ghettos also came a string of Protestant and Catholic missionaries, establishing churches and schools and trying to convert and assimilate the Chinese, as well as a steady stream of political factions and reformers from China, advancing their agendas for modernizing China and recruiting Chinese Americans to support and work for their causes. Both were agents of change, but they worked on different constituencies and at cross purposes: one tried to assimilate them, while the other tried to instill in them a cultural and political loyalty to China.

Virtually all major Christian churches established missions and schools in San Francisco's Chinatown, the largest in the United States and the center of cultural, economic, and political life of Chinese in North America. Among the most enduring institutions were the YMCA and YWCA, the St. Mary's Chinese Mission School, and the Cameron House, a Presbyterian home for "rescued" Chinese prostitutes. The churches, in general, were more successful in winning converts among the American-born generation.

Proportionally smaller in number, those Chinese Americans who were exposed to a segregated but American education very quickly became aware of their inferior status. Many became ashamed of their appearance, status, and culture. Self-hatred and the need to be accepted by white society became their primary obsession. In practice this meant the rejection of their cultural and linguistic heritage and the pursuit of thoroughgoing Americanization: adoption of American values, personality traits, and social behaviors and conversion to Christianity.

Denying their racial and cultural identity failed to gain them social acceptance in the period before World War II. Most found themselves still shut out of the mainstream and were prevented from competing for jobs, even if they were well qualified. Some were compelled to choose between staying in the United States as second-class citizens and going to China, a country whose language and culture had, ironically, become alien to them on account of their attempted assimilation.

For the immigrant generation, there was only one choice: staking their future in China. China's modernization occupied their attention and energy because they attributed their inferior status in the United States to the impotence of China as a nation under Western domination. Reformers from opposing camps in China invariably found an eager audience and generous supporters among the Chinese in the United States. Among the political reformers who frequented Chinatowns across the United States to raise funds and recruit supporters were Kang Youwei, Liang Qichao, and Sun Yat-sen before the 1911 Revolution. During the Sino-Japanese War (1937-41), several leaders of the ruling Kuomintang also toured the United States to mobilize Chinese American support; among them were General Cai Tingkai and Madame Chiang Kai-shek. The factional dispute between the pro-China and pro-Taiwan forces is very much a part of this political legacy. In essence, China's political factionalism became an integral part of Chinese American life.

Between efforts of the missionaries and political reformers, many churches and political parties were established and sectarian schools and newspapers founded. Schools and newspapers became some of the most influential and enduring institutions in Chinese America. Together they played an important role in perpetuating the Chinese culture among the Chinese and in introducing Chinese to ideas of modernity and nationalism.

## CUISINE

Chinese tea was a popular beverage in eighteenth- and nineteenth-century America. Since the 1960s, Chinese cuisine has been an integral part of the American diet as well. Chinese restaurants are found in small towns and large cities across the United States. Key ingredients for preparing authentic Chinese dishes are now found in all chain supermarkets, and lessons in Chinese cooking are regular features on national television. Chinese take-outs, catering, and chain restaurants have become commonplace in major cities, and Chinese *dim sum*, salads, and pastas can be found in cocktail lounges and exclusive clubs and resorts. Gone are such pre-1960 dishes as chop suey, chow mien, egg fooyung, and barbecue spareribs. In fact, many Americans have mas-

tered the use of chopsticks and acquired the taste for sophisticated Chinese regional cuisines, such as Cantonese, Kejia (Hakka), Sichuan (Szechuan), Shangdong, Hunan, Mandarin (Beijing), Taiwan (Minnan), Chaozhou (Teo-Chiu), and Shanghai. American households now routinely use Chinese ingredients, like soy sauce, ginger, and hoisin sauce in their food; employ Chinese cooking techniques, such as stir frying; and include Chinese cooking utensils, like the wok and the cleaver, in their kitchens.

## TRADITIONAL COSTUMES

Very few Chinese Americans now wear traditional Chinese clothing. On special occasions, some traditional costumes are worn. For example, on the wedding day, a bride might wear a Western wedding gown for the wedding ceremony and then change into a traditional Chinese wedding gown, called *gua,* for the tea ceremony and banquet. In some traditional families, the elders sometimes wear traditional Chinese formal clothes to greet guests on Chinese New Year's Day. Sometimes, young Chinese American women wear the tightly fitted *cengsam* (*chongsam*), or *qipao,* for formal parties or banquets. Occasionally, Chinese styles find their way into American high fashion and Hollywood movies.

## SONGS AND DANCES

Chinese opera and folk songs are performed and sung in the Chinese American community. Cantonese opera, once very popular in Chinatown, is performed for older audiences, and small opera singing clubs are found in major Chinatowns in North America. Rarer is the performance of Peking opera. Among the well-educated Chinese, concerts featuring Chinese folk and art songs are well attended and amateur groups singing this type of music can be found in most cities with significant Chinese American populations. Similarly, both classical and folk dances continue to find some following among Chinese Americans. The Chinese Folk Dance Association of San Francisco is one of several groups that promotes this activity. Most American-born Chinese and younger new immigrants, however, prefer either American popular music or Cantonese and Mandarin popular music from China, Taiwan, and Hong Kong.

## HOLIDAYS

Most Chinese Americans today observe the major holidays of the Chinese lunar calendar (*yin li*).

Today, Chinese calendars routinely provide both the solar (*yang li*) and lunar calendars, and Chinese daily newspapers provide both kinds of dates. The most important holiday is the Chinese New Year or the Spring Festival (*chun jie*), which is also a school holiday in San Francisco.

Family members get together for special feasts and celebrations. The Feast of the Dead (*qing ming* or *sao mu*), the fifteenth day of the third lunar month, is devoted to tidying tombs and worshiping ancestors. The Dragon-boat Festival (*duan wu* or *duan yang*), on the fifteenth day of the fifth lunar month, commemorates the death of renown poet, Qu Yuan, who threw himself into the River Milu Jiang in 277 B.C. Usually a dragon-boat race is held and a special dumpling (*zong zi*) is served. For the August Moon Festival (*zhong jiu*), the ninth day of the eighth lunar month, family and friends gather to admire the moon and eat "moon cakes" (*yue bing*).

The founding of the People's Republic of China (*guo qing jie*), October 1, 1949 of the solar calendar, is observed by Chinese Americans with banquets and cultural performances in major cities in the United States. Likewise, the founding of the Republic of by Dr. Sun Yat-sen, October 10, 1911, is commemorated each year in Chinatowns by groups closely associated with the Nationalist government in Taiwan. Not as widely observed are the Children's Day (*er tong jie*) on June 1, Woman's Day (*fu nu jie*) on March 8, and May Day (*lao dong jie*) on May 1.

## HEALTH AND MENTAL HEALTH ISSUES

Prewar housing and job discrimination forced the Chinese to live within American ghettos. Discrimination also denied Chinese Americans access to health care and other services. Most relied on traditional Chinese herbal medicine, and the community had to found its own Western hospital, Chinese Hospital, in the early twentieth century. By the time the postwar immigrants arrived in large numbers in the 1960s, Chinatown was bursting at the seams, burdened with seemingly intractable health and mental health problems.

Chinatowns in San Francisco and New York are among the most densely populated areas in the United States. Housing has always been substandard and overcrowded. Throughout the 1960s and 1970s, Chinatown in San Francisco had the dubious distinction of having the highest tuberculosis and suicide rates in the Unites States. High unemployment and underemployment rates exposed

Chinese American performers carry a red and gold dragon while celebrating the Chinese New Year.

thousands of new immigrants to severe exploitation in sweatshops and restaurants. School dropouts, juvenile delinquency, and gang wars were symptoms of underlying social pathology.

However, it is wrong to assume that health and mental health problems exist only in the Chinatown ghettos. The overwhelming majority of Chinese Americans no longer live in historic Chinatowns, as mentioned above. While many of the health and mental health-related problems in Chinatown are class-based, many others, such as the language barrier, cultural and generational conflict, and attitudes toward illness and soliciting help, are peculiar to Chinese Americans regardless of their class position, education, and place of residence. Mental health service agencies, like the Richmond Maxi Center, in the middle-class Richmond district of San Francisco and the Asians for Community Involvement in the Silicon Valley of California, have been established to meet the needs of Chinese Americans and other Asian Americans. Today, both Chinese and Western medicines are widely used by Chinese Americans, although some use exclusively Chinese medicine while others only Western medicine.

# LANGUAGE

Most prewar Chinese arrived in the United States knowing only the various dialects of Cantonese (*Yue*), one of the major branches of Chinese spoken in the Zhujiang delta. The maintenance of Chinese has been carried out by a strong network of community language schools and Chinese-language newspapers. However, with the arrival of new immigrants from other parts of China and the world after World War II, virtually all major Chinese dialects were brought to America. Most prominent among these are Cantonese, Putonghua, Minnan, Chaozhou, Shanghai, and Kejia. Fortunately, one common written Chinese helps communication across dialects.

Today, Chinese is maintained through homes, community language schools, newspapers, radio, and television, and increasingly, through foreign language classes at mainstream schools and universities. The rapid increase of immigrant students since 1965 also gave rise to growing demand for equality of educational opportunity in the form of bilingual education, a demand that resulted in a 1974 U.S. Supreme Court decision in *Lau vs. Nichols*, a case brought by Chinese American parents in San Francisco. Hand in hand with this trend is the teaching of Mandarin or *Putonghua*, China's national spoken language, in public and community schools.

### GREETINGS AND OTHER POPULAR EXPRESSIONS

Cantonese greetings and other popular expressions include: *Nei hou ma?* (How are you?); *Hou loi mou gin* (Long time no see); *Seg zo fan mei?* (Have you eaten?); *Zoi gin* (Good-bye); *Zou tao* (Good night); *Deg han loi co* (Let's get together again); *Do ze* (Thank you); *M'sai hag hei* (Don't mention it); *Gung hei* (Congratulations); and *Gung hei Fad coi* (Have a prosperous New Year). Mandarin greetings and other popular expressions include: *Ni hao* (How do you do); *Xiexie* (Thank you); *Bu yong xie* or *Bu yong keqi* (Don't mention it); *Dui bu qi* (Excuse me); *Mei guanxi* (It's Okay); and *Zaijian* (Good-bye).

# FAMILY AND COMMUNITY DYNAMICS

Since most Chinese before 1882 came as contract laborers to perform specific tasks, the Chinese population in the United States in the nineteenth century was predominantly young males, either not yet married or married with their wives and children left in the villages in southern China. According to the 1890 census, there were 107,488

Chinese in the United States. Of these 103,620, or 96.4 percent, were males and only 3,868, or 3.6 percent, were females. Among the male population, 26.1 percent were married, 69 percent single, and 4.9 percent were either widowed or divorced. The male-female ratio was not balanced until 1970.

This uneven sex distribution gave rise to an image of Chinatown as a bachelor society, vividly captured in the pictures taken by Arnold Genthe in San Francisco before the 1905 earthquake and in the description by Liang Qichao during his 1903 travel to the United States. Normal family life for most Chinese Americans did not begin until after World War II, when several thousand war brides were brought in by Chinese American GIs.

The exclusion and anti-miscegenation laws forced most Chinese in the United States to maintain their families across the Pacific. Only the privileged merchant class was able to bring over their wives and children. Under such circumstances, the Chinese population in the United States declined steadily, dipping as low as 61,639 in 1920, before it started to rise again. The Chinese American population therefore had to wait until after World War II for the emergence of an American-born political leadership.

The abnormal conditions also contributed to widespread prostitution, gambling, and opium smoking, most of which were overseen by secret societies, known as *tongs*, often with the consent of both the Chinatown establishment and corrupt local law-enforcement agencies. The struggle for control of these illicit businesses also gave rise to frequent intrigues, violence, and political corruption and to sensational press coverage of the so-called tong wars.

It was not until the second decade of the twentieth century that a significant, but still proportionally small, American-born generation began to emerge. According to the 1920 census, only 30 percent of Chinese in America were born in the United States, and therefore, American citizens. The ratio of American born to foreign born was finally reversed in 1960, only to be reversed again in 1970 with the massive influx of new immigrants. Unlike the prewar immigrants, the new immigrants came to the United States with their families, and they came to stay permanently.

Today, most middle-class Chinese Americans place the highest priority on raising and maintaining the family: providing for the immediate members of the family (grandparents, parents, and children), acquiring an adequate and secure home

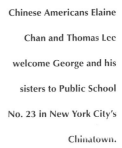

Chinese Americans Elaine
Chan and Thomas Lee
welcome George and his
sisters to Public School
No. 23 in New York City's
Chinatown.

for the family, and investing comparatively greater amounts of time and annual income in their children's education. Even among the poorer families, which have neither financial security nor decent housing, keeping the family intact and close and doing all they can to support their children are also priorities. This is why Chinese Americans continue to perform well in education across all income levels, even if the success rates among the poor are less impressive than those among the better off. Across the nation, Chinese American educational achievement is well known. In particular, Chinese Americans are disproportionately represented among the top research universities and the elite small liberal colleges. In graduate and professional schools, they are overrepresented in certain areas, but underrepresented in others. In addition to Chinese American students, there are thousands of Chinese foreign students from China, Taiwan, and Hong Kong.

However, it is wrong to assume that all Chinese Americans are living in happy, intact, suc-

cessful families and raising obedient, motivated, and college-bound children. Traditional Chinese concepts of family and child-rearing, for both the rich and poor, have undergone drastic changes in America due to job status, income levels, living arrangements, and neighborhood conditions, as well as the social and cultural environment of the United States. Chinese Americans face their share of family break-ups, domestic violence, school drop-outs, drug addiction, gang activities, etc.

### INTERACTIONS WITH OTHER ETHNIC MINORITIES

Racism and past policies of racial segregation have kept Chinese Americans largely separated from the mainstream of the society. Nevertheless, there has been contact between Chinese and other racial groups. For example, some Chinese established small general stores in poor black communities in the rural areas along the Mississippi valley after the Civil War. White missionaries and prostitutes found nineteenth-century Chinatowns to be productive places to carry out their business. Some Chinese laborers married American Indian and Mexican women during the period of exclusion, in spite of anti-miscegenation laws in virtually every state.

Since the Civil Rights movement of the 1960s, intermarriage has become more common as U.S. society becomes more open and Chinese Americans more affluent and desirable. However, racial prejudice and traditional racist stereotypes persist, contributing to racial distrust and conflict between Chinese Americans and whites, as well as between Chinese Americans and African Americans. For example, in the late 1960s and early 1970s, a large number of Chinese American parents in San Francisco mobilized to oppose court-ordered school integration. Chinese American engineer Vincent Chin was brutally murdered in Detroit in 1982 by two unemployed white auto workers because he was assumed to be Japanese and somehow responsible for their loss of jobs. Chinese American Jim Loo of Raleigh, North Carolina, was killed in 1989 by a white person because he was presumed to be a Vietnamese responsible for American deaths in Vietnam.

# RELIGION

All kinds of religions are practiced in the Chinese American community today. There are Christians of all denominations as well as Buddhists, Taoists, and Confucianists. Chinese churches and temples (*miao*) are found wherever there are Chinese Americans. Most of the old temples are found in historic Chinatowns. For example, in San Francisco's Chinatown in 1892, no fewer than 15 temples were present. Some of the temples were dedicated to the Goddess of Heaven (*Tienhou*)—also the god of seamen, fishermen, travelers, and wanderers—while others to Emperor Guangong (*Guandi*), a warrior god. Modern temples, such as the one in Hacienda Heights, California, were built by more recent Chinese immigrants from Taiwan. Likewise, Christian churches, organized by dialects, are found in old Chinatowns as well as in the suburbs.

The majority of Chinese Americans could be characterized as irreligious by Western standards of religion. This does not mean, however, that most of them are devoid of any religious feeling or that they do not practice any religion at all. The majority, in fact, practice some form of Buddhism or Taoism, folk religions, and ancestral worship.

Generally speaking, Chinese are pragmatic in their approach to life and religion. They are somewhat superstitious: they believe in the doctrines of *fengsui*, which are intended to help in the organization of a home, and they do not want to do anything they personally think is likely to offend the gods or the ways of nature. Toward this end, they choose who they want to worship and they worship them through certain objects or locations in nature. They also worship through their ancestors, folk heroes, animals, or their representations in idols or images, *as if* they are gods. To these representations, they offer respect and ritual offerings, burning incense, ritual papers, and paper objects to help maintain order and to bring good luck. This is, perhaps, why Chinese rarely become religious fanatics, evangelical, or driven to convert others. Above all, Chinese respect other people's religions as much as they respect their own.

Like most religions, there are rituals and moral teachings. Rituals are observed, learned, and practiced at home and in community temples or village ancestral halls. In the absence of ancestral halls in the United States, they perform rituals at miniature altars at home and in the place of business and in sanctuaries found in district and family associations in Chinatowns. Festivals and important dates in one's family are observed through rituals and banquets. Beliefs or teachings, to most Chinese, are simply ethical wisdom or precepts for living right or in harmony with nature or gods. They are taught through deeds, moral tales, and ethical principles, at home and in temples. Over the centuries, these teachings have combined major ideas and wisdom from Confucianism, Buddhism, and Taoism with local folk religions and village lores.

# EMPLOYMENT AND ECONOMIC TRADITIONS

Before the 1882 Chinese exclusion law, Chinese could be found in all walks of life. However, with the rise of anti-Chinese movements and the enactment of anti-Chinese laws, Chinese were effectively driven out of most jobs and businesses competitive with whites. Until World War II, Chinese were left with jobs in laundries, Chinese restaurants, sweatshops, gift shops, and grocery stores located in Chinatowns. Even those who were American-born and college educated were unable to find jobs commensurate with their training.

World War II was a turning point for Chinese Americans. Not only were they recruited into all branches of military service, they were also placed in defense-related industries. In spite of racial prejudice, young Chinese Americans excelled in science and technology and made substantial inroads into many new sectors of the labor market during the war. Two significant postwar developments changed the fortune of Chinese Americans. First, the rise of the military industrial complex in suburban areas created opportunities for Chinese Americans in defense-related industries. Second, there was the arrival of many highly educated Chinese immigrants from China, Taiwan, and Hong Kong, whose talents were immediately recognized; they were quickly recruited by the military industrial complex and leading research centers and universities.

In general, the intellectual immigrants settled down in middle-class suburbs near new industrial or research centers, such as Silicon Valley in Santa Clara county, California and NASA Johnson Space Center outside of Houston, Texas. Likewise, affluent pockets of Chinese Americans can be found in such metropolitan areas as Seattle, Minneapolis, Chicago, Los Angeles, Pittsburgh, San Diego, and Dallas. Since the 1970s, some even used their talents to start their own businesses in the highly competitive high-tech industries. Among the best known are An Wang of Wang Laboratories, David Lee of Qume Corporation, Tom Yuen of AST, and Charles Wang of Computer Associates International. Many of the intellectual immigrants also became leading scientists and top engineers in the United States, giving rise to the false impression that the prewar oppressed Chinese working class had finally pulled themselves up by their own bootstraps. This is the misleading "model minority" stereotype that the media originated and has fiercely maintained since the late 1960s. These highly celebrated intellectuals, in fact, have little, politically, economically, or socially in common with the direct descendants of the prewar Chinese communities in big cities.

Among the post-1965 immigrants were also thousands who came to be reunited with their long-separated loved ones. Most of them settled in well-established, but largely disenfranchised, Chinese American communities in San Francisco, New York, Boston, Chicago, Philadelphia, Oakland, and Los Angeles where they became the new urban working class. Many also became small entrepreneurs in neighborhoods throughout these cities, concentrating mostly in laundries, restaurants, and grocery stores. In fact, their presence in these three areas of small business has made them an integral part of the cityscape of American cities. Usually with little or no English, they pursued their "American dream" by working long hours, often with free labor from family members or cheap labor from relatives.

The Chinese American population is, therefore, bifurcated between the poor (working class) and the middle class (professionals and small business owners). The interests of these two groups coincide with each other over such issues as racism and access to quality education, but most of the time, they are at odds with each other. There is much debate over the China-Taiwan conflict, and, regarding housing and employment, their relations are frequently those of landlord-tenant and management-labor, typified by the chronic struggle over land use (e.g., the International Hotel in San Francisco's Chinatown) and working conditions in Chinatowns (e.g., the Chung Sai Sewing Factory, also in San Francisco's Chinatown) since 1970.

# POLITICS AND GOVERNMENT

Unlike European immigrants and African Americans since the Civil War, Chinese immigrants were denied citizenship, systematically discriminated against and disenfranchised until after World War II. Numerically far smaller than Euro-Americans and African Americans, Chinese Americans posed no political threat to the entrenched power, even after they were granted the right of naturalization after the war. They were routinely denied, de jure and de facto, political and civil rights. It was not until the late 1960s, under the militant leadership of younger Chinese Americans, that they began to mobilize for equal participation with the help of African Americans and in coalition with other Asian American groups.

Three key elements shaped the formation and development of the Chinese American community: racism, U.S.-China relations, and the interaction between these two forces. The intersection of American foreign policy and domestic racial politics compelled Chinese Americans to live under a unique structure of dual domination. They were racially segregated and forced to live under an apartheid system, and they were subject to the extraterritorial domination of the Chinese government, condoned, if not encouraged at times, by the U.S. government. Chinese Americans were treated as aliens and confined to urban ghettos and governed by an elite merchant class legitimated by the U.S. government and reinforced by the omnipresent diplomatic representatives from China. Social institutions, lifestyles, and political factionalism were reproduced and institutionalized. Conflict over homeland partisan disputes—including the dispute between the reform and revolutionary parties at the turn of the century and between the Nationalists led by Chiang Kai-shek and Communists led by Mao Tsetung in China—kept the community deeply divided. Such divisions drained scarce financial resources and political energy from pressing issues within the community and left behind a legacy of preoccupation with motherland politics and deep political cleavage to this date. During the Cold War, the extraterritorial domination intensified, as military dictators in Taiwan, backed by the United States, extended their repression into the Chinese American community in an effort to insure political loyalty and suppress political dissent.

The African American civil rights movement inspired and inaugurated a new era of ethnic pride and political consciousness. Joined by other Asian American groups, American-born, college-age Chinese rejected both the racist model of forced assimilation and the political and cultural domination of the Nationalist government in Taiwan. They also rejected second-class citizenship and the option of returning to Asia. Instead, they demanded liberation from the structure of dual domination. These college students and, later, young professionals contributed most significantly to raising the ethnic and political consciousness of Chinese Americans and helped achieve civil rights. Furthermore, they founded many social service agencies and professional, political, and cultural organizations throughout the United States. They also joined forces with other Asian American college students to push for the establishment of Asian American studies programs in major universities and colleges across the nation.

The politicization of Chinese Americans soon led to the founding of new civil rights and partisan political organizations. Most notable was the founding of Chinese for Affirmative Action (CAA) in San Francisco in 1969, a civil rights organization that has been at the forefront of all major issues—employment, education, media, politics, health, census, hate crime, etc.—affecting Chinese Americans across the nation. By the 1970s, two national organizations, the Organization of Chinese Americans (OCA) and the National Association of Chinese Americans (NACA), were formed in most major cities to serve, respectively, middle-class Chinese Americans and Chinese American intellectuals. Likewise, local partisan clubs and Chinese American Democrats and Republicans were organized to promote Chinese American participation in politics and government.

By the 1980s, some middle-class Chinese Americans began to take interest in local electoral politics. They enjoyed with modest success in the races for less powerful positions, such as school boards and city councils. Among the notable political leaders to emerge were March Fong Eu, Secretary of State of California, S. B. Woo, lieutenant governor of Delaware (1984-88), Michael Woo of Los Angeles City Council (1986-90), and Thomas Hsieh and Mabel Teng of the San Francisco Board of Supervisors in 1988.

With increased interest in electoral politics came the demand for greater participation in other branches of government. In 1959 Delbert Wong became the first Chinese American to be appointed a municipal judge in Los Angeles. In 1966 Lim P. Lee was appointed Postmaster of San Francisco, and Harry Low, a municipal judge. Low was later appointed to the Superior Court and the California Appellate Court. Also appointed to the municipal bench were Samuel Yee, Leonard Louie, Lillian Sing, and Julie Tang in San Francisco and Jack Bing Tso, James Sing Yip, and Ronald Lew in Los Angeles. Thomas Tang was appointed to the ninth circuit court in 1977 and Elwood Lui to the federal district court in 1984.

Chinese Americans have been predominantly an urban population since the late nineteenth century. Their community has long been divided between the merchant elites and the working-class, and the influx of both poor and affluent immigrants since the late 1960s has deepened the division in the community by class, nativity, dialect, and residential location, giving rise not to just conflicting classes and public images, but also to conflicting visions in Chinese America. The sources of this open split can be traced to the changes in U.S. immigration laws and Cold War policies and to the arrival of diverse Chinese immigrants from China, Taiwan, Hong Kong, and Southeast Asian countries throughout the Cold War. The division has had serious political and social consequences as Chinese Americans from opposing camps seek political empowerment in cities with a deeply entrenched, white ethnic power structure and emerging African American forces.

# Individual and Group Contributions

Chinese American contributions are significant and far-reaching. In general, it can be said that they contributed in labor to the economic development in the West in the second half of the nineteenth century and to science and technology in the second half of the twentieth century. Even though the nineteenth-century immigrants to the West Coast were mostly peasants working as contract laborers, their collective contribution to the building of the West has long been recognized by historians. Most notable was the completion of the transcontinental railway over the Sierra Nevada and the deserts of Nevada and Utah, and the building of the railroad network throughout the Southwest and into the Deep South. Less known, but no less significant, was the labor they provided for the mining of not just gold but also other minerals from the Pacific Coast to the Rocky Mountains; the construction of the canals, irrigation systems, and land claims that lay the foundation for the well-known and prosperous agribusiness of California; the groundbreaking work in fruit and vegetable farming and fishing industry; and the labor-intensive manufacturing industries, such as garments, shoes, woolen mills, and cigars, which provided the necessities of life in the developing West. Chinese labor was so timely, dependable, and efficient that Stanford historian Mary R. Coolidge, writing in 1909, concluded that "without [it] her [California's] material progress must long be postponed." Likewise, the UCLA historian Alexander Saxton, in a more recent book (1971), characterized the Chinese laborers as the "indispensable enemy" in California's economic development and politics in the nineteenth century.

## LITERATURE

In the world of literature, Maxine Hong Kingston and Amy Tan have captured the imagination of the United States with their writings based in part on their personal experiences and stories told in their families. Kingston is best known for her *Women Warrior* (1976), *Chinamen* (1977), and *Tripmaster Monkey* (1989), while Tan is known for her *Joy Luck Club* (1989) and *The Kitchen God's Wife* (1991). Other accomplished writers, to name a few, include Gish Jen (*Typical American*), David Wong Louie (*Pangs of Love*), and Faye Myenne Ng (*Bone*). Equally successful, in the world of Chinese-language readers, are literary works written in

Chinese by Chinese American writers like Chen Ruoxi, Bai Sienyong, Yi Lihua, Liu Daren, and Nie Hualing, who are also widely read in Hong Kong, Taiwan, China, and Southeast Asia.

## SCIENCE AND TECHNOLOGY

Equally important are the contributions Chinese Americans made to postwar U.S. accomplishments in science and technology. As mentioned above, one of the most outstanding features of the postwar Chinese immigration is the migration of Chinese intellectuals from China, Taiwan, and Hong Kong. Not only did they boost the large pool of scientists and engineers needed in the military-industrial complex throughout the Cold War, they also emerged as leading scientists and engineers in virtually all major disciplines in research laboratories in industries and research universities. For example, Chinese American scientists and engineers constitute a significant work force in the Silicon Valley and in aerospace centers in Seattle, Los Angeles/Long Beach, and San Diego, as well as in the national research laboratories of Lawrence Livermore, California; Los Alamos, New Mexico; Argonne Laboratory in Illinois; Jet Propulsion Laboratory in Pasadena, California; and NASA Space Centers in Houston, Texas, and Cape Canaveral, Florida. Chinese Americans are also employed in the laboratories of IBM, RCA, Bell Lab, GE, Boeing, 3M, Westinghouse, and in major research universities, from MIT to the University of California, Berkeley.

Many distinguished Chinese American scientists and engineers have received national and international recognition. For example, Chinese Americans who have received Nobel Prizes include: Chen-ning Yang, Cheng-tao Lee, and Tsao-chung Ting in physics and Yuan-tse Lee in chemistry. In mathematics, Shiing-shen Chern, Sing-tung Yao, and Wu-I Hsiang are ranked among the top in the world. In the biological sciences, Cho-hoe Li, Ming-jue Zhang, and Yuet W. Kan have all received honors and awards. The leading American researcher in superconductivity research is Paul Chu. In engineering, T. Y. Lin, structural engineer, received the Presidential Science Award in 1986. Others include Kuan-han Sun, a radiation researcher with Westinghouse; Tien Chang-lin, a mechanical engineer and Chancellor of the University of California, Berkeley; Henry Yang, an aerospace engineer and the Chancellor of the University of California, Santa Barbara; and Steven Chen, the leading researcher on the next generation of supercomputers.

Among the Chinese American women with national and international reputations in science are Ying-zhu Lin in aeronautics and aeronautical engineering, recipient of the Achievement Award for women engineers in 1985, and Chien-Hsiung Wu in physics.

## THEATER, FILM, AND MUSIC

Frank Chin, Genny Lim, and David Henry Hwang have all made lasting contributions to the theater. Among the best known plays of Hwang are *FOB*, *The Dance and the Railroad*, *Family Devotions*, and *M. Butterfly*. Several films of Wayne Wang, *Chan is Missing*, *Dim Sum*, *Eat a Bowl of Tea*, and *Joy Luck Club*, have received critical acclaims. Less famous, but no less important, are the unique Chinese American themes and sounds of jazz compositions and recordings of Fred Ho in New York and Jon Jang in San Francisco.

## VISUAL ARTS

Besides their enormous contributions to science and technology, many Chinese Americans also excel in art and literature. Maya Ying Lin is already a legend in her own time. At 21, while an architecture student at Yale University, she created the Vietnam Veterans Memorial in Washington, D.C., the most frequented national monument. After this enormous success, she went on to design the Civil Rights Memorial in Arkansas, a giant outdoor sculpture commemorating the twentieth anniversary of the admission of women into her alma mater, and a monumental sculpture at the New York Pennsylvania Railroad Station.

Just as impressive, are the architectural wonders of I. M. Pei. Among his best known works are the East Wing of the National Art Gallery in Washington, D.C., the John F. Kennedy Library at Harvard University, the Boston Museum and the John Hancock Building in Boston, Dallas Symphony Hall, the modern addition to the Louvre in Paris, the Bank of China in Hong Kong, and the Xiangshan Hotel in Beijing.

# MEDIA

## PRINT

Chinese-language newspapers have always played an important role in the Chinese American community. Newspapers may be found in most major Chinatowns, from Honolulu to New York. San Francisco, however, has long been the national center for Chinese American newspapers.

The *Gold Hills News*, the first weekly periodical to be published in San Francisco, was founded in April 1854. The following year, Rev. William Speer, a Presbyterian missionary to Chinatown, published the first bilingual weekly, *Tung Ngai San-Luk* (*The Oriental*). A year later, in 1856, the *Chinese Daily News*, the first Chinese daily in the world, began circulation in Sacramento, California.

Unfortunately, technical and financial difficulties made success in print medium elusive. Most did not survive long. It was not until the turn of the century, under the influence of Chinese nationalism and opposing political parties seeking support among Chinese in the United States, that newspapers in Chinatown flourished and endured for several decades. The factions with influential papers in San Francisco were Hongmen's *Datung Ribao* (*Chinese Free Press*), *Chung Sai Daily*, a neutral daily, edited by Ng Poon Chew, *Shaonian Zhongguo Zhen Bao* (*Young China Morning Paper*), founded by Sun Yat-sen, and *Shijie Ribao* (*The Chinese World*), a pro-reform party paper.

The next round of blossoming Chinese-language papers began modestly in the early 1970s and, aided by computers, satellite telecommunication, and new printing technology, grew into a major battle in the early 1980s among giant national dailies. The national dailies, printed and distributed simultaneously in major cities in the United States, included *The World Journal* (*Shijie Ribao*), *China Times* (*Zhongguo Shibao*), *International Daily News* (*Guoji Ribao*), *Sing Tao Daily*, and *Centre Daily* (*Zhong Bao*). To be added to this list are two other types of dailies: local dailies and dailies transmitted from Hong Kong and Taiwan. In addition to these nationally distributed dailies are numerous local dailies and weeklies and monthlies distributed both locally and nationally. The most notable weeklies in San Francisco have been *Chinese Pacific Weekly* (*Taipingyang Zhoubao*), *East-West Chinese American Weekly* (*Dongxi Bao*), an independent bilingual paper, and *Asian Week*, an English-only weekly.

Stiff competition for a small pool of Chinese readership and advertising dollars soon eliminated the first of several local dailies and weeklies and some of the national dailies by the late 1980s. However, satellite-transmitted dailies from Hong Kong continue to thrive in major cities in the United States.

### Chinese American Citizens Outlook.

Newsletter of the Chinese American Citizens Alliance; features news of interest to Chinese Americans.

**Contact:** Munson Kwok, Editor.
**Address:** 1044 Stockton Street, San Francisco, California 94108.

### The Chinese Press.

**Address:** 15 Mercer Street, New York, New York 10013.
**Telephone:** (212) 274-8282.

### Sampan.

The only bilingual newspaper in New England serving the Asian community.

**Contact:** Catherine Anderson, or Carmen Chan.
**Address:** Chinese American Civic Association, 90 Tyler Street, Boston, Massachusetts 02111.
**Telephone:** (617) 426-9492.
**Fax:** (617) 482-2315.

### Sing Tao Daily.

**Address:** 215 Litlefield Avenue, South San Francisco, California 94080.
**Telephone:** (415) 872-2299.

### World Journal.

**Address:** 231 Adrian Road, Millbrae, California 94030.
**Telephone:** (415) 692-9936.

### RADIO

Global Communication Enterprises, New York; Huayu Radio Broadcast, San Francisco.

### TELEVISION

Chinese World Television, New York; Hong Kong Television Broadcasts, U.S.A., Los Angeles; United Chinese TV, San Francisco; Hua Sheng TV, San Francisco; Pacific TV Broadcasting Co., San Francisco; and Channel 26, San Francisco.

# ORGANIZATIONS
# AND ASSOCIATIONS

Nineteenth-century Chinese immigrants established most traditional Chinese social organizations in Chinatowns. Most notable were the district associations (*huiguan*) and family name associations (*gongsuo*). Together, they formed the Consolidated Chinese Benevolent Association (CCBA) or the Chinese Six Companies. Before World War II, they were recognized as the leaders and spokesmen of the Chinese American community. Most of these organizations remain today. However, with the passage of time and the rise of new needs and interests, several modern organizations have emerged. Most notable among these are Christian churches of different denominations, secret societies (*tongs*), Chinese schools for different interest groups, trade organizations, guilds, and unions (laundry, garment, cigar, shoes, restaurant, etc.), recreation and youth clubs (YMCA and YWCA), political parties in China (earlier, Chee Kong Tong, Baohuanghui, Tungmenghui, and later, Kuomintang and Xienzhengdang), social and cultural societies, and newspapers. The Chinese Chamber of Commerce was founded in 1908, and the Chinese Hospital was established in 1925. Since the 1960s, new types of organizations have risen and proliferated.

### Chinese American Citizens Alliance (CACA).

A national organization founded early in the century to fight for Chinese American rights, with chapters in different Chinatowns.

**Contact:** Yvonne Lee, Director.
**Address:** 1044 Stockton Street, San Francisco, California 94108.
**Telephone:** (415) 982-4618.

### Chinese American Forum (CAF).

Cultivates understanding among U.S. citizens of Chinese American cultural heritage. Publishes a quarterly.

**Contact:** S. Yen Lee, President.
**Address:** 606 Brantford Avenue, Silver Spring, Maryland 20904.
**Telephone:** (301) 622-3053.

### Chinese Consolidated Benevolent Association (CCBA).

The oldest national Chinese organization in Chinatown, with affiliates in all Chinatowns.

**Address:** 843 Stockton Street, San Francisco, California 94108.
**Telephone:** (415) 982-6000.

### Chinese Culture Foundation of San Francisco.

A community-based cultural and educational facility, this organization provides space for exhibits, performing arts, conferences, classrooms, and meetings.

**Contact:** Vivian Chiang, Director of Administration.
**Address:** 750 Kearney Street, San Francisco, California 94108.
**Telephone:** (415) 986-1822.

### Chinese for Affirmative Action (CAA).

The leading civil rights organization of Chinese in the United States.

**Contact:** Henry Der, Executive Director.
**Address:** 17 Walter U. Lum Place, San Francisco, California 98108.
**Telephone:** (415) 274-6750.

### Chinese Historical Society of America.

Ethnic and historical interests of the Society are published in its bulletin.

**Address:** 650 Commercial Street, San Francisco, California 94111.
**Telephone:** (415) 391-1188.

### Organization of Chinese Americans (OCA).

A national organization committed to promoting the rights of Chinese Americans, with chapters throughout the United States and a lobbyist office in Washington, D.C. Publishes newsletter *OCA Image*.

**Contact:** Daphne Quok, Executive Director.
**Address:** 10001 Connecticut Aven, N.W., Suite 707, Washington, D.C. 20036.
**Telephone:** (202) 223-5500.

# MUSEUMS AND RESEARCH CENTERS

### Chinese Historical Society of America.

Devoted to the study of the Chinese people in the United States and the collection of their relics.

**Address:** Commercial Street, San Francisco, California 94108.

### New York Chinatown History Project, Chinese American Collection.

Located in the Asia American Studies Library, this collection is the largest single collection of Chinese American primary and secondary sources in the United States. Included is the most exten-

sive collection of Chinese-language newspapers in the United States.

**Contact:** Ms. Wei Chi Poon, Librarian.
**Address:** University of California, Berkeley, California 94720-2574.

# SOURCES FOR ADDITIONAL STUDY

*Entry Denied: Exclusion and the Chinese Community in America, 1882-1943*, edited by Sucheng Chan. Philadelphia: Temple University Press, 1991.

Kwong, Peter. *Chinatown, NY: Labor & Politics, 1930-1950*. New York: Monthly Review Press, 1979.

Lowen, James W. *The Mississippi Chinese: Between Black and White*. Cambridge, Massachusetts: Harvard University Press, 1971.

Lydon, Sandy. *Chinese Gold: The Chinese in the Monterey Bay Region*. Capitola, California: Capitola Book Co., 1985.

Ma, L. Eve Armentrout. *Revolutionaries, Monarchists, and Chinatowns: Chinese Politics in the Americas and the 1911 Revolution*. Honolulu: University of Hawaii Press, 1990.

McClain, Charles. *In Search of Equality: Chinese in the 19th Century Courts*. Berkeley & Los Angeles: University of California Press, 1994.

Nee, Victor G., and Brett de Barry. *Longtime Californ': A Documentary Study of an American Chinatown*. New York: Pantheon Books, 1972.

Saxton, Alexander. *The Indispensable Enemy: Labor and the Anti-Chinese Movement in California*. Berkeley and Los Angeles: University of California Press, 1971.

Tsai, Shih-shan Henry. *China and the Overseas Chinese in the United States, 1868-1911*. Fayetteville: University of Arkansas Press, 1983.

Wu, William F. *The Yellow Peril: Chinese Americans in American Fiction, 1850-1940*. Hamden, Connecticut: Archon Book, 1982.

# CHOCTAWS

by
**D. L. Birchfield**

Choctaws are an ancient people, but by their own account, they were the last of earth's inhabits to appear.

## OVERVIEW

The Choctaw nation occupies several non-contiguous blocks of land east of the Mississippi River. Larger than Massachusetts, the land area is located primarily in east-central Mississippi, site of the Choctaw ancestral homeland, and in a large contiguous block of land west of the Mississippi River, where the majority of the Choctaws were moved in the early 1830s. Here, the nation takes in the southeast portion of Oklahoma that encompasses ten and one-half counties. Choctaw communities are also located in Louisiana and Alabama.

The Choctaw nation is divided into separate governmental jurisdictions, each operating under its own constitution. The largest of these, and the only two formally recognized by the U.S. government, are the Choctaw Nation of Oklahoma and the Mississippi Band of Choctaw Indians. Other Choctaw groups, such as the Mowa Choctaws of Alabama, are seeking federal recognition. Since the United States proposed Article IV of the Treaty with the Choctaw in 1820, the official policy of the United States has been to attempt to abolish the Choctaw nation, confiscate its land, and assimilate its people. Article IV states that "the boundaries hereby established between the Choctaw Indians and the United States, on this side of the Mississippi river, shall remain without alteration until the period at which said nation shall become so civilized and enlightened as to be made citizens of the United States." By 1907, when Oklahoma achieved statehood, the federal government had adopted the position that the Choctaw nation had ceased to exist. Not until the present generation did the courts begin to uphold some of the Choctaw claims to national sovereignty. Making rulings about Choctaw claims has been complicated by competing claims of several state governments and those of the U.S. government.

## CHOCTAW SOVEREIGNTY

During the 1890s and the first years of the twentieth century, the U.S. government forcibly moved the Choctaws and other Indian nations into the region that is now the state of Oklahoma. Each nation was forced to accept individual allotments from a tribal land base, their nations were dissolved, and they were forced to become citizens of the new state.

The Choctaw paid a high price to maintain sovereignty. In an 1820 treaty with the United States, the Choctaw acquired new land west of the Mississippi to replace the ancestral homelands east of the Mississippi from which they had been removed. The nation bargained for its right to security within its own government, on its own land in 1830, giving the U.S. government more than ten million acres of land—all of the nation's remaining land in Mississippi and Alabama—in exchange for that right.

In Article IV of the 1830 treaty with the Choctaw, the nation secured this guarantee from the U.S. government: "The Government and people of the United States are hereby obliged to secure to the said Choctaw Nation of Red People the jurisdiction and government of all the persons and property that may be within their limits west, so that no Territory or State shall ever have a right to pass laws for the government of the Choctaw Nation of Red People and their descendants; and that no part of the land granted them shall ever be embraced in any Territory or State."

Few Americans know about the treaty or its contents, and those who do are not eager to acknowledge it. The Oklahoma public education system, for example, does not include this aspect of the state's history in its public school curriculum. Prejudice against indigenous people runs high in Oklahoma, where its citizens do not like to be reminded that their state was founded upon land guaranteed to "Indians."

## FIRST CHOCTAWS IN AMERICA

Choctaws are an ancient people, but by their own account, they were the last of earth's inhabits to appear. According to Choctaw belief, the first people to appear upon the earth lived a great distance from what would become the Choctaw homeland. These people emerged from deep beneath the earth's surface through a cave near the sacred mound, *Nanih Waiya*. They draped themselves on bushes around the cave to dry themselves in the sunshine, and then went to their distant homes. Many others followed the same pattern, finding homes closer and closer to the cave. Some of the last to emerge were the Cherokees, Creeks, Natchez, and others, who would become the Choctaw's closest neighbors. Finally, the Choctaws emerged and established their homeland around the sacred mound of *Nanih Waiya*, their mother.

Another Choctaw legend holds that they migrated to the site of *Nanih Waiya* after a great long journey from the northwest, led by a *hopaii* who carried a sacred pole that was planted in the ground each evening. Every morning the people continued their journey toward the rising sun, according to the direction in which the pole leaned. Finally, they awoke one morning to find the pole standing upright. They built *Nanih Waiya* on that site and made their home there.

In another version of the migration story, two brothers, Chahta and Chicksa, led the migration. After arriving at the site of *Nanih Waiya*, the group following Chicksa became lost for many years and became the Chickasaws, the Choctaws' nearest northern neighbors. Today, *Nanih Waiya* is a state park near the headwaters of the Pearl River in the east-central portion of Mississippi. "Mississippi," from the Choctaw word *Misha sipokni*, means "older than time," the Choctaw name for the great river of the North American continent.

It is not known whether there is a connection between the Choctaws, who have a great affection for the sacred mound of *Nanih Waiya*, and a mound-building civilization that flourished in North America about 2,000 years ago. This civilization constructed approximately 100,000 mounds in the greater Mississippi River Valley, some of which are among the most colossal structures of antiquity. The base of the Great Temple Mound at Cahokia, Illinois, for example, is three acres larger than the Great Pyramid of Egypt. Archaeologists believe *Nanih Waiya* was probably constructed around 500 B.C.

In the early eighteenth century the Natchez, one of the Choctaw's nearest neighbors, were still practicing a temple mound culture when Europeans first made intimate contact with Indians of that area. Many of the mounds were obliterated by farmers before they could be subjected to scientific study, and others were destroyed by eager amateurs. Remarkably, Americans have shown little interest in the mounds, limiting most exploration to hunting for pots.

In her doctoral dissertation in Choctaw history at the University of Oklahoma in 1934 (published as *The Rise and Fall of the Choctaw Republic*), historian Angie Debo attempted to summarize the characteristics of the ancient Choctaws: "They seem to have been distinguished for their peaceful character and their friendly disposition; their dependence on agriculture and trade; the absence of religious feeling and meaningful ceremonial; and their enjoyment of games and social gatherings. A mild, quiet, and kindly people, their institutions present little of spectacular interest; but to the very extent that they were practical minded and adaptable rather than strong and independent and fierce, they readily adopted the customs of the more advanced and more numerous race with which they came in contact."

## CHOCTAWS BEFORE EUROPEAN CONTACT

The Choctaws were one of the great nations of the Western hemisphere, with a population of an estimated 20,000 people living in more than 100 agricultural centers. The Cherokees and the Creeks had a population of comparable size. Choctaw territory encompassed more than 23 million acres in present day Mississippi and portions of Alabama and Louisiana.

Choctaws enjoyed the reputation of a peaceful, agricultural people. Their large numbers provided them with a measure of security from attack by their neighbors, and they are not known to have been disposed to seek military conquest. In fact, disputes among tribes in the region were sometimes settled by a game of ball. In one famous recorded instance, the Creeks and the Choctaws agreed to settle a disagreement about hunting rights to a watershed that lay between them based on the outcome of a game of ball. Tragically, the game ended in bloodshed and may have marked the last instance in which such disputes were decided in that manner. It is said that a Choctaw player became enraged and grabbed a weapon during play. When he attacked some of the Creek players, everyone took up their weapons. Many of the best players from both nations lay dead before elders could intervene. Because outbreaks of violence were unheard of in such games before this incident, it has been said that the Creeks and Choctaws were in shock that such an event could occur.

## FIRST RECORDED CONTACT WITH EUROPEANS

The Choctaws entered European historical records when the Spaniards in the expedition of Hernando DeSoto encountered them in the 1540s—an unhappy encounter for both parties. DeSoto, who had been Francisco Pizarro's cavalry captain in Peru, came to the southeastern portion of North American seeking another civilization as rich in gold and silver as the Incas. When he demanded women and baggage carriers of chief Tuscaloosa at the Choctaw town of Moma Bina, a battle ensued, and the Spaniards' baggage train was burned in a fire that also destroyed Moma Bina. The armored Spanish war horses struck terror in the Choctaws, who had never seen horses before, and Choctaw losses in the battle were heavy. The Choctaws nonetheless inflicted a reported 644 arrow wounds on the Spaniards, piercing their skin wherever armor did not protect it. After a period of rest and recovery, DeSoto's expedition passed through Choctaw country without further incident and wintered among the Chickasaws, who trapped them in a fire so hot that the Spanish had to build a forge and re-temper the steel in their swords before crossing the Mississippi and leaving the lands of the southeastern Indians.

## CHOCTAW RELATIONS WITH THE COLONIZERS

Following the establishment of Louisiana in 1700, the Choctaws and the French became acquainted and maintained an amicable relationship until 1763, when the French were expelled from North America at the conclusion of the French and Indian War. The Choctaws were the pivotal Indian nation with whom the French had to maintain good relations for the security of the Louisiana colony. The French were helped immeasurably in this regard by the depredations of English slave raiders who operated out of the Carolinas and took thousands of Choctaws into slavery in the early eighteenth century.

Choctaw relations with other Indians in the region were greatly affected by the presence of the French. In the 1730s the French waged a war of extermination against the Natchez, close neighbors of the Choctaws. The surviving Natchez fled to the Chickasaws for protection, and the Choctaws were drawn into a war against the Chickasaws that would rage on and off until the French left Louisiana.

The Choctaws experienced the devastating Choctaw Civil War of 1747-1750 when the nation was divided between those who wanted to maintain trade relations exclusively with the French and those who wanted to enter into trade relations with the English. Along with the removal of the Choctaws to the West, the civil war ranks as one of the most catastrophic events in recorded Choctaw history. The war's depopulation of entire villages severely weakened the Choctaws. Eventually, they realized that they were killing themselves for the benefit of the European colonial powers and concluded a peace.

An argument about who was responsible for failing to adequately supply the English faction of the Choctaws has come down to us from the eighteenth century by people deeply involved in attempting to persuade the Choctaws to trade with the English. Among them are James Adair, the English trader among the Chickasaws, in the 1775 British publication *History of the American Indians*, and his one-time business partner Edmond Atkin, in "Historical Account of the Revolt of the Choctaw Indians," a 1753 manuscript in the British Museum.

After the French were expelled from North America in 1763, the Choctaws maintained relations with the British and Spanish, both of whom courted their allegiance. One result of the Choctaw Civil War was that the Choctaws became very cautious, skilled diplomats at dealing with European colonial powers, an attribute of Choctaw political life that would carry over to dealings with the Americans.

During the Revolutionary War, the Choctaws sided with the Americans, providing scouts for Generals Morgan, Sullivan, Wayne, and Washington, and in 1786, entered into their first formal treaty with the Americans—a treaty of peace and friendship. In their second treaty with the Choctaws in 1801, the Americans secured Choctaw permission to build a wagon road through the Choctaw nation. Shortly afterward, Americans began appearing in Choctaw country in increasing numbers and demanding land, by

treaty, with a frequency that alarmed the Choctaws. In 1805, at the negotiations for the Treaty of Mount Dexter, the Americans began pressuring the Choctaws to accept President Thomas Jefferson's idea of removing themselves to new homes west of the Mississippi River.

Despite these pressures, the Choctaws maintained friendly relations with the United States. In 1811, the Choctaws expelled Tecumseh from their nation when he tried to enlist them in his Indian confederacy, and fought against the Red Stick faction of the Creeks in the ensuing war between the United States and the Creeks, who had chosen to join Tecumseh's alliance. The Choctaw war chief Pushmataha led 800 Choctaw troops, who became a part of General Andrew Jackson's army. Pushmataha also led Choctaw troops against the British in support of Jackson's army at the Battle of New Orleans. Despite Choctaw loyalty, the United States demanded further land cessions in 1816.

In 1820, the Choctaws finally agreed to trade a substantial portion of their land for a huge track of land west of the Mississippi River; however, they retained more than ten million acres of their original homeland east of the Mississippi River and did not agree to remove themselves to the West. But in 1830, after Andrew Jackson had become president, the Choctaws were forced to cede the remaining land east of the Mississippi River in a treaty with the Choctaw—also known as the Treaty of Dancing Rabbit Creek, or the Choctaw removal treaty—and remove as a nation to the West.

In *Chief Pushmataha, American Patriot*, published in 1959, historian Anna Lewis, revealed that General Andrew Jackson secured the signature of Chief Puckshenubbee, of the Okla Falaya Choctaw division, to the treaty of 1820 by means of blackmail. Puckshenubbee's daughter had married an American soldier who had deserted. When Jackson learned of this, he threatened to have Puckshenubbee's son-in-law shot if Puckshenubbee did not sign the treaty. The Americans candidly reported the blackmail to the U.S. State Department. The reports were preserved in the State Department files where Lewis eventually found them.

## CHOCTAW REMOVAL

The Choctaws were the first Indians to be removed as a nation by the U.S. government to new land in the West. For the most part, the removal was accomplished in three successive, brutal winter migrations during which 2,500 Choctaws died, many from exposure and starvation. In 1831, the newly created Bureau of Indian Affairs conducted the first removal. The government decided that the removal had been too costly, even though by the terms of the removal treaty the Choctaws were to pay the cost of removal out of profits from the sale of their lands in Mississippi. The U.S. Army was placed in charge of the 1832 and 1833 removals, they cut costs by severely reducing both rations and blankets. When the Choctaws ran out of food and attempted to purchase supplies, the citizens of Arkansas reacted by raising the price of corn. By 1834, 11,500 Choctaws had been removed to the west.

About 6,000 Choctaws remained in Mississippi where, by the terms of Article 14 of the removal treaty, they were to be allowed to choose individual land holdings of 640 acres for each head of household, 320 acres for children over the age of ten, and 160 acres for younger children; however, only 69 Choctaw heads of households were allowed to register for land in Mississippi. Finding themselves dispossessed of everything they owned, they became squatters in their former land. Many took to the swamps where they lived as furtive refugees until they were finally provided with a small reservation near Philadelphia, Mississippi, in the early twentieth century. Throughout the nineteenth century, Mississippi Choctaws continued to remove to the West, often at the urging of official Choctaw delegations sent from the West to induce them to join them.

## CHOCTAW NATION

In 1820 (modified by the treaty of 1824) the Choctaws purchased from the United States what amounted to the southern half of the present day state of Oklahoma, an area that included at its western edge the very heartland of the Comanche nation. But because the Choctaws were unable to find a volunteer to break the news to the Comanches, the Choctaws settled in the eastern portion of their new land in what is now southeast Oklahoma. Upon their arrival in the West in 1834, the Choctaws immediately adopted a written constitution. The constitution was modified in 1837 when the Chickasaws once again became a part of the Choctaw nation, having been removed from their homeland and allowed to chose homes among the Choctaws. They were given a quarter of the votes in the Choctaw legislature. In 1855, the Chickasaws became a separate nation again,

purchasing from the Choctaws what is today the central section of southern Oklahoma.

In the West the Choctaws soon recovered from the trauma of removal and established a republic that flourished for a generation. During this generation of peace and prosperity, the Choctaw nation built a stable economy, established its own public school system, governed itself under its own laws, and adopted many of the habits of its American neighbors.

The Choctaw remained largely free from the encroachments of the advancing American frontier until they were caught between warring American factions and drawn into the Civil War. At its outbreak, the Union removed its troops from Indian Territory, leaving the Choctaws defenseless. The Choctaw were surrounded by Confederates and held long-standing grievances against the United States. In addition, a small percentage of the population, predominantly wealthy mixed-blood Choctaws, owned some slaves. Therefore, the Choctaws entered into formal, diplomatic relations with the Confederacy, at which point the United States considered them in rebellion.

The Choctaw nation was little touched by the war. Two minor engagements were fought within the nation, and the nation was not occupied by troops. Very few Choctaws participated in the war on either side; however, the nation was overrun by refugees from the Creek and Cherokee nations, which were occupied by troops. As a result, they all suffered severe food shortages.

In their last treaty with the United States in 1866, the Choctaws were forced to sell their western lands as punishment for having sided with the Confederacy. The Choctaws also adopted a new constitution, which they explicitly patterned explicitly after the American form of government. It provided for a bi-cameral legislature, and executive and judicial branches.

The most profound effect of the treaty of 1866 was its granting of a railroad right of way, which had the same effect on the Choctaw nation in the last half of the nineteenth century as granting a right of way for a wagon road had in the early part of the century: Americans flooded into the country. By 1890, the Choctaws were outnumbered by Americans within their own country by more than three to one. The Americans did not have the right to own land, were not allowed representation within the nation, and were not allowed to send their children to the Choctaw public schools. They were required to pay taxes, which the Americans considered intolerable. Rather than leave, they clamored for Congress to abolish the Indian nations.

The U.S. Congress had already decided, unilaterally, that the United States need no longer enter into treaties with Indian nations and that the Congress would legislate Indian affairs. In 1893, Congress authorized the president to seek the dissolution of the nations of the Five Civilized Tribes by persuading them to either allot their land to their individual citizens or cede it to the United States. Under the auspices of the so-called Dawes Commission that resulted, the government spent three years attempting to pressure the Indians into agreeing to allot their lands. Finally, under the threat that Congress would allot the lands for them, the Choctaws negotiated and signed the Atoka Agreement of 1897, providing for the allotment of the tribal estate. In this way they avoided being subjected to the much harsher terms they were being threatened with if they did not negotiate. In 1906, enrollment of tribal members for allotment was closed by the Congress, and in 1907, the Choctaw nation was absorbed into the new state of Oklahoma.

### MODERN ERA

The U.S. government virtually ignored the Choctaws, who had remained in Mississippi until after the turn of the century. Then, in 1908 and 1916, the U.S. Congress commissioned studies on the people's condition. Although these Choctaws had remained isolated—living on the margins of the dominant society for generations—they retained their language and culture.

In 1918, the Bureau of Indian Affairs established the Choctaw Indian Agency in Philadelphia, Mississippi, with an initial budget of $75,000. The agency established schools in Choctaw communities and, in 1920, began purchasing land, which totaled 16,000 acres by 1944.

For the Choctaws in Oklahoma, allotment proved to be disastrous. Within a generation, most of the allotted land passed from Choctaw ownership to white ownership, often by fraudulent means. Enrolled Choctaw did not receive payment for the sale of the nation's public land until 1920, and for the sale of mineral resources until 1949. The President of the United States appointed a chief for the Choctaws until 1948, to administer these last remaining matters of tribal affairs.

# ACCULTURATION AND ASSIMILATION

Throughout the twentieth century, Indians have been both overwhelmed and ignored in Oklahoma. In the 1930s, Angie Debo completed the manuscript of her book *And Still the Waters Run*, which details the fraudulent acquisition of Indian land by people then prominent in Oklahoma politics. Debo reported that the dispossession of Indian land allotments was often achieved under the guise of guardianship. Although the University of Oklahoma Press refused to publish the work, it was finally published in 1940 by Princeton University Press. Shortly before her death, Debo read from the University of Oklahoma Press a rejection letter for a documentary film, quoting a characterization of one of her chapters as "dangerous." In fact, the fraud Debo reported was so widespread and perpetuated so openly, that hearing such cases made the Eastern District federal court of Oklahoma the second busiest federal district court in the United States.

Oklahoma has attempted to project the self-image of a state infused with a "pioneer spirit" that sets it apart from other places. Whether in Oklahoma or Hollywood, Americans usually refer to Indians in the past tense, apart from contemporary American culture. For most of the twentieth century, the media in Oklahoma has ignored Indians altogether, with the exception of an occasional piece deploring high rates of alcoholism among Indians or focusing on Indian dances as a means of attracting tourist dollars to the state.

The changes in media focus that have begun are in large part due to recent court rulings that allow Indian nations to operate gambling facilities on tribal land within Oklahoma: the mass media could not ignore the state's vigorous opposition to these rulings. Ironically, such attention has contributed to Oklahomans' slowly growing awareness that Indian nations are still intact and maintain their rights as sovereign nations.

## TRADITIONS, CUSTOMS, AND BELIEFS

Observers have characterized the Choctaw attitude toward life as one that illustrates their belief that they do not exist for the benefit of any political, economic, military, or religious organization. Choctaws also did not favor spectacular ceremonies, religious or otherwise, showing a nearly complete lack of public display, except in the area of oratory.

Choctaws relished and excelled in public oratory, causing some observers to draw comparisons between the Choctaw communities and the small republics of Greek antiquity. When an occasion for public debate presented itself, a large brush arbor was constructed with a hole in the center of the roof. Whoever wanted to speak stood beneath the hole in the full heat of the Mississippi sun while the audience remained comfortably seated in the shade. The Choctaws said they could bear to listen as long as the speaker could bear to stand in the heat and speak.

Oratory skill provided an avenue to upward mobility in Choctaw society. Each district chief appointed a *tichou mingo* as the official spokesperson. The *tichou mingo* had a more visible presence in official life than did the chief. Aiahockatubbee, spokesman for the Okla Falaya district chief Moshulatubbee, is recognized as one of the greatest orators in Choctaw history. It is said that in the 1820s, when Christian missionaries had only been among the Choctaws for a few years, Aiahockatubbee gave them eloquent enunciations of traditional Choctaw beliefs, much to their consternation, although Choctaws gathered from far and wide to hear him. His presence is largely credited with enabling the missionaries to make headway among the Okla Falaya, where district chief Puckshenubbee was an early convert.

Choctaw chiefs were also skilled orators. Okla Hannali war chief Pushmataha was the most persuasive Choctaw public speaker of his generation, with only Aiahockatubbee as his peer. In open debate, Pushmataha persuaded the Choctaws not to join Tecumseh when Tecumseh visited their country seeking their enlistment in his pan-Indian alliance in 1811. The debate was witnessed and later recalled by John Pitchlynn, United States interpreter to the Choctaws.

A brief speech by Homassatubbee, district chief of the Okla Tanap, was recorded by the Americans at the negotiations for the Treaty of Fort Adams in 1801: "I understand our great father, General Washington, is dead, and that there is another beloved man appointed in his place, and that he is a well wisher of us. Our old brothers, the Chickasaws, have granted a road from Cumberland as far south as our boundary. I grant a continuance of that road which may be straightened. But the old path is not to be thrown away entirely, and a new one made. We are informed by these three beloved men that our father, the President, has sent us a yearly present of which we know nothing. Another thing our father, the President, has promised, without our asking, is that he would send women among us to teach our women to spin and weave. These women may first go among our half-breeds. We wish the old boundary which separates us and the whites to be marked over. We came here sober, to do business, and wish to return sober and request therefore that the liquor we are informed our friends have provided for us may remain in the store."

In traditional Choctaw society, serious personal disputes were resolved by an institution called a Choctaw duel. In such a duel, the disputants faced one another while their assistants, usually a brother or close friend appointed for the occasion, split their heads open with an ax. Both died, the dispute was resolved, and the community was spared the incessant bickering of people who could not get along with one another. One could not decline the challenge to a Choctaw duel without suffering everlasting disgrace within the community. Needless to say, Choctaws became adept at getting along with one another.

Observers of Choctaw habits consider ball play the most important social event in the life of the Choctaws. Called *Ishtaboli*, the game has been described in greatest detail by H. B. Cushman, the son of Choctaw missionaries who grew up among the Choctaws in the 1820s. Men and women had teams, and when two villages met on the field of play, every item of any value in the villages was riding on the outcome.

The object of the game was to sling a ball made of sewn skins from the webbed pocket at the end of a *kapucha* stick—a slender, stout stick made of hickory—and propel it so that it struck an upright plank at the end of the playing field, which was often a mile long or longer. There were dozens of players on each side, and there appeared to be no rules. Whatever means one might employ to stop the progress of the opponent toward the goal, including tackling, was allowed. Although Choctaws preferred that each player use two sticks to play the game, the Sioux, used only one. The games demonstrated great skill at handling, throwing, and passing a ball, but the rough game often resulted in serious injury or death, for which there was no punishment. Today a version of *Ishtaboli*, called stickball, is still played by the Choctaws.

# LANGUAGE

Linguists classify the Choctaw language as Muskogean. It is closely related to the Creek language of the same classification. The Muskogean languages belong to the great Algonkian language family. Of the so-called Five Civilized Tribes (Choctaws, Chickasaws, Creeks, Seminoles, and Cherokees), only the Cherokee, whose language is classified as Iroquoian, speak a non-Muskogean language. Unlike the other tribes, the Cherokees migrated to the southeast from the north, and over time their culture became similar to that of the southern neighbors with whom they have come to be identified among the Five Civilized Tribes.

Linguists theorize that many of the native peoples of the Southeast who had separate identities had at some time in the past been Choctaws. For example, the language of the Alabamas of the Muskogee Confederation (Creeks) is still identifiably Choctaw, although it is a distinctive dialect. The same is true of a number of smaller groups who lived in the region, many of whom did not survive contact with Europeans and the endemic diseases that accompanied European colonization. It appears that groups of people began leaving the Choctaw and establishing separate residences and separate identities many years ago, a process that has continued into recent times. The Chickasaw language is still so similar to Choctaw, for instance, that linguists surmise that the separation of two could not have occurred very long ago.

Language is also a key to gaining some understanding of how influential the Choctaws were among the native people of North America at the time of early European contact. Ancient trading paths radiated throughout the continent, facilitating commercial intercourse between greatly distant peoples. A pidgin version of the Choctaw language was used along many of the trading paths as the universal medium of trade communication among a wide assortment of diverse peoples. The trading paths were spread over a vast region that encompassed most of what is now generally referred to as the South and extended to other areas.

The missionaries used the Okla Falaya dialect of the Choctaw language to translate ancient myths of the Hebrews for hymns and other proselytizing materials, which in time made the Okla Falaya dialect the standard dialect of the Choctaw language among the Choctaws who were removed to the West. Within 20 years after the missionaries' arrival among the Choctaws, their printing activity had become feverish. In 1837 alone, Presbyterian minister Cyrus Byington published 576,000 pages of text in the Choctaw language. The effect was comparable to the way in which the printing activity of Thomas Caxton helped to make the dialect of London the standard dialect of the English language.

# FAMILY AND COMMUNITY DYNAMICS

Europeans and Americans universally failed to appreciate or report the powerful and predominant role of women in Choctaw traditional life. Choctaw culture is matrilineal and, in many respects, matriarchal. Choctaw males were conspicuous in their roles as warriors, and war chiefs exercised a good deal of authority in time of war and conducted the diplomatic business of the nation. Likening such practices to those of their own patriarchal models, European observers failed to appreciate that the real decision-making power in times of peace was found among the women within the nation. Modern Choctaws have adjusted to the expectations of their colonizers regarding gender roles in visible positions of leadership, but in Choctaw family and social life, and in many organizations, a mature female is found at the very center of the life of the group, whether visible to outsiders or not.

Geographic divisions among ancient Choctaw tribes were roughly decided according to the crests of watersheds. In present-day east-central Mississippi, the headwaters of three rivers can be found: the Pearl, which drains toward the southwest before turning south to empty into the Gulf of Mexico near Lake Pontchartrain, where the Pearl forms the border with Louisiana; the Chickasawhay, an upper tributary of the Pascagoula, which flows toward the south into the Gulf of Mexico near the Alabama border; and the Noxubee, an upper tributary of the Tombigbee, which flows southeast before turning south to flow into Mobile Bay.

The villages of the Okla Falaya (Long People) lived along the headwaters of the Pearl on the western side of the nation. On the eastern side of the nation, along the headwaters of the Noxubee, lived the Okla Tanap (People of the Opposite Side). And the villages of the Okla Hannali (The Six Town People) were along the headwaters of the Chickasawhay at the southern side of the nation.

The Okla Falaya's relations with the Chickasaws, their nearest northern neighbors, were more congenial than those of other Choctaw divisions. Likewise, the Okla Tanap were generally on good terms with their eastern neighbors, the Choctaw-speaking Alabamas of the Muskogee Confederation, and the Okla Hannali enjoyed frequent contact with the Indians around Mobile Bay. In addition, the Choctaws had chiefs within their nation who served as spokesmen and apologists to neighboring tribes. Called *fanni mingoes*, or squirrel chiefs, they provided individual Choctaws with an opportunity to seek redress for some grievance or an injury caused by an outsider from the *fanni mingo*, rather than seek revenge against the offending tribe. The *fanni mingo* held counsel with the tribe whose interests he represented and tried to resolve the matter to the satisfaction of all parties.

Choctaw towns were divided into peace towns and war towns—called white towns and red towns—and chiefs were either peace chiefs or war chiefs. Neither Europeans nor Americans became well enough acquainted with the inner workings of Choctaw society to accurately describe the duties of the various participants in Choctaw public life. Most observers made assumptions based on models from European government, which were frequently at great variance with Choctaw practice.

Tribal divisions of the Choctaw nation operated with virtual independence. The republic was, in fact, a loose confederation. Within tribal divisions, villages also exercised a great deal of local autonomy. And individual Choctaws exercised such a large degree of personal freedom that the system bordered on anarchy. It was able to function successfully only because Choctaws exercised remarkable restraint regarding encroachment upon the rights of others within the group.

The premiere annual event of the Mississippi Choctaws is the Choctaw Indian Fair, a four-day event in July. Established in 1949, the fair draws more than 20,000 visitors each year and features the Stickball World Championship, national entertainers, and traditional Choctaw costumes and food (Choctaw Indian Fair, Choctaw Reservation, P.O. Box 6010, Philadelphia, Mississippi 39350).

The largest annual celebration in the Oklahoma nation is the four-day Labor Day Celebration at Tuskahoma, which dates from the early 1900s and now draws thousands of Choctaws each year. It includes a viewing of the tribal buffalo herd; softball, horseshoe, volleyball and checkers tournaments; national entertainers; a mid-way carnival and exhibition halls featuring dozens of crafts booths; all-night gospel singing on Sunday night; and a parade, a State of the Nation address by the Principal Chief, and a free barbecue dinner on Monday.

# EMPLOYMENT AND ECONOMIC TRADITIONS

The Mississippi Choctaws have lured industry to the reservation in recent years. With the construction of an industrial park in 1973, at the Pearl River community, a division of General Motors Corporation established the Chata Wire Harness Enterprise, which assembles electrical components for automobiles. Shortly thereafter, the American Greeting Corporation's Choctaw Greeting Enterprise began production, and the Oxford Investment Company started manufacturing automobile radio speakers at the Choctaw Electronics Enterprise. These companies and others currently employ more than 1,000 Choctaws on the reservation.

Recent decades have also brought a construction boom to the reservation of the Mississippi Choctaws. In 1965, the Choctaw Housing Authority constructed the first of more than 200 modern homes on the reservation. In 1969, the Chata Development company, which builds and remodels homes, and constructs offices and buildings for the nation, was established. The Choctaw Health Center, a 43-bed hospital, opened in 1976.

The Oklahoma Choctaws have built community centers and clinics in towns throughout the nation. The Choctaw Housing Authority has pro-

vided thousands of Choctaws with low-cost modern homes. The nation operates the historic Indian Hospital at Talihina, which it acquired from the Indian Health Service; it purchased the sprawling Arrowhead Resort on Lake Eufaula from the state of Oklahoma and operates it as a tourist and convention facility. Tribal industries include the Choctaw Finishing Plant and the Choctaw Village Shopping Center in Idabel, and the Choctaw Travel Plaza in Durant.

The buildings and grounds at the historic Choctaw Council House at Tushkahoma, in the center of the nation, have been restored, and the stately three-story brick Council House has been converted into a museum and gift shop. The Choctaw Tribal Council holds its monthly meetings in the new, modern council chamber nearby. Also constructed on the grounds were a large, roofed, outdoor amphitheater, and softball fields for the tremendously popular fast-pitch softball tournaments. Exhibition buildings, a cafeteria, showers and toilets, campgrounds, and parking facilities have been added.

By far the greatest economic gain in the nation has been through the inauguration of high stakes Indian bingo. Charter buses bring bingo players daily from as far away as Dallas, Texas, to the huge Choctaw Bingo Palace in Durantto.

# POLITICS AND GOVERNMENT

In 1945, the U.S. Secretary of the Interior granted the Choctaws formal federal recognition, approving a constitution and bylaws for the Mississippi Band of Choctaw Indians. The constitution provided for the election of a tribal council, which then appointed a tribal chairman. The land that had been acquired for them became a reservation.

The reservation remains outside of the political and judicial jurisdiction of the state of Mississippi. A 1974 revision of the Choctaw Nation's Constitution provides for the popular election of the chief to a four-year term. The Indian Reorganization Act of 1934, allowed the Choctaws in Oklahoma to elect an advisory council, and in 1948, they were allowed to elect their own principal chief. Impetus toward reorganizing the nation met another shift in federal policy in 1953, when the U.S. Congress enacted House Concurrent Resolution 108, under which the federal government sought to terminate its relationship with all Indian nations in the United States. The Indian Self-Determination and Education Assistance Act of 1975 finally allowed the Choctaws a measure of self-government within the state of Oklahoma.

In 1976, the Choctaws purchased the campus of the former Presbyterian College in Durant, Oklahoma, as their national capitol and in 1978 adopted a new constitution—their first since the constitution of 1866 had been abrogated in 1906. Designating themselves The Choctaw Nation of Oklahoma, they adopted a tribal council form of government led by a principal chief elected by popular vote of the entire nation and council members elected by popular vote of council districts.

Since the mid-1970s, the tribal estate has steadily increased, along with the nation's administrative activities, enabling the Oklahoma Choctaw to exercise more vestiges of sovereignty. A recent federal court ruling stated that the state of Oklahoma could no longer exercise police powers on Indian land within the state. As a result, the Choctaw Nation Police were organized. The Choctaw nation and the state of Oklahoma signed a pact to cross-deputize all law enforcement officers of both governments for the welfare and protection of all citizens.

# INDIVIDUAL AND GROUP CONTRIBUTIONS

## ACADEMIA

Anna Lewis was an historian, whose doctoral dissertation, *Along The Arkansas*, is a study of French-Indian relations on the lower Arkansas River frontier in the eighteenth century; in 1930, Lewis became the first woman to receive a Ph.D. from the University of Oklahoma; she pursued a distinguished teaching career at the Oklahoma College for Women, now the University of Science and Arts, in Chickasaha, Oklahoma, while devoting her life to researching a biography of Pushmataha (a war chief of the Okla Hannali Choctaw tribal division and the most influential Choctaw leader of the early nineteenth century), *Chief Pushmataha, American Patriot*, published in 1959. Clara Sue Kidwell, formerly a professor at the University of California at Berkeley, now works for the Museum of American History at the Smithsonian Institution; she co-authored the

invaluable study *The Choctaws: A Critical Bibliography* in 1980; her detailed history of early missionary activity among the Choctaws is scheduled for publication. Muriell Wright was the granddaughter of Allen Wright, Principal Chief of the Choctaw Nation in the nineteenth century; for two decades, she served as editor of *The Chronicles of Oklahoma*, the quarterly historical scholarly journal of the Oklahoma Historical Society; in 1959, she produced *A Guide to the Indian tribes of Oklahoma*, which provides a summary of the history, culture, and contemporary status of the 65 Indian nations that were either original residents of, or were removed to the area before statehood.

## LITERATURE

M. Cochise Anderson is a poet whose work has appeared in *World of Poetry Anthology* (1983) and in *Nitassinan Notre Terre* (1990). Jim Barnes is a poet and editor of *Chariton Review* at Northwest Missouri State University, Kirksville, Missouri; Barnes won the Oklahoma Book Award for his *The Sawdust War* (1993), a volume of poetry. He was awarded a Fulbright fellowship to the University of Lausanne in Switzerland (1993-1994); among Barnes' other verse collections are *American Book of the Dead* (1982), *A Season of Loss* (1985), *La Plata Cantata* (1989), *The Fish on Poteau Mountain* (1980), and *This Crazy Land* (1980). Roxy Gordon has published more than 200 poems, articles, and short fiction in *Rolling Stone*, *Village Voice*, *Texas Observer*, *Greenfield Review*, *Dallas Times Herald* and *Dallas Morning News*; his fiction has appeared in anthologies including *Earth Power Coming*, edited by Simon J. Ortiz in 1983; Gordon's poetry is collected in *Unfinished Business*, *West Texas Midcentury*, and *Small Circles*. Beatrice Harrell has contributed memoirs of her mother's experiences in the Choctaw boarding schools in such publications as *The Four Directions: American Indian Literary Quarterly*. *The Choctaw Story of How Thunder and Lightning Came to Be* is one of several books in which Harrell recounts traditional Choctaw stories. LeAnn Howe is a widely published poet, essayist, short story writer, and playwright; her poetry has appeared in anthologies such as *Gatherings IV: The En'owkin Journal of First North American People* and *Studies in American Indian Literatures*; her short stories have appeared in many collections, including *A Stand Up Reader* (1987), *Coyote Papers* (1987), and the anthology *Earth Song, Sky Spirit: Short Stories of the Contemporary Native American Experience* (1993); Howe is perhaps best known for her saucy essay, "An American in New York," in *Spiderwoman's Granddaughters*, edited by Paula Gunn Allen and published in 1989; a recent radio broadcast of her play *Indian Radio Days* (co-authored with Roxy Gordon) was transmitted by satellite to stations as far away as Alaska. Gary McLain's nonfiction works include *Keepers of the Fire* (1987), *Indian America* (1990), and *The Indian Way* (1991). Louis Owens is a novelist and co-editor of the American Indian Literature Series of the University of Oklahoma Press; currently an English professor at the University of New Mexico, Owens formerly taught at the University of California at Santa Cruz; his novels include *Wolfsong* (1991), *The Sharpest Sight* (1992), and *Bone Game* (1994); Owens' *Other Destines: Understanding The American Indian Novel* (1992) is a critical study. Ronald Burns Querry, a descendant of Okla Hannali Choctaws, was an English professor at the University of Oklahoma and was former editor of horse industry magazines; a professional farrier (horseshoer); Querry is the author of *The Death of Bernadette Lefthand* (1993), which received both the Border Regional Library Association Regional Book Award and the Mountains and Plains Booksellers Association Award as one of the best novels published in 1993; Querry is also the editor of *Growing Old at Willie Nelson's Picnic, and Other Sketches of Life in the Southwest* (1983), and author of his "unauthorized" biography, *I See By My Get-UP* (1987). In 1992, Wallace Hampton Tucker became the first three-time winner of the Best Play Prize of the Five Civilized Tribes Museum in Muscogee, Oklahoma, for his play *Fire On Bending Mountain;* Tucker also won the first two prizes awarded by the biennial competition in 1974 and in 1976.

### JOURNALISM

Judy Allen is a long-time editor of *Bishinik*, the official monthly publication of the Choctaw Nation of Oklahoma, which is mailed to every registered voter of the nation. Len Green, the late newspaperman, was the first editor of *Bishinik*, where he set a high standard for others to follow; Green was also managing editor of the *McCurtain Gazette*, in Idabel, Oklahoma, for 30 years; early issues of *Bishinik* contain his scholarly writings about Choctaw history and treaties; for the bicentennial celebration, Green published *200 Years Ago In The Red River Valley* (1976), a study of Choctaw country in the West two generations before the Choctaws moved there. Scott Kayla Morrison collaborated with LeAnn Howe on the

investigative article "Sewage of Foreigners" (*Federal Bar Journal & Notes*, July, 1992), a detailed expose that focuses on contract negotiations by the Mississippi Band of Choctaw Indians to allow for toxic waste dumps on Choctaw lands in Mississippi; the winter 1994 *News from Indian Country* reported that Morrison, an attorney, and Howe, a journalist and playwright, had signed a contract with the University of Oklahoma Press to expand the article into a book; Morrison has worked as a legal services attorney among the Choctaws in Mississippi, and is now director of the Native American Office of Jobs in the Environment; in the summer of 1993, *Oklahoma Today* named her in its "Who's Who in Indian Country" in recognition of her environmental work; her short stories and essays have appeared in publications including *The Four Directions: American Indian Literary Quarterly* and *Turtle Quarterly* (Native American Center for the Living Arts, Niagara Falls, New York), and in the anthology *The Colour of Resistance* (1994); she is currently editing an anthology of Native American environmental writings.

# MEDIA

### PRINT

**Bishinik.**
Official monthly publication of the Choctaw Nation of Oklahoma.

**Address:** P.O. Drawer 1210, Durant, Oklahoma 74702.

**Choctaw Community News.**
Official monthly publication of the Mississippi Band of Choctaw Indians.

**Contact:** Julie Kelsey, Editor.
**Address:** Communications Program, P.O. Box 6010, Philadelphia, Mississippi 39350.

# ORGANIZATIONS AND ASSOCIATIONS

**United South and Eastern Tribes (USET).**
Promotes strength and unity of American Indian tribes and assists tribes in dealing with relevant issues.

**Contact:** James G. Sappier, Executive Director.
**Address:** 1101 Kermit Drive, Suite 302, Nashville, Tennessee 37217.
**Telephone:** (615) 361-8700.

# SOURCES FOR ADDITIONAL STUDY

*After Removal: The Choctaw in Mississippi*, edited by Samuel J. Wells and Roseanna Tubby. Jackson: University Press of Mississippi, 1986.

Baird, David. *Peter Pitchlynn: Chief of the Choctaws*. Norman: University of Oklahoma Press, 1972.

Benson, Henry C. *Life Among the Choctaw Indians, and Sketches of the Southwest*. Cincinnati, Ohio: R. P. Thompson Co., 1860.

Brescia, William, Jr. "Choctaw Oral Tradition Relating to Tribal Origin" in *The Choctaw Before Removal*, edited by Carolyn Keller Reeves. Jackson: University Press of Mississippi, 1985.

Crane, Verner W. *The Southern Frontier*. Greenwood Press: Greenwood, Connecticut, 1969.

Debo, Angie. "Indians, Outlaws, and Angie Debo," *The American Experience*, PBS Video, 1988.

———. *The Rise and Fall of the Choctaw Republic*, second edition. Norman: University of Oklahoma Press, 1961.

Densmore, Frances. *Choctaw Music* (Bulletin 136 of the Bureau of American Ethnology). DaCapo Press, 1972 (originally published in 1936).

DeRosier, Arthur H., Jr. *The Removal of the Choctaw Indians*. Knoxville: University of Tennessee Press, 1970.

Farb, Peter. "Natchez: People of the Sun," in his *Man's Rise to Civilization*, 1968.

Foreman, Grant. *The Five Civilized Tribes*. Norman: University of Oklahoma Press, 1934.

Halbert, Henry S. "The Choctaw Creation Legend," *Publications of the Mississippi Historical Society* 2, 1901; pp. 223-234.

———. "A Choctaw Migration Legend," *American Antiquarian and Oriental Journal* 16, 1894; pp. 215-226.

———. "District Divisions of the Choctaw Nation," *Publications of the Alabama Historical Society, Miscellaneous Collections*, Vol. 1 1900; pp. 375-385.

———. "Nanih Waiya, the Sacred Mound of the Choctaws," *Publications of the Mississippi Historical Society* 2, 1899; pp. 223-234.

Jordan, H. Glenn, "Choctaw Colonization in Oklahoma," in *America's Exiles: Indian Colonization in Oklahoma*, edited by Arrell Morgan Gibson, 1976.

Kappler, Charles J. *Indian Affairs, Laws, and Treaties*, four volumes (Vol. 2 contains all the treaties between the United States and the Choctaws). Washington, D.C.: U.S. Government Printing Office, 1929.

Kidwell, Clara Sue, and Charles Roberts. *The Choctaws: A Critical Bibliography*. Bloomington: Indiana University Press for the Newberry Library, 1980.

Lewis, Anna. *Chief Pushmataha, American Patriot: The Story of the Choctaws' Struggle for Survival*. New York: Exposition Press, 1959.

Lincecum, Gideon. "Life of Apushimataha," *Publications of the Mississippi Historical Society* 9, 1905-1906; pp. 415-485.

McKee, Jesse O., and Jon A. Schlenker. *The Choctaws: Cultural Evolution of a Native American Tribe*. Jackson: University Press of Mississippi, 1980.

O'Brien, Sharon. *American Indian Tribal Governments*. Norman: University of Oklahoma Press, 1989.

Swanton, John R. *Indian Tribes of the Lower Mississippi Valley and Adjacent Coast of the Gulf of Mexico*, 1911.

———. *Source Material for the Social and Ceremonial Life of the Choctaw Indians*. Bulletin No. 103. Washington, D.C.: U.S. Government Printing Office, 1931.

Motivated by ethnic
pride and a desire to
circumvent legal,
racial, and cultural
obstacles
encountered in
American life,
Colombian
Americans have
maintained a distinct
identity in the
United States.

# COLOMBIAN AMERICANS

by
Pamela Sturner

## OVERVIEW

Colombia lies in the northwest corner of South America and covers an area of 439,735 square miles (1,138,914 square kilometers). It is bounded to the north by the Caribbean Sea, to the northeast by Venezuela, to the southeast by Brazil, to the south by Peru, to the west by Ecuador and the Pacific Ocean, and to the northwest by Panama. It embraces the northernmost point in South America, Point Gallinas, and is the only country on the continent with both Caribbean and Pacific coasts. The Andes run the length of the country in three ranges called the Cordillera Occidental, the Cordillera Central, and the Cordillera Oriental, which comprise the highland core where most of the population lives. Some of the richest farmland lies between the western and central ranges along the Cauca River. The Magdalena River valley, between the central and eastern ranges, is densely populated and the site of the capital, Bogotá. The eastern plains, or *llanos*, account for 60 percent of the country's territory and are sparsely populated, as are the coastal lowlands. To the southeast lie the undeveloped tropical rainforests of the Amazon basin. The economy depends largely on such agricultural products as coffee (the leading export), bananas, cotton, rice, corn, sugarcane, and tobacco. Colombia produces more than 90 percent of the world's emeralds and also exports gold, iron, nickel, copper, lead, salt, coal, natural gas, and petroleum. Manufacturing, a growing sector of the economy, employed about 20 percent of the population in the early 1990s.

The country's highly diverse population of 33 million includes at least 15 distinct cultural and regional groups. The major ethnic groups include: descendants of Indians, who are concentrated in the Andes; persons of solely European descent, who have traditionally held most of the country's wealth and power and account for less than 20 percent of the population; *costeños*, persons of mixed African, Indian, and Spanish descent living primarily on the coasts; and mestizos, or persons of Indian and Spanish descent, who account for about 58 percent of the population. Most Colombian Americans are Roman Catholic; a few are Protestant, Jewish, Muslim, Buddhist, or Hindu. About 65 percent live in urban areas.

## HISTORY

The civilization of the first inhabitants of what is now Colombia occupied much of the Andean interior until European colonization. Christopher Columbus probably explored the mouth of the Orinoco River in 1498; Alonso de Ojeda led another expedition in 1509, and in 1525 the first Spanish city, Santa Marta, was founded on the Caribbean coast. In 1536 the conquistador Gonzalo Jiménez de Quesada sailed up the Magdalena River to search for the mythical city of El Dorado and, after defeating the Chibcha, founded Bogotá in 1538. During the years of the Spanish Main, the Caribbean port city of Cartagena (founded 1533) was a point of embarkation for shipments of gold and other minerals bound for Spain. The Spanish relied increasingly on the labor of slaves to maintain the expanding colony, and Colombia soon had one of the largest African populations on the continent. After 1740 the colony formed the center of New Granada, a territory that included the greater part of what is now Colombia, Panama, and Venezuela. A movement for independence from Spain began in 1810; in 1812 the territory came under the direction of Simón Bolívar, who waged a series of campaigns that ended with the surrender of the Spanish in 1819. Bolívar renamed the territory Greater Colombia and annexed Ecuador to it in 1822; political differences led Venezuela to secede in 1829, followed by Ecuador in 1830.

The 1830s were marked by the rise of the Partido Conservador and the Partido Liberal as the most powerful rivals in national politics. Their struggles fueled unrest throughout the century and resulted in a civil war from 1899 to 1902 that left 100,000 dead and brought the Conservatives to power. In 1902 crisis beset the country again when the United States seized the zone where the Panama Canal was being built. After rejecting the treaty establishing American control, the Colombian government sent troops to Panama where, with American support, local forces revolted and won independence in 1903. In the wake of this defeat, a president with dictatorial powers assumed office in Colombia during the following year, ushering in more than four decades of peace. Hostilities between the Liberals and Conservatives led again to civil war in 1948, and in 1953 General Gustavo Rojas Pinilla seized power through a military coup; he was removed by the military in 1957 after Liberals and Conservatives joined together to oppose his regime, and political order was restored in 1958 when the two parties formed a coalition government, the National Front. Under its leadership the country began its recovery from the war, known as "La Violencia," which in the course of a decade had left between 200,000 and 300,000 dead and had displaced numerous others by forcing the rural population into the cities and that of small cities into the largest urban centers.

Since the 1960s, attempts have been made to address longstanding social, political, and economic problems. Under President Carlos Lleras Restrepo (1966-1970) inflation slowed, the economy was diversified, and land reforms were instituted. After a period of gradual transition toward full democracy, the government of the National Front ended when elections were held in 1974. Extreme disparity between the wealthy and the poor contributed to widespread disillusionment that kindled a Marxist guerrilla movement dedicated to revolution. Social problems worsened as the birth rate rose and farmers displaced by new technology moved to the cities, where they found their skills inapplicable in an industrial economy. During the 1980s, producers of illegal drugs flourished, banded together in cartels, and threatened the country's political and social stability through campaigns of bombings, abductions, murders, and the assassinations of officials, judges, and newspaper editors. Undocumented immigration to Venezuela increased: by some estimates 200,000 Colombian Americans without work permits found employment there during this time. Years of steady growth in Colombia came to a close as the economy stagnated under the weight of foreign debt in the mid 1980s.

In the face of an escalating social and political crisis, President Virgilio Barco Vargas launched a campaign in 1989 to suppress the drug trade, which resulted in hundreds of arrests, the confiscation of property worth millions of dollars, and violent retaliations by the cartels. Several presidential candidates were assassinated before the election of 1990; victory nonetheless went to César Gaviria Trujillo, a well-known opponent of the drug trade. During his first years in office, he sought to restore the population's faith in the government by pursuing an aggressive policy against the cartels, encouraging the formation of new political parties, and offering a role in national affairs to Indians and former guerrillas. Agreements reached with foreign creditors eased the burden of debt, allowing Colombia to achieve a trade surplus, and in the 1990s negotiations began for new trade arrangements with other countries.

## IMMIGRATION

The first Colombian immigrants were probably among the few South Americans who settled in the United States during the nineteenth century (the federal census did not specify the country of origin for South Americans until 1960). Little is known about these settlers, who maintained no ties with their native countries and within a few generations identified themselves only as Americans. The first Colombian community formed when several hundred white professionals, including nurses, accountants, laboratory technicians, pharmacists, and bilingual secretaries, moved to New York City after World War I; the population was later augmented by students who stayed on after earning their degrees. Most immigrants made their homes in Jackson Heights, a middle-class neighborhood in Queens, attractive for its proximity to employment in Manhattan and for its churches, comfortable houses, large yards, and fine schools. Known by residents as "El Chapinerito" (after Chapinero, a middle-class suburb of Bogotá), the neighborhood did not grow much until the 1940s, when New York City and Venezuela surpassed Panama in popularity as destinations among Colombian emigrants.

The number of Colombians entering the United States each year increased only slightly until the early 1950s, when it rose from a few hundred to more than a thousand, owing in part to upheaval associated with the civil war of 1948. Nor did the rate decline with the restoration of civil order in Colombia. As a result of land reforms and the introduction of agricultural machinery during the 1960s, the population became concentrated in the metropolitan areas and a deep economic recession set in, forcing many Colombian Americans to leave the country in search of work. The number that settled in the United States continued to grow rapidly: according to the annual reports of the Immigration and Naturalization Service 116,444 Colombians entered the country between 1960 and 1977, the first large influx driven by purely economic reasons. These immigrants were far more racially and economically diverse than their predecessors, and with their admittance, skilled and semiskilled laborers gradually displaced professionals as the majority.

In the postwar years, Colombian Americans were among the national groups at the center of a political debate about immigration that reached a peak when immigrants from Asia, Africa, and Latin America outnumbered those from Europe. Calls for stricter controls culminated in the Immigration Act of 1965, the first legislation to place a limit on the western hemisphere, for which only 120,000 visas were to be reserved annually. The law also sought to bar entry to all but the most needed and highly qualified workers, including professionals, technicians, and domestic servants. These measures presented a host of obstacles for Colombian Americans. The quota was so small relative to demand that families could wait 20 months for permission to be reunited. Pressure on the allotted visas was further exacerbated by unemployment and underemployment in Colombia, which escalated to between 20 and 25 percent by the mid 1970s. Patterns of settlement changed as a result of these conditions. In part because they had little hope of establishing legal residency, most Colombians who arrived after the mid 1960s planned to stay in the United States only temporarily, and the rate of undocumented immigration soared: estimates of those living in the country without permanent residency status ranged from 250,000 to 350,000 in the mid 1970s. Discouraged by the law, some immigrants settled in Ecuador, which in 1973 had a Colombian population of 60,000.

Despite a succession of stringent immigration laws, the Colombian population in the United States continued to grow. New York remained the most popular destination. While those who could afford to do so moved to Jackson Heights, other Colombian neighborhoods took shape in nearby Corona, Elmhurst, Woodside, Rego Park, and Flushing. Smaller communities formed in Los

Angeles, San Francisco, Houston, and Washington D.C. During the 1970s, an enclave of a few thousand professionals developed on the North Side of Chicago. After the late 1970s, many Colombians chose to settle in Miami, which they found attractive for its climate, growing economy, and tradition of tolerance dating from the establishment of a Cuban community there. Initially they took up residence in Little Havana, the largest Cuban neighborhood, and many engaged in business related to the brisk trade between Miami and Latin America; a few worked in factories or as domestic servants. The area also became a haven for the wealthy, who moved there to receive medical care, send their children to school, and escape from social, economic, and political turmoil in Colombia. By 1987 Colombian Americans were one of the fastest-growing Latin American groups in Miami.

By the early 1990s, overcrowding, crime, and the high cost of urban living led Colombian Americans to leave metropolitan centers for the suburbs. This trend was perhaps first noticed in the coastal towns of Connecticut and New York, where, since the 1980s, many Colombian Americans and other Latin Americans have taken jobs in service industries left unfilled by the local population; they also had a better choice of housing, which was much more affordable than that in New York City. One of the fastest-growing communities took shape in Stamford, Connecticut, which in the mid-1990s had a Colombian population of more than 7,000. Enclaves in northern New Jersey also grew during these years, including those in Bergenline, a town dominated by immigrants and entrepreneurs, and in Englewood. Jacksonville and such suburbs as Kendall, Florida, attracted a growing number from Miami, and Skokie, Evanston, Arlington Heights, and Park Ridge, Illinois, became fashionable alternatives to the North Side of Chicago. The largest concentrations nonetheless remained in New York City, Miami, and their environs: in 1994 there were 86,000 Colombian Americans in New York City (mainly in Queens), 56,000 in northern New Jersey, and 84,000 in Dade County, Florida.

With other immigrants from developing countries, Colombian Americans have faced serious obstacles to achieving success in the United States in the 1990s. As American society became more technologically advanced, much of the work traditionally performed by immigrants disappeared, leaving only dangerous, undesirable, poorly paid positions that offered no health care benefits and little promise for the future. Language was a definitive barrier against advancement, as most Colombian Americans lacked proficiency in English and the opportunity to gain it. Those living in cities often inherited abandoned neighborhoods, substandard schools, and a crumbling infrastructure. Perhaps the most pressing issue was the rising tide of hostility toward immigrants, especially Latin Americans and Asians, that swept the country on the heels of the economic recession during the late 1980s and early 1990s. After years of being virtually ignored by the larger society, Colombian Americans found themselves a target for American resentment over problems ranging from drug-related crime to a decline in the standard of living. According to the federal census bureau, 19,700 Colombians were admitted to the United States in 1993, more than from any other South American country; they also accounted for the third-largest group of undocumented immigrants (after those from Mexico and Central America). Such statistics figured prominently in debates about the effects of immigration on the economy and even on society itself.

"[In Colombia] my surroundings and the narrow-mindedness of the people always bothered me. In the United States, on the other hand, I could be myself without worrying that others would think ill of me and work at whatever was most profitable without having others think that it was degrading."

Julia de Riano, cited in Ramiro Cardona Gutiérrez, *El éxodo de colombianos,* 1980.

Colombian Americans were also subject to concern about the growth of the Latino population, which was perceived as a threat by those who considered immigrants, particularly the undocumented, an economic burden and resented Latinos' efforts to preserve their language and culture within American society. Such sentiments fueled a political backlash against immigrants that led to the passage of Proposition 187 in California, a law denying services and education to undocumented immigrants. In 1994 the fate of even documented immigrants remained uncertain after the Republican congressional leadership proposed to deny them benefits and services as part of its Contract with America.

## ACCULTURATION AND ASSIMILATION

Motivated by ethnic pride and a desire to circumvent legal, racial, and cultural obstacles encountered in American life, Colombian Americans have maintained a distinct identity in the United States. In light of immigration laws that allow few to expect citizenship, they usually consider their stay in the United States temporary and retain strong ties to Colombia, where they plan to resettle permanently; those with American permanent resident status return for visits as frequently as possible and above all at Christmas. Colombian Americans struggle daily with racial and economic discrimination and also with American culture, which many find both insipid and alienating. Some preserve their own culture by operating within Latin American social and economic networks as much as possible; they nonetheless reject the notion of assuming a larger Latino identity, seeking instead to remain distinct from other groups, especially Puerto Ricans.

Since the 1970s, Colombian Americans' efforts to be accepted in American society have been impeded by the prevalence of stereotypes of them based on news of the drug trade. Reports on escalating drug abuse and related arrests in the United States and the growing chaos in Colombia during the 1980s fueled American fears that the violence and terrorism associated with the cartels would spread to the United States; these reached a peak after the murder of Manuel de Dios Unanue, the editor of *El Diario/La Prensa* and an outspoken critic of the Calí cartel, in a café in Queens on March 11, 1992. To protect against reprisals for American intervention in the drug trade, the state department restricted travel to Colombia by Americans. Sensationalism tinged much of the news reporting on these affairs, and since the mid-1980s, stereotypes of ruthless drug lords supported by unlimited funds, sophisticated weapons, and armies of loyal thugs have captured the public's imagination. These images were perpetuated in Hollywood, where a growing number of motion pictures were based on stories about American efforts to destroy Colombian drug operations; some critics even suggested that with the close of the Cold War in the late 1980s, Colombian drug lords had become the new stock villain of the film industry. Like spy thrillers of earlier times, these films ended with the triumph of American virtue over the machinations of a clever but morally inferior opponent. In the shadow of such characterizations, Colombian Americans have found themselves objects of suspicion and have experienced more intense discrimination in housing and employment. Although by most estimates only a small proportion worked in the drug trade in the mid-1990s, the widespread

## HOLIDAYS

An important holiday is Colombian Independence Day on July 20 (celebrated on November 11 by immigrants from the Caribbean coast), which is marked with traditional foods such as tamales, chorizos, empanadas, Colombian coffee, *yuca congelada, tapas, arepas* (thick cornmeal patties sometimes served with cheese), *obleas* (a confection made with two wafers and a layer of caramel in between), a chilled, blended drink made of milk, sugar, and a fruit known as *curuba,* and the alcoholic beverage *aguardiente cristal;* creole specialties including *ajiaco,* a hearty soup made with chicken, several varieties of potato, capers, herbs, avocado, and corn on the cob; and Andean beans, plantains, fried pork skins, and rice. Colombian Americans also share in the celebration of other Latin American independence days and in cultural festivals held from time to time in major cities.

## MUSIC AND DANCE

Latin American dancing is a central activity at festivals and in local clubs. Since the late 1980s, the Colombian dance known as cumbia has grown in popularity. Developed on the Caribbean coast by slaves, it consists of intricate, restrained steps that reportedly trace the limits of the dancers' shackles.

Colombian music has gained an international audience largely through the efforts of Antonio López Fuentes, who formed the first Colombian record company, Disco Fuentes, in 1934 and made well-received recordings of indigenous music using modern instrumentation. One style, the cumbia, is written in 2/4 time and performed with a button accordion, drums, maracas, and horns. A related form, *vallenato,* traditionally consists of vocals, an accordion, a cane scraper, a drum, and a curved flute. Versions of *vallenato* songs, put to rock instrumentation by Carlos Vives, have enjoyed tremendous success throughout the Americas. Colombian musicians tour the United States frequently, among them the accordionist Lisandro Meza and the bands Las Mantas, Grupo Niche, and Los Macondos, which was formed by seven musicians from the Caribbean coast. Styles known as *porro* and *mapale* are performed to a lesser extent.

## HEALTH AND MENTAL HEALTH ISSUES

Obtaining health care poses a serious problem for many Colombian Americans. Those in poorly paid jobs rarely receive health benefits and cannot afford to pay for a health plan or leave their families long enough to receive treatment; in addition to these problems, undocumented immigrants are burdened with the fear that through the medical establishment, their status might become known to the immigration authorities. As a result, Colombian Americans often seek medical care only in emergencies or confine themselves to facilities available within Latin American networks.

Like other immigrants, Colombian Americans sometimes suffer from stress disorders associated with cultural adjustment; few seek out mental health services, owing to longstanding taboos in Colombia against seeking help for mental illness. By the early 1990s, a few social service centers and programs catered to Latin Americans, including La Familia in Marin County, California, and the Fordham Tremont Mental Health Center in New York, which in June 1993 launched a counseling service to provide not only mental health care, but also information about such matters as housing and employment. The Women's Rights and Information Center in Bergenline, New Jersey, offers counseling to help Latinas take advantage of opportunities open to them, in part by providing advice about work, education, housing, and legal matters.

# LANGUAGE

Colombian Americans traditionally consider themselves the stewards of the most elegant Spanish spoken in South America. After the 1500s, the upper class sought to preserve pure Castilian as the language of the colony; they succeeded largely because the rugged terrain made travel and communication between regions virtually impossible. Some Indian and African words were adopted by the middle and lower classes and eventually became standard in Latin American Spanish, including several of Caribbean origin (*ají, arepa, bagre, batata, bejuco, bohío, cacique, caimán, caníbal, canoa, ceiba, cocuyo, colibrí, guacamaya, guanábana, guayacán, guayaba, maíz, mangle, múcura, papaya, tabaco*) and from Chibcha (*curuba, guadua, toche, tatacoa*) and Tupí-Guaraní (*cámbulo, chamán, maraca, mandioca, anana*). The geographic isolation and diverse populations of the colonial departments encouraged at least nine regional dialects to develop. Certain characteristics are common to many or most of them. Colombians, especially those from coastal areas, tend to speak more quickly than other South Americans, and their speech is also noted for its lyrical intonation. In certain areas some letters are omitted (a "d" occurring in the second-to-last syllable is suppressed in Antioquia and on the plains around Boyacá) or substituted for others, such as "j" for "s" on the Caribbean coast and in the Cauca River valley and "ch" for "tr" in Cundinamarca.

Spanish is the language of most Colombian households in the United States, where it serves as perhaps the surest means of preserving traditions. Professionals and other members of the middle and upper classes worry about the deterioration of Colombian Spanish in American cities, where it is subject to the influences of English and the Spanish of other countries. They tend to use formal address in more situations than other Latin Americans and commonly call only well-known acquaintances by their first names.

For Colombian Americans, as for other immigrants, learning English is a compelling desire, because without advanced language skills they remain ineligible for most kinds of work; many find that achieving fluency nonetheless remains an elusive goal. They are often unable to afford the time and money necessary for intensive courses and, lacking other options, resort to night school, where classes tend to be large and conditions vary widely. Opportunities to use the language are also limited. Aside from those employed in English-speaking households, most Colombian Americans have little exposure to English, and when they do use it are usually received rudely by native speakers. In the face of these difficulties, Colombian Americans often gravitate to Latin American networks, particularly in large cities, where there is little or no need to know English in either business or social life; families sometimes rely on bilingual children for outside transactions. They consider Miami exceptionally hospitable: Spanish is the second official language of government and also dominates business and cultural affairs.

With the children of other immigrants, Colombian students are at the center of a debate about the future of bilingual education. Studies have shown that even after acquiring fairly advanced English skills, non-native speakers are unable to compete with their English-speaking classmates for several years. Some educators argue that bilingual programs are essential to help students of English as a second language build confidence and keep up with their peers; their approach has aroused anger among Americans who believe that English should be the country's only language and consider wide use of other languages a threat to American culture.

# FAMILY AND COMMUNITY DYNAMICS

A focal concern for Colombian immigrants is to preserve their families intact against pressures encountered in American society. In Colombia traditional values define the home: the husband is the wage-earner and head of house; the wife sets the tone of the household and rarely holds outside employment; children are taught to obey their parents and respect authority. Families prefer to immigrate together but have increasingly been prevented from doing so by restrictive immigration laws. They are often forced to separate for months or even years while one member, usually a parent or an older child, finds work and establishes residency before sending for the rest. Undocumented immigrants go for years without seeing their families, as they cannot return to the United States if they leave. Once reunited, families discover that the conditions of American life undermine traditional roles and values. Lacking access to well-paid jobs, nearly all rely on two incomes to meet living expenses and are forced to adjust to the entrance of women into the work force. In earning their own salary for the first time women gain a measure of independence virtually unknown in Colombia; they also have more opportunities for education. By contrast, men usually have more difficulty finding work and often take more responsibility for household chores than they do in Colombia. These changes sometimes tear families apart: despite strong cultural prohibitions, immigrants divorce far more often than their counterparts in Colombia. In other cases, families are strengthened in uniting against such pressure and transmitting traditional values to their children.

Colombian Americans value education highly and often move to the United States for the chance to educate their children through high school and beyond, a privilege reserved in Colombia for the wealthy. Such ready access offers a crucial advantage to immigrants from the middle and lower classes, for whom an American degree represents an end to the cycle of limited education and poorly paid work that inhibits economic mobility in Colombia. During the late 1980s, the rising costs of higher education threatened the hopes of many families, who found themselves unable to afford their children's college tuition. Among all cities, New York remains the most popular destination, in part because of its colleges and universities, especially those of the city system, which were tuition-free until the early 1970s

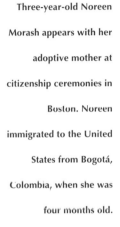

Three-year-old Noreen Morash appears with her adoptive mother at citizenship ceremonies in Boston. Noreen immigrated to the United States from Bogotá, Colombia, when she was four months old.

and remain less expensive than others. Most parents are nonetheless disappointed by American public schools; they consider the curriculum lacking and are disturbed by the informal tone of the classroom, the rate of delinquency among American students, and the wide availability of drugs. They usually look to Catholic schools for an environment that emphasizes values in keeping with their own and enroll their children as soon as they can afford to do so.

Family networks are the primary source of aid in both Colombia and the United States. Relatives, godparents, and friends already living in the United States are often the only source of support for immigrants; they provide not only money and housing but also advice about work and legal and cultural matters. Once financially independent, most immigrants remit a large portion of their salaries to family left behind. On several occasions they have also united in the wake of disaster in Colombia. They responded quickly to a volcanic eruption in the northern part of the country that killed more than 20,000 and destroyed untold

property in November 1985; through campaigns nationwide they mounted one of the world's largest relief efforts on behalf of the victims.

Colombian social networks are extensive and difficult to categorize. Doctors' associations in New York City and Chicago were probably the first Colombian organizations in the United States, and other professional societies soon followed. Social clubs based on regional identity became another community institution. According to Gutiérrez, about a dozen formed in New York during the 1970s, their membership drawn mostly from among poor immigrants; they serve as a soccer league during the warm months and meet indoors in cold weather. Colombian Americans also develop strong ties with other Latinos through more informal networks. To some degree they share a common culture through Spanish-language media, which provide news, entertainment, and music from Latin America unavailable elsewhere. Social events draw immigrants from throughout Latin America and are often held at neighborhood restaurants and nightclubs. Soccer is also widely popular; many Colombian Americans take part in local games and also closely observe the fortunes of Latin American teams.

# RELIGION

Under Spanish rule, Roman Catholicism spread quickly throughout Colombia and displaced native religions. The country's patron saint, the Virgin of Chiquinquira, nonetheless represents a synthesis of Catholicism and indigenous beliefs: the population named St. Mary their champion in impossible matters after the prayers of a poor woman supposedly restored an abandoned painting of her in Chiquinquira in 1586. From colonial times, the church hierarchy cultivated a close alliance with the elite, and for the poor, stressed the promise of an afterlife achieved through obedience and endurance. This system was condemned by Protestant missionaries, who first arrived during the nineteenth century and concentrated on helping the poor. Their efforts met with swift retaliation from the establishment, which persecuted Protestant ministers and closed their churches. These attacks were especially violent during the civil war of 1948-1958 and abated only after Pope John XXIII took office in 1958.

Catholicism in Colombia faced an even more serious challenge during the 1960s with the rise of Liberation Theology, a movement within the church that sought to focus on the needs of the poor. Its agenda was articulated at a conference of Latin American bishops in Medellín in 1968 and solicited strong opposition from the Vatican and the Latin American elite, which waged a campaign of terror against priests and nuns known or suspected of being activists. Marxist guerrilla groups took up the cause of Liberation Theology, but modified its goals of education and political action to allow for warfare. The movement was weakened throughout Latin American by opposition from the military, the government, and the church, which appointed conservative bishops to fill vacated positions; it also lost the support of guerrilla leaders, who abandoned Marxism in favor of democratic solutions.

Colombia has one of the most conservative church hierarchies in Latin America and one of the highest percentages of regular churchgoers. In addition to Christmas and Easter, religious holidays include Corpus Christi Day (June 21), the celebration of Saints Peter and Paul (June 29), the Procession of Our Lady of Carmen (Cartagena, July 16), All Saints Day (November 1), All Souls Day (November 2), and Immaculate Conception Day (December 8); not all are observed throughout the country. Despite efforts at reconciliation, the country's Protestants and Catholics remain divided.

The Catholic church in New York City was slow to respond to the needs of its Colombian parishioners. Like other Latinos, Colombian Americans in Jackson Heights during the 1960s and 1970s were largely ignored by the local Catholic clergy, which was predominantly Irish and Italian and did not acknowledge the changing ethnicity of the neighborhood. As few priests spoke Spanish, Latinos had difficulty obtaining information about services and programs offered by the church. Enrollment in parochial schools was a charged issues; most parents initially failed to secure their children's enrollment because they were unaware of registration dates and the requirement to make donations at Sunday mass for a year before applying for admission (Gutiérrez, p. 224). In response to such problems, the diocese of Queens and Brooklyn sponsored the Instituto de Comunicación Internacional, a program for teaching Latin American culture and Spanish to the clergy. Even after Spanish-language services were introduced, tension remained between the Hispanic congregation, which was assigned to hold its services in the church basement, and the English-language one, which was composed primarily of Italians and Irish and met in the body of the church. The shortage of Spanish-speaking priests persisted, and from the mid 1970s, about a dozen Colombian priests not formally affiliated with the diocese operated within the neighborhood. Some parishes sought to attract Hispanic congregants by offering masses that featured Latin American music. In Queens a few hundred Colombian Americans led by a Colombian priest established a church based on charismatic Catholicism.

The Catholic church provides crucial support to Latin Americans throughout the United States. Religious ceremonies are closely tied to important customs and traditions, such as *compadrazgo*, the establishment of kin networks through the choice of godparents (usually the man and woman who acted as the best man and the maid of honor at the parents' wedding); their preservation has been assured in recent years as parishes have added Spanish-language services in not only large cities, but also a growing number of suburbs. The church is also one of the few venues that offer respite from the isolation, loneliness, and hostility that immigrants encounter in American society.

## EMPLOYMENT AND ECONOMIC TRADITIONS

Since 1960 Colombian Americans have moved to the United States primarily to work. With the deterioration of the Colombian economy after the civil war, the rate of emigration increased as some sought to escape rising unemployment, underemployment, and inflation. In the United States they pursued professional careers, took employment as laborers, factory workers, and domestic servants, and opened small businesses, often catering to Latin Americans. In New York City those who could afford to buy property did so as soon as possible. As immigration restrictions tightened, fewer Colombian Americans planned to remain permanently in the United States; more frequently they sought only to work long enough to improve their financial status before returning to Colombia, where inflation made investment and saving nearly impossible. During the 1970s and 1980s, plans for temporary settlement were common among professionals, who in the United States found opportunities unavailable in Colombia to use their skills, earn salaries commensurate with their education, and enhance their professional standing through advanced training. In the mid 1990s Colombian Americans had one of the highest average incomes among Latinos. Many have prospered in business, especially in ventures in Miami related to trade with Latin America.

Conditions of employment have often brought Colombian Americans into conflict with other groups and exerted pressure on Colombian traditions. According to Gutiérrez, in New York City Colombian Americans developed somewhat strained relations with Cubans, who they felt dominated business, even in El Chapinerito. In Miami they have experienced racial tension with blacks over such issues as competition for work and provisions for more extensive measures to help the poor. They have also had to deal with cultural stigmas attached to the work open to them, which, although remunerative by Colombian standards, often requires far less skill and education than they possess. In New York City during the 1960s and 1970s, they took positions in manufacturing whenever possible, particularly in the garment and textile industries, which were considered most desirable among the kinds of work available. For members of the middle class, especially those without resident status, accepting such work represents a decline in social status; many do not discuss their work with friends and family in Colombia. The problem is severest for women, who in Colombia are held in contempt or deemed disreputable for working at all. With other immigrants, Colombian Americans also face growing uncertainty about their position in the work force. After the economy entered a recession during the late 1980s, they became a target of hostility among Americans who sought to bar immigrants from working, arguing that their jobs should go to the American-born; those without work papers were some of the first to be dismissed.

Work is the focus of Colombian households. While men usually find their earning power diminished, women have many more opportunities than in Colombia, and despite a longstanding tradition of *machismo*, their husbands offer little or no resistance to their employment because their salaries are needed to repay sponsors, meet daily expenses, support family members who stayed behind, and save money toward children's education, trips to Colombia, and other investments. Husbands and wives often operate small businesses together, and many people hold more than one job.

## POLITICS AND GOVERNMENT

Colombian Americans have traditionally devoted themselves to politics in Colombia rather than the United States. Most believe that they will not remain abroad and see little point in becoming involved in American politics; a large proportion do not have the right to vote. In New York City, notes Gutiérrez, strong regional identities have impeded efforts to organize: four associations designed to unite Colombian Americans during the 1970s quickly failed, as did efforts by the Democratic Party to open a Hispanic headquarters in Queens in 1974. By contrast, the power of the community as a voting block in Colombian elections has become so well known that Colombian politicians often campaign in the neighborhood and buy advertisements in *El Diario,* the city's main Spanish-language newspaper. Colombian Americans in Miami have joined with other Latinos to achieve common political goals such as electing mayors, councilmen, and congressional representatives and engaging lobbyists to represent them in political circles. They have also organized to address the increasingly urgent issues of immigration and discrimination. In 1994 Colombian Americans in New Jersey mounted citizenship drives in response to a Republican plan to deny legal immigrants their Supplemental Security Income on retirement. Throughout the country they fight to correct prevailing stereotypes concerning their relationship to the drug trade.

# INDIVIDUAL AND GROUP CONTRIBUTIONS

### BUSINESS

Perhaps the best-known Colombian in American business is the entrepreneur María Elena Ibanez (born in Barranquilla); after helping to manage her father's orchards as a child she moved to Miami in 1973, where she earned a degree in computer science and later formed International High-Tech Marketing, a firm that sells computer equipment in more than 100 developing countries. Andrés Mejia is the world's largest supplier of Paso Fino horses and maintains stables in Miami and Colombia.

### LITERATURE

The works of Gabriel García Márquez (born in Aracata, Colombia, March 6, 1928) were among the first from Latin America widely read by an English-speaking audience; their critical acclaim stimulated interest in other Latin American artists. A number of Colombian writers living in the United States have also enjoyed success. Silvio Martínez Palau (born in Calí, 1954) moved to the United States in the late 1960s and published the play *The English-only Restaurant*, a collection of short stories titled *Made in USA*, and the novel *Disneylandia*. The playwright Enrique Buenaventura has had his work performed in several American cities; his best-known play, ¡*Por Mi Madre Que Es Verdad!* (*I Swear on My Mother's Grave!*), is set in the southern Bronx. Alister Ramirez lives and writes in New York City.

### MEDICINE

Pilar Bernal de Pheils, an assistant clinical professor of nursing at the University of California San Francisco, has promoted educational exchange programs allowing Latin American nurses to study and teach in the United States.

### MUSIC

Several Colombian composers work in the United States. Jaime Leon was named music director of the American Ballet Theater and composes lyrical songs. Juan Carlos Quintero (born in Medellín) grew up in Brussels and in Freehold, New Jersey, and attended the Berklee School of Music and the New England Conservatory before moving to Los Angeles, where he developed a distinctive style combining jazz and pop with cumbia, salsa, and samba. Freddie Ravel is known for the versatility of his compositions. Colombian musicians based in the United States include the opera singer Martha Senn and the salsa performer Yari More, who works primarily in Los Angeles.

### PERFORMING ARTS

The best-known Colombian in the performing arts is the actor and comedian John Leguizamo (born in Bogotá, 1965), who has written and performed one-man comedies based on his childhood in Jackson Heights, including *Spic-O-Rama* and *Mambo Mouth*; he also appeared in the motion pictures *Die Hard II* and *Hangin' with the Homeboys*. Rosario Vargas helped to form the Aguijon II Theater Company, the first Spanish-language theater company in Chicago, and remains one of its artistic directors. The dancer Ricardo Bustamente made his debut as a soloist with the American Ballet Theater in June 1989.

### SPORTS

The race car driver Roberto Guerrero (born in Medellín) won the title of rookie of the year after the Indianapolis 500 in 1984; at the same race in 1992 he set a record qualifying speed of 232.482 miles per hour (371.971 kilometers per hour).

### VISUAL ARTS

The artist Fernando Botero (born in Medellín, 1932) has gained international renown for his paintings, drawings, and sculptures of obese figures; after presenting his first solo exhibition of watercolors in Mexico City as a young man, he lived in New York City during the 1960s, where his painting *Mona Lisa, Age 12* was shown at the

Museum of Modern Art; although decried by members of the academy, his work was enthusiastically received by a wide audience; in 1994 the city of Chicago showed 17 of his bronze sculptures in an outdoor exhibition. Another Colombian artist who has exhibited his work widely in the United States is Enrique Gran, who was born in Panama, spent his childhood in Cartagena, Colombia, and studied painting at the Art Students League in New York City from 1940 to 1943. María Fernanda Cardoso is known for her haunting sculptures dealing with violence in Colombia.

# MEDIA

## PRINT

### El Diario/La Prensa.
Primary Spanish-language newspaper of New York City; founded in 1913.

**Contact:** Carlos D. Ramirez, Publisher.
**Address:** 143-155 Varick Street, New York, New York 10013.
**Telephone:** (212) 807-4600.
**Fax:** (212) 807-4617.

### El Nuevo Herald.
Spanish-language edition of the *Miami Herald*. Founded in 1976, it has a circulation of 103,000, and focuses on Latin America.

**Contact:** Carlos Verdecia, Editor.
**Address:** Miami Herald Publishing Co., 1 Herald Plaza, Miami, Florida 33132.
**Telephone:** (305) 376-3535.
**Fax:** (305) 376-2099.

## RADIO

### KDHX-FM (88.1).
Public radio.

**Contact:** Emeric A. Martin, General Manager.
**Address:** 3504 Magnolia, St. Louis, Missouri 63118.
**Telephone:** (314) 664-3955.

### KLAX-FM (97.8).
Hispanic format.

**Contact:** Alfredo Rodriges, General Manager.
**Address:** 5700 Sunset Boulevard, Los Angeles, California 90028.
**Telephone:** (213) 466-3001.
**Fax:** (213) 466-8259.

### KMPQ-AM (980).
Hispanic format.

**Contact:** Paul Mougel, General Manager.
**Address:** P.O. Box 832, Rosenberg, Texas 77471.
**Telephone:** (713) 342-6601.
**Fax:** (713) 232-3437.

### WOJO-FM (105.1).
Hispanic format.

**Contact:** Lucy Diaz.
**Address:** 625 North Michigan Avenue, Third Floor, Chicago, Illinois 60611-3110.
**Telephone:** (312) 649-0105.
**Fax:** (312) 664-2472.

### WQBA-AM (1140), FM (107.5).
Hispanic format.

**Contact:** Maria Elena Llansa, Station Manager.
**Address:** 2828 Coral Way, Miami, Florida 33145.
**Telephone:** (305) 441-2073.
**Fax:** (305) 445-8908.

## TELEVISION

### Telemundo (Channel 44 in Chicago).
**Contact:** Donald M. Travis.
**Address:** Telemundo Group, Inc., 1740 Broadway, 18th Floor, New York, New York 10019.
**Telephone:** (212) 492-5691.

### WXTV-TV (Channel 41).
**Contact:** Richard P. Ramirez.
**Address:** 24 Meadow Parkway, Secaucus, New Jersey 07094.
**Telephone:** (201) 348-4141.
**Fax:** (201) 348-4104.

# ORGANIZATIONS AND ASSOCIATIONS

### Cartagena Medical Alumni Association.
Established in the late 1960s by costeño physicians.

**Address:** Chicago, Illinois.

### Colombian American Association (CAA).
Objectives are to facilitate commerce and trade between the Republic of Colombia and the U.S.; and to foster and advance cultural relations and goodwill between the two countries.

**Contact:** Paul E. Calvet, Secretary/Treasurer.

**Address:** 150 Nassau Street, Room 2015, New York, New York 10038.

**Telephone:** (212) 233-7776.

**Colombianos Unidos para Labor Activista.**

A political club that holds monthly meetings to discuss problems of a social, political, or economic nature.

**Address:** Chicago, Illinois.

# MUSEUMS AND RESEARCH CENTERS

**Center for Arts and Culture.**

Located at the Eugenio Maria de Hostos Community College, New York City, this research center attracts performing artists from throughout Latin America.

# SOURCES FOR FURTHER STUDY

Birnabaum, Larry. "Colombia's Vallenato Up North," *Newsday*, August 24, 1994 (Nassau and Suffolk County edition), p. B 7.

Booth, William. "Miami Auditions for Lead in Latin American Affairs; As Leaders Gather for Summit, America's Southern Trade Hub Tries to Shed Vice-squad Image," *Washington Post*, December 9, 1994, p. A1.

Feldman, Claudia. "It Is a Source of Irritation to Some, a Matter of Cultural Pride to Others. Either Way, It Is a Fact of Life in Houston: Spanish Spoken Here," *Houston Chronicle*. November 20, 1994, p. 1.

Garza, Melita Marie. "Census Puts Latinos in Bittersweet Light," *Chicago Tribune*. October 20, 1994, p. 1.

# COSTA RICAN AMERICANS

by
Cida S. Chase

Costa Ricans who have emigrated and settled in the United States do not exhibit the same characteristics as many other Hispanic groups.

## OVERVIEW

Slightly smaller than West Virginia, Costa Rica has an area of 19,652 square miles (51,032 square kilometers). Its terrain is rugged and divided from north to south by a central mountain range that separates the eastern and western coastal plains. Costa Rica is located in the southern end of Central America and bordered to the north by Nicaragua and to the south by Panama. Its climate is tropical and subtropical, varying according to altitude and distance from the coasts.

Costa Rica has a population of 3,000,000 with an annual growth rate of 2.5 percent. Almost 30 percent (890,434) of its population lives in the capital city of San José. Ninety-six percent of the total population is from European stock, including some *mestizos*, while three percent is of black descent and one percent is indigenous; a small percentage of its inhabitants are Asian. Ninety-five percent of the Costa Rican population is Roman Catholic, although the Mormon, Christian, Baptist, and other Protestant churches are gaining significant numbers of members. In addition, Costa Rica is home to a small number of Jews. The country's official language is Spanish, although a Jamaican dialect of English is spoken in some areas of the Atlantic coast, especially Puerto Limón. The Costa Rican flag comprises two blue horizontal stripes (top and bottom), two white inner stripes, and a wide red central band with the national coat of arms in the center. The latter portrays the geography of the country; the central massif is signified by three mountain peaks in the center of two oceans, each featuring a Spanish ship. A rising sun to the left and a blue sky crowned by seven stars represent the seven provinces of the country: Alajuela, Cartágo, Guanacaste, Heredia, Limón, Puntarenas, and San José.

## HISTORY

Europeans first set foot in Costa Rica in 1502, when Christopher Columbus arrived during his fourth and last voyage to the New World. Formal settlement of the territory began in 1522, and for 300 years the Spanish administered its colony under a military governor as part of the Captaincy General of Guatemala.

Costa Rica acquired its name when the Spanish, expecting to find an abundance of gold, named it "Rich Coast." However, as there was little gold and few other valuable minerals in the area, the new settlers turned to agriculture for survival. Moreover, as the indigenous population was rather small, the Spanish were unable to establish an extensive forced labor system. Consequently, Costa Rica developed differently from other Latin American nations. The small landowners' modest standard of living, the people's ethnic and linguistic homogeneity, and the isolation from the large colonial centers of Mexico and South America produced a rather independent, individualist agrarian society.

Costa Rica obtained its independence from Spain on September 15, 1821, without bloodshed, after other Central American colonies had fought the Spanish to gain it. In fact, Costa Ricans learned about their independence months after it had been declared. Costa Rica joined the other Central American provinces in an 1821 joint declaration of independence from Spain. These newly created nations formed a confederation, which border disputes soon dissolved. Costa Rica acquired Guanacaste, its northernmost province, from Nicaragua after one of these border disputes. Since 1838, when it declared itself a sovereign nation, Costa Rica has enjoyed an independent existence, which it has zealously maintained. In 1856 the country was invaded by 240 filibusters commanded by William Walker, who had decided to conquer Central America on his own accord, and the Costa Ricans promptly took up arms to defend their territory. The Costa Rican national hero, Juan Santamaría, emerged when he burned down the filibusters' headquarters in Santa Rosa.

## MODERN ERA

Costa Rica's egalitarian traditions have subsisted throughout its history. Even though the introduction of banana and coffee plantations in the nineteenth century gave rise to a small oligarchy, the nation has been able to maintain a strong middle class that sustains the nation's democratic ideals. The modern era of democracy in Costa Rica began after the elections of 1889, which are considered the first free elections in the country's history. This democratic tradition has experienced problems only twice: once in 1917 and 1918 when Federico Tinoco declared his government a dictatorship; and again in 1948 when a disputed election brought forth a civil war in which more than 2,000 people lost their lives. After the civil war, a junta drafted a new constitution, which guaranteed free elections with universal suffrage and the abolition of the army. José Figueres, who emerged as a hero during the Civil War, became the first president under the new constitution.

The most prominent Costa Rican of the modern era is probably Oscar Arias Sánchez, who was president of Costa Rica from 1986 to 1990, a significantly troublesome time in Central America, with disturbances in El Salvador, Nicaragua, and Panama. Although Costa Rica enjoyed peace within its borders, it was not insulated from regional conflicts. The instability in the neighboring countries at this time discouraged investment and tourism. Moreover, the country experienced a flood of Nicaraguan and Salvadoran refugees, which drained the economy and burdened educational and health institutions.

In 1987 President Sánchez designed a regional peace plan—the Esquipulas Process, which became the basis for the peace agreement signed by the presidents of most of the other Central American nations. This peace plan brought about free and open elections in Nicaragua and the subsequent end of the civil war in that country. Arias' peace accomplishments in the region earned him the Nobel Peace Prize in 1987. The Nobel prize money was used to establish the Arias Foundation for Peace and Human Progress, which maintains three centers of funding: the Center for Human Progress, funding programs for the advancement of women; the Center for Peace and

Reconciliation, working for Central American conflict resolution and prevention programs; and the Center for Philanthropy, promoting the participation of non-profit organizations in the building of just and peaceful societies.

## COSTA RICANS IN THE UNITED STATES

Costa Ricans who have emigrated and settled in the United States do not exhibit the same characteristics as many other Hispanic groups. They have not had to flee their country as refugees from political oppression or from extreme economic circumstances. Consequently, there have never been waves of Costa Rican emigrants. U.S. Immigration and Naturalization Service records show that very few Costa Ricans have tried to enter the country illegally.

Costa Ricans who have decided to immigrate to the United States include the following general categories: they have married Americans and raised their families in the United States; they have been hired to work in the United States after completing a degree in an American university, they have come seeking research opportunities which are not so readily available in their country; or they have come to various jobs and trades in the United States.

Only 57,661 Costa Ricans have immigrated to the United States since 1931. Hence, the number of Costa Rican emigrants has been increasing at an extremely slow rate, which is significantly different from the pattern of emigration from most other Central American countries. The other two countries in this region that show a continuously slow rate of emigration are Belize and Panama.

## SETTLEMENT

As Costa Ricans immigrate to the United States, they tend to establish their residences in the states of California, Florida, Texas, and the New York City/New Jersey area. The geographical preferences of Costa Ricans, evident in the statistics from the Immigration and Naturalization Service, are consistent with the findings of the 1990 census. The latter reports the largest concentration of Costa Rican Americans in Los Angeles and its surrounding areas (23,625). The next largest group is located in the New York City area, including parts of Connecticut, New Jersey, and Long Island (12,985). The third largest group is in Miami and surrounding areas, in the Hialeah district, and in Fort Lauderdale (9,987). The concentration of Costa Rican Americans in the Houston and Galveston area of Texas (2,534) is also evident in the 1990 census. There is also a significant Costa Rican American population in the Chicago and Gary areas of Illinois (1,845).

# ACCULTURATION AND ASSIMILATION

Since there are relatively fewer Costa Rican Americans than other Hispanic groups in the United States, they normally do not form communities or *barrios,* as is usually the case with Mexican Americans, Puerto Rican Americans, and other Central American Hispanic groups, such as Salvadoran Americans and Guatemalan Americans. Costa Ricans tend to disappear in the English-speaking multitudes or form working and friendly relationships with other Hispanics, celebrating with them when the occasion arises.

Although Costa Rican Americans tend to maintain their heritage, they also tend to integrate and adjust to their environment quickly, especially if they want to join a church or if they have children in the public school system. If both parents speak Spanish, chances are that the children will be raised bilingually. However, if only one parent speaks Spanish, the children will usually grow up speaking only English.

Since Costa Ricans did not suffer ethnic persecution during the colonial period, nor did they have a violent war of independence, they are not as self-conscious about their ethnicity as other Hispanic groups. Therefore, they usually acculturate and assimilate rather rapidly.

## TRADITIONS, CUSTOMS, AND BELIEFS

Costa Rica has a number of traditions that have survived. Every year in the month of December, the Costa Rican people enjoy their *fiestas cívicas,* which are similar to the state fairs in the United States. In addition to the varied types of food available and the usual midway entertainment, there are simulated bullfights, in which youths try their luck "fighting" balloon decorated *toros guacos* (mean bulls), by pulling their tails and touching their rumps.

Many of the Costa Rican traditions are religious. The small towns hold *Semana Santa* (Holy Week) processions, during which people contemplate Jesus in his suffering. The most impressive procession takes place on Good Friday, for it is the day on which people are able to see Jesus in his *Santo Sepulcro* (Holy Sepulcher). Every year on August 2, Costa Rican people celebrate the *romería de la Virgen de los Angeles* (the pilgrimage of the Holy Mother of the Angels) by making a 20-kilometer trip on foot from San José to Cartágo, where the sanctuary of the patron saint of the country is located.

Although these traditions have not been transported to the United States, Costa Rican Americans try to maintain several other traditions. Such is the case of the tradition of the *Rosario del Niño*, wherein families prepare a special nativity scene for Christmas that does not display the Christ Child figure in the manger until December 25. The nativity scene remains in its place until January 6, the Epiphany (the twelfth night after Christmas). After that date, families celebrate the rosary with a group of friends who bring over their small children. After the recitation of the rosary, the families have a party that includes ice cream and cake and, if possible, Costa Rican foods.

Costa Ricans believe in calling upon Jesus and the saints for assistance when they are in need or in danger. Each saint is thought to have a special mission or to be able to satisfy a particular need. Costa Ricans pray to Saint Anthony, for example, if something has been lost or misplaced.

Not all the Costa Rican popular beliefs are religious in nature, however. Costa Rican people are believers in herbal medicine. Many of them know that gargling with a solution of boiled rue (a strong-scented plant of the genus *Ruta*) leaves will cure a sore throat. Liquefied and strained raw eggplant is thought to lower the cholesterol level and purify the blood. A popular cure for stomach discomfort is to drink liquid in which rhubarb or camomile has been boiled. Costa Ricans also prepare a variety of herbal teas to soothe the nerves. Teas prepared with linden, orange, and lemon blossoms are supposed to relax a person and allow him or her to fall asleep at night.

Conservative Costa Ricans bring many of these customs and beliefs with them to the United States and continue to practice them as long as they can. However, as they assimilate into American society, many of their original popular cultural beliefs become less important. Consequently, second- and third-generation Costa Rican Americans may have minimal knowledge about them.

## TRADITIONAL COSTUMES

If the opportunity arises, Costa Ricans share with others their native costume, which for women consists of a white peasant blouse decorated with embroidery or ribbon work and a colorful ankle-length full skirt. Men wear white peasant shirts and long white pants. In addition, they frequently wear a colorful handkerchief around the neck and a straw hat. Both men and women wear sandals and women braid colorful ribbons into their hair. Costa Rican Americans also celebrate all the American holidays, adopting typical American customs and holiday food.

## PROVERBS

Numerous Costa Rican proverbs come from the Spanish culture and hence they exist in many other Hispanic countries. However, there are some colorful sayings that seem to be typically Costa Rican or appear to be favorite phrases of the people's language: "At night all cats are grey" (People can get away with things that they would not normally do in the daytime); "Between husband and wife not even a pin's head should intervene;" "When times become difficult put on a happy face;" "An egg-eating dog will not break his habit even if one burns his mouth;" "Tuesday is not a good day to make serious decisions or to adventure away from home;" "Skinny dogs get fleas;" "A full tummy gives you a happy heart;" and "A guilty party is afraid of being caught."

Costa Rican expressions are often used to imply definite ideas about something or someone. For example: "To become smoke" means to disappear as when someone goes out of sight; "To be as if travelling between Bagaces and Liberia" (two cities from the northern Costa Rican province of Guanacaste) means to be idle—another expression for this same idea is "To be combing the snake's hair;" "To find someone with his hands in the dough" means to find someone in the act of doing something wrong; "To be walking with lead feet" is to be acting very cautiously about something. In addition, people refer to a lady who has never married as someone who has "missed the train" by saying *la dejó el tren* or, "The train left her." Many other picturesque proverbs and sayings enrich Costa Rican Americans' Spanish.

## CUISINE

Costa Rican cuisine is mild, free of hot and spicy sauces, and usually seasoned with herbs. Black pepper is used sparingly, but fresh cilantro, thyme, oregano, onion, garlic, pimento, and tomato are fundamental ingredients in the preparation of meats, soups, and vegetable hashes. A variety of beef cuts, including tongue and kidneys, are baked or simmered for long periods of time in herbal sauces until they are tender and flavorful. Chicken and pork are prepared in similar ways.

Complete daily meals may include a meat dish, a vegetable hash, white rice, black or red beans, a lettuce and tomato salad, corn tortillas or crusty white bread, and a fresh fruit drink. If the meal includes dessert, it is probably fruit; cakes, pastries, caramel flan, and ice cream are reserved for special occasions, holidays, or the afternoon tea. The traditional salad dressing is made of oil and vinegar, but mayonnaise is a favorite dressing for heart of palm and fresh pea salad. Vegetable hashes, which include a small amount of beef, are made of cubed potatoes, chayote squash with fresh corn, and green plantains. Beef or vegetable soups are also popular in Costa Rica. Black bean soup served with fresh herbs, and a boiled egg with white rice is a favorite side dish.

Holiday meals include meat tamales—meat-flavored cornmeal and mashed potatoes stuffed with meat, saffron rice, olives, a few garbanzo beans, green peas, pimentos, a wedge of boiled egg, and prunes or raisins. These tamales usually come in four-by-six-inch rectangles wrapped in banana leaves; each one is a meal in itself. Holiday meals also include a main dish of chicken and rice prepared with added vegetables and raisins. *Ensalada rusa*, Russian salad, is also a must at a holiday meal. It consists of diced potatoes, fresh beets, and green peas all cooked separately and brought together with a mayonnaise sauce, which sometimes includes diced canned heart of palm. This salad, which is very similar to what the Russians call "vinaigrette," must have come to Costa Rica via some of the early European settlers. During Holy Week, Costa Rican cuisine includes a variety of vegetarian dishes, including small sweet tamales and a dessert called *dulce de chiverre* prepared with a variety of spaghetti squash.

## COSTA RICAN DANCES AND SONGS

Like many Costa Rican folk dances, the Costa Rican national dance, the *punto guanacasteco*, comes from the province of Guanacaste. Couples wear traditional costumes and follow a melody played with a *marimba* (a type of wooden xylophone) and several guitars. This dance, like other popular dances, portrays the courting traditions of the past. The male dancer always follows his female partner and the latter, while smiling, pretends to get away from him. The male dancer periodically stops the music by shouting "*¡Bomba!*" so that he may recite humorous praises, called *bombas*, to his lady. A traditional *bomba* goes as follows: "Dicen que no me quieres / porque no tengo bigote / mañana me lo pondré / con plumas de zopilote." (They say that you don't love me / because I don't have a mustache / tomorrow I shall put one on / made out of buzzard feathers.)

Costa Rican folk songs are nostalgic, featuring ballad-like melodies. The lyrics praise the beauty of the country's women and the landscape as they tell of the sorrows of love. Costa Rican Americans enjoy sharing their songs and dances during community or school Hispanic festivities.

## HEALTH AND MENTAL HEALTH ISSUES

Costa Rica's government-sponsored health-care system deserves much of the credit for the good health of Costa Ricans. Medical attention in that country is not only superior to that of most of Latin America, but surpasses the health services available in many communities in the United States. According to Tom Barry in his book *Costa Rica: A Country Guide*, infant deaths are fewer than 18 per 1,000 compared with 79 per 1,000 in Guatemala. Moreover, life expectancy is 74 years for males and 76 for females—the highest in Central America.

During the 1980s, Costa Ricans were able to arrest the spread of illnesses brought into the country by the flood of Salvadoran and Nicaraguan refugees thanks to their health facilities and their effective methods of disseminating information regarding health issues. Malaria and tuberculosis, which had been eradicated from the country years before, began to appear with the arrival of refugees, but the immediate medical attention given to this issue brought an end to the problem.

Since Costa Rican emigrants customarily follow the rules established by the United States Immigration and Naturalization Service, they have formal documentation on their good state of health upon entering the country. In addition, they acquire medical insurance, looking after their health and the health of their children. There is no evidence of physical or mental health problems unique to Costa Rican Americans.

# LANGUAGE

Costa Ricans are sometimes called *ticos* because of their insistence on using the diminutive forms of Spanish words, which often end in "ico," such as *chiquitico*, coming from *chico* meaning "small." When used with the "ico" suffix, the meaning becomes "tiny, very tiny." The Costa Rican word *chirrisco* or *chirrisca* means "very small," but many people, dissatisfied with conveying the idea of just "very small" add the suffix "ico" or "ica," making the word *chirrisquitico* or *chirrisquitica*—meaning "extremely small." Moreover, Costa Rican oral Spanish exhibits the regional characteristic called *el voseo*, also found in the southern parts of South America. *El voseo* is the use of "*vos*" instead of "*tú*" as the second person singular familiar of the language. Speakers make the verbs agree with the form "*vos*" as in "*Vos vivís en los Estados Unidos*" (You live in the United States), instead of saying "*Tú vives en los Estados Unidos*," as one says in most of the Hispanic world. Although this form is more prominent in the spoken language, increasingly more Costa Rican writers are using it. Costa Rican Americans are likely to lose the use of *el voseo* as they relate to Hispanics of other origins, who do not use it in their speech. Also, Spanish courses in the United States usually do not study this regional form.

Costa Rican Spanish is also marked by a softly pronounced double "r," which means that the prominently trilled initial "r" or "rr" of the Spanish language is missing in the language of most Costa Ricans. However, Costa Ricans generally are careful speakers of Spanish. They pronounce distinctly all the letters in the words, and sound out the final "s," which is not always the case in the speech of other regions of Latin America and Southern Spain.

As has happened in many lands of Latin America, indigenous languages have enriched Costa Rican Spanish with a number of vocabulary items. There are words ending in "ate," "te," and "tle," such as *zacate* (grass), *mecate* (rope), *chayote* (a type of squash), *quelite* (tender ends of the chayote vine) and *tepeizcuinte* or *tepeizcuitle* (paca or spotted cavy, a rodent larger than a rabbit), which are part of the everyday speech of the people. Although this type of vocabulary is not as abundant in Costa Rica as it is in other Central American countries and Mexico, its presence in Costa Rica stands as a trace of the country's ancient indigenous past.

# FAMILY AND COMMUNITY DYNAMICS

Costa Ricans have generally conservative family values and relationships. A family, to many of them, must have a father, a mother, and children. Like many other Hispanic groups, the Costa Rican families tend to be patriarchal in nature, and extended family members have authority roles. The father is the undisputed head of the household, and the elderly members of the extended family are both respected and obeyed.

A traditional Costa Rican home usually has the presence of an elderly grandmother, grandfather, aunt, or uncle, who assists in the rearing of the children when their health allows them to do so. However, as modern life has become more complicated for women, and it is sometimes not possible to keep an elderly relative in the home, residential homes and condominiums for the elderly and the retired are becoming fashionable in Costa Rica. Costa Ricans are a gregarious people. They get together with their relatives and friends as often as possible.

The weekend and holiday afternoon tea is an institution in Costa Rica. Extended family members and friends invite each other for five o'clock tea in order to celebrate birthdays, anniversaries, and other special occasions. This afternoon tea, which constitutes almost a complete meal, including a main dish and a dessert, is also a favorite activity for wedding showers and class reunions. The afternoon tea has become a substitute for supper in modern Costa Rica and occasionally; instead of taking place in the home, as it was in the past, people may gather in a restaurant.

As young Costa Ricans immigrate to the United States, however, they tend to lose their cultural heritage. Once they have a family of their own, however, they often reclaim their ancestral customs. They form close-knit family ties and may experience disappointment when their children grow up and seek early independence, following the example of peers of other ethnic backgrounds. In addition, Costa Ricans, as many other Hispanics, frequently receive in their homes visiting relatives from Costa Rica, who come for the holidays to see their American children and grandchildren. They also provide a temporary home for relatives' children, whose parents send them to spend the summer in the United States.

## BAPTISMS

Babies are baptized in the church when they are newly born, receiving a first and a middle name, one of which is normally a saint's name. The baby's parents select the godparents from among their relatives or their closest friends. The godparents will take responsibility for raising the child within the guidelines of the church if for some reason the baby's parents lose their lives. Godparents are also obliged to look after the child if he or she should be in need.

## FUNERALS

Holding a wake for someone who has died is an important Costa Rican custom. People believe that the deceased must not be left alone while lying in state, and relatives and friends pray devoutly for his soul during the wake and thereafter. The deceased's family offers refreshments to the visitors who call throughout the night of the wake. After a relative's funeral, families and their friends pray the rosary for nine evenings, offering refreshments after each night's prayers. Masses are said for the deceased's soul at the ninth day and also after the first month has passed. Relatives and friends also attend subsequent anniversary masses for the deceased.

Costa Ricans gather with friends for civic celebrations. It is customary to celebrate Independence Day in Costa Rica (September 15) with parades and school assemblies. Costa Rican Americans welcome the opportunity of celebrating with friends whether they are countrymen or people from other ethnic backgrounds. They also join other Hispanics in their celebrations, such as *cinco de mayo* (May 5) and September 16, which are Mexican American holidays.

## RELIGION

Roman Catholicism is the official, traditional, and dominant religion in Costa Rica. After the government, the Catholic church is the most powerful institution in the country. Monsignor Sanabria, the Archbishop of San José in the 1940s, organized and strengthened the modern church, guiding it toward social activism. His work promoted the foundation of church-oriented social organizations such as the Catholic Action, Young Catholic Workers, and a labor union called the Rerum Novarum. This religious social orientation was weakened somewhat during the 1950s when the Partido Liberación Nacional, characterized by its conservatism, dominated the political arena and frowned on liberal social organizations.

Although they have great respect for the church, most Costa Ricans, especially those belonging to the middle class, maintain an independent, personal view of church policies in regard to sensitive issues such as birth control and abortion. Barry describes Costa Ricans' personal attitude: "Catholics in Costa Rica are eclectic believers, whose most fervent expressions of faith are evoked during Holy Week and at the baptism, marriage, or death of family members. Over 80 percent of Costa Rican Catholics do not attend mass regularly." Although people have deep religious beliefs, they follow the dictates of their own conscience in church matters.

Members of other denominations, such as the Mormon, Baptist and other evangelical churches, are also numerous in Costa Rica. Churches whose membership has been rising are the Assemblies of God, Seventh-Day Adventists, Pentecostal Holiness Church, Church of the Nazarene, Association of Bible Churches of Costa Rica, and the Association of Christian Churches.

Costa Rican immigrants to the United States maintain the religious practices of their childhood. They look for a church in which they feel welcome. If the church offers services in Spanish, they are happy to worship with members of the Hispanic community.

## INDIVIDUAL AND GROUP CONTRIBUTIONS

### LITERATURE

Rima de Vallbona, born March 15, 1931 in San José, Costa Rica, has taught Latin American Literature and Civilization at the University of St. Thomas in Houston, Texas, since 1964; her novels and short stories depict feminine characters trying to understand the world: *Mujeres y agonías* (*Women and Grief*, 1982), *Mundo, demonio y mujer* (*World, Demon and Woman*, 1991) *Los infiernos de la mujer y algo más* (*Women's Inferno and Something Else*, 1992) are three of her most acclaimed works. Victoria Urbano, born June 4, 1926, taught Spanish literature at Lamar University in Beaumont, Texas, from 1966 until her death on October 8, 1984; in addition to founding the *Asociación de literatura femenina hispánica* (Association of Hispanic Feminine Literature) in the United States, Urbano published numerous short stories and poems; her *Los nueve círculos* (*The Nine Circles* 1970) and *Exodos incontables* (*Innumerable Exodus* 1982), published in Spain and Uruguay, are frequently studied in Spanish American centers.

## SCIENCE

Franklin Chang-Díaz, born in San José, Costa Rica, April 5, 1950, is a physical scientist; after graduating from the University of Connecticut in 1973 with a degree in mechanical engineering, he obtained a doctorate in applied plasma physics from the Massachusetts Institute of Technology in 1977; at the University of Connecticut he helped design and construct high-energy atomic collision experiments; as a graduate student he worked in the United States' controlled fusion program, doing intensive research in the design and operation of fusion reactors; after obtaining his doctorate, he joined the technical staff of the Draper Laboratory, working on the design and integration of control systems for fusion reactor concepts and experimental devices; in 1979, he developed a concept to guide and target fuel pellets in an inertial fusion reactor chamber; since then he has been working on the implementation of a new concept in rocket propulsion based on magnetically confined high-temperature plasmas. Chang-Díaz became an astronaut in August 1981 and continues to do research work for the National Aeronautics and Space Administration (NASA).

# SOURCES FOR ADDITIONAL STUDY

Barry, Tom. *Costa Rica: A Country Guide*. Albuquerque: Inter-Hemisphere Education Resource Center, 1991.

Biesanz, Richard, Karen Zubris Biesanz, and Mavis Hiltunen Biesanz. *The Costa Ricans*. New Jersey: Prentice-Hall, 1982.

*Costa Rica in Pictures*. Minneapolis: Lerner Publications Company, 1987.

*Costa Rica and Uruguay*, edited by Simon Rottenberg. Oxford: Oxford University Press, 1993.

# CREEKS

by
Loretta Hall

Tribal legend traces
Creek ancestry to
the sky, where the
ancestors lived in
spirit form before
descending to earth
as physical beings.

## OVERVIEW

When Europeans arrived on the North American continent, the Creek Indians occupied major portions of what are now the states of Alabama and Georgia. James Adair, a trader who dealt with the Creeks for three decades, described them in 1770 as the most powerful Indian nation known to the English. They were actually not so much a nation as a confederacy that welcomed new member tribes, even those of a different linguistic and cultural background. Those who joined blended their own traditions into the basic Creek governmental and social structure.

In the early 1830s, the Creek population was about 22,000. Forced relocation to Indian Territory in what is now Oklahoma took a terrible toll, and by 1839 the population had decreased to 13,500. The Civil War further decimated the Creek people, reducing the number to 10,000 by 1867. In 1990 their population of 43,550 placed them tenth among Native American tribes.

### HISTORY

The Creek Indians called themselves Muscogees, or Muscogulges, names that in their language identified them as people living on land that was wet or prone to flooding. During the American colonial period, they received their modern name from English traders who noted that their towns always sat on the banks of picturesque creeks.

Tribal legend traces Creek ancestry to the sky, where the ancestors lived in spirit form before descending to earth as physical beings. They originally lived in the West; their oral tradition tells of a journey toward the sunrise, crossing mountains so large they were called the "backbone of the world," traversing a wide, muddy river, and conquering their new homeland.

Settling in the East, the ancestral Creeks separated into two groups. Settlements along the Coosa, Tallapoosa, and Alabama Rivers became known as the Upper Towns, while communities along the Flint, Chattahoochee, and Ocmulgee Rivers were called the Lower Towns. This partition was merely geographical at first, but as interaction with European colonists developed, the Lower Towns were more accessible to foreign influence. The Upper Towns tended to retain more traditional, political, and social characteristics.

Annual spring floods provided the Creeks with favorable agricultural conditions. They cultivated a variety of crops and gathered wild fruits, roots, and herbs. Grass and the inner bark of trees provided material for making the shawls with which the women clothed themselves. The Creeks were also skillful hunters, depending on animals for both meat and clothing.

Although the Creeks had contact with non-Indians as early as 1540 as a result of Spanish explorer Hernando De Soto's expedition, regular interactions did not begin until the late 1600s when the English moved into South Carolina and the Spanish settled in Florida.

### RELATIONSHIP BETWEEN CREEKS AND NON-INDIANS

"To other Indians the Creeks offered war or friendship with proud indifference," wrote Angie Debo in *The Road to Disappearance*. "To the whites they showed a sturdy sense of equality and independence, tempered by a genuine appreciation of European goods." The Creeks were reputed to be a hospitable people skilled in diplomacy. They traded actively with all of the European colonies, though they generally preferred to deal with the English, who offered a greater variety and better quality of goods, as well as lower prices and better credit terms than the Spanish or the French. In fact, the Creeks allied themselves with the English in 1702, fighting in Queen Anne's War against the French and Spanish. In 1734 a Creek delegation led by Chief Tomochichi traveled to England to see King George II and sign a treaty.

Intermarriage between Creek women and foreign trading partners was common. Creek wives acted as interpreters and taught their European husbands the language and customs of their people. Because they understood both the Indian and white cultures, many of the multiracial children of these marriages became tribal leaders as adults. One such *métis* (mixed-blood) leader was Alexander McGillivray, the son of a Creek/French mother and a Scottish father. He became chief of the dominant Wind Clan in the late 1700s, and for two decades he worked to unify the Creek nation as an ally of the new United States of America.

The Creeks had traditionally welcomed all non-Indians in a spirit of equality, but they did come to accept the concept of black slavery as an economic practicality. Because captured enemy Indians had sometimes become Creek slaves, the practice was not without precedent. European colonials encouraged the Creeks to think of blacks as slaves in order to prevent runaways from seeking refuge within Creek towns. Furthermore, expert Creek hunters were often paid to track and capture runaway slaves.

Immediately after the Revolutionary War, the United States began trying to expand onto Indian homelands, and by 1840 virtually all of the Creeks were relocated to Indian Territory in what is now east-central Oklahoma. They tried to maintain their traditional identity in their new surroundings by reestablishing their former towns: the Upper Creeks settled along the Deep Fork, North Canadian, and Canadian Rivers, while the Lower Creeks located their towns farther to the north along the Arkansas and Verdigris Rivers. The city of Tulsa evolved from a Creek relocation settlement built on sacred ashes brought from the old eastern town of Talsi.

### KEY ISSUES

In addition to job availability and training issues that confront all Americans, Creeks face the problem of tribal economic independence and the struggle to retain their cultural identity. The Muscogee (Creek) Nation of Oklahoma actively seeks to assume and assert the rights and responsibilities of a sovereign nation through the retention of existing tribal lands, acquisition of additional land, and improved access to significant places outside tribal lands.

# ACCULTURATION AND ASSIMILATION

## TRADITIONAL CULTURE

Rebuilding their towns in Oklahoma meant much more to the Creeks than simply erecting buildings. The full meaning of the word *idalwa* is diluted when the English word "town" is substituted. An *idalwa* had the autonomy of a Greek city-state and was the primary cultural unit of Creek society. Each town had its own traditions and its own versions of ceremonies, and the Creeks drew more of their identity from the town than from familial relationships. A child was considered a member of the town of his or her mother.

The town square, the heart of the Creek community, was used for warm-weather council meetings, dances, and rituals. The square was an open space defined by four rectangular structures, each with one open side that faced the square. A ceremonial fire was kept burning in the center of the open space.

Adjacent to the square were two other important facilities: the *chokofa,* or rotunda, and the chunkey yard. The *chokofa* was a circular structure about forty feet in diameter that served as a meeting place for the town council during the winter. It was also used for social gatherings where the entire town could enjoy singing and dancing during inclement weather.

The chunkey yard was a field two to three hundred yards long that was recessed into the ground so that spectators could sit on the surrounding banks. On it was played a ball game that resembled lacrosse. The game was an important part of Creek culture, offering recreation during games, either among the town members or against a team from a friendly town. Known as "brother to war," it also provided a forum for settling disputes between unfriendly or enemy towns.

In addition to the partitioning of the nation into Upper and Lower communities, the confederacy's fifty towns were divided into two categories. Red, or War, towns took the lead in declaring and conducting war operations; councils addressing topics of diplomacy and foreign relations would meet in one of these towns. White, or Peace, towns were cities of refuge; councils seeking to establish peace or enact laws governing internal affairs of the Creek nation met in these towns. The *moiety*, or nature, of each town was easily identifiable, as its color was painted on buildings and ceremonial articles, and was used as body decoration by its people. There was an atmosphere of camaraderie among towns of the same *moiety*, and definite rivalry between towns of opposite natures.

## TRANSFORMATION OF CULTURE

The Creeks were one of the Five Civilized Tribes, along with the Seminoles (who were actually affiliated with the Creek Confederacy until they formed a separate government in 1856), Cherokees, Chickasaws, and Choctaws. The title derived from the fact that these tribes began to assimilate European ways from the earliest phases of contact. The Creeks eagerly traded deerskins for brightly colored cotton cloth. They used their hunting skills to obtain metal tools. Included among these tools were guns, which transformed their methods of hunting, making them increasingly reliant on continual trading. While the acquisition of new goods improved their lifestyle, it also eroded their traditional self-sufficiency.

The Creeks voluntarily modified their way of life in response to interaction with white traders, but the American government went one step further, undertaking an official effort to assimilate them completely into white culture. An early phase of this process involved the 1796 appointment of Benjamin Hawkins as principal agent to the tribe. Hawkins believed that the Creek people would benefit from being taught and equipped to adopt white culture. He devoted the last twenty years of his life to this effort, encouraging the women to become skilled at making cotton cloth and the men to adopt modern farming techniques.

White Americans in the eighteenth century had little appreciation for Indian cultures, assuming that the Indians would prefer white culture if they could be induced to learn about it. Hawkins was uncomfortable with the idea that the Indians might not want to abandon their own traditions to embrace the white way of life. In fact, some Creeks did want to keep their culture intact, but others thought it would be better for them to adopt the culture of the European settlers. In a March 1992 *Progressive* essay Creek author Joy Harjo recalled her great-grandfather, Marsie Harjo, a Creek Baptist minister: "He represents a counterforce to traditional Muscogee culture and embodies a side of the split in our tribe since Christianity, since the people were influenced by the values of European culture. The dividing lines are the same several hundred years later."

Like other Native American groups, the Creeks still encounter a mainstream culture that generally lacks understanding and appreciation for their values. For example, Creeks traditionally shared their possessions readily and relied mainly on current food supplies. These basic inclinations conflict with prevailing American values of acquisition and saving for the future. Such differences in values can cause difficulties when Indians attend white schools. In 1988, Native American students exhibited a dropout rate of 35.5 percent, and they are significantly overrepresented in special education programs. Among teenagers, Indians have the highest suicide rate of any minority group.

The Indians' attitude toward land ownership was another cultural difference that profoundly affected federal acculturation efforts. The Creeks viewed land as belonging to the community; the Dawes Act of 1887 stripped the tribe of all common land and apportioned it to individuals for private ownership. As Harjo wrote in the March 1992 issue of the *Progressive*, "This act undermined one of the principles that had always kept the people together."

With continued attacks on their lifestyle, many Creeks found ways to adapt their traditional ways into the new societal context. Christian missionaries had worked among them since 1735, and by the time the tribe moved to Oklahoma, many Creeks belonged to Baptist, Methodist, or Presbyterian churches. Under governmental pressure to abandon the tribal town structure, they simply shifted their community's center from the square to the church. Each congregation chose from among its members a preacher who would serve for life; it was a natural substitution for the town *micco*, or chief.

### MISCONCEPTIONS AND STEREOTYPES

"From the minds of the earliest English colonists ... who because of their own reverence for the institution of private property expected violent opposition to their intrusion, came the image of the Indian as an uncooperative, hostile, savage, treacherous, murderous creature," wrote historian Florette Henri in *The Southern Indians and Benjamin Hawkins: 1796-1816;* "and the Indians' disinclination to destroy the handful of colonists, but rather to shelter, feed, and aid them, was interpreted as proof of their guile." The Creeks have been victims of the general prejudices that are directed at all Native Americans. In contrast, however, to the stereotype of the reserved, stoic Indian, Creeks respected impassioned public speakers, and lengthy oration was common at council meetings. They were an industrious, happy people, often singing and joking while working.

The Creeks' introduction to liquor caused both real and perceived damage to their society. Traditionally, they drank only water, even at feasts. The drinks they did concoct that may have had an intoxicating effect were generally used only at rare ceremonial rites. Having no tradition of social sanctions against drunkenness, many Indians imbibed freely. The whites with whom they interacted also tended to get drunk. Henri discussed the different perceptions of this activity: "As a rule, it was Indian drinking that was stressed, and when both white and Indian drinking were mentioned, different terms were used for them. When Indians drank excessively, they were said to become noisy, rude, insolent, and violent; but when the garrison got drunk, gouging eyes and biting noses, Price [Hawkins' friend who managed a government trading post in Georgia] characterized the brawl as a 'drunken frolic'."

In 1937 University of Oklahoma professor Morris E. Opler wrote in an unpublished report that many people found it incongruous that Indians who belonged to one of the Five "Civilized" Tribes would want to retain any of their old ways. He further observed that "So far as the whites of Creek country (in Oklahoma) are concerned they have no intention of accepting the Creeks into the main stream of their social and political life." For their part, the Creeks kept to themselves, interacting with the whites only as necessary for trade.

### CUISINE

Corn was the staple food of the Creeks. Two yearly crops of early corn were eaten as they ripened, and a harvest of late corn was dried and stored for winter use as hominy. Each family compound contained a large wooden mortar and pestle used to process corn into meal or grits after it had been hulled by cooking with lye or mixing with ashes. The cornmeal was then cooked with lye and water, and the gruel was left to sour for two or three days. The resulting soup was called *sofkey*, and it was such a basic part of the diet that each household kept a bowlful at the door so visitors could partake as they entered. Corn was used in other ways as well. Burned shells of the field pea were mixed with cornmeal to make blue dumplings. *Apuske*, a drink, was made by sweetening a mixture of parched cornmeal and water. Sweet potatoes, pumpkins, peaches, and apples were eaten fresh or dried for storage. The Creeks also commonly ate vegetable stews, either with or without meat. After relocation to Oklahoma, salt was available from a natural creek-side deposit. Hickory nuts were used both as a cooking ingredient and as a source of oil. Bear fat was prized as a seasoning.

Creek diets included deer, wild hog, turkey, and smaller game such as opossum and squirrel. Beef, venison, and bison meat could be smoked for storage or cut into strips and dried. Meat and fish might be cooked by boiling or roasting. They employed several methods for catching fish, including nets, traps, and spears. During the summer, the population of an entire town gathered at a favorable spot where a stream could be dammed or fenced to trap fish. Appropriate roots were prepared and thrown into the water to drug the fish; as they floated to the surface, the men showed their marksmanship by shooting them with bows and arrows. The women then cooked *sofkey* and fried the fish for a feast.

## CLOTHING

Traditional clothing for men consisted of a breechcloth, deerskin leggings, a shirt, and, in winter, moccasins. Women wore shawls and deerskin skirts. Children generally went unclothed until puberty. During the winter, additional warmth was provided by bear skins and buffalo hides.

Both men and women wore their hair long. The men plucked their facial hair and also removed hair around their heads, leaving a long central lock that they braided with decorative feathers, shells, and strings. Sometimes they made turbans from strips of deerskin or cloth. The women, whose hair might reach to their calves, wound it about their heads, fastening it with silver jewelry and adorning it with colorful streamers.

The men used extensive tattooing to decorate their trunks, arms, and legs. The indigo designs included natural objects, animals, abstract scrollwork, and even hunting and battle scenes. Both men and women employed body paint and wore earrings and other jewelry.

Trade with Europeans brought colorful woven fabrics to the Creek people. They quickly incorporated these into their customary fashions, and began to decorate clothing and moccasins with trade beads. The women liked to wear clothing fashioned from calico and other printed cloth, and silk ribbons became popular hair ornaments. Creek women also bought the scrap threads of scarlet cloth that traders cleaned out of the bottoms of their packs; they boiled them to remove the dye, which they then added to berry juice and used to color other cloth.

## THE GREEN CORN FESTIVAL

The major annual holiday was the Green Corn Festival, which celebrated the beginning of the corn harvest in late July or early August. Depending on the size of the town, the festival lasted from four to eight days. It involved a number of traditions, including dancing and moral lectures given by town leaders.

To prepare for the festival, the entire town was cleaned, and the square refurbished with fresh sand and new mats for its buildings. Women made new clothing for their families, as well as new pottery and other household furnishings. The town piled old clothing and furnishings together with the collected rubbish and burned them, along with all remaining food supplies that had been stored from the previous year. All fires in the town were extinguished, and a new fire was started in the town square by the ancient method of rubbing sticks together. Each family carried some of this new fire home to relight their household fire.

The festival was also called the *busk*, especially among whites. The name derived from the Creek word *boosketah*, meaning a fast. The men cleansed themselves with ceremonial bathing and by fasting and drinking a strong emetic potion which they called "medicine." The beverage, which Europeans called the "black drink," was also used on other occasions, but it was a central element of the Green Corn Festival. As time passed, women were allowed to join in the festival dancing; by the late 1800s they occasionally partook of the "medicine." At the end of the festival, when spiritual appreciation had been given for the new crop, the people joined in a feast.

Inspired by the ripening of the new corn, the festival was a time of renewal and forgiveness. Drinking the "medicine" purged the body physically and purified it from sin. A general amnesty was conferred for all offenses committed in the past year, with the exception of murder. If a guilty person was able to hide between the time a crime was committed and the time of the Green Corn Festival, he or she would escape punishment entirely. The festival marked the beginning of the new year and as such became the official date for such events as marriages, divorces, and periods of mourning. It was also the occasion for young men's initiation rites.

### HEALTH AND MENTAL HEALTH ISSUES

According to traditional beliefs, illness was the result of an animal spirit or a conjurer placing some foreign substance in the victim's body. An *owala*, or shaman, would affect a cure by concocting an appropriate medicine out of roots, herbs, and other natural substances. While brewing the potion, he would sing appropriate songs and blow into the mixture through a tube. The afflicted person would take the medicine internally and also apply it externally.

After establishing contact with the Europeans, the Creeks were affected by periodic outbreaks of smallpox, measles, and other imported diseases; the number of fatalities went undocumented. During removal to Indian Territory, emigrating Creeks were subjected to difficult traveling conditions including exposure to weather extremes. Overcrowded conditions on boats during waterborne portions of the journey, coupled with dietary changes and unclean drinking water from the Mississippi River, left the travelers vulnerable to illness. Maladies such as dysentery, diarrhea, and cholera contributed to the many casualties en route.

Health problems did not end with arrival in Indian Territory. Streams behaved differently in the West than they did in the East; unexpected flooding destroyed new homes and crops, while in dry spells the streams turned into breeding grounds for mosquitos, and many Creeks fell victim to malaria. During western winters, periods of mild days alternated with sudden bouts of extremely cold weather; Creek shelters and clothing were inadequate for this climate, and many people perished from pneumonia. During the first year in Indian Territory, 3,500 Creeks died of disease or starvation.

Even in more recent times, health care furnished through the Indian Health Service has sometimes been inadequate. The Muscogee Nation now manages its own hospital to better serve its people. Creeks experience a relatively high incidence of diabetes, which may be related to the poor economic conditions they have endured in modern times; alcoholism may also play a role.

## LANGUAGE

Most Creeks spoke dialects of the Muscogean language. In *Deerskins & Duffels: The Creek Indian Trade with Anglo-America, 1685-1815*, Kathryn E. Braund has asserted that "it was still the English who were forced to learn the melodious Muskogee tongue, for few Creeks expressed any willingness to adopt the harsh and strident tones of their new friends." Creeks who avoided relocation to Oklahoma tended to stop speaking the Muscogean language so they would not be recognized as Indians and therefore forced to leave their homes. In 1910, 72 percent of Creeks over the age of ten could speak English. By 1980, 99 percent of Creek adults could speak English well; 15 percent of them still spoke their native language at home.

Historically an oral language, Creek was reduced to a phonetic written form by John Fleming, a Presbyterian missionary, with the help of James Perryman, a Creek student. In 1835 they published a primer called *I stutsi in Naktsokv (The Child's Book)* and a book of hymns. Another missionary published a Creek dictionary and grammar book in 1890.

The language's vowels and their sounds are: "v" (as the vowel sound in but), "a" (as in sod), "e" (as in tin), "o" (as in toad), "u" (as in put), and "i" (as in hate). Most consonants are pronounced as in English, except that "c" sounds like "ts" or "ch," while "r" sounds like "hl" (made by blowing while pronouncing an "l").

### GREETINGS AND OTHER POPULAR EXPRESSIONS

Some of the basic words of the Creek language are *Hes'ci* ("hihs-jay")—hello; *henk'a* ("hihn gah")—yes; *hek'us* ("hihg oos")—no; *Mvto'* ("muh doh")—thank you.

## FAMILY AND COMMUNITY DYNAMICS

### CLAN AND FAMILY STRUCTURE

Creek society was based on a clan system, with each person's identity determined by the clan of his or her mother. Clan membership governed social interactions, ranging from whom members could joke with to whom they could marry (marriage within one's clan was considered incest). Each town included members from about six clans.

The family home was actually a collection of several rectangular buildings constructed of a framework of wood poles, with walls of mud and straw plaster, and a roof of cyprus bark shingles. These buildings were arranged in a smaller version of the town square, with a courtyard in the center. One building was used for cooking and eating, one for sleeping in winter (sleeping and eating were done outdoors in warm weather), and one for storing food supplies. Another building was provided for women's retreats, used during menstruation as well as for a four-month period at childbirth. Each homesite included a small garden plot where the women of the family raised some vegetables and tobacco.

The town maintained a large field of fertile land for farming, with a section reserved for each family. The townspeople worked together on the entire field, and at harvest time each family gathered the produce from its section. All were expected to contribute to a communal stockpile that would be used to feed visitors and needy families in the town.

Traditionally, Creeks buried the dead under the earthen floor of the home, though by the late 1800s it was more common to bury them in the churchyard or in a family cemetery near the home. A widower was expected to mourn his dead wife for four months, during which time he would not bathe, wash his clothes, or comb his hair. The same mourning practices were required of a widow; she, however, was obligated to mourn for four years. The period of mourning for a widow could be decreased by the dead husband's clan if they so chose. Often, after the mourning period, the widow would marry a brother of her deceased husband.

## MARRIAGE

Although marriages could be arranged by clan leaders, they were usually initiated by the prospective husband, who solicited the permission of the woman's family. During courtship, the man might woo the woman by playing plaintive melodies on a flute made either of hardwood or a reed.

Sexual activity before marriage was allowed, and it was not unusual for travelers to hire Creek women as bed companions. Once a marriage became final, however, adultery was not tolerated. Punishment was harsh, including severe beatings and cutting off the hair, ears, and sometimes noses of both offenders. A woman committing adultery was rejected by her husband and children, but she could marry her lover.

When a couple married, the husband went to live with his wife in the home of her parents. The marriage was finalized only after the husband had built his wife a home and proven his ability to support her by planting and harvesting a crop and successfully hunting game. During the trial period of the marriage, the couple could decide to separate, and infidelity would not be punished. With the permission of his wife, a man could take a second wife, for whom he provided a separate home. Divorce was allowed but rarely occurred in families with children; when it did, the woman retained the children and the family possessions.

## CHILDREARING

The father fasted for four days after the birth of his child, and he maintained an interest in his family. Raising the child, however, was primarily the responsibility of the mother and the leader of her clan. Babies spent their first year secured to cradle boards; boys were wrapped in cougar skins, while girls were covered with deerskins or bison hides.

A daughter was called by a kinship term or named after some object or natural occurrence associated with her birth. A son was called by the name of his totem, such as bird or snake; as he grew, he might be given a nickname based on some personality trait. At the age of puberty, a boy was initiated into adulthood in his town and was given an actual name. His first name, which served as a surname, was that of his town or clan, while his second, or personal, name was descriptive of something about him.

## EDUCATION

Creek girls learned from their mothers and maternal aunts the skills they would need as adults. Boys were instructed primarily by their maternal uncles, though they also felt their father's influence. Christian missionary schools established in 1822 were the first to formally educate Creeks in American culture; a few earlier attempts at founding schools had been unsuccessful. In recent years, Creek students have generally attended public schools, with a few attending boarding schools. The 1980 census found that 65 percent of Creek adults were high school graduates and 11 percent were college graduates.

A branch of Oklahoma State University at Okmulgee serves the Creek community in Oklahoma. The Poarch Creek Tribe in Alabama has an education department and offers on-the-job training through a Job Training Partnership Act (JTPA) program.

# RELIGION

The traditional Creek religion revered *Esaugetu Emissee* (Master of Breath) as the supreme being. He was believed to live in an upper realm that had the sky as its floor. The sun, moon, and planets were seen as messengers to this deity. The Creeks also worshiped animal spirits. The Green Corn Festival was the principal religious celebration.

Although many Creek myths have been lost to history, some were documented by Frank G. Speck in 1904 and 1905. He reported that the myths told of animal spirits in the sky world who were responsible for the earth's origin. Master of Breath then placed his own innovations on creation, making the earth as it is now. Speck wrote in *Memoirs of the American Anthropological Association:* "The Creeks assert that they were made from the red earth of the old Creek nation. The whites were made from the foam of the sea. That is why they think the Indian is firm, and the white man is restless and fickle."

Each Creek town kept certain sacred objects. The most famous were copper and brass plates held by the town of Tuckabatchee. The five copper plates were oblong, with the largest being about 18 inches by seven inches. The two brass plates were circular, the larger being 18 inches in diameter, and one was stamped with the mark Æ. Although one legend indicated that the objects had been given them by the Shawnee, who may have obtained them from the Spanish, the plates were widely believed to have been bestowed on the Creeks by the Master of Breath.

Contact with European cultures brought a succession of missionaries to the Creek people. Gradually, many of the people began to espouse Christianity. They continued to observe the Green Corn Festival, although those who had become Baptist or Methodist no longer participated in ceremonial dancing. With this decrease in participation, the festival began to lose its former significance, and it deteriorated into little more than a wild party. Christianity became dominant among the Creeks after the removal to Oklahoma. Although some missionaries continued to work among them, most Creek churches were led by preachers who emerged from within the community. As Debo described: "The Creeks had found in Christianity a means of expressing the strong community ties, the moral aspiration, the mystic communion with nature, the deep sense of reverence that had once been expressed by the native ceremonials."

# EMPLOYMENT AND ECONOMIC TRADITIONS

The early Creeks enjoyed a comfortable living based on agriculture and hunting. Their homeland was fertile and game was plentiful. With the emergence of European contacts, the Creek hunting industry changed from a subsistence operation to a commercial enterprise. Trade expanded, and they began to sell not only venison, hides, and furs, but also honey, beeswax, hickory nut oil, and other produce. They also found markets for manufactured goods including baskets, pottery, and decorated deerskins.

As white settlers continued to move into Creek territory, the Indians were crowded into progressively smaller land areas. This process began in 1733 when a cession of two million acres of Creek land was given to the new colony of Georgia so it could be sold to satisfy debts to British traders. In order to attract additional colonists, the land was sold at bargain prices.

An extensive series of other land cessions followed, and eventually the Creek economy collapsed. According to *Indians of the Lower South: Past and Present*, in 1833 Lieutenant Colonel John Abert wrote to the United States Secretary of War that during the last three years the Creek people had gone "from a general state of comparative plenty to that of unqualified wretchedness and want."

The Removal Treaty of 1832 gave land to Creeks who chose to emigrate to Indian Territory in exchange for tribal lands in Alabama. To encourage the Indians to move westward, the government also promised a variety of benefits, including a cash payment of $210,000—to be distributed according to tribal laws over a fifteen year period—two blacksmith shops in the new territory, an educational annuity, and another cash payment of $100,000 to help the Creeks settle their debts and ease their economic hardship. In addition, each warrior would receive a rifle, ammunition, and a blanket; families' expenses would be paid during the migration and throughout the first year in the West.

Today, some full-blooded Creeks still farm land in the area of Oklahoma that was settled by the Upper Creeks. The Muscogee Nation operates a bingo hall and stores that sell tobacco products. Broadening their economic development efforts is a high priority for the tribe.

Many of the mixed-blood Creeks live in Tulsa, Eufaula, or other Oklahoma cities, working in a variety of occupations. Census data from 1980 indicates that about two-thirds of the Creek Indians were living in urban settings at that time.

At the time of Indian removal, a segment of the Creek people apparently entered into an agreement with the government that enabled them to remain in the East. They were business people who operated ferries, served as guides and interpreters, and raised cattle. Their descendants are the Poarch Creeks, whose tribal headquarters are located in Atmore, Alabama.

During the early 1900s, some Poarch Creeks began to work in the timber and turpentine industries. Some also became tenant farmers or worked as hired farm laborers. Beginning in the 1930s, the pulpwood industry became an important element in the Poarch Creek economy. Since the 1950s, Poarch Creeks have been working in other non-agricultural jobs.

According to 1980 statistics, 61 percent of Creeks over the age of 16 were in the labor force. Of those who were employed, 19 percent were in managerial or professional specialty occupations, and 26 percent were in technical, sales, and administrative support occupations. Looking at major industry groups, approximately six percent worked in the agricultural, forestry, fisheries, and mining areas; nine percent worked in public administration; 12 percent worked in retail trade 19 percent were involved in manufacturing and 22 percent worked in professional and related services, including health and education.

# POLITICS AND GOVERNMENT

Throughout their history, the Creeks governed themselves democratically. Each town elected a chief who served for life, though he could be recalled. Members of each town were informed about issues and participated actively in decision making. Town leaders met in daily council sessions, and when broader councils were called, each town sent several representatives to speak

Creek actor Will Sampson (right) starred with Jack Nicholson in the award-winning movie *One Flew Over the Cuckoo's Nest* (1975).

and vote on its behalf. Although there was no specific law fixing a penalty for misrepresenting constituents, leaders who did so faced severe consequences; for example, after signing a 1783 treaty that ceded good hunting grounds to Georgia, a chief returned home to find his house burned and his crops destroyed.

The society was matrilineal, but most positions of tribal leadership were filled by men. While women did not vote, they did enjoy full economic rights including property ownership, and they exerted significant influence on decisions by discussing their opinions with the men of the town. Each town may also have appointed a Beloved Woman who communicated with her counterparts in other towns. The roles of the Beloved Woman and perhaps other female leaders have been lost to history since European observers ignored them and omitted them from written accounts.

### TREATIES

The Creeks supported the British in the American Revolutionary War. In 1790, a delegation of Creek leaders traveled to New York to negotiate a treaty with President Washington. It was the first in a long series of treaties that ceded tribal land to the United States; with each cession, the tribe was guaranteed unending ownership of their remaining land. In some cases, treaties were obtained by such fraudulent means as purposely negotiating with a non-representative group of minor chiefs after being refused by the official delegation, or forging the names of chiefs who refused to cooperate.

In 1812 the Shawnee chief Tecumseh, whose mother was Creek, organized a rebellion against the United States. The Creek nation split over whether to join the uprising; most of the Lower Creeks supported Tecumseh while the Upper Creeks were rather evenly divided in their allegiance. This division resulted in the Red Stick War, a devastating civil war within the tribe. Under terms of the peace treaty signed in 1814, the tribe relinquished to the United States 22 million acres of land, including the townsites of some of the Upper Creeks who had fought alongside Andrew Jackson's forces against the rebels.

In addition to gradually obtaining ownership of tens of millions of acres of Creek land, federal and state governments placed a succession of restrictions on the Indians. Alabama law, for example, prohibited an Indian from testifying against a white man. According to Grant Foreman in *Indian Removal: The Emigration of the Five Civilized Tribes of Indians*, a Creek delegation to the United States Secretary of War in 1831 complained, "We are made subject to laws we have no means of comprehending; we never know when we are doing right."

The Removal Treaty of 1832 guaranteed the Creeks political autonomy and perpetual ownership of new homelands in Indian Territory in return for their cession of remaining tribal lands in the East. It specified that each Creek could freely choose whether to remain on his homeland or move to the West. Those who decided to stay in the East could select homesteads on former tribal land. Land speculators eager to profit from the anticipated influx of white settlers devised a variety of ways to cheat the Indians out of their land, either by paying far less than its true value or by forging deeds. After an Indian attack on a mail stage—which a white man was later convicted for inciting—a brief civil war pitted Creeks who wanted to remain in the East against those who accepted the concept of relocation. Finally the federal government ordered forcible removal of all remaining Creeks in 1836.

Emigrants were subjected to horrible conditions during the government-subsidized trips to Indian Territory. One group began their journey in December 1834, barefoot and scantily clothed; 26 percent of them died during the four-month journey. Leaders pushed onward as quickly as they could, not allowing the Indians to conduct funeral services to ensure the dead an afterlife, and sometimes not even allowing the survivors to bury the dead. In July 1836, a party of 1,600 Creeks departed for the West with the warriors handcuffed and chained together for the entire journey.

Upon arrival in Indian Territory, the Five Civilized Tribes faced opposition from plains Indians who would now have to share diminished hunting grounds with 60,000 new residents. Although the Creeks were capable of defending themselves against attack, they took the lead in conducting negotiations between the immigrant tribes and the indigenous people to establish peaceful coexistence.

## GOVERNMENT AFTER RELOCATION

As they settled into their new homeland, the Creeks discovered that the United States' promises of assistance went largely unfulfilled. Tools and farm implements did not come in time to build homes and plant crops. Weapons and ammunition did not arrive, so the men had to relearn bow and arrow hunting techniques. In order to maximize profits from their government contracts, food suppliers delivered partial shipments and rancid provisions. Especially during the first few years after relocation, annuity payments guaranteed by the treaty were made primarily in goods rather than in cash, and most of the items to be delivered were either useless to the Indians or were lost in shipment.

By the 1850s the Creek people had begun to achieve a relatively prosperous life in their new territory. Then the Confederate States of America seceded from the United States. The Creeks tried to remain neutral in the conflict but were drawn into hostilities by attacks on their people. Loyalties were once again divided. The Lower Towns generally favored retention of slavery and sided with the South, while the Upper Towns chose to abide by their treaties with the North. What ensued was another civil war within the Creek nation. In retribution for the failure of the entire tribe to support the Union, the post-war treaty required the cession of 3.2 million acres, or about half of the Creek land in Indian Territory.

## GOVERNMENT DISSOLUTION AND LAND ALLOTMENT

The Creeks attempted to formalize their government after arriving in the West. Opothle Yahola, a chief who led Creeks loyal to the United States during the Red Stick War and the Civil War, oversaw an effort to record Creek law into written form. A written constitution providing for elected tribal officers was adopted about 1859; after the Civil War, it was replaced with a new one modeled closely after the U.S. Constitution.

Acting on recommendations of the Dawes Commission, Congress passed the Curtis Act in 1898. As a result, tribal lands were removed from common ownership and distributed among individual Indians for private ownership. In 1906, the U.S. government declared the Creek tribal government dissolved. These federal policies were reversed by the 1934 Wheeler-Howard Act, which encouraged tribal cultural and economic development. Two years later, Congress passed the Oklahoma Indian Welfare Act, providing Indian tribes with a mechanism for incorporating. It also provided benefits such as a student loan program and a revolving fund to be used for extending credit to Indians.

Today, the 37,000 members of the Muscogee Nation are governed by an elected principal chief, a bicameral legislature, and a judicial branch. The 2,000 Poarch Creeks in Alabama are governed by an elected tribal council that selects a tribal chairman from among its nine members.

# INDIVIDUAL AND GROUP CONTRIBUTIONS

Listed below are some of the Creek people who have made notable contributions to American society as a whole. It is difficult to arrange their names by area of contribution, since some individuals attained prominence in several fields.

## ACADEMIA

Edwin Stanton Moore attended Chilocco Indian School and Oklahoma A & M College, where he played football from 1938 to 1940; he was awarded the Department of the Interior Meritorious Service Medal upon retirement as the Director of Indian Education in 1979.

## FILM AND BROADCAST MEDIA

Will Sampson (1934-1987) was an actor who appeared in several motion pictures, including *The Outlaw Josie Wales* and *One Flew Over the Cuckoo's Nest*, which won an Academy Award for Best Picture in 1976. Gary Fife is the producer and host of "National Native News," which airs on over 160 public radio stations around the country.

## GOVERNMENT AND PUBLIC INVOLVEMENT

Enoch Kelly Haney is an Oklahoma state senator who is nationally recognized for his political involvement and proactive stance for Native American rights; he is also an accomplished artist on canvas and in bronze. Gale Thrower (1943- ) received the Alabama Folk Life Heritage Award for her contributions toward preserving her tribe's traditions and culture.

## LITERATURE

Alexander (Alex) Lawrence Posey (1873-1908) was a poet and a writer of prose; he was elected to the House of Warriors, the lower chamber of the Creek National Council; at various times he served as superintendent of two boarding schools and the Creek Orphan Asylum, and as superintendent of public instruction for the Creek Nation of Oklahoma; he helped draft the constitution for the proposed State of Sequoia, a document on which the constitution for the state of Oklahoma was later based. Louis (Littlecorn) Oliver (1904-1990) wrote *Chasers of the Sun: Creek Indian Thoughts*, and two books of poetry: *The Horned Snake* and *Caught in a Willow Net*. Joy Harjo (1951- ) wrote "Northern Lights" a short story about Whirling Soldier, a Vietnam veteran, published in *Talking Leaves: Contemporary Native American Short Stories*; she has also written four books of poetry, including *The Last Song* and *Secrets from the Center of the World*.

## MILITARY

Ernest Childers (1918- ) was awarded the Congressional Medal of Honor for "exceptional leadership, initiative, calmness under fire, and conspicuous gallantry" on September 22, 1943, at Oliveto, Italy. John N. Reese was awarded the Congressional Medal of Honor for "his gallant determination in the face of tremendous odds, aggressive fighting spirit, and extreme heroism at the cost of his life" on February 9, 1945, at Manila in the Philippine Islands.

## SPORTS

Allie P. Reynolds was a baseball pitcher with the Cleveland Indians from 1942 to 1946 and the New York Yankees from 1947 to 1954; he had the best earned run average (ERA) in the American League in 1952 and 1954, and he led the league in strikeouts and shutouts for two seasons; he was named America's Professional Athlete of the Year in 1951. Jack Jacobs played football for the University of Oklahoma from 1939 to 1942; he also played professional football for 14 years with several teams including the Cleveland Rams, the Washington Redskins, and the Green Bay Packers.

## VISUAL ARTS

Acee Blue Eagle (1908-1959) was an acclaimed Creek painter. Fred Beaver (1911-1980) and Solomon McCombs (1913-1980) were painters who served with the U.S. Department of State as goodwill ambassadors, using their art as a means of bridging the communications gap around the world. Jerome Tiger (1941-1967), a painter and sculptor, was also a Golden Gloves boxer. His brother Johnny Tiger, Jr., is a master artist at the Five Civilized Tribes Museum. Joan Hill is a Creek/Cherokee painter who has received numerous recognition awards, grants, and fellowships in the art world. She has done a series of paintings depicting the various treaties of the Five Civilized Tribes, and another portraying the women of the tribes.

# MEDIA

## PRINT

### Muscogee Nation News.
A monthly English-language publication of the Muscogee Nation.

Contact: Jim Wolfe.
Address: Department of Communications, P.O. Box 580, Okmulgee, Oklahoma 74447.
Telephone: (918) 756-8700.

### Poarch Creek News.
A monthly English-language publication of the Creek tribe in Alabama.

Contact: Daniel McGee.
Address: HCR 69, Box 85-B, Atmore, Alabama 36502.
Telephone: (205) 368-9136.

## RADIO

### WASG-AM and FM.
Operated by the Poarch Creek Tribe. Programming is in English and features country music, local news, and community events.

Contact: Nathan Martin.
Address: HCR 69, Box 85-B, Atmore, Alabama 36502.
Telephone: (205) 368-2511.

# ORGANIZATIONS AND ASSOCIATIONS

### Muscogee (Creek) Nation.
Contact: Principal Chief Bill Fife.
Address: Tribal Offices, P.O. Box 580, Okmulgee, Oklahoma 74447.
Telephone: (918) 756-8700.

### Poarch Battle Creek Indians.
Contact: Tribal Chairman Eddie Tullis.
Address: Tribal Office, HCR 69, Box 85-B, Atmore, Alabama 36502.
Telephone: (205) 368-9136.

# MUSEUMS AND RESEARCH CENTERS

### Creek Council House Museum.
A museum and library of tribal history.

Contact: Debbie Martin.
Address: P.O. Box 580, Okmulgee, Oklahoma 74447.
Telephone: (918) 756-2324.

### Calvin McGee Library.
A cultural center and library for the eastern Creeks.

Contact: Gale Thrower.
Address: HCR 69, Box 85-B, Atmore, Alabama 36502.
Telephone: (205) 368-9136.

### Five Civilized Tribes Museum.
Displays Indian artifacts and art work, with separate sections devoted to each of the Five Civilized Tribes.

Contact: Lynn Thornley.
Address: Agency Hill on Honors Heights Drive, Muskogee, Oklahoma 74401.
Telephone: (918) 683-1701.

# SOURCES FOR ADDITIONAL STUDY

Braund, Kathryn E. Holland. *Deerskins & Duffels: The Creek Indian Trade with Anglo-America, 1685-1815.* Lincoln: University of Nebraska Press, 1993.

Corkran, David H. *The Creek Frontier: 1540-1783.* Norman: University of Oklahoma Press, 1967.

Debo, Angie. *The Road to Disappearance.* Norman: University of Oklahoma Press, 1941.

Foreman, Grant. *Indian Removal: The Emigration of the Five Civilized Tribes of Indians.* Norman: University of Oklahoma Press, 1932.

Green, Donald Edward. *The Creek People.* Phoenix: Indian Tribal Series, 1973.

Green, Michael D. *The Politics of Indian Removal.* Lincoln: University of Nebraska Press, 1982.

Harjo, Joy. "Family Album," *Progressive*, March 1992; pp. 22-25.

Henri, Florette. *The Southern Indians and Benjamin Hawkins: 1796-1816.* Norman: University of Oklahoma Press, 1986.

*Indians of the Lower South: Past and Present*, edited by John K. Mahon. Pensacola, Florida: Gulf Coast History and Humanities Conference, 1975.

Speck, Frank G. "The Creek Indians of Taskigi Town," *Memoirs of the American Anthropological Association 1907-1915*, Vol. 2, No. 8. Lancaster, Pennsylvania: New Era Printing Co., 1915.

The identification of
a Creole was, and is,
largely one of self-
choice.

# CREOLES

by
**Helen Bush Caver**
**and Mary T. Williams**

## OVERVIEW

Unlike many other minority groups in the United States, Creoles did not migrate from a native country. The term Creole was first used in the sixteenth century to identify descendants of French, Spanish, or Portuguese settlers living in the West Indies, Latin America, and the southern part of what is now the United States. A single definition sufficed in the early days of European colonial expansion, but as Creole populations established divergent social, political, and economic identities, the term acquired different meanings. In the West Indies, Creole refers to a descendant of any European settler. In Louisiana, it identifies French-speaking populations of French or Spanish descent. These populations are variously defined as pure white or a mixture of Spanish or French with some African ancestry. The latter were generally products of miscegenation in a seignorial society.

Opinions differ about the derivation of the term Creole. Some scholars hold that Creole comes from the Spanish verb *crear*, which means to create or to be born. Others point to the Portuguese *crioulo*, which means a slave born in the master's household.

### HISTORY

The era of French domination in the United States began in the late seventeenth century, as

French explorers and settlers moved into the New World with their customs, language, and government. Their control continued until 1768 when France ceded Louisiana to Spain. Even with Spanish control, French language and customs continued to prevail.

The majority of Creoles, however, are descendants of French colonials who fled Saint-Dominique (Haiti) for North America's Gulf Coast when a slave insurrection (1791) challenged French authority. According to Thomas Fiehrer's essay "From La Tortue to La Louisiane: An Unfathomed Legacy," Saint-Dominque had more than 450,000 black slaves, 40,000 to 45,000 whites, and 32,000 *gens-de-couleur libres*, who were neither white nor black. As Fiehrer explained, "Money doubtless bleached some pedigrees." By 1815, over 11,000 refugees had settled in New Orleans. These people, somewhat vaguely known as Creoles, owed their existence to the overseas expansion of France and, during the seventeenth and eighteenth centuries, had developed a loose ethno-cultural identity.

Saint-Dominique's Pierre Dominique Toussaint L'Ouverture (1743-1803), a self-educated slave, established a formal government in 1801, sending more refugees to the Gulf Coast. Some exiles went directly to present-day Louisiana; others went to Cuba. Of those who went to Cuba, many came to New Orleans in the early 1800s after the Louisiana territory had been purchased by the United States (1803). This influx from Saint-Dominque and Cuba doubled New Orleans' 1791 population. Some refugees moved on to St. Martinville, Napoleonville, and Henderson, rural areas outside New Orleans. Others traveled further north along the Mississippi waterway.

In Louisiana, the term Creole came to represent children of black or racially mixed parents as well as children of French and Spanish descent with no racial mixing. Persons of French and Spanish descent in New Orleans and St. Louis began referring to themselves as Creoles after the Louisiana Purchase to set themselves apart from the Anglo-Americans who moved into the area. Today, the term Creole can be defined in a number of ways. Louisiana historian Fred B. Kniffin, in *Louisiana: Its Land and People*, has asserted that the term Creole "has been loosely extended to include people of mixed blood, a dialect of French, a breed of ponies, a distinctive way of cooking, a type of house, and many other things. It is therefore no precise term and should not be defined as such."

Louisiana Creoles of color were different and separate from other populations, both black and white. These Creoles of color became part of an elite society; in the nineteenth century they were leaders in business, agriculture, politics, and the arts, as well as slaveholders. Nonetheless, as early as 1724 their legal status had been defined by the *Code Noir* (Black Code). According to Violet Harrington Bryan in *The Myth of New Orleans in Literature, Dialogues of Race and Gender,* they could own slaves, hold real estate, and be recognized in the courts, but they could not vote, marry white persons, have contact with slaves, and had to designate themselves as *f.m.c.* or *f.w.c.* (free man or color or free woman of color) on all legal documents.

### FIRST CREOLES IN AMERICA

According to Virginia A. Dominguez in *White By Definition*, much of the written record of Creoles comes from descriptions of individuals in the baptismal, marriage, and death registers of Catholic churches of Mobile, (Alabama) and New Orleans, two major French outposts on the Gulf Coast. The earliest entry is a death record in 1745 wherein a man was described as the first Creole in the colony. The use of Creole in reference to colored individuals appears in local Louisiana documents as early as 1779.

# ACCULTURATION AND ASSIMILATION

Misconceptions about Creoles persist. The greatest controversy stems from the presence or absence of African ancestry. In an 1886 lecture at Tulane University, Charles Gayarre ("Creoles of History and Creoles of Romance," New Orleans: C. E. Hopkins, c. 1886) and F. P. Poche (in a speech at the American Exposition in New Orleans, *New Orleans Daily Picayune*, February 8, 1886) both stated that Louisiana Creoles had "not a particle of African blood in their veins." In "A Few Words About the Creoles of Louisiana" (Baton Rouge: Truth Books, 1892), Alcee Fortier repeated the same defense. These three men were probably the most prominent Creole intellectuals of the nineteenth century. Lyle Saxon, Robert Tallant, and Edward Dreyer continued this argument in 1945 by saying, "No true Creole ever had colored blood."

Sister Dorothea Olga McCants, translator of Rodolphe Lucien Desdunes' *Our People and Our*

*History* (Baton Rouge: Louisiana State University Press, 1973), gives attention to the term Creole. She says that the free mixed-blood, French speaking descendants from Haiti living in New Orleans came to use the word to describe themselves. The phrase "Creole of color" was used by these proud part-Latin people to set themselves apart from American blacks. These Haitian descendants were cultured, educated, and economically prosperous as musicians, artists, teachers, writers, and doctors. In "Louisiana's 'Creoles of Color'," James H. Dorman has stated that the group was clearly recognized as special, productive, and worthy by the white community, citing an editorial in the *New Orleans Times Picayune* in 1859 that referred to them as "Creole colored people." Prior to the Civil War, a three-caste system existed: white, black, and Creoles of color. After the Civil War, however, the Creoles of color—who had been part of the free black population before the war—were merged into a two-caste system, black and white.

The arrival of Anglo-Americans in the northern areas of the Louisiana territory changed the civilization of the many Creoles already residing in present-day Missouri, particularly in architecture; the horizontal log cabin of the American frontiersman superseded the French cabin built of vertical logs. French geographical names were likewise displaced, and the festive Gallic Sunday was frowned upon by the incoming Protestant settlers. By the time Missouri became a state, much of the French culture had been erased and the Creoles were quickly assimilated into the dominant European culture. However, some traces of French culture survive to the present day.

Acadians (Cajuns) are another ethnic population in Louisiana who are sometimes confused with Creoles. Both groups are French Catholics; yet there the similarity ends. The Cajuns have a distinct identity derived from their common French background, their frontier experience, and their relocation from Canada to Louisiana. During their intracontinental sojourn, Cajuns had to cope with diverse Native American groups and immigrants from various national areas to maintain their separate status. Cajuns settled west of the Mississippi and pursued occupations close to the land, like farming and fishing. Creole identity was manifested in New Orleans or small cities where the people engaged in occupations not involving manual labor. Creoles, including Creoles of color, have tended to self-isolation, even in cities, by educating their children in private schools and keeping to themselves.

Some Creole and Cajun groups have long been in contact. Cajuns have historically been a white ethnic population and have interacted with Creoles of color according to racial dictates of the era in which they lived. In the 1970s Cajuns underwent a revitalizing movement, which sometimes included Creoles. To counter such inclusion and to revitalize group identity, an organization called Creole, Inc., has been formed to specifically recognize the black French/Creole minority in southern Louisiana. Other indications of a renewed interest in Creole group identity are the popularization of Zydeco music, the Festival Internationale in Lafayette, Louisiana, and the publication, since 1990, of *Creole Magazine*.

The identification of a Creole was, and is, largely one of self-choice. Important criteria for Creole identity are French language and social customs, especially cuisine, regardless of racial makeup. Many young Creoles of color today live under pressure to identify themselves as African Americans. Several young white Creoles want to avoid being considered of mixed race. Therefore, both young black and white Creoles often choose an identity other than Creole.

## TRADITIONS, CUSTOMS, AND BELIEFS

With imported furniture, wines, books, and clothes, Creoles once existed in a total French atmosphere. Part of Creole social life has traditionally centered on the French Opera House; from 1859 to 1919, it was the place for sumptuous gatherings and glittering receptions. The interior, graced by curved balconies and open boxes of architectural beauty, seated 805 people. Creoles loved the music and delighted in attendance as the operas were great social and cultural affairs.

Sometime after First Communion, girls made their initial appearance in society at the French Opera House in a gown imported from Paris. However, no Creole girl's picture was ever to be published in the newspapers, and nothing was ever to be printed in the newspapers about her.

## INTERACTION WITH OTHER ETHNIC MINORITIES

Creoles clung to their individualistic way of life, frowned upon intermarriage with Anglo-Americans, refused to learn English, and were resentful and contemptuous of Protestants, whom they considered irreligious and wicked. Creoles generally succeeded in remaining separate in the rural sections but they steadily lost ground in New Orleans. In 1803, there were seven Creoles to every Anglo-American in New Orleans but these figures dwindled to two to one by 1830.

Anglo-Americans reacted by disliking the Creoles with equal enthusiasm. Gradually, New Orleans became not one city, but two. Canal Street split them apart, dividing the old Creole city from the "uptown" section where the other Americans quickly settled. To cross Canal Street in either direction was to enter another world. These differences are still noticeable today.

## CUISINE

Creole cooking is the distinguishing feature of Creole homes. It can be as subtle as Oysters Rockefeller, as fragrantly explicit as a jambalaya, or as down to earth as a dish of red beans and rice. A Creole meal is a celebration, not just a means of addressing hunger pangs.

New Orleans was Spanish before it was French, and French before it was American. The Europeans who settled there found not only the American Indians, whose filé (the ground powder of the sassafras leaf) is the key ingredient of Creole gumbos, but also immense areas of inland waterways and estuaries alive with crayfish, shrimp, crab, and fish of many different varieties. Also, the swampland was full of game. The settlers seized what they found and produced a cuisine based on good taste, experimentation, and spices. On the experimental side, it was in New Orleans that raw, hard liquor was transformed into the more sophisticated cocktail, and where the simple cup of coffee became café Brulot, a concoction spiced with cinnamon, cloves, and lemon peel and flambéed with cognac. The seasonings used are distinctive, but there is yet another essential ingredient—a heavy black iron skillet.

Such dexterity produced the many faceted family of gumbos. Gumbo is a soup or a stew, yet too unique to be classified as one or the other. It starts with a base of highly seasoned roux, scallions, and herbs, which serves as a vehicle for oysters, crabs, shrimp, chicken, ham, various game, or combinations thereof. Oysters may be consumed raw (on the half-shell), sauteed and packed into hollowed-out French bread, or baked on the half-shell and served with various garnishes. Shrimp, crayfish, and crab are similarly starting points for the Creole cook who might have croquettes in mind, or a pie, or an omelette, or a stew.

## CREOLE DANCES AND SONGS

Creoles are a festive people who enjoy music and dancing. In New Orleans, public balls were held twice weekly under Spanish rule, and when the French took over, they continued the practice. Cotillions presented by numerous academies provided young ladies and gentlemen with the opportunity to display their skills in dancing quadrilles, valses á un temps, valses á deux temps, valses á trois temps, polkas, and polazurkas. Saturday night balls and dances were a universal institution in Creole country. The community knew about the dances by means of a flagpole denoting the site of the dance. Families arrived on horseback or in a variety of wheeled carriages. The older adults played vingt-et-un (Twenty-one) or other card games while the young danced and engaged in flirtations until the party dispersed near daybreak. During the special festive season, between New Year's and Mardi Gras, many brilliant balls were scheduled. Only the most respected families were asked to attend with lists scrutinized by older members of the families to keep less prominent people away.

Creole songs lacked religious elements and were often short. They contained elements of satire, ridicule, or mockery, sometimes a suggestive vulgarity, and frequently mentioned food. Some typical songs include "Mo l'aime toi, chere;" "Fais do-do, fais do-do;" and "Youn, tou tou." The "Fais do-do" accompanies a dance similar to the Virginia Reel.

## PROVERBS

A rich collection of Creole proverbs can be found in several references. One of the best is from Lafcadio Hearn's Gombo Zhebes, Little Dictionary of Creole Proverbs (New Orleans: deBrun, n.d.): the monkey smothers its young one by hugging it too much; wait till the hare's in the pot before you talk; today drunk with fun, tomorrow the paddle; if you see your neighbor's beard on fire, water your own; shingles cover everything; when the oxen lift their tails in the air, look out for bad weather; fair words buy horses on credit; a good cock crows in any henhouse; what you lose in the fire, you will find in the ashes; when one sleeps, one doesn't think about eating; he who takes a partner takes a master; the coward lives a long time; conversation is the food of ears; it's only the shoes that know if the stockings have holes; the dog that yelps doesn't bite; threatened war doesn't kill many soldiers; a burnt cat dreads fire; an empty sack cannot stand up; good coffee and the Protestant religion were seldom if ever seen together; it takes four to prepare the perfect salad dressing—a miser to pour the vinegar, a spendthrift to add the olive oil, a wise man to sprinkle the salt and pepper, and a madcap to mix and stir the ingredients.

### HEALTH AND MENTAL HEALTH ISSUES

Health conditions among Creoles during the early history of America was deplorable. Many of the diseases that plagued the European colonies were prevalent. Pleurisy, pneumonia, skin diseases, dental problems, children's diseases, epilepsy, dysentery, diseases of the stomach, and malaria were the most common. Due to better housing and dietary conditions, these diseases and the ravages of tuberculosis, declined in the twentieth century. Today, Creoles have Catholic hospitals, general hospitals, private doctors, and medical insurance benefits.

# LANGUAGE

French has always been the language of the Creole; it should not be confused with the language known as Louisiana Negro Creole. Morphologically and lexically Louisiana Negro Creole resembles Haitian Creole; it is usually thought to have been derived from the language spoken by the slaves of the refugees from Saint-Dominque who came to Louisiana at the beginning of the nineteenth century. For many years, Louisiana Negro Creole was predominantly a language of rural blacks in southern Louisiana.

French continues to be the language of Creoles but is not as widespread as it once was. As Americans from other states began to settle in Louisiana in large numbers after 1880, they refused to learn French. Yet because many Anglo-American children taunted Creole children, they soon wished to speak English rather than French. Most Creole families, white and black, send their children to private schools or to schools within the Creole district. The curriculum at these schools usually includes instruction in the French language. French is also frequently the language spoken in homes, at family gatherings, and at fes-

tivals. The state of Louisiana supports this bilingual heritage by supplying teachers of French for most schools. Differences can be noted in the pronunciation of certain words depending upon the locality from which the speaker comes.

Older Creoles complain that many young Creoles today do not adhere to the basic rules of language propriety in speaking to others, especially to older adults. They claim that children walk past homes of people they know without greeting an acquaintance sitting on the porch or working on the lawn. Young males are particularly criticized for greeting others quickly in an incomprehensible and inarticulate manner.

### GREETINGS AND OTHER POPULAR EXPRESSIONS

Creoles have some unusual sayings. According to Leonard V. Huber in "Reflections on the Colorful Customs of Latter-Day New Orleans Creoles," an ugly man who has a protruding jaw and lower lip had *une gueule de benitier* (a mouth like a holy water font), and his face was *une figure de pomme cuite* (a face like a baked apple). A man who stayed around the house constantly was referred to as *un encadrement* (doorframe). The expression *pauvres diables* (poor devils) was applied to poor individuals. Anyone who bragged too much was called *un bableur* (a hot air shooter). A person with thin legs had *des jambes de manches-á-balais* (broomstick legs). An amusing expression for a person who avoided work was that he had *les cotes en long* (vertical ribs). Additional Creole colloquialisms are: *un tonnerre a la voile* (an unruly person); *menterie* (lie or story); *frou-frou* (giddy); *homme de paille, pistolet de bois* (a man who is a bluff).

# FAMILY AND COMMUNITY DYNAMICS

Traditionally, the father in a Creole family was the absolute head of his household. His word was final in all matters. He was also generous, devoted, and kind unless a family member did something to invite scandal; then his wrath knew no bounds. Providing for a household of people was not the least of his problems. There were limitations to the kind of employment open to him. Manual work was for common people. He had to have a job requiring a coat and tie. Most Creoles worked for banks, cotton firms, and sugar and coffee importers, or sought governmental positions in the courts, city hall, or mortgage offices. They were also professionals, doctors, notaries, and lawyers. A Creole man was judged by his appearance and he maintained it regardless of conditions at home.

Creole women were concerned with their appearance and their families. They loved fine clothes and would never leave home unless they were completely attired, including gloves and veil. For evening, the more affluent wore imported gowns from Paris, which were usually enhanced with jewelry. The young wife was usually a beauty but age and increasing numbers of children altered her appearance. Creole mothers dedicated their lives to home and family. They were excellent housekeepers, hostesses, and conversationalists. They also took the lead in prodding the family toward the church. In the nineteenth century the Creole wife remained loyal to her husband despite his mistresses and other absences from home, and she rarely remarried after the death of her husband. Widowers did remarry, and relatively soon, to provide a mother for their children. Often the new mother was a spinster sister of the deceased wife.

The Creoles also felt it a duty to take widowed cousins and orphaned children of kinspeople into their families. Unmarried women relatives (tantes) lived in many households. They provided a much-needed extra pair of hands in running the household and rearing the children. Children sometimes loved them as much as they did their mothers. Creoles today are still closely knit and tend to marry within the group. However, many are also moving into the greater community and losing their Creole ways.

## WEDDINGS

In the old days, Creoles married within their own class. The young man faced the scrutiny of old aunts and cousins, who were the guardians and authorities of old family trees. The suitor had to ask a woman's father for his daughter's hand. The gift of a ring allowed them to be formally engaged. All meetings of young people were strictly chaperoned, even after the engagement. Weddings, usually held at the St. Louis Cathedral in New Orleans, were opulent affairs with Swiss Guards meeting the wedding guests and preceding them up the aisle. Behind the guests came the bride, accompanied by her father, and then the groom, escorting the bride's mother. The groom's parents

followed, and then all the relatives of both bride and groom. A relative's absence was interpreted as a silent protest against the wedding. The bride's gown was handed down through generations or purchased in Paris to become an heirloom. Unlike today's weddings, there were no ring bearers, bridesmaids, or matrons of honor, or any floral decorations in the church. Ceremonies were held in the evenings. Some things do remain the same. St. Louis Cathedral is still the place for New Orleans' Creole weddings, and many relatives still attend, though in fewer numbers.

Plantation weddings in the nineteenth century were even more elaborate. Everything came from New Orleans and was shipped by boat to the plantation. Five hundred guests at a wedding were not unusual, nor was chartering a steamboat to bring guests to the plantation.

## BAPTISMS

Baptisms usually took place when the child was about a month old. The godfather (parrain) and the godmother (marraine) were always relatives, usually from each side of the family. It was a decided honor to be asked to serve as a godparent. The marraine gave the infant a gift of a gold cross and chain, and the parrain offered either a silver cup or a silver knife and fork. The godfather also gave a gift to the godmother and paid for the celebration that followed the baptism. It was an expensive honor to be chosen parrain.

## FUNERALS

Upon someone's death each post in the Creole section of town bore a black-bordered announcement informing the public of the death and the time and place of the funeral. Usually the notices were put in the neighborhood where the dead person had lived, but if the deceased had wealth, notices would be placed all over the Vieux Carré. These notices were also placed at St. Louis Cathedral on a death notice blackboard. Invitations were issued for the funeral, and funeral services were held in the home.

The wearing of mourning was a rigorous requirement. The deceased's immediate family put on grand deuil (full mourning). During the six months of full mourning it was improper to wear jewelry or anything white or with colors. Men wore a black tie, a black crepe band on the hat, and sometimes a black band on the arm. After six months, the widow could wear black clothes edged with a white collar and cuffs. Slave or black Creole funeral processions often lasted an hour and covered a distance of less than six squares or one-third mile. News of the deaths were received through the underground route by a system of telegraph chanting. In New Orleans today, there are great processions with bands playing when black Creoles die.

Cemeteries held an important place in Creole life. A family tomb received almost as much attention as a church. To not visit the family tomb on All Saints' Day (November 1) was unforgivable. Some outstanding cemeteries are St. Louis Number One, the oldest in Louisiana, and St. Louis Number Two. St. Roch Cemetery, which is noted for its shrine, was built by Father Thevis in fulfillment of a vow to Saint Roch for protection for the congregation of Holy Trinity Church from the yellow fever epidemic of 1868. Cypress Grove, Greenwood, and Metairie cemeteries are among the most beautiful burial grounds in Louisiana. Large structures resembling churches with niches for life-like marble statues of the saints may be found in Metairie Cemetery.

## EDUCATION

Creole children receive a thorough French education. Traditionally, the selection of a school brought in many unwritten laws of caste. Where the children were sent reflected the social standing of the family. During antebellum days, the boys frequently went to school in Paris while girls attended convents under the watchful eyes of French nuns. Some girls were sent to boarding schools, particularly to the Ursuline Convent or to one of the Sacred Heart Academies located at Grand Coteau, the St. Michael's Academy at Convent, or in New Orleans to the Holy Angels Academy or St. Mary's Academy of the Dominicans. French thought, literature, and art comprised the major part of the curriculum.

Most Creoles, black or white, sent their children to parochial schools. The Ursuline Order and the Sacred Heard Order educated girls and Jesuits provided education for boys. Although schools segregated by color are no longer present, most Catholic schools attended by Creoles are still separated by gender.

# RELIGION

Roman Catholicism is strongly associated with Creoles. French and Spanish cultures from which Creoles originate are so closely associated with Catholicism that some people assume that all Louisianans are Catholic and that all people in Louisiana are of French and/or Spanish ancestry. Records from churches in Mobile, New Orleans, and other parts of the area indicate the presence of both black and white Creoles in church congregations very early in the eighteenth century.

After segregation of the Catholic church in 1895, certain churches became identified with Creoles of color. In 1916 Corpus Christi Church opened in the seventh ward, within walking distance of many Creoles of color. St. Peter Claver, Epiphany, and Holy Redeemer are also associated with black populations. Each church has a parish school run by the Blessed Sacrament Sisters. St. Louis Cathedral and St. Augustine's Church are prominent in the larger Creole society, with women predominating in attendance. Today, only about half of the people in Louisiana are Catholics but the early dominance of Catholicism has left its mark on people of other denominations. In the southern part of the state, especially in New Orleans, place and street names are often associated with particular saints.

Almost all of the material written about Creoles describes a devotion to the Virgin Mary, All Saint's Day (November 1), and the many activities associated with the observance of Lent and Holy Week, especially Mardi Gras. Other important religious figures are St. Jude (the patron saint of impossible cases), St. Peter (who opens the gates of Heaven), and St. Anthony (who helps locate lost articles).

Holy Week is closely observed by Creoles, both as a religious celebration and as a time of customs and superstition. On Holy Thursday morning, housewives, when they heard the ringing of church bells, used to take pots from the stove and place them on the floor, making the sign of the cross. Also, nine varieties of greens were cooked—a concoction known as *gumbo shebes*. On Good Friday Creoles visited churches on foot and in silence to bring good fortune.

Few Protestants and no known Jews are found in the white Creole community, which seems unusual given the frequency of intermarriage in the eight or ten generations of Creole life in the area. Today, many Creoles are nonpracticing Catholics with some agnostics, some atheists, and a very few professing a non-Catholic faith.

## EMPLOYMENT AND ECONOMIC TRADITIONS

The Creoles' image of economic independence is rooted in the socioeconomic conditions of free people of color before the Civil War. Creoles of color were slave owners, land owners, and skilled laborers. Of the 1,834 free Negro heads of households in New Orleans in 1830, 752 owned at least one slave. New Orleans persons of color were far wealthier, more secure, and more established than blacks elsewhere in Louisiana.

Creole occupations vary widely. In general, they require a strong educational background. Creole people of color and their descendants have carved out their own occupational niche over time. Carpentry, cabinet making, cigar manufacturing, masonry, housepainting, and plastering are all tasks that have been traditionally dominated by Creoles of color. More recently, Creoles of color have been pursuing careers that require more schooling.

Economic independence is highly valued in the colored Creole community. Being on welfare is a source of embarrassment, and many of those who receive government aid eventually drop out of the community. African Americans with steady jobs, respectable professions, or financial independence frequently marry into the community and become Creole, at least by association.

The Creoles have been quick to adapt strategies that maintain their elite status throughout changing economic conditions. Most significant is the push to acquire higher education. Accelerated education has allowed Creoles to move into New Orleans' more prestigious neighborhoods, first to Gentilly, then to Pontchartrain Park, and more recently to New Orleans East.

## POLITICS AND GOVERNMENT

When the Constitutional Convention of 1811 met at New Orleans, 26 of its 43 members were Creoles. During the first few years of statehood, native Creoles were not particularly interested in national politics and the newly arrived Americans were far too busy securing an economic basis to seriously care much about political problems.

Many Creoles were still suspicious of the American system and were prejudiced against it.

Until the election of 1834, the paramount issue in state elections was whether the candidate was Creole or Anglo-American. Throughout this period, many English-speaking Americans believed that Creoles were opposed to development and progress, while the Creoles considered other Americans radical in their political ideas. Since then, Creoles have actively participated in American politics; they have learned English to ease this process.

### MILITARY

During the War of 1812, many Creoles did not support the state militia. However, during the first session of Louisiana's first legislature in 1812, the legislature approved the formation of a corps of volunteers manned by Louisiana's free men of color. The Act of Incorporation specified that the colored militiamen were to be chosen from among the Creoles who had paid a state tax. Some slaves participated at the Battle of New Orleans, under General Andrew Jackson, and he awarded them their freedom for their valor. Many became known as "Free Jacks" because only the word "Free" and the first five letters of Jackson's signature, "Jacks," were legible.

## INDIVIDUAL AND GROUP CONTRIBUTIONS

### CHESS

In 1858 and 1859 Paul Morphy (1837-1884) was the unofficial but universally acknowledged chess champion of the world. While he is little known outside chess circles, more than 18 books have been written about Morphy and his chess strategies.

### LITERATURE

Kate O'Flaherty Chopin (1851-1904) was born in St. Louis; her father was an Irish immigrant and her mother was descended from an old French Creole family in Missouri. In 1870 she married Oscar Chopin, a native of Louisiana, and moved there; after her husband's death, she began to write. Chopin's best-known works deal with Creoles; she also wrote short stories for children in *The Youth's Companion*. *Bayou Folk* (1894) and *The Awakening* (1899) are her most popular works. Armand Lanusse (1812-1867) was perhaps the earliest Creole of color to write and publish poetry. Born in New Orleans to French Creole parents, he was a conscripted Confederate soldier during the Civil War. After the war, he was principal of the Catholic School for Indigent Orphans of Color. There he, along with 17 others, produced an anthology of Negro poetry, *Les Cenelles*.

### MILITARY

Pierre Gustave Toutant Beauregard (1818-1893), is perhaps the best known Louisiana Creole. He was born in New Orleans, educated in New York (unusual for the time), graduated from West Point Military Academy, and served with General Scott in the War with Mexico (1846). Beauregard was twice wounded in that conflict. He served as chief engineer in the draining of the site of New Orleans from 1858 to 1861. He was also a Confederate General in the Civil War and led the siege of Ft. Sumter in 1861. After the Civil War, Beauregard returned to New Orleans where he later wrote three books on the Civil War. He was elected Superintendent of West Point in 1869.

### MUSIC

Louis Moreau Gottschalk (1829-1869), was a pianist and composer born in New Orleans. His mother, Aimée Marie de Brusle, was a Creole whose family had come from Saint-Dominique. Moreau went to Paris at age 13 to study music. He became a great success in Europe at an early age and spent most of his time performing in concerts to support members of his family. His best known compositions are "Last Hope," "Tremolo Etudes," and "Bamboula." Gottschalk is remembered as a true Creole, thinking and composing in French. An important figure in the history and development of American jazz, "Jelly Roll" Ferdinand Joseph Lementhe Morton (1885-1941), was a jazz musician and composer born in New Orleans to Creole parents. As a child, he was greatly influenced by performances at the French Opera House. Morton later played piano in Storyville's brothels; these, too, provided material for his compositions. His most popular works are "New Orleans Blues," "King Porter Stomp," and "Jelly Roll Blues."

# MEDIA

### PRINT

**The Alexandria News Weekly.**
Founded in 1975, this general newspaper for the African American community contains frequent articles about Creoles.

**Contact:** Rev. C. J. Bell, Editor.
**Address:** 1746 Wilson, Alexandria, Louisiana 71301.
**Telephone:** (318) 443-7664.

**Bayou Talk.**
A Cajun creole newspaper.

**Address:** Jo-Val, Inc., Box 1344, West Covina, California 91793-1344.

**Creole Magazine.**
Published since December 1990 by Creole, Inc., it contains articles about African American Creoles in southwestern Louisiana and includes advertisements, a calendar of events, and organizations.

**Contact:** Ruth Foote, Editor.
**Address:** P.O. Box 91496, Lafayette, Louisiana 70590.
**Telephone:** (318) 269-1956.
**Fax:** (318) 332-4775.

**Louisiana Weekly.**
Black community newspaper published since 1925, which contains frequent articles about Creoles.

**Contact:** C. C. Dejoie, Jr., Publisher.
**Address:** 616 Barone Street, New Orleans, Louisiana 70150.
**Telephone:** (504) 524-5563.

**The Times of Acadiana.**
A weekly newspaper with Acadian/Creole emphasis.

**Address:** P.O. Box 3528, Lafayette, Louisiana 70502.
**Telephone:** (318) 237-3560.

### RADIO

**KAOK-AM.**
Ethnic programs featuring Cajun and Zydeco music.

**Contact:** Ed Prendergast.
**Address:** 801 Columbia Southern Road, Westlake, Louisiana 70669.
**Telephone:** (318) 882-0243.

**KVOL-AM/FM.**

Features a weekly Creole broadcast with African American programming, news, and Zydeco music.

**Contact:** Roger Canvaness.

**Address:** 123 East Main Street, Alexandria, Louisiana 70501.

**Telephone:** (318) 233-1330.

## ORGANIZATIONS AND ASSOCIATIONS

**Creole American Genealogical Society (CAGS).**

Formerly Creole Ethnic Association. Founded in 1983, CAGS is a Creole organization which promotes Creole American genealogical research. It provides family trees and makes available to its members books and archival material. Holds an annual convention.

**Contact:** P. Fontaine, Executive Director.

**Address:** P.O. Box 3215, Church Street Station, New York, New York 10008.

## MUSEUMS AND RESEARCH CENTERS

**Beau Fort Plantation Home.**

Collects Louisiana Creole period furnishings, furniture, and ornaments for display in a 1790 Creole house.

**Contact:** Jack O. Brittain, David Hooper, or Janet LaCour.

**Address:** P.O. Box 2300, Natchitoches, Louisiana 71457.

**Telephone:** (318) 352-9580.

**Bayou Folk Museum.**

Collects furniture, furnishings, and artifacts relating to the educational, religious, social, and economic life of Creoles. Contains agricultural tools, doctor's office with instruments, and a blacksmith shop. Guided tours, lectures for study groups, and permanent exhibits.

**Contact:** Marion Nelson or Maxine Southerland.

**Address:** P.O. Box 2248, Natchitoches, Louisiana 71457.

**Telephone:** (318) 352-2994.

**Louisiana State University.**

Contains local history and exhibits, tools for various trades, and historic buildings. Conducts guided tours, provides lectures, and has an organized education program.

**Contact:** John E. Dutton.

**Address:** 6200 Burden Lane, Baton Rouge, Louisiana 70808.

**Telephone:** (504) 765-2437.

**Melrose Plantation.**

Collects furnishings dating from 1796 to the early 1900s. Contains plantation gardens with the African and Yucca Houses. Museum sponsors an annual historic tour of Natchitoches and the Can River Country in October.

**Contact:** Maxine Southerland.

**Address:** Box 2248, Natchitoches, Louisiana 71457.

**Telephone:** (318) 379-0055.

## SOURCES FOR ADDITIONAL STUDY

Ancelet, Barry Jane, Jay D. Edwards, and Glen Pitre. *Cajun Country*. Jackson: University Press of Mississippi, 1991.

Bryan, Violet Harrington. *The Myth of New Orleans in Literature: Dialogues of Race and Gender*. Knoxville: University of Tennessee Press, 1993.

Davis, Edwin Adams. *Louisiana: A Narrative History*. Baton Rouge: Claitor's Book Store, 1965.

Dominguez, Virginia R. *White by Definition: Social Classification in Creole Louisiana*. New Brunswick: Rutgers University Press, 1986.

Dorman, James H. "Louisiana's 'Creoles of Color': Ethnicity, Marginality, and Identity," *Social Science Quarterly* 73, No. 3, 1992: 615-623.

Eaton, Clement. *A History of the Old South: The Emergence of a Reluctant Nation*, third edition. New York: Macmillan, 1975.

Ebeyer, Pierre Paul. *Paramours of the Creoles*. New Orleans: Molenaar Printing, 1944.

Fiehrer, Thomas. "From La Tortue to La Louisiane: An Unfathomed Legacy," in *The Road to Louisiana: The Saint-Dominique Refugees, 1792-*

*1809*, edited by Carl A. Brasseaux and Glenn R. Conrad. Lafayette, Louisiana: Center for Louisiana Studies, University of Southwestern Louisiana, 1992; 1-30.

Huber, Leonard V. "Reflections on the Colorful Customs of Latter-day New Orleans Creoles," *Louisiana History*, 21, No. 2, 1980; 223-235.

Kniffin, Fred B. *Louisiana: Its Land and People*. Baton Rouge: Louisiana State University Press, 1968.

Saxon, Lyle, Robert Tallant, and Edward Dreyer. *Gumbo Ya-Ya: A Collection of Louisiana Folktales*. Boston: Houghton Mifflin, 1945.

# CROATIAN AMERICANS

by
Edward Ifkovic

Despite their small, low-profile population, Croatian Americans have made distinguished individual contributions to American literature, music, science, and business.

## OVERVIEW

The newly independent republic of Croatia is located on the Balkan peninsula in southeastern Europe. Throughout much of the twentieth century, Croatia was one of five republics within Yugoslavia, an amalgam of ethnicities and religions tenuously held together by dictatorship and economic feasibility.

Croatia, which runs along the Adriatic to Montenegro, has a distinctive elongated geography that is largely the result of demarcations imposed upon it throughout this century. Occupying 21,829 square miles, Croatia is bordered by Bosnia-Hercegovina on the south, by Italy on the west, by Slovenia to the north and northwest, by Hungary to the north and northeast, and by Vojvodina, an autonomous Serbian province, to the east.

According to a 1981 census, Croatia has a population of more than 4.6 million people, 75 percent of whom are ethnic Croatian. Ethnic Serbians comprise another 11.5 percent of the population, and the remaining 13.5 percent includes Slovenians, Hungarians, Italians, and Czechs. Among Croatians, the predominant religion is Roman Catholicism, although some practice Islam.

### HISTORY

Croatia's long, turbulent history has been affected

by the control of empires that have included the Ottoman, Hapsburg, and Venetian empires. During the fifth century B.C., nomadic Slavic tribes from beyond the Carpathian Mountains of Poland and Russia drifted down into the Balkans, pushing out the Romans. Among the migrating South Slavic people, new religious ethnic identities evolved. The Croatians and Slovenians were strongly influenced by the Roman Catholic Church, and the Serbians, Montenegrins, and Macedonians by the Eastern Orthodox Church. The small independent countries of Slovenia and Croatia did not survive the Middle Ages. After a period of self-rule under King Tomislav and King Peter Kresimir IV, Croatia fell under the governance of Hungary in 1102.

During the fourteenth century, the Ottoman Turks began invading the Balkans. A powerful people, the Ottomans had gradually taken the region of Asia Minor now known as Turkey from the Byzantines, who had controlled a great empire there since before the fall of Rome. By 1350 the Ottomans had begun their invasion of the Balkan Peninsula. After the legendary battle of Kosovo in 1389, Serbia fell under Turkish rule.

With the defeat of the Serbians, the Turks began to make inroads into Croatian territory. The Croatians turned to the Austrians for military support, but with the rise of the Austro-Hungarian Empire, the Croatians found themselves in a slave-like condition. For generations, the Croatians were used as a military buffer between Europe and the Turks. In 1573 Matija Gubec led an inspiring if disastrous rebellion against the Austrian nobles, but Austro-Hungarian control of the Croatians continued until 1918.

During the nineteenth century, Slavic nationalism grew in proportion to the decline of the Austro-Hungarian Empire. World War I erupted as a result of conflict between independent Serbia and the Austro-Hungarian Empire, and with the 1918 defeat of Austria-Hungary and its German allies, European geography was restructured.

U.S. President Woodrow Wilson advocated independence for various nationalities, and South Slavs seized the opportunity for freedom. Based on the "Yugoslav Idea," a Serbo-Croatian Coalition issued a Declaration of Yugoslav Independence and the Kingdom of Serbs, Croats, and Slovenes was formed on July 20, 1917, under the rule of Serbian Prince Alexander. Eight years later, Alexander changed the country's name to Yugoslavia.

## MODERN ERA

Internal dissension and ethnic rivalries persisted in the new Yugoslavia. Serbians conceived of the country as a Greater Serbia with a centralist government, while Federalist Croatians and Slovenians demanded that each republic have a strong voice in the government. When Stejpan Radic, the respected head of the Croat Peasant Party, was assassinated in Parliament in 1928, the king dissolved Parliament and made himself dictator. The king was himself assassinated by right-wing Croatian sympathizers in Marseilles, France, in 1934 and his cousin, Prince Paul, assumed control of the country.

On March 27, 1941, Yugoslavia (under fascist dictator Ante Pavic) signed a pact allying itself with Germany. When the Yugoslavian people revolted against this government action with chants of "Better war than pact, better grave than slave," the military assumed control of the country and proclaimed young Peter II king. In retaliation, Adolf Hitler ordered an attack on Belgrade on April 6, 1941. After a bloody battle, the Nazis conquered Yugoslavia and set up a puppet government in Croatia. The fascist Ustashe eliminated thousands of Jews, Serbians, and unsympathetic Croatians. Underground resistance to the Germans included the Partisans, under the command of Croatian Communist Marshal Tito, and the Chetniks, who supported the monarchy in exile and, some believe, later collaborated with the Germans.

The Partisans viewed the war as an opportunity to create a Communist government in postwar Yugoslavia. Tito's forces wrested large sections of the country from German control, ultimately winning the support of Communists and non-Communists, including the Allies. When the war ended, the Socialist Party assumed control of the government and abolished the monarchy.

The 1945 Partisan massacre of thousands of Croatians alarmed the many Croatian Americans who wanted to support the new Titoist government. Despite such tactics, Tito used his personality and power to help placate ethnic and religious rivalries within Yugoslavia. Refusing to allow Yugoslavia to become a puppet of the Soviet Union, Tito asserted Yugoslav independence from Russian control in 1948, thus establishing Yugoslavia as one of the most liberal and progressive Socialist countries of Eastern Europe. Upon Tito's death in 1980, Yugoslavia was ruled by a collective state presidency and party presidium, which immediately suffered severe economic difficulties and saw the resurgence of nascent rivalries.

The breakdown of Communism in Eastern Europe, most dramatically illustrated by the 1989 dismantling of the Berlin Wall, toppled a number of Communist governments and affected still others, including Yugoslavia-where old rivalries and long-buried aspirations for independence resurfaced. Following the lead of Slovenia, Croatia challenged growing Serbian hegemony. In Yugoslavia's first postwar free elections, held in 1990, the Croatian Democratic Union (HDZ) ran on an anti-Communist platform and won 205 of 356 seats in Parliament.

Despite Croatia's first real independence in 1,000 years, many feared a rise in nationalistic fascism under the leadership of Franjo Tudjman, who viewed Greater Croatia as a means of countering Greater Serbia. Government corruption and censorship added to these fears and overall dissatisfaction. On June 25, 1991, Croatia and Slovenia issued declarations of independence.

Although Croatia was recognized by the international community, including the EC, its secession from Yugoslavia was not smooth. Serbian forces attacked Croatia, with long sieges of Dubrovnik, Vukovar, and other Croatian cities. The 1991 and 1992 seven-month war against the combined forces of the Yugoslav army and Serbian paramilitaries left thousands dead and many villages destroyed. The Serbians instituted policies of "ethnic cleansing" in Croatian villages and throughout Bosnia. With control of one-third of Croatian territory, the Serbians attacked ethnic Croatians in Bosnia and Croatia proper.

Independent Croatia is now recognized by 53 nations, including the United States; however, the war in the Balkan Peninsula continues to spread despite United Nations peace efforts. The future stability of Croatia can only be addressed within the greater context of peace in the Balkans.

## THE FIRST CROATIANS IN AMERICA

During the Middle Ages, the Adriatic ports of Croatia's "Dalmatian Coast" were thriving centers of commerce and trade. The Italian ports of Venice and Genoa fought for control of the high seas, as did the small but powerful independent Republic of Ragusa, a city-state in Croatia now known as Dubrovnik.

Skilled Ragusan navigators and seaman were in great demand, as well as crew members on most European ships. Many scholars believe Dalmatian sailors were on Columbus' ships to the New World. An often-repeated Croatian legend has it that one of Columbus' sailors amassed considerable wealth in gold and returned to his native Ragusa to build a beautiful palace at Bonda.

In 1494 Ragusa signed a treaty with Spain, which allowed Ragusan ships to trade with Spanish colonies. Because Ragusa's government had banned slavery in 1416, the Ragusan ships were not allowed to transport slaves from Africa to the colonies. Many Ragusan sailors remained in the colonies, married English women, and changed their names. It is documented, for example, that brothers Mato and Dominko Kondjevic sailed to America in 1520 and remained for 30 years before returning home with substantial wealth.

Legend and early American history unite in the story of John White, who in 1587 established an English colony on Roanoke Island off the coast of North Carolina. When poverty and disease threatened the survival of the settlement, White returned to England to seek aid. The colonists had agreed to leave a sign on a tree if trouble developed or they were forced to leave. Upon his return to the island, White found the houses in ruins and no sign of life, but discovered the word Croatan deeply etched into the bark of a tree. It has been theorized that the Ragusan ship Croatian, believed to have left for America in the 1580s, touched the shore at Roanoke, picked up the surviving English colonists, and was later lost at sea. Another story tells of survivors of a sunken Ragusan ship who were helped by friendly Native Americans who later became known as the Croatians. Years later, a visitor noted that some of the Croatian Indians had light skin, fair hair, and blue eyes—characteristic of Ragusans.

These stories remain undocumented legend; however, a letter sent by the government of Dubrovnik to its diplomatic representative in Madrid, states that by 1600, "many Ragusans" were already living in America.

## THE MISSIONARIES

The work of Croatian and Slovene missionaries in America is well documented. Priests and members of religious orders ventured into the American wilderness. One of the first was Baron Ivan Ratkay (Ratkaj), a wealthy Croatian nobleman, who early in life rejected the comfortable existence into which he was born to commit himself to doing God's work. After joining the Jesuit Order, he underwent rigorous training in Rome and Madrid and was named a missionary to the uncharted regions of New Spain.

Ratkay arrived in America in 1673 and began teaching and baptizing the Taramuhara Indians of the Southwest. A scholar, he also pursued interests that included the study of the area's physical geography. Detailed records of his travels through the New Mexican region proved valuable to many of the pioneers who followed him. In 1683 Ratkay died at age 36 at the hands of Native Americans—supposedly poisoned for forbidding drinking and dancing.

Another missionary, Father Ferdinand Konscak, worked in the unsettled regions of California and Mexico under the name Padre Consago Gonzales. The son of an army officer, Father Konscak was born in 1703 in Verazdin, Croatia, and attended the Jesuit College in Budapest, Hungary. For more than 22 years he remained in California at the San Ignacio Mission. A traveler, Father Konscak also discovered that Lower (Baja) California was a peninsula rather than an island and constructed an accurate, detailed map of the region. In 1770 J. Baegert copied the map in his pioneer guidebook *Nachrichten von Kalifornien*. Father Konscak also founded the village of San Antonio Real.

Croatian missionary Josip Kundak worked in the Midwest with Native Americans and growing German and Swiss immigrant populations. In 1854 he established the Benedictine Abbey in St. Meinhard, Indiana. He also founded a mission in Jasper, Indiana, and the town of Ferdinand. Honoring the centennial of his death, the governor of Indiana proclaimed December 8, 1957 "Father Kundak Day" to show, in his words, "tribute to a great missionary, pioneer, and citizen who left Croatia, the land he loved, to come and colonize the wilderness of this great state, for which we owe him a huge debt of gratitude."

## DALMATIANS IN THE SOUTH AND WEST

When the Civil War began, Dalmatian colonies (Dalmatia is a region in Croatia) had spread into Mississippi and Alabama. U.S. Census records of the 1850s and 1860s reveal hundreds of Dalmatian saloonkeepers, grocers, tugboat operators, and restaurant owners. By 1880 an estimated 20,000 Croatians lived in the United States, primarily in the South and the West. Not surprisingly, many fought on the side of the Confederacy during the Civil War, forming the Austrian Guards and two Slavonian rifle units.

Throughout the nineteenth century, Dalmatian sailors jumped ship at major American ports, especially at favored locations such as New Orleans. The former seamen found the oyster business a natural transition. Some, like Luka Jurisich, who arrived in Bayou Creek, Louisiana, from Duba, in 1855, are credited with building the trade in the region. Dalmatians also became early developers of oyster fisheries in Biloxi, Mississippi. Today, the huge fishing industry in these regions is heavily populated by descendants of the early Dalmatian settlers.

Many Dalmatians moved from New Orleans to ports in the Far West, establishing large colonies such as the one that grew in and around San Francisco. Some arrived as early as 1835, predating settlers from the Eastern states. Although gold enticed many Croatians to move west, those who settled in California were captivated by the climate, which they likened to that of their sunny Adriatic homeland. Most made their living, not from gold, but by operating businesses. According to one study, more than 50 Dalmatian businesses occupied a single San Francisco street in the 1850s and 1860s.

In 1857 the Slavonic Illyrian Mutual and Benevolent Society was formed in San Francisco as the first Slavic charitable society of its kind in America. In 1861 the Society purchased land for the first Croatian-Serbian cemetery in the United States. Vincent Gelcich, president of the Society in 1860, was a physician who served as a surgeon and colonel in the Union Army during the Civil War. This society, which helped immigrants survive in the new land, is still in existence today.

Perhaps the most important Dalmatian contribution to America was made in agriculture. Mateo Arnerich, a sailor from Brac, arrived in San Francisco in 1849, the year after gold was discovered at Sutter's Mill. One of the first Dalmatians to settle in the Santa Clara Valley, Arnerich bought land and established the vineyards that made his wealth. His two sons became lawyers and one, a member of the State Legislature, was the first Croatian to hold public office in the United States. In the 1870s, Mark Rabasa introduced the apple industry to northern California. Another Dalmatian, Steve Mitrovich, imported the Dalmatian fig to Fresno and displayed the "Adriatic fig" at the Columbian Exposition in Chicago in 1893, winning first prize.

Because of Dalmatian success at growing and developing a superior quality of grapes, figs, plums, apples, and apricots in Pajaro Valley, the region was called New Dalmatia. Although the novelist Jack London feared "alien" control, he described the flourishing 12,000-acre apple paradise of the Dalmatians in his 1913 novel *Valley of* the Moon: "Do you know what they call Pajaro Valley? New Dalmatia. We're being squeezed out. We Yankees thought we were smart. Well, the Dalmatians came along and showed they were smarter.... First, they worked at day labor in the fruit harvest. Next, they began, in a small way, buying the apples on the trees. The more money they made, the bigger became their deals. Pretty soon they were renting the orchards on long leases; and now they own the whole valley, and the last American will be gone."

The discovery of silver in the Nevada Territory in the late 1850s inspired the influx of Croatian settlers into towns like Virginia City, Carson City, Austin, and Reno. These Slavs were commonly referred to as "Sclavonians" or "Slavonians." The successful Slavonian Gold and Silver Mining Company at Resse River, Nevada, was organized in 1863, but most settlers made their living in businesses that served miners. The largest food provision house in Nevada in the 1860s was owned by Dalmatians, and Marco Medin, one of the first men to arrive in Nevada during the silver fever, grew rich in the fruit and saloon businesses.

The lives of Antonio Mazzanovich, Antonio Milatovich, and Captain John Dominus illustrate a more colorful side of Croatian history. Mazzanovich enlisted as a bugler in the U.S. 6th Cavalry when he was 11 years old and helped pursue the famous Apache Geronimo through the Southwest, which he recalled in his memoirs, *Trailing Geronimo* (1931). Milatovich sued the Republic of Mexico when a revolutionary change of government deprived him of more than one million acres of Mexican land he had acquired. He lost his fortune when the new government refused his claim on the basis of his Austrian citizenship. The Croatian Captain John Dominus, who sailed to America in his own ship, subsequently settled in Hawaii, where he built a lavish mansion that was later used as the official residence of the Governor. Captain Dominus disappeared at sea while attempting to reach China. His son, John Owen Dominus, married the Hawaiian princess Lydia Kamekaha Kapaaka in 1862. She became Queen Liliuokalani, the last reigning queen of Hawaii, and Dominus served as her Prince Consort until his death in 1891.

## THE GREAT MIGRATION: AFTER 1880

From 1880 through 1914, Croatians and other Eastern European peasants immigrated to the United States in large numbers. Fleeing from poverty brought on by changes in land inheritance laws, blight, and deteriorating farming soil quality, and a decreasing infant mortality rate that increased the population, a young generation looked to America *trbuhom za kruhum* ("with belly after bread").

Because statistics were so poorly kept in general, and Slavs were so often lumped together or confused with other groups, it is not known how many Croatians entered the United States during the Great Migration. In the 1930s Croatian historian Ivan Mladineo estimated that approximately half a million Croatians were living in America at that time.

The first wave of immigrants consisted of primarily illiterate, unskilled male laborers who came to the United States to make their fortunes and then return home. Many made frequent trips between the United States and Eastern Europe, and became known as "birds of passage." These men sent money to their villages, markedly improving the economic conditions of the Croatians who remained at home. In 1938 the *South Slav Herald* reported that two thirds of the new homes built in Croatia during the previous 30 years had been built with American money.

According to the 1907 Immigration Commission survey, about 66 percent of Croatians who came to America returned home. Between 1899 and 1924, the rate was nearly half. The thousands who returned to Croatia took new ideas with them, including ideas about democracy. In 1906 Croatian writer Antun Matos wrote "America is presently the most important factor in the creation of Croatian democracy."

Following World War II, millions were left homeless, and the rise to power of Communist regimes in Yugoslavia and other parts of Eastern Europe meant that others could not return home. Of the 400,000 Displaced People initially admitted into the United States, 18,000 were "Yugoslavs."

Laws like the Refugee Relief Act of 1953 and the Refugee Escape Act of 1960, and the demise of the quota system in 1965, facilitated more Croatian emigration. This new wave included many educated professionals. In "A Clash of Two Immigrant Generations," Bogdan Raditsa discussed the sharp contrast between the earlier, unskilled Croatian immigrants and their later counterparts, revealing the "bitterness that divides the Croatians who came here as displaced persons after 1945 from the Croatian American families established in this country for four or five decades." According to the 1990 U.S. Census, there are an estimated 544,000 Croatian Americans living in the United States.

Croatian Americans take great pride in their ethnic heritage.

## SETTLEMENT PATTERNS

Today, Pennsylvania's Croatian population of nearly a quarter million is the largest in the country. During the Great Migration, most Croatians settled in the industrial cities of the Midwest in already established immigrant communities. In places like Ohio, Pennsylvania, Illinois, Michigan, Minnesota, Wisconsin, and Indiana, they worked in coal mines, and in the iron and steel mills. California also supports a sizable Croatian population. There settlers found employment in fishing and mining. In San Francisco Croatian Americans introduced new methods of drying fruits, packaging, and shipping.

The traditional patriarchal Croatian family structure, which emphasized control and rigid discipline, remained a part of the early immigrant lifestyle and contributed to the Slavs reputation as a dependable hard worker. Aside from arrests for drunkenness, there was little crime among the Croatians in America. Industrialists struggling against labor unions often exploited the new immigrants, making them scabs during worker strikes.

# ACCULTURATION AND ASSIMILATION

Although events since the breakup of Yugoslavia in the early 1990s have made Croatia more visible internationally, Croatians are still mislabeled and subsumed into larger classifications such as Austrian-Hungarian or Yugoslavian. Croatians have also been the object of discrimination.

During the period of the Great Migration, Croatians and other Slavs were often lumped together and assessed as an uninspired, stolid, sluggish people who were only useful as drudges and unskilled grunts. They were called derogatory names like "Hunkies," "modgies," and "strams" and labeled "Bo hunks" or "dumb Polacks."

The unskilled, often illiterate early immigrants gave little thought to assimilation. They clustered together, often in cooperative boarding-houses called *drustvo*, and worked at unskilled labor 12 to 16 hours a day, and in the process, resisted acculturation. One Slavic commentator wrote, "My people do not live in America; they live underneath America. America goes on over their heads."

During and after World War I, when many Croatians who had planned to return to Europe could not, the number who became American citizens increased sharply. By 1919 a study showed that 60 to 65 percent of the immigrants had taken out naturalization papers. The Jugoslav Central organization—formed in Detroit in 1932 to promote unity among Slovenians, Serbians, and Croatians—had as one of its chief goals the encouragement of U.S. citizenship.

## THE ROLE OF THE NEWSPAPER

Even though many Croatian immigrants were illiterate, newspapers assumed an importance in the "Little Croatias" of America. They reported changes in American immigration law, carried employment opportunities, and kept up with major European events.

The most popular newspaper among early immigrants was *Narodni List* (1898), published in New York by Frank Zotti, a colorful and controversial Croatian figure of the time. Zotti's tabloid featured gutsy topical reporting, melodramatic fiction and popular peasant poetry. The Croatian Fraternal Union's *Zajednicar* (Unity) began in 1905 in Pittsburgh, and is still published today with a circulation of 70,000.

## TRADITIONAL MUSIC AND FOLK DANCE

The popular *kolo* or circle dance is performed to the accompaniment of the tamburitsa, a traditional mandolin-like stringed instrument. The tamburitsa is a modern version of the one-stringed *gusle* used for centuries by the village poets. A tamburitsa band performed at the White House during Theodore Roosevelt's presidency and in concert at Carnegie Hall in 1900. Today, Duquesne University supports tamburitsa orchestras and festivals and runs the Tamburitsa School of Music the only one of its kind in America.

Singing societies, which have also been popular, are patterned after an early group called "Zora" (Dawn), which was founded in Chicago in 1903 to keep old folk songs and past experiences alive.

## TRADITIONS, CUISINE, AND FOLK CULTURE

For Croatians, food, tradition, and folk culture are interconnected, especially as a part of holiday celebrations. In many Croatian households, the Christmas celebration begins on Christmas Eve with a meal of (cod fish). On Christmas Day, *sarma* (cabbage and sauerkraut) and *orehnjaca* (nut cake) are traditional favorites.

St. Nicholas Day and Easter are also important holidays to Croatians. St. Nicholas Day, December 6, is a children's holiday for giving presents. Lamb and ham are central to celebrating Easter, a celebration of eating following a meatless Lent. *Pogaca* is an Easter bread that is braided and decorated with painted eggs. Food is blessed in the church and sometimes broken egg shells are scattered throughout the household.

In Croatia, name days paid homage to the saint for whom you were named. As immigrants and later generations gradually adopted the American custom of celebrating birthdays, this traditional celebration disappeared.

## TRADITIONAL COSTUMES

Traditional Croatian dress is distinguishable by its fine embroidery. Women wear long linen dresses, often white, covered by a colored apron and a shawl over the shoulders. They usually cover their heads with a kerchief. Croatian men wear white shirts topped with a colored vest or jacket. Their pants are often dark linen or wool, worn with high leather boots or knee-socks. The outer garments are embroidered in red or gold with geometric designs or images such as birds or flowers. Today, such costumes are only worn on holidays or during special occasions.

## HEALTH AND MENTAL HEALTH ISSUES

In the early days of settlement Croatians relied on home health care. The local midwife, a Croatian woman, most often handled childbirth in the home. Because there were no labor compensation laws then, men injured on the job had no benefits for hospitalization. Folk remedies, the use of practiced "bonesetters," and superstitions often were used in place of English-speaking doctors (dropping hot coals in water to dispel headaches from evil eyes, for example), but there was little involvement with the American medical establishment. Those involved with settlement houses in cities—as with Jane Addams' in Chicago—became conversant with doctors and health care—matters of ventilation and cleanliness, for example. Croatians were hesitant to accept welfare. In New York before World War I one charity group reported that it had never had one application from a Croatian. There have been no studies done of mental health conditions among Croatian immigrants, and little on their health care. Successive generations, of course, have adopted American ways for dealing with the medical community.

# LANGUAGE

The Croatian language spoken by early immigrants was largely dialect, identifiable by the region from which the immigrant came. The three primary dialects of Croatian are *cakavski*, from Dalmatia, *kajkavski* from the far northwest near Zagreb, and two varieties of *stokavski* (*stokavski ijekavski* is the literary variant for Croatians). These dialects are often so various that Croatians in America sometimes have difficulty understanding each other.

Writers like Louis Adamic and Clement Mihanovich have pointed out the manner in which Croatians have added familiar endings to English words. Some linguists distinguish this as a "new" dialect. For example, the Croatian word for automobile is *kola* and the Americanized-Croatian word is *kara* (car); *novine* (paper) has become *papir*; *Soba* (room) is now *rum*. This bastardization of the language has alarmed many purists.

"In Croatia I enjoyed my godparents as really my real parents. They never talked about my mother and father in America. So, in other words, I didn't know that there was somebody in America. I didn't even know where America was or heard of America. Nothing."

Louis Zauneker in 1923, cited in *Ellis Island: An Illustrated History of the Immigrant Experience,* edited by Ivan Chermayeff et al. (New York: Macmillan, 1991).

Croatian and Serbian are, for the most part, the same language. Serbian, however, uses a Crylic alphabet, while Croatian uses a Latin alphabet. Until the breakup of Yugoslavia, the official language was Serbo-Croatian (*Srpsko-hrvatski*) or Croato-Serbian (*Hrvasko-srpski*). In America, many Croatians refuse to use the term "Serbo-Croatian," an issue which became less significant when Croatia gained independence in 1990. Several American colleges and universities teach Serbo-Croatian, including Stanford University, Yale University, and Northwestern University.

### GREETINGS AND OTHER POPULAR EXPRESSIONS

Common Croatian expressions include: *Dobro jutro* ("dobro yootro")—Good morning; *Dobar dan* ("dobahr dahn")—Good afternoon; *Dobro vece* ("dobro vehcheh")—Good evening; *Laku noc* ("lahkoo noch")—Good night; *Zbogom* ("zbogom")—Good-bye; *Kako stje* ("kahko steh")—How are you?; *Hvala* ("fahlah")—thank you; *sretan bozic* ("srehtan bozich")—Merry Christmas.

# FAMILY AND COMMUNITY DYNAMICS

Because most of the early immigrants were single men, the saloon became their most important social institution. More than a place to drink, the Croatian saloon provided a place to exchange news about the Old Country, translate letters, and do banking.

Immigrants also organized benevolent fraternal associations for protection in the event of on-the-job injury or unemployment. These included the Slavonian Mutual and Benevolent Society, organized by Croatians and Serbians in San Francisco in 1857; the United Slavonian Benevolent Association, founded in New Orleans in 1874; and the Austrian Benevolent Society (later the First Croatian Benefit Society), established in New York in 1880, among others.

As more and more men decided to settle in America, they sent for their wives and marriageable women. Coming from a pre-industrial, Roman Catholic peasant culture, these women were occupied with housekeeping and child rearing. The rural concept of the godmother and godfather (*kum* and *kuma*) survived for some time in America The parents of a newborn child selected family members, or friends considered part of the extended family (*zadruga*) to care for the child in the event that something happened to the parent and to take charge of the child's spiritual well-being, a responsibility that was taken seriously.

Communal Croatian life and the tradition of taking in as many boarders as possible to earn money had socialized women to serve large numbers of people. Men went into the workplace and, thus, the larger American society, and children went to American schools where they learned the language and mores, but women remained isolated in the home. Divorce was uncommon, but did occur. Although both partners were ostracized by the larger community, the woman was more harshly treated.

Over time, however, the woman's subservient position in America changed, largely because women ran most of the boarding houses and achieved some measure of economic security from doing so. As Croatian American women became more "Americanized," some men argued that once "a Croatian woman becomes Americanized and accepts the liberalization policy of American women ... permissiveness with the children develops." Some Croatian women countered that because they bore fewer children and were free of the patriarchal restraints and demands of the Old Country, successive generations of mothers maintained better relationships with their children.

As the educational and economic lives of second- and third-generation Croatians improved, most left the Little Croatia ghettoes and the parochial schools where Croatian nuns taught in Croatian, and these communities began to die.

## INTERACTION WITH OTHER ETHNIC GROUPS

Croatian interaction with Serbians and Slovenians grew out of a similarity of language and the fact that they often settled near one another. Croatians also interacted with other Slavic peoples who emigrated from Austria-Hungary, as well as with Germans, Italians, and Hungarians, with whom they shared the common bond of Roman Catholicism. Although immigrant men attend Catholic Mass with their Irish foremen, they had little social contact.

Alliances with Serbians were temporary and topical as old enmity persisted. There is a saying that "There is no putting history behind one's self in the Balkans; the battles one's ancestors fought are today's battles as well." Fights and flare-ups still erupt today.

# RELIGION

Devout Roman Catholics, the Croatians organized the first U.S. Croatian parish in 1895 in Allegheny City, Pennsylvania. Despite California's large Croatian population in the nineteenth century, a Croatian parish was not organized there until 1903. As late as 1912, there were still only 12 Croatian parishes and four parochial schools in America. The number doubled within the next decade. By the 1970s only 30 Croatian parishes and two dozen parochial schools remained for a declining Catholic Croatian population. Today's Croatians are heavily disaffected with religion, and with the clergy in particular.

Most of the small number of Protestant Croatians came from Slovakia and Slovenia. Croatian Muslims who emigrating to America largely from the Croatian section of Bosnia arrived after World War II and settled in Cleveland and Chicago.

# EMPLOYMENT AND ECONOMIC TRADITIONS

Many companies paid immigrants' passage to America in return for a guaranteed period of servitude. Although this practice was outlawed in 1885, industrialists found ways around the law and Croatians were sent to coke foundries, iron mines, lumber camps, and factories across America.

A 1910 study revealed that Croatians in Pennsylvania were the lowest paid of the immigrant groups, and their unemployment rates the highest, with only 34 percent full-time, full-year employees. When Croatians arrived in industrialized American cities, manufacturers coerced them into replacing striking workers. Uneducated and often unaware of the dynamics of American labor-management politics, the immigrants were happy to have jobs. Manufacturers were adept at pitting one ethnic group against another. Railroad magnate Jay Gould once declared: "I can hire one half of the working class to kill the other half."

By 1900 when labor unions were gaining power, Croatians and other Slavs played a role in establishing the viability of the United Mine Workers of America, which helped break the cycle of using immigrants as scabs and strikebreakers. In 1909 Anton Pavisic was a leader in a coal miners' strike at McKees Rocks, Pennsylvania, where more than 2,000 fellow Croatians followed him. The first miners' compensation law introduced into the Michigan legislature was introduced by Anthony Lucas, a Croatian.

# POLITICS AND GOVERNMENT

Politically, Croatian Americans have been torn between concern for Croatia and involvement in American democracy. Early immigrants were more preoccupied with the former, and this concern persisted for many generations. Croatian organizations formed in America campaigned for political goals abroad. These organizations ranged from conservative to radical.

During the years of the Great Migration, groups like the National Croatian Society (NCS) and the Croatian League combated the tyrannical Austria-Hungary rule. In 1912 the Reverend Nikola Grskovic founded the Croatian Alliance, calling for complete Croatian independence from the Hapsburgs and advocating an alliance with the other South Slavs.

Influential South Slavic Americans, like Serbian American Michael Pupin, worked on committees dedicated to the formation of the new nation of Yugoslavia after World War I. Michael Pupin and other high-profile South Slavs were joined by Reverend Grskovic, Joseph Marohnic, and other leaders to create the South Slavic National Council of Chicago, with its main goal being the formation of Yugoslavia. When the Kingdom of Serbs, Croats, and Slovenes was realized in 1918, Croatian Americans were dissatisfied with the pan-Serbian centralist Yugoslav government and appealed in vain to the League of Nations for more encompassing ethnic representation.

During World War II, the Yugoslav Relief Committee was created to aid those living under a Nazi-installed puppet government in Croatia. After the war, American South Slavs—often under the guidance of high profile leaders like Slovenian American Louis Adamic—compelled the American government to lend its support to the Partisan cause in Yugoslavia. Increasingly, Americans were supporting Tito and his partisan forces. At a 1943 meeting, the Congress of American Croatians advocated support of Tito, a momentous decision called for by the more than 700 affiliates of the Congress.

With the installation of Communism in Yugoslavia by Tito after 1945, and rumors of mass killings of Croatians by Tito's command, many Croatians withdrew their support. The émigrés who came to America at that time included many radicals expelled from Yugoslavia. They organized in America and perpetrated terrorist acts to advance the cause of an independent Croatian state. The majority of Croatians in America condemn such extremists.

Although interest in the homeland and its politics continues, the intensity of this interest has gradually diminished. Represented prominently in the Democratic Party, Croatian Americans have won local legislative seats, governorships, and positions in Congress. Active as voters and local campaigners, Croatians have become an integral part of American life.

### RELATIONS WITH INDEPENDENT CROATIA

The majority of American Croatians have supported the newly independent Republic of Croatia. In fact, as the old Yugoslav federation began to crumble, American Croatians mounted letter campaigns and fund raising events to support the creation of a new government. In particular, when Germany recognized the new Republic in 1990, many Croatian Americans wrote to the American government to do likewise. Since independence, there has been the on-going war with old guard Serbian nationalists, both in Croatia proper and from without. Croatian Americans have worked to raise funds for war relief, health care, and for political action groups. The casualties in human life have alarmed many here, as has the wanton destruction of venerable old landmarks, like those in Dubrovnik. Some organizations, like the Croatian New Yorker Club, a group of business and professional people, organized a traveling exhibit of art work done by Croatian and Bosnian children in refugee camps in Croatia— to heighten awareness of the war in Croatia and Bosnia and to raise money to aid some displaced children, many orphaned by the war.

# INDIVIDUAL AND GROUP CONTRIBUTIONS

Despite their small, low-profile population, Croatian Americans have made distinguished individual contributions to American literature, music, science, and business.

### ACADEMIA AND JOURNALISM

Dr. Henry (Zucalo) Suzzallo (1873-1933) was born in San Jose, California, and earned degrees from Stanford, Columbia, and the University of California. During World War I, he advised President Wilson, and was appointed to the War Labor Policy Board in 1918. Suzzallo assumed the presidency of the University of Washington in 1915, a position he held until 1926. During his tenure at Washington, Suzzallo helped increase enrollment, raise academic standards, and create new programs. In 1927 he became chair of the Carnegie Foundation for the Advancement of Teaching and served as president of the foundation until his death. His books (such as *Our Faith in Education*) are examples of the commitment he always felt to the children of America. Other notable Croatian Americans include: historian Francis Preveden who did comprehensive studies of Croatians; Ivo Banac, a professor of comparative literature at Yale University; and Clement S. Mihanovich, St. Louis University sociologist. George Prpic has done extensive writing on Croatian culture in both America and Croatia. Vlaho S. Vlahovic, a Dalmatian, edited the *Slavonic Monthly*. Bogdan Raditsa was a columnist and journalist for years.

## FILM, TELEVISION, AND THEATER

Actor Peter Coe (Knego) left a football career with the Detroit Lions to play "touch-guy" roles in numerous motion pictures. Silent screen star Laura La Plante reached her peak during the 1920s. Walter Kray was one of the stars of the television series "The Roaring Twenties." Slavko Vorkapic (1884-?) acted throughout the 1920s and later became a director who worked with film montage and special effects. John Miljan was in more than four hundred movies, playing lead opposite such actresses as Joan Crawford and Virginia Bruce. Gene Rayburn is a television emcee. Michael Lah brought a new sensitivity and artistry to the animated cartoon.

## INDUSTRY AND AGRICULTURE

Hugo Tomich was a metal manufacturer and Marcus Nalley (Marko Narancic) a food-processing manufacturer. Samuel Zorovich, who came from Dalmatia in 1923, built an empire manufacturing cement. Nick Bez (Nikola Bezmalinovic) emigrated from the island of Brac in 1910 and eventually owned a fleet of salmon vessels, ultimately controlling much of the industry in Alaska. Paul Marinis, entrepreneur, was called "The King of Salmon" in the 1950s. John Slavich was owner of Del Monte Fruit Company, one of the largest in America. Nikola Sulentic was the inventor of the first valve-spring lifter.

In 1901 Anthony Lucas (Lucic) became the first man to discover oil in Texas. In 1936 the American Institute of Mining and Metallurgical Engineering established the Anthony F. Lucas Medal, an award for "distinguished achievement and practice in finding and producing petroleum."

## LITERATURE

Works like Ivan Mladineo's *Zetva* (*Harvest*) remain inaccessible to the English-reading audience. The popular almanac (*kalendar*), filled with popular poetry, written in the ever-present decameter, was the wellspring for the start of a Croatian American literature. Zdravko Muzina, an influential journalist, issued *Hrvastko-Amerikanska Danica za Godinu 1895*. Josip Marohnic, "the founder of popular Croatian literature in America," published the first book of Croatian poetry in America, *Amerikanke*.

In 1937 Gabro Karabin published the autobiographical "Honorable Escape" in *Scribner's*. The tale of his psychological journey from the steel mills that were his home, the story promised a literary career that never materialized. Victor Vecki wrote *Threatening Shadows* (1931), the story of a Croatian American doctor in California. Antun Nizeteo's *Bez Povratka* (*Without Return*, 1957). and Nada Kestercanek-Vujica's *Short Stories*, 1959, were written in Croatian. The poet Boris Maruna, who lived in America, also wrote in Croatian. Joseph Hitrec, a Croatian whose works do not deal with Croatian experience, came to America after years of travel, mostly in India. In 1946 he published *Ruler's Morning and Other Stories*, tales set in India. Other works by Hitrec include *Son of the Moon* (1948) and *Angel of Gaiety* (1951). George Vukelich wrote short stories and a novel. Edward Ifkovic wrote *Anna Marinkovich* (1980), the story of a Croatian immigrant family living on a farm in Connecticut during the Depression.

## MUSIC

Milka Ternina (1863-1920), an operatic soprano, sang for nine seasons with the Metropolitan Opera Company in New York. She premiered in the United States in the opera *Tosca* with Enrico Caruso. Hailed by Italian conductor Toscanini as the "world's greatest artist," Ternina returned to Zagreb in 1906, where she discovered the young Zinka Milanov. Ternina coached Milanov for three years. Milanov made her Met debut in *Il Trovatore* and for three decades remained as the Metropolitan's in-house coloratura. Violinist Louis Svecenski (1862-?) studied in Zagreb and Vienna, and in 1885 accepted a bid to become first violinist for the Boston Symphony Orchestra. He performed in the United States for 33 years Guy Mitchell was a popular recording artist in the 1950s and had his own television series in 1957. His recordings include "The Roving Kind," "Singing the Blues," and "My Heart Cries for You." Tony Butala was one of The Lettermen, whose most famous recording was "Can't Take My Eyes Off of You."

## POLITICS

Rudolph G. Perpich, a dentist who began a career in politics in 1956, served two terms in the Minnesota state senate. Elected lieutenant governor in 1970, he became governor of Minnesota in 1976 when Governor Wendell Anderson resigned. Perpich was elected to two more terms in 1982 and 1986.

Mike Stepovich, the first governor of the state of Alaska, had earlier helped establish a colony in Alaska. Nick Begich, of Alaska, was elected to the House of Representatives in 1970. Michael A. Bilandic was elected mayor of Chicago in 1977 after the death of Richard Daley. Dennis J. Kucinich served as mayor of Cleveland in the 1970s.

## SPORTS

Teodor Beg, a wrestler from Croatia, won eight gold medals for wrestling. Baseball players of Croatian descent include Walt Dropo of the Baltimore Orioles, Joseph Beggs of the Cincinnati Reds, and Roger Maras and Mickey Lolich, stars of the 1968 World Series. Joseph L. Kuharich coached the Washington Redskins football team from 1954 to 1958 and in 1955 was named coach of the year. "Pistol" Pete Marovich had a nationally publicized career with the New Orleans Jazz. Elcanor Laich was one of Olson's All-American Redheads. Mike Karakas played hockey for the Chicago Black Hawks, and Johnny Polich for the New York Rangers. Helen Crienkovich won world diving championships. Fritzie Zivich was the world welterweight boxing champ in 1941.

## VISUAL ARTS

Ivan Mestrovic (1883-1962) showed his marble sculptures in one-man shows in Belgrade, Zagreb, and London, before establishing a studio in Paris in 1907. After World War I, he joined the art faculty of Syracuse University in New York, and then taught at Notre Dame University, where he lived until his death. Mestrovic's work demonstrated a consciousness of the suffering of people in Austria-Hungary. His work also shows the influence of Michelangelo, whose art he studied for four years in Rome. The first artist to hold a one-man exhibit at the Metropolitan Museum of Art in New York, Mestrovic has left a legacy of works that can be found throughout the United States in churches, parks, and institutions that include Grant Park in Chicago and the Mayo Clinic in Minnesota.

The painter Vlaho Bukovac (1865-1963) studied art in Paris and worked in San Francisco. His home in his native Cavtat is now a museum. Another painter, Maksimiljan (Makso) Vanka, studied painting in Zabreb and Brussels. He came to the United States in 1934 with his American wife and attracted fame when he painted the towering frescoes for St. Nicholas' Catholic Church in Millvale, Pennsylvania. Louis Adamic's novel *Cradle of Life* (1936) is based on Bukovac's life.

# MEDIA

### PRINT

*American Croat/Americki Hrvati.*
**Contact:** Peter Radielovic, Editor and Publisher.
**Address:** P.O. Box 3025, Arcadia, California 91006.
**Telephone:** (213) 795-3495.

*Croatian Almanac.*
Published by the Croatian Franciscan Press.

**Address:** Croatian Ethnic Institute, 4851 Drexel Boulevard, Chicago, Illinois 60615.
**Telephone:** (312) 268-2819.

*The Croatian Voice.*
**Contact:** Steven Varga, Publisher.
**Address:** P.O. Box 14278, Cleveland, Ohio 44114.
**Telephone:** (216) 431-0811.

*Ragusan Press.*
**Contact:** Adam Eterovich, Publisher.
**Address:** 2527 San Carlos Avenue, San Carlos, California 94070.
**Telephone:** (415) 592-1190.

*The Trumpeter.*
Published quarterly by the Croatian Philatelic Society (CPS).

**Contact:** Ekrem Spahich, Editor.
**Address:** 1512 Lancelot Road, Borger, Texas 79007.

*Zajednicar (CFU Junior Magazine).*
Weekly magazine published by the Croatian Fraternal Union.

**Contact:** Bernard M. Luketich, President.
**Address:** 100 Delaney Drive, Pittsburgh, Pennsylvania 15235.
**Telephone:** (412) 351-3909.

### RADIO

**WKBN-AM (57).**
Youngstown, Ohio. "The Croatian Radio Hour," a two-hour weekly show, is hosted by Milan Brozovic.

**WKTX-AM (830).**

"Croatian Cultural Radio Program," airs weekly for two hours, with host Zvonimir Dzeba.

**Address:** P.O. Box 1432, Akron, Ohio 44309

**WNWK-FM (105) and WNYE-AM (91.5).**

"Croatian Radio Club."

**Address:** 37-18 Astoria Boulevard, Astoria, New York 11103.

**Telephone:** (201) 947-9754.

## ORGANIZATIONS AND ASSOCIATIONS

**Croatian Academy of America (CAA).**

Sponsors lectures for members and the public on Croatian literature, history, and culture.

**Contact:** Diane Gal, Executive Secretary.
**Address:** P.O. Box 1767, Grand Central Station, New York, New York 10163-1767.

**Croatian American Association.**

**Address:** 818 18th Street, N.W., Suite 950, Washington, D.C. 20006.
**Telephone:** (202) 429-5543.

**Croatian American Society.**

**Contact:** Dr. Slobodan Lang, President.
**Address:** Odranska 6, 41000, Zagreb, Croatia.
**Telephone:** 011 385 41/538-006.

**Croatian Genealogical Society (CGS).**

Encourages Croatia genealogical and heraldic research.

**Contact:** Adam S. Eterovich, Director.
**Address:** 2527 San Carlos Avenue, San Carlos, California 94070.
**Telephone:** (415) 592-1190.

**Croatian New Yorker Club.**

**Contact:** Anton Angelich.
**Address:** 4705 Henry Hudson Parkway, Apartment 7J, Riverdale, New York 10471.

**National Federation of Croatian Americans.**

**Address:** P.O. Box 11538, Washington, D.C. 20008.
**Telephone:** (412) 343-4534

## MUSEUMS AND RESEARCH CENTERS

**Croatian Heritage Museum and Library.**

**Address:** Lakeshore Blvd. and Route 91, Eastlake, Ohio 44094.

**Immigrant Archives.**

Managed by Hrvatska Matica Iseljenika (Croatian Homeland Association).

**Contact:** Ivo Smoljan, Director.
**Address:** Trnjaska bb. 41000 Zagreb, Croatia.
**Telephone:** 011 385 41/530-002.

**Museum of the Croatian Fraternal Union.**

**Address:** 100 Delaney Drive, Pittsburgh, Pennsylvania 15245.

## SOURCES FOR ADDITIONAL STUDY

Balch, Emily Greene. *Our Slavic Fellow Citizens.* New York: Charities, 1910.

*Croatia: Land, People, and Culture*, edited by Francis H. Eterovich and Christopher Spalatin. Toronto: University of Toronto Press, 1964.

Gorvorchin, Gerald G. *Americans from Yugoslavia.* Gainesville: University of Florida, 1961.

Preveden, Francis. *A History of the Croatian People.* New York: Philosophic, 1962.

Prpic, George. *The Croatian Immigrants in America.* New York: Philosophic, 1971.

Raditsa, Bogdan. "Clash of Two Immigrant Cultures," *Commentary*, January 1958, pp. 8-15.

Shapiro, Ellen. *The Croatian Americans.* New York: Chelsea House, 1989.

"South Slavic American Literature," in *Ethnic Perspectives in American Literature*, edited by Robert Di Pietro and Edward Ifkovic. New York: MLA, 1983.

> The driving
> ideological force
> behind most Cuban
> American political
> activity has been
> opposition to the
> Marxist regime in
> Cuba.

# CUBAN
by
**Sean Buffington**

# AMERICANS

## OVERVIEW

Cuba is an island nation located on the northern rim of the Caribbean Sea. It is the largest of the Greater Antilles islands. To Cuba's east is the island of Hispaniola, shared by Haiti and the Dominican Republic. Off the southeastern coast of Cuba lies Jamaica, and to the north is the state of Florida. In 1992 Cuba had an estimated population of nearly 11 million. Since 1959, Cuba has been led by President Fidel Castro, whose socialist revolution overthrew dictator Fulgencio Batista. In the years before the breakup of the Soviet Union, Cuba maintained a close political and economic relationship with that nation. Cuba has had a distant and antagonistic relationship with the United States. Sugar is the principal export of Cuba, but the Cuban economy, by most accounts, is weak.

The Cuban people are descendants of Spanish colonizers and of African slaves once employed in the sugar industry. Two-fifths of the Cuban population is Roman Catholic. Nearly half report no religious affiliation. Many of those who call themselves Catholics are also adherents of an Afro-Cuban religious tradition known as *santeria*. The official language of Cuba and the language spoken by nearly all Cubans is Spanish.

The capital of Cuba is Havana, located on the northwestern coast of the island. Nearly 20 percent of Cubans are city dwellers; most live in the capital city. The United States, which has limited diplomatic relations with Cuba, nonetheless maintains, against the Cuban government's wishes, a significant military presence in Cuba at the Guantanamo Bay base on the southeastern coast of the island.

## HISTORY

Cuba was colonized by the Spanish in 1511. Before colonization, the island was inhabited by Ciboney and Arawak Indians. Shortly after colonization, the native population was ravaged by disease, warfare, and enslavement, causing their eventual extinction. Throughout the sixteenth and seventeenth centuries, Cuba, like most of Spain's Caribbean possessions, received little attention from the imperial government. Especially in the sixteenth and seventeenth centuries, Spain lavished attention on its mainland colonies in Central and South America and ignored its island colonies. By the end of the seventeenth century, Spain itself had begun to decline as a world power through financial mismanagement, outmoded trade policies, and continued reliance on exhausted extractive industries. Spain's colonies suffered during this period. Then the British captured Havana in 1762 and encouraged the cultivation of sugar cane, an activity that would dominate the economy of the area for centuries to come.

## SLAVERY

The need for labor on the sugar and tobacco plantations and in raising livestock, which had been the area's first major industry, resulted in the growth of African slavery. Lasting only ten months before Spain resumed control, Britain's rule was of short duration. However, in this brief period North Americans had become buyers of Cuban goods, a factor that would contribute greatly to the well-being of the island population.

In the next 60 years, trade increased, as did immigration from Europe and other areas of Latin America. The introduction of the steam-powered sugar mill in 1819 hastened the expansion of the sugar industry. While the demand for African slaves grew, Spain signed a treaty with Britain agreeing to prohibit the slave trade after 1820. The number entering the area did decrease, but the treaty was largely ignored. Over the next three decades, there were several slave revolts, but all proved unsuccessful.

## REVOLUTION

Cuba's political relationship with Spain during this period became increasingly antagonistic. Creoles on the island—those of Spanish descent who had been born in Cuba and were chiefly wealthy landowners and powerful sugar planters—bridled at the control exercised over them in matters political and economic by colonial administrators from Europe. These planters were also concerned about the future of slavery on the island. They wanted to protect their investment in slaves and their access to the cheap labor of Africa from zealous imperial reformers. At the same time, black slaves in Cuba and their liberal white allies were interested both in national independence and in freedom for the slaves. In 1895, independence-minded black and white Cubans joined in a struggle against Spanish imperial forces. Their rebellion was cut short by the intervention of U.S. troops who defeated the Spanish in the Spanish-American War (1898) and ruled Cuba for four years. Even after the end of direct U.S. rule, however, the United States continued to exercise an extraordinary degree of influence over Cuban politics and the Cuban economy. U.S. interventionist policy toward Cuba aroused the resentment of many Cubans as did the irresponsible and tyrannical governance of the island by a succession of Cuban presidents.

## MODERN ERA

That anger finally exploded in the late 1950s when a socialist guerrilla army led by Fidel Castro launched an uprising against the brutal, U.S.-supported dictator, Fulgencio Batista. Castro formed a socialist government after taking control of the island, and, in the polarized world of geopolitics during the Cold War, turned to the Soviet Union for support. Cuba's relationship with the United States has been cool at best since Castro's victory. The 1961 U.S.-sponsored Bay of Pigs invasion, an unsuccessful attempt by the U.S. government and Cuban exiles in the United States to overthrow Castro, was the first of many clashes. The Cuban missile crisis of 1962, in which the United States successfully resisted an attempt by the Soviet Union to place nuclear weapons in Cuba, is also noteworthy.

Castro's Cuba has over the years supported socialist revolutions throughout the world. At home, Castro has used a heavy hand against dissidents, imprisoning, executing, and exiling many who have opposed him. Today, since the collapse of the Soviet Union, Cuba has lost its most

important trading partner and supporter. Castro's Cuba is in dire economic straits, and many wonder about the future of Castro's regime.

### SIGNIFICANT IMMIGRATION WAVES

The famous Cuban poet and dissident, Jose Martí, lived in exile in the United States before returning to Cuba to lead the 1895 rebellion against Spanish forces. In New York City, he strategized with other Cuban opposition leaders and planned their return to Cuba as liberators. Not more than 60 years later, Fidel Castro himself was an exile in the United States. He too plotted a revolution in the country that would soon become his enemy.

Cubans have had a long history of migrating to the United States, often for political reasons. Many Cubans, particularly cigar manufacturers, came during the Ten Years' War (1868-1878) between Cuban nationals and the Spanish military. Yet the most significant Cuban migrations have occurred in the last 35 years. There have been at least four distinct waves of Cuban immigration to the United States since 1959. While many, perhaps most, of the earlier migrants were fleeing Cuba for political reasons, more recent migrants are more likely to have fled because of declining economic conditions at home.

The first of these recent migrations began immediately after Castro's victory and continued until the U.S. government imposed a blockade of Cuba at the time of the Cuban missile crisis. The first to leave were supporters of Batista. They were later joined by others who had not been prominent Batista allies but who nonetheless opposed Castro's socialist government. Before the U.S government imposed its blockade, almost 250,000 Cubans had left Cuba for the United States.

The second major migration started in 1965 and continued through 1973. Cuba and the United States agreed that Cubans with relatives residing in the United States would be transported from Cuba. The transportation of migrants began by boat from the northern port of Camarioca and, when many died in boat accidents, was later continued by plane from the airstrip at Varadero. Almost 300,000 Cubans arrived in the United States during this period. The third migration, known as the Mariel Boat Lift, occurred in 1980 after Castro permitted Cubans residing in the United States to visit relatives in Cuba. The sight of well-to-do Cuban Americans coupled with an economic downturn on the island prompted many to line up at the Peruvian Embassy, which Castro had opened for emigration. The sheer numbers of Cubans clamoring to leave led Castro to permit any Cubans wishing to emigrate to leave by boat from the port of Mariel. Some 125,000 Cubans took advantage of this opportunity.

As economic conditions have worsened since the fall of Cuba's principal economic supporter, the Soviet Union, more Cubans have left Cuba in makeshift boats for Florida. Since Castro decided not to impede the departure of aspiring migrants, thousands of Cubans have left, many perishing on the boat journey. U.S. President Bill Clinton has initiated a policy of intercepting these migrants at sea and detaining them in centers at Guantanamo Bay and elsewhere in Latin America, a policy that has outraged many in the Cuban American community.

These four migrations have brought substantial numbers of Cubans to the United States. Over the years, just as the migration "push factors" have changed, so has the composition of the migrant population. While the earliest migrants were drawn from the highly educated and conservative middle and upper classes—those who had the most to lose from a socialist revolution—more recent migrants have been poorer and less educated. In the past several decades, the migrant population has come to look more like the Cuban population as a whole and less like the highest socioeconomic stratum of that population.

## SETTLEMENT PATTERNS

According to the 1990 U.S. Census, there are nearly 860,000 persons of Cuban descent in the United States. Of these, 541,000, or almost 63 percent of the total, live in Florida. Most of these live in Dade County, where Miami is located. There are also sizable communities in New York, New Jersey, and California. Together, these three states account for 23 percent of the Cuban American population. Florida, and Miami specifically, is the center of the Cuban American community. It is in Florida that the most significant Cuban American political organizations, research centers, and cultural institutions make their homes. The first Cubans to arrive in Florida settled in a section of Miami known among non-Cubans as "Little Havana." Little Havana was originally that area to the west of downtown Miami, bounded by Seventh Street, Eighth Street, and Twelfth Avenue. But the Cuban American population eventually spread beyond those initial boundaries, moving west, south, and north to West Miami, South Miami, Westchester, Sweetwater, and Hialeah.

Many Cuban migrants moved even farther afield with the encouragement and assistance of the federal government. The Cuban Refugee Program, established by the Kennedy administration in 1961, provided assistance to Cuban migrants, enabling them to move out of southern Florida. Almost 302,000 Cubans were resettled though the Cuban Refugee Program; however, many have begun to return to the Miami area.

Return to Cuba has not been an option for Cuban Americans for political reasons. Many early migrants hoped to return quickly after Castro was ousted, but that ouster never happened. There are prominent and powerful political organizations dedicated to ridding Cuba of Castro and setting up a non-socialist government in Cuba. Recent surveys, however, have shown that most Cuban Americans today do not wish to return to Cuba. Fully 70 percent have said that they will not go back.

# ACCULTURATION AND ASSIMILATION

The Cuban American community is well assimilated in the United States. Because of its size, they have significant political influence. In 1993, the Cuban American National Foundation lobbied against and successfully prevented the Clinton administration from appointing an undersecretary of state for Latin American affairs whom it opposed. Fully 78 percent of Cuban Americans had registered to vote in 1989 and 1990, compared to 77.8 percent of non-Hispanic white Americans. Moreover, 67.2 percent of Cuban Americans reported that they voted in the 1988 presidential election, compared to 70.2 percent of Anglo-Americans, 49.3 percent of Mexican Americans, and 49.9 percent of Puerto Ricans.

Cuban Americans also enjoy greater economic security than other Hispanic groups. In 1986, the median family income of Cuban Americans was $26,770—$2,700 less than the median for all U.S. family incomes but $6,700 more than the median for all Hispanic American family incomes. Cuban Americans are also highly educated; fully 17 percent of the Cuban American population has completed college or college and some graduate schooling, compared with eight percent of Puerto Ricans, six percent of Mexican Americans, and 20 percent of the total U.S. population. In other significant ways too, Cuban Americans closely resemble the total U.S. population. Two-parent households account for 78 percent of all Cuban American households and 80 percent of all U.S. households. The average U.S. family has 3.19 members, while the average Cuban American family has 3.18 members.

Despite the overwhelming success of early Cuban immigrants, many of the more recent migrants to the United States have not enjoyed as warm a reception from their adopted country as their predecessors. This is partially due to the fact that, as a group, they have less business or professional experience and are less educated. More likely, it is because Castro sent some mentally disturbed individuals and convicted criminals to the United States along with other Cubans in the Mariel Boat Lift. While the vast majority of Cubans who migrated to the United States during this period were not social deviants, they were nonetheless labeled as such by the media. The challenges presented to these migrants serve to remind us that Cuban Americans are not a monolithic community. Rather, they are quite diverse; generalizations about Cuban American politics and conservatism or about Cuban American wealth and business success must therefore consider the full complexity of the Cuban American community.

## EDUCATION

In Cuba, a sixth-grade education is compulsory and the illiteracy rate, in 1981, was 1.9 percent. There is a strong emphasis on math and science, and Cuba has become a center for preparing medical personnel, generating scores of young doctors. In the United States, Cubans and Cuban Americans are equally concerned about education and their children are often well-educated. The overwhelming majority of U.S.-born Cuban Americans have completed high school and some form of further education (83 percent). More than 25 percent have gone to post-secondary schools, compared to less than 20 percent of Cuban Americans born abroad, less than 16 percent of native-born Puerto Ricans, and ten percent of native-born Mexican Americans. More than any other Hispanic migrant group, Cuban Americans have shown a willingness and the ability to pay for private education for their children. Of native-born Cuban Americans, almost 47 percent have attended private schools. These numbers indicate that education is extremely important to Cuban Americans and that they, more than any other Hispanic migrant group, have the resources to pay for additional schooling and private education.

## CUISINE

Like many recent migrant groups, Cuban Americans enjoy both Cuban and U.S. cuisines. Traditional Cuban food is the product of the mingling of Spanish and West African cuisines in the climate of the Caribbean. Pork and beef are the most common meats in the traditional Cuban diet. Rice, beans, and root vegetables usually accompany such dishes. Necessary ingredients are available in most major cities where there are significant Hispanic populations. Many Cuban Americans, especially those who have been raised in the United States, have easy access to a variety of "American" foods and tend to reserve traditional cooking for special occasions.

## INTERACTIONS WITH OTHER ETHNIC GROUPS

Early Cuban immigrants entered the United States with the blessing of a president and a nation committed to combating communism. These Cubans therefore enjoyed a largely favorable relationship with their host communities. More recently, signs of conflict between Cuban Americans and other American communities have increased. The movement of Cuban Americans beyond the Little Havana enclave was accompanied by a movement of non-Hispanic whites out of the areas into which Cuban Americans were moving. There has also been a longstanding antagonism between Cuban Americans and African Americans in Florida, especially as Cuban Americans have asserted themselves politically and economically in the Miami area, becoming the dominant ethnic community there. African American community leaders often accuse Cuban Americans of shutting them out of the political process and keeping them out of the tourist industry. Recently, black Dade County residents were outraged by five Cuban American mayors' failure to officially welcome South African freedom fighter and president Nelson Mandela; they retaliated by initiating a boycott of tourism-related businesses in the Miami area (Nicole Lewis, "Miami Boycott Anniversary Yields Little Change," Black Enterprise, September 1991, p. 22).

Most Cuban Americans report and perceive a nondiscriminatory relationship with white Americans. A survey of Hispanic Americans conducted from 1989 to 1990 showed that 82.2 percent of Cubans who were U.S. citizens said they had not personally experienced discrimination because of their national origin. Nonetheless, 47 percent of Cuban Americans surveyed said that they thought there was discrimination against Cuban Americans in general.

## HEALTH AND MENTAL HEALTH ISSUES

Cuban Americans are generally healthier than other Hispanic Americans but often less healthy than non-Hispanic white Americans. Several indicators demonstrate the health status of Cuban Americans. The proportion of Cuban American babies with low birth weight is lower than the percentage of all infants in the United States with low birth weight and slightly higher than that of non-Hispanic white Americans. Similarly, the proportion of Cuban American infants born early, while lower than that of Mexican Americans or Puerto Ricans, is nonetheless higher than that of non-Hispanic whites (Fernando S. Mendoza, et al, "Selected Measures of Health Status for Mexican American, Mainland Puerto Rican, and Cuban American Children," *Journal of the American Medical Association* [*JAMA*], 9 January 1991, pp. 228-29).

In other areas, the comparative position of Cuban Americans is similar. Cuban Americans are far more likely than non-Hispanic white Americans to be murdered or to commit suicide. Still, they are less likely to be murdered than black or Puerto Rican Americans and less likely to die in accidents than black, Puerto Rican, or Mexican Americans (Council on Scientific Affairs, "Hispanic Health in the United States," *JAMA*, 9 January 1991, p. 251). When Cuban Americans do seek treatment for injury or disease, they frequently must pay the entire cost of emergency care, since a higher proportion of Cuban Americans than U.S. residents is uninsured (Fernando M. Trevino, and M. Eugene Moyer, et al, "Health Insurance Coverage and Utilization of Health Services by Mexican Americans, Mainland Puerto Ricans, and Cuban Americans," *JAMA*, 9 January 1991, p. 235). Many Cuban Americans turn to the *santeria* tradition for health care, participating in *santeria* healing services and seeking the advice of *santeria* healers.

## LANGUAGE

The national language of Cuba is Spanish and many Cuban Americans have some facility with Spanish. In 1989 and 1990, among Cuban Americans born in the United States, 96 percent said that they could speak either Spanish and English equally well or English better than Spanish. Cuban Americans born in the United States tend to be English speakers and have less facility with Spanish. Among those individuals born abroad, 74.3 percent said that they could speak either Spanish or Spanish better than English; however, while those born abroad have greater facility with Spanish, more than half have some English ability as well.

These numbers do not capture the phenomenon of "Spanglish." Among many Cuban Americans born in the United States who speak English at school and in other public domains but speak some Spanish at home with relatives and neighbors, "Spanglish," or a linguistic mixture of Spanish and English, is a common alternative. Many Cuban Americans—especially younger Cuban Americans—use Spanglish to talk with friends and acquaintances, incorporating English words, phrases, and syntactic units into Spanish grammatical structures. Facility with Spanglish, however, does not necessarily imply lack of facility with either English or Spanish, though such a lack of facility *may* characterize the Spanglish speaker.

## FAMILY AND COMMUNITY DYNAMICS

The Cuban American family is different in significant ways from the Cuban family. The Cuban family is characterized by patriarchy, strong parental control over children's lives, and the importance of non-nuclear relationships for the nuclear family. In the United States, these elements have become less characteristic among families of Cuban descent. For example, the Cuban tradition of selecting godparents for a child who will maintain a close and quasi-

"Sometimes I have dreams, and I see myself walking to my grantparents' house in Cuba ... It brings back a lot of memories. The States is home. I have no qualms about it, but I'm still attracted to that little island, no matter how small it is. It's home. It's your people. You feel, if it's ever possible again, you'd like to reconstruct what was there. You want to be a part of it."

Ramon Fernández in 1961, cited in *American Mosaic: The Immigrant Experience in the Words of Those Who Lived It,* edited by Joan Morrison and Charlotte Fox Zabusky (New York: E.P. Dutton, 1980).

parental relationship with the child has begun to decline in the United States. *Compadres,* or godparents, are less likely to play a significant role in the lives of Cuban American children.

Similarly, Cuban American women are more likely to have greater authority in the family than in Cuba. This is in part attributable to the greater workforce participation of Cuban American women. These women, because they contribute to the household income and to the overall security and independence of the family, claim a greater share of authority and power within the household. Authority in Cuban American families has changed in other ways too. Children have greater freedom in the United States than in Cuba. For example, in Cuba young people are traditionally accompanied by an adult chaperon when dating. This is less true in the United States where young people go out unaccompanied or accompanied by an older sibling.

### MARRIAGE AND CHILDBEARING

There are significant changes in patterns of marriage and childbearing within the U.S. Cuban community as Americans of Cuban descent raised in the United States have begun to depart from traditional Cuban familial patterns. Although 63 percent of foreign-born Cuban Americans over the age of 18 are married, only 38 percent of similarly aged U.S.-born Cubans are married. Also, almost 50 percent of U.S.-born Cuban Americans are single, compared with 10.7 percent of Cuban Americans born in Cuba. Cuban Americans born in the United States are also less likely to become parents than Cuban Americans born abroad. Finally, nearly 30 percent of native-born Cuban Americans who are married are married to Anglo-Americans, compared to 3.6 percent of Cuban-born Americans.

# RELIGION

Most Cubans living in Cuba identify themselves either as Roman Catholics or as nonreligious. The large number of nonreligious people is a consequence of the antireligious bias of the current socialist government in Cuba. The most recent statistics reflecting the religious affiliations of Cubans come from before the Castro Revolution. In 1954 more than 70 percent called themselves Roman Catholic, and six percent called themselves Protestant. There were also small numbers of *santeria* adherents and Jews at that time.

Recent figures demonstrate that Americans of Cuban descent overwhelmingly identify themselves as Roman Catholics. Almost 80 percent of those born in Cuba and 64 percent of those born in the United States are Catholic. Fourteen percent of Cuban migrants and ten percent of U.S.-born Cubans follow some form of Protestantism.

Fully one-quarter of native-born Cuban Americans say they either have no preference or have another religious affiliation.

Among Protestant Cubans in Florida, most belong to mainline Protestant denominations, the most common being Baptist, Methodist, Presbyterian, Episcopal, and Lutheran. However, there are increasing numbers of independent church members, including Pentecostals, Jehovah's Witnesses, and Seventh-Day Adventists. This growth parallels the growth of charismatic, fundamentalist, and independent churches throughout Latin America and in the United States. Jewish Cuban Americans, while few, are also notable. The Miami Jewish Federation reported in 1984 that there were 5,000 Jewish Cubans in the Miami area. The Miami Cuban Hebrew Congregation and Temple Moses are two of the largest Miami area Cuban synagogues.

The Cuban religious tradition that has received the greatest publicity in recent years is *santeria*. *Santeria* has been portrayed in movies and television since the mid-1980s as a form of Afro-Caribbean "black magic" similar to Haitian vodun, popularly known as "voodoo." These media portrayals, which have been largely negative and frequently inaccurate, have led to a public misunderstanding of the nature of *santeria*. The tradition is, like vodun, a synthesis of West African and Roman Catholic religious vocabularies, beliefs and practices. *Santeros*, or adherents of *santeria*, seek the guidance, protection, and intervention in their lives of *orishas*—divine personages who trace their lineage both to Yoruba West African gods and Roman Catholic saints. The practice of *santeria* involves healing rituals, spirit possession, and animal sacrifice. This last aspect of *santeria* practice caused controversy when leaders of a *santeria* church recently challenged a local Miami area law prohibiting animal sacrifice. The U.S. Supreme Court later struck down that law as unconstitutional. The same *santeria* church that challenged that law has incorporated itself and plans to establish a national church similar to other national religious organizations (Russell Miller, "A Leap of Faith," *New York Times*, 30 January 1994, p. 8).

# EMPLOYMENT AND ECONOMIC TRADITIONS

Most Cuban Americans, both foreign-born and U.S.-born, were employed in 1989 and 1990. Their rates of unemployment were lower than those of Puerto Ricans and Mexican Americans though somewhat higher than those of non-Hispanic white Americans. Almost 18 percent of Cuban Americans were professionals or managers. Although only 15 percent of Anglo-Americans were so employed, more than one-third of Cubans who were U.S. citizens were employed in technical, sales, or administrative support positions.

Cuban Americans are better off financially than other Hispanic Americans and nearly as well off as the average American. Their economic and employment profiles look very little like those of other recent Hispanic Caribbean immigrant groups (e.g., Puerto Ricans and Dominicans). In the Miami area, the center of the Cuban American community, Cuban Americans are prominent in virtually every profession. In 1984 Cuban Americans headed a third of the Miami area private companies that returned sales of at least 12.5 million. There are approximately 2,000 Cuban American medical doctors in the Miami area, and the Cuban Medical Association in Exile claims more than 3,000 members nationwide (Manuel Viamonte, with Adolfo Leyva, "The Contributions of Cuban Physicians to the State of Florida," in *Cuban Exiles in Florida: Their Presence and Contribution* [Miami: Research Institute for Cuban Studies, University of Miami, 1991], pp. 292-93).

Cubans are regarded as a successful migrant group. They are reputed to be excellent and dedicated entrepreneurs who came to the United States with nothing and built profitable industries. Scholars report that later immigrants have built upon the connections and resources of the Cuban community already here. And many of the wealthiest Cuban American business people built their businesses by catering to the Cuban community or by using their connections to or knowledge of it. Nonetheless, there are many exceptions to this portrait of Cuban Americans. More than 33 percent of Cuban American households earn less than $20,000 per year, and while this proportion is close to the proportion of Anglo-Americans in the same income category, it still represents an extraordinary number of Cuban Americans who have not yet achieved the "American Dream" of security and prosperity.

# POLITICS AND GOVERNMENT

Cuban Americans are reputed to be conservative politically and to vote overwhelmingly for the

Republican Party in elections. The validity of this reputation is suggested by the voting patterns of Cuban Americans in the 1992 election. Voting returns from Dade County, Florida, showed that 70 percent of Hispanic Americans there voted for then-President George Bush (Dario Moreno and Christopher L. Warren, "The Cuban Community in the 1992 Presidential Election," in *Harvard Journal of Hispanic Policy*, 1992, p. 29). Another survey indicated that, of Cuban Americans who voted in 1988, almost 78 percent voted for Republican candidates. That same survey showed that, in the 1988 elections, most Cuban Americans were registered to vote and voted. Thus, Cuban Americans seem to share many basic political values and a willingness to exercise their voting power to advance these values.

The driving ideological force behind most Cuban American political activity has been opposition to the Marxist regime in Cuba. Some of the most powerful Cuban American political organizations are dedicated to shaping U.S. policy toward Cuba and to ridding Cuba of Castro. Perhaps the most important of these organizations is the Cuban American National Foundation (CANF). Headed by Jorge Mas Canosa, a wealthy Miami businessman who participated in the 1961 Bay of Pigs invasion attempt, CANF squelched the Clinton administration's nomination of a Cuban American lawyer for Latin American undersecretary at the State Department because it judged him too sympathetic to the current Cuban regime. CANF also pushed for the passage of the 1992 Cuban Democracy Act, which imposed further restrictions on trade with Cuba. The Foundation has also supported U.S. anticommunist ventures elsewhere in the world. CANF is active in several areas: it sponsors research on Cuba and Cuban Americans; it raises money for political purposes; and it lobbies elected officials. Many regard the organization as representative of the Cuban American community. Some, however, have charged that the foundation tries to stifle dissent within the community.

The Cuban American community's political activities have been very successful in certain areas. It has elected Cuban Americans to Congress and have dominated the local political scene in the Miami area. Consequently, candidates have courted them as a group in the last two presidential elections. Change may lie in the community's political future, however. Mas Canosa, a staunch Republican, gave some support to Bill Clinton in the 1992 campaign, and CANF donated $275,000 to the Democrat's coffers. Voices within the community have raised questions about the conservatism that has guided Cuban Americans since the 1960s. Indeed, Bill Clinton received more Hispanic support in the Miami area than any of his predecessors (Michael Dukakis, Walter Mondale, and Jimmy Carter), suggesting that political preferences in the Cuban American community may be changing.

### RELATIONS WITH CUBA

Since the start of Cuban migration to the United States, Cuban Americans have been greatly concerned with the political status of Cuba and many are committed to Cuba's political transformation. In the United States, they have been staunchly conservative, supporting candidates who have taken a hard line against Cuba. However, Cuban Americans are becoming less committed to the struggle against Castro; or at least, the anti-Castro struggle is becoming less central to Cuban American identity. A principal challenge facing the Cuban American community in the years ahead is a reconsideration of what it means to be Cuban American. Perhaps that definition will become more elastic and accommodating, and the Cuban American community will embrace ever greater internal diversity. What had once seemed a politically united community is divided on issues like migration, Castro, and U.S. Republicanism. However, these internal divisions should not weaken the community, and may even strengthen the Cuban American community, making it more vital.

*

# INDIVIDUAL AND GROUP CONTRIBUTIONS

### ACADEMIA

Lydia Cabrera (1900-1991) was one of Cuba's most prominent scholars and writers. Born in Havana, she studied Afro-Cuban folklore and edited many collections of folk literature; she was also a prolific fiction writer. She lived in exile in Spain and Miami.

### BUSINESS

Born in Havana, Cuba, Roberto Goizueta (1931- ) is the chief-executive of Coca-Cola. Jorge Mas Canosa (1939- ) is a Miami businessman and chairman of the Cuban American National Foundation. Born in Santiago, Cuba, he is currently president of his own company, the Mas Group, and chair of the advisory board of Radio Marti, the U.S. government-sponsored radio station that broadcasts to Cuba.

### FILM, TELEVISION, AND THEATER

Desi Arnaz (1917-1986) was an actor and musician who is perhaps best remembered for his role in the popular 1950s TV series "I Love Lucy," which he helped create with his wife Lucille Ball. Cuban American dancer Fernando Bujones (1955- ) danced with the American Ballet Theatre from 1974 to 1985. Maria Conchita Alonso (1957- ), a singer and film actress, was born in Cuba; she has appeared in films such as *Moscow on the Hudson* and *House of the Spirits*, and was nominated for a Grammy Award for a solo album. Andy Garcia (1956- ), a television and film actor, was born in Cuba; he has starred in such films as *The Untouchables, Internal Affairs, Godfather III,* and *When a Man Loves a Woman,* and was nominated for an Oscar for best supporting actor for his role in *Godfather III.* Elizabeth Pena (1959- ), a television and movie actress, was born in New Jersey; she has appeared on stage and in such films as *Jacob's Ladder, Blue Steel, La Bamba,* and *The Waterdance,* as well as in the television series "Hill Street Blues" and "L.A. Law."

## LITERATURE

Cristina Garcia (1958- ), a journalist and a fiction writer, was born in Havana; she earned a B.A. from Barnard College and a master's degree from Johns Hopkins University; she served as a bureau chief and correspondent for *Time* magazine, and was a National Book Award finalist for her *Dreaming in Cuban*. Oscar Hijuelos (1951- ), a Cuban American born in New York City, won the Pulitzer Prize for fiction in 1990 for *The Mambo Kings Play Songs of Love*, a novel that was later made into a movie of the same name. One of the leading voices in contemporary American literature, he is the author of several novels and short stories that address his Cuban American heritage.

## MUSIC

The popular salsa musician Celia Cruz had a cameo role in the film *The Mambo Kings Play Songs of Love*. Gloria Estefan (1958- ), a Cuban-born singer/songwriter, enjoyed top-ten popularity during her stint with the Miami pop band Miami Sound Machine and during her solo career; she fronted Miami Sound Machine from 1975 to 1987; the song "Conga" propelled her and the band to national prominence.

## SPORTS

Baseball outfielder Tony Oliva (1940- ) played for Minnesota from 1962 to 1976. During that period, he won the American League batting tittle three times. Tony Perez (1942- ) was an infielder, mostly with the Cincinnati Reds, from 1964 to 1986. He was a seven-time National League All-Star. Cuban-born José Canseco (1964- ) began playing for Oakland as an outfielder in 1985. In 1986 he was proclaimed rookie of the year and in 1988 he became the first player to have 40 home runs and 40 stolen bases in one year.

## POLITICS

Lincoln Diaz-Balart (1954- ), a Florida Republican member of Congress since 1993, was born in Havana; he earned a law degree from Case Western Reserve University and served in the Florida State Senate. Robert Menendez (1954- ), the first Cuban American Democratic representative to the national legislature, was born in New York City and represents New Jersey in Congress; he was also a member of the New Jersey State Assembly and was mayor of Union City, New Jer-

sey, from 1986 to 1993. Ileana Ros-Lehtinen (1952- ), a Republican member of Congress from Florida, was born in Havana; first elected in 1989, she was the first Hispanic woman to serve in the U.S. Congress. She has also been a school principal and a Florida State Senator. Xavier Suarez (1949- ) was born in Las Villas, Cuba; he earned a law degree from Harvard before chairing Miami's Affirmative Action Commission; he serves as mayor of the City of Miami. Bob Martinez (1934- ) served as the first Hispanic governor of Florida from 1987 to 1991. In 1991 he was appointed director of the Office of National Drug Control Policy by President George Bush.

# MEDIA

## PRINT

### *Diario Las Americas.*

Though not precisely a Cuban American paper, it has been one of the principal forums for Cuban American expression since 1953, and has a readership of 70,000.

**Contact:** Mario Gonzalez, Editor.
**Address:** 2900 Northwest 39th Street, Miami, Florida 33142.
**Telephone:** (305) 633-3341.

### *El Nuevo Herald.*

The Spanish-language subsidiary of *The Miami Herald*, it was founded in 1976 and has a circulation of 120,000.

**Contact:** Carlos Verdecia, Editor.
**Address:** 1 Herald Place, Miami, Florida 33132-1693.

### *El Nuevo Patria.*

Originated in 1959, it has a circulation of 28,000.

**Contact:** Carlos Diaz-Lujan, Editor.
**Address:** 850 North Miami Avenue, No. 102, Miami, Florida 33136.
**Telephone:** (305) 530-8787.

### *Linden Lane Magazine.*

A literary magazine founded in 1982.

**Contact:** Belkis Cuza Male, Editor.
**Address:** P.O. Box 2384, Princeton, New Jersey 08543-2384.
**Telephone:** (609) 921-7943.

*Mariel.*

A literary magazine founded in 1986.

**Address:** P.O. Box 452304, Shenandoah Station, Miami, Florida 33245.

### RADIO

### WQBA-FM (107.5), AM (1140).

Programs news and talk on its AM station and contemporary music on its FM station.

**Contact:** Oscar Haza, AM News Director; or Maria Cristina Ruiz, FM Programming Director.
**Address:** 2828 Coral Way, Miami, Florida 33145.
**Telephone:** (305) 441-2073.

### WAQI-AM (710).

A Spanish-language news and talk station.

**Contact:** Tomas Regalado, News Director.
**Address:** 2690 Coral Way, Miami, Florida 33145.
**Telephone:** (305) 445-4040.

### WRHC-AM (1550).

Programs Spanish talk and news shows.

**Contact:** Lazaro Asencio, News Director.
**Address:** 330 Southwest 27th Avenue, Second Floor, Miami, Florida 33135.
**Telephone:** (305) 643-1121.

### TELEVISION

Two of the most prominent Spanish-language television stations serving the Cuban American population in the Miami area provide diverse programming created by Cuban American journalists and administrators.

### WSCV-Channel 51 (Telemundo).

**Contact:** Myrna Senoro, News Director.
**Address:** 2340 West Eighth Avenue, Hialeah, Florida 33010.
**Telephone:** (305) 884-0101.

### WLTV-Channel 23 (Univision).

**Contact:** Alina Falcon, News Director.
**Address:** 9405 Northwest 41st Street, Miami, Florida 33178.
**Telephone:** (305) 470-2323.

# ORGANIZATIONS AND ASSOCIATIONS

### Cuban American Committee.

Works to improve interaction between the U.S. and Cuba.

**Contact:** Alicia Torrez, Executive Director.
**Address:** 1601 Connecticut Avenue, Suite 500, Washington, D.C. 20009.
**Telephone:** (202) 667-6367.

### Cuban American Foundation.

Comprises Americans of Cuban descent and works for the restoration of democracy in Cuba.

**Contact:** Marilyn Kalusin, Executive Vice President.
**Address:** 7300 Northwest 35th Terrace, Suite 105, Miami, Florida 33122.
**Telephone:** (305) 477-1202.

### Cuban American Legal Defense and Education Fund.

Fights discrimination against Cuban Americans in education, employment, and housing and works to combat stereotypes of Cuban Americans.

**Contact:** Graciela Beecher, Chair.
**Address:** 2119 Webster Street, Ft. Wayne, Indiana 46802.
**Telephone:** (219) 745-5421.

### Cuban American National Council (CNC).

Aims to identify the socioeconomic needs of the Cuban population in the U.S. and to promote needed human services.

**Contact:** Guarione M. Diaz, President and Executive Director.
**Address:** 300 Southwest 12th Avenue, Third Floor, Miami, Florida 33130.
**Telephone:** (305) 642-3484.

### Cuban American National Foundation.

Spreads information about Cuba and works for the restoration of democracy there.

**Contact:** Tom Cox, Executive Director.
**Address:** 1000 Thomas Jefferson Street, Suite 505, Washington, D.C. 20007.
**Telephone:** (202) 265-2822.

### Cuban Medical Association in Exile.

This association supports and represents the interests of Cuban physicians working in the United States.

**Address:** 811 Ponce de Leon Boulevard, Coral Gables, Florida 33134.

**Telephone:** (305) 445-1429.

**Cuban Representation of Exiles.**

This organization raises funds to support, and coordinates efforts to initiate, the liberation of Cuba.

**Address:** 1784 West Flagler, Suite 21, Miami, Florida 33135.

**Telephone:** (305) 642-3256.

**National Association of Cuban American Women of the U.S.A.**

Addresses current issues, concerns, and problems affecting Hispanic and minority women.

**Contact: Dr. G. F. del Cueto Beecher, President.**

**Address:** 2119 South Webster, Fort Wayne, Indiana 46802.

**Telephone:** (202) 544-6246.

# MUSEUMS AND RESEARCH CENTERS

**Center for Cuban Studies (CCS).**

Organizes conferences and maintains a speakers' bureau and library.

**Contact:** Sandra Levinson, Executive Director.

**Address:** 124 West 23rd Street, New York, New York 10011.

**Telephone:** (212) 242-0559.

**Institute of Interamerican Studies, University of Miami, North-South Center.**

Sponsors a lecture series and publishes the *Journal of Interamerican Studies and World Affairs*.

**Contact:** Dr. Jaime Suchlicki, Executive Director.

**Address:** 1531 Brescia, Coral Gables, Florida 33124.

**Latin American and Caribbean Research Center, Florida International University.**

Besides supporting and encouraging research on Cuba, it also sponsors an annual teacher training workshop and a journalist workshop.

**Contact:** Dr. Mark B. Rosenberg, Director.

**Address:** University Park, DM 353, Miami, Florida 33199.

# SOURCES FOR ADDITIONAL STUDY

Boswell, Thomas D., and James R. Curtis. *The Cuban American Experience: Culture, Images, and Perspectives*. Totowa, New Jersey: Rowman and Allanheld, 1983.

de la Garza, Rodolfo O., Louis DeSipio, F. Chris Garcia, John Garcia, and Angelo Falcon. *Latino Voices: Mexican, Puerto Rican, and Cuban Perspectives on American Politics*. Boulder, Colorado: Westview Press, 1992.

Jorge, Antonio, Jaime Suchlicki, and Adolfo Leyva de Varona, Editors. *Cuban Exiles in Florida: Their Presence and Contribution*. Miami: Research Institute for Cuban Studies, University of Miami, 1991.

Morganthau, Tom. "How Can We Say No?" *Newsweek*, 5 September 1994, p. 29.

Peterson, Mark F., and Jaime Roquebert. "Success Patterns of Cuban American Enterprises: Implications for Entrepreneurial Communities," in *Human Relations* 46, 1993, p. 923.

Schwartz, Joe. "Hispanics in the Eighties," *American Demographics*, January 1988, p. 44.

Stone, Peter H. "Cuban Clout," *National Journal*, February 20, 1993, p. 449.

# CZECH

**by**
**Christine Molinari**

# AMERICANS

## OVERVIEW

Under Communist rule until 1989, the Czech Republic (Ceská Republika), which shared a common federal government with Slovakia until 1992, is now an independent state with democratic, multiparty institutions. Located in central Europe and occupying a territory of 78,864 square kilometers, it is bordered on the northwest and southwest by the Federal Republic of Germany, on the south by Austria, on the southeast by Slovakia, and on the north by Poland.

The Czech Republic has a population of 10,339,000. Of that number, 81.3 percent claim to be of Czech ethnic origin; 13.2 percent are Moravian; and the remaining 4.5 percent belong to other groups, notably Slovak, Polish, German, Silesian, Romany (Gypsy), Hungarian, or Ukrainian. The majority of Czechs (39.2 percent) are Roman Catholic, with a smaller number (4.1 percent) adhering to Protestant denominations. Czech is the official language. The capital city, Prague, preserves one of the oldest and richest architectural traditions in Europe, with many buildings, such as the Romanesque Church of St. George and the Gothic St. Vitus Cathedral, dating back to the Middle Ages. The flag of the Czech Republic, designed and first flown in New York to honor the visit of the World War I patriot Tomas G. Masaryk, consists of a blue triangle on a rectilinear background of white and red.

## HISTORY

The Czechs are a Slavic people, closely related to the Slovaks in speech and custom, but with a distinct history and national identity. The term "Czech" denotes the inhabitants of historic Bohemia, Moravia, and Silesia, while "Slovak" is reserved for those people who settled on the southern slopes of the Carpathian Mountains and who historically were dominated by the Hungarians.

Between the fifth and seventh centuries, the Slavic ancestors of the Czechs swept across the region that subsequently became known as Bohemia. Although for a time assimilated into the neighboring Moravian Empire, Bohemia emerged as the stronger power and absorbed Moravia in the eleventh century. Under its ruling dynasty, the Přemsylides, Bohemia became Christian in the ninth century and a member of the Holy Roman Empire in the eleventh century, led by the German kings but retaining its own monarchy. Two prominent rulers of the House of Přemsyl were Wenceslas the Holy (c. 907-929) and Otaker II (1253-78), who extended Bohemia's territorial borders to the Adriatic. After the decline of the Přemsylides, Bohemia was ruled for a time by the House of Luxembourg. The union of King John of Luxembourg with the Czech princess Elizabeth produced a son, Charles IV (1346-1378), who, as emperor of the Holy Roman Empire, established Bohemia as the center of the empire and made Prague its cultural center. He founded the University of Prague in 1348. In the fifteenth century the university became the center of a church reform movement led by Jan Hus (1369-1415), who was burned as a heretic in 1415. Divided between the followers of Hus—the Hussites—and the Catholics, the country was attacked by crusaders and plunged into turmoil.

Through a dynastic union with the Jagiello family in Poland, the kings of Bohemia eventually became linked to the House of the Austrian Habsburgs, which ruled there from 1526 to 1918. Favoring monarchical control over the Protestant Reformation, the Habsburgs opposed the Bohemian estates, a struggle that resulted in the defeat of the Bohemian Protestant insurgents at the Battle of the White Mountain in 1620. Many thousands of noblemen were expelled from the country, and Bohemia was completely absorbed into the Habsburg empire, with German becoming the primary language of instruction in the schools. However, a national awakening in the nineteenth century, culminating in the political protest movement of 1848, reestablished a sense of Czech identity.

After the Austrian declaration of war on Serbia and Russia in 1914, the Czechs and Slovaks, in a struggle to establish a common republic, joined the side of the Allies. Under the leadership of Masaryk, Eduard Beneš (1884-1948), and Milan Rastislav Stefánik, they were able to persuade the Allied governments to dissolve the Habsburg Empire. With the surrender of Austria on October 28, 1918, a revolutionary committee in Prague declared the establishment of the Czechoslovak Republic.

## MODERN ERA

The Czechoslovak Republic, a parliamentary democracy, was governed from 1918 to 1935 by Masaryk, who was succeeded by his pupil Benes. But after occupation by the invading forces of Adolph Hitler in 1939, the republic never completely regained autonomy. In the aftermath of World War II, the Soviet Union began to tighten its control over central Europe, and in February 1948 it staged a governmental crisis in Czechoslovakia that solidified Communist control over the Czech government. A trend toward democratic liberalization in the 1960s culminated in the events of the Prague Spring in 1968, when a cultural revolution headed by the reformer Alexander Dubček was suppressed by the military intervention of the Soviet Union. Under Soviet leader Mikhail Gorbachev, a further period of liberalization began in the 1980s that led to the downfall of Communism in 1989, when largely peaceful strikes and demonstrations in Prague swept aside the old regime and elevated dissident playwright Vaclav Havel to the presidency. After a brief coexistence in a federation with Slovakia, the Czech Republic became fully independent in 1992.

## THE FIRST CZECHS IN AMERICA

Prior to the nineteenth century, few Czechs had immigrated to the United States, and evidence of their presence during the colonial and revolutionary periods is sketchy. Hermann Augustine (1605-1686), one of the founders of the Virginia tobacco trade and compiler of the first map of Maryland and Virginia, is thought to be the first Czech immigrant. In 1638 Czech Protestant exiles, who had set sail for America in the service of the Swedish army, assisted in the building of Fort Christina on a tributary of the Delaware River.

The first major immigration wave occurred in 1848 when the Czech "Forty Eighters" fled to

These Czech emigrants are waving from the S.S. *President Harding,* which landed in New York City on May 25, 1935. They later joined relatives in Ohio.

the United States to escape political persecution by the Habsburgs. This year also saw the arrival of Vojta Náprstek, a radical free thinker and a vocal opponent of the Austrian government who, as part of a general amnesty extended to political refugees, returned in 1857 to his native land where he opened an American museum to acquaint European Czechs with America.

By the late 1850s there were an estimated 10,000 Czechs living in the United States. Chicago, tied to the West by rail and more readily accessible to the immigrants, became the most populous Czech settlement. By 1870, other cities with Czech concentrations included St. Louis, Cleveland, New York, and Milwaukee.

At the turn of the century, Czech immigrants were more likely to make the journey to the United States with their families. This marks a contrast with the immigration patterns of other ethnic groups, such as the Germans, English, Poles, and Slovaks, who tended to come over individually, as exhibited by the high ratio of male to female immigrants in the U.S. demographic statistics of the period. Moreover, it was not uncommon in large families for the head of the household to make more than one trip to the United States, bringing along one or more children each time. In addition, many of those who immigrated in the late nineteenth century were of Moravian ancestry. One important characteristic of this group was their staunch adherence to the Catholic faith at a time when membership among Czech Americans was declining and a distinct anti-Catholic spirit prevailed.

### RECENT IMMIGRATION

By the turn of the century, a widening gap between the first and second generations was already in evidence. In 1900 there were 199,939 American-born Czechs as opposed to 156,640 Czechs who had been born in Europe. The number of Czechs entering the country was further reduced by the temporary Emergency Quota Act, legislated by Congress in 1921, and the National Origins Act of 1924. Settlement patterns were also changing. Perhaps as a reflection of the growing trend toward urbanization in the United States, two-thirds of Czech Americans now lived in urban areas.

The next major immigration to the United States occurred during the dismemberment of Czechoslovakia, when approximately 20,000 fled to escape Nazi persecution. About one-quarter of these were professionals, including scholars and artists.

Between 1946 and 1975, 27,048 Czechs immigrated to the United States. With the Communist takeover in 1948, a large number of refugees, many of them students, teachers, journalists, and professional people, began pouring into the United States. Financial support for these refugees was provided by the American Fund for Czechoslovakia, established with the assistance of Eleanor Roosevelt. Subsequent immigration of refugees was supported by the Displaced Persons Act of 1948, which permitted the admission of refugees of Communist countries.

In 1968 the relaxed atmosphere in Czechoslovakia under the Dubček regime was conducive to the immigration of hundreds of refugees to the United States. Many of them were middle-aged, skilled, and educated; consequently, they had little difficulty finding employment. Although they made significant contributions to American society, this recent community of immigrants has been characterized more by its capacity for assimilation than by its ability to stimulate a resurgence in Czech American culture.

According to the 1990 U.S. Census, 1,296,000 Americans reported themselves to be of Czech ancestry, with 52 percent residing in the Midwest, 22 percent in the South, 16 percent in the West, and ten percent in the Northeast. The number of foreign-born Czechs in the United States has been steadily decreasing, and with the collapse of Communism in Eastern Europe, Czech immigration to the United States has significantly slowed.

### SETTLEMENT PATTERNS

The oldest significant Czech colony in the United States is in New York, which by 1854 had about 40 families. In Texas, the first Czech settlement was established at Catspring in 1847. In 1848 the Czechs settled alongside Germans, Irish, and Norwegians in Wisconsin, mainly in the counties of Adams, Kewaunee, Manitowok, Marathon, and Oconto, with the first major Czech farming town established at Caledonia, north of Racine. Other settlements followed in Iowa, Kansas, and Nebraska. The first Czech settlers to arrive in Chicago in 1852 settled in what is today the Lincoln Park area, assisting in local building by cutting trees and loading lumber. Minnesota Territory was populated by the first Czechs in 1855, while the Dakota Territory saw its first Czech settlements in 1870. Czech Americans also lent names to several U.S. towns and cities in which they settled, including New Prague and Litomysl in Minnesota, and Pilsens, Iowa, to name a few.

# ACCULTURATION AND ASSIMILATION

The Czechs were uniquely suited to assimilate into American society. Although they lacked direct experience with democratic institutions, the first generation—many of whom left their homeland to escape the oppression of the Austrian Habsburgs—nevertheless brought with them a love of liberty and social equality. A relatively large proportion of nineteenth-century Czech immigrants were literate, a result of the educational policies of the Austrian regime that made education compulsory to age fourteen throughout Bohemia and Moravia.

On arrival, many Czechs Americanized their last names. Some last names were translated into English (e.g., Jablečník became Appleton or Krejčí became Taylor), while others were changed to American-sounding equivalents (e.g., Červeny became Sweeney, and Vlk became Wolf).

The years between 1914 and 1941 marked a turning point for the Czech community in two important ways. First, as a result of World War I, the Czech community had become less isolated. A growing trend toward Americanization could be seen in the second and third generations, which were already moving out of the Czech communities and marrying into families with ethnic backgrounds that differed from their own. Second, perhaps partially in response to this trend, the Czech American community was becoming more protective of its traditions, emphasizing the study of Czech language and culture.

As relatively recent arrivals in the United States, the Czechs were forced to deal with prejudice as they established their homes in the midst of other immigrant communities. The self-sufficiency of Czech urban settlements, with their assemblage of Czech-owned banks, theaters, amusement halls, and shops, may have contributed to a perception of Czechs as "clannish." Despite the Czechs' insistence that they be referred to as "Czechs," many Americans persisted in calling them by the pejorative "Bohunks" or by the less pejorative, but equally unacceptable "Bohemians." When the Czechs began moving out of urban neighborhoods into the suburbs after World War II, their search for new homes was not always greeted with enthusiasm. Some efforts at community expansion were met with strong prejudice, as when a Czech real-estate developer attempting to purchase land in a Chicago suburb returned home to find a burning cross on his land.

To many early twentieth-century observers, the Czechs were a relatively "successful" immigrant community. They were perceived as law-abiding and family- and community-oriented, and because they were dedicated to becoming fully Americanized, their assimilation into American culture was relatively smooth and complete.

### TRADITIONS, CUSTOMS, AND BELIEFS

Community festivals such as polka celebrations and *houby* (mushroom) hunting contests continue to play a prominent role in Czech American culture. Some traditions celebrated in the early days of immigration were centered around the church. At box-supper church fund raisers, women baked their fanciest dinners and put them into boxes decorated with crepe paper, hearts, and ribbons to be auctioned off to the highest bidder.

Customs frequently were derived from old pagan traditions. On Palm Sunday, children created an effigy of *Smrt* ("death"), a lifesize straw doll that might be dressed in rags and have a necklace of eggs. The straw woman, who symbolized the end of winter, was then cast into a river as the children sang a welcome to the beginning of spring. On New Year's Eve, young men would gather in circles and fire their rifles into the air three times, a practice known as "shooting the witches."

Czech superstitions include the belief that a bird that flies into a house is an omen of death. A dream about a body of water could also mean that a death would occur. Pebbles were placed inside eggshell rattles made for children, to drive away evil spirits. A garnet that dimmed while worn on the body was thought be a sign of melancholy.

### PROVERBS

Czech proverbs express popular wisdom on themes such as the family, labor, fortune, and benevolence. Common proverbs among Czech Americans in the United States include: Father and mother have taught us how to speak, and the world how to keep quiet; Too much wisdom does not produce courage; A pocketful of right needs a pocketful of gold; The poor are heaven's messengers; He who has daughters has a family, and he who has sons has strangers; If there were no children, there would be no tears; All the rivers do what they can for the sea; Better a lie that heals than a truth that wounds; As long as the language lives, the nation is not dead.

### CUISINE

Czech American cooking boasts a range of savory meat dishes and rich, flavorful desserts that can be prepared with simple ingredients. Potatoes, mushrooms, and cabbage are the staples of Czech cooking. Czech cooks in Minnesota prepared a potato strudel; flour was added to mashed potatoes to form a stiff dough, which was then sprinkled with cinnamon and melted goat's milk butter and baked in the oven. Mushrooms picked during autumn field trips were brought home in bushels and set out in neat rows to dry. They were then turned into a sour mushroom soup which contained sauerkraut juice and fried onions. Sauerkraut, made from boiled cabbage, could also be mixed with pork and rice to make a cabbage roll.

The best-known Czech dessert is *koláče*, a sweet, squared-shaped dough bread filled with cheese; stewed prunes, apricots, or other fruit; or a mixture of poppy seed, custard pudding, and honey. Traditional at Christmas time was *vánočka*, a Christmas twist loaf flavored with mace, anise, and lemon and sprinkled with almonds and seedless raisins.

### TRADITIONAL COSTUMES

Czech American traditional costumes were worn as everyday apparel in some parts of the country until the twentieth century, when they were worn only on ceremonial occasions. Women's billowy skirts, multicolored or solid, were topped by gold-trimmed black vests and blouses with full puffed sleeves that might be trimmed in gold or lace and embroidered with a floral geometric motif. Women's bright caps were worn flat on the head and had flaps on either side. Men's trousers were

of a solid hue but often decorated according to individual taste. Men wore a black vest over a full embroidered shirt.

Bridal costumes were particularly ornate. The bride wore a crown covered with rosemary wreaths made by the groom; this crown might also be strewn with long, flowing ribbons. Her white vest was covered with light sea beads or with red, yellow, or green streamers. The groom wore a close-fitting blue or red vest and a plumed hat.

## CZECH DANCES AND SONGS

Most Americans are familiar with the *polka*, but few of them know that it is a Czech courtship dance. The polka originated in Prague in 1837. Derived from the Czech word for "half," it is danced with a half step to music written in two-quarter time, with the accent on the first three eighth notes. Another popular Czech dance is the *beseda*, a collection of mazurkas, polkas, and waltzes arranged according to local tradition and performed at festivals.

Czech melodies, strongly Western European in character, were usually composed to accompany dances. The *koledy*—ritual carols that were sung at Christmas, the New Year, and Easter—date back to the fourteenth and fifteenth centuries. A typical rustic band included a clarinet, violins, and the *dudy*, a shepherd's bagpipe that had a goat's head on top. Another traditional Czech instrument

played in the United States is the *tamburash*, a stringed instrument similar to the lute.

## HOLIDAYS CELEBRATED BY CZECH AMERICANS

For Czech Americans, Christmas began on December 24 with a Christmas dinner that was served as soon as the first stars came out. Before dining, it was customary to eat consecrated bread dipped in honey; extra place settings were made for deceased members of the family, who were said to be present in spirit. Christmas Day, December 25, was celebrated at church in an extended ceremony where the women and girls stood in front of the altar for the duration of the service. New Year's Eve (sometimes called St. Sylvester's) was celebrated in the streets, with revelers spending all night in song and dance. Also commemorated were Epiphany (January 6), to honor the journey of the Magi; St. Valentine's Day; and Whitsunday, in remembrance of the Ascension. On Sprinkling Day, the first Monday of Easter week, boys would go through the town spraying the girls with little homemade "spritzers" or, if lucky enough to abduct one of them, would throw her into the river; the girl was required to show her gratitude for this treatment by baking the boy a homecooked meal. Czechs also observe St. Joseph's Day (March 19), a day honoring their national heritage.

Mother's Day was more than just the promotional holiday it is today. It was celebrated either at church, if it fell on a Sunday, or at a separate festival, and was marked by the wearing of red and white carnations grown especially for the occasion, a red carnation signifying that one's mother was living, the white carnation that she was no longer living.

A festival celebrated by Czech Americans in Iowa and Minnesota is the Rogation Days—the Monday, Tuesday, and Wednesday before the Feast of the Ascension. After the mass, the congregation would follow the priest through the fields, reciting the Litany of the Saints and praying for a good harvest.

## HEALTH AND MENTAL HEALTH ISSUES

Czech immigrants sometimes turned to home remedies to cure common ailments. A wedding ring tied around the neck of a child was believed to cure fever. Poultices made of bread and milk were used to heal cuts. Concern about scoliosis prompted Czech women to ensure that their babies had adequate calcium, and at one time it was mandatory for newborns to have their hips examined to see whether they would develop the disease. Czech Americans have always been very diet conscious. When fruits were in scarce supply in the winter, they served rosehip tea as well as sauerkraut, a rich source of vitamin C.

Czech Americans believe that there is a strong connection between mental and physical well-being. Their commitment to physical fitness led to the establishment of the Sokol (Falcon) gymnastic organization, which strives to develop a person "perfect physically, spiritually, and morally, of a firm and noble character, whose word is irrevocable, like the law."

# LANGUAGE

Czech is a Slavic language with a declension system based on seven cases. The present orthographic system was introduced in the fourteenth century by the religious reformer Jan Hus, who instituted a system of diacritical markings to eliminate consonant clusters. Thus, the consonants "š," "č," "ř," "ž," "ň," "ť'" and "ď'" stand for "sh," "ch," "rzh," "zh," "ny," "ty," and "dy," respectively. Czech is a phonetic language; every sound is pronounced exactly as it is written, with the accent always on the first syllable.

Because of the differences between Czech and English—Czech is a Slavic language, while

English is Germanic—the acquisition of English as a second language presents a unique challenge to Czech Americans. The U.S. public school system and Czech American benevolent organizations have provided systematic English-language instruction to assist Czech American immigrants in learning English. Numerous American colleges and universities also teach the Czech language, including Stanford University, Yale University, the University of Chicago, the University of Michigan, and Harvard University.

## GREETINGS AND OTHER POPULAR EXPRESSIONS

Greetings and expressions include *dobré jitro*—good morning; *dobry den*—good afternoon; *dobrou noc*—good night; *nazdar*— hello; *s Bohem*—goodbye; *na shle-da-nou*—till we meet again; *prosím*—please; and *děkuji pěkne*—thank you very much. Other polite expressions are *Jak se máte?*—a polite form of "How are you?"), and *Jak se más* (the familiar form); *Jak se jmenujetě?*— What's your name? (polite form), and *Jak se jmenujes* (familiar form); *Těsší mne*—Nice to meet you; and *Dobré chutnání*—Enjoy your meal.

# FAMILY AND COMMUNITY DYNAMICS

The lifestyle of the nineteenth-century Czech immigrants was determined by the region and community in which they settled. Those who came to New York in the 1860s lived in sparsely furnished rented quarters, and it was not uncommon to find two families sharing the same small apartment. Immigrants who came to Chicago in the early 1850s had trouble settling permanently there: driven from place to place, they resided in makeshift housing until they could find permanent lodging. While the men loaded lumber to assist in the new building in the area, the women and children did the chores and went to the slaughterhouse where they could obtain the poorer cuts of meat, often purchased on a cooperative plan.

Hardships also were endured in rural communities. Dwellings in Nebraska, Kansas, and Iowa were simple sod houses—no more than underground burrows. Immigrants to rural Wisconsin built log cabins and lived off meager provisions, in some cases subsisting on cornbread and on the "coffee" that they made from ground roasted corn.

The accumulation of wealth by first-generation families made it easier for the second generation to purchase property. They began by building wood-frame homes and eventually saved enough money to build with brick. In the early twentieth century, an estimated 64 percent of Czech families living in Chicago owned their own dwellings, a high proportion for an immigrant community at that time. Children were sent to college and frequently went on to pursue professional vocations, such as law, education, or medicine.

Historically, the Czechs have been markedly active in community groups that have assisted immigrants and have promoted greater familiarity with Czech culture. In 1854 Czechs in Ripon, Wisconsin, formed the Czech-Slavonic Benevolent Society, the oldest continuous benevolent society in the United States, to provide insurance and aid to immigrants, as well as social services to the young, the elderly, and the poor. The Sokol (Falcon) gymnastic organization, established in St. Louis in 1865, continues to attract people of all ethnic backgrounds to its sponsored gymnastic meets.

Czech American women have played an exceptionally important role in community life, forming a number of active social and political organizations. By 1930 approximately one-third of the membership of Czech American benevolent societies consisted of women. The National Council of Women in Exile, convened in 1948, provided assistance to Czech refugees. Although Czech women were prominent in their communities, the women's suffrage movement in the early twentieth century was viewed with either polite tolerance or outright scorn and had difficulty winning acceptance among Czech Americans.

## WEDDINGS

Traditional Czech weddings were announced by the groom's attendants, who would go from house to house extending the invitations. Food and drink were prepared days in advance. On the day of the wedding, the couple, their parents, and the bridal party would gather for the wedding breakfast. The groom was not allowed to see the bride in her gown until 2:00 in the afternoon, when the sponsor would present the bride and the parents to the groom, admonishing him to be kind, gentle, and worthy, and telling the bride to be moral, obedient, and submissive. After the wedding ceremony, as the guests proceeded to the feast, friends of the couple would stand along the path and tie a ribbon from one side to the other, requesting a donation. This gift was later presented to the couple or was sometimes given to the musicians as a gratuity. At the wedding feast, the bridesmaids would present the guests with sprigs of rosemary, a symbol of fidelity, and a collection would be taken up for the birth of the first child.

## BAPTISMS

Preparation for the birth of a child began even before the wedding, when the bride-to-be would knit a set of white bonnets, boots, jackets, and shawls—sometimes enough for a family of six children—which were then carefully arranged in neat, ribbon-tied bundles and set aside until the arrival of the firstborn. Baptisms occurred a week after birth. They were followed by baptismal parties, where the godfather recited a customary toast and the godmother presented the gifts. Godparents adhered to their pledge to safeguard the child in the event of the parents' death. Six weeks after the baptism, the baby was taken to the church, where the religious officiant joined with the parents at the altar to say prayers of thanksgiving for the baby's arrival and health.

## FUNERALS

In the nineteenth and early twentieth centuries, vigils were still kept in the home, a custom brought over from Europe. The casket might be brought to the home by the undertaker, if the village were prosperous enough to have one; in some villages, the caskets were kept in the general store. Family members would take turns sitting by the side of the deceased, who was waked in the home for a period of days.

On the day of the funeral, the religious officiant came to pray over the coffin with the family. In some rural areas, as in central Texas, businesses might be closed one hour before a funeral. The town bells summoned the townsfolk to the service. After the procession to the cemetery, the family would gather around the grave and sing hymns while the earth was shoveled into the grave. In My Ántonia, a novel about the life of a Czech immigrant family on the Nebraska plain, Willa Cather related the superstition that a suicide could not be buried in the cemetery, but only at a crossroads. In populous areas, the Czechs sometimes established their own national cemeteries; Bohemian National Cemetery in Chicago is one example.

After the funeral, not just the surviving husband or wife, but the entire family would observe a period of mourning, usually for several months. Widows observed the custom of wearing black; other family members, children included, were expected to preserve an atmosphere of deep solemnity, neither laughing nor indulging in games or amusement.

## INTERACTIONS WITH OTHER ETHNIC MINORITIES

The earliest immigrants settled in proximity to ethnic groups for whom they had a strong affinity. In an important early study on Czech immigration, Thomas Čapek noted that many Czech settlements were located near German settlements (e.g., in St. Louis and Milwaukee) and observed that "the Čechs were drawn to the Germans by a similarity, if not identity, in customs and mode of life." By 1900, intermarriages with other nationalities were more common, most of them occurring with Germans, but also with Austrians, Hungarians, and Poles.

During World War II, Czech Americans participated in the national American Slav Congress, which convened in Detroit in 1940 and 1942. The war effort brought them closer to other Slavic ethnic groups, particularly to the Poles, an alliance that had its international parallel in a European concord of November 1940, when Czech and Polish refugees living in Europe agreed to establish friendly relations after the conclusion of the war.

# RELIGION

Many of the Czechs who immigrated to the United States were Roman Catholic when they arrived. But the Czech immigration movement is unique in that as many as 50 percent of the Czechs immigrants broke their religious ties when they arrived to the United States. Their arrival in this country gave many Czechs an opportunity to sever with the Roman Catholic Church, an institution that was closely associated with the oppressive Habsburg regime that they had left behind. Some of them were also influenced by movements that questioned all forms of religious dogma.

The first Roman Catholic church was established in St. Louis. In 1920, *Katolik*, the official almanac of the Czech Benedictines, listed as many as 338 Roman Catholic parishes and related organizations (Kenneth D. Miller, *The Czech-Slovaks in America* [New York: George H. Doran Company, 1922] p. 127). Traditionally, the Roman Catholic Church was strong in Texas, Wisconsin, Nebraska, and Minnesota and had a greater following in rural than urban areas. Among urban centers, Chicago and St. Louis had the strongest Czech Roman Catholic following. The Roman Catholic Church maintained its following by establishing churches or mission stations, founding benevolent chapters, publishing Catholic periodicals, and opening schools, which included a Czech college and seminary: Illinois Benedictine College (formerly St. Procopius), located in Lisle, Illinois.

In the early part of the twentieth century, approximately two percent of the Czechs living in the United States were Protestant. Unlike the Slovaks, who tended to adhere to the old-world Calvinist and Lutheran denominations, Czech Protestants tended to affiliate with American denominations. Common affiliations were Presbyterian, Methodist, the Bohemian Moravian Brethren, and Congregational. The predominantly high number of Presbyterian adherents was due both to the perceived similarities between the Presbyterian Church and the old-world Reformed Church and to early missionary efforts.

The Moravian Brethren, who settled in Bethlehem, Pennsylvania, were descendants of the followers of Jan Hus, the initiator of the reform movement. During the persecution of Protestants by the Habsburg dynasty in the seventeenth century, the Moravians, who had converted many German Waldensians living in Moravia, emigrated to Saxony. In time, members of this group, the majority of whom were German, made their way to Pennsylvania, where they purchased a large tract of land from William Penn. The Brethren established a number of schools; in keeping with the precepts of the educator Comenius, who believed in equal education for women, they founded the first American preparatory school for girls in 1742.

# EMPLOYMENT AND ECONOMIC TRADITIONS

Many of the Czechs who immigrated to the United States in the late 1850s were farmers or laborers. Of the three classes of Czech peasants who lived in Europe—the *sedlák*, or upper-class farmer, who owned 25-100 acres and a farmhouse; the chalupník, or cottager, who owned 5-25 acres and a small cottage; and the nadeníci, or day laborer, who dwelt on the nobleman's estate or on the farm of the sedlák and owned no property—Czech immigrants to the United States most frequently derived from the middle, or cottager, class. This was probably because the sedlák had little to gain by leaving behind his rich farmland, while the nadeníci did not have the means to emigrate.

Settlers who came to the Midwest lived in log cabins; those on the plains resided in dugouts and sod houses. With no tools at their disposal, farmers were constrained to hard manual labor. In the off-season they focused on survival, migrating to the cities or to the lumber and mining camps to find what work they could.

Occasionally, Czechs specializing in a certain industry—such as the cigar-making industry in New York—had emigrated from a particular region, in this case, Kutna Horá, which was pre-eminent in the cigar trade. In the 1870s, 95 percent of the Czechs in New York were employed in the cigar-making industry. Working conditions were harsh, and wages poor. Joseph Chada has noted that it took the average Czech industrial laborer ten years to attain the economic status of the average American laborer. Many women and children were also employed in these factories.

Urban-dwellers were eager to purchase property. Community-minded and thrifty, the Czechs created the building and loan association, an institution which became one of their most significant contributions to U.S. economic life. The building and loan association, introduced in Chicago in 1873, was a small cooperative agency to which shareholders made minimal weekly contributions with an aim toward eventually purchasing a home. So successful were these agencies that during the Great Depression, when other banks were failing, Czech building and loan associations posted a total of $32,000,000 in deposits, a substantial figure for that period.

By the first half of the twentieth century, Czech businesses were flourishing. Czech breweries (Pilsen and Budweiser are both derived from Czech place names) kept pace with the best German establishments. The Bulova watch company, a Czech enterprise, is an example of a successful, well-established Czech American business. And the character of the Czech labor force was changing as well. By the second generation, among Czech laborers, there was a greater preponderance of salesmen, machinists, and white-collar laborers.

# POLITICS AND GOVERNMENT

The Czechs were relatively slow to take part in U.S. political life. By the 1880s, however, Czechs were playing an increasingly active role in government, both at the state and local levels. Most Czechs voted the democratic ticket, in part because of the perception that the democrats favored labor. Some Czechs ran successfully for high public office. Charles Jonás served as senator of Wisconsin in 1883 and as governor of Wisconsin in 1890.

By the 1880s support had grown among Czech American labor for the socialist movement. But in the aftermath of the Haymarket Riot of 1886—a violent confrontation between labor protesters and police in Haymarket Square in Chicago, initially triggered by the crusade for the eight-hour work day—the movement was forced underground. With the emergence of the American Socialist Party, Czech Americans renewed their membership, many of them recruited by appeals in the ethnic press. By 1910, Czech American socialists numbered approximately 10,000. They reduced their activities during World War I, however, as the concerns of nationalism began to loom over those of internationalism. And as the lifestyle of second- and third-generation Czech Americans improved, they became less concerned with the labor situation. By the 1920s the movement had all but come to a standstill.

"The factories in the regions of Seventieth street, New York, are filled with Bohemian women and girls employed in the making of cigars. ... [They] dread going into the cigar factories. The hygiene is bad, the moral influences are not often the best, and the work is exhausting."

Jane E. Robbins, "The Bohemian Women in New York," cited in *The Czechs in America, 1633-1977*, edited by Vera Laska, (Dobbs Ferry, New York: Oceana Publications, 1978; p. 111).

The prospect of establishing Czech independence from Austria led Czech Americans fervently to support the Allied cause during World War I. Prior to the outbreak of the war, Czech Americans openly demonstrated their support for the Serbs and rallied for the establishment of an independent Czech homeland. The Czech National Alliance was established in Chicago to provide political and financial support to the Czech cause in Europe. Also characteristic of this period was the willingness of the Czech American community to band together with the Slovak American community to establish a common political framework that would unite Bohemia, Moravia, and Slovakia under a single government. On October 25, 1915, the Czechs and Slovaks met in Cleveland to agree on such a program. In April 1917, the Czechs succeeded in gaining the introduction of resolutions in Congress supporting the establishment of an independent European homeland.

Czech Americans also played an active role in supporting the cause of Czechoslovakia during World War II. During the Munich Crisis, Czechs organized a protest rally of 65,000 at Chicago Stadium. The war efforts of Czech Americans were coordinated primarily by the Czechoslovak National Council. In addition to publishing *News Flashes from Czechoslovakia*, with a circulation of 5,000-105,000, the council aided soldiers and refugees who participated in the Allied campaign. Czech Americans effectively used propaganda to direct world attention to the Nazi massacre of the village of Lidice.

After the Soviet takeover of Czechoslovakia, Czechs were admitted to the United States under the American Displaced Persons Act. The Czechoslovak National Council assisted these individuals in their struggle to regain their homeland, primarily through the publication of anti-Communist propaganda. In addition to requesting members of the Czech American community to sign affidavits that would assist refugees in obtaining shelter and employment, on June 3, 1949, the Council presented a memorandum to President Harry Truman, requesting that the United States push for United Nations-sponsored free elections in Czechoslovakia.

## MILITARY

Czech Americans on the whole were opposed to slavery and therefore supported the North during the U.S. Civil War, serving at Chancellorsville, Fredericksburg, and Bull Run. Many of those living in the Confederacy (primarily in Texas) avoided conscription into the Southern army at enormous cost to their lives, hiding in the woods or swamps or serving as drivers on perilous journeys to Mexico.

Czech Americans in the First World War either served in the Czechoslovak Army on the Western Front (if they were immigrants) or enlisted as draftees in the U.S. Army. Approximately 2,300 Czech immigrants served in European Czech contingents. During World War II Czech American loyalties were divided between providing active military service to their country and providing moral support to the Czech community in Europe, both duties which they admirably fulfilled. They also made a financial contribution to the war effort by investing substantially in war loans.

# INDIVIDUAL AND GROUP CONTRIBUTIONS

## ACADEMIA

Aleš Hrdlička (1869-1943), curator of the physical anthropology division at the Smithsonian Institution, developed the theory that Native Americans migrated to North America from Asia across the Bering land bridge and did extensive research on Neanderthal man. Jaroslav Pelikan (1923- ) is the author of the five-volume *The Christian Tradition*, an authoritative work on the history of Christian doctrine. Francis Dvorník (1893-1975) was a noted Byzantine scholar affiliated with the Dumbarton Oaks Center for Byzantine Studies. Managed by Harvard University, the center is located in Washington, D.C.

## FILM, TELEVISION, AND THEATER

Milos Forman (1932- ), who immigrated to the United States in 1969, won Academy Awards for best direction for *One Flew over the Cuckoo's Nest* (1975) and *Amadeus* (1984). Actress Kim Novak (1933), who made her screen debut in 1954, starred in such films as *Pal Joey* and *Boys Night Out*. Television and screen actor Tom Selleck (1945- ) is best known for his role in the television series "Magnum P.I." (1980-1988). John Kriza (1919-1975) was a ballet dancer who performed with the American Ballet Theater and the Chicago Opera Ballet.

## JOURNALISM

Charles Jonáš (1840-1896), who served in the Wisconsin state legislature, founded *Pokrok* (Progress), an anticlerical weekly. In 1869 Frank Kořízek (1820-1899) established the weekly

*Slowan Amerikánsky* in Iowa City. Lev J. Palda (1847-1912), the founder of Czech American socialism, established the first Czech social-democratic or socialist newspaper, *Národní noviny* (*National Newspaper*), in St. Louis, Missouri. Josephine Humpal-Zeman (1870-1906), an important figure in the women's suffrage movement, founded the *Ženské Listy* (*Woman's Gazette*).

## LITERATURE

René Wellek (1903- ), a member of the Prague Linguistic Circle, settled in the United States in 1939, where he established the field of comparative literature at Yale University. Bartos Bittner (1861-1912) was an essayist and political satirist. Paul Albieri (1861-1901) wrote stories of military life.

## MUSIC

The composer Antonin Dvořák (1842-1904) lived in the United States from 1892 to 1895, where he wrote the *New World Symphony*, a piece inspired by American folk motifs, particularly Native American rhythms and African-American melodies. Rafael Kubelík (1914- ), son of the violinist Jan Kubelík, studied music at the Prague Conservatory and conducted the Czech Philharmonic (1936-39, 1942-48) and the Chicago Symphony Orchestra (1950-53). In 1973-74 he was musical director of the Metropolitan Opera. Bohuslav Martinu (1890-1950), a contemporary composer whose music exhibits French and Czech influences, wrote the *Double Concerto* (1940), an expression of grief at the partition of Czechoslovakia. Jarmila Novotna Dauberk (1907-1993) was an opera singer with the Metropolitan Opera Company who studied under the renowned Czech opera singer Emmy Destinn; she also performed at the Salzburg Festival and the National Theater in Prague. Ardis Krainik (1929- ) is general director of the Lyric Opera in Chicago. The pianist Rudolf Firkusny (1912-1993) made his first appearance with the Czech Philharmonic in 1922 and played with numerous orchestras in the United States, including those in New York, Philadelphia, Boston, Chicago, and Detroit.

## PUBLIC LIFE

Ray Kroc (1902-1984), founder of McDonald's restaurants, was a pioneer in the establishment of the fast-food industry. Francis Korbel (1830-1920), who entered the United States in cognito to avoid an arrest warrant, purchased redwood forest in northern California and established the Korbel winery. Louis D. Brandeis (1856-1941), descended from a Bohemian Jewish family that immigrated to the United States in 1849, became the first Jewish Supreme Court Justice (1916-39). He helped to draft the Czechoslovak Declaration of Independence, issued in 1918. Anton Joseph Cermak (1873-1933), a mayor of Chicago who established Illinois as a stronghold of support for Franklin D. Roosevelt, was killed in Miami by an assassin intending to kill President Roosevelt. Eugene A. Cernan (1934- ) was copilot on the Gemini 9 mission, lunar module pilot of the Apollo 10 mission, and spacecraft commander of Apollo 17. James Lovell (1928- ) served on the Apollo 8 mission, the first manned flight around the moon.

## SCIENCE AND TECHNOLOGY

Biochemists Gerty Cori (1896-1957) and Carl Cori (1896-1984) won the 1946 Nobel Prize for physiology or medicine, for their studies on sugar metabolism. The physician Joseph Goldberger (1874-1929) discovered a cure for pellagra, which he correctly attributed to diet deficiency, against the prevailing view that it was due to infection. Frederick George Novy (1864-1957) made important contributions to the field of microbiology. Joseph Murgas (1864-1930) was a pioneer in wireless technology who, although never able to amass sufficient resources to carry out his research, shared research with Guglielmo Marconi that contributed to the invention and patenting of the device.

## SPORTS

George Halas (1895-1983) was founder and owner of the Chicago Bears football team. As head coach he led his team to seven championship seasons. Jack Root (1876-1963) was the first world champion lightweight boxer in 1903. Stan Musial (1920- ) was an outstanding baseball hitter and outfielder with the St. Louis Cardinals who won seven batting championships. Martina Navratilova (1956- ) has dominated women's tennis since the 1970s, winning the U.S. Open and Wimbledon numerous times and becoming only the fifth person in history to win the Grand Slam. Ivan Lendl (1960- ) has likewise dominated men's tennis, winning the U.S. Open in 1985 and the Australian Open in 1989. Stan Mikita (1940- )

was an outstanding hockey center with the Chicago Blackhawks, with 541 career goals.

## VISUAL ARTS

Andy Warhol (1927-87) was an artist and film-maker whose name is particularly associated with the Pop art movement. He is perhaps most famous for his paintings of mass-produced images of consumer goods, such as the Campbell's soup can. Alphonse Mucha (1860-1939) was an Art Nouveau decorative artist, recognized for his posters promoting the actress Sarah Bernhardt.

# MEDIA

### PRINT

#### Hlas Národa (Voice of the Nation).
Publishes items related to religious and political topics and events in both the United States and the Czech Republic.

**Contact:** Vojtech Vit, Editor.
**Address:** 2340 South 61st Avenue, Cicero, Illinois 60650-2608.
**Telephone:** (708) 656-1050.

#### Hlasatel.
Publishes general news items in both Czech and English.

**Contact:** Milo R. Tuma, Editor.
**Address:** 1545 West 18th Street, Chicago, Illinois 60608.
**Telephone:** (312) 226-3315.

#### Hospodar.
Prints general news, letters, and features on farm topics.

**Contact:** Jerome Kopecky, Editor.
**Address:** 214 West Oak, West, Texas 76691.
**Telephone:** (817) 826-5282.

### RADIO

#### KMIL-AM (1330).
Broadcasts eight hours weekly in Czech.

**Contact:** Joe Smitherman.
**Address:** Drawer 832, Cameron, Texas 76520.
**Telephone:** (817) 697-6633.

#### WCEV-AM (1450).
"Czechoslovak Sunday Radio Hour" in Chicago is a weekly one-hour broadcast in Czech.

**Contact:** Diana Migala.
**Address:** 5356 West Belmont Avenue, Chicago, Illinois 60641-4103.
**Telephone:** (312) 282-6700.

#### WRMR-AM (850).
"Czech Voice of Cleveland" broadcasts in Czech on Sunday, 11:00 to 12:00 p.m.

**Contact:** Jim Davis.
**Address:** 1 Radio Lane, Cleveland, Ohio 44114.
**Telephone:** (216) 696-0123.

# ORGANIZATIONS AND ASSOCIATIONS

**American Sokol Educational and Physical Culture Organization (ASEPCO).**
Founded in 1865, ASEPCO is a physical fitness organization for children and adults of all ages, with 8,500 adult members and 8,000 gymnasts. It sponsors gymnastic meets and competitions, clinics, workshops, and schools; conducts educational activities; and offers lectures and films.

**Contact:** Nancy Pajeau, Secretary.
**Address:** 6424 South Cermak Road, Berwyn, Illinois 60402.
**Telephone:** (312) 795-6671.

**Czech Catholic Union (CCU).**
Founded in 1879, the CSU is a Catholic fraternal benefit life insurance society that makes an annual donation to the Holy Family Cancer Home, bestows awards, participates in local civic and cultural events, and provides services for children.

**Contact:** Mary Ann Mahoney, Secretary-Treasurer.
**Address:** 5349 Dolloff Road, Cleveland, Ohio 44127.
**Telephone:** (216) 341-0444.

**Czechoslovak Genealogical Society (CGS).**
Founded in 1988, CGS supports research in Czechoslovakian culture and genealogy, hosts workshops, and maintains a research library.

**Contact:** Mark Bigaouette, President.
**Address:** P.O. Box 16225, St. Paul, Minnesota 55116.
**Telephone:** (612) 426-1222.

**Czechoslovak Society of America Fraternal Life (CSA).**
Founded in 1854, CSA is a fraternal benefit life insurance society that hosts contests, including a Miss National CSA competition; bestows awards;

and coordinates scholarship programs. The CSA also maintains a museum, biographical archives, and a library of Czech books and periodicals.

**Contact:** Vera A. Wilt, President.

**Address:** 2701 South Harlem Avenue, Berwyn, Illinois 60402.

**Telephone:** (708) 795-5800.

**Czechoslovak Society of the Arts and Sciences (CSAS).**
Founded in 1958, CSAS sponsors lectures, concerts, and exhibitions. It promotes the activities of professors, writers, artists, and scientists interested in Czech or Slovak concerns.

**Contact:** F. Marlow.

**Address:** 4064 Woodcliff Road, Sherman Oaks, California 91403.

**Telephone:** (818) 784-0970.

## MUSEUMS AND RESEARCH CENTERS

**Czechoslovak Heritage Museum and Library.**
Founded in 1854, the museum houses a large collection of books, periodicals, and historic documents, as well as costumes, dolls, and antiques.

**Contact:** Dagmar Bradac.

**Address:** 2701 South Harlem Avenue, Berwyn, Illinois 60402.

**Telephone:** (708) 795-5800.

**Moravian Historical Society.**
Hosts guided tours through its collection of art and artifacts on the history of the Moravian Church. The museum also exhibits paintings by John Valentine Haidt, as well as early musical instruments.

**Contact:** Rev. Charles Zichman, President.

**Address:** 214 East Center Street, Nazareth, Pennsylvania 18064.

**Telephone:** (215) 754-5070.

**National Czech and Slovak Museum and Library.**
Located in the restored home of a Czech immigrant, this museum preserves national costumes, as well as porcelain ethnic dolls, handwork, wood-carved items, paintings, prints, maps, and farm tools. There is also a library with reference materials and oral history videotapes.

**Contact:** Patty Hikiji, Executive Director.

**Address:** 10-16th Avenue, S.W., Cedar Rapids, Iowa 52404.

**Telephone:** (319) 362-7173.

**The Western Fraternal Life Association.**
Houses a library and archives and sponsors educational lectures on Czech language and culture.

**Contact:** Charles H. Vyskocil.

**Address:** 1900 First Avenue, N.E., Cedar Rapids, Iowa 52402.

**Wilber Czech Museum.**
Maintains a collection of dolls, dishes, murals, pictures, laces, costumes, and replicas of early homes and businesses.

**Contact:** Irma Ourecky.

**Address:** 102 West Third Street, Wilber, Nebraska 68465.

**Telephone:** (402) 821-2485.

## SOURCES FOR ADDITIONAL STUDY

Čapek, Thomas. *The Čechs (Bohemians) in America*. Boston and New York: Houghton Mifflin, 1920.

Cather, Willa. *My Ántonia*. Boston: Houghton Mifflin, 1918.

Chada, Joseph. *The Czechs in the United States*. Chicago: SVU Press, 1981.

Dvornik, Francis. *Czech Contributions to the Growth of the United States*. Washington, D.C., 1961.

Laska, Vera. *The Czechs in America, 1633-1977*. Dobbs Ferry, New York: Oceana Publications, 1978.

Miller, Kenneth D. *The Czech-Slovaks in America*. New York: George H. Doran Company, 1922.

Writers' Program of the Work Projects Administration in the State of Minnesota. *The Bohemian Flats*. St. Paul, Minnesota: Minnesota Historical Society Press, 1986.

The majority of the Danes who immigrated to the United States looked to agriculture for a livelihood.

# DANISH AMERICANS

by
**John Mark Nielsen**
**and Peter L. Petersen**

## OVERVIEW

Denmark is geographically the southernmost of the Nordic nations, which also include Finland, Iceland, Norway, and Sweden. Its land mass includes Jutland, a peninsula extending north from Germany, and more than 480 islands. Denmark consists of 16,630 square miles (43,094 sq. km.). With the exception of its 42-mile southern border with Germany, Denmark is surrounded by water. Sweden lies to the east across the Oresund, a narrow body of water that links the North and Baltic Seas; Norway lies to the north; and the North Sea to the west. Denmark has nearly 4,500 miles of coastline, and no part of the nation is more than 30 miles from the sea. Denmark also possesses Greenland, the world's largest island, and the Faeroe Islands, both of which are semiautonomous. Denmark means "field of the Danes." The Danish national flag, the oldest national banner in the world, is a white cross on a red field. Legend has it that the banner, called *Dannebrog,* descended from the heavens in the midst of a battle between the Danes and the Estonians on June 15, 1219.

Although the smallest of the Nordic countries in terms of land mass, Denmark, with 5.2 million people, is second in population after Sweden. The Danish people are among the most homogeneous in the world. Almost all Danes are of Nordic stock, and most are members of the Lutheran church. In 1990 foreigners made up less than 2.5 percent of the population. Because of the ancient practice called patronymics, whereby Peter, the son of Jens, became Peter Jensen, many Danes have the same surname. Although a government decree in 1856 ended patronymics, some 60 percent of all present day Danish names end in "sen" with Jensen and Nielsen being the most common. Approximately one out of every four Danes lives in the capital of Copenhagen (*København*) and its suburbs on the eastern island of Sealand. Other major cities include Århus, Odense, and Ålborg. The country's official language is Danish, but many Danes, especially the young, also speak English and German.

## HISTORY

It was not until the Viking Era of the ninth and tenth centuries that Danes, along with Swedes and Norwegians—collectively known as Norsemen or Vikings—had a significant impact upon world history. Sailing in their magnificent ships, Vikings traveled west to North America, south to the Mediterranean, and east to the Caspian Sea. They plundered, conquered, traded, and colonized. For a brief period in the eleventh century, a Danish king ruled England and Norway.

While Vikings roamed far and wide, those Danes who stayed at home cleared fields, built villages, and gradually created a nation. After a king with the colorful name of Harald Bluetooth (d. 985) was baptized in circa 965, Christianity began to spread across Denmark. Many Vikings encountered the religion on their voyages and were receptive to it. The current Queen of Denmark, Margrethe II (1940- ), traces her sovereignty back to Harald's father, Gorm the Old (d. 950), thus making Denmark one of the oldest monarchies in the world. Slowly the forces of Crown and Church helped make Denmark a major power in northern Europe. Under the leadership of Margrethe I (1353-1412), Denmark, Norway, and Sweden were joined in 1397 in the Kalmar Union. Eventually, the growth of nationalism led Sweden to abandon the union in 1523, but Norway and Denmark remained allied until 1814. Like much of Europe in the early sixteenth century, Denmark struggled with the religious and political issues set in motion by the Protestant Reformation. In 1536 King Christian III defeated the forces of Roman Catholicism, and Denmark embraced Lutheranism.

Growing rivalry with Sweden and various rulers along the north German coast created new problems for Denmark, but the greatest international disaster to befall the country came during the Napoleonic Wars (1804-1814) when an ill-fated alliance with France left the nation bankrupt and Norway lost to Sweden. New threats to Danish territory soon followed from the south. After decades of intrigue and diplomatic maneuvering, Denmark and Prussia went to war in 1864 over the status of the Danish-ruled Duchies of Schleswig and Holstein. The Prussians quickly gained the upper hand and Denmark was forced to surrender both Duchies. This meant a loss of about 40 percent of its territory and more than 30 percent of its population. This defeat reduced Denmark to the smallest size in its history and dashed any remaining dreams of international power.

The nineteenth century was also a time of great domestic change for Denmark. A liberal constitution, which took effect June 5, 1849, brought to an end centuries of absolute monarchy. Danes could now form political parties, elect representatives to a parliament, and were guaranteed freedom of religion, assembly, and speech. The country also underwent an economic revolution. Danish farmers found it difficult to compete with the low-priced grains offered in European markets by American and Russian exports and increasingly turned to dairy and pork production. The growth of industry attracted many job-hungry Danes to developing urban centers. But agricultural change and the rise of industrialism were not enough to stop rising discontent and eventually one out of every ten Danes felt compelled to emigrate; most traveled to the United States.

## MODERN ERA

Throughout the first half of the twentieth century Denmark pursued a policy of neutrality in international affairs. While this policy enabled the country to remain a non-belligerent in World War I (1914-1918), it did not prevent a German occupation during much of World War II (1939-1945). It was during this occupation that the Danish people won the admiration of much of the world by rescuing 7,200 of some 7,800 Danish Jews from Nazi forces in 1943. After World War II, Denmark moved away from neutrality, and in 1949, it joined with the United States, Canada, and nine other European nations to form the North Atlantic Treaty Organization (NATO), a pact aimed at containing the expansion of the

Soviet Union. In 1973 Denmark became the first and thus far the only Scandinavian country to join the European Economic Community (EEC).

The twentieth century also witnessed great economic and social change. Danish agriculture became more specialized and moved toward increased exports while industrial development transformed most urban areas. Denmark gradually became a prosperous nation, and with the development of a welfare system which provides education, health care, and social security from cradle to grave, its citizens now enjoy one of the highest living standards in the world. Since 1972, Queen Margrethe II has presided over this small, peaceful, and civilized land whose character is best symbolized by its most famous author, Hans Christian Andersen (1805-1875), a writer of fairy tales with profound psychological depths, and by one of its modern exports—the small, colorful plastic bricks called Lego.

## THE FIRST DANES IN AMERICA

Although it is clear that Vikings reached the coast of Newfoundland early in the eleventh century, it is impossible to determine if there were any Danes among these early voyagers. Jens Munk (1579-1628), a Danish explorer, reached North America in 1619, 12 years after the English first settled at Jamestown. The Danish king, Christian IV (1577-1648), had sent Munk to find a trade route to the Orient via the Northwest Passage. With two ships and 65 men, Munk reached Hudson Bay before winter halted his exploration. Near the mouth of the Churchill River, members of the expedition celebrated a traditional Danish Christmas—the first Lutheran Christmas service in North America. Another Danish explorer, Vitus Jonassen Bering (1681-1741), discovered in 1728 that a narrow body of water separated the North American and Asian continents. Today this strait is named the Bering Sea in his honor. Bering also was the first European to find Alaska in 1741.

Other Danes sought warmer climes. In 1666 the Danish West Indies Company took possession of the island of St. Thomas in the Caribbean. Eventually, Danes took control of nearby St. John (1717) and St. Croix (1733). Danish planters imported slaves from Africa; raised cotton, tobacco, and sugar on the islands; and engaged in a lively commerce with England's North American colonies and, later, the United States. In 1792, Denmark became the first country to abolish the slave trade in overseas possessions. Denmark sold the islands, today called the Virgin Islands, to the United States in 1917 for $25 million.

Individual Danish immigrants reached North America early in the seventeenth century. By the 1640s approximately 50 percent of the 1,000 people living in the Dutch colony of New Netherlands (later New York) were Danes. It has long been believed that Jonas Bronck—for whom the borough of the Bronx was named—was a Dane, but recent research suggests that he may have been a Swede. After 1750 several Danish families who were members of a religious denomination called the Moravian Brethren immigrated to Pennsylvania where they settled among German Moravians in the Bethlehem area.

Most Danish immigrants to North America from colonial times until 1850 were single men, and quickly blended into the general population. Rarely, with few exceptions, does the name of a Danish immigrant appear in the historical annals of this period. Hans Christian Febiger or Fibiger (1749-1796), often called "Old Denmark," was one of George Washington's most trusted officers during the American Revolution. Charles Zanco (1808-1836) gained a degree of immortality by dying at the Alamo in March 1836 during the struggle for Texan independence. A Danish flag stands today in one corner of the Alamo Chapel as a reminder of Zanco's sacrifice. Peter Lassen (1800-1859), a blacksmith from Copenhagen, led a group of adventurers from Missouri to California in 1839, establishing a trail soon to be followed by "forty-niners." Lassen is considered one of the most important of California's early settlers. Today a volcano in northern California, a California county, and a national park bear his name.

## SIGNIFICANT IMMIGRATION WAVES

Between 1820 and 1850, the number of Danes entering the United States averaged only about 60 each year. But soon this trickle became a steady stream. From 1820 to 1990, more than 375,000 Danes came to the United States, the vast majority arriving between 1860 and 1930. The peak year was 1882, when 11,618 Danes entered the country. Converts to the Church of Jesus Christ of Latter Day Saints (Mormons) represent the first significant wave of Danish immigrants to America. Mormon missionaries from Utah arrived in Denmark in 1850, only months after the Constitution of 1849 granted the Danish people religious freedom. Between 1849 and 1904, when Mormons stopped recruiting immigrants, some 17,000 Dan-

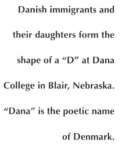

Danish immigrants and their daughters form the shape of a "D" at Dana College in Blair, Nebraska. "Dana" is the poetic name of Denmark.

ish converts and their children made the hazardous journey to the Mormon Zion in Utah, making Danes second only to British in number of foreigners recruited by the church to the state. Many of these Danes settled in the small farming communities of Sanpete and Sevier counties, south of Salt Lake City; today these counties rank second and fifth respectively among all the counties in the United States in terms of percent of Danish ancestry in their population.

Another source of sizable Danish emigration was the Schleswig area of Jutland. As noted earlier, Denmark had been forced to surrender Schleswig to Prussia in 1864. Some 150,000 residents of North Slesvig were thoroughly Danish and many bitterly resented their area's new status. After Wilhelm I, King of Prussia, became Emperor of Germany in 1871, the policy of Prussia in Schleswig was essentially that of Germany. This meant the abolition of the Danish language in the schools and the conscription of young Danish men for the German military. Between 1864 and 1920, when North Schleswig was returned to Denmark as a result of a plebiscite following Germany's defeat in World War I, some 50,000 North immigrated to the United States. Ironically, most of these Danes appear in census statistics as immigrants from Germany rather than Denmark.

Most Danes who immigrated to the United States after 1865 were motivated more by economic than religious or political motives. Like much of nineteenth-century Europe, Denmark experienced a steep rise in population. Better nutrition and medical care had produced a sharp decline in infant mortality, and Denmark's population rose from approximately 900,000 in 1800 to over 2,500,000 by 1910. Denmark's economy was unable to absorb much of this increase, and the result was the rise of restless and dissatisfied elements within the population. For these people, migration to a nearby city or to America appeared to offer the only chance for a better life. Many used the Homestead Act or other generous land policies to become farmers in the United States. The work of emigration agents, often employed by steamship companies and American railroads with land to sell, and a steady stream of American letters (some containing pre-paid tickets) from earlier immigrants, stimulated the exodus. During the 1870s almost half of all Danish immigrants to the United States traveled in family groups, but by the 1890s family immigration made up only 25 percent of the total. Perhaps more than ten percent of these later immigrants, largely single and male, would eventually return to Denmark.

### SETTLEMENT

By 1900 a Danish belt of settlement had spread from Wisconsin across northern Illinois and southern Minnesota and into Iowa, Nebraska, and South Dakota. The largest concentration of these settlers was in western Iowa where today the adjacent counties of Audubon and Shelby rank first and third respectively in the United States in percentage of population with Danish ancestry. Communities with Danish names—Viborg and Thisted in South Dakota; Dannebrog and Nysted, Nebraska; and Ringsted, Iowa—attest to the role of Danes in settling the Midwest.

As the midwestern and eastern Great Plains began to fill with settlers, a variety of immigrant leaders and organizations sought to establish Danish agricultural colonies elsewhere by arranging for land companies to restrict sales in specific tracts to Danes. The *Dansk Folkesamfund* (Danish Folk Society) sponsored several of these colonies, including settlements at Tyler, Minnesota, in 1886; Danevang, Texas, 1894; Askov, Minnesota, 1905; Dagmar, Montana, 1906; and Solvang, California, 1911. Similar colonies were established in Mississippi, North Dakota, Oregon, Washington, and Alberta, Canada. Most of these colonies were quite small and eventually blended into the surrounding community. An exception is Solvang, 45 miles north of Santa Barbara, which has become a major tourist attraction and bills itself today as "A Quaint Danish Village."

Not all Danish emigrants sought land; a significant minority settled in American cities. Chicago led the way in 1900 with over 11,000 Danish-born residents while New York counted 5,621. Omaha, Nebraska, and its neighboring city of Council Bluffs, Iowa, also had sizable Danish populations. Smaller concentrations of Danes could be found in Racine, Wisconsin (the city with the highest percentage of Danes among its population), the Twin Cities of Minneapolis and St. Paul, and in San Francisco. By 1930 political and economic reform in Denmark, along with the closing of the American farming frontier, brought this wave of immigration to an end.

The latest wave of immigrants came during the 1950s and the 1960s when some 25,000 Danes, mostly highly educated young professionals, moved to the United States where they settled in major cities, particularly New York, Chicago, Los Angeles, and San Francisco.

# ACCULTURATION AND ASSIMILATION

Historians agree that the Danes were among the most easily acculturated and assimilated of all American ethnic groups. A variety of studies indicate that in comparison to other immigrants Danes were more likely to speak English, become naturalized citizens, and marry outside their nationality. Several factors explain the relative ease of Danish assimilation. In comparison to people from many other countries, the number of Danish immigrants to the United States was quite small. In the census of 1990, 1,634,669 Americans listed Danish as their ancestry group. This represents only 0.7 percent of the total population of 248,709,873. Even in Iowa, which had more Danish American residents than any other state from 1890 to 1920, people born in Denmark made up little more than two percent of the total population. Danes were generally literate and understood the democratic process, were Protestant in their religion, and easily blended with the northern and western European majority. Because Danes offered little challenge to the more established Americans, they seldom encountered resistance.

## TRADITIONS, CUSTOMS, AND BELIEFS

Danes have a variety of traditions and customs that have been adapted or preserved in Danish American society. Everyday life customs include men and women shaking hands with everyone when entering or leaving a group. Danes and Danish Americans take great pleasure in setting a proper table and following a proper etiquette. This often means using fine Danish porcelain from one of the two famous Danish porcelain makers, Royal Copenhagen or Bing and Grøndahl. Being a guest requires that one bring flowers for the hostess. When a guest meets the host or hostess shortly after being entertained, the proper greeting is *Tak for sidst* ("tuck for seest")—Thanks for the last time.

Entertaining and tradition merge in the many customs surrounding Christmas. Because of the dark Scandinavian winter nights, Christmas, with its message of hope, light, and love, is especially welcomed and celebrated in Denmark. Danish Christmas customs are also celebrated by Danish Americans. December begins with baking. No home is without at least seven different kinds of Christmas cookies. These treats are shared with guests, and it is customary to take decorated plates of cookies to friends and relatives. This custom is the origin of the well known porcelain Danish Christmas plates that can be found in many homes.

These Danish Americans are sampling the food at a 1995 ethnic festival.

The celebration of Christmas culminates on Christmas Eve, a holiday traditionally shared with close family. Usually the family attends church in the late afternoon and then returns to a feast of roast goose and all the trimmings. A special dessert is prepared: *risengrød* ("reesingroidth"), a rice pudding in which one whole almond is placed. The person who discovers the almond will have good luck throughout the coming year. After dinner, the family sees the decorated Christmas tree for the first time. It is lit with candles and decorated with paper cuttings of angels, woven straw ornaments, heart-shaped baskets, and strings of Danish flags. In Danish American homes, the tree is decorated earlier and lit with electric lights. The family joins hands and dances around the tree, singing favorite carols. Gifts are exchanged, and the family enjoys coffee and cookies. To assure happiness and good fortune, before the family goes to bed it is important to take a bowl of porridge to the *nisse* ("nisa")—the mythical little people of Denmark who inhabit the lofts and attics of homes.

## CUISINE

Danes love to eat, and often do so six times a day. This includes morning and afternoon coffee and cookies and *natmad* ("nat-madth"), a snack eaten before going to bed. Many Danish Americans continue this routine. A Danish breakfast consists of an array of breads, cheeses, jellies and plenty of butter. This is often topped off with pastry that in no way resembles what has come to be known in America as a "Danish." This pastry is baked fresh, with flaky, golden brown crust, and rich fillings.

Lunch often includes open-faced sandwiches, or *smørrebrød* ("smoorbroidth"). These are artfully created to be both a feast for eye and palate. Combinations include: sliced, smoked beef, fried onions and a mayonnaise topping; carrots and peas mixed with mayonnaise topped with mushrooms; parboiled egg slices topped with anchovies or smoked eel; and a children's favorite, liverpaste and slices of pickled red beets, which is eaten like peanut butter and jelly sandwiches in the United

States. Beer, *sodavand* ("soda-van")—soda, and coffee are popular beverages.

The most important and time-consuming meal of the day is *middag* ("mid-da")—midday, though it is eaten in the evening. Danes linger for at least an hour over this meal. *Middag* might include stuffed pork, fish (often plaice or cod) or *frikadeller* ("fre-ka-della")—Danish meatballs of pork, beef, flour, and egg. The meal would also include *brunede kartofler* ("bru'-na-the-car-tof-ler")—potatoes browned in butter and sugar; *rød-kål* ("roidth-coal")—red cabbage; marinated fresh cucumbers; beer or a glass of red wine; and a dessert of cookies and fruit pudding, *rød grød med fløde*.

Other popular Danish dishes served in Danish American communities are: *rullepølse* ("rol'-la-poolsa")—spiced, pressed veal; *medisterpølse* ("ma-dis'-ta-poolsa")—pork sausage; *sød suppe* ("sooth soopa")—sweet soup made with fruit; *æbleskiver* ("able skeever")—Danish pancake balls; and *kringler* ("cringla")—almond filled pastry.

Danes and Danish Americans welcome any excuse for gathering together and eating. Formal dinners are held at Christmas, confirmations, wedding anniversaries and "round" birthdays—birthdays that can be divided by ten. Formal dinners normally last at least four to five hours and include toasts, light-hearted speeches, singing, and much conversation.

### TRADITIONAL COSTUMES

Danish peasant costumes were colorful, yet practical. A woman's costume consisted of headdress, scarf, outer bodice, knitted jacket, apron, shift, and leather shoes with clasps of silver or pewter. The scarf was often embroidered in bright colors of red and yellow on one side and with more somber, mourning colors on the other so that it could be reversed depending on the occasion. The cut and design of headdress, scarf, and apron reflected regional identities. Men wore hats or caps, a kirtle or knee-length coat, shirt, waistcoat, trousers, woolen stockings, and shoes or high boots. By the 1840s, these folk costumes of rural Denmark became a thing of the past. On special occasions in the Danish American community, some will dress in "traditional" costumes, but these often reflect a nostalgic recreation of the past rather than a true authenticity.

### DANISH DANCES AND SONGS

Danish folk dancing mirrors other northern European countries with both spirited and courtly dances. On the Faeroe Islands, a stately line dance dates back to the time of the Vikings. Singing is a part of many Danish and Danish American gatherings. Popular are songs from the period of Danish Romanticism (1814-1850), which celebrate former national greatness or the gently rolling Danish countryside. The two Danish national anthems capture these important themes: *"Kong Christian stod ved højen mast"* (King Christian Stood by Lofty Mast) by Johannes Ewald (1743-1781) and *"Der er et yndigt land"* (There is a Lovely Land) by Adam Oehlen-schlager (1779-1850).

### INTERACTIONS WITH OTHER ETHNIC MINORITIES

Danish immigrants often interacted first with other Scandinavians and with the German American community. Because they shared beliefs, attitudes, and general customs similar to the dominant culture in America, they made the transition to life in the United States without having to change many of their traditions.

# LANGUAGE

Danish is a North Germanic language closely related to Norwegian and Swedish, and is also related to the West Germanic languages, including German and English. Contemporary Danish has adopted many English and American words such as weekend, handicap, film, and hamburger. Danish, however, has also had an influence on English. When Danish Vikings settled in England in the ninth century and established the Danelaw, many of their words became a part of English. Examples are: by, fellow, hit, law, sister, take, thrive, and want. The English town of Rugby is Danish for "rye town," and the word "bylaw" means "town law." Modern Danish has three vowels not found in English: "æ" (pronounced as a drawn-out "ei" in eight); "ø" (pronounced as "oi" in coil or as "oo" in cool), and "å," formerly spelled "aa" (pronounced as "o" in or).

There is a popular saying among Danes that "Danish is not a language at all; it's a throat disease." Unlike the other Scandinavian languages, Danish makes use of the guttural "r" and the glottal stop, a sound produced by a momentary closure of the back of the throat followed by a quick release. The language is not as melodic as Norwegian or Swedish. Danes or Danish Americans challenge people who do not speak the language to say the name of a popular dessert, a fruit pudding made from raspberries or currants called, *rød grød med fløde* ("roidth groidth meth floodthe")—literally: red gruel with cream. The guttural "r"s and the "ø" sound, made deep in the back of the throat, make this phrase virtually impossible to say for someone who does not speak Danish.

Because the Danish language is similar to English in syntax and the use of regular and irregular verbs, Danish immigrants did not have as much difficulty learning English as many other immigrants did. Almost all Danish immigrants were literate when they arrived which also contributed to rapid linguistic assimilation.

## GREETINGS AND OTHER POPULAR EXPRESSIONS

Though Danes quickly acquired English, many phrases and expressions remain popular and are understood within the Danish American community. Common greetings and other expressions include: *goddag* ("go'·day") good day; *godmorgen* ("go'-mo'-ren")—good morning; *godaften* ("go'-af-ten")—good evening; *farvel* ("fa'-vel")—goodbye; *på gensyn* ("po gen-soon")—see you later; *værsgo* ("vairs-go")—please; or, would you be so kind!; *til lykke* ("til looka")—congratulations; *tak* ("tuck")—thanks; *mange tak* ("monga tuck") many thanks; *velkommen* ("vel-komin")—welcome; *glædelig jul* ("gla-le yool")—Merry Christmas; *godt nytår* ("got newt'-or")—Happy New Year. When toasting each other, the Danes, like other Scandinavians, use the word *skål* ("skoal") which literally means "bowl." One popular tradition suggests that the expression was used when Vikings celebrated victory by drinking from the skulls of their enemy. A more civilized Danish word for which there is no exact English equivalent is *hyggelig* ("hoo'-ga-le"). *Hyggelig* describes a warm, cozy environment in which friends eat, drink and converse.

# FAMILY AND COMMUNITY DYNAMICS

## EDUCATION

Education has played an important role in the Danish American community. A significant early influence were folk high schools. Inspired by the writings of Bishop Nicolai Frederik Severin Grundtvig (1783-1872)—a Danish poet, pastor and educator—these schools offered an education that sought to instill a love of learning in its students, though they offered no diplomas and no tests or grades were given. Folk schools were established in Elk Horn, Iowa (1878-1899); Ashland, Michigan (1882-1888); West Denmark, Wisconsin (1884); Nysted, Nebraska (1887-1934); Tyler, Minnesota (1888-1935); Kenmare, North Dakota (1902-1916); and Solvang, California (1910-1931). Because the educational philosophy differed from many American institutions, folk high schools eventually ceased to exist. Grundtvig's philosophy lives on in adult education programs and in the work of the Highlander Research and Education Center in Tennessee which played an important role in the civil rights movement of the 1950s and 1960s. Elderhostel, a popular program offering one-week educational experiences on college and university campuses for senior citizens, has roots in the folk high school experience and the thoughts of Grundtvig. Two liberal arts colleges founded by Danish Americans are Dana College in Blair, Nebraska, and Grand View College, in Des Moines, Iowa.

## HOLIDAYS CELEBRATED BY DANISH AMERICANS

In addition to Christmas, many Danish Americans celebrate *Grundlovsdag,* or Constitution Day on June 5, marking the date in 1849 when the modern Danish state was born. An unusual celebration held on the fourth of July in Denmark and attended by many Danish Americans is *Rebildfest.* It was begun by Danish Americans in 1912 and is billed as the largest celebration of American independence held outside the United States.

# RELIGION

With the exception of the Mormons in Utah and small numbers of Methodists, Baptists, and Seventh Day Adventists, most Danish immigrants were Lutheran and at least nominal members of the *Folkekirke,* the Danish National Church. After the adoption of the liberal constitution of 1849, the Church of Denmark was no longer a state church; however, it has always been state-supported. For many years there was no established Danish Lutheran organization in the United States, and those immigrants who were religiously inclined frequently worshiped with

Norwegian or Swedish Lutherans. Eventually two clergymen from Denmark and some laymen met in Neenah, Wisconsin, in 1872 and organized what became the Danish Evangelical Lutheran Church. The church faced many difficulties, including slow growth. By one estimate, only about one out of every ten Danish immigrants joined a Danish Lutheran church.

A second problem involved the development within the Danish National Church of a factionalism which immigrants carried to the United States. On one side were the followers of the aforementioned Grundtvig, the Danish educator and church leader, who emphasized the Apostle's Creed and the sacraments. These people were called Grundtvigians. Their opponents were identified as members of the Inner Mission. They stressed Biblical authority, repentance, and the development of a personal faith. Eventually the theological disputes within the Danish Church in the United States grew so serious that in 1892 it was forced to close its seminary at West Denmark, Wisconsin. Two years later many of the Inner Mission members left the church and formed their own organization. In 1896 they joined with another Inner Mission group that had started a small Danish Lutheran church headquartered at Blair, Nebraska, in 1884. This new body called itself the United Danish Evangelical Lutheran Church. The divisions among Danish Lutherans

"He who can do a little of everything gets along best. He must not shirk hard work, and he must not shirk being treated like a dog. He must be willing to be anyone's servant, just like any other newcomer here."

Peter Sørensen, in a letter dated April 14, 1885.

in the United States weakened the church's role as a rallying point, thus contributing to the immigrant's rapid assimilation.

The Danish Church (*Grundtvigian*) was more inclined than the United Danish Church to stress its immigrant heritage. It opened Grand View Seminary in Des Moines, Iowa. The seminary also offered non-theological courses and in 1938 it became an accredited junior college. Its seminary function ceased in 1959 and Grand View continues today as a four-year liberal arts college. The Danish Church and its 24,000 members joined with three non-Danish Lutheran bodies in 1962 to form the Lutheran Church in America.

The United Church (Inner Mission) operated Trinity Seminary (founded 1884) and Dana College on the same campus at Blair, Nebraska. In 1956 Trinity moved to Dubuque, Iowa, where four years later it merged with Wartburg Seminary. In 1976 Queen Margrethe II of Denmark came to Dana and gave the spring commencement address in recognition of the American Bicentennial. The 60,000-member United Church joined with German and Norwegian churches to form the American Lutheran Church in 1960.

In 1988, when the Lutheran Church in America and the American Lutheran Church merged to create the Evangelical Lutheran Church in America, the century-long organizational division among Danish Lutherans in the United States came to an end.

# EMPLOYMENT AND ECONOMIC TRADITIONS

The majority of the Danes who immigrated to the United States looked to agriculture for a livelihood. Many who were farm laborers in Denmark soon became landowners in the United States. Danish immigrants contributed to American agriculture, particularly dairying, in a variety of ways. Danes had experience with farmers' cooperatives and helped spread that concept in the United States. The first centrifugal cream separator in the United States was brought to Iowa by a Dane in 1882. Danes worked as buttermakers, served as government inspectors, and taught dairy courses at agricultural colleges.

Young, single women often took jobs as domestic servants, but few remained single very long as they were in demand as spouses. Men who sought non-farm work found it in construction, manufacturing, and various business enterprises. Other than small concentrations in a Danish owned *terra cotta* factory in Perth Amboy, New Jersey, and in several farm equipment manufacturing companies in Racine, Wisconsin, urban Danes were rarely identified with a specific occupation.

# POLITICS AND GOVERNMENT

Given their small numbers and widespread distribution across the United States, Danes have seldom been able to form any kind of voting bloc beyond local elections in a few rural areas. Nevertheless, politicians of Danish descent have served as governors of Iowa, Minnesota, Nebraska, and California. Several others have served in the United States Congress. In every election these Danish American politicians have had to depend upon non-Danish voters for a majority of their support. Danes have not displayed any collective allegiance to a particular political party.

Two events in the twentieth century involving Denmark have attracted significant political interest among Danish Americans. The first of these was the status of Schleswig after World War I. Danish Americans organized to lobby the administration of President Woodrow Wilson to ensure that a provision granting Schleswigers the right to vote on their status be included in any peace treaty with Germany. Accordingly, in February 1920, residents of North Schleswig voted to return to Denmark after 56 years of foreign rule. Danish Americans expressed considerable concern about the German occupation of Denmark during World War II. After the war many Americans sent relief parcels to their Danish relatives.

## MILITARY

By one estimate nearly 30,000 Danish Americans served in the armed forces of the United States during World War I. During World War II, 195 members of the United Danish Evangelical Lutheran Church died in the service of their country—a sizable number for a church that had less than 20,000 adult members and only 192 congregations. Generally, it appears that Danish Americans were no more or less willing to serve in the military than other Americans.

## RELATIONS WITH DENMARK

Relations between Denmark and the United States have been unusually cordial. In 1791 Denmark became the eighth nation to recognize the independence of the United States, and it has maintained uninterrupted diplomatic relations since 1801, longer than any other country. In 1916, by a margin of nearly two to one, Danes voted to approve sale of the Danish West Indies (the U.S. Virgin Islands) to the United States. During World War II the United States and Denmark signed a treaty authorizing the United States to build two air bases in Greenland. After the war the United States provided Denmark with $271 million in Marshall Plan aid. In 1949 both nations

joined the North Atlantic Treaty Organization (NATO) and thereafter jointly operated several military installations in Greenland.

# INDIVIDUAL AND GROUP CONTRIBUTIONS

### ACADEMIA

Peter Sørensen "P.S." Vig (1854-1929), church leader and teacher, wrote six books on the Danish immigrant experience and contributed to and edited the two-volume *Danske i Amerika* (*Danes in America*), published circa 1908. Marcus Lee Hansen (1892-1938), who studied under the renowned American historian Frederick Jackson Turner, is acclaimed as a scholar who early understood the importance of the immigrant experience in American life; his book, *The Atlantic Migration*, was awarded the Pulitzer Prize for history in 1941. The preeminent historian, Henry Steele Commager (1902- ) has written of the influence his maternal grandfather, the Danish born Adam Dan, had on him as a child; Dan was one of the founders of the Danish Lutheran Church in America and an important writer in the immigrant community. Alvin Harvey Hansen (1887-1975), a Harvard economist influenced by the economic theories of John Maynard Keynes, played a role in the formation of the Social Security System in 1935 and the Full Employment Act of 1946 that established the Council of Economic Advisors.

### FILM, TELEVISION, AND THEATER

The most famous Danish American entertainer is Victor Borge (1909- ). Fleeing Copenhagen after the Nazi occupation of Denmark in 1940, Borge came to New York; in 1941, a successful guest appearance on Bing Crosby's Kraft Music Hall radio program launched his career. Known as "The Clown Prince of the Piano," Borge has since entertained audiences with a unique blend of music and humor. Jean Hersholt (1886-1956) appeared in over 200 films between 1914 and 1955; he is best remembered for his creation in the 1930s of the popular radio character, "Dr. Christian." Another well-known actor of Danish descent is Buddy Ebsen (1908- ), who starred in three long-running television series, "Davy Crockett," "The Beverly Hillbillies," and "Barnaby Jones." More recently, Leslie Nielsen (1926- ), a descendant of Danish immigrants to Canada, has gained wide popularity in the *Naked Gun* films.

## JOURNALISM

Jacob A. Riis (1849-1914), the most important Danish American journalist, fought for the rights of the poor; his work, *How the Other Half Lives* (1890), described the impoverished conditions of laborers in New York City. Riis had a powerful ally in the person of President Teddy Roosevelt. Two important newspaper men in the Danish American community were Christian Rasmussen (1852-1926) and Sophus Neble (1862-1931). Rasmussen, a Republican, founded or purchased a number of papers in Minnesota, Wisconsin, and Illinois, and his printing company, headquartered in Minneapolis, published magazines and books as well. Neble's newspaper, *Den Danske Pioneer* (*The Danish Pioneer*), published in Omaha, championed the Democratic Party and had the largest circulation of any Danish American newspaper, reaching an estimated readership of 100,000.

## LITERATURE

A number of writers have described the Danish immigrant experience. Most, however, have written in Danish. Kristian Østergaard (1855-1931) wrote both poetry and fiction; his five novels combine fantastic tales of Indians, horse thieves, and bank robbers with accounts of Danish immigrants struggling to create Danish communities on the prairies. The poet, Anton Kvist (1878-1965), found audiences through the Danish American press; many of his poems were set to music and sung within Danish immigrant circles. Enok Mortensen (1902-1984) published several collections of stories, novels, and an important history, *The Danish Lutheran Church in America* (1967); his novel, *Den lange plovfure* (*The Long Plow Furrow*), published in Denmark in 1984, is the last novel by an immigrant who participated in the major wave of Danish immigration. The most important Danish American novelist writing in English was Sophus Keith Winther (1893-1983); three of his novels, *Take All to Nebraska* (1936), *Mortgage Your Heart* (1937), and *This Passion Never Dies* (1937), portray the struggles of the Grimsen family who arrives in Nebraska in the 1890s; the novels illustrate the darker side of the rural experience as fluctuating grain prices drive the family into bankruptcy. Julie Jensen McDonald's novel, *Amalie's Story* (1970), recounts the story of an immigrant woman whose poor parents are forced to give her up for adoption. Later she finds success as an immigrant in the Danish American community in Iowa.

## MUSIC AND DANCE

Lauritz Melchior (1890-1973), the great heroic tenor, won world-wide acclaim on European and American stages for his roles in the operas of Richard Wagner. Born in Copenhagen, Melchior began his career with the Metropolitan Opera in 1926; shortly before World War II, he immigrated to the United States with his German-born wife, settling in California where he starred in a number of films; he continued to perform with the Metropolitan Opera until his retirement in 1950. Peter Martin (1946- ) first appeared as a guest artist with the New York City Ballet; he became the company's principal dancer in 1970, and in 1983 he was named ballet master and co-director of the company. Libby Larsen (1950- ), an award-winning composer and the granddaughter of Danish immigrants, was named composer-in-residence with the Minnesota Orchestra in 1983.

## POLITICS AND GOVERNMENT

Several Danish Americans have served multiple terms in the United States Congress. For example, Ben Jensen (1892-1970) represented Iowa's Seventh District from 1938 to 1964 while voters in Minnesota's Second District sent Archer Nelsen (1904- ) to Congress for eight terms between 1958 and 1974. Lloyd Bentsen (1921- ), the grandson of a Danish immigrant to South Dakota, was elected to the House of Representatives from Texas in 1948; at the age of 27 he was then the youngest member of Congress. In 1970 Bentsen won election to the Senate, and in 1988, he was the vice-presidential candidate on the Democratic ticket headed by Michael Dukakis. President Bill Clinton appointed Bentsen as Secretary of the Treasury in 1992. Another high-profile member of the Clinton Cabinet, Attorney General Janet Reno (1938- ), is also of Danish descent; her father, Henry Reno, was an immigrant who changed his surname from Rasmussen to Reno after his arrival in the United States; prior to her appointment, Reno had served as State Attorney in Dade County, Florida. Although she never reached full Cabinet rank, Esther (Eggertsen) Peterson (1906- ), has held a variety of important governmental posts. An outspoken consumer advocate, Peterson was named by President John F. Kennedy as assistant Secretary of Labor and director of the Women's Bureau in the United States Department of Labor; in 1977 President Jimmy Carter appointed her as Special Assistant to the President for Consumer Affairs.

## SCIENCE AND TECHNOLOGY

Max Henius (1859-1935), a chemist, specialized in fermentation processes; proud of his Danish heritage, he was the prime mover in founding the Danes Worldwide Archives in Ålborg, Denmark, and establishing the Rebild Celebration of the Fourth of July in Denmark. Niels Ebbesen Hansen (1866-1950), a horticulturist, did pioneering work in the development of drought resistant strains of alfalfa. Peter L. Jensen (1886?-1961) and an American partner invented the loudspeaker system and founded the Magnavox Company; later, he established the Jensen Radio Manufacturing Company, which makes Jensen Speakers. A Danish born blacksmith who settled in Nebraska, William Petersen (1882-1962) invented and registered the name VISE-GRIP which is manufactured by the Petersen Manufacturing Company. William S. Knudsen (1879-1947), who was born in Copenhagen, became president of General Motors in 1937 and was chosen by President Franklin D. Roosevelt to lead the development of defense production programs during World War II.

## SPORTS

While there have been a number of Danish Americans of later generations who have played in professional sports, the most famous recent Danish American immigrant to play professionally is Morten Andersen (1960- ), the kicker for the New Orleans Saints. Born in Denmark, Andersen came to the United States at the age of 17 as a high school exchange student; before coming to this country, he had never kicked a football. After the 1993 NFL season, Andersen was already fifteenth among the NFL's all-time leading scorers.

## VISUAL ARTS

One of the most important monuments in the United States is Mount Rushmore National Memorial in South Dakota. The heads of presidents Washington, Jefferson, Lincoln and Theodore Roosevelt were sculpted by Gutzon Borglum (1867-1941), the son of Danish immigrants. Christian Guldager (1759-1826), the earliest of Danish American artists, painted George Washington's portrait in 1789. A Danish Mormon, Carl Christian Anton Christensen (1831-1912), created a panorama of works depicting important events in the history of the Mormon trek to Utah. Benedicte Wrensted (1859-1949), born in Hjørring, Denmark, photographed many Native Americans at her studio in Pocatello, Idaho. More recently, two artists, Olaf Seltzer (1877-1957) and Olaf Wieghorst (1899-1988) have been recognized for their depictions of the Old West. Marshall Fredericks (1908- ) is a contemporary, award-winning sculptor of Danish descent who has exhibited in the United States and Europe.

# MEDIA

## PRINT

A comprehensive study of the role of the press in Danish immigrant life is Marion Marzolf's book, *The Danish-Language Press in America*, published by the Arno Press of New York in 1979. Marzolf explores the history of the two existing Danish language newspapers *Bien* and *Den Danske Pioneer* as well as a number of others which have ceased publication, illustrating how stories and readership reflected an assimilating ethnic group.

### Bien (The Bee).

The only weekly Danish newspaper printed in the United States. Founded in 1882 in California, it continues to print stories in Danish and English on international news and news of Denmark and the United States. A special focus is on Danish American lodges and organizations on the west coast.

**Contact:** Poul Dalby Andersen, Editor.

**Address:** 1527 West Magnolia Boulevard, Burbank, California 91506.

**Telephone:** (818) 845-7300.

### Church and Life (originally Kirke og Folk).

A monthly publication by the Danish Interest Conference of the Evangelical Lutheran Church in America. Articles often reflect the influence of the Danish church reformer, N.F.S. Grundtvig, and are published in both English and Danish.

**Contact:** Thorvald Hansen, Editor.

**Address:** 1529 Milton, Des Moines, Iowa 540316.

**Telephone:** (515) 262-5274.

*Den Danske Pioneer (The Danish Pioneer).*
The oldest Danish newspaper published in the United States, it was founded in Omaha, Nebraska, in 1872. Because of its liberal agenda it was banned in Denmark between 1887 and 1898. In 1958, the paper was sold and moved to Illinois where today it is published bi-weekly and carries news of the Danish American community and stories of interest from contemporary Denmark in both Danish and English.

**Contact:** Chris Steffensen, Editor.
**Address:** Bertlesen Publishing Company, Glen Lake Road, Hoffman Estates, Illinois 60195.
**Telephone:** (708) 882-2552.

### RADIO AND TELEVISION

While there has been no radio or television program devoted specifically to a Danish speaking audience, individuals of Danish descent have made important contributions to American media. The A. C. Nielsen Company, founded in 1923 by Arthur C. Nielsen, Sr., pioneered media market listener surveys for radio and television. The Nielsen Ratings have become an integral part of programming decisions both by the networks and cable companies. Bill and Scott Rasmussen, a father and son team with roots in Chicago's Danish American community, founded the Entertainment and Sports Programming Network (ESPN) in 1979.

# ORGANIZATIONS AND ASSOCIATIONS

**Danish American Chamber of Commerce and Danish American Society (DACC and DAS).**
The DACC is an organization of over 200 business leaders, firms, and institutions that promotes commercial relations between the United States and Denmark and seeks to avoid duplication of governmental activities. The DAS is an affiliated society sponsoring cultural events. Separate organizations of the Chamber of Commerce exist in Chicago and Los Angeles.

**Contact:** Werner Valeur-Jensen, DACC Board Chairman; or Mrs. Neel Halpern, DAS President.
**Address:** 1 Dag Hammarskjold Plaza, 885 Second Avenue, 18th Floor, New York, New York 10017.
**Telephone:** (212) 980-6240.

**Danish American Heritage Society (DAHS).**
Founded in 1977, the DAHS has a membership of 650 individuals across the United States. Its purpose is to promote an interest in Danish culture, heritage, and language and to encourage research in the life, culture, and history of Danish Americans. The society publishes a journal, *The Bridge,* and a newsletter.

**Contact:** Gerald Rasmussen, President.
**Address:** 29681 Dane Lane, Junction City, Oregon 97448.
**Telephone:** (503) 998-8562.

**Danish Brotherhood in America (DBA).**
Founded in 1882 in Omaha, Nebraska, the DBA is a fraternal association of 8,000 members, featuring social activities celebrating the Danish American heritage and offering life and health insurance to members. In 1995 the DBA is proposing a merger of its insurance functions with a larger fraternal benefit society while retaining its name and independent lodge structure.

**Contact:** Jerome Christensen.
**Address:** 1323 Wright Street, Blair, Nebraska 68008.
**Telephone:** (402) 426-5894.

**Danish Interest Conference of the Evangelical Lutheran Church of America (DIC).**
Founded in 1962 when the Danish Evangelical Lutheran in America merged with several other Lutheran synods, the DIC seeks to preserve Danish contributions to the Lutheran heritage. A meeting is held annually at the Danebod Folk High School in Tyler, Minnesota.

**Contact:** Roland Jespersen, President.
**Address:** 116 North Seventh Street, Box 376, Eldridge, Iowa 52748.
**Telephone:** (319) 285-4693.

**Danish Sisterhood in America (DSA).**
Founded in 1883 at a time when the Danish Brotherhood did not accept women as members, the DSA continues as an active social organization of 3,200 members, celebrating Danish heritage and supporting education through scholarships.

**Contact:** Karen Favero, National Secretary.
**Address:** 3002 192nd Street, N.E., Seattle, Washington 98155.
**Telephone:** (206) 364-0994.

**Rebild National Park Society, Inc.**

Founded in 1912, this society of over 1,000 members supports what is acclaimed as the largest observation of American independence outside the United States. The festival is held annually on the Fourth of July in Rebild National Park, just outside the city of Ålborg, Denmark.

**Contact:** Erik Meyer, Corporate Secretary.

**Address:** 1788 North Fern Street, Orange, California 92667.

**Telephone:** (714) 637-8407.

**Society for the Advancement of Scandinavian Studies.**

With more than 600 members in the academic communities in the United States and Scandinavia, it publishes the respected journal, *Scandinavian Studies*.

**Contact:** Dr. Terje Leiren.

**Address:** Department of Scandinavian Studies, DL-20, University of Washington, Seattle, Washington 98195.

**Telephone:** (206) 543-1510.

# MUSEUMS AND RESEARCH CENTERS

**Danes Worldwide Archives.**

Founded by Danish Americans in 1932 to record the history of Danes who immigrated to other countries, the archives contain letters, manuscripts, diaries, biographies, photographs, tape-recorded interviews, and over 10,000 titles related to Danish emigration. Also available are the emigration lists compiled by the Copenhagen police between 1860 and 1940 and microfilms of church records from most Danish parishes. There is a charge of $25 (U.S.) for requests received by mail or telephone.

**Contact:** Birgit Flemming Larsen.

**Address:** Ved Vor Frue Kirke, P.O. Box 1731, DK-9100 Ålborg, Denmark.

**Telephone:** 45 98 12 57 93.

**Danish Immigrant Archives-Dana College.**

Contains an extensive collection of books in Danish published in the United States, as well as periodicals, newspapers, journals, and letters relating to Danish immigration. The religious emphasis is on Danish Lutherans influenced by the more pietistic Inner Mission movement. Special holdings include the Lauritz Melchior, Sophus Keith Winther, and Hansen-Mengers Collections. Genealogy is not a focus of the archives.

**Contact:** Sharon Jensen.

**Address:** 2848 College Drive, Blair, Nebraska 68008-1099.

**Telephone:** (402) 426-7300.

**Danish Immigrant Archives-Grand View College.**

A repository for books, periodicals, letters, documents, and memoirs relating to Danish immigration. The archives' religious emphasis is on those Danish Lutherans influenced by N.F.S. Grundtvig, and the archives include a special N.F.S. Grundtvig Studies Collection. Genealogy is not a focus of the archives.

**Contact:** Rudolph Jensen.

**Address:** 1351 Grandview Avenue, Des Moines, Iowa 50316-1599.

**Telephone:** (515) 263-2800.

**Danish Immigrant Museum.**

Tells the story of the life and culture of Danish immigrants with displays of house furnishings, costumes, tools, church furniture, photographs, and many other items. The collection contains over 8,000 artifacts and includes a family history room for researching genealogy. Situated in Elk Horn, Iowa, the museum is located in an area settled by Danish immigrants during the late nineteenth century.

**Contact:** Director.

**Address:** Box 178, Elk Horn, Iowa 51531.

**Telephone:** (712) 764-7001.

# SOURCES FOR ADDITIONAL STUDY

*Danish Emigration to the U.S.A.*, edited by Birgit Flemming Larsen and Henning Bender. Ålborg, Denmark: Danes Worldwide Archives, 1992.

Hale, Frederick Hale. *Danes in North America*. Seattle: University of Washington Press, 1984.

Hvidt, Kristian. *Flight to America*. New York: Academic Press, 1975.

———. *Danes Go West*. Skørping, Denmark: Rebild National Park Society, Inc., 1976.

MacHaffie, Ingeborg, and Margaret Nielsen. *Of Danish Ways*. Minneapolis: Dillon Press, Inc., 1976.

Mussari, Mark. *The Danish Americans*. New York: Chelsea House Publishers, 1988.

Nielsen, George. *The Danish Americans*. Boston: G. K. Hall & Co., 1981.

Petersen, Peter L. *The Danes in America*. Minneapolis: Lerner Publication Company, 1987.

Riis, Jacob A. *The Making of an American*. New York: Grosset & Dunlap, 1901.

Stilling, Niels Peter, and Anne Lisbeth Olsen. *A New Life*. Ålborg, Denmark: Danes Worldwide Archives, 1994.

# DOMINICAN AMERICANS

by
Sean T. Buffington

Dominican
Americans are one
of the newer
national-cultural
communities in the
United States.

## OVERVIEW

The Dominican Republic shares the island of
Hispaniola with the nation of Haiti. Hispaniola
defines the northern rim of the Caribbean Sea
along with Cuba, which lies just to the west, and
Puerto Rico, Hispaniola's eastern neighbor. The
Dominican Republic occupies the western half of
the island.

The Dominican Republic today is a nation of
approximately 5.5 million people. Its significant
sources of revenue are the tourist industry, remittances sent home by Dominicans abroad, and the
sugar industry. Dominicans speak Spanish as a
first language although increasing numbers also
speak English. The Dominican Republic has traditionally and predominantly been a Roman
Catholic nation. However, there are notable and
historic Protestant, Jewish, and Afro-Christian
religious communities as well. While the Trujillo
government and the Balaguer administration to a
lesser degree have emphasized the Spanish ancestry of Dominicans, the population is diverse in its
origins. African-descended slaves, Spanish colonizers, and Haitian invaders and later laborers, as
well as other Europeans, Middle Eastern and Chinese merchants, and immigrants from neighboring Caribbean islands have all contributed to the
diverse population and culture of the Dominican
Republic.

## HISTORY

The nation now called the Dominican Republic was originally colonized by the Spanish in the late fifteenth and early sixteenth centuries. The previous inhabitants, Taino indigenes, were destroyed by diseases, weapons, and enslavement brought by the Spanish. Like the other Spanish Caribbean colonies, Santo Domingo, as it was called then, was peopled sparsely by Spanish, Spanish creoles (people of Spanish descent born in the Americas), and relatively small numbers of African and African-descended slaves. Isolated from a distant Spanish monarch, underpopulated, and with little investment from the outside, Santo Domingo languished in comparison to her French and British West Indian neighbors. Barbados in the seventeenth century and Saint Dominque (now called Haiti) in the eighteenth century became centers of sugar production and generated great wealth for the British and French planters who worked those lands. It was not until the nineteenth century that Santo Domingo became a central presence in the Western Hemisphere.

In 1822, the newly founded nation of Haiti, which had won its independence from France at the turn of the century and become the first black sovereign nation in the Americas, invaded and occupied the Spanish half of Hispaniola. For the remainder of the century, Santo Domingo passed into and out of sovereignty, winning independence from Haiti in 1844 and then voluntarily resubmitting to Spanish colonial rule in 1861. After regaining independence after several years of colonial rule, the Dominican government discussed the possibilities of annexation with U.S. officials.

At the same time that the government was discussing new political directions, the economy began to move in new directions too. After centuries of slow progress, the Dominican economy experienced new growth: Cuban immigrants, along with others from North America and Europe, brought new capital into the country. They invested heavily in the sugar industry, which soon became the most important productive industry in the nation.

The Dominican Republic's claims to sovereignty, however, did not go unchallenged in the twentieth century. Twice, the United States invaded and occupied the Caribbean island, first from 1916 to 1924, and again in 1965. The second invasion played a more significant role in launching the most recent migration of Dominicans to the United States. The assassination of military ruler Rafael Trujillo in 1961 marked the start of a period of political uncertainty in the Dominican Republic that was ended when U.S. paratroops intervened by order of President Lyndon Johnson. The U.S. troops brought to a close a civil war between supporters of democratically elected President Juan Bosch and his right-wing opponents in the Dominican military and oversaw the election of former Trujillo aide Joaquin Balaguer to the presidency.

That civil war and subsequent intervention by the United States on the side of the conservative military led to an outflux of Bosch supporters and other like-minded political activists from the Dominican Republic in the 1960s (Luis E. Guarnizo, "Los Dominicanyorks: The Making of a Binational Society," Annals of the American Academy of Political and Social Science, Volume 533, 1994, p. 71). Those emigrants, most of whom came to the United States, were the first of many Dominicans who have come in ever-increasing numbers in the past several decades.

## IMMIGRATION

In the 1980s, immigration to the United States from the Dominican Republic rose to unprecedented levels. The number of Dominicans legally entering the United States between 1981 and 1990 was far greater than the number of Cubans: indeed, more Dominicans entered the United States in the last decade than any other Western Hemisphere national group except migrants from Mexico (Ruben G. Rumbaut, "The Americans: Latin American and Caribbean Peoples in the United States" in Americas: New Interpretive Essays, p. 288).

Despite these numbers, however, Dominican immigrants have been relatively unstudied. Systematic research on the Dominican population in the United States is scarce, and newspaper and magazine coverage is sparse compared to the coverage received by other Caribbean immigrant groups (e.g., Cubans and Haitians). Those studies that do exist rely on data from the 1980 census or from studies conducted in the early or mid-1980s. Thus, up-to-date, accurate, and complete information on Dominicans in the United States is difficult to find. As the raw data from the 1990 census is analyzed and studied, more work on this important immigrant group will result.

Most Dominicans in the United States arrived after 1960. Of the 169,147 Dominican-born persons resident in the United States at the time of the 1980 census, only 6.1 percent had come to the United States before 1960. More than a third came during the decade of political instability in the Dominican Republic—the 1960s—and the remaining 56 percent arrived in the 1970s. During the 1980s, however, Dominican immigration soared. In those ten years, more than 250,000 Dominicans were legally admitted to the United States. The number of new immigrants in that ten-year period was 50 percent greater than the entire Dominican-born population of the United States at the start of the decade. The 1990 U.S. Census reported that of the 506,000 persons of Dominican descent in the United States, the vast majority were Dominican-born. Thus the Dominican American community is primarily an immigrant community and, indeed, a community of recent immigrants.

According to the recent census, most Dominicans have settled in the Northeast (86.3 percent). Though the greatest number reside in New York and New Jersey (nearly 390,000), there are significant Dominican communities in Massachusetts (29,000) and Florida (36,000). These communities are predominantly urban: most Dominicans in New York and New Jersey live in New York City (the Washington Heights neighborhood of Manhattan is one prominent location) and its New Jersey suburbs, while Florida and Massachusetts Dominicans tend to reside in Miami and Boston.

No reliable figures on the number of undocumented immigrants in this country exist; however, many who have studied Dominican immigration believe it to be quite high. One scholar writing in 1986 suggested that there were at that time some 300,000 undocumented Dominicans in the United States (John A. Garcia, "Caribbean Migration to the Mainland: A Review of Adaptive Experiences," *Annals of the American Academy of Political and Social Science,* Volume 487, 1986, p. 119). Although that number seems high given the statistics collected by the Census Bureau in 1990, it does suggest the significance of undocumented migrants in the Dominican community in the United States.

A number of Dominican migrants also return to the Dominican Republic either to visit or to resettle permanently. Again, no recent or reliable statistics show exactly how many Dominicans have returned to the Caribbean or for how long. Other indicators, however, suggest that the return movement is significant. For example, the Tourism Secretariat in the Dominican Republic reported in 1985 that 20 percent of all visitors to the island from abroad were Dominicans who had previously emigrated. Moreover, businesses in the Caribbean nation that serve the returned migrant community, and schools, apartment buildings, and discos have been opened especially for returned migrants.

Many *retornados*, or returned migrants, as well as those living overseas have invested heavily in their country of origin, establishing real estate brokerages and grocery stores, among other businesses, on the island. Even those who do not start businesses contribute vitally to the economic life of the Dominican Republic. Remittances, monies sent back to family members still resident on the island, bring more foreign currency into the Dominican economy than any industry except tourism. It is clear from these examples that Dominicans in the United States maintain a strong interest in their country of origin.

The causes of the Dominican immigration are various and have changed over time. As suggested above, the first significant immigration from the Dominican Republic to the United States was in large part the product of political and social instability at home. Those who opposed or had reason to fear the new regime in 1965 and those who were fleeing violence throughout the 1960s came to the United States in notable numbers. As time went on, however, and the political situation stabilized, Dominicans continued to emigrate, now because of limited employment opportunities and poor economic conditions. Studies have shown that those who emigrate are better educated than those they left on the island and were more likely to have been employed when they left the Dominican Republic. These urban, often professional migrants left the Caribbean to find better opportunities elsewhere (Sherri Grasmuck, "Immigration, Ethnic Stratification, and Native Working Class Discipline: Comparisons of Documented and Undocumented Dominicans," *International Migration Review,* Volume 18, No. 3, 1984, p. 695).

Puerto Rico is also a principal destination of Dominicans leaving the Dominican Republic. Many Dominicans find employment in this Caribbean territory of the United States, primarily in the service sector (Maria del Carmen Baerga and Lanny Thompson, "Migration in a Small Semiperiphery: The Movement of Puerto Ricans and Dominicans," *International Migration Review,* Volume 24, No. 4, 1990, pp. 671-677). Many others use Puerto Rico as a stepping stone to the

These Dominican American women are performing in New York City's Hispanic Parade.

mainland United States. Dominicans maintain a significant presence in Puerto Rico and should be considered a small but important stream in the movement of Dominicans to the United States.

### RELATIONSHIP WITH OTHER AMERICANS

The Dominican Republic has had a long and often contentious relationship with the United States, its culture, and its citizens. Because of extended periods of U.S. occupation and because of U.S. cultural and political hegemony in the Caribbean basin, Dominicans are familiar with the United States and American culture. U.S. movies and television programs are shown regularly in the Dominican Republic. Baseball is the most popular sport in the country. And American values are admired and emulated by many Dominicans. Thus, Dominicans coming to the United States already have more than a passing familiarity with the country to which they are immigrating. Moreover, those migrants who return home are disparaged for the degree to which they have adopted American cultural forms.

Nonetheless, the available evidence suggests that Dominican migrants do not have a simple and wholly positive relationship with Americans and American culture. Most Dominicans work in non-unionized workplaces for wages that most "established" Americans would refuse. Many Dominicans have encountered race prejudice in

the United States also. The mixed Afro-Hispanic heritage of many Dominicans has led them to be categorized as black by white Americans; they have encountered the same racial prejudice that African Americans have experienced for centuries. Despite the accusations by their compatriots that they have been assimilated into American culture, Dominicans have tended to be seen by Americans as especially resistant to assimilation and committed to their country, culture, and language of origin.

Dominican Americans are one of the newer national-cultural communities in the United States. They are still in process of creating a unique place for themselves here. Their relationships to the United States and its culture and to the Dominican Republic and Dominican culture are still evolving. The space that Dominicans create for themselves here will surely look in some ways like the spaces other immigrant groups have carved out. However, the Dominican American community will find its own ways of living in the United States, and will make its own unique culture.

## ACCULTURATION AND ASSIMILATION

Dominicans in the United States have neither abandoned their country and culture of origin nor embraced wholly the culture of their adopted land. The accusations of non-migrant Dominicans that migrants are too "American" clearly indicate that migrants have adopted certain highly visible characteristics of American culture. On the other hand, the regular return of migrants to the Caribbean, the settling of migrants in mostly Dominican, localized areas, and the continued presence of Dominicans near the bottom of the U.S. economic ladder, suggest that Dominicans at least for now will sustain their "Dominicanness" and remain distinct from the American population as a whole. Dominicans still resident in the Caribbean who criticize Dominican migrants point to several aspects of Dominican American culture as "foreign" or "un-Dominican." According to Professor Luis E. Guarnizo, "[M]igrants' style of living, their tastes, and their manners, especially those of youngsters and the most prosperous ... are judged as tasteless and revolting especially by the upper classes." This may suggest that migrant children and the children of migrants are abandoning traditional children's roles and adopting American models of proper behavior and attitude for children. At least one young Dominican migrant has noted that American young people behave differently than Dominican youngsters, that they are "too 'liberal'—so preoccupied with boyfriends, clothes, and the latest fads" (David Gonzalez, "New Country Is Like Prison to Asenhat, 18," *New York Times*, 20 April 1993, p. A1). Studies have also shown that the Dominican migrant family as well as the occupational profile of migrants are much different from the island family and the occupational profile of islanders.

Many Americans hold several misconceptions about Dominican migrants. Like many other immigrant groups, Dominican migrants have been regarded as coming from the poorest, least educated segment of their country of origin. They have also been accused of placing a substantial burden on federal and state social services. Research conducted in the 1980s has shown both of these ideas to be false. Researchers have reported that the proportion of highly educated Dominicans is greater among the migrant community than among island Dominicans. In the group of Dominicans who entered the country between 1986 and 1991, there were 15,000 professionals. Dominican migrants have also been shown to have more schooling as a group than island Dominicans. Likewise, 99 percent of undocumented immigrants surveyed in 1981 and 85.9 percent of documented immigrants reported that they had never received welfare payments. A majority of both groups also reported that they had never received unemployment compensation or food stamps. Thus Dominican migrants are neither "the dregs" of their home society nor a drain on national resources.

Little specific information about the Dominican American diet is available. However, many Dominicans operate small independent grocery stores, or *bodegas*, in Dominican neighborhoods. Such grocery stores, in addition to selling toiletries and American food products, also sell Caribbean and Latin American products and ingredients commonly used in Dominican cooking. The presence of these stores indicates that Dominicans in the United States continue, at least with some frequency, to prepare traditional Dominican dishes (Allen R. Myerson, "Thriving Where Others Won't Go," *New York Times*, 7 January 1992, pp. D1, D5).

### HEALTH AND MENTAL HEALTH ISSUES

No sources address the question of the state of Dominican Americans' health in a systematic and complete way. The 1991 report of the American Medical Association on Hispanic health in the United States does not distinguish Dominicans from the group "Central and South Americans" (Council on Scientific Affairs, "Hispanic Health in the United States," *Journal of the American Medical Association* [JAMA], Volume 265, No. 2, 1991, pp. 248-252); however, the findings for Puerto Ricans may be suggestive. Puerto Ricans are also an Hispanic Caribbean migrant group who have settled largely on the East Coast and especially in New York City. Like Dominicans, they are poorer and have less social power than most Americans. A greater proportion of Puerto Rican infants are born premature or with lower birth weights than white American infants. The homicide rate among Puerto Ricans is much higher than among whites, and the proportion of those not insured is also much greater (Fernando S. Mendoza, et al., "Selected Measures of Health Status for Mexican-American, Mainland Puerto Rican, and Cuban American Children," in *JAMA*, Volume 265, No. 2, 1991, pp. 229-230). These few indicators suggest that the health status of Puerto Ricans in the United States is worse than that of white Americans. It is not unreasonable to extrapolate from the Puerto Rican community to the Dominican community and conclude that Dominicans share with Puerto Ricans a lower health status than white Americans.

# LANGUAGE

Dominican migrants are Spanish speakers. The 1980 Census showed that 45 percent of foreign-born Dominicans reported that they could speak English well or very well. More than 52 percent said that they could not speak English well or at all. The large and rapid influx of migrants during the 1980s indicates that a somewhat higher proportion of migrants today might report poor English language capabilities.

# FAMILY AND COMMUNITY DYNAMICS

The Dominican family in America is a different institution than the family in the Dominican Republic. Although kin relationships have continued to be important to migrants in the United States, families have tended to become smaller and more nuclear as migrants remain in the United States longer. Dominican families in the Caribbean are more likely to be large and non-nuclear. A 1981 study showed that while only 1.1 percent of those surveyed resided in nuclear households before emigrating, 30.6 percent did so after more than six months in the United States. Likewise, 43.1 percent of respondents said that they had lived with family members but not with spouses or children before emigrating; after emigration, that proportion was reduced to 23.5 percent (Greta Gilbertson and Douglas T. Gurak, "Household Transitions in the Migrations of Dominicans and Colombians to New York," *International Migration Review*, Volume 26, No. 1, 1992, p. 27). These numbers suggest both that migrants have tended to marry after some period of residence in the United States and that, after marrying, they have tended not to live in extended or non-nuclear families. Other studies have shown that Dominican women in the United States tend to have fewer children than women in the Dominican Republic (Vivian Garrison and Carol I. Weiss, "Dominican Family Networks and United States Immigration Policy: A Case Study," in *Caribbean Life in New York City: Sociocultural Dimensions*, p. 229).

Gender roles within the family seem also to have been transformed in the migration. The Dominican family tends to be patriarchal. Male heads of household exercise control over household budgets and have final authority over family members. Women in households are responsible for domestic tasks and maintenance. Among Dominican migrants, however, this pattern seems to be changing. Dominican women in the United States have demanded greater control over budgets and have wrested some authority from their husbands. Their new role as co-breadwinners seems to have empowered them to challenge male authority in the household more effectively (Patricia R. Pessar, "The Linkage Between the Household and Workplace of Dominican Women in the U.S.," in *Caribbean Life in New York: Sociocultural Dimensions*, pp. 241-245).

These changes in the structure and organization of the Dominican family in the United States suggest that the process of courting and the institution of marriage have changed. While there are no authoritative or specific treatments of these topics, it seems reasonable to conclude from the above evidence about gender relations within marriages that gender relations among dating couples may well be changing also.

Education seems to occupy a place of importance in the Dominican migrant world view. Certainly the migrants themselves are as a group better educated than Dominicans who remain at home. Dominicans in the United States have also fought some of their most significant political battles over education. In the Washington Heights neighborhood of Manhattan, Dominicans organized to gain a voice on the local school board. That board had been dominated by non-Dominicans even though Dominicans represented a majority of school age children in the district. Dominicans campaigned to put representatives of their own community on the board and were successful. The political mobilization around education marked one of the New York Dominican community's early forays into the realm of city politics, and at least one Dominican city leader began his political career on the Washington Heights board of education.

Statistics on the level of education of the native-born Dominican American community as a whole are difficult to find. The Census Bureau currently classifies Dominicans as "Central/South Americans"—along with many other communities of South and Central American communities. These groups, of course, are not comparable: their forebears came from radically different cultures, and they inhabit very different socioeconomic "worlds" in the United States. The 1990 Census showed that 15.6 percent of Americans of Central/South American origin were college graduates. However, it is likely that the percentage of Americans of Dominican descent who had graduated college by 1990 is substantially smaller. The percentage of Dominican migrants that the 1980 Census reported as college graduates was 4.3 percent.

Apparently as important to the community as education is another institution that at first glance seems frivolous. Baseball, however, is far more than sport or recreation to Dominicans both in the Caribbean and in the United States. According to one writer, baseball is integral to Dominican identity: "In the Dominican Republic baseball has a place all out of proportion to the normal one of sport in society. There is nothing comparable to it in the United States.... Americans may love the game of baseball as much as Dominicans do, but they do not need it as much." (Milton Jamail, "Baseball and Latin America" [book review], *Studies in Latin American Popular Culture*, No. 11, 1992, p. 220.)

A recent story on baseball in Washington Heights, New York, suggests that Dominican migrants have retained their love for the game. Players use their earnings to pay for equipment, and mothers make sure that sons do not work on game days. The community gathers to watch the young people on the diamond (Sara Rimer, "Summer's Game and the Ties that Bind," *New York Times*, 6 May 1991, pp. B1, B6). Scholars of baseball in the Dominican Republic have noted that becoming a professional baseball player is the dream of many Dominicans. Baseball represents a way out of poverty for the largely poor population of the Caribbean nation. And, as the national pastime, baseball represents a way to demonstrate the pride Dominicans have in their nation.

# RELIGION

Religion remains little commented upon in the literature on Dominicans in the United States. Dominicans in the Caribbean are overwhelmingly Roman Catholic, and it seems likely that a majority in the United States also profess that faith (Saskia Sassen-Koob, "Formal and Informal Associations: Dominicans and Colombians in New York," in *Caribbean Life in New York: Sociocultural Dimensions*, p. 262). Some Dominicans also participate in Afro-Catholic religious rituals and communities of the tradition known as *santeria*. It is not known how many Dominicans in the United States practice *santeria*, which is primarily associated with Cuban Americans and Puerto Ricans. *Santeria* combines certain aspects of Catholic belief with aspects of West African, chiefly Yoruba, belief and practice. Participating in *santeria* rites does not preclude belonging to a Catholic church and practicing that tradition (Stephen Gregory, "Afro-Caribbean Religions in New York City: The Case of *Santeria*," in *Caribbean Life in New York: Sociocultural Dimensions*, pp. 287-302).

# EMPLOYMENT AND ECONOMIC TRADITIONS

While significant numbers of those who immigrate from the Dominican Republic to the United States were professionals before they emigrated, the vast number once they are in the United States are employed in low-wage, low-prestige jobs. The 1980 census showed that, among foreign-born Dominicans, only 6.9 percent occupied "upper white-collar" positions while 33.5 percent occupied "lower blue-collar" positions. Rates among the U.S. population as a whole were quite different: 22.7 percent upper white-collar and 18.3 percent lower blue-collar; and 22.1 percent of foreign-born Dominican families lived in poverty, compared with 9.6 percent of the total U.S. population.

A study conducted around the same time provides more detailed information about Dominican migrants. That study showed that the proportion of professionals among migrants decreased markedly as migrants moved from the Dominican Republic to the United States. At the same time, the proportion of laborers increased dramatically. That study also showed that among those employed as laborers, the majority worked in manufacturing, with a sizable number of men also working in restaurants and hotels. These laborers worked primarily for smaller firms; 40 percent earned less than $150 each week; and 45 percent worked in non-unionized workplaces. A much larger proportion, in other words, earned less and were less protected at their workplaces than most Americans. According to Guarnizo, more recent treatments of the topic have suggested that things have not changed for most Dominicans in the United States: "Toiling in dead-end, low-paid jobs in the secondary labor market remains the most common path of economic incorporation for Dominicans in the United States." The reasons for the economic position of Dominican Americans are easy to guess at: the language barrier, discrimination, the illegal status of many in the community, and the lower level of education of the Dominican American community as a whole relative to the average level of education of the U.S. population.

The garment industry employs the greatest number of Dominican women in the New York area. Many of these Dominican garment workers are employed in what is called the "informal sector" of the garment industry, in small firms that are not regulated or unionized. Women who work for these firms are paid much lower wages and enjoy little job security or protection while on the job.

Despite the fact that most in the U.S. Dominican community work in low-paid, low-status jobs, a significant number own businesses that often draw many of their customers from the immigrant and ethnic communities. The Ctown Group, a voluntary association of 167 small grocery stores in metropolitan New York, says that half of its stores are owned and operated by Dominicans. Other similar associations in New

In this 1960 photograph, Dominican refugees demonstrate in front of the Spanish-language radio station WHOM. They are voicing their discontent with the Dominican dictator Trujillo.

York report high levels of Dominican ownership as well. The Dominican involvement in the groceries trade goes even farther: many Dominicans own and operate *bodegas* in their neighborhoods that are not affiliated with any grocery association.

# POLITICS AND GOVERNMENT

The U.S. Dominican community has taken up several important political issues both in the United States and in the Dominican Republic. Education, the status of undocumented migrants in the United States, citizenship status, and police violence against Dominicans have been the most important. In the 1970s, a union of several Dominican associations called *Concilio de Organizaciones Dominicanas* (Council of Dominican Organizations) began to push for greater rights for undocumented Dominicans in the Unit-

ed States. In the same decade, a group called *Asociacion Nacional de Dominicanos Ausentes* (National Association of Absent Dominicans) lobbied the Dominican government for the right of migrants in the United States to vote in Dominican elections. More recently, Dominican migrants have pushed the Dominican Republic to permit Dominicans in the United States to retain their Dominican citizenship so that they will be considered citizens when they return home to visit or to live, as many do.

The most significant recent mobilization of Dominicans in the United States was in response to the 1992 police shooting of Dominican Jose Garcia in New York City. The Dominican community was outraged. Already established Dominican organizations joined the mobilization against police violence, and new organizations formed in response to it. Demonstrations were held in the Washington Heights neighborhood, and there were other, less peaceful expressions of anger as well. The *Alianza Dominicana*, a community organization, worked to channel communal anger into positive directions, and Dominican leaders worked with city and police officials. The mobilization attracted the attention of community leaders throughout the city (Maria Newman, "New Leadership Forms in a Crucible of Violence," *New York Times*, 11 July 1992, p. 23). Dominicans have not yet entered the arena of national politics, but they have made impressive strides at the local level. The 1990s have seen the election in New York City of the city's first Dominican city councilor, Guillermo Linares.

# INDIVIDUAL AND GROUP CONTRIBUTIONS

Though Dominicans have been coming to the United States in very significant numbers only for 25 years, they have as a community already contributed immensely to U.S. culture, society, and politics.

## ACADEMIA

Elsa Gomez serves as president of Kean College of New Jersey. Born in 1938 in New York City, she recently faced a controversy at Kean that catapulted her into the national spotlight; Jewish students were outraged when a Nation of Islam speaker made remarks that many regarded as anti-Semitic.

## FASHION

Oscar de la Renta (1932- ), born in the Dominican Republic, is a world-renowned fashion designer and creator of his own line of high-end women's clothing.

## FILM AND TELEVISION

Agustin Rodriguez (1967- ), born in New York City, is frequently seen on network television and in the movies; he has had smaller roles in *Final Analysis* and *Falling Down* and has guest-starred on the television series "Street Justice" and "Sirens." He was a regular on the series "Moon over Miami."

## JOURNALISM AND LITERATURE

Born in the United States and raised in part in the Dominican Republic, Julia Alvarez has already shown herself to be a talented and provocative writer and poet; Alvarez is the author of the much-lauded story collection, *How the Garcia Girls Lost Their Accents*; her work has treated the experience of growing up in two cultures. Tony Marcano (1960- ) has served as a reporter for several nationally known newspapers during his career as a journalist; he was born in New York City and currently serves as editor of the "City Times" section of the *Los Angeles Times*.

## POLITICS

Guillermo Linares (1950- ), born in the Dominican Republic, is a former Washington Heights school board member and the first Dominican city councilor in New York City; he has had a distinguished career as local politician.

## SPORTS

Mary Joe Fernandez (1971- ) was born in the Dominican Republic; she played in her first Grand Slam tennis tournament at the age of 14; she has played in the final of the Australian Open and the semifinals of the U.S. Open; she has also been a winning doubles player, taking eight tournaments; her earnings exceed $2.1 million. Juan Marichal (1938- ), born in the Dominican Republic, is a baseball Hall of Famer and a former pitcher for the San Francisco Giants, the Boston Red Sox, and the Los Angeles Dodgers; he now works as a scout for the Oakland A's.

# SOURCES FOR ADDITIONAL STUDY

*Americas: New Interpretive Essays*, edited by Alfred Stepan. Oxford: Oxford University Press, 1992.

*Caribbean Life in New York: Sociocultural Dimensions*, edited by Constance R. Sutton and Elsa M. Chaney. New York: Center of Migration Studies for New York, 1992.

del Castillo, Jose, and Martin F. Murphy. "Migration, National Identity and Cultural Policy in the Dominican Republic," *Journal of Ethnic Studies*, 15, No. 3, 1987, p. 67.

Klein, Alan M. *Sugarball: The American Game, the Dominican Dream*. New Haven: Yale University Press, 1991.

# DUTCH AMERICANS

by
**Herbert J. Brinks**

*Mainstream culture has either attracted Dutch ethnics out of their enclaves or the surrounding culture has so altered the ethnic communities that they can no longer flourish on ethnic exclusivity.*

## OVERVIEW

Located in northwestern Europe, the Netherlands is bounded to the east by Germany, to the south by Belgium, and to the north and west by the North Sea. The Netherlands has about 16,000 square miles of landmass, making the country roughly equal in size to New Jersey and Maryland combined. The nation supports a population density of about 1,000 people per square mile. A coastal region, incorporating two major harbors (Rotterdam and the Hudson Bay), the Netherlands' economy is heavily dependent upon shipping.

During the New Stone Age (c. 8000-3500 B.C.), the Netherlands' landmass roughly equaled its current 16,000 square miles, but by 55 B.C., when Rome's legions gained hegemony in the area, rising sea levels and erosion from winds, tides, and rivers reduced the coastal areas by at least 30 percent. Since then, the Dutch have employed various strategies to regain the land lost to the sea. Simple earthen hills (village sites) linked by dikes long preceded the complex drainage systems that drain the enclosed lowlands today with electrically powered pumps.

Windmills, preserved currently as historic monuments, pushed water up and out of the Netherlands for some five centuries (1400-1900) because viable habitation of the western provinces (South Holland, Zeeland, and North Holland) required flood control along the Rhine River delta and along the North Sea's shifting shoreline. The massive Delta Works, stretching across the islands of South Holland and Zeeland, was constructed following disastrous floods in 1953 to protect the Netherlands from storms and high water. Because the most productive farm land together with the most populous commercial and industrial districts lie as much as 20 feet below sea level, hydrological science has become a hallmark of Dutch achievement.

## HISTORY

While historians believe that nomadic peoples hunted and fished in the Netherlands as early as 16,000 B.C., the area was not settled until about 4000 B.C. Around 60 B.C., Roman armies under Julius Caesar conquered the Saxon, Celtic, and Frisian groups occupying the Netherlands at that time. The Romans built roads and made improvements to existing dikes in the lowlands. In the A.D. 400s, as Rome weakened, the Germanic Franks conquered the area and later introduced the Dutch to Christianity.

From the 700s to the 1100s, the Dutch were subjected to violent raids by Viking sailors from Scandinavia. During this unstable period, power passed to local nobles, whose arms and castles offered protection in return for rent, labor, and taxes. This system gradually declined when, beginning in the 1300s, much of the Netherlands was taken by the dukes of Burgundy, a powerful French feudal dynasty. In the early 1500s, Charles V, Duke of Burgundy, inherited the thrones of both Spain and the Holy Roman Empire. While he was well-liked by the Dutch, his successors were not. In 1568 the Dutch prince, William the Silent (1533-1584), led a rebellion against the Spanish Habsburgs (Phillip II, 1527-1621), initiating the Eighty Years' War (1568-1648). Although William was assassinated in 1584, his efforts eventually resulted in Dutch independence. For this reason, he is often regarded as the Father of the Netherlands.

Resistance to the Spanish united the lowlanders, who previously had local (rather than national) loyalties. In 1579 the Union of Utrecht unified the seven northern lowland provinces. (Their 1580 agreement, essentially a defensive alliance, served as a national constitution until 1795.) Two years later (1581), those provinces declared the Netherlands an independent country. Meanwhile, Dutch exploration and trade had flourished and by the 1620s, the Dutch shipping

fleet was the world's largest. This "Golden Age" lasted until the 1700s, after which the Netherlands underwent a gradual decline as the balance of colonial power shifted in favor of England. The beginning of this change can be traced to the 1664 sale of New Netherland (New York) to England.

## MODERN ERA

The Netherlands was occupied by the French during the Napoleonic Era (1795-1813). Afterwards, in 1814, descendants of the House of Orange established a monarchy, which was reformed successively in 1848, 1896, and 1919 to create a broadly based democracy. Today, the Netherlands has a constitutional monarchy with a bicameral, multi-party system administered by a premier and a coalition cabinet of ministers. Queen Beatrix (1938- ), the titular head of state, performs largely ceremonial duties.

## THE FIRST DUTCH SETTLERS IN AMERICA

Following English explorer Henry Hudson's 1609 exploration of the Hudson River, a new joint stock company, the Dutch West India Company (1621), gained colonization rights in the Hudson River area and founded New Netherland (New York). The Dutch West India Company was chartered specifically to trade in the New World, where the Dutch had acquired colonies in Brazil, the Caribbean, and the east coast of North America. Pursuing its commercial interest in New Netherland, the company established Fort Orange (Albany), Breuckelen (Brooklyn), Vlissingen (Flushing), and in Delaware, Swanendael (Lewes). In 1624 the company also established the Dutch Reformed Church (the Reformed Church in America) which has exercised a significant influence in the Dutch American community.

In New Amsterdam (New York City) Governor Peter Stuyvesant (1592-1672) attempted to eliminate all worship apart from that of the Dutch Reformed Church, but his governing board in Amsterdam opposed the policy as detrimental to commerce. Like Amsterdam itself, New Amsterdam did not enforce rules which prohibited worship to Jews, Catholics, and others. Thus, New Amsterdam flourished and, as New York City, it continues to host a diverse populace with widely varying religious expressions.

After the British captured New Netherland in 1664, Dutch immigration virtually ceased but England imposed no severe restraints on the

In this 1921 photograph a Dutch woman and her children prepare to depart from the S.S. *Vedic* in New York City.

Dutch and the vast majority remained in New York. By 1790 they numbered about 100,000 and, in addition to New York City, they clustered in towns and villages scattered along the Hudson and Mohawk Rivers. In New Jersey they estab-lished towns beside the Hackensack, Passaic, and Raritan Rivers. In such places they dominated the local culture, spoke Dutch, and established both Reformed churches and day schools. After the American Revolution, the Dutch more rapidly assimilated into the dominant Anglo-American culture by adopting English for worship, by attending public schools, and by attaining social status within the general culture. Consequently, when a new wave of Dutch immigrants came to the United States in the 1840s, they found few in New York or elsewhere who spoke Dutch.

## SIGNIFICANT IMMIGRATION WAVES

Nineteenth-century Dutch immigration, numbering about 200 people annually before 1845, increased that year to 800 and averaged 1,150 annually over the next decade. That movement, which stemmed from religious and economic discontent in the Netherlands; a potato famine (1845-1846) and high unemployment combined with a division in the Reformed Church that pitted conservative Calvinists against the increasingly liberal State Church, forced many Dutch to emigrate. At the same time, three clergymen organized colonies on the Midwestern frontier. In 1848 Father Theodore J. Van den Broek (1783-1851) established a Catholic community in Little Chute, near Green Bay, Wisconsin. Two conservative Reformed pastors, Albertus Van Raalte (1811-1876) and Hendrik P. Scholte (1805-1868) founded respectively, Holland, Michigan (1847) and Pella, Iowa (1847). Once these communities were established, printed brochures and private correspondence triggered a persistent flow of newcomers until 1930, when immigration quotas and the Great Depression closed out that 85-year period of migration. During that era, Dutch immigration followed typical northern European patterns, increasing or decreasing in response to economic prospects at home or in the United States. With peaks in the mid-1870s, the early 1880s and 1890s, and again from 1904 to 1914, a total of about 400,000 Netherlanders immigrated to the United States between 1845 and 1930.

Seventy-five to 80 percent of these immigrants originated from rural provinces surrounding the Netherlands' urban core. They settled mainly in the Midwest, clustering where the original colonies had been established in Wisconsin, Michigan, and Iowa. They also settled in and around Chicago, in Paterson, New Jersey and in Grand Rapids, Michigan. Those with hopes of becoming independent farmers moved West and gained land under the Homestead Act, which encouraged settlement in northwestern Iowa, South Dakota, Minnesota, Montana, Washington, and California. In nearly every settlement, they organized and had prominent roles in local towns where they established churches, private schools, and farm-related businesses of all sorts. After 1900, when the best homestead lands were occupied, the Dutch selected urban industrial locations and formed solid ethnic enclaves in Grand Rapids, Chicago, and Paterson. By 1930 Dutch immigrant communities stretched from coast to coast across the northern tier of states, but they concentrated most heavily around the southern half of Lake Michigan, from Muskegon, Michigan, through Chicago and north to Green Bay, Wisconsin.

After World War II, when a war-ravaged economy and a severe housing shortage caused a third of the Dutch populace to seriously consider emigration, a new wave of 80,000 immigrants came to the United States. The Dutch government encouraged emigration and sought to increase the annual U.S. immigration quota of 3,131. Consequently, under special provisions of the Walter-Pastori Refugee Relief Acts (1950-1956), about 18,000 Dutch Indonesians were admitted to the United States. These Dutch Colonials, who had immigrated to the Netherlands after 1949 when Indonesia became independent, settled primarily in California, the destination of many other postwar Dutch immigrants. The 1970 U.S. Census recorded the highest number (28,000) of foreign-born Dutch in California, while seven other states—Michigan, New York, New Jersey, Illinois, Washington, Florida, and Iowa—hosted nearly the whole 50,000 balance. Apart from Florida, these states had been traditional strongholds for Dutch Americans.

# ACCULTURATION AND ASSIMILATION

During the chief era of Dutch immigration, 1621-1970, religious and ideological viewpoints structured the character of public institutions in the Netherlands. In the Dutch Republic (1580-1795), Reformed Protestants controlled the government, schools, public charities, and most aspects of social behavior. Although both Catholics and Jews practiced their faith without hindrance, they could not hold public offices. Then, beginning in the 1850s, when the national constitution permitted a multiparty system, political parties grew from constituencies identified with specific churches or ideologies. The Reformed, the Catholic, and the

Socialist groups each organized one or more parties. In addition, each group established separate schools, labor unions, newspapers, recreational clubs, and even a schedule of television programs to serve constituencies. Dutch Americans recreated parts of that structure wherever they clustered in sufficient numbers to sustain ethnic churches, schools, and other institutions. Since the 1960s, these enclaved groups have begun to embrace mainstream American institutions more rapidly and they have altered the goals of their private organizations to attract and serve a multicultural constituency.

Religious and cultural separation flourished primarily in the ethnically dense population centers of Reformed Protestants. Dutch Catholics, apart from those in the Green Bay area, were not concentrated in large numbers. Instead they joined other Catholic parishes in Cincinnati, St. Louis, New York City, and elsewhere. Even around Green Bay, Dutch Catholics intermarried readily with Catholics of other ethnicities. Lacking large and cohesive enclaves, Dutch Catholics were neither able nor inclined to re-establish ethnic institutions in America. Similarly, Dutch Jews settled mainly in cities such as New York, Philadelphia, and Boston, where they assimilated the social and religious patterns of much larger Jewish groups from Germany, Russia, and Poland. One prominent Dutch rabbi in New York, Samuel Myer Isaacs (1804-1878), attempted to maintain a Dutch identity by founding a synagogue, a school, and the orthodox periodical *The Messenger*, but these institutions faltered after his death.

Currently, the major strongholds of Dutch American separatism are fragmenting rapidly. Reformed churches, schools, colleges, theological schools and even retirement facilities for the aged are campaigning to gain a full spectrum of non-Dutch clients. Marriage outside of the ethnic group has become common and media-driven popular culture has altered traditional behavior among all age groups. In short, mainstream culture has either attracted Dutch ethnics out of their enclaves or the surrounding culture has so altered the ethnic communities that they can no longer flourish on ethnic exclusivity.

There are no aggressively mean-spirited or demeaning stereotypes of Dutch Americans. They are correctly perceived as valuing property, inclined to small business ventures, and culturally conservative with enduring loyalties to their churches, colleges, and other institutions. The perception that they are exceptionally clannish is also accurate, but that characteristic is demonstrated primarily among Reformed Protestants. Other ethnic stereotypes—financial penury, a proclivity for liquor and tobacco, and a general humorlessness—reflect individual rather than group features.

## CUISINE

The earlier immigrants' plain diets (potatoes, cabbage and pea soup with little meat beyond sausage and bacon) could not compete with America's meat-oriented menu. In general, Dutch foods are not rich or exotic. Potatoes and vegetables combined with meat in a Dutch oven, fish, and soups are typical. The Indonesian rice table, now widely popular in Dutch American kitchens, came from Dutch colonials. Holiday pastries flavored with almond paste are a major component of Dutch baked goods. Social gatherings thrive on coffee and cookies with brandy-soaked raisins during the Christmas season.

## TRADITIONAL COSTUMES

In the Netherlands traditional costumes vary by region, demonstrating local loyalties, once paramount, that still flavor Dutch life. Men often dressed in baggy black pants and colorful, wide-brimmed hats, while women wore voluminous black dresses, colorfully embroidered bodices, and lace bonnets. Such costumes have been replaced by modern clothes in the Netherlands. In the United States, traditional dress is reserved for special occasions.

## HOLIDAYS CELEBRATED BY DUTCH AMERICANS

Dutch Jews and Christians generally celebrate the holidays associated with their particular religious affiliation. However, many postwar immigrants have preserved a distinctive pattern of Christmas observance which separates gift exchanges on St. Nicholas Day (December 6) from the religious celebrations of December 25.

## HEALTH AND MENTAL HEALTH ISSUES

There are no specifically Dutch related medical problems or conditions. Health and life insurance, either private or from institutional sources, has long ago replaced the need for immigrant aid cooperatives which once provided modest death benefits. Reformed churches regularly assisted widows, orphans, and chronically dependent people prior to the Social Security system. In isolated cases, church funds are still used to supplement the incomes of especially needy persons or to assist those with catastrophic needs. For mental diseases, a cluster of Reformed denominations established the Pine Rest Psychiatric Hospital in 1910, but that institution now serves the general public. Other institutions, the Bethany Christian Home adoption agency and the Bethesda tuberculosis sanitorium, have also been transformed to serve a multicultural clientele.

# LANGUAGE

In general, the Dutch language is no longer used by Dutch Americans. The vast majority of postwar immigrants have adopted English and the small number of immigrants who have arrived since the 1960s are bilingual because English is virtually a second language in the Netherlands. Still, some Dutch words and expressions have survived: *vies* ("fees") denotes filth and moral degradation; *benauwd* ("benout") refers to feelings of anxiety, both physical and emotional; *flauw* ("flou") describes tasteless foods, dull persons, and faint feeling; and *gezellig* ("gezelik") is a comfortable social gathering. Typical Dutch greetings, *dag* ("dag"), which means "good day" and *hoe gaat het* ("who gat het") for "how are you doing," are no longer in common usage in the United States.

There are small groups of Dutch Americans—descendants of nineteenth century immigrants—who have maintained provincial Dutch dialects (including dialects from Overijssel, Drenthe, and Zeeland) that have all but disappeared in the modern-day Netherlands. Consequently, some Dutch linguists have traveled to western Michigan and other Dutch American strongholds to record these antiquated dialects.

Formal Dutch remained vital among the immigrants until the 1930s, due partly to its use for worship services, but World War I patriotism, which prohibited the use of German, Dutch and other languages, signaled the demise of Dutch usage in Reformed churches. Long before World War I, however, Dutch Americans, and especially their American-born children, began to reject the ancestral language. It was well understood and frequently asserted among them that economic opportunities were greater for those who spoke English. Consequently, daily wage earners, business people, and even farm hands adopted English as quickly as possible. Formal Dutch is currently used only in commemorative worship services, and in the language departments of several colleges founded by Dutch Americans. Among these, only Calvin College in Grand Rapids, Michigan, offers a major in Dutch language and literature.

# FAMILY AND COMMUNITY DYNAMICS

Colonial New Netherland (New York), like Jamestown and other trading post colonies, attracted single men, few women, and even fewer families. Every account of New Amsterdam (New York City) refers to its rough and raucous social character—the products of an astonishing mixture of people, languages, and behavior which severely tested polite standards of social order. By the time of the British conquest in 1664, however, the arrival of immigrant women and the high colonial birth rate provided a population base for marriages and family life.

When the British took formal control of the colony, the Dutch populace, about 8,000 people, struggled to retain their cultural identity. Until about 1720, Dutch ethnics married within the group, worshiped together, and joined hands for economic and political objectives. Family cohesion was at the core of this ethnic vitality, but by 1800, Dutch ethnicity had weakened because economic and cultural bonds were established outside of the ethnic subculture. These bonds eventually led to marriages across ethnic lines.

Apart from New York City, in the many towns founded by the Dutch (such as Albany and Kinderhoek, New York, and Hackensack and New Brunswick, New Jersey) ethnic solidarity persisted well into the nineteenth century. In such places Dutch families adhered to the values instilled by Reformed churches and their day schools. Men dominated all the public institutions, while women managed typically large households with six or seven children. Domestic life, including the education of girls, depended largely on Dutch homemakers. Girls and boys gained basic skills from part-time teachers who were also expected to indoctrinate their students for church membership. Formal education continued for boys, who excelled academically, usually in the form of an apprentice relationship with lawyers, pastors, and business firms. Women received the bulk of their training from mothers

and older female relatives. By 1800 most of the parochial schools were replaced by public instruction, which led to an increase in the level of formal education for girls.

In the nineteenth century, most Dutch immigrants to America had family members who had preceded them. The newcomers (80 percent) came largely from rural areas and resettled in rural America where extended families were frequently reconstituted. Siblings, parents, and even grandparents regularly joined the first settlers, contributing to the family-oriented character of that ethnic subculture. The original colonies in Michigan, Iowa, Illinois, and Wisconsin spawned more than one hundred similarly rural towns and villages which attracted successive waves of farmers, farm hands, and craftspeople. When Dutch immigration shifted from rural to urban destinations (1890-1930), the newcomers clustered in enclaves that grew once again when extended families reunited in places like Paterson, New Jersey; Grand Rapids, Michigan; and the Chicago area. These Dutch American communities still exist, but the urban enclaves have regrouped in suburban areas, while many farmers have moved either to ethnic towns or suburban neighborhoods. Throughout its history, the Dutch subculture has been sustained by a complex institutional structure of churches, schools, homes for the aged, recreational organizations, and small businesses.

Private schools, which were especially attractive to devoted traditionalists, provided educational opportunities without a notable gender bias, but most women became housewives and supported the male-dominated institutions which served the ethnic subculture. Since the 1960s, Dutch American women have moved beyond the teaching, secretarial, nursing, and homemaking professions into medicine, law, business, and ecclesiastical positions.

The new infusion of 80,000 Dutch immigrants, who arrived after World War II (1946-1956), reinvigorated Dutch ethnicity across the continent. It is more from them than their nineteenth-century predecessors that ethnic foods and customs have been introduced to the Dutch American community.

## RELIGION

Neither Dutch Catholics nor Jews have retained discernible ethnic practices in their religious exercises. Both groups are part of international organizations which, because they used either Latin or Hebrew in formal rituals, were not drawn into major controversies regarding vernacular language usage in worship. Furthermore, due to their general dispersion, Dutch Catholics and Jews have had few opportunities to dominate either a parish or a synagogue. Instead they have worshiped and intermarried readily within multi-ethnic religious communities. Furthermore, Dutch Jews and Catholics have not acted in concert to support particular branches of Judaism or specific viewpoints within the Roman Catholic Church. Even the Dutch Catholic stronghold around Green Bay, Wisconsin, has become ethnically diverse, including French, German, and Flemish Catholics. One village, Little Chute, however, does continue to promote its Dutch ethnicity with a mid-September celebration (*kermis*), featuring a Dutch-costume parade, games, and craft exhibits. And Holland, Michigan, hosts its annual tulip festival in the spring.

By contrast, Dutch Protestants, most of whom affiliated with a cluster of Reformed churches, have spawned a long history of controversy regarding language usage, doctrinal interpretations, and liturgical expressions—all issues that were intimately related to cultural adaptation. In the Colonial Era the Dutch Reformed Church experienced crippling divisions (1737-1771) due to conflicting views of ordination and theological education. One group favored continued interdependence with church authorities in the Netherlands (the Classis of Amsterdam), that the American party, led by Theodore Frelinghuysen (1692-1742), promoted education and clerical ordination at "home" in the colonies. Then, in 1792, the Dutch Reformed Church became an independent denomination known as the Reformed Protestant Dutch Church (RCA). With that the RCA moved toward mainline status by adopting English, cooperating with other major church groups (Presbyterian, Methodist, and Episcopal), and participating in interdenominational campaigns to establish churches on the Midwestern frontier.

In the late 1840s about 3,000 Dutch Protestant immigrants settled in Michigan, Illinois, and Wisconsin, and by 1850 a large majority of these newcomers became affiliated with the New York-based RCA. The immigrants' spiritual patriarch, Albertus Van Raalte, had contacted the RCA's leaders before immigrating, and because he found them both helpful and doctrinally compatible, he and his followers united with the RCA. Some Midwestern immigrants, however, objected to this fusion; they initiated a separatist movement in 1857 which became the Christian Reformed Church (CRC).

Throughout the next hundred years, the two denominations pursued different strategies for cultural adaptation. The RCA acquired American church programs, including the revival, the Sunday school movement, and ecumenical cooperation, while neglecting its Netherlandic connec-

tions and traditions. The CRC, however, remained loyal to its religious cohorts in the Netherlands. That posture was marked by its general use of Dutch until the 1920s, and by the CRC's efforts to recreate Calvinistic schools and other institutions on the Dutch model. In this practice they followed the views of Dr. Abraham Kuyper (1837-1920), the most prominent Reformed leader in the Netherlands. Consequently, the CRC attracted a majority of the Reformed immigrants who arrived between 1880 and 1920.

Since the 1960s and especially during the period from 1985 to 1995, the RCA and CRC have become increasingly similar. Netherlandic theology and culture no longer influence the CRC significantly and the denomination increasingly emulates the liturgical and theological ethos of conservative evangelical groups affiliated with the National Association of Evangelicals. Although the RCA, with membership in the World Council of Churches, is more broadly ecumenical than the CRC, the two denominations have appointed a joint committee to encourage cooperation. At the same time, the growing tide of congregationalism has diminished denominational cohesion among them so that, like American political parties, the two denominations contain a wide spectrum of viewpoints. Neither denomination, then, can be labeled exclusively liberal or conservative.

The prospect for an eventual reunification of the RCA and CRC is good. At present their respective clergymen, theological professors, and parishioners move freely across denominational boundaries, and their parishioners have a long history of acting jointly to establish nursing homes, retirement facilities, and mental health institutions. The two denominations proclaim identical confessions of faith and no barriers restrict their mutual participation in sacramental rites. They are divided primarily by traditions, which are becoming increasingly irrelevant due to a rapid assimilation of America's mainstream religious attitudes and values.

# EMPLOYMENT AND ECONOMIC TRADITIONS

Free enterprise capitalism was introduced to the United States by the joint stock companies that colonized the eastern seaboard. The New Netherland Colony (New York) exemplified that phenomenon just as obviously as Jamestown and the

New England Company. Understandably, then, Dutch immigrants have never been seriously disoriented by economic procedures in the United States. Virtually the whole populace of New Amsterdam and its surrounding areas was defined by its relationship to the joint stock company. Early Dutch immigrants were stockholders, officers, and employees, or traders operating illegally on the fringes of the company's jurisdiction. In all these cases, including the farmers who provisioned the trading posts, small and large businesses dominated daily life in New Amsterdam.

Like others with roots in the Colonial Era, Dutch merchants, farmers, and land speculators benefited from being among the first to invest in the New World. Families such as the Van Rensselaers, Schuylers, and Roosevelts quickly joined the ranks of prominent Americans. By contrast, Cornelius Vanderbilt left a small farm to become a captain of great wealth 150 years after his ancestors immigrated to America in 1644. In fact, for all of the early Dutch Americans, as well as nineteenth-century immigrants, self-employment and economic security were major objectives.

**"We all have our pet notions as to the particular evil which is `the curse of America,' but I always think that Theodore Roosevelt came closest to the real curse when he classed it as a lack of thoroughness."**

Dutch immigrant Edward Bok, from his Pulitzer Prize-winning account of his editorial career, *The Americanization of Edward Bok,* 1920.

Throughout most of the nineteenth century, Dutch immigrants preferred agriculture as the means to economic independence. Because 80 percent of them were farm hands, day laborers, small farmers, and village craftsmen, they readily became self-employed farmers either on inexpensive government land or, after 1862, on free homestead land until about 1900.

Dutch immigrants arriving in the twentieth century were frequently employed in factories, the construction trades, and garden farming. But during the prosperous 1950s, many if not most Dutch Americans developed small family businesses—construction, trucking, repair shops, and retailing. They ranged from door-to-door vendors of eggs and garden farm produce to developers of supermarket chains. Few were unionized shop workers. Supported by the G.I. Bill of Rights (1944), many

Dutch American veterans acquired college and professional training to enter law, medicine, dentistry, and teaching so that today nearly every Dutch American family has post graduate professionals among its children and grandchildren. Those who remain in agriculture (less than ten percent) cultivate large farms. For non-professionals, incomes average about $30,000 and for the 50 percent who have attended college and professional schools, incomes are between $30,000 and $100,000. Home ownership, usually in suburbs or small towns, is a common feature of the Dutch American community.

## POLITICS AND GOVERNMENT

The vast majority of Dutch Americans are Republicans but they are usually not political activists. During the Anglo-Boer War (1899-1902), Dutch Americans organized to influence U.S. foreign policy in favor of the South African Boers. Because they distrusted Great Britain, the Dutch resisted Woodrow Wilson's pro-British policies prior to World War I. But when war broke out, they did not resist the draft. Instead, to demonstrate their loyalty, they enlisted, bought war bonds, and adopted English. During that era, religious and educational leaders promoted patriotism, which has remained vibrant to the present.

In places where the Dutch are concentrated, especially in western Michigan and northwestern Iowa, they have elected Dutch Americans to local, state and national offices. With few exceptions, Republican loyalty has not been breached by ethnic cohesion.

## INDIVIDUAL AND GROUP CONTRIBUTIONS

### BUSINESS

Major business leaders stretching from the railroad builder, Cornelius Vanderbilt (1794-1877), to Wayne Huizenga (1938- ), co-founder of Waste Management Inc. and the Blockbuster Video chain, demonstrate that Dutch Americans have reached the highest levels of commercial success. But again, apart from its early engagement in establishing world-wide capitalism, Netherlandic culture has had little to do with the specific endeavors of its most prominent Dutch American entrepreneurs. Others in this category—Walter Chrysler (1875-1940) of auto fame, retail innovator Hendrik Meijer (1883-1964), and the Amway Corporation's co-founders—Jay Van Andel (1924- ) and Richard De Vos (1926- )—have created uniquely American institutions.

Among less prominent entrepreneurs, the Hekman brothers and several book publishers have adapted ethnic business ventures to gain national markets. John Hekman (1866-1951), his brother Jelle (1888-1957), and Jan Vander Heide (1905-1988) both inherited and purchased small-scale bakeries which currently market nationally under the Keebler and Dutch Twin labels. A third Hekman brother, Henry (1890-1962), developed his furniture company with an upscale inventory of office and home furniture. In this he joined several other Dutch-owned furniture companies in western Michigan—such as Bergsma Brothers, Hollis Baker, and especially Walter D. Idema, who with others founded the metal office furniture giant, Steelcase Inc. Doubtless the area's large number of Dutch immigrants with woodworking skills has contributed to Grand Rapids' long-standing identity as the furniture city.

## ENTERTAINMENT

Pop culture icons like film producer Cecil B. de Mille (1881-1951) and rock star Bruce Springsteen (1949- ) are Dutch American.

## LITERATURE

Americans of Dutch descent have contributed significantly to American literature but, while firmly embedded in the literary canon, the works of Walt Whitman (1819-1892), Herman Melville (1819-1891) and Van Wyck Brooks (1885-1963) demonstrate little or nothing that reflects a Dutch American ethos. Well-known authors whose Dutch ethnicity shaped and informed their works include Peter De Vries (1910-1993), David (1901-1967) and Meindert De Jong (1906-1991), along with Frederick Manfred (1912- ), and Arnold Mulder (1885-1959). Both De Vries' *The Blood of the Lamb* and Manfred's *The Green Earth* draw deeply from the wells of ethnic experience. Unlike Arnold Mulder's characters, who trade ethnic culture for that of the American mainstream, Manfred's *Englekings* and De Vries' *Don Wanderhope* incorporate their ethnicity and struggle with its meaning.

David De Jong's *With a Dutch Accent* highlights conflicts between settled and newly arriving immigrants within Dutch enclaves, while Meindert De Jong crafted his widely acclaimed children's literature from recollections of his Netherlandic (Frisian) boyhood.

## POLITICS

Dutch American political activists who achieved national prominence—Martin Van Buren (1782-1862), Theodore Roosevelt (1858-1919), Anna Eleanor Roosevelt (1906-1975), and Franklin Delano Roosevelt (1882-1945)—achieved nothing of significance that can be ascribed to their Netherlandic backgrounds. In contrast, Senator Arthur Vandenberg (1884-1951) and current U.S. Representatives Peter Hoekstra (1954- ) and Vern Ehlers (1934- ) owe much of their political success to the large percentage of Dutch ethnic support they attract in their districts. Similar correlations are evident in northwestern Iowa or in Whatcom County, Washington where the executive director, Shirley Van Zanten, receives crucial support from ethnic cohorts. The Dutch, wherever they cluster together—in western Michigan, in the Chicago area, in Washington State, and in Iowa—are pervasively conservative and Republican. Of 41 Dutch Americans holding national, state, and local offices, 35 are Republican. Thus, socialist Daniel de Leon (1852-1914) and pacifist A. J. Muste (1885-1967) are clearly atypical among their ethnic cohorts.

## PUBLISHING

Grand Rapids, Michigan, has also become a center for the publication of religious books, led by the William B. Eerdmans Publishing Company. Eerdmans (1882-1966) and Louis Kregel (1890-1939) began by printing and reprinting Dutch and English books, catechisms, and pamphlets for the Reformed community. Since then, the Kregel firm has continued to feature the republication of standard religious works, while Eerdmans issues an inventory of new studies in theology, literature, and history aimed at a wide spectrum of religious interest groups. The Baker Book House, founded by Louis Kregel's son-in-law, Herman Baker (1912-1991), publishes primarily for traditional religious groups. Peter J. Zondervan (1909-1993) left Eerdmans in 1931 to organize the Zondervan Corporation which, with a chain of Midwestern book stores, has created a market among Christian fundamentalists. Edward Bok (1863-1930) came to America from Holland as a small child; he became editor of *Ladies' Home Journal* and addressed it to America's homemakers—a revolution in publishing.

### THEOLOGY, PHILOSOPHY, MEDICINE, AND HISTORY

Due largely to their abiding interest in Reformed religious perspectives, Dutch Americans are prominent in theology, philosophy and in some facets of history. They have founded theological schools in Grand Rapids, Michigan (Calvin Theological Seminary, 1876), in New Jersey (New Brunswick Theological Seminary, 1784), and in Holland, Michigan (Western Theological Seminary, 1866). Graduates Lewis B. Smedes (1921- ) and Richard Mouw (1941- ), both currently at Pasadena's Fuller Theological Seminary, have gained national acclaim from their publications and lectures. Robert Schuller (1926- ) is the most widely known preacher with a Dutch Reformed heritage. Among theological school professors, Ira John Hesselink (1928- ) at Western, Cornelius Plantinga (1946- ) at Calvin, James Muilenburg (1896-?) at Union, and Simon De Vries (1921- ) at the Methodist Theological School in Delaware, Ohio, have gained wide acclaim due to their classroom teaching and many publications. In philosophy, Yale's Nicholas Wolterstorff (1932- ) and Alvin Plantinga (1932- ) from Notre Dame have reinvigorated religious discussions throughout the international community of philosophers. Both William Bousma (1923- ), in his re-examination of John Calvin (1509-1564), and Dale Van Kley (1941- ), with revisionist studies of the French Revolution, have rekindled and directed an interest in the historical significance of religion in Western history. Famed pediatrician Benjamin Spock (1903- ) guided millions of young parents with his baby books.

# MEDIA

Dutch-language journalism, vibrant between 1870 and 1920, included over 50 periodicals, but none have survived without adopting English. *De Wachter* (*Watchman*) persisted from 1868 to 1985 with subsidies from the Christian Reformed Church. Two bilingual periodicals, *D.I.S.*—published by the Dutch International Society—and the *Windmill Herald,* retain an audience from among the postwar immigrants, but with the passing of that generation, even bilingual periodicals will probably cease to exist.

*The Windmill Herald.*
Bi-weekly newspaper for Dutch and Flemish communities; first published in 1958.

**Contact:** A. A. Van der Heide, Editor.

**Address:** Vanderheide Publishing Co. Ltd., P.O. Box Bag 9033, Surrey, British Columbia, Canada V3T 4X3.

**Telephone:** (604) 597-2144.

# ORGANIZATIONS AND ASSOCIATIONS

**The American Association for Netherlandic Studies.**
Sponsors biennial interdisciplinary conferences on the study of the Dutch language and of Netherlandic culture around the world. It publishes the biennial journal *PAANS* and biannual *Newsletter.*

**Contact:** Margriet Lacy, President.

**Address:** Butler University, Dean's Office, LAS, 4600 Sunset Avenue, Indianapolis, Indiana 46208.

**Telephone:** (317) 283-9678.

**Association for the Advancement of Dutch American Studies (AADAS).**
Sponsors biennial conferences on nineteenth and twentieth century Dutch ethnic history in North America.

**Contact:** Larry J. Wagenaar, President.

**Address:** Joint Archives of Holland, Hope College Campus, Holland, Michigan 49423.

**Telephone:** (616) 394-7798.

**The Dutch American Historical Commission.**
Composed of representatives from Calvin College, Calvin Theological Seminary, Hope College, the Netherlands Museum, and the Western Theological Seminary, the commission publishes significant studies of nineteenth- and twentieth-century Dutch American history and coordinates the preservation of historical source materials.

**Contact:** John Huisken, President.

**Address:** Hope College, Holland, Michigan 49423.

**Dutch Family Heritage Society (DFHS).**
Gathers and disseminates information on Dutch history, culture, and genealogy in the United States, Canada, and Netherlands.

**Contact:** Mary Lynn Spijkerman Parker, President.

**Address:** 2463 Ledgewood Drive, West Jordan, Utah 84084.

**Telephone:** (801) 967-8400.

### The Dutch International Society.

With a North American and Netherlandic membership, the society maintains international relationships by travel tours, the quarterly *D.I.S. Magazine*, and sponsoring cultural programs and events.

**Contact:** Peter Wobbema, President.

**Address:** 5370 Eastern Avenue, S.E., Grand Rapids, Michigan 49508.

**Telephone:** (616) 531-2298.

### The Holland Society of New York.

Organized to collect and preserve information about the history of Colonial New Netherlands, membership consists primarily of Colonial Era descendants.

**Contact:** Peter Van Dyke, President.

**Address:** 122 East 58th Street, New York, New York 10022.

**Telephone:** (212) 758-1675.

### Netherland-America Foundation (NAF).

Works to advance educational, literary, artistic, scientific, historical, and cultural relationships between the United States and the Netherlands.

**Contact:** Wanda Fleck, Administrator.

**Address:** 1 Rockefeller Plaza, 11th Floor, New York, New York 10020.

**Telephone:** (212) 767-1616.

# MUSEUMS AND RESEARCH CENTERS

### Calvin College and Theological Seminary Library Archives.

Contains manuscripts, books, microfilm, and periodicals for the study of nineteenth- and twentieth-century Dutch American history, religion, and culture in the United States, Canada, and the Netherlands. Its publications include: *Origins*, a biannual historical journal; the annual *Newsletter*; and *Heritage Hall Publication Series*.

**Contact:** Zwanet Janssens, Archivist.

**Address:** 3207 Burton Street, S.E., Grand Rapids, Michigan 49546.

**Telephone:** (616) 957-6313.

### Dutch Heritage Center.

Contains books, manuscripts, microfilm, and periodicals for the study of Dutch American history and culture in the greater Chicago area.

**Contact:** Hendrik Sliekers, Curator.

**Address:** Trinity Christian College, 6601 West College Drive, Palos Heights, Illinois 60463.

**Telephone:** (708) 597-3000.

### Holland Society of New York.

Included in its collection are books, manuscripts, films, and paintings related to Dutch American culture, history, and genealogy. The society publishes *De Halve Maen*, a quarterly journal.

**Contact:** Margaret Hutchinson, Librarian.

**Address:** 122 East 58th Street, New York, New York 10022.

**Telephone:** (212) 758-1878.

### The Joint Archives of Holland.

Contains the combined archival resources of Hope College, the Western Theological Seminary, and the Holland, Michigan, community, and centers on the general history of Dutch Americans in the nineteenth and twentieth centuries.

**Contact:** Larry J. Wagenaar, Director.

**Address:** Hope College Campus, Holland, Michigan 49423.

**Telephone:** (616) 394-7790.

### Northwestern College Library Archives.

Provides manuscripts, books, microfilm, and periodicals for the study of nineteenth- and twentieth-century Dutch American history in northwestern Iowa, Orange City, and Northwestern College.

**Contact:** Nella Kennedy, Archivist.

**Address:** Orange City, Iowa 51041.

**Telephone:** (712) 737-7000.

# SOURCES FOR ADDITIONAL STUDY

Balmer, Randall, H. *A Perfect Babel of Confusion: Dutch Religion and English Culture in the Middle Colonies*. New York: Oxford University Press, 1989.

Bratt, James H. *Dutch Calvinism in Modern America: A History of a Conservative Subculture*. Grand

Rapids, Michigan: Eerdmans Publishing Co., 1984.

Brinks, Herbert J. *Dutch Immigrant Voices, 1850-1930: Correspondence from the USA.* Ithaca, New York: Cornell University Press, 1995.

De Jong, Gerald F. *The Dutch in America, 1609-1974.* Boston: Twayne Publishers, 1975.

Fabend, Firth H. *A Dutch Family in the Middle Colonies, 1660-1800.* New Brunswick, New Jersey: Rutgers University Press, 1991.

Goodfriend, Joyce D. *Before the Melting Pot: Society and Culture in Colonial New York City, 1664-1730.* Princeton, New Jersey: Princeton University Press, 1992.

Kroes, Rob. *The Persistence of Ethnicity: Dutch Calvinist Pioneers in Amsterdam, Montana.* Chicago: University of Illinois Press, 1992.

Lambert, Audrey M. *The Making of the Dutch Landscape: An Historical Geography of The Netherlands.* London: Academic Press, 1985.

Lucas, Henry. *Netherlanders in America: Dutch Immigrants to the United States.* Ann Arbor: University of Michigan Press, 1955.

Swierenga, Robert P. *The Dutch in America: Immigration Settlement and Cultural Change.* New Brunswick, New Jersey: Rutgers University Press, 1985.

Van Hinte, Jacob. *Netherlanders in America: A Study of Emigration and Settlement in the Nineteenth and Twentieth Centuries of the United States of America.* Grand Rapids: Baker Book House, 1985.

# ECUADORAN AMERICANS

by
Jeremy Mumford

Ecuadoran
Americans are
ambivalent about
assimilation. It eases
the difficulties of
immigrant life, yet it
steals what remains
of home.

## OVERVIEW

Ecuador is a small country on the northwestern coast of South America. It measures 280,000 square kilometers—roughly the size of Colorado. It is bordered by Colombia on the north, Peru on the south and east, and the Pacific Ocean on the west. The earth's equator, for which the country is named, runs through Ecuador only a few miles from its capital, Quito. Ecuador's flag consists of horizontal stripes—a wide yellow stripe above narrower blue and red stripes—surmounted by the national seal. This seal contains various national symbols, including a huge bird of prey with wings outspread, the sun in the sky, a white mountain and a boat on a river.

Geography divides Ecuador into three regions, western, central, and eastern. In the west is the coast, or *costa*. Flat and streaked with rivers, this region is a lush, hot jungle. East of that are the Andes, or the *sierra*. For centuries this was the most populous and dominant region. The highest peaks fall into two ranges that run parallel to each other, north and south; between them is a long, fertile plateau, which the nineteenth century explorer Alexander von Humboldt called "the Avenue of the Volcanoes." This "avenue" and the lower slopes of the great mountains are crowded with history and human settlement. Below the mountains on the eastern side is the Amazonian area, or the *oriente*. While similar in climate to the *costa*, it has a denser jungle, greater rivers, and is in every way more isolated from the outside world. Only two percent of Ecuador's population lives in the *oriente*. In much of this region, Spanish is not spoken. Of the three this region has the loosest ties to the Ecuadoran state. Yet it is here that Ecuador's greatest wealth in recent times is found: its oil, its "black gold."

Ecuador's population is about 11 million. The majority are descended from Spaniards and Indians. In the last 30 years, between 200,000 and 500,000 Ecuadorans—between about two and five percent of the national population—have immigrated to the United States.

Ecuador's history has long been shaped by empires from outside, and its identity as an independent unified nation is of recent origin. Historically, Ecuador has had to struggle against both external and internal forces threatening its national identity. On the one hand, larger neighbors have at various times absorbed part or all of its territory. On the other hand, Ecuador's three regions have such separate geographical and social characteristics that a sense of common nationality is difficult.

## HISTORY

Many civilizations have inhabited Ecuador over the millennia, but there is little continuity between most of these groups and modern Ecuadorans. Coastal Ecuador has been called the cradle of South America because the earliest evidence of advanced human society was found here. A shroud of mystery covers the first settlement of the continent. Most historians assume its first inhabitants were migrants from northeast Asia who crossed the Bering Strait and worked their way south. Others think settlers may have reached South America by sea from Japan or elsewhere. In any case, the earliest South Americans whose artifacts have survived were coastal Ecuadorans—the Valdivian civilization in Manabí province, whose pottery dates from 3500 B.C. Later Ecuadorans *costeños* (people of the *costa*) produced finely worked gold and platinum ornaments; their descendants may have carried their pottery and metal-working skills into the Andean highlands and beyond.

While the earliest settled societies in Ecuador were on the coast, in later centuries the most powerful and advanced societies were found in the mountains. Various ethnolinguistic groups, with varying degrees of political organization, divided the highlands between them, sometimes at war, sometimes at peace.

During the middle of the fifteenth century A.D., the Inca state in what is now southern Peru began to expand rapidly under a series of gifted leaders. In the 1460s the Inca army penetrated the southern part of what is now Ecuador. The Incas were able to transform their conquered lands in a short amount of time. They built excellent roads, leading to rapid and efficient communication within their empire. And they forced whole villages to relocate, placing speakers of their own language (Quechua) on the conquered soil while moving their new subjects to where they had no roots or allies. In a short time, the Incas virtually obliterated the political entities that had preceded them in Ecuador. Although Inca rule in Ecuador was brief, a descendant of Quechua remains the most common Indian language in Ecuador.

By the early sixteenth century, the Inca conquest of what is now Ecuador was complete. Ironically, it was soon after this first foreign conquest that Ecuador had its one moment of ascendancy over Peru. After the death of the emperor Huanya-Capac, his two sons were rivals for the throne. Huascar was born in the Inca heartland of Cuzco, the child of his father's sister. Atahualpa was born in Quito, the child of the emperor and a local princess. After a grueling civil war, Atahualpa prevailed, and by 1530 the portion of the aristocracy that had settled in Ecuador controlled the empire.

It was just at this moment that Spanish conquistadors entered the picture—one of the strangest moments in the history of warfare and cruelty. A minor nobleman named Francisco Pizarro, with an army of less than 2,000, was able to conquer an empire of half a million in ten years. The civil war, which had just ended, left the army and the emperor exhausted and demoralized. With little information about the invaders, and fearing that they would ally with his defeated brother, Atahualpa did not attack the Spaniards but sought to negotiate with them. He put himself into a position where they were able to make him their prisoner; this crucial advantage, skillfully exploited, eventually allowed Pizarro to defeat and all but exterminate the Inca ruling class by 1540.

This conquest led to a 300-year Spanish empire in South America. During this period, the region known as the *audiencia* of Quito (modern Ecuador) was semi-autonomous but remained a lesser sibling to its larger neighbors. Until 1720 Ecuador was a section of the viceroyalty of Peru; after that date, it was grouped with what is now Colombia in the viceroyalty of New Granada.

At the time of South America's independence in the early nineteenth century, Ecuador was again a pivotal territory, and was again contested by outside powers. Two great generals shared the glory of South America's liberation: Bolívar, a Creole from Venezuela; and San Martín, a Spanish officer, born in Buenos Aires, who defected to serve his native land. Starting at opposite ends of the continent, each achieved a series of stunning victories by moving soldiers quickly and unexpectedly across mountains and jungles. After Bolívar had advanced as far as Quito, and San Martín took Peru from Spain, the two generals met in Quayaquil—the chief city of coastal Ecuador.

That meeting in 1822 between the continent's two greatest heroes has become legendary. Nobody knew how the great talents and plans of the two men would accommodate one another; and no one knows what they said to each other that day in Quayaquil. But after the meeting, San Martín left South America forever, while Bolívar became known as the continent's liberator. Historians from the southern part of South America charge that Bolívar denied San Martín reinforcements he needed, thus forcing his abdication. Northern historians, siding with Bolívar, say San Martín simply recognized Bolívar's superior greatness. In any case, an Ecuadoran city was the point where two movements of liberation met and where the continent's destiny was decided.

After independence Ecuador joined with what are now Colombia, Panama, and Venezuela to form a nation called Gran Colombia. Once again Ecuador was made a lesser section of a larger unit. But centrifugal forces pulled the nation apart. When Bolívar's chosen successor, the Ecuadoran Antonio José de Sucre, was assassinated the union collapsed and Bolívar left for Europe.

In modern times the uncertainty of Ecuador's national identity, with regard to its powerful neighbors, has persisted. In 1941 Peru seized in war more than one-third of Ecuadoran territory in the south and east. Most of this land was thinly inhabited Amazonian forest; and most of the people living there had little sense that they were Ecuadoran to begin with. Although Ecuadorans have never forgiven the seizure, their government at the time signed a treaty legitimizing it.

## GEOGRAPHY

As well as being threatened from the outside, Ecuador's national identity is threatened by deep internal divisions. The country's three regions feel little affinity with one another. Each is markedly different from the others in geography, ethnic makeup, accent and language, and culture.

The people of the *costa* are descended from Europeans, Indians, and—in the northern state of Esmeraldas—from Africans. But not much traditional Indian culture survives, and very few speak any language other than Spanish. They inhabit a land that is sparsely populated, flat, fertile, and covered by a dense tropical forest that resists cultivation at every step. Most live in great poverty. Many poor people own their own land but few become rich off it. Many farmers practice a primitive slash-and-burn agriculture, seldom pushing the encroaching jungle more than an arm's length away. In temperament the *costeños* are thought to be cheerful and egalitarian, giving little thought to the future. Led by the firebrand politicians of Quayaquil, the *costeño* political inclination is liberal, if not socialist.

The *sierra* is a very different land—dry, mountainous, and crowded. There is fertile land on the Andean plateau but not in abundance. The people are *mestizos* and Indians, many of whom live in ancient, traditional villages. Many *serranos* speak the Indian language Quichua (descended from the Quechua of the Incas) and some speak no Spanish. The soil in the *sierra* is of poorer quality than that on the *costa*, but the methods of farming are more sophisticated and it requires less struggle to keep the land in cultivation. Families may have farmed the same plot of land for many generations. Unlike on the *costa*, there is a strong sense of social hierarchy in the *sierra*, where one family may have run the village and farmed the most fertile land for a hundred years. There is also a greater tradition of handicrafts such as weaving in the *sierra* than the *costa*. The temperament of the people is believed to be far more serious, even melancholy, than on the *costa*. Politically, *serranos* tend to be conservative.

The third region of Ecuador is the *oriente*, the Amazonian rainforest. This region is far less populous than the other two, containing just two percent of the national population. Like the *costa*, it contains dense forests but the soil is far less fertile than on the *costa*, and the farming is primitive or non-existent. Most of the people of the *oriente* are Indians living in traditional communities. Many preserve an ancient economy of hunting and gathering. About half speak neither Spanish nor Quichua and have little affinity with either the *mestizos* or the Indians to the west. Far less than either the *costeños* or the *serranos*, these people have little sense of themselves as Ecuadorans. With transistor radios, this has changed but only slowly.

Traditionally, the uncontested dominance of the *sierra* held Ecuador together. The *sierra* held the bulk of the population, the *costa* was lesser, and the *oriente* was mere territory to be owned. Recently, however, this situation has begun to change. According to John Martz in *Ecuador: Conflicting Political Culture and the Quest for Progress*, recent decades have seen a gradual but continuous population shift from *sierra* to *costa*. In 1875 the *sierra* had three times as many inhabitants as the *costa*; by the 1970s the two regions were approximately equal in population. The fertile areas of the *sierra*, however, continue to be more crowded than almost any area of the *costa*.

As the two regions have become equal in population, their political rivalry has become more serious. Each side is unwilling to accept a leader from the other. Furthermore, the *oriente* is rising slightly from its subservient position. Since the early 1970s Ecuador's greatest wealth has been its oil, which is nearly all under the soil of the *oriente*. While the local people have so far received little benefit from this, they have been forced to become more aware of the outside world as foreigners and Ecuadorans have plunged into these forests to drill for oil. As serious oil spills threaten the ecology and even the survival of the people of the *oriente*, they have begun to claim a voice in national decisions, consideration for their way of life, and a share of the wealth of their land. Indian groups have even sued Texaco, the oil company whose pipeline has spilled an estimated 17 million gallons of crude oil into the forest, in United States court.

### THE PEOPLE

Ecuador's 11 million people are descended from Spaniards, Indians, Africans, and other Europeans. About 40 percent of the country is *mestizo*, or of mixed Indian and Spanish ancestry, and 40 percent is Indian. Traditionally, Indians are at the bottom of the social order, are less likely to own their own land, and work at the most menial jobs. In traditional communities, whites and *mestizos* call Indians by first names, while Indians must treat whites and *mestizos* with deference.

Identity as an Indian or a *mestizo* has less to do with ancestry, skin color, and features than with social identity. On rare occasions people move back and forth between the two communities. An Indian may move to the city, improve his Spanish, and wear *mestizo* clothes; or a *mestizo* may return to his grandparents' village and the protection of the community, and adopt Indian clothes and habits.

### ECUADORAN AMERICANS

Until the 1960s very few Ecuadorans immigrated to the United States. In the late 1960s, however, Ecuadorans began to emigrate in large numbers. The 1990 census found 191,000 Ecuadorans in the United States, but there are so many undocumented Ecuadoran Americans that the true number is much larger. The Ecuadoran consulate in Manhattan estimates there are 300,000 Ecuadorans in New York and New Jersey, and 500,000 in the United States.

Several factors helped cause this large immigration. First, United States immigration law changed. Before 1965, national quotas on immigrants strongly favored Europeans; after that year, changes in the law made it easier for Latin Americans and others to immigrate. Furthermore, emigration was physically easier as air travel became affordable to ordinary people for the first time in history.

Another factor in Ecuadoran emigration—which, unlike those mentioned above, was specific to Ecuador—was the land reform of the mid-1960s. In 1964 Ecuador passed the Land Reform, Idle Lands, and Settlement Act. An attempt to end the feudal system that had existed in the *sierra* for centuries, the law redistributed land from absentee landlords to the peasants who farmed it. According to *Ecuador: A Country Study*, this act improved the lives of tens of thousands of poor Ecuadorans, and brought a measure of social justice to the countryside. But it also shook up what had been a stable society, causing far-reaching and unpredictable changes. Without credit or experience, many new small landowners had to sell their land. Peasants left the land their forefathers had farmed for generations. Large sections of the population left the *serrano* countryside for the cities, the *costa*, and foreign lands such as Venezuela and the United States.

Once Ecuadoran immigration to the United States began, it accelerated through a snowball effect. More than anything else, what makes emigration possible is having contacts in the new country. As immigrants send money home and encourage others to join them, the immigrant community builds on itself, causing its own growth. Ecuadorans come to the United States in many ways. Many immigrate according to the rules and procedures laid out by United States law: a close relative or a prospective employer petitions for them and they wait in Ecuador until a visa becomes available. But this means complex paperwork and often years on a waiting list. Others follow the correct procedures but stay illegally in the United States while awaiting their papers. Still others follow no legal procedure, but live in the United States for years without documentation. These may smuggle themselves across the border without papers—either by foot from Mexico, or by boat into Puerto Rico. Most often, they fly in with a limited-stay tourist visa and never leave. A study done in New York found that undocumented Ecuadorans are one of the three largest groups of illegal immigrants in the city (Deborah Sontag, "Study Sees Illegal Aliens in New Light," *New York Times*, September 2, 1993, p. B1).

Many people make their living by helping Ecuadorans immigrate illegally. This is one industry where nationality counts. Immigrants from different Latin American countries may read the same newspapers and watch the same television shows, but for immigration help, Ecuadorans seek out other Ecuadorans. Immigrant smuggling ventures usually involve people who are all from the same country, even from the same city or village. There are businesses that advise Ecuadorans how to answer questions so as to obtain a tourist visa, and others that simply sell green cards. There are shipping workers who smuggle Ecuadorans as stowaways on commercial vessels. There are even businesses that falsely guarantee success in the INS green card lottery (Deborah Sontag, "You Don't Need a Tout for This Race," *International Herald Tribune*, June 21, 1994).

Ecuadoran Americans come from every part of Ecuador. In the early period of immigration most came from the northern and central *sierra*, including the area around Quito. Later, large numbers came from the *costa*. During the early 1990s the largest numbers have come from the southern *sierra*, near the border with Peru. An estimated five percent of the Ecuadoran states of Cañar and Azuay immigrated to the United States.

The majority of Ecuadoran immigrants come to one destination: New York City. According to the 1990 census, 60 percent of Ecuadorans live in the New York area; the second-largest group, ten percent, lives in Los Angeles. This concentration is due partly to the snowball effect mentioned above: the more Ecuadorans there are in one place, the more will come there. It is also due partly to New York's unusual hospitality to immigrants. New York has always been a city of newcomers, and in recent decades the city's growth has been largely dependant on immigrants. At a time when public opinion all over the country has turned against immigrants, including legal ones, New York has not followed suit. City officials emphasize getting illegal aliens into the taxpaying mainstream, not deporting them or denying them services.

Ecuadorans in New York cluster in neighborhoods, usually in the same ones where other South Americans live. The greatest number live in the borough of Queens, especially in the swath of northern Queens covering Astoria, Jackson Heights, and Flushing. Roosevelt Avenue in Jackson Heights is lined with Ecuadoran travel agencies, restaurants, and telephone and money-wiring services. Signs in local bars advertise South American soccer matches on cable television. Another group of Ecuadorans settled in the Bronx, in the Morris Hills and Highbridge neighborhoods north of Yankee Stadium. Still other Ecuadoran neighborhoods are found in Brooklyn, in New Jersey cities such as Newark and Jersey City, and in working class towns in Connecticut.

# ACCULTURATION AND ASSIMILATION

Like most immigrants, Ecuadoran Americans are ambivalent about assimilation. It eases the difficulties of immigrant life, yet it steals what remains of home. New Ecuadoran immigrants do not tend to embrace a new American identity to the extent that some immigrant groups do. Many return home after a few years, or hope to do so. For those who stay, however, assimilation is difficult to resist. Older immigrants often complain that their grown-up children speak better English than Spanish, marry outside of the community, get divorced, abandon their religion, and ignore their parents.

Part of the assimilation that Ecuadoran Americans experience is not toward mainstream American culture, but toward the culture of the Latino American community. For instance, in Mexican American families a girl's fifteenth

Civic committee officials lead the annual Ecuadoran Day Parade in Queens, New York.

birthday, or *quinceaño*, is an extremely important occasion. She will wear a white dress and attend mass, surrounded by her friends in formal, matching outfits. Her party afterwards may be the fanciest occasion of her life before her wedding. Her parents will spend a lot of money, may even hire a live band. This custom has never been a common one in Ecuador. Among Ecuadoran Americans, however, it has become current, just as it is among other Americans of Latino background ("Today I Am a Señorita: In Latin American Tradition, the Quinceañera Marks a Girl's Transition to Womanhood," *The Record* [Bergen County, New Jersey], February 2, 1995, p. D1).

One difficult issue related to assimilation is whether or not to become a naturalized U.S. citizen. Only a minority of Ecuadoran Americans do so. Those who are undocumented aliens cannot become citizens, of course, and even those who have legally obtained a green card must wait five years before they are eligible to become citizens. However, even of those Ecuadorans who are eligi-

ble for citizenship, no more than 20 percent choose to become citizens. The number for immigrants generally is 37 percent (Deborah Sontag, "Immigrants Forgoing Citizenship While Pursuing American Dream," *New York Times*, July 25, 1993, p. 1). This is partly because the naturalization process can be intimidating, involving a battery of paperwork, an English language test, and obscure civics questions such as: "In what order did the 13 original states enter the union?"

Furthermore, many Ecuadorans see U.S. citizenship as a betrayal of their own country. Recently, Ecuador began to permit expatriates to become citizens of other nations without losing their Ecuadoran citizenship. On an emotional level, however, many Ecuadorans feel uncomfortable swearing allegiance to the United States. Naturalization and assimilation, however, can be a defense against the discrimination that Ecuadoran Americans experience. Immigrants venturing into the wrong neighborhoods may be beaten by assailants shouting "Speak English!" (Ann Costello, "Ecuadorian Immigrants Finding Obstacles in Their Path," *New York Times*, October 3, 1993, Section 13WC, p. 23; cited hereafter as Costello). Many English-speakers have negative stereotypes about Latinos: that they are stupid, lazy, and destined for low-status jobs. A mother whose son joined the army and received advanced training in electrical engineering was proud that he had disproved a city official, who once told her Ecuadoran immigrants were good for nothing except being dishwashers and waiters (Ken Yamada, "A Dream Dies in Desert Sand: Queens Family Mourns Soldier Slain by Mine," *Newsday*, March 2, 1991, p. 12).

## CUISINE

Each of the different regions of Ecuador has its own cuisine. Perhaps the most distinctive and highly prized Ecuadoran dish, or what most closely approaches a national dish, is the *ceviche* of the *costa*. The dish is consumed in many regions of Latin America, but Ecuadorans claim to have invented it. *Ceviche* is raw seafood marinated in the juice of citrus fruits and served cold. The acidic juice causes a chemical reaction in the meat: it toughens it, keeps it from going bad, and changes its flavor. *Ceviche* can be made with many different fish in lemon, lime, or even orange juice; but shrimp is most commonly used. The *ceviche* may also have vegetables such as onions and peppers, and roasted peanuts may be sprinkled on top. This dish can be found in any Ecuadoran American restaurant.

Besides fish, the other staple food of the *costa* is bananas. Ecuador was one of the original "banana republics," depending utterly on banana exports. Bananas have always been at the heart of lowland Ecuadoran agriculture and cuisine and are a major part of the diet both in the *costa* and in the *oriente*. There are many *costeños* in New York, and these New Yorkers eat a lot of bananas. A wide variety of bananas grow in Ecuador: *guineos* (the yellow bananas known in the United States); *magueños* (short, plump red bananas); *oritas* (tiny bananas); *platanos* (green plaintains for cooking). These and others are all available in South American specialty groceries and are prepared by Ecuadoran Americans in many different ways—whole, sliced and pulped, raw, boiled, fried, and baked.

Where *costeños* use bananas, *serranos* use potatoes. The potato, which was first domesticated by ancient Andean farmers, has been a staple in the region ever since. Like the banana, the potato has many forms in Ecuador, and is prepared in many ways. Ecuadoran Americans from the *sierra* must seek out specialty groceries to find the various different potatoes they are used to. Besides potatoes, *serranos* also love corn, which can be eaten on the cob or in tamales. Much of *serrano* cooking takes the form of soups. Before the Spaniards came, Ecuadorans did not have ovens so they boiled a large part of their food. This custom has continued. The ordinary Ecuadoran meal will center on a *sopa* or *caldo*—a thin soup with potatoes and other vegetables and meat.

The ordinary diet in Ecuador has very little meat. One traditional meat is the *cuy*, or guinea pig. Many Indian families in rural Ecuador keep guinea pigs, which they kill and eat on special occasions. The meat is delicious, but there is very little of it. Ecuadorans in the United States have trouble getting *cuy* meat. But beef, chicken, and pork are more affordable in the United States than in Ecuador and have been more widely incorporated in Ecuadoran American cooking.

In Ecuador one of the most popular drinks is *chicha*, a fermented liquor from the yucca tubor. In villages in the *costa*, the drink is still made by women who chew the yucca up and spit it out. Chemicals in the saliva help to ferment the yucca. In the United States, this drink is difficult to obtain. Most Ecuadoran Americans drink wine or beer. Ecuadoran Americans still drink their coffee in the traditional way, which requires boiling the coffee down to a thick sludge known as *esencia* and bringing it to the table in a small pitcher or bottle. It is then blended in the cup with hot water, milk, and sugar. The final product has an odd, burnt taste quite different from the coffee most Americans drink. Ecuadorans prefer it.

## MUSIC

Music is an important part of Ecuadoran culture. The Ecuadoran *sierra*, along with Peru and Bolivia, is the heartland of Andean music. This is an ancient and highly evolved musical style, mainly played by Indians. Like all American musical forms, it has European and African influences; but musicologists believe that Andean music in its most basic form has remained the same since before the arrival of the Spaniards.

The essential components of Andean music are winds and percussion. The wind instruments are flutes or panpipes—a row of pipes of various lengths attached together; the percussion is drums and rattles. From the Spaniards, Andean Indians adopted string instruments: some violins, but more often guitars and small ukulele-like instruments. With these instruments, musicians produce a sound that is both emotional and danceable. The mood, carried by the winds and strings, is generally plaintive, even melancholy. The percussion carries the music forward at a steady pace, inviting dancing. The typical musical group is large (six or more different musicians) and is usually all male. To those unfamiliar with it, Andean music can sound monotonous with slight variations on a theme by the flutes. But to those who appreciate it, the long Andean song is a hypnotic exploration of a musical idea.

In recent years there has been a renaissance of traditional music throughout the Andes. In the past, traditional music was a local phenomenon, and musicians were seldom heard outside of their own region. Today, recordings of traditional music are widely available, groups tour, and certain musical groups have become famous throughout the whole Andean region. For instance, the Bolivian group Los Kjarkas won a wide following throughout Ecuador when they toured there, and their songs are now widely played in Ecuador. The listening public, both in the cities and countryside, has become more sophisticated about traditional music. Certain songs have become standards, and are played throughout the region. Panpipes from the southern Andes, called *zamponas*, are becoming popular in Ecuador.

Traditional Andean music has also become popular in the United States. Many Ecuadoran Americans of *serrano* Indian background perform in traditional groups, often with Peruvians and Bolivians. Some play on university campuses and in halls, but many more play in the streets and subways of New York and other cities. Such groups may tour in a bus to play in the streets of different cities: with their long, straight hair, homburg hats and brightly colored *serrano* ponchos, they create a spectacle anywhere they have not been seen before, and may earn good money in spontaneous gifts. These musicians wear working clothes that emphasize their Indian background but that they would probably not wear at home, either in New York or Ecuador.

Traditional Andean music is by no means the only Ecuadoran music. Even in Ecuador, that music is less popular than so-called *musica nacional*, a style of music that uses amplified and electronic instruments, and blends elements of traditional and popular Latin music. This music is played at weddings and other festivities, and is also called *sanjuanitos*, after the festival of San Juan. Ecuadorans in the *costa* play a musical style closely related to the coastal Colombian *cumbia* style, with strong Afro-Caribbean influences. While traditional Andean music is Ecuador's most distinctive cultural export, Ecuadoran Americans at home are more likely to listen to *sanjuanitos* or the various other Latin styles that have come together in the Latino American community.

### HOLIDAYS

The most important holiday for Ecuadorans is August 10, the anniversary of the *primer grito* or "first cry" of independence in Ecuador and South America. In New York this day is Ecuador Day and is marked by a parade on 37th Avenue in Queens. Ecuadoran New Yorkers also participate in the Desfile de Hispanidad, a parade of Latin American immigrants on the day before Columbus Day.

Many Ecuadoran Americans also celebrate the festivals of the Christian year, such as Christmas, Carnival, and Holy Week. In addition, individual saints have their festivals, which are associated with certain towns or regions of Ecuador. The feast of Saint John the Baptist (San Juan), celebrated on June 24, is of special importance to Otavaleños, and is celebrated by all-night music and dancing throughout the northern *sierra*. The feast of the Virgin of Carmen, on July 16, is marked by people from the town of Cuenca. Among immigrants, these religious holidays are generally celebrated in private and with friends, and not in public festivals as in Ecuador.

# LANGUAGE

Ecuador is a bilingual country. Spanish is the country's primary language, but it shares its position with the Indian language Quichua.

Most Ecuadorans speak Spanish. In the *costa*, few people speak anything else. In the *sierra*, Spanish is also the dominant language, spoken with a very different accent from on the *costa*. However, in traditional Indian communities in the *sierra*, the first language is Quichua, although they may also speak Spanish. Quichua was the language of the Inca empire, and was carried to Ecuador by Peruvian populations whom the Incas brought in to consolidate their position. Many of the Incas' subjects learned Quichua as the language of government and trade. Ironically, the Spaniards continued the spread of Quichua; Spanish missionaries taught Christianity in the Quichua language, prompting other Indian communities to learn it. In the *sierra*, Quichua is the only surviving Indian language. It has several dialects, and is no longer mutually comprehensible with the Indian language of Peru, called Quechua.

In the Amazonian *oriente*, about half the Indians speak Quichua. Their ancestral culture was destroyed by European diseases, and the survivors were gathered together by Spanish missionaries. The rest of the Amazonian Indians speak the languages of their separate tribes, such as the Shuur and the Achuar. These more traditional groups live mainly in the southern part of eastern Ecuador.

Nearly all Ecuadorans who immigrate to the United States speak Spanish. Only a minority of immigrants come from traditional Indian communities, and they lack sufficient numbers to maintain a Quichua-speaking community. But while Ecuadoran immigrants cannot avoid Spanish, the same does not hold true for English. The cohesive Ecuadoran American community allows many to avoid learning fluent English, even after ten years or more in the United States.

# FAMILY AND COMMUNITY DYNAMICS

Ecuadorans have two models of family life: the Spanish and *mestizo* model, and the Indian model. In the first model the father rules the family. He has few responsibilities at home, spends much of his leisure time away from his family, and is tacitly permitted to see other women. The mother does the work within the family. Children are taught to be obedient to their parents. Daughters are allowed little freedom outside the house. In the Indian family, on the other hand, husband and wife have a more equal relationship. The wife plays a greater economic role and has more decision-making authority within the family. Sexual infidelity is socially unacceptable for either spouse.

Mainstream American society, meanwhile, exhibits a third model of family life. The position of the two parents is relatively equal, there is more sexual freedom than in either style of Ecuadoran family, and children have great free-

dom and independence. As do all immigrants, Ecuadoran Americans must grapple with the cultural differences in family life between their home and their adopted country; and they must decide whether to resist or to embrace American norms.

Many Ecuadoran Americans believe that child-rearing in the United States is too lax, and they worry that the culture will be a bad influence on their own children. The children themselves experience culture shock at the freedom and informality of American childhood. But some Ecuadorans seek out American norms of family life. One woman filed an application for asylum in the United States, saying that she would be in danger from her abusive husband if she went home. She felt protected from him in America, but was afraid that if she went back to Ecuador he could hurt her without fear of punishment because the authorities would not object to a husband disciplining his wife. If they were divorced in Ecuador, she feared that the state would grant him full custody of their two-year-old daughter (Dan Herbeck, "Asylum Request Here Might Set Precedent," *Buffalo News*, January 3, 1995, p. 1).

Immigration inevitably brings change to family life, whether one accepts or rejects it. This is due not only to new cultural norms, but also to the ways in which immigrating separates and rearranges families. Often men immigrate alone leaving their wives and children in Ecuador. In this respect, Ecuadoran immigrants differ from other South American immigrants, among whom women outnumber men. Such men may plan to get settled in the United States and then send for their families, or they may intend to return home after earning some money. Often such immigrants will first send for their older sons, and only later for their wives and other children. In working-class Ecuadoran neighborhoods in the United States, there is a predominance of men. For the same reason, many Ecuadoran villages are currently made up mainly of women (Costello, p. 23).

Some immigrants, however, are young single women who may have a freedom and independence they would not experience in Ecuador. Among the community of immigrant Indian street peddlers from the Otavalo region, for instance, there are single women. Alone in an American city, they have a more free and independent life from the one they would have at home with their families. Interestingly, these women tend to be more culturally conservative than single Otavaleño men, and less likely to adopt North American clothing and values (Jonathan Kandell,

"Shuttle Capitalism: an Ecuadorean Indian Community Turns a Traditional Craft into a Tool for Cultural Survival and Takes It to the Street Corners of the World," *Los Angeles Times Magazine*, November 14, 1993, p. 30).

## COMMUNITY INSTITUTIONS

The Ecuadoran American community's most important institution is the regional association, established to unite fellow-immigrants from the same province or town. For the Ecuadoran, loyalty to village, city or region often looms larger than national loyalty. An Ecuadoran may identify himself first as a resident of the city of Ambato, second as a *serrano*, and only third as an Ecuadoran. Outside of New York, an immigrant may join an organization for Ecuadorans generally; but in New York, where there are many Ecuadorans, an immigrant will join an association of his hometown or region. These associations, many of which have very little formal organization but join in federations with those from other regions, are a vital part of immigrant social life.

Regional associations allow immigrants to surround themselves with others who not only share their country and language, but their cultural background, their regional accent, and even perhaps friends in common at home. They provide an extended family to immigrants who may be homesick or lonely, a pool of credit for an immigrant to start a business, and an informal channel for news and information as well as gifts and money. Mail may be slow, there may be no telephone at home, but at any given moment someone from the club is about to visit or return from Ecuador.

One important outward function of a regional association is charity. Individually, Ecuadoran immigrants send money to family and relatives. They join regional associations partly to extend this generosity beyond their family. Regional associations send large amounts of money to Ecuador every year—to schools, libraries, youth sports clubs, orphanages, and soup kitchens. One fundraiser will be to renovate a hometown church, another to bring a sick child to the United States for an operation.

The associations use a variety of fund-raising techniques, including raffles, fund drives, and radio promotions, but the most popular method is the fund-raising party. Members will rent an appropriate space, perhaps a community center, dance-club or South American restaurant; or they will convince a community businessperson to let them use the space for free. They will advertise the event in community newspapers and with flyers in Ecuadoran neighborhoods and businesses. The party will have an admission price, often between $10 and $15, and will feature food, drink, music and disco-style lighting. The band will be Ecuadoran, and will play a mix or traditional Ecuadoran folk music, romantic ballads, modern Ecuadoran dance music, and other Latino music. Those who dance to any one variety of music will probably not dance to the others (Evelyne Delori, "The Function of Voluntary Associations in the Ecuadoran-American Community in the New York-New Jersey Area," senior essay in anthropology, Columbia University, 1992).

Besides the regional associations, Ecuadoran Americans rely heavily on a range of services within the community. They depend on Ecuadoran groceries, restaurants, travel agencies, telephone services, and undertakers: the patchwork of services that make sections of Queens a little Quito, where one never has to feel like a foreigner. One of the most important of these services is Spanish-language banking. New York banks are notoriously unfriendly and will refuse to open accounts for those without much money, a job, or a social security number. Banks such as First Bank of the Americas, a Colombian-owned bank with branches in Queens, mean a great deal to Ecuadoran immigrants.

While Ecuadoran American community institutions are important, they do not aim to embrace every aspect of life, to keep their members separate from society, or to replace American government in the lives of immigrants. Regional associations do not undertake to provide work or housing for new arrivals, as the institutions of some immigrants from other countries do. Ecuadorans are not insular, and willingly seek out the benefits and services of society at large. For instance, 11 to 12 percent of Ecuadoran American families receive government welfare benefits (George Borjas, "Refugees More Likely to Be On Welfare," *Minority Markets Alert*, December, 1994).

## SPORTS

Ecuadorans play soccer, popular throughout Latin America; and young Ecuadoran Americans play football, basketball, and all the other games played in American high schools. But the games at which Ecuadorans truly excel are net games: tennis and especially volleyball. Unlike in

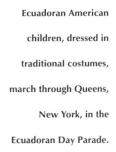

Olympic volleyball, with six-person teams, Ecuadorans play the game with three-person teams, and with a net over nine feet high. Each player must cover a lot of ground, and jump high. Without spiking, volleys are longer. The game is very arduous. On summer Saturdays, Ecuadorans play at Riverside Park in Manhattan's Upper West Side. Though Ecuadorans are shorter on average than most Americans, non-Ecuadoran challengers do not fare well in these hotly contested matches (Eric Pooley, "Sports: Little Ecuador," *New York*, September 16, 1985, p. 32).

## RELIGION

Ecuadorans are about 95 percent Roman Catholic, and five percent Protestant. However, the proportions of the two faiths are slightly more equal among immigrants to the United States.

Over the centuries, the Roman Catholic church in rural Ecuador incorporated elements of Indian religions. In the *sierra*, and especially in villages, Ecuadoran Catholic practice centers around *fiestas* honoring the various saints' days of the Christian year. Individuals in the community make a religious commitment, known as a *cargo*, to sponsor these *fiestas*. They proceed upward through increasingly complicated and expensive affairs, to make a name for themselves as leaders of the community. These and other traditional practices have less to do with Catholic dogma than with ancient Indian customs.

In recent decades, evangelical Protestant missionaries have converted many in Ecuador, especially in the countryside and urban slums. These missionaries, mainly of North American origin, have had the most success in the southern *sierra*, including Cañar, Azuay, and Chimborazo provinces. In Chimborazo province, nearly 40 percent of the population was Protestant by 1980. During the 1980s and 1990s the southern *sierra* provinces contributed the largest number of Ecuadoran immigrants to the United States. For this reason, the number of Ecuadoran American Protestants is a greater proportion of the whole than among Ecuadorans in general. Furthermore, many Ecuadorans associate the United States with the Protestant missionaries who originate there, so Protestants are more likely to emigrate than Catholics are. There are no reliable statistics on this subject, but some community members estimate that one-third of Ecuadoran Americans are Protestant.

## EMPLOYMENT AND ECONOMIC TRADITIONS

Due to the lack of hard statistics, it is difficult to generalize about the employment patterns of Ecuadoran Americans. Also, the community has a more diverse economic profile than that of other Latino immigrant groups. Mexican and Central American immigrants, for instance, have generally come from the working class; immigrants from certain South American countries, such as Argentina and Chile, have come largely from the professional class. Ecuadoran immigrants, however, come from both classes. Ecuador shares with other South American countries the problem of "brain drain" emigration: Ecuadorans who graduate from universities, often in a technical field such as engineering, come to the United States hoping for a more affluent lifestyle. But there are also large numbers of Ecuadorans for whom emigration is simply the only alternative to grinding poverty at home.

Many Ecuadorans join the immigrant underclass of greater New York. They work not just with other Ecuadorans, but surrounded by other arrivals from Latin America, Asia, and Africa, often without a shared language. They work in the garment industry sweatshops, restaurant and hotel kitchens, and taxicabs. They frequently must work for less than minimum wage. Accustomed to a more activist labor movement at home, Ecuadorian Americans have often taken a lead in union organizing, but face frustration.

Another group of Ecuadoran Americans consists of the entrepreneurs. Many immigrants with initiative and capital start businesses catering to the Ecuadoran community. These include Ecuadoran restaurants, travel agencies, and telephone and money-wiring services. Such community-oriented businesses also provide jobs for other Ecuadorans.

A third group of Ecuadorans contains the professionals. Of all the immigrants, the members of this group occupied the highest status in Ecuador, received the most education there, and are often the unhappiest in the United States. Immigrating with great ambitions, they meet great disappointments. To resume their profession in their new country, doctors, lawyers, architects, and social workers must receive new training and pass new tests. They must become fluent in English even to begin this process. In the meantime, they must support themselves in a country where their savings from home have little buying power, and must often take menial jobs such as cleaning houses and waiting tables. Many never succeed and permanently enter a lower social class. Those who succeed tend to be the most assimilated of immigrants and participate the least in community organizations (Suzanne Bilello, "Here, Suddenly, I Am No One," *Newsday*, July 9, 1989, p. 1).

## THE OTAVALEÑOS

The Ecuadoran immigrants who have made a unique contribution to the American economy and society are the Otavaleño Indians. Living in the northern *sierra* near the modern town of Otavalo this group has for centuries preserved its economic role: textile weaving for sale to outsiders. Even before the Inca conquest, Otavaleños produced wool clothing and peddled it throughout the region. When the Spaniards came, they enslaved the Otavaleños and forced them to weave Spanish-style clothing in *obrajes*, or forced-labor workshops. After the end of slavery, white landowners kept control of the weaving by means of debts owed them by the weavers, which were passed down through the generations.

Finally, in the 1960s, this debt-slavery was outlawed and large amounts of land were redistributed to tenant farmers. Otavaleños finally began to earn real profits from their centuries of hard work. Otavaleños are both weavers and farmers, and they benefited from the land redistribution. They left the workshops and took their weaving home. Otavaleños were determined no longer to allow others to reap the reward from their skill and traditions. Returning to a pre-Inca model, they sent members of their own community to market their textiles in other countries. While other Indian communities practice traditional weaving, the Otavaleños are unique in their resourcefulness and success in selling their wares, without middlemen, on the international market.

In small factories in or near Otavalo, the Indians make heavy wool sweaters, ponchos, hats and blankets, all in bright colors and traditional designs. They send these clothes to Quito and other South American cities, to Mexico City, New York, and other North American cities, and to Europe and Asia to be sold in the streets. At any given time 6,000 Otavaleños, or ten percent of the whole community, live abroad as itinerant salespeople. The sellers may be the grown children of the manufacturer, who are working in the family business and seeing the world at the same time. Even if they are not related, all the people involved are Otavaleños. The profits do not leave the community.

Otavaleño street-sellers in New York, though relatively few in number (about 300 by one estimate), are highly visible with their traditional dress and appearance in outdoor shopping areas such as Canal Street. The men wear their long straight hair in braids and wear blue ponchos and white pants. The women wear embroidered white blouses, red wristbands, and heavy dark wraps around their shoulders and skirts. Otavaleño clothing is very traditional; in fact, the women's clothing has changed only slightly from the time of the Incas. The appearance that Otavaleño peddlers project helps them to sell their inventory, because it adds to the apparent authenticity of the product.

Of course, the outfit an Otavaleño peddler would wear in the streets of New York is not necessarily what he would wear at home. Furthermore, the product sold is not timeless. Each year Otavaleño street-sellers send home samples of the latest fashions, and the manufacturers make changes in style and color, even introducing new products such as headbands. Many of the street-sellers hold licenses from the city while others are unlicensed. Some sellers cannot afford the license fee while others only intend to stay in the city for a short time, and so do not buy the license. Laws against unlicensed street-selling are often only loosely enforced, but at times such street-sellers must face having all their goods confiscated by police. Furthermore, like all people who do business out of doors, Otavaleño merchants must operate within the complex society of the street. They are subject to the whims of police, the maze of city regulations, the unwritten laws of those who sell clothes, food, stolen goods, sex, and drugs, and the extortionists and predators of the street. But the international marketing of their clothes has brought the Otavaleños great rewards.

Most Otavaleños abroad ultimately return home, often to attend university and enter a profession. Otavaleños have become wealthy and influential in their home province; indeed, the *mestizo* community of Otavalo is poorer than the Otavaleño Indians. The Otavaleños have converted that money into education and opportunities for their children. They have refused to allow wealth to steal their culture and traditions. While most Otavaleños today speak Spanish, most also speak Quichua. They have not changed the style of their clothes as they became richer, although some have improved the materials used, perhaps from rough cotton to velvet (Jonathan Kandell, "Shuttle Capitalism: an Ecuadorean Indian Community Turns a Traditional Craft into a Tool for Cultural Survival and Takes It to the Street Corners of the World," *Los Angeles Times Magazine*, November 14, 1993).

### CHINESE ECUADORANS

One small but significant segment of the Ecuadoran American community is the Chinese Ecuadorans. People from southern China immigrated in the nineteenth century to every American country, including Ecuador. When Ecuadorans began immigrating to the United States in large numbers, after the mid-1960s, many Chinese Ecuadorans joined the migration—probably a disproportionate number compared to their numbers in the general Ecuadoran population. This was partly because the Chinese Ecuadorans had less deep roots in Ecuador than others, and had experienced discrimination there; and partly because New York, where most Ecuadorans went, had a large and established Chinese community. Today there are several thousand Chinese Ecuadorans in the United States, or about one percent of the Ecuadoran American community. Chinese Ecuadorans are more likely to be in commerce or the professions than other Ecuadorans, but in general are not demographically different from the rest of the community. Most have some familiarity with both Chinese and Spanish, but most are more fluent in Spanish. They typically live in Latino neighborhoods, not Chinese ones; most live in New York.

# POLITICS AND GOVERNMENT

Ecuadoran Americans are not extremely politically active. Ecuador does not encourage its expatriates to cast absentee ballots in elections at home. While taking a keen interest in the news from home (Ecuadoran papers in the United States carried extensive news and analysis of the 1995 border hostilities between Ecuador and Peru) the immigrants seldom organize around specific policy issues at home. On the other hand, few Ecuadoran Americans are U.S. citizens with the right to vote. And because so many Ecuadorans plan to return home one day, they do not concern themselves much with American politics.

One of the few legislative acts for which Ecuadoran Americans actively lobbied was the passage, in Ecuador, of a dual citizenship law. The Ecuadoran congress passed the measure in response to vigorous and coordinated efforts by the Ecuadoran American organizations—in particular, by the New York umbrella group Comite Cívico Equatoriano. Ecuadoran Americans no longer have to choose between being an Ecuadoran citizen and being an American citizen, but can embrace both sides of their identity.

When Ecuadoran Americans do take a political stand it is often linked to their region of origin. *Costeños* tend to be liberal, while *serranos* are conservative. This difference can be seen in the different attitudes in *serrano* immigrant neighborhoods in Queens and *costeño* neighborhoods in the Bronx. Yet overall, Ecuadorans from all regions are socially conservative by U.S. standards. For instance, they are among the most outspoken proponents of the death penalty, long an object of controversy in the state of New York.

In general, however, Ecuadoran Americans are a non-citizen, non-voting community, which may hurt them. Elected officials have less incentive to address their concerns than those of voting citizens. Many Ecuadoran New Yorkers live in state Assembly districts with Latino majorities; but even there, politicians focus attention on the needs of Puerto Ricans and other voting Latinos, and ignore the Ecuadoran American community (Nicholas Goldberg, "District Boosts Hispanic Clout," *Newsday*, June 12, 1992, p. 8). Non-citizens become ever more vulnerable as politicians across the nation advocate anti-immigrant measures. Concern over such measures is now prompting more Ecuadorans to file for citizenship.

# INDIVIDUAL AND GROUP CONTRIBUTIONS

Because large-scale emigration from Ecuador to the United States began only recently, there are not many famous Ecuadoran Americans. However, there are Ecuadorans who have made a mark on American society.

## ART

Oswaldo Guayasamin (1919- ), born to an Indian father and a *mestizo* mother, has forged a powerful art that addresses what it means to be Indian, to be *mestizo*, to be Ecuadoran. His semi-abstract paintings are generally figurative, and feature rugged faces and bodies of Indians at work or at home; they often illustrate scenes from Ecuadoran history and express his left-wing views, his spirit of protest, and his sense of sadness at social injustice. His work is internationally acclaimed and has been exhibited all over the world.

In 1988, Guayasamin caused controversy in the United States by painting a mural in the Ecuadoran hall of Congress. One of the panels in the mural—intended to summarize Ecuador's history—showed a skeleton's head in a helmet, with the letters "CIA." Despite his frustration with aspects of American policy, Guayasamin was an Ecuadoran American during the 1950s, when Nelson Rockefeller arranged an official invitation for him to come to the United States. He lived for several years with his family in the Bayside neighborhood of Queens, New York. In 1960, however, a visit to communist China earned him official hostility in the United States, and he returned with his family to Ecuador.

## BUSINESS

One Ecuadoran American who made an important contribution to American business is Napoleon Barragan, founder of Dial-a-Mattress in Queens, New York. Recognizing that speed and convenience matter the most to some people, he sold mattresses over the telephone and delivered them immediately. In 1994 his business was the ninth largest minority-owned business in the New York area. However, some of the company's sales, as well as some of its payments to employees, were cash-only, which skirted reports and payments to the government. Barragan pleaded guilty to tax fraud and paid $1 million to the state.

## FEMINISM

Lorena Bobbitt (1970- ) was born in Bucay, Ecuador, and moved with her family to Venezuela at a young age, but always considered herself an Ecuadoran. As a young woman she moved to the United States, where she met and married John Wayne Bobbitt. During their stormy relationship, she accused her husband of beating and raping her; she severed his penis with a kitchen knife while he slept. Although her husband was tried and acquitted of rape, Lorena faced the charge of malicious wounding. As Lorena's trial approached, women throughout America protested the prospect of Lorena's conviction and Ecuadoran women took to the streets in her defense, in Quito and in Manassas, Virginia (the site of her trial). She was found not guilty by reason of temporary insanity. Although widely criticized as a tabloid media event, the Lorena Bobbitt trial forced the nation to address the issues of wife-beating and marital self-defense. For this reason, feminists welcomed it as consciousness-raising, and considered Lorena a hero.

## MILITARY

Mario Fajardo, an Ecuadoran New Yorker, was the first soldier from the borough of Queens to die in the Gulf War.

## POLITICS

In 1993, Ecuadoran immigrant Aida Gonzalez was named director of cultural affairs to Queens Borough President Claire Shulman; she is one of a handful of Ecuadoran New Yorkers who are acquiring power and influence in the Democratic Party establishment.

## SPORTS

Probably the most famous Ecuadoran athlete is Andres Gomez, the world-class tennis player; many of his great matches have been played in the United States and he has been a source of inspiration to Ecuadoran Americans and all lovers of tennis. Another important Ecuadoran tennis player is Francisco Segura (1921- ), who has made the United States his home; an unorthodox but highly successful player in his youth, "Panco" Segura surprised the professional tennis world with his powerful two-fisted forehand; former tennis director at the La Costa Resort and Spa in California, he retired from pro tennis and coached both Jimmy Connors and Andre Agassi.

# MEDIA

## PRINT

Various weekly, monthly, or occasional newspapers have been produced and distributed to the Ecuadoran American community in New York. Most do not last long. The monthly newspaper *Amazonas*, produced in Queens, falls into this category; it contains news, analysis, and opinion pieces about affairs in Ecuador, along with advertisements for local Ecuadoran American businesses.

Magazines and daily and weekly newspapers from Quito and Quayaquil are also available in newsstands in Queens, with a lagtime of several days. These are rather expensive, and do not contain local news or advertisements.

For most of their local, national, and international news, Ecuadoran Americans rely on the general Spanish-speaking press, especially New York's *El Diario* and *Noticias del Mundo*.

These papers were originally founded for a Puerto Rican readership; but in recent decades, the growing New York population of Ecuadorans, Colombians, Cubans, and Dominicans has forced the New York Spanish press to broaden its focus. These papers now contain news from various Latin American countries, as well as local news that is relevant to the new arrivals.

## RADIO

There are several radio shows in the New York area geared toward Ecuadoran Americans.

### WADO-AM (1280).

Broadcasts "Presencia Ecuatoriana" ("Ecuadoran Presence"), a talk show discussing news, art, sports and culture from Ecuador, hosted by Homero Melendez, president of the Tunguahua regional association on Sunday from 2:00 to 3:00 p.m.

### WHBI-FM (105.9).

Broadcasts two shows: "Así Canta el Ecuador" ("This is How Ecuador Sings"), a music show on Saturdays at 9:00 a.m.; "Pentagrama Sentimental Ecuatoriano" ("Sentimental Ecuadoran Musicsheet"), a news, music and culture show on Mondays from 7:30 to 8:30 a.m.

# ORGANIZATIONS AND ASSOCIATIONS

**Alianza Ecuatoriana Tungurahua.**

Contact: Homero Melendez, President.

Address: 465 41st Street, Brooklyn, New York 11232.

Telephone: (718) 854-1506.

**Asociación Chino Ecuatoriana.**

Contact: Mirna Chiang, President.

Address: 3007 36th Avenue, Queens, New York 11106.

Telephone: (718) 937-3291.

**Club Social Salitre.**

Contact: Gaston Sanchez, President.

Address: 421 Menham Street, Brooklyn, New York 11237.

Telephone: (718) 366-8467.

**Comite Cívico Ecuatoriana.**

**Contact:** Srowell Ugalde, President.

**Address:** 7312 35th Avenue, Suite 261, Queens, New York 11372.

**Telephone:** (718) 476-2851.

**Confraternidad Ecuatoriana.**

**Contact:** Antonio Pinargote, President.

**Address:** 47 Duncan Avenue, No. 45, Jersey City, New Jersey 07306.

**Telephone:** (201) 332-7285.

# MUSEUMS AND RESEARCH CENTERS

**Hillman Library.**

Contains a general collection of Latin American literature with strong holdings on Ecuadoran literature.

**Contact:** Eduardo Lozano, Bibliographer.

**Address:** 171 Hillman Library, Pittsburgh, Pennsylvania 15260.

**Telephone:** (412) 624-4125.

# SOURCES FOR ADDITIONAL STUDY

*Ecuador: A Country Study*, third edition, edited by Dennis Hanratty. Washington, D.C.: Federal Research Division, Library of Congress, 1991.

*Insight Guide: Ecuador*, edited by Tony Perrottet. New York: Apa Publications, 1994.

Martz, John. *Ecuador: Conflicting Political Culture and the Quest for Progress*, Boston: Allyn and Bacon, 1972.

Thompson, Mortitz. *The Farm on the River of Emeralds*. Boston: Houghton Mifflin, 1978.

Winsberg, Morton. "Specific Hispanics," *American Demographics*, February 1994.

# EGYPTIAN
by
Mona Mikhail

# AMERICANS

## OVERVIEW

Situated in northeast Africa, Egypt (known since 1971 as the Arab Republic of Egypt) occupies an area of 390,000 square miles (1,010,100 sq. km.). With 90 percent of the land covered by desert, only a small portion of it, about 14,000 square miles, is arable, and it is here that the majority of Egyptians live. Egypt is bordered by Israel to the northeast, the Red Sea to the east, the Sudan to the south, Libya to the west, and the Mediterranean Sea to the north. The majority of people in Egypt are Muslim, although some Egyptians belong to the Coptic Church and practice Christianity and an even smaller percentage are Jews.

## HISTORY

Ancient Egypt was the cradle of Western Civilization. Here, as early as 4000 B.C., people had come together and formed organized societies. By 3100 B.C., the pharaoh Menes had united the peoples of the Nile delta with those living southward along the river into a single empire. During Egypt's height, its people thrived in the Nile valley; they constructed massive pyramids, created world-renowned art, established an advanced writing system, made advancements in science, built irrigation systems, and developed trade with Middle Eastern and Asian powers. But by 1085 B.C., the

Egyptian empire had begun to decay and again divided into Upper and Lower kingdoms—that of the delta and that of the river. Many sought to conquer the valley and claim its riches: Greeks, Romans, Aragians, North Africans, Turks, French, and, most recently, the British. All these people contributed to the rich culture of Egypt.

For centuries, the majority of arable land in Egypt was possessed by a select few. This land was worked by the *fellahin,* who wielded two to three crops each season, usually keeping one-fourth to one-half of the harvest for themselves. Agricultural reform did not take place until the latter half of the nineteenth century, when Egyptians began to grow cotton in an attempt to establish a market economy rather than simply growing food products. However, when other world markets began producing cotton as well, the market suffered and the well-being of the Egyptian rural class greatly deteriorated.

In 1882 the British assumed economic control of the country and built roads, railways, telegraph systems, and canals. Egypt's royal family and the already wealthy landowners greatly benefitted from British occupation. Although the rural class was heavily taxed, many prospered as well, thus creating a new social class. It was this newly established middle class, along with the nation's armed forces, that instigated Egypt's 1952 Revolution, which freed the country from British occupation and initiated land reform, thus altering the social, economic, and political power of Egypt's ruling families.

In 1956 Egypt elected Gamal Abdal Nasser as its first president. Under Nasser's leadership, in 1962, the newly established national charter limited the amount of land held by farm owners to 100 acres. The remaining land was confiscated by the government, divided into plots, and awarded to the middle and lower classes. Improved housing, transportation, and health care resulted in a significant increase in Egypt's population. Despite the efforts of such leaders as Nasser (who tried to industrialize the country) and Anwar Sadat (who created an open economy) to modernize Egypt, inflation, overpopulation, and the general unrest in the Middle East have hindered the nation's progress.

Modern Egypt is the most populous and most advanced of the Arab nations. Traditionally allied with the Arab cause, it is the seat of the League of Arab States. Egypt has also played a leadership role among the African nations, with Egyptian president Hosni Mubarak presiding over the Organization of African Unity. Egypt's social

order is partially composed of intellectuals, government officials, urban businessmen, and landowners. It is this segment of the population that has emigrated the most, largely for economic or educational purposes. The vast majority of Egypt's population is composed of rural laborers and factory workers.

### SIGNIFICANT IMMIGRATION WAVES

Egyptian Americans are among the more recent groups to have immigrated to the United States. Unlike other peoples of Arab descent who settled in the Americas in large numbers as early as the mid-nineteenth century, the Egyptians, regarded as one of the most sedentary ethnic groups, began to emigrate in significant numbers only during the latter part of the twentieth century. While the majority left for economic or educational reasons, many Copts, Jews, and conservative Muslims emigrated because they were concerned about the political developments in Egypt. Still, thousands of others left after Egypt's 1967 defeat in the Arab-Israeli War; approximately 15,000 Egyptians immigrated to the United States from 1967 to 1977. The past three decades have witnessed unprecedented movements of large Egyptian populations not only to the United States and Canada but also to Australia, Europe, and the Gulf Arab countries.

The majority of the first Egyptian immigrants to the United States comprised educated professionals and skilled workers. Their immigration was eased by the 1965 Immigration and Nationality Act, which welcomed certain professionals, especially scientists. Estimates of the number of Egyptian immigrants to the United States have varied from 800,000 to two million, with the largest concentration of Egyptians living in New Jersey, New York, California, Illinois, Florida, and Texas. Climate has had an important influence on the settlement patterns of Egyptian Americans. Accustomed to the warm and temperate climate of their homeland, many Egyptians have gravitated toward America's southern states.

# ACCULTURATION AND ASSIMILATION

Egyptian immigrants and their American-born children have had little difficulty adjusting to American culture. This is largely due to the strong educational background of most Egyptian Americans. Numerous Egyptian Americans have also married outside their ethnic community, which has further eased their assimilation. Still, Egyptian Americans have united to establish numerous secular organizations, many of which have a professional, academic, or business orientation. These include the Egyptian American Professional Society, the Egyptian Physicians' Association, and the Egyptian Businessmen's Association. Several have also joined the numerous organizations of the more established Arab American community such as the Arab American University Graduates, the American-Arab Relations Committee, and the American-Arab Anti-Discrimination Committee (ADC).

## CUISINE

Egyptian cuisine is a mixture of Middle Eastern cuisine and a modified continental (French-style) cuisine. Traditional Egyptian dishes include *mullkhia*, a thick green soup made from chicken or meat broth (sometimes rabbit). *Squab* (stuffed pigeon) and *fatta*, a rice-and-bread dish, are among the many favorites. What came to be known in the United States as *falafel* is also a favorite, as is *baklava*. Another popular food is *kahk*, a sweetbread baked for special feasts. To make *kahk*, a well-kneaded dough of flour and rarified butter is filled with honey or a mixed-nut filling. The dough is beautifully decorated by a special tool, a *minkash*, then is baked and sprinkled with powder sugar. *Kakh* can be purchased at bakeries.

During Lent and Advent, Egyptian Copts do not eat meat or dairy products, a practice that has given rise to many delicious nondairy and meatless grain-based meals that are a delight to the vegetarian and the health-conscious. Muslims are prohibited from eating pork and therefore buy their meats at *hallal* or kosher butcher shops. In Brooklyn, on Atlantic Avenue, a large concentration of Arab and Muslim shops cater to the needs of the Middle Eastern community at large. Jersey City also has a growing community of Egyptians where one can find most of the specifically Egyptian ingredients to prepare native dishes. Middle Eastern specialty items can be found at grocery stores in almost every major U.S. city., and some staple items—such as pita bread—are found at supermarkets across North America.

## TRADITIONAL COSTUMES

Egyptian Americans who live in urban areas do not wear traditional garments. Since the turn of the century, urbanized Egyptians have adopted Western-style clothing, and the vast majority who have come to the United States have retained this custom. It is only in approximately the past two decades that Muslim women have chosen to dress in a traditional Islamic garment consisting of a floor-length, long-sleeved dress and a head covering. Many Muslim women adhere only to the tradition of covering the head, while the vast majority of Egyptian Americans wear the usual Western-style wardrobe. The men wear suits, though on rare occasions they wear a *gallabiyya*, a long white robe, for prayers or at home.

## HOLIDAYS CELEBRATED BY EGYPTIAN AMERICANS

Most Egyptian holidays are religious observances. There are two major Muslim holidays: *Eid al Fitr* falls at the end of Ramadan; *Eid al-Adha* (Feast of Sacrifice), which follows soon after, commemorates the slaughtering of the lamb by the Prophet Abraham and is followed by a pilgrimage. The Islamic New Year as well as the birthday of the Prophet are also important holidays for Muslims. Major holidays are celebrated at the mosques and among friends. Traditionally, children wear new clothes and receive monetary gifts (*iddiyya*).

Christian Copts celebrate Christmas according to the Gregorian calendar, usually on January 6-7 of every year. Easter is a week-long observance of strict religious rituals culminating in Good Friday, a midnight mass on Holy Saturday, and a mass at dawn on Easter Sunday. A secular holiday, the New Year is celebrated by Muslims and Christians.

Another important holiday is *Sham al-Nassim*, a rite of spring dating to ancient times that is celebrated on the Monday after Easter Sunday. Egyptians go out into the fields or onto the beaches and eat a specially prepared salted fish (*fisikh*), onions or shallots, colored hard-boiled eggs, fruits, and sweets. This tradition is dying out in the United States because Monday is a workday. Since *Sham al-Nassim* is a moveable feast, Egyptians sometimes celebrate it on Easter Sunday so that everyone can participate. It is an occasion when all Egyptians, irrespective of religious faith, can get together and enjoy themselves.

## HEALTH AND MENTAL HEALTH ISSUES

Traditional health care practices and beliefs are rarely practiced by urban dwellers in Egypt.

Because the majority of immigrants to the United States are from urban centers, there is no evidence that such practices are being carried over to the United States. A large percentage of the first wave of immigrants were trained as physicians in Egypt and acquired additional fields of specialty in the United States. Many of these physicians serve people in their own communities, who turn to them for advice and medical care and who also find Egyptian American medical doctors a source of comfort, especially if they are still in the midst of overcoming the language barrier.

# LANGUAGE

Ancient Egyptians developed a pictographic and ideographic writing system known as hieroglyphics. With the fall of the Egyptian empire, the language was lost altogether until the recent discovery of the Rosetta Stone. Scientists have since established that this writing system, which functioned both vertically and horizontally in either long or abbreviated forms, has qualities similar to an alphabet.

Arabic has been the common language of all Egyptians since the eighth century. The dialect most often spoken in Egypt is Cairene Arabic, which is also the Arabic dialect most widely known throughout the Arabic-speaking world. Cairene Arabic is widely used by all Egyptian Americans at informal social gatherings. The great popularity of Egyptian singers and movies assists the dissemination of this dialect. Formal Arabic is used in religious services by Muslims and Copts. Recently, Copts have introduced English into their church services (usually in sermons) to maintain the participation of new generations of American-born Egyptians.

# FAMILY AND COMMUNITY DYNAMICS

The nuclear family is the basic social unit of Egyptian society. Although the extended family also continues to play a dominant role in the intricate family grid, familial ties are beginning to loosen, even in Egypt. Some of these changes have become more accentuated in the United States. Wide distances may separate children from their parents, brothers, and sisters and from other members of the extended family. Whereas once people would grow up and spend their lives in the same neighborhood and would die and be buried in the same city, today things have changed so that families are scattered throughout the 50 states. More often than not, most Egyptian Americans opt for burial in the United States.

The growing prevalence of intermarriage between Egyptians and Americans—most commonly between Egyptian-born men and American women—has challenged the family structure. A Muslim woman's husband is required by religion and law to convert to Islam, while a Muslim man's wife may retain her Christian or non-Muslim faith. In either case, the children must be raised as Muslims. Christian Egyptians experience relatively fewer difficulties integrating into American society, although Egyptian Copts tend to be conservative and prefer that their children marry within the Coptic church.

## COURTSHIP

Having been raised in a conservative and traditional society, Egyptian Americans—particularly Muslims—worry about their offspring's dating habits and urge their children to marry someone of Egyptian descent or to choose someone from the larger community of Arab peoples. Families commonly send their children back to Egypt to immerse them within Egyptian society in the hope that they will choose a bride or groom there. Some Egyptian Americans encourage marriage between cousins, a practice common in Egypt.

For these reasons, the role of the mosque as a social center and as a religious gathering place is changing from what it was in Egypt. Today, for instance, women not only pray at the mosque but also participate in social activities there. The custom of women praying at the mosque has now become prevalent in Egypt, having been brought back there by returning Muslim Americans.

## CHILDREN

Boys are often treated differently than girls and are given more leeway when it comes to curfews and dating. However, because education is highly esteemed by Egyptians, and because many members of the first generation of Egyptian Americans possess advanced college degrees, children—both boys and girls—are encouraged to attend college. Children who decide to attend school out of state generally obtain their parents' blessing, although some parents still prefer to have their children—especially their daughters—nearby. In some cases, mothers will move to another state just to live with their children. Some parents encourage their children to return to Egypt to obtain a degree, not only because it is less costly to do so (medical students receive free education in Egypt), but also because it ensures that their children will be supervised by members of the extended family.

## EDUCATION

Because the majority of first generation of Egyptian Americans are highly educated professionals, they have a tendency to apply to the best schools, private or public. In rare cases their children attend religious-affiliated schools; there are a few Muslim schools in New Jersey and Washington, D.C. However, because of the emphasis on higher education, Muslims attending these schools tend to join regular school systems beyond the primary level. The vast majority of Egyptian Americans go on to four-year colleges. There is still a premium on the traditional professional disciplines such as medicine, engineering, and accounting. Yet growing numbers of Egyptian Americans are now enrolled in business or law schools or are pursuing degrees in the humanities. Many Egyptian Americans are enrolled in Ivy League schools, especially if their parents can afford the high cost of tuition, but larger numbers are entering state schools. It is not unusual to find young Egyptian Americans working their way through school to help pay for their tuition. Some opt to work after high school for a few years before going on with their studies. While some Egyptian Americans do not complete high school, they represent a very small percentage of the Egyptian American population.

## THE ROLE OF WOMEN

Since the nineteenth century, women in Egypt have come to play a more prevalent role in improving their status and in increasing the degree of their participation within society. World War I and World War II brought radical change in the status of women in Egypt. By the 1920s women began to enroll in universities and entered the workforce as physicians, lawyers, and educators. They became fuller participants in the workforce after the 1952 Revolution and after the implementation of the National Charter in 1962, which stipulated that "women must be regarded as equal to men, and must shed the remaining shackles that impede their free movement." Consequently, they have enjoyed a relatively long tradition of active participation in the public domain. Many Egyptian American women carried this tradition to their new home in the United States.

Whether they immigrated to the United States or are American-born, most Egyptian women are active within American society on several levels. Women tend to participate within the workforce, even those who are raising families. This is especially true of the second wave of immigrants, some of whom have not acquired employment on a par with their college backgrounds. These underemployed immigrants work in jobs as foodstand operators, baby-sitters, or waitresses either in family-run restaurants or in the catering trade. Many Egyptian American women have created lucrative catering businesses that specialize in preparing foods for Egyptian households. Many others have successful careers in medicine and accounting, with a high number of them in academia.

# RELIGION

The majority of Egyptians are Muslim, while Copts (Orthodox Christians), the largest religious minority, are believed to form approximately eight percent of the religious community in Egypt. Both Egyptian Muslims and Egyptian Copts have settled in the United States. Within this immigrant community, the number of Egyptian Christians possibly surpasses the number of Egyptian Muslims, although Egyptian Muslims in the United States have increased their numbers steadily in the past two decades.

Islam, which was introduced to Egypt by Arab Muslim invaders in A.D. 641, is a religious system that permeates Egyptian society at every level. Islam means submission to the will of God. A Muslim is one who has submitted to Allah and who acknowledges Muhammad as God's Prophet. Islamic tradition takes into account the doctrines of both Judaism and Christianity, and Muslims consider their Prophet Muhammad the last in a series of prophets that included Abraham, Moses, and Jesus.

Muslims believe in one God and in the afterlife as do Christians and Jews. Islam also acknowledges Jews and Christians as "people of the Book" or *Bible* (*ahl al-Kitab*) and has granted them privileged status from the early days of the Islamic Empire. For this reason, religious minorities throughout the Arab world have survived and flourished during periods of severe cultural and religious repression elsewhere.

Islamic acts of devotion and worship are expressed in the five Pillars of Islam. The first Pillar is the profession of faith, "There is no God but God, and Muhammad is his Prophet," or the *Shahada*, which requires the believer to profess the Unity of God and the mission of Muhammad. The assertion forms part of every prayer.

The second Pillar is prayer, or *Sala,* required five times a day: at dawn, noon, mid-afternoon, sunset, and dusk. It may be performed in a state of ritual purity. The worshipper has the choice of praying privately in open air, in a house, with a group, outdoors, or in a mosque. Because Islam opposes the practice of withdrawing into ascetic life, there is no priesthood. There are, however, *Ulama,* or learned men who are well versed in Islamic law and tradition. Muslims also pray in mosques on Friday, their holy day of the week.

The third Pillar is almsgiving, or *Zakat.* This embodies the principle of social responsibility. The fourth Pillar is fasting, or *Saum,* which is observed during the month of Ramadan when God sent the *Qur'an* to the angel Gabriel who in turn revealed it to the Prophet. Fasting demands complete abstinence from food and drink from sunrise to sunset. Ramadan is followed by *Iftar,* a sumptuous banquet where friends and family gather to celebrate the break of fast. Dearly cherished by Egyptians in Egypt, this tradition is observed closely in America where it is celebrated with Christian Egyptians and American friends alike.

The fifth Pillar is the pilgrimage to Mecca, which should be made by every able-boded Muslim who can afford to do so at least once in a lifetime. Attached to the experience of the pilgrimage is an added status: the person will henceforth be addressed as *al-Haj* or *al-Hajjah,* a title which carries great prestige. Many Egyptian Muslims living in the United States go on a *Haj,* or pilgrimage, as well as an *Umrah,* a modified pilgrimage which can take place at different times of the year and not necessarily at the officially specified time.

The other significant group of Egyptian Americans are the Coptic Christians. The Copts are native to Egypt, having converted to Christianity from their Ancient Egyptian religions as early as the first century A.D. After the Arab conquest of Egypt in 642, the Coptic language began to give way to Arabic; however, Coptic is still used as the liturgical language in church services,

is taught in Sunday schools, and is employed in some daily communications among *Ulama.*

Today, Coptic is still used in church services in the United States where large congregations of Egyptian Copts are found. There is an archdiocese in Jersey City, New Jersey, where one of the first American Coptic churches was founded in the early 1960s.

There are well-developed cordial and reciprocal social relations between Egyptian Copts, Egyptian Muslims, and the general American public. In Egypt, many Copts have adopted a number of Islamic customs, just as some Egyptian Muslims have adopted certain Coptic customs, and this has carried over to the United States. Egyptian Copts sometimes share in the festivities of Ramadan, while Muslim Egyptians celebrate certain aspects of Christmas and the New Year.

## EMPLOYMENT AND ECONOMIC TRADITIONS

The first wave of immigrants consisted of individuals who either had obtained a professional degree or had come seeking further education. They pursued careers as doctors, accountants, engineers, and lawyers, and a good number joined the teaching faculties of major universities. The second wave held college degrees but had to accept menial jobs. When they first arrived many drove taxicabs or waited on tables in restaurants. The economic recession and corporate downsizing undoubtedly have affected Egyptian Americans. Some enterprising citizens have gone into business for themselves. Because of the stigma attached to being unemployed or on welfare, Egyptian Americans have resisted receiving these benefits, but as time goes on their participation in social aid programs will become an increasing fact of life.

## POLITICS AND GOVERNMENT

Egyptian Americans are only now beginning to show interest in municipal and national politics. As with every immigrant group, they first had to establish themselves in society before venturing into the political arena. Unlike other groups of Arab Americans who have been in the United States for more than a century and who are only now coming into their own by being elected to positions in national and local government, Egyptian Americans are just beginning to get involved politically, by exercising their right to vote and supporting their preferred candidates. Because significant numbers of them do not belong to trade unions, they have not had a perceptible influence on union politics. Egyptian Americans are politically conservative and tend to vote Republican, although a growing number who have been in the United States for more than 20 years are beginning to lean toward the Democratic Party or to vote independent. A few Egyptian Americans have volunteered for the armed forces, especially physicians.

## RELATIONS WITH EGYPT

Only recently have there been attempts at involvement in the politics of Egypt. The Egyptian government is interested in its expatriate communities and maintains good relations with them by encouraging them to invest in its economy. For instance, in the past few years the Egyptian American Businessmen's Association has taken official tours to Egypt, meeting with officials and advising the country on various economic matters. The Union of Egyptians is a loosely structured organization that claims to meet Egyptian needs abroad by securing links with the homeland. Other organizations, such as the Egyptian American Professional Organization, prefer to avoid political matters, instead focusing on educational and cultural ties between Egyptian Americans and their home country.

# INDIVIDUAL AND GROUP CONTRIBUTIONS

## FILM, TELEVISION, AND THEATER

In Hollywood, Egyptians who have made a name for themselves include the sitcom director Asaad Kelada.

## INDUSTRY AND FINANCE

Fayz Sarofim is an investment banker and financier who is one of the wealthiest people in the world. Many prominent Egyptians work in Washington-based organizations such as the World Bank and the International Monetary Fund, notably Ibrahim Shehata, Vice President of the World Bank.

## INTERNATIONAL RELATIONS

Boutros Boutros Ghali is the Secretary General of the United Nations. Dr. M. Sherif Bassiouni, who was born in Cairo Egypt in 1937, has written a number of books on International Criminal Law; he is the founder and first Vice-President of the Association of Egyptian American Scholars.

## MUSIC

Halim al Daabi', composer and musician, has written scores for ballets of Martha Graham.

## SCIENCE AND TECHNOLOGY

Farouk Al Baz was born in Egypt in 1938. Since 1975 he has been the Research Director of the Center for Earth and Planetary studies at the National Air and Space Museum at the Smithsonian Institution in Washington, D.C.; Baz was one of the principal scientists involved in the NASA lunar-landing project. Dr. Samy Farag, who was born in Egypt in 1942, served as U.S. delegate to the Congress of Rheumatology in Paris in 1981.

# MEDIA

## PRINT

*American Research Center in Egypt Newsletter.*
Reports quarterly on the Center's activities, plans, and projects. Covers archaeology, history, culture, and language of Egypt in all periods from pre-history to contemporary times.

**Contact:** Monique Bell, Editor.
**Address:** American Research Center in Egypt, New York University, 50 Washington Square South, New York, New York 10012.
**Telephone:** (212) 998-8890.

## RADIO

**WJPF-AM (1340).**
Formerly WJPF-AM and WHPI-AM, broadcasts continuously and offers 40 percent local programming.

Contact: Robert A. Ferrari, Program Manager.

Address: Egyptian Broadcasting Co., Box 550, Herrin, Illinois 62948.

Telephone: (618) 942-2181.

Fax: (618) 988-8111.

## ORGANIZATIONS AND ASSOCIATIONS

Prominent Egyptian American Organizations include: Association of American Muslims; Coptic Association of New Jersey in Jersey City; Egyptian American Businessmen's Association in Greenwich, Connecticut; Egyptian American Physicians' Association; Egyptian American Professionals' Society in Westchester, New York.

## SOURCES FOR ADDITIONAL STUDY

Brugman, J. *An Introduction to the History of Modern Arabic Literature in Egypt*. Leiden: E. J. Brill, 1984.

Marsot, Afaf Lutfi Al-Sayyid. *A Short History of Modern Egypt*. London: Cambridge University Press, 1985.

Orfalea, Gregory. *Before the Flames: A Quest for the History of Arab Americans*. Austin: University of Texas Press, 1988.

Stevens, Georgiana G. *Egypt Yesterday and Today*. 1963.

# ENGLISH AMERICANS

by
**Sheldon Hanft**

*The descendants of English expatriates are so numerous and so well integrated in American life that it is impossible to identify all of them.*

## OVERVIEW

England, a country slightly larger than New York State, occupies 50,363 square miles (130,439 square kilometers) of the southern end of the largest island off the Atlantic coast of Europe. A land of rolling hills, moderate climate, abundant rainfall, fertile plains, many navigable rivers, and nearly 2,000 miles of ocean coastline, it is mineral rich and very arable. From the southwestern plateau of Cornwall and southeastern marshy downs through the gentle plains, the Pennine uplands, and the lake country, to the Cambrian mountains and Cheviot Hills, which shapes its western and northern borders with Wales and Scotland, no point is more than 75 miles from the seas that brought commerce, migrations, and invasion throughout much of England's early history.

While 80 percent of its 50 million people are native born, England has large communities of Scots (nearly ten percent), Irish, and Welsh in its border counties and about two million Asian Indians, Pakistani, West Indians, and other non-white peoples in its large cities. These Asian and Caribbean groups settled in England during and after the collapse of the British empire in the last half century. London, with a population approaching seven million, is the capital of England and the United Kingdom. The government is a constitutional monarchy with a Parliament and a cabinet system dominated by the Conservative and Labour parties. Seventy-eight percent of the English population belong to the Church of England (the Anglican Church, or the COE), which is legally established (tax supported) and officially governed by the monarch and the Archbishop of Canterbury. There are also sizable groups of Methodists, Evangelicals, Roman Catholics, Muslims, Jews, and Quakers in England. The national flag, commonly called the "union jack," has a broad red English cross (of St. George) with white borders imposed over the Scottish cross (of St. Stephen), shown as thinner red diagonals with thin white borders traversing from corner to corner on a field of royal blue.

## HISTORY

The English descend from the Celtic tribes who brought iron age technology and Druid ceremonies, reflected in such monumental megaliths as Stonehenge, to the British isles in the first millennium. Their language and heritage are reflected in Welsh and Gaelic more strongly than in the English language. Roman conquests, begun by Emperor Claudius, brought England and Wales under Roman control by the end of the first century. During the next three centuries, England developed as a typical Roman colony, protected by the 73-mile-long Hadrian's Wall in the north and policed by the legions, who also constructed roads. During their occupation, Romans promoted commerce, established their institutions, and introduced Christianity in England.

The collapse of Roman rule in the early fifth century ended urban life, as groups of Germanic Angles, Jutes, and Saxons carved the country into tribal enclaves and later created the heptarchy. This diverse group of seven Anglo-Saxon kingdoms vied among themselves for control of the island and later resisted the waves of Viking invaders from the eighth to the eleventh centuries. The most famous Anglo-Saxon ruler was Alfred the Great, who defeated the Danish Vikings, began the English navy, and made Roman Catholicism dominant.

In 1066 William of Normandy conquered England, ending a century of instability, and imposed systemic feudalism by constructing hundreds of castes. During the next three centuries, the institutions of Common Law and Parliamentary government developed, Henry II created a large Angevin empire, Richard the Lionhearted won fame on the Crusade of Kings, and his brother John provoked a baronial revolt that led to the signing of the Magna Carta—the first serious limitation on monarch's power in England. Royal power was further weakened by England's defeat in the Hundred Years' War (1337-1453), depopulation caused by the Black Death, and the baronial War of the Roses, which brought the Tudor dynasty to the throne in 1485.

Henry VII's victory at Bosworth restored strong central government, began transatlantic exploration, developed fiscal reform, and reasserted strong kingship. Henry VIII patronized the Renaissance, separated the Church of England from papal control, and furthered the Tudor revolution in government administration. After "Bloody" Mary's brief effort to return to Catholicism during the middle of the sixteenth century, her younger sister, Queen Elizabeth, restored Henry's church and defended it from the Spanish Armada of 1588. Her prosperous reign supported explorers like Sir Francis Drake and Sir Walter Raleigh, a cultural revival led by William Shakespeare and Francis Bacon, and let merchant adventurers settle England's first permanent American colony.

Between 1603 and 1714 a succession of Stuart rulers encountered Parliamentary opposition to their religious, tax, social, and constitutional policies, which resulted in massive emigration, three civil wars between 1642 and 1649, the public execution of Charles I, and Oliver Cromwell's republican Commonwealth. While Charles II was restored in 1660, the Glorious Revolution ensued in 1688-1689, establishing a Bill of Rights and making England the chief opponent of Louis XIV's wars during the reigns of William and Mary and Queen Anne.

In 1715, eight years after England united with Scotland, the present dynasty, the Hanoverian Windsors, ascended to the throne. During the eighteenth century, England compiled a vast empire, defeated the French in the Seven Years' War (1756-1763), and dominated international trade, notwithstanding having lost the 13 American colonies. Led by such English writers as John Locke and Sir Isaac Newton, the Enlightenment constituted the century's main cultural movement. The English organized the alliance that eventually defeated Napoleon in 1815.

Strengthened by electoral reforms, the Industrial Revolution, and imperialistic expansion in Africa and Asia, Britain remained a dominant world power throughout most of the nineteenth century. Although troubled by the Potato Famine, which began in Ireland, the reign of Queen Victoria (1837-1901) has become synonymous with the expansion of imperialism and the cosmopolitan culture of the age. While creating an empire on which the sun never set, as it was said, England adopted social and economic reforms that made the government more democratic despite challenges to England's economic and political leadership.

The burden of fighting two world wars, the loss of much of its empire, and the demands of its new "welfare state" policies diminished England's political importance in the second half of the twentieth century. To accommodate these changes, Britain strongly allied itself with the United States and reluctantly increased its involvement in the European Common Market, a policy reflected in the difficult struggle to complete the channel tunnel connecting England with France in 1994. Yet the policy continues to meet strong resistance in Parliament and among the peoples of the British Isles. The challenges of surrendering their historical independence and cooperating with the policies and obligations of Common Market membership remain among the most difficult problems facing England and Great Britain at the end of the twentieth century.

## CONTEMPORARY ENGLAND

Contemporary England is at the center of the United Kingdom of Great Britain and Northern Ireland, which also includes Scotland, Wales, the Sea Islands, and the Channel Islands. Presently, the United Kingdom is composed of several distinctive areas that maintain their national churches and ethnic traditions and harbor a reluctance to be absorbed into a "greater England." In the 1960s the desire for greater independence led to national referenda in Wales and Scotland and erupted into sustained violence in Northern Ireland. These movements have declined considerably in recent decades. Less than ten percent of the people of the United Kingdom live in Scotland, while 5.5 percent inhabit Wales and under three percent live in Northern Ireland. The Channel Islands, mainly Jersey and Guernsey (off the French coast) and the Isle of Man (in the Irish Sea), historically considered part of England, have received self-government and dependency status in the last half century.

Scotland, directly north of England, has nearly five million inhabitants who occupy the northern 37 percent of the main island. It is a diverse area of over 30,414 square miles of land (78,772 square kilometers) that includes the Inner and Outer Hebrides and other islands in the Irish Sea and the Orkney and Shetland Islands in the North Sea. Edinburgh is its capital and three-quarters of its population live in its southern lowlands. This region makes use of inexpensive hydroelectric power and North Sea oil, which sustain an industrial complex and the textile, fishing, herding, and whiskey industries traditional in this region. The English language is spoken throughout Scotland, but Scottish accents are strongly divergent from those in England. Nearly 100,000 Scots speak Gaelic in addition to English.

The principality of Wales is 8,018 square miles (20,768 square kilometers) of generally mountainous terrain and nearly 2.8 million residents. While English is the official language, about 12 percent of its residents are bilingual in Welsh and English and about two percent speak only Welsh. Although the Church of England is established, it never won the loyalty of the general populace. During the nineteenth-century Industrial Revolution, Welsh "Calvinistic Methodists" gained the support of most of the working class and added a religious dimension to the social and economic issues separating working-class Welsh from the wealthier social groups who accepted the established Church. Administratively, Wales remains part of England, and, while Welsh nationalism has declined as a political force, it remains an important cultural and social expression of the Welsh character.

While England occupied parts of Ireland since the Middle Ages and conquered the whole island in the sixteenth century, deep religious loyalties, punitive economic legislation, and cultural differences left native Irish Catholics resentful of the transplanted Protestant minority who enjoyed great privilege. This division fueled periodic rebellions and led, in 1920, to a division of the island into a predominantly Catholic republic in the south and a predominantly Protestant Northern Ireland, which stayed part of the United Kingdom. These six Ulster counties with an area of 5,452 square miles (14,121 square kilometers) and over 1.5 million people were given semiautonomous local government centered in Belfast under the supervision of a royal governor and a Parliamentary committee. The eruption of sectarian violence in 1969 prompted London to resume direct control of local government. Negotiations in the 1990s provided hope for a solution to "the troubles."

Elizabeth II, of the House of Hanover-Windsor is the reigning sovereign. She married a Greek prince, Philip Mountbatten, and succeeded her father, George VI, to the throne in February 1952 and was crowned on June 2, 1953 in a ceremony televised worldwide. Her husband was made Duke of Edinburgh in 1947 and added the title of Prince of the United Kingdom and Northern Ireland a decade later. Prince Charles Philip Arthur George, born November 14, 1948, was created Prince of Wales and is the heir apparent. His son, William Philip Arthur Lewis, born June 21, 1982, is next in the line of succession.

The Sovereign is the titular head of government and summons the meeting of Parliament—the national legislature, the members of which sit for five years or less. The House of Lords, empowered only to delay legislation, is composed of the two archbishops and 24 bishops of the Church of England, 763 hereditary nobles, and 314 life peers who are nominated by the government and created by the monarch. The House of Commons has 650 members directly elected by universal suffrage from 516 districts in England, 71 in Scotland, 36 in Wales, and 12 in Northern Ireland. Scottish, Welsh, and Irish nationalist parties elect some members to Parliament, and a Social Democratic Party has emerged to weakly challenge the Conservative and Labour parties. Asian and West Indian members of Parliament were returned from urban constituencies in every election since 1987.

Executive power is exercised by the Prime Minister and his or her cabinet, who are appointed by the monarch from among the members of the party receiving a majority in the House of Commons. Cabinet members must sit in Parliament, and they, individually and collectively, are responsible to the Crown and the Parliament whose support they must have in order to frame legislation, tax, and determine domestic and foreign policy.

While no longer an economic superpower, England remains a major manufacturing, food-producing, and commercial nation that has regained a favorable balance of trade. London remains one of the premier financial markets in the world, and its universities, museums, scientific establishment, and tourist attractions draw millions of people to England, especially from former colonies that remain affiliated through the British Commonwealth of Nations.

## IMMIGRATION, SETTLEMENT, AND EMPLOYMENT

The English were the first non-Native Americans to settle the area that became the United States of America. From the first permanent colonies established at Jamestown, Virginia, in 1607 and at Plymouth and Massachusetts Bay in 1620-1622 to James Oglethorpe's settlement in Savannah, Georgia, in 1732, English joint-stock companies, proprietors, and Crown officials sought to create a modified version of their native society in their American colonies. While many Englishmen came to America to exercise their own religion, and others sought liberation from the religious intolerance on both sides of the Atlantic—as did Roger Williams, fonder of Rhode Island—most English settlers were drawn by the economic opportunities and cheap land. Despite their diverse origins, the majority of colonies came under royal control, established the Church of England Episcopal Church after 1776, and created laws that adapted and imposed the English systems of law, governmental administration, education, commercial and financial management, and agriculture, as well as the arts and popular entertainment.

The group of single men sent by the Virginia company in 1607 to find gold and create a profitable trade failed, and the survival of the colony was doubtful, even under royal proprietorship, for two decades. It was not until the late 1620s, when stability agriculture and a profitable tobacco export began attracting an annual English immigration of several thousand men and women, that the success of Jamestown was assured. This rate of English immigration to the Chesapeake area was maintained until the early part of the next century, when it expanded as England suffered economic difficulties. After Maryland and Delaware were founded, the latter by Catholics, indentured Englishmen and working-class families constituted a majority of the new English settlers.

In addition to the small number of gentry, clergy, lawyers, officials, and minor aristocratic families who settled in the Chesapeake basin to develop plantations, over 30,000 male and female prisoners convicted of serious felonies were transported to Virginia, Maryland, and southern Pennsylvania between 1717 and 1776. Most of the prisoners and indentured servants, as well those as those who paid their passage to the Chesapeake, were young men with some training, possessions, and vocational skills. Although all colonies from Virginia to Georgia received a stream of English prisoners and indentured servants, many were successful in attracting the younger sons and poorer cousins of gentry and merchant families. In the late-seventeenth and eighteenth centuries sizable numbers of Scots, Germans, French, Irish, and Scotch-Irish settled in the South, and they accepted the culture and institutions already established.

Pilgrim and Puritan settlement in Massachusetts Bay attracted over 20,000 settlers from East Anglia and the counties west of London between 1620 and 1642. During these decades English settlements were planted in New Hampshire and Maine, and several English communities were established in Rhode Island and Connecticut by religious reformers who were not tolerated in Massachusetts. Unlike the southern colonies, most of the New England settlers were older and came to America with their family, friends, and assorted relatives. In some instances whole congregations immigrated to New England in this period. The influences of the clergy and the government was strong throughout the region, and successful efforts were made to convert Indians to Christianity.

English settlers from Virginia migrated into North Carolina in the seventeenth century, and English immigrants settled in all of the colonies between Connecticut and Maryland in the middle decades of the century. When an English fleet captured New Amsterdam in 1664 renaming it New York, their countrymen already comprised a majority of the city's population and were well established in New Jersey. While Pennsylvania, founded by English Quakers, attracted large numbers of German, French, Welsh, Scottish, and Scotch-Irish settlers, the colony retained its English character throughout the colonial period.

In the late seventeenth century most English immigrants were younger men who came from the rural areas of southern and south central England. Unlike the New England farming families, most who settled in the region from the Chesapeake to Charleston came as indentured servants and had training as farmers, skilled tradesmen, laborers, or craftsmen. By the last decade of the century, when the English and their descendants comprised 90 percent of the European settlers, Southern planters began importing slaves and the number of new indentured servants decreased. In the eighteenth century, many of those who indentured themselves to get to America were older than those who came before them and were accompanied by their family or related to the families in whose employ they remained.

In the eighteenth century, people from London and the northern counties comprised the majority of English immigrants. The percentage of women increased slightly, from about 15 percent to nearly 25 percent of the English settlers. English Americans began to intermarry more frequently than any other European group. This was partly due to the increased numbers of mobile tradesmen, craftsmen, and merchants among the new English Americans. After the government began transporting felons to the colonies after 1717, the number of unskilled settlers increased in the New England and middle colonies that were willing to accept them. Economic and political troubles brought new spurts of English immigration in the 1720s and in the decades preceding the American Revolution. Americans cited the writings of John Locke, the defender of England's Glorious Revolution, to condemn George III for abusing their "rights as Englishmen."

While English settlers and their descendants constituted only about 60 percent of the European settlers and half of the four million residents living from Maine to Georgia, according to the 1790 census, they had ensured the dominance of English institutions and culture throughout the new republic. This was reflected in the leaders of the national and state governments as well as in the movement to add an English-style Bill of Rights to the new Constitution. While Massachusetts had the largest number of English Americans, only in Pennsylvania, New Jersey, and the Northwest Territory were they a plurality. A cadre of English-trained officials, educated clergymen, wealthy merchants, landlords, and professionals dominated the governments and social structure in all of the colonies, despite the growing influx of immigrants from other parts of Great Britain and Europe.

English immigration to America sharply decreased between 1780 and 1815, as a consequence of English involvement in India and Latin America, events surrounding the French Revolution and Napoleonic conquest, and a "second war of independence" with the United States. During the War of 1812 British aliens were forced to register with local marshals; many English merchants were kept from their trade and forced to relocate; and for the duration of the war English aliens were treated with suspicion, and their freedom of movement was severely restricted.

In the decades preceding the war, London prevented English craftsmen from immigrating to America and restricted the number of settlers each ship could transport. Despite the general decline in immigration to America, several short spurts of English immigration to America occurred. One such increase developed at the end of the Revolutionary War, and another resulted from the monarchy's suppression of English radicals in 1793.

Although German, Irish, Scandinavian, Mediterranean, and Slavic peoples dominated the new waves of immigration after 1815, English settlers provided a steady and substantial influx throughout the nineteenth century. The first wave of increasing English immigration began in the late 1820s and was sustained by unrest in England until it peaked in 1842 and declined slightly for nearly a decade. Most of these were small farmers and tenant farmers from depressed areas in rural counties in southern and western England and urban laborers who fled from the depressions and from the social and industrial changes of the late 1820s-1840s. While some English immigrants were drawn by dreams of creating model utopian societies in America, most others were attracted by the lure of new lands, textile factories, railroads, and the expansion of mining.

"We were put on a barge, jammed in so tight that I couldn't turn 'round, there were so many of us, you see, and the stench was terrible." Eleanor Kenderdine Lenhart in 1921, cited in *Ellis Island: An Illustrated History of the Immigrant Experience,* edited by Ivan Chermayeff et al. (New York: Maxmillan, 1991).

The Chartist movement in the late 1840s, with its massive urban protests, spurred another period of English immigration, which peaked in 1854 and coincided with the waves of Germans and central Europeans who fled to America after the failed revolutions of 1848. With this new influx, as with the previous one, there was a preponderance of English people traveling with one or more family members, and the number of industrial workers, tradesmen, and craftsmen outnumbered farmers more than three to one. Along with its economic appeal, America attracted English settlers because of its similar language and customs and the popular admiration for "things English," especially in its large cities and in the South. A number of English labor unions, Poor Law authorities, charitable organizations, and utopian colonization schemes also encouraged English resettlement in America.

During the last years of 1860s, annual English immigration increased to over 60,000 and continued to rise to over 75,000 per year in 1872, before experiencing a decline. The final and most sustained wave of immigration began in 1879 and lasted until the depression of 1893. During this period English annual immigration averaged more than 80,000, with peaks in 1882 and 1888. The building of America's transcontinental railroads, the settlement of the great plains, and industrialization attracted skilled and professional emigrants from England. Also, cheaper steamship fares enabled unskilled urban workers to come to America, and unskilled and semiskilled laborers, miners, and building trades workers made up the majority of these new English immigrants. While most settled in America, a number of skilled craftsmen remained itinerant, returning to England after a season of two of work. Groups of English immigrants came to America as missionaries for the Salvation Army and to work with the activities of the Evangelical and Mormon Churches. The depression of 1893 sharply decreased English immigration, and it stayed low for much of the twentieth century.

Throughout the nineteenth century, England was the largest investor in American land development, railroads, mining, cattle ranching, and heavy industry. Perhaps because English settlers gained easy acceptance, they founded few organizations dedicated to preserving the traditions of their homeland. While the English comprised only 15 percent of the great nineteenth-century European migration to American, those going to America from England made up less than ten percent of the people leaving England between 1820 and 1920. These migrations in the late nineteenth century were important in that they altered the distribution of English settlers in America. By the end of the century the middle-Atlantic states had the largeest number of English Americans, followed by the north-central states and New England. The growing number of English settling in the West and Pacific Coast regions left the South with the smallest percentage of English Americans by the end of the century.

In the twentieth century, English immigration to America decreased, a product of Canada and Australia having better economic opportunities and favorable immigration policies. English immigration remained low in the first four decades of the century, averaging about six percent of the total number of people from Europe. English culture, literature, and family connections became widely coveted in the early decades of the twentieth century, due to a number of well-publicized marriages of wealthy Americans to children of English aristocrats and to the introduction of Western history and literature courses stressing America's English heritage in colleges and in the public school curriculum after World War I. During the decade of the Great Depression of the 1930s more English returned home than immigrated to the United States. For the first time, more English women than men immigrated.

This decline reversed itself in the decade of World War II when over 100,000 English (18 percent of all European immigrants) came from England. In this group was a large contingent of war brides who came between 1945 and 1948. In these years four women emigrated from England for every man. Although total English immigration increased to over 150,000 (the level maintained in the 1920s) it was less than 12 percent of the European influx during the 1950s. In the 1960s English immigration rose by 20,000 (15.5 percent of all Europeans migrating) and continued in the next decade because of the so-called brain drain of English engineers, technicians, medical professionals, and other specialists being lured to America by multinational corporations. In the three decades since 1970, English immigrants, who were about 12 percent of the total arriving from Europe, were usually unmarried, professionally trained men and women. While the average age of immigrants rose in the last decades of the twentieth century, the number of married people and children continued to decline, and immigrants continued to merge almost imperceptibly into American society.

The periods of increased English immigration in this century are notable because they involved more people from middle and upper-class groups whose migrations raised political issues in England, not because the level of immigration was significant. For most of the period between 1921 and 1969, when immigration quotas were based on the country of origin, England did not fill the generous quotas granted to it. Despite the slight decline in English immigration under the current immigration structure adopted in the 1970s, 33 million Americans identify themselves as being of English descent in the 1990 census. They constitute the third largest ethnic group in the United States, and despite the fact that the Southeast is the region of the nation with the largest number of Americans of English descent, the states currently having the largest number of English Americans are California, Texas, Florida, New York, and Ohio.

# ACCULTURATION AND ASSIMILATION

Since all but two of the original colonies were founded by Englishmen, were administered by English officials, were protected by England's army and navy, and were led by English-trained clergy, lawyers, and educators, they adapted English models in their laws, constitutions, educational system, social structure, and cultural pursuits. From the colonial period it remained fashionable for wealthy Americans to send their sons to England for a year of college, and English styles in literature, poetry, music, architecture, industry, and clothing were the models to emulate until the twentieth century. Throughout the colonial period Americans supported England's wars enthusiastically, and when resentment and resistance to English policies developed in America in the 1760s and 1770s, Americans looked to Parliament for redress of their grievances, which they perceived as emanating from a tyrannical King and his corrupt ministers. Numerous colonial towns created in this period were named in honor of William Pitt and John Wilkes, two popular English Parliamentarians who opposed George III.

While differences developed, it is not surprising that English immigrants had little difficulty in assimilating to American life. Although some loyalists left the United States for England and other colonies after the revolution, the American resentment against the policies of the English government was rarely transferred to English settlers who came to American in the first decades of the nineteenth century. This separation is seen in the sharp rise in English imports in the two decades after the American Revolution. As British naval policies and practices, adopted in their long struggle against Napoleonic France, kindled new conflicts with America, which culminated in the War of 1812, popular resentment against English immigrants intensified. In such states with large German, French, and Celtic communities as Maryland, Pennsylvania, New York, and the Carolinas, broadsides and pamphlets such as *Niles' Weekly Register*, rebuked English immigrants for their "assumed superiority," their poverty, and their provincialism. During the War of 1812, English merchants, primarily in Charleston, Baltimore, and New York, were relocated and prevented from conducting their business, and recent English immigrants were required to register with local government agencies.

In 1820, English immigration again increased and the new settlers found an easy acceptance, though some resentment remained in the Northeast and in the cities of the Atlantic seaboard with large Irish and Scotch-Irish communities. Faced with few language barriers and a familiar legal and political system at the local level and American variants of nearly every English religious denomination, they had little inclination to establish their own churches, newspapers, or political organizations. While the immigrants often confined their socializing to friends and relatives from their own county (shire) or region of England, their children found easy acceptance, resettled comfortably, and merged into the general population virtually unnoticed by all but their parents.

The only English social organizations to endure for several generations were the assorted groups of Odd Fellows, English fraternal societies for the working class recreated in America by Thomas Wildey and John Welch in Baltimore in 1819 and James B. Barnes in Boston the following year. These lodges appealed to the more skilled immigrant tradesmen and craftsmen because they provided the companionship of English pubs, employment connections, and shelter from critics of English immigrants. Despite difficulties in the 1830s and 1860s, the fraternity survived by accepting immigrants from other parts of Britain and Americans of mixed lineage. Its appeal to waves of English immigrants from 1870 to 1893 was limited, and at the turn of the century there were fewer than three dozen chapters, mostly in New England and the northern states. The organization survived to the present by opening its membership to all Americans and by devoting its activities to civil affairs.

While a few social organizations and newspapers were established for English immigrants in the early nineteenth century, they all failed to gain significant support and did not last long. New York was the home of the first newspaper published in 1827 for English American readers. Named *Albion; or, the British and Colonial Foreign Gazette*, it survived until 1863 and outlasted its rivals, the *Old Countryman* (1830-1835), the *Emigrant* (1835-1838), and the *Anglo-American* (1843-1847). Inexpensive editions of English newspapers became available in the 1840s and undermined the three efforts made in the 1870s and 1880s to publish dailies for the expanding communities of English residents in Massachusetts and New York.

In comparison with other new immigrants, the English immigrants in the decades preceding the Civil War were more prone to separate from the community of their fellow immigrants, more willing to intermarry, and more enthusiastic in embracing the culture of their new land. For most groups of English immigrants throughout the century their ethnic identity was expressed by their participation in the Episcopal Churches in most states and in the Methodist and Baptist Churches in the rural South. Throughout the century, such groups as the Domestic and Foreign Missionary Society of the Episcopal Church of England, the Society for the Propagation of the Gospel, and the Salvation Army sent ministers and missionaries to English congregations in America. With funds raised in England and in English immigrant communities along the Atlantic seaboard, Kenyon College and Jubilee College were established in Ohio and Illinois, respectively, to train Episcopal ministers for service in towns in the middle and far western states where numerous English immigrant communities of miners, craftsmen, and farmers had settled. In many of these states, English immigrants avoided political office beyond the local level and were more reluctant than members of other ethnic groups to apply for American citizenship.

The tendency to adapt and integrate increased in the second half of the century. One study concluded that less than 20 percent of children from the turn of the century's largest community of English immigrants eventually married someone of English descent. While a number of

English immigrant groups in the second half of the nineteenth century, like the textile workers in Lowell, Massachusetts, the cutlery workers in Connecticut, and English miners in West Virginia, may have lived close together and established distinctly English denominational congregations, they were absorbed into the mainstream of American life within a generation. While some communities of English miners, mill workers, and agricultural settlers in the Midwest established libraries, social clubs, and musical societies to provide English culture, most, including the chapters of the St. George's Society in Madison, Wisconsin, and in Clinton, Iowa, rarely survived for more than a decade.

While English immigrants unsuccessfully tried to establish local labor unions, labor exchanges, and political pressure groups in this period, small groups of English skilled workers in industrial and mining communities in the East and Midwest were able to maintain some social cohesion and community identity in the periods of heightened immigration. These groups were able to maintain, for as long as two decades, the self-help associations, buying cooperatives, fraternal lodges, and sporting associations common in English communities in the late Victorian era.

The English immigrants in the last three decades established their own groups of working-class fraternal, social, political, and literary organizations. The Sons of St. George was one of the most durable of these groups and survived until the Great Depression. Originally excluding all but native born English and their descendants, the lodges developed insurance services, secret rituals, and special social functions that were characteristic of other groups. The organization declined as English immigration decreased and America became more isolationist in the two decades following World War I.

A major stimulus for English immigrants to organize was the emergence of the Irish as a major constituency in American politics. In order to increase their political influence, English American groups encouraged the reluctant English immigrants to become citizens in the last decades of the century. While a smaller percentage of English renounced their loyalty to their homeland than did immigrants from other parts of Europe, the census of 1900 showed a significant increase in the percentage of English Americans becoming citizens of the United States. This trend continued and grew in the twentieth century until the rate of English immigrant assimilation matched that of other European settlers.

One result of this trend was the organization of English American and British American political clubs in Philadelphia, Boston, and New York, as well as in smaller industrial towns including Elizabeth, New Jersey, and Stanford, Maine; and in Ohio, Iowa, and California, where communities of English miners, artisans, and industrial workers asserted their political muscle, predominantly on behalf of the Republican party. These activities escalated after an 1887 banquet celebration of Queen Victoria's Golden Jubilee in Boston's Faneuil Hall was disrupted by thousands of angry Irish protesters, who tried to prevent the entry of the 400 ticket holders. When only a few British politicians condemned the protest, English American and Scottish American leaders organized a federation of more than 60 political action clubs and launched a number of periodicals. Massachusetts, New York, Pennsylvania, and Illinois each had a dozen or more English communities that organized politically, and New Hampshire, Connecticut, New Jersey, Ohio, Michigan, Iowa, and California each had several chapters. These clubs had little impact on the elections of 1888 and 1892, and most were absorbed into a broader anti-Catholic confederation, the American Protective Association, an offshoot of the nativism and populist movements of the 1890s.

Three publications launched in the late 1880s—the British-American Citizen, published in Boston between 1887 and 1913; the Western British American, published in Chicago between 1888 and 1922; and the British-American, published in New York and Philadelphia between 1887 and 1919—attained a limited degree of success by appealing to immigrants from all parts of Britain. They were not successful in uniting Americans of Scottish, English, Irish, and Welsh descent into a single effective political action group, but they did serve to sharpen the ethnic identity of their readers and underscore the importance of the British contribution to American society. The survival of these periodicals after the collapse of the political clubs was due in part to improved diplomatic relations between the United States and Britain after 1895, which led to an alliance in World War I.

The Anglo-American partnership begun in World War I has endured to the present. Britain's actions and policies throughout the century, represented in the American consciousness by the Tommies in the trenches of World War I, Prime

Minister Winston Churchill's resistance to Hitler, and Prime Minister Margaret Thatcher's support of America in the Persian Gulf War, has increased the popularity and general acceptance of English immigrants.

### COMMON STEREOTYPES AND MISCONCEPTIONS

Derived from stage plays, BBC television shows, and novels, many of which have been made into Hollywood movies, a number of overdrawn stereotypes abound that exaggerate class distinctions and distort the social attitudes of English Americans. The long-lasting series, "Masterpiece Theater," and the many movies made from Noel Coward plays and Agatha Christie mysteries have reinforced the cartoonish view of the English aristocracy as a rather stuffy, humorless, reserved, and insensitive group of social relics living hollow lives and wasting their remaining resources on trivial pursuits. They survive the traumas of modern life only with the assistance of their ever-dependable gentlemen's gentleman. English rulers and political leaders are unrealistically portrayed as charismatic, cosmopolitan, and solely responsible for all of the grand achievements in English history. From the craftiness of Henry VIII and Queen Elizabeth to the architects of the British Empire and such gifted orators like Pitt and Churchill, English leaders emerge as incorruptible patriots with unerring policies and a love of their citizens not matched in the history books. Despite its inaccuracy, this image is the one with which American presidents from John Fitzgerald Kennedy to Bill Clinton have tried to associate themselves in the course of their relations with England.

The stereotypes of middle-class English Americans keep alive an unreal idealization of the Victorian era. This depiction of the irascible and hardworking English detective, lawyer, professor, or businessman with an idiosyncratic personality has become a stock figure on both sides of the Atlantic. They are the more respectable versions of such working-class bounders as the comic strip character Andy Capp, lazy sports zealots inclined to violence, alcoholism, and womanizing. Working-class women, typified by the cheerful movie heroine Mary Poppins, are just the opposite; English nannies, secretaries, and junior executives are perceived as extremely hardworking and efficient and are in great demand in the homes of elite families and in the offices of American corporations.

### HEALTH AND MENTAL HEALTH ISSUES

There are no particular health problems or psychological conditions that are specifically associated with British Americans. A number of descendants of British Americans were among the founders of medical societies and others have been prominent in the health insurance industry. England expatriates brought the cooperative movement to America in the early nineteenth century and were early supporters of group health insurance. The success of the National Health system in Britain created benefits for employers, making British multinational corporations advocates of national health insurance in the United States.

# LANGUAGE

The popularity in America of English music—both classical and contemporary—movies, television, and theater, and of English performers might suggest that the only distinction between the speech of England and America is in the accents. Pronunciation in England, however, is an important indicator of social class and region of origin, as it is in America. Yet Americans make little distinction between the working-class cockney staccato of the east end of London and the slower, precise articulation of well-educated professional. After living in the United States for several decades, most English immigrants are not identifiable by their accents, and their descendants are indistinguishable from other native born Americans.

The sharper distinction between English of the immigrant generation and those born in the United States is a vocabulary of several hundred words and phrases. While some newer English words, especially slang words, are popularized in America by English musicians and actors, the names of ordinary items distinguish the immigrant English from other Americans. While an American might guess that petrol powers an automobile, he might be hesitant to open the car's bonnet (hood) or eat some crisps (potato chips) or ring off (hang up) the telephone. The English refer to sausages as bangers and call the toilet the "loo" or the "W.C." (for water closet).

# FAMILY AND COMMUNITY DYNAMICS

As in other areas of American society, it was the English pattern of the nuclear family—focused on

English Morris Dancers

perform at the Red Lion

Inn in Stockbridge,

Massachusetts.

the husband, wife, and children with an occasional relative family living in close proximity—that set the pattern of early life in the colonial era. While women were in short supply in the early decades of the colonial era, the majority of Puritan settlers came to New England with their families, as whole congregations and sizable groups of religious dissidents transferred their hopes of a "Godly commonwealth" to America. They set the pattern for establishing Sunday "blue laws," to sanctify the Sabbath by prohibiting public drinking, dancing, and work-related activities and encouraging prayer and charitable and missionary activities, especially among family members. Outside New England the pastimes described in King James' *Book of Sports* (1681) were more prevalent; and modest displays of entertainment, especially dancing, singing, and athletic competitions among family groups were common and often held under the auspices of the local Episcopal congregation. As noted above, English immigrants, especially those who were part of the larger waves of migration in the nineteenth century,

usually settled in small towns with other English miners, metal workers, farmers, and skilled textile specialists and recreated English-style pubs, choral groups, sporting clubs, self-help societies, unions, and fraternal organization, few of which endured for very long beyond the lifetime of the founders.

In all social classes, to differing degrees, English American women dominated the domestic and social life of family as well as its relations with friends and extended family as completely as men dominated the public aspects of family life and business. As in the land of their birth, family celebrations and the maintenance of connections with the prominent relatives or members of "cadet" branches of the family were left to women, especially in more affluent and socially prominent families. Among middle- and upper-class families, care was taken to educate and discipline the older children and to encourage them to continue family businesses and social obligations. Their greater reliance on family, kinsmen, and contacts from their native regions of England and the ease with which they blended into American society, may help explain why English immigrants were last among the new settlers to embrace American citizenship.

This may partially explain the greater proclivity of their children to eventually marry spouses who were not of English ancestry and their willingness to leave the communities in which they were reared. They found that they could be "at home" anywhere in America and that their heritage was not an obstacle, but rather an asset, in finding a mate who could improve their social and economic status.

For most groups of English immigrants throughout the century, the church was central to ethnic identity. The literature and scriptures of the Episcopal, Methodist, and Baptist churches across the country were nearly the same as those in the communities of their birth. Many of these congregations maintained and supported projects of the Episcopal Church of England, the Society for the Propagation of the Gospel, and the Salvation Army, making it easy for descendants of English immigrants to transfer their loyalties from their parents' congregation to one in the community to which they had moved to create their own family. This pattern may change in the future, as the acceptance of the ordination of women and negotiations for a reconciliation with the Vatican and the Church of England proceed and as the Episcopal Church worships with its own "modern" Prayer Book.

From the colonial era, English Americans were concerned about higher education and the need for a trained ministry. A large percentage of the early colleges in America were founded and supported by English immigrants and their descendants especially in New England and the southeast. A number of traditional English sports such as sculling (team rowing) and rugby are still supported at colleges founded by English Americans, but the three English aristocratic pastimes that enjoy the greatest popularity in America, and have shed their English identity, are "lawn" tennis, horse racing, and sailing. In a scattering of communities in America, rugby, cricket, and English football (soccer) fields—where teams wearing traditional outfits of long socks, short pants, and shirts with broad horizontal stripes—keep alive a uniquely English sports heritage.

While many groups, including the New England Puritans and the English Quakers in Pennsylvania, were among the earliest advocates of free public education at all levels, the wealthy and professional classes of English settlers favored private schools and colleges, often affiliated with their particular denomination. When they could, they provided their older sons with a junior year abroad at a British university, as a substitute for the "grand tour" of the continent provided by their own parents. Many endowments were provided to subsidize the education of the children of expatriates in England, the most famous of which is the Rhodes scholarship program, named for the English financier and colonial official Cecil Rhodes. Throughout the United States, English immigrants and their descendants were among the leading philanthropists, supporting museums, colleges, and cultural organizations and many donated facilities in England to enable American colleges to conduct exchange and study-abroad programs. After World War II, Americans of English descent raised millions of dollars for the restoration of churches, schools, and other public buildings in England and that they had visited or attended.

Few particularly English holidays are celebrated by English Americans. In some communities small Guy Fawkes Day commemorations are held on November 5 to remember the deliverance of the King and Parliament from a plot in 1605 to destroy them by gunpowder. The English equivalent of July 4, it is celebrated in a similar fashion, with games, fireworks, and a large meal. Among some royalist families, St. Charles Day, marking the martyrdom of King Charles I on January 29, 1649 is celebrated with a somber ritual resembling a wake but featuring the imbibing of spirits, flag waving, and the reading of Charles's final speech from the gallows.

Because of their shared heritage, the family structure and community dynamics of English Americans have differed little from the rest of mainstream American. The mass media have continued to shape the culture of English and American societies in similar ways in the late twentieth century.

# RELIGION

Beginning in the colonial era, the Church of England was active in every colony, despite the fact that many groups of English immigrants came to America to escape that institution and enjoy the freedom to practice other forms of Christianity. In the federalist period, as the Church of England became the Episcopal Church of America, other evangelical denominations including Quaker and Methodist ended their affiliation with their English counterparts and joined the American religious establishment. Throughout the history of the United States, there was little need for English expatriates to found separate churches, as virtually all English denominations found support in the American religious establishment. The exceptions to this situation were the groups of mill workers, miners, and tradesmen who settled in distinct enclaves in small towns in the 1870s and 1880s. A half dozen of these communities formed small congregations affiliated with less prominent English evangelical sects but were absorbed by other mainstream denominations within a decade. The Episcopal and Methodist-Episcopal churches remained an important segment of American Protestantism, and English immigrants and their descendants make up a significant and influential part of their membership.

# POLITICS AND GOVERNMENT

The histories of England and America were inseparable during the colonial period, and English settlers dominated all aspects of colonial government and society. The American colonies successfully fought a war of rebellion against Britain from 1776 to 1783, after which several thousand English loyalists migrated to other Crown colonies, while others returned home. Several diplomatic problems, American aspirations to annex Canada, and the impressment of American sailors by the British navy led to the War of 1812. After America defeated Britain in 1815, a nationalist spirit swept the victorious nation, resulting in harsh public criticism of England, a brief period during English immigration was discouraged, and a number of conflicts renewed tension between the two countries.

Diplomatic relations began to improve as Britain promised naval support for the Monroe Doctrine, sealing off the American continent from colonial settlements by European powers, and as disputes over the Canadian border were settled. While new problems arose during the American Civil War and the period of Western expansion, cordial relations developed in the last part of the nineteenth century as the interests of Britain and America were challenged by other imperialist nations. Throughout the twentieth century a special relationship has endured, through alliances in two world wars and the Cold War. Britain was America's strongest supporter the Persian Gulf War, and the United States supported Britain in its war against Argentina to retain the Falkland Islands.

# INDIVIDUAL AND GROUP CONTRIBUTIONS

During all of American history English immigrants and their descendants were prominent on every level of government and in every aspect of American life. Eight of the first ten American presidents and more than that proportion of the 42 presidents, as well as the majority of sitting congressmen and congresswomen, are descended from English ancestors. The acronym WASP, for white Anglo-Saxon Protestant, is used to describe the dominant political and cultural demographic segment in America.

The descendants of English expatriates are so numerous and so well integrated in American life that it is impossible to identify all of them. While they are the third largest ethnic nationality identified in the 1990 census, they retain such a pervasive representation at every level of national and state government that, on any list of American senators, Supreme Court judges, governors, or legislators, they would constitute a plurality if not an outright majority.

# MEDIA

**PRINT**

*Albion.*

An interdisciplinary quarterly journal that features scholarly articles and reviews of books dealing with English history and culture. It is published by the North American Conference on British Studies and Appalachian State University.

**Contact:** Michael J. Moore, Editor.

**Address:** Department of History, Boone, North Carolina 28608-3906.

**Telephone:** (704) 262-6004.

*British-American Trade News.*

Monthly publication that provides a variety of information, statistics, and projections for the purpose of fostering trade between the two countries. It is published by the British-American Chamber of Commerce.

**Address:** 10 East 40th Street, New York, New York 10016.
**Telephone:** (212) 889-0680.

*British Record.*
A free bimonthly newsletter published by the British Information Services that provides a brief listing of British news items, cultural events, and short feature articles on people and places of general interest.

**Address:** 845 Third Avenue, New York, New York 10022.
**Telephone:** (212) 752-8400.

*In Britain.*
Monthly magazine published by the British Tourist Authority that includes an abundance of pictures and special features of tourists attractions, festivals, and historical and architectural monuments.

**Address:** 680 Fifth Avenue, New York, New York 10019.
**Telephone:** (212) 581-4708.

*Manchester Guardian Weekly.*
North American edition of *The Guardian*. It summarizes the news of the week in England and contains a variety of features, book reviews, international news, advertisements aimed at expatriates, and selections extracted from the Parisian *Le Monde* and the *Washington Post*. It has the largest circulation of any English newspaper in America.

**Address:** 19 West 44th Street, Suite 1613, New York, New York 10036-6101.
**Telephone:** (212) 944-1179.

*Union Jack.*
Brings news of Britain to the British community in the United States.

**Contact:** Ronald Choularton, Editor.
**Address:** Box 1823, La Mesa, California 91944-1823.
**Telephone:** (619) 466-3129.

### RADIO AND TELEVISION

**British Broadcasting Corporation (BBC).**
Publishes *London Calling*, a program guide for several shortwave radio programs broadcast by the BBC to the United States and other countries.

Also distributes such BBC television series such as "The East-Enders," "Mystery Theatre," and "Are You Being Served," which are featured on America's Public Broadcasting System.

**Address:** 630 Fifth Avenue, New York, New York 10017.
**Telephone:** (212) 507-1500; or, (212) 507-0033.

# ORGANIZATIONS AND ASSOCIATIONS

**British Social and Athletic Club.**
Founded in 1966 and centered in California, it has a dozen branches in the state and abroad. It provides a range of social and recreational activities and teaches and promotes cricket and soccer. It sponsors group flights to important matches around the world and has branches in Australia and New Zealand.

**Address:** 13429 Tiara Street, Van Nuys, California 91401.
**Telephone:** (713) 787-9985.

**Daughters of the British Empire in the United States of America National Society.**
Founded during World War I, this charitable society maintains facilities for aged British men and women.

**Address:** 4703 Ivanhoe Road, Houston, Texas 77027.
**Telephone:** (713) 626-7221.

**English Speaking Union of the United States.**
Founded in 1920 to promote British American friendship and understanding it sponsors debates, lectures, and speakers. It provides scholarships and travel grants and has over 70 branches throughout the United States. It publishes a quarterly newsletter.

**Address:** 16 East 69th Street, New York, New York 10021.
**Telephone:** (212) 879-6800.

**International Society for British Genealogy and Family History (ISBGFH).**
Strives to foster interest in the genealogy and family history of persons of British descent, improve U.S.-British relations, increase the educational opportunities and knowledge of members and the public, and encourage preservation of historical records and access to records.

Contact: Hazel M. Tibbitts, Corresponding Secretary.

Address: P.O. Box 3115, Salt Lake City, Utah 84110-3115.

Telephone: (801) 240-4314.

## North American Conference on British Studies.

Founded in 1951, it is a national scholarly group that promotes scholarly research and discussion of British history and culture. It has seven regional branches, publishes *Albion* and the *Journal of British Studies,* and awards several prizes for the best new works in British Studies.

Contact: Reba Soffer, President.

Address: History Department, California State University, Northridge, California 91330.

## St. George's Society of New York.

Founded in 1770, it is a charitable organization whose membership is limited to British citizens, their descendants, and members of Commonwealth nations. It provides assistance for needy British expatriates in the New York area.

Contact: John A. Ford, President.

Address: 15 East 26th Street New York New York 10010.

Telephone: (212) 532-2816.

# MUSEUMS AND RESEARCH CENTERS

## The Folger Shakespeare Library.

Maintains a collection of over 300,000 volumes and rare manuscripts on Shakespeare, drama, history, and government in Tudor and Stuart England. Founded in 1932, it provides scholarships, seminars, and evening colloquia for scholars and students of Renaissance Britain. It supports a diverse publication program, research projects, and traveling exhibits.

Contact: O. B. Hardison, Jr., Director.

Address: 201 East Capital Street, Washington, D.C. 20003.

Telephone: (202) 546-4800.

## Paul Mellon Center for British Art and British Studies.

Founded in 1968, the center is part of Yale University. It includes the Mellon collection of British art and rare books, and it features a gallery, lecture, and seminar rooms and a library of over 100,000 volumes. It is affiliated with the under-

graduate and graduate programs at the University and provides scholarships for research projects.

Address: Box 2120, Yale Station, New Haven, Connecticut 06520.

Telephone: (203) 432-4594.

# SOURCES FOR ADDITIONAL STUDY

Berthoff, Roland T. *British Immigrants in Industrial America, 1790-1950.* New York: Russell and Russell, 1968.

Bridenbaugh, Carl. *Vexed and Troubled Englishmen, 1590-1642.* London: Oxford University Press, 1976.

*The British in America: 1578-1970,* edited by Howard B. Furer. Dobbs Ferry, New York: Oceana Publications, 1972.

Bryson, Bill. *The Mother Tongue: English and How It Got to Be That Way.* New York: Morrow, 1990.

Cohen, Robin. *Frontiers of Identity: The British and the Others.* London: Longmans, 1994.

Erickson, Charlotte. *Invisible Immigrants: the Adaptation of English and Scottish Immigrants in Nineteenth Century America.* Coral Gables, Florida: University of Miami Press, 1972.

*To Build a New Land: Ethnic Landscapes in North America,* edited by Allen G. Noble. Baltimore: Johns Hopkins University Press, 1992.

# ESTONIAN AMERICANS

by
Mark A.
Granquist

## OVERVIEW

Located on the east coast of the Baltic Sea, the Republic of Estonia is the northernmost of the three Baltic Republics. The country measures 17,413 square miles (45,100 sq. km.), including some 1,500 islands in the Baltic Sea. The population is approximately 72 percent urban in character, and the capital city is Tallinn. Estonia is bordered on the north by the Gulf of Finland, on the east by Lake Peipus and Russia, on the south by Latvia, and on the west by the Baltic Sea.

The 1992 census estimated the population of Estonia at 1,607,000. Of these inhabitants 65 percent are Estonian, while 30 percent are Russian, and the rest are Ukrainian and Byelorussian. The ethnic Russian immigration intensified during the Soviet period (1940-1991) and is concentrated in the east, especially around Narva. Lutherans constitute the largest religious group, although there are other Protestant denominations (principally Baptist) and a significant number of Eastern Orthodox Christians. The official language is Estonian, with Russian also widely spoken. The Estonian flag consists of three evenly spaced horizontal bands—blue on the top, black in the middle, and white on the bottom.

### HISTORY

The Estonians are a Baltic-Finnish group related

These Estonian refugees, who sailed to Florida to escape Russian domination, were granted immigration visas by President Truman on November 2, 1946.

to the Finno-Ugric peoples. Their first significant historical contact was with the Vikings, who in the ninth and tenth centuries conquered the Estonian homeland, bringing trade and cultural exchange. In the Middle Ages the Swedes, Danes, and Russians all attempted to conquer the land and to introduce Christianity, but it was not until the thirteenth century that the Germans prevailed and introduced Christianity by force. The Teutonic Order, a German order of crusading knights and priests, won control of Estonia by 1346, subjugating the native population and establishing a tradition of German rule that would extend into the twentieth century. As the power of the Teutonic Knights began to wane in the fifteenth century, Poland, Lithuania, and Russia all laid claim to Estonian territory, but it was Sweden who won control after the dissolution of the Teutonic Order in 1561. With Russia's defeat of Sweden in the Great Northern War, Estonia was transferred to Russian rule in 1721. Although some Estonians looked favorably to Russian rule as a way to free their country from German and Swedish domination, Russian government proved to be a mixed blessing. During the eighteenth century rural Estonians lost many of their traditional liberties. Serfdom was finally eliminated by 1819, and other social reforms followed. Imperial attempts at the "Russification" of Estonian life in the late nineteenth century broke the grip of the Baltic-Germans over the country, but these efforts came into conflict with an ascendant wave of Estonian nationalism.

The January 1905 Revolution in Russia spread to Estonia, with Estonian leaders demanding national autonomy. When the revolution was crushed by imperial forces, many Estonian revolutionary leaders fled abroad. With the collapse of imperial government in 1917, Estonia won first autonomy and then independence. This was opposed by the Communists, who backed down only with the advance of German troops into the Baltic States in 1918. From 1917 to 1920, with British and Finnish aid, Estonians fought for independence from Russia. By 1920 Estonian troops had forced all remaining Soviet troops out of Estonia, and the country was finally independent. Between the World Wars, the newly emerging state had to contend externally with continued pressure and intrigue from the Soviets and internally with economic and political instability. In 1940, with the secret compliance of the Germans, Soviet troops took over Estonia and incorporated it into the Soviet Union. From 1941 to 1944, Estonia was occupied by the Nazis, and when Soviet troops reentered Estonia in 1944, large numbers of Estonians (perhaps ten percent of the total population) fled the country. Estonia continued as a Soviet Republic until 1991, undergoing another wave of Russification in the 1950s and 1960s. With the breakup of the Soviet Union,

Estonia declared its independence in 1991, and a new Estonian government was elected in 1992.

## SIGNIFICANT IMMIGRATION WAVES

During the period of Swedish rule over Estonia in the seventeenth century, a few Estonians assisted the Swedes in establishing the colony of New Sweden on the Delaware River. Estonian immigration to the United States was nevertheless quite limited until the late nineteenth century. The first Estonian immigrants were fortune hunters or seamen who jumped Russian sailing vessels. Immigration records do not identify them as Estonians, referring to them instead as "Russians," a practice that continued until 1922. In 1894, one group settled near Fort Pierre, South Dakota, while others settled in New York and San Francisco.

The first significant wave of immigration came after the failure in Estonia of the 1905 Revolution. This wave brought a strong Socialist contingent to the United States that led to the formation of many Estonian American Socialist and Communist organizations. Population estimates of the Estonian American community during this period vary widely and are difficult to reconcile. By 1930, official immigration and census records reveal that there were only about 3,550 Estonian Americans in the United States. Other sources, however, including government estimates, suggest that this number was much larger, recording 5,100 Estonian Americans in 1890, 44,100 in 1910, and 69,200 in 1920. The establishment of an independent Estonia in 1920, combined with the tightening of American immigration laws in the 1920s, dramatically slowed Estonian immigration to the United States. After World War II, there was a tremendous exodus of Estonians from Soviet rule; most Estonians made their way to Sweden or Germany, although about 15,000 of them came to the United States. Unlike the group that arrived in 1905, this group was strongly anti-Socialist and nationalistic; it spanned a larger exile community and was connected by a web of international organizations. The U.S. Census of 1990 lists 26,762 Americans claiming Estonian as a first or second ancestry.

## SETTLEMENT PATTERNS

Early settlements arose on both coasts, in New York City and around San Francisco and Astoria, Oregon. In the late nineteenth century, there were rural, agricultural colonies of Estonian Americans in Fort Pierre, South Dakota; Bloomville, Wisconsin; Dickenson, North Dakota; and Chester, Montana, among other places. But these rural Midwestern settlements did not represent the bulk of Estonian immigrants. Rather, the two major waves of Estonian immigration in the twentieth century were mainly urban in nature. Major Estonian American settlements were located in the northeastern United States (Boston, Connecticut, New York City, New Jersey, Baltimore, and Washington), in the Midwest (Detroit and Cleveland), and on the West Coast (San Francisco and Los Angeles). More than half of Estonian Americans lived in the Northeast, with 20 percent concentrated in California and 15 percent in the Midwest. There was limited reverse migration back to Estonia in the 1920s, but this never became a significant trend. During the period of German and Russian occupation from 1940 to 1991, there was virtually no reemigration.

## RELATIONS WITH SETTLED AMERICANS

Estonian immigrants have not stirred much reaction from the dominant culture in America, as the group is rather small in number. Because they share many characteristics with their white, middle-class urban neighbors, they quickly assimilate into their surroundings and have become part of their local communities. These immigrants tend to be literate, skilled, and hardworking and have made successful lives in the United States. One possible source of tension was the emergence of a radical socialist and communist movement among Estonians from 1905 to 1920. Instigated by refugees who took flight from Estonia during the 1905 Russian Revolution, this radicalizing movement captured and transformed many Estonian American institutions, causing great turmoil within the immigrant community. Coming at a time when Estonians were considered Russian in the popular mind, and when fear of communism was rampant, this did not go far to create a positive image of the Estonian immigrant. Nevertheless, the events of World War II, the Russian invasion of Estonia, and the flood of refugees out of the country created a swell of popular recognition for all the Baltic countries, including Estonia.

# ACCULTURATION AND ASSIMILATION

Estonian immigrants in the United States have generally assimilated well into the mainstream of American society, especially after 1945. Before World War II, the Estonians did not push hard to become American citizens; in 1930 only 42 percent of immigrants had citizenship (a pace behind Finnish and other Baltic immigrants). In the late twentieth century, however, Estonian Americans have rapidly climbed the social and economic ladder, specializing in areas of technical expertise. A number of factors have contributed to a high degree of assimilation among Estonian Americans: the size of the community, its rapid educational and social success, and the wide geographical dispersion of the immigrants.

Estonian Americans have created a large network of social and cultural organizations, schools, churches, and clubs to keep alive the language and culture of their homeland. This network is coordinated by the Estonian American National Council, headquartered in New York City. A major goal of these institutions is to retain and transmit the Estonian heritage to succeeding generations. A network of 14 Estonian schools in the United States teaches Estonian language, history, and culture to the children of the community. Estonian American scouting is a national program with sponsored activities. Local Estonian American groups include women's and veterans' organizations and literary and cultural circles. Before 1992 and the establishment of the independent Republic of Estonia, many groups were dedicated to the opposition of communism and the eventual freedom of the Baltic states.

The tensions inherent in acculturation and assimilation are best displayed in the lives of the refugees who fled Estonia after World War II. On the one hand, they were glad to be in the United States and emphasized success within the American culture. On the other hand, as with many political refugees from Soviet communism, they held a strong passion for the overthrow of communism in Estonia and maintained hope that they would someday return to their native land. This refugee status created internal turmoil for some Estonian Americans, as they tried to balance the demands of their homeland and heritage with feelings of patriotism for the United States and a desire to assimilate into American society. Today, much of the active Estonian American community is composed of these first- and second-generation immigrants.

## INTERACTION WITH OTHER ETHNIC GROUPS

Estonian Americans are closely affiliated with immigrants from other Baltic countries (Latvia, Lithuania, and Finland). Not only did these groups arrive in the United States at roughly the same time, they share a common history in Europe. Since the Soviet takeover of the Baltic Republics in 1940, Americans of Baltic descent have joined in common action toward securing independence for their ancestral homelands. A number of groups were formed around this issue, including the Joint Baltic American National Committee (1961) and the Baltic World Council (1972). There are also joint cultural and educational efforts and celebrations, and a Baltic Women's Council (1947).

## CUISINE

Estonian cooking combines the culinary influences of Scandinavia, Germany, and Russia with native traditions. The raw ingredients come from the forests, farms, and coastal waters of Estonia: berries, pork, cabbage, sour cream, and seafood (salmon, herring, eel, sprat) are staples. From Scandinavia and Finland come the traditional foods of the smorgasbord; from Germany come sauerkraut and various cold potato salads. Russian influences also abound. *Rossolye* is a cold mixed salad of potatoes, vegetables, diced meat, and herring, with a sour cream-vinegar dressing. *Mulgikapsad* is a pork and sauerkraut dish that takes its name from an Estonian province. Other salads, common to the Baltic region, include a preserved mixed fruit salad and a sour cream-cucumber salad.

## TRADITIONAL COSTUMES

Estonian Americans do not wear a distinctive everyday garment that would set them apart as being Estonian. As with many other European groups, Estonians have colorful regional costumes that immigrants sometimes brought with them, but these are worn only on special occasions, such as ethnic celebrations or festivals.

Traditional costumes for women include a tunic shirt, a full colorful skirt, and an embroidered apron. The headdresses worn by women vary according to region and village. In southern Estonia, the traditional headdress for a married woman is a long, linen, embroidered kerchief worn around the head and down the back. In northern Estonia, small, intricately designed *coifs* (hats) adorn women's folk costumes. Heavy necklaces are also common. Men's costumes generally consist of wide-legged pants gathered at the knee and loose-fitting shirts. The principal headdress for men is a high, stiff felt hat or fur cap with earflaps, the latter of which is worn during the winter months. Both men's and women's traditional costumes include a decorative broach used to fasten shirts and blouses. During the winter, traditional Estonian costumes included high felt boots called *valenka* to protect them from the cold.

### HOLIDAYS CELEBRATED BY ESTONIAN AMERICANS

Along with the traditional Christian and American holidays, there are certain festival days that are of special significance to the Estonian American community. February 24 is celebrated as Estonian Independence Day, marking the formal declaration of Estonian independence in 1918. A two-day holiday in June combines two separate celebrations, St. John's Eve (Midsummer) on June 23, and Victory Day on June 24. Reaching far back into history, Midsummer is a common festival in the Scandinavian and Baltic countries. Victory Day commemorates the defeat of the Soviet Armies in the Estonian War of Independence (1918-1920). In their celebration of Christmas, Estonians extend the holiday a day or two after December 25; the first few days after Christmas are devoted to visiting friends and family.

A feature of resurgent Estonian nationalism during the nineteenth and twentieth centuries has been national song festivals, celebrated for a period of days during the summer. Estonians in Europe and North America continue to celebrate these festivals, organizing mass gatherings to honor Estonia and to maintain national identity. In North America Estonians from Canada and the United States gathered in such celebrations from 1957 to 1968, twice in New York and twice in Canada. The Estonian World Festivals, a series of worldwide Estonian gatherings, began in 1972. The first such event was in Toronto, followed by Baltimore, Maryland, and Stockholm.

### HEALTH AND MENTAL HEALTH ISSUES

Estonian Americans have embraced medicine as it is practiced in the United States and have been eager to become medical practitioners. A 1975 survey by the *Väliseestlasea kalendar* (*Almanac for the Estonian Abroad*) listed over 100 Estonian American doctors or dentists, of whom 25 percent were women.

# LANGUAGE

The Estonian language is a branch of the Baltic-Finnish group of the Finno-Ugric family, related to Finnish. Most ethnic Estonians speak Estonian, but ethnic Russians and others in Estonia continue to speak Russian because Estonian is considered to be a difficult language to learn. Historically, there have been a number of dialects, but the one spoken around the capital of Tallinn has come to dominate literary expression, thus ruling the development of modern Estonian. Another form of Estonian is spoken by Estonian war refugees in Sweden and has absorbed some Swedish influences. The written language uses the Roman alphabet and consists of 14 consonants and nine vowels ("a, ä, e, i, o, ö, õ, u," and "ü"). The consonants ("c, f, q, w, x, y," and "z") are generally used only in names and words of foreign origin. The language has a musical quality and employs a great number of diphthongs and other vowel combinations.

The Estonian American community has made strong attempts to maintain the language, with mixed success. A number of schools, publications, congregations, and learned societies within the community still use Estonian as a means of discourse. This is somewhat problematic within the larger community because new generations and the non-Estonian spouses of mixed marriages have a hard time understanding Estonian. Still, Estonian is taught at Indiana University, Kent State University, and Ohio State University, and a number of public libraries throughout the United States offer Estonian language collections, including the Boston Public Library, the New York Public Library, and the Cleveland Public Library.

### GREETINGS AND OTHER POPULAR EXPRESSIONS

Common Estonian greetings and other expressions include: *Tere hommikut* ("tere hommikoot")—Good morning; *Tere õhtut* ("tere erhtut")—Good evening; Jumalaga ("yoomahlahgah")—Good-bye; *Kuidas käsi käib* ("kooydahs kasi kayb")—How are you?; *Tänan hästi* ("tanahn haysti")—Fine, thanks; *Palun* ("pahloon")—Please; *Tänan* ("tanahn")—Thanks; *Vabandage* ("vahbahndahge")—Excuse me; *Jah* ("yah")—Yes; *Ei* ("ey")—No; and *Nägemieseni* ("nagesmiseni")—See you later.

# FAMILY AND COMMUNITY DYNAMICS

Before 1920 the Estonian American community tended to be dominated by young single men and women who came either to look for work or to escape the religious and political repression of tsarist Russia. Because the vast majority lived in cities on the East or West Coast, a stable immigrant community, with a predominance of families and other social and cultural institutions, was slow to develop. But the 1920s and 1930s saw the appearance of a strong immigrant community that was augmented after 1945 by the arrival of war refugee families. A significant degree of educational and economic advancement, a high rate of intermarriage, and the dispersal of this relatively small community have moved the Estonians well into the mainstream of American life. In addition, research has shown a considerable degree of ethnic consciousness among the contemporary Estonian Americans that will help hold the community together.

## EDUCATION

Education has played an important role in shaping the Estonian American community and in moving these immigrants into mainstream American life. Because Estonia in the nineteenth century was more advanced in literacy than many other parts of the Russian Empire, many of the early immigrants were literate. Likewise, a significant number of the political refugees who fled Estonia after the abortive 1905 Revolution were educated, and the Socialist ferment within the community produced journals, newspapers, and reading rooms. However, the emphasis on education was nowhere more apparent than in the refugees who arrived in the United States after 1945. Many of them were members of the educational and political elite of Estonia, and in the United States they pushed for their children to get a good education. Studies of the second generation of these Estonian Americans have shown that a large majority have at least some college education, a modest majority have completed college, and a sizable number have graduate degrees. Also among this last group of immigrants were a number of Estonian intellectuals and academics who took positions in the American educational system. Estonian Americans have tended to specialize in science and technology, moving into fields such as engineering and architecture.

The Estonian American community has established a number of institutions to promote advancement in scholarship and education. These include Estonian academic fraternities and sororities, as well as an Estonian Students Association in the United States that promotes students' knowledge of Estonian language and culture and Estonian study abroad (especially in Finland). Learned societies, such as the Estonian Educational Society and the Estonian Learned Society in America, sponsor publications and conferences. A number of other specialized educational groups have a broader membership that extends throughout North America and Europe.

Estonian schools, located in major centers of the Estonian American community, are designed to supplement the education of Estonian youth by teaching them Estonian language, geography, history, and culture. These schools are interlinked in a regional and national network.

"After I got my citizenship, I sponsored two Estonian immigrant families. And a few years ago, I married a man from one of those families. So I have a new life. I feel that I have been blessed, really. This country has given me many things: a home, friendship, a chance to live again."

Leida Sorro in 1951, cited in *American Mosaic: The Immigrant Experience in the Words of Those Who Lived It*, edited by Joan Morrison and Charlotte Fox Zabusky (New York: E.P. Dutton, 1980).

## THE ROLE OF WOMEN

Since the advent of the Estonian American community, women have traditionally worked outside the home, pursuing education and careers. In 1932 an anonymous Estonian American writer commenting in his journal *Meie Tee* (quoted in *The Estonians in America, 1627-1975: A Chronology and Factbook*, p. 83) remarked about his community: "Estonian women here have always worked, even though the husband might have a well-paying job. Perhaps this is ... an established tradition." A 1968 survey of young Estonian American women showed that only 14 percent had ended their education at the high school level, whereas 61 percent were college graduates. The advanced level of women's education and work outside the home partly explains the swift rise in socioeconomic status of the Estonian American community. Estonian American women have also formed numerous local, national, and international women's organizations centered on educational, cultural, and social concerns and have banded with other Baltic-American women's groups to achieve common goals.

# RELIGION

In Estonia the dominant form of Christianity is Lutheranism, with smaller numbers of Baptist and Orthodox adherents. In Estonian American communities Lutheranism continues to be the dominant religious force. Headquartered in Stockholm, the Estonian Evangelical Lutheran Church is easily the largest organized religious group within the Estonian American community, with 38 congregations and 12,032 members across North America. The Estonian American Baptists came to the United States before World War I to escape persecution in Estonia and have maintained a number of congregations. The Baptist congregation in New York City, one of the first congregations formed, was an important early institution within the immigrant community. Estonian Orthodox parishes are active in Los Angeles, San Francisco, Chicago, and New York City. There are also several Estonian Pentecostal congregations.

This is not to say, however, that religious belief and affiliation have been universally important for Estonian immigrants in America; indeed, many Estonians were ambivalent or even hostile toward religious belief, especially early in this century. There are a number of reasons for these negative feelings, which spring from religious faith and practice in Estonia. The Lutheran Church in Estonia had traditionally been dominated by the Baltic-Germans, who monopolized many aspects of Estonian national life; not until 1860 did ethnic Estonians serve as Lutheran pastors. Thus, to many nineteenth-century Estonians Lutheranism represented a "foreign" presence. Another factor in the ambivalence of early Estonian immigrants toward religion was their adherence to socialist and communist ideologies that opposed organized religion. These dynamics proved to be very difficult for early Estonian American pastors to overcome, as they clashed with anticlerical and socialist immigrant groups.

The first religious leader in the Estonian American community was the Reverend Hans Rebane, who arrived in New York in 1896. Rebane had been invited by the American denomination, the German Missouri Lutheran Synod, to establish a mission for Estonian and Latvian Lutheran immigrants. Rebane established a small congregation in New York City and visited other Estonian settlements in the East and Midwest. Rebane also established a newspaper, *Eesti Amerika Postimees* (*Estonian American Courier*), the first Estonian publication in the United

States. Rebane used this newspaper to push his religious views and feuded with Estonian socialist groups until his death in 1911. Though the congregation in New York survived, and the Missouri Synod continued mission work among Estonian immigrants, this work was not particularly successful. During the period before World War II only two other Estonian American congregations took hold: a Baptist congregation formed in 1919, and a Pentecostal congregation formed in 1928, both in New York City.

After 1945 the influx of Estonian war refugees resulted in the construction of a number new Lutheran congregations, all linked with the Estonian Evangelical Lutheran Church (EELC). Established in 1954, the EELC has Lutheran congregations in most major Estonian settlements in North America. The other religious force to appear after 1945 was Estonian Orthodox Christianity, establishing several regional parishes. Orthodoxy took root in Estonia during the nineteenth century, winning Estonian converts who were discontent with German-dominated Lutheranism and Russian inducements. The first Estonian Orthodox parish was formed in New York City in 1949.

Especially since 1945 religion has come to play an important role in the life of the Estonian American community and has helped maintain a sense of group identity and cultural cohesion.

# EMPLOYMENT AND ECONOMIC TRADITIONS

The large majority of early immigrants settled in cities on the East and West Coasts, seeking jobs in labor and industry. Many Estonian men worked in the construction trades, and some rose to the level of independent contractors. Many women worked as domestics or in small retail or industrial operations. In the 1920s and 1930s numbers of Estonians were employed as building attendants and superintendents in apartments and office buildings, especially in New York. Other Estonians started small businesses, some of which were fairly successful.

An early conflict within the Estonian American community was over socialism and communism. Many of the refugees from the failed 1905 Revolution were socialists who were influential in establishing a strong socialist-oriented urban worker's movement among the Estonian Americans. Workers' societies were formed in centers of Estonian settlement, and in 1908 a central committee was organized to coordinate their activities. These organizations were often the only collective Estonian bodies in the community and thus came to be influential. However, the leadership of these organizations proved to be more radical than the American socialists and the majority of Estonian American workers. Between 1917 and 1920 the Estonian workers' movement was split over the issue of whether to support the Soviet military takeover of the newly independent Republic of Estonia. Many of the movement's leaders adopted a communist platform that supported inclusion of Estonia within the Soviet Union, whereas the majority of the rank and file opposed the move. The split shattered the effectiveness of the immigrant institutions and the Estonian American workers' movement as a whole. The communists were eventually absorbed into the American Communist Party, losing any particular ethnic identity.

After 1945 the employment and economic status of the community shifted in response to the new wave of political refugees, many of whom were well-educated professionals. A strong emphasis on education, professionalism, and the two-income family brought prosperity and socioeconomic mobility to the Estonian American community, which became predominantly middle class. Education, engineering and applied technology, medicine, science, and music and the arts were the leading professions. In 1962 a study of young Estonian American professionals found that 43 percent worked in the fields of engineering and technology; 18 percent in the sciences; 16 percent in the humanities and social sciences, respectively; and seven percent in medicine. Some Estonians have gone into business, often starting small- to medium-sized businesses within the Estonian American community.

# POLITICS AND GOVERNMENT

Political activity within the Estonian American community has been responsive to events within Estonia itself. Fluctuations in Estonia's status as an independent country have had a significant impact on this activity.

Because of Estonia's dependent status in the nineteenth century, many Estonian immigrants had not formed a clear consciousness of their national identity. But the rise of Estonian nationalism, coupled with the socialist struggle against the tsarist government, prompted the Estonian American community toward greater involvement in the affairs of the homeland. As political refugees began streaming into the country after the 1905 Revolution, the leadership of the immigrant community and many of its institutions passed into socialist hands. The communist revolution and the struggle to free Estonia (1917-1920) split the Estonian American community between those who supported a free Estonia and those who supported its inclusion into the Soviet Union. The Estonian nationalists prevailed because of a growing sense of national pride and because of the arrival (after 1920) of many veterans of the Estonian struggle for independence. In the wider sphere of American politics, the immigrant community was not particularly active unless the Republic of Estonia's affairs were directly involved. The number of immigrants seeking citizenship during this period was lower than for other Baltic nationalities.

The Soviet invasion of Estonia in 1940, along with the arrival of the war refugees after 1945, dramatically changed the face of the Estonian American community and its political efforts. The major concern now was Estonian independence from Soviet control. Many Estonian and Baltic-American groups formed to support their Estonian homeland in achieving this goal. Their initial activities centered on lobbying both the U.S. government and the United Nations to prevent the legal recognition of the Soviet conquest of Estonia. Because of their efforts (in concert with Latvian and Lithuanian Americans), the U.S. government never formally recognized the annexation of the three Baltic countries by the Soviet Union in 1940 and again in 1944 until 1991 when these countries regained their independence. Consequently, in the post World War II years, all three Baltic nations maintained consulates in the United States. Estonian Americans, as well as other Eastern European immigrant groups, were particularly outraged by the 1945 U.S.-Soviet agreement at Yalta, which they viewed as a sellout of the nations under communist domination.

After 1945 most Estonian Americans supported the Republican Party, faulting the Democrats for the Yalta agreement and viewing the Republicans as more sympathetic to their concerns. This trend of support for the Republican

Estonian Americans demonstrate in New York City in December 1988 while Mikhail Gorbachev delivers a speech in the United Nations building nearby.

Party has continued. In 1970 the Estonian American National Republic Committee was formed, with a network of Estonian American Republican clubs established in geographic centers of the immigrant community. Socialist influence in the community has diminished.

### UNION ACTIVITY

Estonian American involvement in organized labor grew with the rise of the workers' movement in the early twentieth century. Support for this movement saw the rise many local workers' and socialist organizations and a number of newspapers and periodicals. Many of the activities of the workers' movement went beyond economic and union concerns to include social and cultural activities as well as political mobilization. However, the socialist leaders of the movement tended to be more radical than either the rank and file or the American labor movement, and this was the cause of much friction. With the drift toward communism and agitation over Estonian independence, the worker's movement became divided and lost much of its vitality.

### ARMED FORCES

Estonian Americans have served in the U.S. armed forces in every significant military conflict in the twentieth century. There was a small Estonian American presence during the two World Wars, while a larger group fought in the Korean and Vietnam Wars. In 1951 an Estonian American, Kalju Suitsev, was awarded a Silver Star and Purple Heart for bravery in Korea. In Vietnam many Estonian youth participated, including a number who were killed or decorated for bravery. Given the fervent patriotic and anticommunist stance of the Estonian American community during this period, support for military service was strong.

### RELATIONS WITH ESTONIA

The intense support given to the Republic of Estonia during the 1920s and 1930s, and the agitation for a free Estonia after 1940, galvanized the immigrant community and created a course of common action. The drive toward nationalism has not always won universal support, however, the most notable example being the Estonian American communists who favored Soviet rule over Estonia. It remains to be seen how Estonian independence, achieved in 1991, will shape the activities of the Estonian American community.

# INDIVIDUAL AND GROUP CONTRIBUTIONS

Although small in number, Estonian Americans have played a significant part in their communities and in the United States. Their most striking accomplishments have been in the fields of education, engineering and technology, architecture and applied arts, and music.

## ARCHITECTURE

The most prominent of all Estonian Americans is probably the architect Anton Hanson, who was born in Estonia in 1879 and immigrated to the United States in 1906. Hanson was one of the designing architects of the Seattle World's Fair, for which he was awarded the grand prize.

## EDUCATION

Herrman Eduard von Holst (1841-1904) studied in Estonia and received his doctorate from the University of Heidelberg in Germany. He became the first chair of the history department at the University of Chicago and wrote a number of important works on American and European history. He also held academic positions in Germany and France. Theodore Alexis Wiel was born in Estonia in 1893 but attended college in America. After being decorated for service in France in World War I, Wiel earned a doctorate in international relations and taught at American International College, where he also served as dean. Ragnar Nurske (1907-1959) studied in Estonia and England before coming to the United States, where he taught Economics at Columbia University. Nurske authored a number of works on international economics and also served on the League of Nations prior to World War II. Ants Oras was an English professor at the University of Tartu, Estonia. He came to America via England after World War II and taught at the University of Florida. Arthur Vööbus (1909-1990) obtained his doctorate in Estonia in 1943 and came to the United States after the war. A biblical scholar and expert on early Syrian Christianity, Vööbus taught at the Lutheran School of Theology in Chicago.

## FILM AND THEATER

Miliza Korjus was born in Estonia to Estonian and Polish parents. A soprano, Korjus performed the leading role in the film *The Great Waltz* (1938), a biography of the waltz king, Johann Strauss. Korjus later settled in California to continue her singing career. Ivan (John) Triesault, born in Estonia, was a film actor who made over 25 films, from *Mission to Moscow* (1942) to *Von Ryan's*

*Express* (1965). He specialized in playing character roles, including German military officers.

## GOVERNMENT

William Leiserson (1883-1957), born in Estonia, received his Ph.D. from Columbia University in 1911. A specialist in labor affairs, he was employed by the U.S. Department of Labor and was appointed by President Franklin Roosevelt to the Labor Arbitration Commission in 1939.

## INDUSTRY

Carl Sundbach, born in Estonia in 1888, invented a freezer that greatly reduced the time required to bulk freeze fish. William Zimdin (1881-1951) was an international businessman and millionaire. Zimdin began his career in the United States in 1920 by arranging transactions between the United States and the Soviet Union; he eventually settled in California. Otto Lellep, born in Estonia in 1884, was a metallurgical engineer who came to the United States in 1917. Working in the United States and Germany, he developed a cement baking oven and made advancements in the processing of steel, iron ore, and nickel. Lellep went into business manufacturing his ovens in the United States after World War II. John Kusik, born in Estonia in 1898, rose to become director and senior vice president of the Baltimore and Ohio Railroad and served on a number of other corporate boards.

## JOURNALISM

Edmund Valtman (1914- ) came to the United States in 1949. A political cartoonist with the *Hartford Times*, Valtman received the Pulitzer Prize for his drawings in 1961.

## MUSIC

Ludvig Juht (1894-1957), an Estonian-born musician, specialized in the contrabass. Juht had an international career in Estonia, Finland, and Germany until he was brought to America in 1934 by Serge Koussevitzky to be principle contrabass with the Boston Symphony Orchestra. In addition, Juht taught at both the New England Conservatory of Music and Boston University, and worked as a composer. Evi Liivak was born in Estonia in 1925 and studied the violin. In 1951 she joined her American husband in the United States and has enjoyed an international career.

## SCIENCE AND TECHNOLOGY

Elmar Leppik, a biologist educated in Estonia and Europe, came to America in 1950. He taught at a number of American universities and then worked as a research scientist with the U.S. Department of Agriculture in Maryland. Igor Taum, born in Estonia in 1922, came to the United States in 1945 and has served as a research physician at Rockefeller University, New York City, where he specializes in the study of viruses. Richard Härm, born in 1909, was educated in Estonia and Germany prior to coming to the United States after World War II. He taught mathematics at Princeton University. Rein Kilkson (1927- ) was born in Estonia, and received his doctorate at Yale University in 1949. A physicist, he did research in the areas of biophysics and virology and taught at the University of Arizona. Lauri Vaska (1925- ), a chemist, discovered a new chemical compound, which was eventually named the "Vaska compound." Vaska taught at Clarkson College of Technology, Potsdam, New York. Harald Oliver, Jyri Kork, and Rein Ise have participated as scientists in the U.S. space program on the Apollo moon project and the Skylab space station.

## VISUAL ARTS

Voldemar Rannus (1880-1944) came to the United States in 1905. A sculptor, Rannus studied at the National Academy of Design in New York, and later in Europe. He molded a bas-relief of Albert Beach (the designer of the New York City subway) for the subway station near the New York City Hall. Andrew Winter (1893-1958) painted realistic winter scenes and seascapes. Born in Estonia, he came to the United States and studied here, eventually settling in Maine.

# MEDIA

## PRINT

### Journal of Baltic Studies.

Published by the Association for the Advancement of Baltic Studies (AABS), this quarterly provides a forum for scholarly discussion on topics regarding the Baltic Republics and their peoples.

Contact: William Urban or Roger Noel, Editors.

Address: 111 Knob Hill Road, Hacketstown, New Jersey 07844.

### Meie Elu.

Estonian weekly newspaper in Canada, established in 1950.

Contact: Tony Parming, Editor.

Address: Estonian Publishing Co., 958 Broadview Avenue, Toronto, Ontario, Canada M4K 2R6.

Telephone: (416) 466-0951.

Fax: (416) 461-0448.

### Meie Tee (Our Path).

Estonian American monthly journal, established in 1931, with general information about the American and worldwide Estonian community. Published by the World Association of Estonians.

Address: 243 East 34th Street, New York, New York 10016.

Telephone: (212) 684-9281.

### Vaba Eesti Sõna (Free Estonian Word).

Estonian American weekly newspaper, established in 1949. Known for its staunch anti-communist and nationalist views.

Contact: Harald Raudsepp, Editor.

Address: Nordic Press, Inc., 243 East 34th Street, New York, New York 10016.

Telephone: (212) 686-3356.

### Väliseestlase Kalendar (Calendar for Estonians Abroad).

Annual publication for the immigrant community, established in 1953.

Address: The Nordic Press, P.O. Box 123, New York, New York 10156.

Telephone: (212) 686-3356.

### Yearbook of the Estonian Learned Society in America.

Published by the Estonian Learned Society in America to advance and disseminate scholarly knowledge for and about Estonia and Estonians.

Address: 243 East 34th Street, New York, New York 10016.

# ORGANIZATIONS AND ASSOCIATIONS

Estonian American National Council (EANC). Founded in 1952, this umbrella organization represents all Estonian Americans and major Estonian American organizations. Coordinates the efforts of the member groups; supports political, cultural, and social activities; provides grants for study; and maintains a library and archives at its headquarters in New York City.

**Contact:** John J. Tiivel, Secretary General.

**Address:** 243 East 34th Street, New York, New York 10016.

**Telephone:** (212) 685-0776.

### Estonian Evangelical Lutheran Church (EELC).

Founded in 1954. Ecclesiastical structure for all Estonian Lutherans outside of Estonia, headquartered in Sweden. Promotes religious education and outreach in the immigrant communities, conducts religious services, and maintains congregations. The North American branch of the EELC consists of 38 congregations in the United States and Canada.

**Contact:** Rev. Udo Petersoo, Archbishop for North America.

**Address:** 383 Jarvis Street, Toronto, Ontario, Canada M5B 2C7.

**Telephone:** (416) 925-5465.

### Estonian Heritage Society (EHS).

Promotes and seeks to preserve Estonian cultural heritage.

**Contact:** Mart Aru, Chair.

**Address:** P.O. Box 3141, 200090 Tallinn, Estonia.

**Telephone:** (142) 449216.

### Estonian Learned Society in America.

Founded in 1950, this scholarly organization represents Estonian Americans with graduate degrees; it seeks to encourage Estonian studies, especially in English and supports translation of Estonian literary works. Publishes a yearbook every three to four years.

**Contact:** Viktor Koressaar, President.

**Address:** 243 East 34th Street, New York, New York 10016.

### Estonian Relief Committee, Inc.

Founded in 1941, this committee assists Estonians with settlement and employment in the United States. It also supports Estonian American activi-

ties and groups, especially Estonian American scouting programs.

**Contact:** Alfred Anderson, Secretary-General.

**Address:** 243 East 34th Street, New York, New York 10016.

**Telephone:** (212) 685-7467.

### Federated Estonian Women's Clubs.

Founded in 1966, this club coordinates and encourages ties between Estonian women's organizations throughout the world. It also sponsors scholarship and cultural activities, such as folk art, language training, Estonian handicrafts, and camping.

**Contact:** Juta Kurman, President.

**Address:** 243 East 34th Street, New York, New York 10016.

### United Baltic Appeal (BATUN).

Serves as an information center dealing with events and circumstances pertinent to Estonia, Latvia, and Lithuania.

**Contact:** Baiba J. Rudzifis-Pinnis, President.

**Address:** 115 West 183rd Street, Bronx, New York 10453.

**Telephone:** (718) 367-8802.

# MUSEUMS AND RESEARCH CENTERS

### Estonian Archives in the United States.

The main archives for documents on the immigrant settlements and their development. Located in the Estonian American community of Lakewood, New Jersey, this institution is particularly valuable to the study of Estonian Americans.

**Address:** 607 East Seventh Street, Lakewood, New Jersey 08701.

### Estonian Educational Society (EHS).

Maintains school of Estonian language and history and library of 3,000 volumes in Estonian.

**Contact:** Rudolf Hamar, Manager.

**Address:** Estonian House, 243 East 34th Street, New York, New York 10016.

**Telephone:** (212) 684-0336.

**Estonian Society of San Francisco.**
A cultural, educational, and social foundation for Estonian Americans on the West Coast. It sponsors ethnic scouting, dancing, and scholarship and maintains a library and reading room.

**Contact:** August Kollom, President.
**Address:** 537 Brannan Street, San Francisco, California 94107.
**Telephone:** (415) 797-7892.

**Immigration History Research Center.**
Located at the University of Minnesota, this is a valuable archival resource for many of the immigrant groups from Eastern and Southern Europe, including the Estonians. In addition to newspapers and serials, the center also has a collection of books and monographs, along with the records of Estonian American groups in Minnesota and Chicago.

**Contact:** Dr. Rudolph Vecoli, Director.
**Address:** 826 Berry Street, St. Paul, Minnesota 55114.
**Telephone:** (612) 627-4208.

**Office of the Estonian Consulate General.**
Representing the Republic of Estonia in the United States, it is a valuable resource for general information on Estonia and the Estonian American community.

**Address:** 9 Rockefeller Plaza, New York, New York 10020.

# SOURCES FOR ADDITIONAL STUDY

Balys, J., and Uno Teemant. "Estonian Bibliographies: A Selected List," *Lituanus: The Lithuanian Quarterly*, 19, No. 3, 1973; 54-72.

Brown, Francis, and Joseph Slabey Roucek. *One America: The History, Contributions, and Present Problems of Our Racial and National Minorities*, revised edition. New York: Prentice-Hall, 1945.

*The Estonians in America, 1627-1975: A Chronology and Factbook*, edited by Jaan Pennar, et al. Ethnic Chronology Series, No. 17. Dobbs Ferry, New York: Oceana Publications, Inc., 1975.

Parming, Marju, and Tönu Parming. *A Bibliography of English-Language Sources on Estonia*. New York: Estonian Learned Society in America, 1974.

Raun, Toivo. *Estonia and Estonians* (Studies in Nationalities of the U.S.S.R.). Stanford, California: Hoover Institution Press, 1987.

Tannberg, Kersti, and Tönu Parming. *Aspects of Cultural Life: Sources for the Study of Estonians in America*. New York: Estonian Learned Society in America, 1979.

Walko, M. Ann. *Rejecting the Second Generation Hypothesis: Maintaining Estonian Ethnicity in Lakewood, New Jersey*. New York: AMS Press, 1989.

# ILIPINO AMERICANS

by
**H. Brett Melendy**

## OVERVIEW

The Philippine Islands, off the east coast of Asia, are part of the Pacific Ocean's fiery volcanic rim. The Philippine archipelago, consisting of about 7,100 islands, lies along a north-south arc of 1,152 miles. From east to west, its widest dimension is 682 miles. Most islands, large and small, have high mountains, and many are surrounded by coral-reef shorelines.

The Philippines' land area is 115,831 square miles, slightly larger than the state of Nevada. Eleven islands comprise about 95 percent of the land mass of the Philippines, with the two largest, Luzon and Mindanao, accounting for 65 percent of the total. The national capital, Quezon City, and the de facto capital and largest city, Manila, are both situated on Luzon, on which over 25 percent of the country's population lives. Thirty-five percent inhabits the Visayan Islands, a cluster of islands—Samar, Leyete Bohol, Cebu, Negros, Panay, and Masbate—that lie between Luzon and Mindanao. Cebu has the highest population concentration with more than 400 people per square mile. The country's total population in 1992 was about 67,144,000. Malays are in the majority; major ethnic minorities are Chinese, Americans, and Spanish. Eighty-three percent of the population is Roman Catholic, nine percent is Protestant, and five percent is Muslim. Mindanao has the greatest Islamic concentration.

Climatic conditions, which are about the same throughout the archipelago, help determine the islanders' lifestyle. The climate, both tropical and maritime in nature, usually has high humidity and high temperatures. Monsoons and typhoons, overriding normal conditions, bring periods of heavy rain. All of these factors have determined where and how Filipinos have cultivated their land. Agriculture, ranging from subsistence farming to export plantations, remains the basis of the islands' economy. Even so, given the mountainous terrain, only about 15 percent of the land is cultivated. Major domestic crops are rice and corn; important export crops are abaca (Manila hemp), copra (dried coconut meat, from which coconut oil is made), pineapple, sugar, and tobacco.

One of the persistent problems for Philippines islanders has been inequitable land distribution. A share tenant system has made most farmers captives of landlords, or *caciqueors*. At the time of independence in 1946, over 70 percent of the crops went to *caciqueors*. Share tenancy has brought considerable political and social unrest. Historically, limited economic opportunities tied to tenancy and a high birthrate led to immigration to Hawaii and the mainland United States.

### HISTORY

The islands have seen the arrival of different peoples over the centuries leading to the evolution of the present diverse cultures. Among the earliest immigrants were the Little People, shorter than five feet tall. They are dark skinned, have Negroid features, and were named Negritoes by the Spanish. They may have arrived about 25,000 years ago, and they lived throughout the islands. In recent decades, they occupied the mountain interiors of Luzon, Mindanao, and Palawan, living in isolation and not mixing with later arrivals.

Sometime between 4000 B.C. and 3000 B.C., the first Indonesians arrived from the Asian continent. A second Indonesian influx occurred about 1000 B.C. and lasted about 500 years. Both waves of Indonesians settled throughout the islands, and over the centuries assimilated with subsequent immigrants. Present-day Ilongots are one result of tribal intermixing.

The Malays, an Iron Age people, began arriving in the third century A.D. Peak influxes started in the thirteenth century and continued well into the next. The Bontoks, Igorots, and Tinguians are descendants of the Malays. Tribes that in time became dominant were the Visayans, Cebunos, and Ilocanos. European and American colonists discovered some of these groups were "head-hunting pagans." Those Malays who came in the later waves had elements of an alphabet and metal tools. More peaceful than earlier arrivals, they were the ancestors of most present-day Filipino Christians. While considered primitive by Western standards, these Malays were in fact far advanced over the earliest immigrants. During the fourteenth century, Islamic Arab traders arrived; their descendants, the Moros, populated the southern islands and remained militant Muslims.

The Chinese and Japanese have had a major impact in the twentieth century, although trade between the Philippines and South China began to develop as early as the fourteenth century as Chinese emigrants became successful merchants and traders. Descendants of Filipino and Chinese marriages continued this domination of island businesses, gaining economic successes and power. Their virtual monopoly of the nation's big businesses in the twentieth century led some Filipinos, particularly those in urban areas, to resent the Chinese and to engage in occasional hostile activities. Japanese immigration occurred after 1900; emigrants from Japan settled first on the island of Mindanao, and they developed several large abaca plantations. Unlike the Chinese and earlier Malay emigrants, the Japanese remained largely a homogeneous group, rarely intermarrying. At the outbreak of World War II, Japanese could be found throughout the islands, working mostly at such crafts as cabinetmaking and photography.

### SPANISH RULE, 1565-1898

The first European immigrants did not intend to settle permanently in the Philippines. Spanish settlement proved transitory during the 400 years of Spain's colonial occupation. The first contact between Spain and the Philippines occurred in March of 1521, when Ferdinand Magellan's fleet reached the island of Samar on its circumnavigation of the earth. Magellan claimed the archipelago for Spain and the Catholic church, but Spain did not make his claim official until 1565. The country was named the Philippines in the 1550s after King Philip II of Spain.

In 1565, nine years after ascending to the Spanish throne, Philip II sent a royal governor to the Philippines. The governor, from his first seat of government on Cebu, sent expeditions to other islands and imposed Spanish rule. From the outset, colonial officers exerted forceful and lasting control, using the colonial methods used in the Americas as their model.

As royal governors gained greater dominion over the islands, they moved the colonial capital to Manila, with its superior harbor. Endorsing European ideas of mercantilism and imperialism, Spain's monarchs believed that they should exercise their power in the Philippines to enrich themselves. In the course of almost four centuries, Spanish settlers and their descendants in the islands came to own large estates and to control the colonial government.

The Catholic church, supported by the colonial powers, controlled large areas of land and held a monopoly on formal education. The church and the Spanish language were major Spanish cultural institutions imposed upon Filipinos. By 1898, over 80 percent of the islanders were Catholics. Most young Filipinos, migrating to Hawaii and the mainland before World War II, came from Catholic backgrounds.

The Spanish, in installing an autocratic imperialism that alienated Filipinos, created a class society and a culture that many Filipinos later tried to imitate. Some of the Spanish, who made the islands their home, married Filipinos; the descendants of these marriages were known as mestizos. By the nineteenth century, mestizos had inherited large areas of agricultural lands. This Filipino upper class found that the lighter their skin color, the easier it became to mingle with Europeans and Americans. They also learned to control local politics through power and corruption. This economic-political dominance came to be known as *caciquism*.

Local revolts against Spanish imperial corruption, *caciquism*, and racial discrimination began late in the nineteenth century. These first revolts called for reform of the economic-political system but not for independence. An early leader, Jose Rizal, who formed *La Liga Filipina* (the Filipino League), called for social reform. After the Spanish banished Rizal, more radical leaders emerged. When Rizal returned to the islands, the Spanish colonial government arrested, tried, and executed him in 1896, thus unwittingly creating a martyr and national hero.

Twenty-seven-year-old Emilio Aguinaldo became the next leader of the insurrectionists—now fighting openly against the Spanish. In 1898, Aguinaldo conferred with American officials in Hong Kong and Singapore. He was led to understand that the Filipinos would become allies with the United States in a war against Spain, the anticipated outcome of which would be an independent Philippine nation. Admiral George Dewey and Consul General E. Spencer Pratt, with whom Aguinaldo met, later denied that they had made such a promise. In 1898, the United States declared war against Spain, and as a result of the ensuing Spanish-American War, the United States gained control of the Philippines. The Treaty of Paris, approved on February 6, 1899, made the United States an imperial power and started a 47-year relationship with the Philippines.

Filipinos, following Aguinaldo's lead, protested the arrival of American imperialism, and the insurrection first launched against the Spanish continued. After annexation of the Philippines by the United States, the U.S. Army fought to quell uprisings throughout the islands. With his capture on March 23, 1901, Aguinaldo advised his followers to swear allegiance to the United States. On July 4, 1902, the Army declared the insurrection to be at an end, even though the Moros, who had become largely independent under Spanish rule, continued to fight until 1913.

## AMERICAN COLONIAL PERIOD, 1898-1946

U.S. President William McKinley sent several commissions to the Philippines even as the U.S. Army fought the Filipinos. William Howard Taft, president of the Philippine Commission, began installing American control on September 1, 1900. A year later, he became the first governor-general of the Philippines. Between 1901 and 1913, American officials, controlling executive, legislative, and judicial offices, rebuilt the islands' government from the village to the national level. An elected lower house, the Philippine Assembly, soon participated in national affairs. Both the judicial system and the civil service, modeled after American counterparts, replaced the Spanish system.

Undoubtedly, the great American impact came in education, with primary schools set up in most communities and high schools in each province. Nationwide vocational schools and teacher colleges were established, as was the University of the Philippines in Manila, founded in

1908 as the capstone of the islands' education program. Religious freedom was guaranteed, and government support of the Catholic church as the state religion ended. Most of the provincial colleges remained under Catholic control with a curriculum reflecting the church's traditional education. A major cause of Filipino unrest under Spanish imperialism was church-controlled Friar lands. To ease this crisis, the United States bought about 400,000 acres from the Catholic church. This land was then sold, mostly to former tenants at low prices and with easy payment terms.

While American administrators tended to be benevolent authorities, Filipinos still desired independence. From the outset of American rule, the leaders of the *Nacionalista* party called for immediate independence. From 1907 on, the *Nacionalistas* gained and held control of elective offices in villages, provinces, and the Philippine Assembly. A small number of wealthy party members, drawn from among large landowners, used *caciquism* to control the *Nacionalista* party. Early major political leaders were Sergio Osmena and Manuel Quezon. By 1917, these two men had concentrated national political power under their absolute control. Most immigrants to the United States and the Territory of Hawaii were *Nacionalistas*.

In 1916, U.S. President Woodrow Wilson, committed to making the Philippines an independent nation, supported passage of the Jones Act, which promised that the Philippines would be free as soon as a stable government was established. The act provided that during a transitional period, executive power would remain with an American appointed governor-general while Filipinos elected members to the Assembly and to the newly established Senate. The Jones Act helped Osmena's and Quezon's political machine entrench itself. In 1921, with the election of a Republican administration in the United States, independence was no longer strongly advocated, as Republican governor-generals insisted that the islands were not ready to be set free.

During the late 1920s, concerns over the large influx of Filipinos into the West Coast of the United States and falling agricultural prices for certain American commodities led to agitation that called for change in the relationship between the islands and the United States. American farmers wanted an end to free trade of commodities from the islands while exclusionists wanted to stop Filipino immigration. These two political forces began calling for Philippine independence.

In December 1931, Congress passed the Hare-Hawes-Cutting bill, which was intended to grant independence to the islands after a ten-year period. It then overrode President Herbert Hoover's veto, and the bill became law. The new law provided that American goods would be imported into the islands duty free, while Philippine goods exported to the United States would be subject to increasing tariff rates during these ten years. During this period, Filipino immigration would be limited to an annual quota of 50, and general United States immigration laws would apply. The Philippine national legislature had to approve the act, but in October 1933, Quezon-led forces rejected the proposal, which had the backing of Osmena and Manuel Roxas adherents. Quezon then led a delegation to Washington to negotiate with the new American president, Franklin Roosevelt.

Quezon obtained only a slight modification of the Hare-Hawes-Cutting Act; key issues relating to the island economy and immigration to the United States remained unchanged. At the end of the ten-year transition period, the United States was to withdraw its forces from all military and naval bases, something that did not actually happen until the 1990s. The Tydings-McDuffie Act, signed into law on March 23, 1934, promised independence after ten years and created the Commonwealth of the Philippines. The Philippine legislature approved this act on May 1, 1934, and a year later the Filipino people approved a constitution.

## THE COMMONWEALTH OF THE PHILIPPINES, 1934-1946

At the first presidential election in September 1935, Filipinos elected Quezon as president and one of his major rivals, Osmena, as vice president. With their inauguration on November 15, 1935, the Commonwealth of the Philippines came into being, although many Filipinos were ambivalent about the prospect of complete independence. While independence appealed to their sense of nationalism, the hard economic fact was that the islands depended upon tariff-free American markets. Many felt that, in due course, imposition of a tariff upon Philippine products could be disastrous.

With the Tydings-McDuffie Act, independence was to come to the Philippines in 1944, but the Japanese conquest of the islands in 1942 brought a two-year hiatus to the commonwealth. The Quezon government fled, first to Australia with General Douglas MacArthur and then to the United States, where Quezon continued to serve as the commonwealth's president until his death in 1944.

## THE REPUBLIC OF THE PHILIPPINES

After U.S. President Harry Truman proclaimed the independence of the Philippines on July 4, 1946, Manual Roxas was elected the first president of the Republic of the Philippines. However, the Philippine Rehabilitation Act and the Philippine Trade Act, imposed upon the new republic by the United States, created a favorable environment for American corporations at the expense of the Philippine economy. With the growing threat of communism, the United States continued to maintain air and naval bases in the islands.

The new republic struggled to nationhood during the turmoil of the postwar years. Communist-dominated Huks soon confronted Roxas' government with armed resistance in an internal war that lasted until 1954. Since independence in 1946, urban and rural violence have continued; election days in the Philippines are marked by many deaths. Under the leadership of Ramon Magsaysay, who succeeded Roxas, the republic by 1955 came to be seen as a sturdy bastion of democracy in the Far East, one that the United States hoped would be a model for other Asian countries.

In 1965, Ferdinand Marcos was elected president. When several groups conducted terrorist tactics and the Moros continued to fight for their independence, Marcos, declaring martial law in September of 1972, seized dictatorial powers. This state of affairs lasted fourteen years. Early in 1973, Marcos proclaimed a new constitution, naming himself as president. In 1978, he gave his wife, Imelda, extensive powers to control national planning and development. In the face of growing political repression, many of Marcos' political opponents found it expedient to leave the country as caciquism was elevated to the national level. Marcos lifted the decree of martial law in 1981 and turned political power over to the national legislature. He was then elected to another six-year term as president.

Following the 1983 assassination of Benigno S. Aquino Jr., a leading rival of Marcos, political unrest and violence became commonplace until 1986, when Marcos fled the country, and Corazon Aquino, Benigno Aquino's widow, was declared president. The end of the Marcos era did not bring political and economic calm to the nation, however; unsuccessful coups against the government have continued and the national economy has remained weak. Additionally, widespread poverty and communism have posed threats to the unstable central government.

## MAJOR IMMIGRATION WAVES

Filipino arrivals in the Territory of Hawaii and the United States mainland came in four waves. The earliest, starting in 1903 and lasting to the outbreak of World War II, brought many young men to enroll in American universities and colleges and then return to the Philippines. The second influx took place in Hawaii as plantation workers arrived from 1907 to the 1930s, with a parallel movement occurring along the Pacific Coast during the 1920s—an immigration that lasted until enactment of the Tydings-McDuffie Act in 1934. A much smaller influx to American shores occurred following World War II. The fourth and largest immigration wave arrived after passage of the 1965 Immigration Act. Since 1970 the Philippines have been surpassed only by Mexico in the number of immigrants coming to the United States.

The first Filipino immigrants came to the United States seeking higher education. Governor-General Taft's administration prepared an educational plan, the *Pensionado* Act, to send promising young Filipinos to United States' institutions of higher learning. Beginning in 1903, a group of 100 students left for the United States, and by 1910 all had returned. Once home, these new college graduates were met with confusion and jealousy by fellow Filipinos and with hostility by American colonials. However, these men came to play key roles in agriculture, business, education, engineering, and government.

Other students followed; a later estimate indicated that between 1910 and 1938 almost 14,000 Filipinos had enrolled in educational institutions throughout the United States. Most of these came as independent students, apart from the *Pensionado* program. Many of these hopefuls became overwhelmed by the high cost of living, their inadequate academic preparation, insufficient language skills, and an inability to determine what level of American education best suited their state of educational preparation. These Filipinos soon found themselves trapped as unskilled laborers. Those who were successful in graduating from major universities returned to the

Philippines to take their places with *Pensionados* as provincial and national leaders.

### FILIPINO WORKERS IN HAWAII AND THE WEST COAST, 1907-1935

A chance encounter in 1901 between a trustee of the Hawaiian Sugar Planters Association (HSPA) and a band of Filipino musicians en route to the United States led the planter to speculate about Filipinos as potential plantation workers, for he felt that these musicians had a "healthy physique and robust appearance." Even before 1907, Hawaii had begun looking for other pools of unskilled labor on the island of Luzon. During 1907 some 150 workers were sent to Hawaii. Two years later, with Chinese, Japanese, and Koreans now banned from immigrating to the United Sates, the HSPA returned to the Philippines, looking for workers. The Bureau of Census reported that there were 2,361 Filipinos in Hawaii in 1910. Recruiting efforts after 1909 centered on the Visayan Islands, Cebu in particular, and Luzon's Tagalogs.

In 1915 recruiters focused on Luzon's northwestern Ilocano provinces: Ilocos Norte, Ilocos Sur, and La Union. The Ilocanos, suffering greatly from economic hardship and overpopulation, proved willing recruits. The HSPA awarded a three-year labor contract to Filipinos migrating to Hawaii; this paid their passage to Hawaii and guaranteed free subsistence and clothing. If they worked a total of 720 days, they received return passage money. A worker was not penalized for violating his contract, but if he did, he forfeited all guarantees, including his return passage. Plantation owners found the Ilocanos to be the "best workers," and poverty in their provinces provided a stimulant for out-migration. By 1935, young single Ilocano men were the largest Filipino ethnic group in Hawaii.

According to census figures, the Filipino population in Hawaii climbed from 21,031 in 1920 to 63,052 in 1930, but dropped to 52,659 by 1940. The decline in the number of Filipinos during the late 1930s is attributable to the return of many to the Philippines during the Depression years and to others seeking greener pastures on the West Coast. The high point of immigration to Hawaii occurred in 1925, when 11,621 Filipinos arrived in Honolulu. At that point, the HSPA closed active recruiting in the Philippines, relying upon self-motivation to maintain the influx of workers.

In 1910, only 406 Filipinos lived on the United States mainland. The largest group, of 109, lived in New Orleans, the remnants of a nineteenth-century settlement of Filipino sailors who came ashore at that port city, married local women, and found jobs. The state of Washington had 17 and California had only five. In 1920, 5,603 Filipinos lived along the West Coast or in Alaska. California then had 2,674 Filipinos while Washington had 958. The northeastern United States had the second-largest number: 1,844.

The 1920s saw dramatic changes as California's Filipino population, mostly single young men, increased by 91 percent; over 31,000 Filipinos disembarked at the ports of San Francisco and Los Angeles. In 1930, there were 108,260 Filipinos in the United States and the Territory of Hawaii. California had 30,470, and this number rose to 31,408 by 1940. Washington had 3,480 in 1930 and 2,222 in 1940. Apart from the West Coast and Hawaii, the next largest concentration was in New York, which in 1930 had 1,982 and 2,978 in 1940.

### POSTWAR IMMIGRATION

Emigrants in the third wave left the Philippines in increasing numbers during the late 1940s and 1950s. Internal conditions in the new republic contributed to many moving from the islands to the United States. By 1960 Hawaii, which had become a state a year earlier, had 69,070 Filipinos, followed closely by California with 65,459. The two states together accounted for 76 percent of all Filipinos living in the United States. The Pacific Coast states had 146,340 (83 percent of the total), while the East and the South had slightly more than 10,000 each and the Great Lakes states had 8,600. Included in these census numbers were second-generation Filipino Americans.

Changes in American immigration law in 1965 significantly altered the type and number of immigrants coming to the United States. Unlike pre-war immigrants who largely worked as unskilled laborers in West Coast and Hawaiian agriculture and in Alaska's salmon canneries, the fourth wave was composed of larger numbers of well-educated Filipinos between the ages of 20 and 40 who came looking for better career opportunities than they could find in the Philippines. This highly skilled fourth-wave population had a command of the English language, allowing them to enter a wide range of professions.

Unlike earlier arrivals, most of the Filipino immigrants after 1970 came to the United States without intending to return to the Philippines. In

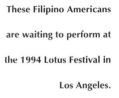

These Filipino Americans are waiting to perform at the 1994 Lotus Festival in Los Angeles.

1970, 98,400 Filipinos lived in the United States; in 1980, the number was 355,000, with 92 percent of these living in urban areas. By 1990, the number of Filipinos had reached 1,450,512. The West, as reported in the 1990 Census, had 991,572, or 68.4 percent of the Filipinos. The other three areas, Northeast, Midwest, and South, ranged from 8.8 to 12.5 percent. California in 1990 had the largest Filipino population, almost 50 percent of the total; Hawaii had fallen to second place. Every state in the union had a Filipino population. Florida, Illinois, New York, New Jersey, Texas, and Washington had Filipino populations in excess of 30,000.

## ACCULTURATION AND ASSIMILATION

From the outset of their arrival in Hawaii and the Pacific Coast, Filipinos, as a color-visible minority, have encountered prejudice and discrimination as they have pursued their economic and educational goals. One major problem for Filipinos prior to 1946 was the issue of American citizenship.

From 1898 to 1946, Filipinos, classified as American nationals, could travel abroad with an American passport and could enter and leave the United States at will, until the Tydings-McDuffie Act limited the number entering as immigrants to

50 a year. The opportunity for most Filipinos to become American citizens before 1946 was closed to them by the United States Supreme Court in its 1925 decision, *Toyota v. United States.* This decision declared that only whites or persons of African descent were entitled to citizenship, thus closing the opportunity for Filipinos to become United States citizens. Those Filipinos, however, who had enlisted and served three years in the United States Navy, Marine Corps, or Naval Auxiliary Service during World War I and who had received an honorable discharge could apply for citizenship. In 1946, Congress passed a law that permitted Filipinos to qualify for American citizenship.

The inability to acquire citizenship, besides being a social stigma, presented serious economic and political implications. Since most states required citizenship to practice law, medicine, and other licensed professions and occupations, Filipinos were prohibited from these occupations. Filipinos had no recognized voice of protest to speak for them, unlike immigrants from other countries who had ambassadors and consuls to support them. The Philippines had a Resident Commissioner in Washington who could protest, but this commissioner generally proved ineffective in dealing with federal and state bureaucracies.

Throughout the Depression years of the 1930s, Filipinos found it difficult to qualify for federal relief. Although the Works Progress

Administration in 1937 ruled that Filipinos were eligible for employment on WPA projects, they could not receive preference since they were not citizens. During the 1920s and 1930s, those Filipinos living on the Pacific Coast encountered prejudice and hostilities resulting in hateful discrimination and race riots. A sagging economy made assimilation difficult if not impossible.

At the height of discrimination in California, the California Department of Industrial Relations published in 1930 a biased study, *Facts about Filipino Immigration into California,* claiming that Filipinos posed economic and social threats. On the West Coast, Filipinos were frequently denied service in restaurants and barbershops and were barred from swimming pools, movies, and tennis courts. They found that their dark skin and imperfect English marked them, in the eyes of whites, as being different and therefore inferior. White Californians presented several contradictions that confused Filipinos. Farmers and certain urban enterprises welcomed them because they provided cheap labor. However, discriminatory attitudes relegated them to low-paying jobs and an inferior social existence. Consequently, many other Californians criticized the Filipinos' substandard living conditions and attacked them for creating health problems and lowering the American standard of living. Faced with discrimination in real estate, Filipinos were forced into "Little Manilas" in California cities. Filipinos in cities such as Chicago, New York, and Washington, D.C., also clustered together.

Discrimination against Filipinos has persisted into the late twentieth century, but civil rights legislation, affirmative action, and equal opportunity laws have improved the daily lives of most Filipinos who have arrived in recent decades. A perhaps unexpected form of discrimination for immigrants arriving after 1965 was the hostility that they met from second-generation Filipinos who saw the new arrivals as snobs and upstarts who were benefiting from advances made by the older group. At the same time, more recent Filipino immigrants have treated their older compatriots with disdain, considering them the equivalent of "hillbillies."

As the fastest-growing Asian group in California, Filipino Americans have demanded a greater leadership role in solving social problems of concern to them. While ethnically and culturally different from other Asian immigrants, they have been lumped by government agencies into one East Asian group. They have, with some success, particularly in Los Angeles County, demanded to be separated from the concept of an Asian American panethnic group. Filipino social workers have insisted that Filipino Americans deserve a larger share of available social-service money because of their numbers. In comparison to Chinese and Japanese Americans, Filipino Americans appear to be at a greater disadvantage in the labor market. Second-generation Filipino American, in addition to recent arrivals who are not trained professionally as well as Americans, have usually earned much less than white Americans. In Hawaii, newly arrived Filipinos moved into Honolulu's ghettos or to outlying farming centers, where they paid $30 a month to live in shacks made of scrap lumber and sheet iron. The state of Hawaii provided special training programs for unskilled Filipinos to prepare them for entry-level jobs.

## ENTERTAINMENT

The Filipinos who came to Hawaii and the West Coast during the 1920s and 1930s sought a range of leisure-time entertainment activities to relieve the monotony of unskilled labor. They attended and enjoyed spectator sports, bet on prize fights and wrestling matches, and gambled at poker, blackjack, and dice. During the 1930s they increased the profits of Stockton gambling operators and prostitutes by about $2 million annually. Gambling, dance halls, and prostitution gave credence to white Americans' complaints that Filipinos were immoral and lawless. Many in California traveled to Reno, Nevada, looking for the proverbial "pot of gold." Pool halls in the "Little Manilas" provided both recreation and gambling. Cockfighting, a major source of entertainment and gambling, was imported from the Philippines. The fighting of cocks, although illegal, continues to attract Filipinos in Hawaii and on the mainland.

## CUISINE

Filipino Americans, like other immigrants, brought with them cuisine from their native country. As with many Eastern Pacific Rim countries, rice is the basic staple. Three favorite foods are Lumpia, Kare Kare, and Chicken and Pork Adobo. Lumpia is an egg roll—a lumpia wrapper filled with pork, shrimp, cabbage, beans, scallions, and bean sprouts and fried in peanut oil. Kare Kare is a peanut-oil-flavored, stewed mixture of oxtail and beef tripe mixed with onions and tomatoes. Chicken and Pork Adobo consists of these two meats boiled in vinegar and soy sauce and flavored with garlic and spices. This dish is then served over rice.

## HEALTH AND MENTAL HEALTH ISSUES

Second-wave Filipinos incurred severe health problems as they aged. One illness that seemed almost endemic was gout arthritis, coupled with an excessive amount of uric acid in the blood. Doctors have speculated that a genetic characteristic makes these Filipinos unable to tolerate the American diet. Unmarried men also had a high rate of venereal disease. Complicating these health problems was the fact that these men did not or could not obtain regular health care when they had good health.

There is evidence, according to a study conducted in Hawaii, that Filipino women have a higher rate of heart disease and circulatory problems than does that state's general population. The same study noted that Filipino men suffered more from lateral sclerosis than other men did. Other diseases of high incidence were liver cancer and diabetes. The more highly educated fourth-wave Filipinos know the value of good health care and have utilized medical services available to them.

# LANGUAGE

The official languages in the Philippines are Pilipino (a derivative of Tagalog) and English. Linguists have identified some 87 different dialects throughout the country. At the time of Philippine independence, about 25 percent of Filipinos spoke Tagalog, the language of central Luzon. About 44 percent spoke Visayan dialects; Visayans in the United States generally spoke Cebuano. The language most commonly spoken by Filipinos in Hawaii and the United States mainland is Ilocano, although only 15 percent of those in the Philippines speak this language. The coming of the fourth wave of Filipinos brought more Talagog speakers. However, the high number of university graduates in the fourth wave communicated easily in English. Others, however, did not know English or spoke it poorly. In Hawaii, social service centers taught English by showing Filipinos how to shop in supermarkets and how to order in restaurants.

# FAMILY AND COMMUNITY DYNAMICS

The distinct migration patterns of the Filipinos have led to unique community dynamics. The vast majority of the second wave of Filipinos migrating to Hawaii and the West Coast, as noted, were single young men. Only a very few married and had families in the United States. The dream that most Filipinos never realized—of returning to the Philippines—led in time to disillusionment as these young men grew old, trapped as unskilled laborers. Many of these "birds of passage" sent money to the Philippines to help their families pay taxes, buy land, finance the education of relatives, or meet obligations owed by the Philippines' family alliance system.

Relatively few Filipinos of the second wave who returned to the Philippines came from the West Coast. Many more from Hawaii's plantations were able to do so. Those who did return were called *Hawaiianos*. In comparison to those in their Philippine villages, they had a degree of affluence. Filipino American philanthropy aimed mostly to benefit relatives in the Philippines. Filipinos sent funds to their families in Philippine *barrios*. Several mayors of villages in the Ilocos Norte reported that about $35,000 a month was received through the pension checks of returned Ilocanos workers and from remittances sent by fourth-wave immigrants. During the Marcos regime the Philippine government offered inexpensive airfares and incentives to foster return visits by recent immigrants, who in turn furnished information about life in America and provided money, as had earlier immigrants, to pay taxes, buy land, and finance college education.

While some Americans believed that Filipinos of the second wave were headhunting savages, others feared that they were health hazards because of a meningitis outbreak in the early 1930s. However, the greatest concern came from the attention that these young men lavished on white women. Given that in 1930 the ratio of Filipino males to females was fourteen to one, it was only natural that the men would seek companionship with white women. Young men frequented taxi-dance halls (where white girls, hired to dance with male customers, were paid ten cents for a one minute dance) during the 1920s and 1930s, seeking female companionship. Many white citizens believed that meetings between the young Filipinos and white women, whose morals were assumed to be questionable, led to inappropriate behavior by these men. In addition to these urban dance halls, "floating" taxi-dancers followed the Filipino migrant workers from California's Imperial Valley to the central and coastal valleys. Coupled with white hatred of Filipino attention to white women was an economic motive—the fear of losing jobs to the migrant labor force.

Filipino Americans came from a society where families, composed of paternal and maternal relatives, were the center of their lives. The family provided sustenance, social alliances, and political affiliations. Its social structure extended to include neighbors, fellow workers, and ritual or honorary kinsmen, called *compadres*. All of these people were welded together by this *compadrazgo* system. Through this system, which stemmed from the Roman Catholic church's rituals of weddings and baptisms, parents of a newborn child selected godparents, and this in turn led to a lifelong interrelated association. This bound the community together while excluding outsiders. Given the tightly knit villages or *barrios*, the *compadrazgo* system created obligations that included sharing food, labor, and financial resources. This system assured the role of the individual and demanded loyalty to the group.

To offset the absence of kin in the Philippines or to compensate for the lack of Filipina immigrants, Filipino Americans sought out male relatives and *compadres* from their *barrios* to cook, eat, and live together in bunk houses. Thus they formed a surrogate family, known as a *compang*, with the eldest man serving as leader of the "household."

A few Filipinos in California married Filipinas or Mexicans, while those living in Hawaii married Filipinas, Hawaiians, Puerto Ricans, or Portuguese. These women who married Filipinos in mixed marriages came from cultures whose value systems were similar to those of the men. However, large weddings, common in the *barrios*, did not occur because of the lack of family members. The birth of a child saw the duplication of the *compadrazgo* system. The rite of baptism gave an opportunity for those of the same *barrio* to come together for a time of socializing. As many as 200 sponsors might appear to become godparents, but there was not the same sense of obligation as there was in the Philippines. Marriages and funerals were also occasions that brought Filipino Americans together to renew their common ties.

Recent immigrants, unlike the agricultural workers of the 1920s and 1930s, have moved to major metropolitan areas of the United States,

finding that urban areas provided better employment opportunities. They came with their families or sent for them after becoming established in the United States. These recent arrivals also brought with them the *barrio* familial and *compadrazgo* structures. Having complete families, they found it much easier to maintain traditional relationships. Those in the greater New York area settled in Queens and Westchester County in New York and in Jersey City, Riverdale, and Bergen County in New Jersey. A part of New York City's Ninth Avenue became a Filipino center, with restaurants and small shops catering to Filipinos' needs. Unlike the West Coast, however, there was no identifiable ethnic enclave. Outsiders saw these East Coast Filipinos merely as part of the larger Asian American group. They were largely professionals: bankers, doctors, insurance salesmen, lawyers, nurses, secretaries, and travel agents.

Filipinos have organized community groups representing a wide range of concerns, but the tendency to fragment has made it difficult to present a common front on issues of mutual concern. Organizations may be based upon professions or politics, but most have evolved from a common religion, city or *barrio*, language, school, or church in the Philippines. In 1980 California had more than 400 cultural and social organizations representing Filipinos.

Second-wave Filipinos in California, finding white society closed to them, organized three major fraternal organizations: *Caballeros de Dimas-Alang, Legionairos del Trabajo,* and *Gran Oriente Filipino* (Great Filipino Lodge). The first, organized in 1921, honored Jose Rizal, the Philippine national hero (his pen name while writing revolutionary tracts was Dimas-Alang). This fraternal lodge at one time during the 1930s had 100 chapters throughout the United States and was one of many that commemorated Rizal's execution on Jose Rizal Day, December 30. *Legionairos del Trabajo,* organized in San Francisco in 1920, originated in the Philippines. Centered in the Bay City, it had about 700 members, some of whom were women. Filipinos established *Gran Oriente Filipino* in San Francisco in 1924. At one time it had 3,000 members in 46 states and in the Territories of Alaska and Hawaii. All lodges sponsored beauty pageant contests and dances in their various communities. Such pageants continue, and now often include a Mrs. Philippines pageant.

Besides these formal organizations, Filipinos gather with others from their province for ritualistic and religious ceremonies and festivals. Most Filipinos, from the first wave of immigrants, were either nominal or practicing Roman Catholics, and in the United States, they participated in church celebrations. Some Filipinos have, however, become members of evangelical churches.

As second-wave Filipinos grew old and remained in California, various organizations started looking after their welfare. *Caballeros de Dimas-Alang,* using federal and city agencies, built the Dimas-Alang House in San Francisco to care for elderly and low-income Filipinos. The United Farm Workers Organizing Committee established the Paulo Agbanyani Retirement Village near Delano for older Filipino field workers. As younger Filipinos worried about the fate of these aging agricultural workers, the organization Pilipino Bayanihan built in 1972 the largest federally funded community located in Stockton; subsequently, branches were built in Tulare County, Cochella, Brawley, and Ventura. Pilipino Bayanihan hoped to fulfill the needs of the unemployed, underemployed, and senior citizens.

## RELIGION

The vast majority of Filipino Americans are Roman Catholic, although about five percent are Muslim. Both Roman Catholicism and Islam, however, are heavily influenced by a belief in the intervention of spirits, reminiscent of religious beliefs that existed in the Philippines prior to European and Asian settlement. Because the majority of early Filipino immigrants to the United States were single males, few Catholics attended church with any regularity. Once families began settling in the United States, however, religion became a central component of family and community life.

## EMPLOYMENT AND ECONOMIC TRADITIONS

Second-wave Filipinos came primarily "to get rich quick"—by Philippine standards—and return to their home provinces to live in affluence. Thus their goal was not to adjust to life in the United States but to find high-paying jobs. They faced severe handicaps because of limited education and job skills, inadequate English, and white racial prejudice.

Filipino Americans pose in traditional dress during the Lotus Festival.

Some found ready but low-paying employment as Pacific Coast migratory field hands and cannery workers. Others were employed in the merchant marine, the United States Navy, and Alaska's salmon canneries. Compared to Philippine wages, agricultural workers' pay seemed high. The workers, however, became ensnared in these jobs due to the higher cost of living in the United States. Consequently, many of the young Filipinos grew old in California, unable to fulfill their dream of returning to their homeland.

California agriculture, with its specialty crops, relied on migratory field workers. From the Imperial Valley to the Sacramento Valley, farmers sought cheap field labor to harvest their crops. Filipino and Mexican workers dominated in harvesting asparagus, cantaloupes, citrus fruits, cotton, lettuce, potatoes, strawberries, sugar beets, and tomatoes. Filipinos returned annually to work as members of an organized work gang headed by a *padrone* who negotiated contracts with growers. The *padrone* supervised the gang's work and provided housing and meals, charging a fee against wages. These gangs followed the harvest season north from California into Oregon's Hood River Valley and Washington's Wenatchee Valley. As late as the 1950s, Filipinos provided the largest number of migrant workers for western agriculture.

Migrant jobs ended after the harvest season. Filipinos then moved to cities in the late fall and winter in search of employment. But most usually had to return to the fields in the spring. By 1930,

Los Angeles, San Francisco, Stockton, and Seattle each had "Little Manilas," as discriminatory real estate covenants restricted Filipinos to congested ghettos. The number living in these racial enclaves varied depending on the time of year, with the population highest in the winter months. A few Filipinos catered to their countrymen's needs—barbershops, grocery stores, pool rooms, dance halls, restaurants, and auto-repair garages. Others found employment in hotel service jobs, working as dishwashers, bellhops, and elevator operators. Some worked in various unskilled restaurant jobs or as houseboys.

Second-generation Filipino Americans, descendants of immigrants of the 1920s and 1930s, worked in unskilled and skilled jobs. California trade unions remained closed to them, keeping them out of many industrial jobs. Second-generation Filipinos in Hawaii found employment on plantations and in the islands' urban centers. Unions there became open to all Asians during the New Deal years. Many who immigrated to the United States after 1970 with limited education entered the unskilled labor market and soon found themselves joining second-generation Filipinos on welfare.

## THE LABOR MOVEMENT

Declining market prices for agricultural produce in the late 1920s and during the Great Depression of the 1930s seriously affected the Filipinos. As migrant workers saw their wages fall lower and lower, they threatened strikes and boycotts. Given the American Federation of Labor's antipathy to non-white workers, minority workers, such as Filipinos, sought to organize ethnic unions. In 1930, an Agricultural Workers Industrial League tried without success to organize all field workers into a single union. California's Monterey County saw two short-lived unions emerge in 1933—the Filipino Labor Supply Association and the Filipino Labor Union.

The Filipino Labor Union, utilizing the National Industry Recovery Act's collective bargaining clause, called on the Salinas Valley lettuce growers to recognize the union. The lettuce workers struck, leading to violence, white vigilante action, and defeat for the workers time and time again. The Filipino labor movement generally failed during the Depression years and well into the 1950s as growers used strikebreakers and court injunctions to quash union activities.

During the 1920s many Filipinos spent summer seasons in Pacific Northwest and Alaskan salmon canneries. Again, Filipinos worked in labor gangs under a contractor for seasonal work lasting three or four months. In 1928 there were about 4,000 Filipinos employed in Alaska canneries but at low wages. Wages remained in dispute each season. This conflict continued until 1957 when Seattle's Local 37 of the International Longshoremen's and Warehousemen's Union (ILWU) became the sole bargaining voice for cannery workers in California, Oregon, and Washington.

In 1959, the AFL-CIO formed the Agricultural Workers Organizing Committee (AWOC) to organize grape pickers in California's lower San Joaquin Valley. About the same time, Cesar Chavez founded the National Farm Workers Association (NFWA). Both unions were ethnically integrated, but Larry Itliong led the largely Filipino AWOC union. Itliong, born in the Philippines in 1914, campaigned during the 1960s to improve the lot of Filipinos and other minorities. Other Filipino union leaders were Philip Vera Cruz, Pete Velasco, and Andrew Imutan.

Both AWOC and NFWA spent their initial energy recruiting members. In 1965, the unions protested the low wages being paid to grape pickers. On September 8, at the height of the picking season, AWOC struck against 35 grape growers in the Delano, Kern County, area. Domestic pickers, including Filipinos and Mexicans, demanded $1.40 an hour plus 20 cents a box. They argued that domestic pickers were receiving $1.20 an hour while Braceros, under a United States Department of Labor order, received $1.40. Chavez's NFWA joined the strike, which lasted for seven months.

In August of 1966 AWOC and NFWA joined forces to end any unnecessary conflict between themselves. The merger resulted in the formation of the United Farm Workers Organizing Committee (UFWOC). Some major grape growers recognized this union as the bargaining agent for workers in the vineyards. Itliong was instrumental in securing three contracts with a $2.00 minimum wage for field workers. The battle between the growers and their workers continued as the UFWOC challenged California's agriculture strongholds.

Filipinos were also instrumental in Hawaii's labor union movement. The key figure during the 1920s was Pablo Manlapit (1892-1969), who organized the Filipino Federation of Labor and the Filipino Higher Wage Movement. His organizations ran head long into the Hawaiian Sugar Planters Association (HSPA), which refused to meet the Filipinos' demands. This led to a 1920 sugar strike that lasted about six months. To rebuild his union, Manlapit continued to organize Filipinos as they arrived from the Philippines. A second confrontation between Manlapit's followers and plantation owners caused a strike in 1924 which resulted in a bloodbath in Hanapepe, Kauai, where sixteen workers and four policemen were killed. During the 1930s, the Filipinos' ethnic union, *Vibora Luviminda*, failed to make headway against the powerful HSPA. The ILWU started organizing dock and plantation workers in the 1930s and gained economic and political power after World War II. An important ILWU president was Filipino Carl Damsco. Another key labor leader was Pedro dela Cruz, born in Mindanao. He was a leading spokesman for the workers on the island of Lanai who worked in Dole's pineapple fields.

By 1980, Filipinos constituted 50 percent of the Hawaii branch of the ILWU. Agricultural workers were not the only union members; Filipinos also formed 40 percent of the Hotel and Restaurant Workers' Union.

Many of those Filipinos arriving during the 1970s and after created a "brain drain" for the Philippines. By 1980, the Philippines had replaced all European countries as the leading foreign provider of accountants, engineers, nurses, physicians, teachers, and technical workers. It is noteworthy that the Philippines have had a higher number of college and university graduates per capita than any other country. In the early 1970s, one-third of all immigrants seeking licensure in the United States were Filipino, and many found employment easy to obtain. Such was often not the case for physicians, pharmacists, dentists, lawyers, and teachers. These professionals ran into the highly protective bureaucratic screens that had been enacted by western state legislatures in earlier years. A Filipino dentist, who had served in the United States Navy for eight years, found it took him three years to gain a California license. A physician, licensed in the Philippines in 1954, had been in practice for 16 years before moving to Hawaii, where he was denied a license and forced to take a job as a janitor in a drive-in restaurant. He eventually found employment as a meat cutter. His employer thought he "was very good at separating the meat from the bone." Those professionals who settled in eastern and middle states found it easier to start careers

because these states had less stringent laws or had reciprocity agreements.

By the 1990s, with affirmative action and equal opportunity programs, the lot of Filipino American professionals improved greatly, and they were able to employ their talents in the skills for which they were trained. Doctors and nurses found ready employment once they gained certification. In most urban areas with a high concentration of Filipino businessmen, Filipino chambers of commerce were organized. The purpose of such organizations was to stimulate business, but these chambers also provided support groups for small businessmen.

# POLITICS AND GOVERNMENT

During the Depression years, discrimination against Filipinos led to efforts by exclusionists to bar further emigration from the Philippines. Some Filipino organizations, concerned about the economic hardships confronting their fellow countrymen, suggested a program of repatriation to the Philippines. Several members of Congress tried to enact a repatriation measure, but did not gain much support until Representative Richard Welch of San Francisco introduced his repatriation bill. This bill provided that the federal government would pay repatriation expenses of those wishing to return to the Philippines. These repatriates could only return to the United States as one of the annual quota of 50 immigrants. When this program ended in 1940, 2,190 of the 45,000 Filipinos living in the United States had elected to be repatriated. Many who took this opportunity for free transportation across the Pacific were university graduates who had already planned to return to assume leadership roles in the Philippines.

Repatriation did not satisfy California's exclusionists, who attempted to demonstrate that Filipinos were taking scarce jobs. However, Los Angeles County reported that of the 12,000 Filipinos who lived in the county in 1933, 75 percent could not find work. At the time, they were not eligible for federal relief programs. During the Depression, not only did Filipinos face legal discrimination in obtaining licenses to practice their professions, but they found that restrictive housing covenants prohibited them from living where they wished. During the New Deal era, Filipinos registered for relief projects only to be denied positions by the Civil Works Administration. In 1937, the United States Attorney General restated that Filipinos were American nationals and thus eligible for employment on Works Progress Administration projects. However, they could not receive preference because they were not citizens.

## MISCEGENATION LAWS AIMED AT FILIPINOS

Filipinos found that miscegenation laws denied them the right to marry white women. In 1901, the California legislature had enacted a law forbidding whites to marry blacks, Mongolians, or mulattos. In the early 1930s, California Attorney General U. S. Webb ruled that Filipinos were Mongolians, but since his opinion did not have the force of law, it was up to each of the 58 county clerks to make his/her interpretation as to the racial origin of Filipinos. By 1936, Nevada, Oregon, and Washington had enacted laws prohibiting marriages between Filipinos and whites. Consequently, white women became common-law wives. In 1948, the California Supreme Court ruled in *Perez v. Sharp* that the miscegenation law violated individual civil rights, thus freeing Filipinos to marry whomever they pleased.

## MILITARY SERVICE

During World War I, some Filipinos enlisted in the United States Navy and the Marine Corps. Men who had served three years and had received an honorable discharge could apply for American citizenship, and several did so. Following the Japanese attack on Pearl Harbor and the Philippines in 1941, which triggered America's involvement in World War II, Filipinos tried to volunteer for military service and/or work in defense factories. Existing law had no provisions to enlist nationals, thus denying Filipinos employment in war industries. However, given the need for Army personnel, Secretary of War Henry Stimson on February 19, 1942, announced the formation of the First Filipino Infantry Battalion, which began training at Camp San Luis Obispo in California. It was activated on April 1, 1942, but in July the Army reformed the unit as the First Filipino Regiment. A few weeks later, President Franklin Roosevelt issued an executive order that opened the way for Filipinos to work in government and in war industries. He also ordered a change in the draft law, reclassifying Filipinos from 4-C to 1-A, making them eligible for Army service.

The First Filipino Regiment, after training in several California Army posts, transferred to Camp Beale near Marysville, California. The citizenship of the troops remained a major issue. On February 20, 1943, Army officers on Camp Beale's parade grounds administered the oath of allegiance, granting citizenship to 1,000 Filipinos. Many in the First Regiment believed that citizenship gave them the right to marry their common-law wives, thus providing family allowances and making these women their federal insurance beneficiaries. An appeal from the miscegenation law fell upon deaf ears, leading the regimental chaplain and the Red Cross to obtain emergency leaves so that couples could travel to New Mexico to become legally married before the regiment went overseas.

A second Army unit, the Second Filipino Infantry Battalion, was formed in October 1942 and reorganized in March 1944, training at Camp Cooke, California. This battalion and the First Infantry were sent to Australia and fought in New Guinea before landing in the southern Philippines. The First Infantry Regiment also went to Australia and then to New Guinea. They fought in Mindanao, the Visayan Islands, and northern Luzon. From the First Infantry Regiment came the First Reconnaissance Battalion, organized in 1944, to undertake pre-invasion intelligence in Luzon. Some 1,000 went ashore from submarines to work undercover as civilians.

The First Filipino Infantry Regiment earned the prestige of fighting bravely and with honor, closely paralleling the record of the more widely known Japanese American 442 Regimental Combat Team. At the war's end, 555 soldiers returned to the United States, 500 of whom reenlisted; 800 of the regiment remained in the Philippines. Altogether, more than 7,000 Filipinos served in the United States Army.

The United States Navy began early to recruit Filipinos in the Philippines, Hawaii, and the mainland. By the end of World War I, about 6,000 Filipinos had served in the Navy or the Marine Corps. During the 1920s and 1930s, enlistments totaled about 4,000. However, the only billet open to these men was mess steward, for the Navy had determined during World War I that this was the best assignment for Filipinos. During World War II, the Navy continued its mess-boy policy and denied these men the opportunity to secure other ratings and privileges.

In 1970, over 14,000 Filipinos served in the Navy. Most had sea duty as personal valets, cabin boys, and dishwashers. Captains and admirals had Filipino stewards assigned directly to them. Others worked at the White House, the Pentagon, the United States Naval Academy, and at naval bases. At the same, the Navy discovered that its ships' galleys had become "Filipino ghettos." The Navy then provided opportunities for a few to train for other ratings. Some 1,600 Filipinos gained new assignments. The Navy continued to recruit mess stewards in the Philippines. Of the some 17,000 Filipinos in the Navy in 1970, 13,600 were stewards. Those in the Navy did not complain quite as much as did outsiders. The steward's entry-level pay of $1,500 equalled the salary of a lieutenant colonel in the Philippine Army. Naval service was an important way for Philippine nationals to gain American citizenship.

## FILIPINOS IN AMERICAN POLITICS

Over the decades, linguistic groups, religious affiliations, and *barrio* relationships have prevented Filipinos from engaging in American politics to any large extent. This changed to a degree after 1960, with Filipinos in Hawaii taking the lead. By the 1990s, Filipino Americans had become more aware of the need to align themselves politically to improve their place in American society. Older Filipinos in the United States, with inadequate education and low levels of employment, generally remained uninvolved in American politics. During the 1930s and 1940s they were vitally interested in the issue of independence for the Philippines. Filipinos saw a need for political unity, but efforts in this direction usually floundered because of their tendency to fragment into self-interest groups based generally upon family and provincial affiliations. In 1969, delegates from local cities from the San Francisco Bay area to San Diego formed the Filipino American Political Association to work on civil rights issues; Larry Itliong was elected president. Another organization was the Filipino American Coordinating Committee. Neither of these two groups, nor other similar ones, endured for long.

# INDIVIDUAL AND GROUP CONTRIBUTIONS

## EDUCATION

James Misahon was a prominent administrator at the University of Hawaii and served as the chair-

person of the 1969 Governor's Statewide Conference on Immigration in Hawaii. Many other Filipinos are active in public and higher education.

## LITERATURE

Two prominent authors of earlier years were Manuel Buaken, who wrote *I Have Lived with the American People* and Carlos Bulosan, author of *America Is in the Heart*.

## POLITICS AND LAW

Several Filipinos have entered politics and won election to office. Those in Hawaii have had the most success, in part because of large Filipino enclaves and because of their strength in the ILWU, a strong arm of the Democratic Party in Hawaii. In 1954, the Democratic Party gained control of the legislature and won the governorship in 1962; Democrats have controlled Hawaii's politics ever since. Between 1954 and the winning of statehood in 1959, three Filipinos were elected to the House of Representatives. Peter Aduja, born in Ilocos Sur, received his education in Hilo, Hawaii, and graduated from the University of Hawaii before completing his law degree at Boston University. He was elected to one term in 1955 but was defeated in his bid for a second term. After statehood, Aduja was elected to three terms, starting in 1966. Bernaldo D. Bicoy, another of the five Filipino lawyers in the Territory of Hawaii, was elected in 1958. He was defeated in 1959 for a seat in the new state senate, but he won election for one term to the House in 1968. The third pioneer Filipino legislator was Pedro dela Cruz of Lanai, a longtime ILWU labor leader who was first elected to the House in 1958 and served 16 years until his defeat in 1974. In his later years in the House, he served as vice speaker. During the 1970s Emilio Alcon and Oliver Lunasco served as representatives from the island of Oahu.

Alfred Lareta became Hawaii's first Filipino director of the Department of Labor and Industrial Relations. Born in Hawaii on May 21, 1924, he graduated from the University of Hawaii in 1947 and then received his law degree from Fordham University. Governor John Burns appointed him to the directorship in 1963 and then in 1969 appointed him judge of Hawaii's Circuit Court One. A second Filipino, Joshua C. Agsalud, gained appointment to the same directorship in 1975.

In 1974 Benjamin Menor, born in the Philippines on September 27, 1922, became the first Filipino appointed to the Hawaii State Supreme Court. He migrated to Hawaii in 1930 and graduated from the University of Hawaii in 1950, later earning his law degree from Boston University. After practicing law in Hilo, he served for a time as Hawaii county attorney. In 1962 he was elected to the Hawaii State Senate, becoming the first Filipino in the United States to be elected as a state senator.

Two other Filipino firsts also occurred in Hawaii. In 1975, Eduardo E. Malapit, who had served several terms on the Kauai County Council, was elected mayor of Kauai. In 1990, Benjamin Cayetano, a member of the Hawaii legislature, was elected lieutenant governor of Hawaii.

Only a few Filipinos have achieved political success outside of Hawaii. In California, Maria L. Obrea has served as Los Angeles municipal judge; G. Monty Manibog served as mayor of Monterey Park; Leonard Velasco held the same office in Delano. Glenn Olea was a councilman in the Monterey Bay community of Seaside.

## SPORTS

Most American sports enthusiasts remember Roman Gabriel, who gained national recognition as quarterback for the Los Angeles Rams football team.

# MEDIA

### PRINT

From the early 1920s to the late 1980s, several Filipino newspapers were published, although their existence was generally short-lived. In Hawaii, the *Kauai Filipino News* became the *Filipino News* in 1931. In California, early papers were the *Philippine Herald* of 1920, the *Commonwealth Courier* of 1930, and the *Philippine Advocate* of 1934. In 1930, the *Philippine Mail* began publishing in Salinas, California. It succeeded the *Philippine Independent News*, started in Salinas in 1921. The *Philippine Mail* is still published in Salinas, making it the oldest Filipino newspaper in the United States. Over the years, it has reported news from the Philippines as well as news stories about Filipinos in the United States. In the 1990s, Filipino publications included the *Philippine News*, printed in South San Francisco, the *Filapinas Magazine* of San Francisco, and *The Philippine Review* of Sacramento and Stockton, California.

*California Examiner.*
Bi-weekly newspaper for Filipino communities.

**Contact:** Mas Alvarez, Editor.
**Address:** 2901 West Beverly Boulevard, Los Angeles, California 90057.
**Telephone:** (213) 380-3980.

*Filipino-American Herald.*
**Contact:** Emiliano A. Francisco, Editor and Publisher.
**Address:** 508 Maynard Avenue South, P.O. Box 14240, Seattle, Washington 98114.
**Telephone:** (206) 725-6606.
**Fax:** (206) 723-2530.

*Heritage.*
Magazine of Filipino culture, arts and letters, and the Filipino American experience.

**Contact:** Victor P. Gendrano, Editor.
**Address:** 20218 Tajauta Avenue, Carson, California 90746.

*Los Angeles Philippine News.*
Weekly newspaper for Filipino communities.

**Contact:** Gat Santos, Editor.
**Address:** 1052 West Sixth Street, Suite 420, Los Angeles, California 90017.
**Telephone:** (213) 482-7611.
**Fax:** (213) 482-5362.

*Mosaik: Multicultural News and Views.*
Monthly newspaper for Filipino Canadians and Latin Americans (Filipino, Spanish, and English).

**Contact:** Ted Alcuitas, Editor and Publisher.
**Address:** 696 Buckingham Road, Winnipeg, Manitoba, Canada R3R 1C2.

*Philippine American News.*
Weekly newspaper for Filipino communities.

**Contact:** Jilroy Gorre, Editor.
**Address:** 1250 Wilshire Boulevard, Suite 101, Los Angeles, California 90017.
**Telephone:** (213) 481-0258.

***Philippine Liberation Courier.***

Journal of the International Association of Filipino Patriots.

**Contact:** Joel Rocamore, Editor.

**Address:** Box 64, Oakland, California 94668.

***Philippine News.***

Weekly newspaper for the Filipino community with six U.S. editions.

**Contact:** Alex A. Esclamado, Publisher.

**Address:** 156 South Spruce Avenue, Room 207, South San Francisco, California 94080.

**Telephone:** (415) 872-3000.

**Fax:** (415) 872-0217.

## ORGANIZATIONS AND ASSOCIATIONS

**Filipino American National Historical Society.**
Gathers, maintains, and disseminates Filipino American history.

**Contact:** Dorothy Cordova, Director.

**Address:** 810 18th Avenue, Room 201, Seattle, Washington 98122.

**Telephone:** (206) 322-0203.

## MUSEUMS AND RESEARCH CENTERS

Asian American Studies Center at the University of California, Los Angeles; Asian American Studies Department at the University of California, Davis; Institute of Asian Studies at the University of the Philippines in Quezon City, Philippines; the Oakland Museum History Department in Oakland, California; and the Social Science Research Institute of Hawaii at the University of Hawaii in Honolulu.

## SOURCES FOR ADDITIONAL STUDY

Ave, Mario P. *Characteristics of Filipino Organizations in Los Angeles.* San Francisco: R & E Research Associates, 1974.

Cabezas, Amado, et al. "New Inquiries into the Socioeconomic Status of Pilipino Americans in California," *Amerasia Journal,* 13, 1986; pp. 1-21.

Chan, Sucheng. *Asian Americans* (Golden State Series). San Francisco: MTL/Boyd & Fraser, 1991.

Dorita, Mary. *Filipino Immigration to Hawaii.* San Francisco: R & E Research Associates, 1975.

Dunne, John. *Delano.* New York: Farrar, Straus & Giroux, 1971.

Lasker, Bruno. *Filipino Immigration to the Continental United States and to Hawaii.* New York: Arno Press, 1969 (first published in 1931).

*Letters in Exile: An Introductory Reader on the History of Pilipinos in America,* edited by Jesse Quinsaat. Los Angeles: UCLA Asian Studies Center, 1976.

McWilliams, Carey. *Brothers Under the Skin,* revised edition. Boston: Little, Brown and Co., 1951.

Melendy, H. Brett. *Asians in America: Filipinos, Koreans and East Indians.* New York: Hippocrene Books, Inc., 1981.

Navarro, Jovina. "Immigration of Filipino Women" in *Asian American Women.* Stanford: Stanford University Press, 1976.

# INNISH AMERICANS

by
**Marianne
Wargelin**

## OVERVIEW

Finland, a nation-state created in the closing days of World War I, is located in the far northern reaches of Europe. It is bounded by Sweden to the west, Russia to the east, Norway to the north, and the Gulf of Finland to the south. About 90 percent of Finns are Lutheran; the Russian Orthodox church (two percent) is the second largest in the nation. Finnish people continue to maintain a unique language spoken today by only about 23 million people worldwide.

The nearly five million people of contemporary Finland reflect the traditional groups who settled in the nation centuries ago. The largest group consists of Finns who speak Finnish; the second largest group, some six percent, are Finland-Swedes (also known as Swede Finns) who speak Swedish; the most visible minority groups are the Sami (about 4,400), who speak Sami (or Lappish) and live in the North, and the Gypsies (about 5,500), who live in the South.

### HISTORY

The ancestors of these peoples came under the domination of the Swedes in the twelfth century, when Finland became a province of Sweden. While the Swedish provinces operated quite independently for a time, efforts to centralize power in the kingdom in the sixteenth century made Finns citizens of Sweden. Sweden was the primary power in the Baltic region for more than a hundred years, until challenged by Russia in the eighteenth century. By 1809 Sweden was so weakened that she was forced to cede her entire Baltic holdings, including Finland, to Russia.

Russia gave Finland a special status as a "Grand Duchy," with the right to maintain the Lutheran religion, the Finnish language, and Finnish constitutional laws. This new status encouraged its leaders to promote a sense of Finnish spirit. Historically a farming nation, Finland did not begin to industrialize until the 1860s, later than their Nordic neighbors; textile mills, forestry, and metal work became the mainstays of the economy. Then, in the final days of the nineteenth century, Russia started a policy of "Russification" in the region, and a period of oppression began.

Political unrest dominated the opening years of the twentieth century. Finland conducted a General Strike in 1906, and the Russian czar was forced to make various concessions, including universal suffrage—making Finland the first European nation to grant women the right to vote— and the right to maintain Finland's own parliament. The oppressive conditions returned two years later, but Finland remained a part of Russia until declaring its own independence in the midst of the Russian Revolution of 1917. A bitter civil war broke out in Finland as the newly independent nation struggled between the philosophies of the bourgeois conservatives and the working class Social Democrats. In 1919 the nation began to govern itself under its own constitution and bill of rights.

## MODERN ERA

With basic democratic rights and privileges established, the 1920s and 1930s emerged as a period of political conservatism and right wing nationalism. Then, in 1939, the Soviet Union invaded Finland. War between the two nations ensued— first in a war known as the Winter War, then in the so-called Continuation War. When it ended, Finland made major concessions to the Soviets, including the loss of a considerable portion of its eastern territory.

In the 1950s Finland continued its transformation from a predominantly agricultural economy into a modern industrial economy. By the 1960s it had established itself as a major design center in Europe, and by the end of the 1970s it maintained a post-industrial age culture with a stable economy that continued to produce premier quality work in the arts. Throughout the rest of the twentieth century, Finland maintained a strict policy of neutrality toward its neighbors to the east and west.

## THE FIRST FINNS IN AMERICA

The first Finns in North America came as colonists to New Sweden, a colony founded along the Delaware River in 1638. The colony was abandoned to the Dutch in 1664, but the Finns remained, working the forest in a slash-and-burn-style settlement pattern. By the end of the eighteenth century, their descendants had disappeared into a blur amidst the dominant English and Dutch colonist groups. However, many Finnish Americans believe that a descendant of those Finnish pioneers, John Morton, was a signer of the Declaration of Independence. Few material signs—other than their distinctive log cabin design and place names—remain to mark their early presence.

A second colonial effort involved Finns in the Russian fur trading industry. In Sitka, Alaska, Finns mixed with Russian settlers in the 1840s and 1850s, working primarily as carpenters and other skilled craftsmen. Two of Alaska's governors were Finnish: Arvid Adolph Etholen (1799-1876) served from 1840 to 1845, and Johan H. Furuhjelm (1821-1909) served from 1859 to 1864. A Finnish pastor, Uno Cygnaeus (1810-1888), who later returned to Finland to establish the Finnish public school system, also served the Finnish American community. Today, this Finnish presence is represented in the Sitka Lutheran church, which dates from that period. After 1867, when Alaska was transferred to the United States, some of the Sitka Finns moved down to communities developing along the northwest coastline—places like Seattle and San Francisco.

Colonial settlers were small in number. Similarly, according to Reino Kero in *Migration from Finland to North America in the Years Between the United States Civil War and the First World War*, the Finnish sailors and sea captains who left their ships to enter the California Gold Rush or to establish new lives in American harbor cities like Baltimore, Galveston, San Francisco, and New York, numbered only several hundred. One sailor, Charles Linn (Carl Sjodahl; 1814-1883), became a wealthy southern merchant who ran a large wholesale business in New Orleans and later established Alabama's National Bank of Birmingham and the Linn Iron Works. He is credited with opening the immigration from southern Finland to the United States when, in 1869, he brought 53 immigrants from Helsinki and Uusimaa to work for his company.

## SIGNIFICANT IMMIGRATION WAVES

Finnish immigration is considered to have occurred primarily between 1864 and 1924. Early Finnish immigrants to the United States were familiar with agricultural work and unskilled labor and were therefore new to industrial work and urban life. Later, skilled workers like carpenters, painters, tailors, and jewelers journeyed to the States, but the number of professionals who immigrated remained small until after 1965. Most scholars have estimated that, at the most, some 300,000 Finnish immigrants remained to become permanent residents and citizens of the United States of America. Of these, about 35,000 were Finland Swedes and about 15,000 Sami.

The first immigrants arrived in 1864, when Finns from northern Finland and Norway settled on homestead prairie lands in south central Minnesota. The next year 30 Finnish miners living in Norway went to work in the copper mines in Hancock, Michigan. These Finns, originally from northern Finland, developed the first permanent Finnish American communities in the American Midwest. Continued economic depression in Finland encouraged others to leave their homeland; the number of immigrants grew to 21,000 before 1887.

Those from northern Norway and Finland who traveled as family groups were part of the Great Laestadian Migration of 1864-1895, a migration that began shortly after the death of founder Lars Levi Laestadius (1800-1861). Looking for ways to maintain a separatist lifestyle as well as to improve their economic standing, Laestadian families began a migration that has continued in some form to the present day. Finnish American Laestadian communities formed in the mining region of Michigan and in the homestead lands of western Minnesota, South Dakota, Oregon, and Washington. These Laestadians provided a sense of community stability to the additional immigrants, single men who had left their families in Finland and who migrated from job to job in America. Some of these men returned to Finland; others eventually sent for their families.

After 1892 migration shifted from northern to southern Finland. Most emigrants from this phase were single and under the age of 30; women made up as much as 41.5 percent of the total. A very large increase in the birthrate after 1875 added to the pool of laborers who left home to work in Finland's growing industrial communities. This wave of internal migration to the city foreshadowed an exodus from Finland. "Russification" and a conscription for the draft added even further to the numbers after 1898.

Twentieth-century emigration from Finland is divided into three periods: before the General Strike; after the General Strike and before World War I; and between World War I and the passage of the Immigration Restriction Act. Before the General Strike, the immigrants who settled in the States were more likely to be influenced by the concepts of Social Democracy. After the General Strike, the immigrants were largely influenced by the use of direct force rather than political action to resolve social problems. Immigrants after World War I—now radicalized and disenchanted from the experience of the bloody civil war—brought a new sense of urgency about the progress of socialism.

Two immigration periods have occurred since the 1940s. After World War II, a new wave of immigration, smaller but more intense, revitalized many Finnish American communities. These Finns were far more nationalistic and politically conservative than earlier immigrants. A more recent wave of immigration occurred in the 1970s and 1980s, as young English-speaking professionals came from Finland to work in high-tech American corporations.

## SETTLEMENT

Finnish American communities cluster in three regions across the northern tier of the United States: the East, Midwest, and West. Within these regions, Finland Swedes settled in concentrations in Massachusetts, New York City, Michigan, Wisconsin, Minnesota, Oregon, Washington, and California. Sami peoples settled predominantly in Michigan, Minnesota, the Dakotas, Oregon, and Washington.

The 1990 U.S. Census Bureau report confirms that these regions still exist for the 658,870 Americans who claim Finnish ancestry. The five states with the largest populations are Michigan, with 109,357 (1.2 percent of the total state population); Minnesota, with 103,602 (2.4 percent);

California, with 64,302 (.02 percent); Washington, with 44,110 (0.9 percent); and Massachusetts (0.5 percent). Half of all Finnish Americans—310,855—live in the Midwest, while 178,846 live in the West. Three further regions—the southeastern United States (Florida and Georgia), Texas, and the Southwest (New Mexico and Arizona)—have developed as retirement communities and as bases for Finnish businesses selling their products to an American market.

Reverse immigration occurred both in the nineteenth and twentieth centuries. In the nineteenth century, many men came without families and worked for a while in mining (especially copper and iron ore mining) and lumber, in fishing and canning, in stone quarries and textile mills, and on railroads and docks; they then returned to the homeland. Others came and worked as domestics, returning to Finland to retire. The most significant reverse immigration occurred in the late 1920s and early 1930s, when 10,000 Finnish American immigrant radicals and their families sold all their belongings and left to settle in the Finnish areas of the Soviet Union. They took their dreams of creating a workers' paradise with them, as well as solid American currency, American tools, and technical skills. Today, reverse migration occurs primarily among the Laestadians who may marry and move to Finland.

Like the Swedes and Norwegians, Finns in America were tolerated and accepted into the communities of "established" Americans during the first wave of mass immigration. Their early competitors for work in the mines were the Irish and the Cornish, two groups with whom they had ongoing strained relations.

Finnish Americans soon developed a reputation for clannishness and hard work. Work crews of strictly Finnish laborers were formed. As documented in *Women Who Dared*, Finnish domestics were always sought after because they worked so hard and excelled at cooking and homemaking. Reputations for good and hard work were tarnished, however, when the second wave of immigrants began to organize themselves and others to fight poor wages and working conditions. Finns became known as troublemakers for organizing strikes and leading protests. They were blacklisted and efforts were made to deport them. Racist slurs—epithets like "Finn-LAND-er" and "dumb Finn"—developed, and some Finns became victims of violent vigilantism. Specific efforts to single them out from other working-class immigrants as anti-American put them on the front pages of local, regional, and national newspapers.

By the end of the twentieth century, Finnish Americans had essentially become invisible. They worked hard to be indistinguishable from other Euroamericans and, as descendants of white Europeans, fit easily into the mass culture. Many do not visibly identify with any part of their heritage.

Key issues facing Finnish Americans in the future relate to their position as a culture on the margin. Recent generations seem to be drawn more strongly to America's hegemonic culture and therefore continue to move away from their unique heritage.

# ACCULTURATION AND ASSIMILATION

Finnish Americans themselves are a multicultural society. Being a part of the Laestadian, Finland-Swede, or Sami minorities is different than being part of the Finnish American hegemony. Early Finnish Americans had a reputation for being clannish. Reported by sociologists studying Finns in the 1920s and 1930s, this impression was echoed by those citizens who lived beside them. Reinforcing this belief was their unusual language, spoken by few others anywhere. Finnish immigrant children, who spoke their native language in the grade schools of America, were marked as different; Finnish was difficult for English speakers to learn to use, a fact that encouraged American employers to organize teams of "Finnish-only" workers. And the "sauna ritual," an unheard of activity for Anglo-Americans, further promoted a sense that Finns were both exotic and separatist.

Once in the United States, Finnish immigrants recreated Finnish institutions, including churches, temperance societies, workers' halls, benefit societies, and cooperatives. Within those institutions, they organized a broad spectrum of activities for themselves: weekly and festival programs, dances, worship services, theater productions, concerts, sports competitions, and summer festivals. They created lending libraries, bands, choirs, self-education study groups, and drama groups. Furthermore, they kept in touch with each other through the newspapers that they published—over 120 different papers since the first, *Amerikan Suomalainen Lehti*, which appeared for 14 issues in 1876.

Finnish immigrants used these recreated Finnish institutions to confront and ease their entrance into American culture. The activities helped them assimilate. For example, Finnish American socialists created their own Socialist Federation that functioned to organize Finns; then, the federation itself joined the Socialist Party of America's foreign-language section, which then connected them with the struggle for socialist ideas and actions being promoted by "established" Americans. In a similar manner, the Finnish Evangelical Lutheran Church in America wrote their Sunday school readers in Finnish, yet used the reader to teach American citizenship and history, including stories of American role models like Abraham Lincoln, together with Finnish cultural heroes.

To help maintain their own identities in America, early Finnish immigrants also developed at least two institutions that had no counterpart in Finland. The first was a masonic-type lodge called the Knights of Kaleva, founded in 1898, with secret rituals based on the ancient Finnish epic *The Kalevala*. (A women's section called the Ladies of Kaleva followed in 1904.) Local chapters, called a *tupa* for the knights and a *maja* for the ladies, provided education in Finnish culture, both for the immigrants and for the larger "established" American community. The second institution, directed toward the immigrants' children, was based on the American Sunday school movement. Both the Church Finns and the Hall Finns

published materials specifically for use in Sunday schools. They taught their children the ways of Finnish politics and religion in Finnish-language (and later in English-language) Sunday schools and summer camps.

Finnish American businesses and professional services were developed to serve Finnish communities. In big cities like Minneapolis, Detroit, and Chicago, immigrants created Finntowns, while in small cities like Worcester and Fitchburg, Massachusetts, or Astoria, Oregon, they created separate institutions. In some cities—like those on the Iron Range in Minnesota—Finns became the largest foreign-born population group. Finns actually made up more than 75 percent of the population of small towns like Wakefield, Michigan, and Fairport Harbor, Ohio.

The immigrants were quick to adopt American ways. Almost off the boat, young women would discard the triangular cotton scarf (*huivi*) worn over their hair or the heavy woolen shawl wrapped around their bodies and begin to wear the big wide hats and fancy puffed sleeve bodices so popular in the States at the end of the nineteenth century. Men donned bowler hats and stiff starched collars above their suit coats. Those Finnish immigrant women who began their lives in America working as domestics quickly learned to make American style pies and cakes. And the Finns' log cabins, erected on barely cleared cutover lands, were covered with white clapboard siding as soon as finances permitted.

Recent emigrants from Finland have been quick to adopt the latest in American suburban living, becoming models of post-modern American culture. Privately, however, many Finnish Americans maintain the conventions of the homeland: their houses contain the traditional sauna, they eat Finnish foods, they take frequent trips to Finland and instruct their children in the Finnish language, and their social calendar includes Finnish American events. In the process, they bring new blood into Finnish American culture, providing role models for Finnishness and reenergizing Finnish language usage among the third and fourth generations.

## MISCONCEPTIONS AND STEREOTYPES

Finnish Americans became the victims of ethnic slurs after socialist-leaning Finnish immigrants began to settle in the United States at the turn of the twentieth century. Finnish immigrant promoters of labor activism prompted racist responses directed at all Finnish Americans. The racist response reached its apex in 1908, when "established" Americans turned to the power of federal law, bringing to federal district court the deportation trial of one John Swan, a Finnish immigrant worker. According to Carl Ross in *The Finn Factor*, the unusual argument that Finns were actually of Mongolian descent—and therefore subject to the Asian Exclusion Act—hit many Finnish Americans hard and polarized the community into two camps, one conservative, identifying itself as "True Finns," and the other socialist, promoting American citizenship to its membership. In spite of efforts on both sides, various vigilante activities continued against Finnish Americans even into the late 1930s, as the 1939 wrecking of the Finn Hall in Aberdeen, Washington, attests. Being called a "Finn-LAND-er" became "fighting words" to both first and second generation Finnish Americans.

Stereotyping hastened Finnish assimilation into the American mainstream. As white Europeans, they could do just that. Some Finnish Americans anglicized their names and joined American churches and clubs. Others, identifying themselves as indelibly connected to America's racial minorities, entered into marriages with Native Americans, creating a group of people known in Minnesota and Michigan as "Finndians."

## TRADITIONS, CUSTOMS, AND BELIEFS

In this drive to assimilate, Finnish customs that could remain invisible to the outside world were maintained in the States. Such diverse activities as berry picking, hunting, trapping, woodworking, knitting, and weaving can all be traced to the homeland. And many Finns in America have not lost their love for the sauna.

Today, the institutions of the immigrants are, for the most part, gone. For example, except for the Laestadians, few Finnish Lutheran churches offer a glimpse into the rituals of the Church of Finland. Yet an identifiable Finnish American culture remains. Beginning in the 1950s, older institutions began to be replaced by a Finnish American club movement, which includes such organizations as the Finlandia Foundation, the Finnish American Club, and the Finnish American Historical Society. Some organizations from the former days, like the Saima Society of Fitchburg and the Knights of Kaleva in Red Lodge, Montana, have been recycled to serve a new generation's club needs. Meanwhile, large Finnish American populations like the one in greater Detroit have created a new Finn Hall tradition that unifies all the various political and religious traditions.

FinnFest USA and Salolampi Language Village further strengthen Finnish traditions and customs in the States. An annual national summer festival, FinnFest USA, founded in 1983, brings Finnish Americans from all political and religious camps together for three days of seminars, lectures, concerts, sports events, dances, and demonstrations. The festival's location revolves each year to a different region of the Finnish American geography. Salolampi, founded in 1978, offers a summer educational program that allows young people to immerse themselves in Finnish language and culture. Part of the Concordia College Language Villages Program in northern Minnesota, the school serves children from throughout the United States.

A Finnish American renaissance has also blossomed. The movement began in the 1960s, when third and fourth generation Finnish Americans looked to their own past for models that could help solve the social crises in America. It expanded to include efforts to define and express themselves as members of a culture of difference. The renaissance, which includes cultural revival and maintenance as well as new culture creativity, has nurtured new networks between Finland and the United States.

Within the new social history movement, the renaissance gave rise to a new generation of scholars and creative writers who focused on Finnish American history. By the 1970s, in response to the folk music movement of a decade earlier, musicians also turned to their Finnish American heritage for inspiration. The renaissance includes the visual arts as well.

While this collective renaissance activity can be found throughout the various regions of Finnish America, its center is in Minnesota, most specifically the Twin Cities, where the University of Minnesota has provided a home at the Immigration History Research Center (IHRC) and Finnish Department. The IHRC helped to direct the "Reunion of Sisters Project: 1984-1987," a unique cultural exchange program that brought women and men together from Finland and the United States to consider their common cultural heritage. Then, in 1991, the IHRC co-sponsored the first conference organized to examine this renaissance, a conference entitled "The Making of Finnish America: A Culture in Transition."

### CUISINE

The Finnish diet is rich in root vegetables (carrots, beets, potatoes, rutabagas, and turnips) and in fresh berries (blueberries, strawberries, and raspberries in season). Rye breads (*ruisleipa* and *reiska*) and cardamom seed flavored coffee bread (*pulla* or *nisu*) are absolute necessities. Dairy products—cheeses, creams, and butters—make the cakes, cookies, pancakes and stews quite rich. Pork roasts, hams, meat stews, and fish—especially salmon, whitefish, herring, and trout, served marinated, smoked, cooked in soups, or baked in the oven—complete the cuisine. At Christmas, many Finnish Americans eat *lutefisk* (lye-soaked dried cod) and prune-filled tarts. The traditional, meatless Shrove Tuesday meal (the day before Lent) centers on pea soup and rye bread or pancakes. Plainness, simplicity, and an emphasis on natural flavors continue to dominate Finnish and Finnish American cooking even today. Spices, if used, include cinnamon, allspice, cardamom, and ginger. One beverage dominates: coffee (morning coffee, afternoon coffee, evening coffee). "Coffee tables," as the events are called, served with the right assortment of baked goods, are central to both daily life and entertaining.

More recent Finnish immigrants favor foods that gained popularity after World War II—foods often associated with Karelia, the province lost to the Soviets in the Winter War. Among these are *karjalan piirakka* (an open-faced rye tart filled with potato or rice); *uunijuusto* (an oven-baked cheese, often called "squeaky cheese"); and *pasties*, (meat, potato, and carrot or rutabaga pies).

### TRADITIONAL CLOTHING

Finnish immigrants who landed on American soil in the nineteenth and early twentieth centuries as workers wore heavy woolen stockings, shirts, and skirts. Women wore a triangular scarf, called a *huivi*, over their heads. However, no traditional clothing was worn for special events and ceremonies. By the 1930s, as Finnish Americans became more affluent, the popularity of Finnish national folk costumes increased. (By this time, members of the middle-class were in a position to travel to Finland to purchase costumes.)

### HOLIDAYS CELEBRATED BY FINNISH AMERICANS

Finnish Americans observe a number of holidays celebrated in Finland. On December 6, many communities commemorate Finnish Independence Day. Christmas parties known as *Pikku Joulut* are central to the holiday season, just as *Laskiainen* (sliding down the hill) is celebrated on Shrove Tuesday. Some communities also hold programs in honor of the Finnish epic *The Kalevala* on Kalevala Day each February 28. Festive midsummer celebrations, featuring a *kokko* or large bonfire, occur every year.

Finns in the United States invented St. Urho's Day, a humorous takeoff on St. Patrick's Day, a traditional Irish holiday celebrated on March 17. St. Urho's Day, observed in Finnish American communities each March 16, purportedly commemorates the saint's success in driving the grasshoppers out of Finland.

### HEALTH AND MENTAL HEALTH ISSUES

According to some commentators, Finnish Americans are people with a high propensity for heart disease, high cholesterol, strokes, alcoholism, mental depression, and lactose intolerance.

Many Finnish people believe in natural health care. Immigrants in both the nineteenth and early twentieth centuries used such traditional healing methods as massage and cupping (or bloodletting). The sauna is a historic part of healing rituals. When Finns are sick, they take a sauna. Even childbirth was handled by midwives in the sauna. A Finnish proverb, *Jos ei sauna ja viina ja terva auta niin se tauti on kuolemaksi*, states that if a sauna, whiskey, and tar salve do not make you well, death is imminent. Saunas treat respiratory and circulatory problems, relax stiff muscles, and cure aches and pains. Modern Finnish Americans often turn to chiropractors and acupuncturists for relief of some ailments, but the family sauna remains the place to go whenever a cold hits.

## LANGUAGE

As late nineteenth- and early twentieth-century immigrants, Finns spoke either Finnish or Swedish. Those who spoke Swedish used a form known as Finland-Swedish; those who spoke Finnish used a non-Indo-European language, part of a small language group known as Finno-Ugric. Immigrants to America most likely spoke a regional form of Finnish: most nineteenth-century Finns spoke a northern rural Finnish, while later immigrants spoke a southern rural Finnish. An entirely new language was born in the United States—dubbed "Finglish." Finns arriving in America at the close of the twentieth century tend to speak in a Helsinki dialect.

Assimilation issues often revolved around the maintenance of language. John Wargelin (1881-1970), past president of Suomi College, lost his presidency in 1928 largely because he advocated using English at the college. The Finnish Socialist Federation exploded over orders that they "Americanize" their cultural practices, including their use of Finnish. Various churches vacillated on the language question, most of them finally giving in to using English after World War II. The Laestadians, however, have moved more slowly. Some groups still do all their preaching in Finnish; others use simultaneous translation.

### GREETINGS AND OTHER POPULAR EXPRESSIONS

Typical greetings in Finnish include the following: *Hyvä paivä* ("huv-vaeh pa-e-vaeh")—Good day; *Hyvä ilta* ("huv-vaeh ill-tah")—Good evening; *Tervetuloa* ("terr-veh-too-loh-ah")—to welcome someone; *Tervesiä* ("terr-veh-see-ah")—a general response to a greeting; *Näkemiin* ("nah-keh-mean")—Good-bye, until we meet again; *Kiitos* ("key-tohs")—Thank you; *Hauska Joulua* ("how-skah yo-lu-ah")—Merry Christmas; *Onnellista*

*Uutta Vuotta* ("own-nell-ee-stah oo-tah vu-oh-tah")—Happy New Year; *Mitä kuuluu* ("mi-taah koo-loo")—How are you?; *Kyllä* ("kyl-lah")—Yes; *Hyvä huomenta* ("huv-vaeh who-ow-men-tah")—Good morning; *Olkaa hyva* ("ol-kah huv-vaeh")—please; *Oma tupa, oma lupa*—Your own cottage, your own independence. All Finnish words are pronounced with the accent on the first syllable.

## FAMILY AND COMMUNITY DYNAMICS

Typical family structure among Finnish immigrants was patriarchal. Rural Finnish families were usually large, but in the urban areas, where both husband and wife worked, families often had only one child. Today only the Laestadians continue the tradition of large families.

Since immigrants were separated from their parents and extended families, Finnish American communities developed among immigrants from the same village or region. The 1920 U.S. Census Bureau records indicate that Finnish Americans mostly married other Finnish Americans, both in the first and second generations. By the 1990s, however, Finnish Americans of the third and fourth generations were marrying outside their ethnic group. One exception is the American Laestadian community, whose members prefer courtships within the community and who travel to Finland to meet suitable members of their faith.

### EDUCATION

Education is highly valued by Finnish Americans. Even early immigrants were largely literate, and they supported a rich immigrant publishing industry of newspapers, periodicals, and books. Self-education was central. Thus, immigrant institutions developed libraries and debate clubs, and immigrant summer festivals included seminars, concerts, and plays. That tradition continues today in the three-day FinnFest USA festival, which maintains the lecture, seminar, and concert tradition.

In spite of economic hardship, many immigrant children achieved high school and college educations. Two schools were founded by the Finns: the *Työväenopisto*, or Work Peoples College, in Minnesota (1904-1941), where young people learned trades and politics in an educational environment that duplicated the folk school tradition in Finland; and *Suomiopisto*, Suomi College, in Hancock, Michigan (1895), which began by duplicating the lyceum tradition of Finland. The only higher education institution founded by Finnish Americans, Suomi provides a Lutheran-centered general liberal arts curriculum to its students. The college continues to honor its Finnish origins by maintaining a Finnish Heritage Center and Finnish American Historical Archives. Suomi started as an academy and added a junior college in 1923 and a four-year college in 1994. The Finnish Evangelical Lutheran Church in America (Suomi Synod) established and maintained a seminary there from 1904 to 1958.

Although parochial education never was part of the Finnish tradition, Finnish Americans did develop a program of summer schools and camps where young people learned religion, Finnish culture, politics, and cooperative philosophies. Camps teaching the ideals and practice of cooperativism ran until the late 1950s.

### THE ROLE OF WOMEN

Finnish women have played leading roles in family affairs and community life. In the old country, they ran and organized the household. In addition, immigrant women oversaw the farms while the men found work in the cities, mines, and lumber camps. The women also found daytime employment outside the home, working in laundries and textile manufacturing. In the evenings, they were active in choirs, theaters, politics, and the organization of religious events.

### PHILANTHROPY

Finnish Americans practice group-organized philanthropy. Together, they raise barns, build community halls and churches, and do the ritual spring cleaning. Finnish Americans have also supported famine relief in Finland, assisted the Help Finland Movement during the Winter War, and even held a fund-raising drive for microfilming Finnish language newspapers in 1983.

# RELIGION

Over 90 percent of Finnish American immigrants are Lutherans—some more devout than others. Baptized into the church so that their births were recorded, they were also confirmed so that they could marry and be buried—all with official state records.

During the nineteenth century, within the State Church of Finland, four different religious revivals occurred: the Awakenists, the Evangelicals, the Laestadians, and the Prayers movement. These movements operated within the church itself. In addition, socialism—a secular movement with all the fervor of a religion—also developed. During the immigration process, many Finns left the church entirely and participated only in socialist activities. Those who remained religious fell into three separate groups: Laestadians, Lutherans, and free church Protestants.

The Laestadians, who came first, called themselves "Apostolic Lutherans" and began to operate separately in the heady atmosphere of America's free religious environment. However, they could not stay unified and have since divided into five separate church groups. These congregations are led by lay people; ordained ministers trained in seminaries are not common to any of the groups.

In 1898 the Finnish National Evangelical Lutheran church was formed as an expression of the Evangelical movement. The Finland Swedes, excluded from these efforts, gradually formed churches that entered the Augustana Lutheran Synod (a Swedish American church group). In recent years, the Suomi Synod became part of an effort to create a unified Lutheran church in the United States. They were part of a merger that created first the Lutheran Church in America in 1963, and then the Evangelical Lutheran Church in America in 1984.

The Suomi Synod maintained the Church of Finland "divine worship" service tradition and continued the practice of a clergy-led church. However, a new sense of power resting in the hands of the congregation developed, and the church evolved into a highly democratic decision-making institution. Although women were not yet granted the right to be ordained, they were given the right to vote in the affairs of the church in 1909. In addition, they were elected to high leadership positions on local, regional, and national boards. Pastors' wives were known to preach sermons and conduct services whenever the pastor was serving another church within his multiple-congregation assignment. The rather democratic National Synod also granted women the right to vote in the affairs of the congregation. This became an issue when the National

Synod merged with the Lutheran Church-Missouri Synod, which did not allow women to vote.

In addition to Lutherans, Finnish immigrants also organized a variety of free Protestant churches: the Finnish Congregational church (active mainly in New England, the Pacific Northwest, and California), the Finnish Methodist church, the Unitarian church, and the Pentecostal churches.

# EMPLOYMENT AND ECONOMIC TRADITIONS

In the Midwest and the West, early Finnish immigrant men worked as miners, timber workers, railroad workers, fishers, and dock hands. In New England, they worked in quarries, fisheries, and in textile and shoe factories. When single women began to settle in the United States, they went into domestic work as maids, cooks, and housekeepers. In the cutover lands across northern Michigan, Wisconsin, and Minnesota, and in the farmlands of upstate New York and New England, immigrant families left work in industry to raise grain crops and potatoes and run dairy and chicken farms. In the cities, Finnish American immigrants worked in several crafts—as carpenters, painters, tailors, and jewelers.

Later generations who have had the advantage of an American education have chosen professions that expand on the worklife of the immigrants. Men frequently specialize in agriculture-related subjects, such as natural resources management, mining engineering, and geology. A large percentage of women study nursing and home economics, working as both researchers in industry and as public managers in county extension agencies. The fields of education, medical research, the arts, music, and law have also attracted Finnish American students.

# POLITICS AND GOVERNMENT

Finnish Americans are a politically active people. As voters in American politics, they overwhelmingly supported the Republican party until the 1930s. After Franklin Delano Roosevelt became president in 1933, Finnish Americans became known as Democratic voters.

Early immigrants emphasized Temperance Societies as a political action force. In 1888 they organized the *Suomalainen Kansallis Raittius Veljeysseura* (the Finnish National Temperance Brotherhood), which later had as many as 10,000 members. Many immigrants after 1892 had socialist leanings, and itinerant Finnish agitators found many converts in the States. In 1906 the *Amerikan Suomalaisten Sosialistiosastojen Järjestö* (the Finnish American Socialist Federation) was formed; two years later, the organization became the first foreign-language affiliate within the Socialist Party of America. (Over the next decade, however, the federation began to lose members because of its increasing alignment with the Communist party.)

At the turn of the twentieth century, Finnish Americans worked to change U.S. national policy toward Finland. In 1899 a Finnish American delegation presented a petition to President William McKinley asking for aid to Finland in its fight against czarist Russia. They also lobbied for early recognition of the Finnish Republic and for relief support to the homeland.

Finnish American immigrant women organized feminist-based groups as early as 1895 for the purpose of self-education and the improvement of conditions for women. After 1906—when women in Finland were granted the right to vote—Finnish Americans became heavily involved in American suffrage politics, passing petitions throughout the Finnish American community, participating in suffrage parades, and appearing at rallies. They organized into two wings: one aligned with the temperance movement, which promoted suffrage per se; the other aligned with the socialist movement, which promoted working women's issues. Each published a newspaper, the *Naisten Lehti* (*Women's Newspaper*), and the *Toveritar* (*The Working Woman*). Both worked to improve conditions for all American women through political action.

Finns have been very active in union organizing, working often as leaders of strikes that developed in the mining and timber industries. Their workers' halls were centers of union activity and headquarters for strikes, notably in the Copper Country Strike of 1913-1914 and the two Mesabi Range strikes of 1907 and 1916. After World War II, Finnish Americans were central to the organizing of iron miners into the Steelworkers Union on the Marquette Range in Michigan. In addition, Detroit auto workers used the Wilson Avenue Finn Hall to develop their union organizing.

Finnish American
proponents of socialism
pose with their families
outside their Glassport,
Pennsylvania,
meeting hall.

Finns have been elected to political positions, mainly on local and regional levels, serving as postmasters, clerks, sheriffs, and mayors. As of 1995, no Finn had been elected state governor, and only one Finn, O. J. Larson, had been a member of the U.S. Congress. (He was elected to the House in 1920 and again in 1922.) However, Finnish Americans have served in state Houses in Michigan, Minnesota, Wisconsin, and Alaska. Barbara Hannien Linton, who represents a northern Wisconsin district, is one of the most prominent and progressive members of the Democratic Party in the Wisconsin state legislature. The first woman elected to the office of mayor of Ohio Amy Kaukkonen—was a Finnish American medical doctor. She beat her opponent on a prohibition platform in 1922.

During the effort to win support for U.S. entry into World War I, the administration of President Woodrow Wilson orchestrated a loyalty movement among the Finns. In spite of their anti-draft stance in World War I, Finns have readily served in the U.S. armed forces, beginning with the Civil War, when former Finnish sailors and recent immigrants signed on. Finns served in the Spanish-American War, World Wars I and II, and the Spanish Civil War. Finnish American nurses—mostly female—also contributed to the American war effort over the years.

### RELATIONS WITH FINLAND

Finnish Americans have long been involved in the political issues of Finland. The American Finnish Aid Committee gathered considerable funds for famine relief in 1902. After the General Strike occurred in 1906, a number of Finnish agitators sought a safe haven in the Finnish American community. After Finland declared itself a republic, Finnish Americans worked with Herbert Hoover to provide food to famine-stricken Finland. Later, they lobbied effectively in Washington, D.C., to get official recognition from the

American government for the new nation-state. Their most concerted effort on behalf of the Finns, however, occurred in 1939 and 1940, after the Winter War broke out. They mobilized efforts at such a level, again with Hoover's assistance, that they were able to send $4 million in aid to the war-torn country. Individual family efforts to collect food and clothing for relatives continued well into the end of the decade. In the 1990s Finnish Americans worked actively as volunteers and fund-raisers, promoting religion in the Finnish sections of the former Soviet Union.

# INDIVIDUAL AND GROUP CONTRIBUTIONS

Finnish Americans as a group tend not to promote the concept of individual merit. (*Oma kehu haisee*—a Finnish proverb often quoted by Finnish Americans—means "self-praise smells putrid.") The following sections list contributions made by Finnish Americans:

## ARTS AND ARCHITECTURE

The father and son architectural team of Eliel (1897-1950) and Eero (1910-1961) Saarinen is closely associated with Michigan's Cranbrook Institute, where Finnish design theory and practice were taught to several generations of Americans. Eero Saarinen designed a number of buildings, including the Gateway Arch in St. Louis; the General Motors Technical Center in Warren, Michigan; the TWA terminal at New York's Kennedy International Airport; and Dulles International Airport near Washington, D.C.

Painters include Elmer Forsberg (1883-1950), longtime professor at the Chicago Institute of Arts and a significant painter in his own right. Religious painter Warner Sallman (1897-1968), a Finland Swede, is most famous for his "Head of Christ," the mass-produced portrait of a Nordic-looking Jesus that became an icon of American Protestantism.

Photojournalist Kosti Ruohomaa, a second generation Finnish American from Maine, created a portfolio of photographs after working more than 20 years for *Life* and other national magazines. Rudy Autio (1926- ), also a second generation Finnish American, is a fellow of the American Crafts Council whose work is in the permanent collections of major museums. Minnesota-born sculptor Dale Eldred (1934-1993) became head of the Kansas City Institute of Arts and creator of monumental environmental sculptures that are displayed throughout the world.

## BUSINESS AND INDUSTRY

The earliest successful Finnish American businessman was Carl Sjodahl (Charles Linn; 1814-1883) who began as a sailor and became a wealthy wholesaler, banker, and industrialist in New Orleans and Birmingham, Alabama. Another early Finnish seaman, Captain Gustave Niebaum (1842-1908), established the Inglenook winery in California.

Vaino Hoover, former president and chief executive officer of Hoover Electric Company, designed and manufactured electric actuators and power flight control system components for aircraft and deep sea equipment. An important figure in the American defense industry of the 1950s and 1960s, he was a member of President Dwight D. Eisenhower's National Defense Advisory Committee. Yrjö Paloheimo (1899-1991) was a philanthropist as well as a rancher in New Mexico and southern California. He organized Help Finland activities in the 1940s, founded a farm and garden school for orphans in Finland in 1947, and established the Finlandia Foundation in 1952. In addition, he and his wife organized the Old Cienaga Village, a living history museum of early Hispanic life in New Mexico. Finnish American Armas Christian Markkula, co-founder of the Apple Computer Co., is listed as one of the 500 richest men in America.

## EDUCATION

Finnish Americans in education include Margaret Preska (1938- ). One of the first women in the United States to head an institution of higher learning, she was president of Mankato State University from 1979 to 1992. Robert Ranta (1943- ) is dean of the College of Communication and Fine Arts at the University of Memphis and also serves as a freelance producer of such television specials as the Grammy Awards.

## GOVERNMENT

Among the best-known Finnish Americans in government is Emil Hurja (1892-1953), the genius political pollster who orchestrated Franklin Delano Roosevelt's victorious presidential elections. Hurja became a member of the Democratic National Committee during the 1930s. O. J. Larson was a U.S. representative from Minnesota in the early 1920s. Maggie Walz (1861-1927), publisher of the *Naisten Lehti* (*Women's Newspaper*), represented the Finnish American suffragists in the American suffrage and temperance movements. Viena Pasanen Johnson, co-founder of the Minnesota Farmer Labor Party, was the first woman member of the Minnesota State Teachers' College board of directors. She later became a national leader in the Women's International League for Peace and Freedom. Gus Hall (1911- ) remains president of the Communist Party of America.

### LITERATURE

Jean Auel (1936- ), author of *Clan of the Cave Bear* and other bestselling novels dealing with prehistoric peoples, is a third generation Finnish American. Less well known but still significant to American letters is Shirley (Waisanen) Schoonover (1936- ), whose *Mountain of Winter* (1965) has been translated into eighteen languages. Anselm Hollo (1934- ), the renowned translator and writer with more than 19 volumes of verse to her credit, teaches at the Naroba Institute. Pierre DeLattre, author of two novels, *Tales of a Dalai Lama*, 1971, and *Walking on Air*, 1980, has been published in some 50 magazines. Recent writers emerging from the small press movement include poet Judy Minty, fiction writer and poet Jane Piirto, and fiction writers Lauri Anderson, Rebecca Cummings, and Timo Koskinen.

### MUSIC

Composer Charles Wuorinen (1938- )—the youngest composer to win a Pulitzer Prize—was named a MacArthur fellow in 1986. His music is performed by major symphony orchestras throughout the United States. Tauno Hannikainen was the permanent director of the Duluth Symphony and associate conductor of the Chicago Symphony Orchestra. Heimo Haitto was a concert violinist who performed as soloist with major philharmonics in Europe and the United States. Legendary virtuoso accordionist Viola Turpinen (1909-1958) became a recording artist and professional musician. Jorma Kaukonen (1942- ) played lead guitar for Jefferson Airplane. Elisa Kokkonen, a young emerging solo violinist, performs with major orchestras in the United States and Europe.

### RELIGION

Finnish America's major contributor to American Lutheran theology was renowned professor of theology Taisto Kantonen (1900-1993) of Wittenburg University. Melvin Johnson (1939- ), an administrator at the Evangelical Lutheran Church in America headquarters in Chicago, and retired theologian Raymond W. Wargelin are among the most prominent living church leaders of Finnish descent in America.

### SCIENCE AND TECHNOLOGY

Olga Lakela, a former professor of biology at the Duluth campus of the University of Minnesota and the author of numerous scientific papers on plant and bird life in Minnesota, had her name inscribed on the Wall of Fame at the 1940 New York World's Fair as one of 630 Americans of foreign birth who contributed to the American way of life. Ilmari Salminen, a research chemist with Eastman Kodak, specialized in color photography. Vernen Suomi, now an emeritus professor at the University of Wisconsin-Madison, was responsible for several inventions currently used in the exploration of outer space. A younger generation of scientists includes Donald Saari (1940- ), a Northwestern University mathematician in astronomy and economics; Markin Makinen (1939- ), a biophysicist at the University of Chicago; and Dennis Maki (1940- ), a medical doctor who serves as an infectious disease specialist in the Medical School at the University of Wisconsin-Madison.

### SPORTS

Finnish American sports figures have achieved recognition in track, cross country skiing, ski jumping, and ice hockey. The Finnish American Athletic Club was one of the strongest organizations in U.S. track and field competition. U.S. Olympic hockey and ski jumping teams have included Finnish Americans. Midwestern American sports teams in the 1930s were often called "Flying Finns," after legendary Finnish runner Paavo Nurmi, whose tour of the United States during the 1920s caused a sensation among American track and field enthusiasts. Waino Ketonen was world champion middleweight wrestler from 1918 to 1927. Rick Tapani, pitcher for the Minnesota Twins, and sportscaster Dick Engberg are both third generation Finnish Americans.

## THEATER AND FILM

Stage actor Alfred Lunt (1892-1977), who teamed with his actress-wife Lynn Fontanne from the 1920s through the 1950s was a second generation Finnish American from Wisconsin; he showed his Finnish pride when he chose Robert Sherwood's poignant *There Shall Be No Night* as a touring vehicle and a significant way for the duo to present the plight of Finns fighting in the Winter War in Finland. Bruno Maine was scenic art director for Radio City Music Hall, and Sointu Syrjälä was theater designer for several Broadway shows. Movie actor Albert Salmi (1928-1990) began his career in the New York City Finnish immigrant theater, and Maila Nurmi, who once used the stage name Vampira, hosted horror movies on television in the late 1950s in Los Angeles. She also starred in Ed Wood's immortal alien flick *Plan 9 from Outer Space*, considered by many critics to be the worst movie of all time. Other Finnish American actresses include Jessica Lange (1949- ) and Christine Lahti (1950- ), granddaughter of early Finnish American feminist Augusta Lahti.

# MEDIA

## PRINT

### Amerikan Uutiset.

A weekly newspaper in Finnish with some English; it has a long tradition of providing a national forum for nonpartisan political and general news from Finnish American communities across the country. Founded in 1932, the paper was later bought by Finland-born entrepreneurs interested in creating a more contemporary Finland news emphasis. It has the largest Finnish American readership in the nation.

**Contact:** Sakri Viklund, Editor.

**Address:** P.O. Box 8147, Lantana, Florida 33462.

**Telephone:** (407) 588-9770.

**Fax:** (407) 588-3229.

### Baiki: The North American Sami Journal.

A quarterly journal published since 1991 by descendants of Sami peoples. It explores their own unique heritage.

**Contact:** Faith Fjeld, Editor.

**Address:** 3548 14th Avenue South, Minneapolis, Minnesota 55407.

**Telephone:** (612) 722-0040.

**Fax:** (612) 722-3844.

### Christian Monthly.

Published by and for the members of the national organization serving Finnish Apostolic church congregations, this periodical features religious articles and information about upcoming religious services both for regional and national audiences.

**Contact:** Alvar Helmes, Editor.

**Address:** Apostolic Lutheran Book Concern, P.O. Box 2126, Battle Ground, Washington 98604-2126.

### Finnish Americana.

founded in 1978, this English-language annual journal features creative writing as well as scholarly articles. The journal reflects the growth of a new group of Finnish Americans interested in Finnish American history and culture. *Finnish Americana* is the major forum for the new generation of Finnish American intellectuals.

**Contact:** Michael G. Karni, Editor.

**Address:** P.O. Box 120804, New Brighton, Minnesota 55112.

**Telephone:** (612) 636-6348.

**Fax:** (612) 636-0773.

### Finnish American Reporter.

A newsprint journal featuring personal essays, Finnish American community news, and brief news articles reprinted from and about Finland. Founded in 1986, this monthly has gradually built itself into the leading publication for readers seeking an American-oriented presentation of Finnish American cultural life. It is published by the Työmies Society, the left-wing political movement of Finnish America.

**Contact:** Lisbeth Boutang, Editor.

**Address:** P.O. Box 549, Superior, Wisconsin 54880.

**Telephone:** (715) 394-4961.

**Fax:** (715) 392-5029.

### New Yorkin Uutiset.

A weekly independent newspaper featuring news from Finland and Finnish American communities. Founded in 1906 as a daily, the paper—written primarily in Finnish with some English articles—is now a weekly. *New Yorkin Uutiset* takes a nationalistic and politically conservative position on issues.

**Contact:** Leena Isbom, Editor.

**Address:** The Finnish Newspaper Co., 4422 Eighth Avenue, Brooklyn, New York 11220.

**Telephone:** (718) 435-0800.

**Fax:** (718) 871-7230.

### Norden News.

A weekly newspaper featuring news from Finland and Finland-Swede American communities. This Swedish-language paper provides the only current information on the Finnland-Swede community in the United States.

**Contact:** Erik R. Hermans, Editor.

**Address:** P.O. Box 2143, New York, New York 10185-0018.

**Telephone:** (212) 944-0775.

**Fax:** (212) 944-0763.

### Raivaaja (Pioneer).

A weekly newspaper featuring news from Finland and Finnish American communities. Founded in 1905 as a daily, the newspaper provides a voice for Social Democratic Finnish Americans.

**Contact:** Marita Cauthen, Editor.

**Address:** P.O. Box 600, Fitchburg, Massachusetts 01420-0600.

**Telephone:** (508) 343-3822.

### Työmies/Eteenpäin.

A weekly newspaper of the Finnish American left wing. Published since 1903, it continues to present Finnish American communist views. Readership remains small and largely Finnish-language directed. The newspaper features both news from Finland and news about the United States, written from a politically radical perspective.

**Address:** P.O. Box 549, Superior, Wisconsin 54880.

**Telephone:** (715) 394-4961.

**Fax:** (715) 394-7655.

### Voice of Zion.

A monthly periodical published by the Association of American Laestadian Congregations. This bilingual publication provides devotional articles as well as news articles about religious events occurring in the United States, Canada, Finland, and Sweden.

**Contact:** Jon Bloomquist, Editor.

**Address:** 10911 Highway 55, Suite 203, Plymouth, Minnesota 55441.

**Telephone:** (612) 544-8118.

**Fax:** (612) 544-8229.

## RADIO

### KAXE-FM, Northern Minnesota.

"Finnish Americana and Heritage Show," In Bemidji, 94.7 FM; in Brainerd, 89.5 FM; in Grand Rapids, 91.7 FM. This English-language program—presented the first Sunday of each month—includes Finnish folk and popular music as well as information about Finnish music events in Minnesota.

### KUSF-FM (90.3), San Francisco, California.

"Voice of Finland," a weekly one-hour program in the Finnish language provides music, news, interviews, and information about Finnish activities occurring in the region.

### WCAR-AM (1900), Detroit, Michigan.

"Finn Focus," a light entertainment program in Finnish provides music, news, notice of local activities and interviews.

### WLVS-AM (1380), Palm Beach County, Florida.

"Hyvät Uutiset" (Good News), sponsored by the Lake Worth Finnish Pentecostal Congregation, is a weekly half hour broadcast in Finnish featuring religious music and talk. "American Finnish Evening Hour" provides light entertainment, music, and information about happenings in the listening area and in Finland. "Halls of Finland," a program broadcast in Finnish, includes news reports about local events and activities occurring in the United States and in Finland. "Religious Hour" is sponsored by the Apostolic Lutheran church.

### WYMS-FM (88.9), Milwaukee, Wisconsin.

"Scandinavian Hour," broadcast once a month, this program provides news from Finland and the local region, interviews, and Finnish music. Broadcast in two languages. "Scenes from the Northern Lights" originates in Bloomington, Indiana, and is offered through syndication on National Public Radio (NPR). It features a wide variety of Finnish music (rock, pop, classical, folk, opera).

## TELEVISION

### WLUC, Marquette, Michigan.

"Suomi Kutsu" (Finland Calling) is telecast weekly on Sundays from 10:00 to 11:00 a.m. The first half hour is a newsmagazine about Finland and Finnish America, featuring interviews, music, news, and video essays. The second half hour is a Finnish language devotional worship service led by area Lutheran clergy.

# ORGANIZATIONS AND ASSOCIATIONS

## Finlandia Foundation.

Founded in 1952, this national philanthropic organization's mission is to cultivate and strengthen cultural relations between the United States and the Republic of Finland. Finlandia Foundation distributes over $70,000 annually for cultural programs, grants, and scholarships.

**Contact:** Carl W. Jarvie, President.

**Address:** 607 Third Avenue, Suite 610, Seattle, Washington 98104.

**Telephone:** (206) 285-4703.

**Fax:** (206) 781-2721.

## Finnish American League for Democracy (FALD).

Promotes the study of Finnish American history and culture.

**Contact:** Marita Cauthen, Executive Officer.

**Address:** P.O. Box 600, 147 Elm Street, Fitchburg, Massachusetts 01420.

**Telephone:** (508) 343-3822.

# MUSEUMS AND RESEARCH CENTERS

## Finnish American Historical Archives of the Finnish American Heritage Center, Suomi College.

Features the best collection of materials that predate the twentieth century, as well as modern materials, including records of the Help Finland Movement, the Finnish Evangelical Lutheran Church in America (Suomi Synod), and the celebration of the 300th anniversary of the Delaware Colony. A small uncataloged and unsystematic collection of material objects has accumulated; parts of this collection are usually on display. A large photograph collection, an oral history collection, and microfilm archives of newspapers and records stored in Finland round out the resources.

**Address:** 601 Quincy Street, Hancock, Michigan.

**Telephone:** (906) 487-7347.

**Fax:** (906) 487-7366.

## Immigration History Research Center of the University of Minnesota.

This collection—one of the largest available anywhere—is part of a larger collection of 24 late immigration groups. The Finnish section includes materials from the Finnish American radical and cooperative movements, Finnish American theater, and music.

**Address:** 826 Berry Street, St. Paul, Minnesota 55114-1076.

**Telephone:** (612) 627-4208.

**Fax:** (612) 627-4190.

Other archival collections of Finnish American materials are more regional. For example, the Iron Range Research Center in Chisholm, Minnesota, has a rich northern Minnesota collection, and the Finnish Cultural Center at Fitchburg State College in Fitchburg, Massachusetts, has been trying to reconstitute materials from the New England region.

Finnish Americans have not developed any major museums. The most systematically catalogued collection of Finnish American materials can be found at the Michigan State University Museum in East Lansing, Michigan; the Nordic Heritage Museum in Seattle, Washington, includes an interesting display of Finnish culture, collected and organized by the local Finnish American community.

Finnish Americans have preserved their cultural landscape history at two significant sites listed on the National Register of Historic Places. The Hanka Homestead in Arnheim, Michigan, provides an example of a small backwoods farmstead, while the town of Embarrass, Minnesota, is an excellent example of an entire Finnish American farming community.

# SOURCES FOR ADDITIONAL STUDY

*Finnish Diasporaii: United States*, edited by Michael G. Karni. Toronto: The Multicultural History Society of Ontario, 1981.

The Finnish Experience in the Western Great Lakes Region, edited by Michael G. Karni, Matti E. Kaups, and Doublas J. Ollila, Jr. Vammala, Finland: Institute for Migration, Turku, 1972.

The Finns in North America: A Social Symposium, edited by Ralph Jalkanen. East Lansing: Michigan State University Press, 1969.

Hoglund, A. William. Finnish Immigrants in America, 1880-1920. Madison: University of Wisconsin Press, 1960.

Jalkanen, Ralph. The Faith of the Finns: Historical Perspectives on the Finnish Lutheran Church in America. East Lansing: Michigan State University Press, 1972.

Jutikkala, Eino, and Kauko Pirinen. A History of Finland. New York: Dorset Press, 1988.

Ojakangas, Beatrice A. The Finnish Cookbook. New York: Crown, 1964.

Ross, Carl. The Finn Factor in American Labor, Culture, and Society. New York Mills, Minnesota: Parta Publishing, 1977.

Sampo: The Magic Mill—A Collection of Finnish American Writing, edited by Aili Jarvenpa and Michael G. Karni. Minneapolis: New Rivers Press, 1989.

Women Who Dared: The History of Finnish American Women, edited by Carl Ross and K. Marianne Wargelin Brown. St. Paul: Immigration History Research Center, University of Minnesota, 1986.

Wuorinen, John. The Finns on the Delaware, 1638-1655: An Essay in American Colonial History. New York: Columbia University Press, 1938.

———. A History of Finland. New York: Columbia University Press, 1965.

# FRENCH

by
**Laurie Collier
Hillstrom**

# AMERICANS

Despite their
relatively small
numbers, French
immigrants have
tended to be more
successful and
influential than
other groups in
America.

## OVERVIEW

The French Republic (République Française)—
more commonly known as France—occupies
212,918 square miles, making it the largest country in Western Europe and slightly smaller than
the state of Texas. It is hexagonal in shape, with
half its borders, or 1,920 miles, made up of coastline. It borders on the Atlantic Ocean to the
west, the English Channel to the northwest, Belgium and Luxembourg to the north, Germany to
the northeast, Switzerland to the east, Italy to the
southeast, the Mediterranean Sea to the south,
and Spain to the southwest. The topography of
France includes the Pyrenees mountains along
the southern border and the Alps along the
southwest border. The remaining terrain varies
from mountain ranges to plains to forests, and
includes four major river systems.

The population of France was approximately
55.5 million in 1987, and it has remained relatively stable over time. The capital and major
cultural center is Paris, where about one-fifth of
the total population resides. France has held a
prestigious position in Western culture since the
Middle Ages, showing particular influence in art,
architecture, philosophy, and literature. The
country became a leading member of the European Economic Community (EEC) and later the
European Community (EC) and is one of the five

permanent members of the United Nations Security Council. The French national flag consists of three wide vertical stripes of blue, white, and red.

About 80 percent of French people consider themselves Roman Catholic, though only 20 percent of French Catholics attend church regularly. According to Jonathan Harris in *The Land and People of France*, French discord with the Catholic church dates back to the eighteenth century, when the church reached the height of its wealth and power. Since then, anticlericalism has been a pervasive attitude in French society. France is also home to about 800,000 Protestants, who, despite their minority status, enjoy a strong influence in business and the government. In addition, with 700,000 Jewish residents, France has the largest Jewish community in Europe besides Russia. About 1.5 million Muslims—mostly emigrants from the former French colonies of Algeria, Morocco, and Tunisia—comprise another sizable religious minority in France.

Since conditions in France historically have been considered humane and prosperous, relatively few French citizens have decided to emigrate. On the contrary, an estimated four million people from other lands have chosen to immigrate to France in the past 150 years. The most prevalent sources of immigrants to France in modern times include Portugal, Spain, Italy, eastern Europe, northern Africa, and Asia. The foreign population in France grew by 4.5 percent annually throughout the 1970s. Although this rate slowed to 0.7 percent during the 1980s, immigrants comprised seven percent of the population of France by the early 1990s. One estimate suggested that up to 500,000 of these immigrants had remained in the country illegally. While France has faced some problems in assimilating such large numbers of immigrants from different cultures, some experts claim that the French have largely succeeded in forging a sense of national identity.

### HISTORY

The history of France dates back to about 1000 B.C., when Celtic tribes moved into large areas of northern Europe. The Celts who remained in the area that eventually became France were known as Gauls. Around 600 B.C., Greek colonists settled in the Mediterranean area of Marseilles, and their civilized ways had a strong influence on the Gauls. In 59 B.C., however, Julius Caesar led Roman forces in conquest of the area, which the Romans ruled for the next 500 years. During this time they built the foundation of many modern French roads and cities and ensured that Latin would form the basis of the French language. After the fall of the Roman Empire in 476 A.D., France was ruled as an absolute monarchy by four successive dynasties. By the time King Henry IV established the Bourbon dynasty in 1589, France had developed a strict system of social hierarchy known as feudalism. Wealthy aristocrats owned the land and participated in government, while the poorer people worked the land and had few rights.

The stage was set for French immigration to North America in the early 1500s, during a religious movement known as the Reformation. At this time, many citizens of France and other European nations protested against some of the doctrines and corrupt practices then prevailing in the Roman Catholic church. The Reformation caused conflict throughout Europe, eventually dividing the church into two separate factions, Catholics and Protestants. John Calvin, a French priest, was instrumental in the spread of Protestantism. His followers, called Huguenots, built 2,000 churches in France by the mid-1500s, though they also became the targets of persecution by French Catholics during 30 years of civil war. King Henry IV, who was born a Protestant but converted to Catholicism, stopped the conflict temporarily in 1594 by enacting the Edict of Nantes, which granted political rights and freedom of religion to French Protestants. After spending several years unsuccessfully pressuring Protestants to convert, however, King Louis XIV revoked the Edict of Nantes in 1685. This sudden loss of rights and status caused thousands of Huguenots to leave France for North America. The majority of Huguenot immigrants were skilled, well-educated, and prosperous.

Another important event in French history that affected immigration to North America occurred in 1763, with the conclusion of the Seven Years' War (also known as the French and Indian War) between France and England. These traditional enemies had clashed repeatedly over expansionist policies and colonization in Europe, North America, and India. After losing this conflict, France relinquished to England control of its colonies, through the Treaty of Paris. According to Jean-Baptiste Duroselle in *France and the U.S.: From Beginnings to Present* (1976), French Americans "nursed the knowledge that they had been abandoned by a country that was no longer their homeland, and of which they today retain nothing but the language." Duroselle goes on to state that

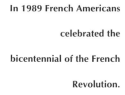

this event marked the end of French political power in the land that would become the United States. The American Revolution began just 12 years later, however, and France was persuaded to provide invaluable military aid to the American side. In fact, many historians claim that the French support enabled the United States to form.

France became embroiled in its own revolution in 1789. As the French middle class, or bourgeoisie, became more prosperous and powerful, they began to resent the feudal system and demanded equal rights and tax reform. King Louis XVI accepted some of the people's demands, but later brought troops into Paris to try to crush the rebellion. On July 14, crowds of armed protesters destroyed the Bastille, a fortress that was used to hold political prisoners and that gradually had become a symbol of oppression. This event marked the end of the old regime and the beginning of the French Republic, and it has been celebrated ever since as a national holiday—Bastille Day. France soon adopted a constitution that ensured equal rights for all citizens and limited the powers of the monarchy and the church. The French Revolution continued, however, as conservative and radical forces vied for control of the new government. These factions staged reciprocal campaigns of violence against one another that came to be known as the Reign of Terror.

In the meantime, France entered into war with a coalition of European nations determined to halt the revolution and its radical ideas.

Napoleon Bonaparte gained prominence as a French military leader and then overthrew the government of France in 1799, granting himself dictatorial powers as Emperor Napoleon I. Although Napoleon scored many popular military victories and initiated lasting reforms to the French educational and legal systems, he also severely limited individual rights. His rules made it virtually impossible for French citizens to emigrate, for example, so only a few immigrants came to the United States until the end of his reign in 1815.

Public opinion in the United States, which had been generally positive toward France since the American Revolution, gradually became negative during the Reign of Terror. The United States ended up claiming neutrality during the French Revolution and refused to provide assistance during the resulting war in Europe. Relations with France became the subject of intense debate among the leaders of the U.S. Congress and in the newly influential American press. Negative attitudes toward France peaked in 1797 with the XYZ Affair, when three unnamed French diplomats demanded a huge bribe before they would agree to speak with American delegates about a new treaty. This perceived insult caused the United States to begin preparing for a war with France.

During this time, French Americans—especially those who had come to the United States as refugees from the French Revolution—were viewed by some American leaders as a potential threat to national security. In 1798 the U.S. government passed the controversial Alien and Sedition Acts, which were intended to monitor and limit the power of immigrant groups. For example, the Acts increased the residency requirement from five to 14 years before immigrants were allowed to vote, forced ships to compile dossiers on immigrant passengers, and granted the government the power to deport anyone it considered "dangerous." The Acts became the subject of considerable public outrage and were allowed to expire two years later. Shortly thereafter, the 1803 purchase of the Louisiana Territory from Napoleon helped relax the tension over immigration. This vast tract of land doubled the size of the United States and provided a new frontier for a large wave of new immigrants.

After Napoleon was defeated at Waterloo in 1815, France was ruled first as a constitutional monarchy and then as a republic. In 1848, Napoleon's nephew Louis Napoleon Bonaparte was elected president of the republic, but he soon overthrew the government and proclaimed himself Emperor Napoleon III. He was soundly defeated in the Franco-Prussian War in 1870, however, which resulted in the loss of the French provinces Alsace and Lorraine to the German Empire. Thousands of Alsatians chose to immigrate to the United States at this time rather than live under German rule. France approved the democratic constitution of the Third Republic in 1875.

World War I helped improve relations between France and the United States when French and American soldiers fought together. In the period between the World Wars, France endured a weak government and low birth rates. These conditions contributed to the fall of France in 1940, shortly after the beginning of World War II, and to its occupation by German troops for the next four years. The Fourth Republic was established in 1946, but the government was unstable and faced constant conflict with French colonies seeking independence. Charles de Gaulle was elected president of the Fifth Republic in 1958 and managed to bring peace and economic recovery to France.

## PARADOXES OF FRENCH IMMIGRATION

The history of French immigration to the United States involves a number of paradoxes. In only a few cases did groups of French citizens make a collective decision to leave France for the United States. Instead, typical French immigrants came as individuals or families seeking change or economic opportunity. Some analysts attribute this lack of group movement to the humane climate of France, while others claim that in general the French are reluctant to organize into groups. As a result, the number of immigrants to the United States from France has always been smaller than from other European countries.

According to the *Statistical Abstract of the United States,* for example, immigrants from France accounted for only 0.46 percent of total American immigrants over the 30-year period from 1961 to 1991—or 78,300 out of a total 16.98 million. In addition, only 18,000 people came to the United States from France between 1980 and 1988, compared to 112,000 from England and 56,000 from Germany ("French American Relations: Rapprochement," *Economist,* March 16, 1991). In total, approximately 740,000 immigrants from France have settled in the United States since 1820, and between 30,000 and 40,000 came earlier. In 1990, 119,233 people living in the United States told the U.S. Census Bureau that they had been born in France. The flow of French immigrants to the United States also has been very stable in comparison to other countries, ranging from a high of 77,000 during the decade of the 1840s to a low of 18,000 during the 1970s.

While these figures provide useful information about the trends of French immigration, demographers admit that counting French Americans has been problematic since U.S. colonial times. For many years U.S. officials tended to overestimate the number of French immigrants because they equated immigrants' nationality with their last place of domicile before arrival. This policy meant that many people who actually hailed from Germany or Eastern Europe and had settled in France temporarily in order to facilitate their eventual passage to the United States were regarded as French Americans. Another problem in the U.S. immigration figures involves inconsistent treatment of the French speaking people who came to America from Canada or the Caribbean. French Canadian Americans, Acadians (or Cajuns), and Creoles form distinct U.S. ethnic groups but are not always distinguished from French Americans in census figures. Compounding the problems with U.S. immigration figures, for many years French officials tended to underestimate the number of emigrants because they wished to downplay any outflow of French citizens. However, most sources agree that French immigration to the United States has been small and steady over time.

Despite their relatively small numbers, French immigrants have tended to be more successful and influential than other groups in America. French immigrants are generally urban, middle-class, skilled, and progressive, and they are most likely to be employed as artisans or merchants. The U.S. Census of 1910 showed that French Americans were more literate, more concentrated in liberal professions, and had fewer children and larger living spaces than other immigrant groups. In the 1930s, moreover, French Americans accounted for ten percent of the entries in *Appleton's Encyclopedia of American Biography*, although they made up only two percent of the overall population. In typically paradoxical style, however, many French immigrants returned to France despite their high rate of success in the United States. In fact, a 1980 estimate showed that only one-third of registered French immigrants ultimately decided to seek U.S. citizenship.

## THE FIRST FRENCH AMERICANS

Many of the earliest French settlements in North America were mainly intended as trading outposts. Jean Ribaut, a French Huguenot sailor, established two of the first French colonies near Beaufort, South Carolina, and Jacksonville, Florida, in the 1550s. He settled in these locations in order to compete with the Spanish for control of trade in the Caribbean region. In 1534, French explorer Jacques Cartier became the first to travel the length of the St. Lawrence River. Although he failed to find the gold he was seeking, by 1542 he did reach the area that would become Quebec, including Montreal, in Canada. After forming an alliance with the powerful Algonquin Indians, Samuel de Champlain founded the first permanent French settlement in Quebec in 1608.

Originally, French colonial policy allowed only Catholics to emigrate, but most French Catholics were reluctant to leave their homes. As a result, the few people who came to North America from France were mostly explorers, traders, or Jesuit missionaries seeking to convert the Indians. These individuals tended to spread out and travel far into the wilderness. In fact, by the time the Pilgrims arrived in New England in 1620, the French had already discovered three of the Great Lakes. This migration to the Midwest later led to French bases in Detroit and St. Louis.

Robert Cavelier de La Salle traveled the length of the Mississippi River to the Gulf of Mexico in 1682, and upon completion of his journey founded Louisiana by claiming the entire Mississippi Basin in the name of King Louis XIV of France. Jean-Baptiste Bienville followed by forming a successful French colony in New Orleans in 1717.

## SIGNIFICANT IMMIGRATION WAVES

There have been several notable waves of French immigrants to the United States based upon economic, religious, or political factors. For the most part, however, French immigration has been a result of individual decisions rather than a mass movement. The earliest flow of French immigrants began around 1538 and consisted of Huguenots who felt alienated from mainstream French society due to their Protestant faith. The Huguenots' emigration peaked after King Louis XIV revoked the Edict of Nantes in 1685, outlawing the Protestant religion and forcing the Huguenots to either convert to Catholicism or face death. According to Albert Robbins in *Coming to America: Immigrants from Northern Europe*, the king's official decree gave orders to "kill the greatest part of the Protestants that can be overtaken, without sparing the women, to the end that this may intimidate them and prevent others from falling into a similar fault."

Many Huguenots decided to flee from France, but it was still illegal for Protestants to emigrate. Those who managed to leave often had to pay bribes or use connections to acquire false passports. As a result, the majority of the 15,000 Huguenots who arrived in North America were wealthy and skilled, and they eventually gained prominence as craftsmen and merchants. The Huguenots established a strong presence in New York with settlements in Harlem, Staten Island, New Rochelle, and New Paltz. In fact, the first child born in New York City was Jean Vigné, the son of a Huguenot immigrant. Pennsylvania, Virginia, South Carolina, and Massachusetts also became the sites of successful Huguenot settlements. Since the Huguenots could not settle among French Catholics and felt alienated from France, most accepted North America as their new homeland and changed their names to sound more English.

With the beginning of the French Revolution, a wave of Roman Catholic refugees emigrated from France to the United States. Many of these immigrants were either wealthy aristocrats or working-class people, such as chefs and hairdressers, who depended upon the aristocrats for their livelihood. Another important group of refugees to arrive at this time included 100 French priests. Since there were only 25 priests in the American colonies prior to their arrival, these immigrants had a strong influence on the development of the American Catholic church. Missionary work carried the Roman Catholic refugees to far-ranging French colonial areas, such as Michigan, St. Louis, and Louisiana.

About 10,000 political refugees managed to leave France during the French Revolution, and many of these immigrants traveled through French colonies in the Caribbean to reach the United States. This group included about 3,000 people of mixed black and French ancestry who settled in Philadelphia. Following Napoleon's defeat in 1815, a large wave of French immigration began, which lasted through the start of the American Civil War. Napoleon's brother Jérome came to the United States at this time with several hundred former soldiers and tried unsuccessfully to establish settlements in Texas, Alabama, and Ohio.

The California Gold Rush, which began in 1848, convinced a record number of French immigrants to make their way to the United States. About 30,000 people arrived between 1849 and 1851, with an all-time high of 20,000 coming in 1851 alone. Unfortunately, few of these immigrants ever found the riches they were seeking. According to Abraham P. Nasatir in *French Activities in California*, the following letter written by Montes Jean—one of the French immigrant "forty-niners"—describes the conditions immigrants encountered in San Francisco in December 1849: "It is twenty-four days since we arrived in California, but in what condition.... We have been very fortunate being in a country where a great deal is earned and where work is not lacking. I say 'work'; that is to say, go to the dock of San Francisco, become a working man, carry bales of merchandise to various stores and you will be quite well paid. For carrying a trunk weighing about a hundred livres for a distance of fifty meters or more one is paid three dollars (about sixteen francs); and in this way we have lived up to now, when I am writing you. But at present, since people are arriving in large numbers, prices are diminishing greatly. One cannot go to the mines at this time on account of the rising waters and because the routes are miry and submerged.... Food is very expensive in this country. Bread, for example, costs a half-dollar a livre,

and meat twenty-six sous de France. Work is not progressing very much at present, although there are two hundred vessels in the harbor."

In 1871 a group of Alsatian Jews settled in Los Angeles, after the Franco-Prussian War put the French provinces Alsace and Lorraine under German rule. Immigration slowed significantly during the American Civil War, and the years immediately following saw a larger percentage of unskilled workers from France moving to the United States. A number of French Jews immigrated after the fall of France to the Germans in 1940. From the end of World War II onward, a strong cultural and economic recovery in France caused the flow of French immigrants to slow considerably. Most French immigrants in the second half of the twentieth century came to the United States because they married an American citizen or simply wanted to try something different, rather than out of religious, economic, or political necessity.

## SETTLEMENT PATTERNS

French American settlement patterns reflect the fact that French immigrants typically came to the United States as individuals or families seeking economic opportunity. Rather than joining groups of previous French settlers or establishing French American communities, these immigrants most often scattered to the areas where new opportunities seemed likely to be found. For example, the number of ethnic French living in Louisiana dropped from 15,000 in 1860 to half that number by 1930 as the prosperity of the South declined. In the meantime, the French population of California rose from 8,000 in 1860 to 22,000 by 1970 as immigrants pursued new opportunities in the West. According to *We the People: An Atlas of America's Ethnic Diversity*, in 1980 more immigrants directly from France lived in California, New York, New Jersey, and Pennsylvania than in any other states. Many of these French immigrants possessed professional skills that were most valuable in urban environments. Less than 40 percent of French Americans immigrated directly from France, however, as the majority came from French speaking parts of Canada. In general, these groups came from different French social classes and tended to avoid contact with each other despite their shared language.

According to the U.S. Census of 1980, the counties with the largest number of people of French ancestry—including those whose ancestors immigrated to the United States directly from France as well as those whose ancestors immigrated from Canada or the Caribbean—were Worcester, Massachusetts, with 90,332; Providence, Rhode Island, with 72,461; Middlesex, Massachusetts, with 66,911; Los Angeles, California, with 65,263; and Hillsborough, New Hampshire, with 58,278. The counties (parishes) with the highest percentage of their population claiming French ancestry were all in Louisiana: Vermillion, with 43.13 percent French ancestry; St. Martin, with 37.67 percent; Evangeline, with 36.22 percent; Lafourche, with 36.2 percent; and Avoyelles, with 33.48 percent.

# ACCULTURATION AND ASSIMILATION

Historically, the people who immigrated to the United States from northern Europe—including France—were more readily accepted than some other immigrant groups. For example, when the U.S. Congress passed a law restricting immigration in the 1920s, northern European groups received the most liberal quotas. This favored status allowed northern European immigrants to assimilate more easily into American culture. The type of individual who was most likely to leave France for the United States, moreover, had a particularly strong propensity toward assimilation. For instance, a high percentage of French immigrants were professionals or merchants who earned their livings among the greater population and within an urban environment. At the same time, very few French farmers—who would have lived in rural areas and been more isolated from the dominant culture—decided to emigrate. Typical French immigrants were also modernists who felt estranged from mainstream French culture and viewed the United States as a progressive, classless, secular, and innovative society. "Given this background of alienation and yearning," Patrice Louis René Higonnet explains in the *Harvard Encyclopedia of American Ethnic Groups,* "it is hardly surprising that French immigrants, self-selecting and at odds with the national ethos, should have been assimilationists."

Higonnet also attributes the absence of group spirit among French Americans to their geographic dispersion, a general French distaste for group interaction, and the fact that French immigrants came to the United States seeking new forms of society and culture. One early example of assimi-

lation among French immigrants was when the Huguenots chose to join the less-extreme Anglican Church in North America. In the modern era, despite the strong cultural nationalism found in France, French Americans have shown a higher rate of intermarriage than any other non-English-speaking immigrant group. In fact, French Americans tend to assimilate so quickly and completely that most sources can only cite their overall impact on American culture. As James S. Pula confirmed in *The French in America,* "Place names and linguistic quirks remain as a lasting testimony to the influence of France on American culture, but the people have all but disappeared into an abyss of assimilation. Unlike many other national groups, the French generally held no special reluctance toward Anglicizing their names and their speech."

## TRADITIONAL BELIEFS, ATTITUDES, AND CUSTOMS

The rapid assimilation of French immigrants into American society ensured that few traditional customs were carried over and practiced by French Americans. Instead, Americans studied and emulated French culture, manners, cuisine, fashion, art, and literature. French Americans mainly disseminated information and acted as role models. French culture first gained widespread popularity in the United States in the early nineteenth century—shortly after the Revolutionary War—when Americans followed the events and supported the principles of the French Revolution. French chefs and restaurants bolstered the popularity of French cuisine, while the influence of French impressionists on American art became apparent. Several U.S. presidents also ordered French furniture and silverware for use at the White House.

## CUISINE

French immigrants introduced a wide range of interesting foods to America. For example, French Americans made the first yeast breads in North America and brought technical farming skills that vastly improved American rice and wines. Huguenots grew and prepared the first okra, artichokes, and tomatoes. The popularity of French cuisine took off in the 1780s, following the alliance between France and the United States during the American Revolution. Many respected French chefs, such as Arthur Goussé in

Los Angeles, immigrated to the United States and established restaurants. Even non-French Americans began to prepare buns and rolls, omelettes, and delicate soups. A number of French culinary terms remain prominent in modern times, including *bouillon*, *purée*, *fricassée*, *mayonnaise*, *pâté*, *hors d'oeuvres*, *bisque*, *fillet*, *sauté*, *casserole*, *au gratin*, and *à la mode*.

### FASHION

Imported French attire gained popularity in the early nineteenth century as well, particularly items such as gloves and lace. Around 1850, the French custom of wearing beards swept across the United States. In 1908, several women wearing imported French skirts and fishnet stockings were arrested for indecent exposure. France has maintained its position on the leading edge of world fashion through the present day.

### HOLIDAYS CELEBRATED BY FRENCH AMERICANS

The French national holiday of Bastille Day—which commemorates the uprising that destroyed a major symbol of oppression in Paris and led to the formation of the First Republic in 1789—is celebrated in some communities throughout the United States on July 14. In addition, the New Orleans tradition of Mardi Gras—a week-long series of parades and parties usually held in February—was first organized in 1827 by French American students.

### HEALTH AND MENTAL HEALTH ISSUES

The average life expectancy in France is exactly the same as in the United States—70 years for men, and 78 years for women. Although there are no known congenital diseases specific to French Americans, the French have shown a higher than average susceptibility to lung and throat cancers, mainly because they tend to smoke and drink heavily. In fact, with four million alcoholics in its population, France has one of the highest rates of alcoholism in the world.

## LANGUAGE

French is a Romance language derived from Latin. It has enjoyed a prestigious position in world cul-

ture for over three centuries. French was the official language of diplomatic negotiations, and the preferred language among the upper classes of Western civilization, beginning around 1650. By about 1920, however, English began to gain popularity, and it eventually surpassed French in terms of international status. In 1975 the French National Assembly, reacting to what it viewed as an encroachment of English slang upon the French language (commonly called "franglais"), passed a law restricting the use of untranslated English words in advertising materials. They also hoped to discourage the French public from using English words when an equivalent French term existed.

As of 1990, an estimated 1.93 million people in the United States spoke the French language at home. The influence of French is also apparent in American English. For example, since French explorers often served as guides for other settlers after the United States purchased the Louisiana Territory, French words were used to describe many aspects of the frontier experience, such as *portage*, *rapids*, *bayou*, *butte*, *peak*, *gopher*, *prairie*, *pass*, and *cache*. French explorers also left a legacy of American place names, including Baton Rouge, Sault Ste. Marie, Detroit, Couer d'Alene, Marquette, Joliet, Lake Champlain, Lake Pontchartrain, Des Moines, Eau Claire, Fon du Lac, Charlevoix, and Terre Haute. Finally, numerous French words occur in everyday American usage, such as *croquet*, *poker*, *roulette*, *automobile*, *garage*, *lingerie*, *restaurant*, *crayon*, *bouquet*, and *boutique*.

### GREETINGS AND POPULAR EXPRESSIONS

Common French greetings and other expressions include: *Bonjour*—Hello, Good morning, Good afternoon; *Comment allez-vous*—How do you do; *Au revoir*—Good-bye; *Très bien*—Very good; *Oui, c'est ça*—Yes, that's right; *Merci beaucoup*—Thank you very much; *À votre service*—You're welcome; or, Don't mention it.

## FAMILY AND COMMUNITY DYNAMICS

### EDUCATION

The French educational system, which was initiated during Napoleon's rule, has had a marked influence on schooling in the United States since the early 1800s. The French system features innovative nursery and primary schools, followed by

*collèges*, the equivalent of American junior high schools. Students then must decide whether to complete their secondary education at an academic or a vocational *lycée*—a three-year preparatory school similar to American high schools. Admission to French universities is based upon a rigorous, competitive examination in a specific subject area. Only top students may attend the *grandes écoles*, or elite schools, that serve as a prerequisite for top jobs in business and government. Educators in the United States emulated the French system of progressive schooling culminating in admission to a private or municipal university. In France, however, the entire educational system is administered by the Ministry of National Education, while in the United States education is controlled by states or local communities. Proponents of the French system claim that it is superior, in that it demands students' best efforts and rewards exceptional performance. On the other hand, some detractors claim that the system works to maintain a social class system in France, since the vast majority of students at the *grandes écoles* hail from upper-class backgrounds.

## RELIGION

The majority of French immigrants to the United States have been Roman Catholic. This fact is so partly because Catholics form a majority in France, and partly because during colonial times only Catholics were allowed to emigrate. Descendants of the 15,000 French Huguenots who came to the United States tend to be Anglican. More recently, the United States became a refuge for French Jews during and after World War II.

## EMPLOYMENT AND ECONOMIC TRADITIONS

On the whole, French immigrants have been highly successful and have made a lasting impact in the United States. According to *We the People*, the French immigrants who remained in the United Stated tended to be "less traditional and more enterprising, ambitious, and forward-looking" individuals who typically "adjusted without much apparent stress to American ways." In contrast to other immigrant groups, only 12 percent of French Americans were farmers. Instead, French immigrants most often worked as professionals, clerical workers, cooks, waiters, artists, and managers.

Specific French immigration waves contributed different labor practices to American society. For example, the Huguenots introduced a number of skilled crafts to the United States, including sophisticated techniques of weaving, leather dressing, lace making, and felt manufacture. Some historians claim that the Huguenots' stylish ways helped transform crude frontier settlements into civilized cities and towns. Refugees from the French Revolution and the fall of Napoleon who came to the United States tended to be former army officers or aristocrats. These educated individuals often taught the French language or such elite activities as fencing and dancing. A number of French chefs, hairdressers, dress designers, and perfumers accompanied the wave of aristocrats and introduced French cuisine and fashion to America.

# POLITICS AND GOVERNMENT

Americans of French ancestry began to influence politics in the United States during colonial times. Most French immigrants rapidly became "Americanized," however, and participated in government as individuals rather than as a group. Four U.S. presidents—John Tyler, James B. Garfield, Theodore Roosevelt, and Franklin D. Roosevelt—were of French Huguenot descent.

## MILITARY SERVICE

Many descendants of French Huguenots, including Paul Revere, were distinguished patriots during the American Revolution. In addition, the French government provided invaluable support to the American cause. One French army captain in particular, Marquis de Lafayette, had an important influence on the events at this time. Lafayette fought brilliantly as a major general in George Washington's army, and later returned to France to convince King Louis XVI to formally recognize the independence of the United States and to provide military aid against the British. French immigrants fought passionately on both sides of the American Civil War. For example, Brigadier General Benjamin Buisson, a veteran of the Napoleonic Wars, formed troops out of French volunteers to defend New Orleans for the Confederacy. A number of all-French American groups, known as Zouave units, fought for both the North and the South, wearing uniforms in the French colonial tradition.

# INDIVIDUAL AND GROUP CONTRIBUTIONS

## ARTS AND LEISURE

Pierre Charles L'Enfant (1754-1825), a civil engineer by training, fought with Lafayette during the American Revolution. He later became the architect of the United States capital city in Washington, D.C. His designs of majestic buildings and tree-lined squares were considered visionary. French artist Régis François Gignoux came to the United States in 1844. He served as the first president of the Brooklyn Art Academy and had a vast influence on American landscape painting. In 1876, John La Farge painted the first mural in America to decorate Trinity Church in Boston. He later went on to develop techniques that allowed stained glass to be used on a large scale for decorative purposes. Marcel Duchamp, the French Dadaist painter and conceptual artist, lived in New York from 1942 until his death in 1968.

Celebrated poet Henry Wadsworth Longfellow (1807-1882), of French descent, was perhaps best known for his epic *Song of Hiawatha*, published in 1855. John Greenleaf Whittier (1807-1892) became a prominent abolitionist as well as poet. French American author and naturalist Henry David Thoreau (1817-1862) gained renown with the 1854 publication of *Walden*, a diary of his two years in the wilderness near Concord, Massachusetts. Two other respected French American writers were Edna St. Vincent Millay (1892-1950), who won the Pulitzer Prize in 1923 for *The Harp Weaver, and Other Poems*, and Stephen Vincent Benét (1898-1943), who won the 1929 Pulitzer Prize for his epic poem "John Brown's Body."

Among the French American actors to gain prominence in the United States were Leslie Caron (1931- ), Charles Boyer (1899-1978), and Claudette Colbert (1905- ). After making her American debut in 1924, Colbert won an Academy Award as best actress for her role in *It Happened One Night* in 1934. Actor Robert Goulet made his debut in the Broadway production of *Camelot* in 1960, and went on to appear in many feature films and receive both Tony and Emmy Awards. Composer Maurice Jarée won several Academy Awards for the musical scores he wrote for such classic American films as *Lawrence of Arabia*, *Dr. Zhivago*, *Grand Prix*, and *The Longest Day* in the 1960s. In sports, French American jockey Ron Turcotte rode the most famous American racehorse of all time, Secretariat, to victory in the Triple Crown of horse racing.

## EDUCATION

Thomas Gallaudet (1787-1851) founded the first American school for the deaf in Hartford, Connecticut, in 1817. He also established teachers' training schools and promoted advanced education for women. Gallaudet College, a national institute for the deaf, was established in Washington, D.C. in 1855. French American Edouard Seguin (1812-1880) was responsible for significant developments in the education of mentally retarded individuals. In 1842, Father Edward Sorin, a French priest, founded a seminary which later became the University of Notre Dame. Finally, James Bowdoin served as governor of Massachusetts and first president of the American Academy of Arts and Letters. He also founded Bowdoin College and established the Massachusetts Humane Society.

## GOVERNMENT

One of the most influential French Americans in the history of U.S. government was John Jay (1745-1829). Among his many contributions, Jay acted as president of the Continental Congress, negotiated the treaty with England that ensured American independence, and served as the first Chief Justice of U.S. Supreme Court.

## INDUSTRY

One of the most famous French Americans, partly due to the variety of his contributions, was Paul Revere (1735-1818). The son of Huguenot Apollos Revoire de Romagnieu, Revere led several protests against British rule of the American colonies, including the Boston Tea Party. He also made the legendary "midnight ride" to warn Massachusetts residents that British soldiers were approaching at the start the American Revolution. In his time, however, Revere was also known as a talented silversmith who developed a distinctly American style. He designed and engraved the plates for the first paper money in Massachusetts and established the first mill for rolling copper sheets. Pierre Faneuil, who belonged to a wealthy and influential family of merchants, donated to the city of Boston the public market and meeting place known as Faneuil Hall.

Eleuthère Irénée Dupont de Nemours (1772-1834), who was considered a radical in France, came to the United States after losing his publishing business during the French Revolution. He opened a gunpowder mill in 1799, which grew rapidly during the War of 1812. Eventually, under the management of his heirs, his holdings grew into the Dupont Chemical-General Motors complex, one of the largest industrial concerns in the world. In 1851, French American John Gorrie invented an ice machine and received the first U.S. patent for mechanical refrigeration. Philip Danforth Armour, whose Armour brand meats are still sold in the United States, first entered the meat-packing business in 1863. His contributions to the industry included the development of advanced slaughtering and modern refrigeration techniques.

## SCIENCE AND MEDICINE

Civil engineer Octave Chanute came to the United States from France at the age of six. He conducted numerous experiments in aeronautics and created the wing design that became the basis for the Wright Brothers' successful airplane. John J. Audubon (1785-1851), the son of a French immigrant who fought in the American Revolution, is remembered as America's premier naturalist. His comprehensive study *Birds in America,* which included over 1,000 illustrations drawn or painted by Audubon, appeared beginning in 1827. Matthew Fontaine Maury is credited as the founder of the modern science of hydrography. He was the first person to chart the flow of the Gulf Stream, to conduct deep-sea soundings, and to imagine the potential of a transoceanic cable. His best-known work, *The Physical Geography of the Sea,* was published in 1856. Marine explorer Jacques Cousteau (1910- ) contributed to the invention of the aqualung in 1943 and won an Academy Award in 1957 for his documentary film feature *The Silent World.*

In medicine, surgeon François Marie Provost performed the first successful cesarean sections in Louisiana in 1809. Alexis Carrel (1873-1944) became famous during his tenure at the Rockefeller Institute as the first doctor to sew blood vessels together, transplant animal organs, and keep human tissue alive in jars. He wrote the seminal work *Man, the Unknown,* and won the Nobel Prize for Medicine in 1912.

# MEDIA

## PRINT

### *France-Amérique.*

Published by Trocadero Publishing, Inc., this weekly periodical is a French language tabloid established in 1943 by prominent refugees. It covers news from France and Franco-American life in the United States.

**Address:** 330 West 42nd Street, Suite 2600, New York, New York, 10036.
**Telephone:** (212) 629-4460.

### *France Today.*

Published ten times annually by France Press, Inc., *France Today* covers contemporary issues, events, trends, and travel in France.

**Address:** 1051 Divisadero, San Francisco, California, 94115.
**Telephone:** (415) 921-5100.

### *Journal Français d'Amérique.*

Published bi-weekly by France Press, Inc., this periodical covers French history, politics, culture, and travel.

**Contact:** Anne Prah Perochon, Editor.
**Address:** 1051 Divisadero, San Francisco, California, 94115.
**Telephone:** (415) 921-5100.

# ORGANIZATIONS AND ASSOCIATIONS

### Federation of French American Women (FFFA).

Also known as Federation Feminine Franco-Americaine. Founded in 1951, the 8,000-member FFFA promotes French culture; conducts an oral history program; sponsors French speaking contests, youth festivals, ethnic vacations, and an annual scholarship for outstanding students of French; compiles statistics; and maintains an archive and a hall of fame.

**Contact:** Marthe W. Whalon, President.
**Address:** 240 Highland Avenue, Fall River, Massachusetts, 02720.
**Telephone:** (508) 678-1800.

### French American Foundation (FAF).

Founded in 1976, FAF works to strengthen relations between the United States and France by creating opportunities for French and American pro-

fessionals to discuss problems of concern to both societies. FAF sponsors exchanges of specialists, internships, study tours, conferences, and fellowships, including the Tocqueville Grant Program for U.S. doctoral candidates and a continuing Chair in American Civilization at a university in Paris.

**Contact:** Diantha D. Schull, Executive Director.
**Address:** 41 East 72nd Street, New York, New York, 10021.
**Telephone:** (212) 288-4400.

### French Institute/Alliance Française (FIAF).

Formed in 1971 through the merger of Alliance Française de New York (founded 1898) and French Institute in the United States (founded 1911), FIAF encourages study of French language and culture among its 8,600 members and fosters friendly relations between French and American peoples. FIAF also offers a program of French lectures, films, concerts, theater, and art; operates a school of French for adults; and maintains a library of 40,000 volumes in French.

**Contact:** Jean Vallier, Director.
**Address:** 22 East 60th Street, New York, New York, 10022-1077.
**Telephone:** (212) 355-6100.

### National Association of Franco-Americans (AFA).

Also known as Assemblée Nationale des Franco-Americains. Founded in 1977, AFA works to provide a cultural identity and create a forum for the exchange of ideas among its 7,000 members, who share a French linguistic heritage or belong to a French speaking population in the United States. AFA also represents Franco-Americans in legislative matters, conducts research on Franco-American history and culture, and publishes a bimonthly newsletter.

**Contact:** Real Gilbert, President.
**Address:** 83 Amherst Street, P.O. Box 2000, Manchester, New Hampshire, 03105.
**Telephone:** (603) 627-0505.

### Societé Historique Franco-Americaine (SHFA).

Founded in 1899, SHFA studies and honors the role played by people of French ancestry in the evolution of the United States. SHFA also compiles documents, statistics, and archives; presents historical lectures; and sponsors research.

**Contact:** Marthe Biron Peloquin, President.
**Address:** 1 Leyland Road, Westford, Massachusetts, 01886.
**Telephone:** (508) 692-6370.

# MUSEUMS AND RESEARCH CENTERS

**The American and French Research on the Treasury of the French Language (ARTFL) Project.**

Cooperative effort of the University of Chicago and the Centre National de la Recherche Scientifique that is involved in the development of an online database covering French language and literature from the Middle Ages to the present, including more than 150 million words of major literary, technical, and philosophical texts.

**Contact:** Dr. Robert Morrissey, Director.

**Address:** Department of Romance Languages and Literature, 1050 East 59th Street, Chicago, Illinois, 60637.

**Telephone:** (312) 702-8488.

**The Center for French and Francophone Studies.**

Located at Louisiana State University, the center conducts research into French and francophone culture of the southern United States and the Caribbean, including studies of mores and customs, work, law and commerce, role of women, Creole languages, and literature.

**Contact:** Professor Edouard Glissant, Director.

**Address:** Department of French and Italian, Louisiana State University, 225 Prescott Hall, Baton Rouge, Louisiana, 70803.

**Telephone:** (504) 388-6589.

**The Centre for Research on French Canadian Culture.**

An integral unit of the University of Ottawa, the center conducts research into all aspects of French culture in Canada and North America, including history, literature, fine arts, social sciences, and education. It also maintains a reference library of 5,200 books and an archive containing manuscripts, photographs, audio- and videotapes, and periodicals that is open to the public.

**Contact:** Yolande Grise, Director.

**Address:** Lamoureux Hall, Room 274, 145 Jean-Jacques Lussier Street, Ottawa, Ontario, Canada, K1N 6N5.

**Telephone:** (613) 564-6847.

**The Centre for the Study of the Language, Art, and Culture of Francophones in North America.**

An integral unit of Laval University, the center maintains a folklore archive center containing 10,000 iconographic records and 200,000 documents of songs, legends, and memoirs concerning French culture and identity in North America.

**Contact:** Jocelyn Letourneau, Director.

**Address:** Pavillon Charles De Koninck, Cite universitaire, Quebec, Canada, G1K 7P4.

**Telephone:** (418) 656-5510.

**The Henri Peyre Institute for the Humanities.**

An integral unit of the graduate school of the City University of New York, the institute conducts research into French literature, philosophy, politics, film, and the arts with the support of the French government.

**Contact:** Dr. John W. Kneller, Co-director.

**Address:** 33 West 42nd Street, New York, New York, 10036.

**Telephone:** (212) 790-4481.

# SOURCES FOR ADDITIONAL STUDY

Bernstein, Richard. "The Myth of the Anti-American," *Fragile Glory: A Portrait of France and the French* New York, Knopf, 1990.

Brasseaux, Carl A. *The "Foreign French": Nineteenth-Century French Immigration into Louisiana*. Lafayette: University of Southwestern Louisiana, Center for Louisiana Studies, (n.d.).

Duroselle, Jean-Baptiste. "The Hereditary Enemy," *France and the United States: From Beginnings to Present*, translated by Derek Cotton. Chicago: University of Chicago Press, 1976.

Harris, Jonathan. *The Land and People of France*. New York: Lippincott, 1989.

Maisel, Albert Q. "The French," *They All Chose America*. New York: Thomas Nelson, 1955.

Nasatir, Abraham P. *French Activities in California*. Stanford: Stanford University Press, 1945.

Pula, James S. *The French in America, 1488-1974: A Chronology and Fact Book*. Dobbs Ferry, New York: Oceana, 1975.

Robbins, Albert. *Coming to America: Immigrants from Northern Europe*. New York: Delacorte Press, 1981.

# FRENCH-CANADIAN AMERICANS

by
Marianne
Fedunkiw

## OVERVIEW

Canada, with an area encompassing just over six million square miles, is the largest country in the world. This American neighbor to the north is bordered on the other three sides by oceans: the Pacific to the west, the Atlantic to the east, and the Arctic to the north. At 5,525 miles, the border with the United States is the longest unde-fended border in the world.

More than half of the 26.9 million people in Canada are concentrated in the corridor between Windsor, Ontario, and Québec City, Québec. Much of the remaining population live in the southern areas of each of the nation's ten provinces and two territories. The country's largest cities are Toronto, with 3.8 million residents, Montréal with 3.1 million, and Vancouver with 1.6 million. Although there are French Canadians in each of the provinces, by far the greatest number can be found in the province of Québec. In 1991, 81 percent of the population of Québec cited French as their "mother tongue" (the first language spoken as a child and still understood), compared to about nine percent for English. The next-highest concentration of French-speaking Canadians is in New Brunswick (33 percent). All of the remaining provinces reported figures of less than five percent, ranging from 0.4 to 4.6 percent. Overall, 6.5 million

Canadians, or 24 percent of the population in 1991, reported French as their "mother tongue." English-speaking Canadians numbered 16.5 million, or almost 61 percent of the total population.

There is also a strong and growing trend of bilingualism in Canada. According to the 1986 census, 16 percent of the population spoke both English and French, again with the province of Québec leading the way. In Québec almost 60 percent of anglophones, more than 30 percent of francophones, and close to half of all allophones (those whose mother tongue is neither English nor French) were bilingual. For comparison, outside Québec only about five percent of anglophones and 80 percent of francophones were bilingual.

Québec was by far the leading point of departure for French-Canadian immigration to the United States, although there were those who travelled south from Nova Scotia, New Brunswick, Manitoba, and Ontario. Québec is the largest province, making up almost 16 percent of Canada's total area and over one-fourth of its population. The provincial motto is *Je me souviens* (I remember), and the flower is the fleur-de-lis. Both motto and flower are featured prominently on the provincial coat of arms.

## HISTORY

The man who is credited with discovering the Canadian mainland was French explorer Jacques Cartier (1491-1557). He was seeking gold and riches via the famed Northwest Passage to the East, but reached Newfoundland instead in May 1534. He made another journey to Canada in 1535 and, unlike earlier explorers, continued west along the St. Lawrence River as far as modern-day Québec City, and then pressed on even farther to the future site of Montréal. This first foray into the interior was difficult—particularly because of the harsh winter conditions in Québec City and the rampant scurvy that killed many men. The remainder were said to be saved by a native tea made from the bark of the white spruce tree.

Cartier's third voyage to Canada was a failure in terms of establishing a settlement. Permanent settlement would have to wait until the fur trade gave reason to send more than the occasional fishing vessel. Samuel de Champlain (1567-1635) finally established the first trading post on the site of Québec City in 1608. Champlain, too, had sought the Northwest Passage, but he soon realized that beaver pelts would be responsible for the

survival of any settlements. He set up a system of company monopolies to systematically hunt and sell pelts and, in exchange for 300 settlers coming to the new land annually, to serve as the area's government from 1627 until 1642.

Unfortunately, Champlain's early settlement was attacked by English and Iroquois Confederacy rivals. The Catholic church, an integral part of French settlement, also suffered during the mid-seventeenth century at the hands of those opposed to French colonization. Groups such as the Jesuit missionaries, who were sent to convert the natives, were often attacked, and many missionaries and their followers were tortured and killed.

In addition to founding Québec, Champlain ventured into northern New York (he discovered the lake named for him in 1609), and explored the Atlantic coast as far as Massachusetts, including many of the larger rivers in Maine. However, Champlain's efforts to establish a successful French colony were thwarted by weather, battles with the English and certain native groups, and limited support from France. He died in Québec in 1635, at the age of 68.

## NEW FRANCE

For all of the hardships, the King of France, Louis XIV, did not give up. In 1665 he sent two ships to Québec containing the first regular troops to be sent to Canada, in addition to Alexandre de Prouville, the Marquis de Tracy (1596-1670), who was made lieutenant-general for all French possessions in North America. The government changed from Champlain's company monopolies to a Sovereign Council composed of the governor of New France, a bishop, and an intendant—the latter being the chief representative of royal power in a French colony. France shipped boatloads of *demoiselles bien choisies* (women of good health and upbringing), or *filles du roi* (king's girls), to raise the numbers and help settle New France. Jean Talon (1626-1694), the first intendant of New France, was instrumental in doubling the population between 1666 and 1678, to 7,605 settlers. He was joined in his efforts by the first bishop, François de Montmorency-Laval (1623-1708), who established a seminary that would become the University of Laval, and the governor of New France, Louis de Buade, Comte de Frontenac (1622-1698).

Talon also successfully implemented the seignorial system, in which feudal land tenures were granted to settlers free of charge in exchange for clearing the land and pledging loyalty to the King of France. The seigneur would, in turn, subdivide his acreage to tenants who paid a nominal rent, cleared, and farmed the land. These *habitants* were the first French Canadians. Soon the settlements had, at their center, a parish church and an established *curé* (priest) to meet their religious needs. In addition to the *habitants*, there were the *coureurs de bois*, traders who negotiated for furs with the Indians in the upper reaches of the Ottawa River and in the Great Lakes.

### SETTLEMENTS OUTSIDE QUÉBEC

The French settled in other parts of North America as well. By the Treaty of Utrecht (1713), France ceded Hudson Bay, Newfoundland, and Acadia to England. The French, however, retained control of present-day Cape Breton Island on the east coast of Nova Scotia where they built the fortress of Louisburg (1720-1740) to defend its remaining territory. In addition to Acadia, or the Maritime provinces of Canada, the French could be found in the coastal region of northern Maine. The first Acadian settlement was established in 1604 by Pierre du Gua, Sieur de Monts at St. Croix Island in the Bay of Fundy. In 1755, 6,500 Acadians were deported to the American colonies of the Atlantic Seaboard for having refused to take an oath to the king of England. Many of them would later find their way to Louisiana where they became known as Cajuns, a derivation of the word Acadian. Other early French towns in the United States included Detroit, Michigan, founded by Antoine de Lamothe Cadillac (1658-1730) in 1701. Cadillac also served as colonial governor of the Louisiana territory.

Finally, outside of Québec, the major concentration of French settlers was in what are now Louisiana, Mississippi, Missouri, and Illinois. The Louisiana Territory was claimed for France in 1682 and named by explorer Robert Cavelier, Sieur de la Salle (1643-1687), after King Louis XIV. French forts along the Mississippi River spread northward from New Orleans. A pair of French Canadians founded and helped to colonize this southern French territory. Pierre le Moyne d'Iberville (1661-1706) established the city of Biloxi, Mississippi, in 1699, and Jean-Baptiste le Moyne de Bienville, established New Orleans in 1718. In 1803 the United States bought the land, which spread from the Mississippi River to the Rocky Mountains, from France for $15 million in the Louisiana Purchase.

There are many other place names in the United States that tell the tale of French influence and settlement. The state of Maine is said to have been named for the province of Mayne in France, and Vermont comes from the French words *vert mont*, which mean "green mountain." Duluth, Minnesota, is named for Daniel Greysolon, Sieur Du Lhut (1636-1710), who won the Lake Superior and upper Mississippi region for France. Likewise, Dubuque, Iowa, is named for Julien Dubuque (1762-1810), a pioneer settler of Iowa. Vestiges of the French connection remain in Minnesota's motto, *L'Étoile du Nord* (The star of the north).

### WAR WITH THE ENGLISH

The English, French, and Spanish all wanted to claim North America for their own. After a series of smaller skirmishes, the French and Indian Wars of 1689-1763 (between the French and the English) finally led to the fall of the French colonies. These battles, offshoots of various European wars, culminating in the Seven Years' War, saw the French and native peoples aligned against the British and their American colonists. In 1745 English forces captured the fort at Louisburg. (It was returned to France in 1748.) The most renowned battle, however, took place on the Plains of Abraham in modern-day Québec City in 1759. By the time the assault was over, both the French General, Louis-Joseph de Montcalm (1712-1759), and the British commander, Brigadier General James Wolfe (1727-1759), lay dead on the battlefield. The Treaty of Paris was signed in 1763 and France ceded her Canadian and American territories east of the Mississippi to England, as well as much of French Louisiana to Spain as compensation for Florida, which Spain yielded to Great Britain. This temporarily ended immigration from France to the Canadian colonies—the French numbered around 60,000 in 1763. During the American Revolution, some French Canadians moved to the United States to escape British rule, while many American Loyalists (who were British sympathizers) were granted land in Québec and the Maritime Provinces.

In recognition of the differing interests of English and French Canadians, what are now the provinces of Ontario and Québec became Upper Canada and Lower Canada, respectively, in 1791. Lower Canada had its own legislature, and French Canadians were allowed to practice their Roman Catholic religion. Nevertheless, tensions culminated in a revolt in 1837, when Britain tried to unite the two Canadas. After the rebellion was quelled, the two halves were successfully joined in 1840. Many of the French rebels fled to the United States, particularly to New England. Finally, the Dominion of Canada was established in 1867.

## THE RIEL REBELLION

The battle to maintain French Canadian culture and language in a land under British rule also surfaced outside of Québec. Resentful of the encroaching power of the English from the East, Louis Riel led a group of French Canadian Métis (individuals who are part French and part American Indian) settlers in an attack on Upper Fort Garry, the main camp of the Hudson Bay Company, in 1869. Riel was one-eighth native Canadian and seven-eighths French Canadian, and his Métis followers were of similarly mixed native and French ancestry. They captured the fort and used it as leverage to bargain for special rights for the French and the Métis in Manitoba.

Riel's actions—including the execution of Thomas Scott, a Protestant who fought the French Canadians and Métis—led to a growing hatred on the part of the English in the East. Although Manitoba entered the Canadian confederation in 1870, Riel was banished from Canada in 1875. He settled in Montana temporarily, but returned to Canada in 1884 to participate in the fight for French Canadian and Métis independence. He was charged with treason and later executed for his part in the Saskatchewan Rebellion of 1885.

## MODERN-DAY FRENCH CANADA

French Canadians continued to resent having to subordinate themselves to British rule throughout the twentieth century. When World War I broke out in 1914, French Canadians fought against conscription to fight in what they perceived to be Britain's war. French-speakers also fought to have their culture and language recognized and maintained. The 1960s saw a resurgence in the "Quiet Revolution" to preserve "Québec for the French Canadians." In 1976, the Parti Québecois (PQ), a group of militant separatists, was elected to national office for the first time. Their leader was René Lévesque (1922-1987). The year after gaining power, the PQ declared French to be the official language of the province of Québec, but this was overturned by the Supreme Court of Canada in 1979.

A number of referenda have been taken in Québec to gauge popular support for the idea of separating from Canada. In 1980 the vote was against separating, but just a year later the province refused to acknowledge the new Canadian constitution. To address this issue, the premiers of the provinces met in 1987 and drew up the Meech Lake Accord (named for the site of the meetings). The Accord recognized Québec as a "distinct society," but changes to the constitution were not forthcoming, since many English Canadians were opposed to special treatment for Québec. The Accord failed to be ratified by all the provinces. In 1994 Québec once again voted in favor of the PQ, which has renewed its call for independence. Separatism, therefore, remains by far the most significant issue facing French Canadians in Québec during the later decades of the twentieth century.

## EARLY SETTLEMENT IN THE UNITED STATES

Exploration by the French was not limited to Canada. Jesuit missionaries travelled south along the Mississippi River, and in 1673 Louis Joliet (1648-1700) and Jesuit Priest Jacques Marquette (1637-1675) explored the Mississippi River. Robert Cavelier, Sieur de la Salle (1643-1687), discovered the mouth of the Mississippi in 1682.

## MAJOR IMMIGRATION WAVES: 1830-1870

Small groups or individuals of French Canadian descent have decided to settle in the United States since the major periods of exploration in the seventeenth century. Some fled the aftermath of the Patriote Rebellion of 1837, when hostility toward the French was high. The large number who crossed the border in the nineteenth century, particularly to the New England states, made their choice to seek a better life. These were predominantly young adults, some with families and others who were single. Traditionally, French-Canadian Americans had large families, and these numbers, coupled with dismal economic conditions, drove them south. Some estimates put the extent of the migration at 600,000, which had the effect of draining Canada of a generation.

Work in textile mills and the logging industry—anything besides the backbreaking farm work in Québec—was what drew them. For example, six mills opened in the Lewiston area of the state of Maine alone between 1819 and 1869. When they did settle, French-Canadian Americans sought to build a sense of community much like what they were used to "back home"—centered about a parish church and school, thus combining both the nuclear family and the extended family of the ethnic community. By 1850 about 20,000 French Canadians had settled in the New England area, with the majority living in Vermont. By 1860 there were another 18,000, including clusters in Massachusetts, Rhode Island, and New Hampshire.

### THE WAVE CONTINUES: 1865-1920

The influx of French Canadians in the years following the American Civil War resulted from the initiative of American businessmen to expand the textile and shoe industries. Although the French Canadian population was largest in Vermont throughout the 1850s and 1860s, since 1870 Massachusetts has claimed the majority. In his book *The French-Canadian Heritage in New England,* Gerard J. Brault notes that the French Canadians "have the distinction of being the only major ethnic group to have immigrated to the United States in any significant number by train." Most French Canadians settled in a circular pattern around Boston—in towns such as Lewiston, Maine, Manchester, New Hampshire, and Lowell, Massachusetts, to the north; Worcester and Holyoke, Massachusetts, to the west; and Woonsocket, Rhode Island, and Fall River, Massachusetts, to the south. New York State also attracted some settlers as did the Midwestern states of Michigan, Illinois, and Minnesota. The majority of Franco-American settlements were established from the 1860s to the 1880s, though some areas of Vermont had high numbers of French-Canadian Americans as early as 1815.

Québec did not enjoy losing its youth. Starting in 1875, the Canadian government made fairly successful efforts to bring them back by offering either free or cheap land. In fact, up to half of those who had travelled south returned to Canada by 1900. In the first two decades of the twentieth century, recessions in the United States and relative prosperity meant that immigration to the United States fell off from previous years and some French Canadians returned home.

French Canadian settlers in the United States maintained a high level of concentration and a low level of mobility. By 1900 towns such as Woonsocket, Rhode Island (60 percent French-Canadian American), and Biddeford, Maine (also at 60 percent), were very much French Canadian. The most outstanding example is the area in Maine, along the Canadian frontier, known as the St. John Valley, which was almost entirely Franco-American. This level of concentration heightened the sense of community for the new immigrants and facilitated getting French Canadian priests to serve the thriving parishes. Spiritual guidance and a sense of community became all the more important because, for those who toiled in tedium at the mills, "home" was no longer fresh air and open land but crowded, dingy tenement houses.

### 1920 TO 1960: EDUCATION KEEPS THINGS ALIVE

According to *The Canadian Born in the United States,* a book published in 1943 using American census data, 47 percent of those reporting themselves as "French Canadian born" immigrated to the United States earlier than 1900. Almost 16 percent of those in the United States through the year 1930 came from 1901 to 1910, while about ten percent came between 1920 and 1930.

The 1920s and 1930s were decades of strength for French-Canadian Americans—organizations had been established, French-language newspapers were thriving, and there were successful battles against attempts to abolish teaching in French. Mount Saint Charles Academy, a Franco-American diocesan high school in Woonsocket, Rhode Island, was established in 1924 and hailed as a strong academic school. Assumption College in Worcester, Massachusetts, continues to offer Franco-American studies as well as French-language instruction. Founded in 1904, it was built upon the model of the French Canadian *collège classique,* in which liberal arts were taught with traditional values and Catholic doctrine.

Elementary schools were set up in great numbers in the 1920s and 1930s. These were parochial schools, supported by the parishes, and they offered a half-day of exposure to the French language and culture. By the 1960s, however, these schools, faced with the increased cost of having to pay lay teachers, were forced to close.

Maintaining French identity became more of a challenge after World War II. The initial immigrants had established a vibrant community of

French-language parishes, schools, press, and fraternal organizations, but the group was slowly assimilating and there was no large wave of immigration to keep up the enthusiasm. Immigration to the United States dropped off after the Great Depression of the 1930s. At the same time, many French-Canadian Americans took advantage of the proximity of their home country and lived where the economic conditions or political situation was better for them.

The French were also regarded differently in Canada than in the United States—in Canada they represented one of the two founding nations, while in the United States they were just one of many ethnic groups to arrive in America after much of the country had been settled. After World War II, the original incentives to remain a tight community faded away. More French-Canadian Americans had the opportunity to get an education, for example, and their economic situations improved so that they no longer had to huddle in tenement houses while working long, hard hours in the textile and shoe mills. As a result, many began to drift outside of traditional Franco-American enclaves. For example, most of the once-numerous French-speaking parochial schools near Albany, New York, had ceased to exist by the 1960s, having been demolished for urban renewal or sold to other denominations.

This trend reversed in the 1970s and 1980s, however, with a move toward reviving French Canadian traditions and language. Many books have been written, in both English and French, on the Franco-American experience, and a number of historical centers, such as the French Institute at Assumption College in Worcester, Massachusetts, support Franco-American studies.

## SETTLEMENT PATTERNS IN 1990

Historically, most of the French Canadian immigrants settled in the New England states, geographically closest to the province of Québec. Some, however, travelled further to settle in Illinois, Minnesota, New York, Wisconsin, Michigan, and even California. By 1990, the state with the highest number of French-Canadian Americans was Massachusetts, with 310,636, followed by Michigan with 174,138, California with 156,625, New York with 155,531, New Hampshire with 118,857, Connecticut with 110,426, Florida with 110,221, and Maine with 110,209. All other states have less than 100,000.

Although California ranks third, the Northeast predominates as home to French-Canadian Americans—that region alone makes up 45 percent of the total of 2.16 million who cited French Canadian ancestry in the 1990 census. This total is a small percentage of the American population—just under one percent of the total 248.7 million—but it ranks French-Canadian Americans at sixteenth on a tally of the most frequently reported ancestry groups. Franco-American New England is often divided into three regions: central and southeastern New England, which includes southern Maine; western Vermont and upper New York State; and northern Maine, particularly the area known as the St. John Valley.

It is interesting to note that the number of individuals citing French Canadian as their ancestry for the 1990 census was substantially larger than for the census a decade earlier. One possible explanation cited by census takers was that French Canadian was listed among sample response categories—intended to help those who were uncertain of their ethnic origin—in 1990, but not in 1980.

# ACCULTURATION AND ASSIMILATION

## TRADITIONS, CUSTOMS, AND BELIEFS

French Canadian life, in Canada and in the United States, centered around the community—first that of the family (which tended to be large), and then that of the larger French-speaking community. One thing French-Canadian Americans had in common with their French Canadian ancestors was resistance to other ethnic influences. In Canada, French-speakers long opposed all things British, and in the United States, Irish or English Americans often viewed the newest immigrants as interlopers. This lack of acceptance helped to draw Franco-Americans closer together and resulted in maintaining traditions, customs, and language through the generations. Many of the traditions and beliefs are also tied to a strong sense of religion. To be a Franco-American immigrant was to be a strict Catholic, especially for the early settlers.

## PROVERBS

Many French Canadian proverbs can be interpreted as similar to those found today in English, although several are French Canadians in origin. Some well-known examples include: Each to their own taste; God dictates and women decide; Better to prevent than to heal; If the young knew and if the old could...; To leave is to die a little; Speech is silver, but silence is golden; Better late than never; Slow but sure; After the storm comes good weather; Tell me with whom you associate, and I will tell you who you are; and, One you have is worth more than two you think you may get.

## CUISINE

French Canadian farmers ate hearty, simple meals. Breads and other carbohydrates were popular and readily available. Breakfast items included pancakes, fried eggs, salt pork spread on slices of bread, coffee, and tea. Soup, made from peas, cabbage, or barley, was a staple for lunch and dinner meals; also on the daily menu might be potatoes, bread and butter covered in maple syrup, pork, and seasonal vegetables. In the Roman Catholic tradition, no meat was served on Fridays.

More elaborate meals were prepared for special religious holidays and celebrations. *Tourtière* (pork and spice pie), *cretons* (pork terrine), *ragoût boulettes* (a stew of chicken, beef, or veal), *boudin* (blood sausage) and sugar pies are some of the dishes associated with French Canadians. In fact, one French Canadian dish, *poutine* (french fries covered with gravy and cheese curds) is now being served in North American fast-food restaurants.

## TRADITIONAL COSTUMES

Traditional French Canadian costumes harken back to the days when the *coureurs de bois* hunted for beaver pelts and the *voyageurs* explored Canada. Most recognizable were the brightly colored, woven sashes, or *ceintures fléchées*.

As Brault explains, more common were the clothes worn by the farmers. They wore flannel shirts over loose-fitting pants fashioned of *droguet*, or drugget, a durable and coarse woolen fabric. The pants would be held up by suspenders or a broad leather belt. On his feet, a man would wear stockings and moccasin-style boots. To combat the cold, the French Canadian farmer would add a vest or sweater, a *tuque* (woollen cap), and an overcoat made of wool or animal skins fastened about his waist with a *ceinture flechee*.

Women made many of their materials, such as the drugget. They, too, would wear woolen stock-

ings and moccasins in addition to a flannel skirt over a heavy slip or *jupon*, as well as a long-sleeved bodice and sturdy apron. In the winter, women would wear heavier blouses and skirts, shawls, and a cotton or woollen *capuche* on their heads to keep warm. Since most French-Canadian Americans today live in towns or cities rather than on farms, these clothes are worn only on festive cultural occasions. Part of the assimilation process was to adopt clothing that was "American."

## FRANCO-AMERICAN SONGS AND DANCES

Rounds were a popular form of song for French Canadians. Round dances, in which the participants, often children, danced in a circle making certain actions as they sang, were also popular.

Among the most popular traditional folk songs were those that told stories of settlers, voyageurs, or kings, and courtships between maidens and young men. For example, "À Saint Malo" told the tale of ladies and sailors who argued over the price of grain until the women eventually won and got the grain for nothing. Perhaps the best-known song is "Alouette," which came from France but is identified with Québec. It can be sung as a round and tells the tale of a lark.

Traditional French Canadian dances include the *quadrille* and the *gigue* (or jig). Square dances, with many of the calls in French, also became popular in the twentieth century. All of these involved musical accompaniment, with fiddles, harmonicas, and later accordions. As part of the tight family and community structures in French Canadian life, music and dancing was featured at any celebration.

## HOLIDAYS CELEBRATED BY FRENCH-CANADIAN AMERICANS

Some of the major holidays are part of the Christmas season, from Advent (a time of fasting and prayer) to Christmas and its midnight mass followed by a *réveillm* (a repast designed to "wake you up"). There is also the feast on New Year's Day (a holy day of Obligation for Catholics that includes family visits and the *bénédiction paternelle* in which the father blesses all of his children and grandchildren) and finally Epiphany (called *la Fête des Rois*) on January 6. For the evening meal on January 6 it was a French Canadian tradition to serve the Twelfth Night Cake (*le gâteau des Rois*—"the cake of kings"). Inside the cake were a pea and a bean; whoever got the slice with the bean was deemed king and whoever found the pea was named queen. *La Chandeleur* or Candlemas, another winter holiday held on February 2, included a candlelit mass and pancake parties in the evening.

In addition to the religious liturgies and worship of Holy Week and Easter, there is Saint-Jean-Baptiste day on June 24. John the Baptist was declared the patron saint of French Canadians by the Pope in 1908. A society was established in the saint's name in 1834 to promote patriotic celebrations. November featured both All Saints' Day and Saint Catherine's Day, during which it was a French Canadian custom to pull taffy.

## HEALTH AND MENTAL HEALTH ISSUES

There are no ailments specific to French Canadians in the United States, with the exception of occupational maladies related to the fact that many of the newly arrived immigrants worked in dusty, grimy mills or quarries. Dr. Paul Dufault (1894-1969) and Dr. Gabriel Nadeau (b. 1900), both French Canadian immigrants, were leaders in the treatment of tuberculosis, spending the better part of their careers at the Rutland, Massachusetts State Hospital, the first State Hospital for tuberculosis patients in the United States.

# LANGUAGE

French belongs to the Latin and Romance group of Indo-European languages. In *The French Canadian Heritage in New England*, Brault notes that "correct" speech was a sign of status, but that did not stop the evolution of syntactical and phonological differences. One French Canadian "dialect," called *joual*, is synonymous with the lower classes, or at least with loose pronunciation. Brault goes on to summarize some of the most obvious phonetic differences in the French spoken by French Canadians in Canada and the United States compared to France. A computerized dictionary called *Trésor de la langue française au Québec* (*The Treasures of the French Language in Québec*) documents Canadian French.

## GREETINGS AND OTHER POPULAR EXPRESSIONS

Some of the most common French Canadian sayings are similar to those of France. Greetings and popular expressions include: *Bonjour,* or *Salut*— each of which can be translated as "hello" depending on what degree of formality is intended; *Au revoir*— Good bye; *Bonne chance*—Good luck; *Merci*—Thank you; *De rien* or *Il n'ya pas de quoi*—You're welcome, or (literally in the first case), It was nothing; *Félicitations*—Congratulations; *Bonne Fête* or *Joyeux Anniversaire*—Happy Birthday; *Bonne Année*—Happy New Year; *Joyeux Noël*—Merry Christmas; and *À votre šanté*—To your health.

# FAMILY AND COMMUNITY DYNAMICS

The family is at the center of the French-Canadian American's world. In previous decades this meant not only the nuclear family but the extended clan who would come together to eat, play card games, sing, drink, and dance.

## INTERACTIONS WITH OTHER ETHNIC MINORITIES

Some tension has existed historically between French immigrants and French Canadians because, while French immigrants tended to be well-educated, most of the first French Canadian immigrants were farmers and received little if any formal education.

Although the French-Canadian Americans worked with Irish Americans in the mills and had a common religion in Catholicism, the language barrier and the sense that the Irish were established immigrants, having come a generation earlier, led to tension. In his 1943 account of New England immigrants, *The Shadows of the Trees*, Jacques Ducharme writes that "many were to feel the *caillou celtique*, or 'Kelly Biscuit,' for in the early days the Irish were not averse to violence by way of showing their distaste for the newcomers." There was opposition to French teaching in schools, and it spilled over into the workplace, where there was favoritism based upon background, and the church, where it took years before American bishops brought French-speaking priests to Franco-American parishes.

There was also rampant prejudice against Catholics and Jews in New England in the 1920s. By 1925 the Ku Klux Klan numbered more than half a million. It supported the Protestants in the area and their efforts to "take back what was their own." This resulted in cross burnings and hooded Klansmen fighting with French-Canadian Americans throughout New England. Many French Canadian immigrants hid in their houses while the Klan stormed through the streets.

## WEDDINGS

The tradition for immigrants at the turn of the century was a conservative courtship where a potential suitor might visit a young girl's home on Sunday evenings to spend time with the entire family. After a series of visits that became more private—although always in public pursuits, such as buggy rides or swinging on the porch—the young man, or *cavalier,* would ask the father for the hand of his *blonde* in marriage. Often the young man was at least 21, although his fiancée could be as young as 16.

The wedding itself was a festive affair marked by feasting and dancing. In parishes, the bans would be read for three consecutive Sundays, naming the intention of that particular couple to marry. With all parishioners being so informed, if any impediments to the upcoming marriage existed, they could be announced then. Brault notes that in rural Québec, the bans might only be read once, because this procedure was viewed as embarrassing to the couple.

Much like today, the groom was given a stag party in his honor. In this case it was called the *enterrement de la vie de garçon,* or "burial of the bachelor life," and was symbolized by a mock funeral in which the groom lay on planks while a eulogy, sincere or in fun, was read over him. The bride, in turn, might be honored with a shower.

Wedding attire was influenced by the fashion of the time. The elaborateness of the ceremony was dictated by the wealth of the participants. The church bells pealed for the morning nuptial mass and a reception followed. Honeymoons often meant a few days' stay at a relative's home. Brault says that after marriage, French Canadian women were often expected to dress more conservatively and in darker colors, while men displayed their marital status by growing a mustache or wearing a gold watch and chain. Today, many of the marriage practices reflect a greater assimilation into American culture as well as a move away from a predominantly rural way of life.

## BAPTISMS

Until recently, French-Canadian Americans tended to have large families, often with ten or more children. Baptisms, as a religious rite, were an integral part of life. As Brault describes, if there was any risk that the newborn might not survive, the priest was called immediately to baptize the baby. Otherwise the ceremony was performed within the first week. Traditionally, boys were given, as part of their name, Joseph, and girls given the name Marie, in addition to being named by the parents. Often one of the other given names was that of a godparent.

The role of godparent, as in other cultures, is filled by close relatives or friends. They are responsible for bringing up the child if the parents die, part of which includes ensuring that the child is brought up in the Catholic faith. After the baptismal ceremony, the parents, godparents, child, and guests returned to a family home for a celebratory meal. Godparents would bring gifts for the child, and, in the past, for the mother and the church sexton, who would ring the church bells to mark the occasion.

## FUNERALS

Brault states that French Canadians feared sudden death or *la mort subité* most because it meant there would be no time to prepare for death, particularly for the administering of the last rites by a priest. When a person died, the church sexton signalled the death by ringing the church bells. This, Brault says, not only told all those in the town that there had been a death, but also revealed who had died: one stroke signalled a child, two a woman, and three a man.

The wake took three days, during which visitors greeted the family in their home. Until it became the practice to carry out wakes in "funeral parlours," the dead were laid out in the family home. Flowers were not part of the setting, although it was customary to shroud the room in white sheets so it resembled a chapel and to hang a cross between a pair of candles at the person's head. The visitors came to pray with the family and gathered once an hour to recite the rosary.

After the wake, a morning funeral was held, complete with a mass in church, and then the body was taken to the cemetery for burial. The priest accompanied the family and other mourners and said a prayer as the casket was lowered into the burial plot. Everyone then returned to the family's home for a meal in honor of the dead person.

# RELIGION

Religion is at the heart of French Canadian life. While in Canada, French Canadians were staunch Roman Catholics; this did not change when they immigrated to the United States. In fact, as was true in Canada, the church was an integral part of the early settlements—often the priest acted as counselor in secular matters, in addition to spiritual leader. Some of the earliest parishes were established in the 1830s and 1840s in rural northern Maine. By the turn of the century, there were 89 Franco-American parishes.

In his book *Ethnic Diversity in Catholic America*, Harold J. Abramson states that the completeness with which French-Canadian Americans transplanted their religion, especially to the New England area, was partly due to being close to Canada. Basically, the immigrants set up the same sort of parish-centered social organization that had existed in the home country. In his book about Franco-American life in New England, *The Shadows in the Trees*, Jacques Ducharme wrote: "The Franco-Americans are profoundly attached to their parish church, and there one may see them every Sunday.... From Maine to Connecticut these churches stand, forming a forest of steeples where men, women and children come to pray in French and listen to sermons in French. When the tabernacle bell rings, know that it proclaims the presence of *le bon dieu*."

Despite their proximity to Canada, French Canadians in New England experienced many of the trials typical to new immigrants, including discrimination by religion and language. The church offered them a place where their language could be freely spoken and celebrated. But in the early days, mass was often conducted by priests who spoke little or no French. Because of this, many attendees could not understand sermons, risked getting their meatless days wrong, and gave little for special collections because they did not understand what they were for.

The fight for French masses began in earnest in the late nineteenth century. For example, in October of 1884 parishioners at the Notre-Dame-de-Lourdes Church in Fall River, Massachusetts, began a two-year struggle against the Irish American Bishop of Providence, Rhode Island, to gain a French-speaking priest after the death of their French Canadian pastor. Their battle successfully ended what became known as "the Flint Affair."

Often it was the Irish Americans who opposed French-language services. In May 1897, for example, French-Canadian Americans in North Brookfield, Massachusetts, wrote to the Papal Delegate to tell him that their Irish American priest would not allow religious services or teaching in French. It was not until 1903 that a French priest and French services were permitted. Such fights also went on in Rhode Island, Connecticut, and Maine communities. It was also a matter of some time before French Canadians assumed positions of power within the Catholic church. The first Franco-American bishop was Georges-Albert Guertin (1869-1931), named Bishop of Manchester in 1906. He was followed by, among others, Ernest J. Primeau (1960-1974) and Odore J. Gendreau (1975- ).

These battles with the Irish Americans over religious issues continued into the 1920s. One of the most notable was the "Sentinelle Affair" of 1924-1929. A group of French-Canadian Americans, most from Woonsocket, Rhode Island, had been concerned about their religion, language, and culture surviving in the United States. They resented the hierarchy of the Catholic church in the United States, which was mostly Irish, and militantly defended the Franco-American parochial schools and the fragile autonomy of the French-language parishes.

Religion played another role in Franco-American communities through religiously affiliated fraternal organizations. Like other ethnic groups, the French-Canadian Americans set these up to offer insurance as well as language and cultural activities to new and recent immigrants. The oldest of the two most prominent mutual benefit and advocacy organizations is the Association Canado-Américaine, founded in 1896, followed by the Union St. Jean Baptiste in 1900. Both still exist today, although the Union has since become affiliated with Catholic Family Life Insurance.

# EMPLOYMENT AND ECONOMIC TRADITIONS

Immigration to the United States in the late nineteenth and early twentieth centuries effectively drained Québec of a large number of its young

The majority of individuals in this photograph, taken around 1900, are French-Canadian American coal and ice workers in Manchester, New Hampshire.

adults. Economic times were tough in Canada, and the newly opened mills in New England offered employment for both women and men—although this was hard, back-breaking, and often unhealthy work. Many children joined the labor force in the mills as well. Women also earned money by taking in boarders. Another group of French Canadians settled near the forest of northern Maine to work in the logging industry.

Although the first major wave of immigrants was made up predominantly of farmers, mill workers, and lumbermen with little education, there was also a select group of educated individuals, such as priests, doctors, and lawyers who came to serve the needs of their people. Of course, as Franco-Americans became more established, the numbers of professionals grew. There is a rich history of French-language journalism, particularly in the nineteenth and early twentieth centuries. For example, in the early 1870s, Hugo Dubuque (1854-1928) of Fall River, Massachusetts, led the way in refuting Labor Commissioner Carroll D. Wright's description of French-Canadian Americans as "the Chinese of the Eastern States;" Dubuque became a Massachusetts Superior Court Justice after serving for ten years (1888-1898) in the Massachusetts House of Representatives. Another judge, Alfred J. Chretien, (b. 1900), who was born in Fall River, Massachusetts, attended Harvard University after spending his adolescence in Québec. After graduating, he established a law practice in Manchester, New Hampshire,

and went on to be named Chief Justice of the Manchester Municipal Court in 1940. He played an active role in the formation of the Legal Aid Society of New Hampshire and was a member of the National Council of Juvenile Court Judges.

A number of French-Canadian Americans have distinguished themselves in labor unions and syndicates. J. William Belanger (1902-c.1992), born in Newmarket, New Hampshire, began his working career at the age of 14 in the Hamlet Mills. As an employee of the Hope Knitting Company in Central Falls, Rhode Island, he founded a union affiliated with the American Federation of Labour (AFL) during the Great Depression, and later became director of the Textile Union of Massachusetts, affiliated with the Congress of Industrial Organizations (CIO). In 1948 he was elected president of the Massachusetts CIO.

The first financial institution controlled by French Canadians in New England, the Banque Coopérative Lafayette, was set up in 1894 in Fall River, Massachusetts. Not long afterwards, the first Franco-American Credit Union in the United States, La Caisse Populaire Sainte-Marie, opened in Manchester, New Hampshire on November 24, 1908. Credit Unions were founded in most of the important Franco-American centers of New England. Initially parish-based, they later became independent entities that did much to support small businesses and to encourage home ownership.

## POLITICS AND GOVERNMENT

In his study of Franco-American life in New England, Gerard J. Brault states Franco-Americans have supported the Democratic presidential candidate since the election of 1928 when the Catholic Al Smith was defeated by Herbert Hoover. Franco-Americans also voted for Franklin Delano Roosevelt, but by 1952 and 1956 most voted for the Republican Dwight D. Eisenhower. There are also regional trends: most today are Democrats, with the exception French-Canadian Americans in New Hampshire and Vermont, where many are "dyed-in-the-wool Republicans." The Franco-American elite has also supported Republican candidates in the past. Even the working class has voted the Republican ticket, as in Rhode Island, to elect one of their own, Aram Pothien, as governor or to distinguish themselves from the Irish who usually voted the Democratic ticket, as in Worcester, Massachusetts. Brault adds, however, that no recent comprehensive study has addressed the issue of historical voting patterns for the group at large. Patterns usually take into account religious and economic considerations, with French-Canadian Americans choosing the candidate who, on these two counts, is most supportive of their views.

In addition to being involved in local politics—Maine alone boasts of more than 500 Franco-American mayors and state legislators in a single century. According to Brault, there have been a number of Franco-Americans in state and federal politics as well. Aram J. Pothier (1854-1928), a Republican, was chosen governor of Rhode Island in 1908 and served two terms, from 1909 to 1915 and from 1925 to 1928. Subsequent Franco-American governors also served in Rhode Island, including Democrats Emery J. Sansoucy (1857-1936) from 1921 to 1923 and Philip W. Noël (1931- ) from 1973 to 1977.

On a federal level, Franco-American senator Félix Hébert (1874-1969), a Republican, was elected in 1928 and served until 1934. Jean-Claude Boucher (1894-1960) was also a senator. Born in Rivière-Ouelle, Québec, his family moved to Lewiston, Maine, around the turn of the century, and he was elected a senator from Maine in 1935. Journalist Antonio Prince (1894-1973) made a run for the senate in 1935 as a Democratic candidate, but was not successful. Georgette Berube of Lewiston, Maine, a member of the state legislature, also made a run in the Democratic primary of June 1982, but was defeated.

Among those who have been elected U.S. representatives, there have been three French-Canadian Americans from Rhode Island (Louis Monast from 1927-1929; Aime J. Forand with two terms, 1937-1939 and 1941-1961; and Fernand J. St. Germain from 1961-82) and two from New Hampshire (Alphonse Roy from 1938-1939 and Norman E. D'Amours from 1975-1984). Internationally, editor Elie Vézina (1869-1942) was named a special ambassador to Haiti by President Herbet Hoover as a member of a Commission of Inquiry in 1930. Vézina, born in Québec, founded the newspaper Le Devoir in Michigan. Franco-Americans were also named to consular posts in France; Alphonse Gaulin, Jr., (b. 1874) of Woonsocket, Rhode Island, was Consul to LeHavre in 1905 and to Marseilles in 1909, and Eugene-L.Belisle was named Consul to Limoges in 1906.

## MILITARY SERVICE

Franco-Americans have served in all of the major wars, including the American Revolution; some 800 French-Canadian Americans are believed to have fought for American independence. Rémi Tremblay (1847-1926) fought in the Civil War and wrote about his experiences in a novel entitled Un Revenant (1884). There are also many tales of French Canadians being tricked into enlisting in the Union Army. After being offered jobs in the United States and given gifts of money, many signed a document they could not read and travelled south only to find themselves put in uniform and bullied into taking part in the Civil War. For many who survived, it was a natural decision to stay in the United States, and if they were married, they sent for their families as soon as they were able.

One of the most famous images of World War II features a Franco-American, Private René A. Gagnon (1924-1979) of Manchester, New Hampshire, one of three raising the American flag on Mount Suribachi during the battle for Iwo Jima on February 19, 1945. It was captured on film by Associated Press photographer Joe Rosenthal. Gagnon survived the battle and returned from the war to settle in Hooksett, New Hampshire.

## RELATIONS WITH FRENCH CANADA

Because of the proximity of Canada—at least to the large pockets of French-Canadian Americans in New England—many French Canadians in the United States still have strong ties to their home country. However, family ties seem to diminish with each passing generation: many third- and fourth-generation French-Canadian Americans have lost touch with relatives who stayed in Canada. French-language newspapers and Franco-American studies programs help French-Canadian Americans keep abreast of what is going on in Québec.

# INDIVIDUAL AND GROUP CONTRIBUTIONS

## ACADEMIA

Will Durant (1885-1981), raised in Massachusetts and New Jersey, received his Ph.D. from Columbia University at the age of 32. He published the first installment of Story of Civilization in 1935, and the tenth volume, entitled *Rousseau and Revolution* (co-written with his wife Ariel), won the 1968 Pulitzer Prize for general nonfiction.

Maximilienne Tétrault (1884-1959) of Southbridge, Massachusetts, studied at the University of Boston and at the Sorbonne in Paris, after which she taught French at the University of Baltimore, at Notre-Dame in Indiana, and from 1936 to 1944 in Detroit. Her doctoral thesis dealt with the role of the press in the evolution of the Franco-Americans of New England.

Professor Joseph Medard Carrière (1902-1970), whose specific interest was in folklore, published, in 1937, *Tales from the Folklore of Missouri*. He was awarded the Chevalier de la Legion d'honneur by the French government in 1950.

Professor Gérard J. Brault (1929- ) was born in Chicopee Falls, Massachusetts. A specialist in the Middle Ages, he is also interested in the language and culture of Franco-Americans. In 1986 he published *The French-Canadian Heritage in New England*, an important English-language work on Franco-American life in the United States.

Armand Chartier (1938- ), born in New Bedford, Massachusetts, is a professor of French at the University of Rhode Island. He published *Historie des Franco-Américains de la Nouvelle-Augleteure* in 1991, a thorough compendium of facts and figures on Franco-Americans from 1775 to 1990.

Claire Quintal (1930- ) is a professor of French at Assumption College in Worcester, Massachusetts, as well as the founding director of its French Institute. A native of Central Falls, Rhode Island, she is a scholar of Franco-American, French, and French-Canadian culture. Under her direction, the Institute has organized 11 colloquia, publishing the proceedings of these between 1980 and 1995.

Eloise Brière, born in Northhampton, Massachusetts, in 1946, has taught at Rutgers University and the State University of New York in Albany. Among her published work is *The North American French Language in New York State* (1982) and *Franco-American Profiles* (1984).

### FILM, TELEVISION, AND THEATER

Hubert Prior "Rudy" Vallée (1901-1988) earned a doctorate from Yale but is best known for his film and stage career as a bandleader. In 1927 he created the Connecticut Yankees orchestra and later opened the New York cabaret club Villa Vallee. He starred in *The Vagabond Lover* (1939) and later on television. Born in Island Pond, Vermont, he was brought up in Westbrook, Maine, where he is buried in St. Hyacinthe cemetery.

Eva Tanguay (1878-1947), born in Marbletin, Québec, was brought up in Holyoke, Massachusetts. She starred for many years in the *Ziegfeld Follies*. Paul Bunyan (who had a blue bull named "Babe") was a French Canadian made famous by the loggers of Michigan. The "strong man" tradition was once very current throughout French North America. The best known of these were Joe Montferrand and Louis Cyr, who both performed in New England. The name Montferrand became synonymous with strength among Franco-Americans.

### JOURNALISM

Many Franco-Americans have had distinguished careers in journalism, particularly in the early years of immigration to the New England states, when many started up French-language publications. One such individual was Ferdinand Gagnon (1849-1886), often referred to as "the father of Franco-American journalism." Gagnon was born in Saint-Hyacinthe, Québec, and after studying at the seminary there, moved to Manchester, New Hampshire before settling in Worcester, Massachusetts. There he published *Le Travailleur*, the foremost newspaper of its day.

Born in Wottonville, Québec, Philippe-Armand Lajoie (1887-1964) moved to New England with his family in 1889. Lajoie became editor of Fall River's *L'Indépendant* in 1926, which later became one of the four best French-language dailies in New England. In addition to his writings, he was a noted composer of religious music.

Marthe Biron-Péloquin (1919- ) came from a family of journalists. Her father, Louis-Alphonse Biron (1861-1947), was born in Saint-Louis-de-Lotbiniere, Québec, but after moving to Lowell, Massachusetts, he founded *L'Impartial* in 1898 and later acquired *L'Étoile* (1939-1957), a local daily. Marthe wrote for *L'Étoile*, and served as an editor for *Bulletin de la Fédération féminine franco-américaine* (*Bulletin of the Federation of Franco-American Women*) from 1973 to 1986.

Alexandre Bélisle (1856-1923) founded *L'Opinion publique* (*Public Opinion*), in Worcester, Massachusetts, in 1893. Bélisle also published a history of the French-language press in 1911, called *Histoire de la presse franco-américaine*.

Born in L'Epiphanie, Québec, Élie Vézina (1869-1942) immigrated to Michigan in 1890 where he founded the weekly *Le Devoir* in Muskegon. Vézina then worked in Chicago for the *Courrier de l'Illinois*. In 1930 President Herbert Hoover named him to a special commission in Haiti.

Wilford Beaulieu (1900-1978) founded of *Le Travailleur* in Worchester, Massachusetts in 1931. The second newspaper in New England by that name, it honored the memory of Ferdinand Gagnon. A literary and cultural affairs weekly, the paper was an ardent voice in the cause of French *survivance* in New England. It ceased to be published after the death of its owner/publisher.

## LITERATURE

Among the best-known Franco-American authors is "Beat Generation" novelist Jean-Louis "Jack" Kerouac (1922-1969). In addition to *On the Road*, he profiles his youth spent in the French-speaking community of Lowell, Massachusetts, in books such as *Doctor Sax* (1959), *Visions of Gerard* (1963), and *Vanity of Duluoz* (1968). Another famous author is Grace (DeRepentigny) Metalious (1924-1964) of Manchester, New Hampshire, who wrote *Peyton Place* in 1956. The fiction best-seller was made into a film in 1957 and a long-running television series in the 1960s. Two of Metalious' other novels, *The Tight White Collar* (1960) and *No Adam in Eden* (1963), deal with working-class French Canadians in New England.

Josaphat Benôit (1900-1976), in addition to being editor of *L'Avenir national*, a paper in Manchester, New Hampshire, and co-founder of the paper *L'Action* in 1949, wrote a number of books dealing with Franco-Americans, such as *L'Âme franco-américaine* (1935), *Rois ou esclaves de la machine?* (1935), and *Catéchisme d'historie franco-américaine* (1939).

Georges-Alphonse Boucher was born in 1865 at Rivière-Bois-Clair, Québec. Trained as a physician, he settled in Brockton, Massachusetts, in 1890. His first work of poetry was titled *Ode à Québec*, which was followed by three editions of *Je me souviens* and then *Sonnets de guerre* (1943), inspired by World War II. Other works include *Chants du nouveau monde* and his memoirs, *Vie abrégée*, published after his death in 1956.

Rémi Tremblay (1847-1926) was author of *Un Revenant*, one of the earliest novels published by a Franco-American, which dealt with the Civil War battle of Cold Harbor. Rosaire Dion-Lévesque (1900-1974), another Franco-American poet, translated Walt Whitman's *Leaves of Grass*. Novelist and journalist Camile Lessard-Bissonette (b. 1883) was the author of *Canuck* (1936). Poet, novelist, and critic Louis Dantin (1865-1945), who was born Eugene Seers in Québec but later lived in Boston, wrote *Les Enfances de Fanny*.

Novelist Gérard Robichault, who spent his childhood and youth in Maine, writes such autobiographical novels as *Papa Martel* and *The Apple of His Eye*. Annie Prouex won the National Book Award (1993) and the Pulitzer (1994) for *The Shipping News*. The novel also received the Heartland Prize from the *Chicago Tribune* and the *Irish Times International* Fiction Prize. Prouex was awarded a Pen/Faulkner Award in 1993 for her first novel *Postcards*. Annie David Plante (1940- ), who was born in Providence, Rhode Island, is a prolific writer with nine novels to his credit. Robert B. Perreault, the only Franco-American to publish a French-language novel since 1938, wrote *L'Heritage* (1983). Playwright Grégoire Chabot and poets Paul P. Chassé and Normand C. Dubé are also worthy of mention.

## MUSIC

Composer Calixa Lavallée (1842-1891), born in Verchères, Québec, left for the United States at age 15, in 1857, to participate in the Civil War as part of the Fourth Rhode Island Regiment. After that he studied in Paris and, in 1879, became organist of the cathedral in Boston. Among his compositions are operas, marches, waltzes, and the music for the Canadian national anthem, "O Canada."

Opera singer Albaninée Emma Lajeunesse (1847-1930) moved to Plattsburgh, New York, from Chambly, Québec, in 1852, then back to Montréal before settling in Albany, New York, in 1864. She was a soloist, at age 18, at the cathedral in Albany and went on to sing at Covent Garden in London as well as touring Europe, Russia, Ireland, and the United States in various operatic roles. At the request of Edward VII, she sang at the funeral of Queen Victoria.

The Champagne brothers—Octave (1859-1941), Eusebe (1865-1929), and Philias (1871-1957)—played various instruments in local bands and orchestras in Lowell, Massachusetts where the family had settled. Masterful performers of French Canadian folk music, they also played their own compositions. Octave published and distributed the songs written by the other two.

Violinist Joseph-Émile Chambord Giguère (1877-c. 1957) was the son of French-Canadian musicians who moved to the United States around 1874. Giguère, who was born in Woonsocket, Rhode Island, studied in both Canada and the United States as well as at the Royal Conservatory in Brussels, Belgium. After returning from Europe, he toured North America extensively.

Montréal-born composer and musician Pierre-Amedee Tremblay (1876-c.1949) served as organist at cathedrals in Salt Lake City and Los Angeles. He composed the operetta *L'Intransigeant* and also published, in 1902, a collection of French Canadian folksongs, *Dix-huit chansons populaires du Canada*.

C. Alexander Peloquin (1918- ), born in Northbridge, Massachusetts, is a noted organist and composer of sacred music. He began his career in Woonsocket, Rhode Island, and has for more than 40 years been organist at the Catholic Cathedral in Providence, Rhode Island. Named Director of Choral Activities at Boston College in 1955, he also founded the Peloquin Chorale in Rhode Island after World War II.

### SCIENCE AND TECHNOLOGY

Inventor Victor Bélanger (1856-1918), the founder of the Worcester, Massachusetts, newspaper *Le Courrier de Worcester* is credited for developing a rotating coil for spinning cotton. Another inventor was John C. Garand (1888-1974). Born in St. Remi, Québec, Garand moved to Jewett City, Connecticut. He is credited with the design of the .30 caliber Springfield rifle, which was used by American troops during World War I. His M1 rifle, which eliminated manual operation of the bolt mechanism, was adopted as standard equipment by the Army, Navy, and Marines in 1936 and was a staple weapon during World War II and the Korean War.

### SPORTS

Napoléan ("Larry" or "The Big Frenchman") Lajoie (1875-1959), a member of the Cleveland Indians baseball team, was a contemporary of Ty Cobb. Lajoie still ranks as the player with the seventh-highest batting average in major league history, averaging .339 in his 21 years in the major leagues, which ended in 1919. He was elected to the Baseball Hall of Fame in 1937. Another Cleveland Indian was Louis Boudreau, born in Harvey, Illinois, in 1917. He was with the Cleveland team from 1938 to 1950, as both player and manager, during which time he was the youngest manager in the major leagues. Boudreau went on to play for and manage the Boston Red Sox (1950-1955) and then moved on to the Kansas City Athletics (1955-1957). He was nominated to the Hall of Fame in 1970. A third famous Franco-American in baseball is Leo Durocher (1905-1982), born in Springfield, Massachusetts. Durocher spent 41 years in the major leagues, first as a player and later as a manager. He led the Brooklyn Dodgers and then the New York Giants to three National League pennants in the years 1941, 1951, and 1954, and the Giants to a World Series victory in 1954.

Other Franco-American athletes include marathon runner and Olympic gold medalist Joan Benoit (1957- ); boxer George "Kid" Lavigne (1869-1936); and Henri Renaud, the first Franco-American to win the Boston Marathon on April 19, 1909.

### VISUAL ARTS

Sculptor Lucien Gosselin (1883-1940) was born in Whitefield, New Hampshire. The nephew of French-Canadian sculptor Louis-Philippe Hébert, he studied in Paris from 1911 to 1916 and is known for his statues, monuments, and designs for commemorative medals. Another artist of the period was Lorenzo de Nevers (1877-1967), born in Bai-du-Febure, Québec. He spent ten years in Paris (1902-1912) at the Ecole des Beaux-Arts and upon his return, he established his studio in Central Falls, Rhode Island, where his family had prospered in the furniture business. He is known for his religious paintings, portraits, and landscapes.

Born in Old Town, Maine, Bernard Langlais (1921-1977) is known for his large and somewhat whimsical carvings of animals. The Ogunquit Museum of American Art has three of his sculptures—"Seated Bear," "Horse in Field," and "Lion"—in its permanent collection. Another Franco-American sculptor, Armand Lammtague (c. 1940- ), who was born in Central Falls, Rhode Island, is known for his life-size statues of sports figures, especially Larry Bird, the basketball star, and Bobbie Orr of hockey fame.

Woodcarving is a celebrated art in Franco-American culture. One of the most famous woodcarvers was Adelard Côté (1889-1974), originally from St. Sophie, Québec. Côte moved to Biddeford, Maine, in his early twenties. Although a blacksmith by trade, he began whittling in his fifties and was a prolific artist, creating elaborate primitive carvings, many with moving parts.

Photographer Ulric Bourgeois (1874-1963) received his first camera at age 11. This artist, born in Fulford, Québec, moved to Manchester, New Hampshire, soon after he married in 1899, and opened up a studio. His work documents Franco-American life in New England and Québec, which he visited often. His life provided inspiration for the Québec film *J.A. Martin, photographe.*

# MEDIA

## PRINT

The first French Canadian newspaper published in the United States was *Le Patriote Canadien*, the first issue of which was printed in Burlington, Vermont, on August 7, 1839. The Franco-American press served not only to disseminate news, but also as a forum for ideas. French-language and bilingual papers flourished in the United States until the 1930s, when many were abandoned by readers in favor of English-language dailies. Some of those available today follow.

### Le F.A.R.O.G. Forum.

A bilingual quarterly, first printed in 1972, it comes out of the University of Maine's Center for Franco-American Studies with a circulation of more than 4,500. The Center also publishes the bilingual quarterly newspaper *Le Forum*, which offers articles on the activities of prominent Franco-Americans, book reviews, genealogy information, and scholarly pieces on Franco-American studies.

**Contact:** Rhea Côté-Robbins.
**Address:** Center Franco-Américain, University of Maine, 126 College Avenue, Orono, Maine 04469.
**Telephone:** (207) 581-3775.

### Femmes D'Action.

Magazine addressing the social, educational, and health issues of French-Canadian women.

**Contact:** Marie-Lyne Renaud, Marketing Director.

**Address:** Federation Nationale des Femmes Canadiennes-Françaises, 325, rue Dalhouse, piece 525, Ottawa, Ontario, Canada K1N 7G2.
**Telephone:** (613) 232-5791.
**Fax:** (613) 232-6679.

### Le Journal de Lowell.

Founded in 1975, the journal has a circulation of about 4,200, mostly in Massachusetts. This French-language monthly features news on the New England region as well as news from Québec and France.

**Contact:** Albert V. Côté.
**Address:** P.O. Box 1241, Lowell, Maine 01853.
**Telephone:** (508) 453-1780.

### La Revue Canado-Américaine.

Published by the Association Canado-Américaine.

**Contact:** Paul Paré.
**Telephone:** (603) 622-2883.

### Le Soleil de la Floride.

This monthly, founded in 1983 with a circulation of 65,000, reaches French-speaking readers throughout Florida, Québec, and parts of the Caribbean, especially French-Canadian "snowbirds" who spend winter in warmer climates.

**Contact:** Jean Leurac.
**Address:** 2020 Scott Street, Hollywood, Florida 33020.
**Telephone:** (305) 923-4510.

### L'Union.

This bilingual quarterly newspaper, which is free to its members, is sent to some 16,000 households. It is published by the Union Saint-Jean-Baptiste (USJB), a fraternal life insurance organization for French-Canadian Americans with 44,000 members.

**Contact:** Joseph Gadbois (English); or, Bernard Theroux (French).
**Address:** 68 Cumberland Street, P.O. Box F, Woonsocket, Rhode Island 02895-9987.
**Telephone:** (401) 769-0520.

## RADIO
### WCUW-FM (91.3).
"L'Heure Française" Airs every Saturday from noon to 1:30 p.m.

Contact: Marcel Raymond.

Address: 297 Pleasant Street, Worcester, Massachusetts 01609.

Telephone: (508) 753-0711.

## WFAU-AM (1340).

"La Boite à Chansons" airs every Sunday from 10:00 a.m. to noon.

Contact: Jean-Paul Poulain.

Address: 160 Bangor Street, Augusta, Maine 04330.

Telephone: (207) 623-5044.

## WFEA-AM.

"Franco-American Hour" broadcasts music and information from 9:00 a.m. to 11:00 a.m. on Sundays.

Contact: Joe Maltais.

Address: 500 Commercial Street, Manchester, New Hampshire 03101.

Telephone: (603) 669-5777.

## WHTB-AM (1400).

Broadcasts every Sunday from 5:00 to 6:00 p.m.

Contact: Bernard Theroux.

Address: Fall River, Massachusetts.

Telephone: (508) 678-9727.

## WKRI-AM (1400).

"The French Program," airs on Sundays from noon to 1:00 p.m.

Contact: Roger Laliberte.

Address: 1585 Centerville Road, Warwick, Rhode Island 02893.

Telephone: (401) 821-6200.

## WLAM-AM (1740).

"L'Heure Farnçaise," broadcast on Sundays from 8:00 to 10:00 a.m.

Contact: Constance Cote.

Address: P.O. Box 929, Lewiston, Maine 04240.

Telephone: (207) 784-5401.

## WMHB-FM (90.5).

"Mondo Franco."

Contact: Paul Gregorie.

Address: Bates College, Lewiston, Maine 04240.

Telephone: (207) 784-5044.

## WMOU-AM (1230).

"Le Programme Canadien-Français," broadcast every Sunday from 7:00 a.m. to noon.

Contact: Robert Barbin.

Address: 38 Glen Avenue, Berlin, New Hampshire 03570.

Telephone: (603) 752-1230.

## WNRI-AM (1380).

Broadcast on Saturdays and Sundays from 10:00 a.m. to noon.

Contact: Roger Laliberte.

Address: 786 Diamond Hill Road, Woonsocket, Rhode Island 02895.

Telephone: (401) 769-0600.

## WSMN-AM (1590).

"The French Program," broadcast every Sunday from 9:00 a.m. to noon.

Contact: Maurice Parent.

Address: 502 West Hollis Street, P.O. Box 548, Nashua, New Hampshire.

## WWON-AM (1240).

Airs every Sunday from 9:00 a.m. to 10:00 a.m.

Contact: Normand Vaillancourt.

Address: 187 Madeline Avenue, Woonsocket, Rhode Island 02895.

Telephone: (401) 762-1240.

### TELEVISION

### "Bonjour."

This half-hour program is produced in Manchester, New Hampshire on the Cable Network and re-broadcast on the public broadcasting system in Maine, is repeated a number of times each week. It includes interviews of French-Canadian Americans on topics from music to cooking. Broadcast in French, it serves local audiences in New England and New York. It is also broadcast in the Canadian provinces of New Brunswick, Nova Scotia, Ontario, and Québec.

Contact: Paul Paré.

Address: Association Canado-Americaine, 52 Concord Street, P.O. Box 989, Manchester, New Hampshire 03105-0989.

Telephone: (603) 625-8577.

# ORGANIZATIONS AND ASSOCIATIONS

In addition to the organizations listed below, there are many local historical societies and genealogical societies for Franco-Americans throughout the United States. See *Le Répertoire de la vie française en Amérique,* a sourcebook of French Canadian organizations in the United States and Canada, for more information.

### Action for Franco-Americans in the Northeast.

**Contact:** Yvon A. Labbé.

**Telephone:** (207) 581-3775.

### Association Canado-Américaine.

Supports 45,000 members and local branches in many states, including Connecticut, Maine, Massachusetts, New Hampshire, and Rhode Island, as well as in Canada. Its interests include life insurance, cultural excursions, a summer camp, and a French-language cable television program for the New England region.

**Contact:** Eugene Lemieux.

**Address:** 52 Concord Street, P.O. Box 989, Manchester, New Hampshire 03105-0989.

**Telephone:** (603) 625-8577.

### Conseil de la Vie Francaise en Amerique/The Council for French Life in America (CVFA).

Founded in 1937 to promote the interests of French Canadians throughout North America. Among its membership is the Société Canadienne-Française du Minnesota and other such local groups for French-Canadian Americans, as well as groups that more generally promote French language and culture. They publish the annual reference guide to French-language organizations in North America and sponsor various awards, such as the Bourse Archibald Lemieux for Franco-Americans. The head office for this North American council is in Canada.

**Contact:** Paul Paré, President.

**Address:** 56 Saint-Pierre Street, 1st Floor, Québec City, Québec, Canada G1K 4A1.

**Telephone:** (418) 692-1150.

### Fédération Féminine Franco-Américaine de la Nouvelle-Angleterre.

Consists of some 5,000 women in 49 local associations who organize conferences, projects for seniors, cultural exchanges, and aid for students in French programs in a bid to promote French cultural interests in the New England region. Among the local associations are branches in Bristol, Connecticut; Lowell, Massachusetts; Manchester, New Hampshire; Woonsocket, Rhode Island; and New Bedford, Massachusetts.

**Contact:** Claire Quintal, President.

**Address:** Assumption College, 500 Salisbury Street, Worcester, Maine 01615-0005.

**Telephone:** (508) 767-7415.

### Société Historique Franco-Américaine (SHFA).

Founded in 1899. This institution holds regular lecture meetings and publishes a bulletin that contains the texts of the lectures and articles on its notable members.

**Contact:** Marthe B. Peloquin.
**Telephone:** (508) 692-6370.

### Union St. Jean Baptiste.

This organization, which serves over 40,000 members, has local branches throughout New England.

**Contact:** Joe Gadbois.
**Telephone:** (401) 769-0520.

# MUSEUMS AND RESEARCH CENTERS

### Center Franco-Américain.

Established in 1991, the Center is loosely affiliated with the fraternal organization Association Canado-Américaine. This resource center has an art gallery with featured exhibitions, a library, and offers French-language classes. The Center is also affiliated with the Federation Americaine Franco-American des Aînés/Francophone American Federation of the Elderly (FAFA), founded in 1981 to promote the interests of Franco-American seniors in both local affairs, as well as on a state and national scale.

**Contact:** Adele Baker, Director.
**Address:** 52 Concord Street, P.O. Box 989, Manchester, New Hampshire 03105-0989.
**Telephone:** (603) 669-4045.

**Center Franco-Américain de l'Université du Maine.**
Part of the University of Maine since 1972. Resources here include library and video materials on Franco-Americans and their publications, *F.A.R.O.G. Forum* and *Maine Mosaic*.

**Contact:** Yvon A. Labbé, Director.
**Address:** 126 College Avenue, University of Maine, Orono, Maine 04469.
**Telephone:** (207) 581-3775.


**Conseil International d'Etudes Francophones.**
Founded in 1981, this research center conducts studies of Franco-American literature, history, culture and language. Although its headquarters are at Montclair State University in New Jersey, it includes in its membership 300 individuals and 25 organizations.

**Contact:** Maurice Cagnon, President.
**Address:** French Department, Montclair State University, Upper Montclair, New Jersey 07043.
**Telephone:** (201) 655-4000.


**Fédération Franco-Américaine du New York.**
Sponsors lectures on the French in America, Québec films, language courses, the *Fête du Roi* (Twelfth Night) a winter cultural celebration, and exchanges with Québec. These activities, mostly in English, are for the public as well as members. Founded in Cohoes, New York in 1980, this organization, with about 140 members, also publishes a bulletin, *Franco-Nouvelles*, at least nine times a year.

**Contact:** Bernard Ouimet.
**Address:** Box 12-942, Albany, New York 12212.
**Telephone:** (518) 692-2690.


**Institut Français.**
Founded in 1979, the institute is associated with Assumption College. It has organized 11 collo-quia and published 12 books dealing with the French experience in New England. These include *The Little Canadas of New England*, as well as books on schools, religion, literature, the press, women, and folklore. The center collects documents on Franco-Americans and its holdings contain such archival materials as manuscripts, newspapers, and books.

**Contact:** Claire Quintal, Director.
**Address:** Assumption College, 500 Salisbury Street, Worcester, Massachusetts 01615-0005.
**Telephone:** (508) 752-5615.


# SOURCES FOR ADDITIONAL STUDY

Brault, Gerard J. *The French-Canadian Heritage in New England.* Hanover: University Press of New England, 1986.


Doty, C. Stewart. *The First Franco-Americans: New England Life Histories from the Federal Writers' Project, 1938-1939.* Orono: University of Maine at Orono Press, 1985.


Ducharme, Jacques. *The Shadows of the Trees: The Story of French-Canadians in New England.* New York: Harper & Brothers, 1943.


*French America: Mobility, Identity, and Minority Experience across the Continent*, edited by Dean R. Louder and Eric Waddell, translated by Franklin Philip. Baton Rouge: Louisiana State University Press, 1993.


Parker, James Hill. *Ethnic Identity: The Case of the French Americans.* Washington: University Press of America, Inc., 1983.

# GERMAN

by
La Vern J. Rippley

# AMERICANS

German immigrants to the United States have distinguished themselves in virtually every field of endeavor.

## OVERVIEW

Situated in the heart of Europe, Germany today adjoins nine neighbors: Denmark to the north; Poland and the Czech Republic to the east; Austria and Switzerland to the south; and the Netherlands, Belgium, Luxembourg, and France to the west. With a population of nearly 80 million, Germany follows Russia as the most populous nation in Europe. In size, however, Germany is smaller than either France or Spain and equates roughly with the combined area of Minnesota and Wisconsin. With an average of 222 people per square kilometer, Germany has one of the highest population densities in Europe.

### HISTORY

Recorded German history begins with the battle between the Roman legions and Arminus, a prince of the Germanic Cherusci tribe, recounted in the chronicles of Tacitus. *Deutschland,* the Germans' name for their country, came into use in the eighth century when Charlemagne incorporated German and French speakers into a common nation. As cohesion among the population of the eastern realm increased, the term *Deutschland* applied to all German speakers. Once confined west of the Elbe River, Germans gradually penetrated father east into former Slavic territory, often peacefully, but sometimes by force.

Almost from the time of Charlemagne, Germany bore versions of the name Holy Roman Empire of the German Nation, beginning with the Salian dynasty and proceeding with the rule of the Hohenstaufens, the Habsburgs, and the Hohenzollerns. Germany suffered religious schism when Martin Luther proposed reforms in 1517, which led to the pillaging of the country by those who profited from the weakened central political, religious, and social ruling structures. The religiously motivated Thirty Years' War (1618-1648), which erupted a century after Luther's death, devastated Germany's territory and its moral fiber until the age of French absolutism. During this period, also known as the Enlightenment, Prussian king Frederick the Great (1740-1786) became a patron of the American Revolution. Frederick sent Baron von Steuben, Johannes DeKalb, and others to train American military novices at Valley Forge and elsewhere.

During the Napoleonic period, the Holy Roman Empire dissolved in favor of the *Deutscher Bund* (German Confederation), a loose confederation of individual sovereign states that functioned with a single participatory government unit, the *Bundestag,* a delegated parliament in Frankfurt. The *Bundestag* often behaved like a monarchical oligarchy, suppressing freedom, enforcing censorship, and controlling the universities and political activity.

Arguments arose among the liberals over whether to establish a "greater Germany," along the lines of Great Britain, or a "smaller Germany," which would include only the more traditionally German principalities without Austria. Because Austria wanted to bring into the union its more than a dozen ethnic groups, the National Assembly opted for a smaller Germany, for which they offered a constitution to King Friedrich Wilhelm IV of Prussia. The king's rejection of the constitution triggered popular uprisings in the German states, which were in turn met by military suppression. A large group of German intellectual liberals, known as the Forty-eighters, immigrated to the United States during this period to escape persecution. The contemporary flag of Germany with its black, red, and gold stripes derives from the flag of the Forty-eighter parliament.

Following three short wars in 1864, 1866, and 1870, the new Prussian chancellor Bismarck united the remaining German states into the smaller German Reich, which lasted until World War I. German industry grew during the late nineteenth century. Domestic unrest erupted when Kaiser Wilhelm I attempted to suppress the domestic socialist working class. In the early twentieth century, Germany struck up alliances with Austria and the age-old Ottoman Turkey, triggering fear abroad. Ultimately, the entente between France, England, and Russia led to Germany's defeat in World War I in November 1918.

## MODERN ERA

With the framers of the Versailles Treaty, German Social Democrats and the Catholic Center Party succeeded in writing a constitution dubbed the Weimar Republic. The Republic was doomed from the outset by its struggles with burdensome war reparations, inflation, foreign military occupation west of the Rhine, a war guilt clause in the Versailles Treaty, and heavy losses of territory. In 1925 Field Marshal von Hindenburg, a hero on the Eastern Front in World War I, was elected president. Stricken by the political-economic disaster of 1929, Hindenburg in 1933 appointed to the chancellorship Adolf Hitler. Hitler promptly banned parties, expelled Communists from the government, and restructured the military. Hitler's goals were to purify Germany by removing people with all but the purest Teutonic blood and to expand German territory throughout Europe. In 1940 Germans occupied France, Czechoslovakia, Poland, Austria, and Hungary, and acted on the policy of extermination of unwanted peoples that nearly resulted in destroying the Jews and Gypsies of Europe.

Hitler's troops rounded up Jews in Germany and in other countries, forcing them to give up their lands and property. Systematically, Jews and political prisoners in Western Europe were shipped from Belgium, France, Germany, Greece, Italy, and Holland to forced-labor camps and to prisons. Concentration camps, which held Jews captive without regard for the accepted norms of arrest, appeared in France, Germany, and Austria, as well as Poland and Czechoslovakia. There were camps built to exterminate the Jews; most were gassed, and some were shot, drowned, or starved to death. Nearly six million people were killed by Nazi command, although there was some national resistance. When Germany was defeated in World War II, the country was divided into several parts governed by the various countries of the opposing armies. Eventually the Western countries that had opposed the Germans combined their sections into a European-influenced West Germany. This part of Germany was established as a democratic republic in 1949. The territory of Germans in the east was formed into a Russian satellite, and East Germany became a communist people's republic. For nearly 40 years distrust among Germans was encouraged by the Soviet Union on the one hand and by the West on the other. Both feared a united Germany. Finally in 1990 a revolution in East Germany deposed the communist regime there and the leaders sought reunification with West Germany. The two German states agreed to reunite under a two-house parliament and the pattern of free elections that had been developed by West Germany. Germany has worked to balance the economies of an agriculturally entrenched east and a west with a long-standing industrial sector.

## THE FIRST GERMANS IN AMERICA

With their arrival at Jamestown in 1607 and for nearly four centuries afterward, Germans have been one of the three largest population components of American society. When Columbus arrived in America in 1492, he did so in the name of Ferdinand and Isabella of Spain, that is, with the entitlement of the Habsburgs who also ruled Germany as part of the Holy Roman Empire. It was a German cosmographer, Martin Waldseemüller, who suggested that the New World be designated "America."

German immigration began in the seventeenth century and continued throughout the postcolonial period at a rate that exceeded the immigration rate of any other country; however, German immigration was the first to diminish, dropping considerably during the 1890s. Contrary to myth, the first German immigrants did not originate solely in the state of Pfalz. Although emigrants from Pfalz were numerous from 1700 to 1770, equally high percentages came from Baden, Württemberg, Hesse, Nassau, and the bishoprics of Cologne, Osnabrück, Münster, and Mainz. During the American pre-Revolutionary War period, immigrants came primarily from the Rhine valley, an artery that gives access to the sea. German emigration during this period was almost exclusively via French or Dutch ports like LeHavre or Rotterdam.

## SIGNIFICANT IMMIGRATION WAVES

Between 1671 and 1677 William Penn made trips to Germany on behalf of the Quaker faith, result-ing in a German settlement that was symbolic in two ways: it was a specifically German-speaking ward, and it comprised religious dissenters. Pennsylvania has remained the heartland for various branches of Anabaptists: Old Order Mennonites, Ephrata Cloisters, Brethren, and Amish. Pennsylvania also became home for many Lutheran refugees from Catholic provinces (e.g., Salzburg), as well as for German Catholics who also had been discriminated against in their home country.

By 1790, when the first census of Americans was taken, more than 8.6 percent of the overall population of the United States was German, although in Pennsylvania more than 33 percent was German. During the Revolutionary War, these German Americans were numerically strengthened by the arrival of about 30,000 Hessian mercenaries who fought for England during the hostilities, of whom some 5,000 chose to remain in the New World after the war ceased.

In addition to those who had arrived for political and religious reasons until about 1815, Americans and some foreign shippers brought many Germans to America under the redemptioner system. The scheme was that a German peasant traveled on a sailing vessel without charge and on arrival at an Atlantic port was sold to an American businessman to work from four to seven years to redeem his passage and win his freedom. Some of the early sectarians—Baptist Dunkers, Schwenkfelders, Moravian Brethren, and others—were only able to reach America in this way.

Populous as German immigrants to America were by the end of the eighteenth century, the major waves of immigration came after the conclusion of the Napoleonic Wars in 1815. Germany's economy suffered in several ways. Too many goods were imported, especially cloth from industrialized England. Antiquated inheritance laws in southwestern Germany caused land holdings continuously to be divided, rendering farms too minuscule for assistance. A failing cottage industry collapsed when faced by a flood of foreign products. Finally, the population had grown artificially large because of growing dependence on the potato. Like Ireland, rural Germany in the 1840s was suddenly hit by famine precipitated by the potato blight.

Because the 1848 revolutions in Europe failed to bring democracy to Germany, several thousand fugitives left for America in addition to the nearly 750,000 other Germans who immigrated to America in the following years. While a

In this 1949 photograph, a two-year-old girl waits for her parents to complete their customs inspection in New York City following the family's arrival from Germany.

mere 6,000 Germans had entered the United States in the 1820s, nearly one million did so in the 1850s, the first great influx from Germany. Despite annual fluctuations, especially during the Civil War period when the figure dropped to 723,000, the tide again swelled to 751,000 in the 1870s and peaked at 1,445,000 in the 1880s.

During the nineteenth century religious and political refugees were numerous. During the

1820s, for example, Prussia forced a union of the Reformed and Lutheran congregations, which by the late 1830s caused many Old Lutherans to emigrate. Saxon followers of Martin Stephan came in 1839 to escape the "wickedness" of the Old World. Other refugees were the Pietists, who founded communal societies in America (including Harmony and Economy Pennsylvania—established by the Rappists—as well as Zoar in Ohio, St. Nazianz in Wisconsin, and Amana in Iowa).

Societies sponsored by German princes sought to use emigration as a solution to social problems at home. For example, the Central Society for German Emigrants at Berlin (1844), the National Emigration Society at Darmstadt (1847), the Giessener Emigration Society (1833), and the Texas Braunfels Adelsverein (1843) operated on the principle that a one-way ticket for the downtrodden was cheaper than a long-term subsidy. Also influential in unleashing a tidal wave of German emigration were writers like Gottfried Duden whose book (1829) about Missouri became a best-seller.

During the 1850s small farmers and their families dominated the first major wave of immigrants, who often came from southwest Germany. Soon after artisans and household manufacturers were the main arrivals from the more central states of Germany, while day laborers and agricultural workers from the rural northeast estates characterized subsequent waves of German immigrants. Not until German industrialization caught up with the English in the late nineteenth century did German emigrants no longer have to leave the country to improve their lives. Beginning in the late 1880s and for several decades thereafter, migrants from depressed German agricultural regions were destined less for America than for the manufacturing districts of Berlin, the Ruhr, and the Rhine in Germany itself.

Interspersed among these waves of economic emigrants were fugitives from oppression, including thousands of German Jews who left because of economic and social discrimination. Young men sometimes fled to avoid serving in the Prussian military. Organized industrial laborers also fled the antisocialist laws enacted when a would-be assassin threatened the life of Germany's Kaiser Wilhelm I, who blamed socialist labor leaders for the attempt. Catholics, too, were oppressed by Bismarck's infamous May Laws during the 1870s, which suppressed the influence of the Catholic Center Party and its drive for greater democracy during the first decade of the new emperor's reign.

Also during the latter half the nineteenth century, a host of agents fanned out across Germany to drum up emigration. Some were outright recruiters who were technically outlawed. More often these agencies took the form of aid societies working to better the lot of the emigres in Germany, such as the Catholic Raphael Society, the Bavarian *Ludwigsmissionsverein,* the Leopoldinen *Stiftung* in Vienna, the Pietist society of Herrnhut in Saxony, and the Lutheran support groups at Neuendettelsau of Franconia in northern Bavaria. Frankenmuth, Michigan, for example, traces its roots to the latter organization. Aiding the immigrants on this side of the Atlantic were such agencies as the Catholic Leo House in New York and the Central-Verein in St. Louis. Much better funded promoters were those established by the north-central states (most prominently, Michigan, Wisconsin, and Minnesota) as they joined the Union, many of which had ample support from their legislatures for their Immigration Commissioners. Even more influential were transcontinental railroads that sent agents to the ports of debarkation along the Atlantic and Germany to recruit immigrants to either take up their land grants or supply freight activity for their lines. Especially active was the Northern Pacific during the time when German immigrant Henry Villard headed the corporation and sought to populate his land grant with industrious German farmers.

In the latter phases of German immigration, newcomers joined established settlers in a phenomenon called "chain migration." Chain migration is defined as the movement of families or individuals to join friends and family members already established in a given place. Chain migration strengthened the already existing German regions of the United States. One such concentrated settlement pattern gave rise to the phrase "German triangle," that is, St. Paul, St. Louis, and Cincinnati, with lines stretching between them so that the triangle incorporates Chicago, Milwaukee, Indianapolis, Fort Wayne, Davenport, and other strongly German cities. Other descriptors include the more accurate "German parallelogram," which stretches from Albany westward along the Erie Canal to Buffalo and farther westward through Detroit to St. Paul and the Dakotas, then south to Nebraska and Kansas, back to Missouri, and eastward along the Ohio River to Baltimore. Except for large settlements in Texas, San Francisco, and Florida, German American settlement is still largely contained within the German belt.

The number of German Americans has remained constant. From 1850 to 1970 German was the most widely used language in the United States after English. In the 1990 U.S. census, 58 million Americans claimed sole German or part-German descent, demonstrating the persistence of the German heritage in the United States.

"We were stationed in Hamburg in a tremendous big place. It was sort of an assembly building where you got processed. There was an exodus from Europe at that time, and they had all races in this place. You could see people from Russia, Poland, Lithuania, you name it. I can't describe the way I felt—it was part fear, it was exciting. It's something I'll never forget." Ludwig Hofmeister in 1925, cited in *Ellis Island: An Illustrated History of the Immigrant Experience,* edited by Ivan Chermayeff et al. (New York: Macmillan, 1991).

### SETTLEMENT

Germans settled in different locations depending upon when they arrived and where the best locations for economic opportunity were situated. When France, which had attempted to colonize Louisiana in the early eighteenth century with the help of Germans, assumed an important role in the cotton trade, German immigrants arrived in New Orleans and made their way up the Mississippi, Ohio, and Missouri rivers. Others arrived in New York and travelled the Erie Canal and the Great Lakes to the Midwest. The primary port of arrival for early immigrants was Philadelphia and many Germans chose to settle in Pennsylvania. The German American population of 58 million breaks down demographically as follows: 39 percent live in the Midwest, 25 percent in the South, 19 percent in the West, and 17 percent in the Northeast. With regard to specific states, Americans reporting German ancestry are the most numerous in California, followed by Pennsylvania, Ohio, Illinois, and Texas. In terms of absolute numbers, the Germans have always been at their largest in New York City. The German Americans are nowhere more densely settled than in Wisconsin, Minnesota, North Dakota, South Dakota, Nebraska, and Iowa—in the traditional German belt.

# ACCULTURATION AND ASSIMILATION

In many respects, the Germans were slower to assimilate than their fellow immigrants from other countries. This was due in part to their size and in part to their overall percentage of the population. When a cross-section of basic needs can be supplied within an ethnic community, the need to assimilate in order to survive is less urgent. Germans had their own professionals, businesses, clergy, churches, and especially schools. However, second generation German immigrants were drawn more quickly into the mainstream and the survival of German communities depended upon immigration.

### TRADITIONS, CUSTOMS, AND BELIEFS

The true picture of German culture differs substantially from that presented in the popular media where Germans are presented as either brutal or as jolly, overweight, and beer-guzzling. Equally enigmatic is post-World War II German Americans' perception of their heritage as inseparable from certain icons and costumes, notably, beer mugs, fast high-quality cars, sausage and sauerkraut—enlivened by the spirit of Bavarian folk music. In the United States Bavarian culture is regarded as synonymous with all German culture, even though Bavarian customs and language are confined to the regional state of Bavaria and its capital, Munich. German Day festivals almost always feature Bavarian dance and clothing such as the *lederhosen* (men's shorts with suspenders) and the *dirndl* (women's full skirt). Replicas of German cities—such as Leavenworth, Washington, or Frankenmuth, Michigan—invariably assume an air of Alpine Bavaria.

### HOLIDAYS

In addition to traditional American holidays, Catholic communities celebrate the feast of Corpus Christi in which there are outdoor processions to altars decorated with flowers. At the Epiphany, neighbors visited from house-to-house and young men adorned with paper crowns would sing in exchange for treats. The German Christmas served as the basis for the American celebrations; it emphasizes the family and the exchange of gifts; often, the Christmas tree is not illuminated until Christmas eve. December 6 was the traditional time of St. Nicholas' visit. Another tradition that has survived from German American communities is the greeting of the New Year by gunfire—young men would ride horses through the neighborhood and fire their shotguns when midnight arrived.

This German American Tricentennial Multicycle from Philadelphia, Pennsylvania, is traveling along Fifth Avenue in New York City during the 1988 Steuben Day Parade.

## LANGUAGE

The German language is related to Danish, Norwegian, Swedish, Dutch, and Icelandic, as well as to English. High German, the dialect spoken in the east-west central geographic elevation, differs linguistically from the language spoken in the lower-lying geographic regions of northern Germany, where once Low German was in everyday usage. It is also radically different from Bavarian and Swiss German which typically is voiced in the southern, more Alpine regions. Spoken natively by 100 million people, German is the mother tongue of thousands of people who live beyond all of Germany's current borders. Ten percent of all books published in the world are in German.

## FAMILY AND COMMUNITY DYNAMICS

There was a low rate of tenancy among early German immigrants, who purchased homes as early as possible. German Americans have traditionally placed a high value upon home ownership and prefer those made of brick. The traditional German American family was essentially patriarchal with women assuming subservient roles. Because many German immigrants were from agricultural areas, they brought with them a traditional concept of the family. Farm families were, of necessity, large and family members worked together for the good of all. Wives and daughters worked together with husbands and sons to manage the harvests. In families whose work was not farm-centered, though, wives worked with their husbands in small family operated businesses. Children frequently left school early with the boys entering family businesses and the girls entering domestic service. According to 1880 census figures, though, a smaller proportion of German American women were part of the work force than other immigrant groups. Those who were employed outside the home did not work in factories or in jobs in which a knowledge of English was necessary; instead, they labored in janitorial work or the service industry.

## EDUCATION

To emphasize the importance of their language in the transmission of cultural values, German Americans strove to maintain their own German-language schools, first by establishing private institutions and later, after 1849, by pressuring school districts to offer German or bilingual education where parents requested it. In addition to the German-language instruction offered in the public schools, there was the instruction in the parochial schools operated especially by Catholics and Lutherans, which enrolled thousands of the children of German immigrants.

Parochial schools started in colonial times and continued through the nineteenth century, sometimes sponsored by nonreligious organizations such as a local German school society which functioned as legal owner of the school. Some of these schools operated according to new pedagogical principles and had a lasting impact on the American school system. For example, they introduced kindergarten. At all school levels sports programs, which had their origin in the German socialist *Turner* societies, became an integral aspect of American training for physical fitness. A few German American leaders dreamed of having their own university with German as the language instruction, but in spite of *Kultur* enthusiasm, it never came to fruition.

At the lower levels Germans achieved success in the political arena. When the question of teaching subjects in German drew the attention of truancy alarmists in Wisconsin and Illinois around 1890, the Wisconsin legislature passed the infamous Bennett Law, which required that children attend school more faithfully and which added the stipulation that at least some of the subjects be taught in English. In Illinois a similar measure was called the Edwards Law. As a result, the Lutheran and Catholic constituents of these states campaigned to defeat Wisconsin's governor William Dempster Hoard and to free the German language schools of state intervention. Over time, however, German faded in favor of English.

To supply teachers for these many schools, German Americans maintained a teachers' college while the *Turner* gymnastic societies developed their own teacher preparation institute for the production of scholars who would educate pupils. After the turn of the twentieth century, a special three-million-strong organization, the German American Alliance, actively promoted the cause of German. They did so in part to preserve their culture and in part to maintain a clientele for German products like newspapers, books, and beer. In 1903 the Alliance urged in its *German-American Annals*, "Only through the preservation of the German language can our race in this land be preserved from entire disappearance. The principal aim should be the founding of independent parochial schools in which the language of instruction would be German, with English as a foreign language."

Elementary German language school enrollments reached their zenith between 1880 and 1900. In 1881 more than 160,000 pupils were attending German Catholic schools and about 50,000 were in Missouri Synod Lutheran schools. Of the roughly one-half million people attending school with a curriculum partly or all in German, as counted by the German American Teachers Association around the turn of the century, 42 percent were attending public schools, more than a third were in Catholic schools, and 16 percent were in Lutheran private schools.

However, when World War I broke out, the German element was so discredited in the United States that when Congress declared war in April 1917, within six months legal action was brought not only to dampen considerably German cultural activities but also to eliminate the German language from American schools. The flagship case was the Mockett Law in Nebraska, which anti-German enthusiasts repealed. Eventually, 26 other states followed suit, banning instruction *in* German and *of* German. When the Missouri Synod Lutherans of Nebraska brought the test case, *Meyer v. Nebraska*, the ban on German was reconfirmed by all the courts until it reached the U.S. Supreme Court. On June 4, 1923, the Supreme Court held that a mere knowledge of German could not be regarded as harmful to the state, and the majority opinion added that the right of parents to have their children taught in a language other than English was within the liberties guaranteed by the Fourteenth Amendment. Nevertheless, as a language of instruction in schools, during church service, and at home, German gradually drifted into oblivion as assimilation accelerated.

# RELIGION

Religious differences have characterized the German people. Most of the population is Protestant and practice a form of Lutheranism—the Protestant Reformation church created by the German religious leader Martin Luther. Religion was important to German immigrants and the lack of ministers attracted Moravian missionaries in the early eighteenth century. The success of these churches strengthened the established Reformed churches, which rejected the ecumenical stance of the Moravians. In the eighteenth century the language, doctrine, and rituals of some of the established synods of the Reformed church had become Americanized and they were unable to attract new immigrants. The conservative synods, such as the Missouri Synod, were more successful, however.

Many German immigrants were Catholic; but because the Catholic church was controlled essentially by the Irish there was much friction between the two groups. Many parishes were established by lay people, which resulted in frequent friction between the pastors and trustees in pioneer churches. The German American churches, which used the German language exclusively, featured a liturgy rich with ritual and music and offered its parishioners a variety of associations and societies. They also addressed numerous social needs by supporting and operating orphanages and hospitals. By the twentieth century, however, many of the German American Catholic parishes underwent severe attrition when many of its members moved to suburban mixed parishes.

# POLITICS AND GOVERNMENT

On the whole, Germans in America have been reluctant to participate in politics. They arrived without the necessary language skills, even if they had *not* lacked a tradition that conditioned them for political participation. Thus, at the national level, the first and most prominent German figure in American politics was Carl Schurz, who was influential in the election of Abraham Lincoln, served as ambassador to Spain, became a general in the Civil War, later was elected U.S. senator from Missouri, and finally was appointed Secretary of the Interior under Rutherford Hayes. At the state level, too, the Germans seem to have avoided public office. Except for John P. Altgeld, the German-born governor of Illinois from 1893 to 1897, no German was ever elected to head an American state. Even in the U.S. Senate, few German-born and a surprisingly small number of German Americans have ever entered that upper house.

Not until Dwight D. Eisenhower was there an American president with a German surname.

Eisenhower's ancestors were colonial Pennsylvania Germans who had moved to Texas and then Kansas, but certainly this president was no friend of Germans. Political scientists have shown how strongly the Germans came to resent Franklin Roosevelt and General Eisenhower for their defeat of Germany during World War II. This resulted in a fading from Democratic Party support until the candidacy of President Harry Truman in 1948. During that campaign the German American electorate returned in droves to their traditional Democratic Party, handing Truman a surprise victory over Republican Thomas E. Dewey. Apparently, Truman's strong stand against Stalin at Potsdam, his subsequent anti-Communist actions in Greece, and his May 1948 decision to save Berlin by airlift aided his November reelection chances with German Americans. There was no similar outpouring for Eisenhower in 1952, who won in spite of only mild German support.

## LABOR UNIONS

Occupationally, the Germans were skilled in such trades as baking, carpentry, and brewing. They were also laborers, farmers, musicians, and merchants. According to the 1870 census figures, 27 percent of German Americans were employed in agriculture, 23 percent in the professions, and 13 percent in trades and transportation. By 1890, however, some 45 percent reportedly were laborers or servants, perhaps as a result of industrial workers' migration rather than a farmers' migration. This may explain why the labor movement in the United States gained considerable impetus from its German component.

The mid-nineteenth century witnessed the introduction of the communist ideologies of Wilhelm Weitling (1808-1871) and Joseph Weydemeyer (1818-1866), which gave impetus to early struggles for social and economic reform. The International Workingmen's Association in America was founded in 1869 as the first of the communist and socialist groups in America; and its membership was predominantly German American. And in 1886, German American anarchists were also instrumental in the forming of the labor movement implicated in the infamous Chicago Haymarket bombing during the labor strikes of that period. Had it not been for the greater need for workers to unite against their employers and join the American Federation of Labor (AFL), German trade unions might have been consolidated in the late 1880s. In future years many leaders of American labor were German American, including Walter

Reuther, who fought on the picket lines during the 1930s before becoming president of the AFL-CIO following World War II. For German immigrants, labor union membership enabled them to not only improve working conditions, it helped them to form a solidarity with workers from other ethnic backgrounds.

### RELATIONS WITH GERMANY

During the period from 1945 to 1990, the United States, with allies Great Britain and France, officially occupied West Germany, each in a special zone. The Americans occupied Bavaria, the Rhine-Main Frankfurt, and Palatinate areas. Each country was also allocated a sector in the capital of Berlin. During the Cold War, dramatic confrontations focused on Berlin because it lay 110 miles from the Iron Curtain. For 11 months in 1948 and 1949, the Soviets noosed a land blockade around the city, only to have the Allies supply the needs of two million inhabitants by air. For example, when the city's electrical power supply was severed, West Berliners lived in darkness until an entire generating plant could be flown in and assembled on site.

After Khrushchev met John F. Kennedy at a June summit in Vienna, East German border police erected the Berlin Wall on August 13, 1961. Throughout the Cold War, the wall was an important political symbol. It figured in the political phraseology of each U.S. president, most prominently in Kennedy's "Ich bein ein Berliner" speech at the City Hall, which endeared him to Berliners for all time. After the collapse of Communism the wall was dismantled in 1990. Today a small portion of the wall stands as a museum. Before unification of the two Germanies on October 3, 1990, the four World War II Allied victors' flags were lowered from the *Komandatura* palace in Berlin. Thus ended four centuries of control, returning Germany to full international autonomy, which further restored the confidence of Americans in their German descent. With its strong economy and continuous universal military conscription, Germany remains the linchpin of NATO and the core member in the European Community.

# INDIVIDUAL AND GROUP CONTRIBUTIONS

German immigrants to the United States have distinguished themselves in virtually every field of endeavor. John Roebling (1806-1869) is still known from his prowess with bridges, although the once famous empire builder, John Jacob Astor (1763-1848), is little remembered for his American Fur Company. Baron Friedrich von Steuben (1730-1794) commands respect as a military hero, but cartoonist Thomas Nast (1840-1902) is all but forgotten, although his elephant and donkey mascots for the Republicans and Democrats and his Santa Claus are not. With the arrival of the computer screen, Ottmar Mergenthaler's (1854-1899) famous Linotype printing system has met oblivion. Even Wernher von Braun's (1912-1977) pioneer rocketry, which still carries Americans and their satellites into outer space, is fading from consciousness.

### BUSINESS

In business John August Sutter (1803-1880) is remembered less for his Pacific trading prowess than for the fact that gold was found on his California land holdings in 1848. Claus Spreckels developed sugar refining in California and Hawaii, while Frederick Weyerhaeuser masterminded the Northwest timber industry. Henry Villard, born Heinrich Hilgard, completed the Northern Pacific Railroad. Prominent brewers include Philip Best, Valentin Blatz, Frederick Miller, Joseph Schlitz, and the Coors and the Anhaeuser-Busch families.

### MUSIC

In music there were the father and son Walter Damrosch (1862-1950) and Leopold Damrosch, Erich Leinsdorf (1912- ), and Bruno Walter Schlesinger, all conductors in New York; opera singers Ernestine Schumann-Heink (1861-1936) and Lotte Lehmann (1888-1976); and the composers Paul Hindemith (1895-1963), Kurt Weill (1900-1950), and Arnold Schoenberg (1874-1951).

### SCIENCE AND TECHNOLOGY

In atomic energy Albert Einstein (1879-1955) is the most prominent scientist. In the laboratories it was his German-born colleagues, Nobel laureates James Franck (1882-1964), Otto Loewi (1873-1961), Victor Hess (1883-1964), Felix Bloch (1905-1983), Otto Stern (1888-1969), and Hans Bethe (1906- ) who mattered. On the Manhattan Project they worked with two German-educated

Hungarians, Edward Teller (1908- ) and Leo Szilard (1898-1964), all under the command of Julius Robert Oppenheimer (1904-1967), the American-born son of Forty-cighter immigrants, who had taken his Ph.D. at the University of Goettingen before engineering the bomb. Szilard and the German-born scientists Erwin Schrödinger (1887-1961) and Max Delbrück (1906-1981) later worked closely with colleagues to develop the Crick-Watson model of DNA. George Westinghouse (1846-1914) invented, among many other things, the air brakes to stop trains. For his electric motors, Charles Steinmetz (1865-1923) became known as the wizard of Schenectady.

## SPORTS

George Herman Erhardt Ruth (1895-1948), better known as the Babe, and Lou Gehrig, both the sons of German immigrants, continue to enjoy sports fame.

## VISUAL ARTS

In architecture there was the famous Bauhaus School headed by Walter Gropius (1883-1969) at Harvard and Ludwig Mies van der Rohe (1886-1969) in Chicago. Marcel Breuer and Josef Albers (1888-1976) created the designation "modern design," overshadowed now by the so-called postmodern style.

# MEDIA

## PRINT

### Amerika Woche.

Newspaper with text in English and German.

**Contact:** Werner Baroni, Editor.
**Address:** 4732 North Lincoln Avenue, Chicago, Illinois 60625.
**Telephone:** (312) 275-5054.

### Der Deutsch-Amerikaner/German American Journal.

Newspaper published by the German American National Congress; promotes the organization's efforts to maintain German culture, art, and customs.

**Contact:** Ernst Ott, Editor.
**Address:** 4740 North Western Avenue, Second Floor, Chicago, Illinois 60625.

**Telephone:** (312) 275-1100.
**Fax:** (312) 274-4010.

### IGAR News.

Monthly publication of the Institute for German American Relations; promotes friendly German American relations through education.

**Contact:** Dr. Bruce D. Martin, Editor.
**Address:** 9380 McKnight Road, Suite 102, Pittsburgh, Pennsylvania 15237-5951.
**Telephone:** (412) 364-6554.

### Nordamerikanische Wochen-Post.

Published in Troy, Michigan, this weekly carries a front page directly from Germany, reports on many German American organizations, and includes coverage of business activity in Germany. It is currently the best-edited and most widely distributed such publication in America.

**Contact:** Regina Bell, Editor.
**Address:** Detroit Abend-Post Publishing Co., 1120 East Long Lake Road, Troy, Michigan 48098.
**Telephone:** (313) 528-2810.
**Fax:** (313) 528-2741.

### Society for German-American Studies— Newsletter.

Quarterly publication of the Society; focuses on German immigration and settlements in the United States and on German American history and culture.

**Contact:** LaVern J. Rippley, Editor.
**Address:** St. Olaf College, Northfie, Minnesota 55057.
**Telephone:** (507) 663-3233.

New Yorker Staats-Herold is the oldest and among the best North American German-language publications. America Woche, Wächter und Anzeiger, California Staats-Zeitung, and similar publications typify efforts of regional German-language newspapers to continue their noble traditions. Such organizations as the Deutsch-Amerikanische Nationalkongress, headquartered in Chicago, publishes its own monthly, as do a number of its chapters.

## RADIO

German-language programs on radio stations abound. There are at minimum one-hour radio programs on perhaps a dozen radio stations in Chicago, and several radio programs in Milwaukee; Pittsburgh; Detroit; Saginaw; St. Paul;

Cleveland; Toledo; Cincinnati; Denver; Seminola, Florida; New Braunfels, Texas; and on the West Coast.

## ORGANIZATIONS AND ASSOCIATIONS

Throughout the German belt there continue to exist hundreds of German societies. In Michigan alone where the *Wochen-Post* carries a listing, there are 28 ranging from the Arion singers and the *Berlin Verein* to *Schwäbischer Männerchor* and the *Verein der Plattdeutschen* (Low German speakers). In other states there are dozens more, some representing Germans from beyond the borders of the nation, such as the German-Bohemian Society of New Ulm, the Germans from Russia Heritage Society in Bismarck, and the Transylvanian Saxons in Cleveland. New York City alone has perhaps 100 German clubs, listed periodically in the local German newspaper. So, too, hundreds of once German-language churches offer services routinely but not regularly, sometimes weekly, more often monthly for a persistent but waning German-language clientele.

### German American Information and Education Association (GIEA).

Patriotic conservative organization seeking to improve the public image of "Germanity" and to publicize contributions to American culture made by German Americans.

**Contact:** Stanley Rittenhouse, President.
**Address:** P.O. Box 10888, Burke, Virginia 22015.
**Telephone:** (703) 425-0707.

### German American National Political Action Committee (GANPAC).

Seeks to represent what the committee considers to be the interests of German Americans.

**Contact:** Hans Schmidt, Chair.
**Address:** P.O. Box 1137, Santa Monica, California 90406.

## MUSEUMS AND RESEARCH CENTERS

The Society for German American Studies, headquartered at the University of Cincinnati, func-

tions as a scholarly umbrella for many others that have a more social or genealogical orientation. The Pennsylvania German Society in Philadelphia has a major library, while research centers with the name Max Kade Institutes recently have sprung up on university campuses, notably, at Madison, Wisconsin; Lawrence, Kansas; Indianapolis; and Penn State. There is no semblance of a German American museum, although local historical societies in the "German" states have much material.

## SOURCES FOR ADDITIONAL STUDY

Allen, James Paul, and Eugene James Turner. *We the People: An Atlas of America's Ethnic Diversity*. New York: Macmillan, 1988.

*America and the Germans: An Assessment of a Three-Hundred-Year History*, two volumes, edited by Frank Trommler and Joseph McVeigh. Philadelphia: University of Pennsylvania Press, 1985.

Conzen, Kathleen Neils. "Germans," *Harvard Encyclopedia of American Ethnic Groups*, edited by Stephan Thernstrom. Cambridge, Massachusetts: Belknap Press of Harvard University Press, 1980.

Kloss, Heinz. *Atlas of German-American Settlements*. Marburg: Elwert, 1974.

*News from the Land of Freedom: German Immigrants Write Home*, edited by Walter D. Kamphoefner, Wolfgang Helbich, and Ulrike Sommer, translated by Susan Carter Vogel. Ithaca, New York: Cornell University Press, 1991.

O'Connor, Richard. *The German-Americans*. Boston: Little, Brown, 1968.

Piltz, Thomas. *The Americans and the Germans*. Munich: Heinz Moos, 1977.

Pond, Elizabeth. *Beyond the Wall: Germany's Road to Unification*. Washington, D.C.: Brookings Institution, 1993.

Rippley, La Vern J., and Eberhard Reichmann. *The German-Americans: An Ethnic Experience*, translated by Willi Paul Adams. Indianapolis: Max Kade German-American Center, 1993.

Totten, Christine M. *Roots in the Rhineland: America's German Heritage in Three Hundred Years of Immigration, 1683-1983*. New York: German Information Center, 1988.

Walker, Mack. *Germany and the Emigration, 1816-1885*. Cambridge: Harvard University Press, 1964.

Wittke, Carl. *Refugees of Revolution: The German Forty-eighters in America*. Philadelphia: University of Pennsylvania Press, 1952.

Wust, Klaus. *Three Hundred Years of German Immigrants in North America, 1683-1983: A Pictorial History*. Baltimore and Munich: Heinz Moos, 1983.

# GREEK

by

**Jane Jurgens**

# AMERICANS

## OVERVIEW

Officially known as the Hellenic Republic, Greece is a mountainous peninsula located in southeastern Europe, between the Aegean and Mediterranean Seas. With a landmass of 51,000 square miles (132,100 square kilometers), Greece is bordered to the north by Bulgaria and Macedonia. Nearly 2,000 islands surround its eastern, southern, and western borders. The nine major land areas that constitute Greece include Central Pindus, Thessaly, the Salonika Plain, Macedonia/Thrace, Peloponnesus, the Southeastern Uplands, the Ionian Islands, the Aegean Islands, and Crete.

The capital city, Athens, and the cities of Thessaloniki (Salonika), Patras, Volos, and Larissa have the largest populations in Greece, which has a total population of approximately ten million. Ninety-seven percent of the ethnically and linguistically homogeneous nation speaks Greek, and one percent, Turkish. The Eastern Orthodox church is the dominant religion; only about 1.5 percent of the population is Muslim, and a small percentage is Roman Catholic, Greek Catholic, or Jewish.

Traditionally, Greeks referred to themselves as "Hellenes" and to the country of Greece as "Hellas." The word "Greek" comes from the Latin

*Graeci*, a name given to the people of this region by the Romans.

The Greek flag features a small white cross in the upper left corner flanked to the right and bottom by alternating white and blue stripes. The white cross symbolizes the Greek Orthodox religion, while the blue stripes stand for the sea and sky, and the white stripes for the purity of the Greek struggle for independence. The national anthem is "The Hymn to Freedom" (*"Imnos pros teen elefteeriahn"*). The basic monetary unit is the drachma.

## HISTORY

Greece is an ancient country that was continuously occupied from 6000 B.C., the beginning of its Neolithic period, until the nineteenth century. The Bronze Age, traditionally divided into early, middle, and late phases, dated from 2800 B.C. to 1000 B.C. It was during this period that Minoan civilization of Crete and the Mycenean civilization of mainland Greece flourished. These civilizations were destroyed around 1000 B.C. just as the individual city-state or "polis" was beginning to experience rapid growth. In 479 B.C. the city-states united to defeat Persia, a common enemy, but national unity proved to be short-lived. The power struggle between Athens and Sparta, the principal city-states, dominated the period.

Athens reached its zenith during the fifth century B.C., a period known as its Golden Age. At this time Athens experimented with a form of internal democracy unique in the ancient world, achieved a singular culture, and left enduring literary and architectural legacies. Socrates, Plato, Xenophon, Herodotus, Sophocles, Euripides, and Aeschylus came into prominence, and in 432 B.C. the Parthenon on the Acropolis was completed. The Peloponnesian War fought between Athens and Sparta from 431 to 404 B.C. and a plague that raged through Athens in 430 contributed to bring the Golden Age to an end. For a time Sparta dominated the Greek world, but war and severe economic decline hastened the decline of all of the city-states.

Greece came under Macedonian domination between 338 and 200 B.C. The Macedonian king, Alexander the Great, conquered Greece, Persia, and Egypt to create an empire, and he carried the idea of Hellenism to places as far away as India. The Hellenistic Age that followed Alexander's rule lasted until 146 B.C., As a Roman state from 127 B.C. to A.D. 330, Greece and its city-states had no political or military power. When the Roman Empire was divided in A.D. 395, Greece became part of the Eastern Empire, which continued as the Byzantine Empire until 1453. That year the Turks captured Constantinople, the capital of Byzantium, and Greece became part of the Ottoman Empire.

## MODERN PERIOD

Greece's declaration of independence from the Ottoman Empire on March 25, 1821, resulted in the Greek War of Independence, which lasted until 1829, and began the history of independent modern Greece. Great Britain, France, and Russia assisted Greece in its struggle for independence, and Greece came under the protection of these powers by the London Protocol of 1830. In 1832 the Bavarian Otto I became the first king of Greece, and in 1844 a conservative revolutionary force established a constitutional monarchy. George I, who succeeded Otto I, created a more democratic form of government with a new constitution in 1864.

During the 1880s and 1890s, transportation, education, and social services rapidly improved. Then in 1897 a revolt against the Turks in Crete led to war between Greece and the Ottoman Empire and to eventual self-governance for Crete. A revolt by the Military League in 1909 prompted the appointment of Eleuthérios Venizélos as Prime Minister of Greece. Between 1910 and 1933 Venizélos enacted major financial reforms.

During World War I Greece joined the Allied forces in opposing Germany. After the war Greece regained much of the territory it had lost to the Ottoman Empire. But in 1921 Greece began a war against the Turks in Asia Minor and suffered a crushing defeat in 1922. In 1923, under the Treaty of Lausanne, more than 1.25 million Greeks moved from Turkey to Greece, and more than 400,000 Turks in Greece moved to Turkey.

Between the World Wars, the Greek population vacillated between the establishment of a republican form of government and the restoration of monarchy. In 1936 Greece became a military dictatorship under General Ioannis Metaxas, who remained in power until 1944. The Germans occupied Greece during World War II, and the country did not recover until the 1950s, when it began slowly to regain economic and political stability. In 1952 Greece joined the North Atlantic Treaty Organization and also granted women the right to vote and to hold political office. During

1952 to 1963 Alexander Papagos and Konstantinos Karamanlis each held the office of prime minister.

On April 27, 1967, Colonel George Papadopoulos led a military coup, resulting in the suspension of constitutionally guaranteed rights and the imposition of harsh social controls. Papadopoulos declared Greece a republic in 1973 and put an end to the monarchy before his government was overthrown. In November 1974 Greece held its first free elections in more than a decade. Parliament adopted a new constitution in 1975, and a civilian government was established.

The first Socialist government in Greece gained control in 1981, the year Andreas Papandreou—the son of George Papandreou and a member of the Panhellenic Socialist movement—succeeded conservative Georgios Rallis as prime minister. In 1989 a conservative-communist coalition formed a new government, and pledging that Greece would be an active participant in the greater European community, Papandreou was reelected.

### THE FIRST GREEKS IN AMERICA

According to official records, the Greek sailor Don Teodoro or Theodoros, who sailed to America with the Spanish explorer Panfilio de Narvaez in 1528, was the first Greek to land in America. The names of other Greek sailors who may have come to America during this period are John Griego and Petros the Cretan. There is some speculation that Juan De Fuca, who discovered the straits south of Vancouver Island, may have been a Greek named Ionnis Phocas.

One of the first Greek colonies was at New Smyrna near Saint Augustine, Florida. Andrew Turnball and his wife Maria Rubini, daughter of a wealthy Greek merchant, persuaded approximately 450 colonists to journey to America and settle. With the promise of land, Greek colonists primarily from Mani in the south of Greece, as well as Italians, Minorcans, and Corsicans, began arriving in Florida on June 26, 1768. The colony was an overwhelming failure and was officially disbanded on July 17, 1777, but many of the colonists had already moved to neighboring Saint Augustine, where they were becoming successful as merchants and small businessmen. A small community of Greeks also built a chapel and school there.

### SIGNIFICANT IMMIGRATION WAVES

The first wave of Greek immigrants included about 40 orphans who had survived the Greek Revolution of 1821 and who were brought to the United States by American missionaries; survivors of the 1822 massacre of Chios by the Turks; and merchant sailors who settled in the Americas. Most of these Greeks were from islands such as

Chios, and others came from Asia Minor, Epirus, and Macedonia. By 1860 about 328 Greeks were living in the United States, with the majority residing in California, Arkansas, New York, and Massachusetts.

The U.S. Greek population remained small until the 1880s, when poor economic conditions in Greece prompted many Greeks to immigrate to the United States. During the 1880s most who came were from Laconia (notably, from the city of Sparta), a province of the Peloponnesus in southern Greece. Beginning in the 1890s, Greeks began arriving from other parts of Greece, principally from Arcadia, another province in the Peloponnesus. The largest numbers arrived during 1900-1910 (686) and 1911-1920 (385). Most were young single males who came to the United States to seek their fortunes and wished to return to Greece as soon as possible. About 30 percent of those who came before 1930 did return, some of whom went to fight in the Balkan Wars of 1912-1913.

The Immigration Acts of 1921 and 1924 reversed the open-door policy of immigration and established quotas. The Act of 1921 limited the number of Greek admittants to 3,063, while the Act of 1924 limited the number to 100. Legal petition increased the quota, and during 1925-1929 about 10,883 Greeks were admitted. Another 17,000 Greeks were admitted under the Refugee Relief Act of 1953, and 1,504 were accepted as a result of further legislation in 1957.

The Immigration Act of 1965 abandoned the quota system and gave preference to immigrants with families already established in the United States. The new Greek arrivals usually were better educated than their predecessors and included men and women in equal numbers, as well as family groups.

From 1820 to 1982 a total of 673,360 Greeks immigrated to the United States. After 1982, the number of Greeks entering the United States is as follows: 1983 (3,020); 1984 (2,865); 1985 (2,579); 1986 (2,512); 1987 (2,653); 1988 (2,458); 1989 (2,157); 1990 (2,742); 1991 (1,760); 1992 (1,790). The 1990 Census reports the number of people claiming at least one ancestry as Greek at 1,110,373.

## SETTLEMENT

During the 1890s Greeks began settling in major urban areas, including the industrial cities of the Northeast and Midwest. The first immigrants settled in Massachusetts and southern New Hampshire. The city of Lowell, Massachusetts, attracted the majority of Greeks, and by 1920 it had the third largest Greek community in the United States. Greeks also settled in the New England towns of Haverhill, Lynn, Boston, Peabody, and Manchester. The largest Greek settlement in the twentieth century was in New York. Greeks also settled in western Pennsylvania, particularly Pittsburgh, and in the Midwestern cities of Detroit, Milwaukee, Cleveland, Youngstown, and Chicago.

Small Greek communities existed in Galveston, Texas, and Atlanta, Georgia, but the largest concentration of Greeks in the South was at Tarpon Springs, Florida. In the first half of the twentieth century, this unique settlement of Greeks made its living by sponge diving.

Attracted to mining and railroad work, large numbers of Greeks settled in Salt Lake City, with smaller numbers inhabiting Colorado, Wyoming, Idaho, and Nevada. The heaviest early concentration on the Pacific Coast was in San Francisco. Today, Greeks live primarily in urban areas and are increasingly moving to the South and West. The 1990 Census reveals that New York State still has the largest population of Greeks, with the highest concentration in the Astoria section of the borough of Queens. The next largest populations are in California, Illinois, Massachusetts, and Florida.

# ACCULTURATION AND ASSIMILATION

Few negative Greek stereotypes persist. Greeks share the American work ethic and desire for success and are largely perceived as hardworking and family-oriented. They are also said to possess a "Zorba"-like spirit and love of life. However, many Greek Americans perceive the recent Greek immigrants as "foreign" and often as a source of embarrassment.

### TRADITIONS, CUSTOMS, AND BELIEFS

Greeks have an assortment of traditional customs, beliefs, and superstitions to ensure success and ward off evil and misfortune. Old beliefs persist in some communities in the United States. For example, belief in the "evil eye" is still strong and is supported by the Greek Orthodox church as a generalized concept of evil. Precautions against the evil eye (*not* endorsed by the church) include wearing garlic; making the sign of the cross behind the ear of a child with dirt or soot; placing an image of an eye over the lintel; wearing the *mati*, a blue amulet with an eye in the center; and recitation of a ritual prayer, the *ksematiasma*. Greeks may also respond to a compliment with the expression *ptou, ptou*, to keep the evil eye from harming the person receiving the compliment. Greeks also "knock wood" to guard against misfortune, and reading one's fortunes in the patterns of coffee dregs remains popular.

## PROVERBS

The Greeks "have a saying for it": In wine there is truth; You make my liver swell (You make me sick); God ascends stairs and descends stairs (Everything is possible for God); An old hen makes the tastiest broth (Quality improves with age); He won't give her any chestnuts (He wouldn't cut her any slack); I tell it to my dog, and he tells it to his tail (To pass the buck); I went for wool, and I came out shorn (To lose the shirt off one's back); Faith is the power of life.

## CUISINE

Greek food is extremely popular in the United States, where Greek American restaurants flourish. In Greek restaurants and in the home, many of the traditional recipes have been adapted (and sometimes improved on) to suit American tastes. In Greece meals are great social occasions where friends and family come together and the quantity of food is often impressive. Olive oil is a key ingredient in Greek cooking and is used in quantity. Traditional herbs include parsley, mint, dill, oregano (especially the wild oregano *rigani*), and garlic. You will find on most Greek tables olives, sliced cheese (such as feta, *kaseri*, and *kefalotiri*), tomato, and lemon wedges, along with bread. Fish, chicken, lamb, beef, and vegetables are all found on the Greek menu and are prepared in a variety of ways. Soup, salad, and yogurt are served as side dishes. Sheets of dough called *phillo* are layered and filled with spinach, cheese, eggs, and nuts. Greeks create such masterpieces as *moussaka*, a layered dish of eggplant, meat, cheese, and bread crumbs sometimes served with a white sauce. Other popular Greek dishes in the United States include *souvlakia*, a shish kabob of lamb, vegetables, and onions; *keftides*, Greek meatballs; *sagana-*

*ki*, a mixture of fried cheese, milk, egg, and flour; *dolmathes yalantzi*, grape leaves stuffed with rice, pine nuts, onions, and spices; and gyros, slices of beef, pork, and lamb prepared on a skewer, served with tomatoes, onions, and cucumber yogurt sauces on pita bread.

Soups include *psarosoupa me avgolemono*, a rich fish soup made with egg and lemon sauce; *spanaki soupa*, spinach soup; *mayeritsa*, an Easter soup made with tripe and/or lamb parts and rice; and *fasolatha*, a white bean Lenten soup made with tomatoes, garlic, and spices. Salads always accompany a meal. The traditional Greek salad (*salata a la greque*) is made with lettuce or spinach, feta cheese, tomatoes, onions, cucumbers, olives, oregano, and olive oil.

The national drink of Greece is *ouzo* ("oozoh"), an anise-flavored liquor that tastes like licorice and that remains popular with Greek Americans. Traditionally, it is served with appetizers (*mezethes*) such as olives, cheese, tomato, and lemon wedges. A popular Greek wine, *retsina*, is produced only in Greece and is imported to the United States.

## TRADITIONAL COSTUMES

Greek traditional costumes come in a variety of styles, some dating back to ancient times. Women's clothing is heavy, with many layers and accessories, designed to cover the entire body. The undergarments include the floor-length *poukamiso* (shirt) made of linen or cotton and the *misofioni* (underskirt) and *vraka* (panties), usually of muslin. The outer garments consist of the *forema-palto*, a coatdress of embroidered linen; the *fousta* (shirt) of wool or silk; the *sigouni*, a sleeveless jacket of embroidered wool worn outside the *forema-palto*; the *kontogourni* or *zipouni*, a short vest worn over the *fousta*; the *apodia*, an apron of embroidered wool or linen; and finally the *zonari*, a long belt wrapped many times around the waist. Buckles on these belts can be very ornate.

Traditionally, men's costumes are less colorful than women's costumes. Men's urban and rural clothing styles vary by region. The *anteria* is a long dress coat with wide sleeves once worn in the city. In rural areas, men wore the *panovraki* (or its variation, the *vraka*), white or dark woolen pants, narrow at the bottom and wide at the waist, with the *poukamiso*, a short pleated dress. The *foustanela* is a variation on the old style and soon became the national costume of Greece. The *foustanela* is a short white skirt of cotton or muslin with many folds that is worn above the knee. It is worn with the *fermizi*, a jacket of velvet or serge with long sleeves that is thrown over the back; waist-high white stockings; and a shirt with wide sleeves made of cotton, muslin, or silk. The *foustanela* is a common sight on Greek Independence Day.

## HOLIDAYS AND CELEBRATIONS

Greeks celebrate many Greek Orthodox holy days throughout the year, in addition to Christmas Day, Easter Day, and New Year's Day. Greeks in the United States also celebrate Greek Independence Day on March 25, commemorating their independence from the Ottoman Empire in 1821. In Chicago and New York, cities with a sizable Greek population, people dress in traditional costumes and sing the national anthem. The program of events also includes a parade, public address, folk dance, song, and poetry recitation.

## MUSIC AND DANCE

Greek music and dance are an expression of the national character and are appreciated by people of all ethnic backgrounds. As Marilyn Rouvelas stated in *A Guide to Greek Traditions and Customs in America*: "To the uninitiated, the music invites images of intriguing places, food and people. For the Greeks, the sounds and rhythms express their very essence: their dreams, sorrows and joys. Add dancing and nothing more need be said."

Varieties of Greek popular music include *dimotika* (*thimotika*), *laika*, and *evropaika*. *Dimotika* are traditional rural folk songs often accompanied by a clarinet, lute, violin dulcimer, and drum. *Laika* is an urban style of song, developed at the turn of the century, which may feature the bouzouki, a long-necked stringed instrument. *Evropaika* is Eurostyle music set to Greek words that is popular with the older generation.

Traditional Greek dances may be danced in a circle, in a straight line, or between couples. The *kalamatianos* is an ancient dance with many variations in which both men and women participate. It has 12 basic steps and is danced in a semicircle to 7/8 time. All variations are performed by the leader who stands facing the semicircle. The *sirtos*, perhaps the most ancient dance, is similar to the *kalamatianos*, but it is more controlled, performed to 2/4 time. First danced in the mountainous region of Epirus in northwestern Greece, the

tsamiko, traditionally danced by men, is today performed by both men and women. It was danced by the fighters and rebels in the Greek Revolution of 1821. The *hasapiko* is a popular folk dance for both men and women that is danced in a straight line, with one dancer holding the shoulder of the other. The *sirtaki*, a variation of the *hasapiko*, culminates with the "Zorba" dance popularized in the movie *Zorba the Greek*. Although the Zorba has no roots in Greek dance history, it does capture the mood and temperament of the Greek spirit. Originating in the Middle East, the *tsifteteli* is a seductive dance performed by one or two people. The *zeibekiko* is a personal dance traditionally danced only by men, either singly or as a couple. It is a serious, completely self-absorbed dance in which the dancer freely improvises the steps.

# LANGUAGE

Greek is a conservative language that has retained much of its original integrity. Modern Greek is derived from the Attic Koine of the first century A.D. During Byzantine times, the language underwent modifications and has incorporated many French, Turkish, and Italian words. Modern Greek retained the ancient alphabet and orthography of the more ancient language, but many changes have taken place in the phonetic value of letters and in the spelling. Although about 75 percent of the old words remain from the ancient language, words often have taken on new meanings. Modern Greek also retains from the ancient language a system of three pitch accents (acute, circumflex, grave). In 1982, a monotonic accent (one-stress accent) was officially adopted by the Greek government.

Greeks are fiercely proud of the continuity and relative stability of their language and much confusion and debate persists about "correct Greek." Two separate languages were once widely written and spoken in Greece: demotic Greek (*Demotiki*), the more popular language of the people, and *Katharevousa*, the "pure" archaic language of administration, religion, education, and literature. In 1967 demotic Greek was recognized as the official spoken and written language of Greece and is the language adopted for liturgical services by the Greek Orthodox church in the United States.

Modern Greek contains 24 characters with five vowels and four vowel sounds. It is traditionally written in Attic characters; the letters, their names, transliterations, and pronunciations are: "Aα"—alpha/a ("ah"); "Bβ"—beta/v ("v"); "Γγ"—gamma/g ("gh," "y"); "Δδ"—delta/d, dh ("th"); "Eε"—epsilon/e ("eh"); "Zζ"—zeta/z ("z"); "Ηη"—eta/e ("ee"); "Θθ"—theta/th ("th"); "Iι"—yiota/i ("ee"); "Κκ"—kappa/k, c ("k"); "Λλ"—lambda/l("l"); "Mμ"—mu/m ("m"); "Nν"—nee/n ("n"); "Θξ"—kse/x ("ks"); "Oo"—omicron/o ("oh"); "Ππ"—pee/p ("p"); "Pρ"—rho/r ("r"); "Σσ"—sigma/s ("s"); "Ττ"—taf/t ("t"); "Υυ"—ypsilon/y ("ee"); "Φφ"—fee/ph ("f"); "Χχ"—khee/h ("ch" [as in "ach"]); "Ψψ"—psee/ps ("ps" [as in "lapse"]); "Ωω"—omega/o ("oh").

Today Greek language schools continue to encourage the study of Greek, and new generations are discovering its rich rewards.

### GREETINGS AND OTHER POPULAR EXPRESSIONS

Some of the more common expressions in the Greek language include: Οχι ("ohchi")—No; Ναι ("neh")—Yes; Ευχαρσμετω (efcharisto)—Thank you; Καλημερα ("kahleemera")—Good morning; Καλησπερα ("kahleespehrah")—Good afternoon/night; Γειασου/σαζ ("yah soo/sahs")—Hello/Good-bye (informal); Χαιρετε ("chehrehteh")—Greetings/Hello (formal); Οπα! ("ohpah")—Hooray! Toasts may include Για χαρα ("yah chahrah")—For joy; Καλη τυχη ("kahlee teechee")—Good luck. Other popular expressions are Χρονια πολλα ("chrohnyah pohllah")—Many years/Happy birthday; Καλη χρονια ("kahlee chrohnyah")—Good year; Καλη Σαρακοστι ("kahlee sahrahkohstee")—Good Lent; Καλα Χριστουγεννα ("kahlah christooghehnna")—Merry Christmas. Expressions used at Easter are Καλο Πασχα ("kahloh pahschah")—Happy Easter (used before Easter); Καλη Αναστаση ("kahlee ahnahstahsee")—Good Resurrection (said after the Good Friday service); Χριστο ανεστι ("christohs ahnehstee")—Christ has risen (said after the Good Friday service) and its response, Αγηθω ανεστι ("ahleethohs ahnehstee")—Truly he has risen.

# FAMILY AND COMMUNITY DYNAMICS

If there is one self-defining concept among Greeks, it is the concept of *philotomo*, which may be translated as "love of honor." *Philotomo* is a highly developed sense of right and wrong involving personal pride and honor and obligation to family and community. It shapes and regulates an individual's relationships as a member of both a family and the community. Because the acts of each individual affect the entire family and community, each person must work to maintain both personal and family honor. It is *philotomo* that "laid the foundation for Greek success in America," wrote G. Kunkelman in *The Religion of Ethnicity*.

The idea of family and attachment to the Greek Orthodox church remains strong among Greek Americans. In many communities, the ideal family is still a patriarchy where the man, as husband and father, is a central authority figure and the woman a wife and mother. Children are highly valued, and frequently parents will sacrifice a great deal to see that their children accomplish their goals. Elderly parents may still move in with their children, but "Americanization," with accompanying affluence, assimilation, and mobilization, has rendered this arrangement less practicable.

Another change from traditional Greek custom is the rising number of marriages between Orthodox and non-Orthodox Greeks. The 1994 *Yearbook* of the Greek Orthodox Archdiocese of North and South America reports that between 1976 and 1992, the number of marriages between Orthodox Greeks was 35,767, while the number between Orthodox and non-Orthodox Greeks was 53,790; the divorce rate is 6,629 and 5,552, respectively.

### WEDDINGS

The wedding service conducted by a Greek Orthodox priest may be said in both Greek and in English, but the traditional elements of the Greek wedding remain unchanged. The hour-long ceremony is conducted around a small table on which two wedding crowns, the book of the Gospels, the wedding rings, a cup of wine, and two white candles are placed. The two-part Greek Orthodox wedding includes the betrothal and the wedding proper. During the betrothal the rings are blessed to signify that the couple is betrothed by the church. The priest first blesses the rings and then, with the rings, blesses the couple, touching their foreheads with the sign of the cross. The rings are placed on the bride's and groom's right hands, and the official wedding sponsors (*koumbari*) exchange the rings three times. During the wedding ceremony the bride and groom each hold a lighted white candle and join right hands while the priest prays over them. Crowns (*stephana*) joined with a ribbon are placed on their heads, and the *koumbaros* (male) or *koumbara* (female) is responsible for exchanging the wedding crowns three times above the heads of the couple during the service. Traditionally read are the Epistle of Saint Paul to the Ephesians and the second chapter of the Gospel of Saint John, which stress the mutual respect and love the couple now owe each other and the sanctity of the married state. After the couple shares a common cup of wine, they are led around the table by the priest in the Dance of Isaiah, which symbolizes the joy of the church in the new marriage. The *koumbaros* follows, holding the ribbon that joins the crowns. With the blessing of the priest, the couple is proclaimed married, and the crowns are removed.

The wedding reception reflects the influence of both Greek and American tradition and is notable for its abundance of food, dancing, and singing. The wedding cake is served along with an assortment of Greek sweets that may include baklava and *kalamatianos*, and *koufeta*—traditional wedding candy—is often distributed in candy dishes or in *bonbonieries* (small favors given to guests after the wedding).

## BAPTISM/CHRISMATION

The *koumbari* who act as wedding sponsors usually act as godparents for a couple's first child. The baptism begins at the narthex of the church, where the godparents speak for the child, renouncing Satan, blowing three times in the air, and spitting three times on the floor. They then recite the Nicene Creed. The priest uses the child's baptismal name for the first time and asks God to cleanse away sin. The priest, the godparents, and the child go to the baptismal font at the front of the church, where the priest consecrates the water, adding olive oil to it as a symbol of reconciliation. The child is undressed, and the priest makes the sign of the cross on various parts of the child's body. The godparents rub olive oil over the child's body, and the priest thrice immerses the child in the water of the baptismal font to symbolize the three days Christ spent in the tomb. The godparents then receive the child and wrap it in a new white sheet. During chrismation, immediately following baptism, the child is anointed with a special oil (*miron*), which has been blessed by the Ecumenical Patriarch of Constantinople. The child is dressed in new clothing, and a cross is placed around its neck. After the baptismal candle is lighted, the priest and godparents hold the child, and a few children walk around the font in a dance of joy. Finally, scriptures are read, and communion is given to the child.

## FUNERALS

The funeral service in the Greek Orthodox church is called *kithia*. Traditionally, the *trisayion* (the three holies) is recited at the time of death or at any time during a 40-day mourning period. In the United States the *trisayion* is repeated at the funeral service. At the beginning of the service, the priest greets the mourners at the entrance of the church. An open casket is arranged so that the deceased faces the altar. During the service mourners recite scriptures, prayers, and hymns, and they are invited by the priest to pay their last respects to the deceased by filing past the casket and kissing the icon that has been placed within. The family gathers around the casket for a last farewell, and the priest sprinkles oil on the body in the form of the cross and says a concluding prayer. After the priest, friends, or family members deliver a brief eulogy, the body is taken immediately for burial (*endaphiasmos*). At the cemetery the priest recites the *trisayion* for the last time and sprinkles dirt on the casket while reciting a prayer. After the funeral guests and family share a funeral meal (*makaria*), which traditionally consists of brandy, coffee, and *paximathia* (hard, dry toast). A full meal may also be served, with fish as the main course.

## THE ROLE OF WOMEN

As stated in the introduction to *American Aphrodite*, "Greek-American women have been without a voice since the first Greek immigrants arrived here as wives, mothers, sisters and daughters, usually, but not always, some months behind the menfolk, making no sound, proclaiming no existence." Traditionally, the lives of Greek women have centered on the home, the family, and the Greek Orthodox church. Since the earliest period of settlement in the United States, the burden of preserving Greek culture and tradition has been the responsibility of women. Women among the first and second generations of immigrants became the traditional keepers of songs, dances, and other folk customs and often cut themselves off from the *xeni*, the foreigners, who were essentially anyone outside the Greek community.

Today many Greek women are seriously challenged in their efforts to accommodate the values of two different worlds. The pressure to remain part of the community, obey parents' rules, and be "good Greek girls" who marry "well" and bear children is still strong. The conflict arises between family loyalty and self-realization, between duty to parents and community and the pursuit of the "American way of life." Many Greek American girls are given less freedom than their male counterparts and tend to remain close to their mothers even after marriage. The pursuit of education and a career is secondary and may even be perceived as "un-Greek" or unwomanly.

Although Greeks tend to be a highly educated ethnic group, the pursuit of higher education remains the province of men. The 1990 Census reports that twice as many Greek men as women received university degrees, with a significantly higher proportion of men going on to receive advanced degrees.

"I felt grateful the Statue of Liberty was a woman. I felt she would understand a woman's heart." Stella Petrakis in 1916, cited in *Ellis Island: An Illustrated History of the Immigrant Experience,* edited by Ivan Chermayeff et al. (New York: Macmillan, 1991).

## RELIGION

Theodore Salutos in *The Greeks in the United States* wrote: "Hellenism and Greek Orthodoxy—the one intertwined with the other—served as the cord that kept the immigrant attached to the mother country, nourished his patriotic appetites and helped him preserve the faith and language of his parents." The Greek Orthodox church helped to meet the emotional and spiritual needs of the immigrant. The early churches grew out of the *kinotitos* (community) where a *symvoulion* (board of directors) raised the money to build the church. The first Greek Orthodox church in the United States was founded in New Orleans in 1864. As Greek communities grew, other churches were established in New York (1892); Chicago (1893); Lowell, Massachusetts (1903); and Boston (1903). By 1923, there were 140 Greek churches in the United States.

Today, the liturgy and spirit of the Greek Orthodox church help to keep alive Greek ethnic cultural traditions in the United States. According to Kunkelman, to a Greek American, "ethnicity is synonymous with the church. One is a Greek not because he is a Hellene by birth; indeed many of Greek parentage have abandoned their identities and disappeared into the American mainstream. Rather one is Greek because he elects to remain part of the Greek community and an individual is a member of the Greek community by virtue of his attachment to the Greek Orthodox church, the framework on which the community rests."

For many, the Greek Orthodox church is the center of community life. In the United States all dioceses, parishes, and churches are under the ecclesiastical jurisdiction of the Archdiocese of North and South America, an autonomous self-governing church within the sphere of influence of the Ecumenical Patriarch of Constantinople and New Rome. The Ecumenical Patriarch has the power to elect the archbishop and the bishops, directs all church matters outside the American church, and remains the guiding force in all matters of faith. Founded in 1922, the Archdiocese is located in New York City. It supports 62 parishes in the Archdiocesan District of New York, as well as the parishes in ten dioceses across the Americas.

"Orthodox" comes from the Greek *orthos* (correct) and *doxa* (teaching or worship). The Greek Orthodox share a common liturgy, worship, and tradition. In its fundamental beliefs, the church is conservative, resistant to change, and allows little flexibility. The Orthodox tradition is an Eastern tradition with the official center of Orthodoxy at Constantinople. After the tenth century Eastern and Western traditions grew apart on matters of faith, dogma, customs, and politics. East and West finally divided on the issue of papal authority.

The basic beliefs of the Orthodox are summarized in the Nicene Creed dating back to the fourth century. The Orthodox believe that one can achieve complete identification with God (*theosis*). All activities and services in the church are to assist the individual in achieving that end. The most important service is the Divine Liturgy in which there are four distinct liturgies: St. John Chrysostom (the one most frequently followed), St. Basil (followed ten times a year), St. James (October 23), and the Liturgy of the Presanctified Gifts (Wednesdays and Fridays of Lent and the first three days of Easter Holy Week). The church uses Greek Koine, the language of New Testament

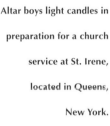

Altar boys light candles in preparation for a church service at St. Irene, located in Queens, New York.

Greek, as its liturgical language. The seven sacraments in the church are Baptism, Chrismation, Confession, Communion, Marriage, Holy Unction (Anointing of the Sick), and Holy Orders. The Greek Orthodox calendar has many feast days, fast days, and name days. The most important feast day ("the feast of feasts") is Holy Pascha (Easter Sunday). In addition to Easter, the "twelve great feasts" are the Nativity of the Mother of God, the Exaltation of the Holy Cross, the Presentation of the Mother of God in the Temple, Christmas, Epiphany, the Presentation of Jesus Christ in the Temple, Palm Sunday, Ascension of Jesus Christ, Pentecost, the Transfiguration of Jesus Christ, and the Dormition (death) of the Mother of God.

The Greek Orthodox church also follows the Byzantine tradition in its architecture. The church is divided into the vestibule (the front of the church representing the world), the nave (the main area where people assemble), and the sanctuary. The sanctuary is separated from the nave by an iconostasis, a screenlike partition. Only the priests enter the sanctuary. Icons (images of saints) decorate the iconostasis in prescribed tiers. The service takes place in the sanctuary, which contains an altar table and an oblation (preparation) table. The Greek Orthodox church is filled with symbols, including crosses and icons, which create an aura of heaven on earth.

The church today continues to face the process of Americanization. The American Orthodox church has many American elements: an American-trained clergy, the introduction of English into the service, modern music written for organ, modern architecture and architectural features (pews, choir lofts, separate social halls). The limited role of women in the church is being questioned. Until the second century, women fully participated in the church as teachers, preachers, and deacons. After that period, however, their roles were limited by official decree. Today women are taking more active leadership roles; however, the question of ordaining women to the priesthood has not been seriously considered.

## EMPLOYMENT AND ECONOMIC TRADITIONS

The first immigrants were for the most part young single men who had no intention of remaining permanently in the United States. They came to work in the large industrial cities of the Northeast and Midwest as factory laborers, peddlers, busboys, and bootblacks. Those who went to the mill towns of New England worked in textile and shoe factories, while the Greeks who went West worked in mines and on the railroads. These Greeks often were subject to the *pardone* system, a form of exploitative indentured servitude employed in many of the larger industrial cities of the North and in the large mining corporations of the West.

Greeks in America have stressed individual efforts and talent and have had a long tradition of entrepreneurship in the United States, and many who were peddlers and street merchants in the United States became owners of small businesses. First-generation Greeks who were fruit and vegetable peddlers became owners of grocery stores; flower vendors opened florist shops. Greeks in Lowell, Massachusetts, became successful in numerous businesses. By 1912, according to a publication of the National Park Service, *Lowell: The Story of an Industrial City*, they owned "seven restaurants, twenty coffee houses, twelve barber shops, two drug stores, six fruit stores, eight shoeshine parlors, one dry-goods store, four ticket agencies, seven bakeries, four candy stores [and] twenty-two grocery stores."

In the 1920s Greeks owned thousands of confectionery stores across the country and usually owned the candy-manufacturing businesses that supplied the stores. When the candy businesses collapsed, Greeks became restaurant owners. By the late 1920s several thousand Greek restaurants were scattered across the country. Many immigrants of the 1950s and 1960s went into the fast-food restaurant business.

The Greek professional class remained small until the 1940s. During the first quarter of the twentieth century, most Greek professionals were doctors. The next largest group comprised lawyers, dentists, pharmacists, and chemists. A few became professors of literature, philosophy, and the classics. Although the Greeks were slow to develop an academic tradition in this country in part because of low economic incentive, a new professional class began to emerge after World War I. Today Greek Americans engage in many professional academic endeavors. Instead of remaining in family-held businesses, third- and fourth-generation Greek Americans increasingly are pursuing professional careers.

Currently, Greeks are found in almost every occupation and enterprise and constitute one of the wealthier economic groups in the United States. The average per capita income of all persons with Greek ancestry according to the 1990 Census is $18,361.

## POLITICS AND GOVERNMENT

Numerous Greek American political and social organizations have existed since the 1880s. These organizations often were made up of Greeks who had come from the same region in Greece. They had a shared sense of Hellenism and a common religion and language and often aligned themselves with native Greek concerns. The *kinotitos* (community) was an organization similar to the village government in Greece. Although the *kinotitos* helped to preserve Greek traditions, it sometimes hindered assimilation.

In 1907 the Pan-Hellenic Union was founded to coordinate and incorporate local organizations; to provide a means of helping Greece obtain more territory from the Ottoman Empire; and to support the return of Constantinople to Greece and the consolidation of all Greek colonies in the Eastern Mediterranean under Greek authority. It also helped Greeks to adapt to their new home in the United States. Many Greek immigrants were slowly beginning to accept the fact that they would not be returning to Greece and that the United States was their permanent home. In 1922 the American Hellenic Educational Progressive Association (AHEPA) was founded. Although the AHEPA supported the assimilation of Greeks to the American way of life, it did not relinquish its strong attachments to Greece. During World War II, the AHEPA was a major contributor to the Greek War Relief Association.

The one issue that mobilized the Greek American community to political action was the Turkish invasion of Cyprus on July 15, 1974. The efforts of well-organized lobby groups to effect an arms embargo against Turkey were impressive. The AHEPA played a leading role in these activities, along with other lobby groups—the American Hellenic Institute and its public affairs committee, the influential United Hellenic American Congress, and the Hellenic Council of America. The Greek Orthodox church and local community organizations also assisted. Primarily because of the successful lobbying of these groups, the United States imposed an arms embargo on Turkey on February 5, 1975.

Greek political figures are almost overwhelmingly Democratic. They include Michael Dukakis, Paul Tsongas, John Brademas, Paul Spyro Sarbanes, and George Stephanopoulos. Although Greek Americans traditionally have voted Democratic, their increasing wealth and status have led to an even division within the Greek American community between Republicans and Democrats.

## MILITARY

Greek Americans have participated in large numbers in all major wars fought by the United States. Greek American men with veteran status number 90,530; women number 2,635.

# INDIVIDUAL AND GROUP CONTRIBUTIONS

Greek Americans have made significant contributions in virtually all of the arts, sciences, and humanities, as well as in politics and business. Following is a sample of their achievements.

## ACADEMIA

Aristides Phoutridis, a distinguished professor at Yale University, established Helikon, the first Greek student organization, in 1911 in Boston. George Mylonas (1898-1988) had a distinguished career in the fields of Classical and Bronze Age art and archaeology. His numerous books include *Mycenae, the Capital City of Agamemnon* (1956), *Aghios Kosmas* (1959), *Eleusis and the Eleusinian Mysteries* (1961), *Mycenae and the Mycenean Age* (1966), *Mycenae's Last Century of Greatness* (1968), *Grave Circle B of Mycenae* (1972), *The Cult Center of Mycenae* (1972), and *The West Cemetery of Eleusis* (1975). Theodore Salutos (1910-1980) was a professor of history at the University of California, Los Angeles, who is well known for his studies of the Greek immigration experience. His most important work, *Greeks in*

*the United States* (1964), became a model for other works on this topic.

## EDUCATION

John Celivergos Zachos (1820-1898), one of 40 orphans who came to the United States during the Greek Revolution of 1821, was associate principal of the Cooper Female Seminary in Dayton, Ohio (1851-1854), principal and teacher of literature in the grammar school of Antioch College in Yellow Springs, Ohio (1854-1857), a surgeon during the Civil War, a teacher at Meadville Theological School (1866-1867), and a teacher and curator at Cooper Union in New York until 1898. Michael Anagnos (1837-1906) became the director of the famous Perkins Institute for the Blind in Boston where he promoted vocational training and self-help.

## FILM, TELEVISION, AND THEATER

Olympia Dukakis (1931- ), a well-known film actress and the cousin of politician Michael Dukakis, has appeared in a number of roles since the 1960s. Selected films include *Lilith* (1964), *Twice a Man* (1964), *John and Mary* (1969), *Made for Each Other* (1971), and *The Idolmaker* (1980). Her most recent films are *Steel Magnolias* (1989) and *Moonstruck* (1987), for which she won an Academy Award for Best Supporting Actress. John Cassavetes (1929-1989) was a well-known stage, screen, and television actor, director, playwright, and screenwriter. His many film appearances include *Fourteen* (1951), *Affair in Havana* (1957), *The Killers* (1964), *The Dirty Dozen* (1967), and *Rosemary's Baby* (1968). He directed and produced many films including *Too Late Blues* (1962), *A Child Is Waiting* (1963), *A Woman under the Influence* (1974), and *Big Trouble* (1986). George Tsakiris (1933- ), a singer, dancer, and actor, has been in films since the 1940s. He starred in roles in *Gentlemen Prefer Blondes* (1953); *White Christmas* (1954); *West Side Story* (1961), for which he won a Golden Globe Award and an Academy Award for Best Supporting Actor; *Diamond Head* (1962); and *Is Paris Burning?* (1963). Elia Kazan (1909- ) was born Elia Kazanjoglou in Constantinople. He is well known as a director, producer, actor, and writer. His best-known productions include *A Streetcar Named Desire* (1951), *A Face in the Crowd* (1957), *Splendor in the Grass* (1961), *America, America* (1963), and *The Arrangement* (1969). He directed such films as *A Tree Grows in*

*Brooklyn* (1945), *Gentlemen's Agreement* (1947), *On the Waterfront* (1953), and *East of Eden* (1954). His writings include *America, America* (1962), *The Arrangement* (1969), *The Assassins* (1972), *The Understudy* (1974), *Acts of Love* (1978), and *The Anatolian* (1982). Katina Paxinou (1900-1973), born Katina Constantopoulos, was a popular actress who starred in many films, including *For Whom the Bell Tolls* (1943), *Confidential Agent* (1945), *Mourning Becomes Electra* (1947), *The Inheritance* (1947), and *Prince of Foxes* (1945). Telly Savalas (1923-1994), a popular film and television actor, is best known for his role as Theo Kojack in the National Broadcasting Corporation's television series "Kojack" (1973). Born in Garden City, New York, Savalas starred in several films including *The Young Savages* (1961), *Birdman of Alcatraz* (1962), *The Greatest Story Ever Told* (1965), and *The Dirty Dozen* (1967).

### JOURNALISM

Constantine Phasoularides published the first Greek American newspaper in New York in 1892, the *Neos Kosmas* (*New World*). Nicholas Gage (1939- ), born in Lia, is a journalist and writer, associated with the *Worcester Telegram and Evening Gazette*, *Boston Herald Traveler*, Associated Press, *Wall Street Journal*, and the *New York Times*. He left the *New York Times* in 1980 to write *Eleni*, a work detailing the events surrounding the execution of his mother by Communist guerrillas in Greece in the 1940s.

### LITERATURE

In 1906 Mary Vardoulakis wrote *Gold in the Streets*, the first Greek American novel. Olga Broumas (1949- ), born in Syros, is a feminist poet who writes a poetry of the "body" with distinct lesbian-erotic motifs. Many of her poems capture the spirit of the Greek homeland. Her works include *Beginning with O* (1977), *Sole Savage* (1980), *Pastoral Jazz* (1983), and *Perpetua* (1985). Kostantinos Lardas (1927- ) writes both poetry and fiction. His major works are *The Devil Child* (1961) and *And In Him Too; In Us,* which was nominated for a Pulitzer Prize in 1964. Henry Mark Petrakis (1923- ) is a major figure in Greek American fiction. His novels include *Lion of My Heart* (1959), *The Odyssey of Kostas Volakis* (1963), *The Dream of Kings* (1966), *In the Land of Morning* (1973), and *Hour of the Bell* (1976). Petrakis writes of the immigrant experience of the conflict between the old and new generations.

### MILITARY

Captain George Partridge Colvocoresses (1816-1872) distinguished himself as commander of the *Saratoga* in the Civil War. His son Rear Admiral George P. Colvocoresses fought in the Spanish-American War was appointed the commandant of midshipmen at the U.S. Naval Academy.

### MUSIC

Dimitri Mitropoulos (1896-1960), a well-known composer-conductor, conducted the Minneapolis Symphony (1937-1949) and the New York Philharmonic. Maria Callas (1923-1977), born Mary Kalogeropoulou, was a noted operatic soprano. Callas made her film debut in *Tosca* (1941). She is remembered as a true artist for her original interpretations of Bellini, Donizetti, and Cherubini and in her roles as Norma, Medea, Violetta, and Lucia, as well as Tosca.

### POLITICS

The first Greek American to be elected to the U.S. Congress was Lucas Miltiades Miller (1824-1902). Miller, a Democrat from Wisconsin, served in Congress from March 4, 1891, to March 3, 1893. Spiro Agnew (1918- ), a Republican who served as governor of Maryland in 1966, became vice president of the United States under Richard Nixon on November 5, 1968, and was reelected as vice president on November 7, 1972. John Brademas (1927- ), a Democrat from Indiana, served in Congress from 1959 to 1981. He became president of New York State University in 1981 until his retirement in 1992. Michael Dukakis (1933- ) was governor of Massachusetts in 1975-1979 and 1983-1991 and was Democratic candidate for president in 1988. Paul Efthemios Tsongas (1941- ), congressman from Massachusetts, served in the House of Representatives during 1974-1979 and in the U.S. Senate during 1979-1985. Paul Spyro Sabannes (1933- ) was a Democratic congressman from Maryland who was reelected to the Senate in 1982. Gus Yatron (1927- ), Democratic congressman from Pennsylvania, served in the U.S. House of Representatives during 1969-1989. George Stephanopoulos (1961- ) was director of communications for President Bill Clinton's administration during 1992-1993 before becoming senior advisor to the president for policy and strategy.

## SCIENCE AND TECHNOLOGY

George Papnicolaou (1883-1961) was professor emeritus of anatomy at Cornell Medical College. His research led him to develop the "pap smear," a test designed to detect cervical cancer. Polyvios Koryllos was a professor of medicine at the University of Athens and Yale University. He is well known for his work in diagnosing tuberculosis. John Kotzias was a neurologist who discovered the drug L-dopa for the treatment of Parkinson's disease.

## SPORTS

Alex Karras (1935- ) was a well-known football player (a two-time All-American) for the Detroit Lions from 1958 to 1971. He hosted the National Football League's Monday Night Football and has made numerous television appearances. Alex Grammas (1926- ) was a professional baseball player between 1954 and 1963 who played with the St. Louis Cardinals, Cincinnati Reds, and the Chicago Cubs. He was a baseball manager in 1969 and 1976-1977. Harry Agganis (1930-1955) distinguished himself in baseball, football, and basketball. Although he was drafted by the Cleveland Browns football team on graduation from Boston University in 1953, he signed with the Boston Red Sox. Jimmy Londos (c. 1895-1975), born Christopher Theophilus, won the world heavyweight wrestling championship on June 25, 1934.

# MEDIA

## PRINT

Historically, the Greek ethnic press in the United States has kept pace with the needs of Greek Americans, and its presence has contributed to a strong ethnic cohesion in the Greek community. The first Greek American newspaper in the country was *Neos Kosmos* (*New World*), first published in New York by Constantine Phasoularides in September 1897. It was followed by the *Thermopylae*, published by John Booras in 1900. The *Ethnikos Keryx* (*National Herald*), which began publication in New York on April 2, 1915, was one of the few newspapers to have a significant influence on the Greek reading public. Its serious competitors in New York are *Proini* (*Morning News*), which publishes only in Greek, and the *Greek American*, which publishes only in English. In Chicago the *Greek Star* (*Hellenikos Aster*) and the *Greek Press*

(*Hellenikos Typos*), both published in Greek and English, still hold a sizable readership.

Currently, there are 27 Greek American newspapers in the United States; seven are published in either Greek or English, respectively, and 14 are published in both languages. The majority focus on community events and church news, as well as on news from Greece and the lobbying activities of Greek American politicians.

### Campana.

Founded in 1917, *Campana* is published semi-monthly in Greek and English and features the news from Greece, with information about Greeks abroad. Covers local and community events.

**Contact:** Costas Athansasiades, Editor.

**Address:** 30-96 42nd Street, Long Island City (Astoria), New York 11101.

**Telephone:** (718) 278-3014.

### Ethnikos Keryx (The National Herald).

Begun in 1915, the *Herald* is the oldest daily newspaper in the Greek language in the United States. Features international, national, and local news and items about Greece of interest to the community.

**Contact:** Anthony Diamataris, Editor

**Address:** 41-17 Crescent Street, Long Island City, New York 11101.

**Telephone:** (718) 784-5255.

### The Greek American.

Widely read English-language publication that focuses on the political events in Greece and in the United States. Publishes a national calendar of events that lists activities taking place in the larger Greek community.

**Contact:** Tina Maurikos, Editor.

**Address:** 25-50 Crescent Street, Astoria, New York 11102.

**Telephone:** (718) 626-7676.

**Fax:** (718) 956-8076.

### Greek Press (Hellenikos Typos).

Founded in 1929 and published bi-weekly in English and Greek, *Greek Press* covers political, educational, and social events, as well as local and international news of interest to the Greek community.

**Contact:** Helen Angelopoulos, Editor.

**Address:** 808 West Jackson Boulevard, Chicago, Illinois 60607.
**Telephone:** (708) 766-2955.
**Fax:** (708) 766-3069.

### Greek Star (Hellenikos-Aster).

Founded in 1904, *Greek Star* is the oldest continuously published Greek newspaper in the United States. A bi-weekly publication of the United Hellenic American Congregation, it appears in Greek and English and features local and international news of interest to the Greek community in Chicago. Covers news from Cyprus and Greece.

**Contact:** Nicholas Philippidis, Editor.
**Address:** 4715 North Lincoln, Chicago, Illinois 60625.
**Telephone:** (312) 878-7331.

### The Hellenic Chronicle.

A weekly English-language publication dedicated to the promulgation of American, Hellenic, and Orthodox ideals. Features political, national, international, and local news of interest to the Greek community. Contains an Entertainment Arts and Social section.

**Contact:** Nancy Agris Savage, Editor.
**Address:** 324 Newbury Street, Boston, Massachusetts 02115.
**Telephone:** (617) 262-4500.

### Proini.

Competing with *The National Herald*, this daily publishes community news and news from Greece and Cyprus, sporting events, artistic and cultural events, and editorials.

**Contact:** Fanny Holliday Petallides, Publisher.
**Address:** 25-50 Crescent Street, Astoria, New York 11102.
**Telephone:** (718) 626-7676.

### RADIO

### WEDC-AM.

"Hellenic American Radio Hour" airs every Saturday, 7:00 to 8:00 p.m. One of the oldest Greek radio shows in the Chicago area (75 years). Features community events, discussion of family problems, religious issues, music, and news from Greece.

**Contact:** Tom Chiampas and Katina Chiampas.
**Address:** 5413 North Nagle Avenue, Chicago, Illinois 60630.
**Telephone:** (312) 775-6577.

### WEEF-AM.

"Greek Orthodox Hours of the Chicago Diocese" airs every Tuesday and Wednesday, 11:00 p.m. to 12:00 a.m. Discusses topics related to the Greek Orthodox church.

**Contact:** Paula Rekoumis and Sotirios Rekoumis.
**Address:** 7902 Maple Street, Morton Grove, Illinois.
**Telephone:** (708) 967-8798.

### WLYN-AM.

"Soul of Greece" programs are scheduled daily Monday through Friday (3:00 p.m. to 7:00 p.m.), Saturday (2:00 p.m. to 6:00 p.m.), Sunday (8:00 a.m. to 12:00 p.m.; and 1:00 p.m. to 2:00 p.m. Features local, community, and international news; cultural events; sports; and music. Broadcasts about 95 percent in Greek (with the news in English).

**Contact:** Oscar Papanastasiou or Pauline Papanastasiou.
**Address:** 427 Union Street, Lynn, Massachusetts 01910.
**Telephone:** (617) 592-3002.

### WNTN-AM.

"Greek Cultural Radio Program of Boston," a noncommercial, one-hour program that broadcasts twice a week. Features topics relating to Greek heritage, customs, and history. In Greek and English.

**Contact:** Athanasios Vulgaropoulos.
**Address:** 26 Tudor Street, Waltham, Massachusetts 02154.
**Telephone:** (617) 894-7666.

### WUNR.

"The Other Program," a talk show where people can call in with questions; "The Athenian Hour," featuring cultural and news events; "Hellenic Voice of Massachusetts"; "Let Us Sing," playing selections of Greek music.

**Address:** 160 North Washington, Boston, Massachusetts 02114.
**Telephone:** (617) 367-9003.

### TELEVISION

### Cable Television Network (CTN) of New Jersey, Inc.

A 24-hour cable network service available to more than 1.7 million homes in New Jersey. The cable service currently airs "Greek Orthodox," produced by Greek Orthodox Communications, Inc.

**Contact:** James DeBold, Information Manager.

**Address:** 128 West State Street, Trenton, New Jersey 08608.

**Telephone:** (609) 392-8682.

### "Grecian Spotlight," Channel 26, Chicago.

A weekly show that highlights community events in the Chicago area, sports, news, and music of Greece.

**Contact:** Ernest Panos, Producer.

**Address:** 168 North Michigan Avenue, Chicago, Illinois 60601.

**Telephone:** (312) 906-8888.

### "The Greek Spirit," WYBE, Channel 35, Philadelphia.

The program broadcasts on Sundays, 10:00 p.m. to 11:00 p.m. About 80 percent of the program is in the Greek language. It features dance, local and community events, news from Greece (through ERT-1, Channel 1, from Athens). Through cable services, the program is seen in New York and New Jersey. Channel 35 also broadcasts "Hellenic World" (in English), on Sundays, 4:30 p.m. to 5:00 p.m. It features items on the history, historical personalities, and antiquities of Greece and Greek life.

**Contact:** George Burlotos.

**Address:** Cooper Landing, Suite 4E, Cherry Hill, New Jersey 08002.

**Telephone:** (609) 482-5681.

### "Hellenic Television Program," Channel 47, New York.

The program broadcasts one and one-half hours every week, on Sundays. It includes documentaries, sports, dances, news from Greece, and local and community events. It can be seen in the tristate area of New York, Connecticut, and New Jersey.

**Contact:** Takis Paralikas.

**Address:** 32-09 31st Avenue, Astoria, New York 11106.

**Telephone:** (718) 956-3434.

### "National Greek TV Show," Channel 26, Chicago, and Channel 47, New York.

A weekly variety show (one hour in Chicago; one and one-half hours in New York) that features local events, national and international news, sports, interviews, and music. The show is part of the *Greek Channel* distributed by Time Warner Cable (serving Queens, New York, and West Brooklyn), which broadcasts Greek programming for 19 hours a day.

**Contact:** Demitrios Kastanas, Producer.

**Address:** 30-97 Steinway Street, No. 206, Astoria, New York 11103.

**Telephone:** (718)726-0900.

# ORGANIZATIONS AND ASSOCIATIONS

### Greek Orthodox Ladies Philoptochos Society.

Founded in 1931. The Society promotes the values of the family and the Greek Orthodox faith and engages in many charitable, educational, and religious activities on behalf of the church. Its membership of more than 400,000 includes women 18 years and older.

**Contact:** Terry Kokas, Director.

**Address:** 345 East 74th Street, New York, New York 10021.

**Telephone:** (212) 744-4390.

### Greek Orthodox Youth Adult League.

Conducts workshops on religious education for Greek youth. Assists the church both nationally and locally, with 6,000 to 10,000 members.

**Contact:** Tom Kanelos.

**Address:** 80 East 79th Street, New York, New York 10021.

**Telephone:** (708) 295-7924

### Order of American Hellenic Educational Progressive Association (AHEPA).

Founded in 1922. The AHEPA is dedicated to the preservation of the Greek national identity in the United States. The oldest Greek fraternal organization in the United States has a membership of more than 500,000 members, with many chapters across the county. It engages in numerous charitable, publishing, and educational activities. It includes the Daughters of Penelope, a women's auxiliary; the Maids of Athens, a girls' organization; and the Sons of Pericles, a boys' organization. Publishes *AHEPAN*, a bimonthly.

**Contact:** Constantine Gekas, Executive Director.

**Address:** 1909 Q Street, N.W., Suite 500, Washington, D.C. 20009.

**Telephone:** (202) 232-6300.

**United Hellenic American Congress (UHAC).**
Founded in 1974. The UHAC was established to preserve the cultural traditions of Greece. It coordinates many of the cultural activities of the Greek community in the Chicago area. Every year the UHAC issues a Greek Heritage Calendar of Events and is active in promoting the Greek Independence Day parade. The UHAC was a prominent lobbyist in the Greek American protest against the Turkish invasion of Cyprus.

**Contact:** Andrew Athens.

**Address:** 40 North Franklin, Suite 215, Chicago, Illinois 60610.

**Telephone:** (312) 822-9888.

## MUSEUMS AND RESEARCH CENTERS

**Greek-American Folklore Society.**
Founded 1983. Society members conduct classes and workshops on traditional dances and songs from every region of Greece. The Society presents hundreds of performances throughout the year and offers exhibits of and lectures on traditional Greek costumes. It coordinates the *Panegyri,* an annual conference of Greek folklore societies, as well as the Hellenic Folk Music Festival. The Society has 50 to 60 members.

**Contact:** Paul Ginis.

**Address:** 29-04 Ditmars Boulevard, Astoria, New York 11105.

**Telephone:** (718) 728-8048.

**Hellenic Cultural Museum at Holy Trinity Cathedral.**
Opened on May 3, 1992. The museum is considered to be the first Greek cultural museum in the United States. This "people's museum" contains important collections of scrapbooks, diaries, letters, artifacts, newspapers, and photographs documenting the lives of the Greeks who settled in Utah from 1905 to the present. The museum contains a unique display of mining operations.

**Contact:** Chris Metos.

**Address:** 279 South 300 West, Salt Lake City, Utah 84101.

**Telephone:** (801) 328-9681.

**Hellenic Museum and Cultural Center.**
Opened 1992. The center preserves original documents, artifacts, and other archival source materials relating to the Greek American immigrant experience. It also collects the artistic works (crafts, embroideries, furniture) of Greek Americans.

**Contact:** Elaine Kollintzas, Executive Director.

**Address:** 400 North Franklin Street, Chicago, Illinois 60610.

**Telephone:** (312) 467-4622.

**Immigration History Research Center.**
Located at the University of Minnesota, this center contains important primary source materials on many aspects of the life of Greek immigrants in the United States. The collection includes the papers of the immigrant historian Theodore Salutos.

**Contact:** Joe Whorl.

**Address:** 826 Berry Street, St. Paul, Minnesota 55114.

**Telephone:** (612) 627-4208.

**Saint Photios Foundation.**
Founded in 1981. A Greek fraternal organization dedicated to preserving a shrine in Saint Augustine, Florida, commemorating the Greeks of New Smyrna, the first Greeks immigrants to arrive in America in 1768. The museum has a small library and cultural exhibit.

**Contact:** Father Dimitrios Couchell.

**Address:** 41 Saint George Street, Post Office Box 1960, Saint Augustine, Florida 32085.

**Telephone:** (904) 829-8205.

## SOURCES FOR ADDITIONAL STUDY

Callincos, Constance. *American Aphrodite: Becoming Female in Greek America.* New York: Pella, 1990.

Kunkelman, Gary. *The Religion of Ethnicity: Belief and Belonging in a Greek-American Community.* New York: Garland, 1990.

Moskos, Charles C. *Greek Americans: Struggle and Success,* second edition. New Brunswick, New Jersey: Transaction, 1989.

Mouzaki, Rozanna. *Greek Dances for Americans.* Garden City, New York: Doubleday, 1981.

Pappas, Susan. "The Greek-American Press Marks Its 100th Anniversary This Year," *Editor and Publisher,* September 1992, pp. 18-19.

Rouvelas, Marilyn. *A Guide to Greek Traditions and Customs in America.* Bethesda, Maryland: Attica, 1993.

Salutos, Theodore. *The Greeks in the United States.* Cambridge: Harvard University Press, 1964.

Scourby, Alice. *The Greek Americans.* Boston: Twayne, 1977.

*Treasured Greek Proverbs,* compiled, edited, and translated by Elaine G. Bucuvalas, Catherine G. Lavrakas, and Poppy G. Stamatos. (1980).

U.S. Department of Commerce, Economics and Statistics Administration. *Ancestry of the Population in the United States, 1990.* Washington, D.C.: Government Printing Office, 1990.

U.S. Department of the Interior, National Park Service, Division of Publications. *Lowell: The Story of an Industrial City.* Washington, D.C.: Government Printing Office, 1990.

Although Guatemalan Americans constitute a very small percentage of the American population and are one of the most recently established American ethnic groups, they have contributed significantly to American life through political and cultural organizations and as individuals.

# GUATEMALAN AMERICANS

by
Maria Hong

## OVERVIEW

The most populous country in Central America, Guatemala is located in the northern part of the Central American region. Its land mass encompasses 42,042 square miles (108,889 square kilometers), bordered by Mexico to the north and west, El Salvador and Honduras to the south and east, the Pacific Ocean along its West Coast, and Belize and the Caribbean Sea to the north and east. The southern half of the Republic of Guatemala mainly consists of beautiful mountain highlands and plateaus, which are susceptible to devastating earthquakes. The northern region contains the department of the Petén, a sparsely populated lowland tropical jungle. There is also a narrow Pacific coastal plain and a small Caribbean lowland area. Most of Guatemala's population and its major cities, including the capital, Guatemala City, are located in the southern region.

Guatemala has a population of about ten million people, and the largest indigenous population in Central America. Although estimates of the indigenous population vary greatly from as low as 40 percent of the total population to as high as 85 percent, most sources estimate it at over 50 percent. Most of the indigenous groups are Mayan, although small numbers of Pipil Aztecs live in the southern and eastern areas and Xincas in the east. More than a racial classification, the term *indigena* (indigenous) refers to cultural and linguistic groups. The population of Spanish-speaking *ladinos* consists of the small Caucasian elite class; the substantial number of *mestizos* of mixed Spanish and indigenous race; minorities of African, Chinese, and Arab descent; and indigenous people who no longer consciously identify themselves as such. Guatemala's smallest ethnic group is the Garifuna, descendants of African and Carib people formerly from the island of St. Vincent who reside along the Caribbean coast.

Guatemala's official language is Spanish. However, the Maya speak over 20 distinct languages and numerous dialects, and many do not speak Spanish. The four main Mayan languages—Quiché, Mam, Cakchiquel, and Kekchi—are spoken by about 40 percent of the population. Other indigenous languages include Kanjobal, Chuj, Jacalteco, Ixil, Achi, Pocomchi, Central Pocomam, Eastern Pocomam, and Tzutuhil. These languages are spoken by distinct indigenous groups.

Although Roman Catholicism is the dominant religion, many Mayan Guatemalans have traditionally practiced a syncretist form of Catholicism, blending Catholic and Mayan rites and beliefs. Since the 1950s, Evangelical Pentecostal Protestantism has been on the rise in Guatemala, and it surged in popularity during the 1980s. Two recent presidents have been Evangelical Pentecostal Protestants and up to one-third of the population now practices this religion.

Guatemala's national symbol of independence and pride is the quetzal, a brilliantly colored tropical bird native to Central America. According to legend, the quetzal lost its voice after the Spanish Conquest in the sixteenth century.

## HISTORY

Guatemala's roots lie in the great Mayan civilization, concentrated in separate city-states established throughout what is now southern Mexico and Central America. From 2000 B.C. through 900 A.D., Mayan civilization accomplished much in the areas of astronomy, written language, architecture, the arts, and religion. Some of these achievements remain for us to appreciate today, such as the immense stone temples and pyramids at Tikal in the Petén.

However, the Mayan city-states were also very militaristic, usually warring with each other and devoting much of their energies and resources to military efforts. This penchant for warfare may have contributed to the mysterious disappearance of Mayan civilization by 900 A.D. By the time the Spanish arrived, there were about one million indigenous people whose violent feuding facilitated their conquest. By 1650, most of the indigenous people had been wiped out by disease, war, and exploitation, and their numbers had dwindled to about 200,000.

From 1523 to 1524, the Spanish, led by Pedro de Alvarado, colonized many Mayan city-states. De Alvarado became the first captain general of Guatemala, which then encompassed most of Central America. In 1821, Guatemala gained independence from Spain, and in 1824 it joined the Central American Federation. In 1838, the Federation disbanded, due mostly to a revolt against it led by an indigenous general, Rafael Carrera, who then seized control of the newly independent nation of Guatemala.

In 1871, a liberal *caudillo* or military dictator, Justo Rufino Barrios, took power and ruled as president from 1873 to 1885. Barrios enacted anti-clerical legislation, began to establish a national education system, and fostered the inception of Guatemala's coffee industry. Guatemala was ruled by a succession of military dictators until the last *caudillo*, Jorge Ubico, was overthrown in 1944. Shortly thereafter, Juan Jose Arevalo, a university professor exiled to Argentina, was called back and elected president. Arevalo instituted political democracy in Guatemala, encouraging organized labor, the formation of a social security system, and industrialization.

Arevalo's successor, Colonel Jacobo Arbenz Guzman, introduced a radical agrarian reform program that redistributed land from wealthy landowners and much of the holdings of the U.S.-based United Fruit Company. United Fruit had dominated the commercial banana industry and exploited peasant workers since the early twentieth century. Arbenz's challenge to United Fruit and his support of Guatemala's Communist party resulted in conflict with the company and U.S. President Dwight D. Eisenhower's administration. In mid-1954, Arbenz was overthrown by a U.S.-supported, largely CIA-directed revolt, led by Colonel Carlos Castillo Armas.

During the next 30 years, most of the agrarian and labor reforms achieved under Arevalo and Arbenz were undone by a succession of mostly military rulers. Since the 1960s, leftist guerrillas have attempted to undermine these regimes, while right-wing paramilitary death squads have fought back against the guerrillas by brutally repressing the civilian population. According to Amnesty International, at least 20,000 civilians were killed by the death squads from 1966 to 1976.

During the late 1970s, a popular resistance movement to the military governments began to operate through a collaboration among *ladinos*, *indigenas*, peasants, labor leaders, students, journalists, politicians, and Catholic priests. In response, the army and paramilitary counterinsurgency units stepped up their repression efforts. From 1980 to 1981, guerrilla forces encouraged and sometimes coerced large numbers of highland *indigenas* to join them in their armed revolutionary efforts. The army retaliated by massacring whole indigenous villages; kidnapping, torturing, and murdering people suspected of supporting the guerrillas; and scorching peasant crops and homes.

Although the army's terrorism techniques affected all sectors of the resistance movements, indigenous communities suffered the brunt of the violence of the 1980s. Most authorities have called the military efforts an ethnic genocide campaign, stemming from pervasive discrimination against *indigenas* in Guatemalan society. In addition to destroying indigenous villages, the government army forced more than one million indigenas into military-controlled "model villages" and "reeducation camps," and conscripted men into the army's civil defense patrols.

Violence in the villages peaked under Efrain Rios Montt, a Pentecostal Protestant, who became president through a military coup in 1982. By the army's own count, the counterinsurgency movement destroyed 440 villages and damaged numerous others between 1980 and 1984. Widespread terrorism continued under Rios Montt's successor Brigadier General Oscar Humberto Mejia Victores, who became president in 1983. In 1984, the Guatemalan Supreme Court reported that around 100,000 children had lost at least one parent in the massacres.

In 1985, Marco Vinicio Cerezo Arevalo, a Christian Democratic Party leader, won the presidential election, initiating a transition from military to civilian government. Cerezo tried unsuccessfully to carry out reforms, and political killings by the right-wing death squads continued. He was succeeded in 1991 by Jorge Serrano Elias, an Evangelical Protestant and former member of the Rios Montt regime.

Although right-wing violence persisted, Serrano's government reached a tentative accord with the major guerrilla coalition, the Guatemalan National Revolutionary Unity (URNG) and police and military men were arrested for death-squad activity for the first time. In 1993, Serrano and military leaders attempted to dissolve Guatemala's Congress and suspend the constitution. After a short period of political turmoil, the Congress elected Ramiro de Leon Carpio, a former human rights ombudsman, as president.

De Leon Carpio resumed the peace talks between the government and the URNG, which had been going on intermittently since 1991, and he has made significant breakthroughs in the peace process. On March 29, 1994, the government and the URNG signed three peace agreements brokered by the United Nations. Among other provisions, the agreements call for human rights investigations and monitoring, guerrilla demobilization, and prosecution of human rights violators. Fragile peace process negotiations are still going on.

Despite the achievements of the peace accords, however, widespread violence, including abductions, torture, and executions by army and paramilitary men, continues in Guatemala. In the political arena, the Guatemalan Republican Front, the right-wing party of Rios Montt, gained many seats in the Congress and Rios Montt himself was elected to the Congress in August of 1994. Members of the Party of National Advancement, another conservative party that opposes de Leon Carpio, also won many Congressional seats.

Guatemala today remains a country in crisis. Sixty-three percent of the population lives in extreme poverty. In this mostly rural, agrarian country, two percent of the population owns over 64 percent of the arable land. Peasants survive by farming sub-subsistence land or by doing seasonal migratory work on coastal coffee, sugar, and cotton plantations. Among Central American nations, Guatemala has the highest infant and child mortality rates, the lowest life expectancy, and most malnourished population, with rampant severe hunger.

The efforts of activists such as Guatemalan Nobel Peace Laureate Rigoberta Menchú Tum have focused international attention on the oppression of indigenous people in Guatemala. However, an apartheid-type of oligarchic system remains entrenched with the government and other power centers controlled by a small European-descended minority. The long armed conflict has resulted in the disappearance or murder of tens of thousands of people and the displacement of over a million more. Although several hundred thousand Guatemalans remain uprooted within Guatemala, hundreds of thousands have fled to the United States and Mexico to escape the violence since the late 1970s.

## IMMIGRATION TO THE UNITED STATES

Until 1960, the United States did not keep separate statistics on the number of immigrants from Guatemala, and figures reflect migration from the entire Central American region. However, it is fair to conclude that few Guatemalans immigrated to the United States before 1960, since the numbers for all Central American immigrants were small.

During the 1830s, only 44 arrivals of Central Americans were recorded. Between 1890 and 1900, 500 Central Americans immigrated to the United States according to records of legal migration. The numbers increased during the next two decades, with 8,000 arriving from 1900 to 1910 and 17,000 migrating between 1910 and 1920. Emigrants from Guatemala may have been seeking a better life following a devastating earthquake in 1917.

During the 1930s, the number of immigrants fell to less than 6,000 in the decade, due in part to quotas on immigration from Western Hemisphere nations enacted in the 1920s. However, since the mid-1950s the annual number of legally admitted Central Americans has steadily risen, with 45,000 arriving from 1951 to 1960.

Due to political upheavals and related economic crises throughout the region, large numbers of undocumented Guatemalans and other Central Americans have been coming to the United States since the late 1970s. During the early 1970s, several factors, including inflation, political turmoil and violence, unemployment, low wages, land scarcity due to inequitable land allocation, and the population explosion, especially among indigenous people, precipitated the mass internal and external displacement of Guatemalan *campesino* peasants, *indigenas,* and professionals. In February of 1976, an earthquake destroyed much of Guatemala City, causing some to emigrate. From 1967 to 1976, 19,683 Guatemalans immigrated to the United States, and the 1970 U.S. Census recorded a Guatemalan American population of 26,865 persons. The 1980 U.S. Census recorded 62,098 Guatemalan Americans, with 46 percent arriving from 1975 to 1980.

However, the vast majority of the Guatemalan American population has arrived since 1980. Offi-

cial immigration statistics do not reflect the true number of immigrants from Guatemala since most arrivals are undocumented refugees. In 1984, there were an estimated one million Guatemalan refugees, with many displaced within Guatemala and hundreds of thousands fleeing to Mexico and the United States. Thousands also escaped to neighboring Belize, Costa Rica, Nicaragua, and Honduras.

Since the 1920s or earlier, Mayan Guatemalans had traveled annually to southern Mexico to work on seasonal coffee harvests, attracted by the wages and low cost of living. Others possibly planned to sell contraband items upon their return home. By the late 1950s, ten to fifteen thousand men and women were crossing the border into Mexico and back every year. In the 1960s and 1970s, the number increased to around 60,000 annually; some of these settled in the state of Chiapas in southern Mexico, where Mayan communities also reside. After the massacres of Mayan villages in Guatemala, *indigenas* from the departments of Quiché, Alta Verapaz, Huehuetenango, Itzabal, and the Petén fled to this region, and many seasonal workers remained in Mexico. Refugee camps were established in Chiapas and in Campeche and Quintana Roo. Due to the desperate economic and health conditions in these camps many Guatemalan refugees moved on to the United States, often enduring great hardships on the way. Migration spurred by these circumstances continues today.

This Guatemalan boy's family arrived in Brownsville, Texas, seeking asylum in the United States.

Since they must cross the border illegally, the emigrants usually hire guides called *coyotes*, who facilitate the crossings for high fees costing up to $1,500 per person. During the trips many experience graft, robbery, rape, or imprisonment by people who exploit their precarious status. Some are smuggled to the United States by religious workers who also give them sanctuary once they arrive. Due to the expense of the trip, those who migrate to the United States are not generally the poorest of the poor.

According to the 1970 U.S. Census, 90 percent of Guatemalans in the United States were white. During the 1950s and 1960s most Guatemalan immigrants were middle class. Before the 1980s, most Guatemalan political emigrants were *ladino* activists and politicians from urban centers. After 1980 large numbers of indigenous people and *campesinos* fled to the United States from counter-insurgency campaigns in the western highland areas. Significant numbers of schoolteachers, student activists, journalists, and other professionals accused of being guerrilla sympathizers also migrated for political reasons. More than 300,000 Guatemalans have entered the United States illegally since 1980.

The United States has not recognized Guatemalans as political refugees. Most recent immigrants from Guatemala are considered economic migrants, and only one to two percent of Guatemalan requests for political asylum are granted. Many sources state that immigration officials view Guatemalan asylum cases less favorably than those from applicants from other countries where human rights abuses are common, because U.S. refugee policy is politicized. They say that the United States has historically granted asylum to people fleeing communist regimes rather than those from countries the United States is friendly with. Immigration officials deny bias in assessing asylum cases.

Illegal migrants who are caught by the Immigration and Naturalization Service are usually deported back to Guatemala, where they may face dangerous situations as repatriates. Some Guatemalan migrants travel to Canada, where they can receive refugee status. Despite the threat of deportation, the difficulty of the trip to the United States, and problems here as undocumented persons, Guatemalans have continued to arrive in the United States and are one of the fastest growing American immigrant groups.

## SETTLEMENT PATTERNS

According to the 1990 U.S. Census, there are 268,779 persons of Guatemalan origin in the United States. The 1990 Census also lists 225,739 foreign-born persons from Guatemala, reflecting the large portion of recent immigrants among Guatemalan Americans. However, the actual number of Guatemalan Americans is higher than the Census figures, since many are migratory and/or undocumented and thus reluctant to have contact with officials. In reality, there are probably over half a million Guatemalan Americans, and they are the second largest group among Central Americans after Salvadorans.

Guatemalan Americans have settled primarily in cities with large existing Latino communities. The greatest number—probably over 100,000—are in Los Angeles, where the biggest concentration of Central Americans in the United States resides. There are also significant numbers of Guatemalan Americans in Houston, Chicago, New York City, Washington D.C., southern Florida, and San Francisco. Smaller enclaves are found in Miami, New Orleans, Phoenix/Tucson, and other cities in Texas and North Carolina.

During the early 1980s, Phoenix/Tucson became an important center for the Sanctuary Movement, a group of mostly Christian religious organizations that provided sanctuary to illegal migrants from Guatemala and El Salvador. These groups supported migrants in their efforts to gain legal status and helped them obtain work and housing. However, most Guatemalans moved on to other areas cities or towns outside of Arizona.

The communities in Chicago and New York expanded considerably during the mid- to late-1980s. In these cities, Guatemalan Americans tend to be inconspicuous, blending in with the more established Mexican or Cuban American populations, for fear of being detected by the Immigration and Naturalization Service (INS). In the San Francisco Bay area and Washington D.C., Central Americans predominate among Latinos. A number of wealthy Guatemalan Americans live in Miami, the commerce gateway to Latin America.

Many of the Guatemalan Americans in Los Angeles live in or near the Central American-dominated Pico-Union district. Once primarily a Mexican American area, Pico-Union is now characterized by businesses that cater to Central Americans, including bakeries, restaurants, grocery stores, and social service organizations. A substantial portion of the Guatemalan Americans in Los Angeles and in southern Florida are Kanjobal Mayans. In Houston, there are over a thousand Mayans from the provinces of Totonicapan and Quiché. These indigenous communities represent the best-documented Guatemalan American populations.

Guatemalan Americans have met with both hostility and empathy from the general American public. Many of the negative reactions by "established" Americans have focused on immigration issues. During recent recessions and concurrent waves of anti-immigrant sentiment, Guatemalans and other Central Americans have been depicted as economically threatening migrants who overwhelm government social services and undermine American labor by taking low-paying jobs. However, others have described newly arrived Central Americans as resourceful contributors to the economy.

The U.S. government's refusal to designate Guatemalan emigrants as political refugees and its persecution of Sanctuary Movement workers can also be interpreted as an unsympathetic stance toward Guatemalan Americans. On the other hand, grassroots supporters and many major city governments have defended recent Guatemalan immigrants. In the mid-1980s some members of Congress and at least a dozen cities, including Los Angeles, St. Paul, and Chicago criticized President Ronald Reagan and his administration's federal policy concerning illegal Central Americans and limited city cooperation with INS officials.

Relations with other Latino groups near whom Guatemalan Americans often live have been similarly mixed. The more established Chicano communities have expressed both resentment and support for the newer residents. Sometimes there is rivalry among Central American and Mexican groups for jobs, and cultural differences can preclude social interaction among people of different national origin. A number of Native American groups have been very supportive of indigenous Guatemalan immigrants to United States and empathize with their struggle against genocide and cultural obliteration.

Although there are many Guatemalan Americans whose ancestors came to America generations ago, the key issues facing the group in the near future are generally linked with immigration and their previous lives in Guatemala, since the majority of Guatemalan Americans have arrived within the last 15 years. Most Guatemalan Americans face a host of challenges in the areas of work, health, and cultural preservation due to their undocumented status and the terrible economic and political conditions they left behind.

# ACCULTURATION AND ASSIMILATION

Guatemalan Americans comprise a very culturally diverse group of people. Within Guatemala there are about 23 distinct ethnic groups that speak different languages and maintain unique cultural traditions. The majority of these groups are Mayan; and *ladinos*, or Hispanic Guatemalans, constitute a separate population as persons of Spanish language and culture. Guatemalan Americans represent a broad cross-section of this multicultural society, and assimilation processes, traditional beliefs, and customs vary from group to group. Given the diversity of the Guatemalan American population, it is impossible to generalize about the group as a whole.

Immigrant Mayan American communities have maintained their traditional practices the most visibly. Hispanic Guatemalans have tended to blend in more with other Latino cultures and very little information about them or third-, fourth-, and fifth-generation Guatemalan Americans exists. For instance, no studies have been conducted on how traditions are being passed on beyond the second generation. Further inquiry into these areas is needed and will probably occur as the recent wave of immigrants matures into second- and third-generation adults.

Certain practices like the celebration of *quinceñeros*, the formation of soccer leagues, and the organization of patronal fiestas have been maintained in most of the newer Guatemalan American neighborhoods. Specific Guatemalan American groups in Los Angeles, Houston, and southern Florida have received the most attention from sociologists and the media. The following sections on these three communities illustrate how some Guatemalan traditions are being preserved, transformed, and lost through the process of acculturation.

## GUATEMALAN AMERICANS IN LOS ANGELES

Until the late 1970s, Los Angeles's Pico-Union district was populated by Mexican immigrants, Chicanos, African Americans, and European

Americans. Some Central and South Americans began arriving in the mid-1950s, and after 1980 an influx of Central Americans settled the neighborhood. These Central American immigrants, including university students, teachers, clergy, and *campesinos*, came from all classes and political persuasions. New residents could shop at Latino-owned businesses such as grocery stores, *botánicas* selling religious articles and herbs, dance halls, informal vendors, and record companies specializing in Latino music.

Among the Guatemalan immigrants were Mayan Chujes, Quichés, and Kanjobals. The Kanjobals from the highlands of Huehuetenango near Mexico constitute the largest Mayan group in Los Angeles, with a population of about 4,000 in 1984. Many call themselves *Migueleños* after their hometown of San Miguel Acatán. The first Kanjobal immigrants to Los Angeles came during the late 1970s in search of work, and large numbers followed during the early 1980s, when Kanjobals were targeted as guerrilla sympathizers, and both guerrillas and the army pressured men and boys to fight on their sides.

Coming from an agrarian society, the Kanjobals have made many adjustments to living in urban Los Angeles. Many had not used electricity or cars before. Women who had washed their clothes by hand in rivers became accustomed to coin laundromats. Both men and women encountered unfamiliar appliances such as refrigerators and strange products like hot dogs and commercial cleaning agents in the supermarkets.

To avoid deportation to Guatemala, many have become inconspicuous by passing for Mexican American. For example, women generally do not wear traditional clothing such as the bright embroidered blouses called *huipils* outside the home. Rather than using colorful cloth *rebozos* to carry infants on their backs, they now use baby carriages.

Deeper forms of integration into American society may be more elusive. Jacqueline Maria Hagan, who researched Houston's Mayan community, noted that assimilation can be intimately tied to legalization. Legal status affords the opportunity to develop bonds with the established society in areas like higher education, sports, stable jobs, and access to banks and other institutions. As undocumented immigrants, many Guatemalan Americans cannot interact with mainstream society in these areas.

A few organizations in Los Angeles have formed to promote and preserve Guatemalan and Mayan American culture. A group called Integración de Indígenas Mayas (IXIM), sponsors a range of political and cultural activities to foster community solidarity among Mayans in southern California.

## FROM TOTONICAPAN TO HOUSTON

There are approximately 30,000 Guatemalan Americans living in Houston. As in Los Angeles, most Guatemalans emigrated after 1980 to escape political violence and economic repression. Both Hispanics and *indigenas* migrated to Houston, including Mayans from Quiche and Totonicapan in the southwestern highlands.

The thousand or so Mayans have maintained many of their traditional social and cultural customs, and *indigenas* from Totonicapan can depend on a well-developed community for support upon arrival. Life-cycle events such as birthdays, baptisms, weddings, and funerals are celebrated with the involvement of the whole group.

One such event is *quinceñeros*, which is like an elaborate coming-out party for girls celebrating their fifteenth birthdays. *Quinceñeros* is observed by most Guatemalan American groups, although only wealthier families may be able to afford it. Sometimes *padrinos*, or godparents, of the celebrant from the same locale but of higher social standing participate in the event. *Padrinos* have traveled from Totonicapan to Houston to honor *quinceñeros* celebrants and to give away brides.

The marimba, an ancient Mayan instrument made of hormiga wood native to Guatemalan forests, is played by bands at Guatemalan American holiday fiestas and special events throughout the United States. Marimba bands play both popular songs and sacred music and may play all night during certain occasions. The music is often accompanied by festive folk dancing. Another instrument native to the highlands is the flutelike *chirimías*.

Sports and church activities also spur much communal interaction in Guatemalan American communities. Soccer is the most popular national sport, and Guatemalan American men have formed soccer leagues in Los Angeles, Houston, San Francisco, and other cities. In Houston, the Community Soccer Club has played against other immigrant soccer teams on a weekly basis and the sports events have served to raise funds for fiesta in San Cristobal Totonicapan. In Los Angeles,

Mayan Americans also play basketball, and both men's and women's tournaments are organized.

Some traditions have been lost upon settlement in the United States. Totonicapan is known as the capital of artisan production in Guatemala, and most of the male immigrants to Houston were previously craft tailors, weavers, or bakers. Since those skills were not transferable to the Houston workplace they have had to make the transition from cottage industry production to wage labor. Women, however, still buy traditional garments from Totonicapan for special events.

Close relations between Guatemalan home villages and Mayan American communities also sustain cultural practices on both ends. Many Guatemalan Americans have close family members remaining in Guatemala. Often they communicate regularly with them by sending letters and cassette tapes back and forth. In the 1980s, couriers traveled monthly between Houston and San Cristobal Totonicapan to deliver news, money, and goods. As they have achieved temporary or permanent residency status, some Guatemalans in Houston have been able to make the trips themselves. Items typically transported include traditional clothing, Guatemalan foods and spices, and occasionally things like wedding bands or other special celebratory objects.

Some families have moved out of the Houston Totonicapan community after gaining legal status and saving enough money. Researcher Hagan saw this as part of a shift toward adopting American Texan culture, which included buying new types of cars and women modernizing their hairstyles and clothes.

## KANJOBALS IN SOUTHERN FLORIDA

A small farming town 25 miles inland from the East Coast of Florida called Indiantown is home to several thousand Guatemalan refugees. Along with other migrant workers, the Guatemalan Americans here harvest sugar, oranges, cucumbers, and other crops during the winter growing season. Indiantown derived its name from the Seminole Native Americans who used to inhabit the area, and is the center of the Guatemalan American population of southern Florida, which extends to other small towns like Immokalee.

Most of the Guatemalans in Indiantown are Kanjobals, although there is a small non-Kanjobal speaking group from the mostly *ladino* town of Cuilco. The Kanjobals first arrived in late 1982, when a Mexican American crew boss brought some refugees from Arizona to Indiantown to pick crops. These workers subsequently led family and friends from Kanjobal communities in Los Angeles and Guatemala to the area, and the town became a refuge from both the civil war and urban environments.

As in other Mayan American communities, the tradition of going to the weekly market to exchange news and gossip and buy fresh fruit, meat, and vegetables has been supplanted by going to supermarkets. However, other customs remain intact and the Kanjobals maintain a visible ethnic presence.

Kanjobal marimba players from Indiantown played at the U.S. Folk Festival in 1985 and they also received a grant to teach Kanjobal American teenagers traditional music. The local Catholic Church and Mayan American associations sponsor an annual fiesta in honor of the patron saint of San Miguel Acatán. Committees of men and women organize entertainment, sports, and the election of festival queens who give speeches in Kanjobal, Spanish, and English. Participants wear traditional clothing and teach children how to dance to marimba music. The dances traditionally involve costumed performances with masks made from paper maché, but in the first year of the masked dances, the masks were purchased from a local store. The patronal fiesta functions as an important gathering of Kanjobals who must work and live outside of Indiantown, and as an affirmation of identity.

Although many Mayan Americans have strived to preserve traditions such as these, others eschew former customs. Since acculturation is ultimately a personal choice, degrees of assimilation will vary from individual to individual. As in every other ethnic group, there are many like Mateo Andres, a first-generation Kanjobal American farmworker who told *New York Times* reporter Larry Rohter that he sees no need to pass on Mayan languages or practices and hopes that his newborn son grows up "100 percent American."

## STEREOTYPES AND MISCONCEPTIONS

Guatemalan Americans face the stereotypes that have historically plagued almost all immigrant groups in the United States. Like the Irish, Eastern European, Asian, and other groups that have preceded them, Guatemalan Americans have been scapegoated as new immigrants by nativists who depict them as docile, ignorant workers who do not mind being exploited, overwhelm American economic and social resources, and are of little value except as workers in undesirable jobs. During economic recessions, politicians have exploited this anti-immigrant bias to curry favor with constituents who want to blame their financial woes on vulnerable targets rather than coming to terms with the real sources of the problem.

Guatemalan Americans are also generally lumped together with other Central American and Latino groups as indistinguishable from one another. Although there is great diversity within and among the different Central American and Latino groups, the American populace tends to perceive them as one entity, and subjects Guatemalan, Nicaraguan, Salvadoran, Honduran, Mexican, Cuban, and Puerto Rican Americans to the same stereotypes.

### CUISINE

Savory sometimes spicy Guatemalan cuisine has its origins in pre-Hispanic foods. Mayan staples such as corn, beans, hot chile peppers, and tomatoes are still the staples of Guatemalan cooking. During the Spanish conquest rice and other European and Asian ingredients were introduced into the cuisine. Guatemalan cooking falls into three categories: the highland indigenous cuisine; the Spanish colonial style cultivated by *ladinos*; and the food of the Caribbean coast town Livingston. The last style of cooking developed with the culinary input of indentured laborers from India and Africa and it resembles the cuisine of Belize. Unlike the other two kinds of Guatemalan cooking, this type is tropical and uses a lot of seafood, coconut, and bananas in its recipes.

The indigenous and Spanish styles are much more prevalent and are somewhat intermixed. They make use of many of the vegetables and fruits native to the New World. Some of the most popular ingredients include *chayote* or *huisquil*, a pear-shaped vegetable with firm, deep to pale green skin, which can be boiled, fried, mashed, baked, or used in salads and deserts; *cilantro* or *culantro*, a green, leafy herb otherwise known as Chinese parsley or fresh coriander; and *cacao*, a chocolate made from local cacao beans sold in small cakes or tablets, which is used in cooking and to make hot chocolate.

*Tortillas* and black beans are among the most common foods in Guatemala. In indigenous villages, women often make the *tortillas* the traditional way by grinding corn with a rounded pestle on a flat lava stone called a *piedra* or *metate* and baking the flat corn disks on a dry, clay platter known as a *comal*. (This process is very time-consuming and generally cannot be sustained in the United States.) The black beans, which are difficult to find in the United States, are prepared whole, pureed, as soup, or paste and can be eaten at all meals. On the Caribbean coast and in cities the beans may be eaten with rice.

There are many varieties of *tamales*, which are essentially dough with meat and/or vegetables wrapped and steamed in a corn husk, leaf, or other wrapping. The dough can derive from cornmeal, flour, potatoes, or green bananas. In Guatemalan towns, women sell home-made *tamales* in markets. *Chuchitos* are a delicious type of cornmeal *tamale* made with chicken, pork, or turkey, tomatoes, and chiles.

*Chilaquiles/as* consist of *tortillas* stuffed with cheese or other ingredients dipped in a batter and then fried or baked. They can be served with a savory tomato sauce. In the chilly Guatemalan highlands, *caldos* or soups are frequently made and consumed. Soup ingredients can include beef, chicken, lamb, potatoes, carrots, *chayotes*, onions, mint, eggs, tomatoes, beans, garlic, cilantro, and *epazote*, a mildly antiseptic herb, which also has medicinal purposes.

Turkey is native to the Americas and was raised, eaten, and sacrificed as a ceremonial bird in Mayan times. In Guatemala, turkey is still prepared and eaten during fiestas and national holidays. Another festive meat dish is *pepián*, which is eaten on Corpus Christi Day in June. *Pepián* consists of beef stewed with rice, spices, and vegetables such as tomatoes, green snap beans, chiles, and black peppercorns.

Plantains or *plátanos* are commonly eaten in the cities and in the more tropical areas. This very versatile fruit/vegetable, which looks like a banana, can be eaten ripe or green (but always cooked) and is alternately boiled, mashed, pan-fried, and deep-fried. Ripe plantains are sweet and can be prepared as a dessert with chocolate, cinnamon, or honey.

Sweets are quite popular in Guatemala and there is a wide variety of desserts and sweet breads like *pan dulce*, a sweet corn bread. *Hojuelas* are fried flour crisps drizzled with honey, which are sold in cities and in village markets. There are also prepared drinks like *boj*, a fermented sugar cane liquor drunk by Kekchi *indigenas* in Cobán. *Atol de maíz tierno* is a popular beverage made by boiling the paste of young corn, water, cinnamon, sugar, and salt.

This photograph shows a

Guatemalan in traditional

costume.

## TRADITIONAL CLOTHING

Since the 1930s, most men have worn European-style clothing, but women of the highlands still wear the brightly colored garments distinct to each Mayan village. The wearing of traditional clothing or *traje típico* has evolved into a way to preserve ethnic identity and pride in both Guatemala and in the United States. Mayan American women may wear *traje* at home and especially at cultural events like fiestas, church meetings, and weddings. The *huipil* is a multicolored, intricately embroidered blouse. The *corte* is an ankle-length brightly woven skirt that may also be embroidered. Traditionally, hair is kept long and worn in a braid or ponytail. On festive occasions women may also wear colorful beaded or silver necklaces and sparkly earrings. The cloth for *traje típico* is traditionally hand-woven on a loom, but today machine-produced cloth is widely available in Guatemala, although the hand-woven might be preferred for special occasions.

## HOLIDAYS CELEBRATED BY GUATEMALAN AMERICANS

Guatemalan Americans celebrate Thanksgiving, Christmas, and New Year's Day, as well as Guatemalan holidays like *Semana Santa* and patronal festivals. Totonicapan immigrants in Houston sometimes travel to San Cristobal to celebrate their town's patron saint fiesta *La Fiesta de Santiago*, Christmas, and *Semana Santa*. *Semana Santa* is based on the Catholic Holy Week. The week-long festivities reflect the blending of Mayan and Catholic rites and include costumed allegorical dramas that depict the Spanish conquest. During the week, participants cover the streets with *alfombras*, literally carpets, made of colored sawdust arranged in intricate patterns. The celebration reaches its climax on the last day when the parish priest leads a procession of the townspeople across the *alfombras*.

Although they are not national holidays, preparations for fiestas that honor a town's patron saint are elaborate, and Guatemalan Americans dynamically maintain these traditions. Kanjobals in both Los Angeles and southern Florida celebrate the fiesta of the patron saint of San Miguel Acatán on September 29th every year.

In 1990, more than 900 people attended the patronal festival in Los Angeles, which involved the coronation of festival queens, serving traditional Guatemalan food, the awarding of trophies to athletes, and a Deer Dance. The ancestral Deer Dance is performed by people dressed as animals and different types of people. In Guatemala, 60 to 80 dancers participate in the dance. The costumes have religious meaning and prayers are said before the dance commences. Celebrants set off firecrackers and rockets and play music on the marimba and on a drum made of wood and deer skin during the dance.

## HEALTH AND MENTAL HEALTH ISSUES

The theory of health and illness common in Mesoamerica is based on a humoral dichotomy of hot and cold, which should be in balance. The idea is derived from the Spanish importation of the Hippocratic quadratic that also considered the forces of wet and dry. In her study of the health practices of Mayan Americans in Florida, Maria Miralles observed that they sometimes attributed their illnesses to an imbalance in hot and cold or to the weather and heat.

Many of the indigenous and rural refugees are not accustomed to relying on modern American medicine to cure their health problems. In rural Guatemala and in some cities, *curanderos*, or traditional curers, use teas, herbs, and other natural remedies to heal the sick. *Curanderos* are also consulted as spiritual diviners and healers. Some *curanderos* are specialists trained in bone-setting or the treatment of tumors. In Los Angeles, the Kanjobals can go to local *curanderos* for problems like stress or depression. However, *curanderos* have been mostly supplanted by U.S. doctors, because they cannot get licenses to practice medicine here. *Promotores de salud* or health promoters trained by Catholic Action missionaries to know first-aid and preventative medicine also work in Guatemalan villages.

In many Mayan cultures, birth ceremonies are extremely important and the infant is received as a part of the community. Babies are traditionally delivered by midwives, and it is considered scandalous to go to a hospital to give birth. However, in the United States women may go to hospitals to deliver in order to obtain birth certificates for their newborns, despite their preferences.

Curative herbs can be consumed or used in medicinal steam baths. In Guatemala, the herbs can be bought from herb vendors; here they can found at *botánicas*, although not all of them are available. Some of the herbs used are *manzanilla* or chamomile and *hierba buena*, a mixture from Mexico. These can be taken for stomach disorders or headaches. Medicines can also be purchased without a prescription at pharmacies in Guatemala. Guatemalan immigrants who relied on traditional curative practices may prefer them to those of the American medical establishment. However, many also go to clinics and hospitals to cure their ailments.

## HEALTH PROBLEMS AMONG REFUGEES

The journey from Guatemala to the United States is usually traumatic for emigrants escaping persecution or extreme poverty. Traveling by foot for up to thousands of miles with little money and few possessions, many become dehydrated, malnourished, and exhausted. Most refugees travel through Mexico, where they may stay in overcrowded refugee camps that provide little food and shelter and have poor sanitary conditions. Under these circumstances, refugees are susceptible to serious diseases like malaria and tuberculosis as well as parasites, gastrointestinal disorders, severe malnutrition, cracked and damaged feet, and skin infections.

Many refugees are also surviving the shock of experiencing extreme violence and subsequently suffer from mental health problems. Physical and mental health problems from conditions in Guatemala and the journey are compounded by the precariousness of the refugees positions once they settle here. Poor housing, underemployment, fear of deportation, and drastic changes can induce stress-related ailments such as ulcers and high blood pressure. Anxiety, depression, and alcohol abuse (among men) have also afflicted survivors.

Undocumented refugees usually do not receive insurance from employers, Medicaid, or other government health-care benefits, and often do not have access to affordable health care. However, in Los Angeles and Indiantown, health clinics have been established for Guatemalan and other immigrants without papers. In Indiantown, a county-sponsored health clinic known as *el corte* operates a Woman, Infant, and Child program for family planning and gives vaccinations to migrant workers' children. A privately run clinic known as *la clinica* provides screening, acute episode care, chronic disease management, and laboratory and x-ray services on a sliding fee basis. Kanjobal immigrants use both clinics, although they may also use traditional remedies at home.

In 1983, several social service and ecumenical religious groups created the Clinica Monsenor Oscar A. Romero as a free health care center for Central American refugees in Los Angeles. It was formed to address the special needs of refugees who cannot go to public medical facilities where they risk being deported and who contend with language and financial barriers that keep them from going to other clinics.

# LANGUAGE

Spanish is the official language of Guatemala and is spoken by most first-generation Guatemalan Americans. However, some indigenous immigrants, especially women from the rural areas, speak exclusively Mayan languages and are unfamiliar with Spanish. Many first- and second-generation Mayan Americans are trilingual, and can communicate in Spanish, English, and a Mayan dialect. The Mayan languages spoken by Guatemalans in the United States include Kanjobal, Quiché, Mam, Cakchiquel, Chuj, Jacaltec, and Acatec. In Los Angeles, several dialects of Kanjobal are spoken, according to what village the person originates from.

The Mayan Americans in Houston speak both Quiché and Spanish. However, Hagan noted that the use of Quiché is diminishing both in Houston and in Guatemala, due to the predominance of Spanish in both areas. Children in Latino communities in Houston and Los Angeles learn Spanish in school and in their neighborhoods. Since Spanish is the language of access in Guatemala and in Latino areas, parents may encourage children to learn Spanish so they can interpret for them in various situations.

Language issues can be intimately linked with assimilation, as children sometimes reject both their Mayan language and customs. In Los Angeles, some second-generation Kanjobal Americans attend a Spanish-language church rather than one that holds services in Kanjobal, espousing the larger Latino community.

Guatemalan American refugees sometimes learn to speak Mexican Spanish to disguise their national origin. By passing for Mexican, they may be able to evade detection by the immigration authorities. For example, they may use Mexican terms such as "*lana*" instead of the Guatemalan term "*pisto*" for money. In some cities, Guatemalan immigrants learn to speak Puerto Rican Spanish for the same reasons. As one Guatemalan refugee aid worker put it: these more established Latino groups have "provided us with the tools to get along in an environment that doesn't accept us."

## GREETINGS AND OTHER POPULAR EXPRESSIONS

Popular Guatemalan greetings and expressions include: *Buenos días* ("bwe'nos de'âs")—good morning, good day, hello; *buenas noches* ("bwe'nâs no'ches")—good night; *gracias* ("grâ'syâ"s)—thank you; *con mucho gusto* ("kon mü'cho gus'to")—with much pleasure, often used as "You're welcome," and as "It's a pleasure to meet you;" *sí pues* ("se pwes")—It's okay; or, Yeah, you're right; *con permiso* ("kon per me'so")—excuse me; *que rico, que riquíssimo* ("ke rre'ko, ke rreke'semo")—How rich, delicious, great!; *¡Salud!* ("sâ luth'")—To your health! Cheers!; and *¡Buen provecho!* ("bwen pro ve'cho")—literally "Good digestion!" Said before a meal as in *bon apetit* or Enjoy!

In Cakchiquel, common sayings include: *Raxnek, seker, xseker*—good morning; *xocok'a', xok'a*—good night; *nuch' ocob'a'*—I'm sorry; *matiox*—thank you; *ja'e*—with pleasure (like *con gusto*); and *rutzil, ruwech*—hello.

# FAMILY AND COMMUNITY DYNAMICS

The family is very important among Guatemalan Americans. In many cases, large extended kinship groups maintain close bonds of loyalty, obligation, and social support. The family group traditionally includes grandparents and fictive kin such as *comadres* or godmothers.

However, among immigrants, many family members are now separated, since it is generally impossible for everyone to immigrate at the same time. Many men were forced to flee without their families because they were in immediate danger of being killed or conscripted into the fighting. Undocumented migrants usually have traveled to the United States alone, because they cannot afford to pay the *coyotes* for everyone at once and because their chances of making the crossing and surviving in the new environment are better.

After establishing their lives here, immigrants generally try to bring the rest of their families over. Spouses, children, and siblings frequently reunite with the original migrant. However, elderly parents and grandparents often cannot make the difficult trip north, which can require withstanding physical dangers and hardships. Children are sometimes left with grandparents in Guatemala, because both parents must work long hours and cannot afford day care or similar services.

Separation and reunification after long periods of living apart can strain family relations. Housing conditions may also change family dynamics. In refugee enclaves like Indiantown, families live in very crowded, tenement apartments due to low wages and the lack of adequate housing. In these situations, a family may share a one-room apartment with other families. Because of the lack of privacy and pressures these conditions create, many families move out of the community if they can save enough money to do so.

Despite the difficulty of finding work and making a living as undocumented persons, most Guatemalan Americans do not receive public assistance. Illegal aliens are not eligible for public assistance and are usually wary of government institutions. Citizen children may be eligible for welfare and food stamps, but undocumented parents are often afraid to apply for it. There are no official statistics on the percentage of Guatemalan American families who receive public assistance.

As in all immigrant communities, younger family members adjust much more quickly to American life, and may become alienated from older members. In urban Latino neighborhoods, adolescents may conflict with their parents if they assume *cholo* identities. *Cholo* refers to an originally Chicano teenage subculture that involves the use of slang, a street-wise pose and walk, activities like low-riding, using marijuana, and a specific style of dress—pressed Chinos, plaid shirts, and oversized brimmed hats for boys, and lots of make-up for girls.

Attitudes toward marriage have also changed in several Guatemalan American communities. Divorce and couples living together without being married are more common in the United States than they are in Guatemala. The absence of older generations in some communities may lead to a decline in the observance of traditional customs. In general, there is little intermarriage with other ethnic groups among the first-generation. Immigrant men are more likely to date or marry non-Guatemalans than women, and second-generation girls may be encouraged more than boys to date only Guatemalan Americans.

## THE ROLE OF WOMEN IN FAMILY AND COMMUNITY

Guatemalan American women occupy complex and important positions within their families and communities. Guatemalan society is patriarchal and patrilineal, with men controlling most of the major institutions. However, within the last two decades women have garnered more leadership roles in all areas of society and they have led and played crucial parts in many of the popular resistance movements. During the 1980s, organizations like CONAVIGUA, composed mostly of indigenous widows of murdered or disappeared men, formed and fought for women's and human rights.

In many cases, women take on a larger economic role in the family when they immigrate to the United States. In migrant worker communities, women as well as men do wage field work. In addition, women are often expected to do all the domestic labor—child-rearing, cooking, and cleaning. Given the large size of households in some neighborhoods, this can involve an enormous amount of work, cooking and cleaning for ten to 20 people.

Immigrant women tend to transmit and sustain traditional culture more than the men, especially in Mayan Guatemalan groups. By maintaining religious practices and language, preparing foods, and wearing traditional clothes and hairstyles, women preserve the cultural fabric of their group. Women also frequently organize church-related or community-oriented events like fiestas.

## EDUCATION

Education is a high priority for many Guatemalan American parents. In urban areas, like Los Angeles and Houston, the available public schools often have poor reputations, and parents prefer to send their children to private Catholic schools. In Guatemala, schoolchildren generally attend private or boarding schools, if their parents can afford it. Guatemalan American parents whose children remain in Guatemala will often pay for their education there through wages earned here.

Children who were previously educated in Guatemalan schools in which the curriculua are rigorous generally adjust easily to American schools once they learn English. However, a good number of refugee children have not had prior access to much education, since many Guatemalan schools were closed during recent decades due to poverty or violence. In southern Florida, two schools have been set up to address the needs of the migrant workers' children, who may not yet speak English and must deal with other challenges. The Migrant Head Start Program and the Hope Rural School are attended by Guatemalan American and many other children from Indiantown's diverse community. No statistics on the number of Guatemalan Americans who go to four-year universities and graduate schools are available. Undocumented refugee students cannot apply for financial aid for college and therefore it is almost impossible for them to attend institutions of higher learning.

Organized religion has greatly influenced the lives of Guatemalans and Guatemalan Americans in various ways. Since the time of the Spanish conquest, Guatemalans have practiced Roman Catholicism, while maintaining Mayan religious customs and beliefs. The Roman Catholic church is still dominant in Guatemala and has been involved with all aspects of life there, including politics, community development, social services, and internal refugee relief.

During the early 1980s when two Evangelical Pentecostal Protestant presidents ruled, the Catholic clergy were associated with rebel forces and became targets for violence. In some areas it was dangerous to identify with Catholicism. Protestant Evangelism grew dramatically during this time, as the U.S. church sent missionaries to convert people. The rise in Pentecostal and other types of Protestant religions is evident in some Guatemalan American communities, where a large percentage are Protestants.

Norita Vlach, who interviewed Guatemalan refugee families in San Francisco, observed that many Catholic families switch to the Pentecostal church during their first years in that city. The churches offer women's groups, youth groups, and Spanish language classes. In Houston, La Iglesia de Dios, the Protestant Evangelical church, is similarly active among the Totonicapan community, holding bible readings for women and multiple services during the week, and hosting cultural events like *quinceñeros* for church- and non-church-goers alike. The Evangelical Protestant church forbids dancing and drinking.

Other Protestant religions and Catholicism are practiced by the majority of Guatemalan Americans in Houston. In Indiantown and Los Angeles, the Kanjobal are Catholics, Seventh Day Adventists, Catholic Charismatics and Protestants, and many do not practice any religion although they may be nominally Catholic. A few practice traditional Mayan rituals of *costumbre*. Some *cofradias* or indigenous village elders who interpreted Catholicism in villages, mixing Mayan and Catholic customs, have immigrated to the United States, but they often have a diminished role in their new environments. It is difficult to maintain all Mayan religious practices here since some depend on being in sacred places in Guatemala. *Catequistas* or followers of the Catholic Action Movement seek to remove indigenous practices from Catholicism.

The Catholic church has provided asylum and many social services for Guatemalan American refugees. In Indiantown, the Holy Cross Church funded a social service center that helped process asylum and immigration papers, and supplied emergency relief, health referrals, and organizational help. Services are in Spanish and Kanjobal, and the annual patron saint's festival is held there. The Presbyterian Church's Office of World Service and World Hunger has also the supported the formation of local cultural groups.

# EMPLOYMENT AND ECONOMIC TRADITIONS

Although Guatemalan Americans with legal resident or citizen status work in any number of professional fields such as law, teaching, and medicine, the large percentage of undocumented recent immigrants have little access to decently paying jobs. Since they have not been granted refugee status that would enable them to work here legally, these Guatemalan Americans have been forced to take low-paying jobs in the service sector, manufacturing, and agriculture. These are the same jobs that have historically been held by other new immigrant groups upon arrival in the United States. In rural areas throughout the United States Guatemalan immigrants work as migrant harvesters, picking fruit, flowers, vegetables, and commodities like tobacco in places like the San Joaquin Valley. The Kanjobal in Los Angeles and southern Florida frequently do migrant work when they first come to United States.

Field work of this type is often dangerous because of accidents and exposure to pesticides that can cause rashes and burns, and it demands long hours of physical exertion and a lifestyle of constant mobility. Exploitation of migrant workers is also common, as it is easy for agricultural contractors to pocket their Social Security payments or refuse to pay them altogether. If legal status is obtained, Guatemalan Americans usually move on to other types of work such as construction, or jobs where they can apply their professional skills in areas like education or social services. Many Guatemalan immigrants worked as trained professionals in Guatemala but cannot obtain the same type of work here because of their undocumented status.

The Mayan American men and women of southern Florida and Los Angeles sometimes work in garment factories during the off-season. In 1984, less than one percent of the undocumented garment workers in Los Angeles belonged to unions, although they legally have a right to unionize to demand better working conditions and wages. There have been a few successful efforts at unionizing illegal workers (including Guatemalan Americans) in agriculture and manufacturing, but most attempts have not gotten off the ground. The difficulty of organizing itinerant laborers, language differences, lack of experience with unions, and fear of being deported may all contribute to the lack of union activity.

Other Guatemalan Americans in Los Angeles and Florida work as gardeners in nurseries, landscapers on golf courses, and in restaurants and hotels. During the last few years, a textile cooperative was developed in Indiantown to create safe, year-round work in the Kanjobal neighborhood. The cooperative produces women's clothing that incorporates Mayan-style weaving.

Men may also do odd jobs as carpenters, roofers, or as informal vendors. Women often work as domestics throughout the United States, cooking, cleaning, or looking after children for individual families with whom they live. Women may also earn money by baby-sitting, doing laundry by hand, or cooking for people within their community.

In an unusual situation, many of the Totonicapan American men in Houston work as maintenance or stock workers in one retail chain. The employers who hired the original migrants from Totonicapan think of the Mayans as hard-working, responsible, and loyal. As more Totonicapan immigrants arrived, they obtained jobs with the company, creating a steady labor supply for the chain. This situation and the legalization of community members has made the acculturation process relatively smooth for this group.

Most of the work available to immigrants without legal papers is sporadic, and underemployment is a problem for many. However, the same people who have limited access to nonexploitative work are also ineligible for unemployment benefits. (There are no statistics on the number of Guatemalan Americans who receive unemployment, since figures are not categorized by national origin/individual ethnic groups.) The need for reliable, fairly paid employment is the most pressing issue in many Guatemalan American communities.

# POLITICS AND GOVERNMENT

Since immigration in general and refugee status in particular are at the heart of the issues affecting many Guatemalan Americans, changes in federal immigration law have influenced the group. Since the 1980s, there have been several key pieces of federal legislation regarding immigration.

The 1980 Refugee Act mandates that immigration officials judge political asylum cases individually, rather than by national origin and that the rulings be independent of the government's relations with the country the applicant has come from. However, critics of asylum processes say that the INS still bases asylum decisions on national origin. This criticism is borne out by the fact that so few Guatemalan applicants receive asylum (fewer than two percent) when compared with applicants from countries the United States does not support like Nicaragua or the former Eastern Bloc countries. Although the act did not immediately change the way asylum decisions are made, it paved the path for later legislation and court decisions. The complex Immigration Reform and Control Act (IRCA) of 1986 enabled immigrants living in the United States continuously since January 1, 1982 and arriving before that date to apply for legalization status. This provision helped the small percentage of Guatemalan emigrants who arrived before 1982. Another provision of IRCA called for employer sanctions that penalize employers who hired unauthorized workers after November 6, 1986. Observers noted that this provision could reduce the demand for undocumented workers, force repatriation, and restrict immigration, but it is difficult to ascertain what the results of this part of IRCA have been. Some Guatemalan American migrant workers benefited from the farmworker amnesty portion of IRCA that provided resident alien status to farmworkers. Farmworkers who did agricultural labor for at least 90 days from 1985-1986 were eligible for this status under SAW or the Seasonal Agricultural Worker provision.

Several court cases have questioned the government's handling of political asylum proceedings for people from Central America and have prohibited discriminatory practices in these hearings. In February 1991, a Federal district judge in San Francisco approved a settlement that blocked deportation of up to 500,000 Salvadoran and Guatemalan immigrants and allowed them to reopen their asylum cases. Under the decision, the INS had to reconsider an estimated 150,000 cases of Guatemalan and Salvadoran refugees whose asylum cases had been denied since 1980 but who had not yet been deported.

Refugee advocacy groups are currently lobbying for Temporary Protected Status (TPS) for Guatemalan refugees in the United States under the Immigration Act of 1990. The act authorizes TPS where there is an ongoing armed conflict that would seriously threaten the safety of an individual upon return, or where conditions prevent nationals from returning safely. Advocates state that Guatemala should meet these requirements due to the ongoing civil war in Guatemala. The Clinton administration may also be considering granting Deferred Enforced Departure to Guatemalan immigrants, which would postpone forced repatriation as an alternative to TPS. Guatemalan American refugee aid groups would welcome the temporary safe haven and legal status that both TPS and Deferred Enforced Departure provide.

## INVOLVEMENT IN U.S. POLITICS AND GOVERNMENT

Since Guatemalan Americans comprise a small and largely unestablished group, they have not yet been very involved with American politics. However, a number of grass-roots refugee advocacy groups have lobbied for immigrant rights. There are no statistics on Guatemalan American voting patterns, the number of elected officials, or participation in the armed forces. The National Association of Latino Elected and Appointed Officials in Houston does not categorize their listing of Latino politicians by national origin. However, there are at least two Guatemalan American city officials in California.

Veronica Cardenas-Jaffe helped to incorporate Mission Viejo into the City of Mission Viejo in 1988. She was subsequently elected to the charter city council in 1988 and has served as Mayor pro tem since 1990. Jim Gonzalez was appointed to City and County Supervisor on the San Francisco Board of Supervisors in 1988. He has also worked as a special assistant to former San Francisco Mayor now Senator Dianne Feinstein from 1981 to 1986.

## RELATIONS WITH GUATEMALA

Most Guatemalan Americans have family or close friends remaining in Guatemala, and the majority are very concerned about the state of affairs there. While many Guatemalan Americans do not have the resources or time to address the conditions they fled from, there are already several Guatemalan American organizations that actively strive for an end to violence and corruption in Guatemala. These groups include many refugee aid organizations, since political and economic turmoil in Guatemala continues to have a direct impact on the situation of refugees here.

# INDIVIDUAL AND GROUP CONTRIBUTIONS

Although Guatemalan Americans constitute a very small percentage of the American population and are one of the most recently established American ethnic groups, they have contributed significantly to American life through political and cultural organizations and as individuals. Personal contributions have been especially numerous in the arts and sciences. The following subsections list some notable Guatemalan Americans and their accomplishments.

## BUSINESS

Marta Ortiz-Buonafina (1933- ) is an associate professor of marketing at Florida International University. She has published many articles and books, including the second edition of *Profitable Export Marketing* in 1992. Luis Alfredo Vasquez-Ajmac (1961- ) is president of MAYA, a marketing communications firm targeting Latinos in Washington, D.C., that he established in 1990. He has also served as an advisory member to the Corporation for Public Broadcasting.

## MEDICINE, SCIENCE, AND MATHEMATICS

In 1990, Hermann Mendez (1949- ), associate professor of pediatrics at the State University of New York-Health Science Center at Brooklyn, received awards from the Department of Health and Human Services and the Assistant Secretary of Health for his outstanding contributions to the fight against AIDS. He was also named as one of the Best Doctors in New York by *New York Magazine* in 1991 and as one of the Best Doctors in America by Woodward/White Inc. in 1992.

John Joaquin Munoz (1918- ) is a scientist emeritus at the National Institute of Health's Rocky Mountain Laboratories. He served as chairman of the immunology section of the American Society of Microbiology (1980-1981), and received an NIH Director's Award in 1979. He has also published many papers and is the co-author of *Bordetella Pertussis: Immunological and Other Biological Activities* (1977).

Psychiatrist Julio Alfredo Molina (1948- ) is the founder and director of the Anxiety Disorders Institute of Atlanta. Psychologist and government official Carmen Carrillo (1943- ) is the director of Adult Acute Services at San Francisco's Department of Public Health. She has earned many awards for her work in education, psychology, mental health, and Latino issues, including the City and Council of San Francisco Distinction and Merit Award in 1988, the National Women's Political Caucus Public Service Award in 1989, and the California School Boards Association Service Award in 1991.

Sergio Ramiro Aragón (1949- ), a professor of chemistry at San Francisco State University, established a supercomputer center at California State University in 1989. Sergio Roberto López-Permouth (1957- ), assistant professor of math at Ohio University, has published several articles and co-edited a book called *Non-Commutative Ring Theory* with S. K. Jain in 1990. Victor Perez-Mendez (1923- ) has edited two books, written over 300 articles, and is a professor of physics and faculty senior scientist at the University of California at Berkeley. Statistician Jorge Huascar del Pinal (1945- ) is the chief of the U.S. Bureau of the Census's Ethnic and Spanish Statistics Branch. He published *Microcomputer Programs for Demographic Analysis* in 1985.

## MUSIC AND LITERATURE

Aida Doninelli (1898- ), Guatemalan-born and raised daughter of Italian immigrants to Guatemala, made her American debut as an opera singer in Chicago in 1927. A dramatic soprano, she performed in the major concert stages of the United States and Latin America and sang with New York's prestigious Metropolitan Opera from 1928 to 1933. During her tenure at the Met, Doninelli performed in many operatic roles, including Micaela in *Carmen*, Mimi in *La Bohème*, and Cio-Cio San in *Madame Butterfly*. She also appeared in some of the earliest musical films like *La Traviata* and *Tosca*, and introduced Latin American music to a wide U.S. audience by singing in radio shows broadcast from New York.

Several contemporary Guatemalan American authors and academics have augmented the field of American literature. Donald Kenneth Gutierrez (1932- ), a professor of English at Western New Mexico University, has published numerous essays and scholarly books, including *The Dark and Light Gods: Essays on the Self in Modern Literature* in 1987. David Unger (1950- ), a writer, translator, and co-director of the Latin American Writers' Institute, edited *Antipoems, new and selected* (1985) by Nicanor Parra and co-translated *World Alone: Mundo a Solas* (1982). He has received awards for his translation work from the New York State Council on the Arts.

Author Arturo Arias (1950- ) co-wrote (with Gregory Nava and Anna Thomas) the screenplay for *El Norte*, which won the Montreal Prize and was nominated for an Academy Award for best screenplay in 1982. The film portrays the experiences of a Kanjobal brother and sister who flee from persecution in Guatemala and make the arduous journey to Los Angeles. The realistic depiction of their struggles on the way and in the United States was well-received by the Kanjobal American community in Los Angeles, on which it is based. Arias has also written several novels, including *Jaguar en llamas* in 1989, and he is a professor of humanities at Stanford University and San Francisco State University.

Journalist and author Francisco Goldman's first novel *The Long Night of White Chickens* was published in 1992 and received much critical acclaim. The book evokes contemporary Guatemala and is narrated by a Guatemalan American character who travels to Guatemala in search of Guatemalan American friend who was murdered under mysterious circumstances.

# MEDIA

## PRINT

### El Vocero de IXIM: Boletín Informativo de Integración de Indígenas Mayas (IXIM).

Trilingual newsletter in Acatec Mayan, Spanish, and English published by IXIM. Reports on cultural activities, news of interest to the Guatemalan American community, and sometimes features traditional folk tales. Frequency is roughly quarterly.

**Contact:** Pascual Francisco, President.

**Address:** 1432 West Olympic Boulevard, No. 2, Los Angeles, California 90015.

**Telephone:** (213) 384-4134.

### Guatemala Review.

Bilingual Spanish and English publication published by the Guatemalan Education Action Project. Features articles on the political situation in Guatemala and Chiapas.

### Guatemala: The Bulletin of the Guatemala Human Rights Commission/USA.

Quarterly publication that provides information on the human rights situation in Guatemala.

**Contact:** Patricia Davis, Editor.

### Guate-Noticias.

An English-language bi-monthly newsletter published by the Guatemala Support Network. In-depth articles on the peace process in Guatemala and announcements on conferences, events.

**Contact:** Benito Juarez, Director.

**Address:** Guatemala Support Network, 4223 Richmond Avenue, No. 112, Houston, Texas 77027.

**Telephone:** (713) 850-0441.

### La Opinión.

A Spanish-language daily newspaper popular among Central Americans in Pico-Union.

**Contact:** Monica Lozano, Editor.

**Address:** Lozano Enterprises, 411 West Fifth Street, Los Angeles, California 90013.

**Telephone:** (213) 896-2020.

**Fax:** (213) 896-2144.

### Report on Guatemala.

Published quarterly by the Guatemala News and Information Bureau. Focuses on news and analysis of events in Guatemala.

**Contact:** Todd Kolze, Coordinator.

**Address:** GNIB, P.O. Box 28594, Oakland, California 94604.

**Telephone:** (510) 835-0810.

## RADIO

### WZOR-AM (1490).

Broadcasts programs for the Hispanic community in Immokalee, Florida, specifically the large Guatemalan American population in the area.

Contact: Jose Quiatanilla, Station Manager.

Address: 2105 West Immokalee Drive, Immokalee, Florida 33934.

# ORGANIZATIONS AND ASSOCIATIONS

### Casa Guatemala.

A member of Atanasio Tzul-Guatemala Support Network, the umbrella organization for ten Guatemalan refugee services groups in the United States. Provides legal assistance for immigration cases, English as a second language classes, and organizes cultural activities.

Contact: Julio Revolorio, Executive Director.

Address: c/o Atanasio Tzul, 4554 North Broadway, Suite 273, Chicago, Illinois 60640.

Telephone: (312) 561-0842.

Fax: (312) 561-1382.

### La Comité Unidad Guatemalteca.

A mostly *ladino* cultural and political group organized by the Guatemalan American refugee community in San Francisco.

Contact: Mario Ordonez, Coordinator.

Address: 1200 Florida Street, San Francisco, California 94110.

Telephone: (415) 550-9225.

### Grupo Maya.

Promotes the culture of Guatemalan Mayans and indigenous people in the United States through the production of art exhibits, language classes, and traditional dances and ceremonies. It also supports projects in Guatemala.

Contact: Adrian Cuyuzh, Coordinator.

Address: P.O. Box 40892, San Francisco, California 94140.

Telephone: (415) 824-2534.

### Guatemala Education Action Project.

Formed in 1986 by Guatemalan refugees in the United States to build awareness, response, and respect for the people of Guatemala.

Address: GEAP, P.O. Box 2151, Los Angeles, California 90051.

Telephone: (213) 653-4030.

### Guatemala Human Rights Commission/USA.

Monitors and provides current information about human rights in Guatemala.

Contact: Alice Zachmann, Director.
Address: 3321 12th Street, N.E., Washington, D.C. 20017.
Telephone: (202) 529-6599.
Fax: (202) 526-4611.

### Guatemala Project.

Organizes the North American community to work on political issues concerning Guatemala.

Contact: Emily Jones, Coordinator.
Address: P.O. Box 650054, Austin, Texas 78765.
Telephone: (512) 447-9442.

### Guatemala Support Network.

A multichapter organization that works to organize Guatemalan Americans in the Southwest and promote awareness of the political situation in Guatemala. It provides health and social service referrals, legal representation, documentation research, educational workshops, emergency aid, including food, shelter, and advocacy, through conferences, letters, and publications. It also supports a marimba band, Lira Nimazac.

Contact: Dr. Geoffrey A. Grimes, Consultant.
Address: 223 Hanna Avenue, DeSoto, Texas 75115.
Telephone: (214) 333-8624.
Fax: (214) 333-8570.

### Integración de Indígenas Mayas (IXIM).

Founded in 1986, IXIM is a cultural and educational organization that focuses on community development and the cultural expression of Mayan groups, including Quichés, Cakchiquels, Tzutujiles, Chujes, and Kanjobales. It sponsors cultural activities such as the annual fiesta of San Miguel Acatán and a marimba band. IXIM also provides social services and legal support for immigration matters and workshops on workers' rights and health problems. IXIM is the Mayan word for maize or corn.

Address: 1432 West Olympic Boulevard, No. 2, Los Angeles, California 90015.
Telephone: (213) 384-4134.

### International Maya League.

Promotes Mayan thought in the areas of culture, science, technology, and art. It produces brochures and other media and participates in speaking engagements. Headquarters are in Costa Rica, with offices throughout the world, and it serves as the parent organization of Guatemala Watch of Vermont.

**Contact:** Felipe or Elena Ixzot, Coordinators.

**Address:** 11 Cider Mill Road, Weston, Vermont 05161.

**Telephone:** (802) 824-5078.

### Network in Solidarity with the People of Guatemala (NISGUA).

Founded in 1981. NISGUA acts as an umbrella organization for groups that support human rights in Guatemala. Collects and disseminates information about the political, military, and economic situation there.

**Contact:** Michael Willis, Coordinator.

**Address:** 1500 Massachusetts Avenue, N.W., No. 214, Washington, D.C. 20005.

**Telephone:** (202) 483-0050.

### Representacion Unitaria de la Oposicion Guatemaltecam (RUOG).

RUOG lobbies the United Nations and the U.S. Congress to support the peace process in Guatemala.

**Contact:** Raul Molina Mejia, Coordinator.

**Address:** P.O. Box 3007, Grand Central Station, New York, New York 10163.

**Telephone:** (212) 682-3633.

### El Rescate.

Founded in 1981, El Rescate functions as a social services center for Central American refugees in Los Angeles. Provides food, clothing, shelter, education, financial support, and legal advice in political asylum and deportation cases. Also investigates human rights abuses in Guatemala.

**Contact:** Oscar Andrade, Executive Director.

**Address:** 1340 South Bonnie Brae, Los Angeles, California 90006.

**Telephone:** (213) 387-3284.

**Fax:** (213) 382-9189.

# MUSEUMS AND RESEARCH CENTERS

### Dallas Museum of Art.

The museum displays an extensive collection of pre-Columbian and eighteenth- to twentieth-century textiles, censers, and other art objects from Guatemala.

**Contact:** Karen Zelanka, Associate Registrar, Permanent Collection.

**Address:** 1717 Harwood, Dallas, Texas 75201.

**Telephone:** (214) 922-1200.

**Fax:** (214) 954-0174.

### Documentation Exchange.

Formerly known as the Central America Resource Center, the Documentation Exchange maintains a library of information on human rights and social conditions in many countries, including Guatemala, as well as some information on Guatemalan Americans. Also produces biweekly compilations of current news articles on Central America called NewsPaks.

**Contact:** Charlotte McCann, Editor.

**Address:** P.O. Box 2327, Austin, Texas 78768.

**Telephone:** (512) 476-9841.

**Fax:** (512) 476-0130.

### Middle American Research Institute at Tulane University.

The Institute features a collection of pre-Hispanic Mayan Guatemalan textiles and archeological artifacts.

**Contact:** Kathe Trujillo, Assistant Director.

**Address:** Middle American Research Institute, Tulane University, New Orleans, Louisiana 70118.

**Telephone:** (504) 865-5110.

### Nettie Lee Benson Latin American Collection at the University of Texas at Austin.

This internationally renowned library of books and periodicals on Latin America, maintains one of the best collections on Guatemalan Americans and Guatemala.

**Contact:** Laura Gutiérrez-Witt, Head Librarian.

**Address:** Sid Richardson Hall 1.109, General Libraries, University of Texas at Austin, Austin, Texas 78713-7330.

**Telephone:** (512) 471-3818.

### San Antonio Museum of Art.

The museum features a variety of textiles and sculpture from Guatemala.

**Contact:** Dr. Marion Oettinger, Jr., Curator, Latin American Folk Art.

**Address:** 200 West Jones Avenue, San Antonio, Texas 78215.
**Telephone:** (210) 978-8100.
**Fax:** (210) 978-8118.

### Textile Museum.

The museum displays a collection of hand-made historic and ethnographic textiles from Guatemala and other Latin American countries.

**Contact:** William J. Conklin, Research Associate, Pre-Columbian textiles.
**Address:** 2320 South Street, N.W., Washington, D.C. 20008.
**Telephone:** (202) 667-0441.
**Fax:** (202) 483-0994.

### The University of Texas Institute of Texan Cultures at San Antonio.

The multicultural museum and educational resource center maintains a library of books, files, and photographs of 90 ethnic groups in Texas, including Guatemalan Americans.

**Contact:** Diane Bruce, Librarian.
**Address:** 801 South Bowie, San Antonio, Texas 78205.
**Telephone:** (210) 558-2298.

# SOURCES FOR ADDITIONAL STUDY

Ashabranner, Brent. *Children of the Maya: A Guatemalan Indian Odyssey.* New York: Dodd, Mead & Company, 1986.

Goldman, Francisco. *The Long Night of White Chickens.* New York: Atlantic Monthly Press, 1992.

Hagan, Jacqueline Maria. *The Legalization Experience of a Mayan Community in Houston* (Dissertation). University of Texas at Austin, 1990.

Hernandez, Marita. "Kanjobal Indians: Guatemala to L.A.—Bid for Survival," *Los Angeles Times,* September 24, 1984, Part I; pp. 1, 3, 12.

Marks, Copeland. *False Tongues and Sunday Bread: A Guatemalan and Mayan Cookbook.* New York: M. Evans and Company, 1985.

Miralles, Andrea Maria. *A Matter of Life and Death: Health-Seeking Behavior of Guatemalan Refugees in South Florida.* New York: AMS Press, Inc, 1989.

Rodriguez, Nestor P. "Undocumented Central Americans in Houston: Diverse Populations," *International Migration Review* 21, No. 1, 1987; pp. 4-26.

Rohter, Larry. "In a Florida Haven for Guatemalans, Seven Deaths Bring New Mourning," *New York Times,* October 24, 1991; p. A18.

Vlach, Norita. *The Quetzal in Flight: Guatemalan Refugee Families in the United States.* Westport, Connecticut: Praeger, 1989.

# GUYANESE AMERICANS

by
Jacqueline A.
McLeod

Guyanese Americans represent a minuscule percent of America's total population, but they have made significant contributions to American popular culture, the arts, academia, and politics.

## OVERVIEW

The Cooperative Republic of Guyana—formerly the colony of British Guiana—is a country the size of its former colonial master, Great Britain, and slightly bigger than the state of Kansas. As one of many Caribbean nations, Guyana is often assumed to be an island rather than a continental country. Larger than the rest of the English-speaking Caribbean put together, it sprawls across 83,000 square miles of the northeastern coast of South America, bounded on the west by Venezuela, on the southwest by Brazil, and on the east by Suriname. Its northern boundary consists of 250 miles of coastline on the Atlantic Ocean. Of the country's total area, 86 percent is forest, 10.5 percent is savannah grassland, and 3.5 percent is the coastal belt on which nearly all its people live.

Guyana has a population of about three-quarters of a million people; 50 percent are of East Indian descent and about 30 percent are of African ancestry. Amerindian, Chinese, Portuguese, and British peoples all have contributed to the cultural heritage of the land. (The name Amerindian is used to distinguish Guyana's native groups from the immigrant East Indian population.) Primarily because of ambitious missionary activities during the nineteenth century, the Afro-Guyanese are mostly Christian. In fact, more than half of Guyana's people—regardless of race or ethnicity—are classified as Christian: 18 percent of the population is Roman Catholic, and 16 percent is Anglican. Of the non-Christian Guyanese, 35 percent is Hindu, and 9 percent is Muslim. The major religious holidays of each of the three faiths—Christianity, Hinduism, and Islam—are observed nationally.

Guyana's capital city is Georgetown. No other cities or towns rival it in importance. The official language of the country is English, but almost everyone speaks Creolese, a fusion of European and African dialects. Amerindian dialects and East Indian tongues are spoken as well, and three major Indian languages—Hindi, Tamil, and Telugu—are still in use among the Indo-Guyanese. Each of a dozen native groups speaks a different Carib, Arawak, or Warrau dialect. About 91 percent of the Guyanese population is literate—one of the highest rates among new nations of the world. Guyana's national flag consists of five colors: the green background symbolizes agriculture and forests, the golden arrowhead represents mineral wealth, the white border stands for water resources, and the red triangle edged in black signifies the energy and zeal of the Guyanese in building their nation.

### HISTORY

Guyana is an Amerindian word that means "land of [many] waters." The Europeans first used the name to refer to the triangle formed by the Orinoco, Amazon, and Negro rivers. The British used "Guiana"—an English spelling of the same Amerindian name—to refer to their New World colony. Before the arrival of the Europeans, Guyana was inhabited by several native groups. The largest group was the Caribs, who lived in the upper reaches of the Essequibo River, as well as near the Mazaruni, Cuyuni, Pomeroon, and Barima rivers. The Caribs roamed the heavily forested regions of the interior. Between the Corentyne and Waini rivers lived the Arawaks, a friendly, peace-loving native group whose people were the first to greet Christopher Columbus in other areas of the Caribbean. Another native group, the Warrau, inhabited the swampland near the mouth of the Orinoco in present-day Venezuela but eventually moved east into Guyanese territory.

Christopher Columbus was the first European known to have sailed along the coast of Guyana. But during his voyage to the New World in 1498, Columbus only viewed the land's low-lying tropical shore. It was not until 1499 that Alonso de Ojeda became the first Spaniard to actually set foot on the land that would later be known as Guyana. No settlement, however, resulted from this early exploration. Between 1595 and 1616, English explorer Sir Walter Raleigh—who dreamed of "El Dorado" (the mythical land of gold)—led three expeditions to the Guyanese territory. Although Raleigh failed to locate any gold, his efforts resulted in the earliest mapping of the Guyanese coastline.

The Dutch were the first Europeans to gain a real foothold in Guyana. In 1616 Dutch colonists selected a site on an island peak overlooking the junction of the Mazaruni and Cuyuni rivers, about 40 miles upstream from the mouth of the Essequibo River. The settlement was named Kijk-over-al ("Overlooking All"). Early attempts at farming included the growth of coffee, tobacco, and cotton crops. Meanwhile in Europe, the Dutch States-General (governing the provinces of present-day Holland) granted a charter over the Guyana territory to the Dutch West India Company in 1621. The charter gave the company complete political and economic authority, the privilege to undertake pirate raids against Spanish shipping, and the right to carry slaves from West Africa to the New World. By 1770 more than 15,000 Africans were enslaved in Guyana.

With a slave labor force, which consisted of men and women forcibly removed from their native Africa, the farms began to grow in size and in yield. The success of the Dutch venture encouraged the development of sugar plantations in other inland regions of Guyana. Similar settlements sprang up along the Berbice, Demerara, and Pomeroon rivers. The Berbice district became a separate territory in 1732, and a Demerara district was established in 1741.

In 1781 war broke out between the Dutch and the British over ownership of the colony, resulting in a year of British control over Guyana. In 1782 the French seized power and governed for two years, during which time they created the new town of Longchamps at the mouth of the Demerara River. When the Dutch regained power in 1784, they moved their colonial capital to Longchamps and renamed it Stabroek; the city was later renamed again—this time "Georgetown" after the British king, George III.

The Dutch maintained control over the Berbice, Essequibo, and Demerara settlements until 1796, when a British fleet from the Caribbean island of Barbados conquered the country. The British governed until 1802, at which time Guyana was restored to the Dutch under a truce established by the Treaty of Amiens. The next year the British once again conquered the colony, which was finally ceded to them in 1814 under agreements contained in the Treaty of Paris and the Congress of Vienna. In 1831, three years before slavery ended in the region, the British merged Berbice, Essequibo, and Demerara to form British Guiana. After slavery was abolished throughout the British colonies on August 1, 1834, former slaves were subjected to a four-year apprenticeship to facilitate their transition to a wage labor system. However, after emancipation, few former slaves chose to work—even for wages—for the plantation owners who had once enslaved them.

Faced with a critical shortage of workers, planters decided to import workers under a system of indentured servitude. Immigrants under this system included people from Portugal, China, the West Indies, and Africa, but by 1844 indentured servitude in Guyana was almost solely the domain of East Indian laborers. After a five-year indenture period, the East Indians were "free" to return to India at their own expense. This indenture system, which had satisfied the planter aristocracy's demand for workers, was abolished in British Guiana in 1917. But no matter how much headway was achieved by the former slaves or by former indentured laborers, the reins of political power remained in the firm grasp of a European elite.

## MODERN ERA

Guyana's road to independence was a rocky one. In 1953, a new constitution granted universal adult voting rights and established a two-house legislature. But political turmoil followed the first general election. The British government feared the communist leanings of the winning People's Progressive Party (PPP), which was led by Cheddi Berret Jagan (1918- ). Consequently, the British suspended the new constitution and the elected government. (Guyana's constitution did not go into effect until 1961.)

In addition to the PPP's communist stance, the party also advocated independence from Great Britain. From 1954 until the time that new elections were held in 1957, an interim government ruled British Guiana. Meanwhile, Jagan, an East Indian, and his fellow PPP co-founder, Linden Forbes Sampson Burnham (1923-1985), an African, had a major disagreement that ended

their collaboration. Burnham left the PPP in 1957 and formed the People's National Congress (PNC), which eventually became an opposition party to the PPP. The split weakened the party's majority, but the PPP still won the most legislative seats in 1957 and again in 1961.

As head of the PPP, Jagan was elected prime minister of the colonial Guyanese government in 1957 and remained in office until the heavily contested election of 1964. That year, the colonial governor declared Burnham the victor by virtue of his ability to lead a coalition of the PNC and the United Force (UF), a third party led by Portuguese businessman Peter Stanislaus d'Aguiar. Under Burnham's leadership, the nation's long struggle for independence ended on May 26, 1966, when he assumed the office of prime minister of an independent Guyana.

In an attempt to put an end to foreign meddling in Guyanese affairs, Burnham steadfastly positioned Guyana among the world's non-aligned nations in world affairs. With Burnham at the helm, Guyana declared itself a "Cooperative Republic" in 1970. The change meant that Guyana became a socialist nation—a country committed to achieving prosperity by pooling its material and human resources. The Guyanese government also nationalized its industries, including foreign-owned bauxite companies (bauxite is used in the production of aluminum), which produced much of the country's wealth. By 1985, the end of Burnham's 20-year tenure as chief executive and the year of his death, more than three-quarters of the country's economy had been brought under government control.

Immediately following Burnham's death, vice president Hugh Desmond Hoyt was sworn into office. Regularly scheduled elections, criticized as fraudulent, were held in December of 1985. Hoyt and the PNC won a solid but questionable victory. However, in national elections held in October of 1992—under the watchful eyes of the international community—the Jagan-led PPP won, bringing the tenure of the PNC as ruling party to a close after almost three decades.

## FIRST GUYANESE IN UNITED STATES

The Guyanese people were part of the two major waves of British West Indian immigration to the United States. The earlier wave encompassed the first two decades of the twentieth century, showing a steady increase in immigration until the passage of the Immigration Act of 1924. This act placed race and ethnicity restrictions on entry to the States and included the English-speaking Caribbean in the quota allotted to Great Britain, with a visa limit of 800 per year and a preference system for skilled workers and relatives of United States citizens. Throughout the 1940s and 1950s, Guyanese immigrants primarily chose Britain as their destination. However, following the passage of the Immigration and Nationality Act of 1952, also known as the McCarran-Walter Act, which removed race and ethnicity as conditions of entry, the second wave of immigration to the United States began; the Guyanese American migration pattern continued to accelerate in the ensuing decades.

## SIGNIFICANT IMMIGRANT WAVES

Guyanese immigration to the United States increased sharply with the passage of Britain's 1962 Commonwealth Immigration Act, which overturned the British Nationality Act of 1948. The earlier act allowed citizens of Guyana to claim citizenship in the United Kingdom and granted all Commonwealth citizens the same legal rights accorded to British citizens. Many Guyanese took advantage of this opportunity to further their education and improve their economic status. However, the concentration of non-white manual workers and their families in British cities stimulated an outcry against unregulated immigration, culminating in the 1962 Act, which restricted their entry. With the doors of their "mother country" virtually closed to them, many Guyanese, mostly of the professional and technical classes, began to turn to the United States as their new land of opportunity.

In 1965 the McCarran-Walter Act was amended to protect American workers while restricting immigration from the Western Hemisphere. But with the introduction in 1968 of an annual ceiling of 120,000 immigrant visas for the Western Hemisphere, the intent of the Act of 1965 was negated. Skilled laborers from Western Hemisphere countries journeyed to the United States in record numbers. The response from Guyana was immediate and dramatic. The majority of Guyanese applicants fell into the categories of "professional," "technical," and "kindred" (or skilled) workers.

The outward flow from Guyana intensified as the country experienced drastic economic and political changes during the 1970s and 1980s. After declaring itself a "Cooperative Republic" in 1970, Guyana began taking steps toward the nationalization of resources. During this time the country was under progressively heavier stresses and strains, resulting in declining productivity, massive unemployment, and skyrocketing inflation. It was also during this period that the Burnham regime came under increasing fire for its repression of political opposition.

Between 1960 and 1970, more Guyanese entered the United States than ever before. Around this time, the United States experienced labor shortages—especially in the health industry and in private households, traditional areas of employment for women. Guyanese women, like other Caribbean women, met demands in the United States for workers in the health and domestic fields. The first Guyanese to arrive in 1968, either as "private household workers" or as nurses' aides, were of African descent. East Indian Guyanese women were forbidden by custom to venture to the States alone.

Guyanese immigrants no longer fit the traditional immigration pattern, in which the men settle in a new country first and send for their families later. Since the 1960s, female immigrants have assumed the status of "principal alien," the term given to an immigrant worker within a specific or delineated labor force capacity, whose status activates other provisions in the migration process of family members. According to Monica Gordon in *In Search of a Better Life: Perspectives on Migration from the Caribbean*, more Guyanese women than men settled in the United States in the 1960s and 1970s, making them primarily responsible for securing immigrant status for their families. These women, Gordon concluded, tended to see migration as a means to improve their economic and social status and the educational opportunities of their children. U.S. Census Bureau records indicate that of the 48,608 people of Guyanese ancestry living in the United States in 1980, 26,046 were female. By 1990 approximately 81,665 people of Guyanese ancestry had settled in the States.

## SETTLEMENT

Because the overwhelming majority of Guyanese were migrating from urban centers (90 percent of Guyana's population is clustered along the coastal plain), they tended to settle mostly in the northeastern cities of the United States. As of 1990, 80 percent of Guyanese Americans lived in the Northeast. The heaviest concentration of Guyanese Americans can be found in New York (56,462), New Jersey (6,697), and Maryland

(3,106), although a significant portion of the population also settled in Florida, California, Texas, and Pennsylvania.

Guyanese American communities are not localized. There are no clearly demarcated spatial boundaries between them and other Caribbean groups. Rather, a multiplicity of Caribbean peoples tend to settle in the same regions. New York City's immigrant pool from 1982 to 1989 was drawn mostly from the Caribbean. Of the top five source countries, four were the Caribbean nations of the Dominican Republic, Jamaica, Haiti, and Guyana. Seventy percent of all Guyanese immigrants move to New York. In fact, about eight percent of the total population of Guyana moved to New York City—particularly the East Flatbush, Flatbush, and Crown Heights sections of Brooklyn—in the 1980s, according to a *New York Times* report. Of the 46,706 Guyanese immigrants in the United States from 1983 to 1989, a total of 8,912, or approximately 19 percent, settled in these sections of the city.

# ACCULTURATION AND ASSIMILATION

Many immigration studies on the Caribbean focus on the island nations of Jamaica, Haiti, Barbados, and Trinidad and Tobago because of their large populations abroad. Guyana's immigrant population in the United States has only recently increased to a noticeable degree. Guyana first grabbed the international spotlight in November of 1978, after the shocking People's Temple incident involving the mass suicide by poison of more than 900 Americans in the country's interior. The People's Temple, a cult that originated in California, consisted of U.S. citizens under the leadership of Reverend Jim Jones. Members of the Guyanese government found Jones's credentials sound and granted him permission to construct a religious center in Guyana's western region, near Port Kaituma. The enterprise, however, ended in tragedy when Jones—under scrutiny by the U.S. government for his questionable dealings—convinced his followers to kill themselves. For years after, the country of Guyana was associated with the cult members' deaths.

## TRADITIONS, CUSTOMS, AND BELIEFS

Guyanese folklore and traditions date back centuries. Many Guyanese superstitions or belief systems are maintained among Guyanese Americans, especially those who identify with some Caribbean enclave. The following are some examples of Guyanese beliefs: Good Friday is considered a very unlucky day to be involved in outdoor activities if they are not church-related. When entering a house late at night, a person should go in backwards in order to keep evil spirits out. To cure a fever, a sliced potato should be placed on the ill person's forehead. To cure the effects of a stroke (like a twisted mouth), a whole nutmeg should be placed inside of the mouth on the affected side. A woman whose feet have been swept will not get married. A black cat crossing in front of a pedestrian will bring bad luck. A dog howling at a particular house is a sign that death will soon come to someone in that household. A pondfly in the house is a sign of news or correspondence. Stepping over someone's leg will stunt their growth. All references to the dead must be prefaced with the words: "God rest the dead in the living and the looking."

## PROVERBS

A wealth of proverbs from Guyanese culture have survived through the generations: "Hint at Quashiba mek Beneba tek notice" (Pay attention to the hints someone drops); "Wuh is fun fuh school boy is dead fuh crappo" (One man's meat is another man's poison); "Bush gat ears, goobie gat hole" (When you least expect it, people are eavesdropping); "Mouth open, story jump out" (Some people can't keep a secret); "Show me yuh company, I'll tell you who you be" (People judge you by the friends you keep); "Moon run til day ketch he" (Your deeds usually catch up with you); "Greedy man y'eye does yalla twice, fuh he own and he mattie own" (Some people are never satisfied); "Monkey mek he pickney til he spoil'um" (Similar to "Too many cooks spoil the broth"); "Wuh fall from head drop pun shoulder" (Sins of the parents fall on the children); "If yuh guh to crab dance, yuh mus get mud" (What you sow you reap); "Who lif yuh up doan put yuh dung" (Those who get you into trouble don't get you out); "It's a lazy horse that can't carry its own oats" (Your burden is yours to carry); "Hand wash hand mek hand come clean" (More is accomplished through cooperation); "Mocking is ketching" (Don't laugh at another's situation, it might be yours); "Monkey know wuh limb to jump pun" (Bullies know exactly on whom to pick); "Donkey ears long, but he doan hear he own story" (Some people mind other people's business); "Do suh nuh like suh" (Treat others as you would like to be treated); "If yuh nuh gat muhma suck granny" (Make do with what you have).

### CUISINE

Guyanese cuisine is appetizing, spicy, and delicious. Spices and herbs are used in abundance, and one-dish meals occupy an important place in Guyanese cuisine. These dishes, sometimes called "poor man food," are nourishing, inexpensive, and very easy to prepare. Guyanese men and women both enjoy cooking, each trying to outdo the other in excellence. *Pepperpot*, considered a national dish, is a combination of different meats (beef, pork), spices, a dash of sugar, lots of onions, and *cassareep* (a sauce made from fomented juice from the bitter cassava plant); it is eaten with rice or bread. *Cookup rice*, another national dish, is a blend of rice, split peas or black-eyed peas, spices, onions, coconut milk, and meats. Also central to the repertoire of Guyanese recipes is the array of Indian curried dishes, made with curry powder, an East Indian spice with a distinctive flavor. *African Metemgee*, an inexpensive dish that is very filling, is made from coconut milk, meat or fish, onions, spices, plantains, and dumplings. *Souse* is a very spicy and tangy dish made from boiled pig ears and pig feet, flavored with cucumber, hot pepper, scallions, and lemon juice. Portuguese garlic pork is highly spiced pork pickled in garlic and vinegar. It is served fried, and eaten with bread. *Dahl* is a blend of boiled split peas, onions, garlic, curry powder, and cumin. This can be served over rice or eaten with *roti*, a pancake-like bread. Guyanese cuisine is not complete without Chinese noodles and chow mein, and black pudding, also called blood pudding, which is served with a tangy hot sauce.

*Konkee* is a sweet dish made from corn flour, sugar, spices, grated coconut, and raisins. The mixture is then wrapped in a banana leaf and boiled. *Foofoo*, one of several substitutes for rice, is simply boiled plantains pounded in a mortar with a pestle. This is usually served with some type of stew. *Coocoo*, another substitute for rice, is a corn meal mush blended with seasoned boiled okra. *Cutty Cutty soup*, a "poor man" dish, is made with okra, salt beef, pig tail, tripe (stomach tissue, usually of a cow), onions, green plantains, and dumplings. *Salt fish cakes*, also called codfish cakes, are made from shredded salted codfish mashed together with boiled potatoes, onions, and pepper, then placed in a batter and fried. Black cake is Guyanese fruit cake, usually made at Christmas or for weddings. It is a very dark and very rich fruit cake made with rum. Ginger beer is a non-alcoholic homemade drink made from grated ginger and sweetened water.

### TRADITIONAL DRESS

Many Indo-Guyanese women wear their traditional *sari* for special occasions such as weddings or East Indian holidays. *Saris* are garments made from long pieces of light cloth: one end is wrapped around the waist to form a skirt and the other is draped over the shoulder or the head. Some Afro-Guyanese wear the African *booboo* and *head wrap*. During the 1970s, when Guyana became a socialist republic, Prime Minister Burnham formally declared the official business attire for men to be *shirtjacks* and pants, instead of the European suit and tie.

### GUYANESE DANCES AND SONGS

Guyana's National Dance Company—a multiethnic troupe—performs East Indian and African dances during national holidays, including Independence Day; *Deepavali*, the Hindu celebration of lights; *Phagwah*, the Hindu festival to welcome spring; and the Republic celebrations.

### HOLIDAYS CELEBRATED BY GUYANESE AMERICANS

In addition to Christmas Day, New Year's Day, and Easter Sunday, Guyanese Americans celebrate Guyana's Independence on May 26, and to a lesser degree "August Monday," the first Monday in August, symbolizing Emancipation Day. At Independence Day celebrations, the national anthem, "Dear Land of Guyana," is sung.

### HEALTH AND MENTAL HEALTH ISSUES

There are no documented health problems or medical conditions that are specific to Guyanese Americans. Many families have health insurance coverage through their employers. Like most Americans, Guyanese American business owners and professionals in private practice are insured at their own expense.

# LANGUAGE

Guyanese generally speak and understand Creole or Creolese, which is a linguistic fusion of African dialects and English. Standard English is used for formal communication, although it is spoken in a definite Guyanese vernacular. For the first generation of immigrants who settled (as most did) among other Caribbean enclaves, there was no real attempt to alter their speech patten, since others in their community could understand them. For those immigrants who moved away from their Caribbean neighbors and integrated socially into the host society, their speech pattern gradually lost its distinctive Guyanese sound. Some immigrants, however, chose to hold onto their speech pattern as a way of maintaining their identity.

## GREETINGS AND OTHER POPULAR EXPRESSIONS

Common Guyanese words and expressions include: Howdy—How are you?; God spare life—an expression used after promising to do something; God rest the dead—expression used before speaking the name of the dead; *Beannie*—referring to a young female; *Banna*—referring to a young male; *Jert*—to eat; *Tassay*—to get lost; *Ahgee*—grandmother; *Bambuy*—leftovers; *Eye wata*—tears; *Mamoo*—uncle (Indo-Guyanese); *Pagaly*—silly; "Don't mek yuh eyes pass me"—meaning don't disrespect me.

# FAMILY AND COMMUNITY DYNAMICS

The first wave of Guyanese immigrants in the early decades of the twentieth century were typically single males who had left their families and possibly a fiancee behind temporarily in the hopes of sending for them later; in the interim, they supplemented the income of the family back home. Many married men did not immigrate ahead of their families, since their jobs at home provided the only income the family had. In the case of the Indo-Guyanese, some husbands and wives came together, leaving children with grandparents or other relatives. Recently there has been an increase in the numbers of Indo-Guyanese women who have immigrated without their families, but these numbers are still minuscule in comparison to the Afro-Guyanese women, who began moving to the States alone in the 1960s. Typically these newcomers first stayed for a short time with friends or relatives. After finding work, however, they usually rented rooms in crowded boarding houses (often occupied by other Guyanese and Caribbean immigrants).

Like typical first generation immigrants, the Guyanese worked hard and saved most of their earnings, doing without the simplest of pleasures. Their primary goal was to facilitate the passage of their family members to the United States. Many of the males worked around the clock and went to night classes to better themselves educationally; women typically performed "sleep in" work—living six days per week at their place of employment and returning to the boarding house for one day, usually beginning Saturday night and ending Sunday night. That one day off was spent in church and at stores shopping for things to "pack a barrel" for their kin back home.

After acquiring permanent resident status and securing their family's passage to the States, Guyanese immigrants then concentrated on improving their economic and educational status. Many women pursued nursing degrees part-time while holding multiple jobs.

The core of the social network of the Guyanese is the family. Other Guyanese are preferred as marriage partners, but many Guyanese marry persons from other Caribbean nations, or Americans of Caribbean parentage. The percentage of marriages between Guyanese and Americans—black or white—is low.

## INTERACTIONS WITH OTHER ETHNIC MINORITIES

From their first arrival, the Guyanese began to interact with other ethnic groups, particularly Jamaicans, Trinidadians, Barbadians, Grenadians, and people from other English-speaking Caribbean nations. This nurturing of a Caribbeanness contributes to the resistance to marry outside of the Caribbean group. Guyanese American cultural traditions have been preserved by the religious observances of weddings, baptisms, and funerals.

## WEDDINGS

The bridal shower is a social custom practiced in Guyana among many Christians and non-Christians. Many Guyanese Hindus, for example, have simultaneous Christian celebrations to include their Christian friends. For Christian weddings, bans are usually announced in the church for three consecutive Sundays so that impediments to the marriage—if any—can be brought to the attention of the priest. During this period the priest counsels the couple on the duties of marriage. As in the United States, the couple selects a best man, maid (or matron) of honor, bridesmaids, and attendants. In most cases the best man and maid/matron of honor serve as godparents to the couple's first child. The godmother then becomes the couple's *mac mae* ("mac may"), and the godfather the *com pae* ("com pay").

On the night before the wedding, in a celebration of song and dance called a *kweh kweh*, the bride is feted by the older women of her family. The actual wedding ceremony mirrors the traditional American church wedding. Silver coins are also blessed by the priest and given to the bride and groom for good luck and prosperity. The priest wraps a robe around the bride and groom, symbolizing their union, and blesses them before concluding the ceremony.

Most Guyanese American weddings are held at a private home or at a Caribbean catering hall to ensure a Guyanese menu. Gifts are usually delivered before the day of the wedding. Toasting or paying respects to the newlyweds is the focal point of the reception. The best man gives his blessings and advice first, then directs the parents of the couple to speak, then any elders in the audience. The bridegroom then speaks, thanking everyone for attending. The reception is accompanied by Caribbean music and dancing. Two weeks after the wedding, the couple entertains family and friends at a gala called a "Second Sunday."

### BAPTISMS

The Guyanese American community is a dispersed one, but family members often travel hundreds of miles for celebrations such as baptisms. According to Guyanese tradition, a female child will have two godmothers and one godfather, and a male child will have two godfathers and one godmother. The godparents are responsible for purchasing the baptismal gown for the child; however, if the mother still has her wedding dress, she may choose to make a baptismal dress from it for her first born. The godparents take the child to church; the priest then confers the grace of God on the baby by placing his hand on his or her head. The godparents promise to lead the child in the way of the Lord. Then, the priest blesses the child in the name of the Holy Trinity while rubbing incense on the forehead and chest; pours holy water over the child's forehead; and finally offers the child up to God.

After the baptism, it is customary to have a large gathering with lots of music, dancing, and food. Family members and friends shower the child with gifts, and money is pinned on the child for good luck and prosperity. Guyanese custom dictates that the child be given a piece of gold jewelry for good luck soon after birth. Girls usually are given a pair of gold bangles (bracelets) and a pair of gold earrings, and boys are given a gold ring and a gold bracelet.

### FUNERALS

Among the Guyanese, a death in the family is announced by word of mouth. In Guyana, the body of the dead is usually washed and dressed by family members, but because of health regulations this tradition is not practiced in the United States. The deceased is remembered and mourned during a wake, which is followed by a gathering of loved ones and friends. Food and liquor abound, tall tales are told, and folksongs are sung.

After the funeral service at church, prayers are said by the priest at the cemetery, and family members are invited to place flowers on the coffin. Before the deceased is lowered into the grave, the priest sprinkles soil on top of the coffin and while saying: "Ashes to ashes, dust to dust." The congregation then returns to the home of the deceased where friends and relatives have gathered bearing food and beverages. Nine days after the death of a loved one, there is another wake—called "Nine Night"—held in memory of the deceased.

For many days before and after the burial, the family of the deceased is never left alone. Mirrors in the house are covered, for fear of seeing the deceased. Homes are not swept out for days after the burial, for fear of the dead taking more family members with him or her.

# RELIGION

Guyanese Americans generally maintain an affiliation with the religious denomination of their homeland. The vast majority of Guyanese American churchgoers are Episcopalian. Priests from Guyana who immigrate to the States often go on to lead Guyanese American churches. These churches also serve as network centers for newly arrived immigrants. Many Caribbean-led Episcopalian churches in the New York City area have established schools that cater to the educational demands of Caribbean parents and are staffed by former Caribbean schoolteachers. Guyanese parents view education as a combination of learning and discipline; many opt to pay for private schooling for their children, feeling assured that they will be taught in the "home way."

Beginning in the 1970s, a surge of non-denominational churches were established by the Guyanese in the New York and New Jersey areas. These "churches," which are more like teaching centers, have attracted many newly settled Guyanese Americans. So-called "Unity Centers" serve as community centers and teach positive thinking and ways to attain a closer relationship with God. The congregation reflects the many faces of the nations in the Caribbean, although Guyanese usually predominate in those Unity Centers run by Guyanese priests and priestesses.

# EMPLOYMENT AND ECONOMIC TRADITIONS

Because the early Guyanese immigrants settled in the northeastern region of the United States, particularly New York, they found work in the health care, domestic labor, banking, clerical, and physical security fields. They were paid the lowest wages, and—like members of other immigrant groups—many worked several jobs at a time. After accumulating work experience and permanent resident status, many Guyanese advanced to better paying positions.

Some Guyanese established their own small, family-run businesses, such as bakeries and take-out restaurants catering to the tastes of a Caribbean community. Others who could not afford to rent business space in Caribbean neighborhoods sold Guyanese food out of their homes on weekends. As the Guyanese immigrants became more established, they opened real estate offices, guard services, small grocery stores (specializing in food products from home, like *cassareep*), neighborhood law offices (specializing in immigration and real estate law), beauty salons, and travel agencies.

# POLITICS AND GOVERNMENT

Guyanese are active in the organizations of the larger Caribbean region. There are many Guyanese nurses' and police associations. Guyanese Americans have not yet made a collective impact on political activity nationally. Locally, however, they have organized through their churches with other ethnic groups to call attention to problems in their neighborhoods. They have also entered politics on a local level.

### RELATIONS WITH GUYANA

Guyanese Americans maintain close ties to their homeland and its people and provide significant financial support to their native country. During the late 1970s and 1980s—when Guyana was experiencing a terrible economic crisis owing to the further devaluation of the Guyanese dollar, skyrocketing prices for consumer goods, and shortages of basic necessities—Guyanese organizations pooled their resources from fund-raising and made generous donations of money, food, clothing, and equipment to Guyanese hostels, orphans, almshouses, schools, and hospitals. High school alumni associations furnished their alma maters and other schools with chairs, desks, books, and office supplies. Nurses' organizations donated syringes, bed sheets, thermometers, penicillin, and other scarce supplies to hospitals.

There is a steady flow of scholarly exchanges between Guyana and the United States in the form of academic conferences. In almost every college or university with a sizable Caribbean student body, there are Caribbean associations that encourage the connections with home through guest lecturers, trips, and networking. In the United States, academic organizations such as the Association of Caribbean Historians, the Caribbean Studies Association, and the Caribbean Writers Association cater to scholars from the Caribbean.

# INDIVIDUAL AND GROUP CONTRIBUTIONS

Guyanese Americans represent a minuscule percent of America's total population, but they have made significant contributions to American popular culture, the arts, academia, and politics:

### LITERATURE AND THE ARTS

Guyana has long provided a theme for literary expression. Popular Guyanese authors include Jan Carew (1925- ), Wilson Harris (1921- ), Denis

Williams (1923- ), O. R. Dathorne (1934- ), Christopher Nicole (1930- ), Gordon Rohlehr, and E. R. Braithwaite (1920- ). Braithwaite's memoir *To Sir With Love* details his experiences as a black high school teacher in a white London slum. The work was praised for its hopeful view of difficult race relations and was adapted for a 1967 film of the same name.

Edgar Mittelholzer (1909-1965) became well known outside of Guyana for such novels as *Corentyne Thunder, Shadows Move Among Them* (which won high critical acclaim in America and Britain), *Morning at the Office, The Life and Death of Sylvia, The Piling of Clouds,* and a three-part novel known as the *Kaywana Trilogy* (*Children of Kaywana, Kaywana Stock,* and *Kaywana Blood*). This trilogy follows the fortunes of a Dutch planter family, the Van Groenwegels, over three centuries of Guyanese history and attempts to capture the raw and violent spirit of those times.

*Miramy,* a full-length Guyanese comedy by Frank Pilgrim, is set on an imaginary island in the West Indies. It became the first locally written play to be performed outside of Guyana. The works of Jan Carew include *Black Midas,* a picaresque novel acclaimed for its vivid portrayal of raw and roguish types in the diamond fields of Guyana; *The Wild Coast,* a sensitive study of a young man's difficult passage from puberty to manhood; and *The Last Barbarian,* a study of West Indian and African life in Harlem. Works by Wilson Harris include a series of poems entitled *Eternity to Season* and the novel *The Palace of the Peacock,* about the journey of a river crew through the jungles of Guyana. Among his other works are *The Far Journey of Oudin, The Whole Armour,* and *The Secret Ladder.*

Gregory A. Henry, a Guyana-born artist, draws upon the endemic storytelling traditions of his culture for his paintings and sculpture. His work, which has been featured in several travelling exhibits and solo and group shows, has been praised by art critics who number him among a select group of artists projected to come to national prominence in the 1990s.

## MUSIC

Alvin Chea is a member of Take 6, a Grammy Award-winning, all-male, *a cappella* gospel-pop group. Chea is first generation Guyanese American, born to a Guyanese mother.

## POLITICS

Colin Moore is a Guyanese American who has made a name for himself in New York politics. An attorney in private practice in Brooklyn, Moore is known for representing many Guyanese Americans and other Caribbean immigrants throughout the New York area. He sought election to the office of governor of New York in 1994, ran unsuccessfully in the past for New York City councilman and district attorney, and—with a group of politically active African Americans—helped found the Freedom Party.

# MEDIA

## RADIO

WLIB in New York City focuses on information of interest to Guyanese Americans; owned by the Inner City Broadcasting Corporation. One of station's best-known personalities is Claude Tate, a Guyanese American.

# SOURCES FOR ADDITIONAL STUDY

*The Caribbean Exodus,* edited by Barry B. Levine. New York: Praeger, 1987.

*Caribbean Immigration to the United States,* edited by Roy S. Bryce-Laporte and Delores M. Mortimer. Washington, D.C.: Research Institute on Immigration and Ethnic Studies, 1983.

*In Search of a Better Life: Perspectives on Migration from the Caribbean,* edited by Ransford W. Palmer. New York: Praeger, 1990.

Sontag, Deborah. "A City of Immigrants Is Pictured in Report," *New York Times,* July 1, 1992.

Udeogalanya, Veronica. *Demographic and Socio-Economic Characteristics of Caribbean Immigrants and Non-Immigrant Population in the United States.* Brooklyn, New York: Caribbean Research Center, Medgar Evers College, 1989.

# GYPSY

by
**Evan Heimlich**

# AMERICANS

Gypsies value luck
and health. Ideas
about health and
illness among the
Rom are closely
related to a world
view (*romania*),
which includes
notions of good and
bad luck, purity and
impurity, inclusion
and exclusion.

## OVERVIEW

Ethnic Gypsies are descendants of an ancient Indian caste that roamed westward. Ethnic Gypsies in the United States from eastern and southern Europe call themselves Rom; those from Great Britain are Romnichals (who may be related to Irish tinkers and travelers); and those from Spain or Mexico may be known as Gitanos. Each group of ethnic Gypsies draws its own line to determine which other groups they consider Gypsy, and which not. Estimates of the total population of ethnic Gypsies in the United States range from 250,000 to one million.

## HISTORY

The Gypsies originated in India as the *Dom*, a caste of strolling entertainers who beat drums, sang, and danced. According to Angus Frazier's *The Gypsies*, they spoke a branch of Hindi. Among the vegetarian Hindus (as among the Punjabi and other tribes of India) they constituted a low-caste of meat-eating, dark-skinned, menial workers. Near the end of the ninth century B.C. an Indian King, Shangul, sent 10,000 *Dom* to Persia (now Iran) as minstrel musicians. According to Jean Paul Clébert (*The Gypsies*, translated by Charles Duff [Harmondsworth: Penguin, 1967], p. 40) their remarkable story is recorded in the Persian nation-

al epic poem, *Shah Nameh* (*Book of Kings*), by poet Firdawsi. In the poem, Bahram Gur, the Persian monarch, has declared that everyone in his kingdom should work only half a day and should spend the other half listening to music, eating, and drinking. He seeks lute players and other Indians to ease the burdensome existence and the tedium of work of his people and requests the Indian King to gather and send 10,000 musicians, which the Indian King does. When the Persian monarch receives his itinerant musicians (male and female), he attempts to turn them into farmers. He assigns them wheat and cattle and the necessary land to provide their own sustenance while amusing his people. However, when the musicians fail to plant the wheat or breed the cattle, and consume the stock instead, the king rebukes them and orders them to pack their possessions onto their asses and support themselves by travelling the countryside.

According to Marlene Sway's *Familiar Strangers,* the name that Gypsies use to refer to themselves, "Rom" originates from the Sanskrit word *Dom.* Literally translated, *Dom* means "a man of low caste who gains his livelihood by singing and dancing." Sway posits that *Dom* probably derived from the sound that a drum makes, and that the "first pariahs may have been the *Dom,* as the term originally described a despised people who were hereditary drum-beaters."

Linguistic evidence indicates that after a hundred years or so of entertaining Persians in the tenth century the *Dom* began to roam far afield. They separated into two major groups and lived as nomads. The first group to leave wandered into Syria, Palestine, and Egypt, eventually spreading throughout the Middle East and North Africa. The second group traveled northward from Persia into Armenia, where they stayed for a long time; after passing through Byzantine Greece, the Northerners reached Eastern Europe. They traveled across Europe, often moving because of harsh treatment. According to Sway, "The inhospitality of the Balkans caused a band of three hundred [of these nomads] to explore more western regions.... Promising reports given by their pioneers inspired massive migrations of these nomads into northern, central, and southern Europe."

The Gypsies approached Europe from Turkish-occupied lands. By the fifteenth century, when Gypsies had reached Western Europe, populations of that region still feared the Turkish domination of the Ottoman Empire. It was in Western Europe that some of these people became known as Gypsies. The term itself probably derives from 'Gypcian, and results from an early confusion of Egypt with Epirus, or Little Egypt, in the Western Byzantine Empire. Eventually, Europeans used "Gypsies" or related words to name not only a particular ethnic group of people, but also other groups of people, unrelated by blood, whose traveling lifestyles made them resemble ethnic Gypsies. For the most part, Gypsies kept to themselves as a people; however, as Matt Salo suggests in his introduction to *Urban Gypsies,* "The existence of a number of Gypsy-like peripatetic groups, some of which (such as British Travellers) have intermarried with Gypsies ... complicate our attempts at classification" of who should not count and who should count as Gypsies. Although purists tend to define the group narrowly, loose classifications of ethnic Gypsies include all nomads who live and identify themselves as Gypsies.

During the fifteenth century, nomadic descendants of the *Dom* spread throughout and beyond Europe. The migrations widely dispersed the small groups, which lost contact with one another; and Matt Salo reports that sufficient cultural and linguistic differentiation occurred so that the groups lost consciousness of themselves as a single people. Around the middle of the nineteenth century, more Gypsies left Eastern Europe, constituting the second wave of migrations westward, northward and southward from there. Crossing many political borders, Eastern European Gypsies began migrating to Mexico, Central and South America, and to a lesser extent, countries in the Caribbean basin. Many of these Gypsies or their descendants arrived in the United States via this Latin American route. Some who came to the United States left, especially after the United States passed restrictive immigration legislation in 1924. Currently, Gypsies live in at least 40 different countries, and may number as many as ten million worldwide.

The two groups of Gypsy Americans about whom scholars know the most are the Rom and the Romnichals. Many of the Rom came to the New World from Russia, or Eastern or Central Europe; the Romnichals came from Great Britain. Although these two groups have much in common, they also are divided by the cultural differences and prejudices between Great Britain and Eastern Europe; the derision with which some Romnichals refer to the Rom reflects this split. The Romnichals came to the United States earlier than the Rom, and ran successful horse-trading operations in New England. The Rom arrived in the United States during the late nineteenth century and filled an American need for fortunetellers. It is uncertain how many Gypsies are in the United States primarily because many Gypsies entered the country illegally, leaving few records, and were not counted on statistical tables of immigrants. Those who did immigrate legally were recorded by their country of origin and not as Gypsies. Because Gypsies are historically rooted in no nation, mutual mistrust has grown between Gypsies and governments. Gypsies tend to avoid the census taker and are justifiably wary of record-collecting, especially since records on Gypsies enabled the Nazis them to round up and kill one million of them during World War II. According to Rom Gypsy and scholar Ian Hancock, estimates that there are half a million Rom in America. In an October 1994 interview, Sheila Salo, another leading scholar of Gypsy Americans, estimated that America may have as few as 100,000 Rom and perhaps as many Romnichals.

Almost all Gypsies in the United States originated from some part of Europe, although there are a few small groups from elsewhere, such as parts of Asia. Some "black Dutch," from Germany, the Netherlands, and Pennsylvania, intermarried with Romnichals, and pass as white Anglo-Americans. Besides the Eastern Europeans who make up the large group of Rom, there are in the United States two other large groups of Gypsies: the Baschalde (from Slovakia, Hungary, and Carpagia), who may number close to 100,000; and the Romungre (from Hungary and Transylvania) who may number as many as 60,000. There are also some Horchanay, who are historically Muslims from the South Balkans, and a small population of Sinti Gypsies, who came from Northern Europe—Germany, Netherlands, France, Austria, Hungary—where they, like other Gypsies, were targets of the Nazis. There are also Bosnian and Polish Gypsies present in the United States Within the category of Rom Gypsies, there are several subgroups in the United States, such as the Kalderash and Machwaya. One of the most recent immigrations of a Gypsy group is that of the Lovara, which arrived in the 1990s. There are also a few small groups of Romanian Ludar, who may be Gypsies, in addition to the population of Gypsy Americans who emigrated from the Gypsy stronghold within the nation of Romania.

## IMMIGRATION WAVES TO THE UNITED STATES

Gypsies have come to the United States for reasons similar to those of other immigrants; however, since European powers have tended to oppose Gypsies, this hostility has hastened Gypsy emigrations. Some Gypsies, though, came before those from Eastern Europe. According to Sway, "Gypsy deportations from England, France, Portugal, and Spain created the genesis of Gypsy life in the New World." Gypsies' social marginality left them little institutional power in Europe. To the deporting nations, sending Gypsies to the colonies let them remove what was seen as a "Gypsy problem." Sway adds that England deported some Gypsies to Barbados and Australia, and by the end of the seventeenth century, every European country with New World holdings followed the practice of deporting Gypsies to the Americas.

Ill will between Gypsies and established powers of civilizations spurred Gypsy emigration, also. Christian churches of Europe institutionalized hostility toward Gypsies, prompting their deportation. Sending Gypsies home was not an option—no nation welcomed them since their origin in India was unknown to the Western world until the eighteenth century. As Sway states, "After wandering in Europe for two hundred years, the Gypsies were citizens of no country and members of no church." Near the end of the nineteenth century, Eastern European emigrants spread throughout Europe and the Western Hemisphere; within this mass movement came the biggest immigrant waves of Gypsies to the United States.

Although Europeans have historically treated Gypsies poorly, Gypsies tended to fare better in Western Europe than in Eastern Europe, where they suffered the extremes of racial prejudice, including enslavement. Still, the New World society extended hope for alleviating social oppression. Some came to the United States via indirect routes. Of Gypsies deported to South American colonies, some migrated North. Some Gypsies were annexed into America with territory itself: for example, Napoleon transported hundreds of Gypsy men to Louisiana during the two-year period before selling the Louisiana Territory to the United States in 1803. More recently, toward the end of the twentieth century, the collapse of communism in Eastern Europe has enabled Gypsies to emigrate more freely, and has generated new waves of Eastern European Gypsies to the United States. Currently, of the estimated ten million Gypsies worldwide, the United States hosts between 250,000 and a million.

## SETTLEMENT PATTERNS

Gypsies have resisted pressures from any civilization, including the United States, to have a single name or address. Nomadic Gypsies travel to avoid permanent settlement. By keeping their populations on the move and thinly spread, Gypsies decrease their visibility. They often go where they can make money and balanced nomadism allows groups of Gypsies to maintain their own economic territories. Rather than wander, they tend to travel purposefully from one destination to another. Historically, some families have reportedly traveled in regular circuits, often returning to the same places; others have ranged more widely, following no set route. Hardly ever, though, has travel been either continuous or completely random. Awareness of the best cities, small towns, or rural areas for exploitation has guided all travel. A group might camp for weeks, sometimes months, at especially productive urban areas, returning to these spots year after year.

Gypsy Americans might maintain a sequence of home bases; they often live in mobile homes, settling indefinitely in a trailer park. Gypsy Americans, unlike their European counterparts, tend to remain mobile despite a somewhat restricted range of mobility. Gypsies frequently tear down walls or and enlarge doorways of their homes to combine rooms or make them larger to create a wide open space suitable for the large social gatherings that occur in Rom homes. In *Urban Gypsies,* Carol Silverman notes that Gypsies frequently pass along the houses, apartments, or trailers that they modify to a succession of Gypsy families.

According to Anne Sutherland's essay in *Gypsies, Tinkers and Other Travellers*, "Because they no longer travel in caravans or pitch their tents in the fields of America, many Rom claim that they are no longer nomadic, and they speak with nostalgia about the 'good old days' when they were 'on the road.'" Relative to other Americans, however, many Gypsy Americans tend to travel and to change residences frequently; by non-Gypsy standards, they remain an itinerant people.

The Gypsy population has been participating in American migrations from countryside into cities. Yet, estimates tend to support that the Gypsy American population at any given time is evenly divided between urban and rural areas. Generally, as noted by Silverman, the urbanization of the Rom began as early as the end of the eighteenth century when various groups began to spend the winter months camping in vacant lots on the outskirts of cities, and intensified when "a large number of *Rom* flocked to the cities during the 1920s and 1930s to take advantage of various relief programs, and remained there because of gas rationing and because of increasing business opportunities within the city."

Because Gypsies tend to follow economic opportunities, the most populous cities, such as Los Angeles, San Francisco, New York, Chicago, Boston, Atlanta, Dallas, Houston, Seattle, and Portland, have the largest concentrations of Gypsies. Currently, there are Romnichal strongholds of very conservative Gypsies who reside in Texarkana, southern Arkansas, and other predominantly rural regions. Gypsies also have joined American movement westward. Many live in California.

## REVERSE IMMIGRATIONS

Gypsy Americans who can do so often travel to other parts of the Western Hemisphere and to Europe. Many repeatedly visit certain places as part of a set route, including places where their kinfolk lived for generations. Gypsy Americans largely consider Eastern Europe their peoples' home. "In 1933 at the first International Conference on Gypsy Affairs held in Bucharest, Romania," states Sway, "the United Gypsies of Europe asked for a piece of land in Bucharest where Gypsies in trouble could settle. Later in 1937, Janus Kwiek, the 'Gypsy King of Poland,' asked Mussolini to grant the Gypsies a strip of land in Abyssinia (present-day Ethiopia) so they might escape persecution in various host societies."

Many Americans have romanticized Gypsies as exotic foreigners. Some Americans draw on the supposedly romantic appeals of Gypsy traditions—especially traditions of dancing and music-making, lives on the road, and maintaining a traveling culture. Often, established Americans maintain or adopt European prejudices against Gypsies and treat Gypsy immigrants poorly. Just as Europeans have often attributed the fortune-telling skills of Gypsies to "black magic," Gypsy traders have been accused of fencing stolen goods, and of stealing their goods themselves. Laws attempting to deter, prevent, and punish fortune-tellers and thieves in America have singled out Gypsy Americans. According to Sway, until 1930, Virginia legally barred Gypsies from telling fortunes. And in New Jersey in the middle 1980s, special regulations and licensing requirements applied to Gypsies who told fortunes. Gypsy households have been labeled as "dens of thieves" so that charges brought against one resident may apply to any and all. In Mississippi in the middle 1980s, such application of liability "jointly-and-severally" is law. There have also been recent cases in the Pacific Northwest. Police, moreover, tend to regard Gypsies with vigilance and disfavor. As recently as the 1970s, New Hampshire expelled some Gypsies from that state on the grounds merely that they were Gypsies.

The fearsome shadow of attempted genocide of Gypsies in Europe still menaces Gypsies. Gypsy Americans are concerned about worsening oppression of fellow Gypsies, most severely in Eastern Europe. This concern is understandable in light of the first two genocidal massacres: during World War I, Turks killed Gypsies and Armenians; and during the Holocaust, Nazis massacred Gypsies alongside Jews. Because too few people know about the Gypsy victims of the Nazis, Gypsies advocate public recognition of that loss. They attempt to draw attention, too, to the current plight of Eastern European Gypsies. Though the collapse of communist regimes—especially that of Ceaușescu, which conducted sterilizations and other genocidal persecutions of Gypsies—has alleviated some of the worst oppression, "ethnic cleansing" in Eastern Europe is a cause for Gypsy concern.

# ACCULTURATION AND ASSIMILATION

Groups of Gypsies are supremely resistant to assimilation. Traditional Gypsy Americans continue to resist the inroads of acculturation, assimilation, and absorption in the United States Even groups such as the Gitanos or Romnichals, despite having lost most of their original language, still maintain a strong sense of ethnic identity and exclusiveness. A major issue facing Gypsy Americans since the 1980s is a worldwide Christian Fundamentalist revival that has swept up Gypsies around the world. As masses of Gypsies practice versions of Pentecostal Christianity, currents of Gypsy culture may be undergoing a sea-change.

Gypsies maintain a powerful group identity, though. Their travelling itself sets them apart from other cultures, as does their common rejection of international borders. Travels of Gypsies and exclusivity of Euro-American cultures have helped maintain a group-identity for Gypsies. Travel itself helps keep Gypsies separate from any settled society, and unrestricted by national boundaries. Gypsy American separation from mainstream America is best evidenced by their general lack of attendance at schools. Until recently, many Gypsies sent their children to schools only until the age of ten. Although Gypsies have adapted to American business ways, many try to limit their acculturation to only those necessary business practices.

Prejudice against Gypsies has strengthend their insolation. One might suppose that economic interactions would disperse the group insularity of Gypsies, if insular social techniques did not pull Gypsies together. These opposing tensions give Gypsies a flexible identity. Gypsy people may seem split between their business life, which focuses outwardly on non-Gypsies, and on the other hand, their social life, which focuses inwardly on only Gypsies.

Gypsy Americans—especially the Romnichals, who can pass as Anglo-Americans—seem to have been more successful in resisting assimilation than other groups. As Silverman notes, some Gypsy Americans may pass as Puerto Ricans, Mexicans, Armenians, Greeks, Arabs, and as other local ethnics in order to obtain jobs, housing, and welfare.

Contemporary urban Rom usually live interspersed among the non-Gypsy population, establishing *ofisi* (fortune-telling parlors) in working areas or in their homes. Their businesses may make many Gypsies seem quite assimilated, and at other times the same Gypsies may seem very traditional. Gypsies have tended to maintain two distinct standards of public behavior, one among themselves, another among outsiders, and Sway points to a "form of body language and interactional style" that Gypsies often use when interacting with non-Gypsies. "A Gypsy's very survival among non-Gypsies often depends on his [or her] ability to conceal as well as exaggerate his Gypsiness at appropriate times," observes Silverman. For example, an appropriate time for a Gypsy to exaggerate Gypsiness is while performing as a musician or fortune-teller for audiences who are known to value Gypsies' exoticism. On the other hand, Silverman adds that "a large part of behaving appropriately as a Gypsy involves knowing when to conceal one's Gypsiness." By passing as someone from a less stigmatized group, one can circumvent anti-Gypsy prejudice. For many, notes Silverman, "the process of boundary crossing [is] a performance strategically enacted for survival."

Gypsies and non-Gypsy Americans tend to have bad impressions of each other. To many Americans, Gypsy Americans seem to be sinister foreigners. To the Gypsies, Sway observes, "non-Gypsies seem cold, selfish, violent," as well as defiled or polluted. However, because Gypsies depend economically on non-Gypsies as customers for their services, they cannot afford to isolate themselves physically from non-Gypsies. Instead, social techniques enable Gypsies to maintain their cultural separateness from the people near whom they live, and with whom they do business. Basically, these techniques consist of taboos. A Gypsy court system enforces the taboos, to effectively limit social interactions with non-Gypsies. Gypsy Americans may bend their taboos by eating in a restaurant with non-Gypsies, and then attend to the taboos by remarking that some uncleanliness made them sick or unlucky.

## IMAGES OF GYPSY AMERICANS

Stereotypes of Gypsies have targeted their nomadism, fortune-telling, and their trading. Ethnically, non-Gypsies have stereotyped Gypsies, their cultures, and their skills as exotically different. Non-Gypsies have described Gypsies as a harmful other, lurking within the body of society, with rhetoric that often portrays them as parasites, reproducing uncontrollably. Mainly, Europeans and Americans have stereotyped Gypsies as criminals. As a result, English-speakers say that to defraud, swindle, or cheat someone is to "gyp" them. This sensational image of Gypsies as criminals does not find support from statistical analysis of court records, since conviction rates of Gypsy Americans seem to be lower than rates of other ethnic Americans for rape and murder; and the conviction rate of Gypsies for theft is no higher than the rate for other Americans. However, Hancock points out in his *The Pariah Syndrome* that the association of Gypsies with crime goes deep and is sometimes justified since Gypsies have resorted to theft as a means of survival; but, "much of it is not justified, however, and is the result of exploitation of a stereotype by a popular press which is less interested in the honest Gypsies."

Western stereotypes of Gypsies as criminals arose when Gypsies first entered Europe. Confusion reigned over Europe's attempts to know who the Gypsies were. Matt Salo states in his introductory essay to *Urban Gypsies* that "many early [European] accounts describe Gypsy bands as conglomerations of various segments of the underclass of society," adding that Gypsies were widely thought to be "a motley assemblage of rogues and vagabonds." European Christians, especially, tended to believe that dark-skinned people were evil. Sway suggests that because the Gypsies were dark, strangely dressed, and spoke a language believed to be "a kind of gibberish used to deceive others" lent credence to the fear that they were spies for the Turks and enemies of Christendom.

Their obscure origins, plus their lack of geographic and institutional ties, have made the Gypsy people seem mysterious. Europeans sometimes thought that Gypsies' differences were all part of their scam. Matt Salo recounts that "they were accused of painting their faces with walnut juice to appear darker and to have invented an argot to disguise their speech for criminal purposes." Gypsies' dark skin and language were authentic—the stories about them were invented. Sway points out that "Gypsies themselves have participated in building and spreading myths about themselves, either from a desire to confuse non-Gypsies or through actual ignorance."

Many Europeans and Americans have romanticized Gypsies in literature, music, and folklore; part of the strength of the Gypsy-figure's appeal was that s/he seemed free from the constraints of life in contemporary industrial society. This stereotypical figure's popularity has captured audiences and helped to conceal ethnic Gypsies. In addition to their supposed criminality and freedom, the Gypsies have been portrayed as beautiful, loose, loose-bodied, flexible, and insolent—as in British novelist D. H. Lawrence's portrayal of a Gypsy man in *The Virgin and the Gipsy*, first published in 1931. Desire for the other tends to represent itself culturally as the other's desire; as Hancock notes, "Gypsy women have long been represented as sexual temptresses, and Gypsy men as a sexual threat to non-Gypsy women, in both song and story."

Conversely, the roles of non-Gypsies as customers for Gypsy businesses have contributed to Gypsies' negative stereotypes of non-Gypsies. Primarily, non-Gypsies may be seen as gullible "suckers." To fortune-tellers, furthermore, non-Gypsies tend to seem depraved. "Many regular customers are lonely, mal-adjusted, or both," writes Sway. "They reveal aspects of *gaje* (non-Gypsy) life to the fortune-teller which sound deviant to her; in turn, she tells her family everything she has heard."

Until relatively recently, when some Gypsy activists and scholars have begun to try to present their people in a better light, stereotypes faced little or no opposition. Most Gypsies have resisted attempts to reveal how they "really" are, and lacked the resources (such as literacy) to publish denials of specific claims.

However, many Gypsy Americans are actively trying to debunk oppressive stereotypes of Gypsies and promote a new public image. The film, *King of the Gypsies*, which was "suggested by" the best-selling book by Peter Maas, focuses on the squalor of Gypsy life from the perspective of a Gypsy-born boy who reviles Gypsies. Gypsies have protested the inaccurate and garish portrayals in this film. At the other end of the film spectrum is *Latcho Drom*—a "musical journey from India to Iberia, a seamless anthology of Gypsy music as played by an assortment of professionals on a variety of stringed instruments—sitars, zithers, violins, guitars—against means of percussion that range from small drums to brass vases to paired spoons to castanets," writes J. Hoberman (*Village Voice*, July 26, 1994, p. 47). "The vocals are as wailing and soulful as the rhythms are hypnotic and infectious." Community scenes feature children in Istanbul; an old man sings of the fall of Ceaușescu; a woman sings a lament of Auschwitz. The film ends in Western Europe, with singers, players, and dancers performing in France and Spain.

## TRADITIONS AND TABOOS

Gypsies' patterns of kinship structures, traveling, and economics characterize them as an ancient people who have adapted well to modern society. Much scholarship on U.S. Gypsies treats only the Rom; and although other groups differ in some ways, Silverman states that the folk belief or folk religion of all ethnic Gypsies consists mainly of "the taboo system, together with the set of beliefs related to the dead and the supernatural."

Gypsy taboos separate Gypsies—each group of Gypsies—from non-Gypsies, and separate the contamination of the lower half of the adult Gypsy's body (especially the genitals and feet) from the purity of its upper half (especially the head and mouth). The waist divides an adult's body; in fact, the *Romani* word for waist, *maskar*, also means the spatial middle of anything. Since a Gypsy who becomes polluted can be expelled from the community, to avoid pollution, Gypsies try to avoid unpurified things that have touched a body's lower half. Accordingly, a Gypsy who touches his or her lower body should then wash his or her hands to purify them. Similarly, an object that feet have touched, such as shoes and floors, are impure and, by extension, things that touch the floor when someone drops them. Gypsies mark the bottom end of bedcovers with a button or ribbon, to avoid accidentally putting the feet-end on their face.

To Gypsies, it seems non-Gypsies constantly contaminate themselves. Non-Gypsies might neglect to wash their hands after urinating in public restrooms, they may wash underwear together with face towels and even tablecloths, or dry their faces and feet with the same towel. According to Silverman, when non-Gypsies move into a home, "they often replace the entire kitchen area, especially countertops and sinks, to avoid ritual contamination from previous non-Gypsy occupants."

Taboos apply most fully to Gypsies who become adults when they marry. Childbearing potential fully activates taboos for men and especially for women. At birth, the infant is regarded as entirely contaminated or polluted, because s/he came from the lower center of the body. The mother, because of her intensive contact with the infant, is also considered impure. As in other traditional cultures, mother and child are isolated for a period of time and other female members will assume the household duties of washing and cooking. Between infancy and marriage, taboos apply less strictly to children. For adults, taboos, especially those that separate males and females, relax as they become respected elders.

### CUISINE

Hancock generalizes that for mobile Gypsies, methods of preparing food have been "contingent on circumstance." Such items as stew, unleavened bread, and fried foods are common, whereas leavened breads and broiled foods, are not. Cleanliness is paramount, though; and, "like Hindus and Muslims, Roma, in Europe more than in America, avoid using the left hand during meals, either to eat with or to pass things" (Ian Hancock, "Romani Foodways," *The World and I*, June 1991, p. 671; cited hereafter as Foodways).

Traditionally, Gypsies eat two meals a day—one upon rising and the other late in the afternoon. Gypsies take time from their "making a living in the *gadji-kanó* or the non-Gypsy milieu," in order to have a meal with other Gypsies and enjoy *khethanipé*—being together (Foodways, p. 672). Gypsies tend to cook and eat foods of the cultures among which they historically lived: so for many Gypsy Americans traditional foods are Eastern European foods. Those who have adopted Eastern Orthodox Catholicism celebrate holidays closely related to the *slava* feast of southeastern Europe, and eat *sarmaa* (cabbage rolls), *gushvada* (cheese strudel), and a ritually sacrificed animal (often a lamb). Gypsies consider these and other strong-tasting foods *baxtaló xabé*, or lucky.

For all Gypsies, eating is important. Gypsies commonly greet an intimate by asking whether or not s/he ate that day, and what. Any weight loss is usually considered unhealthy. If food is lacking, it is associated with bad living, bad luck, poverty, or disease. Conversely, for men especially, weight gain traditionally means good health. The measure of a male's strength, power, or wealth is in his physical stature. Thus a Rom *baro* is a big man physically and politically. A growing awareness of the health risks of obesity tempers some Gypsies' eating.

Eating makes Gypsy social occasions festive, and indicates that those who eat together trust one another. Taboos attempt to bar anybody sickly, unlucky, or otherwise disgraced from joining a meal. Because of these taboos, it is more than impolite for one Gypsy to refuse an offer of food from another. Such refusal would suggest that the offerer is *marimé*, or contaminated. Since Gypsies consider non-Gypsies unclean, in Gypsy homes they serve non-Gypsies from special dishes, utensils, and cups that are kept separate, or disposed of and replaced. Though some Gypsies will eat in certain restaurants, traditionally Gypsies cook for themselves.

### CLOTHING

Gypsies have brightly colored costumes often using brilliant reds and yellows. Women often wear dresses with full skirts and men wear baggy pants and loose-fitting shirts. A scarf often adorns a woman's hair or is used as a cumberbund. Women wear much jewelry and the men wear boots and large belts. A married Gypsy woman customarily must cover her hair with a *diklo*, a scarf that is knotted at the nape of the neck. However, many Gypsy women may go bareheaded except when attending traditional communal gatherings.

### HOLIDAYS AND FESTIVALS

In addition to religious holidays, Gypsy funerals are the biggest community holidays. Groups of Gypsies travel and gather to mark the passing of one of their own. Marriages are also important gatherings.

### HEALTH AND MENTAL HEALTH ISSUES

Gypsies value luck and health. Ideas about health and illness among the Rom are closely related to a world view (*romania*), which includes notions of good and bad luck, purity and impurity, inclusion and exclusion. Sutherland, in an essay entitled "Health and Illness Among the Rom of California," observes that "these basic concepts affect everyday life in many ways including cultural rules about washing, food, clothes, the house, fasting, conducting rituals such as baptism and the slava, and diagnosing illness and prescribing home remedies." In Gypsy custom, ritual purification is the road to health. Much attention goes to avoiding diseases and curing them.

The most powerful Gypsy cure is a substance called *coxai*, or ghost vomit. According to Gypsy legends, *Mamorio* or "little grandmother" is a dirty, sickness-bringing ghost who eats people, then vomits on garbage piles. There, Gypsies find and gather what scientists call slime mold, and bake it with flour into rocks. Gypsies also use *asafoetida*, also referred to as devil's dung, which has a long association with healing and spiritualism in India; according to Sutherland, it has also been used in Western medicine as an antispasmodic, expectorant, and laxative.

Sutherland also recounts several Gypsy cures for common ailments. A salve of pork fat may be used to relieve itching. The juice of chopped onions sprinkled with sugar for a cold or the flu; brown sugar heated in a pan is also good for a child's cold; boiling the combined juice of oranges, lemons, water, and sugar, or mashing a clove of garlic in whiskey and drinking will also relieve a cold. For a mild headache, one might wrap slices of cold cooked potato or tea leaves around the head with a scarf; or for a migraine, put vinegar, or vinegar, garlic, and the juice of an unblemished new potato onto the scarf. For stomach trouble, drink a tea of the common nettle or of spearmint. For arthritis pain, wear copper necklaces or bracelets. For anxiety, sew a piece of fern into your clothes. Sutherland notes that elder Gypsies tend to "fear, understandably, that their grandchildren, who are turning more and more to American medicine, will lose the knowledge they have of herbs and plants, illnesses, and cures."

When a Gypsy falls sick, though, some Gypsy families turn to doctors, either in private practices or at clinics. As Sutherland notes in her essay in *Gypsies, Tinkers and Other Travellers*, "The Rom will often prefer to pay for private medical care with a collection rather than be cared for by a welfare doctor if they feel this care may be better." The Romnichals seem to have been historically prone to respiratory illnesses. In general, Gypsy culture seems to facilitate obesity, and thus heart trouble.

# LANGUAGE

Most Gypsies are at least bilingual, speaking the language of the country in which they live as well as some branch of the Gypsy language, *Romani*. Sway observes that "since the Gypsy language has [almost] never been written, it has been easily influenced by the sounds of local languages." The Armenian language strongly influenced that of the Gypsies in their sojourns. Next, modern Greek contributed words to the vocabulary.

The language of the Gypsies was the key that unlocked the mystery of their supposed origin. Sway reports that the discovery that Gypsies originated in India was made by a scholar who noticed a close similarity between the language of the Hungarian Gypsies and the Sanskritized Malayalam of subcontinent Indians. This discovery, by a Hungarian theology student, Istvan Valyi, did not come until the middle of the eighteenth century. Matt Salo suggests that "from the realization that Gypsies indeed had their own language, the step to the recognition of their separate ethnicity followed automatically." Linguistics remains the science that can advance the most defensible claims about genealogies of peoples, including Gypsies.

Matt Salo points to linguistic histories that help account for Gypsies who do not speak *Romani*: groups of Gypsies split when they left the Balkans, leaving behind others, including those who were enslaved. Frazier indicates that currently, some dialects of *Romani* are classified as Armenian, others as Asiatic (other than Armenian), and the rest as European. Groups from each of the language branches are now widespread. And, according to Frazier, the English word, "pal," (first recorded in 1681) is one of the few *Romani* words to have entered the English lexicon.

When non-Gypsies ask Gypsies speaking *Romani* to identify the foreign language, explains Silverman, "Gypsies usually answer Romanian, Greek, or Yugoslavian," to minimize curiosity and prejudice toward them. Among themselves, Gypsies are also said to use a sort of sign language, *patrin*—marks meaningful to themselves but unintelligible to others. They seemingly used these symbols to describe conditions of camps for future campers, as well as to provide information about people in the area that might be useful for those practicing fortune-telling. Furthermore, Gypsies usually use their Gypsy name only among other Gypsies, and adopt an Americanized name for general and official uses. Particularly because many Gypsies pick common names, they are hard to trace.

## GREETINGS

*P'aves Baxtalo/Baxtali!* ("pah-vis bach-tah-low/ bach-tah-lee")—May you be lucky (to a male/ female).

A gypsy wedding party poses for the camera in this 1941 photograph.

## FAMILY AND COMMUNITY DYNAMICS

Traditionally Gypsies maintain large extended families. Clans of people numbering in the scores, hundreds, or even thousands gather for weddings, funerals, other feasts, or when an elder falls sick. Although Gypsy communities do not have kings, as such, traditionally a group will represent a man as king to outsiders when it needs one to serve as a figurehead or representative. Often, too, a man and his family will tell hospital staffers that he is "King of the Gypsies" so that he will receive better treatment—the title can help provide an excuse for the hospital to allow the large family to make prolonged visits.

In units bigger than a family and smaller than a tribe, Gypsy families often cluster to travel and make money, forming *kumpanias*—multi-family businesses. During recent decades in the United States, on the other hand, Gypsies have been acculturating more closely to the American model by consolidating nuclear families. Currently, after the birth of their first child, some Gypsy couples may be able to move from the husband's parents' home into their own. This change has given more independence to newly wedded women as daughters-in-law.

Gypsy families and communities divide along gender lines. Men wield public authority over members of their community through the *kris*—

the Gypsy form of court. In its most extreme punishment, a *kris* expels and bars a Gypsy from the community. For most official, public duties with non-Gypsies, too, the men take control. Publicly, traditional Gypsy men treat women as inferiors.

The role of Gypsy women in this tradition is not limited to childbearing: she can influence and communicate with the supernatural world; she can pollute a Gypsy man so that a *kris* will expel him from the community; and she makes and manages most of a family's money. Fortune-tellers, all of whom are female, when successful provide the main income for their families. Men of their families will usually aid the fortune-telling business by helping in some support capacities, as long as they are not part of the "women's work" of talking to customers.

### MARRIAGE AND CHILDREN

Gypsies of marriageable age may travel with their parents to meet prospective spouses and arrange a marriage. In making a good match, money, and the ability to earn more of it, tend to be factors more important than romance. A Gypsy who marries a non-Gypsy can expect her community to expel her, permanently. A Gypsy man, however, may eventually get permission to return to his people with his wife. Once married, a new daughter-in-law must subject herself to the commands of her husband's family, until her first pregnancy. With the birth of her first child, she fully enters womanhood.

Gypsy cultural practices attempt to prevent Gypsy children from learning non-Gypsy ways, and to facilitate raising them as Gypsies. Gypsy children, or at least post-adolescents, generally do not go to school, day-care centers, or babysitters who are not friends or relatives. Furthermore, Gypsy culture forbids them to play with non-Gypsies. Instead, they socialize with Gypsies of all ages. Formal schooling, as such, is minimal. Traditionally, Gypsies devalue education from outside their own culture. They educate their own children within extended families. An important reason Gypsies do not like to send their children to school is that they will have to violate Gypsy taboos: they will have to use public restrooms, and the boys and girls will come into contact too closely in classrooms and on playgrounds. Many Gypsy Americans send their children to schools until the age of ten or 11 years, at which time the parents permanently remove them from school.

Children are expected to watch and act like their elders. Rather than bar children from adult life, Gypsies often include them in conversations and business. Children learn the family business, often at home. Many Gypsies marry and become partners in family businesses by their late teens. For example, daughters, but not sons, of a fortune-teller train early to become fortune-tellers. Boys may train to sell cars.

# RELIGION

Gypsy spirituality, part of the core culture of Gypsies, derives from Hindu and Zoroastrian concepts of *kintala*—balance and harmony, as between good and evil. When that balance is upset, ancestors send signals to keep people on track. Mysticism of fortune-tellers and tarot readers—though services to non-Gypsies are not the same as Gypsies' own spirituality—has a basis in Gypsy spirituality. Many Gypsies are Christians. Despite the fact that some Gypsies may use Christian symbols and Christian identity for self-preservation and advantage, Gypsy faith in Christianity need not necessarily be doubted.

Historically, toward the beginning of the second millennium B.C., Gypsies invented a story of their origins in Egypt—hence the name, "Gypsies"—which gave many of them safe passage in a hostile Europe. The story claimed that they had been oppressed and forced into idol-worship in Egypt, and that the Pope had ordered them to roam, as penitence for their former unchristianity. This story also played on legends of a common heritage of Gypsies and Jews, which were partly based on actual overlap of these two ethnic cultures in marginal trades and ghettos. Sway indicates that the story of an Egyptian origin convinced Europeans until the early sixteenth century when the church became convinced these "penitents" were frauds. The church moved to isolate its followers from Gypsies: "As early as 1456 excommunication became the punishment for having one's fortune told by a Gypsy.... More effective than the policy of excommunication was the assertion by the Catholic Church that the Gypsies were a cursed people partly responsible for the execution of Christ."

Although European churches have a long history of condemning Gypsies, their magic, and their arranged marriages, most Rom Gypsy Americans are Eastern Orthodox. They celebrate the *pomona* feast for the dead, at which the feasters invite the dead to eat in heaven. Also, preparation for their *slava* feast requires thorough cleaning of the interior of the host's house, its furniture, and its inhabitants, as the host transforms a section of the house into a church. The feast ceremony begins with coffee for the guests, prayer and a candle for the saints.

Today, around the world Christian fundamentalist revival movements have been sweeping through Rom, Romnichal, and other groups of Gypsies. Since the mid-1980s, through Assemblies of God, various American groups have formed Gypsy churches. In Fort Worth, Texas, for example, a church integrates traditional Gypsy faith with Christian Pentecostal ritual.

Gypsies have tended to syncretize or blend their ethnic Gypsy folk religion with more established religions, such as Christianity. Gypsy religious beliefs are mostly unrelated to the business of fortune-telling. Silverman points out that while Gypsies may disbelieve Gypsy "magic," and "often joke about how gullible non-Gypsies are," in some ways, others act as believers; fortune-tellers generally treat their reading room as sacred and may "consult elder Gypsy women who are known to be experts in dream interpretation, card reading, and folk healing". Gypsies use codenames to mention certain evil-spirits to other Gypsies; and Gypsies sometimes cast curses on other Gypsies (or ward them off). Also, states Silverman, Gypsy fortune-tellers use diverse religious iconography to create impressions out of a belief "that good luck and power can come from any the symbols of any religion."

# EMPLOYMENT AND ECONOMIC TRADITIONS

Quite often, Gypsy Americans have found their economic niche by making money from other members of the lower classes of U.S. society, usually other ethnic minorities, such as Hispanic Americans, African Americans, and immigrants to America from Eastern and Central Europe.

Mobility and adaptation characterize Gypsy trades. By serving populations they encounter, Gypsies have succeeded in various times and places. From their beginnings, their traditional occupations have kept them dependent on other groups, and at the same time maintained Gypsies' separation. The *Dom* were never agricultural; they were musicians, dancers, and entertainers in ancient India, states Sway, adding that they were also were metalworkers—"the only group in ancient India to work with iron, a metal considered dangerous according to Indian religious belief."

The need for mobility shaped their livelihoods. In their essay in *Urban Gypsies*, Matt and Sheila Salo explain that "the main features of all occupations were that they were independent pursuits, required little overhead, had a ubiquitous clientele, and could be pursued while traveling" in urban and rural areas. Moreover, Gypsies have adapted to different locales and periods. Silverman discusses a change in occupations in twentieth century America that parallels the urbanization of the Rom. After their arrival in the 1880s, the Rom followed nomadic European trades such as coppersmithing, refining, and dealing in horses for the males, and begging or fortune-telling for the females. They would camp in the country and interact mostly with the rural population, venturing into the cities only to sell their services and purchase necessities. As the automobile supplanted horse travel, the Rom became used-car dealers and repairmen, occupations that they still pursue. When metalworking skills became less important, Gypsies learned new trades, including the selling of items such as watches and jewelry.

As Sutherland points out in *Gypsies, Tinkers and Other Travellers*, "In the *kumpania* men and women cooperate with each other in exploiting the economic resources of their area." Although jobs may be exploited by an individual, the Rom prefer to work in groups called *wortacha*, or partners. These groups always comprise members of the same sex, however, women often take along children of either sex. *Wortacha* may also include young unmarried Gypsies who learn the skills of the adults. Adults work as equals, dividing expenses and profits equally. As a token of respect for an elder, an extra amount may be given, but unmarried trainees receive only what others will give them. The Rom do not earn wages from another Rom. As a rule, Gypsies profit from non-Gypsies only. In the United States and other countries (including England and Wales), Gypsy Americans divide geographic territories to minimize competition between Gypsy businesses.

Gypsies, supremely mobile and profit-making traders, became dealers of vehicles. Romnichals took an early American role as horse traders, and achieved particular success in Boston. According to Matt and Sheila Salo, "During World War I, Gypsies brought teams of their horses to the Great Plains to help harvest crops. For a while at least, the label 'horse trader' or 'horse dealer' seemed almost synonymous with 'Gypsy.' The colorful wagons used by Romnichals to advertise their presence to any community they entered further reinforced this identification by the professionally painted side panels depicting idealized horses and the horse trading life." The pride of Romnichals in their ability to trade horses is reflected in the carved figures of horses on the tombstones of horse dealers, say Matt and Sheila Salo. Many of the Rom, who arrived in America after the horse trade's heyday, sell cars. Other mobile service contributions of the Gypsies have included driveway blacktopping, house painting, and tinsmithing. Gypsy tinkers, who were mostly Romanian-speaking Gypsies, were essential to various industries such as confectioneries, because they re-tinned large mixing bowls and other machinery on-site. They also worked in bakeries, laundries, and anywhere steam jackets operated.

By the 1930s the Rom group of Gypsy Americans virtually controlled the business of fortune-telling. Their advertisements and shop windows have their undeniable place on American boardwalks, roads, and streets. Gypsy mysticism, as represented in fortune-teller costumes and props such as the crystal ball and tarot deck, have impacted on American culture directly, and through their media representations and imitations, such as the likes of commercially produced Ouija boards. Gypsies have maintained a presence and influence in America's quasi-religious, commercially mystical functions.

## MUSIC AND MINSTRELSY

Worldwide, Gypsies are most famous for their contributions as musicians. In the United States, Hungarian Slovak Gypsies, mostly violists, have played popular Hungarian music at immigrant weddings. Historically, Gypsies have contributed to music Americans play. Flamenco, which Gypsies are credited with creating in Spain, has its place in America, particularly in the Southwest. Django Rheinhardt, a well-known European Gypsy who contributed to American culture is perhaps the all-time greatest jazz guitarist. Furthermore, Klezmer music of Jewish immigrants overlaps with music of Eastern European Gypsies, especially in oriental, flatted-seventh chords played on a violin or clarinet.

There are intriguing parallels between Gypsies and African Americans in European and American cultural history. The rhythmic innovations that Gypsies brought to Europe were not only Asiatic and Middle Eastern, but also African, at least North African; similarly, African Americans brought innovations of African music to America. Some Gypsies owned slaves or employed African American laborers and stevedores (loaders/unloaders). According to legend, some of these men had eloped with Gypsy daughters. When African American ex-slave minstrels first attempted to taste the freedom of the road in post-Reconstruction America, some claimed to adopt the ethnicity, or at least the title, of Gypsies (Konrad Bercovici, "The American Gypsy," *Century Magazine*, 103, 1922, pp. 507-519). In popular American musical traditions of jazz, blues, and rock, the Gypsy has remained a powerful referent.

### FORTUNE-TELLERS

In the United States, Rom Gypsies have dominated a niche for fortune-tellers, who are also known as palmists, readers, or advisers. "Fortune-telling actually includes elements of folk psychotherapy and folk healing," made into a business to serve non-Gypsies, writes Silverman, who adds that one fortune-teller describes her relationship with her customers in this way: "All they need is confidence and strength and a friend and that's what I am." Some customers come only once, and others make themselves more valuable by returning. A reader will try to establish a steady relationship with the customer, whether in person, by telephone, or by mail. Readers will also try to use the customer's language, usually English or Spanish. Moreover, readers often adopt and advertise names for themselves that help them claim the ethnicity of their clientele; and/or, they choose an ethnicity renowned for mystical perception, such as an Asian, African, or Native American one. Fortune-tellers set up shop where they can make money. Often, they serve a working-class clientele composed of other ethnic minorities. They tend to choose visible locales where they can operate freely: New York supports a great many fortune-tellers, while Los Angeles (where more Gypsies sell real estate and cars) has relatively few because of strict laws governing fortune-telling. Daughters of successful fortune-tellers traditionally become

fortune-tellers whether or not they are interested. Their family business is part of their household.

### PUBLIC ASSISTANCE

It is difficult to determine with much accuracy the percentage of Gypsy Americans on public assistance. For Rom Gypsy Americans, receiving public assistance is part of what they do, the role they perform. Gypsy community leaders can control any Gypsy's access to public assistance in their territory by reporting renegades or outsiders for fraud.

# POLITICS AND GOVERNMENT

Aside from benefits it provides, American government tends to hinder Gypsies. Some states and districts maintain policies and statutes that prohibit fortune-tellers, require them to pay hundreds of dollars for annual licenses, or otherwise control activities in which Gypsies engage. Despite the unconstitutionality of such measures, some rules apply specifically to Gypsies, by name. One excuse for this discrimination is the confusion between ethnic Gypsies and vagrants. Additionally, Silverman indicates that many police have little toleration for Gypsies. Truant officers, too, bother Gypsies by continually trying to locate Gypsy children.

# INDIVIDUAL AND GROUP CONTRIBUTIONS

### CULTURE

Brian Vessey-Fitzgerald, who authored *The Gypsies of England;* Jane Carlisle, Thomas's wife; Rita Sackville West; David Birkenhead Smith; and scholar Ian Hancock.

### PERFORMING ARTS

Many Gypsy contributors to American culture have been performers. Among Romnichal (English Gypsies) who lived some in America, we can count Charlie Chaplin and Rita Hayworth. Ava Gardner, Michael Cain, and Sean Connery are reported to have Gypsy ancestry. Freddy Prince, the late singer of rock group Queen, was on one side Hungarian Gypsy.

# MEDIA

**PRINT**

*Gypsies and Travelling People.*

**Contact:** Don Kennington or David Barton, Editors.

**Address:** Capital Planning Information Ltd., 52 High Street, Stamford, Lincolnshire PE9 2LG, England.

**Telephone:** 780-57300.

**Fax:** 780-54333.

*The World and I.*

**Contact:** Dr. Ian F. Hancock.

**Address:** P.O. Box 822, Manchaca, Texas 78652-0822.

**Telephone:** (512) 282-1286.

# ORGANIZATIONS AND ASSOCIATIONS

**Baschalde.**

**Contact:** Bill Douna.

**Telephone:** (612) 926-8281.

**Gypsy Folk Ensemble.**

Also performs for school assemblies.

**Contact:** Preston Ashbourne.

**Address:** 3265 Motor Avenue, Los Angeles, California 90034.

**Gypsy Lore Society.**

Publishes the *Journal of the Gypsy Lore Society*.

**Contact:** Sheila Salo, Treasurer.

**Address:** 5607 Greenleaf Road, Cheverly, Maryland 20785.

**Telephone:** (301) 341-1261.

**International Romani Church.**

**Address:** P.O. Box 17222, Wichita, Kansas 67217.

**International Romani Union (IRU).**

Works to foster unity among members; promotes human rights and obligations; advocates protection and preservation of Romani culture and language. Publishes the quarterly *Buhazi*, the bimonthly *Lacio Drom*, the bi-weekly *Nevipens Romani*, the monthly *Romano Nevipen*, the monthly *Rrom po Drom*, and the quarterly newspaper *Scharotl*.

**Contact:** Dr. Ian F. Hancock, President.

**Address:** P.O. Box 822, Manchaca, Texas 78652-0822.

**Telephone:** (512) 282-1286.

**U.S. Romani Council.**

**Address:** 528 Madeira, S.E., Suite 1, Albuquerque, New Mexico 87108.

# MUSEUMS AND RESEARCH CENTERS

**Texas Romani Archives, University of Texas at Austin.**

**Address:** Calhoun Hall 501, Austin, Texas 78712.

**Victor Weybright Archives of Gypsy Studies.**

**Contact:** Sheila Salo, Manager.

**Address:** 5607 Greenleaf Road, Cheverly, Maryland 20785.

**Telephone:** (301) 341-1261.

# SOURCES FOR ADDITIONAL STUDY

Frazier, Angus. *The Gypsies*. Cambridge, Massachusetts: Blackwell, 1992.

*Gypsies and Travelers in North America: An Annotated Bibliography*, compiled by William G. Lockwood and Sheila Salo. Cheverly, Maryland: The Gypsy Lore Society, 1994.

Hancock, Ian. *The Pariah Syndrome: An Account of Gypsy Slavery and Persecution*. Ann Arbor, Michigan: Karoma Publishers, 1987.

Miller, Carol. "The American Rom and the Ideology of Defilement," in *Gypsies, Tinkers and Other Travellers*, edited by Farnham Rehfisch. New York: Harcourt, Brace Jovanovich, 1975; pp. 41-54.

Salo, Matt, and Sheila Salo. "Romnichal Economic and Social Organization in Urban New England 1850-1930," *Urban Gypsies* (special issue of *Urban Anthropology*), Volume 11, No. 3-4 (fall-winter) 1982.

Silverman, Carol. "Everyday Drama: Impression Management of Urban Gypsies," *Urban Gypsies* (special issue of *Urban Anthropology*), Volume 11, No. 3-4 (fall-winter) 1982.

Sutherland, Anne. "The American Rom: A Case of Economic Adaptation," in *Gypsies, Tinkers and Other Travellers*, edited by Farnham Rehfisch. New York: Harcourt, Brace Jovanovich, 1975; pp. 1-40.

——. *Gypsies: The Hidden Americans*. London: Tavistock Publications, 1975.

——. "Health and Illness Among the Rom of California," *The Journal of the Gypsy Lore Society*, February 1992.

Sway, Marlene. *Familiar Strangers: Gypsy Life in America*. Chicago: University of Illinois Press, 1988.

Tyrner-Stastny, Gabrielle. *The Gypsy in Northwest America*. Olympia: Washington State American Revolution Bicentennial Commission, 1977.

*Urban Gypsies* (special issue of *Urban Anthropology*), introduction by Matt Salo, Volume 11, No. 3-4 (fall-winter), 1982.

Yoors, Jan. *Crossing* (autobiography). New York: Simon and Schuster, 1971.

Haitian Americans are very traditional by nature. They have a strong belief in the culture, traditions, and mores of their homeland.

# HAITIAN AMERICANS

by
**Felix Eme Unaeze
and Richard E.
Perrin**

## OVERVIEW

Haiti, an independent republic since 1804, is the oldest black republic in the world. It is located in the West Indies on the western third of the Island of Hispaniola, which lies between Cuba and Puerto Rico in the Caribbean Sea. The eastern two-thirds of the island is the Dominican Republic. Haiti, which occupies a total area of 10,714 square miles (27,750 sq. km.), is slightly larger than the State of Maryland. Mostly rough and mountainous in terrain with Massif de la Selle and La Hotte among the main ranges, Haiti also contains a few plateaus and plains such as the Northern Plain, Artibonite, and Cul-de-Sac. Haiti has a tropical climate with temperatures that vary between 70 and 90 degrees all year, although December and January can be quite cool. There are two rainy seasons, one beginning in April and ending in May, and the other beginning in October and ending in November. Tropical thunderstorms are frequent during the summer.

In 1992, Haiti's population was estimated to be about 6.5 million inhabitants, with approximately 71 percent living in rural areas and about 29 percent in urban centers. Haiti records one of the highest population densities in the world, with about 600 persons per square mile. The birth rate is about 44.6 per 1000 people and the fertility rate is about six children per woman. The death rate is about 15.6 deaths per 1000 persons. Life expectancy at birth is 53 years for males and 55 years for females.

The people of Haiti are primarily of African descent, although a smaller percentage is mulatto and therefore of European and African descent. Creole is the main language spoken with about ten percent of the population fluent in French. The literacy rate is 23 percent. About 80 percent of the population is Roman Catholic and ten percent is Protestant; Voodoo is practiced by a majority of the people. The capital city is Port-au-Prince, the country's largest city, which boasts a population of about 1,148,000 people. Other major cities are Cap-Haitien, Gonaives, Les Cayes, Jeremie, and Jacmel. The national flag is horizontally blue over red with the national arms on a centered white panel. The national anthem is *La Dessalinienne: Pour le pays, pour les ancêtres,* which translates as "for the country, for the ancestors," with lyrics by J. Lherisson and music by N. Geffrand (1903).

## HISTORY

The island, which was first inhabited by Indian tribes—the Arawaks, the Tainos, and lastly the Caraibes—called their country "Quisqueya" and later "Haiti," which means "the body of land." The island has had a turbulent and bitter history. When Christopher Columbus landed at the Mole St. Nicholas Bay on December 5, 1492, he claimed the island in the interest of the Spanish rulers who had financed the expedition—Ferdinand and Isabella—and called it "Hispaniola," which means "Little Spain."

Although the Indians welcomed the new settlers, the discovery of gold in the riverbeds sent the Spaniards into a frenzied search for the coveted nuggets. The Indians died by the thousands from diseases introduced by the Spaniards, who also enslaved the natives, treated them with extreme cruelty, and massacred them. The Indian population was reduced from about 300,000 to less than 500. In 1510, the Spaniards began to import their first African slaves from the West Coast of Africa to work in the gold mines. The French, who came in 1625 and changed the name of the island to Saint Domingue, fought the Spaniards to keep a hold on part of the territory. After Spain signed a treaty in 1697 in which it conceded the western part of the island to France, the colony developed rapidly under French rule. The 700,000 slaves who worked on the cotton,

sugar cane, and coffee plantations generated great wealth for the plantation owners; Saint Domingue became a prosperous colony in the New World and was called "the Pearl of the Caribbean."

After the French Revolution in 1789, the slaves revolted against the colonists and the movement spread to the north and then to the west and the south. Under the leadership of such famous generals as Toussaint L'Ouverture, the slaves made significant progress in their struggle. Self-educated, Toussaint served first in the Spanish army and then in the French army. He was one of the main instruments of Haiti's independence, defeating the English who had invaded Saint Domingue. He also administered and divided the country into districts without the approval of the mainland "Metropole." The French later grew angry with General Toussaint and placed him in a French prison where he died on April 7, 1803 from hunger and lack of medical care. Although disheartened, the indigenous army fought under Generals Dessalines and Petion, and beat the French army at every turn. French General Leclerc died of yellow fever on November 2, 1803; his successor, General Rochambeau, took refuge. Dessalines surrounded his officers and proclaimed the independence of Saint Domingue in Gonaives on January 1, 1804, and restored the former name of Haiti. Independence was won and the country became the second, after the United States, in the Western Hemisphere to become an independent republic.

## MODERN ERA

Dessalines became Haiti's first head of state. Following the elaboration and ratification of a constitution, full powers were given to Dessalines on September 2, 1804. He proclaimed himself Emperor and took the name Jacques the First. He redistributed the country's wealth and converted most of the colonist plantations to state property. He made many political enemies who later resented his manner of governing. Ambushed on his way to Port-au-Prince, he was killed on October 17, 1806. After his death, a constituent assembly amended the Constitution and limited the powers of the president. General Henri Christophe, who had started a power struggle with General Alexandre Petion, withdrew to the northern part of the country and formed a new government; Petion was elected president in March of 1807, thus dividing the new nation.

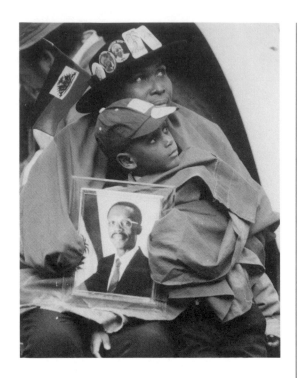

Two Haitian Americans hold a photo of deposed Haitian president Jean-Bertrand Aristide while listening to Aristide speak in New York City in 1992. Aristide returned to Haiti as president in 1994.

Petion governed the West and South while Christophe ruled the North. In March of 1811, Christophe proclaimed himself king and took the name of Henri the First. Because of his strict regulations, the Kingdom of the North became prosperous, and he erected monuments, which became symbols of power and authority. For example, the Citadel Laferriere, a monument to human endurance, was constructed by the labor of 20,000 men between 1805 and 1814 as a center of resistance against any attempt by foreigners to conquer the island. His ornate palace at Sans Souci near Cap Haitien and his vast citadel, though in ruins, are likewise marvels of massive masonry. When Christophe died in an apparent suicide in 1820, the North and South were reunited with Jean-Pierre Boyer succeeding Petion.

Twenty different presidents headed the Haitian government from 1867 to 1915, and Haiti's unstable political and economic conditions made it vulnerable to outside intervention. Haiti's rising external debt caused European countries to threaten force to collect. At this time, World War I was at its peak in Europe and in July of 1915, the United States Marines landed on Haiti's coast and occupied the country. Under the Monroe Doctrine—a document stating U.S. opposition to European involvement in the Western Hemisphere—the U.S. Marines remained in Haiti for 19 years from 1915 until 1934. The Haitian people resented American occupation and wanted to restore their national sovereignty. Guerrilla resistance movements were in place but were crushed. In 1946, a popular movement brought forth a rising middle class whose members asked for the sharing of power and liberalization of governmental institutions. The movement was aborted, which contributed to the fall of then-President Elie Lescot (1941-1946), and Dumarsais Estime was elected president. From that period on, all Haitian presidents, with the exception of François "Papa Doc" Duvalier, have been deposed by military coup d'état.

In 1957, Francois Duvalier was elected president. He became a dictator, enforcing a reign of terror with his secret police, sometimes referred to as *tonton macoute*. Duvalier proclaimed himself President-for-Life in 1964 and his reign of terror continued. The Haitian economy began to deteriorate and the people were suffering seriously in the 1960s. He died in 1971 and his son, Jean-Claude "Baby Doc" Duvalier, who was only 19 years old, succeeded his father. Both Duvaliers ruled for nearly 30 years. It was during this period that many Haitians fled Haiti. Jean-Claude followed in his father's footsteps, maintaining the same policies of hate and oppression. He was ousted by the Haitian people on February 7, 1986. From 1986 until 1990, four different provisional governments were put into power with the sole purpose of holding general elections, but popular discontent forced them out. Free elections were held on December 16, 1990; and, although the Reverend Jean-Bertrand Aristide was elected by a majority of 67 percent, he was overthrown by the army on September 30, 1991, and took refuge in the United States. He was restored to his position through peaceful negotiation; he returned to Haiti under a United States military escort and was reinstated on October 15, 1994.

## THE FIRST HAITIANS IN AMERICA

During the 1790s, Haiti was the most affluent of the French colonies. It was then that the black populace of the island revolted against slavery and there was a panicked exodus. Thousands of whites, free blacks, and slaves fled to American seaports, culminating in large French-speaking communities in New Orleans, Norfolk, Baltimore, New York City, and Boston. Immigrants from Haiti who arrived in the United States during the eighteenth and nineteenth centuries were determined to survive in their new land. Jean-Baptiste Point du Sable, a trapper who settled on the shore of Lake

Michigan was an early Haitian arrival; he settled and established a trading post on the river at a point that would later become the City of Chicago. Pierre Toussaint, a devout Catholic who came to New York as a slave of a French family in 1787, became a prominent hair dresser to wealthy New York patrons and also became a fund-raiser who helped the poor and destitute. France was a safe haven for many educated Haitians, and only a few middle-class Haitians chose to go to the United States. Many of them stayed to receive a university education. A renowned poet and playwright, Felix Morisseau-Leroy was one of the post-World War II immigrants.

## SIGNIFICANT IMMIGRATION WAVES

According to the United States Census of 1990, there were about 290,000 people who claimed Haitian ancestry; however, this figure does not include the tens of thousands who were in the United States illegally. Moreover, there are second- and third-generation Haitian Americans who simply identify themselves as black; also, some legal immigrants may find it difficult to admit to roots that go back to a Caribbean nation so often associated with superstition and poverty. However, anthropologists estimate that about 1.2 million people in the United States are of Haitian ancestry.

There are four major documented periods of Haitian immigration to the United States: the period of French colonization; the Haitian revolution (1791-1803); the United States occupation of Haiti (1915-1934); and the period of the Duvaliers (1957-1986). For almost three decades, from 1957 to 1986, when François "Papa Doc" and Jean-Claude "Baby Doc" Duvalier were in power, political persecution caused Haitian professionals, the middle class, and students to leave the island in large numbers. Haitians emigrated in search of political asylum or permanent residence status in various countries such as the United States, Mexico, Puerto Rico, Jamaica, France, Dominican Republic, French Guyana, and Africa.

In the United States, Haitian immigrants arrived in large numbers, some by air but the majority by boat. Known as the "boat people," they reached the shores of Florida and settled in such cities as Miami, Chicago, New Orleans, Los Angeles, Boston, and New York City. Some refugees were detained and deported to Haiti due to policies of the U.S. government, which at the time supported the Duvalier government. Michel S. Laguerre has documented that with the help of some volunteer lawyers and local activists, and through the generosity of various humanitarian organizations, many refugees have been able to remain in their adopted country. However, Laguerre in his book *American Odyssey: The Haitians in New York City* has also recorded that some refugees attempted suicide while in detention. Some of the Haitian refugees were thought to have left their homeland because of economic rather than political reasons. Despite the odds, the Haitian refugees had the energy and determination to survive in the United States. In her book, *Demele: "Making It"*, social anthropologist Rose-Marie Chierici, herself a Haitian American, has recounted how Haitian immigrants used the Creole word "demele" to manage life in the face of hardship.

Every wave of migration from Haiti has come during political turmoil there; however, economic malaise has always accompanied such turmoil so it has been difficult to distinguish political from economic migrants. Early Haitian immigrants stayed in cities in the United States where they could work and maintain contact with their homeland. The greatest concentration of immigrants are found in New York City, Miami, Chicago, New Orleans, Los Angeles and Boston. Until 1977, Brooklyn was the heart of Haitian America; however, between 1977 and 1981, 60,000 Haitian boat people landed in South Florida, and the center of the Haitian Diaspora moved south to a community of stucco cottages and mom-and-pop businesses anointed "Little Haiti."

In the early 1980s, thousands of Haitian doctors, teachers, social workers and entrepreneurs moved from New York to Miami. Restaurants serving conch and goat meat and record shops blaring Haitian meringue music sprang up on 54th Street and Northeast Second Avenue. The Tap Tap Haitian Restaurant in Miami Beach also serves as a Haitian hangout.

Haitian immigrants are employed in all types of fields. Deborah Sontag reported in the *New York Times* on June 3, 1994 that among the early immigrants, Haitian workers include not only migrant workers in Homestead, Florida, but also wealthy doctors on Long Island, not only taxi drivers in Manhattan but college professors in Washington, D.C.

# ACCULTURATION AND ASSIMILATION

Like most immigrants in the United States, Haitians are busy in the pursuit of the American dream. Almost every Haitian American wishes to buy a home as a matter of status and security. This is implied in the saying, "Se vagabon ki loue kay," which means, "Respectable people don't rent." However, behind the facade of pride and achievement, there is a litany of social problems—battered women, homeless families, and economic exploitation. The problems that face Haitian immigrants are enormous and complex. Moreover, the problem of undocumented immigrants who live in constant fear of being deported and thrown into Haitian jails has also led to stress-related emotional disorders, which frequently keep the immigrants from using such facilities as public hospitals. Instead, they rely on folk medicine to cure ordinary aliments or they seek a private clinic with Haitian medical personnel. Marc Abraham, a Haitian who has lived on Long Island for 37 years, has said, "I think Americans see Haitians as desperate people instead of decent people who struggle." Abraham continues: "I have to understand that hostility, I guess, to take it off my heart. I mean, this country has enough problems without ours too."

According to Father Thomas Wenski, director of Pierre Toussaint Haitian Catholic Center in Miami, Haitians have been specifically and harshly excluded because of "America's endemic 'negrophobia' and inherent racism." Haitians have been excluded because of their race and economic condition. "Thus," says Wenski, "one must ask: will the Haitians be able to assimilate into American society as other immigrant groups of the past? Again, Haitians are black and can Haitians hope for a 'piece of the American pie' while native-born American blacks still fight for crumbs? Many would see an eventual amalgamation into the African American community but does such a view give too much importance to race as a determinant and underrate such values as religion and culture?" (Fr. Thomas Wenski, "Haitians in South Florida," unpublished research done in Miami, Florida, July 1991.)

### TRADITIONS, CUSTOMS, AND BELIEFS

Haitian Americans are very traditional by nature. They have a strong belief in the culture, traditions and mores of their homeland. Haitian Americans believe, for example, that several types of illness are of supernatural origin and caused by angry spirits. Most believe that a Voodoo family has a spirit protector whose role is to protect its members from the malevolent powers of other spirits.

The institution of the family has made possible their enclaves in the United States. It is here that a bond with the old country is maintained, consciously or unconsciously. Laguerre has noted, "The family provides a niche within which a cultural continuity can be adapted to the exigencies of the new environment. Through the medium of the family, which influences the behaviors of its members through the mechanism of socialization, immigrants were able to retain some of their cultural heritage and develop an awareness of their ethnic legacy."

Haitian families spend their leisure time within their own family and friendship groups. Visits are made to friends and relatives especially on the weekends. It is important to be warm and hospitable to visitors by offering them food and drink. Visitors are usually parents, other relatives, in-laws, and friends. Haitian social circles commonly celebrate birthdays, first communions, and baptisms among other special occasions and holidays. Larger numbers of people attend weddings and funerals.

### PROVERBS

Haitians have a keen sense of humor which is reflected in many of their proverbs: Beyond the mountains there are more mountains; A dog has four paws, but it can go only one way; Little by little the bird makes its nest; Only the knife knows what is in the heart of the yam; The goat looks at the home owner's eyes before entering his house; Every vein affects the heart; An empty sack cannot stand up; With patience you will see the belly button of an ant; All that you do not know is greater than you; The big water pot is not a spring; You can hurry as much as you like, but being in too big a hurry will not make the day dawn.

### CUISINE

Haitian cooking is a unique blend of many cultural influences. It is a mixture of the traditions of Europeans, West African slaves, and indigenous people of the island. The most common ingredients used in Haitian cuisine are black-eyed peas, squash, pumpkins, cassava, rice, cornmeal, and plantain. The meat served tends to be high in salt and fat and is spicy. In the United States, Sunday dinners often consist of spicy chicken and goat, rice and djondjon, a dried mushroom.

*Pois et ris* is a combination of kidney beans and rice and is considered the national dish of Haiti. *Kabrit boukannen ak bon piman* is a traditional favorite both in Haiti and the United States. It is barbecued goat with hot pepper. *Soup joumou* is a pumpkin soup. *Kasav ak manba* is homemade peanut butter, made with or without spices and hot peppers; it is often eaten with cassava bread. *Griyo ak bannan* is deep-fried pork and fried plantain. *Pwason fri* is a fried fish often sold with fried plantain and fried sweet potatoes. *Accra* or *calas* are black-eyed pea patties and the tradition of eating them on New Year's Eve means luck for the coming year.

## HOLIDAYS CELEBRATED BY HAITIAN AMERICANS

Haitians celebrate Christmas Day, New Year's Day, Carnival or Mardi Gras, All Saints' Day, and All Souls' Day on the days that are traditionally celebrated in other parts of the world. Flag and University Day is the most celebrated national holiday and is held on May 18. Other important holidays are Independence Day (January 1), Ancestors Day (January 2), the Anniversary of Dessalines' Death (October 17), and Discovery of Haiti Day (December 5).

## HEALTH AND MENTAL HEALTH ISSUES

Health care beliefs vary widely among Haitian Americans. Immigrants from rural areas usually do not seek help from a physician but rely instead on folk healers. Immigrants from the cities are more likely to go to a physician or other professional health care provider. Social class and education also influence the type of medical help sought. Those from a lower social class or those who have not attained legal status in the United States rely on health care that is readily available to them such as home remedies, family recommendations, folk healers, and Voodoo medicine. The mother or grandmother is usually responsible for diagnosing symptoms and keeping alive the traditions of the family in treating sickness. First-generation Haitian Americans initially try home remedies prepared by members of the older generation; if these are unsuccessful, the person is advised to seek help from a physician, folk healer, or Voodoo priest. The use of folk healers is often limited because the medicinal preparations and elements of traditional health care are not available locally. The size of the local Haitian group affects the number of traditional healers.

The Voodooist folk healer is a Voodoo priest who has studied the mythology of spirits and which plants have the properties necessary for home remedies. Treatment involves prayers and herbal remedies. Neighborhood licensed pharmacies specialize in herbal remedies and French medications. They have Haitian personnel and sell the type of products from home which are familiar to Haitian Americans. Haitians consider eating well, good personal hygiene, and keeping regular hours as important qualities for maintaining good health. Fat people are considered healthy and happy, whereas thin people are believed to be in poor health caused by psychological and emotional problems.

The following statements may be used by a Haitian American when he is ill: *Kom pa bon* (I do not feel well)—indicates a temporary situation and that the person will soon be well; *Dan tan zan tan moin malad* (I feel sick from time to time)—indicates how the person feels about his/her general health; *Moin an konvalesans* (I am convalescing)—indicates that the person was sick and is now getting better; *Moin malad* (I am sick)—indicates the person is ill but the illness will not lead to death; *Moin malad ampil* (I am very sick)—indicates that the person is in a critical condition; *Moin pap refe* (I will never get well again)—indicates that the person is going to die from the illness.

Haitians from rural areas believe that illness can be of supernatural origin or natural origins. Natural illnesses are called *maladi pei* (country diseases) or *maladi bon die* (diseases of the Lord). Natural illnesses last for only a short time. Supernatural illnesses appear suddenly and the person does not feel any previous signs of illness. Angry Voodoo spirits are believed to cause several types of illness. This occurs when a person offends the family's Voodoo spirit protector in some manner. A Voodoo priest is consulted to help in diagnosing the illness. The priest attempts to contact the spirit to find out the reason for the spirit's unhappiness, what the person must do to make the spirit happy, and what medications the ill person must take.

Another belief commonly held by Haitians of all classes is that of the effect of blood irregularities on causing dangerous illnesses. Terms such as *san cho* (hot blood) and *san fret* (cold blood) are used to describe various conditions. Blood is believed to control the hot or cold state of the body. Various "blood" terms are used to describe what condition or state of health a person is in during certain types of activity.

*Gaz* (gas), a common complaint, can cause pain and anemia. It can occur in the head, shoulder, back, legs, or appendix. It is believed to cause *kolik* (stomach pain) and *van nan tet* (gas in the head), which causes headaches. A tea made of garlic, cloves, and mint or solid foods, such as corn, is used to treat these conditions. The milk of a nursing mother is believed to cause certain illnesses if it becomes "too thick" or "too thin." If a mother becomes frightened, the belief is that the milk moves to her head and causes a bad headache. It may also cause depression in the nursing mother and diarrhea in the baby.

Foods may be divided into hot, cold, or neutral categories and are believed to affect the health of an individual. Anything that creates an imbalance between "hot" and "cold" factors may cause illness or discomfort. Treatments which must be used to treat these illnesses are the opposite of the class of the disease. "Hot" medicines are used to treat "cold" conditions. Patent or herbal medicines are also used to treat these diseases. Cough medicines ("hot") are used to treat coughs and colds ("cold").

The following home remedies are used: *Asorousi* is a tea boiled from leaves that will restore a person's appetite; *Fey korosol* is used to bathe a child's head to cure insomnia; a variety of leaves are used for gas or if a child's stomach is swollen; and warm oils are used in combination with massage to solve a number of problems from aching or sprained bones to displaced organs.

Haitian Americans often believe that only traditional healers have the knowledge and skills to treat particular illnesses so that it does not make sense to take these complaints to an American doctor. Haitian Americans often have problems with the behavior of American physicians during an office visit. The patient expects the physician to receive him or her with a few moments of conversation about the patient's life in general and then a straightforward, hands-on examination of the patient. The examination should not include a long list of questions by the doctor; it is the doctor, not the patient, who is supposed to determine what is wrong. Patients respect doctors who try to learn about their cultural beliefs and practices.

# LANGUAGE

Two languages are spoken in Haiti: Creole and French. French is the official language and is spo-ken by the educated elite. The great majority of Haitians, however, speak only Creole.

## HAITIAN CREOLE

The term Creole derives from the Portuguese word "*crioulo*" meaning an individual of European ancestry who was born and reared abroad. Haitian Creole developed when slaves who were taken to the Caribbean island of Saint Domingue from various areas of the west coast of Africa interacted with each other and with Europeans. Although predominantly French, some Spanish and Amerindian (Carib and Arawak) words have entered the language. While Haitian Creole has a French word base, the two languages are distinct. The sentence structure of Creole is basically African, but it has its own grammar, morphology, and syntax.

Haitian immigrants to the United States, especially the more recent ones, communicate best in Creole. This causes problems in interaction with Americans who have little knowledge of Creole and believe that all Haitians speak French.

## GREETINGS AND OTHER POPULAR EXPRESSIONS

Common Haitian greetings and other expressions include: *Allo* ("ah-low")—Hi!; *Bonjou* ("boon-ZHEW")—Good morning/day; *Bonswa* ("bon-SWA")—Good afternoon/evening; *Ki jan ou rele?* ("kee jan oo ray lay")—What is your name?; *M rele ...* ("m ray lay ...")—My name is ...; *Kote ou rete?* ("ko TAY oo ray TAY")—Where do you live?; *Ki numewo telefon ou?* ("kee new meh-wo tele FON OO")—What is your telephone number?; *Suple* ("soo-PLAY")—Please; *Chita!* ("SHEE-tah")—Sit down!; *Kanpe!* ("kan PAY")—Stand up!; *Mesi* ("MAY-see")—Thank you; *Orevwa* ("oh-ray-VWAH")—Goodbye.

# FAMILY AND COMMUNITY DYNAMICS

The family is the nucleus of Haitian society; within it, individuals are dependent upon each other. The traditional Haitian family is a composed of father, mother, children, and grandparents. The family is involved in all decision-making for its members. The patriarchal system is prevalent, but many women rear children without the consistent presence of the father. By tradition, the father is the breadwinner and authority figure. The mother is the household manager and disciplinarian.

Family honor is of utmost importance. Family reputation is so important that the actions of a member of the family are considered to bring either honor or shame to the entire family. A family's reputation in society is based on honesty and former family history. Offspring of the *grandes familles* are considered excellent prospects for marriage.

From birth, males are granted more freedom and educational opportunities than females. Transgressions in behavior are more readily overlooked in males, and the male "macho" image is admired since men play the dominant role in society. Females in urban areas of Haiti lead a sheltered and protected life. The family and educational system prepares them for marriage and respectability. Social mobility outside the home is usually limited. Adolescent girls do not go out alone and their activities are closely controlled. They are expected to help with chores and care for siblings at home. Women in rural areas have always worked. They farm as well as perform household tasks. They are the backbone of the economic stability of the family. Traditionally, clear distinctions have existed between male and female roles. These are changing due to economic conditions. More urban women are working outside the home, enjoying some degree of freedom, and are less willing to play a subservient role to the male. This is especially true in the United States. Many women want a greater voice in the decision-making processes of their homes.

Haitian American parents are generally strict with their children, as is customary in Haiti. The children are regulated and monitored by the adults of the family. Adult rules are to be respected and obeyed without question. Children are expected to live at home until they are married. Haitian American children seem to accept these customs and values despite the freer attitudes and lifestyles they see in their American counterparts. Haitian parents have immigrated to seek a better standard of life for their children and they want to obtain a good formal education for them. They want their children to grow up to be obedient, responsible, and close to the family.

Treatment of the elderly in Haiti differs from that in the United States. Senior citizens are highly respected because they have wisdom that can only come from living a long life. Sending an aged parent to a nursing home is unthinkable for Haitians. Children vie with each other as to whom will be granted the privilege of caring for the parents.

Haitian families maintain regular contact with relatives in Haiti by visiting them during winter or summer vacations. Some also return during the carnival period and for relatives' funerals. Still others return for familial Voodoo gatherings. The Voodoo believers, who cannot return to the island because they do not have resident status, often help pay for such ceremonies. Haitian Americans keep in regular contact with family members in Haiti and even send money home for child care and other family matters. There is a common belief that once you take in a Haitian there will come other Haitians.

Haitian Americans also maintain contact with a network of friends and neighbors. This network enables them to know what is happening around their communities and to help each other. Old friends in Haiti have a common background and maintain their relationships in the United States. The immigrants try to maintain survival contacts with neighbors in the same apartment buildings. The more interaction the family has with other Haitian immigrants, the more the community is able to maintain its cultural tradition, its folklore, the Creole language, and other aspects of social life.

## WEDDINGS

The most common marital relationship among the rural and urban lower class was *plasaj*, an arrangement not recognized by the state. The man and woman often make an explicit agreement about their economic relationship at the beginning of the marriage. The husband is required to cultivate at least one plot of land for the wife and to provide her with a house. The wife is expected to perform most household tasks. The *plasaj* previously would take place with beautiful traditional ceremonies and secret ritualistic sacrifices to the ancestors. Because weddings were expensive, many couples waited several years before having them. Due to the expense, however, few of these ceremonies remain today. The upper class traditionally had civil and religious marriage ceremonies, which were arranged mainly for prestige rather than legality. The "best" families could trace legally married family members back to the nineteenth century.

## FUNERALS

To Haitians, death goes far beyond the immediate family. It includes the various *loa* (lesser deities) and the many dead relatives and ancestors. Some Haitians believe that the dead live in close proximity to the loa, in a place called "Under the Water." Others hold that the dead have no special place after death. Many believe that a dead person will become a loa. Sometimes the spirits of the dead do not go quietly but remain behind to annoy the living.

Burial ceremonies vary according to local tradition and the status of the person. Relatives and friends expend considerable effort to be present when death is near. The family does not express grief aloud until most of the deceased's possessions have been removed from the home. Persons who are knowledgeable in the funeral customs wash, dress, and place the body in a coffin. Mourners wear white clothing which represents death. A priest may be summoned to conduct the burial service. The burial usually takes place within 24 hours.

## INTERACTIONS WITH OTHER ETHNIC MINORITIES

Haitians face a identity dilemma in the United States. Although they are different in national origin, they are almost physically indistinguishable from other black Americans. They cannot easily merge with the rest of the black population because of their language and culture. Haitian Americans perceive differences between themselves and other blacks. Most seek a middle ground between being merged with the rest of the black population and complete isolation. Haitian language and culture are preserved at home, which makes it possible for Haitian immigrants to separate themselves from the Afro-American culture around them. Traditional Haitian values are carefully guarded. They adapt to the dominant American culture while retaining their distinctive lifestyle at home.

# RELIGION

Religion is a basic force in the lives of Haitians who have migrated to the United States and they continue the beliefs that they brought with them from Haiti. Religious groups and churches serve as a powerful unifying element in the lives of the immigrants.

The national religion of Haiti is Roman Catholicism. The first missionaries were Catholic, and the schools that they established are still highly regarded for their educational standards; it is common for even the non-Catholic children to attend Catholic schools. Protestant churches are strong and vigorous in Haiti. Protestant missionaries have increased substantially and represent Baptist, Methodist, and Pentecostal as well as other evangelical denominations.

## VOODOO

An important focus of Haitian religious life centers around Voodoo, which blends elements of Catholicism with those of diverse African beliefs resulting in Haitian Voodoo. It appears throughout the art, music and social customs of Haiti. Voodoo is a set of beliefs and practices that deals with the spiritual forces of the universe and attempts to keep the individual in harmonious relation with them as they affect his life.

A key to understanding the relationship and interplay between Catholicism and Voodooism is the fusion of the two belief systems. Children born into rural families are generally baptized twice, once into the Voodoo religion and once in the Catholic church. Voodoo means many things. It means an attitude toward life and death, a concept of ancestors and the afterworld, and a recognition of the forces which control individuals and their activities.

Those who practice Voodooism believe in a pantheon of gods who control and represent the laws and forces of the universe. In this pantheon, there is the Supreme Deity, the master of all gods, the loa who are a large group of lesser deities, and the twins known as marassas. Twins are believed to have special powers and once a year special services are held for them.

In Voodoo the major gods are classified into the four natural elements: water, air, fire and earth. There is also a god of love, of death, etc. These lesser gods (loas) are analogous to the saints of the Catholic Church and those of African gods. These gods are not only expected to protect people, but they are also expected to accord special favors through their representatives on earth which are the *hougans* (priests) and *mambos* (priestesses). In Voodoo, the soul continues to live on earth and may be used in magic or it may be incarnated in a member of the dead person's family. This belief is similar to Catholicism in that the soul is believed to be immortal. Elaborate burial customs have been established to keep the dead buried in the ground. It is believed that corpses that have been removed from their tombs may be turned into zombies, who then serve the will of their masters.

Voodoo worship centers in family groups and cult groups headed by a *hougan* or *mambo*. Ceremonies are performed annually for such events as Christmas and the harvest and also for specials occasions such as initiations and memorial services. Believers have obligations for the worship of their loa and their ancestors. Expert help is called in to help with the ceremonies which consist of Roman Catholic prayers, drumming and dancing, and the preparation of feasts. Each group of worshipers is independent and there is no central organization, religious leader, or set of beliefs. Beliefs and ceremonies often vary depending upon family traditions.

# EMPLOYMENT AND ECONOMIC TRADITIONS

When François Duvalier came to power in 1957, many dissident politicians, middle-class professionals, and tradespeople left Haiti and headed for New York City. The most recent wave of immigrants has included the poorer people of Haiti, who have entered the migrant workforce or the menial jobs in the New York City area. Haitian Americans are hard-working and use the lower-status jobs as springboards to better, more permanent positions. Many businesses dependent on trade with Haiti have been hurt by the international embargo against the country. This is especially true in Little Haiti in Miami where unemployment is running about 30 percent. From an analysis of the 1990 U.S. Census data, about six percent of the nation's Haitian households or about 5,300 individuals collect welfare benefits, compared to about five percent of households generally.

Haitian Americans are accustomed to using rotating credit associations as an avenue of saving. Such associations are called in Creole "sangue," "min," or "assosie." They rotate money to members of the association from a lump-sum fund into which each member has contributed an amount of money. It is assumed that the Haitians adapted this system of contribution from their West African friends who call it "esusu." Haitian immigrants, especially undocumented ones who have no banking accounts, use the sangue to buy homes and finance various business ventures.

# POLITICS AND GOVERNMENT

New York City has traditionally been the center for Haitian opposition politics. More than 30 political groups opposed to the dictatorship of François Duvalier have been in existence there since 1957. Some have had to operate secretly because of fear of reprisals against family members back home in Haiti. Political activities in New York have occurred during three periods. The first period was from 1956 to 1964 when former Haitian officials dominated and hoped to install a new president and to introduce reforms in the Haitian government system. Several attempted invasions of Haiti occurred during this period. The next period of activity occurred during the years from 1965 through 1970. The Haitian American Coalition (La Coalition Hatienne) was formed in 1964, composed of the groups Jeune Haiti, Les Forces Revolutionnaires Haitiennes, Le Mouvement Revolutionnaires du 12 Novembre, and followers of ex-President Paul-Eugene Magloire. The Coalition published a newspaper *Le Combattant Haitien* and broadcast messages to Haiti on Radio Vonvon. In 1970 the coalition was dissolved and La Resistance Haitienne was organized, which had more popular support. In 1971, the Comité de Mobilisation was formed to attempt to overthrow Jean-Claude Duvalier. This group was dissolved and in 1977, Le Regroupement de Forces Democratiques was formed to force Duvalier from power after he had completed his six-year term. Involvement in the American political process began in earnest in 1968 when Haitian Americans formed the Haitian American Political Organization. This organization was formed to lobby on behalf of the Haitian American community. Haitian Americans have worked in various elections to increase their presence as political force to obtain public services to be provided to the community.

On April 20, 1990, more than 50,000 Haitian Americans marched across the Brooklyn Bridge to City Hall to protest the action of the Centers for Disease Control and the American Red Cross. These organizations had ruled that no Haitian could donate blood because all Haitians were AIDS risks. This was one of the largest demonstrations of its type and encouraged local

Haitian exiles celebrate in Miami's "Little Haiti" after hearing that Haitian president Jean-Claude Duvalier had fled the country.

leaders to find a Haitian candidate for the city council from Brooklyn.

Currently, an increasing amount of political activity has involved attempts to help the "boat people" who have tried to escape oppressive conditions in Haiti. The Haitian Refugee Center in Miami and the National Coalition for Haitian Refugees work to help those refugees trapped in the American legal system and facing possible deportation.

### MILITARY

The American Revolution saw the participation of freedmen from Saint Domingue who fought under General Lafayette at Savannah in 1779. From 1814 to 1815, Joseph Savary headed the Second Battalion of Freemen of Color which fought under General Andrew Jackson. Savary was the first black to hold the rank of major in the U.S. Army.

Since the largest number of immigrants arrived in the United States after World War II, there was not a great involvement on their part in earlier wars. Many Haitian Americans, however, served in Vietnam. Haitian Americans currently serve in the U.S. armed forces; indeed, many of them were sent to Haiti to serve as Creole interpreters during the efforts to reinstate President Jean-Bertrand Aristide.

# INDIVIDUAL AND GROUP CONTRIBUTIONS

### ACADEMIA

Michel S. Laguerre, an anthropologist in the Department of Afro-American Studies, University of California at Berkeley, has researched many aspects of Haitian American life and has published numerous books and articles. Tekle Mariam Woldemikael, a sociologist in the Department of Sociology and Anthropology at Whittier College in Whittier, California, has written several studies concerning Haitian Americans. Carole M. Berotte Joseph, who was born in Port-au-Prince and came to the U.S. in 1957, is the Assistant Dean and Director of the Office of Student Services at the City College School of Education in New York City where she is an authority on bilingual and foreign language teaching; she is a founder of the International Alliance for Haiti, Inc. Michaelle Vincent, the District Supervisor Binlingual and Foreign Language Skills of the Dade County (Florida) Public Schools, is a consultant on Haitian culture and the Creole language, developing and implementing seminars on Haitian culture; she also hosted a daily radio show in Haitian Creole on WLRN in Miami.

### JOURNALISM AND BROADCASTING

Joel Dreyfuss, editor of *PC Magazine*, emigrated from Haiti in the 1950s; he has published extensively in computer magazines as well as the *New York Times*. Marcus Garcia is the editor and publisher of *Haiti En Marche*, a weekly newspaper published in Miami; most articles are published in French but there is a section in Creole for Creole language speakers. Raymond Cajuste is a filmmaker and host of a program on Radio Tropicale. Ricot Dupuy is the station manager of Radio Soleil which was created after the 1991 coup in Haiti; he also helps new refugees with their needs upon arriving in New York.

### MUSIC

The migration of Haitians to the United States has caused a boom in its music. Haitian music serves as an anchor connecting individuals with their country, one another, and themselves. Music functions as a sanctioned means of social protest. Theodore Beaubrun is the lead singer and composer of the Boukman Eksperyans whose songs assault

Haiti's evildoers; the music is steeped in the symbolism of Voodoo and Haitian history. Dieudonne Larose, a composer who lives in Montreal, is transforming Haitian music and writes in the style of the old favorites of compas, Haiti's well-known dance music; he criticizes whites for racist attitudes toward black governments and warns Haitians to work hard and to respect the law.

## SCIENCE AND TECHNOLOGY

John James Audubon (1785-1851) was born in Cayes. His drawings of birds in America are an invaluable source of information for naturalists and anthropologists.

## VISUAL ARTS

Marc Jean-Louis emigrated to the United States at a very young age. He lives in South Florida and has made many contributions to Haitian art.

# MEDIA

## PRINT

### Haiti en Marche.

Published weekly in French. There is a section in Creole for Creole speakers.

**Address:** Miami, Florida.

### Haiti Observateur.

Published weekly in French, Creole, and English.

**Address:** 50 Court Street, Brooklyn, New York 11201.

### Haiti Progrès.

Published weekly in French.

**Address:** 1398 Flatbush Avenue, Brooklyn, New York 11210.

## RADIO

### WKCR-FM (89.9).

"L'Heure Haitienne" is broadcast on Sunday mornings.

**Address:** Columbia University, 208 Ferris Booth Hall, New York, New York 10027.

### WLIB-AM (1190).

"Moment Creole" is broadcast every Sunday from 10:00 a.m. to 4:00 p.m.

**Contact:** Claude Tait.
**Address:** 801 Second Avenue, New York, New York 10017.

### WNWK-FM (105.9).

"Eddy Publicité" is broadcast every Saturday from 8:00 p.m. to 10:00 p.m. It features a mix of Haitian music, news, and discussion of community issues.

**Contact:** Otto Miller.
**Address:** 449 Broadway, Second Floor, New York, New York 10013.

### WNYE-FM (91.5).

This station broadcasts various programs daily aimed at the Haitian American audience.

**Address:** 112 Tillary Street, Brooklyn, New York 11201.

Radio Tropical and Radio Soleil d'Haiti are sub-carrier stations that broadcast 24 hours a day over special radios sold to listeners. They broadcast talk, call-in shows, news, gossip, and social announcements.

## TELEVISION

Several cable companies offer programs aimed at their local Haitian American communities. Programs air political debates and instructions on coping with life in the United States.

# ORGANIZATIONS AND ASSOCIATIONS

**The Association of Haitian Educators of Dade.**
Founded in 1989, the Association champions the educational rights of the Haitian Community. Its purpose is to promote education throughout the Haitian Community of South Florida, to ensure educational equity for Haitians, to encourage the adoption/study of Haitian Creole, to preserve Haitian culture, and to obtain statistical information and conduct research related to the educational needs of the Haitian community.

**Contact:** Gepsie Metellus.
**Address:** P.O. Box 38011, Miami, Florida 33238.
**Telephone:** (305) 751-7499.

**Caribbean Haitian Council (CAHACO).**

Provides cultural normalization of and advocacy for Haitians and other Caribbean groups.

**Address:** 26 Ashland Avenue, East Orange, New Jersey 07017.

**Telephone:** (201) 678-5059.

**Friends of Haiti (FOH).**

Founded in 1971, FOH attempts to generate support for the Haitian national liberation struggle. It distributes information on the Haitian social structure and the liberation process, with an emphasis on U.S. economic, political and military involvement. Friends of Haiti maintains a data center on Haiti and has a library of 3,000 volumes.

**Contact:** Mauge Leblanc, Coordinator.

**Address:** 1398 Flatbush Avenue, Brooklyn, New York 11210.

**Telephone:** (718) 434-8100.

**Haitian American Foundation, Inc. (HAFI).**

Founded in 1990, HAFI works to help, educate and assist Haitian immigrants and other ethnic groups become self-sufficient. It sponsors programs that provide acculturation, vocational skills training, English classes, counseling, food distribution, and technical assistance to small business.

**Contact:** Ringo Cayard, President.

**Address:** 8340 Northeast Second Avenue, Suite 103, Miami, Florida 33138.

**Telephone:** (305) 758-3338.

**Haitian Coalition on AIDS (HCA).**

Founded in 1983, the HCA works to educate the public concerning the discriminatory classification of Haitians as a group that runs a high risk of contracting AIDS. It seeks to heighten AIDS awareness in the Haitian community. Social services are provided for AIDS victims and their families. Conferences and seminars are given at churches and universities.

**Contact:** Yvon Rosemond, Executive Director.

**Address:** 50 Court Street, Suite 605, Brooklyn, New York 11201.

**Telephone:** (718) 855-0972.

**Haitian Refugee Center (HRC).**

Founded in 1974, the Center provides free legal support and educational services to indigent Haitian aliens in their political asylum proceedings. It works to impede deportations and to publicize the plight of refugees.

**Contact:** Rolande Dorancy, Executive Director.

**Address:** 119 Northeast 54th Street, Miami, Florida 33137.

**Telephone:** (305) 757-8538.

**Haitian Studies Association.**

Encourages research and interest in Haiti, the Haitian people, and their culture.

**Contact:** Dr. Leslie G. Desmangles, President.

**Address:** Trinity College, McCook Hall, 300 Summit Street, Hartford, Connecticut 06106.

**Telephone:** (203) 297-2407.

**National Coalition for Haitian Refugees (NCHR).**

Founded in 1982, NCHR attempts to obtain humane treatment, due process of law, and legal status for Haitians seeking asylum in the United States. Its goals are to obtain fair treatment for Haitians in their quest for asylum; convince the public of the need for legal status for refugees; stop the U. S. Coast Guard interdiction of Haitian boats; and increase the awareness of the social, economic, and political causes of the Haitian flight from Haiti.

**Contact:** Jocelyn McCalla, Executive Director.

**Address:** 16 East 42nd Street, Third Floor, New York, New York 10017.

**Telephone:** (212) 867-0020.

# MUSEUMS AND RESEARCH CENTERS

**The Afro-American Historical and Cultural Museum.**

The museum maintains a vast collection of African sculpture and artifacts relating to Africa and diaspora as well as the slave trade. Haiti is represented in the collection.

**Contact:** Nannette A. Clark, Executive Director.

**Address:** 701 Arch Street, Philadelphia, Pennsylvania 19106-1557.

**Telephone:** (215) 574-0380.

**Amistad Research Center.**

The Center contains material relating to ethnic history and race relations in the United States, with concentration on blacks, Native Americans, Chicanos, Asian Americans, Puerto Ricans, and Haitians. E-mail: LB21ILS@MUSIC.TULANE.

**Contact:** Frederick Stielow, Director.

**Address:** Tulane University, Tilton Hall, New Orleans, Louisiana 70118.

**Telephone:** (504) 865-5535.

**The Black Heritage Museum.**

The museum has a vast collection of art and artifacts from the Caribbean and Haiti.

**Contact:** Priscilla G. Stephens Kruize, President.

**Address:** Miracle Center Mall, 3301 Coral Way, Miami, Florida 33257.

**Telephone:** (305) 252-3535.

**The Museum for African Art.**

The museum has an extensive collection of art from all over Africa and the Caribbean including Haiti.

**Contact:** Susan M. Vogel, Executive Director.

**Address:** 593 Broadway, New York, New York 10012.

**Telephone:** (212) 966-1313.

**The Museum of African American Art.**

The museum has preserved a large collection of African and African descendant peoples, including Haiti.

**Contact:** Belinda Fontenote-Jamerson, President.

**Address:** 4005 Crenshaw Boulevard, Third Floor, Los Angeles, California 90008.

**National Museum of African Art, Smithsonian Institution.**

The museum has over 6,000 objects of African art. It preserves black heritage and has some of its collection on Haiti.

**Contact:** Dylvia H. William, Director.

**Address:** 950 Independence Avenue, S.W., Washington, D.C. 20560.

**Telephone:** (202) 357-4600.

**Schomburg Center for Research in Black Culture (Harlem).**

This is a reference library devoted to material by and about black people throughout the world, with major emphasis on Afro-America, Africa, and the Caribbean, especially Haiti. Among its Haitian holdings is the Kurt Fisher and Eugene Maximilien Collection of Haitian manuscripts.

**Contact:** Howard Dodson, Chief Librarian.

**Address:** 515 Malcolm X Boulevard, New York, New York 10037-1801.

**Telephone:** (212) 491-2200.

# SOURCES FOR ADDITIONAL STUDY

Beard, John Reilly. *The Life of Toussaint L'Ouverture the Negro Patriot of Hayti, Comprising an Account of the Struggle for Liberty in the Island, and Sketches of Its History to the Present Period.* London: Ingram, Cook & Co., 1853.

Chierici, Rose-Marie Cassagnol. *Demele: "Making It": Migration and Adaptation Among Haitian Boat People in the United States.* New York: AMS Press, 1980; pp. 1-12.

Davison, Robert B. *West Indian Migrants; Social and Economic Facts of Migration From the West Indies.* London: Oxford University Press, 1962.

Deren, Maya. *Divine Horsemen: The Living Gods of Haiti.* New York: Chelsea House, 1953.

Diederich, Bernard, and Al Burt. *Papa Doc: The Truth About Haiti Today.* New York: McGraw-Hill, 1969.

Dreyfuss, Joel. "The Invisible Immigrants: Haitians in America Are Industrious, Upwardly Mobile and Vastly Misunderstood," *New York Times Magazine,* May 23, 1993; pp. 20-21, 80-82.

*General Information on Haiti,* Washington, D.C.: Embassy of Haiti.

Gollab, Caroline. *The Impact of Industrial Experience on the Immigrant Family: The Huddled Masses Reconsidered.* Charlottesville: University Press of Virginia, 1977.

*Harvard Encyclopedia of American Ethnic Groups,* edited by Stephan Thernstrom et al. Cambridge, Massachusetts: Harvard University Press, 1980.

Healy, David. *Gunboat Diplomacy in the Wilson Era: The U.S. Navy in Haiti, 1915-1916.* Madison: University of Wisconsin Press, 1976.

Herskovits, Melville J. *Life in a Haitian Valley.* New York: Alfred A. Knopf, 1937.

Laguerre, Michel S. *American Odyssey: Haitians in New York City.* New York: Cornell University Press, 1984.

————. *The Complete Haitiana: A Bibliographic Guide to the Scholarly Literature, 1900-1980.* Mill-

wood, New York: Kraus International Publications, 1982.

Sontag, Deborah. "Haitian Migrants Settle In, Looking Back," *New York Times,* June 3, 1994; p. A1.

*The Statesman Yearbook,* 129th edition, 1992-93. New York: St. Martin's Press, 1992.

U.S. Bureau of the Census. *Detailed Ancestry Groups for States, 1990.* Prepared by the Economic and Statistics Administration, Bureau of the Census, Washington, D.C., 1992.

# HAWAIIANS

by
**Elaine Winters**
**and Mark Swartz**

While native Hawaiians almost invariably suffered as their homeland underwent its transformations, it is also true that the Hawaiian culture greatly affected the attitudes and perspectives of many immigrant groups.

## OVERVIEW

The Pacific Ocean surrounds the Hawaiian archipelago. There are eight major and 124 minor islands, volcanic in origin, with a total land mass of 6,425 square miles (16,641 square kilometers). The eight major islands are Niihau, Kauai, Oahu, Molokai, Maui, Kahoolawe, Lanai, and Hawaii. Honolulu, the capital, is located on Oahu, and is 6,200 kilometers southwest of San Francisco. The islands' topography includes such diverse features as active volcanos, grassy pastures, and endless stretches of beach.

According to U.S. Census Bureau figures (1990), the population of the entire state is 1,108,229, with 836,231 persons living within the incorporated city of Honolulu and its immediate environs. Seventy-three percent of the entire population of the state lives on Oahu. Statewide, 135,263 persons identify themselves as native Hawaiians, though it is not known how many of these people are of mixed race. There has been a widespread diaspora of native Hawaiians, largely to the west coast of the United States and also to other Pacific Island nations.

### HISTORY

The islands in the triangle formed (roughly) by Tahiti, New Zealand, and Hawaii are inhabited by people who possess prominent genealogical traits in common, speak related languages, and live similar lifestyles. They are descendants of Polynesians (Polynesia is Greek for "many islands"), who began settling in the South Pacific islands around 1100 B.C. They are believed to have reached the Hawaiian islands sometime between A.D. 300 and 500. They called the largest island *Havaiki* after one of the major islands of their former home. Dogs, pigs, chickens, tuber (taro), coconuts, bananas, breadfruit, yams, and sugar cane comprised much of the traditional Polynesian diet. The mulberry plant called *wauke* was pounded and bleached to make *kapa* or barkcloth. Ti, a lily, provided leaves for *hula* skirts and roots to weave into matting or brew into a liquor called *okolehao*.

The population of native Hawaiians has diminished considerably since Western contact, usually dated from the arrival of the English seaman Captain James Cook in 1778. From an estimated 300,000 that year, the population fell to 71,019 in 1853. This dramatic decrease was largely due to the introduction of various diseases (including cholera, chicken pox, influenza, measles, mumps, and syphilis), for which the immune systems and medical expertise of the natives were completely unprepared. Furthermore, Cook and those who came after him introduced firearms to the archipelago, making tribal conflicts much deadlier.

## EUROPEAN SETTLEMENT IN THE HAWAIIAN ISLANDS

January 18, 1778 marked the arrival of Captain Cook and the crews of his two ships, H.M.S. *Resolution* and H.M.S. *Discovery*, off the coast of the island Kauai. The British visitors recorded trading iron nails for fresh water, pigs, and sweet potatoes. Captain Cook named the archipelago the "Sandwich Islands," after his patron, the Earl of Sandwich. Cook was killed by natives on the island of Hawaii one year after his arrival in a skirmish over a small boat that had been stolen from him.

Prior to European settlement, native Hawaiians viewed land as the common property of everyone. The economic interests of the common people, the king, and the chiefs were collaborative, mutually beneficial, and intertwined. The arrival of settlers and their Western ideas of title and ownership, however, terminated that approach to government.

In 1780, Kamehameha, the first and mightiest of four leaders with the name, began a campaign to unite the islands under a single chiefdom. Hawaiian chiefs had traditionally clashed over land and the resources of the sea, but many of their disputes were settled in ritualized combat, which resulted in relatively few casualties. Kamehameha, however, adapted the modern weapons and armaments of the British visitors to suit his own purposes and hired two of Cook's seamen as war advisors. By 1795 he had obtained complete power over the eight main islands.

With the technological know-how introduced by foreigners, called *haoles*, (a term that later came to apply exclusively to white people), Kamehameha was able to take advantage of political and economic opportunities. He established a trade advantage and created a personal monopoly over foreign commerce. He used *Kapu*, the existing system of religious and social customs, to exclude both commoners and lesser chiefs from engaging in commerce with ships that passed by, and brought fresh provisions to these ships personally. As soon as he realized the value that foreigners placed on pearls, he reserved pearling in Pearl Harbor for himself and employed commoners to dive. Furthermore, he exacted tolls for the privilege of using Honolulu's harbor. In these ways, Kamehameha accumulated enormous wealth and power over the Hawaiian people and lesser royalty.

Westerners ventured to the Sandwich Islands in large numbers. Missionaries from various Protestant sects, particularly Calvinism, were the first major group of *haoles*, followed by Norwegian whalers, Mormons, diplomatic representatives from various countries, plantation owners, and Filipino, Japanese, and Chinese workers.

Sandalwood became a trading commodity as soon as it became known that the Chinese held it in high regard and were willing to pay virtually any price. Kamehameha incorporated sandalwood into his tribute demands from commoners and left the collection process to lesser chiefs. The sandalwood trade, however, required substantial labor, thus drawing workers from food production. Moreover, demand for provisions by ships stopping in Hawaii drew on local food supplies, causing a famine in 1810 that significantly weakened the small nation. Hawaii's position further degenerated when all the sandalwood was sold and trade ceased altogether.

In 1794 George Vancouver, a British navigator, drafted an agreement with island chiefs to transfer ownership of the islands to Great Britain.

He believed the chiefs had formally granted the islands to Great Britain, while the chiefs thought they had a defense agreement. Although Britain did not ratify the agreement, the English Empire, which held sway over lands in Asia, the Middle East, and Africa, established a dominant presence in Hawaii.

In 1819 *Kapu* was overthrown and abandoned when Kamehameha II violated one of its cardinal rules by accepting an invitation to dine alongside women. In the ensuing chaos, many temples and works of sacred art were destroyed. As Christianity, fueled by the influx of missionaries, supplanted *Kapu*, such cultural hallmarks as *hula* dancing, surfing, and kite flying were forbidden along with other so-called pagan practices.

### U.S. INVOLVEMENT IN THE HAWAIIAN ISLANDS

U.S. President William McKinley, acting according to the national spirit of Manifest Destiny, supported a policy of amplified political, military, and economic activity in the Pacific. Citing such reasons as resolving racial unrest on the islands, arresting the influence of Japan, and boosting American shipping and commerce, the United States officially annexed Hawaii in 1893, a few months after an unofficial coup d'état (supported by white plantation owners and enforced by U.S. Marines) and the imprisonment of Queen Liliuokalani. For her refusal to go along with annexation and her support of an attempted uprising against American domination, Liliuokalani is remembered by politically liberal native Hawaiians as a freedom fighter, whereas Kamehameha is regarded as an opportunist and an accomplice in the decline of native Hawaiian culture.

U.S. involvement with Hawaii reached a new plateau after Japan bombed Pearl Harbor on December 7, 1941. The islands were placed under martial law for the duration of the war and were used extensively as bases, bombing practice sites, and rest and recreation spots for soldiers and sailors. The memorial at the site of the sunken battleship *Arizona* attracts many visitors each year, as does the national cemetery at Punchbowl (an extinct volcanic crater), with its spectacular view of Honolulu and the harbor. Hawaii joined the union in 1959, thus becoming the fiftieth state. The current flag of the State of Hawaii has eight horizontal stripes (red, white, and blue), to symbolize the eight major islands, and a Union Jack in the upper left corner, to symbolize the occupation of the islands by the British.

# ACCULTURATION AND ASSIMILATION

Writing in 1916, W. Somerset Maugham described Honolulu, in a story of the same name: "It is the meeting of East and West. The very new rubs shoulders with the immeasurably old." The ethnic variety of immigrants since the arrival of Captain Cook has created many opportunities for cultural exchange and hybridization. Of the 1,108,229 people living in Hawaii, 23 percent describe themselves as white, 22 percent as Japanese, 20 percent as part Hawaiian, 11 percent as Filipino, four percent as Chinese, two percent as black, and about one percent each as Korean and pure Hawaiian. Such clear-cut terms blur when faced by another statistic, however; about half of all Hawaiian marriages now occur between men and women of different races.

While native Hawaiians almost invariably suffered as their homeland underwent its transformations, it is also true that the Hawaiian culture greatly affected the attitudes and perspectives of many immigrant groups. The most striking example of this is the spirit of *aloha*, which is found on all the islands and among all ethnic groups. Although many consider the term to have been corrupted by colonialist opportunism and the tourist industry, it remains an important aspect of the culture of the State of Hawaii. The word *aloha* means many things: hello, good-bye, peace, and, perhaps most importantly, a sense of welcome and identity within the larger community.

### TRADITIONS, CUSTOMS, AND BELIEFS

Storytelling is a great Hawaiian tradition. Before the Hawaiian language was written, the literature was spoken. The Hawaiian legend of the King of *Ku-ai-he-lani* is similar to the western tale of *Cinderella*; and *Au-ke-le* recalls Rip Van Winkle, or perhaps Odysseus. *Menehunes* are small people, rather like Irish leprechauns. Legends of their mischievous ways abound. For example, *menehunes* are held to be responsible when something is misplaced. In various locations, on all the islands, there are elaborate fish ponds that do not appear to have been formed naturally. Native Hawaiians believe *menehunes* built them, and there are strict rules about these ponds. Nothing

Canoes have figured prominently in the marine culture of native Hawaiians.

must be removed or the *menehunes* will come at night and take it back. The implication is that the retrieval will be unpleasant.

Many of the old superstitions and traditions in Hawaii are still observed in modern form; ti leaves, for example, are still reputed to ward off evil spirits. Today, students in dormitories decorate entries and windows with ti leaves when they think there is an evil spirit afoot. Hawaiians bring ti leaves to football games and wave them like pom-poms to keep bad spirits away from a favorite team. Feasts, or *luaus*, are a native Hawaiian tradition still held on every important occasion. The traditional practice involves roasting a pig in a large oven (*imo*) dug into the ground. Weddings, childbirth, the completion of a canoe or a house, and a good catch or an abundant harvest are typical occasions for a native Hawaiian *luau*. Today, *luaus* are held everywhere in Hawaii. Churches frequently hold *luaus* as fundraising events, and the entire community joins in the festivities and the eating. Tourists expect to enjoy a *luau* before leaving the islands.

## AGRICULTURE

The Hawaiian farmer of ancient times was a superior cultivator who systematically identified and named plants—both those cultivated as well as the wild species gathered for use when crops failed. Procedures for cultivation at every arable location on an island (approximately 15 percent of the land), for the variety of altitudes, exposures, and weather conditions were likewise developed by farmers. They practiced organic farming, meaning that the unused leaves of plants were combined with plants that grew during fallow periods in a "green" manure; that is, no animal excrement was used.

Elaborate systems of aqueducts and ditches brought water from dammed springs to planted terraces, demonstrating engineering and building skills as well as planning and organizing abilities. The remnants of these systems can still be seen from the air. Plants cultivated for food included such staples as taro, breadfruit, and yam, as well as foods that offered variety and additional nutrients, including banana, sugarcane, coconut, candelnut, arrowroot, and ti.

About three hundred varieties of taro are known to have existed in Hawaii. Early natives used the entire taro plant. The leaves were steamed alone or used to wrap potatoes or fish for steaming. The root was steamed in an *imo* and then peeled and pounded into a stiff paste handy for traveling when wrapped in pandanus leaves. Adding water to this paste produces *poi*, a starchy thick paste sometimes allowed to ferment. The entire coconut was used as well. Unripe coconuts provided nourishing liquid for journeys when no fresh water was available. The flesh of the mature nut was grated and pressed to produce a cream. Pudding was made by mixing this cream with arrowroot. The husks were halved when the mature coconut was harvested and, when empty, were used as drinking or baking cups. The fibers on the outside of the husks were pounded and then woven into rope. The leaves of the plant were sometimes used for thatching houses.

In addition to attracting laborers from China, Japan, and elsewhere, sugar production has been a major source of employment for native Hawaiians. In 1873, for instance, more than half the native male population was engaged in cultivating sugar. Women were employed stripping, grinding, and boiling cane and were paid half the wages of male natives.

## MARINE CULTURE

Fish has traditionally supplied most of the protein in the Hawaiian diet. It is also a crucial and highly developed trade. Early Hawaiian fishermen were often accompanied by an individual responsible for actually finding the fish—the fish watchman. This skill involved understanding the sea floor, both inside and outside of the reef; the shape of the reef, including where the fish liked to hide; and what kind of net, hook, and bait were appropriate for each fish. Various traps were also devised for catching fish and other marine animals that lived in streams. Not everyone was allowed to eat every species of fish; certain fishes were for special events and then only for royalty. Priests were consulted every step of the way when it came to consumption of various foods. Rarely did women consume fish; rather, they were permitted shrimp and other shellfish.

Nautical culture was an important aspect of early Hawaiian life. There were freshwater ponds and shore ponds. The shore ponds were enclosures built of stone that encompassed both shallow and deep water; some ponds were as large as 60 acres. The walls had sluice gates made of wood. Native Hawaiians have long believed in the conservation of fresh water. In early times, after growing fish, the water was used to irrigate crops. Waste from ponds, a rich source of calcium, provided for an excellent fertilizer. (Hawaiian soil is low in calcium.) Some of these early conservation traditions have been revived and are practiced by native Hawaiians today.

Canoes were built for either transportation or racing. Racing is believed to have been reserved for royalty, and the large double canoes are thought to have been used for major inter-island travel and trading. The elaborate process of building a canoe began with a priest selecting the appropriate lumber. Suitable animal sacrifices (pigs or chickens) were offered and incantations and ceremonies accompanied each step of the process. For example, ti leaves were wrapped around the tree at various stages of the carving and building to ward off evil spirits. Canoe racing remains an active sport in modern Hawaii. One organization devoted to perpetuating the tradition of building and racing canoes is the Hawaiian Canoe Racing Association in Honolulu.

## CUISINE

Hawaii's patchwork past is most apparent in its varied cuisine. Japanese *manju* (sweet black bean pastry), Portuguese sweet bread, Chinese noodles or crispy duck, and spicy Korean *kim chee* are as easy to find as Hawaiian *poi*, which is served as the traditional island staple. Hawaiians eat about twice as much fish as residents of any other state, as well as more fresh fruit. Mangoes, papayas, bananas, pineapples, oranges, and avocados are grown locally. Different areas are famed for specialty crops: open-air markets on Oahu overflow with Kahuku watermelons, Maui onions, Waimanalo corn, Manoa lettuce, and Puna papayas. During a *luau*, a pig is roasted in a pit lined with wood, lava rocks, and banana stumps. The pig is stuffed with hot rocks, wrapped in leaves, and buried along with pieces of fish, taro, yams, and breadfruit. A festive banquet for friends and extended family, the *luau* has absorbed many non-Hawaiian elements. In the 1800s, missionaries brought cakes, Chinese brought chicken, and Norwegian whalers brought salmon marinated with onion and tomato (lomi salmon). All are now standard *luau* dishes.

## TRADITIONAL COSTUMES

Because of Hawaii's tropical climate, early natives usually wore no more than a strip or two of barkcloth (*kapa*). Many Hawaiians also covered much of their bodies with tattoos. Warriors ornamented themselves with spectacular yellow and gold capes and helmets of woven feathers. Today, Hawaiians continue to dress casually. Some Hawaiian women wear the *muumuu*, a voluminous dress originally designed by modest missionaries for Hawaiian women. Today these dresses are printed in bright and colorful cotton or silk. More firmly grounded in Hawaiian culture is the *lei*, a colorful wreath of fresh flowers or other decorative objects worn around the neck. Originally an artful offering to the gods, *leis* have become an emblem of Hawaiian hospitality and warmth.

## HAWAIIAN DANCE AND MUSIC

Although it has long been associated with Hawaii, the ukulele originated in Portugal. "Aloha Oe," a song written by Queen Liliouokalani, is a perennial favorite on this small, four-stringed, guitar-like instrument. Instruments native to Hawaii include beating sticks, bamboo pipes, and rattles and drums of various kinds. According to historians, native Hawaiians also played a bamboo nose flute, a whistle made from a gourd, and an instrument having one string that was played with a bow. A variety of Jew's harp was also used.

Singing, drumming, and the *hula* dance are sacred forms of worship and remain integral to the daily life of some native Hawaiians. Certain superstitions continue to be observed with regard to modern *hula*; for example, while black can be used to ornament a costume, one never dresses totally in black for *hula*, since black is the traditional color of mourning. It is believed that ancient Hawaiians blackened their faces and limbs when in mourning.

## HOLIDAYS CELEBRATED BY NATIVE HAWAIIANS

Ancient religious holidays are not known, owing to the determination on the part of missionaries to enforce the celebration of only the Christian holidays. In addition to federal holidays observed by the entire United States, Hawaii also celebrates Kuhio Day (Kuhio was a prince) on March 26, and Kamehameha Day on June 11. Hawaiians also observe "Aloha Friday" each week. On Fridays Hawaiians wear especially bright clothing and women wear a flower tucked behind one ear and perhaps a *lei* around their neck. The occasion is marked by a celebratory attitude and a sense of good fun.

## HEALTH AND MENTAL HEALTH ISSUES

Religion and medicine were closely related in traditional native Hawaiian life. People expected prayer to heal most things. There were several classes of *Kahuna lapa'au* (medical priest/healer) who treated physical and mental ailments according to a variety of traditions now mostly lost to history.

Drinking seawater followed by fresh water was considered a universal remedy. Various native plants were used as compresses for relieving pain or injury, and the leaves of plants were brewed in teas and used for healing purposes. *Piper methysticum* (the source of the intoxicating *awa* or *kava*) was used in many ways. Today, this species is a sedative given in mild form to infants during teething and is used in commercial diuretics. Seasonal changes and extremes of humidity and dryness produced many respiratory problems among native Hawaiians. There were as many as 58 herbal remedies for asthma, many of which have been studied or adapted by modern medical science.

In addition to the diseases brought over by the first wave of immigrants to Hawaii, leprosy, whose origin is not known and for which there has never been a cure, had a profound effect on the public health of native Hawaiians. Because of the social stigma attached to the diseases (it was mistakenly thought to be a venereal disease) as well as its extreme contagiousness, lepers were isolated on the island of Molokai beginning in 1886. For 16 years, a Belgian priest named Demian Joseph de Veuster provided medical care for these patients, whom the medical community refused to treat, before succumbing to the illness himself in 1889.

Compared to Hawaiians of European and Asian ancestry, native Hawaiians have continued to bear the brunt of the archipelago's health problems. Whereas Hawaii as a whole boasts of the longest average life span of any state (males live an average 75.37 years, females, 80.92 years), the death rates of native Hawaiians at all ages are above average. Economic factors undoubtedly play the most important role in this situation.

## LANGUAGE

Polynesian-based Hawaiian is dying out as a spoken language. Today, it survives mostly on the island of Niihau, in some religious services, and in words and phrases used by English-speakers (the predominant group of Hawaiians), rather than as a language of everyday use. Traditionally unwritten, Hawaiian had no alphabet until the arrival of the *haole*. The Hawaiian alphabet was Romanized and first written by early missionaries. It contains twelve letters: "a," "e," "i," "o," "u," "h," "k," "l," "m," "n," "p," and "w." In general, vowels are pronounced separately, except for diphthongs such as "*ai*" ("eye"), "*au*" ("ow"), and "*ei*" ("ay"). Thus, Kamehameha is pronounced "kah may hah MAY hah." Fewer than 2,500 people speak Hawaiian as their mother tongue, most of whom are older people. It is estimated that within 30 years, Hawaiian will survive only in isolated phrases and in place names throughout the islands. All the languages of Oceania, and particularly those of Polynesia, are linguistically related. New Zealand, Tahiti, Fiji, Samoa, and Hawaii share many words, with slight variations. Some representative words in Hawaiian are *ali'i* (chief or royalty); *kahuna* (priest and/or expert healer); *kapu* (taboo or sacred); *mahalo* (thank you); *mana* (energy or spiritual power); and *ohana* (extended family).

## FAMILY AND COMMUNITY DYNAMICS

Although for centuries women had to endure cultural and domestic oppression, the segregation of men and women under the *Kapu* system provided women with a good deal of autonomy. They led their own lives, cooked food for themselves, had their own deities, and had their own function in matters of royal inheritance and social stature. Women's status depended on social position and birth order. Older sisters were respected and generally wielded greater authority than junior siblings, including males. Older women continue to command respect in the community, relative to younger men and women.

Traditionally, the differences in raising native Hawaiian boys and girls center around their eventual roles as adults. Boys learn to plant, cultivate, cook, and fish; girls learn to cook and are taught how to prepare *tapa* for decoration or clothing. In the past, children were raised by the entire extended family, a practice called *hanai*. Grandparents usually had more to say in the upbringing of children than did parents. When the first child was a boy, it was taken by the father's parents and raised by them and the father's siblings—the child's aunts and uncles. If the first child was a girl, it was raised by the mother's parents and her extended family. Childless couples were unheard of in the social sense; there were always children who needed attention and instruction.

Among native Hawaiians today, the old ways, while fragmented, are still observed. For example, in neighborhoods that are predominantly Hawaiian, children move in and out of houses freely, and adults are clearly watching out for all the children in view. The concept of children belonging to and being the responsibility of the larger extended family remains vital.

### WEDDINGS

Hawaiian chiefs created political alliances by marrying both commoners and other royalty. Most chiefs had many wives and provided for adopted as well as biological children. Engagements were arranged by the parents of the prospective bride and groom during their late childhood or early adolescence. When arrangements were settled by the parents, the young people were consulted, and once agreement to the match was obtained from all parties, the engagement became binding. The extended community that constituted the couple's family gave the bride and groom away. Hawaiian weddings were traditionally, and continue to be, associated with flowers. Both the bride and groom wear elaborate *leis*—necklaces of flowers, nuts, seeds, and other plant material woven together. Traditional Hawaiian weddings are still performed with the addition of whatever civil or religious sanction is necessary for legal purposes.

There are also superstitions linked with weddings: The bride and groom are not wished good luck on their wedding day, as this can result in bad luck. The only way this unfortunate situation can be reversed is for the individual who was offered the wish to cross his or her fingers immediately after it is offered, thus counteracting the curse. In addition, pearls should not be worn on the wedding day, as they resemble tears and will cause the marriage to be filled with sorrow.

## FUNERALS

When someone died, the *kahuna aumakau* (priest of the appropriate ancestral deity) of the dead person came and ritually sacrificed a pig or a chicken to ensure that the soul would live with its ancestors. There were several ways of disposing of the dead. Burial in the ground was the most common method; there are ancient graveyards found on all the major islands. In another disposal ritual, the corpse was eviscerated, filled with salt, and burned. Sometimes, the flesh was scraped off the bones, and the skull, femur, and humerus were saved. The rest of the body was taken by boat far out to sea and dumped. Those in the boats were not permitted to look back once the remains were deposited into the sea, or the soul would follow them back to the land and thus not rest properly. Remnants of special, woven caskets have been found, and it is believed they were used to hold the bones of kings. Such caskets are considered extraordinary works of art and are unique to Hawaii.

The bones of the dead are revered among native Hawaiians. Water is sprinkled in the house of the deceased so the soul will not return. After attending a funeral, it is important to sprinkle one's body with water so that the soul will not follow a mourner home.

## PRIMARY EDUCATION

Many bilingual programs exist to accommodate children for whom English is not a first language. Many classes are given in Hawaiian, which is the second official language of the State of Hawaii. For native Hawaiian children there are the well-endowed Kamehameha Schools, which were established in perpetuity by the estate of Bernice Pauahi Bishop, the last descendant of Kamehameha. The schools were intended to provide native Hawaiian children with a place where they could learn together, away from the influences of the children of various immigrant groups.

## HIGHER EDUCATION

The University of Hawaii has two major campuses (Manoa and Hilo), and several smaller ones, which provide both education and employment to various strata of the native Hawaiian population. There are also several community colleges. The 1990 Census revealed that 22 percent of those between 18 and 24 years old who identify themselves as native Hawaiians are enrolled in school. There were 318 people under the age of 24 identifying themselves as native Hawaiians who had a bachelor's degree or higher. Of those native Hawaiians aged 25 or older, 1,549 are reported as having graduate or professional degrees.

# RELIGION

The ancient religion of Hawaii incorporates hundreds of deities as well as magical and animist beliefs. Hawaiians worshipped both in their homes and in open-air temples called *heiau*. Ruins of these temples are still visible on all the islands. The largest were *heiau waikaua*, or war temples, at which sacrifices occurred. Chief gods were *Ku* (god of war and male fertility), *Kane* (the creator and chief god), *Lono* (god of thunder and agriculture), and *Kanaloa* (god of the ocean and winds). With the arrival of other immigrant groups, particularly early explorers in the early 1800s, ancient Hawaiian religious practices disappeared completely. Today, many Hawaiians practice Buddhism, Shinto, and Christianity.

# EMPLOYMENT AND ECONOMIC TRADITIONS

Before tourism and the establishment of the U.S. military on the islands, agriculture was the biggest industry in Hawaii. Sugar, coconut, and pineapple formed the core of the plantation system. When the large plantations were established in the 1820s and 1830s, native Hawaiian men were employed as farm workers while Hawaiian women worked in the houses of white immigrants as maids and washerwomen.

Wage labor first developed to meet foreign demand and was centered in Honolulu and Lahaina. Beginning around 1820, commoners were enticed to work for wages (although records show that such payment was usually practiced to avoid taxation). By the mid-1840s there existed a group of landless native Hawaiian laborers in Honolulu; these people were paid about a dollar a day in 1847, less than half of what *haoles* earned. Plantation owners, in fact, set wages at different levels for each of the different racial groups, in order to maintain distrust among them and thereby prevent workers from organizing.

A statement made by the plantation kingpin Sanford B. Dole (who also served for a time as president of the Hawaiian Republic) at a planter's convention in the 1880s captures the disregard in

These Hawiians are celebrating the Lotus Festival.

which the planters held their native Hawaiian employees: "I cannot help feeling that the chief end of this meeting is plantation profits, and the prosperity of the country, the demands of society ... the future of the Hawaiian race only comes secondarily if at all." Even to those commoners who were conscious of their exploitation, however, working for wages on plantations seemed a better way of life than working to pay tribute to chiefs. Plantation workers, for example, had taxes paid for them by plantation owners, and an early strike forced plantations to pay workers directly rather than through the chief.

Emigration of male native Hawaiians to the west coast of the United States occurred during the California Gold Rush. The growing absence of local labor resulting from this exodus, as well as from the dwindling native Hawaiian population, encouraged the importation of Chinese, Japanese, and Portuguese farm workers; a total of 400,000 came between 1850 and 1880. Smaller numbers of European workers came from Germany, Norway, and other countries.

From the time of the missionaries until the beginning of World War II, Hawaii was economically controlled by five powerful companies: Castle and Cooke, Alexander and Baldwin, Theodore Davies, C. Brewer, and American Factors (Amfac). About one-third of the Directors of these five companies were direct descendants of missionary families or immediately related to them by marriage. Collectively, these companies formed an alliance that, by 1930, controlled 96 percent of the islands' sugar industry and every business associated with that crop. They therefore manipulated virtually all the sizable businesses and institutions on the islands: banking, insurance, utilities, transportation, wholesale and retail sales, marketing, and inter-island and mainland shipping. In 1932, the Big Five gained control of the pineapple industry, Hawaii's second most important agricultural crop prior to World War II. After the war, in which many Japanese Americans served with great distinction, the Japanese vote broke the political power of the planter elite.

Today the economy of the State of Hawaii is based on tourism. Visitors to Hawaii spent almost $10 billion in 1990. The second largest employer is the U.S. Department of Defense, which spent more than $3 billion in 1990. Native Hawaiians often take jobs as domestic servants or serve in other, often menial, capacities to meet the needs of those who are staying on the islands for a short time. As agriculture diminishes in magnitude and economic importance, opportunities are becoming scarce for native Hawaiians who have traditionally worked in the fields and canneries.

Statistics gathered for the 1990 census indicate that 57,185 persons over the age of 16 who identify themselves as native Hawaiians are employed. Median income for a native Hawaiian family living in Honolulu was $37,960. (No family size is given with this statistic.) That many native Hawaiian families may live on public assistance is surmised by the percentages who are reported as living below the poverty line; 14 percent of the native Hawaiian population is given as living below the standard U.S. poverty line. Some impoverished families are taken care of by those who honor the tradition of supporting extended family; many are not so fortunate. Unemployment for the entire state was calculated at 15 percent by the census taken in 1990. No figures are available for native Hawaiians as a separate category.

# POLITICS AND GOVERNMENT

Native Hawaiians have expressed a mix of determination and apprehension as they face the beleaguered state of their centuries-old culture. The Hawaiian language, considered a crucial aspect of cultural identity, has been the object of renewed attention. In 1978, Hawaiian won recognition as an official state language. For many, cultural survival is inextricably linked to having a political voice. More than a century after the overthrow of the last Hawaiian monarch, the issue of sovereignty has resurfaced. The organization Ka Lahui Hawai'i (The Nation of Hawaii), founded in 1987, is dedicated to mobilizing support for this objective, thus galvanizing anti-*haole* sentiment that dates back to the age of Captain Cook. Chief among their complaints is that native Hawaiians are the only indigenous people living within the borders of the United States not recognized as a separate nation by the federal government. Rather, they are regarded as "wards" of the State of Hawaii. Informed by the Civil Rights movement of the 1960s and encouraged by sovereignty movements around the globe, Ka Lahui Hawai'i asks that native Hawaiians be treated as other Native Americans and be given their own lands (in addition to homestead lands), as well as rights of self-governance.

The sovereignty movement maintains that the independent and internationally recognized government of the Hawaiian islands was illegally overthrown by the government of the United States. It is further argued that acculturation—produced by intermarriage and lack of attention to native traditions, customs, and language—is a form of racial genocide. Because native Hawaiian religion, traditions, and values are closely associated with 'aina (the land) and respect for the environment, many native Hawaiians feel that American desecration of the environment, resulting from military and commercial exploitation, constitutes a grievous crime. The island of Kahoolawe, which was rendered uninhabitable after its use as target practice by the U.S. military, is cited as a prime example of these destructive policies—as are the crowds of tourists.

## RACE RELATIONS

The circumstances surrounding the alleged rape of Thalia Massie in 1931 represent for many native Hawaiians the racial injustice of the present as well as the past. Massie testified that two Japanese, two Hawaiians, and a Chinese Hawaiian had attacked her near Waikiki, but the trial resulted in a hung jury. Massie's husband took matters into his own hands and killed one of the Hawaiians—a crime that brought him a sentence of only one hour. In a separate instance, a convicted murderer named Keanu was purposely infected with leprosy.

For a long time after annexation, Hawaii's politics were dominated by conservative men of European descent who served the interests of the plantations. In the wake of World War II and statehood, the labor unions, especially the International Longshoremen's and Warehousemen's Union, exerted a strong political influence, creating a tradition of support for the Democratic party and a politically liberal climate. The presence of Hawaiians of Japanese descent in the political arena has created the impression of progressive attitudes regarding race. Nevertheless, native Hawaiians have not always benefited from liberal politics. "On the issue of the original Hawaiians," wrote Francine Du Plessix Gray in her book, Hawaii: The Sugar-Coated Fortress, "the most far-sighted men would tend to maintain their paternalism."

# INDIVIDUAL AND GROUP CONTRIBUTIONS

## ACADEMIA

Haunani-Kay Trask, a political theorist, is professor of Political Science at the University of Hawaii and author of From a Native Daughter: Colonialism and Sovereignty in Hawaii (1993).

## ART AND ENTERTAINMENT

Keanu Reeves (1964- ), whose film credits include Bill and Ted's Excellent Adventure (1989), My Own Private Idaho (1991), Point Break (1991), Much Ado about Nothing (1993), and Speed (1994), is partially Hawaiian. The artist Polani Vaughan has produced a work of his photos and verse called Na leo. Don Ho (1930- ), Hawaii's beloved singer, achieved fame for his recording "Tiny Bubbles" (1967).

## LITERATURE

John Dominis Holt is a playwright and author of fiction and nonfiction. Dana Naone Hall is the author of Malama: Hawaiian Land and Water (1985).

## POLITICS

In the political arena, Mililani Trask is Kia'aina (governor) of Ka Lahui Hawai'i (The Hawaiian Nation). Congressman Daniel Akaka (1924- ) was elected to the U.S. Senate in 1990 and John Waihee (1926- ) became Governor of the State of Hawaii in 1987.

# MEDIA

## PRINT

**Literary Arts in Hawaii.**
A quarterly newsletter covering topics relating to Hawaiian literature.

**Address:** Box 11213, Mioluili Station, Honolulu, Hawaii 96828.
**Telephone:** (808) 955-2362.

## RADIO

**KCCN-FM (100.3).**
Plays ethnic-contemporary Hawaiian music.

**Contact:** Michael Kelly, Manager.
**Address:** 900 Fort Street, Honolulu, Hawaii 96813.
**Telephone:** (808) 536-2728.

**KPOA-FM (93.5).**
Plays ethnic Hawaiian music.

**Contact:** Chuck Bergson, Manager.
**Address:** 658 Front Street, Lahaina, Hawaii 96761.
**Telephone:** (808) 667-9110.

**KUAI-AM (720).**
Plays ethnic Hawaiian music.

Contact: William Dahle, Manager.
Address: 4469 Waiald Road, Eleele, Hawaii 96705.
Telephone: (808) 355-3171.

### TELEVISION
**Hawaiian Cable Vision Co.**
Founded in 1969, this station serves Lahaina and West Maui with 31 channels, two community access channel, and 30 hours per week of community access programming.

Contact: Jim McBride, General Manager.
Address: Daniels Communications Partners, 910 Honoapiilani Highway, Suite 6, Lahaina, Hawaii 96761.
Telephone: (808) 661-4607. Fax: (808) 661-8865.

# ORGANIZATIONS AND ASSOCIATIONS

**Congress of the Hawaiian People.**
A coalition of organizations seeking to preserve the heritage of traditional Hawaiian culture and to improve the social and economic condition of native Hawaiians and their communities.

Address: 98-1364 Akaaka Street, Aiea, Hawaii 96701.
Telephone: (808) 488-6905.

**Daughters of Hawaii.**
An organization of native Hawaiian women working to perpetuate the memory and spirit of old Hawaii; preserves the nomenclature and pronunciations of the Hawaiian language. Offers classes in Hawaiian.

Address: 2913 Pali Highway, Honolulu, Hawaii 96817.
Telephone: (808) 595-6291.

**Halau Mohala Ilima.**
A group of professional dancers offering instruction in *hula* and traditional Hawaiian culture.

Address: 1110 Aalappa Drive, Kailua, Hawaii, 96734.
Telephone: (808) 261-0689.

**Hale Naua, Society of Hawaiian Art.**
A group which serves contemporary native Hawaiian artists with exhibits, lectures, and historical tours.

Address: 99-919 Kalawiea Place, Aiea, Hawaii 96701.
Telephone: (808) 487-6949.

**Hana Cultural Center.**
Community facility which mounts exhibits about Hana history.

Address: P.O. Box 27, Hana, Hawaii 96717.
Telephone: (808) 248-8622.

**Hawaiian Canoe Racing Association.**
An organization devoted to perpetuating the tradition of canoe racing and the building of traditional Hawaiian canoes.

Address: 169 South Kuhio Street, Honolulu, Hawaii 96813.
Telephone: (808) 526-1969.

**Naimi Nolau.**
A group of artists dedicated to fostering and preserving Native Hawaiian arts and crafts.

Address: 1210 Laukahi Street, Honolulu, Hawaii 96821.
Telephone: (808) 373-3730.

**Native Hawaiian Culture and Arts Program (NHCAP).**
Works to research, recover, and develop native practices and ceremonies; fosters personal pride among Native Hawaiians and enhances awareness and appreciation of Native Hawaiian history among all peoples.

Contact: Lynette Paglinawan, Executive Director.
Address: 680 Iwilei Road, Suite 560, Honolulu, Hawaii 96817.
Telephone: (808) 532-5630.

**Royal Hawaiian Band.**
An organization of professional musicians which has been performing traditional Hawaiian music for 150 years. Tours worldwide on a regular basis.

Address: 2805 Monsarrat Avenue, Honolulu, Hawaii 96815.
Telephone: (808) 922-5331.

**State Council on Hawaiian Heritage.**
State-funded agency which sponsors seminars in dance and presents the annual King Kamehameha *hula* Competition. Also sponsors conferences and seminars on traditional storytelling and ancient legends of Native Hawaiians.

Address: P.O. Box 3022, Honolulu, Hawaii, 96807.
Telephone: (808) 536-6540.

# MUSEUM AND RESEARCH CENTERS

## Bernice P. Bishop Museum.
Founded by Charles Bishop in memory of his wife, Bernice (the last known surviving member of the Kamehameha family), it is one of the most significant scientific and cultural facilities in the Pacific Region. The collection of ancient Hawaiian artifacts is world famous. The Museum owns extensive collections and mounts frequent exhibits related to the cultural and natural history of Hawaii. There is also an Immigrant Preservation Center which houses collections and permits scholarly research of immigrant artifacts from all the major ethnic groups.

**Contact:** Siegfried Kagawa, President.
**Address:** 1525 Bernice Street, Honolulu, Hawaii 96817-0916.
**Telephone:** (808) 847-3511.

## Brigham Young University: Institute for Polynesian Studies.
Center for interdisciplinary research in anthropology, sociolinguistics, ethnomusicology, and ethnopharmacology. Its publication is *Pacific Studies*.

**Contact:** Dr. Jerry Loveland, Director.
**Address:** Laie, Hawaii 96762.
**Telephone:** (808) 293-3665.

## Hawaii State Library, Hawaii and Pacific Section.
Hawaiiana; books and official state documents, bound periodicals.

**Contact:** Joyce Miyamoto, Librarian.
**Address:** 634 Pensacola Street, Honolulu, Hawaii 96814.
**Telephone:** (808) 586-3535.

## Hawaiian Newspaper Agency Library.
Collection of Hawiiana in print and microfilm, dating back to the mid-nineteenth century.

**Contact:** Beatrice Kaya, Librarian.
**Address:** 605 Kapiolani Boulevard, Honolulu, Hawaii 96813.
**Telephone:** (808) 525-7669.

## Lyman House Memorial Museum.
Historical residence containing both modern native Hawaiian history and Pre-Cook history. There is also information about native flora and fauna, geology, and local family genealogies.

**Contact:** Gloria Kobayashi, Curator.
**Address:** 276 Haili Street, Hilo, Hawaii 96720.
**Telephone:** (808) 936-5021.

## Polynesian Cultural Center.
Presents, preserves, and perpetuates the arts, crafts, culture, and lore of Fijian, Hawaiian, Maori, Marquesan, Tahitian, Tongan, Samoan, and other Polynesian peoples.

**Contact:** Lester W. B. Moore, President.
**Address:** 55-370 Kamehameha Highway, Laie, Hawaii 96762.
**Telephone:** (808) 293-3333.

## Queen Emma Summer Palace.
Historical building that houses ancient Hawiiana, including tapa, quilts, furniture, and other artifacts belonging to Queen Emma and her family.

**Contact:** Mildred Nolan, Regent.
**Address:** 2913 Pali Highway, Honolulu, Hawaii 96813.
**Telephone:** (808) 595-3167.

## University of Hawaii at Manoa: Hawaiian, Asian and Pacific Studies.
Umbrella center for ten research programs and centers on the main Manoa campus, including Hawaiian Studies. Their publication is *Journal of Contemporary Pacific*.

**Contact:** Mark Juergensmeyer, Dean.
**Address:** Moore Hall, Room 315, University of Hawaii, Honolulu, Hawaii 96822.
**Telephone:** (808) 956-8818.

# SOURCES FOR ADDITIONAL STUDY

Beckwith, Martha Warren. *Hawaiian Mythology.* Honolulu: University of Hawaii Press, 1970.

Daws, Gavan. *Shoal of Time: A History of the Hawaiian Islands.* New York: Macmillan, 1968.

Gray, Francine Du Plessix. *Hawaii: The Sugar-Coated Fortress.* New York: Random House, 1972.

*A Hawaiian Reader*, edited by A. Grove Day and Carl Stroven. New York: Appleton-Century-Crofts, 1958.

Michener, James A. *Hawaii.* New York: Random House, 1959.

# HMONG AMERICANS

by
Carl L. Bankston III

*Hmong Americans generally have a very positive view of their new country and younger generations tend to understand both cultures quite well.*

## OVERVIEW

Social scientists estimate that there are between six and seven million Hmong in the world. Until recently, almost all of these people lived in the mountains of southern China, Laos, Thailand, and northern Vietnam. Chinese oppression during the nineteenth century and the rise of communism in Vietnam following World War II pushed many Hmong into Laos, where about 300,000 Hmong lived peacefully during the 1960s. After the royal Laotian government was overthrown by Communist forces in 1975, about one-third of the Laotian Hmong were killed, another third fled to Thailand, and the remaining third stayed in Laos. Many of those who took refuge in Thailand found homes in France, Australia, or the United States. Overall, about 95,000 Hmong have settled in the United States. The Hmong are sometimes referred to by outsiders as the *Meo* (also spelled *Miao*), meaning savage, a name that the Hmong consider insulting.

The Hmong are divided into five major tribes: the White Hmong, the Black Hmong, the Flowery Hmong, the Red Hmong, and the Blue (also known as Green) Hmong. Most Hmong in the United States are from the White or Blue tribes. According to Hmong legend, these tribes were developed by ancient Chinese conquerors who forced the Hmong to divide into different groups and to identify themselves by wearing distinctive colors of clothing. However, clans, or large extended family groups, are more important to the Hmong than tribal membership. In Laos, there are about 20 of these clans, all identified by family names. While marriages between different clans are acceptable, marriage between individuals who share the same family name is considered incestuous and is strictly forbidden.

In Southeast Asia, the Hmong live in villages with economies based on raising livestock and growing crops. They practice *swidden* (slash and burn) agriculture, meaning that the Hmong clear fields by burning, thereby fertilizing the ground with ashes. Since this kind of agriculture exhausts soil rapidly, Hmong villages must constantly be on the move. Their principal crops are corn and opium poppies, which they use for medicines and spiritual ceremonies, and sell to foreigners.

## HISTORY

Chinese historical sources indicate that the Hmong have lived in China since 2000 B.C. Many scholars believe that they may have lived in Siberia prior to this date because blond hair and blue eyes are occasionally found among the Hmong.

For centuries, the Hmong, who lived in the mountainous regions of southern China, struggled against the Chinese government to maintain their distinctive ethnic identity. In the 1700s Chinese generals convinced Sonom, the last Hmong king, to surrender, promising him that the Hmong would be treated well and that his surrender would bring an honorable peace to the mountains. Instead, Sonom was taken to Beijing where he, his officers, and his advisors were tortured to death in the presence of the Chinese Emperor.

After China was defeated by the British in the first Opium War (1842), the imperial Chinese government was forced to pay indemnities to the victors. To raise money, the government of China levied heavy taxes on its subjects, thus increasing tension between Chinese authorities and the Hmong minority. Between 1850 and 1880, the Hmong waged a series of wars against the Chinese. Unsuccessful in their rebellion, the Hmong fled southward; the majority of these emigrants settled in Laos, although many Hmong also migrated to Vietnam and Thailand.

## THE HMONG IN LAOS

In Laos, the Hmong met new oppressors—the French—who had claimed Vietnam, Laos, and Cambodia as part of their vast Indochinese Empire. French taxation led to two major revolts against the French by the Hmong, one in 1896 and one in the 1920s. (The second revolt was initiated by Pa Chay, who called for the establishment of an independent Hmong kingdom and remains a hero to many Hmong today.)

In an effort to pacify the Hmong, the French established an autonomous Hmong district that was allowed to partake in self-government. However, this created competition between the heads of two major clans in the district, the Lo clan and the Ly clan. In 1922 a feud broke out between the two clans over who would become head of the district. To defuse the perilous situation, the French organized a democratic election for chief of the district in 1938 and two cousins, one a member of the Lo clan and the other a member of the Ly clan, ran for the office. Touby Lyfong of the Ly clan won the election, defeating Faydang Lobliayao of the Lo clan. The subsequent rivalry between these two men and their clans led to the permanent political separation of the Hmong in Laos. Touby Lyfong made common cause with the French and later allied himself with the Americans in their fight against the North Vietnamese. Faydang Lobliayao, on the other hand, joined forces with the Lao nationalists, who favored total independence from France, and later became an important leader of the Lao Communist forces.

## UNITED STATES INVOLVEMENT IN SOUTHEAST ASIA

The United States became involved in Southeast Asia to preserve a non-Communist regime in South Vietnam. Because the *Pathet Lao*, the communist guerrillas of Laos, were allied with North Vietnam's *Viet Minh* (later known as the *Viet Cong*), the United States provided economic and tactical support to the royal Lao government to fight the guerrillas as well as North Vietnamese troops. Many of the individuals recruited by the U.S. government were Hmong tribesmen led by Vang Pao, an anti-Communist Hmong military leader who had earlier assisted the French. According to many sources, the Central Intelligence Agency (CIA) officials who organized the Hmong army promised the soldiers, who numbered 40,000 by 1969, that the United States would resettle the Hmong if they were defeated.

After American troops were withdrawn from Indochina in 1973, the Lao government was forced to negotiate with its enemies and to bring the pro-North Vietnamese leftists into a coalition government. Following the fall of South Vietnam in April 1975, the leftists in Laos consolidated their political power, the royal government crumbled, the king abdicated his throne, and the Lao People's Democratic Republic was proclaimed. Despite General Vang Pao's insistence that the United States resettle all of the Hmong soldiers, the U.S. government evacuated only about 1,000 Hmong in the first year.

The new Laotian government sent many Hmong to harsh reeducation camps. Others continued to fight against the new government and there are reports that the Lao People's Democratic Republic has used biological and chemical poisons in attempts to exterminate the Hmong rebels. Still other Hmong made their way across the border into Thailand, where they stayed in refugee camps for months or, in some cases, years. It has been estimated that some 55,000 Hmong are living in such camps today.

"Being an American is really espousing the founding principles of freedom, no matter whether you speak the language or not.... And I think the Hmong ... know in their hearts that these principles are what they have fought for, even in Laos—the basic principles of freedom."

Mouachou Mouanoutoua in 1988, cited in *Hmong Means Free: Life in Laos and America*, edited by Sucheng Chan (Philadelphia: Temple University Press, 1994).

### SIGNIFICANT IMMIGRATION WAVES

In December 1975 the United States agreed to begin resettling the Hmong in America and Congress admitted 3,466 individuals. In 1976, 10,200 refugees from Laos (who had fled across the border into Thailand) were admitted to the United States; some of these immigrants were Hmong, although there is no official record of them. The number of Laotian immigrants then dipped to only 400 in 1977, but climbed to 8,000 in 1978. By the early 1980s, about 50,000 Hmong were living in the United States. By the time of the 1990 U.S. Census the number of Hmong in the United States had doubled to almost 100,000 people. Of the foreign-born Hmong in the United States in 1990, 75 percent had arrived during the 1980s, the majority of whom had arrived in the first half of the decade.

### GEOGRAPHIC DISTRIBUTION OF HMONG AMERICANS

In 1990 the majority of Hmong Americans lived in California (43,000), Minnesota (17,000), and Wisconsin (16,000). When the Hmong began arriving in the United States in the mid- to late-1970s, American refugee resettlement agencies dispersed the 12 traditional clans all over the country, placing small groups in 53 different cities and 25 different states, where voluntary agencies such as churches could be found to sponsor the refugees. Between 1981 and 1985, however, the Hmong reassembled through massive secondary migration, making their way across the country in small family groups. Drawn by the lure of reforming their clan-based society and by the moderate climate of the Pacific Coast, the majority congregated in farming towns and small cities in California, primarily in Fresno (18,000), Merced (7,500), Sacramento (5,000), Stockton (5,000), and Chico, Modesto, and Visalia (6,000).

# ACCULTURATION AND ASSIMILATION

Hmong Americans generally have a very positive view of their new country and younger generations tend to understand both cultures quite well. However, there is a general ignorance of the Hmong on the part of most Americans. Many Americans find it difficult to distinguish them from the Vietnamese or other Asian groups. Insofar as stereotypes have arisen, the Hmong are often seen as hard-working, but also extremely foreign. Many Americans are also perplexed by the colorful rituals of the Hmong and by the music that often accompanies them. Nonetheless, Hmong Americans tend to be friendly to members of other groups and welcome attempts on the part of outsiders to learn more about their culture. The Hmong themselves are rapidly becoming an American minority, rather than an alien group in American society. As of 1990, about one-third of the Hmong in the United States were born in this country. Since Hmong Americans tend to be very young, the proportion of Hmong who have personal memories of Laos is decreasing rapidly.

Many Hmong customs are not practiced in the United States, especially by those who have converted to Christianity. As might be expected in a group that has experienced such rapid social change, Hmong Americans are still trying to sort

Young Hmong American couples play ball games during the Hmong New Year.

out which traditions may be retained in the new land, and which traditions must be left behind.

## MYTHS, LEGENDS, AND FOLKTALES

Hmong folktales and legends have traditionally been passed orally from generation to generation. In recent years, efforts have been made to record and preserve these ancient stories as younger members of the ethnic group are drawn into the mass media-based American culture. One of the most comprehensive collections is the large, bilingual volume *Myths, Legends, and Folktales from the Hmong of Laos* (1985), edited by Charles Johnson.

The stories told by the Hmong date back to before they became part of the Chinese Empire. Magic, supernatural events and spirits occupy a prominent place in these stories and, as in the folktales of other nations, animals can often talk. People are occasionally transformed into animals, or animals into people. Reincarnation is common and characters may reappear after their deaths. Many Hmong stories convey moral lessons, relaying happy outcomes for honest, hard-working, and virtuous individuals, and unfortunate outcomes for the evil, lazy, or selfish.

Hmong literature in America is largely preserved by older Hmong. Young Hmong Americans, like young Americans of many ethnic groups, are frequently more familiar with the lore of pop culture than with the lore of their ancestors. The Hmong and those familiar with them, however, recognize the oral literature as a unique repository of spiritual values and hope that some of it may be saved.

## HOLIDAYS CELEBRATED BY HMONG AMERICANS

The New Year Festival (*noj peb caug*) is the most important Hmong American holiday. In Laos, this holiday begins with the crowing of the first rooster on the first day of the new moon in the twelfth month, or harvest time, and lasts four to seven days. The scheduling is somewhat more flexible in America and does not usually last as long, but it always takes place around the time of the new moon in December. The New Year festival is the only holiday shared by the entire Hmong community and is an important occasion for bringing different Hmong families together.

The purpose of the New Year ceremonies is to get rid of the evil influences of the old year and to invoke good fortune for the new. One of the central rituals of the New Year ceremonies is the "world renewal ritual." This involves a small tree traditionally brought in from the forest (although Hmong Americans may use a green stick, or other symbolic tree), which is placed in the ground at the celebration site. One end of a rope is tied to the top of the tree and the other end is held by one of the participants or tied to a rock. An elder stands near the tree holding a live chicken. The elder chants while the people circle the tree three times clockwise and four times counter-clockwise. The chanting during the clockwise movement is intended to remove the accumulated bad fortune of the previous year and the chanting during the counter-clockwise movement is intended to call out good fortune. The evil fortune, in the traditional perspective, is believed to accumulate in the blood of the chicken. After the participants have finished circling the tree, the elder is supposed to take the chicken to a remote place in the forest and cut its throat to take away the evil influences, but this practice is frequently not carried out in the United States.

Other rituals associated with the New Year ceremonies involve calling home the ancestral spirits to enjoy the festivities with the living and offering sacrifices to the guardian spirits of each house. For American Hmong, the New Year serves as an opportunity to reaffirm their culture and to teach their children about their traditions. For this reason, New Year celebrations in the United States usually involve displays of traditional cultural practices, such as dances, intended to educate Hmong children born in the United States. Aspects of western culture, such as performances by rock bands, have been integrated into the ceremonies. Many New Year exhibitions and practices show a merging of custom with newly acquired cultural practices, as when young Hmong women participate in beauty pageants wearing their elaborate traditional dresses.

Because the New Year holiday brings together people from different clans, it is considered an important occasion for young couples to meet one another. Ball games, in which long lines of young unmarried men and women toss a ball back and forth with their favorites, are a colorful tradition brought to America that may be seen at each New Year celebration.

### HEALTH AND MENTAL HEALTH ISSUES

Traditional Hmong methods for healing are based on shamanism, which includes the use of herbal medicines and massage. Shamanistic health practices stem from the belief that illness is essentially spiritual in nature. For this reason, some western students of Hmong shamanism have characterized it as a form of psychotherapy.

The shamanistic view of the world considers reality as being composed of two parts: the visible and the invisible. The visible part of the world is the material reality that we see around us. The invisible part of the world is the realm of spirits, including the souls of the living, the spirits of the dead, care-taker spirits, malevolent spirits, and others. The shaman is a person capable of making contact with the spirit-world and dealing with it on the behalf of others.

The Hmong recognize that illness can result from many causes, including natural causes, but they consider the chief cause of illness the loss of one's spirit or soul. The soul may become disconnected from the body and wander away from it, so that an individual may become alienated from his or her spiritual essence. Fear, loneliness, separation from loved ones, and other emotional stresses can rip the soul away from the body. This leads to a variety of physical symptoms, such as loss of weight and appetite, that usually lead to more serious diseases.

The "soul-caller" is one of the most important roles of traditional Hmong health care experts. There are many methods of calling a wandering soul back to its body. In less serious illnesses, parents or other family members may be able to perform the rituals needed. If a baby cries during the night, for example, an adult family member may go to the door and swing a burning stick back and forth to light the way for the baby's soul to return. In more serious illnesses, a shaman will be needed to perform rituals that typically include animal sacrifices.

Lost souls may also be found by someone who has a *neng*, a healing spirit in his own body. The *neng* and the healing skills that accompany it must be inherited from a clan member. A healer who has a *neng* can not only find lost souls, but he can also cure illnesses caused by evil spirits, frequently by engaging in battle with the evil spirit that has brought the sickness.

The Hmong have a great knowledge of curative herbs and most Hmong households in the United States have small herbal gardens. Women are almost always experts in herbal medicines. Herbs and massages are often combined to treat ailments such as stomach aches.

While the Hmong are, generally speaking, a healthy people, during the late 1970s and 1980s, Hmong Americans attracted nationwide attention as victims of Sudden Unexpected Nocturnal Death Syndrome. Similar to Sudden Infant Death Syndrome, the illness strikes during sleep. The mysterious fatalities occurred almost exclusively among men, most of whom showed no prior signs of illness. Physicians have connected the disease to breathing difficulties, but many Hmong ascribe it to an evil spirit that sits on the chests of victims during slumber.

Western-style health care professionals often have difficulty winning the confidence of Hmong patients because their concepts of illness are so different. Those who have written on the subject feel that doctors, nurses, and other health-care providers who work with the Hmong must try to better understand the Hmong approach. Some have also pointed out that the Hmong, with their intimate knowledge of herbal medicines, have much to teach American doctors.

# LANGUAGE

Two tribal dialects of the Hmong language are spoken by Hmong in the United States: Blue Hmong and White Hmong. Hmong is monosyllabic and tonal, meaning that it consists mainly of one-syllable words and words spoken with different tones take on different meanings. Hmong uses more tones than other major Asian tonal languages; White and Blue Hmong each have eight different tones.

After joining the Chinese Empire, the Hmong lost their original writing system and any Hmong caught using the Hmong alphabet was punished with death. Women of the tribes tried to keep the alphabet alive by sewing the letters into the patterns of their traditional clothes. Portions of this alphabet can be found on Hmong clothing today, but few people are capable of reading these carefully preserved designs.

Prior to the mid-twentieth century, those Hmong who could write their language usually did so with Chinese characters. In the 1950s, American and French missionaries in Laos developed the Romanized Popular Alphabet (RPA), a means of writing Hmong with a version of the alphabet used by English and other western European languages. Because the Hmong language is substantially different from European languages, however, some characteristics of the RPA are not familiar to English speakers.

Each of the eight tones is indicated by a consonant written at the end of the word. When the letter "b," for example, is written at the end of a word, it is not pronounced. It serves merely to indicate that this word is spoken with a high

tone. The letter "j" at the end of a word indicates a high-falling tone, a bit like the sound of "day-o" in the popular Caribbean song. A word ending in "v" is to be spoken with a mid-rising tone, similar to the intonation at the end of a question in English. Moreover, "s" indicates a mid-low tone, "g" indicates a mid-low breathy tone, and "m" at the end of a word is spoken with a low, glottalized tone, a tensing of the throat. Words ending in "d" have a low-rising tone.

Most of the vowels and consonants that do not occur at the ends of words have pronunciations similar to those of western European languages, but there are some differences. The consonant "x" is pronounced like the English "s," while "s" is pronounced like the English "sh." Likewise, "z" in the RPA has the sound of the "c" in "leisure." The Hmong "r" has no equivalent in English, but is closer to the English "t" or "d" than to the English sound "r." The consonant "c" in this writing system has a sound similar to the sound that "t" and "y" would make if we pronounced the words "quit you" very rapidly. The consonant "q" is like the English "k" or "g" but is pronounced further back in the throat. Finally, "w" has a sound that linguists call the "schwa," the vowel sound in the word "but," and "aw" is a longer version of this sound, somewhat like the vowel sound in "mud."

### GREETINGS AND OTHER POPULAR EXPRESSIONS

The White Hmong phrases given here are written in the Romanized Popular Alphabet described above. Therefore, in words that end in consonants, the final consonant is not pronounced. It indicates the tone with which the word should be spoken.

Common greetings include: *Koj tuaj los?*—You've come?; *Kuv tuaj*—I've come; and *Mus ho tuaj*—Come again. It is not usually regarded as polite to ask a stranger's name but a Hmong may turn to someone else and ask *Tus no yog leej twg tub?*—Whose son is this?; *Tus no yog leej tus ntxhais?*—Whose daughter is this?; *Tus no yog leej tus pojniam?*—Whose wife is this?; or *Tus no yog leej tus txiv?*—Whose husband is this? It is both polite and common to ask where someone lives: *Koj nyob qhov twg?*—Where do you live? If a visitor starts to leave, a Hmong host may say *Nyob. Wb tham mentsis tso maj*—Stay, and we'll chat a little first, since it is considered polite to try and keep visitors from leaving. A useful phrase for anyone wanting to learn a little Hmong is *Lub no lus Hmoob hu li cas?*—What is this called in Hmong?

# FAMILY AND COMMUNITY DYNAMICS

Adjusting to life in a highly industrialized society has not been easy for the Hmong. In 1990, almost two-thirds of Hmong Americans (63.6 percent) lived below the poverty level, compared to seven percent of white Americans, and just over 23 percent of black Americans. Their median household income of $14,276 was one of the lowest of any ethnic or racial group in the United States. As a result, about three out of every four Hmong families (74.1 percent) were receiving public assistance in 1990.

Many of the difficulties faced by Hmong Americans result from inadequate educational preparation. Having lived in a society based on agriculture and hunting, formal education was simply not a part of the traditional Hmong upbringing. Most adults, therefore, have very few educational credentials. Nearly 55 percent of Hmong over the age of 25 in the United States have less than a fifth grade education, and nearly 70 percent are not high school graduates. Despite these handicaps, however, young Hmong (those born or raised in the United States) have shown surprisingly high rates of college attendance. Almost 32 percent of Hmong aged 18 to 24 were in college in 1990, a rate of college attendance that is slightly below that of white Americans (39.5 percent) and slightly above that of black Americans (28.1 percent).

According to the 1990 U.S. Census, the average Hmong family has 6.38 individuals, compared to 3.73 individuals for the average Asian American family, 3.06 for the average white American family, and 3.48 for the average African American family. Over 60 percent of Hmong Americans were below the age of 18 in 1990 and the median age of Hmong Americans was 12.7 years, compared to 30.4 years for other Asian Americans and 34.1 years for Americans in general. The size of Hmong families, therefore, contribute to the economic difficulties of the group, since adults must use their incomes to support more children than are found in most American households. However, while the extreme youth of Hmong Americans may complicate family economic situations at present, this youth, combined with the educational achievement of young Hmong people, is a source of great potential for future upward mobility.

Hmong families in America generally regard men as the head of the family and chief decision-maker. Nonetheless, women often wield a great deal of power in the family, since they usually have primary responsibility for the household. This is partially due to the fact that Hmong homes are viewed as "child-centered" places, where small children are regarded as treasures. As chief caregivers for children, Hmong-American women can be extremely influential in their communities.

Hmong parents tend to exercise a high degree of control over their children, which provides for a sharp contrast with American beliefs about personal freedom. Moreover, young Hmong sometimes have difficulty in seeing the relevance of cultural values important to their parents. As a result of this generation gap, some social workers and people who work with agencies serving the Hmong say that teenaged runaways have become a major issue among Hmong Americans and other Southeast Asian refugee groups.

While the extended family is the basic unit of social organization for the Hmong in Asia, those in the United States often find difficulty in maintaining the tradition of the extended family. It is not possible for large numbers of people to live together under one roof in the new country due to landlord and government regulations on fire and housing codes. Hmong Americans, therefore, have had to break up into nuclear-style families. However, extended family members almost always live in close proximity to one another and assist newcomers with living expenses, child care, and adaptation to American society.

Although clans are still recognized in the United States, they have become less important to Hmong Americans. Clan elders previously took their functions from the rituals they performed in traditional ceremonies. Since the conversion of some Hmong to Christianity, however, these traditional ceremonies have become less important and less common. Also, many of the ceremonies require the sacrifice of animals, which is often illegal and typically frowned upon by other Americans. Many clan elders are gradually being replaced by newer and younger leaders who are well-educated and fluent in English and are, therefore, better able to help their families and other Hmong with the complexities of modern American society. However, clan leaders are still held in high regard and receive deference from the young. Newer leaders rely on the moral authority and blessings of the elders.

These Hmong Americans
are participants in New
Year's activities in
Detroit, Michigan.

## CUSTOMS RELATING TO BIRTH

It is the traditional Hmong belief that when a man dies he will be reborn as a woman and that when a woman dies she will be reborn as a man. Thus, every child born is seen as a reincarnated soul. The child is believed to join human society three days after he or she is born. Therefore, if a child dies within three days, no funeral ceremonies are held since the child did not yet have a soul. After three days of life, a shaman evokes a soul to be reincarnated in the baby's body. The family's ancestors are called upon to join the living family members in blessing the incarnation and in protecting the baby. The baby is then given a silver necklace that is supposed to keep the newly reincarnated soul from wandering.

## MARRIAGE CUSTOMS

Hmong marriage customs, as well as popular attitudes toward marriage, have undergone rapid change as a result of the move to America. In Laos, members of the same clan who share the same family name are not allowed to marry. However, men and women with different family names may engage in marriage, even if they are first cousins or otherwise closely related. Most often, young people in Laos met potential mates at the New Year's Festival, which brought together people from different villages. At the Festival, young women wore their most colorful skirts and showed off their sewing and embroidery skills, while young men displayed their horse-riding and other skills, and sometimes played musical instruments to serenade the young women. Men generally married at any age between 18 and 30 years, while women often married between 14 and 18 years.

Traditional Hmong marriages required the prospective groom to secure a go-between, most often a relative, who bargained with the young woman's family for a bridal price, usually paid in silver bars. Marriages were made public by a two-day feast, featuring a roasted pig. This feast symbolically joined the clans of the bride and groom as well as the bride and groom themselves.

When a suitor could not reach an agreement on bridal price with the woman's family, the couple sometimes eloped. This practice became especially common after World War II when the social disruptions of war loosened parental control. Following the elopement, outside arbitrators helped to find an acceptable bridal price to pay in settlement. If the young woman did not want to elope, the suitor would sometimes kidnap her with the help of his friends and, following payment to her family, she would be recognized as his wife.

Although most Hmong men had one wife, polygyny, or marriage with several women, was an accepted practice. During the war, polygyny became common due to the custom that required Hmong men to marry the widows of their dead brothers in order to provide a means of support for the brothers' families. Wealthy men often had several wives as symbols of affluence. Moreover, clan leaders sometimes married several times to establish political alliances.

American culture and law has made it necessary for the Hmong to change many of their attitudes and practices with regard to family. On occasions, those who have failed to drop older practices have found themselves in conflict with the American legal system. There have been a few instances of young Hmong American men kidnapping and sexually assaulting young females. While they may have considered this a culturally acceptable way to enter into marriage, American law defines this kind of activity as illicit abduction and rape. Some of the young women who have been abducted have viewed the events from an American perspective and have pressed charges.

The use of negotiators to arrange a marriage remains fairly common among Hmong Americans. However, many young women wait until their late teens or early twenties to marry. Surveys of Hmong Americans indicate that the majority believe that it is best for women to delay marriage until they are at least 18 years of age. Polygyny is rarely found among Hmong Americans.

## FUNERALS

Before the Hmong came to America, the death of a family member was announced by firing three shots into the air. This action was thought to frighten away evil spirits. Today, this tradition is rarely followed by Hmong in the United States because of laws regulating the use of guns in populated areas.

The deceased is washed, dressed in new clothes, and left to lie in state. Mourners bearing gifts visit the home of the deceased, where they are fed by the family of the departed. A shaman makes an offering of a cup of alcohol to the dead person and tells the soul that the body has died. Colorful bits of paper, representing money for use in the spirit world are burned and the shaman tells the soul the route it must follow to get to the ancestors and how to avoid dangers during the journey.

## INTERACTIONS WITH OTHER ETHNIC MINORITIES

Hmong Americans interact most closely with ethnic Laotian Americans, with whom they work in a number of Southeast Asian refugee assistance organizations. Most Hmong speak Laotian, facilitating interaction. The Hmong also maintain friendly relations with members of most other groups, but intermarriage is still relatively rare because of the continued importance of clan and family.

# RELIGION

The cult of spirits, shamanism, and ancestor worship compose the three major parts of traditional Hmong religion. It is a pantheistic religion, teaching that there are spirits residing in all things. According to Hmong religious beliefs, the world consists of two worlds, the invisible world of *yeeb ceeb*, which holds the spirits, and the visible world of *yaj ceeb*, which holds human beings, material objects, and nature.

The shaman is important because he can make contact with the world of the spirits. Each shaman has a set of spirits that serve as his allies in intervening with the unseen world on behalf of others. Some spirits, particularly those of ancestors, also make themselves accessible to people who are not shamans. Every householder, for example, feeds the spirits of the ancestors at feasts by placing a spoonful of rice and a spoonful of pork in the center of the table and inviting the ancestors to share in the feast. Because women are most often in charge of medicinal herbs, they are responsible for propitiating the spirits of medicine on special altars.

Some Hmong Americans adhere to the *Chao Fa* (in Lao, literally, "Lord of the Sky") religion.

This religion is said to have begun in Laos in the 1960s when a Hmong prophet, Yang Chong Leu (sometimes written as Shang Lue Yang), announced that the Hmong would be sent a king who would lead them to salvation from their enemies provided the Hmong rejected lowland Laotian and western ways, and returned to the ways of their ancestors. Yang Chong Leu also taught an original system of writing known as *Pahawh Hmong*, which is still used by adherents to *Chao Fa* today. The prophet was killed in 1971, but his followers continued to grow in numbers and were active in the fight against the new Laotian government after 1975.

Missionaries from a wide variety of Christian denominations converted many Hmong in Laos. Even more Hmong converted to Christianity after their arrival to the United States. Baptists, Presbyterians, members of the Church of Christ, Mormons, and Jehovah's Witnesses have all been energetic in seeking converts among the Hmong in America. Since religion is regarded as the foundation of life among the Hmong, conversion has been among the most drastic social changes. In many cases, conversion to Christianity has split families, with some members taking up the new faith and some members adhering to traditional beliefs. Marriage practices, in particular, have been affected by religious conversion since many traditional Hmong practices, such as the bridal price, arranged marriage, bride kidnapping, and the marriage of girls, are strongly discouraged by Christian churches.

# EMPLOYMENT AND ECONOMIC TRADITIONS

Since most Hmong in Asia practice agriculture, early arrivals had few transferable skills, considering America's vast industrial economy. Hence, of the 40,649 Hmong Americans who were over the age of 16 in 1990, only 11,923 had participated in the American labor force; 18.3 percent of this group were unemployed. Almost 80 percent of the Hmong Americans who are employed have blue-collar, or manual, occupations.

Employers who hire Hmong Americans generally hold high opinions of them. Most employers and managers who have experience with members of this group praise them for their hard work and honesty. Some supervisors have remarked that the Hmong have a more flexible concept of time than the American majority, and

that this can sometimes lead to minor difficulties in the workplace. Most of the problems faced by Hmong Americans, though, appear to result from an inadequate command of the English language.

One of the most interesting aspects of Hmong adaptation to the American economy has been their discovery of a demand for traditional handicrafts in the American market. For centuries, Hmong women have practiced an elaborate needlecraft known as *paj ntaub* (also frequently spelled *pa ndau*). This art combines the techniques of embroidery and applique to produce colorful, abstract, geometric designs. The needlecraft is done entirely by hand, without the use of instruments for measurement.

During the 1980s, a cottage industry of *paj ntaub* emerged in large Hmong communities, especially in California. Responding to the American marketplace, Hmong artisans have begun to produce bedspreads, pillow cases, wall hangings, and other items appealing to buyers. This emerging industry confirms Hmong cultural value, while demonstrating the economic importance of women to their families and communities.

# POLITICS AND GOVERNMENT

Adaptation to American society is a matter of overriding concern to Hmong organizations, most of which are geared toward helping Hmong Americans with housing, employment, language issues, and other immediate problems. The Hmong National Development is one of the largest organizations of this kind and, as such, functions as an advocate in obtaining funding for local Hmong organizations.

Hmong Americans are also passionately concerned with political events in their native land, where the Communist party that overthrew the Laotian government remains in power today. Although the government of Laos appears to have moderated its position toward political opponents in recent years, most Hmong remain strongly opposed to the regime. In fact, some American Hmong communities provide economic aid for small groups of Hmong in Laos who are still fighting the government. It has been suggested that Hmong Americans have been coerced into making contributions to anti-Communist forces in their homelands by groups operating in the United States, but this has not been definitely established.

# INDIVIDUAL AND GROUP CONTRIBUTIONS

Despite the fact that the Hmong have lived in the United States for only a short period of time, many members of the Hmong American community have made significant contributions to American society. The following list represents only a few such individuals:

### MEDICINE

Dr. Bruce (Thow Pao) Bliatout is Director of the International Health Center in Portland, Oregon. Dr. Bliatout first came to the United States in 1966, as a young exchange student. He returned to Laos, where he worked for the Laotian government until 1975. He then returned to the United States and earned a Ph.D. in public health. Dr. Bliatout is an authority on Sudden Death Syndrome (SUDS), and has written widely on the subject.

Dr. Xoua Thao arrived in the United States in 1976 at the age of 14. Dr. Thao's mother is a traditional herbalist and his father is a shaman. As a result of this family background in healing, Dr. Thao developed an interest in medicine and attended medical school at Brown University, where he received his medical degree in 1989. He is currently president of Hmong National Development and is studying for a law degree.

### SOCIOLOGY

Dr. Dao Yang lives in St. Paul, Minnesota. Dr. Yang became the first Hmong to receive a Ph.D. when he received a doctorate in social economics in France. He was one of the co-founders of Hmong National Development and remains active in social issues, such as the prevention of teen-age pregnancy.

Community leader Vang Pao lives in Santa Ana, California. He was leader of the Hmong army in Laos and is still widely respected, especially among older Hmong Americans.

# MEDIA

### PRINT

*California Hmong Times.*
The chief Hmong publication in the United States, it publishes news and general interest articles, with a focus on the American Hmong community.

**Address:** 1362 North Fresno Street, Fresno, California 93703.

# ORGANIZATIONS AND ASSOCIATIONS

**Hmong Council.**

A community organization serving America's largest Hmong population. Helps with housing problems, translations, health and social services, and conflict resolution.

**Contact:** Houa Yang, President.

**Address:** 4753 East Olive Avenue, Suite 102, Fresno, California 93702.

**Telephone:** (209) 456-1220.

**Hmong National Development (HND).**

A national, non-profit organization that promotes the interests of Hmong Americans throughout the United States. The HND helps to facilitate communication among local Hmong organizations and to advocate for increased resources to Hmong organizations and communities.

**Contact:** Dr. Xoua Thao, President; or, Lor Mong Lo, Executive Director.

**Address:** P.O. Box 44350, Washington, D.C. 20036.

**Telephone:** (202) 586-7318.

**Lao Coalition of Washington State.**

Coordinates the activities of ten Laotian organizations, including Hmong organizations and organizations of other minority groups from Laos. The Coalition provides such social services as transitional counseling, transportation, and tutoring.

**Contact:** Udong Sayasana, President.

**Address:** 4713 Rainier Ave., Seattle, Washington 98118.

**Telephone:** (206) 723-8440.

**Lao Family Community, Inc.**

Provides English training and vocational education, a variety of youth programs, and a gang prevention program to Hmong, Laotians, and other minorities from Southeast Asia.

**Contact:** Pheng Lo.

**Address:** 807 North Joaquin, Stockton, California 95202.

**Telephone:** (209) 466-0721.

**Lao Hmong Association.**

Provides educational and social services to the Wisconsin Hmong community.

**Contact:** Lo Lee.
**Address:** 214 East Wisconsin Avenue, Appleton, Wisconsin 54911.
**Telephone:** (414) 739-7244.

**Southeast Asia Center (SEAC).**

Grassroots organization seeking to assist Lao, Hmong, Cambodian, Vietnamese, and Chinese refugees from Indochina.

**Contact:** Peter R. Porr, Executive Director.
**Address:** 1124-1128 West Ainslie, Chicago, Illinois 60640.
**Telephone:** (312) 989-6927.

# SOURCES FOR ADDITIONAL STUDY

*Hmong Means Free: Life in Laos and America*, edited by Sucheng Chan. Philadelphia: Temple University Press, 1994.

Quincey, Keith. *Hmong: History of a People*. Cheney: Eastern Washington University Press, 1988.

Sherman, Spencer. "The Hmong in America: Laotian Refugees in the `Land of the Giants,'" *National Geographic Magazine*, October 1988, pp. 586-610.

*Southeast Asian-American Communities*, edited by Kali Tal. Woodbridge, Connecticut: Viet Nam Generation, 1992.

Vang, Pao. *Against All Odds: the Laotian Freedom Fighters*. Washington, D.C.: Heritage Foundation, 1987.

# HONDURAN AMERICANS

by
**William Maxwell**

## OVERVIEW

Honduras is a Central American country bordered on the northwest by Guatemala, on the southwest by El Salvador, and on the southeast by Nicaragua. It has a population of 5.8 million and an area of 43,277 square miles, about the size of Virginia. The population is composed of 89 percent mestizo (people of mixed ancestry, often Indian and Spanish), seven percent pure Indian, two percent black, and one percent Caucasian.

### HISTORY

It is not known when the geographical area that is now Honduras was originally settled by humans. However, archaeologists have recently found evidence of complex society that is at least 3,000 years old. Over the millennia, city-states gradually developed in the vast geographical area that includes large parts of present-day southern Mexico, Guatemala, and western El Salvador and Honduras. These city states had many common cultural characteristics, including a common spoken and written language. People of this region called themselves Maya.

One of the centers of Mayan civilization during its Classic period, between 250 and 900 A.D., was Copán, a metropolis on the Copán river in what is now western Honduras. Copán boasts the largest collection of mural hieroglyphics in the Americas. In recent decades, anthropologists and archaeologists have been able to decipher large parts of the hieroglyphic code. What they formerly assumed to be a collection of astronomical and religious treatises has turned out to be a comprehensive history of Copán.

The Great Hieroglyphic Stairway, on one side of a pyramid in central Copán, is a collection of about 6,000 glyphs, where one glyph is equivalent to a word, idea, or sentence. They tell the story of the 16 god-kings of Copán's Classic period, of their births, ascensions, conquests, defeats, and deaths; and of the significant political, social, and astronomical events during their reign.

The Maya, through these writings, portrayed themselves as a warlike people, with a rigid class system and a very high level of civilization, involving complex religion, science, art, and architecture. For reasons not well understood, the major centers of Maya civilization, Copán, Teotihuacan in Mexico, Utatlan in Guatemala, and many others, lost their populations and became ghost towns in the twelfth century. Christopher Columbus, in 1502, found Honduras to be a land of peoples who lived mostly in small villages and hunted and farmed for their food.

## THE COLONIAL ERA

In 1524, *Conquistador* (conqueror) of the Mexican Aztecs Hernan Cortés sent Cristóbal de Olid to conquer and rule Honduras in the name of the Spanish Crown. When Olid arrived in the region, he decided to rule it for himself and declared independence from Spain. Cortés sent an army to take it back, but Olid was assassinated by rivals before the army arrived. In the meantime, Cortés decided to go to Honduras himself, with another army. When he arrived, he consolidated Spanish power over Honduras and returned to Mexico. Shortly thereafter, Spain appointed Diego López de Salcedo as the first royal governor of Honduras.

The sixteenth, seventeenth, and eighteenth centuries saw relatively little change in this land. In the eighteenth century, gold and other mineral deposits were found in the central mountains and near the Caribbean coast, and the Spanish colonists employed nearby Indians in the mines. As mining expanded, larger numbers of Indians had to be found to work in them, and forced labor, severe working conditions, and forced migration led to the deaths of large numbers of Indians. Indian revolts then led to massacres of many other Indians at the hands of the armies of the Spanish colonists. Mistreatment of and violence against the Indians remains to this day a problem in Honduras.

In the eighteenth century, most colonists settled in the highlands near the Pacific coast, in cities including Tegucigalpa and Comayagua. The Caribbean coast was and is inhabited by the Mosquito and black Carib Indians (and more recently by banana plantation workers, managers, and owners). An island chain off Honduras's Caribbean coast, the Bay Islands, was also settled by the black Caribs, who are part Indian and part descendants of African runaway or emancipated slaves.

## THE INDEPENDENT REPUBLIC OF HONDURAS

In 1823, the Central American provinces of Mexico broke away to form the United Provinces of Central America. Then, after years of interstate tension, squabbling, rewriting of the constitution, and moving of the capital, the Central American states decided to form independent, sovereign nations. Honduras declared independence on October 26, 1838, and adopted a constitution as the Republic of Honduras in January of 1839. The constitution of 1839 provided a single legislative body, a president elected by a majority of the registered male population, and a supreme court whose justices are appointed by the president; thus, it was a constitution in part inspired by the U.S. model.

Wars, military skirmishes, coups, and political intrigues across regional borders have been common in Central America since initial settlement. The Conservative and Liberal parties had been active for some time even before the founding of the Republic. When the candidate of one party was winning a campaign in one country, the presidents of the Central American countries who were members of the other party frequently took political and sometimes military action to prevent his election.

Throughout its history as an independent republic, Honduras has had to cope with an understandably hostile Indian population, a colonist population that was frequently at odds with other cultures within Honduras, meddling neighbors, and a massive U.S. economic, political, and military influence over the country. These are some of the reasons Honduras has one of the world's smallest annual per capita gross domestic products ($1,090 U.S. dollars in 1995), which is the value of what the average Honduran worker produces in a year.

## THE TWENTIETH CENTURY

In 1899, the Vaccaro brothers of New Orleans, Louisiana, founded the Standard Fruit and Steamship Company to ship bananas and other fruit on the Caribbean coast of Honduras to the United States. After a few years, when the company wanted to begin to cultivate its own fruit in Honduras, the Honduran government leased land to the company at a very favorable rate, and the company employed Mosquito Indians to work on the plantations they created. Other fruit companies followed, and Honduras's Caribbean coast has become a vast network of giant plantations owned by U.S. companies. La Ceiba and Trujillo became huge ports where the fruit was and is still today loaded onto ships bound for the United States and countries around the world. To this day, Honduras charges American companies very low taxes for the export of fruit and charges no taxes at all on profits from sales.

Over the last 95 years, the fruit companies have built schools, hospitals, and housing for their workers and connected cities in the region to a railroad network. It has been the region with the country's best infrastructure and standard of living, even for the peasants.

In 1956, the problems with political instability that Honduras had had since its foundation came to a head. The 1954 presidential election was inconclusive; no candidate won a majority of votes. As had happened in 1923 in a similar situation, the Honduran Congress, the arbiter of such dilemmas, was not able to reach a decision on any of the candidates. Lozano Díaz, the vice president in power after the president had had a heart attack and had been flown to Miami, unconstitutionally proclaimed himself president and arrested the leaders of principal parties, labor unions, and farmers' unions. As the political situation became more and more repressive in Honduras under Díaz, the military seized power in a bloodless coup and replaced him with a *junta,* a governing council of military officers. The next 40 years would see a revolving door leadership between the military- and civilian-elected governments.

The situation in Honduras continues to be a product of its past. Political instability is still one of the country's major problems. Throughout the 1980s, for example, the war on Nicaragua's revolutionary Sandinista government by the United States, using Nicaraguan *Contra* rebels stationed and trained in Honduras near the Nicaraguan border, threatened to embroil Honduras itself in a war with Nicaragua.

Today, the democratically elected civilian President Carlos Roberto Reina is attempting reforms in business, education, and in labor policy. However, he is, as others in his place have been, under tight reins from the military.

## IMMIGRATION WAVES

The first Hondurans came to this country in the late eighteenth and early nineteenth centuries during the turmoil of independence from Spain and the founding of the republic of Honduras. Since then, every major period of conflict has seen a minor immigration wave, never exceeding a few thousand people. The turbulence surrounding the 1956 succession dilemma saw another spurt in immigration. The 1980s have seen a steady rise in immigration rates, as the 1986 Immigration Reform and Control Act raised the hopes of potential illegal immigrants that they would eventually gain legal status. Another factor impacting immigration rates has been the hardships created by Central American unrest, including civil wars raging in all of Honduras's neighboring countries throughout the decade, often partially fought or launched from Honduran soil. It is too early to tell what will be the impact of California's Proposition 187, passed in 1994 to bar all government services except emergency medical aid from undocumented immigrants.

Many Honduran Americans are migrant farm laborers, and their number is difficult to measure since many of them are undocumented residents. The 1990 Census records 1,272 working-age people in farming, forestry, and fishing operations, but by all accounts, the actual number is much higher. Of those who have settled into a particular area, the largest numbers are found in New York City (33,000), Los Angeles (24,000), and Miami (18,000). Hondurans have followed the immigration patterns of previous groups; they first settled in the largest cities, in which they found support networks in the large Honduran American communities already present. Cities provide the most accessible market for jobs requiring the kind of basic labor skills most Hondurans possess upon arrival.

## IMMIGRATION ISSUES

The families of the vast majority of Honduran Americans have entered the United States in the last 40 years to seek better economic opportunities and to escape political turmoil or oppression in Honduras. Many have had to leave their families in Honduras and regularly send a large part of their income home to support them. As a new immigrant group, Hondurans are experiencing the same prejudices and suspicions that arrivals have always felt from the longer-established population. Some Americans are under the impression that Hondurans have come here to live off the welfare state and simply take advantage of social services. Proposition 187 can be seen as a legal result of this attitude. It declares that every immigrant without visa and working papers shall be barred from all government services except emergency medical care. Apparently, those who voted for it believe that illegal immigrants take more social services than they pay for through taxes and consumer spending. However, there is substantial evidence that illegal immigrants pay for more social services than they use. This is due to the fact that many immigrants first come alone and attempt to secure working papers before bringing their families over. They need very few government services. Those who do bring their children often do not send them to school because they need the revenue from their work.

If Proposition 187 represents the locking of the door to Honduran undocumented immigrants, the federal Immigration Reform and Control Act of 1986 represents the legal welcome mat. It stipulates that those illegal immigrants who can prove they were in the country before January 1, 1982, may apply for legalization and may legally work until their cases are decided by the Immigration and Naturalization Service. Furthermore, if they have been granted working papers and legal status, they may apply for citizenship after five years.

Honduran Americans are a very diverse group. They include those of Spanish, mixed, Mayan, black Carib, African, Palestinian and Chinese ancestry, among many others. They have made important improvements in their own standards of living, major educational and professional achievements, and important cultural contributions to American society. In the future, they must face the challenges of prejudice from some Americans and overcome a history of poverty.

# ACCULTURATION AND ASSIMILATION

There is no particular stereotype of the Honduran American in this country. However, this lack of specific prejudice is part of the prejudice. More established non-Hispanic Americans, when they exhibit prejudice, like to lump all Hispanic Americans together, contributing to the racist notion that all Hispanics are alike. Some will refer to Latin American immigrants derogatorily as "wetbacks," as economic refugees who "all just swam the Rio Grande to fall into the arms of Sweet Mother United States." So, the fact that Honduran Americans are rarely if ever singled out as an undesirable group does not mean Hondurans are free from prejudice; instead, that fact may only suggest ignorance of Latin American people and differences between their countries.

One notable observation about established American prejudice toward Latin American immigrants is that it is not limited to white Americans. Ladera Heights, California, is a wealthy suburban community primarily comprised of African Americans. Its citizens have attempted to pass an ordinance making it illegal for day laborers to solicit work in public places. They describe the day laborers, who are almost exclusively Hispanic American immigrants, as dirty, loud, disruptive, dangerous, and potentially criminal. While the sheriff's office had no criminal complaints against the day laborers when this case was reported in the *Los Angeles Times* by Robert J. Lopez on March 6, 1994, residents assumed that the Latin American immigrant workers were up to no good. "I do not want welfare. I want work," commented one Latin American day laborer criticizing the proposed ordinance. The issues raised in Ladera Heights reflect broader concerns about illegal immigration, concerns that have led to the passage of California's Proposition 187. Responding to this bill in an August 29, 1994, in a *Los Angeles Times* article by Lorenza Muñoz, one undocumented immigrant named Amanda expressed the often-ignored immigrant perspective: "We do pay taxes—we consume goods and services. This issue of illegal immigration needs to be looked at in a more creative way such as understanding the factors of immigration, and how much immigrants contribute to this country, economically and culturally. It cannot be looked at only in a negative light."

## CUISINE

The staple of the mestizo Honduran diet is rice and beans. Other mainstays include *atól*, corn soup; *mondongo*, tripe soup in a tomato base with corn; and *tamale*, a corn pie stuffed with chicken, olives, and capers, among other ingredients. The diet of the Garifuna is based largely on cassava, a starchy root that is similar in texture, consistency, and taste to the potato. The Garifuna create combinations of cassava, coconuts, plantains, avocado, pineapples, and pigs' feet and tails, sometimes all in the same stew. A favorite is *Machuca*, a stew of fried fish and mashed plantains in a coconut base.

## MUSIC

As a group, Hondurans have made their mark in American music. One important contribution is Garifuna music. Geoffrey Himes described this music in the *Washington Post* (April 2, 1993): "Legend has it that the Garifuna culture sprang from the survivors of a shipwrecked slave vessel who swam ashore on St. Vincent Island in the sixteenth century. There they intermarried with the local Carib and Arawak Indians and created a music that blended West African drumming and Caribbean Indian group singing. The culture then spread to Belize and Honduras." Garifuna is described as an astonishingly melodic and intricate music. The beat is usually carried by two to four large tuba (or hollow log) drums. The tercera drum provides the booming bass notes that establish the foundation rhythm. The primera drum supplies the melodic lead pattern, and the segunda drum shadows the primera with a counter rhythm. These three main patterns are amplified by turtle shells, claves, timbales, bongos, congas, maracas and tambourines. Himes noted: "Because each drum has its own pitch and timbre and because the vocals are woven inextricably into the drumming, the music has a richness you'd never expect from just percussion and voice."

Musical styles popular among Honduran American mestizos include salsa and meringue, both big-band styles of music, with many brass instruments, a driving, steady beat, and a high melody sung over the instruments.

## HEALTH AND MENTAL HEALTH ISSUES

There are problems related to medical care that affect Honduran Americans more than other groups. The mass of Honduran American migrant farm workers suffer from a lack of organized medical care. This class of Honduran American workers is severely damaged by a lack of financial resources to obtain crucial medical care. Officially, New Jersey grants medical care to immigrants, legal or illegal, who demonstrate need and the lack of money for medical care and medicine. However, many illegal aliens from Honduras are

wary of going through a government process like applying for Medicaid. They see the danger of being turned over to the Immigration and Naturalization Service as too great. Compounding this problem is the lack of adequate education for migrant farm workers. The average farm worker, especially the male, has only a few years of formal schooling, if any. There is a general lack of health, nutrition, and medical knowledge, especially as it pertains to the safe-keeping of foodstuffs.

The attitude of Honduran Americans in general to the American medical establishment is suspicious. Most Honduran Americans came to the United States as undocumented immigrants or legally working laborers, and in both categories, the level of medical care has been low, marked by neglect and indifference, especially on the part of government officials.

Psychiatry presents another area in which Honduran Americans, particularly new arrivals, have felt alienated. This is due less to neglect than to different cultural attitudes to psychiatry in Latin American and in the United States: "I thought that if you went to a psychologist, you were crazy," said Maximina Machado of the Bronx, originally from Honduras, as reported by Elaine River in New York *Newsday*, August 24, 1994. Older, traditional therapy in Honduras for psychological problems has included *Santeria*, a Caribbean-based faith that combines elements of African ritual with Catholicism, and *espiritualismo* (spiritualism). Both therapies see the psychological problem as a spiritual problem, an imbalance of supernatural forces. Therapy can then take the form of an attempt to reach a transcendent consciousness by using meditation, concentrating on specific personal objects, or consulting a medium. It can also take the form of an exorcism, where the treatment is meant to drive out an evil spirit or devil from the victim.

Psychiatrists and clinical psychologists in some urban medical centers around the country are seeking to break down cultural barriers to clinical therapy and begin addressing the psychological traumas that particularly affect Latin American immigrants. Dr. Arnold Ruiz's Latin American Immigrant Services program, founded in June 1993 in the Fordham-Tremont Mental Health Center in the Bronx, New York, is one such clinic. Here, Dr. Ruiz and his colleagues treat immigrants for adjustment disorders that arise from culture shock—a sense of confusion due to coming into a culture in which the immigrant does not know the language or the cultural mores. They also treat anxiety disorders and depression due to immigrants' feelings of isolation. Especially acute is post-traumatic stress, caused by witnessing horrors in the immigrants' home countries. Hondurans have had to endure the Horcones Massacre, in which the army slaughtered ten unarmed peasants, two students, and two foreign priests; terrorist groups such as the *Mancha Brava*, a covert group that struck terror into the hearts of all opposition activists from 1963 to 1978; and the 1969 war with El Salvador and part of the Nicaraguan war with the Contra rebels. Fordham-Tremont employees have been successful in breaking down some of the suspicions Honduran American immigrants typically have had toward clinical psychologists and psychiatrists. Most clinic employees are bilingual, and they have a respectful attitude toward the patients, taking their religious beliefs into account during therapy.

The American Psychiatric Association's manual of mental disorders lists some disorders specifically afflicting Latin Americans. They include *Ataque de nervios* (attack of nerves), which is characterized by uncontrollable shouting, trembling, fainting, seizures, and verbal and physical aggression; and *mal de ojo* (evil eye), which afflicts children and some adults and causes fitful sleep, diarrhea, vomiting, and crying spells.

A further example illustrates the confusion that arises from cultural differences in psychological and sexual mores between Hondurans and Americans. Attorney General Janet Reno, a Nevada prosecutor in the early 1990s, prosecuted a Honduran immigrant, Ileana Fuster, for child sexual abuse. Ms. Fuster ran a small day-care center from her home, where she kissed the babies all over their bodies in a non-sexual way when caressing them. Anthropologists commented that this practice is common in rural Latin American communities like the one in which Ms. Fuster grew up. Ms. Reno, with the help of two psychologists, extracted a confession after Ms. Fuster had initially asserted no wrongdoing and after several days of hours-long interrogations. Ms. Fuster's Honduran child-rearing practices had come head-to-head with a different set of cultural practices in suburban Nevada.

Another difference between Hondurans and Americans involves a congenital condition among certain Hondurans that affords them a specific medical immunity. The Garifuna, whose ancestors include black Africans and Caribbean Indians, have an African-component sickle-cell genetic adaptation to malaria. This means that, due to their genes, they are immune to malaria.

# LANGUAGE

The almost universally spoken language of Honduran Americans, besides English, is Spanish. Most Honduran Indians speak it also. In addition, most Maya speak their own language, and the black Caribs speak Garifuna. Far from being a dead or obscure language, Garifuna is a living, vibrant, and growing language in the United States. Some estimates put the number of Garifuna around 10,000 for New York City, the Garifuna nexus in this country. The following are some Garifuna expressions: *Jin!* ("hing")—Hey, you!; *Buiti binafi illawuritei* ("booitey binaffy illawoorittay")—"Good morning, Uncle." *Abau isilledu eiguini, fulesei* ("ab-bow eeseelaydoo aiguiny, foolasay")—A plate of food, please.

Spanish expressions include *Buenos dias* ("buaynos deeass")—Good day; *Feliz navidad* ("feleece navidad")—Merry Christmas; and *¿Donde están mis zabatos?* ("DONday isTAHN meese saBATTose")—Where are my shoes?

# FAMILY AND COMMUNITY DYNAMICS

Since many Hondurans initially come to the United States alone, without their spouse or families, life in the United States can represent a strain on the family. Nonetheless, a sizeable percentage of adult Honduran Americans are married. The 1990 Census shows 20,529 of 44,132, or 46.5 percent, of Honduran American men 15 years and older as being married or having been married and 25,722 of 55,933 Honduran American women, or 46 percent, as being married at least once. These figures paint a picture of the typical Honduran American family as similar to that of the typical American family. The percentage of Honduran Americans married is similar to the percentage of other Americans who are married. The average number of children in Honduran American families is also similar to the average number of children in American families in general. The average married Honduran American woman aged 25 to 34 years old has 1.8 children, while the married Honduran American women 35 to 44 years old will have an average of 2.6 children.

The family experience of black Caribs, or Garifuna, presents a different, unique picture. They first came to Honduras's Bay Islands and Caribbean Coast from St. Vincent in 1797, crossing in ocean-going giant canoes, rowing thousands of sea miles from all over the Western Hemisphere. In ensuing years, young men had to migrate to find work and support their families. This became an accepted and permanent part of the Garifuna family structure. Soon after a young Garifuna couple married, the husband began his travels to find work to support his wife and young children. She would rely on brothers or other male family members to help her with what she herself could not do around the house. And often, she would take another lover to fill the void left by her absent husband. So, the Garifuna immigrant wave to the United States, which peaked in 1975, did not represent a big change for Garifuna society. Nancie González has advanced the thesis that Garifuna immigration to the United States allows the black Caribs in Honduras to retain ancient customs and their traditional family and cultural structure. American dollars earned by Garifuna in the United States are, according to her, helping to preserve the Garifuna way of life in Honduras (Nancie González, "Garifuna Settlement in New York: A New Frontier," *International Migration Review*, 1976). Of the 33,426 Honduran American households, 3,794, or 11.3 percent, are on public assistance.

## EDUCATION AND GENDER

It has been easier for Honduran American girls to stay in school than for Honduran American boys. Especially in working-class families, there is tremendous pressure for boys, once they turn 12 or 14, to start working full time. This pressure is not as strong on the girls. As a result, statistics show Honduran American women to have more years of school than Honduran American men, with 10.9 percent of Honduran American women 25 years and older having a bachelor's degree, while the number drops to 6.4 percent for both women and men are in the same age category. In terms of high school education, 22.4 percent of the women 25 and older have a diploma, while the figure is 20.9 percent for the general Honduran American population according to the 1990 Census. The numbers even out, however, when it comes to advanced degrees. Of the 43,482 women 25 years and older, 602 have a master's degree, 411 have a professional degree, and 60 have a doctoral degree. For the total Honduran American population in

the age category, the figures are 1,091 for a master's degree, 862 for a professional degree, and 151 for a doctoral degree.

Due to economic circumstances, it is likewise easier for girls to stay in school through college. However, young men are more encouraged than women to seek advanced degrees consequently means that those men who do go to college are more likely to stay in school. Women, however, when they reach 22 or 23, experience strong pressure to marry, settle down, have a family, and focus their ambitions on their children.

Honduran American women are more likely to pursue professional careers than to complete advanced degrees. As a matter of fact, 11.3 percent of employed females 16 years and over, according to the 1990 Census, work in managerial and professional specialty occupations, versus 10.4 percent for the population as a whole.

Honduran American women have also become active in the community, fighting for their rights and the rights of their families. Mugama: Garifuna Women on the March, for example, is an organization dedicated to working with young Garifuna in New York City, giving them counseling and support and guiding them on their educational and professional paths. The organization also fights for the rights of Garifuna women, organizing rallies and creating banners for Hispanic parades.

# RELIGION

An overwhelming majority of Hondurans are Catholic. The church exerts less influence than in the past. Honduran Americans are active in their church communities, and women take major responsibility for church affairs, such as attending Sunday church suppers and helping to organize parish charity drives. Yet, the move to the United States has brought with it a new phenomenon for the Honduran community. More and more Honduran Americans are exploring Protestant religions, with a sizeable number converting. Particularly popular are the storefront churches opening across the country. These storefront churches allow virtually anybody to take an active role in religion, even to become a minister. In particular the evangelical and Pentecostal churches stress energetic recruitment and a very close, equal relationship between minister and flock.

Storefront churches are a common sight in Latin neighborhoods across the Northeast. In New York, they can be found in Jackson Heights, Queens, and in the Lower East Side of Manhattan. The service, especially in Pentecostal churches, is typically very high-energy, with the reverend building to a shouting rant and the congregation responding in turn with a unified "amen." Sometimes, a parishioner will collapse in a type of "seeing" trance and experience a religious epiphany or rebirth. Such worship links Pentacostals closely to southern evangelical Baptists.

# EMPLOYMENT AND ECONOMIC TRADITIONS

While new arrivals have traditionally entered fields involving basic labor, established Honduran American immigrants have shown impressive success in moving into more lucrative professions. Of the 34,220 Honduran Americans who came to this country between 1980 and 1990, according to the U.S. Census, 33.7 percent described themselves as being in service occupations, which include waitering, other restaurant work, janitorial work, and work in laundries and retail stores. Only 24.2 percent of the immigrants who arrived before 1980 are in that industry. Of those who came during the 1980s, 27.3 percent were operators, fabricators, and laborers; for those who came before, only 18.7 percent fit in that category. Those who came before 1980 are more heavily represented in managerial and professional specialty occupations, 14.6 percent as opposed to 5.6 percent for the newer arrivals. The contrast in public administration is similar, with a ratio of three percent for established Honduran Americans to one percent for newer arrivals; the same is true of educational services, the ratio being 4.9 percent to 2.4 percent. These figures demonstrate the trend towards self-improvement as Honduran Americans establish themselves in the United States.

# POLITICS AND GOVERNMENT

Being a relatively new immigrant group from a country that has seen its share of political turmoil, Honduran Americans have not been very conspicuous in American politics or unions, nor has there been much overt action on the part of Honduran Americans to influence politics in the mother country. For the most part, the overriding political issue for Honduran Americans has been the right to participate in the political process. As reported by Jorge Zarazua and Marty Gra of *The Houston Post* on July 10, 1994, a recently naturalized citizen represents a case in point: "Mario Casildo no longer wants to be one of the thousands of voiceless immigrants in America ... as soon as he takes the oath of citizenship, the 60-year-old Honduran immigrant intends to register to vote."

To address problems of the undocumented alien community, a group of Honduran American and other Central American undocumented aliens formed the Aliens for Better Immigration Laws in February 1994. At that time the group filed a class-action law suit in federal court to allow undocumented aliens to work while they are on a decade-long waiting list for green cards. This grassroots lobbying organization has fought to bring the issues of undocumented immigrants to the forefront, not only in the courts, but also in the consciousness of the American public.

### MILITARY SERVICE

Honduran Americans have taken an active role in defending the United States. Of all the native (U.S.) Honduran American males 16 years old and over, 13.7 percent are military veterans. Even 769 Honduran American male non-citizens are veterans. The percentage of naturalized Honduran American male civilians 16 years old and over who have served in the armed forces is 13.2 percent. For those who came to the United States before 1980, this number jumps to 18.4 percent, almost one-fifth.

# INDIVIDUAL AND GROUP CONTRIBUTIONS

### ART

Julian Albert Touceda is a New Orleans artist and supporter of Latin art who was born and lived the first years of his life in Honduras. Born in the early 1940s, Touceda has been instrumental in preserving Latin American culture and exposing the local community to Latin artists. Touceda's main influences are the Spanish painters Francisco Goya and Diego Balasca, Mexican muralist

Diego Rivera, and painter Rufino Tamayo. Since 1976, Touceda has had 23 exhibits in Louisiana, Mississippi, Florida, and New York. Among more than 50 prominent artists, he was the only Hispanic artist selected to exhibit his works at the Louisiana World Exposition in 1984.

### MUSIC

Chatuye is a ten-man Garifuna band of Belizean and Honduran immigrants in Los Angeles.

### PUBLISHING

One Honduran American who has contributed significantly to the United States is Julio Melara, a second-generation Honduran American who grew up in Kenner, Louisiana, before establishing himself in New Orleans. As a freshman in college, Melara worked as a courier at a local business newspaper. A graduate of the University of New Orleans, Melara was only 28 years old when he became the top sales executive at WWL radio in New Orleans and the only million-dollar producer in the radio industry in Louisiana. Determined and committed to excellence, Melara became the publisher of *New Orleans Magazine*. He joined the New Orleans Publishing Group in 1993 as vice president for sales and training. He also owns Action Inc., a sports marketing firm, and is writing a book called *Do You Have Time for Success?* In addition, he publishes *Arriba*, a magazine in Spanish for tourists coming to New Orleans from Latin America and Spain.

# MEDIA

### PRINT

*Noticias de Honduras Internacional*
(International News from Honduras).

Covers headlines from the home country and gives first-person accounts of the Honduran American experience.

**Contact:** Mario Ramos, Publisher.

**Telephone:** (718) 446-2523.

### TELEVISION

*"Abriendo brechas"* (Opening Gaps).

This three-hour weekly program on Cable Channel 69 is also known as BronxNet, a New York City public access cable channel.

**Contact:** Murphy Valentine, Producer.

**Address:** 1465 Fulton Avenue, Apartment 5B, Bronx, New York 10456.

**Telephone:** (718) 538-2244.

*"Conversando con Antonieta Máximo"* (Conversing with Antonieta Máximo).

Airs on Manhattan Neighborhood Network Channel 16 for three hours each week. The program features prominent Honduran and other Latin American community and cultural leaders discussing current issues.

**Contact:** Antonieta Máximo.

**Address:** 484 West 43rd Street, Apartment 9-M, New York, New York 10036.

**Telephone:** (212) 947-5712.

# ORGANIZATIONS AND ASSOCIATIONS

**Comité Cultural Folklorico Garifuna.**

Sponsors concerts, dance concerts, and potluck suppers of traditional Garifuna cuisine.

**Contact:** Francisco Rivas, President.

**Address:** 889 Dawson Street, No. 1E, Bronx, New York 10459.

**Telephone:** (718) 893-7356.

**Federation of Honduran Organizations in New York (FEDHONY).**

Founded by Myriam DeMéndez and others as a response to the 1990 Happy Land Social Club fire in the Bronx that killed 87 people, most of whom were Honduran American. The Federation is a valuable resource for contacts of every kind for Honduran American communities.

**Contact:** Walter Krochmal, President.

**Address:** 100 East 175th Street, First Floor (NYNEX Building), Bronx, New York 10453.

**Telephone:** (718) 716-4882.

**Fax:** (718) 716-4964.

**Honduran American Cultural Association.**
A nexus for news of the local Honduran American communities and sponsor of concerts and other cultural events.

**Contact:** Jorge Cotto, President.
**Address:** 41-42 42nd Street, Sunnyside, New York 11104.
**Telephone:** (718) 784-7517.

**Sociedad Hondureña Hijos y Amigos del Progreso (Society of Honduran Children and Friends of Progress).**
A general-purpose Honduran American cultural and support organization.

**Contact:** Adriana Panchamé Kruger.
**Address:** 2305 Summit Avenue, Union City, New Jersey.
**Telephone:** (201) 348-6934

**Sociedad Honduras—New York, Inc.**
The Honduran American equivalent of the Junior League, sponsoring social events and organizing charity drives.

**Contact:** Myriam de Méndez, Chair.
**Address:** 7 Meadow View Drive, Hartsdale, New York.
**Telephone:** (914) 686-0117.

# SOURCES FOR ADDITIONAL STUDY

Fash, William L. *Warriors and Kings: The City of Copán and the Ancient Maya*, London: Thames and Hudson, 1991.

González, Nancie. "Garifuna Settlement in New York: A New Frontier," *International Migration Review* 13, No. 2, 1975.

Himes, Geoffrey. "Chatuye: Upholding the Garifuna Beat," *Washington Post*, April 2, 1993.

*Honduras: A Country Study*, edited by James D. Rudloph. Washington, D.C.: The American University, 1994.

River, Elaine. "Erasing a Stigma—Mental Health Center Deals with Latinos' Special Needs," *Newsday*, August 24, 1994.

By the 1920s, most immigrants had resolved to stay permanently in the United States. They established families, had American-born children, and became intimately involved in the social lives of their churches, fraternal societies, and cultural institutions that in the past served as their extended families.

# HUNGARIAN AMERICANS

by
**Steven Béla Várdy**
and
**Thomas Szendrey**

## OVERVIEW

Hungary is a small landlocked country in the Carpathian Basin of Central Europe. It is about the size of Indiana (35,919 square miles, or 93,030 square kilometers) with twice the latter's population. It is bounded by Slovakia in the north, Ukraine in the northeast, Romania in the east, the former Yugoslavia (Serbia, Croatia, Slovenia) in the south, and Austria in the west.

Hungary is inhabited almost exclusively by Hungarians (Magyars), who constitute 96.1 percent of its population. The remaining 3.9 percent is made up of Germans, Slovaks, South Slavs, Gypsies, and Romanians. Since the dismemberment of Greater Hungary after World War II— complemented by several waves of overseas emigration—about one-third of all Hungarians live abroad. The majority of them live in parts of former Greater Hungary in such newly created or enlarged neighboring states as Romania (more than two million), Slovakia (700,000), the former Yugoslavia (500,000), Ukraine (200,000), and Austria (50,000). Another two million reside in Western Europe, the Americas, and Australia— the majority of them in the United States.

According to statistics compiled in 1992, 67.8 percent of Hungarians are Catholic, 20.9 percent Calvinist (Reformed), and 4.2 percent Lutheran (Evangelical). The three religious groups together make up 92.9 percent of the population. Of the remaining portion, 2.3 percent belong to several minor denominations (Greek or Byzantine Catholic, Orthodox Christian, Baptist, and Adventist), while 4.8 percent claim no religious affiliation. Jews, who in 1941 constituted 4.3 percent of Hungary's population, do not show up in these statistics. This is in part because the Holocaust or subsequent emigration to Israel decimated their ranks and in part because of the reluctance of some to identify themselves as Jews. Learned estimates, however, put their numbers close to 100,000 (about one percent of the country's population), which still makes them the largest Jewish community in East Central Europe. As the result of half a century of communist rule, relatively few people practice their religion in Hungary. The religious revival following the collapse of communism, however—which includes the return of organized religious education—is in the process of changing this lack of attention to religion.

## HISTORY

Medieval Hungarian traditions count even the fifth-century Huns among the Magyars' ancestors, but their immediate forebears arrived in the Carpathian Basin as late as the seventh century. Known as the "late Avars," they established the center of their empire in the region that is part of modern Hungary. The last of several Magyar migratory waves took place in the late ninth century, when under the leadership of Prince Árpád, they conquered this region, gradually extending their rule over the entire Carpathian Basin.

In A.D. 1000, one of Árpád's successors, Stephen I (king of Hungary 997-1038; canonized 1083) Christianized his people and made Hungary part of the Western Christian world. During the next four centuries, the Hungarians continued to expand beyond the Carpathian Basin, especially into the northern Balkans. At the end of the eleventh century they conquered and annexed Croatia as an autonomous kingdom, while in the twelfth and thirteenth centuries they extended their influence over Bosnia, Dalmatia, and northern Serbia—largely at the expense of the declining Byzantine Empire. Moreover, in the fourteenth century, under the Angevin rulers Charles Robert (who ruled from 1308 until 1342) and Louis the Great (who ruled from 1342 to 1382), they expanded their control over the newly formed Vlach (Romanian) principalities of Wal-

lachia and Moldavia and for a brief period (1370-1382) even over Poland. With the expansion of the Ottoman Turkish Empire into the Balkans in the late fourteenth and fifteenth centuries, Hungarian influence over the northern Balkans declined and was replaced by that of the Turks. Even so, Hungary still experienced moments of greatness, particularly under Regent John Hunyadi (who ruled from 1444 to 1456) and his son King Matthias Corvinus (who ruled from 1458 to 1490). Matthias even conquered Moravia and eastern Austria (including Vienna) and also established a brilliant Renaissance royal court at Buda (now part of Budapest).

Medieval Hungary's greatness ended with its defeat at the hands of the Ottoman Turks at the Battle of Mohács in 1526. Turkish conquest was followed by the country's trisection, which lasted for nearly two centuries. Western and northwestern Hungary ("Royal Hungary") became part of the Habsburg Empire ruled from Vienna; central Hungary was integrated into the Ottoman Turkish Empire; and eastern Hungary evolved into the autonomous principality of Transylvania, whose semi-independence under Turkish suzerainty ended with the country's reconquest and reunification by the Habsburgs of Vienna in the late seventeenth and early eighteenth centuries.

Although dominated by Vienna throughout the eighteenth and nineteenth centuries, Hungary retained considerable autonomy within the Habsburg Empire. In the mid-nineteenth century the Habsburgs and the Hungarians clashed in the Hungarian Revolution and War of Independence (1848-1849), and two decades later they united in the Austro-Hungarian Compromise of 1867. This compromise—engineered by Francis Deák (1803-1876) and Emperor Franz Joseph (who ruled from 1848 to 1916)—resulted in the dual state of Austria-Hungary, which played a significant role in European power-politics until nationality problems and involvement in World War I on the German side resulted in its dissolution in 1918-1919.

The demise of Austria-Hungary was accompanied by the dismemberment of historic Hungary, codified in the Peace Treaty of Trianon in 1920. This treaty turned Hungary into a small truncated country, with only 28.5 percent of its former territory (35,900 square miles versus 125,600 square miles) and 36.5 percent of its former population (7.6 million versus 20.9 million). Trianon Hungary became "a kingdom without a king" under the regency of Admiral Nicholas

These Hungarian refugees were part of the U.S. Navy's "sea lift," which helped Hungarians fleeing their homeland after the 1956 Soviet military crackdown.

Horthy (who ruled from 1920 to 1944), who devoted most of the country's energies to the effort to regain at least some of Hungary's territorial losses. These efforts did result in temporary territorial gains in 1938-1941, but as these gains were achieved with German and Italian help, they landed Hungary in the unfortunate German alliance during World War II.

After the war Hungary again was reduced in size and became one of the communist-dominated Soviet satellite states under the leadership of the Stalinist dictator, Mátyás Rákosi (who ruled from 1945 to 1956). Communist excesses and the relaxation that followed Stalin's death in 1953 led to the Hungarian Revolution of 1956, the most significant anti-Soviet uprising of the postwar period. Put down by Soviet military intervention, it was followed by a brief period of retribution and then by a new communist regime under János Kádár (who ruled from 1956 to 1988), who initiated a policy of political liberalization (1962) and economic reform (known as the New Economic

Mechanism of 1968). By the 1970s these reforms—supported by generous Western loans—made Hungary and its system of "goulash communism" the envy of the communist world. In the 1980s, however, the system began to flounder, and economic problems resurfaced. These problems, together with Mikhail Gorbachev's reforms in the Soviet Union, undermined the Kádár regime. Kádár was ousted in 1988, and in 1989 Hungary came under the control of reform communists, who, unable to control the situation, relinquished power in 1990. They were replaced by a new multiparty government under the leadership of the Hungarian Democratic Forum (HDF), headed by József Antall (who ruled from 1990 to 1993). The HDF regime immediately began to transform Hungary from a communist to a democratic state, but the economic and social problems it encountered—rapid social polarization, the collapse of the protective social welfare system, and pauperization of a large segment of the society—proved to be too much. The HDF government was also plagued by amateurism in leadership. Voted out of office in May 1994, it was replaced in July of the same year by a coalition of the Hungarian Socialist Party and the Federation of Free Democrats. The new prime minister is the ex-Communist Gyula Horn (1932- ), who had served as Hungary's foreign minister during the peaceful transition from communism to democracy in 1989-1990.

## HUNGARIANS IN THE UNITED STATES

According to Hungarian tradition, the first Hungarian to reach the shores of America was a certain Tyrker who had arrived with the Viking chief Eric the Red around A.D. 1000. This is alleged to have happened concurrently with Stephen I's transformation of Hungary into a Christian kingdom. If the Tyrker story is discounted, the first documented Hungarian to land in America was the learned scholar Stephen Parmenius of Buda (c. 1555-1583), who participated in Sir Humphrey Gilbert's expedition in 1583 and later drowned off the coast of Newfoundland.

The next two and one-half centuries belonged to the explorers, missionaries, and adventurers who came to North America in increasing numbers during the colonial and early national periods. The most noted among the latter was Colonel Michael de Kováts (1724-1779), a member of the Pulaski Legion during the Revolutionary War, who is generally credited with being one of the founders of the American cavalry. The late eighteenth and early nineteenth century also saw the arrival of the first sporadic settlers, most of whom came from the middle and upper classes, were motivated by personal reasons to immigrate, and usually settled in such coastal cities as Boston, New York, Philadelphia, Charleston, and New Orleans. In the 1830s and 1840s came a number of learned travelers, including Sándor Bölöni-Farkas (1795-1842) and Ágoston Haraszthy (1812-1869), both of whom wrote influential books about their experiences in the New World under the identical title *Journey to North America* (published in 1834 and 1844, respectively). In 1844 Haraszthy returned permanently with his family and became the founder of California viticulture. The two decades prior to the Hungarian Revolution of 1848 also saw the initial scholarly contacts between the Hungarian Academy of Science and the American Philosophical Society.

The long period of individual migration was replaced in 1849-1850 by the first Hungarian group immigration to America. These were the so-called "Forty-niners," who emigrated to escape retribution by Austrian authorities after the defeat of the Hungarian Revolution of 1848. Several thousand strong, the numbers included only educated men, many of them from the gentry class (middle nobility), who found it difficult to adjust to America's frontier society. A large number of them joined the Union armies during the Civil War, and a few of them returned to Hungary during the 1860s and 1870s, but most of them became a part of American society. Many of the latter rose to important positions, usually in fields other than their original calling.

The next wave was the turn-of-the-century "Great Economic Immigration" that landed about 1.7 million Hungarian citizens, among them 650,000-700,000 real Hungarians (Magyars), on American shores. These immigrants came almost solely for economic reasons, and they represented the lowest and poorest segment of the population.

"When we were getting off of Ellis Island, we had all sorts of tags on us. Now that I think of it, we must have looked like marked-down merchandise in Gimbel's basement store or something."

Anna Vida in 1921, cited in *Ellis Island: An Illustrated History of the Immigrant Experience,* edited by Ivan Chermayeff et al. (New York: Macmillan, 1991).

The outbreak of World War I in 1914 halted mass migration, while the exclusionary U.S. immigration laws of 1921 and 1924 pushed the Hungarian quota down to under 1,000 per year. This situation did not change until the new Immigration Law, the Hart-Celler Act of 1965, ended the quota system. Yet, during the intervening four decades, there were a number of nonquota admissions, which brought completely different types of Hungarian immigrants to American shores. These included the refugee intellectuals (2,000 to 3,000) of the 1930s, who were fleeing the spread of Nazism; the post-World War II political immigrants or the so-called displaced persons or DPs (17,000), who came under the Displaced Persons Acts of 1948 and 1950; and the "Fifty-sixers" or Freedom Fighters (38,000), who left Hungary after the failed Revolution of 1956. Although the combined numbers of these last three groups (60,000) were less than 10 percent of that of the turn-of-the-century economic immigrants, their impact on American society was much more significant.

## SETTLEMENT PATTERNS

Although the turn-of-the-century economic immigrants were from rural areas, almost all of them settled in the industrial cities and mining regions of the northeastern United States. According to one set of statistics, of all the Hungarians (Magyars) in the United States in 1920, fewer than 0.2 percent were engaged in agriculture. Virtually all of them worked in mining and industry—most of them in the unskilled or semiskilled category. This was primarily because the majority of them came to America not as immigrants but as migrant workers who intended to repatriate to Hungary. Their goal was to return with enough accumulated capital to be able to buy land and thus become prosperous farmers. To do this, however, they had to work in industry, where work was readily available, because during the Gilded Age the rapidly expanding American industrial establishment was in grave need of cheap immigrant labor.

Most of the immigrants were never able to fulfill their original goal of repatriation, although perhaps as many as 25 percent did return permanently. Factors contributing to this included their inability to accumulate the capital to buy enough land; the difficulties they encountered in readjusting to Hungary's class-conscious society; the influence of their American-born children who viewed Hungary as an alien land; and most important, Hungary's post-World War I dismemberment, which transferred the immediate homelands of most of the immigrants to such newly created states as Czechoslovakia or Yugoslavia or to the much-enlarged Romania. They did not wish to join the ranks of Hungarians who had been forcibly transferred to these states, two of which had gone out of existence twice since their creation (Czechoslovakia and Yugoslavia) and one of which had become the home base of postwar Europe's most oppressive and chauvinistic communist regime (Romania).

According to the 1920 U.S. Census, 945,801 persons in the United States either had been born in Hungary or had Hungarian-born parents, slightly over half of whom (495,845 or 52.9 percent) were Magyars. In 1922 the Hungarian-born Magyars numbered 474,000, of whom 427,500 (90 percent) were concentrated in 10 northeastern states: New York (95,400), Ohio (88,000), Pennsylvania (86,000), New Jersey (47,300), Illinois (40,000), Michigan (26,200), Connecticut (14,800), Wisconsin (11,600), Indiana (10,900), and West Virginia (7,300). They congregated in this region because of the coal mines of Pennsylvania, northern West Virginia, and southeastern Ohio, as well as because of the steel mills, textile mills, and machine factories of Pittsburgh, Cleveland, Youngstown, Chicago, Philadelphia, and the Greater New York area.

This settlement pattern remained unchanged until the 1960s when—partially because of the coming of the more mobile political immigrants, and partially because of the general population shift in previous decades—many Hungarians began to move to the West and to the South. The younger and more daring souls flooded to California and Texas, while the retirees favored Florida. Thus, by 1980 the Hungarian population of these states rose, respectively, to 165,000, 28,000, and 90,000.

## RELATIONS WITH ANGLO-AMERICAN SOCIETY

The relationship of the Hungarians to Anglo-American society varied with the diverse waves of immigrants. The Forty-niners, also known as the "Kossuth immigrants" (after the leader of the revolution, Lajos Kossuth), had been received with awe and respect. Because of their gentry-based background and education, they established the image of the Hungarians as a "nation of nobles." This image was undermined by the turn-of-the-century economic poor and uneducated. They were the ones who unwittingly created the negative "Hunky" image of Hungarians, which then was transferred to all of the East and Southeast European immigrants. This image survived well into the post-World War II period, even though by that time the intellectual immigrants of the 1930s and the political immigrants of the 1950s began to diversify the immigrants' social composition. Although far fewer in number, these newer immigrants were the ones who gave birth to the revised Hungarian image that Laura Fermi, the author of the highly praised study *Illustrious Immigrants* (1968), defined as the "mystery of the Hungarian talent." This was a natural by-product of the fact that many of these intellectual and political immigrants made impressive achievements that had a measurable impact on American society.

## KEY ISSUES FOR THE FUTURE

The key issue at this time is one of survival and of relationship to Hungary. The third-, fourth-, and fifth-generation descendants of the economic immigrants have already melted into American society. Most of them have lost their ability to speak Hungarian and no longer have a true identity of themselves as Hungarians. Most have only a minimal acquaintance with modern Hungary and know very little about Hungarian traditions. This is somewhat true of the post-World War II immigrants as well, even though a sizable percentage of their American-born offspring does speak Hungarian and has some knowledge of Hungarian culture. Moreover, in light of the collapse of communism in 1989-1990, a significant number of them have found their way back to the land of their ancestors. This was and is being done largely in the form of employment with some of the major American or Western European corporations that have established branches in Hungary. This temporary return does create a set of new ties, but because of the radical transformation of Hungarian society during the four decades of communist rule, the experience is not always positive.

Despite renewed contacts with the homeland, Hungarian Americans are losing their struggle to survive as a separate ethnic group in America. This is evident both in their declining numbers, as well as in the decreasing number of their ethnic institutions, churches, cultural organizations, and fraternal organizations. This phenomenon is best seen when comparing the census statistics of 1980 with those of 1990. The number of those who claimed to be fully or primarily Hungarian during those two census years has declined by nearly 11 percent (from 1,776,902 to 1,582,302), while the number of those who speak primarily Hungarian in their families has dropped by almost 18 percent (from 180,000 to 147,902). During the same period Greater Pittsburgh alone lost about half a dozen Hungarian churches; the remaining ones are struggling for survival. The same fate befell Hungarian cultural and social organizations of western Pennsylvania, few of which are active today. This trend appears to be equally true for the entire Northeast, embracing the above-mentioned 10 states. It should be noted here, however, that this decline is not as evident in California and Florida, which experienced a rapid growth of Hungarians from the 1960s through the 1990s. More recently, however, even California experienced a 3.5 percent decline in its Hungarian population (from 164,903 to 159,121), and Florida gained 11.4 percent only because of its extreme popularity with retirees (from 89,587 to 99,822).

# ACCULTURATION AND ASSIMILATION

Notwithstanding earlier immigrations, the Hungarian presence in the United States was established by the large mass of rural immigrants in the three decades before World War I. These immigrants fostered their Hungarian identity and a sense of community because of their social, cultural, and psychological needs and also because of Anglo-American society's unwillingness to accept them. The same cannot be said of their American-born children, who tended to assimilate at a rapid pace. They were driven by the socioeconomic drawing power of American society, as well as by their own conscious desire to separate themselves from the world of their simple immigrant parents. Most of them managed to move up a notch or two in social status, but perhaps for this very reason many of them also left the ethnic communities founded by their parents. Their efforts to assimilate, however, were not fully successful, for although native born, they were still viewed as outsiders by the Anglo-American majority.

The situation changed significantly with the second native-born generation, whose rise to adulthood coincided with the birth of the "ethnic revolution" of the 1960s. Their embracing of this revolution led to the rediscovery of their ethnic roots. It was impeded, however, by their inability to speak Hungarian and by the gradual disintegration of viable Hungarian ethnic communities, a disintegration that began precisely at the start of this ethnic revolution. At present, most self-contained Hungarian American communities are in the process of final dissolution. A few of their cultural and religious institutions still exist, but they serve only the needs of the older generation, and very briefly those of some of the new arrivals. This dying-out process is best demonstrated in the institutional life of the oldest and largest Hungarian Catholic church and parish in the United States, St. Elizabeth of Cleveland (founded in 1892), where the ratio of burials to baptisms is nearly 20 to one.

The turn-of-the-century immigrants and their descendants provided the foundations of Hungarian American life, but their role and influence were much more limited than those of the later waves, who brought with them a high level of learning and a strong sense of historical and national consciousness. The latter were less prone to buckle under assimilative social pressures. Moreover, if they assimilated, they did so consciously. Most of them, however, retained a large degree of dual identity, which they also passed on to their second- and third-generation descendants. The latter usually moved rapidly into American professional and business circles and—

with the exception of those in the vicinity of greater New York, Cleveland, Chicago, and Los Angeles—were forced to live outside the influence of their ethnic communities. Thus, they experienced their Hungarian identity in isolation. This sense of isolation has permeated the lives of most upward-moving professionals, especially since the 1960s. Consequently, their success or lack thereof in passing their traditions on to their offspring depended and still largely depends on their dedication to the idea of dual identity. But because relatively few had the time to deal with this issue, the next generation is rapidly losing its facility to speak Hungarian and along with it its true Hungarian identity.

American-born offspring of the various immigrant waves still practice some of their folk traditions, partially during social events held at their churches and social clubs, but mostly during major folk festivals and "Hungarian Days" that are still celebrated in such large centers of Hungarian life as New Brunswick, New Jersey; Pittsburgh; and Cleveland. Although declining in numbers, the quality of these major performances has actually improved in recent years because of closer contact with Hungary and Hungarian professionals.

Misconceptions about Hungary and the Hungarians abound in the United States, although this is much less true today than in the early part of the century when they were often misidentified as Mongols or Gypsies. This was due in part to American society's minimum knowledge about Central and Eastern Europe and in part to conscious distortions by politically motivated propagandists. Today, the situation has improved significantly because of the impact of the Hungarian Revolution of 1956 and because of the enhanced number and quality of publications about Hungary, produced mostly by the American-educated offspring of the political immigrants. This improvement, however, is more noticeable among the educated classes than among the general public.

### HOLIDAYS

Hungarian Americans generally celebrate three major national holidays: March 15 (Revolution of 1848), August 20 (Saint Stephen's Day), and October 23 (Revolution of 1956). These celebrations may combine patriotic and religious elements. There is no such thing as a specifically Hungarian American holiday, perhaps because

the attention of most unassimilated Hungarian Americans is focused on the mother country.

### HEALTH AND MENTAL HEALTH ISSUES

Hungary has the highest suicide rate in the world (45-48 per 100,000). The factors connected with this suicide rate, however, appear to be limited to Hungarian society, and Hungarian Americans are no more prone to mental health problems than are other ethnic groups in the United States.

The Hungarian medical profession is of high quality, even though it does not have access to much of the modern equipment available in the United States. This does not prevent Hungarian physicians from being among the best educated, as is demonstrated by, among other things, the virtually nonexistent failure rate of Hungarian medical students on American medical examinations. This holds true both for Hungarians who have emigrated after their medical training in Hungary and Hungarian Americans who attend Hungarian medical schools and then return to take their examinations in the United States.

# LANGUAGE

Hungarian is classified as a Finno-Ugric language and is part of the larger Ural-Altaic linguistic family. The most distinctive characteristic of these languages is that they are agglutinative—that is, words are extended into complex expressions through the use of prefixes and suffixes. One example will conveniently serve to illustrate. The meaning of a single word, *szent* (saint), can be changed by adding numerous prefixes and suffixes as follows (hyphens indicate the additions): *szent-ség* (sanctity), *szent-ség-ed* (your sanctity), *szent-ség-eid-del* (with your sanctity), *szent-ség-eid-del* (with your sanctities), *meg-szent-ségel-és-ed* (your sanctification), *meg-szent-ség-telenít-hetetlen-ség-ed-del* (with your ability to withstand desanctification).

The closest linguistic relatives of the Hungarians are the Finns and the Estonians, but the Hungarians are also distantly related to the Turkic peoples. This is due both to their common roots and to the renewal of contacts through the mixing of Finno-Ugric and Turkic tribes during the first nine centuries of the Christian Era.

Before the conquest of Hungary, the Hungarians had their own runic script. After their conversion to Christianity, they borrowed the Latin liturgical language and alphabet and adapted this alphabet to the phonetic properties of the Hungarian language. This was done by doubling up letters to represent a single sound: "cs" ("ch"), "gy" ("dy"), "ly" ("y"), "ny" (soft "n"), "sz" ("s"), "ty" (soft "t"), "zs" ("zh"), "dzs" ("dzh"); or by adding diacritical marks ("á," "é," "í," "ö," "ő," "ü," "ű"). In many instances the accent marks not only signify the pronunciation but also alter the meaning of the word—for example: *sor* (row), *sör* (beer); *bor* (wine), *bör* (skin); *sas* (eagle), *sás* (sedge); *szar* (excrement), *szár* (stem). The meaning of a single word can be changed several times simply by adding or subtracting a diacritical mark—for example: *kerek* (round), *kerék* (wheel), *kérek* (I am requesting), *kérék* (I have requested).

The English language has had an impact on how Hungarian Americans speak Hungarian. This was particularly true for the less educated immigrants, who readily mixed their simple Hungarian with working-class English. Thus, they rapidly developed a language of their own known as "Hunglish" (Hungarian English), which introduced English words into the Hungarian, but transformed them to fit Hungarian pronunciation and orthography: *trén* (train), *plész* (place), *szalon* (saloon), *bedrám* (bedroom), *atrec* (address), *tájm* (time), *szendsztón* (sandstone), *gud báj* (good-bye), *foriner* (foreigner), *fandri* (foundry), *fánesz* (furnace), *bakszi* (box), *burdos* (boarder), *burdosház* (boarding house), *görl* (girl), *groszeri* (grocery).

There was also a reverse version of Hunglish that may be called "Engarian" (English Hungarian), which adjusted the primitive English to the ears of the immigrants. The result was two hodge-podge languages that were barely comprehensible to Hungarians or Americans who did not speak both languages—for example: *Szé, miszter, gimi order, maj hen trók brók!* (Say, Mister, give me the order. My hand truck broke.). Such usage is no longer common, largely because the Americanized offspring of the turn-of-the-century immigrants have switched to English but also because the more educated post-World War II immigrants never really acquired it.

## GREETINGS AND POPULAR EXPRESSIONS

Common greetings are as follows (all words are pronounced with the accent on the first syllable): *Jó reggelt* ("yo reggelt")—Good morning; *Jó napot* ("yo nahpote")—Good day; *Jó estét* ("yo eshtayt") —Good evening; *Jó éjszakát* ("yo aysahkaht")—

Good night; *Kezitcsókolom* ("kezeet choakho-lohm")—I kiss your hand; *Szervusz* or *Szerbusz* ("servoos, serboos")—Hello, Hi; *Szia* ("seeyah") —Hi, Hello; *Viszontlátásra* ("veesoant-lah-tahshrah")—Good-bye, See you again; *Isten áldjon meg* ("eeshten ahldyoan meg")—God bless you. Other popular expressions include: *Boldog újévet* ("bohldogh ooy-ayveth")—Happy New Year; *Kellemes húsvétot* ("kellehmesh hooshvay-toth")—Happy Easter; *Kellemes karácsonyi ünnepeket* ("kellehmesh karahchoanyi ünnepeketh")— Merry Christmas; *Boldog ünnepeket* ("bohldogh ünnepeketh")—Happy Holidays; *Egészségedre* ("eggayshaygedreh")—To your health (spoken when toasting).

# FAMILY AND COMMUNITY DYNAMICS

After the early and predominantly male phases of economic immigration abated, Hungarian American immigrant communities assumed a traditional and stable family structure. By the 1920s, most immigrants had resolved to stay permanently in the United States. They established families, had American-born children, and became intimately involved in the social lives of their churches, fraternal societies, and cultural institutions that in the past served as their extended families. The structure survived almost intact into the 1960s, although with only limited participation by the political immigrants of the interwar and postwar periods. Unable to agree on a common platform with the earlier economic immigrants, the latter usually founded their own organizations and pursued their familial and social activities within these more politically oriented groups.

With the exception of the relatively few immigrants who came during the 1960s through the 1980s—many of them from the Hungarian-inhabited regions surrounding Hungary—very few Hungarians have ever received public assistance. Traditionally, accepting handouts has been perceived in Hungarian society as an admission of failure. This view was much less prevalent among the more recent immigrants, who had become accustomed to state assistance under the communist social system.

Immigrant life and ethnic experience in America transformed basic traditional patterns of family life, resulting in a hybrid set of customs. In terms of everyday existence, Hungarian family life conforms to American patterns, but with a greater emphasis on education. The role of women has been enhanced compared with the still male-dominated Hungarian model. Adjustment to American custom is also evident in the area of dating, marriage, and divorce. Until a generation ago, dating practices were very strict and circumscribed. More recently, they have loosened, as has the commitment to a lasting marriage. Thus, whereas a generation ago divorce among Hungarian immigrants was rare, today it is almost as common as it is for American society as a whole.

Philanthropic activities among Hungarian Americans tend to be aimed at specific groups of Hungarians. During the past three decades, these were oriented almost exclusively toward the Hungarian minorities in the areas surrounding Hungary. There are, of course, exceptions to the rule, but these exceptions are usually connected with the philanthropic activities of the few super-rich, the best-known of whom is the billionaire investor George Soros.

# RELIGION

Hungary has been a Roman Catholic country since its conversion to Christianity in the late tenth and early eleventh centuries. This religious uniformity was shattered only in the sixteenth century, when Protestantism entered the country and spread, especially in its Calvinist form. After a century of intense struggle, Catholicism remained strong in the country's western and central regions, while Calvinism came to dominate its eastern regions. This Catholic-Calvinist rivalry was complicated somewhat by the presence of a significant minority of Lutherans (Evangelicals), Jews, Greek/Byzantine Catholics, and Unitarians, as well as by a few other small Christian sects. Yet, in spite of its losses to rival faiths, Roman Catholicism retained its dominant position as Hungary's only official "state religion" until the communist takeover in 1948.

The religious divisions in Hungary also came to be reflected in Hungarian American society. The Calvinists were the first to establish their pioneer congregations in 1891 in Cleveland and in Pittsburgh, to be followed in 1892 by the Roman Catholics (St. Elizabeth of Hungary Church, Cleveland) and in 1907 by the Lutherans (Cleveland). These early congregations soon sprouted scores of other Hungarian churches throughout the Northeast. As a result, by the 1930s Hungarian Americans had nearly 140 Calvinist, more than 60 Roman Catholic, and about ten Lutheran churches, as well as perhaps two dozen other prayer houses. Although the Calvinists had the greatest number of churches, their congregations were small, and as such they represented only one-third as many faithful as did the Roman Catholics.

Roman Catholics, Calvinists, and Lutherans together constituted slightly over 90 percent of all religious affiliations of Hungarian Americans. The other eight to ten percent was made up of smaller denominations including the Byzantine Catholics, Jews, Baptists, and Adventists. Because of their small numbers, however, none of the latter had more than a limited and passing influence on Hungarian American life.

The religious practices of Hungarian Roman Catholics and Protestants in the United States are basically identical to those of their coreligionists in Hungary and are also similar to the practices of their American counterparts. Although religious practices did not change after emigration, the social significance of the congregations and the position and the role of the parish priests and pastors underwent significant changes. In Hungary the religious congregations and their priests or ministers were supported by their respective mother churches through an obligatory religious tax. As a result these congregations were centrally controlled, with little or no input from the members of the congregations. This was particularly true of the Roman Catholic Church, which had retained its monarchical structure from the Middle Ages. Although Calvinist and Lutheran congregations did elect their pastors even in Hungary, the powers of the presbytery (church council) were much more limited than in the United States. This was true not only because of the somewhat authoritarian nature of traditional Hungarian society but also because the pastors did not depend on the financial support of their parishioners. In Hungary, therefore, it was the priests and the ministers who controlled the congregation, and not vice versa.

After emigration, this relationship changed significantly. Much of the control over church affairs slipped into the hands of the members of the church council. This change in the power relationship was due both to the lack of state support for religion and to the fact that now the members of the congregations were paying for the upkeep of their churches and their pastors.

Just as the role of the church leaders had changed, the function of the church had also changed. Traditionally, American churches have

A Hungarian refugee
reunites with his family in
a New Jersey airport in
1957.

always combined religious and social functions—a phenomenon that was largely unknown in Europe. This American tradition was accepted by the immigrant churches, which consequently ceased to function solely as houses of prayer. They now also assumed the role of social clubs, where members of the congregation combined their search for spiritual salvation with an ongoing attempt to fulfill their earthly social needs. As such, immigrant churches lost some of the sanctity of their Old World counterparts.

The climax of Hungarian religious life in America was reached in the period between the 1920s and 1960s. By the 1970s, however, a process of slow decay had set in, which during the 1980s had accelerated to the point where several Hungarian ethnic churches were closing their doors every year.

During the past 100 years of Hungarian religious life in the United States, all denominations have been plagued by dissension, but none more

so that the Hungarian Calvinist (Reformed) Church. Within the first quarter century after having taken root in America, this dissension has led to the establishment of several competing Calvinist denominations—a process that resulted in a new subdenomination as late as 1982. While some of these conflicts and fragmentations were of an ideological and administrative nature (e.g., their relationship to the mother church in Hungary), most of them were really the result of personal animosity among the clergy. American social practices make it easy for anyone to establish a new church, while personality conflicts and group squabbles often result in institutional divorces. At the moment Hungarian Calvinists are still divided into a half dozen rival and competing churches that are held together only by the awareness of their common roots and by their membership in the Hungarian Reformed Federation (HRF). Founded in 1898 as a fraternal association, the HRF also serves as a force of unity among Hungarian Calvinists.

## Employment and Economic Traditions

Hungarian immigrants have been involved in all facets of American economic life, with the level of their employment depending for the most part on their social background. Those who came before the mid-nineteenth century were individual adventurers who were well prepared for all eventualities in the New World. Although few in numbers, most of those who stayed proved to be successful. Some of them became well-known merchants in Philadelphia, Baltimore, and New Orleans, while others became well-respected professors at American universities. Whatever they did, they did it well, for they could rely on a good education and on the self-assurance common to well-born individuals.

To a large degree this was also true for the 3,000 to 4,000 Forty-niners who immigrated after the defeat of the Hungarian Revolution of 1848. Belonging mostly to the gentry, they had no intention of becoming dirt farmers or laborers in America. They spread Hungary's image as the land of a valiant "noble nation," but only a minority were able to adjust to America's pioneer society. This was true even though a few of them also became involved in the establishment of Hungarian colonies in the West, such as László Újházy (1795-1870), a high-ranking official of the revolutionary government, who founded New Buda in Iowa in 1852. After trying their hands at many things, a thousand of the Forty-niners joined the Union armies in the Civil War, after which a good number of them went into diplomatic service or into various major business ventures in the West.

The next wave of immigrants came during the late nineteenth and early twentieth centuries with the intention of repatriating after four or five years with enough capital to make themselves into prosperous farmers. Few of them achieved this goal, and virtually all of them became unskilled or semiskilled workers in America's bustling industries. They were the peons of America's Gilded Age, who contributed their brawn to American coal mines and steel smelters, and who produced the mythical Hungarian American hero, Joe Magarac, who could bend steel bars with his bare hands.

Each of the next four immigration waves contributed to the abatement of this stereotype. These waves comprised the interwar "intellectual immigrants"; the post-World War II "political immigrants"; the Fifty-sixers; and finally the political-economic immigrants of the past four decades. Given their achievements in Europe, the intellectual immigrants moved immediately into the highest American intellectual and scientific circles and almost overnight created the myth of the uniqueness of Hungarian talent.

The political immigrants, or DPs, represented the military-legal-administrative leadership of interwar Hungary and had few transferable skills; thus, many of them were forced to engage in physical labor. Yet, their learning, cultural background, and personal bearing immediately revealed to their fellow American workers that they were of a different caliber. Many of them eventually did manage to transfer to white-collar work, although it was largely their American-educated children who moved up rapidly into the professions.

The Fifty-sixers differed from the DPs in their relative youth, orientation toward transferable technical and practical skills, and diminished cultural background—the product of a decade of communist restructuring of Hungarian society. Yet they and the American-educated children of the DPs produced a class of professionals that penetrated all aspects of American scientific, scholarly, artistic, literary, and business life.

The final immigration wave began during the 1960s and is still going on today. It is characterized by a slow but gradual influx of professionals and professionally oriented individuals. During the 1960s through the 1980s, political persecution was the ostensible motive for their immigration. Since the collapse of communism, they have come as needed professionals.

According to a recent survey by the *New York Times*, Hungarians are not among the most highly regarded ethnic groups in America, but they are certainly among the most successful. They have also managed to eradicate the Hunky stereotype that was unwittingly transmitted by their less fortunate predecessors.

## Politics and Government

The political activism of the Hungarians in America reaches back to the mid-nineteenth century, when Lajos Kossuth (1802-1894) visited the United States (1851-1852) and in a highly celebrated tour of the country urged Americans to intervene on behalf of defeated Hungary by supporting Hungary's struggle against Austria. Although the Hungarian statesman's presence created a veritable "Kossuth craze" in America, the results were disappointing. Despite its outward expression of sympathy, the U.S. government was unwilling to budge from its policy of isolationism. Although unsuccessful in its political aims, Kossuth's presence did create a positive image of Hungary, as well as stir up pro-Hungarian sentiment among the American public. The image and sentiment survived until the turn of the century. The final blow to the Kossuth-inspired image came during World War I, when Austria-Hungary sided with imperial Germany.

Although the Austro-Hungarian Empire disappeared and historic Hungary was dismembered after the war, anti-Hungarian sentiment resurfaced after Hungary's forced alliance with Italy and Germany during World War II. Following the war, Hungary came to be regarded as a Soviet satellite. The daring anti-Soviet uprising of 1956 once again stirred pro-Hungarian sentiment. The American image of Hungary has been improving ever since, both because Hungary was among the first of the Soviet-dominated nations to liberalize economically and politically during the 1960s and because of the increasingly sophisticated political activism of Hungarian American lobby groups.

Hungarians established several mutual aid societies in the second half of the nineteenth century, but not until 1906 did they create the first successful political organization, the American-Hungarian Federation (AHF), which is still in existence. The twin goals of the AHF were to protect the interests of the Hungarian immigrants and to promote the cause of Hungary in the United States. During the first decade of its existence, the AHF worked toward these goals in close cooperation with Hungary. During World War I, particularly after the United States entered the war on the opposite side, this task became impossible. Following the war the AHF proved unsuccessful in its efforts to influence American foreign policy on postwar treaties. Yet, during the interwar period—in conjunction with the largest Hungarian fraternal organizations (i.e., Verhovay, Rákóczi, Bridgeport, the Reformed Federation)—it conducted a steady propaganda campaign to revise the unfair terms of the Treaty of Trianon (1920). This task became increasingly difficult during the late 1930s, when Hungary began to regain some of its former territory with the help of Germany and Italy.

The darkest and most difficult period in Hungarian political activism came during World War II, when the AHF and the major fraternal organizations were forced to defend Hungary's territorial gains while maintaining their support for the American war effort. To prove their loyalty to the United States, more than 50,000 Hungarians served in the U.S. armed forces, and all Hungarian American organizations bought U.S. defense bonds and made repeated declarations of allegiance. Toward the end of the war, they organized the American-Hungarian Relief Committee, whose members undertook a major effort to send aid to their devastated homeland, as well as to hundreds of thousands of Hungarians who had been trapped in German and Austrian refugee camps. Moreover, in 1948 and 1950, the AHF and the major Hungarian fraternal societies supported the passage of the two Displaced Persons Acts that brought almost 18,000 Hungarian political refugees to the United States.

The appearance of the post-World War II political immigrants—the DPs during the early 1950s and the Fifty-sixers after the Revolution of 1956—created a completely new situation. Much better educated and more involved politically than most of their predecessors, the newcomers created their own organizations. Some of the most vocal and active of these associations included the American branch of the Fraternal Association of Hungarian Veterans (1947), the Cleveland-based Committee for Liberation (1951), and the Hungarian National Committee (1948)—the last of which was viewed by the U.S. government as a virtual government in exile.

The appearance of the Fifty-sixers added a new color to this political spectrum. Although a number of them joined existing DP organizations, many of them also founded their own associations. The most important of these was the Hungarian Freedom Fighter's Federation (1957), although very soon it was joined by others with nearly identical names. During the 1970s several minority-oriented organizations were created specifically to help the cause of the increasingly oppressed Hungarian minorities in the neighboring states. These included the Committee for Human Rights in Romania, the Transylvania World Federation, the Transylvanian Committee, and the Hungarian Human Rights Committee, all of which were especially concerned with the plight of the Hungarian minorities under the oppressive rule of the communist Ceauşescu regime in Romania.

From the late 1950s through the early 1980s, most of the nonminority-oriented organizations were concerned primarily with the liberation of Hungary and then with soliciting U.S. government help to undermine the communist regime. Throughout this period the politically active new immigrants had little concern for American domestic politics; their attention was turned to Hungary. Thus, after becoming citizens, they usually voted with the Republican Party, which they perceived to be tougher on communism. As opposed to them, the turn-of-the-century economic immigrants and their American-born descendants paid only lip service to Hungary. They were much more concerned with domestic politics, and with bread-and-butter issues, than with the problems of communism. Thus, they voted mostly Democratic.

The rise of a new generation among the political immigrants during the 1970s and 1980s also produced some changes. On the one hand, the American-born or American-educated members of the younger generations became involved in U.S. domestic politics in both political parties. On the other hand, they began to assume a much more realistic approach toward Hungary and its "goulash communism." Some of them assumed the leadership of the AHF and carried their pragmatism into its politics. While understandable, this act split the AHF and brought about the foundation of the National Federation of Hungarian Americans (NFHA) in 1984, and subsequently several rival organizations, including the very active and influential Hungarian American Coalition (HAC) in 1992.

The collapse of communism and the rise of a nationalist government under the Hungarian Democratic Forum (1989-90) produced a general euphoria among Hungarian Americans, and also an upsurge in their desire to help their homeland. The euphoria coincided with Hungary's unheard of popularity in the world for its role in undermining communism. This euphoria and popularity, however, did not last. The country's social and economic problems produced a general disillusionment that was also felt by Hungarian Americans, many of whose hopes also remained unrealized.

At present, most Hungarian Americans have become American citizens and are heavily involved in the political life of both U.S. political parties. At the same time they still display considerable interest in Hungary. Even though somewhat disillusioned with the way things are going in Hungary, they continue to pursue pro-Hungarian lobbying efforts through several umbrella organizations (AHF, NFHA, HAC), as well as through their presence in the U.S. Congress. The most visible and active among the Hungarian congressional representatives is the Fifty-sixer Tom Lantos (1928- ) from California (1980- ), who in recent years has become increasingly involved in Hungarian-related political activities.

## MILITARY

Relative to their size as an ethnic group, more Hungarian Americans served in the Civil War than any other nationality. Of the approximately 4,000 Hungarians in the United States (including women and children) at the outbreak of the war in 1861, more than 800—at least three-fourths of the adult male population—served in the Union armies. Among them were two major generals, five brigadier generals, 15 colonels and lieutenant colonels, 13 majors, 12 captains, about four dozen first and second lieutenants, and scores of noncommissioned officers.

The most prominent of the officers was Major General Julius H. Stahel (1825-1912)—known in Hungary before his emigration as Gyula Számvald. General Stahel became a close confidant of President Lincoln and the first Hungarian recipient of the Congressional Medal of Honor. Among the nearly 1,000 Hungarians in the Union Army was the young Joseph Pulitzer (1817-1911), who subsequently became the king of American journalism and the founder of the famous literary prize that bears his name.

# INDIVIDUAL AND GROUP CONTRIBUTIONS

Following Hungary's dismemberment after World War I, many educated Hungarians—engineers, physicians, sociologists, educators, and lawyers—came to the United States to pursue their livelihood. In the 1930s their numbers were increased by those fleeing the spread of fascism in Central Europe. In this category were numerous internationally known scientists, social scientists, musicologists, artists, filmmakers, and other persons of unusual talent.

## ECONOMICS

From the late nineteenth century, Hungarians have made important contributions to U.S. industry and finance. Two of the earliest entrepreneurs were the Black (Schwartz) and Kundtz families. The Black family founded a series of garment factories and department stores, while Tivador Kundtz (1852-1937) established the White Machine factory. These two families employed and aided thousands of fellow immigrant Hungarians.

Modern entrepreneurs include the billionaire financier George Soros (1930- ), who has played a significant role in the transformation of the former Soviet world through philanthropic efforts such as the establishment of the Budapest- and Prague-based Central European University; and Andrew Grove (born András Gróf; 1936- ), who as the founder and president of Intel Corporation created the world's largest manufacturer of computer chips.

## FILM AND ENTERTAINMENT

Two Hungarians were influential in the development of the Hollywood film industry: Adolph Zukor (1873-1976), the founder of Paramount Pictures; and William Fox (1879-1952), the founder of Twentieth Century-Fox. Zukor and Fox transformed the stylish Biedermeier culture of the Austro-Hungarian Empire into the glamorous society portrayed in Hollywood film.

Other pioneers in the film industry included directors/producers Michael Curtiz (born Michael Kertész; 1888-1962), Sir Alexander Korda (1893-1956), George Cukor (1899-1983), and Joseph Pasternak (1901- ), as well as film stars Leslie Howard (born Árpád Steiner; 1893-1943), Bela Lugosi (1883-1956) of Dracula fame, Tony Curtis (born Bernard Schwartz; 1925- ), and the Gabor sisters, Zsa-Zsa, Eva, and Magda. In this category also belongs the magician Harry Houdini (born Erich Weisz; 1874-1926).

## MUSIC

By the time the internationally known composers Béla Bartók (1881-1945) and Ernő Dohnányi (1877-1960) emigrated in the 1940s, the American cultural scene was already peopled by such Hungarian composers as Fritz Reiner (1888-1963), George Szell (1897-1970), Eugene Ormandy (1899-1985), Antal Dorati (1906-1988), and Sir Georg Solti (1912- ). Hungarians were also present on Broadway in popular American musicals. The best-loved of them was Sigmund Romberg (1887-1951), who was perhaps the most successful transplanter of the Viennese and the Budapest operetta. Also significant was the contribution of Miklós Rózsa (1907- ), who worked with Sir Alexander Korda and wrote the music to some of the great American films.

## SCIENCE AND MATHEMATICS

Three Hungarians assisted Enrico Fermi with the breakthroughs in atomic fission that resulted in the development of the atomic bomb: Leo Szilard (1898-1964), Eugene Wigner (1902-1995), and Edward Teller (1908- ). Other major contributors are Theodore von Kármán (1881-1963), father of the heat and quantum theory; mathematician and father of the computer Johann von Neumann (1903-1957); and Zoltán Bay (1900-1992), the pioneer in radar astronomy.

George Pólya (1887-1985) and Gábor Szegő (1895-1985) were responsible for making Stanford University one of the world's premier centers of mathematics. A much younger exponent of finite mathematics and its application, John George Kemény (1926- ) later became the president of Dartmouth College.

Other leading Hungarian scientists included the Nobel laureates Georg Karl Hevesy (1855-1966), Albert Szent-Györgyi (1893-1986), Georg von Békésy (1899-1972), and Dennis Gabor (1900-1979). The list also includes several members of the Polányi family: the social philosopher Karl Polányi (1886-1964), the physicist-philosopher Michael Polányi (1891-1976), as well as the latter's son, John Charles Polányi (1926- ), who won the Nobel Prize for chemistry in 1986.

# MEDIA

### PRINT

*Amerikai-Kanadai Magyar Élet (American-Canadian Hungarian Life).*
Founded in 1959 as *Amerikai Magyar Élet*, this weekly has been under the control of Bishop Tibor Dömötör of the Free Hungarian Reformed Church since 1986.

**Contact:** Elizabeth Schmidt, Managing Editor.
**Address:** 2637 Copley Road, Akron, Ohio 44321.

Telephone: (216) 666-2637.
Fax: (216) 666-4746.

### Amerikai Magyar Szó (American Hungarian Word).

Weekly newspaper printed in Hungarian.

Contact: Z. Deak, Editor.
Address: 130 East 16th Street, New York, New York 10003.
Telephone: (212) 254-0397.

### Californiai Magyarság (California Hungarians).

Founded in 1924 as a middle-of-the-road regional newspaper, it is now a national paper that has retained its moderate stance.

Contact: Mária Fényes, Editor and Publisher.
Address: 207 South Western Avenue, Suite 201, Los Angeles, California 90004.
Telephone: (213) 463-3473.
Fax: (213) 384-7642.

### Hungarian Insights.

A quarterly publication that provides news and information on Hungarian culture, history, and business.

Contact: Lel Somogyi, Editor.
Address: 6020 Pearl Road, Cleveland, Ohio 44130.
Telephone: (216) 842-4651.

### Hungarian Studies Newsletter.

Quarterly publication of the American Hungarian Foundation; publishes news of the Foundation as well as information for English-speaking scholars concerned with Hungarian studies.

Contact: August J. Molnar, Editor.
Address: American Hungarian Foundation, P.O. Box 1084, New Brunswick, New Jersey 08903.
Telephone: (201) 846-5777.

### Magyar Elet (Hungarian Life).

An independent weekly newspaper published in Hungarian and circulated throughout Canada and the United States.

Contact: Laszlo Schnee, Editor.
Address: 21 Vaughan Road, Suite 201, Toronto, Ontario, Canada M6G 2N2.
Telephone: (416) 652-6370.
Fax: (416) 652-6370.

### Magyarok Vasárnapja (Hungarians' Sunday).

Founded in Cleveland in 1894, for its first hundred years this paper was called Katolikus Magyarok Vasárnapja (Catholic Hungarians' Sunday). Since the change in ownership in 1993, it has lost its religious character and has become the voice of populist nationalism.

Contact: Loránt Szász, Editor and Publisher.
Address: P.O. Box 4442, Thousand Oaks, California 91359.
Telephone: (818) 707-1548.
Fax: (818) 597-9867.

### Szabadság (Liberty).

Published for the East Coast readership under the title Amerikai Magyar Népszava (American Hungarian People's Voice), the two papers, which were founded in 1891 and 1899 respectively, were once rivals, but after the owner-editor of Szabadság bought its rival in 1949, they were gradually merged into a single paper under two different titles.

Contact: Eva Nadai, Editor; or, Judith Fliegler, English Editor.
Address: 8140 Mayfield Road, Cleveland, Ohio 44026-2441.
Telephone: (216) 729-7200.
Fax: (216) 729-7250.

### Új Világ (New World).

Founded in 1971, this paper was a neutral middle-of-the-road weekly until the early 1990s, when it became the voice of the right wing.

Contact: Viktor K. Molnár, Editor and Publisher.
Address: 15005 South Vermont Avenue, Gardena, California 90247.
Telephone: (310) 719-1078.
Fax: (310) 719-8918.

### William Penn Life.

Founded in 1965 to replace an earlier Hungarian-language version, Vehovayak Lapj (Verhovay News), it is a small English-language monthly geared toward the William Penn Association, the largest Hungarian fraternal organization in America. Its influence is limited to its membership, which is made up largely of third- and fourth-generation descendants of the turn-of-the-century economic immigrants.

Contact: Elmer E. Vargo, Editor.
Address: William Penn Association, 709 Brighton Road, Pittsburgh, Pennsylvania 15233-1821.

Telephone: (412) 231-2979.
Fax: (412) 231-8535.


**TELEVISION**

**The Nationality Broadcasting Network.**
Located in Cleveland, this network broadcasts Hungarian programs everyday via satellite throughout North America.

Contact: Miklós Kossányi, President.
Address: 11906 Madison Avenue, Cleveland, Ohio.
Telephone: (216) 221-0330.
Fax: (216) 221-3638.


# ORGANIZATIONS AND ASSOCIATIONS

**American Hungarian Federation (AHF)
(Amerikai Magyar Szövetség [AMSZ]).**
Founded in Cleveland in 1906, the AHF is the oldest umbrella organization of Hungarian Americans. After being based in Washington, D.C., from the 1940s to the 1970s, in the early 1980s it transferred its office to Akron. Following an internal controversy that resulted in the formation of the rival National Federation of American Hungarians in 1984, the AHF is now the second-largest Hungarian American umbrella organization, with about 55 member organizations. Like its rival organizations, it conducts lobbying activities on behalf of Hungarian causes.

Contact: Rev. Tibor Dömötör, President.
Address: 2631 Copley Road, Akron, Ohio 44321.
Telephone: (216) 666-9777.
Fax: (216) 666-4746.


**American Hungarian Folklore Centrum
(AHFC).**
Supports and promotes Hungarian studies and folk culture within the scholarly and public life of America.

Contact: Kalman Magyar, Director.
Address: P.O. Box 262, Bogota, New Jersey 07603.
Telephone: (201) 836-4869.


**American Hungarian Reformed Federation
(AHRF) (Amerikai Magyar Református
Egyesület [AMRE]).**
Founded in 1898, the AHRF is the second-largest and only religiously based Hungarian fraternal association in existence. It has about 20,000

members, and although it is now primarily an insurance company, it continues to support Hungarian cultural activities and also engages in some lobbying efforts on behalf of Hungarian causes.

Contact: George Dózsa, President.
Address: 2001 Massachusetts Avenue, N.W., Washington, D.C., 20036-1011.
Telephone: (202) 328-2630.
Fax: (202) 228-7984.


**Hungarian American Coalition (HAC)
(Magyar-Amerikai Koalíció [MAK]).**
Founded in 1992, the HAC is the most recent of the Hungarian umbrella organizations. Politically, it has a moderate-centrist, pragmatic orientation. It attempts to carry out an effective lobbying effort on behalf of Hungarian causes in Washington, D.C.

Contact: Edit Lauer, President.
Address: Suite 850, 818 Connecticut Avenue, N.W., Washington, D.C. 20006.


**Hungarian Association of Cleveland (Cleveland
Magyar Társaság).**
Founded in 1958 in Austria and transferred to Cleveland in 1952, the Hungarian Association has been the most influential organization of the post-World War II immigrants, or DPs. Since 1961 it has organized annual congresses (the proceedings of which are published in its yearbook *Krónika*). In 1965 it sponsored the foundation of the Árpád Academy (*Árpád Akadémia*) to recognize the scholarly, scientific, and artistic achievements of Hungarians throughout the world. In 1990 it was responsible for the establishment of one of the rival umbrella organizations of the American Hungarian Federation, the National Federation of Hungarian Americans (NFHA) (Magyar Amerikaiak Országos Szövetsége [MAOSZ]). The Hungarian Association of Cleveland and its member organizations are ideologically conservative, representing essentially the views of interwar Hungary. The HAC functions and publishes primarily in Hungarian.

Contact: Gyula Nádas, President.
Address: 1450 Grace Avenue, Cleveland, Ohio 44107.
Telephone: (216) 226-4089.


**Hungarian Cultural Foundation (HCF).**
Interested in preserving Hungarian cultural heritage in the United States and elsewhere in the English-speaking world.

**Contact:** Joseph Ertavy-Barath, President.

**Address:** P.O. Box 364, Stone Mountain, Georgia 30086.

**Telephone:** (404) 377-2600.


### Hungarian Scout Association in Exile (HSAE) (Külföldi Magyar Cserkészszövetség).

Founded in 1947 in Germany and transferred to the United States in 1951, the HSAE is a worldwide organization, with well over a hundred scout troops, whose goal is to uphold the traditions of Hungarian scouting in the Hungarian language.

**Contact:** Gábor Bodnár, President.

**Address:** Post Office Box 68, Garfield, New Jersey 07026.

**Telephone:** (201) 772-8810.

**Fax:** (201) 772-5145.


### National Federation of Hungarian Americans (NFAH) (Amerikai Magyarok Országos Szövetség).

Founded in 1984, as a splinter group of the much older American-Hungarian Federation, the NFAH has since grown into the largest umbrella organization of Hungarian Americans, with more than one hundred institutional members. Its primary function is to serve as a lobby group for Hungarian and Hungarian American causes in Washington, D.C., and to aid Hungary's transformation toward democracy.

**Contact:** László Pásztor, National President.

**Address:** 717 Second Street, N.E., Washington, D.C., 20002.

**Telephone:** (202) 546-3003.

**Fax:** (202) 543-8425; or, (202) 547-0392.


### William Penn Association (WPA).

Founded in 1886, as the Verhovay Aid Association, the WPA is the largest Hungarian fraternal association in North America. It assumed its present name in 1955, when it absorbed its largest rival, the Rákóczi Federation of Bridgeport, Connecticut. Although primarily an insurance company, the WPA still sponsors certain Hungarian cultural functions. Recently, the WPA has transferred much of its archives and library to the Hungarian Heritage Center of New Brunswick, New Jersey.

**Contact:** Elmer E. Vargo, National President.

**Address:** 709 Brighton Road, Pittsburgh, Pennsylvania 15233-1821.

**Telephone:** (412) 231-2979.

**Fax:** (412) 231-8538.


# MUSEUMS AND RESEARCH CENTERS

### American-Hungarian Foundation (AHF), Hungarian Heritage Center.

Founded in 1955, the AHF has grown into a major Hungarian cultural foundation that operates the Hungarian Heritage Center in New Brunswick, New Jersey. In addition to its museum and visitors' center, the Hungarian Heritage Center possesses one of the largest collections of archival materials relating to Hungarian Americans, as well as one of the largest Hungarica libraries in the United States (40,000 volumes). The library is by far the best source of material on the Hungarian American past.

**Contact:** August J. Molnar, President.

**Address:** 300 Somerset Street, New Brunswick, New Jersey 08903-1084.

**Telephone:** (908) 846-5777.

**Fax:** (908) 249-7033.


### Hungarian Chair, Department of Uralic and Altaic Studies, Indiana University.

Founded in 1979 within the confines of an internationally known Department of Uralic and Altaic Studies that developed during the 1950s, the Hungarian Chair is in charge of the only Ph.D.-oriented Hungarian Studies program in North America. It draws heavily on the expertise of the other members of the department, as well as on Indiana University's multidisciplinary Russian and East European Institute and its strong library collection in Hungarian (25,000 volumes) and Russian and East European (200,000 volumes) material. It is also in charge of organizing several conferences every year, as well as publishing books and periodicals in the field of Hungarian studies. The only other Hungarian chair in North America is at the University of Toronto and publishes the *Hungarian Studies Review*.

**Contact:** Hungarian Chair Professor.

**Address:** Department of Uralic and Altaic Studies, Indiana University, Bloomington, Indiana 47405-2401.

**Telephone:** (812) 855-2223.

**Fax:** (812) 855-7500.


### Hungarian Institute, Rutgers University.

Founded in 1992 with the financial support of the Hungarian government, the Hungarian Institute is in an early stage of development and at the moment is involved only in undergraduate education. It draws heavily on the intellectual and library resources of Rutgers University (Hungarica, 2,000 volumes), as well as on the library of the nearby American-Hungarian Foundation (Hungarica, 40,000 volumes).

**Address:** Rutgers University, New Brunswick, New Jersey 08903-5049.

**Telephone:** (908) 932-1367.

**Fax:** (908) 932-6723.

Several North American libraries have strong Hungarica collections, the most noteworthy of which are: the Library of Congress (60,000 volumes); Columbia University (50,000 volumes); Indiana University (25,000 volumes); University of Chicago (25,000 volumes, including the newly acquired Szathmáry Library and Archives); Harvard University (20,000 volumes); Stanford University and the Hoover Institution (20,000 volumes); New York Public Library (20,000 volumes); University of Illinois (15,000 volumes); University of Toronto (10,000 volumes); Yale University (10,000 volumes); and at least another half dozen libraries with collections of between 5,000 and 10,000 volumes (Berkeley, Cornell, Duke, Notre Dame, UCLA, University of Washington).

### Hungarian Reformed Federation Library and Archives, Bethlen Home.

The Bethlen Home is the center of American Hungarian Calvinism. Located about 50 miles east of Pittsburgh, it houses an Old Age Home and the Archives of the Hungarian Reformed Church, including the papers of all dissolved congregations. The Bethlen Home also has a significant library of Hungarian American materials. The annual meetings of the Hungarian Reformed Federation (founded in 1898 and based in Washington, D.C.) also take place there, with the representatives of all Reformed congregations, irrespective of their current affiliations, in attendance.

**Contact:** The Reverend Paul Kovács, Director.

**Address:** P.O. Box 657, Ligonier, Pennsylvania 15658.

**Telephone:** (412) 238-6711.

**Fax:** (412) 238-3175.

# SOURCES FOR ADDITIONAL STUDY

Lengyel, Emil. *Americans from Hungary*. Philadelphia and New York: J. B. Lippincott, 1948; reprinted, Westport, Connecticut: Greenwood, 1974.

McGuire, James Patrick. *The Hungarian Texans*. San Antonio: University of Texas, Institute of Texan Culture, 1993.

Papp, Susan M. *Hungarian Americans and Their Communities in Cleveland*. Cleveland: Cleveland Ethnic Heritage Studies, Cleveland State University, 1981.

Puskás, Julianna. *From Hungary to the United States, 1880-1914*. Budapest: Akadémiai Kiadó, 1982.

Tezla, Albert. *The Hazardous Quest: Hungarian Immigrants in the United States, 1895-1920*. Budapest: Corvina, 1993.

Várdy, Steven Béla. *Clio's Art in Hungary and in Hungarian-America*. New York: Columbia University Press, 1985.

————. *The Hungarian-Americans*. Boston: Twayne, 1985.

————. *The Hungarian Americans: The Hungarian Experience in North America*. New York and Philadelphia: Chelsea House, 1990.

Várdy, Steven Béla, and Agnes Huszár Várdy. *The Austro-Hungarian Mind: At Home and Abroad*. New York: Columbia University Press, 1989.

An ethnic group noted for their diverse cultural and religious backgrounds and geographical origins, Indonesians who live in the United States split their affection and loyalty between their newfound country and whatever part of their homeland they or their ancestors once inhabited.

# INDONESIAN AMERICANS

by
Eveline Yang

## OVERVIEW

The Republic of Indonesia is located in Southeast Asia, on an archipelago of more than 17,508 islands near the equator. The total land area is 782,665 square miles, and the sea area covers 1,222,466 square miles; altogether, the nation is approximately the size of Mexico. The name Indonesia is coined from Greek: *indos*, India and *nesos*, islands.

Indonesia consists of an array of island stepping-stones scattered in the sea between the Malay Peninsula and Australia, astride the equator and spanning about an eighth of the world's circumference. By comparison, the continental United States stretches across about a sixth of the world's circumference. The islands and island groups consist of a Pacific set and an Indian Ocean set. The Indian Ocean islands are Sumatra, Java, Bali, and the Lesser Sundas, or, in Indonesian, *Sumatera, Djawa, Bali,* and *Nusa Tenggara*. The Pacific Ocean Islands are Borneo, Celebes, and the Moluccas, or *Kalimantan, Sulawesi,* and *Malukus*.

Indonesia's climate may be described as tropical, though land temperatures and rainfall vary considerably according to altitude and relative exposure to winds sweeping in from the ocean. On the whole, temperatures vary little at any one place, and rainfall is generally heavy.

## HISTORY

By the fifteenth century, when the Renaissance was just pulling Europe from the Middle Ages, the islands of Java and Sumatra already had a thousand-year heritage of advanced civilization, spanning two major empires. From the seventh to the fourteenth century, the Buddhist kingdom of Srivijaya flourished on Sumatra. At its peak, the Srivijaya Empire reached as far as west Java and the Malay Peninsula. By the fourteenth century, the Hindu kingdom of Majapahit had risen in eastern Java. Gadjah Mada, the chief minister who ruled the empire from 1331 to 1364, succeeded in gaining allegiance from most of what is now known as modern Indonesia and much of the Malay archipelago as well.

Islam arrived in Indonesia in the twelfth century and had almost wholly supplanted Hinduism as the dominant religion in Java and Sumatra by the end of the sixteenth century. The island of Bali, however, has retained its Hindu heritage to this day. In the eastern archipelago, both Christian and Islamic proselytizing took place in the sixteenth and seventeenth centuries; currently, there are large communities of both religions on these islands.

Beginning in the early seventeenth century, Indonesia's many kingdoms had become fragmented and the Dutch gradually established themselves on almost all of the islands of present-day Indonesia, controlling the islands' social, political, and economic institutions. The eastern half of the island of Timor was likewise occupied by the Portuguese until 1975. During the 300-year Dutch rule, the region then known as Netherlands East Indies became one of the world's richest colonial territories.

## MODERN ERA

Much of Indonesia's history in the modern era revolves around Sukarno (born Kusnasosro; 1901-1979). The Indonesian independence movement began during the first decade of the twentieth century and continued throughout both World Wars. The Japanese occupied Indonesia for three years during World War II. On August 17, 1945, after Japan had agreed to surrender to the Allied Powers, Sukarno and other nationalists declared national independence and established the Republic of Indonesia. Despite several attempts, the Dutch failed to recapture the territory lost to Japan. The victory over the Dutch strengthened Indonesia's sense of national identity and its citizens' belief in nationalism. In 1950 Indonesia became a member of the United Nations.

During the following decade, Sukarno revised the 1945 Constitution and became the President for Life. The Sukarno government badly mismanaged Indonesia's economy; the government seized foreign-owned plantations but did not train people to operate them, and consequently, economic conditions worsened.

The Communist Party began to grow during the early 1960s, with Sukarno's encouragement. In 1965 a group of Indonesian army officers seized power by killing six generals and other officers. This event precipitated more bloodshed as the Indonesian army and civilian mobs later killed between 200,000 and 300,000 people throughout Indonesia. Some of those killed were not Communists, but foreigners who had once controlled a great portion of the Indonesian economy. Shortly thereafter, Lieutenant General Suharto rose to power, outlawed the Communist Party, and reorganized the government. In 1968 Suharto was elected president and has been the head of the state ever since.

## PEOPLE

The population of the Republic of Indonesia, according to the 1990 census, is 180 million, which makes it the fourth most populous country in the world. The national motto is *Bhinneka Tunggal Ika*, which means "Unity in Diversity," a phrase that captures the people's strong national allegiance despite the variety of ethnicities and cultures.

The physical, cultural, and linguistic diversity of the Indonesian people reflects their country's past history and prehistory. At first, groups of people from the Asian mainland moved southeastward to the islands. Later groups, culturally more advanced than their predecessors, arrived to absorb the earlier immigrants or displace them, pushing them to remoter islands or less favorable habitats. By the early 1990s, Indonesia's society was divided into more than 300 ethnic groups, the largest of which was the Javanese, at 45 percent of the total population. Other groups include the Sundanese (14 percent), followed by the Madurese (7.5 percent), and the coastal Malays (7.5 percent).

Most of those who choose to leave their country for other countries, including the United

States, are from larger urban cities on Java. An ethnic group noted for their diverse cultural and religious backgrounds and geographical origins, Indonesians who live in the United States split their affection and loyalty between their new-found country and whatever part of their homeland they or their ancestors once inhabited.

### IMMIGRATION TO THE UNITED STATES

Few Indonesians immigrated to the United States prior to the 1950s. In the mid-1950s many Indonesian students came to the United States to study at American universities and colleges. In 1953 the ICA (now USAID) started providing scholarships for medical faculty members of the University of Indonesia to study at the University of California at Berkeley. In 1956 the ICA likewise provided scholarships for the teaching staff of the Bandung Institute of Technology to study at the University of Kentucky.

In the 1960s, when a number of political and ethnic skirmishes arose in Indonesia, several thousand Indonesians, the majority of whom were Chinese Indonesian, came to the United States. This immigration wave was short lived, however, due to the rapid reestablishment of peace in Indonesia and the limitations imposed by U.S. immigration quotas. More recent Indonesian immigrants have come to the United States for economic and educational reasons.

Overall, the number of Indonesians entering the United States is relatively low when compared to Chinese, Japanese, and Filipino American immigration figures. According to the 1990 U.S. Census, of the 6,876,394 Asians residing in the United States, only 30,085 (0.4 percent) are Indonesian Americans or Indonesians residing in the United States. The majority of Indonesian Americans reside in such large cities as Los Angeles, San Francisco, Houston, New York, and Chicago. This is partly due to the improved employment opportunities of these areas and to the fact that these cities have established Asian American communities.

# ACCULTURATION AND ASSIMILATION

Unlike other immigrant groups, there are no established Indonesian American ethnic enclaves. This may be attributed to the fact that Indonesia has one of the most ethnically diverse populations in the world; their diversity in social classes, language, religion, ethnic and cultural backgrounds, and geographic location has lessened the possibility of forming a community of common traditions. However, there are numerous organizations, clubs, and religious groups in cities where there is a relatively large concentration of Indonesians, including Dharma Wanita, Ikatan Keluarga Indonesia di AS, and Washington Court Gamelan Ensemble Association.

### TRADITIONS, CUSTOMS, AND BELIEFS

Assimilation for Indonesian American immigrants has been difficult, often causing them to become more attached to the traditions of their homeland. The Indonesians' sense of art is closely related to their mystic sense of identity with nature and with God. Humanity, nature, and art constitute an unbroken continuity. Artistic expression in Indonesian art is particularly evident in their dress. Much of their traditional dress consists of *batik* cloth. *Batik* is a design and art form that can be achieved by two techniques. The older method is called *tjanting* because a crucible of that name is used to draw the design directly on the cotton, by means of hot wax. When cooled, the wax resists the dye into which the cloth is immersed, so that all of the cloth except the area bearing the design accepts the dye. The wax is then removed, and the dyeing process is repeated. The second technique is regarded by some as inferior because the batik it produces is perceived to be machine-made. Actually, the design is made by a *tjap*, a printing stamp that is applied by hand to the cloth.

Other distinctive arts of the Indonesian people are the dance dramas of Bali and the Mataram court tradition. Both are essentially religious in character, though some Balinese dance is frivolous, flirtatious, or playful. Puppet dramas, or *wajang*, have been popular for a long time. The most popular puppets are flat and made of leather, but wooden puppets are also used. The puppeteer sits in back of a white screen and moves the puppets to act out stories. A palm-oil lamp throws the shadows of the puppets onto the screen. The plots usually involve a virtuous hero who triumphs over evil by means of supernatural powers and his own self-conquest.

Many Indonesians practice Western arts, from oil painting to metal sculpture, the subjects of which are often inspired by Indonesian life and

This photograph shows the variety of Indonesian foods served at ethnic festivals.

traditions. The literary arts are also popular. Early Indonesian literature consisted largely of local folk tales and traditional religious stories. The works of classical Indonesian authors, such as Prapantja, are still read today, though modern literature in the Indonesian language began in the 1920s.

## CUISINE

Rice is a central ingredient to the Indonesian diet. Indonesians boil or fry rice in various ways and serve it with a great variety of other foods. Foods are usually cooked in coconut milk and oil and sometimes wrapped in banana or coconut leaves. Fish, chicken, and beef are cooked with spices and served with rice. Indonesians eat little pork, since most of them are Muslims. Tea and coffee are favorite beverages.

At ceremonial occasions, including modern weddings, funerals, or state functions, foods such as *sate* (small pieces of meat roasted on a skewer), *krupuk* (fried shrimp or fish-flavored chips made with rice flour), and highly spiced curries of chicken and goat are commonly served. These foods are often served buffet style and at room temperature. Food is eaten with fingertips or with a spoon and fork. Water is served after the meal. These dietary customs are usually observed by Indonesian Americans during holidays and special events in the United States. For everyday meals, some Indonesians adapt readily to American food, while others prefer Indonesian or Chinese cuisine.

## CULTURAL EVENTS AND HOLIDAYS

Despite their ethnic diversity, there are three major holidays that virtually all Indonesian Americans observe. *Idul Fitri* (in Arabic), which is also known as *Hari Raja* or *Lebaran* (in Indonesian), marks the end to the Muslims' obligatory fast during the 30-day fast of Ramadan. Many Indonesians celebrate with a traditional Muslim feast. The date of this holiday is determined by the lunar calendar; therefore, the date varies from year to year. Christmas and Easter are also national holidays in Indonesia. Independence Day is August 17. On this day, according to officials in the Indonesian Embassy and Consulate Generals, Indonesians in the United States are invited to celebrate along with Indonesian officials in a flag-raising ceremony and reception.

## TRADITIONAL COSTUMES

Both Indonesian American men and women wear sarongs, traditional Indonesian garments with *batik* designs. Indonesian men generally wear sarongs only in the home or during informal occasions. Women wear sarongs on formal occasions, along with the *kebaya*, a tight, low-cut, long-sleeved blouse. Women often tie their hair into a bun or attach a hairpiece. Men may also don *batik* shirts that are worn outside their trousers and a black felt cap, called a *peci,* an item once associated with Muslims or Malays that has acquired a more secular, national meaning in the post-independence period.

### MUSIC AND DANCE

The most popular forms of dance in Indonesia are the Balinese dance and the *wajang kulit.* Though the origins of *wajang kulit* are lost in antiquity, many scholars believe that it is indigenous to Indonesia and that other shadow-drama arts around the world derive from it. This shadow drama is so popular that those who grew up in Indonesia can recognize all the stylized puppets and the episodes of the dramatized epics.

### INDONESIAN STUDENTS IN THE UNITED STATES

In recent years, many Indonesians have immigrated to the United States to attend American colleges or graduate schools. Afterward, many choose to apply for permanent residency or for citizenship. Presently, about 26 percent of the Indonesians residing in the United States are between the ages of 25 and 34. The same percentage of Indonesians have bachelor's degrees.

The attitudes of Indonesian graduate students at selected universities in the United States were reported in Dr. Rustam Amir Effendi's doctoral dissertation of 1983. Students attending the University of Illinois at Urbana-Champaign, the University of Michigan, Michigan State University, the University of Minnesota, Ohio University, the Ohio State University, and the University of Wisconsin were polled about their success with academic adjustment and their overall satisfaction with American education. The study disclosed that approximately 80 percent of Indonesian students are male and that 50 percent of them are between the ages of 31 and 35. Slightly more than 50 percent of them had worked as professionals for several years after they acquired their undergraduate degrees in Indonesia and before they came to America. Most of them are university faculty or government officials. Most studied engineering and the social sciences.

The number of Indonesian students in the United States has grown steadily since 1983. The successful personal adjustments and academic achievements of these students are decided by mainly two factors: language efficiency and the ability to adjust to American society. While some of them return to Indonesia, many choose to remain in the United States to continue their professional pursuits.

# LANGUAGE

With over 300 regional languages and dialects, there is a considerable diversity in the languages used in Indonesia. The major family of Indonesian language is the Austronesian. Bahasa Indonesian, a modified form of Malay, was named by Indonesian nationalists in 1928 as the official language. The majority of educated Indonesians in urban areas speak at least two languages.

Spoken Indonesian varies depending on the rank or status of the speaking partner. Respected elders are usually addressed in a kinship term— *bapak* (father or elder) or *ibu* (mother). Indirect references are usually preferred in conversation.

Most Indonesian names have two parts, although some Indonesians, including President Suharto, use only one name. In most cases it is appropriate to use the last part of the name before the indicator as a second reference. If no such filial indicator appears, the last part of the name is used as a second reference. Names including "Abu" or "Abdul" should use that word plus the word immediately following as a second reference. Some Muslim names include a place name. The part of the name preceding the place name should be used on second reference, for example, Abdullah Udjong Buloh, or Mr. Abdullah.

# FAMILY AND COMMUNITY DYNAMICS

Intermarriage is not uncommon between Indonesians and Americans, especially for the younger generation, though the elder-generation Indonesians prefer that their offspring marry others of Indonesian heritage. According to the *1990 Census of Population: Asians and Pacific Islanders in the United States,* more than 50 percent of adult Indonesians are members of families with two parents.

# RELIGION

The religions in Indonesia are as numerous as the languages. Nearly 90 percent of Indonesians observe Islam, with significantly smaller populations observing Protestantism (six percent), Catholicism (three percent), Hinduism (two percent), and Buddhism (one percent). Many Chinese Indonesians follow Buddhist teachings. All five play significant roles in Indonesian communities in and outside the United States

The high percentage of Muslims makes Indonesia the largest Islamic country in the world. Introduced to Indonesia by traders from India between the twelfth and fifteenth centuries, Islam, or *sharia* (in Indonesian), is a strictly monotheistic religion in which God, Allah, is a pervasive, if somewhat distant, figure. The prophet Muhammad is not deified but is regarded as a human who was selected by God to spread the word to others through the Koran, Islam's holiest book. There are significant variations in the practice and interpretation of Islam in various parts of Indonesia. Overall, a less strict interpretation of Islam is practiced than in the Middle East. There has been constant interaction between the Muslims and the Hindu-Buddhist population in Java Island ever since the initial introduction of Islam, and over time they have blended to form a loosely organized belief system called Javanism, or *agama Jawa*, which was officially recognized in the 1945 constitution.

The most rapidly growing religions in Indonesia are the Christian faiths: Roman Catholicism and Protestantism. The number of Christians in Indonesia is very small compared with the number of Muslims, but Christianity has a long history in Indonesia. It was introduced by Portuguese Jesuits and Dominicans in the sixteenth century. When the Dutch defeated Portugal in 1605, the Calvinist Dutch Reformed Church expelled Catholic missionaries and became the only Christian influence in the islands for 300 years. Because Calvinism was a strict, austere, and intellectually uncompromising variety of Christianity that demanded a thorough understanding of scripture, Christianity gained few converts in Indonesia until the nineteenth century, when German Lutherans introduced evangelical freedom and Jesuits established successful missions, schools, and hospitals on some of the islands, including Timor and Flores.

Membership in Christian churches surged after the 1965 coup attempt, when all nonreligious persons were labeled atheists and were suspected to be Communists. By the 1990s, the majority of Christians in Indonesia were Protestants of one affiliation or another. Catholic congregations grew less rapidly, due to the Church's heavy reliance on Europeans in positions of leadership.

Hinduism is perceived to enforce a rigid caste structure, dividing people into classes: priests, ruler-warriors, and commoners-servants. However, the caste system has never been rigidly applied in Indonesia. The majority of the Hindus are in Bali, and they express their beliefs through art and ritual instead of scripture and law. Ceremonies at puberty, marriage, and, most notably, death are closely associated with the Balinese version of Hinduism.

Chinese Indonesians brought Buddhism to Indonesia, along with Taoism and Confucianism. This unique version of Buddhism was introduced by the founder of Perbuddhi, Bhikku Ashin Jinarakkhita. He claimed that there is a single supreme deity, Sang Hyand Adi Buddha. In the wake of the failed coup in 1965, many Indonesians registered as Buddhists—some simply to avoid being suspected as Communist sympathizers and others sincere enough to construct monasteries.

Although there are various schools of thoughts and practices among Indonesian Buddhists, they each acknowledge the Four Noble Truths and the Eightfold Path. The Four Noble Truths concern the suffering of all living beings, resulting from the craving for worldly belongings. The Eightfold Path leads to enlightenment, teaching purified views, speech, conduct, and mind. In Indonesia, Buddhism is highly individualistic, with each person held accountable for his or her own self. Anyone can meditate alone, anywhere. Temples and pagodas exist only to inspire the proper frame of mind for believers' devotion and self-awareness.

In Dr. Fredy Lowell Macarewa's doctoral dissertation (1988), the author chronicled the efforts by the Seventh-Day Adventists, who practice an evangelical Christian faith, to reach Indonesian Americans. These efforts have not been entirely successful, however, because of the failure to comprehend the belief system unique to Indonesians, which grew out of the long transition from Dutch Indonesian rule to Indonesian independence. Macarewa also recognized that evangelizing Muslims is a difficult task, because of prejudice and antagonism between the followers of Christianity and Islamic Indonesia during the past 14 centuries.

Besides Seventh-Day Adventism, there are other religious establishments for the Indonesian residing in the United States, as there are for

In this photograph, an Indonesian American couple is dressed in traditional costume.

Korean Americans and other Asian Americans. These churches or religious groups serve not only as sites for worship but also as centers for social and cultural activities.

## EMPLOYMENT AND ECONOMIC TRADITIONS

According to the 1990 census, one-third of employed Indonesian adults in the United States are managers; one-third are professionals; and one-third are in technical, sales, and administrative-support occupations. There is a growing number of Indonesians who make their living in the importing and exporting business. Trade between Indonesia and United States has been robust. In the early 1990s, U.S. imports from Indonesia, consisting mostly of oil, rubber, coffee, tin, spices, tea, plywood, and textiles, amounted to nearly $4 billion. Exports to Indonesia totaled $2.5 billion and included agricultural products, resins, aircraft and parts, and earth-moving equipment. To facilitate trade there are commercial trade organizations such as the American-ASEAN (Association of Southeast Asian Nations) Trade Council, the American Indonesian Chamber of Commerce, the Central Indonesian Trading Company, the Indonesian Investment Promotion Office, and the Indonesian Trade Promotion Center, all located in New York City. However, recently there have

been organization branches established in other cities, including Los Angeles and Houston.

## POLITICS AND GOVERNMENT

The immigration bill passed by the Indonesian parliament on March 4, 1993 is greatly impacting the influx of Indonesians to the United States or other countries. The bill bars certain individuals from leaving or re-entering Indonesia if doing so could disrupt development, cause disunity among the Indonesian population, or threaten the individual's life or that of his or her family. Furthermore, a time limit of between six months and two-and-a-half years was set on travel in and out of Indonesia, for those affected. There are no public records showing how many Indonesians are barred from leaving the country.

In November 1994, U.S. President Bill Clinton attended the Asian Pacific Economic Summit meeting in Jakarta. Minimizing restrictions for export and import between United States and Indonesia was a major topic of discussion. It is expected that increased trade between these two countries will bring more Indonesians to the United States.

## MEDIA

### PRINT

*Indonesian Journal.*
Indonesian communities in the United States are linked by this publication—the first such commercial magazine in the United States. Published since 1988, it is a monthly journal distributed, free of charge, to the larger Indonesian communities in the country: New York, Chicago, Houston, San Francisco, and Los Angeles. Free copies are also distributed at Indonesian restaurants, churches, and other social organizations throughout the United States. Advertising revenues are its sole means of support. With the exception of some of the advertisements, the text of the publication is in Bahasa Indonesian. With reports on cultural, social, and even political events in the United States as well as in Indonesia, this publication serves as an important vehicle of communication for Indonesians who reside in the United States.

**Contact:** Mr. Mailangkay, Editor and Publisher.

**Address:** Desktop Designs, P.O. Box 4009, West Covina, California, 91791.

### The Indonesia Letter.

This monthly publication enjoys the largest distribution among its kind. It provides commentary and analysis on the subject of Indonesia and news of its economic, political, and social development.

**Address:** Asia Letter, Ltd., Los Angeles, California.

# ORGANIZATIONS AND ASSOCIATIONS

### American-ASEAN Trade Council.

The Council membership consists of members of the American Indonesian Chamber of Commerce, the Philippine American Chamber of Commerce, and other ASEAN (Association of Southeast Asian Nations).

**Address:** 40 East 49th Street, New York, New York 10017.

### American Indonesian Chamber of Commerce (AICC).

This unofficial and nonpolitical organization was incorporated in the United States in 1949, before Indonesia received full independence, a fact that signified the willingness of U.S. firms to trade directly with emerging Republic of Indonesia. Since then, its mission has been to foster and promote trade and investment between the United States and Indonesia. Currently, the American Indonesian Chamber of Commerce has over 150 members, including banks; energy companies; shipping lines; engineering firms; exporters; manufacturers; legal, public relations, and financial-service firms; and consulting and trading companies. The Chamber works closely with both Indonesians and Americans who are interested in doing export and import business from the United States or from Indonesia.

**Contact:** Wayne Forrest, Executive Director.

**Address:** 711 Third Avenue, 17th floor, New York, New York 10017.

**Telephone:** (212) 687-4505.

**Fax:** (212) 867-9882.

### Asian American Arts Centre (AAAC).

Supports exhibition of traditional and contemporary Asian American, Chinese, Japanese, Indonesian, Indian, Korean, and Filipino arts, including dance, music, performance art, and poetry.

**Contact:** Robert Lee, Director.

**Address:** 26 Bowery Street, New York, New York 10013.

**Telephone:** (212) 233-2154.

### East Timor Project.

This organization seeks to draw public attention to the situations of political prisoners in Indonesia, and to conditions in East Timor. It was formerly named the Emergency Committee for Human Rights in Indonesia and Self-Determination on East Timor.

**Contact:** Arnold S. Kohen, Coordinator.

**Address:** P.O. Box 2197, Washington, D.C. 20013.

### Indonesian Community Association.

This association serves as the central point of networking among Indonesians residing in the United States. The Chair serves as leader and coordinator for Indonesian American community. Considered the official representation of Indonesia in the United States, the association was formed to support such activities as family-oriented events, lectures, sports, and religious holidays. The association publication, *Warta IKI*, is published quarterly and distributed among Indonesian organizations in the United States.

**Contact:** Mr. Muchamad Sukarna, Chair.

**Address:** c/o Embassy of Indonesia, 2020 Massachusetts Avenue, N.W., Washington, D.C. 20036.

**Telephone:** (202) 775-5200.

### Indonesian American Society.

**Address:** c/o Major Hal Maynard, 8725 Piccadilly, Springfield, Virginia 22151.

**Telephone:** (703) 425-5080.

### Indonesian Students Association.

Founded to serve the needs of Indonesian students at colleges and universities in the United States. Branches of the organization are also in San Francisco, Los Angeles and other major cities.

**Address:** c/o Embassy of Indonesia, 2121 Massachusetts Avenue, N.W., Washington, D.C. 20036.

**Telephone:** (202) 293-1745.

# MUSEUMS AND RESEARCH CENTERS

**Cornell Modern Indonesia Project.**
The Center for International Studies at Cornell University conducts research activities in the United States on Indonesia's social and political development. The research efforts have resulted in the publication of monographs, bibliographies, and biographies of Indonesian historical figures. The research scope also includes cultural, military, and foreign affairs of Indonesia.

**Contact:** Professor Benedict Anderson.
**Address:** Cornell University, Ithaca, New York 14853.
**Telephone:** (607) 255-4359.

# SOURCES FOR ADDITIONAL STUDY

Aznam, Suhaini. "Passport Control: New Immigration Law Can Render Citizens Stateless," *Far Eastern Economic Review*, March 26, 1992, pp. 18-19.

Cordasco, Francesco. *Dictionary of American Immigration History*. Scarecrow, 1990.

De Leeuw, Ad'ele. *Indonesian Legends & Folk Tales*. New York: Nelson, 1961.

*Ethnic Information Sources of the United States*, Volume 1, second edition, edited by Paul Wasserman. Detroit: Gale Research, 1983.

*Indonesia: A Country Study*, fifth edition, edited by William H. Frederick and Robert L. Worden. Washington, D.C.: Federal Research Division, Library of Congress, 1992.

Ismail, Arshad bin. *Recollections of the Indonesian Association, San Francisco: Oral History Transcript* (tape-recorded interview conducted by Mona Lohanda). Oral History Project of the National Archives of Indonesia, 1977.

Lubis, Mochtar. *The Indonesian Dilemma*, translated by Florence Lamoureux. Singapore: Graham Brash, 1983.

Neill, Wilfred T. *Twentieth-Century Indonesia*. New York: Columbia University Press, 1973.

Notodiharjo, H. "International Cooperation in the Field of Education," *Prisma* 4, April 1977, p. 24.

Sievers, Allen M. *The Mystical World of Indonesia: Culture and Economic Development in Conflict*. Baltimore: Johns Hopkins University Press, 1974.

Temple, John. *Indonesia: Unity in Diversity* (video recording), produced by John Temple, directed by Arch Nicholson. Chicago: Films, Inc.

Van der Veur, Paul W. *Education and Social Change in Colonial Indonesia* (originally published in *Papers in International Studies*, Southeast Asia Series No. 12). Ann Arbor: University Microfilms International, 1969.

United States Department of Commerce, Economics and Statistics Administration. *1990 Census of Population: Asians and Pacific Islanders in the United States*. Washington, D.C.: Bureau of Census, 1993.

# IRANIAN

by
Mary Gillis

# AMERICANS

Americans are encouraged to confuse the few Islamic radicals who espouse violence with the majority of the adherents of the Islamic religion who reject violence.

## OVERVIEW

The Islamic Republic of Iran occupies 1,648,000 square kilometers on the Asian continent. The country is bounded on the north by the Transcaucasian and Turkistan territories of the former Soviet Union (along with the Caspian Sea), on the east by Afghanistan and Pakistan, on the west by Iraq and Turkey, and on the south by the Persian Gulf and the Indian Ocean. Most of Iran is a geographic plateau located about 4,000 feet above sea level; the plateau is spotted with mountains where the annual snowfall provides much of the water needed for irrigation during the hot spring and summer months.

Although most of the country is arid and desert-like, the majority of the population is located in the area around the Caspian Sea, which has a hot and humid climate. As of the early 1980s, approximately one-third of the population was occupied in agriculture, one-third in the service sector, and another third in manufacturing, mining, construction, and utilities. Unemployment grew throughout the 1980s, however, reaching an estimated 28.5 percent in 1986 due to the nation's faltering economy in the face of the ongoing border war with neighboring Iraq and the drop in worldwide oil prices.

Iran is the nineteenth most populous nation in the world, approaching 50 million people in the late 1980s. Nearly half the Iranian population is ethnically non-Arab, being considered direct descendants of Aryan invaders of the second century B.C. Other significant ethnic groups descend from ancient Arabic and Turkish conquerors; there are also smaller populations of nomadic tribes, including Kurds, Lurs, Bakhtiari, Qashqa'i, Mamasani, Khamseh, Shahsevans, Baluchi, and Turkomans.

The majority of Iran's population converted to the Islamic religion in the seventh century A.D. after invasion by Arab tribes, and the Shi'i sect of Islam has predominated since the sixteenth century. Most of the population (98 percent) is Muslim, and fully 93 percent are members of the Shi'i sect. The remaining Muslims are members of the Sunni sect of Islam. There are minority Christian (about 300,000), and Jewish (about 25,000 in 1984) populations, as well as Zoroastrians (about 30,000) and Baha'i (about 350,000). The latter two religions originated in Iran, but practitioners of both have been subjected to persecution by officials of the regime that came to power with the revolution in 1979. In 1987, there were 270,000 Bahais in Iran and 7,000 in the United States, of whom 1,000 were identified as Iranian immigrants.

In discussing possible reasons for the paucity of material available on the Iranian immigrant community in the United States, Diane M. Hoffman summarized its basic characteristics: "The relative recency of the large-scale influx of Iranians (many of whom arrived in the late 1970s and early 1980s), their relatively affluent socioeconomic background, their great religious, political, and ethnic heterogeneity, and their lack of well-defined geographic communities and internal cohesiveness are characteristics that make their status as a minority community somewhat problematic."

This attitude parallels the traditional self-image of the Shi'ism as a minority that must fight off a hostile majority, a paradigm taken from the martyrdom of Husain, commemorated annually during the month of Muharram. Among Shi'i leadership, this attitude evolved into "a quietist stance," according to David Pinault, which entailed "silent opposition to worldly powers, coupled with spiritual authority among a persecuted and excluded minority." Pinault noted that when the Shi'i leadership took political power in 1979, it was able to tap into the traditional Shi'i stance by "portraying the Iranian nation as a righteous minority menaced by powerful external enemies who seek to deprive it of its proper place in the world." A similarity may be found in Hoffman's description of the attitude of the Iranian high school students in Los Angeles in particular.

## HISTORY

Iran's strategic location, bridging the Middle East and India, has determined its history as one of invasion by foreign armies. Aryan invaders of the second century B.C. established Zoroastrianism as the dominant religion in the area, lending the people their distinctive ethnic heritage as well as their name. Alexander the Great swept through the area in the fourth century on his way to India, followed by Arab invaders in the seventh, who spread the teachings of Muhammad. By the eleventh century, the religion of Islam dominated the plateau and the advanced Persian sciences, literature, and learning had seduced the leaders of more than one invading army, including Genghis Khan in the thirteenth century and Tamerlane in the fourteenth. Various native rulers controlled the region over the next centuries. The Safavids ruled from the early sixteenth century until 1736. Their founder and first ruler, Shah Ismail, tried to unify the conglomeration of loosely united tribes scattered through the land by their conversion to Shi'ism as the state religion. During this era theologians laid the basis of Shi'ite theology as it is currently practiced in Iran; also, since then, Shi'ism has been a badge of Persian identity in the Islamic world. By the end of the eighteenth century, a Turkish tribe called the Qajars ruled the area now known as Iran.

## THE MODERN ERA

The Qajars governed Iran until the 1920s when Reza Shah (1878-1944) took over the government and established the Pahlavi monarchy. Reza Shah, whose sympathies leaned toward the Nazis at the start of World War II, was forced to abdicate to his son, Mohammed Reza Pahlavi (1919-1980), in 1941 by Britain and the Soviet Union, which had established a presence in the country in order to block Nazi influence in the region. Some see the first episode of the Cold War in the Soviets' refusal to remove their troops from Iran until forced to do so by the United States and the newly formed United Nations in 1946. Iran became an even more significant player on the political scene worldwide as oil began to dominate the postwar world market—Iran possesses as much as ten percent of the world's oil reserves. It was through its oil contacts that Iran gradually became Westernized, a process consciously accelerated during the "white revolution" of 1962-1963, when various reforms were enacted (including giving women the right to vote and to hold public office) and opposition—increasingly centered in the religious community—was suppressed.

Prior to 1979, Iran was ruled by a constitutional monarchy; however, it was in name only, not in practice. Shah Mohammed Reza Pahlavi changed the country's name from Persia to Iran in 1935 under a directive of Iran's representative abroad who believed that the province under which Persia was named (Pars) was only a single part of the entire country, while the birthplace of the *Aryan* race was Iran. After 1962, Iran became less a constitutional monarchy and more a one-man dictatorship. After the revolution, which toppled the Western-backed government of the Shah, who had led the country for nearly four decades, Iran officially became an Islamic republic governed by the laws of the Koran and the traditions of the Shi'i religion as interpreted by the Ayatollah Ruhollah Khomeini (1900-1989). Khomeini was the nation's official spiritual guide (*faqhi*) until his death a decade after the revolution; he was replaced by Ayatollah Ali Khamenei in 1989. Iran has experienced severe economic, social, and cultural turmoil throughout the twentieth century, particularly in the years leading up to the 1979 revolution. Since that time, the country has struggled to work out the details of its dedication to the teachings of the prophet Muhammad in everyday life and in specific government policies while fighting an expensive border war with Iraq and seeing several million of its wealthiest and most highly educated citizenry emigrate to the West.

## IMMIGRATION TO THE UNITED STATES

It is difficult to trace immigration to the United States from the region designated by the modern world as the Middle East because of the way in which immigration officials on both sides have kept records. Prior to 1900, the destination of all those leaving the Ottoman Empire was officially Egypt, as the West was considered off-limits; upon arrival in the United States, these immigrants were indiscriminately labelled "Arabs." After 1900, when the popular term became "Syrians," and as late as 1930, all Middle Eastern immigrants were both officially and unofficially designated as Syrians. It appears that more than half of those who immigrated to the United States before 1950 were Lebanese, and 90 percent of the total were Christian, despite the overwhelming predominance of Islam in the Middle East.

The first wave of immigration from Iran to the United States, corresponding to the period 1950-1977, was relatively insignificant in terms of numbers of immigrants. Annually, about 1,500 Iranians entered the United States. as immigrants during this period, along with about 17,000 non-immigrants, including students and visitors. The vast majority of Iran's emigrants left their homeland just prior to or as a result of the 1979 revolution, and are often considered de facto political refugees, though they lack that official designation. For the period 1978-1980, the average number of Iranians entering the United States as non-immigrants annually increased to more than 100,000; it is believed that the difference between the figures for the two waves of immigration is explained by the presence of exiles and refugees from the Islamic fundamentalist regime that overthrew the Shah.

Although non-Muslims form a tiny minority of the Iranian population in Iran, non-Muslim religious minorities appear to be overrepresented among Iranians in Los Angeles, where the largest Iranian population outside Iran is concentrated. The reason for the large number of religious minorities among Iranian immigrants compared to their proportion in the feeder population appears to be fear of or actual religious persecution under the fundamentalist Islamic government. For example, at its height, the Iranian Jewish population numbered 90,000 and enjoyed greater freedom and power than in any other Muslim country. But despite Ayatollah Khomeini's assurances of their safety under his government, several Jewish leaders were killed during the regime's early years, and 2,000 Jews leaving temple after Friday night services in 1983 were rounded up and imprisoned. By 1987, an estimated 55,000 Iranian Jews had received permission to emigrate. In 1992, 35,000 of those potential immigrants had settled in Los Angeles, New York City, and in Europe; however, the stream of Iranian Jewish immigrants had slowed considerably by the early 1990s and a few had even returned to Iran to reclaim their former lives and property as living conditions there eased.

Several sources have noted than an estimated two to three million Iranians have fled their homeland since the 1979 revolution; of the more than one million Iranians scattered across the United States, approximately 400,000 are located in southern California. According to U.S. Immigration and Naturalization Services figures through 1991, estimates on Iranian immigrants are much lower, totalling 200,000 Iranian immigrants

Iranian Americans
demonstrate in New York
City.

entering the United States since 1978. The difference in these figures may be the result of counting only those who entered the country as immigrants, leaving out the large numbers of those entering officially as non-immigrants, including students and visitors. This group is often characterized as the former "elite" of Iran, highly educated and skilled professionals of various religions and ethnic backgrounds, many of whom have been financially successful in the United States.

There is some evidence to support the statement, however, that most Iranians who came to the United States did not intend to stay permanently. Only ten percent of those born in Iran and residing in Los Angeles at the time of the 1980 census had become naturalized citizens, and only 18 percent of those admitted into the country that year were relatives of resident aliens. In 1992, more than 100,000 Iranians had returned to their homeland since 1989, due as much to the economic recession in the United States as a state-sponsored campaign that urged reconciliation with the "secular experts." One Iranian questioned pointed to the reversal in the government's attitude toward secular experts as a recognition that the Iranian economy will never recover under the direction of religious experts alone.

### RELATIONSHIP TO ESTABLISHED AMERICAN POPULATION

The relationship between the Iranian American

population and the surrounding population since the 1979 revolution appears to be one characterized by fear and prejudice on the one side, and by anger and sadness on the other. Those belonging to the Muslim religion in particular are often subjected to a kind of nationwide backlash that identifies all members of their religion as violent fanatics or terrorists. In 1985 a proposed religious and cultural center for Muslims to be built in central Oklahoma was abandoned due to the protests of local citizens who feared the project would establish a site for a terrorist network in their midst. In addition, the U.S. government has often reinforced the stereotype that all Iranians are potential terrorists. According to an article in *Maclean's* magazine in 1984, some in the American State Department feared any attempt by the United States to protect its interests in the Persian Gulf during the Iran-Iraq war of the 1980s would inspire "'sleeping' terrorist cells in the ranks of Iranian exiles and students" living in the United States ("Iran's 'Sleeping' Threat," *Maclean's* [June 4, 1984]). And in 1987, the *Nation* reported that Iranian visa and green-card holders constituted one of the groups targeted by the American Immigration and Naturalization Service (INS) for a proposed "contingency plan" intended to identify "potential alien terrorists and undesirables" and remove them from the country ("The Untouchables," *Nation* [March 21, 1987], p. 348).

In response, many Iranian Americans feel a "deep sense of helplessness and alienation" in a culture that appears to understand them little and care less for their fate, according to Homayoon Moossavi. "We are, for the most part, only the subject of ridicule by political cartoonists and second-rate comics. We are treated as a faceless mob. This drives us mad, makes us angry and bitter," Moossavi concluded. Prior to the 1979 revolution, many Iranians would try to conceal their identity by identifying themselves as Persians or by speaking in English. Although some believe that this was to avoid American discrimination, the primary reason was a fear of Iran's State Organization for Intelligence and Security (SAVAK). This organization operated freely abroad, especially in the United States, to punish so-called dissidents or anti-Shah groups.

## ACCULTURATION AND ASSIMILATION

Although there is little data pertaining specifically to Iranian Americans and their struggle with assimilation into the surrounding culture, most Iranians in the United States are Muslims. Azim A. Nanji has identified several areas of conflict between the traditional Muslim and the secular American cultures. The most significant difference between living in a predominantly Islamic society and living in the United States is the lack of social support for the shariah, the Muslim code of conduct which has evolved over the centuries and which governs every aspect of one's life, from the most private to the most public.

In addition, the place of the extended family network at the center of Muslim life, which traditionally provides one's social identity as well as the all-important comforts of the private domain, is often not possible for immigrants, who may have left most or all of their family behind. Furthermore, Nanji noted, women may experience the greatest changes in the new environment due to the more frequent necessity of working outside the home. "This has meant that the essentially separate worlds of Muslim men and women in the public spheres have now become fused," Nanji remarked, adding that Muslim women in America tend to participate more actively in the mosque, though traditionally women pray primarily in the home.

Finally, Nanji identified Muslim youth in the United States as an area for deep concern among Muslim families. Peer pressure to experiment with drinking, dating, and other aspects of the lives of secular American adolescents which are forbidden by Islam, as well as pressure from the school system to practice individualistic values such as self-reliance and independent thinking—values that contradict the family-centered Muslim tradition—are sources of anxiety to Muslim parents. In response to these concerns, Nanji noted, some Muslims have attempted to recreate a totally Islamic atmosphere in the North American context by building schools, mosques, and communes.

Hoffman suggested that unlike with other immigrant groups, degree of language acquisition and length of residence in the United States indicate only the most superficial identification with the surrounding culture for Iranian Americans. Indeed, most Iranian immigrants speak English with some degree of fluency upon arrival in the United States. The prestige accorded those fluent in a second language—especially French or English—in Iran meant that conversations held in public or on social occasions were rarely conducted in Farsi; this attitude was carried over to the American context, reflecting the longstanding Iranian fascination with Western culture prior to the 1979 revolution. Indeed, despite a statistical downturn in education level of Iranian immigrants pre-and post-revolution, Iranian immigrants as a group display an extremely high incidence of English proficiency, particularly compared to other recent immigrant groups, according to Georges Sabagh and Mehdi Bozorgmehr in their study of the demographic, social, and economic characteristics of the Iranian immigrant community in Los Angeles.

Hoffman noted that since the 1979 revolution, however, and thus for the majority of Iranian immigrants in the United States, the attitude toward use of Farsi has reversed itself. This has resulted in a resurgence of interest among immigrants in traditional Persian culture and literature, and a new insistence on using Farsi in public and in private unless compelled to use English by an authority figure (for example, a teacher), or by the exigencies of the situation itself (for example, if one or more people present do not speak Farsi).

Hoffman argued that the resistance to speaking English among Iranians living in the United States indicates a renewed pride in their own cultural heritage as "a response to the twin threat to cultural identity posed by the revolutionary changes in Iran itself and the stresses of living in the United States." Just as the native population was able to maintain its distinctive culture despite centuries of invading armies, so in the United States, Iranians seem to cling to their ethnic heritage in the face of pressures to assimilate. Hoffman found that Iranian immigrants were often less interested in acquiring knowledge about American culture than they were in learning more about their own cultural heritage. Among Iranian American high school students in Los Angeles, Hoffman found both an acknowledgement of the necessity to acquire proficiency in English in order to achieve scholastically and a resistance of the typical association of language acquisition with value acquisition. Among the Los Angeles students and businessmen studied by Hoffman, "American work culture, and perhaps the notion of work as applied to self, such as in the philosophy of self-help or self-development, were the only domains in which Iranians enthusiastically espoused American values."

## COMMON STEREOTYPES ABOUT IRANIANS

Due to the oil shortage experienced in the United States in the 1970s the romantic or exotic image of the Middle East, based on such fairy tales as "Aladdin and His Magic Lamp" and "Ali Babba and the Forty Thieves," became a negative stereotype of "greedy Arab oilmen" and of terrorists crazed by Islamic fundamentalism, as noted in "Media Blitz" (*Scholastic Update*, October 22, 1993). Iranian Americans in particular have been subjected to the latter stereotype because of the political radicals who held 52 Americans hostage for more than a year in 1979 in the American Embassy in Teheran, Iran's capital city. And when four Muslim immigrants were arrested for the bombing of the World Trade Center in New York City in 1993, one Middle Eastern immigrant remarked in "Media Blitz" that "this trial is not about the guilt or innocence of a few men. All Islam is on trial."

Some Muslims blame the American media and popular culture for propagating negative stereotypes about their culture and religion. For example, Disney's popular film *Aladdin* features a Middle Eastern character who sings about cutting off ears as legal punishment and calls his home "barbaric." Middle Eastern critics of American popular culture point to the recent predominance of Arabs or Muslims in the role of villain in movies and television shows. Furthermore, these critics contend in "Media Blitz" that through the media's reliance on such terms as "Islamic terrorists" and "Islamic fundamentalists," Americans are encouraged to confuse the few Islamic radicals who espouse violence with the majority of the adherents of the Islamic religion who reject violence.

## HOLIDAYS

The most significant Iranian holiday is Muharram, which focuses on the seventh-century martyrdom of Husain, the grandson of the prophet Muhammad, who is considered the rightful heir to the caliphate (leadership of the religion) by Shi'i Muslims. Muharram is a period of mourning and penitence as all Shi'ites grieve the murder of Husain, his family, and followers at Karbala. The first eight days represent the period they were besieged in the desert; the eigth and ninth days of Muharram are thus the most intense days of this holiday. The tenth day, *Ashura*, is the height of Muharram festival.

Muharram festivities include processions during which banners or commemorative tombs are displayed, narrative readings are performed, and most important, *ta'ziyeh khani* (mourning songs)—traditional plays in honor of the martyrs

of Karbala—are enacted in every village. Despite the essentially religious subject matter of the *ta'ziyeh* plays—which traditionally depict the death of Husain and his family or related events, such as the awful fate that awaits their assassins in the afterworld—"they are political as well as religious ceremonies during which a community reaffirms its commitment to the shared set of social values inherent in communally-held religious beliefs," according to Milla C. Riggio. Food is often shared throughout the performance of the play, reinforcing the communal feeling among the audience, and the audience interacts with the players onstage by singing along, crying, and beating their breasts in sorrow or penitence.

In her study of a *ta'ziyeh* performed in the United States, Riggio emphasized the ways in which Mohammed Ghaffari, the play's Iranian American director, altered the original play because of the differences in the American versus the Iranian audience. Because his American audience could not (or would not, given the constraints of Western theater-going) verbally respond to the spectacle onstage, the play's traditional "call for vengeance against the cultural as well as religious enemies of Shi'ism" was not available to Ghaffari. Instead, the community-affirming message of the play was transformed into a personal expression of the director's feelings about his own exile. This was achieved in part by altering the traditional costuming, action, and theme of the play, "which abstracted and universalized the idea of cruelty rather than localizing it in Shi'i martyrdom," argued Riggio. "Replacing the call to martyrdom with a mystical dance which affirms the beauty of his life while recognizing human cruelty, Ghaffari displaced the communal values of the *ta'ziyeh* tradition in favor of the existential experience of the isolated individual," Riggio concluded.

## TRADITIONAL CLOTHING

*Hejab*, modest garb appropriate for women, is a controversial aspect of Islamic culture and public conformity to its dictates is often considered a signal of fluctuations in the political atmosphere. During the reign of the Westernized Pahlevi monarchy, women were discouraged from wearing the *chador*, the enveloping robe that ensures women's hair and skin are hidden from view, and among the upper and middle classes the garment came to be associated with oppression. After the revolution, although the *chador* itself was not mandated, it was required that all women appearing in public obey the dictates of modesty in covering themselves completely except for the skin of the hands and face. Although no data was found on the degree of conformity to *hejab* among Iranian women in the United States, given what is known about the high socioeconomic status of most Iranian Americans before immigration, it is unlikely that wearing the *chador* would be widespread among this group.

# LANGUAGE

The official language of Iran is Farsi, known in the West as Persian, which combines the ancient Persian language with many Arabic words and is written with Arabic characters and script. Turkish and Turkic dialects are also spoken in several areas in the country and the nomadic tribes that migrate vertically every spring and fall from the Zagros mountain range to the surrounding lowland plains speak a variety of other languages and dialects. Iranian immigrants to the United States are more highly educated than most immigrant groups; this fact, along with the prestige associated with the use of such foreign languages as French or English in Iran, has meant that the majority of Iranian Americans report a high level of proficiency in English. Sabagh and Bozorgmehr concluded that "Iranian migrants as a whole probably have a better command of English ... than most other immigrants in Los Angeles."

## GREETINGS AND OTHER POPULAR EXPRESSIONS

Common Farsi greetings and other expressions include: *Salam!*—Greetings!; or, more informally, *Cheh khabar?*—What's new?; and *Cheh khabareh?*—What's happening?; *Khoda Hafez*—Good-bye; *Loftan*—Please; *Mamnoon am*—Thank you; *Khabeli nadereh*—You're welcome. *Inshallah*—If God be willing; *Maashallah*—May God preserve, is often used with expressions of admiration, or by itself to express admiration of someone. Other expressions of admiration include *Cheghadr ghashangeh!*—How beautiful!; *Kheili jaleheh*—Very interesting; and *Aliyeh!*—Great!

# FAMILY AND COMMUNITY DYNAMICS

Although half the Iranian population claims a non-Arab ethnicity, all Muslim Iranians—the vast majority of the population—share a common tradition with other Muslims of the Middle East, Arab or non-Arab. Muslim society in general, according to Nanji, is centered on extended family networks headed by the father. Traditionally, business and political life as well as social life has been determined by the family network. According to *Iran: A Country Study*, "Historically, an influential family was one that had its members strategically distributed throughout the most vital sectors of society, each prepared to support the others in order to ensure family prestige and family status." Thus the family is at the center of the individual's economic and political as well as social and emotional life. The extended family is enlarged through marriage with other Muslims and continues through a strong tradition of family inheritance. "On the whole, this heritage of social grouping and family values characterized the value system of immigrant Muslims."

## DATING, MARRIAGE, AND INTERMARRIAGE

The father, as head of the family, is considered responsible for the family's social, material, and spiritual welfare, and in return expects respect and obedience. Marriage, often within the extended family network, is encouraged at a young age both officially and unofficially, and though multiple marriages (as many as four) are allowed for men by Islamic law, it has often been discouraged both by the government and by the family. In addition, the Shi'i religion, the predominant sect of Islam in Iran, allows the practice of temporary marriage, or *muta*. Muslim women are forbidden to marry non-Muslims, as it is feared the woman and her children will most certainly be lost to Islam, but Muslim men may marry non-Muslims if they are Jewish or Christian. These religions are traditionally considered kin to the Muslims, but intermarriage is nevertheless allowed on the assumption that the woman will convert to Islam and raise the children according to Islamic law.

Changes in the characteristic Middle Eastern family structure in the North American context have resulted in part from the loss of power that had been accorded to elders as purveyors of important cultural knowledge and to the father as head of the family. The knowledge elders possess may not be considered relevant in the context of immigration. Power relations are sometimes reversed when the second generation finds it necessary to instruct the first on various aspects of the new culture or to represent the family to the outside world due to its greater knowledge of English. Furthermore, influenced by the culture around them, members of the second generation often desire greater freedom to determine their own lives while their elders struggle to maintain control over the family. One area that has not changed is adherence to the Islamic law to take care of the elderly when they cannot take care of themselves. Other changes among immigrant families include a decrease in the likelihood that marriages will be arranged.

## WOMEN IN THE FAMILY AND THE COMMUNITY

Women of the middle and upper classes—many of whom had adopted secular, Westernized values—were among those most affected when the conservative Islamic government came to power with the revolution in 1979. Strict enforcement of the traditional dress code might extend to flogging for violations such as wearing make-up or nail polish, even if covered by sunglasses and gloves. Throughout the 1980s, the official attitude toward women as indicated by police enforcement of the dress code through patrols and roadblocks varied somewhat by region (women are more severely restricted in rural areas than in Teheran, the capital city) and with fluctuations in the political realm. Still, a woman may be censured or fined for wearing perfume, letting some hair escape from her *chador*, or for speaking to a man in public in an animated fashion. Although Iranian women believe they are allowed more independence than women in Saudi Arabia, this is still far less than was accorded them before the revolution, and the inconsistency with which the laws have been applied is nerve-wracking.

Nevertheless, the sphere of women's power primarily remains the home, extending only to the initiation of social activities there and in the mosque. Nanji refuted the "stereotype of Muslim women as either concubines or oppressed baby-making machines," stressing that despite the interpretation given the laws of the Koran governing women by the most conservative adherents of Islam, "in the overall context of Muslim history and society, the status and role of women accorded with the larger view of the integrity and vitality of the family as the cornerstone of all social relationships." That is, though the home has traditionally been the seat of women's power

in Islamic cultures, and is frequently perceived to be the only sphere where it is appropriate for women to assert themselves, the role that home life plays in Islamic cultures is central to all other aspects of the social structure.

It has been suggested that, among Iranians in Los Angeles at least, the authority of women within the family actually decreases after immigration. Parvin Abyaneh noted that 66 Iranian families in Los Angeles were surveyed on the following four points: amount of time women spent doing housework; amount of help women received while performing household chores; degree of control women had over family income; and, amount of control women had over major family decisions ("Immigrants and Patriarchy," *Women's Studies*, Volume 17 [1989]). Survey results showed that Iranian American women spend more time doing household chores, receive less help with these chores from their husbands (or others), and have less ability to control the way family income is spent in the United States than when they resided in Iran. Although Iranian women exert little influence outside the home before immigration, that sphere of influence appears to deteriorate after migration to the United States.

# RELIGION

Although Shi'ism predominates, there are several minority religious groups in Iran. Less than ten percent of the Iranian population practices the Sunni version of Islam, a sect that differs from Shi'ism in its attitude toward the imamate, the spiritual descendants of Muhammad. Bahaiism is the second largest religious minority in Iran. Formed in the nineteenth century as an offshoot of Shi'ism, the Bahai religion believes in pacifism and equality of the sexes, and maintains that all people are brothers. Shi'i leadership officially regards the Bahai as heretics and, except during the reign of the Pahlavi dynasty, Bahais have been persecuted in Iran. The country's Christian population includes Catholics, Anglicans, and Protestants of mainly Armenian and Assyrian descent. Although this primarily urban population has not suffered official persecution by the government of the Islamic Republic, it has been subjected to many Islamic-oriented laws and to government oversight in its schools, both of which often impinge on the traditional practice of the Christian religion. The small population of Iranian Jews has an ancient history, and was offi-

cially recognized in the constitution set down by the revolution of 1979. Nevertheless, the Iranian government's unfriendly relations with Israel have influenced the treatment of its native Jewish population, and many have emigrated to the United States and Israel. The small population of remaining Zoroastrians are also officially recognized by the Iranian constitution and have not been officially persecuted by the government.

The Islamic Republic of Iran tolerates some religious variation, as long as it does not act against the government or the sanctity of Islamic values. The vast majority of Iranians practice the Islamic faith, which originated with Muhammad (572-632 A.D.), who came to believe he was the prophet of Allah, the one true God. Islam, which means "submission to God," requires the belief in God and His Prophet, the recitation of prescribed prayers, the giving of alms, the observance of the feast of Ramadan, and the making of a pilgrimage to Mecca.

The Muslim religion is divided into two main sects, the Sunni, which predominates worldwide, and the Shi'i, which is the minority sect except in Iran, Iraq, and in parts of India. The Shi'i sect of Islam was established in the first years after Muhammad's death when a dispute arose over leadership of the religion. The Sunnis restrict accession to the caliphate to members of the tribe of Muhammad; the Shi'ites restrict right of accession to members of Muhammad's family. The origin of the name Shi'i is thus *Shi'at Ali* (supporters of Ali), Muhammad's cousin and son-in-law.

# EMPLOYMENT AND ECONOMIC TRADITIONS

Of Iranian immigrants residing in Los Angeles, nearly 30 percent identified themselves as students in the 1980 census. According to Sabagh and Bozorgmehr, because students are younger than the average Iranian immigrant, generally have greater facility with the English language, tend to work fewer hours than non-students, are less likely to be self-employed, and have a lower occupational profile and consequent lower level of income, their inclusion in a statistical profile of Iranians residing in the United States is believed to distort the group profile. Significantly, this study revealed a higher incidence of self-employment among Iranian immigrants than among Korean Americans, an immigrant group reputed to have one of the highest rates of entrepreneurship in Los Angeles. Fully one-third of the Iranian immigrants in Los Angeles, regardless of when they entered the country, reported that they were self-employed. Furthermore, later immigrants—those who fled Iran due to the revolution—tended to bring a great deal of money into the United States with them, and reported a significant income from interest and rental properties. Fluctuations in the American economy have affected this group to the extent that the downswing in the economy in the late 1980s, along with the relaxation of conditions in Iran, had encouraged as many as 100,000 Iranians to return to their homeland.

# POLITICS AND GOVERNMENT

Shi'ism has traditionally shown a disdain for both secular authority and direct involvement in political life. Iranian leaders of Twelver Shi'ism (*Ithna 'Ashariyah*), the dominant strain of Shi'ism, have followed the ancient tradition of remaining separate from the world's political concerns, avoiding the ministering of justice, and seeking a spiritual victory in defeat. There is also a tradition of revolt against injustice within Shi'ism, however, and an inability to suffer the corruption of political figures except when to protest would put one's life in danger. This stance is known as *taqiyah* ("necessary dissimulation") and is traced back to Ali, Muhammad's son-in-law, who quietly accepted the promotion of three others to the caliphate before him in order to avoid civil war. Pinault identified *taqiyah* as a "guiding principle for any Shiite living under a tyrannous government too powerful to be safely resisted; one may given an external show of acquiescence while preserving resistance in one's interior, in one's heart."

The U.S. government was concerned with the political sympathies of Iranians residing in the United States throughout the 1980s but no material was found implicating Iranians in terrorist acts in this country.

# INDIVIDUAL AND GROUP CONTRIBUTIONS

## ACADEMIA

Vartan Gregorian (1935- ) is a former university professor and president of the New York Public Library who has been president of Brown University since 1989.

## FASHION

Bijan (1940- ) is a fashion designer of exclusive men's apparel and perfumes.

## LITERATURE

Sadeq-i Chubak (1916- ), considered one of the foremost modern Iranian writers, is the author of short stories, novels, and dramatic works.

## THEATER

Lotfi Mansouri (1929- ) is a Canadian theatrical director who directed the Canadian Opera Company from 1976 to 1988, and has directed the San Francisco Opera since 1988.

# MEDIA

## PRINT

*American-Arab Message.*

A weekly religious and political magazine printed in Arabic and English.

**Contact:** Imam M. A. Hussein, Publisher.

**Address:** 17514 Woodward Avenue, Detroit, Michigan 48203.

**Telephone:** (313) 868-2266.

**Fax:** (313) 868-2267.

*Iran Nameh: A Persian Journal of Iranian Studies.*

A quarterly academic publication published by the Foundation for Iranian Studies.

Contact: Hormoz Hekmat, Editor.

Address: 4343 Montgomery Avenue, Suite 200, Bethesda, Maryland 20814.

Telephone: (301) 657-1990.

Fax: (301) 657-4381.


*Iran Post.*

A weekly newspaper in English and Farsi.

Address: Box 3765, Beverly Hills, California 90212.

Telephone: (213) 464-5335.


*Iran Times International.*

A weekly newspaper in English and Farsi.

Contact: Javad Khakbaz, Editor.

Address: 2727 Wisconsin Avenue, N.W., Washington, D.C. 20007.

Telephone: (202) 659-9868.

Fax: (202) 337-7449.


*Iranian Assets Litigation Reporter.*

A semi-monthly journal published by Andrews Publications.

Contact: Edith McFall, Editor.

Address: Box 1000, Westtown, Pennsylvania 19395.

Telephone: (215) 399-6600.

Fax: (215) 399-6610.


*Iranian Studies.*

A quarterly published by the Society for Iranian Studies.

Contact: A. Armat, Editor.

Address: c/o Middle East Institute, Columbia University, 1113 International Affairs Building, New York, New York 10027.

Telephone: (212) 854-3996.


**RADIO**

**KPFT-FM.**

Contact: Mary Helen Merzbacher, General Manager.

Address: 419 Lovett Boulevard, Houston, Texas 77006.

Telephone: (713) 526-4000.


# ORGANIZATIONS AND ASSOCIATIONS

**American Institute of Iranian Studies.**

This organization of educational institutions seeks to improve Iranian studies programs and facilitate the research efforts of Iranian and North American scholars of Iranian studies.

Contact: Dr. Marilyn R. Waldman, President.

Address: c/o Ohio State University, History Department, 106 Dulles Hall, 230 West 17th Avenue, Columbus, Ohio 43210-1311.

Telephone: (614) 292-1265.

Fax: (614) 292-2282.


**Iran Freedom Foundation.**

This organization opposes the Islamic Republic of Iran, and attempts to protect human and civil rights in Iran and help establish a secular, constitutional government there by disseminating information to the media, universities, and political institutions, and at demonstrations and gatherings.

Contact: M. R. Tabatabai, President.

Address: P.O. Box 422, Bethesda, Maryland 20817.

Telephone: (301) 608-3333.

Fax: (301) 608-3333.


**Iranian B'Nei Torah Movement.**

This is an organization for rabbinical students seeking to aid Iranian Jews in the United States and Israel in their religious, charitable, and educational requirements.

Contact: David Zargart, President.

Address: P.O. Box 351476, Los Angeles, California 90035.

Telephone: (310) 652-2115.

Fax: (310) 652-6979.


**National Council of Resistance of Iran.**

This is a coalition of organizations opposed to the rule of Ayatollah Ruhollah Khomeini and his successors in Iran and favoring their replacement with a democratic government. Organizes opposition worldwide through diplomatic efforts and demonstrations and strikes in Iran.

Contact: Dr. Masoud Banisadr.

Address: c/o Representative Office in the U.S., 3421 M Street, N.W., Suite 1032, Washington, D.C. 20007.

Telephone: (202) 783-5200.

**Society for Iranian Studies.**

This is an organization of students and scholars of Iranian studies intended to promote scholarship in the field.

**Contact:** Hamid Dabashi, Executive Secretary.

**Address:** c/o Middle East Institute, Columbia University, SIA Building, Room 1113, 420 West 118th Street, New York, New York 10027.

**Telephone:** (212) 854-5284.

# SOURCES FOR ADDITIONAL STUDY

Bill, James A. *The Eagle and the Lion: The Tragedy of American-Iranian Relations*. New Haven, Connecticut: Yale University Press, 1988.

*Cambridge Encyclopedia of the Middle East and North Africa*. Cambridge: Cambridge University Press, 1988.

*Comprehensive Bibliography for the Study of American Minorities*, two volumes. New York: New York University Press, 1976.

Hoffman, Diane M. "Language and Culture Acquisition among Iranians in the United States," *Anthropology and Education Quarterly*, 1989.

*Iran: A Country Study*, edited by Helen Chapin Metz. Washington, D.C.: U.S. Government, 1989.

Kordi, Gohar. *An Iranian Odyssey*. Serpent's Tail Press, 1993.

Milani, Farzaneh. *Veils and Words: The Emerging Voices of Iranian Women Writers*. Syracuse, New York: Syracuse University Press, 1992.

Moossavi, Homayoon. "Teheran Calling," *Progressive*, August 1988.

Nanji, Azim A. "The Muslim Family in North America," in *Family Ethnicity*. Newberry Park, California: SAGE Publications, 1993.

Pinault, David. *The Shiites: Ritual and Popular Piety in a Muslim Community*. New York: St. Martin's Press, 1992.

Riggio, Milla C. "Ta'ziyeh in Exile," *Comparative Drama*, spring 1994.

Rubin, Barry. *Paved with Good Intentions: The American Experience and Iran*. New York: Oxford University Press, 1980.

Sabah, Georges, and Mehdi Bozorgmehr. "Are the Characteristics of Exiles Different from Immigrants?" *Sociology and Social Research*, January 1987.

Sackville-West, Vita. *Passenger to Teheran* (1926). New York: Moyer Bell, 1990.

Simpson, John. *Inside Iran: Life Under Khomeini's Regime*. New York: St. Martin's Press, 1988.

*Worldmark Encyclopedia of the Nations*, eighth edition, Volume 4: *Asia and Oceania*. Detroit: Gale Research, 1995.

Wright, Robin. *In the Name of God: The Khomeini Decade*. New York: Simon and Schuster, 1989.